724 Headley Drive
London, Ontario
N6H 3V6
471-8021

Forest City Pro
Shoppe Tennis

ACCOUNTING
THE BASIS FOR
BUSINESS
DECISIONS

ACCOUNTING
THE BASIS FOR
BUSINESS
DECISIONS

SECOND CANADIAN EDITION
REVISED

WALTER B. MEIGS, Ph.D., C.P.A.
Professor of Accounting
University of Southern California

A. N. MOSICH, Ph.D., C.P.A.
Professor of Accounting and
Chairman, Department of Accounting
University of Southern California

CHARLES E. JOHNSON, Ph.D., C.P.A.
Late Professor of Accounting
University of Oregon

Canadian Edition prepared by

J. DAVID BLAZOUSKE, M.B.A., R.I.A., F.C.A.
Professor of Accounting
University of Manitoba

McGRAW-HILL RYERSON LIMITED
Toronto   Montreal   New York   London   Sydney   Johannesburg   Mexico
Panama   Düsseldorf   Singapore   Sao Paulo   Kuala Lumpur   New Delhi

ISBN 0-07-082420-7

    5 6 7 8 9 10 D 1 0 9 8

Printed and bound in Canada

CONTENTS

SIX CONTROL PROCEDURES IN A MERCHANDISING BUSINESS

SEVEN DATA PROCESSING SYSTEMS: MANUAL, MECHANICAL, AND ELECTRONIC

EIGHT √THE CONTROL OF CASH TRANSACTIONS

ELEVEN PLANT AND EQUIPMENT: DEPRECIATION

TWELVE PLANT AND EQUIPMENT, NATURAL RESOURCES, AND INTANGIBLES

THIR-TEEN   PAYROLL ACCOUNTING

FOUR-TEEN   √ ACCOUNTING PRINCIPLES

FIF- TEEN ✓ PARTNERSHIPS

SIX- TEEN CORPORATIONS: ORGANIZATION AND OPERATION

SEVEN-
TEEN   CORPORATIONS: EARNINGS PER SHARE, RETAINED
         EARNINGS, AND DIVIDENDS

EIGHT-
EEN CORPORATIONS: BONDS PAYABLE AND INVESTMENTS IN
CORPORATE SECURITIES

NINE-
TEEN CORPORATIONS: CONSOLIDATED STATEMENTS

TWENTY INCOME TAXES AND BUSINESS DECISIONS

TWENTY-ONE ANALYSIS AND INTERPRETATION OF FINANCIAL STATEMENTS

TWENTY-TWO STATEMENT OF CHANGES IN FINANCIAL POSITION: FUNDS FLOW ANALYSIS

TWENTY-THREE RESPONSIBILITY ACCOUNTING: DEPARTMENTS AND BRANCHES

TWENTY-FOUR ACCOUNTING FOR MANUFACTURING OPERATIONS

TWENTY-FIVE COST ACCOUNTING SYSTEMS

TWENTY-
SIX   MANAGERIAL CONTROL: STANDARD COSTS AND BUDGETING

TWENTY-
SEVEN   COST-REVENUE ANALYSIS FOR DECISION MAKING

TWENTY-
EIGHT   OTHER USES BY MANAGEMENT OF ACCOUNTING
        INFORMATION

        SOLUTIONS TO DEMONSTRATION PROBLEMS   883

APPEN-
DIX   SELECTED FINANCIAL STATEMENTS OF WELL-KNOWN
        CORPORATIONS   905

PREFACE

This second Canadian edition follows the format and structure of the latest American edition. Revisions have been made, however, throughout the text to reflect the differences in Canadian law, practice, and terminology. Accounting techniques are fairly similar in Canada and the United States because of the close commercial, cultural, and geographical ties between the two countries. Important differences do exist, nevertheless, and the author has attempted to reflect the unique Canadian characteristics in this edition.

Major revisions were required in sections dealing with notes and interest, corporations, payroll accounting and federal income taxes. Canadian law differs significantly from American law in these areas, and these chapters were re-written to agree with Canadian statutory requirements. The treatment of income taxes is based on the tax reform legislation which became law on January 1, 1972. Where applicable, American terminology and illustrations were replaced by their accepted Canadian counterparts, including extracts from the annual reports of four Canadian corporations.

The chapter on Control of Cash uses forms and illustrations of Canadian chartered banks; and the chapter on receivables uses illustrations of forms generally employed in Canada. References have been made to the published financial reports of Canadian companies in various parts of the text. Current Canadian practice is shown by references to *Financial Reporting in Canada, 1972* (ninth edition). Pronouncements in the *CICA Handbook* published by the Canadian Institute of Chartered Accountants have been quoted with the permission of the Institute to present the currently generally accepted Canadian accounting principles. In particular, the text includes the *Handbook's* recommendations on earnings per share, extraordinary gains and losses, prior period adjustments, consolidated statements and reporting of diversified operations.

Because of the strong influences of American thought on Canadian practice, certain quotations from the statements and opinions of the American Institute of Certified Public Accountants have been retained in the Canadian edition. Students should benefit from an insight into underlying accounting principles and logic which these statements provide.

I wish to acknowledge the helpful and constructive criticism received from many instructors who used the first edition of this text. Most of the improvements in this edition result from their invaluable comments. My special thanks go to Mrs. B. Ryland, my secretary, who provided very able assistance in the preparation of the manuscript.

J. DAVID BLAZOUSKE

ACCOUNTING
THE BASIS FOR
BUSINESS
DECISIONS

ONE

ACCOUNTING THE BASIS FOR BUSINESS DECISIONS

Accounting has often been called the "language of business." People in the business world—owners, managers, bankers, stockbrokers, lawyers, engineers, investors—use accounting terms and concepts to describe the events that make up the day-to-day existence of every business, large or small. Since a language is a man-made means of communication, it is natural that languages should change to meet the changing needs of society. Accounting, too, is a man-made art, one in which changes and improvements are continually being made in the process of communicating business information.

Although accounting has made its most dramatic progress in the field of business, the accounting function is vital to every unit of our society. The federal government, the provinces, the cities, the school districts: all must use accounting as a basis for controlling their resources and measuring their accomplishments. Accounting is equally essential to the successful operation of a university, a fraternity, a church, or a hospital.

In every election the voters must make decisions at the ballot box on issues involving accounting concepts; therefore, some knowledge of accounting is needed by every citizen if he is to act intelligently in meeting the challenges of our society.

THE PURPOSE AND NATURE OF ACCOUNTING

The underlying purpose of accounting is to provide financial information about any economic entity. In this book the economic entity which we shall be concentrating upon is a business enterprise. The financial information provided by an accounting system is needed by managerial decision makers to help them plan and control the activities of the economic entity. Financial information is also needed by *outsiders*—owners, creditors, investors, the government, and the public—who have supplied money to the business or who have some other interest that will be served by information about its financial position and operating results.

A SYSTEM FOR CREATING ACCOUNTING INFORMATION We have referred to the day-to-day events that make up the history of every business. For example, goods and services are purchased and sold, credit is extended to customers, debts are incurred, and cash is received and paid out. These *transactions* are typical of business events which can be expressed in money and must be entered in accounting records. The recording process may be performed in many ways: that is, by writing with pen or pencil, by printing with mechanical or electronic equipment, or by punching holes or making magnetic impressions on cards or tape.

To create accounting information in a form which will be useful to the many people who use this information, we perform three major steps. First, we *record* business events as they occur; second, we *classify* these events into groups so that the mass of detailed information will be in compact usable form; and third, we *summarize* the classified information into financial reports or *financial statements.* These financial statements are concise; perhaps only two or three pages for a large business. They summarize the business transactions of a specific time period such as a month or a year. Financial statements show the financial position of the business at the time of the report, and the operating results by which it arrived at this position.

These three steps we have described—recording, classifying, and summarizing—are the means of creating accounting information. Thus one part of accounting is a system for creating financial information.

USING ACCOUNTING INFORMATION Accounting extends beyond the process of *creating* records and reports. The ultimate objective of accounting is the *use* of this information, its analysis and interpretation. The accountant is always concerned with the significance of the figures he has produced. He looks for meaningful relationships between events and financial results; he studies the effect of various alternatives; and he searches for significant trends that may throw some light on what will happen in the future.

Interpretation and analysis are not the sole province of the accountant. If managers, investors, and creditors are to make effective use of accounting information, they too must have some understanding of how the figures were put together and what they mean. An important part of this understanding is to recognize clearly the limitations of accounting reports. A business manager, an investor, or a creditor who lacks training in accounting may fail to appreciate the extent to which accounting information is based upon estimates rather than upon precisely accurate measurements.

THE DISTINCTION BETWEEN ACCOUNTING AND BOOKKEEPING Persons with little knowledge of accounting may also fail to understand the difference between accounting and bookkeeping. *Bookkeeping* means the recording of transactions, the record-making phase of accounting. The recording of transactions tends to be mechanical and repetitive; it is only a small part of the field of accounting and probably the simplest part. *Accounting* includes the design of accounting systems, preparation of financial statements, development of budgets, cost studies, audits, income tax work, computer applications to accounting processes, and the analysis and interpretation of accounting information as an aid to making business decisions. A person might become a reasonably proficient bookkeeper in a few weeks or months; to become a professional accountant, however, requires several years of study and experience.

The work of accountants

Accountants tend to specialize in a given subarea of the discipline just as do lawyers and members of other professions. In terms of career opportunities, the field of accounting may be divided into three broad areas: (*1*) the public accounting profession, (*2*) private accounting, and (*3*) governmental accounting.

Public accounting

Public accountants are independent professional persons comparable to lawyers or physicians, who offer accounting services to clients for a fee. Regulation of public accounting is a relatively new development in Canada with only five provinces—Quebec, Ontario, Prince Edward Island, New Brunswick and Nova Scotia—licensing the practice of public accounting.

AUDITING A principal function of a public accountant is auditing. To perform an audit, the public accountant makes a careful review of the accounting system and gathers evidence both from within the business and from outside sources. This evidence enables him to issue a report expressing his professional opinion as to the fairness and reliability of the financial statements. Persons outside the business, such as bankers and investors who rely upon financial statements for information, attach great importance to the annual *audit report* by the public accountant. The *independent* status of the public accountant retained to make an annual audit is just as important as his technical competence in assuring outsiders that the financial statements prepared by management disclose all relevant information and provide a fair picture of the company's financial position and operating results.

TAX SERVICES An important element of decision-making by business executives is consideration of the income tax consequences of each alternative course of action. The public accountant is often called upon for "tax planning," which will show how a future transaction such as the acquisition of new equipment may be arranged in a manner that will hold income taxes to a minimum amount. The public accountant is also frequently retained to prepare the federal and provincial income tax returns. To render tax services, the public accountant must have extensive knowledge of tax acts, regulations, and court decisions, as well as a thorough knowledge of accounting.

MANAGEMENT ADVISORY SERVICES Auditing and income tax work have been traditional areas of expertise for public accounting firms, but the field of management advisory services has recently become a rapidly growing new area. When public accounting firms during the course of an audit discovered problems in a client's business, it was natural for them to make suggestions for corrective action. In response, the client often engaged the auditor to make a thorough investigation of the problem and to recommend new policies and procedures needed for a solution.

Public accounting firms gradually found themselves becoming more involved in management consulting work. Although this work often concerned accounting and financial matters, sometimes it dealt with organizational structure, statistical research, and a wide variety of problems not closely related to accounting. In recent years many public accounting firms have created separate management advisory service departments which are staffed with mathematicians, industrial engineers, and other specialists as well as accountants. The experience, reputation, and independence of the public accounting firms have placed them in an advantageous position to render advisory services to management over a broad range of administrative and operating problems. For example, these services might include study of the desirability of a merger with another company, the creation of a pension plan for employees, or the researching of a foreign market for the company's products.

In Canada, a number of professional accounting societies exist to maintain a high level of professional competency and ethical practice. Two leading public accounting groups are the Institutes of Chartered Accountants (whose members are entitled to the designation C.A.) and the Certified General Accountants Associations (C.G.A.). Not all members of these two associations are engaged in public accounting. Approximately fifty per cent of all Chartered Accountants and eighty per cent of all Certified General Accountants are employed in industry, government and other institutions. The Societies of Industrial Accountants offer a program of studies to prepare their students for positions as accountants in industry and government. Their registered members are entitled to the designation R.I.A. (Registered Industrial Accountant).

Private accounting

In contrast to the accountant in public practice who serves many clients, an accountant in private industry is employed by a single enterprise. The chief accounting officer of a medium-sized or large business is usually called the *controller,* in recognition of the fact that one of the primary uses of accounting data is to aid in controlling business operations. The controller manages the work of the accounting staff. He is also a part of the management team charged with the task of running the business, setting its objectives, and seeing that these objectives are met.

The accountants in a private business, large or small, must record transactions and prepare periodic financial statements from accounting records. Within this area of general accounting, or in addition to it, a number of specialized phases of accounting have developed. Among the more important of these are:

DESIGN OF ACCOUNTING SYSTEMS Although the same basic accounting principles are applicable to all types of businesses, each enterprise requires an individually tailored *financial information system.* This system includes accounting forms, records, instruction manuals, flow charts, programs, and reports to fit the particular needs of the business. Designing an accounting system and putting it into operation are thus specialized phases of accounting. With the advent of electronic data processing equipment, the problems that arise in creating an effective financial information system have become increasingly complex. However, computers compile information that would be too costly to gather by hand methods and also increase the speed with which reports can be made available to management.

COST ACCOUNTING Knowing the cost of a particular product, a manufacturing process, or any business operation is vital to the efficient management of that business. The phase of accounting particularly concerned with collecting and interpreting cost data has come to be known as *cost accounting.* Determining the cost of anything is not as simple as it appears at first glance, because the term *cost* has many meanings and different kinds of costs are useful for different purposes.

BUDGETING A budget is a plan of financial operations for some future period, expressed in monetary terms. By using a budget, management is able to make comparisons between *planned operations* and the *actual results achieved.* A budget is thus an attempt to preview operating results before the actual transactions have taken place. A budget is a particularly valuable tool in the controller's kit because it provides each division of the business with a specific goal, and because it gives management a means of measuring the efficiency of performance throughout the company.

TAX ACCOUNTING   As income tax rates have gone up and the determination of taxable income has become more complex, both internal accountants and independent public accountants have devoted more time to the problems of taxation. Tax accounting includes planning business operations in order to minimize the impact of taxes, as well as computing taxable income and preparing tax returns. The term *tax avoidance* includes all legal means of minimizing tax payments; the term *tax evasion* indicates illegal actions. Business managers have the responsibility of operating a business profitably and should therefore have an obligation to plan operations with the objective of *avoiding* income taxes. Although many companies rely largely on public accounting firms for tax planning and the preparation of tax returns, larger companies also maintain their own tax departments.

INTERNAL AUDITING   Most large corporations maintain staffs of internal auditors with the responsibility of seeing that company policies and established procedures are being followed consistently in all divisions of the corporation. The internal auditor, in contrast to the independent or external auditor, is not responsible for determining the overall fairness of the company's annual financial statements.

MANAGEMENT ACCOUNTING   We have already discussed the way business concerns sometimes call upon public accounting firms to render management advisory services. In larger companies, however, we can also recognize *management accounting* as a specialized field of work by the company's own accounting staff. First, we need to emphasize that the accounting system provides information for both external and internal use. The external reporting function of the accounting system has already been touched upon in our discussion of audits of annual financial statements by public accounting firms. The internal reporting function of an accounting system gives managers information needed in planning and controlling day-to-day operations; it also gives managers information needed for long-range planning and for major decisions such as the introduction of a new product or the closing of an older plant.

Management accounting utilizes the techniques of both cost accounting and budgeting to achieve its goal of helping executives formulate both short-range and long-range plans, to measure success in carrying out these plans, to identify problems requiring executive attention, and to choose among the alternative methods of attaining company objectives. At every organizational level of a company, specific problems arise for which accounting information is needed to help define the problem, identify alternative courses of action, and make a choice among these alternatives.

Governmental accounting

Government officials rely on financial information to help them direct the affairs of their agencies just as do the executives of private corporations. Accountants are employed by government to prepare budgets, to audit the accounting records of various government departments, and to examine the millions of income tax returns filed by individuals and corporations. Accountants are also employed by provincial securities commissions to make a critical review of the financial statements of corporations which offer securities for sale to the public. Every agency of government at every level (federal, provincial, and local) must have accountants to carry out its responsibilities.

Research in accounting

Research to develop accounting principles and practices which will keep pace with changes in the economic and political environment is a major activity of professional accountants and accounting educators. The Canadian Institute of Chartered Accountants leads the way with an extensive research program dedicated to improvement in financial reporting and accounting practices. The Society of Industrial Accountants of Canada has an equally extensive research program in management accounting. A large number of important research studies have been issued as a result of this program. In brief, accounting is not a closed system or a fixed set of rules, but a constantly evolving body of knowledge. As we explore accounting principles and related practices in this book, you will become aware of certain problems and conflicts for which fully satisfactory answers are yet to be developed. The need for further research is apparent despite the fact that present-day Canadian accounting practices and standards of financial reporting are equal to those achieved anywhere at any time.

Two primary business objectives

The management of every business must keep foremost in its thinking two primary objectives. The first is to earn a profit. The second is to have on hand sufficient funds to pay debts as they fall due. Profits and solvency are of course not the only objectives of businessmen. There are many others, such as providing jobs for people, creating new and improved products, providing more goods and services at a lower cost. It is clear, however, that a business cannot hope to accomplish these things unless it meets the two basic tests of survival—operating profitably and staying solvent.

A business is a collection of resources committed by an individual or group of individuals, who hope that the investment will increase in value. Investment in any given business, however, is only one of a number of alternative investments available. If a business does not earn as great a profit as might be obtained from alternative investments, its owners will be well-advised to sell or terminate the business and invest elsewhere. A firm that continually operates at a loss will quickly exhaust its resources and be forced out of existence. Therefore, in order to operate successfully and to survive, the owners or managers of an enterprise must direct the business in such a way that it will earn a reasonable profit.

Business concerns that have sufficient funds to pay their debts promptly are said to be *solvent.* In contrast, a firm that finds itself unable to meet its obligations as they fall due is called *insolvent.* Solvency must also be ranked as a primary objective of any enterprise, since a firm that is insolvent may be forced by its creditors to close its doors.

Accounting as the basis for management decisions

How does a business executive know whether his company is earning profits or incurring losses? How does he know whether the company is solvent or insolvent, and whether it will probably be solvent, say, a month from today? The answer to both these questions in one word is *accounting.* Not only is accounting the process by which the profitability and solvency of a company can be measured, but it provides information needed as a basis for making business decisions that will enable management to guide the company on a profitable and solvent course.

Stated simply, managing a business is a matter of deciding what should be done, seeing to it that the means are available, and getting people employed in the business to do it. At every step in this process management is faced with alternatives, and every decision to do something or to refrain from doing something involves a choice. Successful managers must make the right choice when "the chips are down." In most cases the probability that a good decision will be made depends on the amount and validity of the information that the manager has about the alternatives and their consequences. It is seldom that all the information needed is either available or obtainable. Often a crystal ball in good working order would be helpful. As a practical matter, however, information which flows from the accounting records, or which can be developed by special analysis of accounting data, constitutes the basis on which a wide variety of business decisions should be made.

What price should the firm set on its products? If production is increased, what effect will this have on the cost of each unit produced? Will it be necessary to borrow from the bank? How much will costs increase if a pension plan is established for employees? Is it more profitable to produce and sell product A or product B? Shall a given part be made or be bought from suppliers? Should an investment be made in new equipment? All these issues call for decisions that should depend, in part at least, upon accounting information. It might be reasonable to turn the question around and ask: What business decisions could be intelligently made without the use of accounting information? Examples would be hard to find.

In large-scale business undertakings such as the manufacture of automobiles or the operation of nationwide chains of retail stores, and even in enterprises much smaller than these, the top executives cannot possibly have close physical contact with and knowledge of the details of operations. Consequently, these executives must depend to an even greater extent than the small businessman upon information provided by the accounting system.

We have already stressed that accounting is a means of measuring the results of business transactions and of communicating financial information. In addition, the accounting system must provide the decision-maker with *predictive information* for making important business decisions in a changing world.

Internal control

Throughout this book, the fact that business decisions of all types are based at least in part on accounting data is emphasized. Management, therefore, needs assurance that the accounting data it receives are accurate and dependable. This assurance is provided in large part by developing a strong system of *internal control.* A system of internal control comprises all the measures taken by an organization for the purpose of (1) protecting its resources against waste, fraud, and inefficiency; (2) ensuring accuracy and reliability in accounting and operating data; (3) securing compliance with company policies; and (4) evaluating the level of performance in all divisions of the company.

When a public accountant conducts an audit of a company, he will judge the adequacy of internal control in each area of the company's operations. The stronger the system of internal control, the more confidence the public accountant can place in the integrity of the company's financial statements and accounting records. Consequently his audit work can be performed more rapidly, with less detailed investigation of transactions, when internal controls are strong. The internal auditor also regards the study of internal control as a major part of his work. If internal controls are weak, the usual consequences are waste, fraud, inefficiency, and unprofitable operations.

A basic principle of internal control is that no one person should handle all phases of a transaction from beginning to end. When business operations are so organized that two or more employees are required to participate in every transaction, the work of one employee gives proof of the accuracy of the work of another.

FINANCIAL STATEMENTS:
THE STARTING POINT IN THE STUDY OF ACCOUNTING

The preparation of financial statements is not the first step in the accounting process, but it is a convenient point to begin the study of accounting. The financial statements are the means of conveying to management and to interested outsiders a concise picture of the profitability and financial condition of the business. Since these statements are in a sense the end product of the accounting process, the student who acquires a clear understanding of the content and meaning of financial statements will be in an excellent position to appreciate the purpose of the earlier steps of recording and classifying business transactions.

There are two major financial statements, the *balance sheet* and the *income statement.* Together, these two statements (perhaps a page each in length) summarize all the information contained in the hundreds or thousands of pages comprising the detailed accounting records of a business. In this introductory chapter and in Chapter 2, we shall explore the nature of the balance sheet, or statement of financial condition, as it is sometimes called. Once we have become familiar with the form and arrangement of the balance sheet and with the meaning of technical terms such as *assets, liabilities,* and *owner's equity,* it will be as easy to read and understand a report on the financial condition of a business as it is for an architect to read the blueprint of a proposed building.

The balance sheet

The purpose of a balance sheet is to show the financial condition of a business at a particular date. Every business prepares a balance sheet at the end of the year, and many concerns prepare one at the end of each month. A balance sheet consists of a listing of the assets and liabilities of a business and of the owner's equity. The following balance sheet portrays the financial condition of the Westside Cleaning Shop at December 31.

WESTSIDE CLEANING SHOP
Balance Sheet
December 31, 19___

Assets		Liabilities & Owner's Equity	
Cash	$ 6,500	Liabilities:	
Accounts receivable	3,000	Notes payable	$ 6,000
Land	7,000	Accounts payable	4,000
Building	15,000	Total liabilities	$10,000
Office equipment	1,000	Owner's equity:	
Delivery equipment	2,500	J. R. Crane, capital	25,000
	$35,000		$35,000

Balance sheet shows financial condition at a specific date

Note that the balance sheet sets forth in its heading three items: (1) the name of the business (2) the name of the statement "Balance Sheet," and (3) the date of the balance sheet. Below the heading is the body of the balance sheet, which consists of three distinct elements: assets, liabilities, and the owner's equity. The remainder of this chapter is largely devoted to making clear the nature of these three elements.

THE BUSINESS ENTITY The illustrated balance sheet refers only to the financial affairs of the business entity known as Westside Cleaning Shop and not to the personal financial affairs of the owner, J. R. Crane. Crane may have a personal bank account, a home, a car, a cattle ranch, and other property, but since these personal belongings are not a part of his cleaning shop business, they are not included in the balance sheet of this business unit.

In brief, *a business entity is an economic unit which enters into business transactions that must be recorded, summarized, and reported.* The entity is regarded as separate from its owner or owners; the entity owns its own property and has its own debts. Consequently, for each business entity, there should be a separate set of accounting records. A balance sheet and an income statement are intended to portray the financial condition and the operating results of a single business entity. If the owner intermingles his personal affairs with the transactions of the business, the resulting financial statements will be misleading and will fail to describe the business fairly.

If a man owns two businesses, such as a drive-in theater and a drug-store, he should have a completely separate set of accounting records for each. Separate financial statements should also be prepared for each business, thus providing information on the financial condition and profitability of each venture.

The principal forms of business organization are the single proprietorship, partnership, and corporation. A *single proprietorship* is a business owned by one person; a *partnership* is a business owned by two or more persons under a contractual arrangement. A *corporation* is a separate legal entity formed in accordance with provincial or federal statutes; its ownership is divided into transferable shares of stock which may be distributed among a very large number of owners or stockholders. In the first several chapters of this book, our study of basic accounting concepts will use as a model the single proprietorship, which is the simplest and most common form of business organization.

Assets

Assets are economic resources which are owned by a business and are expected to benefit future operations. Assets may have definite physical form such as buildings, machinery, or merchandise. On the other hand, some assets exist not in physical or tangible form, but in the form of valuable legal claims or rights; examples are amounts due from customers, investments in government bonds, and patent rights.

One of the most basic, and at the same time most controversial, problems in accounting is the assignment of dollar values to the assets of a business. Two kinds of assets cause little difficulty. Cash and amounts due from customers represent assets that either are available for expenditure or will be in the near future (when the customers pay their accounts). The amount of cash on hand is a clear statement of the dollars that are available for expenditure. The amount that customers owe the business (after taking into account that some receivables may prove uncollectible) represents the dollars that will be received in the near future.

Other assets such as land, buildings, merchandise, and equipment represent economic resources that will be used in producing income for the business. The prevailing accounting view is that such assets should be accounted for on the basis of the dollars that have been invested in these resources, that is, the *historical cost* incurred in acquiring such property or property rights. In recording a business transaction, it is the transaction price that establishes the accounting value for the property or service received. In accounting terms, therefore, the "value" or "valuation" of an asset ordinarily means the cost of that asset to the entity owning it.

For example, let us assume that a business buys a tract of land for use as a building site, paying $40,000 in cash. The amount to be entered in the accounting records as the value of the asset will be the cost of $40,000. If we assume a booming real estate market, a fair estimate of the sales value of the land 10 years later might be $100,000. Although the market price or economic value of the land has risen greatly, the accounting value as shown in the accounting records and on the balance sheet would continue unchanged at the cost of $40,000. This policy of accounting for assets at their cost is often referred to as the *cost principle* of accounting.

In reading a balance sheet, it is important to bear in mind that the dollar amounts listed do not indicate the prices at which the assets could be sold, nor the prices at which they could be replaced. One useful generalization to be drawn from this discussion is that a balance sheet does not show "how much a business is worth."

WHY SHOW ASSETS AT COST RATHER THAN PRESENT MARKET VALUE? It is appropriate to ask *why* accountants do not change the recorded values of assets to correspond with changing market prices for these properties. One reason is that the land and building used to house the business are acquired for use and not for resale; in fact, these assets cannot be sold without disrupting the business. The balance sheet of a business is prepared on the assumption that the business is a continuing enterprise, a "going concern." Consequently, the present estimated prices at which the land and buildings could be sold are of less importance than if these properties were intended for sale.

Another reason for using cost rather than market values in accounting for assets is the need for a definite, factual basis. The cost of land, buildings, and many other assets purchased for cash can be rather definitely determined. Estimated market values, on the other hand, for assets such as buildings and specialized machinery are not factual and definite. Market values are constantly changing and are largely a matter of personal opinion; of course at the date of acquisition of an asset, cost and value are ordinarily the same because the buyer would not pay more than the asset was worth and the seller would not take less than current market value. The bargaining process which results in a sale serves to establish both the current market value of the property and the cost to the buyer. With the passage of time, however, the current market value of assets is likely to differ considerably from the cost recorded in the owner's accounting records.

The decline in the purchasing power of the dollar in recent years has raised serious doubts as to the adequacy of the conventional cost basis in accounting for assets. Proposals for adjusting recorded dollar amounts to reflect changes in the value of the dollar, as shown by a price index, are receiving increasing attention.[1] Balance sheets showing assets at current appraised values rather than at historical cost are also being advocated by some accountants. Accounting concepts are not as exact and unchanging as many persons assume; to serve the needs of a fast-changing economy, accounting concepts and methods must also undergo continuous evolutionary change. As of today, however, the cost basis of valuing assets is still in almost universal use.

The problem of valuation of assets is one of the most complex in the entire field of accounting. It is merely being introduced at this point; in later chapters we shall explore carefully some of the valuation principles applicable to the major types of assets.

Liabilities

Liabilities are debts. All business concerns have liabilities; even the largest and most successful companies find it convenient to purchase merchandise and supplies on credit rather than to pay cash at the time of each purchase. The liability arising from the purchase of goods or services on credit (on time) is called an *account payable,* and the person or company to whom the account payable is owed is called a *creditor.*

A business concern frequently finds it desirable to borrow money as a means of supplementing the funds invested by the owner, thus enabling the business to expand more rapidly. The borrowed funds may, for example, be used to buy merchandise which can be sold at a profit to the firm's customers. Or, the borrowed money might be used to buy new and more efficient machinery, thus enabling the company to turn out a larger volume of products at lower cost. When a business borrows money for any reason, a liability is incurred and the lender becomes a creditor of the business. The form of the liability when money is borrowed is usually a *note payable,* a formal written promise to pay a certain amount of money, plus interest, at a definite future time. An *account payable,* as

[1] See *Financial Statements Restated for General Price-Level Changes,* Statement No. 3 of the Accounting Principles Board, American Institute of Certified Public Accountants, June, 1969, New York.

contrasted with a *note payable,* does not involve the issuance of a formal written promise to the creditor, and it does not call for payment of interest. When a business has both notes payable and accounts payable, the two types of liabilities are shown separately in the balance sheet. The sequence in which these two liabilities are listed is not important, although notes payable are usually shown as the first item among the liabilities. A figure showing the total of the liabilities may also be inserted, as shown by the illustrated balance sheet on page 10.

The creditors have claims against the assets of the business, usually not against any particular asset but against the assets in general. The claims of the creditors are liabilities of the business and have priority over the claims of owners. Creditors are entitled to be paid in full even if such payment should exhaust the assets of the business, leaving nothing for the owner. The issue of valuation, which poses so many difficulties in accounting for assets, is a much smaller problem in the case of liabilities, because the amounts of most liabilities are specified by contract.

Owner's equity

The owner's equity in a business represents the resources invested by the owner; it is equal to the total assets minus the liabilities. The equity of the owner is a residual claim; as the owner of the business he is entitled to whatever remains after the claims of the creditors are fully satisfied. For example:

The Westside Cleaning Shop has total assets of	*$35,000*
And total liabilities amounting to	*10,000*
Therefore, the owner's equity must equal	*$25,000*

Suppose that the Westside Cleaning Shop borrows $1,000 from a bank. After recording the additional asset of $1,000 in cash and recording the new liability of $1,000 owed to the bank, we would have the following:

The Westside Cleaning Shop now has total assets of	*$36,000*
And total liabilities are now	*11,000*
Therefore, the owner's equity still is equal to	*$25,000*

It is apparent that the total assets of the business were increased by the act of borrowing money from a bank, but the increase in assets was exactly offset by an increase in liabilities, and the owner's equity remained unchanged. The owner's equity in a business is not increased by borrowing from banks or other creditors.

The owner's equity in a business comes from two sources:

1 Investment by the owner
2 Earnings from profitable operation of the business

Only the first of these two sources of owner's equity is considered in this chapter. The second source, an increase in owner's equity through earnings of the business, will be discussed in Chapter 3.

The accounting equation

One of the fundamental characteristics of every balance sheet is that the total figure for assets always equals the total figure for liabilities and owner's equity. This agreement or balance of total assets with total equities is one reason for calling this statement of financial condition a *balance sheet.* But *why* do total assets equal total equities? The answer can be given in one short paragraph, as follows:

The dollar totals on the two sides of the balance sheet are always equal because these two sides are merely two views of the same business property. The listing of assets shows us what things the business owns; the listing of liabilities and owner's equity tells us who supplied these resources to the business and how much each group supplied. Everything that a business owns has been supplied to it by the creditors or by the owner. Therefore, the total claims of the creditors plus the claim of the owner equal the total assets of the business.

The equality of assets on the one hand and of the claims of the creditors and the owner on the other hand is expressed in the equation:

Fundamental accounting equation

Assets   =   Liabilities + Owner's Equity
$35,000 = $10,000   + $25,000

The amounts listed in the equation were taken from the balance sheet illustrated on page 10. A balance sheet is nothing more than a detailed statement of this equation. To emphasize this relationship, compare the balance sheet of the Westside Cleaning Shop with the above equation.

To emphasize that the equity of the owner is a residual element, secondary to the claims of creditors, it is often helpful to transpose the terms of the equation, as follows:

Alternative form of equation

Assets − Liabilities = Owner's Equity
$35,000 − $10,000 = $25,000

Every business transaction, no matter how simple or how complex, can be expressed in terms of its effect on the accounting equation. A thorough understanding of the equation and some practice in using it are essential to the student of accounting.

Regardless of whether a business grows or contracts, this equality between the assets and the claims against the assets is always maintained. Any increase in the amount of total assets is necessarily accompanied by an equal increase on the other side of the equation, that is, by an increase in either the liabilities or the owner's equity. Any decrease in total assets is necessarily accompanied by a corresponding decrease in liabilities or owner's equity. The continuing equality of the two sides of the balance sheet can best be illustrated by taking a brand-new business as an example and observing the effects of various transactions upon its balance sheet.

Effects of business transactions upon the balance sheet

Assume that James Roberts, a real estate broker, decided to start a real estate business of his own, to be known as the Roberts Real Estate Agency. The operations of the business consist of obtaining listings of houses being offered for sale by owners, advertising these houses, and showing them to prospective buyers. The listing agreement signed with each owner provides that the Roberts Real Estate Agency shall receive at the time of sale a commission equal to 6% of the sales price of a house sold.

The new business was begun on September 1, when Roberts deposited $20,000 in a bank account in the name of the business, the Roberts Real Estate Agency. The initial balance sheet of the new business then appeared as follows:

Beginning balance sheet of a new business

ROBERTS REAL ESTATE AGENCY
Balance Sheet
September 1, 19___

Assets		Owner's Equity	
Cash	$20,000	James Roberts, capital	$20,000

Observe that the equity of the owner in the assets is designated on the balance sheet by the caption, James Roberts, capital. The word *capital* is the traditional accounting term used in describing the equity of the proprietor in the assets of the business.

PURCHASE OF AN ASSET FOR CASH The next transaction entered into by the Roberts Real Estate Agency was the purchase of land suitable as a site for an office. The price for the land was $7,000 and payment was made in cash on September 3. The effect of this transaction on the balance sheet was twofold: first, cash was decreased by the amount paid out; and second, a new asset, Land, was acquired. After this exchange of cash for land, the balance sheet appeared as follows:

Balance sheet totals unchanged by purchase of land for cash

ROBERTS REAL ESTATE AGENCY
Balance Sheet
September 3, 19___

Assets		Owner's Equity	
Cash	$13,000	James Roberts, capital	$20,000
Land	7,000		
	$20,000		$20,000

PURCHASE OF AN ASSET AND INCURRING OF A LIABILITY On September 5 an opportunity arose to buy from OK Distributors a complete office building which had to be moved to permit the construction of a freeway. A price of $12,000 was agreed upon, which included the cost of moving the building and installing it upon the Roberts Agency's lot. As the building was in excellent condition and would have cost approximately $20,000 to build, Roberts considered this a very fortunate purchase.

The terms provided for an immediate cash payment of $5,000 and payment of the balance of $7,000 within 90 days. Cash was decreased $5,000, but a new asset, Building, was recorded at cost in the amount of $12,000. Total assets were thus increased by $7,000 but the total of liabilities and owner's equity was also increased as a result of recording the $7,000 account payable as a liability. After this transaction had been recorded, the balance sheet appeared as shown below. Notice that cash is always the first asset listed on a balance sheet.

ROBERTS REAL ESTATE AGENCY

Balance Sheet

September 5, 19___

	Assets		Liabilities & Owner's Equity	
Totals	Cash	$ 8,000	Liabilities:	
increased	Land	7,000	Accounts payable	$ 7,000
equally	Building	12,000	Owner's equity:	
by			James Roberts, capital	20,000
purchase				
on credit		$27,000		$27,000

Note that the building appears in the balance sheet at $12,000, its cost to the Roberts Real Estate Agency. The estimate of $20,000 as the probable cost to construct such a building is irrelevant. Even if someone should offer to buy the building from the Roberts Agency for $20,000 or more, this offer, if refused, would have no bearing on the balance sheet. Accounting records are intended to provide an historical record of *costs actually incurred;* therefore, the $12,000 price at which the building was purchased is the amount to be recorded.

SALE OF AN ASSET After the office building had been moved to the Roberts Agency's lot, Roberts decided that the lot was much larger than was needed. The adjoining business, Carter's Drugstore, wanted more room for a parking area so, on September 10, the Roberts Agency sold the unused part of the lot to Carter's Drugstore for a price of $2,000. Since the sales price was computed at the same amount per foot as the Roberts Agency had paid for the land, there was neither a profit nor a loss on the sale. No down payment was required but it was agreed that the full price would be paid within three months. By this transaction a new asset, Accounts Receivable, was acquired, but the asset Land was decreased by the same amount; consequently, there was no change in the amount of total assets. After this transaction, the balance sheet appeared as follows:

ROBERTS REAL ESTATE AGENCY
Balance Sheet
September 10, 19___

		Assets			Liabilities & Owner's Equity	
No change in totals	Cash	$ 8,000		Liabilities:		
by sale	Accounts receivable	2,000		Accounts payable	$ 7,000	
of land at cost	Land	5,000		Owner's equity:		
	Building	12,000		James Roberts, capital	20,000	
		$27,000			$27,000	

In the illustration thus far, the Roberts Real Estate Agency has an account receivable from only one debtor, and an account payable to only one creditor. As the business grows, the number of debtors and creditors will increase, but the Accounts Receivable and Accounts Payable designations will continue to be used. The additional records necessary to show the amount receivable from each debtor and the amount owing to each creditor will be explained in Chapter 7.

PURCHASE OF AN ASSET ON CREDIT A complete set of office furniture and equipment was purchased on credit from General Equipment Ltd., on September 14. The amount of the transaction was $1,800, and it was agreed that payment should be made later. As the result of this transaction the business owned a new asset, Office Equipment, but it had also incurred a new liability in the form of Accounts Payable. The increase in total assets was exactly offset by the increase in liabilities. After this transaction the balance sheet appeared as follows:

ROBERTS REAL ESTATE AGENCY
Balance Sheet
September 14, 19___

		Assets			Liabilities & Owner's Equity	
Totals increased	Cash	$ 8,000		Liabilities:		
by	Accounts receivable	2,000		Accounts payable	$ 8,800	
acquiring asset on	Land	5,000		Owner's equity:		
credit	Building	12,000		James Roberts, capital	20,000	
	Office equipment	1,800				
		$28,800			$28,800	

COLLECTION OF AN ACCOUNT RECEIVABLE On September 20, cash in the amount of $500 was received as partial settlement of the account receivable from Carter's Drugstore. This transaction caused cash to increase and the accounts receivable to decrease by an equal amount. In essence, this transaction was merely the exchange of one asset for another of equal value. Consequently, there was no change in the amount of total assets. After this transaction, the balance sheet appeared as shown below:

ROBERTS REAL ESTATE AGENCY

Balance Sheet

September 20, 19___

		Assets		Liabilities & Owner's Equity	
Totals	Cash	$ 8,500	Liabilities:		
unchanged by	Accounts receivable	1,500	Accounts payable	$ 8,800	
collection	Land	5,000	Owner's equity:		
of an account	Building	12,000	James Roberts, capital	20,000	
receivable	Office equipment	1,800			
		$28,800		$28,800	

PAYMENT OF A LIABILITY On September 30 Roberts paid $1,000 in cash to General Equipment Ltd. This payment caused a decrease in cash and an equal decrease in liabilities. Therefore the totals of assets and equities were still in balance. After this transaction, the balance sheet appeared as follows:

ROBERTS REAL ESTATE AGENCY

Balance Sheet

September 30, 19___

		Assets		Liabilities & Owner's Equity	
Totals	Cash	$ 7,500	Liabilities:		
decreased	Accounts receivable	1,500	Accounts payable	$ 7,800	
by paying					
a liability	Land	5,000	Owner's equity:		
	Building	12,000	James Roberts, capital	20,000	
	Office equipment	1,800			
		$27,800		$27,800	

The transactions which have been illustrated for the month of September were merely preliminary to the formal opening for business of the Roberts Real Estate Agency on October 1. Since we have assumed that the business earned no commissions and incurred no expenses during September, the owner's equity at September 30 is shown in the above balance sheet at $20,000, unchanged from the original investment by Roberts on September 1. September was a month devoted exclusively to organizing the business and not to regular operations. In succeeding chapters we shall continue the example of the Roberts Real Estate Agency by illustrating operating transactions and considering how the net income of the business is determined.

Effect of business transactions upon the accounting equation

A balance sheet is merely a detailed expression of the accounting equation, Assets = Liabilities + Owner's Equity. To emphasize the relationship between the accounting equation and the balance sheet, let us now repeat the September transactions of Roberts Real Estate Agency to show the effect of each transaction upon the accounting equation. Briefly restated, the seven transactions were as follows:

Sept. 1 Began the business by depositing $20,000 in a company bank account.

3 Purchased land for $7,000 cash.

5 Purchased a building for $12,000, paying $5,000 cash and incurring a liability of $7,000.

10 Sold part of the land at a price equal to cost of $2,000, collectible within three months.

14 Purchased office equipment on credit for $1,800.

20 Received $500 cash as partial collection of the $2,000 account receivable.

30 Paid $1,000 on accounts payable.

In the table below, each transaction is identified by date; its effect on the accounting equation and also the new balance of each item are shown. Each of the lines labeled Balances contains the same items as the balance sheet previously illustrated for the particular date. The final

	Assets					=	Liabil-ities	+	Owner's Equity
	Cash	+ Accounts Receiv-able	+ Land	+ Building	+ Office Equip-ment	= Accounts Payable		+	James Roberts, Capital
Sept. 1	+$20,000								+$20,000
Sept. 3	−7,000		+$7,000						
Balances	$13,000		$7,000						$20,000
Sept. 5	−5,000			+$12,000		+$7,000			
Balances	$ 8,000		$7,000	$12,000		$7,000			$20,000
Sept. 10		+$2,000	−2,000						
Balances	$ 8,000	$2,000	$5,000	$12,000		$7,000			$20,000
Sept. 14					+$1,800	+1,800			
Balances	$ 8,000	$2,000	$5,000	$12,000	$1,800	$8,800			$20,000
Sept. 20	+500	−500							
Balances	$ 8,500	$1,500	$5,000	$12,000	$1,800	$8,800			$20,000
Sept. 30	−1,000					−1,000			
Balances	$ 7,500 +	$1,500 +	$5,000 +	$12,000 +	$1,800 =	$7,800		+	$20,000

line in the table corresponds to the amounts in the balance sheet at the end of September. Note that the equality of the two sides of the equation was maintained throughout the recording of the transactions.

USE OF FINANCIAL STATEMENTS BY OUTSIDERS

Through careful study of financial statements, it is possible for the outsider with training in accounting to obtain a fairly complete understanding of the financial condition of the business and to become aware of significant changes that have occurred since the date of the preceding balance sheet. Bear in mind, however, that financial statements have limitations. As stated earlier, only those factors which can be reduced to monetary terms appear in the balance sheet. Let us consider for a moment some important business factors which are not set forth in financial statements. Some companies have a record of good relations with labor unions, freedom from strikes, and mutual respect between management and employees. Other companies have been plagued by frequent and costly labor disputes. The relationship between a company and a union of its employees is certainly an important factor in the successful operation of the business, but it is not mentioned in the balance sheet. Perhaps a new competing store has just opened for business across the street; the prospect of intensified competition in the future will not be described in the balance sheet.

Bankers and other creditors

Bankers who have loaned money to a business concern or who are considering making such a loan will be vitally interested in the balance sheet of the business. By studying the amount and kinds of assets in relation to the amount and payment dates of the liabilities, a banker can form an opinion as to the ability of the business to pay its debts promptly. The banker gives particular attention to the amount of cash and of other assets (such as accounts receivable) which will soon be converted into cash; he compares the amount of these assets with the amount of liabilities falling due in the near future. The banker is also interested in the amount of the owner's equity, as this ownership capital serves as a protecting buffer between the banker and any losses which may befall the business. Bankers are seldom, if ever, willing to make a loan unless the balance sheet and other information concerning the prospective borrower offer reasonable assurance that the loan can and will be repaid promptly at the maturity date.

Another important group making constant use of balance sheets consists of the credit managers of manufacturing and wholesaling firms, who must decide whether prospective customers are to be allowed to buy merchandise on credit. The credit manager, like the banker, studies the balance sheets of his customers for the purpose of appraising their debt-paying ability. Credit agencies such as Dun & Bradstreet Ltd., make a business of obtaining financial statements from virtually all business concerns and appraising their debt-paying ability. The conclusions reached by these credit agencies are available to businessmen willing to pay for credit reports about prospective customers.

Others interested in financial information

In addition to owners, managers, bankers, and merchandise creditors, other groups making use of accounting data include governmental agencies, employees, investors, and writers for business periodicals. Some very large corporations have more than a million stockholders; these giant corporations send copies of their annual financial statements to each of these many owners. In recent years there has been a definite trend toward wider distribution of financial statements to all interested persons, in contrast to the attitude of a generation or more ago when many companies regarded their financial statements as confidential matter.

The purpose of this discussion is to show the extent to which a modern industrial society depends upon accounting. Even more important, however, is a clear understanding at the outset of your study that accounting does not exist just for the sake of keeping a record or in order to fill out government payroll forms, income tax returns, and various other regulatory reports. These are but auxiliary functions. If you gain an understanding of accounting concepts, you will have acquired an analytical skill essential to the field of professional management. *The prime and vital purpose of accounting is to aid in the choice among alternatives that faces every decision-maker in the business world.*

DEMONSTRATION PROBLEM FOR YOUR REVIEW

An alphabetical list of the various items showing the financial condition of Wilson Company at September 30 appears below. Although the figure for the owner's equity is not given, it can be determined when all the items are arranged in the form of a balance sheet.

Accounts payable	$18,100	Land	$24,000
Accounts receivable	16,400	Notes payable	35,000
Building	39,200	Notes receivable	1,400
Cash	8,500	Office equipment	4,800
Delivery truck	3,000	Ralph Wilson, capital	?

On October 1, the following transactions occurred:
(1) Accounts payable of $8,000 were paid.
(2) The owner, Ralph Wilson, invested an additional $5,000 cash in the business.
(3) Office equipment was purchased at a cost of $1,000 to be paid for within

10 days. This equipment was almost new and was purchased from a lawyer who was closing his office to accept a political appointment overseas. The equipment would have cost $1,500 if purchased through regular channels.
(4) One-quarter of the land was sold at cost. The buyer gave his promissory note for $6,000 due in 30 days. (Interest applicable to the note is to be ignored.)

Instructions
a Prepare a balance sheet at September 30, 19___ .
b Prepare a balance sheet at October 1, 19___ .

QUESTIONS

1 Why is a knowledge of accounting terms and concepts useful to persons other than professional accountants?

2 In broad general terms, what is the purpose of accounting?

3 What is meant by the term *business transaction?*

4 Distinguish between bookkeeping and accounting.

5 What are financial statements and how do they relate to the accounting system?

6 Distinguish between public accounting and private accounting.

7 In general terms, what are the requirements to become a public accountant?

8 What is the principal function of a public accountant? What other services are commonly rendered by a public accountant?

9 Private accounting includes a number of subfields or specialized phases, of which cost accounting is one. Name five other such specialized phases of private accounting.

10 One primary objective of every business is to operate profitably. What other primary objective must be met for a business to survive? Explain.

11 Not all the significant happenings in the life of a business can be expressed in monetary terms and entered in the accounting records. List two examples of significant events affecting a business which could not be satisfactorily measured and entered in its accounting records.

12 Information available from the accounting records provides a basis for making many business decisions. List five examples of business decisions requiring the use of accounting information.

13 State briefly the purpose of a balance sheet.

14 Define assets. List five examples.

15 Define liabilities. List two examples.

16 Roger Kent, owner of the Kent Store, was offered $100,000 for the land and buildings occupied by his business. He had acquired these assets five years ago at a price of $75,000. Kent refused the offer of $100,000 but is inclined to believe that the land and buildings should be listed at the higher valuation on the balance sheet in order to show more accurately "how much the business is worth." Do you agree? Explain.

17 Explain briefly the concept of the business entity.

18 State the accounting equation in two alternative forms.

19 State precisely what information is contained in the heading of a balance sheet.

20 The owner's equity in a business arises from what two sources?

21 Why are the total assets shown on a balance sheet always equal to the total of the liabilities and the owner's equity?

22 Can a business transaction cause one asset to increase or decrease without affecting any other asset, liability, or the owner's equity?

23 If a transaction causes total liabilities to decrease but does not affect the owner's equity, what change, if any, will occur in total assets?

EXERCISES

Ex. 1-1 *a* The assets of Atom Company total $160,000 and the owner's equity amounts to $40,000. What is the amount of the liabilities?

b The owner's equity of Wild Company appears on the balance sheet as $85,000 and is equal to one-third the amount of total assets. What is the amount of liabilities?

c The assets of Hot Line Company amounted to $75,000 on December 31 of Year 1 but increased to $105,000 by December 31 of Year 2. During this same period liabilities increased by $25,000. The owner's equity at December 31 of Year 1 amounted to $50,000. What was the amount of owner's equity at December 31 of Year 2? Explain the basis for your answer.

Ex. 1-2 The following transactions represent part of the activities of Rawhide Company for the first month of its existence. Indicate the effect of each transaction upon the total assets of the business by use of the appropriate phrase: "increase total assets," "decrease total assets," "no change in total assets."

(*a*) The owner invested cash in the business.
(*b*) Purchased a typewriter for cash.
(*c*) Purchased a delivery truck at a price of $4,000, terms $500 cash and the balance payable in 24 equal monthly installments.
(*d*) Paid a liability.
(*e*) Borrowed money from a bank.
(*f*) Sold land for cash at a price equal to its cost.
(*g*) Sold land on account (on credit) at a price equal to its cost.
(*h*) Sold land for cash at price in excess of its cost.
(*i*) Sold land for cash at price less than its cost.
(*j*) Collected an account receivable.

Ex. 1-3 For each of the following categories, state concisely a transaction that will have the required effect on elements of the accounting equation.

a Increase an asset and increase a liability.
b Decrease an asset and decrease a liability.
c Increase one asset and decrease another asset.
d Increase an asset and increase owner's equity.
e Increase one asset, decrease another asset, and increase a liability.

Ex. 1-4 Some of the transactions of Key Club Company are listed below. Show the effect on total assets, total liabilities, and owner's equity of the business entity for each transaction. Prepare your answer in tabular form, identifying each transaction by letter and using the symbols (+) for increase, (−) for decrease, and (NC) for no change. An answer is provided for the first transaction to serve as an example. Note that some of the transactions concern the personal affairs of the owner rather than being strictly transactions of the business entity.

	Total Assets	Liabil- ities	Owner's Equity
a Owner withdrew cash from the business	–	NC	–
b Purchased a delivery truck for cash			
c Paid a liability of the business			
d Owner invested cash in the business			
e Owner gave a typewriter used in the business to his son as a birthday present			
f Owner wrote a cheque on company bank account to pay for his wife's bill at a beauty shop			
g Returned for credit some defective office equip- ment which had been purchased on credit but not yet paid for			
h Obtained a loan from the bank for business use			

Ex. 1-5 The balance sheet items of the Hart Company at December 31, 19___ , are shown below in random order. You are to prepare a balance sheet (with complete heading). Use a similar sequence for assets as in the illustrated balance sheet on page 10.

Accounts payable	$ 3,400	Land	$ 9,000
Accounts receivable	6,500	Lee Hart, capital	38,600
Building	20,000	Office equipment	1,900
Cash	4,600		

PROBLEMS

Group A

1A-1 Selected transactions of the Spur Company for September are summarized below in equation form, with each of the five transactions identified by a letter. Write a sentence explaining the nature of each transaction.

	Cash	+	Accounts Receiv- able	+	Land	+	Building	+	Office Equip- ment	=	Accounts Payable	+	J. Day, Capital
					Assets					**=**	**Liabil- ities**	**+**	**Owner's Equity**
Balances	$3,000		$9,000		$8,000		$21,000		$3,000		$4,000		$40,000
(a)	+500		−500										
Balances	$3,500		$8,500		$8,000		$21,000		$3,000		$4,000		$40,000
(b)									+800		+800		
Balances	$3,500		$8,500		$8,000		$21,000		$3,800		$4,800		$40,000
(c)	−200										−200		
Balances	$3,300		$8,500		$8,000		$21,000		$3,800		$4,600		$40,000
(d)	−300								+900		+600		
Balances	$3,000		$8,500		$8,000		$21,000		$4,700		$5,200		$40,000
(e)	+700												+700
Balances	$3,700 +		$8,500 +		$8,000 +		$21,000 +		$4,700 =		$5,200 +		$40,700

1A-2 Prepare a balance sheet for the North Star Company at December 31, 19___, from the information listed below. Use a similar sequence for assets as in the illustrated balance sheet on page 10. Include a figure for total liabilities.

Accounts payable	$ 2,500	Delivery truck	$3,300
Accounts receivable	4,100	Frank Ryan, capital	?
Land	8,000	Office equipment	2,600
Building	10,000	Cash	4,170
Notes payable	13,000		

1A-3 Show the effect of business transactions upon the balance sheet by preparing a new and separate balance sheet for the TV Repair Shop at each of the four dates listed below. Each balance sheet should reflect all transactions completed to date.

(1) On March 1, Lee Jones deposited $30,000 cash in a bank account in the name of a new business, TV Repair Shop.

(2) On March 3, land and a building were acquired at a cost of $7,000 for the land and $13,000 for the building. Full payment was made on this date.

(3) On March 9, TV Repair Shop purchased tools and equipment to do repair work, for a down payment of $1,200 cash and a final payment of $1,500 due in 30 days.

(4) On April 7, TV Repair Shop bought a delivery truck at a cost of $3,600. A cash down payment of $1,000 was made, with payment of the balance to be made within 60 days. Also on this date, the account payable incurred by the purchase of tools and equipment on March 9 was paid in full.

1A-4 **Instructions** By studying the successive balance sheets in the series shown below, determine what transactions have taken place. Prepare a list of these transactions by date of occurrence. (For example, the transaction leading to the balance sheet of September 1, 19___, could be described as follows: "On September 1, 19___, George Myers invested $68,000 in cash and started the business of Lakeside Marina.

(1)

LAKESIDE MARINA
Balance Sheet
September 1, 19___

Assets		Owner's Equity	
Cash	$68,000	George Myers, capital	$68,000

(2)

LAKESIDE MARINA
Balance Sheet
September 5, 19___

Assets		Liabilities & Owner's Equity	
Cash	$55,000	Liabilities:	
Land	33,000	Accounts payable	$20,000
		Owner's equity:	
		George Myers, capital	68,000
	$88,000		$88,000

(3)

LAKESIDE MARINA

Balance Sheet

September 8, 19___

Assets		Liabilities & Owner's Equity	
Cash	$45,000	Liabilities:	
Supplies	3,000	Accounts payable	$20,000
Land	33,000	Owner's equity:	
Equipment	7,000	George Myers, capital	68,000
	$88,000		$88,000

(4)

LAKESIDE MARINA

Balance Sheet

September 9, 19___

Assets		Liabilities & Owner's Equity	
Cash	$30,000	Liabilities:	
Supplies	3,000	Accounts payable	$16,500
Land	33,000	Owner's equity:	
Equipment	18,500	George Myers, capital	68,000
	$84,500		$84,500

1A-5 The balance sheet items for Gremlin Auto Wash (arranged in alphabetical order) were as follows at August 1, 19___.

Accounts payable	$ 4,000	Land	$25,000
Accounts receivable	300	Notes payable	36,000
Building	20,000	Supplies	2,800
Cash	4,600	Thomas Young, capital	?
Equipment	26,000		

During the next two days, the following transactions occurred:

Aug. 2 Young invested an additional $15,000 cash in the business. The accounts payable were paid in full. (No payment was made on the notes payable.)

Aug. 3 Equipment was purchased at a cost of $9,000 to be paid within 10 days. Supplies were purchased for $500 cash from another car-washing concern which was going out of business. These supplies would have cost $900 if purchased through normal channels.

Instructions

a Prepare a balance sheet at August 1, 19___.

b Prepare a balance sheet at August 3, 19___.

Group B

1B-1 Certain transactions of Purple Sage Company for October are summarized below in equation form, with each of the five transactions identified by a letter. Write a sentence explaining the nature of each transaction.

	Assets					=	Liabilities	+	Owner's Equity
	Cash	+ Accounts Receivable	+ Land	+ Building	+ Office Equipment	=	Accounts Payable	+	R. Ryan, Capital
Balances	$2,000	$3,000	$5,000	$20,000	$4,000		$9,000		$25,000
(a)	−800						−800		
Balances	$1,200	$3,000	$5,000	$20,000	$4,000		$8,200		$25,000
(b)	+600	−600							
Balances	$1,800	$2,400	$5,000	$20,000	$4,000		$8,200		$25,000
(c)					+400		+400		
Balances	$1,800	$2,400	$5,000	$20,000	$4,400		$8,600		$25,000
(d)	+1,000								+1,000
Balances	$2,800	$2,400	$5,000	$20,000	$4,400		$8,600		$26,000
(e)	−500				+1,600		+1,100		
Balances	$2,300 +	$2,400 +	$5,000 +	$20,000 +	$6,000 =		$9,700	+	$26,000

1B-2 The following balance sheet of a business owned by William Madison contains a number of errors in the placement of items and also in the headings. Prepare a corrected balance sheet, using a similar sequence for assets as in the illustrated balance sheet on page 10. Include a figure for total liabilities.

MADISON COMPANY
For the Year Ended December 31, 19___

Assets		Liabilities	
Cash	$ 10,850	Notes payable	$ 40,000
Accounts receivable	52,750	Accounts payable	78,600
Equity of owner	38,700	Delivery trucks	12,750
Land	20,000	Office equipment	25,950
Buildings	35,000		
	$157,300		$157,300

1B-3 Prepare a balance sheet for the Sugarloaf Chalet as of June 30, 19___, from the random list of balance sheet items listed below. Use a similar sequence for assets as in the illustrated balance sheet on page 10. Include a figure for total liabilities.

Accounts payable	$12,500	Snowmobiles	$ 8,200
Charles Finley, capital	?	Notes payable	20,000
Buildings	52,000	Equipment	25,000
Accounts receivable	11,250	Land	25,000
Cash	9,750		

1B-4 By studying the successive balance sheets for Tony's Place in the series below, determine what transactions have occurred. Prepare a list of these transactions by date of occurrence. (For example, the transaction leading to the balance sheet of October 1, 19___, could be described as follows; "On October 1, 19___, Tony Enrico invested $75,000 in cash and started the business called Tony's Place.")

(1)

TONY'S PLACE
Balance Sheet
October 1, 19___

Assets		Owner's Equity	
Cash	$75,000	Tony Enrico, capital	$75,000

(2)

TONY'S PLACE
Balance Sheet
October 4, 19___

Assets		Owner's Equity	
Cash	$60,000	Tony Enrico, capital	$75,000
Land	15,000		
	$75,000		$75,000

(3)

TONY'S PLACE
Balance Sheet
October 26, 19___

Assets		Liabilities & Owner's Equity	
Cash	$46,000	Liabilities:	
Land	15,000	Accounts payable	$16,000
Building	30,000	Owner's equity:	
		Tony Enrico, capital	75,000
	$91,000		$91,000

(4)

TONY'S PLACE
Balance Sheet
November 10, 19___

Assets		Liabilities & Owner's Equity	
Cash	$35,000	Liabilities:	
Land	15,000	Accounts payable	$11,000
Building	30,000	Owner's equity:	
Equipment	6,000	Tony Enrico, capital	75,000
	$86,000		$86,000

1B-5 Prepare a balance sheet at May 31, 19___, from the information listed below for the Wilshire Insurance Agency. Also prepare a new balance sheet after the transaction on June 1, and a third balance sheet after the transactions on June 10.

Accounts Payable	$14,100	Cash	$?
Office equipment	7,200	Accounts receivable	15,400
J. B. Green, capital	52,900	Building	26,000
Land	12,000		

June 1 One-half of the land was sold at a price of $6,000, which was equal to its cost. A down payment of $2,000 in cash was received and the buyer agreed to pay the balance within 10 days.

June 10 Cash in the amount of $4,000 was received from collection of an account receivable as final settlement from the buyer of the land. Also on this date a cash payment of $1,100 was made on an account payable.

BUSINESS DECISION PROBLEM 1

Datamatic Company and Autopair Company are in the same line of business and both were recently organized, so it may be assumed that the recorded costs for assets are close to current market values. The balance sheets for the two companies are as follows at October 31, 19___.

DATAMATIC COMPANY
Balance Sheet
October 31, 19___

Assets		Liabilities & Owner's Equity	
Cash	$ 4,000	Liabilities:	
Accounts receivable	8,000	Notes payable	
Land	30,000	(due in 60 days)	$ 52,000
Building	50,000	Accounts payable	36,000
Office equipment	10,000	Total liabilities	$ 88,000
		Owner's equity:	
		James Matic, capital	14,000
	$102,000		$102,000

AUTOPAIR COMPANY
Balance Sheet
October 31, 19___

Assets		Liabilities & Owner's Equity	
Cash	$20,000	Liabilities:	
Accounts receivable	40,000	Notes payable	
Land	6,000	(due in 60 days)	$12,000
Building	10,000	Accounts payable	8,000
Office equipment	1,000	Total liabilities	$20,000
		Owner's equity:	
		Dale Pair, capital	57,000
	$77,000		$77,000

Instructions

a Assume that you are a banker and that each company has applied to you for a 90-day loan of $10,000. Which would you consider to be the more favorable prospect?

b Assume that you are an investor considering the purchase of one or both of the companies. Both James Matic and Dale Pair have indicated to you that they would consider selling their respective businesses. In either transaction you would assume the existing liabilities. For which business would you be willing to pay the higher price? Explain your answer fully. (It is recognized that for either decision, additional information would be useful, but you are to reach your decisions on the basis of the information available.)

RECORDING
CHANGES
IN FINANCIAL
CONDITION

Many business concerns have several hundred or even several thousand business transactions each day. It would obviously be impracticable to prepare a balance sheet after each transaction, and it is quite unnecessary to do so. Instead, the many individual transactions are recorded in the accounting records, and, at the end of the month or other accounting period, a balance sheet is prepared from these records.

The accounting model

You are already familiar with the use of *models* in many fields. Just as the aerospace scientist builds a model of a spaceship or an urban planner builds a model of a new city, so shall we construct a model of an accounting system. A good model is an accurate portrayal of the real world situation it represents. However, a model usually emphasizes certain key factors and relationships, while deemphasizing details which may vary without affecting the successful working of the system. The accounting model presented in this and following chapters is a miniature portrayal of the factors and key relationships that influence the accounting process in a real-world business enterprise.

Remember that accounting systems may be maintained in some businesses by one person with pen-and-ink methods, or in other companies by hundreds of people with electric accounting machines, or by large-scale electronic computers. By use of a model which emphasizes basic concepts, however, you can gain an understanding of accounting which will be useful in any one of the wide range of real-world business situations. The purpose of our rather simple model is to demonstrate how business transactions are analyzed, entered into the accounting system, and stored for use in preparing balance sheets and other financial reports. The model will enable us to study the interrelationships of the business enterprise; to determine what information is needed, by whom it is needed, how it can be gathered and classified, and how frequently the information in the system should be summarized and reported.

The use of accounts for recording transactions

The accounting system includes a separate record for each item that appears in the balance sheet. For example, a separate record is kept for the asset Cash, showing all the increases and decreases in cash which result from the many transactions in which cash is received or paid. A similar record is kept for every other asset, for every liability, and for owner's equity. The form of record used to record increases and decreases in a single balance sheet item is called an *account*, or sometimes a *ledger account*. All these separate accounts are usually kept in a loose-leaf binder, and the entire group of accounts is called a *ledger*.

Today many businesses use electronic computers for maintaining accounting records, and data may be stored on magnetic tapes rather than in ledgers. However, an understanding of accounting concepts is most easily acquired by study of a manual accounting system. The knowledge gained by working with manual accounting records is readily transferable to any type of automated accounting system. For these reasons, we shall use standard written accounting forms such as ledger accounts as the model for our study of basic accounting concepts. These standard forms continue to be used by a great many businesses, but for our purposes they should be viewed as conceptual devices rather than as fixed and unchanging structural components of an accounting system.

THE LEDGER

Ledger accounts are a means of accumulating information needed by management in directing the business. For example, by maintaining a Cash account, management can keep track of the amount of cash available for meeting payrolls and for making current purchases of assets or services. This record of cash is also useful in planning future operations, and in advance planning of applications for bank loans. The development of the annual budget requires estimating in advance the expected receipts and payments of cash; these estimates of cash flow are naturally based to some extent on the ledger accounts showing past cash receipts and payments.

In its simplest form, an account has only three elements: (1) a title, consisting of the name of the particular asset, or liability, or owner's equity; (2) a left side, which is called the *debit* side; and (3) a right side, which is called the *credit* side. This form of account, illustrated on page 34, is called a *T account* because of its resemblance to the letter T. More complete forms of accounts will be illustrated later.

34 CHAPTER TWO

T account:
a ledger
account in
simplified
form

Title of Account	
Left or debit side	*Right or credit side*

Debit and credit entries

An amount recorded on the left or debit side of an account is called a *debit,* or a *debit entry;* an amount entered on the right or credit side is called a *credit,* or a *credit entry.* Accountants also use the words debit and credit as verbs. The act of recording a debit in an account is called *debiting* the account; the recording of a credit is called *crediting* the account. A debit to an account is also sometimes called a *charge* to the account; an account is debited or *charged* when an amount is entered on the left side of the account.

Students beginning a course in accounting often have preconceived but erroneous notions about the meanings of the terms debit and credit. For example, to some people unacquainted with accounting, the word credit may carry a more favorable connotation than does the word debit. Such connotations have no validity in the field of accounting. Accountants use *debit* to mean an entry on the left-hand side of an account, and *credit* to mean an entry on the right-hand side. The student should therefore regard debit and credit as simple equivalents of left and right, without any hidden or subtle implications.

To illustrate the recording of debits and credits in an account, let us go back to the cash transactions of the Roberts Real Estate Agency as illustrated in Chapter 1. When these cash transactions are recorded in an account, the receipts are listed in vertical order on the debit side of the account and the payments are listed on the credit side. The dates of the transactions may also be listed, as shown in the following illustration:

Cash

Cash trans- actions entered in ledger account

9/1		20,000	9/3		7,000
9/20	7,500	500	9/5		5,000
		20,500	9/30		1,000
					13,000

Note that the total of the cash receipts, $20,500, is in small-size figures so that it will not be mistaken for a debit entry. The total of the cash payments (credits), amounting to $13,000, is also in small-size figures to distinguish it from the credit entries. These *footings,* or memorandum totals, are merely a convenient step in determining the amount of cash on hand at the end of the month. The difference in dollars between the total debits and the total credits in an account is called the *balance.* If the debits exceed the credits the account has a *debit balance;* if the credits exceed the debits the account has a *credit balance.* In the illustrated Cash account, the debit total of $20,500 is larger than the credit total of $13,000; therefore, the account has a debit balance. By subtracting the credits from the debits ($20,500–$13,000), we determine that the balance of the Cash account is $7,500. This debit balance is noted on the debit (left) side of the account. The balance of the Cash account represents the amount of cash owned by the business on September 30; in a balance sheet prepared at this date, Cash in the amount of $7,500 would be listed as an asset.

DEBIT BALANCES IN ASSET ACCOUNTS In the preceding illustration of a cash account, increases were recorded on the left or debit side of the account and decreases were recorded on the right or credit side. The increases were greater than the decreases and the result was a debit balance in the account.

All asset accounts normally have debit balances; as a matter of fact, the ownership by a business of cash, land, or any other asset indicates that the increases (debits) to that asset have been greater than the decreases (credits). It is hard to imagine an account for an asset such as land having a credit balance, as this would indicate that the business had disposed of more land than it had acquired and had reached the impossible position of having a negative amount of land.

The balance sheets previously illustrated in Chapter 1 showed all the assets on the left side of the balance sheet. The fact that assets are located on the left side of the balance sheet is a convenient means of remembering the rule that an increase in an asset is recorded on the *left* (debit) side of the account, and also that an asset account normally has a debit *(left-hand)* balance.

Asset accounts normally have debit balances	*Any Asset Account*	
	(Debit) Increase	*(Credit)* Decrease

CREDIT BALANCES IN LIABILITY AND OWNER'S EQUITY ACCOUNTS Increases in liability and owner's equity accounts are recorded by credit entries and decreases in these accounts are recorded by debits. The relationship between entries in these accounts and their position on the balance sheet may be summed up as follows: (1) liabilities and owner's equity belong on the *right* side of the balance sheet; (2) an increase in a liability or an owner's equity account is recorded on the *right* side of the account; and (3) liability and owner's equity accounts normally have credit *(right-hand)* balances.

Liability and owner's equity accounts normally have credit balances	*Any Liability Account or Owner's Equity Account*	
	(Debit) *Decrease*	*(Credit)* *Increase*

CONCISE STATEMENT OF THE RULES OF DEBIT AND CREDIT The rules of debit and credit, which have been explained and illustrated in the preceding sections, may be concisely summarized as follows:

	Asset Accounts	*Liability & Owner's Equity Accounts*
Mechanics of debit and credit	*Increases are recorded by debits* *Decreases are recorded by credits*	*Increases are recorded by credits* *Decreases are recorded by debits*

EQUALITY OF DEBITS AND CREDITS Every business transaction affects two or more accounts. The *double-entry* method, which is in almost universal use, takes its name from the fact that equal debit and credit entries are made for every transaction. If only two accounts are affected (as in the purchase of land for cash) one account, Land, is debited, and the other account, Cash, is credited for the same amount. If more than two accounts are affected by a transaction, the sum of the debit entries must be equal to the sum of the credit entries. This situation was illustrated when the Roberts Real Estate Agency purchased a building for a price of $12,000. The $12,000 debit to the asset account, Building, was exactly equal to the total of the $5,000 credit to the Cash account plus the $7,000 credit to the liability account, Accounts Payable. Since every transaction results in an equal amount of debits and credits in the ledger, it follows that the total of all debit entries in the ledger is equal to the total of all the credit entries.

Recording transactions in ledger accounts: illustration

The procedure for recording transactions in ledger accounts will be illustrated by using the September transactions of the Roberts Real Estate Agency. Each transaction will first be analyzed in terms of increases and decreases in assets, liabilities, and owner's equity. Then we shall follow the rules of debit and credit in entering these increases and decreases in T accounts. Asset accounts will be shown on the left side of the page; liability and owner's equity accounts on the right side. For convenience in following the transactions into the ledger accounts, the letter used to identify a given transaction will also appear opposite the debit and credit entries for that transaction. This use of identifying letters is for illustrative purposes only and is not used in actual accounting practice.

Transaction (a) Roberts invested $20,000 cash in the business on September 1.

	Analysis	Rule	Entry
Recording an investment in the business	The asset Cash was increased	Increases in assets are recorded by debits	Debit: Cash, $20,000
	The owner's equity was increased	Increases in owner's equity are recorded by credits	Credit: James Roberts, Capital, $20,000

Cash		James Roberts, Capital	
9/1 (a) 20,000			9/1 (a) 20,000

Transaction (b) On September 3, the Roberts Real Estate Agency purchased land for cash in the amount of $7,000.

	Analysis	Rule	Entry
Purchase of land for cash	The asset Land was increased	Increases in assets are recorded by debits	Debit: Land, $7,000
	The asset Cash was decreased	Decreases in assets are recorded by credits	Credit: Cash, $7,000

Cash			
9/1 20,000	9/3 (b) 7,000		

Land	
9/3 (b) 7,000	

Transaction (c) On September 5, the Roberts Real Estate Agency purchased a building from OK Distributors at a total price of $12,000. The terms of the purchase required a cash payment of $5,000 with the remainder of $7,000 payable within 90 days.

	Analysis	Rule	Entry
Purchase of an asset, with partial payment	A new asset, Building, was acquired	Increases in assets are recorded by debits	Debit: Building, $12,000
	The asset Cash was decreased	Decreases in assets are recorded by credits	Credit: Cash, $5,000
	A new liability, Accounts Payable, was incurred	Increases in liabilities are recorded by credits	Credit: Accounts Payable, $7,000

Cash					Accounts Payable	
9/1	20,000	9/3	7,000		9/5	(c) 7,000
		9/5	(c) 5,000			

Building	
9/5 (c) 12,000	

Transaction (d) On September 10, the Roberts Real Estate Agency sold a portion of its land on credit to Carter's Drugstore for a price of $2,000. The land was sold at its cost, so there was no gain or loss on the transaction.

	Analysis	Rule	Entry
Sale of land on credit (no gain or loss)	A new asset, Accounts Receivable, was acquired	Increases in assets are recorded by debits	Debit: Accounts Receivable, $2,000
	The asset Land was decreased	Decreases in assets are recorded by credits	Credit: Land, $2,000

Accounts Receivable	
9/10 (d) 2,000	

Land			
9/3	7,000	9/10	(d) 2,000

Transaction (e) On September 14, the Roberts Real Estate Agency purchased office equipment on credit from General Equipment Ltd., in the amount of $1,800.

	Analysis	Rule	Entry
Purchase of an asset on credit	A new asset, Office Equipment, was acquired	Increases in assets are recorded by debits	Debit: Office Equipment $1,800
	A new liability, Accounts Payable, was incurred	Increases in liabilities are recorded by credits	Credit: Accounts Payable, $1,800

Office Equipment		Accounts Payable	
9/14 (e) 1,800		9/5 7,000	
		9/14 (e) 1,800	

Transaction (f)   On September 20, cash of $500 was received as partial collection of the account receivable from Carter's Drugstore.

	Analysis	Rule	Entry
Collection of an account receivable	The asset Cash was increased	Increases in assets are recorded by debits	Debit: Cash, $500
	The asset Accounts Receivable was decreased	Decreases in assets are recorded by credits	Credit: Accounts Receivable, $500

Cash			
9/1 20,000	9/3 7,000
9/20 (f) 500	9/5 5,000

Accounts Receivable	
9/10 2,000	9/20 (f) 500

Transaction (g)   A cash payment of $1,000 was made on September 30 in partial settlement of the amount owing to General Equipment Ltd.

	Analysis	Rule	Entry
Payment of a liability	The liability Accounts Payable was decreased	Decreases in liabilities are recorded by debits	Debit: Accounts Payable, $1,000
	The asset Cash was decreased	Decreases in assets are recorded by credits	Credit: Cash, $1,000

Cash					Accounts Payable			
9/1	20,000	9/3	7,000		9/30	(g) 1,000	9/5	7,000
9/20	500	9/5	5,000				9/14	1,800
		9/30	(g) 1,000					

Running balance form of ledger account

The T form of account used thus far is very convenient for illustrative purposes. Details are avoided and we can concentrate on basic ideas. T accounts are also often used in advanced accounting courses and by professional accountants for preliminary analysis of a transaction. In other words, the simplicity of the T account provides a concise conceptual picture of the elements of a business transaction. In formal accounting records, however, more information is needed, and the T account is replaced in many manual accounting systems by a ledger account with special rulings, such as the following illustration of the Cash account for the Roberts Real Estate Agency.

Cash   Account No. _/_

	Date	Explanation	Ref	Debit	Credit	Balance
Ledger account with a balance column	19— Sept. 1			20,000 00		20,000 00
	3				7,000 00	13,000 00
	5				5,000 00	8,000 00
	20			500 00		8,500 00
	30				1,000 00	7,500 00

The **Date** column shows the date of the transaction—which is not necessarily the same as the date the entry is made in the account. The **Explanation** column is needed only for unusual items, and in many companies it is seldom used. The **Ref** (Reference) column is used to list the page number of the journal in which the transaction is recorded, thus making it possible to trace ledger entries back to their source (a journal). The use of a **journal** is explained later in this chapter. In the **Balance** column of the account, the new balance is entered each time the account is debited or credited. Thus the current balance of the account can always be observed at a glance.

Although we will make extensive use of this three-column running balance form of account in later chapters, there will also be many situations in which we shall continue to use T accounts to achieve simplicity in illustrating accounting principles and procedures.

The normal balance of an account

The running balance form of ledger account does not indicate specifically whether the balance of the account is a debit or credit balance. However, this causes no difficulty because we know that asset accounts normally have debit balances and that accounts for liabilities and owner's equity normally have credit balances.

The balance of any account normally results from recording more increases than decreases. In asset accounts, increases are recorded as debits, so asset accounts normally have debit balances. In liability and owner's equity accounts, increases are recorded as credits, so these accounts normally have credit balances.

Occasionally an asset account may temporarily acquire a credit balance, either as the result of an accounting error or because of an unusual transaction. For example, an account receivable may acquire a credit balance because a customer overpays his account. However, a credit balance in the Building account could be created only by an accounting error.

Sequence and numbering of ledger accounts

Accounts are usually arranged in the ledger in "financial statement order"; that is, assets first, followed by liabilities, owner's equity, revenues, and expense. The number of accounts needed by a business will depend upon its size, the nature of its operations, and the extent to which management and regulatory agencies want detailed classification of information. An identification number is assigned to each account. A *chart of accounts* is a listing of the account titles and account numbers being used by a given business.

In the following list of accounts, certain numbers have not been assigned; these numbers are held in reserve so that additional accounts can be inserted in the ledger in proper sequence whenever such accounts become necessary. In this illustration, the numbers from 1 to 29 are used exclusively for asset accounts; numbers from 30 to 49 are reserved for liabilities; numbers in the 50s signify owner's equity accounts; numbers in the 60s represent revenue accounts and numbers from 70 to 99 designate expense accounts. The balance sheet accounts with which we are concerned in this chapter are numbered as shown in the following brief chart of accounts.

Account Title	Account No.

Assets:

Cash *1*

Accounts Receivable *2*

Land *20*

Building *22*

Office Equipment *25*

Liabilities:

Accounts Payable *30*

Owner's Equity:

James Roberts, Capital *50*

In large businesses with many more accounts, a more elaborate numbering system would be needed. Some companies use a four-digit number for each account; each of the four digits carries special significance as to the classification of the account.

Flow of information through the accounting system

The term *transaction* was explained in Chapter 1, but a concise definition at this point may be a helpful reminder. *A transaction is a business event which can be expressed in money and must be recorded in the accounting records.* Common examples are the payment or collection of cash, a purchase or sale on credit, and the withdrawal of assets by the owner of a business. Note that a transaction has an accounting value and has an influence on the financial statements. Events such as the opening of a competing business or the retirement of an employee, although possibly of importance to the business, are not entered in the accounts and are not considered to be transactions.

Business transactions are evidenced by business documents such as a cheque, a sales ticket, or a cash register tape. These business documents (or original papers) are the starting point for the flow of accounting information through the accounting system into the financial statements. In our description of the accounting process thus far, emphasis has been placed on the analysis of transactions in terms of debits and credits to ledger accounts. Although transactions *could* be entered directly in ledger accounts, it is much more convenient and efficient in a manual accounting system to record the information shown on business documents first in a journal and later to transfer the debits and credits to ledger accounts.

THE JOURNAL

The *journal,* or book of original entry, is a chronological record, showing for each day the debits and credits from transactions; it may also include explanatory information concerning transactions. At convenient intervals, the debits and credits in the journal are transferred to the accounts in the ledger; as we have already seen, the ledger accounts serve as the basis from which the balance sheet and other accounting reports are prepared. The following flow chart illustrates the sequence of steps by which information flows through the accounting system.

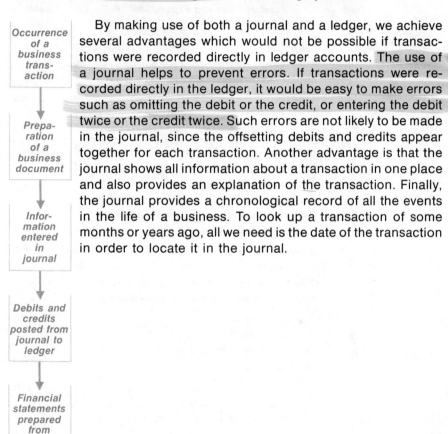

By making use of both a journal and a ledger, we achieve several advantages which would not be possible if transactions were recorded directly in ledger accounts. The use of a journal helps to prevent errors. If transactions were recorded directly in the ledger, it would be easy to make errors such as omitting the debit or the credit, or entering the debit twice or the credit twice. Such errors are not likely to be made in the journal, since the offsetting debits and credits appear together for each transaction. Another advantage is that the journal shows all information about a transaction in one place and also provides an explanation of the transaction. Finally, the journal provides a chronological record of all the events in the life of a business. To look up a transaction of some months or years ago, all we need is the date of the transaction in order to locate it in the journal.

The general journal: illustration of entries

Many businesses maintain several types of journals. The nature of operations and the volume of transactions in the particular business determine the number and type of journals needed. The simplest type of journal, and the one with which we are concerned in this chapter, is called a *general journal.* It has only two money columns, one for debits and the other for credits; it may be used for all types of transactions.

The process of recording a transaction in a journal is called *journalizing* the transaction. To illustrate the use of the general journal, we shall now journalize the transactions of the Roberts Real Estate Agency which have previously been discussed.

General Journal

Page 1

Date			Account Titles and Explanation	LP	Debit	Credit
Sept.	1		Cash	1	20,000	
			James Roberts, Capital	50		20,000
			Invested cash in the business.			
	3		Land	20	7,000	
			Cash	1		7,000
			Purchased land for office site.			
	5		Building	22	12,000	
			Cash	1		5,000
			Accounts Payable	30		7,000
			Purchased building to be moved to our lot. Paid part cash; balance payable within 90 days to OK Distributors			
	10		Accounts Receivable	2	2,000	
			Land	20		2,000
			Sold the unused part of our lot at cost to Carter's Drugstore. Due within three months.			
	14		Office Equipment	25	1,800	
			Accounts Payable	30		1,800
			Purchased office equipment on credit from General Equipment Ltd.			
	20		Cash	1	500	
			Accounts Receivable	2		500
			Collected part of receivable from Carter's Drugstore.			
	30		Accounts Payable	30	1,000	
			Cash	1		1,000
			Made partial payment of the liability to General Equipment Ltd.			

September 19— journal entries for Roberts Real Estate Company

Efficient use of a general journal requires two things: (1) ability to analyze the effect of a transaction upon assets, liabilities, and owner's equity; and (2) familiarity with the standard form and arrangement of journal entries. Our primary interest is in the analytical phase of journalizing; the procedural steps can be learned quickly by observing the following points in the illustrations of journal entries shown above.

1 The year, month, and day of the first entry on the page are written in the date column. The year and month need not be repeated for subsequent entries until a new page or a new month is begun.

2 The name of the account to be debited is written on the first line of the entry and is customarily placed at the extreme left next to the date column. The amount of the debit is entered on the same line in the left-hand money column.

3 The name of the account to be credited is entered on the line below the debit entry and is indented, that is, placed about 1 inch to the right of the date column. The amount credited is entered on the same line in the right-hand money column.

4 A brief explanation of the transaction is usually begun on the line immediately below the last account credited. The explanation need not be indented.

5 A blank line is usually left after each entry. This spacing causes each journal entry to stand out clearly as a separate unit and makes the journal easier to read.

6 An entry which includes more than one debit or more than one credit (such as the entry on September 5) is called a *compound journal entry.* Regardless of how many debits or credits are contained in a compound journal entry, all the debits are customarily entered before any credits are listed.

7 The LP (ledger page) column just to the left of the debit money column is left blank at the time of making the journal entry. When the debits and credits are later transferred to ledger accounts, the numbers of the ledger accounts are listed in this column to provide a convenient cross reference with the ledger.

Remember in journalizing transactions that the exact titles of the ledger accounts to be debited and credited should be used. For example, in recording the purchase of a typewriter for cash, do not make a journal entry debiting "Office Equipment Purchased" and crediting "Cash Paid Out." There are no ledger accounts with such titles. The proper journal entry would consist of a debit to Office Equipment and a credit to Cash.

Posting

The process of transferring the debits and credits from the journal to the proper ledger accounts is called *posting.* Each amount listed in the debit column of the journal is posted by entering it on the debit side of an account in the ledger, and each amount listed in the credit column of the journal is posted to the credit side of a ledger account.

The mechanics of posting may vary somewhat with the preferences of the individual. For example, the debits and credits may be posted in the sequence shown in the journal, or all the debits on a journal page may be posted first. The following sequence is commonly used:

1 Locate in the ledger the first account named in the journal entry.

2 Enter in the Debit column of the ledger account the amount of the debit as shown in the journal.

3 Enter the date of the transaction in the ledger account.

4 Enter in the Reference column of the ledger account the number of the journal page from which the entry is being posted.

5 The recording of the debit in the ledger account is now complete; as evidence of this fact, return to the journal and enter in the LP (ledger page) column the number of the ledger account or page to which the debit was posted.

6 Repeat the posting process described in the preceding five steps for the credit side of the journal entry.

ILLUSTRATION OF POSTING To illustrate the posting process, the journal entry for the first transaction of Roberts Real Estate Agency is repeated at this point along with the two ledger accounts affected by this entry.

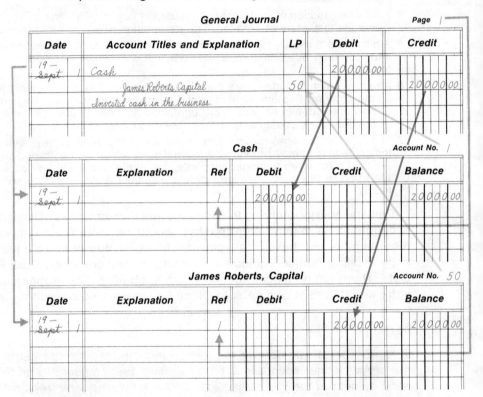

General Journal — Page 1

Date	Account Titles and Explanation	LP	Debit	Credit
19— Sept. 1	Cash	1	20000 00	
	James Roberts, Capital	50		20000 00
	Invested cash in the business.			

Cash — Account No. 1

Date	Explanation	Ref	Debit	Credit	Balance
19— Sept. 1		1	20000 00		20000 00

James Roberts, Capital — Account No. 50

Date	Explanation	Ref	Debit	Credit	Balance
19— Sept. 1		1		20000 00	20000 00

Note that the Ref (Reference) column of each of the two ledger accounts illustrated above contains the number 1, indicating that the posting was made from page 1 of the journal. Entering the journal page number in the ledger account and listing the ledger page in the journal provide a cross reference between these two records. The audit of accounting records always requires looking up some journal entries to obtain more information about the amounts listed in ledger accounts. A cross reference between the ledger and journal is therefore essential to efficient audit of the records. Another advantage gained from entering in the journal the number of the account to which a posting has been made is to provide evidence throughout the posting work as to which items have been posted. Otherwise, any interruption in the posting might leave some doubt as to what had been posted.

Journalizing and posting by hand is a useful method for the study of accounting, both for problem assignments and for examinations. The manual approach is also followed in many small businesses. One shortcoming is the opportunity for error that exists whenever information is being copied from one record to another. In businesses having a large volume of transactions, the posting of ledger accounts is performed by accounting machines or by a computer, which speeds up the work and reduces errors. In these more sophisticated applications, transactions may be recorded simultaneously in both the journal and the ledger.

Ledger accounts after posting

After all the September transactions have been posted, the ledger of the Roberts Real Estate Agency appears as shown below and on page 48. The accounts are arranged in the ledger in balance sheet order, that is, assets first, followed by liabilities and owner's equity.

Ledger showing September transactions

Cash   Account No. 1

Date	Explanation	Ref	Debit	Credit	Balance
19— Sept. 1		1	20 000 00		20 000 00
3		1		7 000 00	13 000 00
5		1		5 000 00	8 000 00
20		1	500 00		8 500 00
30		1		1 000 00	7 500 00

Accounts Receivable   Account No. 2

Date	Explanation	Ref	Debit	Credit	Balance
19— Sept. 10		1	2 000 00		2 000 00
20		1		500 00	1 500 00

Land   Account No. 20

Date	Explanation	Ref	Debit	Credit	Balance
19— Sept. 3		1	7 000 00		7 000 00
10		1		2 000 00	5 000 00

Building   Account No. 22

Date	Explanation	Ref	Debit	Credit	Balance
19— Sept 5		1	12000 00		12000 00

Office Equipment   Account No. 25

Date	Explanation	Ref	Debit	Credit	Balance
19— Sept 14		1	1800 00		1800 00

Accounts Payable   Account No. 30

Date	Explanation	Ref	Debit	Credit	Balance
19— Sept 5		1		7000 00	7000 00
14		1		1800 00	8800 00
30		1	1000 00		7800 00

James Roberts, Capital   Account No. 50

Date	Explanation	Ref	Debit	Credit	Balance
19— Sept 1		1		20000 00	20000 00

THE TRIAL BALANCE

Since equal dollar amounts of debits and credits are entered in the accounts for every transaction recorded, the sum of all the debits in the ledger must be equal to the sum of all the credits. If the computation of account balances has been accurate, it follows that the total of the accounts with debit balances must be equal to the total of the accounts with credit balances.

Before using the account balances to prepare a balance sheet, it is desirable to *prove* that the total of accounts with debit balances is in fact equal to the total of accounts with credit balances. This proof of the equality of debit and credit balances is called a *trial balance.* A trial balance is a two-column schedule listing the names and balances of all the accounts *in the order in which they appear in the ledger;* the debit balances are listed in the left-hand column and the credit balances in the right-hand column. The totals of the two columns should agree. A trial balance taken from the ledger of the Roberts Real Estate Agency appears on page 49.

ROBERTS REAL ESTATE AGENCY
Trial Balance
September 30, 19___

Trial Cash	$ 7,500	
balance at Accounts receivable	1,500	
month-end		
proves Land	5,000	
ledger is Building	12,000	
in balance		
Office equipment	1,800	
Accounts payable		$ 7,800
James Roberts, capital		20,000
	$27,800	$27,800

Uses and limitations of the trial balance

The trial balance provides proof that the ledger is in balance. The agreement of the debit and credit totals of the trial balance gives assurance that:

1 Equal debits and credits have been recorded for all transactions.

2 The debit or credit balance of each account has been correctly computed.

3 The addition of the account balances in the trial balance has been correctly performed.

Suppose that the debit and credit totals of the trial balance do not agree. This situation indicates that one or more errors have been made. Typical of such errors are: (1) the entering of a debit as a credit, or vice versa; (2) arithmetic mistakes in balancing accounts; (3) clerical errors in copying account balances into the trial balance; (4) listing a debit balance in the credit column of the trial balance, or vice versa; and (5) errors in addition of the trial balance.

The preparation of a trial balance does not prove that transactions have been correctly analyzed and recorded in the proper accounts. If, for example, a receipt of cash were erroneously recorded by debiting the Land account instead of the Cash account, the trial balance would still balance. Also, if a transaction were completely omitted from the ledger, the error would not be disclosed by the trial balance. In brief, the trial balance proves only one aspect of the ledger, and that is the equality of debits and credits.

Despite these limitations, the trial balance is a useful device. It not only provides assurance that the ledger is in balance, but it also serves as a convenient steppingstone for the preparation of financial statements. As explained in Chapter 1, the balance sheet is a formal statement showing the financial condition of the business, intended for distribution to managers, owners, bankers, and various outsiders. The trial balance, on the other hand, is merely a working paper, useful to the accountant but not intended for distribution to others. The balance sheet and other financial statements can be prepared more conveniently from the trial balance than directly from the ledger, especially if there are a great many ledger accounts.

Locating errors

In the illustrations given thus far, the trial balances have all been in balance. Every accounting student soon discovers in working problems, however, that errors are easily made which prevent trial balances from balancing. The lack of balance may be the result of a single error or a combination of several errors. An error may have been made in adding the trial balance columns or in copying the balances from the ledger accounts. If the preparation of the trial balance has been accurate, then the error may lie in the accounting records, either in the journal or in the ledger accounts. What is the most efficient approach to locating the error or errors? There is no single technique which will give the best results every time, but the following procedures, done in sequence, will often save considerable time and effort in locating errors.

1 Prove the addition of the trial balance columns by adding these columns in the opposite direction from that previously followed.

2 If the error does not lie in addition, next determine the exact amount by which the schedule is out of balance. The amount of the discrepancy is often a clue to the source of the error. If the discrepancy is divisible by 9, this suggests either a *transposition* error or a *slide.* For example, assume that the Cash account has a balance of $2,175, but in copying the balance into the trial balance the figures are *transposed* and written as $2,157. The resulting error is $18, and like all transposition errors is divisible by 9. Another common error is the slide, or incorrect placement of the decimal point, as when $2,175.00 is copied as $21.75. The resulting discrepancy in the trial balance will also be an amount divisible by 9.

To illustrate another method of using the amount of a discrepancy as a clue to locating the error, assume that the Office Equipment account has a *debit* balance of $420, but that it is erroneously listed in the *credit* column of the trial balance. This will cause a discrepancy of two times $420, or $840, in the trial balance totals. Since such errors as recording a debit in a credit column are not uncommon, it is advisable, after determining the discrepancy in the trial balance totals, to scan the columns for an amount equal to exactly one-half of the discrepancy. It is also advisable to look over the transactions for an item of the exact amount of the discrepancy. An error may have been made by recording the debit side of the transaction and forgetting to enter the credit side.

3 Compare the amounts in the trial balance with the balances in the ledger. Make sure that each ledger account balance has been included in the correct column of the trial balance.

4 Recompute the balance of each ledger account.

5 Trace all postings from the journal to the ledger accounts. As this is done, place a check mark in the journal and in the ledger after each figure verified. When the operation is completed, look through the journal and the ledger for unchecked amounts. In tracing postings, be alert not only for errors in amount but also for debits entered as credits, or vice versa.

Dollar signs

Dollar signs are not used in journals or ledgers. Some accountants use dollar signs in trial balances; some do not. In this book, dollar signs are used in trial balances. Dollar signs should always be used in the balance sheet, the income statement, and other formal financial reports. In the balance sheet, for example, a dollar sign is placed by the first amount in each column and also by the final amount or total. Many accountants also place a dollar sign by each subtotal or other amount listed below an underlining. In the published financial statements of large corporations, however, the use of dollar signs is often limited to the first and last figures in a column.

When dollar amounts are being entered in the columnar paper used in journals and ledgers, commas and periods are not needed. On unruled paper, commas and periods should be used. Most of the problems and illustrations in this book are in even dollar amounts. In such cases the cents column can be left blank, or if desired, zeros or dashes may be used.

DEMONSTRATION PROBLEM FOR YOUR REVIEW

a Drill Company was organized on July 1 and carried out a number of transactions during July before opening for business on August 1. The partially filled in journal for the company appears below. You are to determine the titles of the accounts to be debited and credited to complete these July journal entries.

General Journal

Page 1

Date		Account Titles and Explanations	LP	Debit	Credit
19___					
July	1	Cash	1	50,000	
		Howard Drill, capital	50		50,000
		Howard Drill opened a bank account in the name of the business by making a deposit of his personal funds.			
	2	Land	20	30,000	
		Cash	1		10,000
		Notes Payable	30		20,000
		Purchased land. Paid one-third cash and issued a note payable for the balance.			
	5	Building	22	12,000	
		Cash	1		12,000
		Purchased a small portable building for cash. The price included installation on Drill Company's lot.			
	12	Office equip	25	2,500	
		accounts payable	32		2,500
		Purchased office equipment on credit from Suzuki & Co.			
	28	accounts payable	32	1,000	
		cash	1		1,000
		Paid part of account payable to Suzuki & Co.			

b Post the preceding journal entries to the proper ledger accounts shown below and on page 53. Insert the ledger account number in the LP column of the journal as each item is posted.

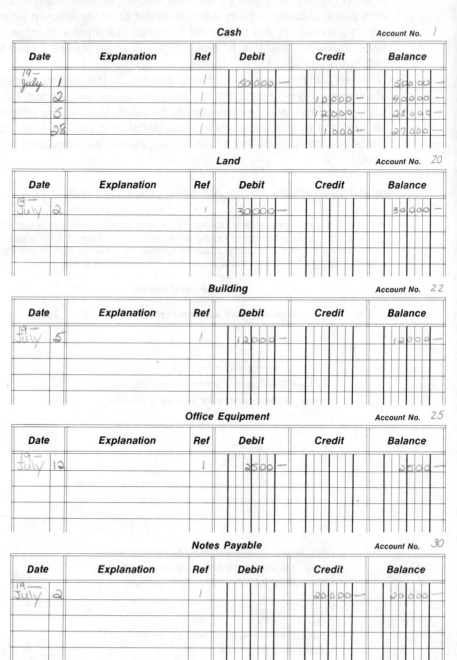

Cash   Account No. *1*

Date	Explanation	Ref	Debit	Credit	Balance
19— July 1		1	50000 —		500 00 —
2		1		10000 —	40000 —
5		1		12000 —	28000 —
28		1		1000 —	27000 —

Land   Account No. 20

Date	Explanation	Ref	Debit	Credit	Balance
19— July 2		1	30000 —		30000 —

Building   Account No. 22

Date	Explanation	Ref	Debit	Credit	Balance
19— July 5		1	12000 —		12000 —

Office Equipment   Account No. 25

Date	Explanation	Ref	Debit	Credit	Balance
19— July 12		1	2500 —		2500 —

Notes Payable   Account No. 30

Date	Explanation	Ref	Debit	Credit	Balance
19— July 2		1		20000 —	20000 —

Accounts Payable   Account No. *32*

Date	Explanation	Ref	Debit	Credit	Balance
19— July 12		1		2500—	2500—
28		1	1000—		1500—

Howard Drill, Capital   Account No. *50*

Date	Explanation	Ref	Debit	Credit	Balance
19— July 1		1		50000—	50000—

c Complete the following trial balance as of July 31, 19___ .

DRILL COMPANY
Trial Balance
July 31, 19___

	Debit	Credit
Cash	$27,000	
Land	30,000	
Building	12,000	
Office equipment	2,500	
Notes payable		$ 20,000
Accounts payable		1,500
Howard Drill, capital		50,000
	$71,500	$ 71,500

QUESTIONS

1 What is an *account* and how does it differ from a *ledger?*

2 Is it true that favorable events are recorded by credits and unfavorable events by debits? Explain.

3 What relationship exists between the position of an account on the balance sheet and the rules for recording increases in that account?

4 In its simplest form, an account has only three elements or basic parts. What are these three elements?

5 State briefly the rules of debit and credit as applied to asset and liability accounts.

6 Does the term *debit* mean increase and the term *credit* mean decrease? Explain.

7 What requirement is imposed by the double-entry method in the recording of any business transaction?

8 Explain precisely what is meant by each of the phrases listed below. Whenever appropriate, indicate whether the left or right side of an account is affected and whether an increase or decrease is indicated.
a A debit of $200 to the Cash account
b Credit balance
c Credit side of an account
d A debit of $600 to Accounts Payable
e Debit balance
f A credit of $50 to Accounts Receivable
g A debit to the Land account

9 For each of the following transactions, indicate whether the account in parentheses should be debited or credited, and give the reason for your answer.
a Purchased a typewriter on credit, promising to make payment in full within 30 days. (Accounts Payable)
b Purchased land for cash. (Cash)
c Sold an old, unneeded typewriter on 30-day credit. (Office Equipment)
d Obtained a loan of $5,000 from a bank. (Cash)
e James Brown began the business of Brown Sporting Goods Shop by depositing $20,000 cash in a bank account in the name of the business. (James Brown, Capital)

10 How does a T account differ from a three-column running balance form of ledger account?

11 For each of the following accounts, state whether it is an asset, a liability, or owner's equity; also state whether it would normally have a debit or a credit balance: (*a*) Office Equipment, (*b*) John Williams, Capital, (*c*) Accounts Receivable, (*d*) Accounts Payable, (*e*) Cash, (*f*) Notes Payable, (*g*) Land.

12 List the following five items in a logical sequence to illustrate the flow of accounting information through the accounting system:
a Information entered in journal
b Preparation of a business document
c Financial statements prepared from ledger
d Occurrence of a business transaction
e Debits and credits posted from journal to ledger

13 Compare and contrast a *journal* and a *ledger.*

14 Which step in the recording of transactions requires greater understanding of accounting principles: (*a*) the entering of transactions in the journal, or (*b*) the posting of entries to ledger accounts?

15 What purposes are served by a trial balance?

16 Are dollar signs used in journal entries? In ledger accounts? In trial balances? In financial statements?

17 What is a *compound* journal entry?

18 State two facts about the sequence of accounts in a journal entry and the use of indentation which make it easy to distinguish between a debit and a credit.

19 A student beginning the study of accounting prepared a trial balance in which two unusual features appeared. The Buildings account showed a credit balance of $20,000, and the Accounts Payable account a debit balance of $100. Considering each of these two abnormal balances separately, state whether the condition was the result of an error in the records or could have resulted from proper recording of an unusual transaction.

20 During the first week of an accounting course, Student A expressed the opinion that a great deal of time could be saved if a business would record transactions directly in ledger accounts rather than entering transactions first in a journal and then posting the debit and credit amounts from the journal to the ledger. Student B agreed with this view but added that such a system should not be called double-entry bookkeeping since each transaction would be entered only once. Student C disagreed with both A and B. He argued that the use of a journal and a ledger was more efficient than entering transactions directly in ledger accounts. Furthermore, he argued that the meaning of double-entry bookkeeping did not refer to the practice of maintaining both a journal and ledger. Evaluate the statements made by all three students.

EXERCISES

Ex. 2-1 Analyze separately each of the following transactions:

    a On May 1, Roger Warren organized Warren Executive Placement, an employment service, by opening a bank account in the company name with a deposit of $30,000 cash.

    b On May 3, land was acquired for $10,000 cash.

    c On May 5, a prefabricated building was purchased at a cost of $11,000 from Speed-bilt Company. A cash down payment of $4,000 was made and it was agreed that the balance should be paid in full within 30 days.

    d On May 8, office equipment was purchased on credit from Randall Office Equipment at a price of $3,600. The account payable was to be paid within 60 days.

    e On May 31, a partial payment of $1,000 was made on the liability to Randall Office Equipment.

Note: The type of analysis to be made is shown by the following illustration, using transaction **(a)** above as an example.

    a (1) The asset Cash was increased. Increases in assets are recorded by debits. Debit Cash, $30,000.

        (2) The owner's equity was increased. Increases in owner's equity are recorded by credits. Credit Roger Warren, Capital, $30,000.

Ex. 2-2 The first six transactions of a newly organized company appear in the following T accounts.

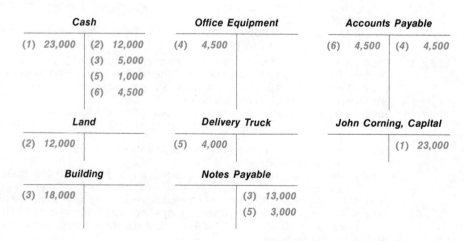

Cash		Office Equipment	Accounts Payable	
(1) 23,000	(2) 12,000	(4) 4,500	(6) 4,500	(4) 4,500
	(3) 5,000			
	(5) 1,000			
	(6) 4,500			

Land	Delivery Truck	John Corning, Capital
(2) 12,000	(5) 4,000	(1) 23,000

Building	Notes Payable
(3) 18,000	(3) 13,000
	(5) 3,000

For each of the six transactions in turn, indicate the type of accounts affected (asset, liability, or owner's equity) and whether the account was increased or decreased. Arrange your answers in the form illustrated for transaction (1), shown here as an example.

	Account Debited		Account Credited	
Transaction	Type of Account	Increase or Decrease	Type of Account	Increase or Decrease
(1)	Asset	Increase	Owner's equity	Increase

Ex. 2-3 The following accounts of Lakeland Real Estate Agency at June 30, 19___, are listed below in alphabetical order. The amount in the account for Notes Payable has been purposely omitted. You are to prepare a trial balance with the proper heading and with the accounts listed in proper sequence. Indicate the balance for Notes Payable.

Accounts payable	$ 2,300	John Jennings, capital	$58,400
Accounts receivable	15,300	Land	14,000
Automobile	4,900	Notes payable	?
Building	28,900	Office equipment	4,300
Cash	7,800		

Ex. 2-4 Enter the following transactions in T accounts drawn on ordinary notebook paper. Label each debit and credit with the letter identifying the transaction. Prepare a trial balance at May 31.
(a) On May 10, Bryant Miller opened a bank account in the name of his new business, World Travel Service, by making a deposit of $20,000 cash.
(b) On May 13, purchased land for cash of $10,000.
(c) On May 18, a prefabricated building was purchased at a cost of $12,000. A cash payment of $3,000 was made and a note payable was issued for the balance.
(d) On May 20, office equipment was purchased at a cost of $3,000. A cash down payment of $1,000 was made, and it was agreed that the balance should be paid within 30 days.
(e) On May 30, paid $1,000 of the $2,000 liability arising from the purchase of office equipment on May 20.

Ex. 2-5 Enter the following transactions in the two-column journal of Crystal Pool Service Company. Include a brief explanation of the transaction as part of each journal entry. Do not include in the explanation amounts or account titles since these are shown in the debit-credit portion of the entry.
June 1 Acquired office equipment from Bell Company for $850 cash.
June 3 Collected an account receivable of $2,000 from a customer, William Rinehart.
June 4 Issued a cheque for $360 in full payment of an account payable to Chemical Supply Company.
June 8 The owner, Ralph James, invested an additional $5,000 cash in the business.
June 8 Borrowed $7,500 cash from the bank by signing a 90-day note payable.
June 9 Purchased an adjacent vacant lot for use as parking space. The price was $12,000, of which $2,000 was paid in cash; a note payable was issued for the balance.

Ex. 2-6 Which of the following errors would cause unequal totals in a trial balance? Give a brief explanatory statement for each paragraph.

a A cheque for $500 issued to pay an account payable was recorded by debiting Accounts Payable $500 and crediting Accounts Receivable $500.

b Collection of an account receivable in the amount of $500 was recorded by a debit to Cash for $500 and a debit to the owner's capital account for $500.

c A payment of $125 to a creditor was recorded by a debit to Accounts Payable of $125 and a credit to Cash of $25.

d A $350 payment for a typewriter was recorded as a debit to Office Equipment of $35 and a credit to Cash of $35.

Ex. 2-7 Williams Company has liabilities to numerous suppliers. The trial balance prepared by the company at December 31 was not in balance. In searching for the error, an employee discovered that a transaction for the purchase of a typewriter on credit for $530 had been recorded by a *debit* of $530 to the Office Equipment account and a *debit* of $530 to Accounts Payable. The credit column of the incorrect trial balance had a total of $85,300.

In answering each of the following five questions, explain briefly the reasons underlying your answer and state the dollar amount of the error if any.

a Was the Office Equipment account overstated, understated, or correctly stated in the trial balance?

b Was the total of the debit column of the trial balance overstated, understated, or correctly stated?

c Was the Accounts Payable account overstated, understated, or correctly stated in the trial balance?

d Was the total of the credit column of the trial balance overstated, understated or correctly stated?

e How much was the total of the debit column of the trial balance before correction of the error?

PROBLEMS

Group A

2A-1 The Opinion Research Company was organized to conduct polls on various issues of interest to political candidates. The following alphabetical list shows the account balances at February 28, 19____ .

Accounts payable	$ 6,809	Notes payable	$52,500
Accounts receivable	1,045	Notes receivable	13,000
Automobiles	6,700	Office building	24,000
Cash	?	Office supplies	552
Computer	23,550	Raymond Jones, capital	40,000
Furniture & fixtures	5,276	Taxes payable	587
Garage building	3,100	Government of Canada bonds	
Land	14,673	(should follow Cash)	5,000

Instructions

a Prepare a trial balance with the above accounts arranged in the usual sequence in which accounts appear in the ledger. (Compute the balance for Cash so that the ledger will be in balance.)

b Prepare a balance sheet.

2A-2 While organizing a new business, to be called Del Amo Beauty Shop, the owner, Jane Campbell, maintained only an informal record of transactions in the form of T accounts. She asks you to develop from the T accounts a ledger using the standard three-column running balance form of account and to determine that the records are in balance. She explains that she will prepare journal entries herself from some rough notes she has kept, but that she needs some assistance in establishing the running balance form of ledger accounts. The T accounts reflecting all February transactions are as follows:

Cash			1
2/1	10,000	2/3	6,000
		2/7	90
		2/22	250

Notes Payable		30
	2/3	21,000

Office Supplies		9
2/7	90	

Accounts Payable			31
2/22	250	2/6	1,800
		2/12	250

Land		20
2/3	7,000	

Jane Campbell, Capital		50
	2/1	10,000

Building		22
2/3	20,000	

Office Equipment		25
2/6	1,800	
2/12	250	

Instructions

a Transfer the information shown by the T accounts to ledger accounts of the three-column running balance type.

b Prepare a trial balance at February 28 from the ledger accounts completed in part (*a*).

2A-3 On October 1 Jon Linden, a real estate broker, decided to organize his own business, to be known as Linden Realty. The following events occurred during October:

Oct. 1 Jon Linden opened a bank account in the name of the business by depositing personal savings of $25,000.

Oct. 2 Purchased land and a small office building at a total price of $36,000. The terms of purchase required a cash payment of $16,000 and the issuance of a note payable for $20,000. The records of the tax assessor indicated that the value of the building was one-half that of the land.

Oct. 4 Sold one-quarter of the land at cost of $6,000 to an adjacent business, Community Medical Clinic, which wished to enlarge its parking lot. No down payment was required. Terms of the sale called for payment of $2,000 within 10 days and the balance within 30 days.

Oct. 10 Purchased office equipment on credit from Swingline Company in the amount of $2,100.

Oct. 14 Received cash of $2,000 as partial collection of the receivable from Community Medical Clinic.

Oct. 19 Paid $1,200 as partial settlement of the liability to Swingline Company.

The account titles and account numbers to be used are:

Cash	11	Notes payable	30
Accounts receivable	15	Accounts payable	32
Land	21	Jon Linden, capital	50
Building	23		
Office equipment	26		

Instructions
a Prepare journal entries for the month of October.
b Post to ledger accounts of the three-column running balance type.
c Prepare a trial balance at October 31.

2A-4 The following T accounts summarize the information contained in the ledger of Ball Company at October 31, 19___.

Cash			Notes Payable	
12,773	13,144			5,000
1,328	831			
3,091				
778				

Accounts Receivable			Accounts Payable	
1,244	3,091		12,144	454
4,318				1,265
34,948				11,965

Land			Taxes Payable	
20,000			731	946

Building			Mortgage Payable	
32,000				28,000

Furniture & Fixtures			Howard Ball, Capital	
2,500	328			50,000
7,300				22,000

Delivery Equipment		
4,747	878

Instructions
a Compute the account balances and prepare a trial balance at October 31, 19___.
b Prepare a balance sheet at October 31, 19___.

2A-5 After several years' managerial experience with a national automobile rental company, Melvin Gray decided to establish his own business, to be known as Economy Car Rental Company. The business transactions during January while the new enterprise was being organized were as follows:

Jan. 1 Melvin Gray withdrew funds from his personal savings account and sold various securities to assemble a total of $80,000 in cash, which he deposited in a bank current account in the name of the business, Economy Car Rental Company.

Jan. 2 The new company purchased land and a building at a cost of $50,000, of which $30,000 was regarded as applicable to the land and $20,000 to the building. The transaction involved a cash payment of $18,000 and the issuance of a note payable for $32,000.

Jan. 4 Purchased 20 new automobiles at $3,500 each from Fleet Sales Ltd. Paid $20,000 cash, the balance to be paid in 90 days.

Jan. 6 Sold an automobile at cost to Gray's brother-in-law, John Blane, who paid $1,500 in cash and agreed to pay the balance within 30 days.

Jan. 7 One of the automobiles was found to be defective and was returned to Fleet Sales Ltd. The amount payable to this creditor was thereby reduced by $3,500.

Jan. 19 Purchased office equipment at a cost of $2,800 cash.

Jan. 25 Issued a cheque for $20,000 in partial payment of the liability to Fleet Sales Ltd.

Instructions

a Journalize the above transactions, then post to ledger accounts. Use the running balance form of ledger account rather than T accounts. The account titles and the account numbers to be used are as follows:

Cash	10	Notes payable	31
Accounts receivable	11	Accounts payable	32
Land	16	Melvin Gray, capital	50
Buildings	17		
Office equipment	20		
Automobiles	22		

b Prepare a trial balance at January 31, 19___.

Group B

2B-1 At March 31, an alphabetical list of the accounts of the Community Theater showed the following balances:

Accounts payable	$ 4,125	Notes payable	$14,100
Accounts receivable	500	Notes receivable	1,500
Building	33,000	Office equipment	2,625
Cash	1,100	Stage equipment	5,545
Land	18,000	Supplies	510
Lighting equipment	5,600	Taxes payable	750
Mortgage payable	20,000	Wayne Ward, capital	?

Instructions

a Prepare a trial balance with the accounts arranged in the normal financial statement order.

b Prepare a balance sheet.

2B-2 The transactions of Valley Ice Skating Rink, a newly formed business, have been recorded by the owner, Casey Gaunt, in informally constructed T accounts. He asks you to transfer this information into ledger accounts of the three-column running balance type. He will prepare journal entries from memoranda and documents in his possession. The T accounts are shown below, with the related debits and credits representing each transaction identified by a letter as well as by date. (In transaction (e) on September 15, a motor originally included in the earlier purchase of equipment was sold on credit to a friend of Casey Gaunt's at its cost of $400.)

Cash				1
9/1	(a) 25,000	9/3	(b) 5,000	
9/25	(f) 300	9/29	(g) 15,000	

Notes Payable		30
	9/3	(b) 35,000

Accounts Receivable				4
9/15	(e) 400	9/25	(f) 300	

Accounts Payable				31
9/29	(g) 15,000	9/6	(c) 20,000	
		9/12	(d) 1,200	

Land		20
9/3	(b) 15,000	

Casey Gaunt, Capital		50
	9/1	(a) 25,000

Building		22
9/3	(b) 25,000	

Equipment				25
9/6	(c) 20,000	9/15	(e) 400	
9/12	(d) 1,200			

Instructions

a Transfer the information shown by the T accounts to ledger accounts of the three-column running balance type.

b Prepare a trial balance at September 30 from the ledger accounts completed in part (*a*).

2B-3 Property Management Company was started on July 1, 19___, by James Harrison to provide managerial services for the owners of apartment buildings. The organizational period extended throughout the month of July and included the transactions listed below.

The account titles and account numbers to be used are:

Cash	11	Notes payable	31
Accounts receivable	15	Accounts payable	32
Land	21	James Harrison, capital	51
Building	23		
Office equipment	25		

July 2 Opened a bank account in the name of the business, Property Management Company, by depositing personal savings in the amount of $35,000.

July 5 Purchased land and an office building for a price of $50,000, of which $24,000 was considered applicable to the land and $26,000 was attributable to the building. A cash down payment of $15,000 was made and a note payable for $35,000 was issued for the balance of the purchase price.

July 8 Purchased office equipment on credit from Malone Office Equipment, $2,750.

July 10 A typewriter (cost $350) which was part of the July 8 purchase of office equipment proved defective and was returned for credit to Malone Office Equipment.

July 12 Sold to Miller's Pharmacy at cost one-third of the land acquired on July 5. No down payment was required. The buyer promised to pay one-half the purchase price of $8,000 within 10 days and the remainder by August 12.

July 20 Paid $1,000 in partial settlement of the liability to Malone Office Equipment.

July 22 Received cash of $4,000 as partial collection of the account receivable from Miller's Pharmacy.

Instructions
a Prepare journal entries for the month of July.
b Post to ledger accounts of the three-column running balance type.
c Prepare a trial balance at July 31.

2B-4 The Moran Stenographic Service is located in a suburban office building and provides typing, duplicating, and other stenographic services to the tenants of the building and to other clients. As of March 31, 19___, the ledger accounts contained entries as follows:

Cash			Notes Payable	
1,890.70	518.60		1,000.00	14,000.00
561.50	1,000.00			
2,465.00	595.00			
315.00	360.00			

Accounts Receivable			Accounts Payable	
3,798.00	260.00		318.60	232.35
263.00	55.00		200.00	318.60
55.00			360.00	890.00
190.50				267.00
2,105.00				511.35

Office Supplies			Taxes Payable	
1,500.00			265.00	1,465.00
250.00			330.00	
250.00				

Office Equipment			Earl Moran, Capital	
13,240.00				15,084.40

Delivery Equipment	
6,200.00	

Instructions
a Determine the account balances and prepare a trial balance as of March 31, 19___.
b Prepare a balance sheet.

2B-5 On October 1, Robert Steel, a public accountant, resigned his position with a CA firm in a large city in order to move to a small town and open his own public accounting practice. His business transactions during October while the new enterprise was being organized are listed below:

Oct. 2 Steel opened a bank current account in the name of his firm, Robert Steel, Chartered Accountant, by depositing $42,000 which he had saved over a period of years.

Oct. 3 Purchased a small office building located on a large lot for a total price of $76,000, of which $40,000 was applicable to the land and $36,000 to the building. A cash payment of $38,000 was made and a note payable was issued for the balance of the purchase price.

Oct. 4 Purchased a used calculating machine for $320, paying cash.

Oct. 5 Purchased office furniture, filing cabinets, and a typewriter from Rogers Office Supply Co. at a cost of $3,300. A cash down payment of $600 was made, the balance to be paid in three equal installments due October 26, November 26, and December 26. The purchase was on open account and did not require the signing of a promissory note.

Oct. 9 Three-quarters of the land purchased on October 4 was sold for $30,000 to Miles Drug Company. The buyer made a down payment of $10,000 cash and agreed to pay the balance within 20 days. Since the land was sold at the same price per foot Steel had paid for it, there was no gain or loss on the transaction.

Oct. 26 Paid Rogers Office Supply Co. $900 cash as the first installment due on the account payable for office equipment.

Oct. 29 Received $20,000 cash from Miles Drug Company in full settlement of the account receivable created in the transaction of October 9.

Instructions

a Journalize the above transactions, then post to ledger accounts. Use the running balance form of ledger account rather than T accounts. The account titles and the account numbers to be used are:

Cash	10	Office equipment	23
Accounts receivable	16	Notes payable	32
Land	20	Accounts payable	35
Building	22	Robert Steel, capital	50

b Prepare a trial balance at October 31.

BUSINESS DECISION PROBLEM 2

Roger Hilton, a college student with several summers' experience as a guide on canoe camping trips, decided to go into business for himself. On June 1 he borrowed $2,000 from his father and signed a three-year note payable which stated that no interest would be charged. He deposited this borrowed money along with $1,000 of his own savings in a business bank account to begin a business known as Wilderness Canoe Trails. Also on June 1, Wilderness Canoe Trails carried out the following transactions:

(1) Bought a number of canoes at a total cost of $4,000; paid $1,000 cash and agreed to pay the balance within 60 days.

(2) Bought camping equipment at a cost of $2,000 payable in 60 days.

(3) Bought supplies for cash, $500.

After the close of the season on September 10, Hilton asked another student, Douglas Ward, who had taken a course in accounting, to help him determine the financial condition of the business.

The only record Hilton had maintained was a chequebook with memorandum notes written on the cheque stubs. From this source Ward discovered that Hilton had invested an additional $1,000 of his own savings in the business on July 1, and also that the accounts payable arising from the purchase of the canoes and camping equipment had been paid in full. A bank statement received from the bank on September 10 showed a balance on deposit of $2,025.

Hilton informed Ward that he had deposited in the bank all cash received by the business. He had also paid by cheque all bills immediately upon receipt; consequently, as of September 10 all bills for the season had been paid.

The canoes and camping equipment were all in excellent condition at the end of the season and Hilton planned to resume operations the following summer. In fact he had already accepted reservations from many customers who wished to return. Ward felt that some consideration should be given to the wear and tear on the canoes and equipment but he agreed with Hilton that for the present purpose the canoes and equipment should be listed in the balance sheet at the original cost. The supplies remaining on hand had cost $25 and Hilton felt that he could obtain a refund for this amount by returning them to the supplier.

Ward suggested that two balance sheets be prepared, one to show the condition of the business on June 1 and the other showing the condition on September 10. He also recommended to Hilton that a complete set of accounting records be established.

Instructions

a Use the information in the first paragraph as a basis for preparing a balance sheet dated June 1.

b Prepare a balance sheet at September 10. (Because of the incomplete information available, it is not possible to determine the amount of cash at September 10 by adding cash receipts and deducting cash payments throughout the season. The amount on deposit as reported by the bank at September 10 is to be regarded as the total cash belonging to the business at that date.)

c By comparing the two balance sheets, compute the change in owner's equity. Explain the sources of this change in owner's equity and state whether you consider the business to be successful. Also comment on the cash position at the beginning and end of the season. Has the cash position improved significantly? Explain.

THREE

MEASURING BUSINESS INCOME

The earning of net income, or profits, is a major goal of most business enterprises. The individual who organizes a small business of his own does so with the hope and expectation that the business will operate at a profit, thereby increasing his equity in the business. In other words, **profit is an increase in the owner's equity resulting from operation of the business.** From the standpoint of the individual firm, profitable operation is essential if the firm is to succeed, or even to survive.

Profits may be retained in the business to finance expansion, or they may be withdrawn by the owner or owners. Some of the largest corporations have become large by retaining their profits in the business and using these profits for purposes of growth: retained profits may be used, for example, to acquire new plant and equipment, to carry on research leading to new and better products, and to extend sales operations into new territories. A satisfactory rate of business profits is generally associated with high employment, an improving standard of living, and a strong, expanding national economy.

Since the drive for profits underlies the very existence of business concerns, it follows that a most important function of an accounting system is to provide information about the profitability of the business. Before we can measure the profits of a business, we need to establish a sharp, clear meaning for **profits.** The word is used in somewhat different senses by economists, lawyers, and the general public. Perhaps for this reason, accountants prefer to use the alternative term **net income,** and to define this term very carefully. At this point, we shall adopt the technical accounting term "net income" in preference to the less precise term "profits."

In Chapter 1, accounting was referred to as the "language of business," and some of the key words of this language such as **assets, liabilities,** and **owner's equity,** were introduced. In the present chapter we want to establish clear working definitions for **revenue, expenses,** and **net income.** Very concisely stated, **revenue minus expenses equals net income.** To understand why this is true and how the measurements are made, let us begin with the meaning of revenue.

Revenue

Revenue is the price of goods sold and services rendered during a given time period. When a business renders services to its customers or delivers merchandise to them, it either receives immediate payment in cash or acquires an account receivable which will be collected and thereby become cash within a short time. The revenue for a given period is equal to the inflow of cash and receivables from sales made in that period. For any single transaction, the amount of revenue is a measurement of the asset values received from the customer.

Not all receipts of cash represent revenue; for example, as shown in Chapter 1, a business may obtain cash by borrowing from a bank. This increase in cash is offset by an increase in liabilities in the form of a note payable to the bank. The owner's equity is not changed by the borrowing transaction.

Collection of an account receivable is another example of a cash receipt that does not represent revenue. The act of collection causes an increase in the asset, cash, and a corresponding decrease in another asset, accounts receivable. The amount of total assets remains unchanged, and, of course, there is no change in liabilities or owner's equity.

As another example of the distinction between revenue and cash receipts, let us assume that a business begins operations in March and makes sales of merchandise and/or services to its customers in that month as follows: sales for cash, $25,000; sales on credit (payable in April), $15,000. The revenue for March is $40,000, an amount equal to the cash received or to be received from the month's sales. When the accounts receivable of $15,000 are collected during April, they must not be counted a second time in measuring revenue for April.

Revenue causes an increase in owner's equity. The inflow of cash and receivables from customers increases the total assets of the company; on the other side of the accounting equation, the liabilities do not change, but the owner's equity is increased to match the increase in total assets. Thus revenue is the gross increase in owner's equity resulting from business activities. Bear in mind, however, that not every increase in owner's equity comes from revenue. As illustrated in Chapter 1, the owner's equity is also increased by the investment of assets in the business by the owner.

Various terms are used to describe different types of revenue; for example, the revenues earned by a real estate broker may be called Commissions Earned; in the professional practice of lawyers, physicians, dentists, and CAs, the revenues are called Fees Earned; a person owning property and leasing it to others has revenue called Rent Earned; and businesses selling merchandise rather than services generally use the term Sales to describe the revenue earned.

Expenses

Expenses are the cost of the goods and services used up in the process of obtaining revenue. Examples include salaries paid employees, charges for newspaper advertising and for telephone service, and the wearing out (depreciation) of the building and office equipment. All these items are necessary to attract and serve customers and thereby to obtain revenue. Expenses are sometimes referred to as the "cost of doing business," that is, the cost of the various activities necessary to carry on a business. Since expenses are the cost of goods and services used up, they are also called *expired costs*.

Expenses cause the owner's equity to decrease. Revenue may be regarded as the positive factor in producing net income, expenses as the negative factor. The relationship between expenses and revenue is a significant one; the expenses of a given month or other period are incurred in order to generate revenue in that same period. The salaries earned by sales employees waiting on customers during July are applicable to July revenues and should be treated as July expenses, even though these salaries may not actually be paid to the employees until sometime in August.

As previously explained, revenues and cash receipts are not one and the same thing; similarly, expenses and cash payments are not identical. Examples of cash payments which are not expenses of the current period include the purchase of an office building for cash, the purchase of merchandise for later sale to customers, the repayment of a bank loan, and withdrawals of cash from the business by the owner. In deciding whether a given item should be regarded as an expense of the current period, it is often helpful to pose the following questions:

1 Was the alleged "expense" incurred in order to obtain revenue of the current period?

2 Does the item in question reduce the owner's equity?

Withdrawals by the owner

The owner of an unincorporated business invests money in the enterprise and devotes all or part of his time to its affairs in hopes that the business will earn a profit. The owner does not receive interest on the money he invests nor a salary for his personal services. His incentive, rather than interest or salary, is the increase in owner's equity that will result if the business earns a net income.

An owner of an unincorporated business usually makes withdrawals of cash from time to time for his personal use. These withdrawals are in anticipation of profits and are not regarded as an expense of the business. The withdrawal of cash by the owner is like an expense in one respect; it reduces the owner's equity. However, expenses are incurred for the purpose of generating revenue, and a withdrawal of cash by the owner does not have this purpose. From time to time the owner may also make additional investments in the business. The investment of cash and the withdrawal of cash by the owner may be thought of as exact opposites: the investment does not represent revenue; the withdrawal does not represent an expense. Investments and withdrawals of cash affect only balance sheet accounts and are not reported in the income statement.

Since a withdrawal of cash reduces the owner's equity, it *could be* recorded by debiting the owner's capital account (James Roberts, Capital, in our example). However, a clearer record is created if a separate *drawing account* (James Roberts, Drawing) is debited to record all amounts withdrawn. The drawing account is also known as a *personal account.*

Debits to the owner's drawing account are required for any of the following transactions:

1 Withdrawals of cash.

2 Withdrawals of other assets. The owner of a clothing store, for example, may withdraw merchandise for his personal use. The debit to the drawing account would be for the cost of the goods which were withdrawn.

3 Payment of the owner's personal bills out of company funds.

The disposition of the drawing account when financial statements are prepared will be illustrated later in this chapter.

Relating revenue and expenses to time periods

A balance sheet shows the financial position of the business at a given date. An income statement, on the other hand, shows the results of operations over *a period of time.* In fact, the concept of income is meaningless unless it is related to a period of time. For example, if a businessman says, "My business produces net income of $5,000," the meaning is not at all clear; it could be made clear, however, by relating the income to a time period, such as "$5,000 a week," "$5,000 a month," or "$5,000 a year."

THE ACCOUNTING PERIOD Every business concern prepares a yearly income statement, and most businesses prepare quarterly and monthly income statements as well. Management needs to know from month to month whether revenues are rising or falling, whether expenses are being held to the level anticipated, and how net income compares with the net income of the preceding month and with the net income of the corresponding month of the preceding year. The term *accounting period* means the span of time covered by an income statement. It may consist of a month, a quarter of a year, a half year, or a year.

Many income statements cover the calendar year ended December 31, but an increasing number of companies are adopting an annual accounting period ending with a month other than December. Generally a business finds it more convenient to end its annual accounting period during a slack season rather than during a time of peak activity. Any 12-month accounting period adopted by a business is called its *fiscal year.* A fiscal year ending at the annual low point of seasonal activity is said to be a *natural business year.* The fiscal year selected by the federal government for its accounting purposes begins on April 1 and ends 12 months later on March 31.

TRANSACTIONS AFFECTING TWO OR MORE ACCOUNTING PERIODS The operation of a business entails an endless stream of transactions, many of which begin in one accounting period but affect several succeeding periods. Fire insurance policies, for example, are commonly issued to cover a period of three years. In this case, the apportionment of the cost of the policy by months is an easy matter. If the policy covers three years (36 months) and costs, for example, $360, the insurance expense each month is $10.

Not all transactions can be so precisely divided by accounting periods. The purchase of a building, furniture and fixtures, machinery, a typewriter, or an automobile provides benefits to the business over all the years in which such an asset is used. No one can determine in advance exactly how many years of service will be received from such long-lived assets. Nevertheless, in measuring the net income of a business for a period of one year or less, the accountant must estimate what portion of the cost of the building and similar long-lived assets is applicable to the current year. Since the apportionments for these and many other transactions which overlap two or more accounting periods are in the nature of estimates rather than precise measurements, it follows that income statements should be regarded as useful approximations of annual income rather than as absolutely accurate determinations.

The only time period for which the measurement of net income can be absolutely accurate is the entire life span of the business. When a business concern sells all its assets, pays its debts, and ends its existence, it would then be possible to determine with precision the net income for the time period from the date of organization to the date of termination. Such a theoretically precise measurement of net income would, however, be too late to be of much use to the owners or managers of the business. The practical needs of business enterprise are well served by income statements of reasonable accuracy that tell managers and owners each month, each quarter, and each year the results of business operation.

Rules of debit and credit for revenue and expenses

Our approach to revenue and expenses has stressed the fact that revenue increases the owner's equity, and expenses decrease the owner's equity. The rules of debit and credit for recording revenue and expenses follow this relationship, and therefore the recording of revenue and expenses in ledger accounts requires only a slight extension of the rules of debit and credit presented in Chapter 2. The rule previously stated for recording increases and decreases in owner's equity was as follows:

Increases in owner's equity are recorded by credits.
Decreases in owner's equity are recorded by debits.

This rule is now extended to cover revenue and expense accounts:

Revenue increases owner's equity; therefore revenue is recorded by a credit.
Expenses decrease owner's equity; therefore expenses are recorded by debits.

Ledger accounts for revenue and expenses

During the course of an accounting period, a great many revenue and expense transactions occur in the average business. To classify and summarize these numerous transactions, a separate ledger account is maintained for each major type of revenue and expense. For example, almost every business maintains accounts for Advertising Expense, Telephone Expense, and Salaries Expense. At the end of the period, all the advertising expenses appear as debits in the Advertising Expense account. The debit balance of this account represents the total advertising expense of the period and is listed as one of the expense items in the income statement.

Revenue accounts are usually much less numerous than expense accounts. A small business such as the Roberts Real Estate Agency in our continuing illustration may have only one or two types of revenue, such as commissions earned from arranging sales of real estate, and commissions earned from the rental of properties in behalf of clients. In a business of this type, the revenue accounts might be called Sales Commissions Earned and Rental Commissions Earned.

RECORDING REVENUE AND EXPENSE TRANSACTIONS: ILLUSTRATION
The organization of the Roberts Real Estate Agency during September has already been described. The illustration is now continued for October, during which month the company earned commissions by selling several residences for its clients. Bear in mind that the company does not own any residential property; it merely acts as a broker or agent for clients wishing to sell their houses. A commission of 6% of the sales price of the house is charged for this service. During October the company not only earned commissions but also incurred a number of expenses.

Note that each illustrated transaction which affects an income statement account also affects a balance sheet account. This pattern is consistent with our previous discussion of revenue and expenses. In recording revenue transactions, we shall debit the assets received and credit a revenue account. In recording expense transactions, we shall debit an expense account and credit the asset Cash, or perhaps a liability account if payment is to be made later. The transactions for October were as follows:

Oct. 1 Paid $120 for publication of newspaper advertising describing various houses offered for sale.

	Analysis	Rule	Entry
Advertising expense incurred and paid	The cost of advertising is an expense	Expenses decrease the owner's equity and are recorded by debits	Debit: Advertising Expense, $120
	The asset Cash was decreased	Decreases in assets are recorded by credits	Credit: Cash, $120

Oct. 6 Earned and collected a commission of $750 by selling a residence previously listed by a client.

	Analysis	Rule	Entry
Revenue earned and collected	The asset Cash was increased	Increases in assets are recorded by debits	Debit: Cash, $750
	Revenue was earned	Revenue increases the owner's equity and is recorded by a credit	Credit: Sales Commissions Earned, $750

Oct. 16 Newspaper advertising was ordered at a price of $90, payment to be made within 30 days.

	Analysis	Rule	Entry
Advertising expense incurred but not paid	The cost of advertising is an expense	Expenses decrease the owner's equity and are recorded by debits	Debit: Advertising Expense, $90
	An account payable, a liability, was incurred	Increases in liabilities are recorded by credits	Credit: Accounts Payable, $90

Oct. 20 A commission of $1,130 was earned by selling a client's residence. The sales agreement provided that the commission would be paid in 60 days.

	Analysis	Rule	Entry
Revenue earned, to be collected later	*An asset in the form of an account receivable was acquired*	*Increases in assets are recorded by debits*	*Debit: Accounts Receivable, $1,130*
	Revenue was earned	*Revenue increases the owner's equity and is recorded by a credit*	*Credit: Sales Commissions Earned, $1,130*

Oct. 30 Paid salaries of $700 to office employees for services rendered during October.

	Analysis	Rule	Entry
Salaries expense incurred and paid	*Salaries of employees are an expense*	*Expenses decrease the owner's equity and are recorded by debits*	*Debit: Office Salaries Expense, $700*
	The asset Cash was decreased	*Decreases in assets are recorded by credits*	*Credit: Cash, $700*

Oct. 30 A telephone bill for October amounting to $48 was received. Payment was required by November 10.

	Analysis	Rule	Entry
Telephone expense incurred, to be paid later	*The cost of telephone service is an expense*	*Expenses decrease the owner's equity and are recorded by debits*	*Debit: Telephone Expense, $48*
	An account payable, a liability, was incurred	*Increases in liabilities are recorded by credits*	*Credit: Accounts Payable, $48*

Oct. 30 Roberts withdrew $600 cash for his personal use.

	Analysis	Rule	Entry
Withdrawal of cash by owner	*Withdrawal of assets by the owner decreases the owner's equity*	*Decreases in owner's equity are recorded by debits*	*Debit: James Roberts, Drawing, $600*
	The asset Cash was decreased	*Decreases in assets are recorded by credits*	*Credit: Cash, $600*

The journal entries to record the October transactions are as follows:

General Journal *Page 2*

<table>
<tr><th colspan="2">Date</th><th>Account Titles and Explanation</th><th>LP</th><th>Debit</th><th>Credit</th></tr>
<tr><td>19__</td><td></td><td></td><td></td><td></td><td></td></tr>
<tr><td>Oct.</td><td>1</td><td>Advertising Expense............</td><td>70</td><td>120</td><td></td></tr>
<tr><td></td><td></td><td>   Cash ....</td><td>1</td><td></td><td>120</td></tr>
<tr><td></td><td></td><td>Paid for newspaper advertising.</td><td></td><td></td><td></td></tr>
<tr><td></td><td>6</td><td>Cash ....</td><td>1</td><td>750</td><td></td></tr>
<tr><td></td><td></td><td>   Sales Commissions Earned ......</td><td>61</td><td></td><td>750</td></tr>
<tr><td></td><td></td><td>Earned and collected commission by selling residence for client.</td><td></td><td></td><td></td></tr>
<tr><td></td><td>16</td><td>Advertising Expense............</td><td>70</td><td>90</td><td></td></tr>
<tr><td></td><td></td><td>   Accounts Payable ....</td><td>30</td><td></td><td>90</td></tr>
<tr><td></td><td></td><td>Ordered newspaper advertising; payable in 30 days.</td><td></td><td></td><td></td></tr>
<tr><td></td><td>20</td><td>Accounts Receivable ....</td><td>2</td><td>1,130</td><td></td></tr>
<tr><td></td><td></td><td>   Sales Commissions Earned ......</td><td>61</td><td></td><td>1,130</td></tr>
<tr><td></td><td></td><td>Earned commission by selling residence for client; commission to be received in 60 days.</td><td></td><td></td><td></td></tr>
<tr><td></td><td>30</td><td>Office Salaries Expense ....</td><td>72</td><td>700</td><td></td></tr>
<tr><td></td><td></td><td>   Cash ....</td><td>1</td><td></td><td>700</td></tr>
<tr><td></td><td></td><td>Paid office salaries for October.</td><td></td><td></td><td></td></tr>
<tr><td></td><td>30</td><td>Telephone Expense ....</td><td>74</td><td>48</td><td></td></tr>
<tr><td></td><td></td><td>   Accounts Payable ....</td><td>30</td><td></td><td>48</td></tr>
<tr><td></td><td></td><td>To record liability for October telephone service.</td><td></td><td></td><td></td></tr>
<tr><td></td><td>30</td><td>James Roberts, Drawing ....</td><td>51</td><td>600</td><td></td></tr>
<tr><td></td><td></td><td>   Cash ....</td><td>1</td><td></td><td>600</td></tr>
<tr><td></td><td></td><td>Withdrawal of cash by owner.</td><td></td><td></td><td></td></tr>
</table>

October journal entries for Roberts Real Estate Agency

The column headings at the top of the illustrated journal page (*Date, Account Titles and Explanation, LP, Debit,* and *Credit*) are seldom used in practice. They are included here as an instructional guide but will be omitted from some of the later illustrations of journal entries.

Sequence of accounts in the ledger

Accounts are located in the ledger in financial statement order; that is, the balance sheet accounts first (assets, liabilities, and owner's equity) followed by the income statement accounts (revenues and expenses). The usual sequence of accounts within these five groups is shown by the following listing.

Balance Sheet Accounts	**Income Statement Accounts**
Assets:	Revenues:
Cash	Commissions earned, (fees earned, rent
Marketable securities	earned, sales, etc.)
Notes receivable	Expenses: (No standard sequence of listing
Accounts receivable	exists for expense accounts.)
Inventory (discussed in Chapter 5)	Advertising
Office supplies, (unexpired insurance, pre-	Salaries
paid rent, and other prepaid expenses dis-	Rent
cussed in Chapter 4)	Telephone
Land	Depreciation
Buildings	Various other expenses
Equipment	
Other assets	
Liabilities:	
Notes payable	
Accounts payable	
Salaries payable (and other short-term lia-	
bilities discussed in Chapter 4).	
Owner's equity:	
John Doe, capital	
John Doe, drawing	

Why are ledger accounts arranged in financial statement order?

Remember that a trial balance is prepared by listing the ledger account balances shown in the ledger, working from the first ledger page to the last. Therefore, if the accounts are located in the ledger in *financial statement order,* the same sequence will naturally be followed in the trial balance, and this arrangement will make it easier to prepare the balance sheet and income statement from the trial balance. Also, this standard arrangement of accounts will make it easier to locate any account in the ledger.

Ledger accounts for Roberts Real Estate Agency: Illustration

The ledger of the Roberts Real Estate Agency after the October transactions have been posted is now illustrated. The accounts appear in financial statement order. To conserve space in this illustration, several ledger accounts appear on a single page; in actual practice, however, each account occupies a separate page in the ledger.

Cash
Account No.

Date		Explanation	Ref	Debit	Credit	Balance
19— Sept.	1		1	20000 00		20000 00
	3		1		7000 00	13000 00
	5		1		5000 00	8000 00
	20		1	500 00		8500 00
	30		1		1000 00	7500 00
Oct.	1		2		120 00	7380 00
	6		2	750 00		8130 00
	30		2		700 00	7430 00
	30		2		600 00	6830 00

Accounts Receivable
Account No. 2

Date		Explanation	Ref	Debit	Credit	Balance
19— Sept.	10		1	2000 00		2000 00
	20		1		500 00	1500 00
Oct.	20		2	1130 00		2630 00

Land
Account No. 20

Date		Explanation	Ref	Debit	Credit	Balance
19— Sept.	3		1	7000 00		7000 00
	10		1		2000 00	5000 00

Building
Account No. 22

Date		Explanation	Ref	Debit	Credit	Balance
19— Sept.	5		1	12000 00		12000 00

Office Equipment
Account No. 25

Date		Explanation	Ref	Debit	Credit	Balance
19— Sept.	14		1	1800 00		1800 00

Accounts Payable

Account No. 30

Date		Explanation	Ref	Debit	Credit	Balance
19— Sept.	5		1		7000 00	7000 00
	14		1		1800 00	8800 00
	30		1	1000 00		7800 00
Oct.	16		2		90 00	7890 00
	30		2		48 00	7938 00

James Roberts, Capital

Account No. 50

Date		Explanation	Ref	Debit	Credit	Balance
19— Sept.	1		1		20000 00	20000 00

James Roberts, Drawing

Account No. 51

Date		Explanation	Ref	Debit	Credit	Balance
19— Oct.	30		2	500 00		500 00

Sales Commissions Earned

Account No. 61

Date		Explanation	Ref	Debit	Credit	Balance
19— Oct.	6		2		750 00	750 00
	20		2		1130 00	1880 00

Advertising Expense

Account No. 70

Date		Explanation	Ref	Debit	Credit	Balance
19— Oct.	1		2	120 00		120 00
	16		2	90 00		210 00

Office Salaries Expense

Account No. 72

Date		Explanation	Ref	Debit	Credit	Balance
19— Oct.	30		2	700 00		700 00

Telephone Expense

Account No. 74

Date		Explanation	Ref	Debit	Credit	Balance
19— Oct.	30		2	48 00		48 00

Trial balance

The trial balance at October 31 was prepared from the preceding ledger accounts.

ROBERTS REAL ESTATE AGENCY
Trial Balance
October 31, 19___

Proving the equality of debits and credits

Cash	$ 6,830	
Accounts receivable	2,630	
Land	5,000	
Building	12,000	
Office equipment	1,800	
Accounts payable		$ 7,938
James Roberts, capital		20,000
James Roberts, drawing	600	
Sales commissions earned		1,880
Advertising expense	210	
Office salaries expense	700	
Telephone expense	48	
	$29,818	$29,818

Recording depreciation at the end of the period

The preceding trial balance includes all the October expenses requiring cash payments such as salaries, advertising, and telephone service, but it does not include any depreciation expense. Although depreciation expense does not require a monthly cash outlay, it is nevertheless an inevitable and continuing expense. Failure to make an entry for depreciation expense would result in understating the total expenses of the period and consequently in overstating the net income.

BUILDING The office building purchased by the Roberts Real Estate Agency at a cost of $12,000 is estimated to have a useful life of 20 years. The purpose of the $12,000 expenditure was to provide a place in which to carry on the business and thereby to obtain revenue. After 20 years of use the building will be worthless and the original cost of $12,000 will have been entirely consumed. In effect, the company has purchased 20 years of "housing services" at a total cost of $12,000. A portion of this cost expires during each year of use of the building. If we assume that each year's operations should bear an equal share of the total cost (straight-line depreciation), the annual depreciation expense will amount to $\frac{1}{20}$ of $12,000, or $600. On a monthly basis, depreciation expense is $50 ($12,000 cost ÷ 240 months). There are alternative methods of spreading the cost of a depreciable asset over its useful life, some of which will be considered in Chapter 11.

The journal entry to record depreciation of the building during October follows:

General Journal

Date		Account Titles and Explanation	LP	Debit	Credit
19...					
Oct.	31	Depreciation Expense: Building	76	50	
		Accumulated Depreciation: Building .	23		50
		To record depreciation for October.			

Recording depreciation of the building

The depreciation expense account will appear in the income statement for October along with the other expenses of salaries, advertising, and telephone expense. The Accumulated Depreciation: Building account will appear in the balance sheet as a deduction from the Building account, as shown by the following illustration of a *partial* balance sheet:

Showing accumulated depreciation in the balance sheet

ROBERTS REAL ESTATE AGENCY
Partial Balance Sheet
October 31, 19___

Building (at cost). $12,000
Less: Accumulated depreciation 50 $11,950

The end result of crediting the Accumulated Depreciation: Building account is much the same as if the credit had been made to the Building account; that is, the net amount shown on the balance sheet for the building is reduced from $12,000 to $11,950. Although the credit side of a depreciation entry *could* be made directly to the asset account, it is customary and more efficient to record such credits in a separate account entitled Accumulated Depreciation. The original cost of the asset and the total amount of depreciation recorded over the years can more easily be determined from the ledger when separate accounts are maintained for the asset and for the accumulated depreciation.

Accumulated Depreciation: Building is an example of a *contra-asset account,* because it has a credit balance and is offset against an asset account (Building) to produce the proper balance sheet valuation for the asset.

OFFICE EQUIPMENT Depreciation on the office equipment of the Roberts Real Estate Agency must also be recorded at the end of October. This equipment cost $1,800 and is assumed to have a useful life of 10 years. Monthly depreciation expense on the straight-line basis is, therefore, $15, computed by dividing the cost of $1,800 by the useful life of 120 months. The journal entry is as follows:

General Journal

Date		Account Titles and Explanation	LP	Debit	Credit
19...					
Oct.	31	Depreciation Expense: Office Equipment . .	78	15	
		Accumulated Depreciation: Office			
		Equipment	26		15
		To record depreciation for October.			

Recording depreciation of office equipment

No depreciation was recorded on the building and office equipment for September, the month in which these assets were acquired, because regular operations did not begin until October. Generally, depreciation is not recognized until the business begins active operation and the assets are placed in use. Accountants often use the expression "matching costs and revenues" to convey the idea of writing off the cost of an asset to expense during the time periods in which the business uses the asset to generate revenues.

The journal entry by which depreciation is recorded at the end of the month is called an *adjusting entry.* The adjustment of certain asset accounts and related expense accounts is a necessary step at the end of each accounting period so that the information presented in the financial statements will be as accurate and complete as possible. In the next chapter, adjusting entries will be shown for some other items in addition to depreciation.

The adjusted trial balance

After all the necessary adjusting entries have been journalized and posted, an *adjusted trial balance* is prepared to prove that the ledger is still in balance. It also provides a complete listing of the account balances to be used in preparing the financial statements. The following adjusted trial balance differs from the trial balance shown on page 77 because it includes accounts for depreciation expense and accumulated depreciation.

ROBERTS REAL ESTATE AGENCY
Adjusted Trial Balance
October 31, 19___

Cash	$ 6,830	
Accounts receivable	2,630	
Land	5,000	
Building	12,000	
Accumulated depreciation: building		$ 50
Office equipment	1,800	
Accumulated depreciation: office equipment		15
Accounts payable		7,938
James Roberts, capital		20,000
James Roberts, drawing	600	
Sales commissions earned		1,880
Advertising expense	210	
Office salaries expense	700	
Telephone expense	48	
Depreciation expense: building	50	
Depreciation expense: office equipment	15	
	$29,883	$29,883

Adjusted trial balance

FINANCIAL STATEMENTS

The income statement

When we measure the net income earned by a business we are measuring its economic performance—its success or failure as a business enterprise. The owner, the manager, and the company's banker are anxious to see the latest available income statement and thereby to judge how well the company is doing. If the business is organized as a corporation, the stockholders and prospective investors also will be keenly interested in each successive income statement. The October income statement for Roberts Real Estate Agency appears as follows:

ROBERTS REAL ESTATE AGENCY

Income Statement

For the Month Ended October 31, 19___

Sales commissions earned		$1,880
Expenses:		
Advertising expense	$ 210	
Office salaries expense	700	
Telephone expense	48	
Depreciation expense: building	50	
Depreciation expense: office equipment	15	1,023
Net income		$ 857

Income statement showing results of operations for October

This income statement consists of the last six accounts in the adjusted trial balance on page 79. It shows that the revenue during October exceeded the expenses of the month, thus producing a net income of $857. Bear in mind, however, that our measurement of net income is not absolutely accurate or precise, because of the assumptions and estimates involved in the accounting process. We have recorded only those economic events which are evidenced by accounting transactions. Perhaps during October the Roberts Real Estate Agency has developed a strong interest on the part of many clients who are on the verge of buying or selling homes. This accumulation of client interest is an important step toward profitable operation, but is not reflected in the October 31 income statement because it is not subject to objective measurement. Remember also that in determining the amount of depreciation expense we had to estimate the useful life of the building and office equipment. Any error in our estimates is reflected in the net income reported for October. Despite these limitations, the income statement is of vital importance, and indicates that the new business has been profitable during the first month of its operation.

Alternative titles for the income statement include *earnings statement, statement of operations,* and *profit and loss statement.* However, *income statement* is still the most popular term for this important financial statement.

The following table[1] shows the terminology in title used for the income statement by major Canadian corporations:

Terminology in Title for the Income Statement

	Number of Companies			Percentage		
Title Used	1970	1969	1968	1970	1969	1968
Income	153	153	140	47	47	43
Earnings	136	129	124	42	40	38
Profit and Loss	17	25	39	5	8	12
Operations	7	7	7	2	2	2
Other	12	11	15	4	3	5
	325	325	325	100	100	100

The balance sheet

Previous illustrations of balance sheets have been arranged in the *account form,* that is, with the assets on the left side of the page and the liabilities and owner's equity on the right side. The balance sheet below is shown in *report form,* that is, with the liabilities and owner's equity sections listed below rather than to the right of the asset section. Both the account form and the report form are widely used.

ROBERTS REAL ESTATE AGENCY
Balance Sheet
October 31, 19___

Assets

Balance sheet at October 31: report form	Cash		$ 6,830
	Accounts receivable		2,630
	Land		5,000
	Building	$12,000	
	Less: Accumulated depreciation	50	11,950
	Office equipment	$ 1,800	
	Less: Accumulated depreciation	15	1,785
			$28,195

[1] Source: *Financial Reporting In Canada,* Ninth Edition, Institute of Chartered Accountants, Toronto, 1971, Table 25, page 125.

Liabilities & Owner's Equity

Liabilities:		
Accounts payable		$ 7,938
Owner's equity:		
James Roberts, capital, Oct. 1, 19___	$20,000	
Net income for October	857	
Subtotal	$20,857	
Less: Withdrawals	600	
James Roberts, capital, Oct. 31, 19___		20,257
		$28,195

The relationship between the income statement and the balance sheet is shown in the owner's equity section of the balance sheet. The owner's original capital investment of $20,000 was increased by reason of the $857 net income earned during October, making a total equity of $20,857. This equity was decreased, however, by the owner's withdrawal of $600 in cash at the end of October, leaving a final balance of $20,257.

Alternative titles for the balance sheet include **statement of financial position** and **statement of financial condition.** Although "balance sheet" may not be a very descriptive term, it continues to be the most widely used, perhaps because of custom and tradition. In 1970, 95% of the major Canadian corporations surveyed by the Canadian Institute of Chartered Accountants used the title "balance sheet."[2]

In the Roberts Real Estate Agency illustration, we have shown the two common ways in which the owner's equity in a business may be increased: (1) investment of cash or other assets by the owner, and (2) operating the business at a profit. There are also two ways in which the owner's equity may be decreased: (1) withdrawal of assets by the owner, and (2) operating the business at a loss.

CLOSING THE ACCOUNTS

The accounts for revenues, expenses, and drawings are **temporary proprietorship accounts** used during the accounting period to classify changes affecting the owner's equity. At the end of the period, we want to transfer the net effect of these various increases and decreases into the permanent account showing the owner's equity. We also want to reduce the balances of the temporary proprietorship accounts to zero, so that these accounts will again be ready for use in accumulating information during the next accounting period. These objectives are accomplished by the use of **closing entries.**

Revenue and expense accounts are closed at the end of each accounting period by transferring their balances to a summary account called Income Summary. When the credit balances of the revenue ac-

[2] *Ibid*, page 24.

counts and the debit balances of the expense accounts have been transferred into one summary account, the balance of this Income Summary will be the net income or net loss for the period. If the revenues (credit balances) exceed the expenses (debit balances), the Income Summary account will have a credit balance representing net income. Conversely, if expenses exceed revenues, the Income Summary will have a debit balance representing net loss.

As previously explained, all debits and credits in the ledger are posted from the journal; therefore, the closing of revenue and expense accounts requires the making of journal entries and the posting of these journal entries to ledger accounts. A journal entry made for the purpose of closing a revenue or expense by transferring its balance to the Income Summary account is called a *closing entry.* This term is also applied to the journal entries (to be explained later) used in closing the Income Summary account and the owner's drawing account into the owner's capital account.

A principal purpose of the year-end process of closing the revenue and expense accounts is to reduce their balances to zero. Since the revenue and expense accounts provide the information for the income statement of *a given accounting period,* it is essential that these accounts have zero balances at the beginning of each new period. The closing of the books has the effect of wiping the slate clean and preparing the accounts for the recording of revenues and expenses during the succeeding accounting period.

It is common practice to close the books only once a year, but for illustration, we shall now demonstrate the closing of the books of the Roberts Real Estate Agency at October 31 after one month's operation.

CLOSING ENTRIES FOR REVENUE ACCOUNTS Revenue accounts have credit balances. Closing a revenue account, therefore, means transferring its credit balance to the Income Summary account. This transfer is accomplished by a journal entry debiting the revenue account in an amount equal to its credit balance, with an offsetting credit to the Income Summary account. The only revenue account of the Roberts Real Estate Agency is Sales Commission Earned, which had a credit balance of $1,880 at October 31. The journal entry necessary to close this account is as follows:

General Journal

Page 3

	Date		Account Titles and Explanation	LP	Debit	Credit
Closing a revenue account	19__ Oct.	31	Sales Commissions Earned	61	1,880	
			Income Summary	53		1,880
			To close the Sales Commissions Earned account.			

After this closing entry has been posted, the two accounts affected will appear as shown below. A few details of account structure have been omitted to simplify the illustration; a directional arrow has been added to show the transfer of the $1,880 balance of the revenue account into the Income Summary account.

Sales Commissions Earned					61
Date	Exp.	Ref	Debit	Credit	Balance
Oct. 6		2		750	750
20		2		1,130	1,880
31	To close	3	1,880		–0–

Income Summary					53
Date	Exp.	Ref	Debit	Credit	Balance
Oct. 31		3		1,880	1,880

CLOSING ENTRIES FOR EXPENSE ACCOUNTS Expense accounts have debit balances. Closing an expense account means transferring its debit balance to the Income Summary account. The journal entry to close an expense account, therefore, consists of a credit to the expense account in an amount equal to its debit balance, with an offsetting debit to the Income Summary account.

There are five expense accounts in the ledger of the Roberts Real Estate Agency. Five separate journal entries could be made to close these five expense accounts, but the use of one *compound journal entry* is an easier, more efficient, timesaving method of closing all five expense accounts. A compound journal entry is an entry that includes debits to more than one account or credits to more than one account.

	General Journal			Page 3
Date	Account Titles and Explanation	LP	Debit	Credit

Closing the various expense accounts by use of a compound journal entry

Date	Account Titles and Explanation	LP	Debit	Credit
Oct. 31	Income Summary	53	1,023	
	Advertising Expense	70		210
	Office Salaries Expense	72		700
	Telephone Expense	74		48
	Depreciation Expense: Building	76		50
	Depreciation Expense:			
	Office Equipment	78		15
	To close the expense accounts.			

(Date: 19___)

After this closing entry has been posted, the Income Summary account has a credit balance of $857, and the five expense accounts have zero balances, as shown on the following page.

Income Summary   Account No. 53

Date		Explanation	Ref	Debit	Credit	Balance
19__						
Oct.	31		3		1,880	1,880
	31		3	1,023		857

Expense accounts have zero balances after closing entries have been posted

Advertising Expense   Account No. 70

Date		Explanation	Ref	Debit	Credit	Balance
19__						
Oct.	2		2	120		120
	16		2	90		210
	31		3		210	-0-

Office Salaries Expense   Account No. 72

Date		Explanation	Ref	Debit	Credit	Balance
19__						
Oct.	30		2	700		700
	31		3		700	-0-

Telephone Expense   Account No. 74

Date		Explanation	Ref	Debit	Credit	Balance
19__						
Oct.	30		2	48		48
	31		3		48	-0-

Depreciation Expense: Building   Account No. 76

Date		Explanation	Ref	Debit	Credit	Balance
19__						
Oct.	31		2	50		50
	31		3		50	-0-

Depreciation Expense: Office Equipment Account No. 78

Date		Explanation	Ref	Debit	Credit	Balance
19__						
Oct.	31		2	15		15
	31		3		15	-0-

CLOSING THE INCOME SUMMARY ACCOUNT The five expense accounts have now been closed and the total amount of $1,023 formerly contained in these accounts appears in the debit column of the Income Summary account. The commissions of $1,880 earned during October appear in the credit column of the Income Summary account. Since the credit entry of $1,880 representing October revenue is larger than the debit of $1,023 representing October expenses, the account has a credit balance of $857—the net income for October.

The net income of $857 earned during October causes the owner's equity to increase. The *credit* balance of the Income Summary account is, therefore, transferred to the owner's capital account by the following closing entry:

General Journal

Page 3

	Date		Account Titles and Explanation	LP	Debit	Credit
Net income	19___					
earned *increases*	Oct.	31	Income Summary	53	857	
the *owner's*			James Roberts, Capital	50		857
equity			To close the Income Summary account for			
			October by transferring the net income to the			
			owner's capital account.			

After this closing entry has been posted, the Income Summary account has a zero balance, and the net income earned during October appears in the owner's capital account as shown below:

Income Summary

Account No. 53

19___						
Oct.	31	Revenue	3		1,880	1,880
	31	Expenses	3	1,023		857
	31	To close	3	857		–0–

James Roberts, Capital

Account No. 50

19___						
Sept.	1	Investment by owner	1		20,000	20,000
Oct.	31	Net income for October	3		857	20,857

In our illustration the business has operated profitably with revenues in excess of expenses. Not every business is so fortunate; if the expenses of a business are larger than its revenue, the Income Summary account will have a debit balance. In this case, the closing of the Income Summary account will require a debit to the owner's capital account and an off-setting credit to the Income Summary account. The owner's equity will, of course, be reduced by the amount of the loss debited to his capital account.

Note that the Income Summary account is used only at the end of the period when the books are being closed. The account has no entries and no balance except during the process of closing the books at the end of the accounting period.

CLOSING THE OWNER'S DRAWING ACCOUNT As explained earlier in this chapter, withdrawals of cash or other assets by the owner are not con-sidered as an expense of the business and, therefore, are not taken into account in determining the net income for the period. Since drawings by the owner do not constitute an expense, the owner's drawing account is closed not into the Income Summary account but directly to the owner's capital account. The following journal entry serves to close the draw-ing account in the ledger of the Roberts Real Estate Agency at Octo-ber 31.

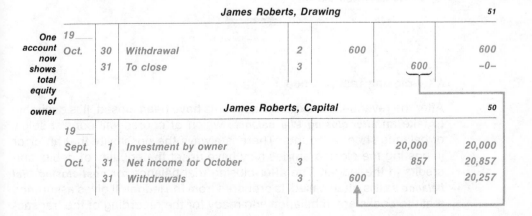

General Journal   Page 3

	Date		Account Titles and Explanation	LP	Debit	Credit
Drawing account is closed to owner's capital account	19__ Oct.	31	James Roberts, Capital	50	600	
			James Roberts, Drawing	51		600
			To close the owner's drawing account.			

After this closing entry has been posted, the drawing account will have a zero balance, and the amount withdrawn by Roberts during October will appear as a deduction or debit entry in his capital account, as shown below:

James Roberts, Drawing   51

One account now shows total equity of owner	19__ Oct.	30	Withdrawal	2	600		600
		31	To close	3		600	-0-

James Roberts, Capital   50

	19__ Sept.	1	Investment by owner	1		20,000	20,000
	Oct.	31	Net income for October	3		857	20,857
		31	Withdrawals	3	600		20,257

SUMMARY OF CLOSING PROCEDURE Let us now summarize briefly the procedure of closing the accounts:

1 Close the various revenue and expense accounts by transferring their balances into the Income Summary account.

2 Close the Income Summary account by transferring its balance into the owner's capital account.

3 Close the owner's drawing account into the owner's capital account. (The balance of the owner's capital account in the ledger will now be the same as the amount of capital appearing in the balance sheet.)

The closing of the accounts may be illustrated graphically by use of T accounts as follows:

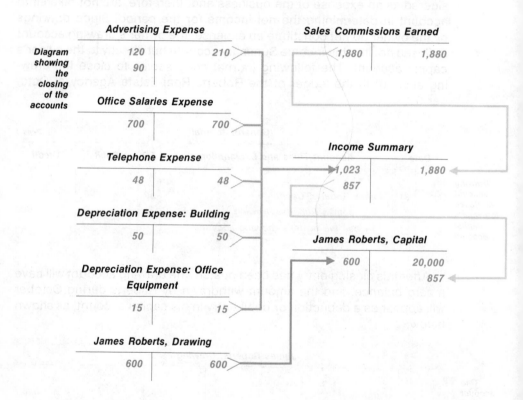

Diagram showing the closing of the accounts

Advertising Expense		Sales Commissions Earned	
120	210	1,880	1,880
90			

Office Salaries Expense	
700	700

Telephone Expense	
48	48

Income Summary	
1,023	1,880
857	

Depreciation Expense: Building	
50	50

James Roberts, Capital	
600	20,000
	857

Depreciation Expense: Office Equipment	
15	15

James Roberts, Drawing	
600	600

After-closing trial balance

After the revenue and expense accounts have been closed, it is desirable to take an *after-closing trial balance,* which of course will consist solely of balance sheet accounts. There is always the possibility that an error in posting the closing entries may have upset the equality of debits and credits in the ledger. The after-closing trial balance, or *post-closing trial balance* as it is often called, is prepared from the ledger. It gives assurance that the books are in balance and ready for the recording of the transactions of the new accounting period. The after-closing trial balance of the Roberts Real Estate Agency follows:

ROBERTS REAL ESTATE AGENCY
After-closing Trial Balance
October 31, 19___

Only the	Cash	$ 6,830	
balance sheet	Accounts receivable	2,630	
accounts	Land	5,000	
remain open	Building	12,000	
	Accumulated depreciation: building		$ 50
	Office equipment	1,800	
	Accumulated depreciation: office equipment		15
	Accounts payable		7,938
	James Roberts, capital		20,257
		$28,260	$28,260

Sequence of accounting procedures

The accounting procedures described to this point may be summarized in eight steps, as follows:

1 Journalize transactions   Enter all transactions in the journal, thus creating a chronological record of events.

2 Post to ledger accounts   Post debits and credits from the journal to the proper ledger accounts, thus creating a record classified by accounts.

3 Prepare a trial balance   Prove the equality of debits and credits in the ledger.

4 Make end-of-period adjustments   Draft adjusting entries in the journal, and post to ledger accounts. Thus far we have illustrated only one type of adjustment: the recording of depreciation at the end of the period.

5 Prepare an adjusted trial balance   Prove again the equality of debits and credits in the ledger.

6 Prepare financial statements   An income statement is needed to show the results of operation for the period. A balance sheet is needed to show the financial condition of the business at the end of the period.

7 Journalize and post closing entries   The closing entries clear the revenue, expense, and drawing accounts, making them ready for recording the events of the next accounting period. They will also transfer the net income or loss of the completed period to the owner's capital account.

8 Prepare an after-closing trial balance   This step ensures that the ledger remains in balance after posting of the closing entries.

Accrual basis of accounting versus cash basis of accounting

A business which recognizes revenues in the period in which they are earned and deducts the expenses incurred in generating those revenues is using the *accrual basis of accounting.* To be meaningful, net income must relate to a specified period of time. Since net income is determined by offsetting expenses against revenues, both the expenses and the revenues used in the calculation must relate to the same time period. This matching or offsetting of related revenues and expenses gives a realistic picture of the profit performance of the business each period. The accrual basis is thus essential to income determination, which is a major objective of the whole accounting process.

The alternative to the accrual basis of accounting is the *cash basis.* Under cash basis accounting, revenues are not recorded until received in cash; expenses are assigned to the period in which cash payment is made. Most business concerns use the accrual method of accounting, but individuals and professionals (such as physicians and lawyers) usually maintain their accounting records on a cash basis.

The cash basis of accounting does not give a good picture of profitability. For example, it ignores uncollected revenues which have been earned and expenses which have been incurred but not paid. Throughout this book we shall be working with the accrual basis of accounting, except for that portion of Chapter 20 dealing with the income tax returns of individuals.

DEMONSTRATION PROBLEM FOR YOUR REVIEW

Lane Insurance Agency began business on April 1, 19____. Assume that the accounts are closed and financial statements prepared each month. The company occupies rented office space but owns office equipment estimated to have a useful life of 10 years from date of acquisition, April 1. The trial balance for Lane Insurance Agency at June 30, 19____, is shown below.

Cash	$ 1,275	
Accounts receivable	605	
Office equipment	6,000	
Accumulated depreciation: office equipment		$ 100
Accounts payable		1,260
Richard Lane, capital, May 31, 19____		6,500
Richard Lane, drawing	1,000	
Commissions earned		3,710
Advertising expense	500	
Rent expense	370	
Telephone expense	120	
Salaries expense	1,700	
	$11,570	$11,570

Instructions

a Prepare the adjusting journal entry to record depreciation of the office equipment for the month of June.

b Prepare an adjusted trial balance at June 30, 19___.

c Prepare an income statement for the month ended June 30, 19___, and a balance sheet in report form at June 30, 19___.

QUESTIONS

1 What is the meaning of the term *revenue?* Does the receipt of cash by a business indicate that revenue has been earned? Explain.

2 What is the meaning of the term *expenses?* Does the payment of cash by a business indicate that an expense has been incurred? Explain.

3 The Milan Company, owned by Robert Gennaro, completed its first year of operation on December 31, 1973. State the proper heading for the first annual income statement.

4 Does a well-prepared income statement provide an exact measurement of net income for the period, or does it represent merely an approximation of net income? Explain.

5 How does depreciation expense differ from other operating expenses?

6 Assume that a business acquires a delivery truck at a cost of $3,600. Estimated life of the truck is four years. State the amount of depreciation expense per year and per month. Give the adjusting entry to record depreciation on the truck at the end of the first month, and explain where the accounts involved would appear in the financial statements.

7 Explain the rules of debit and credit with respect to transactions recorded in revenue and expense accounts.

8 Supply the appropriate term (debit or credit) to complete the following statements.

a The owner's equity account, income summary account, and revenue accounts are increased by _____ entries.

b Asset accounts and expense accounts are increased by _____ entries.

c Liability accounts and owner's equity accounts are decreased by _____ entries.

9 Supply the appropriate term (debit or credit) to complete the following statements.

a When a business is operating profitably, the journal entry to close the Income Summary account will consist of a _____ to that account and a _____ to the owner's capital account.

b When a business is operating at a loss, the journal entry to close the Income Summary account will consist of a _____ to that account and a _____ to the owner's capital account.

c The journal entry to close the owner's drawing account consists of a _____ to that account and a _____ to the owner's capital account.

10 All ledger accounts belong in one of the following five groups: asset, liability, owner's equity, revenue, and expense. For each of the following accounts, state the group in which it belongs. Also indicate whether the normal balance would be a debit or credit.

a Fees Earned

b Notes Payable

c Telephone Expense

d William Nelson, Drawing

e Building

f Depreciation Expense

g Accumulated Depreciation: Building

11 A service enterprise performs services in the amount of $500 for a customer in May and receives payment in June. In which month is the $500 of revenue recognized? What is the journal entry to be made in May and the entry to be made in June?

12 Which of the following accounts should be closed by a debit to Income Summary and a credit to the account listed? (a) James Harris, Drawing, (b) Fees Earned, (c) Advertising Expense, (d) Accounts Receivable, (e) Salaries Expense, (f) Accounts Payable, (g) Depreciation Expense, (h) Accumulated Depreciation.

13 Supply the appropriate terms to complete the following statements. _____ and _____ accounts are closed at the end of each ac-counting period by transferring their balances to a summary account called _____ _____. A _____ balance in this summary account represents net income for the period; a _____ balance represents a net loss for the period.

14 Which of the following accounts are affected by closing entries at the end of the accounting period? (a) Cash, (b) Fees Earned, (c) Income Summary, (d) Accounts Payable, (e) Telephone Expense, (f) James Miller, Drawing, (g) James Miller, Capital, (h) Accumulated Depreciation, (i) Accounts Receivable, (j) Depreciation Expense.

EXERCISES

Ex. 3-1 John Grey & Company, a firm of real estate brokers, carried out the following transactions during the month of May. Which of these transactions represented revenue to the firm during the month of May? Explain.
a John Grey invested an additional $4,000 cash in the business.
b Collected $300 rent for May from a dentist to whom John Grey & Company rented part of its building.
c Arranged a sale of an apartment building owned by a client, James Robbins. The commission for making the sale was $9,000, but this amount would not be received until July 20.
d Collected cash of $1,500 from an account receivable. The receivable originated in April from services rendered to a client.
e Borrowed $8,000 from the National Bank, to be repaid in three months.

Ex. 3-2 A business had the following transactions, among others, during January. Which of these transactions represented expenses for January? Explain.
a Paid $300 salary to a salesman for time worked during January.
b Paid $60 for gasoline purchases for the delivery truck during January.
c Purchased a typewriter for $300 cash.
d Paid $2,000 in settlement of a loan obtained three months earlier.
e The owner withdrew $500 from the business for his own use.
f Paid a garage $200 for automobile repair work performed in November.

Ex. 3-3 Supply the missing figures in the following five independent cases:

a Owner's equity at end of year	$ 77,900
Owner's drawings during the year	12,400
Net income for the year	16,600
Owner's equity at beginning of year	_____
b Net income for the year	$ 20,400
Owner's equity at beginning of year	100,000
Owner's equity at end of year	_____
Owner's drawings during the year	15,500

c Net income for the year . . . . $ _____

   Owner's equity at end of year 32,100

   Owner's equity at beginning of year 26,500

   Owner's drawings during the year 10,400

d Owner's drawings during the year . . . . $ _____

   Owner's equity at end of year 43,400

   Net income for the year 11,800

   Owner's equity at beginning of year 47,500

e Owner's equity at beginning of year $51,700

   Owner's equity at end of year 60,200

   Additional investment by owner during the year 10,000

   Net income for the year . . . . _____

   Owner's drawings for the year 8,100

Ex. 3-4 The income statement prepared by Grayling Company for the month of March showed net income of $18,500. In recording the transactions of the month, however, the accountant had made some errors. Study the following list of March transactions and identify any which were incorrectly recorded. Also give the journal entry as it should have been made. Finally, compute the correct amount of net income for the month of March.

   a Earned a commission of $2,500 by selling a residence for a client. Commission to be received in 60 days. Recorded by debiting Commissions Earned and crediting Accounts Receivable.

   b A payment of $250 for newspaper advertising was recorded by debiting Advertising Expense and crediting Accounts Receivable.

   c Received but did not pay a bill of $285 for October telephone service. Recorded by debiting Telephone Expense and crediting Commissions Earned.

   d Made an error in computing depreciation on the building for October. Recorded as $25. Should have been $250.

   e Recorded the withdrawal of $1,600 by the owner, Howard Grayling, by debiting Salaries Expense and crediting Cash.

Ex. 3-5 Accounts in the ledger of Sky Company are arranged in *financial statement order,* so that a trial balance prepared from the ledger will show the accounts in a convenient sequence for preparing the financial statements. Rearrange the following alphabetical list of account titles in the order in which they are located in the ledger of Sky Company.

(1) Accounts Payable	(11) Marketable Securities
(2) Accounts Receivable	(12) Notes Payable
(3) Accumulated Depreciation: Buildings	(13) Notes Receivable
(4) Advertising Expense	(14) Office Equipment
(5) Buildings	(15) Paul Patroni, Capital
(6) Cash	(16) Paul Patroni, Drawing
(7) Commissions Earned	(17) Rent Expense
(8) Depreciation Expense: Buildings	(18) Salaries Expense
(9) Electricity Expense	(19) Taxes Payable
(10) Land	(20) Telephone Expense

PROBLEMS

Group A

3A-1 The September transactions of the Southern Seas Travel Service are listed below:
  (1) On September 1, Southern Seas Travel Service arranged a round-the-world trip for Mr. and Mrs. Albert Phillips. A commission of $465 cash was collected from the steamship company.
  (2) On September 4, Southern Seas Travel Service placed an advertisement in the Travel section of the *Sunday Chronicle,* payment therefor to be made in 30 days in the amount of $330.
  (3) On September 5, fly-now, pay-later Pacific tours were arranged for several clients. Orient Airlines agreed to pay Southern Seas Travel Service $750 as a commission for arranging the tours, payment to be made as soon as client travel agreements were confirmed.
  (4) On September 15, John Gilbert, owner of Southern Seas Travel Service, withdrew $250 from the business for personal use.
  (5) On September 18, cash in the amount of $750 was collected from Orient Airlines.
  (6) On September 30, an invoice in the amount of $87 was received, payable October 10, for telephone service during September.

Instructions Analyze each transaction, then prepare the necessary journal entry. The following will illustrate an *analysis* of a transaction, using *(1)* above as an example.
  (1) *(a)* The asset Cash was increased. Increases in assets are recorded by debits. Debit Cash, $465.
     (b) Revenue was earned. Revenue increases the owner's equity and is recorded as a credit. Credit Commissions Earned, $465.

3A-2 The Lane Trio was organized on October 1, 19___, by Allan Lane, Lori Lewis, and Donald Terry as a partnership, to provide music at various functions. The following transactions were for the month of October.
  Oct. 1 Lane, Lewis, and Terry each deposited $1,000 in a bank account in the name of the business, the Lane Trio. (Use three separate capital accounts.)
  Oct. 2 Purchased musical instruments from Martin Music Ltd., for $2,000. Cash down payment of $1,000 was made, the balance to be paid in 60 days.
  Oct. 3 Purchased a used automobile for $1,250, paying cash.
  Oct. 4 Retained MBS Booking Service as exclusive agents for the Lane Trio. The arrangement called for a flat $75 monthly retainer fee plus 10% of gross fees earned, to be paid on the last day of every month. The $75 fee was paid this date (debit Promotion Expense).
  Oct. 10 Fees from appearances before various organizations for the first 10 days of October amounted to $825. Cash was collected.
  Oct. 16 Signed an agreement with Seahurst Country Club to provide music for the regular Saturday dances and also at other parties (not to exceed two per month) scheduled by the club. The agreement covered a period of four months, beginning November 1, and provided for a maximum cost to the club of $3,600.
  Oct. 20 Fees from appearances for the second 10 days of October amounted to $600. Cash was collected.
  Oct. 31 Paid gasoline bill for the month, $40.
  Oct. 31 Fees from appearances for the last 11 days of October amounted to $525. Cash was collected.
  Oct. 31 Paid MBS Booking Service 10% of the gross fees earned during the month.

b) **Oct. 31** Each partner withdrew $500 for personal use. (Use a separate drawing account for each partner.)

Instructions

a Journalize the above transactions. (Number journal pages to permit cross reference to ledger.)

b Post to ledger accounts. (Number accounts consecutively, beginning with no. 11.)

c Prepare a trial balance as of October 31, 19____ .

3A-3 MacPherson Auto Repair began business May 1, 19____. The books were closed and financial reports prepared each month. A trial balance as of the succeeding July 31, 19____ , is shown below.

MacPHERSON AUTO REPAIR

Trial Balance

July 31, 19____

Cash	$ 1,260	
Accounts receivable	520	
Land	10,500	
Building	18,000	
Accumulated depreciation: building		$ 120
Repair equipment	2,400	
Accumulated depreciation: repair equipment		80
Notes payable		10,000
Accounts payable		300
Tom MacPherson, capital		21,000
Tom MacPherson, drawing	505	
Repair service revenue		3,400
Advertising expense	55	
Repair parts expense	260	
Utilities expense	50	
Wages expense	1,350	
	$34,900	$34,900

The useful life of the building was estimated at 25 years, and the useful life of repair equipment was estimated at 5 years.

Instructions

a Prepare adjusting entries to record depreciation.

b Prepare an adjusted trial balance.

c Prepare an income statement for the month ended July 31, 19____ , and a balance sheet in report form.

3A-4 The Landis Investment Service offers investment counseling and brokerage services to its clients and earns revenue in the form of commissions. The building and equipment were acquired on March 1 of the current year. Useful life of the building was estimated at 30 years and of the equipment at 8 years. The company closes its accounts monthly; on May 31 of the current year, the trial balance is as follows:

LANDIS INVESTMENT SERVICE
Trial balance
May 31, 19___

	Debit	Credit
Cash	$ 5,400	
Government of Canada bonds	77,320	
Accounts receivable	4,300	
Land	19,000	
Building	54,000	
Accumulated depreciation: building		$ 300
Equipment	19,200	
Accumulated depreciation: equipment		400
Notes payable		60,000
Accounts payable		8,645
Harry Landis, capital		107,659
Harry Landis, drawing	1,500	
Commissions earned		16,120
Advertising expense	500	
News service expense	450	
Salaries expense	11,130	
Telephone expense	324	
	$193,124	$193,124

Instructions From the trial balance and supplementary data given, prepare the following as of May 31, 19___.
a Adjusting entries for depreciation of building and of equipment (building $54,000 ÷ 30 years × $\frac{1}{12}$).
b Adjusted trial balance.
c Income statement for the month of May and a balance sheet at May 31 in report form
d Closing entries
e After-closing trial balance

3A-5 Crandal Music Conservatory was organized on May 1, 19___, to offer instruction to students of music. Account balances on May 31, 19___, are listed below in alphabetical order.

Accounts payable	$ 165	Depreciation expense:		
Accounts receivable	625	building	$ 100	
Accumulated depreciation:		Depreciation expense:		
building	100	musical instruments	100	
Accumulated depreciation:		Land	15,000	
musical instruments	100	Mortgage payable	27,000	
Advertising expense	250	Musical instruments	6,000	
Barry Crandal, capital	26,325	Salaries expense	1,600	
Barry Crandal, drawing	1,100	Telephone expense	42	
Building	30,000	Tuition revenue	2,725	
Cash	1,554	Utilities expense	44	

Instructions

a Prepare a trial balance, rearranging the above accounts in the customary sequence of ledger accounts.

b Prepare an income statement for the month ended May 31, 19___, and a balance sheet in report form.

3A-6 Paul Weiss, M.D., after several years' experience with a medical group, established his own private practice on June 1, 19___. During the first month, the following business transactions occurred:

June 1 Paul Weiss deposited $6,000 cash in a bank account in the name of his practice, Paul Weiss, M.D.

June 1 Paid office rent for June, $350.

June 1 Purchased office equipment for cash, $1,920.

June 2 Purchased medical equipment from Scientific Equipment Company at a cost of $8,100. A cash down payment of $1,100 was made and a note payable was signed which specified a payment of $3,500 on August 2, 19___, and a second payment of $3,500 on October 2, 19___. No interest was charged on the note.

June 3 Retained by Watson Manufacturing Company to be on call for emergency service at a monthly fee of $150. The fee for June was collected in cash.

June 15 Excluding the retainer of June 3, fees earned during the first 15 days of the month amounted to $625, of which $105 was in cash and $520 was in accounts receivable.

June 15 Paid Jane Campbell, R.N., her salary for the first half of June, $450.

June 16 Dr. Weiss withdrew $750 for his personal use.

June 16 Treated James Brant for injuries received in an accident during his employment at Watson Manufacturing Company. Completed medical portions of insurance and industrial accident reports.

June 24 Treated May Douglas, who paid $10 cash for an office visit and who agreed to pay $24 on July 1 for laboratory medical tests completed June 24.

June 30 Excluding the treatment of May Douglas on June 24, fees earned during the last half of the month amounted to $1,060, of which $210 was in cash and $850 was in accounts receivable.

June 30 Paid Jane Campbell, R.N., $450 salary for the second half of the month.

June 30 Received a bill from Grant Medical Supply Company in the amount of $240, representing the amount of medical supplies used during June. (Debit Medical Supplies Expense.)

June 30 Paid utilities bill for the month, $33.

Other information Dr. Weiss estimated the useful life of medical instruments at 9 years and of office equipment at 8 years. The account titles to be used and the account numbers are as follows:

Cash	10	Paul Weiss, capital	40
Accounts receivable	13	Paul Weiss, drawing	41
Medical instruments	20	Income summary	45
Accumulated depreciation:		Fees earned	49
medical instruments	21	Medical supplies expense	50
Office equipment	22	Rent expense	51
Accumulated depreciation:		Salaries expense	52
office equipment	23	Utilities expense	53
Notes payable	30	Depreciation expense:	
Accounts payable	31	medical instruments	54
		Depreciation expense:	
		office equipment	55

Instructions

a Journalize the above transactions. (Number journal pages to permit cross reference to ledger.)

b Post to ledger accounts. (Use the running balance form of ledger account. Number ledger accounts to permit cross reference to journal.)

c Prepare a trial balance as of June 30, 19___.

d Prepare adjusting entries and post to ledger accounts.

e Prepare an adjusted trial balance.

f Prepare an income statement and a balance sheet in report form.

g Prepare closing entries and post to ledger accounts.

h Prepare an after-closing trial balance.

Group B

3B-1 During April a portion of the transactions of Davison Motors, an automobile repair shop, were as follows:

(*1*) On April 1, paid $200 cash for the month's rent.

(*2*) On April 4, made repairs to the car of C. P. Caron and collected in full the charge of $317 (credit Repair Service Revenue).

(*3*) On April 6, at request of National Insurance Ltd., made repairs on the car of Ainsley Dart. Sent bill for $416 for services rendered to National Insurance Ltd.

(*4*) On April 17, placed an advertisement in the *Herald Express* at a cost of $97, payment to be made in 30 days.

(*5*) On April 26, William Davison, owner of Davison Motors, withdrew $330 from the business for his personal use.

(*6*) On April 30, received a cheque for $416 from National Insurance Ltd.

Instructions Write an analysis of each transaction and then prepare the necessary journal entry. An example of the type of analysis desired is as follows:

(*1*) (*a*) Rent is an operating expense. Expenses are recorded by debits. Debit Rent Expense, $200.

(*b*) The asset Cash was decreased. Decreases in assets are recorded by credits. Credit Cash, $200.

3B-2 Listed below in alphabetical order are the account balances required to prepare an adjusted trial balance for Adams Insurance Agency at October 31, 19___.

Accounts payable	$ 414	Depreciation expense:	
Accounts receivable	337	building	$ 55
Accumulated depreciation:		Depreciation expense:	
building	165	office equipment	50
Accumulated depreciation:		Land	12,375
office equipment	150	Lighting expense	178
Advertising expense	198	Notes payable	10,100
Arthur Adams, capital	37,000	Office equipment	6,000
Building	26,400	Salaries expense	1,154
Cash	4,700	Telephone expense	100
Commissions earned	3,718		

Instructions

a Prepare an adjusted trial balance with the accounts arranged in the *customary sequence* of ledger accounts.

b Prepare an income statement for the month ended October 31, 19___ .

c Prepare a balance sheet in report form.

3B-3 During the month of April, 19___ , Ralph Braden organized and began to operate an air taxi service to provide air transportation from a major city to a number of small towns not served by scheduled airlines. The transactions during April were as follows:

Apr. 1 Ralph Braden deposited $400,000 cash in a bank account in the name of the business, Braden Air Service.

Apr. 2 Purchased an aircraft for $297,000 and spare parts for $35,000, paying cash.

Apr. 4 Paid $450 cash to rent a building for April.

Apr. 10 Cash receipts from passengers for the first 10 days amounted to $8,600.

Apr. 14 Paid $625 to Cessna Maintenance Service for maintenance and repair service for April.

Apr. 15 Paid $2,400 to employees for services rendered during the first half of April.

Apr. 20 Cash receipts from passengers for the second 10 days amounted to $10,400.

Apr. 30 Cash receipts from passengers for the last 10 days of April amounted to $16,750.

Apr. 30 Paid $2,400 to employees for services rendered during the second half of April.

Apr. 30 Braden withdrew $1,600 from the business for his personal use.

Apr. 30 Received a fuel bill from Phillips Oil Company amounting to $3,790, to be paid before May 10.

The account titles and numbers used by Braden Air Service are as follows:

Cash	11	*Fares revenue*	51
Spare parts	14	*Maintenance expense*	61
Aircraft	21	*Fuel expense*	62
Accounts payable	31	*Salaries expense*	63
Ralph Braden, capital	41	*Rent expense*	64
Ralph Braden, drawing	42		

Instructions Based on the foregoing transactions

a Prepare journal entries. (Number journal pages to permit cross reference to ledger.)

b Post to ledger accounts. (Number ledger accounts to permit cross reference to journal.)

c Prepare a trial balance as of April 30, 19___ .

3B-4 Robert Gregg received his D.D.S. degree in June, 19___ , and set up his own dental practice on July 1. A trial balance as of July 31, 19___ , and other data are shown on page 100.

ROBERT GREGG, D.D.S.
Trial Balance
July 31, 19___

	Debit	Credit
Cash	$ 2,640	
Accounts receivable	760	
Dental equipment	17,400	
Office equipment	960	
Notes payable		$16,880
Accounts payable		313
Robert Gregg, capital		5,000
Robert Gregg, drawing	950	
Professional fees earned		2,900
Rent expense	300	
Dental supplies expense	370	
Electricity expense	18	
Salaries expense	1,630	
Telephone expense	65	
	$25,093	$25,093

The useful life of the dental equipment was estimated to be 5 years (60 months), and of office equipment 8 years (96 months).

Instructions
a Prepare adjusting entries at July 31 to record depreciation for July of the dental equipment and the office equipment.
b Prepare an adjusted trial balance at July 31.
c Prepare an income statement and a balance sheet in report form.
d Prepare closing entries.
e Prepare an after-closing trial balance.

3B-5 The City Parking System was organized on February 1 to operate a parking lot in a downtown location. The ledger includes the following accounts, with their numbers.

Cash	11	Larry Jensen, drawing	42
Land	21	Parking fees	51
Notes payable	31	Advertising expense	61
Accounts payable	32	Lighting expense	63
Larry Jensen, capital	41	Salaries expense	65

The transactions for the organization of the business and its operations during the month of February were as follows:
Feb. 1 Larry Jensen deposited $85,000 cash in a bank account in the name of the business, the City Parking System.
Feb. 2 Purchased land for $75,000, of which $45,000 was paid in cash. A non-interest-bearing note payable was issued for the balance of $30,000.
Feb. 2 An arrangement was made with Mueller's Restaurant to provide parking privileges for its customers. Mueller's Restaurant agreed to pay $550 monthly, payable in advance. Cash was collected for the month of February.

Feb. 7 Arranged with Playbill Printing Company for a regular advertisement in the *Playbill* at a monthly cost of $95. Paid for advertising during February by cheque, $95.

Feb. 15 Parking receipts for the first half of the month were $1,530, exclusive of the monthly fee from Mueller's Restaurant.

Feb. 28 Electricity bill from the P&L Power Company amounted to $65, to be paid before March 10.

Feb. 28 Paid $600 to the parking attendant for services rendered during the month. (Payroll taxes are to be ignored.)

Feb. 28 Parking receipts for the second half of the month amounted to $1,402.

Feb. 28 Jensen withdrew $900 for his personal use.

Feb. 28 Paid $10,000 cash on the note payable incurred with the purchase of land.

Instructions
a Journalize the February transactions.
b Post to ledger accounts.
c Prepare a trial balance at February 28.
d Prepare an income statement and a balance sheet in report form.

3B-6 The National Moving Company was organized on September 1, 19___, by James Wilbur to provide transcontinental transportation of household goods. During September the following transactions occurred:

Sept. 1 James Wilbur deposited $200,000 cash in a bank account in the name of the business, National Moving Company.

Sept. 2 Purchased land and building for a total price of $122,000, of which $50,000 was applicable to the land and $72,000 to the building. Paid cash for the full amount.

Sept. 3 Purchased three trucks from Bryan Motors at a cost of $28,800 each. A cash down payment of $40,000 was made, the balance to be paid by November 12.

Sept. 6 Purchased office equipment for cash, $4,800.

Sept. 6 Moved furniture for Mr. and Mrs. John Green from Vancouver to Halifax for $3,370. Collected $970 in cash, balance to be paid within 30 days (credit Moving Service Revenue).

Sept. 9 Moved furniture for various clients for $6,470. Collected $3,670 in cash, balance to be paid within 30 days.

Sept. 15 Paid salaries to employees for the first half of the month, $3,020.

Sept. 25 Moved furniture for various clients for a total of $5,400. Cash collected in full.

Sept. 30 Salaries expense for the second half of September amounted to $2,650.

Sept. 30 Received a gasoline bill for the month of September from Midwest Oil Company in the amount of $3,500, to be paid before October 10.

Sept. 30 Received bill of $250 for repair work on trucks during September by Culver Motor Company.

Sept. 30 The owner, James Wilbur, withdrew $1,200 cash for his personal use.

Wilbur estimated the useful life of the building at 20 years, of trucks at 4 years, and of office equipment at 10 years.

Instructions
a Prepare journal entries. (Number journal pages to permit cross reference to ledger.)
b Post to ledger accounts. (Number ledger accounts to permit cross reference to journal.)
c Prepare a trial balance as of September 30, 19___.
d Prepare adjusting entries and post to ledger accounts.
e Prepare an adjusted trial balance.
f Prepare an income statement for September, and a balance sheet as of September 30, 19___, in report form.

g Prepare closing entries and post to ledger accounts.
h Prepare an after-closing trial balance.

BUSINESS DECISION PROBLEM 3

Wendel Ober, owner of a small business called Qwik-Service Company, has accepted a salaried position overseas and is trying to interest you in buying his business. He describes the operating results of the business as follows: "The business has been in existence for only 18 months, but the growth trend is very impressive. Just look at these figures."

*Cash Collections
from Customers*

First six-month period	$12,000
Second six-month period	16,000
Third six-month period	18,000

"I think you'll agree those figures show real growth," Ober concluded.

You then asked Ober whether sales were made only for cash or on both a cash and credit basis. He replied as follows:

"At first we sold both for cash and on open account. In the first six months we made total sales of $20,000 and 70% of those sales were made on credit. We had $8,000 of accounts receivable at the end of the first six-month period.

"During the second six-month period, we tried to discourage selling on credit because of the extra paper work involved and the time required to follow up on slow-paying customers. Our sales on credit in that second six-month period amounted to $7,000, and our total accounts receivable were down to $6,000 at the end of that period.

"During the third six-month period we made sales only for cash. Although we prefer to operate on a cash basis only, we did very well at collecting receivables. We collected in full from every customer to whom we ever sold on credit and we don't have a dollar of accounts receivable at this time."

Instructions

a Do you consider Ober's explanation of the "growth trend" of cash collections to be a well-founded portrayal of the progress of his business? Explain fully any criticism you may have of Ober's line of reasoning.

b To facilitate your reaching a decision, it is suggested that you compile data for each of the three six-month periods under review, using the following column headings for the analysis:

(1) Sales on Credit	(2) Collections on Accounts Receivable	(3) Ending Balance of Accounts Receivable	(4) Sales for Cash	(5) Total Cash Collections from Customers	(6) (1) + (4) Total Sales
First six months					
Second six months					
Third six months					

FOUR

COMPLETION OF THE ACCOUNTING CYCLE

Management makes many important decisions on the basis of information reported in financial statements. Decisions to expand production, to borrow money, and to acquire new plant and equipment are typical of the key moves made in reliance upon the information shown in the income statement and balance sheet. Groups other than management also take action based upon this information. Investors decide to buy or sell securities after a close study of financial statements, and bankers approve or reject applications for loans after intensive study of the financial statements of companies seeking credit.

Apportioning transactions between accounting periods

To serve the needs of management, investors, bankers, and other groups, financial statements must be as complete and accurate as possible. The balance sheet must contain all the assets and liabilities at the close of business on the last day of the period. The income statement must contain all the revenue and expenses applicable to the period covered but must not contain any revenue or expenses relating to the following period. In other words, a precise cutoff of transactions at the end of the period is essential to the preparation of accurate financial statements.

Some business transactions are begun and completed within a single accounting period, but many other transactions are begun in one accounting period and concluded in a later period. For example, a building purchased this year may last for 25 years; during each of those 25 years a fair share of the cost of the building should be recognized as expense. The making of adjusting entries to record the depreciation expense applicable to a given accounting period was illustrated in the preceding chapter. Let us now consider some other transactions which overlap two or more accounting periods and therefore require adjusting entries.

us kinds of transactions requiring adjusting entries at the end of the period may be classified into the following groups:

1 Recorded costs which must be apportioned between two or more accounting periods. Example: the cost of a building.

2 Recorded revenue which must be apportioned between two or more accounting periods. Example: commissions collected in advance for services to be rendered in future periods.

3 Unrecorded expenses. Example: wages earned by employees after the last payday in an accounting period.

4 Unrecorded revenue. Example: commissions earned but not yet collected or billed to customers.

To demonstrate these various types of adjusting entries, the illustration of the Roberts Real Estate Agency will be continued for November. We shall consider in detail only those November transactions relating to adjusting entries. The routine operating transactions during November such as the earning of sales commissions and payment of expenses are not considered individually, but their overall effect is shown in the November 30 trial balance included in the work sheet on page 113.

Recorded costs apportioned between accounting periods

When a business concern makes an expenditure that will benefit more than one period, the amount is usually debited to an asset account. At the end of each period which benefits from the expenditure, an appropriate portion of the cost is transferred from the asset account to an expense account.

PREPAID EXPENSES Payments in advance are often made for such items as insurance, rent, and office supplies. At the end of the accounting period, a portion of the services or supplies probably will have expired or will have been consumed, but another portion will be unexpired or unused. That portion of the economic benefits from the expenditure which *has expired or has been consumed is an expense of the current period.* However, the *unexpired or unused portion of the economic benefits from the expenditure represents an asset* at the balance sheet date which will not become expense (expired cost) until a later accounting period.

INSURANCE On November 1, the Roberts Real Estate Agency paid $180 for a three-year fire insurance policy covering the building. This expenditure was debited to an asset account by the following journal entry:

Expenditure for insurance policy recorded as asset

Unexpired Insurance	180	
Cash		180
Purchased three-year fire insurance policy.		

Since this expenditure of $180 will protect the company against fire loss for three years, the cost of protection each year is $\frac{1}{3}$ of $180, or $60. The insurance expense applicable to each month's operations is $\frac{1}{12}$ of the annual expense, or $5. In order that the accounting records for November show insurance expense of $5, the following adjusting entry is required at November 30:

Portion of asset expires (becomes expense)

Insurance Expense	5	
Unexpired Insurance		5
To record insurance expense for November.		

This adjusting entry serves two purposes: (1) it apportions the proper amount of insurance expense to November operations, and (2) it reduces the asset account so that the correct amount of unexpired insurance will appear in the balance sheet at November 30. What would be the effect on the income statement for November if the above adjustment were not made? The expenses would be understated by $5 and consequently the net income would be overstated by $5. The balance sheet would also be affected by failure to make the adjustment: the assets would be overstated by $5 and so would the owner's equity. The overstatement of the owner's equity would result from the overstated amount of net income transferred to Roberts's capital account when the books were closed at November 30.

OFFICE SUPPLIES On November 2, the Roberts Real Estate Agency purchased a sufficient quantity of stationery and other office supplies to last for several months. The cost of the supplies was $240, and this amount was debited to an asset account by the following journal entry.

Expenditure for office supplies recorded as asset

Office Supplies	240	
Cash		240
Purchased office supplies.		

No entries were made during November to record the day-to-day usage of office supplies, but on November 30 a careful count was made of the supplies still on hand. This count, or physical inventory, showed unused supplies with a cost of $200. It is apparent, therefore, that supplies costing $40 were used during November. An adjusting entry is made on the basis of the November 30 count, debiting an expense account $40 (the cost of supplies consumed during November), and reducing the asset account by $40 to show that only $200 worth of office supplies remained on hand at November 30.

Portion of supplies used represents expense

Office Supplies Expense	40	
Office Supplies		40
To record consumption of office supplies in November.		

The Office Supplies account will appear in the balance sheet as an asset; the Office Supplies Expense account will be shown in the income statement. How would failure to make this adjustment affect the financial statements? In the income statement for November, the expenses would be understated by $40 and the net income overstated by the same amount. Since the overstated amount for net income in November would be transferred into the owner's capital account in the process of closing the books, the owner's equity section of the balance sheet would be overstated by $40. Assets would, of course, also be overstated because Office Supplies would be listed at $40 too much.

When payments for insurance, office supplies, and rent are expected to provide economic benefits for more than one accounting period, the advance payment is usually recorded by a debit to an asset account such as Unexpired Insurance or Office Supplies, as shown in the preceding examples. However, the advance payment *could* be recorded by debiting an expense account such as Insurance Expense. At the end of the period, the adjusting entry would then consist of a debit to Unexpired Insurance and a credit to Insurance Expense. This alternative method would lead to the same amounts in the balance sheet and income statement as the method previously illustrated. Under both procedures, we would be treating as an expense of the current period the cost of the economic benefits consumed, and carrying forward as an asset the cost of the economic benefits applicable to future periods.

DEPRECIATION OF BUILDING   The November 30 journal entry to record depreciation of the building used by the Roberts Real Estate Agency is exactly the same as the October 31 entry explained in Chapter 3.

Cost of building is gradually converted to expense	*Depreciation Expense: Building* *50*	
	Accumulated Depreciation: Building	*50*
	To record depreciation for November.	

This allocation of depreciation expense to November operations is based on the following facts: the building cost $12,000 and is estimated to have a useful life of 20 years (240 months). Using the straight-line method of depreciation, the portion of the original cost which expires each month is $\frac{1}{240}$ of $12,000, or $50.

The Accumulated Depreciation: Building account now has a credit balance of $100 as a result of the October and November credits of $50 each. The book value of the building is $11,900, that is, the original cost of $12,000 minus the accumulated depreciation of $100. The term *book value* means the net amount at which an asset is shown in the accounting records, as distinguished from its market value. *Carrying value* is an alternative term, with the same meaning as book value.

DEPRECIATION OF OFFICE EQUIPMENT   The November 30 adjusting entry to record depreciation of the office equipment is the same as the entry for depreciation a month earlier, as shown in Chapter 3.

Cost of office equipment gradually converted to expense

Depreciation Expense: Office Equipment 15
    Accumulated Depreciation: Office Equipment 15
To record depreciation for November.

Original cost of the office equipment was $1,800, and the estimated useful life was 10 years (120 months). Depreciation each month under the straight-line method is therefore $\frac{1}{120}$ of $1,800, or $15. What is the book value of the office equipment at this point? Original cost of $1,800 minus accumulated depreciation of $30 for two months leaves a book value of $1,770.

What would be the effect on the financial statements if the adjusting entries for depreciation of the building and office equipment were omitted at November 30? In the income statement the expenses would be understated by $65 ($50 depreciation of building and $15 depreciation of office equipment), and net income for the month would be overstated by $65. In the balance sheet the assets would be overstated by $65; the owner's equity would be overstated the same amount because of the $65 overstatement of the net income added to the capital account. If depreciation had not been recorded in either October or November, the overstatement in the balance sheet at November 30 would, of course, amount to $130 with respect both to assets and to owner's equity.

Recorded revenue apportioned between accounting periods

On November 1, James Fortune, a client of the Roberts Real Estate Agency, asked Roberts to accept the responsibility of managing a considerable amount of rental properties. The duties consisted of keeping the buildings rented, arranging for repairs, and collecting rents which were to be deposited in Fortune's bank account. It was agreed that $100 a month would be a reasonable fee to the Roberts Real Estate Agency for its services. Since Fortune was leaving the country on an extended trip, he paid the company for six months' service in advance at the time of signing the agreement. The journal entry to record the transaction on November 1 was as follows:

Commission collected but not yet earned

Cash 600
    Unearned Rental Commissions 600
Collected in advance six months' commissions for management of Fortune properties.

Note that no service had been performed for the customer at the time the $600 was received. As emphasized in Chapter 3, not every receipt of cash represents revenue. In this case the receipt of cash represented an advance payment by the customer which obligated the Roberts Real Estate Agency to render services in the future. Revenue is earned only by the *rendering* of services to a customer, or the *delivering* of goods to him. A portion of the agreed services ($\frac{1}{6}$, to be exact) will be rendered during November, but it would be unreasonable to regard the entire $600 as revenue in that month. The commission is earned gradually over a period of six months as the Roberts Real Estate Agency performs the required services. The $600 collected in advance is therefore credited to an *unearned revenue* account at the time of its receipt. Some accountants prefer the alternative term *deferred revenue.* At the end of each month, an amount of $100 will be transferred from unearned revenue to an earned revenue account by means of an adjusting entry. The first in this series of transfers will be made at November 30 as follows:

Entry to Unearned Rental Commissions *100*
recognize   Rental Commissions Earned. *100*
earning of
a part of Commission earned from Fortune property management in
commission November.

The $500 credit balance remaining in the Unearned Rental Commissions account represents an obligation to render $500 worth of services in future months; therefore, it belongs on the balance sheet in the liability section. An unearned revenue account differs from other liabilities since it will ordinarily be settled by the rendering of services rather than by making a cash payment, but it is nevertheless a liability. The Rental Commissions Earned account is shown in the income statement as revenue for the month.

Unrecorded expenses

Adjusting entries are necessary at the end of each accounting period to record any expenses which have been incurred but not recognized in the accounts. Salaries of employees and interest on borrowed money are common examples of expenses which accumulate day by day but which may not be recorded until the end of the period. These expenses are said to *accrue,* that is, to grow or accumulate.

ACCRUAL OF INTEREST On November 1, the Roberts Real Estate Agency borrowed the sum of $1,000 from a bank. Banks require every borrower to sign a *promissory note,* that is, a formal, written promise to repay the amount borrowed plus interest at an agreed future date. (Various forms of notes in common use and the accounting problems involved will be discussed more fully in Chapter 9.) The note signed by Roberts, with certain details omitted, is shown on page 109.

The note payable is a liability of the Roberts Real Estate Agency, similar to an account payable but different in that a formal written promise to pay is required and interest is charged on the amount borrowed. A Notes Payable account is credited when the note is issued; the Notes

Note payable issued to bank

$1,000	Winnipeg, Manitoba	November 1, 19--

Three months .... after date .... I .... promise to pay

to the order of .... Bank of Montreal ....

.... ————One thousand and no/100———— .... dollars

for value received, with interest at .... 6 per cent ....

.... Roberts Real Estate Agency ....

By .... *James Roberts* ....

Payable account will be debited three months later when the note is paid. Interest accrues throughout the life of the note payable, but it is not payable until the note matures on February 1. To the bank making the loan, the note signed by Roberts is an asset, a note receivable. The revenues earned by banks consist largely of interest charged borrowers.

The journal entry made on November 1 to record the borrowing of $1,000 from the bank was as follows:

Entry when bank loan is obtained

Cash	*1,000*	
Notes Payable		*1,000*
Obtained three-month, 6% loan from bank.		

No payment of interest was made during November, but one month's interest expense was incurred during the month. In practice, interest is computed on a daily basis ($1,000 \times 0.06 \times \frac{30}{365} = \$4.93$). For purposes of this example, however, computation has been made on a monthly basis ($1,000 \times 0.06 \times \frac{1}{12} = \$5.00$). The following adjusting entry is made at November 30 to charge November operations with one month's interest expense and also to record the amount of interest owed to the bank at the end of November.

Entry for interest expense incurred in November

Interest Expense	*5*	
Interest Payable		*5*
To record interest expense applicable to November.		

The debit balance in the Interest Expense account will appear in the November income statement; the credit balances in the Interest Payable and Notes Payable accounts will be shown in the balance sheet as liabilities. These two liability accounts will remain on the books until the maturity date of the loan, at which time a cash payment to the bank will wipe out both the Notes Payable account and the Interest Payable account.

ACCRUAL OF SALARY On November 20, Roberts hired a part-time sales-man whose duties were to work evenings calling on property owners to secure listings of property for sale or rent. The agreed salary was $75 for a five-evening week, payable each Friday; payment for the first week was made on Friday, November 24.

Assume that the last day of the accounting period, November 30, fell on Thursday. The salesman had worked four evenings since being paid the preceding Friday and therefore had earned $60 ($\frac{4}{5} \times$ $75). In order that this $60 of November salary expense be reflected in the accounts before the financial statements are prepared, an adjusting entry is necessary at November 30. Personal income taxes and other taxes relating to payroll are ignored in this illustration.

Salaries	Sales Salaries Expense	60	
expense	Sales Salaries Payable		60
incurred		
but unpaid	To record salary expense and related liability to salesman for last	
at Novem-	four evenings' work in November.	
ber 30		

The debit balance in the Sales Salaries Expense account will appear as an expense in the November income statement; the credit balance in the Sales Salaries Payable account is the amount owing to the sales-man for work performed during the last four days of November and will appear among the liabilities on the balance sheet at November 30.

The next regular payday for the salesman will be Friday, December 1, which is the first day of the new accounting period. Since the books were adjusted and closed on November 30, all the revenue and expense accounts have zero balances at the beginning of business on December 1. The payment of a week's salary to the salesman will be recorded by the following entry on December 1:

Payment	Sales Salaries Payable	60	
of salaries	Sales Salaries Expense	15	
incurred	Cash		75
in two		
account-	Paid weekly salary to salesman.	
ing		
periods		

Note that the net result of the November 30 accrual entry has been to split the salesman's weekly salary expense between November and December. Four days of the work week fell in November, so four days' pay, or $60, was recognized as November expense. One day of the work week fell in December so $15 was recorded as December expense.

No accrual entry is necessary for office salaries in the Roberts Real Estate Agency because Roberts regularly pays the office employees on the last working day of the month.

Unrecorded revenue

The treatment of unrecorded revenue is similar to that of unrecorded expenses. Any revenue which has been earned but not recorded during the accounting period should be recognized in the accounts by means of an adjusting entry, debiting an asset account and crediting a revenue account. *Accrued revenue* is a term often used to describe revenue which has been accumulating during the period but which has not been recorded prior to the closing date.

On November 16, the Roberts Real Estate Agency entered into a management agreement with Henry Clayton, the owner of several office buildings. The company agreed to manage the Clayton properties for a commission of $80 a month, payable on the fifteenth of each month. No entry is made in the accounting records at the time of signing the contract, because no services have yet been rendered and no change has occurred in assets or liabilities. The managerial duties were to begin immediately, but the first monthly commission would not be received until December 15. The following adjusting entry is therefore necessary at November 30:

Entry for commis- sions earned but uncol- lected

Rental Commissions Receivable	40	
Rental Commissions Earned		40
To record revenue accrued from services rendered Henry Clayton during November.		

The debit balance in the Rental Commissions Receivable account will be shown in the balance sheet as an asset. The credit balance of the Rental Commissions Earned account, including earnings from both the Fortune and Clayton contracts, will appear in the November income statement.

The collection of the first monthly commission from Clayton will occur in the next accounting period (December 15, to be exact). Of this $80 cash receipt, half represents collection of the asset account, Rental Commissions Receivable, created at November 30 by the adjusting entry. The other half of the $80 cash receipt represents revenue earned during December; this should be credited to the December revenue account for Rental Commissions Earned. The entry on December 15 is as follows:

Commis- sion applicable to two account- ing periods

Cash	80	
Rental Commissions Receivable		40
Rental Commissions Earned		40
Collected commission for month ended December 15.		

The net result of the November 30 accrual entry has been to divide the revenue from managing the Clayton properties between November and December in accordance with the timing of the services rendered.

Adjusting entries and the accrual basis of accounting

Adjusting entries help make accrual basis accounting work successfully. They bridge the gap between the time of earning revenue and the time of collecting cash. They enable expenses to be recorded in the accounting period in which the benefits from the expenditures are received, even though cash payment is made in an earlier or later period.

THE WORK SHEET

The work necessary at the end of an accounting period includes construction of a trial balance, journalizing and posting of adjusting entries, preparation of financial statements, and journalizing and posting of closing entries. So many details are involved in these end-of-period procedures that it is easy to make errors. If these errors are recorded in the journal and the ledger accounts, considerable time and effort can be wasted in correcting them. Both the journal and the ledger are formal, permanent records. They may be prepared manually in ink, produced on bookkeeping machines, or created by a computer in a company utilizing electronic data-processing equipment. One way of avoiding errors in the permanent accounting records and also of simplifying the work to be done at the end of the period is to use a *work sheet.*

A work sheet is a large columnar sheet of paper, especially designed to arrange in a convenient systematic form all the accounting data required at the end of the period. The work sheet is not a part of the permanent accounting records; it is prepared in pencil by the accountant for his own convenience. If an error is made on the work sheet, it may be erased and corrected much more easily than an error in the formal accounting records. Furthermore, the work sheet is so designed as to minimize errors by automatically bringing to light many types of discrepancies which might otherwise be entered in the journal and posted to the ledger accounts.

The work sheet may be thought of as a testing ground on which the ledger accounts are adjusted, balanced, and arranged in the general form of financial statements. The satisfactory completion of a work sheet provides considerable assurance that all the details of the end-of-period accounting procedures have been properly brought together. After this point has been established, the work sheet then serves as the source from which the formal financial statements are prepared and the adjusting and closing entries are made in the journal.

Preparing the work sheet

A commonly used form of work sheet with the appropriate headings for the Roberts Real Estate Agency is illustrated on page 113. Note that the heading of the work sheet consists of three parts: (1) the name of the business, (2) the title Work Sheet, and (3) the period of time covered. The body of the work sheet contains five pairs of money columns, each pair consisting of a debit and a credit column. The procedures to be followed in preparing a work sheet will now be illustrated in five simple steps.

ROBERTS REAL ESTATE AGENCY
Work Sheet
For the Month Ended November 30, 19___

	Trial Balance		Adjustments		Adjusted Trial Balance		Income Statement		Balance Sheet	
	Dr	Cr	Dr	Cr	Dr	Cr	Dr	Cr	Dr	Cr
Cash	8,600									
Accounts receivable	2,330									
Unexpired insurance	180									
Office supplies	240									
Land	5,000									
Building	12,000									
Accumulated depreciation: building		50								
Office equipment	1,800									
Accumulated depreciation: office equipment		15								
Notes payable		1,000								
Accounts payable		7,865								
Unearned rental commissions		600								
James Roberts, capital		20,257								
James Roberts, drawing	500									
Sales commissions earned		1,828								
Advertising expense	425									
Office salaries expense	400									
Sales salaries expense	75									
Telephone expense	65									
	31,615	31,615								

Trial balance is entered in first pair of columns on work sheet

1 Enter the ledger account balances in the Trial Balance columns The titles and balances of the ledger accounts at November 30 are copied into the Trial Balance columns of the work sheet, as illustrated on page 113. In practice these amounts may be taken directly from the ledger. It would be a duplication of work to prepare a trial balance as a separate schedule and then to copy this information into the work sheet. As soon as the account balances have been listed on the work sheet, these two columns should be added and the totals entered.

2 Enter the adjustments in the Adjustments columns The required adjustments for the Roberts Real Estate Agency have been explained earlier in this chapter; these same adjustments are now entered in the Adjustments columns of the work sheet. (See page 115.) As a cross reference, the debit and credit parts of each adjustment are keyed together by placing a key letter to the left of each amount. For example, the adjustment debiting Insurance Expense and crediting Unexpired Insurance is identified by the key letter (a). The use of the key letters makes it easy to match a debit entry in the Adjustments columns with its related credit. The identifying letters also key the debit and credit entries in the Adjustments columns to the brief explanations which appear at the bottom of the work sheet.

The titles of any accounts debited or credited in the adjusting entries but not listed in the trial balance are written on the work sheet below the trial balance. For example, Insurance Expense does not appear in the trial balance; it is written on the first available line below the trial balance totals. After all the adjustments have been entered in the Adjustments columns, this pair of columns must be totaled. Proving the equality of debit and credit totals tends to prevent arithmetic errors from being carried over into other columns of the work sheet.

3 Enter the account balances as adjusted in the Adjusted Trial Balance columns The work sheet as it appears after completion of the Adjusted Trial Balance columns is illustrated on page 116. Each account balance in the first pair of columns is combined with the adjustment, if any, in the second pair of columns, and the combined amount is entered in the Adjusted Trial Balance columns. This process of combining the items on each line throughout the first four columns of the work sheet requires horizontal addition or subtraction. It is called *cross footing*, in contrast to the addition of items in a vertical column, which is called *footing* the column.

For example, the Office Supplies account is seen to have a debit balance of $240 in the Trial Balance columns. This $240 debit amount is combined with the $40 credit appearing on the same line in the Adjustments column; the combination of a $240 debit with a $40 credit produces an adjusted debit amount of $200 in the Adjusted Trial Balance debit column. As another example, consider the Office Supplies Expense account. This account had no balance in the Trial Balance columns but

ROBERTS REAL ESTATE AGENCY
Work Sheet
For the Month Ended November 30, 19___

	Trial Balance Dr	Trial Balance Cr	Adjustments Dr	Adjustments Cr	Adjusted Trial Balance Dr	Adjusted Trial Balance Cr	Income Statement Dr	Income Statement Cr	Balance Sheet Dr	Balance Sheet Cr
Cash	8,600									
Accounts receivable	2,330									
Unexpired insurance	180			(a) 5						
Office supplies	240			(b) 40						
Land	5,000									
Building	12,000									
Accumulated depreciation: building		50		(c) 50						
Office equipment	1,800									
Accumulated depreciation: office equipment		15		(d) 15						
Notes payable		1,000								
Accounts payable		7,865								
Unearned rental commissions		600	(e) 100							
James Roberts, capital		20,257								
James Roberts, drawing	500									
Sales commissions earned		1,828								
Advertising expense	425									
Office salaries expense	400									
Sales salaries expense	75		(g) 60							
Telephone expense	65									
	31,615	31,615								
Insurance expense			(a) 5							
Office supplies expense			(b) 40							
Depreciation expense: building			(c) 50							
Depreciation expense: office equipment			(d) 15							
Rental commissions earned				(e) 100 (h) 40						
Interest expense			(f) 5							
Interest payable				(f) 5						
Sales salaries payable				(g) 60						
Rental commissions receivable			(h) 40							
			315	315						

Explanatory footnotes keyed to adjustments

*Adjustments:
(a) Portion of insurance cost which expired during November
(b) Office supplies used
(c) Depreciation of building during November
(d) Depreciation of office equipment during November

(e) Earned one-sixth of the commission collected in advance on the Fortune properties
(f) Interest expense accrued during November on note payable
(g) Salesman's salary for last four days of November
(h) Rental commission accrued on Clayton contract in November

ROBERTS REAL ESTATE AGENCY
Work Sheet
For the Month Ended November 30, 19____

Enter the adjusted amounts in columns 5 and 6 of work sheet

	Trial Balance Dr	Trial Balance Cr	Adjustments Dr	Adjustments Cr	Adjusted Trial Balance Dr	Adjusted Trial Balance Cr	Income Statement Dr	Income Statement Cr	Balance Sheet Dr	Balance Sheet Cr
Cash	8,600				8,600					
Accounts receivable	2,330				2,330					
Unexpired insurance	180			(a) 5	175					
Office supplies	240			(b) 40	200					
Land	5,000				5,000					
Building	12,000				12,000					
Accumulated depreciation: building		50		(c) 50		100				
Office equipment	1,800				1,800					
Accumulated depreciation: office equipment		15		(d) 15		30				
Notes payable		1,000				1,000				
Accounts payable		7,865				7,865				
Unearned rental commissions		600	(e) 100			500				
James Roberts, capital		20,257				20,257				
James Roberts, drawing	500				500					
Sales commissions earned		1,828				1,828				
Advertising expense	425				425					
Office salaries expense	400				400					
Sales salaries expense	75		(g) 60		135					
Telephone expense	65				65					
	31,615	31,615								
Insurance expense			(a) 5		5					
Office supplies expense			(b) 40		40					
Depreciation expense: building			(c) 50		50					
Depreciation expense: office equipment			(d) 15		15					
Rental commissions earned				(e) 100 (h) 40		140				
Interest expense			(f) 5		5					
Interest payable				(f) 5		5				
Sales salaries payable				(g) 60		60				
Rental commissions receivable			(h) 40		40					
			315	315	31,785	31,785				

*Explanatory notes relating to adjustments are the same as on page 115.

shows a $40 debit in the Adjustments debit column. The combination of a zero starting balance and $40 debit adjustment produces a $40 debit amount in the Adjusted Trial Balance.

Many of the accounts in the trial balance are not affected by the adjustments made at the end of the month; the balances of these accounts (such as Cash, Land, Building, or Notes Payable in the illustrated work sheet) are entered in the Adjusted Trial Balance columns in exactly the same amounts as shown in the Trial Balance columns. After all the accounts have been extended into the Adjusted Trial Balance columns, this pair of columns is totaled to prove that no arithmetic errors have been made up to this point.

4 Extend each amount in the Adjusted Trial Balance columns into the Income Statement columns or into the Balance Sheet columns Assets, liabilities, and the owner's capital and drawing accounts are extended into the Balance Sheet columns; revenue and expense accounts are extended to the Income Statement columns. The process of extending amounts horizontally across the work sheet should begin with the account at the top of the work sheet, which is usually Cash. The cash figure is extended to the Balance Sheet debit column. Then the accountant goes down the work sheet line by line, extending each account balance to the appropriate Income Statement or Balance Sheet column. The likelihood of error is much less when each account is extended in the order of its appearance on the work sheet, than if accounts are extended in random order.

The extension of amounts horizontally across the work sheet is merely a sorting of the accounts making up the Adjusted Trial Balance into the two categories of income statement accounts and balance sheet accounts. The work sheet as it appears after completion of this sorting process is illustrated on page 118. Note that each amount in the Adjusted Trial Balance columns is extended to one and only one of the four remaining columns.

5 Total the Income Statement columns and the Balance Sheet columns. Enter the net income or net loss as a balancing figure in both pairs of columns, and again compute column totals The work sheet as it appears after this final step is shown on page 119.

The net income or net loss for the period is determined by computing the difference between the totals of the two Income Statement columns. In the illustrated work sheet, the credit column total is the larger and the excess represents net income:

Income Statement credit column total (revenues)	*$1,968*
Income Statement debit column total (expenses)	*1,140*
Difference: net income for period	*$ 828*

Note on the work sheet that the net income of $828 is entered in the Income Statement *debit* column as a balancing figure and also on the

ROBERTS REAL ESTATE AGENCY
Work Sheet
For the Month Ended November 30, 19____

	Trial Balance Dr	Trial Balance Cr	Adjustments Dr	Adjustments Cr	Adjusted Trial Balance Dr	Adjusted Trial Balance Cr	Income Statement Dr	Income Statement Cr	Balance Sheet Dr	Balance Sheet Cr
Cash	8,600				8,600				8,600	
Accounts receivable	2,330				2,330				2,330	
Unexpired insurance	180			(a) 5	175				175	
Office supplies	240			(b) 40	200				200	
Land	5,000				5,000				5,000	
Building	12,000				12,000				12,000	
Accumulated depreciation: building		50		(c) 50		100				100
Office equipment	1,800				1,800				1,800	
Accumulated depreciation: office equipment		15		(d) 15		30				30
Notes payable		1,000				1,000				1,000
Accounts payable		7,865				7,865				7,865
Unearned rental commissions		600	(e) 100			500				500
James Roberts, capital		20,257				20,257				20,257
James Roberts, drawing	500				500				500	
Sales commissions earned		1,828				1,828		1,828		
Advertising expense	425				425		425			
Office salaries expense	400				400		400			
Sales salaries expense	75		(g) 60		135		135			
Telephone expense	65				65		65			
	31,615	31,615								
Insurance expense			(a) 5		5		5			
Office supplies expense			(b) 40		40		40			
Depreciation expense: building			(c) 50		50		50			
Depreciation expense: office equipment			(d) 15		15		15			
Rental commissions earned				(e) 100 (h) 40		140		140		
Interest expense			(f) 5		5		5			
Interest payable				(f) 5		5				5
Sales salaries payable				(g) 60		60				60
Rental commissions receivable			(h) 40		40				40	
			315	315	31,785	31,785				

Extend each adjusted amount to columns for income statement or balance sheet

* Explanatory notes relating to adjustments are the same as on page 115.

ROBERTS REAL ESTATE AGENCY
Work Sheet
For the Month Ended November 30, 19____

Completed work sheet

	Trial Balance Dr	Trial Balance Cr	Adjustments* Dr	Adjustments* Cr	Adjusted Trial Balance Dr	Adjusted Trial Balance Cr	Income Statement Dr	Income Statement Cr	Balance Sheet Dr	Balance Sheet Cr
Cash	8,600				8,600				8,600	
Accounts receivable	2,330				2,330				2,330	
Unexpired insurance	180			(a) 5	175				175	
Office supplies	240			(b) 40	200				200	
Land	5,000				5,000				5,000	
Building	12,000				12,000				12,000	
Accumulated depreciation: building		50		(c) 50		100				100
Office equipment	1,800				1,800				1,800	
Accumulated depreciation: office equipment		15		(d) 15		30				30
Notes payable		1,000				1,000				1,000
Accounts payable		7,865				7,865				7,865
Unearned rental commissions		600	(e) 100			500				500
James Roberts, capital		20,257				20,257				20,257
James Roberts, drawing	500				500				500	
Sales commissions earned		1,828				1,828		1,828		
Advertising expense	425				425		425			
Office salaries expense	400				400		400			
Sales salaries expense	75		(g) 60		135		135			
Telephone expense	65				65		65			
Insurance expense			(a) 5		5		5			
Office supplies expense			(b) 40		40		40			
Depreciation expense: building			(c) 50		50		50			
Depreciation expense: office equipment			(d) 15		15		15			
Rental commissions earned				(e) 100 (h) 40		140		140		
Interest expense			(f) 5		5		5			
Interest payable				(f) 5		5				5
Sales salaries payable				(g) 60		60				60
Rental commissions receivable			(h) 40		40				40	
	31,615	31,615	315	315	31,785	31,785	1,140	1,968	30,645	29,817
Net income							828			828
							1,968	1,968	30,645	30,645

*Explanatory notes relating to adjustments are the same as on page 115.

same line as a balancing figure in the Balance Sheet *credit* column. The caption Net Income is written in the space for account titles to identify and explain this item. New totals are then computed for both the Income Statement columns and the Balance Sheet columns. Each pair of columns is now in balance.

The reason for entering the net income of $828 in the Balance Sheet credit column is that the net income accumulated during the period in the revenue and expense accounts causes an increase in the owner's equity. If the balance sheet columns did not have equal totals after the net income had been recorded in the credit column, the lack of agreement would indicate that an error had been made in the work sheet.

Let us assume for a moment that the month's operations had produced a loss rather than a profit. In that case the Income Statement debit column would exceed the credit column. The excess of the debits (expenses) over the credits (revenues) would have to be entered in the credit column in order to bring the two Income Statement columns into balance. The incurring of a loss would decrease the owner's equity; therefore, the loss would be entered as a balancing figure in the Balance Sheet *debit* column. The Balance Sheet columns would then have equal totals.

SELF-BALANCING NATURE OF THE WORK SHEET Why does the entering of the net income or net loss in one of the Balance Sheet columns bring this pair of columns into balance? The answer is short and simple. All the accounts in the Balance Sheet columns have November 30 balances with the exception of the owner's capital account, which still shows the October 31 balance. By bringing in the current month's net income as an addition to the October 31 capital, the capital account is brought up to date as of November 30. The Balance Sheet columns now prove the familiar proposition that assets are equal to the total of liabilities and owner's equity.

Uses for the work sheet

PREPARING FINANCIAL STATEMENTS Preparing the formal financial statements from the work sheet is an easy step. All the information needed for both the income statement and the balance sheet has already been sorted and arranged in convenient form in the work sheet. The income statement shown on page 121 contains the amounts listed in the Income Statement columns of the work sheet.

ROBERTS REAL ESTATE AGENCY
Income Statement
For the Month Ended November 30, 19___

Data taken from Income Statement columns of work sheet	Revenue:	
	Sales commissions earned	$1,828
	Rental commissions earned	140
	Total revenue	$1,968

Expenses:

Advertising	$425	
Office supplies	40	
Office salaries	400	
Sales salaries	135	
Telephone	65	
Insurance	5	
Depreciation: building	50	
Depreciation: office equipment	15	
Interest	5	
Total expenses		1,140
Net income		$ 828

Balance sheet and statement of owner's equity The balance sheets previously illustrated have shown in the owner's equity section the changes during the month caused by the owner's withdrawals and by the net income or loss from operation of the business. A separate statement, illustrated below, is sometimes used to show the changes in the owner's equity during the period. When a separate statement is used, only the ending amount of the owner's capital account is shown in the balance sheet. The separate statement showing changes in the owner's equity may be used with either the account form or the report form of balance sheet. In this illustration, the report form of balance sheet is used.

ROBERTS REAL ESTATE AGENCY
Statement of Owner's Equity
For the Month Ended November 30, 19___

Net income exceeded withdrawals by owner	James Roberts, capital, Nov. 1, 19___	$20,257
	Net income for November	828
	Subtotal	$21,085
	Less: Withdrawals	500
	James Roberts, capital, Nov. 30, 19___	$20,585

ROBERTS REAL ESTATE AGENCY
Balance Sheet
November 30, 19___

<table>
<tr><td rowspan="12">*Compare these amounts with figures in Balance Sheet columns of work sheet*</td></tr>
<tr><td>Cash ....</td><td></td><td>$ 8,600</td></tr>
<tr><td>Accounts receivable ....</td><td></td><td>2,330</td></tr>
<tr><td>Rental commissions receivable ....</td><td></td><td>40</td></tr>
<tr><td>Unexpired insurance ....</td><td></td><td>175</td></tr>
<tr><td>Office supplies ....</td><td></td><td>200</td></tr>
<tr><td>Land ....</td><td></td><td>5,000</td></tr>
<tr><td>Building ....</td><td>$12,000</td><td></td></tr>
<tr><td>   Less: Accumulated depreciation ....</td><td>100</td><td>11,900</td></tr>
<tr><td>Office equipment ....</td><td>$ 1,800</td><td></td></tr>
<tr><td>   Less: Accumulated depreciation ....</td><td>30</td><td>1,770</td></tr>
<tr><td></td><td></td><td>$30,015</td></tr>
</table>

Liabilities & Owner's Equity

Liabilities:		
Notes payable		$ 1,000
Accounts payable		7,865
Interest payable		5
Sales salaries payable		60
Unearned rental commissions		500
Total liabilities		$ 9,430
Owner's equity:		
James Roberts, capital		20,585
		$30,015

RECORDING ADJUSTING ENTRIES IN THE ACCOUNTING RECORDS After the financial statements have been prepared from the work sheet at the end of the period, the ledger accounts are adjusted to bring them into agreement with the statements. This is an easy step because the adjustments have already been computed on the work sheet. The amounts appearing in the Adjustments columns of the work sheet and the related explanations at the bottom of the work sheet provide all the necessary information for the adjusting entries, as shown on page 123, which are first entered in the journal and then posted to the ledger accounts.

RECORDING CLOSING ENTRIES When the financial statements have been prepared from the work sheet, the revenue and expense accounts have served their purpose for the current period and should be closed. These accounts will then have zero balances and will be ready for the recording of revenue and expenses during the next fiscal period.

The journalizing and posting of closing entries were illustrated in Chapter 3. The point to be emphasized now is that the completed work

General Journal

Adjustments on work sheet are entered in general journal	19__ Nov.	30	Insurance Expense . . . . Unexpired Insurance . . . . Insurance expense for November.	5	5
		30	Office Supplies Expense . . . . Office Supplies . . . . Office supplies used during November.	40	40
		30	Depreciation Expense: Building . . . . Accumulated Depreciation: Building . . Depreciation for November.	50	50

		30	Depreciation Expense: Office Equipment . . .
			    Accumulated Depreciation: Office
			        Equipment . . . .
			Depreciation for November.
				15	15

		30	Unearned Rental Commissions . . . . Rental Commissions Earned . . . . Earned one-sixth of commission collected in advance for management of the properties owned by James Fortune.	100	100
		30	Interest Expense . . . . Interest Payable . . . . Interest expense accrued during November on note payable.	5	5
		30	Sales Salaries Expense . . . . Sales Salaries Payable . . . . To record expense and related liability to salesman for last four evenings' work in November.	60	60
		30	Rental Commissions Receivable . . . . Rental Commissions Earned . . . . To record the receivable and related revenue earned for managing properties owned by Henry Clayton.	40	40

sheet provides in convenient form all the information needed to make the closing entries. The preparation of closing entries from the work sheet may be summarized as follows:

1 To close the accounts listed in the Income Statement credit column, debit the revenue accounts and credit Income Summary.

2 To close the accounts listed in the Income Statement debit column, debit Income Summary and credit the expense accounts.

3 To close the Income Summary account, transfer the balancing figure in the Income Statement columns of the work sheet ($828 in the illustration) to the owner's capital account. A profit is transferred by debiting Income Summary and crediting the capital account; a loss is transferred by debiting the capital account and crediting Income Summary.

4 To close the owner's drawing account, debit the capital account and credit the drawing account. Note on the work sheet that the account, James Roberts, Drawing, is extended from the Adjusted Trial Balance debit column to the Balance Sheet debit column. It does not appear in the Income Statement columns because a withdrawal of cash by the owner is not regarded as an expense of the business.

The closing entries at November 30 are as follows:

General Journal

Page 6

Closing entries derived from work sheet	19__ Nov.	30	Sales Commissions Earned	1,828	
			Rental Commissions Earned.	140	
			Income Summary		1,968
			To close the revenue accounts.		
		30	Income Summary	1,140	
			Advertising Expense.		425
			Office Salaries Expense		400
			Sales Salaries Expense.		135
			Telephone Expense		65
			Insurance Expense		5
			Office Supplies Expense		40
			Depreciation Expense: Building.		50
			Depreciation Expense: Office Equip- ment.		15
			Interest Expense		5
			To close the expense accounts.		
		30	Income Summary	828	
			James Roberts, Capital		828
			To close the Income Summary account.		
		30	James Roberts, Capital.	500	
			James Roberts, Drawing		500
			To close the owner's drawing account.		

Sequence of accounting procedures when work sheet is used

In any business which maintains a considerable number of accounts or makes numerous adjusting entries, the use of a work sheet will save much time and labor. Since the work sheet includes a trial balance, adjusting entries in preliminary form, and an adjusted trial balance, the use of the work sheet will modify the sequence of accounting procedures given in Chapter 3 as follows:

1 Record all transactions in the journal as they occur.

2 Post debits and credits from the journal entries to the proper ledger accounts.

3 Prepare the work sheet. (The work sheet includes a trial balance of the ledger and all necessary adjustments.)

4 Prepare financial statements, consisting of an income statement, a statement of owner's equity, and a balance sheet.

5 Using the information shown on the work sheet as a guide, enter the adjusting and closing entries in the journal. Post these entries to ledger accounts.

6 Prepare an after-closing trial balance to prove that the ledger is still in balance.

Note that the first two procedures, consisting of the journalizing and posting of transactions during the period, are the same regardless of whether a work sheet is to be used at the end of the period.

The accounting cycle

The above sequence of accounting procedures constitutes a complete accounting process, which is repeated in the same order in each accounting period. The regular repetition of this standardized set of procedures is often referred to as the *accounting cycle.*

In most business concerns the books are closed only once a year; for these companies the accounting cycle is one year in length. For purposes of illustration in a textbook, it is convenient to assume that the entire accounting cycle is performed within the time period of one month. The completion of the accounting cycle is the occasion for closing the revenue and expense accounts and preparing financial statements.

Preparing monthly financial statements without closing the books

Many companies which close their books only once a year nevertheless prepare *monthly* financial statements for managerial use. These monthly statements are prepared from work sheets, but the adjustments indicated on the work sheets are not entered in the accounting records and no closing entries are made. Under this plan, the time-consuming operation of journalizing and posting adjustments and closing entries is performed only at the end of the fiscal year, but the company has the advantage of monthly financial statements. Monthly and quarterly financial statements are often referred to as *interim statements,* because they are in between the year-end statements. The annual or year-end statements are usually audited by a firm of chartered accountants; interim statements are usually unaudited.

QUESTIONS

1 Which of the following statements do you consider most acceptable?
  a Adjusting entries affect balance sheet accounts only.
  b Adjusting entries affect income statement accounts only.
  c An adjusting entry may affect two or more balance sheet accounts or two or more income statement accounts, but cannot affect both a balance sheet account and an income statement account.
  d Every adjusting entry affects both a balance sheet account and an income statement account.

2 At the end of the current year, the adjusted trial balance of the Midas Company showed the following account balances, among others:

Building, $31,600

Depreciation Expense: Building, $1,580

Accumulated Depreciation: Building, $11,060

Assuming that straight-line depreciation has been used, what length of time do these facts suggest that the Midas Company has owned the building?

3 The net income reported by Haskell Company for the year was $21,400, and the capital account of the owner, J. B. Haskell, stood at $36,000. However, the company had failed to recognize that interest amounting to $375 had accrued on a note payable to the bank. State the corrected figures for net income and for the owner's equity. In what other respect was the balance sheet of the company in error?

4 Office supplies on hand in the Melville Company amounted to $642 at the beginning of the year. During the year additional office supplies were purchased at a cost of $1,561 and charged to Inventory of Office Supplies. At the end of the year a physical count showed that supplies on hand amounted to $812. Give the adjusting entry needed at December 31.

5 The X Company at December 31 recognized the existence of certain unexpired costs which would provide benefits to the company in future periods. Give examples of such unexpired costs and state where they would be shown in the financial statements.

6 In performing the regular end-of-period accounting procedures, does the preparation of the work sheet precede or follow the posting of adjusting entries to ledger accounts? Why?

7 The Adjustments columns of the work sheet for Davis Company contained only three adjustments, as follows: depreciation of building, $3,600; expiration of insurance, $500; and salaries accrued at year-end, $4,100. If the Trial Balance columns showed totals of $600,000, what would be the totals of the Adjusted Trial Balance columns?

8 Should the Adjusted Trial Balance columns be totaled before or after the adjusted amounts are carried to the Income Statement and Balance Sheet columns? Explain.

9 In extending adjusted account balances from the Adjusted Trial Balance columns to the Income Statement and Balance Sheet columns, is there any particular sequence to be followed in order to minimize the possibility of errors? Explain.

10 Do the totals of the balance sheet ordinarily agree with the totals of the Balance Sheet columns of the work sheet?

11 Is a work sheet ever prepared when there is no intention of closing the books? Explain.

EXERCISES

Ex. 4-1 Rivers Company purchased a three-year fire insurance policy on September 1 and recorded payment of the full three-year premium of $1,080 by debiting Unexpired Insurance. The accounts were not adjusted or closed until the end of the calendar year. Give the necessary adjusting entry at December 31.

Ex. 4-2 The weekly salaries paid by Sampson Company to its sales personnel each Friday for a five-day work week amount to $15,000.
  a Draft the necessary adjusting entry at year-end, assuming that December 31 falls on Tuesday.
  b Also draft the journal entry for the payment by Sampson Company of a week's salaries to its sales personnel on Friday, January 3, the first payday of the new year.

Ex. 4-3 Marin Company adjusts and closes its accounts at the end of the calendar year. Prepare the adjusting entries required at December 31, based on the following information:
  a A six-month bank loan in the amount of $100,000 had been obtained on October 1 at an annual interest rate of 6%. No interest has been paid as yet and no interest expense has been recorded.
  b Depreciation on office equipment is based on the assumption of a 10-year life and no scrap value. The balance in the Office Equipment account is $16,500; no changes have occurred in this account during the current year.
  c Interest receivable on Canadian government bonds owned is $1,200.
  d On December 31, an agreement was signed to lease a truck for 12 months beginning January 1 at a rate of 15 cents a mile. Usage is expected to be 1,500 miles per month and the contract specifies a minimum payment equivalent to 10,000 miles a year.

Ex. 4-4 The Harrison Management Company manages office buildings and apartment buildings for various owners who wish to be relieved of this responsibility. The revenues earned for this service are credited to Management Fees Earned. On December 1, the company received a cheque for $1,800 from a client, James Thurston, who was leaving for a six-month stay abroad. This cheque represented payment in advance for management of Thurston's real estate properties during the six months of his absence. Explain how this transaction would be recorded, the adjustment, if any, to be made at December 31, and the presentation of this information in the year-end financial statements.

Ex. 4-5 The income statement for 1974 for the Martinez Company included the following expenses:

Insurance expense	$ 900
Interest expense	800
Salaries expense	50,000

Listed below are related items taken from two consecutive year-end balance sheets of Martinez Company:

	12/31/73	12/31/74
Unexpired insurance	$ 0	$ 1,800
Interest payable	4,600	0
Salaries payable	8,000	10,000

Instructions Determine the amount of cash
a Paid during 1974 on insurance policies.
b Paid during 1974 for interest.
c Paid during 1974 as salaries.

PROBLEMS

Group A

To simplify calculations, interest should be computed on a monthly basis in the following problems. (Canadian practice requires that interest be computed on a daily basis, but this method of calculation is deferred to Chapter 9).

4A-1 Snow Valley Ski Resort maintains its accounting records on the basis of a fiscal year ending October 31. The following information is available at October 31, as a source for adjusting entries.
   (1) Salaries earned by employees but unpaid amounted to $2,750.
   (2) Depreciation on the ski lodge for the year ended October 31 was $13,600.
   (3) A tractor had been leased from Executive Leasing Ltd., on October 11 at a daily rate of $12. No rental payment had yet been made.
   (4) A six-month bank loan in the amount of $90,000 had been obtained on September 1 at an annual interest rate of 8%. No interest expense has been recorded.
   (5) Among the assets owned by the company were government bonds in the face amount of $15,000. Accrued interest receivable on the bonds at October 31 amounted to $300.
   (6) A portion of the land owned by the company had been leased on July 31 to a service station operator at a yearly rental of $3,600. One year's rent had been collected in advance at the date of the lease and had been credited to Unearned Rental Revenue.
   (7) On October 31 the company signed an agreement to lease a truck from Suburban Leasing Corporation Ltd. for a period of one year, beginning November 1, at a rate of 17 cents a mile.

Instructions
From the information given above, prepare the adjusting entries (including explanations) required at October 31.

4A-2 The schedule presented below shows two pairs of columns taken from the work sheet of Marlin Insurance Agency at September 30, 19___ . The Adjustments columns which would normally appear between the Trial Balance columns and the Adjusted Trial Balance columns have been omitted.

	Trial Balance		Adjusted Trial Balance	
	Debit	Credit	Debit	Credit
Cash	3,000		3,000	
Commissions receivable			700	
Inventory of office supplies	300		140	
Office equipment	5,700		5,700	
Accumulated depreciation: office equipment . . .		2,150		2,230
Accounts payable		775		775
Salaries payable				350
Unearned commissions		200		90
John Marlin, capital		4,925		4,925
Commissions earned		1,950		2,760
Salaries expense	1,000		1,350	
Office supplies expense			160	
Depreciation expense: office equipment			80	
	10,000	10,000	11,130	11,130

Instructions Prepare in journal form the five adjusting entries which explain the *changes* from the amounts in the Trial Balance columns to the amounts in the Adjusted Trial Balance columns. Include an explanation as part of each journal entry.

4A-3 Investors' Advisory Service was organized on June 1, 19___, to provide invest-ment counseling to investors in securities. Some customers paid in advance on a subscription basis; others were billed after services were rendered. Assume that the company's accounts are adjusted and closed each month. The trial balance at October 31 follows:

INVESTORS' ADVISORY SERVICE
Trial Balance
October 31, 19___

Cash	$13,249	
Prepaid rent	1,475	
Inventory of office supplies	495	
Office equipment	3,132	
Accumulated depreciation: office equipment		$ 116
Accounts payable		475
Unearned revenue		6,300
Bruce Bennett, capital		12,000
Bruce Bennett, drawing	225	
Fees earned		4,750
Telephone expense	280	
Travel expense	340	
Salaries expense	4,445	
	$23,641	$23,641

Other data
(a) The monthly rent was $295.
(b) Office supplies on hand October 31 amounted to $325.
(c) The office equipment was purchased on June 1. The useful life was estimated at 9 years.
(d) Services rendered during the month and chargeable to Unearned Revenue (subscription basis) amounted to $1,450.
(e) Investment advisory services (nonsubscription basis) rendered during the month but not yet billed amounted to $280 (debit Advisory Service Receiv-ables).
(f) Salaries earned by employees during the month but not yet paid amounted to $115.

Instructions
a Prepare adjusting entries.
b Prepare an adjusted trial balance.

4A-4 Stanley Wiley organized his own drafting firm on January 1, 19___. At June 30, when the accounts were adjusted and closed for the first time, the following trial balance was prepared.

BLUELINE DRAFTING SERVICE
Trial Balance
June 30, 19____

Cash	$ 9,250	
Prepaid office rent	6,000	
Inventory of drafting supplies	1,200	
Drafting equipment	6,600	
Notes payable		$ 5,000
Unearned fees		13,000
Stanley Wiley, capital		15,100
Stanley Wiley, drawing	4,270	
Fees earned		10,620
Salaries expense	16,200	
Miscellaneous expense	200	
	$43,720	$43,720

Other data
(1) Office rent for one year was paid on January 1, when the lease was signed.
(2) Drafting supplies on hand on June 30 amounted to $240.
(3) Drafting equipment was purchased on January 1. The useful life was estimated at 10 years.
(4) Accrued interest expense on notes payable was $50 as of June 30.
(5) A number of clients obtained during the first six months of the company's operations had made advance payments for services to be rendered over a considerable period. As of June 30, value of services rendered and chargeable against Unearned Fees was $9,500.
(6) Services rendered and chargeable to other clients amounted to $3,700 as of June 30. No entries had yet been made to record the revenues earned by performing services for these clients.
(7) Salaries earned by staff personnel but not yet paid amounted to $500 on June 30.

Instructions
a Prepare adjusting entries as of June 30, 19____.
b Prepare an adjusted trial balance. (*Note:* You may find the use of T accounts helpful in computing the account balances after adjustments.)
c Prepare an income statement for the six-month period ended June 30, 19____, a statement of owner's equity, and a balance sheet.

4A-5 The four-column schedule shown on page 131 represents the first four columns of a 10-column work sheet to be prepared for Miller's TV Repair Service for the month ended April 30, 19____. (The completed adjustment columns have been included to minimize the detail work involved.) These adjustments were derived from the following information available at April 30.
(a) Monthly rent expense, $300.
(b) Insurance expense for the month, $15.
(c) Advertising expense for the month, $150.
(d) Cost of supplies on hand, based on physical count on April 30, $390.
(e) Depreciation expense on equipment, $130 per month.
(f) Accrued interest expense on notes payable, $35.
(g) Salaries earned by employees but not yet paid, $175.
(h) Services amounting to $400 were rendered during April for customers who had paid in advance. This portion of the Unearned Revenue account should be regarded as earned as of April 30.

	Trial Balance		Adjustments	
	Dr	Cr	Dr	Cr
Cash	10,000			
Prepaid rent	900			(a) 300
Unexpired insurance	255			(b) 15
Prepaid advertising	590			(c) 150
Inventory of supplies	630			(d) 240
Equipment	11,700			
Accumulated depreciation: equipment . .		1,040		(e) 130
Notes payable		8,000		
Unearned revenue		1,200	(h) 400	
B. R. Miller, capital		12,665		
B. R. Miller, drawing	1,500			
Revenue from services		4,635		(h) 400
Salaries expense	1,965		(g) 175	
	27,540	27,540		
Rent expense			(a) 300	
Insurance expense			(b) 15	
Advertising expense			(c) 150	
Supplies expense			(d) 240	
Depreciation expense: equipment			(e) 130	
Interest expense			(f) 35	
Accrued interest payable				(f) 35
Salaries payable				(g) 175
			1,445	1,445

Instructions Prepare a 10-column work sheet utilizing the trial balance and adjusting data provided. Include at the bottom of the work sheet a brief explanation keyed to each adjusting entry.

4A-6 Resort Flying Service was organized on June 1, 19___, to offer air service for visitors to a famous island resort. The company follows the policy of adjusting and closing its accounts each month. At December 31, after seven months of operating experience, the trial balance on page 132 was prepared from the ledger.

Other data
(a) Monthly rent amounted to $1,000.
(b) Insurance expense for December was $1,300.
(c) All necessary maintenance work was provided by Ryan Air Services at a fixed charge of $2,500 a month. Service for three months had been paid for in advance on December 1.
(d) Spare parts used in connection with maintenance work amounted to $1,250 during the month.
(e) At the time of purchase the remaining useful life of the aircraft, which were several years old, was estimated at 5,000 hours of flying time. During December, total flying time amounted to 160 hours.
(f) The Chamber of Commerce purchased 2,000 special price tickets for $20,000. Each ticket allowed the holder one flight normally priced at $15. During the month 400 of these reduced-price tickets had been used.
(g) Salaries earned by employees but not paid were $1,100 at December 31.

RESORT FLYING SERVICE
Trial Balance
December 31, 19___

Cash	$ 65,500	
Prepaid rental expense	18,000	
Unexpired insurance	15,600	
Prepaid maintenance expense	7,500	
Spare parts	19,000	
Aircraft	270,000	
Accumulated depreciation: aircraft		$ 25,650
Unearned passenger revenue		20,000
Thomas White, capital		325,920
Thomas White, drawing	4,000	
Passenger revenue earned		63,330
Gasoline expense	4,600	
Salaries expense	28,900	
Advertising expense	1,800	
	$434,900	$434,900

Instructions
a Prepare a work sheet for the month ended December 31, 19___.
b Prepare an income statement and a balance sheet that includes the details of changes in owner's equity.
c Prepare adjusting and closing entries.

Group B

4B-1 The Spyglass Marina maintains its accounts on the basis of a fiscal year ending June 30, and has the following information available as the basis for preparing adjusting entries.
(1) Accrued property taxes, $2,850.
(2) A six-month bank loan in the amount of $60,000 had been obtained on April 30 at an annual interest rate of 6%. No interest had been paid and no interest expense recorded.
(3) Interest receivable on Canadian government bonds owned, $825.
(4) Accrued wages payable, $4,600.
(5) A portion of the land owned had been leased to an amusement park at a yearly rental of $12,000. One year's rent had been collected in advance at the date of the lease (June 16) and credited to Unearned Rental Revenue.
(6) Another portion of the land owned had been rented on June 1 to a service station operator at an annual rate of $2,400. No rent had as yet been collected from this tenant.
(7) Depreciation on the building for the period ended June 30 was $3,000.
(8) On June 30, Spyglass Marina signed an agreement to lease a truck from Leasall Corporation Ltd. for the period of one year beginning July 1 at a rate of 20 cents per mile, with a minimum monthly charge of $200.

Instructions
From the information given above, draft the adjusting entries (including explanations) required at June 30.

4B-2 The four-column schedule shown below consists of the trial balance and the adjusted trial balance of Palisades Realty Company at December 31, 19___. The pair of Adjustments columns which would normally appear between the Trial Balance columns and the Adjusted Trial Balance columns has purposely been omitted.

	Trial Balance		Adjusted Trial Balance	
	Debit	Credit	Debit	Credit
Cash	7,000		7,000	
Commissions receivable	2,130		4,130	
Inventory of office supplies	450		110	
Office equipment	13,200		13,200	
Accumulated depreciation: office equipment . . .		2,880		2,990
Notes payable		10,000		10,000
Accounts payable		1,300		1,300
Salaries payable				1,100
Interest payable				150
Unearned commissions		850		650
Joe Randall, capital		6,500		6,500
Commissions earned		2,350		4,550
Salaries expense	1,100		2,200	
Interest expense			150	
Office supplies expense			340	
Depreciation expense: office equipment			110	
	23,880	23,880	27,240	27,240

Instructions Prepare the six adjusting journal entries which explain the *changes* from the amounts in the Trial Balance columns to the amounts in the Adjusted Trial Balance columns. Include an explanation as part of each journal entry.

4B-3 Sunset Storage Company started business January 1, 19___. Its business consists of renting to others space for storage of various industrial materials. The company makes adjusting entries and closes its books each month. A trial balance and other information needed in making adjusting entries appear on page 134.

Other data
(a) The monthly insurance expense amounted to $85.
(b) The amount of office supplies on hand, based on a physical count on January 31, was $65.
(c) A $24,000, one-year note payable was signed on January 2, with interest at 8% a year.
(d) The useful life of office equipment was estimated at 8 years.
(e) Certain clients chose to pay several months' storage fees in advance. It was determined that $160 of such fees was still unearned as of January 31.
(f) Several clients neglected to send in storage fees amounting to $110 for the month of January. These receivables are considered collectible.
(g) Salaries earned by employees but not yet paid amounted to $80.

SUNSET STORAGE COMPANY
Trial Balance
January 31, 19____

Cash	$32,070	
Unexpired insurance	1,360	
Inventory of office supplies	135	
Office equipment	2,400	
Notes payable		$24,000
Unearned storage fees		450
Robert Laurence, capital		10,300
Robert Laurence, drawing	150	
Storage fees earned		2,950
Rent expense	600	
Telephone expense	45	
Salaries expense	940	
	$37,700	$37,700

Instructions Based on the above trial balance and other information, prepare the adjusting entries (with explanations) needed at January 31.

4B-4 Circle Theater began operations on January 1 of the current year. The company's accounting policy is to adjust and close the accounts each month. Before adjustments at March 31, the account balances were as follows:

Cash	$ 5,125	
Prepaid insurance	850	
Prepaid film rental	4,130	
Projection equipment	4,200	
Accumulated depreciation: projection equipment		$ 100
Notes payable		6,000
Unearned concessions revenue		1,600
Jerry Bowen, capital		4,095
Jerry Bowen, drawing	750	
Admissions revenue		6,320
Salaries expense	2,460	
Building rent expense	600	
	$18,115	$18,115

Other data

(1) A three-year fire insurance policy was purchased on January 2 of the current year for $900.
(2) Film rental expense for the month of March amounted to $2,220.
(3) Projection equipment with an estimated useful life of 7 years was purchased on January 1 of the current year.
(4) Interest expense on notes payable amounted to $30 for the month of March.
(5) Paul Weston, concessionaire, reported that net income from concessions for March amounted to $3,500. Circle Theater's share was 10%, as per agreement. This agreement also provided for semiannual advance payments by Weston based on estimates of future sales. These advance payments were credited to Unearned Concessions Revenue when received.
(6) Salaries earned by employees but not yet paid amounted to $175.

Instructions From the information given, prepare the following:
a Adjusting entries required at March 31.
b An adjusted trial balance.
c An income statement for the month ended March 31.
d A balance sheet in report form, and a statement of owner's equity.

4B-5 Rolling Hills Golf Course obtains revenue from greens fees and also from a contract with a concessionaire who sells refreshments on the premises. The books are closed at the end of each calendar year; at December 31 the data for adjustments were compiled and a work sheet was prepared. The first four columns of the work sheet contained the following account balances and adjustments:

	Trial Balance		Adjustments*	
	Dr	Cr	Dr	Cr
Cash	9,100			
Unexpired insurance	2,100			(a) 700
Prepaid advertising	1,000			(b) 300
Land	375,000			
Equipment	48,000			
Accumulated depreciation:				
equipment		8,000		(f) 4,000
Notes payable		60,000		
Unearned revenue from				
concessions		7,500	(d) 5,000	
Howard Catts, capital		268,000		
Howard Catts, drawing	15,000			
Revenue from greens fees		224,500		
Advertising expense	5,500		(b) 300	
Water expense	10,400			
Salaries expense	78,900		(e) 1,100	
Repairs and maintenance				
expense	17,500			
Miscellaneous expense	5,500			
	$568,000	$568,000		
Insurance expense			(a) 700	
Interest expense			(c) 400	
Accrued interest payable				(c) 400
Revenue from concessions				(d) 5,000
Accrued salaries payable				(e) 1,100
Depreciation expense:				
equipment			(f) 4,000	
			11,500	11,500

* Adjustments:
(a) $700 insurance expired during year.
(b) $300 prepaid advertising expired at end of year.
(c) $400 accrued interest expense on notes payable.
(d) $5,000 concession revenue earned during year.
(e) $1,100 of salaries earned but unpaid at Dec. 31, 19___.
(f) $4,000 depreciation expense for year.

Instructions Using the above data, complete the work sheet by listing the appropriate amounts in the remaining six columns of the work sheet as illustrated on page 119.

4B-6 Oceanside Cinema closes its books each month. At November 30, the trial balance and other information given below were available for adjusting and closing the books.

OCEANSIDE CINEMA

Trial Balance

November 30, 19___

Cash	$ 26,000	
Prepaid advertising	6,200	
Prepaid film rental	26,000	
Land	30,000	
Building	84,000	
Accumulated depreciation: building		$ 1,750
Projection equipment	36,000	
Accumulated depreciation: projection equipment		3,000
Notes payable		15,000
Accounts payable		4,400
L. B. Jones, capital		166,150
L. B. Jones, drawing	4,250	
Revenue from admissions		33,950
Salaries expense	8,700	
Light and power	3,100	
	$224,250	$224,250

Other data
(a) Advertising expense for the month, $3,750.
(b) Film rental expense for the month, $16,850.
(c) Depreciation expense on building, $350 per month; on projection equipment $600 per month.
(d) Accrued interest on notes payable, $100.
(e) The company's share of revenue from concessions for November, as reported by concessionaire, $3,250. Cheque should be received by December 6.
(f) Salaries earned by employees but not paid, $1,500.

Instructions Prepare
a A work sheet for the month ended November 30
b An income statement
c A statement of owner's equity
d A balance sheet
e Adjusting and closing entries

BUSINESS DECISION PROBLEM 4

Mystic Point Marina rents 50 slips in a large floating dock to owners of small boats in the area. The marina also performs repair services on small craft.

Rodger Dunbar, a friend of yours, is convinced that recreational boatin_ become increasingly popular in the area and he has entered into negotiati. to buy Mystic Point Marina.

Rodger does not have quite enough cash to purchase the business at the price the owner has demanded. However, the owner of the marina has suggested that Rodger might purchase the marina with what cash he does have, and turn the net income of the business over to the retiring owner until the balance of the purchase price has been paid. A typical month's income for Mystic Point Marina is determined as follows:

Revenues:		
Slip rentals		$1,500
Repairs		2,800
Total revenues		$4,300
Operating expenses:		
Wages	$1,400	
Insurance	30	
Depreciation expense: docks	800	
Depreciation expense: equipment	100	
Other expenses	100	2,430
Net income		$1,870

Rodger is concerned about turning the whole net income of the business over to the former owner for the next several months, because he estimates that he and his family will need to keep at least $600 a month to meet their living expenses. In coming to you for advice, Rodger explains that all revenues of Mystic Point Marina are collected when earned, and both wages and "other" expenses are paid when incurred. Rodger does not understand, however, when depreciation expense must be paid, or why there is any insurance expense when the insurance policies of the business have more than two years to run before new insurance must be purchased.

Instructions
a Advise Rodger as to how much cash the business will generate each month. Will this amount of cash enable Rodger to withdraw $600 per month to meet his living expenses and pay $1,870 per month to the former owner?
b Explain why insurance expense appears on the income statement of the business if no new policies will be purchased within the next two years.

ACCOUNTING
⌐OR PURCHASES
AND SALES
OF MERCHANDISE

The preceding four chapters have illustrated step by step the complete accounting cycle for a business rendering personal services. In contrast to the service-type business, there are a great many companies whose principal activity is buying and selling merchandise. These merchandising companies may be engaged in either the retail or wholesale distribution of goods. The accounting concepts and methods we have studied for a service-type business are also applicable to a merchandising concern; however, some additional accounts and techniques are needed in accounting for the purchase and sale of merchandise.

Income statement for a merchandising business

An income statement for a merchandising business consists of three main sections: (1) the revenue section, (2) the cost of goods sold section, and (3) the operating expenses section. This sectional arrangement is illustrated in the income statement for a retail sporting goods store on page 139. We shall assume that the business of the Campus Sports Shop consists of buying sports equipment from manufacturers and selling this merchandise to college students. To keep the illustration reasonably short, we shall use a smaller number of expense accounts than would generally be used in a merchandising business.

ANALYZING THE INCOME STATEMENT How does this income statement compare in form and content with the income statement of the service-type business presented in the preceding chapters? The most important change is the inclusion of the section entitled Cost of Goods Sold. Note how large the cost of goods sold is in comparison with the other figures on the statement. The cost of the merchandise sold during the month amounts to $6,000, or 60% of the month's sales of $10,000. Another way of looking at this relationship is to say that for each dollar the store receives by selling goods to customers, the sum of 60 cents represents a recovery of the cost of the merchandise. This leaves a **gross profit** of 40 cents from each sales dollar, out of which the store must pay its operating expenses. In our illustration the operating expenses for the month were $2,800, that is, 28% of the sales figure of $10,000. Therefore, the gross profit of 40 cents contained in each dollar of sales was enough to cover the operating expenses of 28 cents and leave a net income of 12 cents.

CAMPUS SPORTS SHOP
Income Statement
For the Month Ended September 30, 19___

Note distinction between cost of goods sold and operating expenses	Sales		$10,000
	Cost of goods sold:		
	Inventory, Sept. 1	$ 4,400	
	Purchases	9,100	
	Cost of goods available for sale	$13,500	
	Less: Inventory, Sept. 30	7,500	
	Cost of goods sold		6,000
	Gross profit on sales		$ 4,000
	Operating expenses:		
	Salaries	$ 2,230	
	Advertising	450	
	Telephone	60	
	Depreciation	40	
	Insurance	20	
	Total operating expenses		2,800
	Net income		$ 1,200

Of course the percentage relationship between sales and cost of goods sold will vary from one type of business to another, but, in all types of merchandising concerns, the cost of goods sold is one of the largest elements in the income statement. Accountants, investors, bankers, and businessmen in general have the habit of mentally computing percentage relationships when they look at financial statements. Formation of this habit will be helpful throughout the study of accounting, as well as in many business situations.

In analyzing an income statement, it is customary to compare each item in the statement with the amount of sales. These comparisons are easier to make if we express the data in percentages as well as in dollar amounts. If the figure for sales is regarded as 100%, then every other item or subtotal on the statement can conveniently be expressed as a percentage of sales. The cost of goods sold in most types of business will be between 60 and 80% of sales. Conversely, the **gross profit on sales** (excess of sales over cost of goods sold) will usually vary between 40 and 20% of sales. Numerous exceptions may be found to such a sweeping generalization, but it is sufficiently valid to be helpful in visualizing customary relationships on the income statement.

APPRAISING THE ADEQUACY OF NET INCOME The income statement for the Campus Sports Shop shown on page 139 shows that a net income of $1,200 was earned during the month of September. Should this be regarded as an excellent, fair, or mediocre performance? Before reaching a conclusion, let us consider what this item of net income represents in an unincorporated business.

First, let us make the reasonable assumption that the owner of the Campus Sports Shop, Robert Riley, works full time as manager of the business. It is not customary, however, to include any compensation for the personal services of the owner among the expenses of the business. One reason for not including among the expenses a salary to the owner-manager is the fact that he would be in a position to set his own salary at any amount he chose. The use of an arbitrarily chosen, unrealistic salary to the owner would tend to destroy the significance of the income statement as a device for measuring the earning power of the business. Another reason may be that in the owner's own thinking he is not working for a salary when he manages his own business but is investing his time in order to make a profit. The net income of the Campus Sports Shop must, therefore, be considered in part as the equivalent of a salary earned by the owner. If we assume that the owner, Robert Riley, could obtain employment elsewhere as a store manager at a salary of $900 a month, then we can reasonably regard $900 of the net income earned by the Campus Sports Shop as compensation to Riley for his personal services during the month of September.

Secondly, it is necessary to recognize that Riley, as owner of this small business, has invested his own savings, amounting to, say, $20,000. If, as an alternative to starting his own business, he had invested this $20,000 capital in high-grade securities, he might be receiving investment income of perhaps $100 a month.

After deducting from the $1,200 reported net income of the Campus Sports Shop an imputed monthly salary of $900 to the owner and an estimated return on invested capital of $100, we have left a "pure profit" of $200. In judging the adequacy of this amount, we must bear in mind that this residual element of profit is the all-important incentive which induced Riley to risk his savings in a new business venture. The residual profit may also be regarded as the reward for the time and effort which an owner must spend in planning, financing, and guiding a business, apart from the routine aspects of day-to-day management. Moreover, the earning of $1,200 net income in one month provides no assurance that a similar profit, or for that matter any profit, will be forthcoming in another month. It would be somewhat rash to form an opinion about the adequacy of earning power of a business on the basis of such a short period of operating experience.

Economists often use the word *profit* to mean the residual pure profit remaining after deducting from the net income the estimated amounts needed to compensate the proprietor for his personal services and the use of his capital. Confusion over the meaning of technical terms is a major difficulty faced by the accountant in conveying to economists and businessmen the results of his analysis of business operations.

Accounting for sales of merchandise

If merchandising concerns are to succeed or even to survive, they must, of course, sell their goods at prices higher than they pay to the vendors or suppliers from whom they buy. The selling prices charged by a retail store must cover three things: (1) the cost of the merchandise to the store; (2) the operating expenses of the business such as advertising, store rent, and salaries of salesmen; and (3) a net income to the business.

When a business sells merchandise to its customers, it either receives immediate payment in cash or acquires an account receivable which will soon become cash. As explained in Chapter 3, the inflow of cash and receivables from sales of the current period is equal to the revenue for that period. The entry to record the sale of merchandise consists of a debit to an asset account and a credit to the Sales account, as shown by the following example:

Journal entry for cash sale	Cash	*100*
	Sales	*100*
	To record the sale of merchandise for cash.	

If the sale was not a cash transaction but called for payment at a later date, the entry would be:

Journal entry for sale on credit	Accounts Receivable	*100*
	Sales	*100*
	To record the sale of merchandise on credit; payment due within 30 days.	

Revenue from the sale of merchandise is usually considered as earned in the period in which the merchandise is delivered to the customer, even though payment in cash is not received for a month or more after the sale. Consequently, the revenue earned in a given accounting period may differ considerably from the cash receipts of that period.

The amount and trend of sales are watched very closely by management, investors, and others interested in the progress of a company. A rising volume of sales is evidence of growth and suggests the probability of an increase in earnings. A declining trend in sales, on the other hand, is often the first signal of reduced earnings and of financial difficulties ahead. The amount of sales for each year is compared with the sales of the preceding year; the sales of each month may be compared with the sales of the preceding month and also with the corresponding month of the preceding year. These comparisons bring to light significant trends in the volume of sales. The financial pages of newspapers regularly report on the volume and trend of sales for corporations with publicly owned stock.

Accounting for the cost of goods sold

In the illustrated income statement of Campus Sports Shop on page 139, the cost of goods sold for the month of September was computed as follows:

Computing cost of goods sold Inventory of merchandise at beginning of month	$ 4,400
Purchases	9,100
Cost of goods available for sale	$13,500
Less: Inventory at end of month	7,500
Cost of goods sold	$ 6,000

Every merchandising business has available for sale during an accounting period the merchandise on hand at the beginning of the period plus the merchandise purchased during the period. If all these goods were sold during the period, there would be no ending inventory, and cost of goods sold would be equal to the cost of goods available for sale. Normally, however, some goods remain unsold at the end of the period; cost of goods sold is then equal to the cost of goods available for sale minus the ending inventory of unsold goods.

The cost of goods sold is an important concept which requires careful attention. To gain a thorough understanding of this concept, we need to consider the nature of the accounts used in determining the cost of goods sold.

The Purchases account

The cost of merchandise purchased for resale to customers is recorded by debiting an account called Purchases, as illustrated below:

Journal entry for purchase of merchandise Purchases	1,000	
Accounts Payable (or Cash)		1,000
Purchased merchandise from ABC Supply Co.		

The Purchases account *is used only for merchandise acquired for resale;* assets acquired for use in the business (such as a delivery truck, a typewriter, or office supplies) are recorded by debiting the appropriate asset account, not the Purchases account. The Purchases account does not indicate whether the purchased goods have been sold or are still on hand.

At the end of the accounting period, the balance accumulated in the Purchases account represents the total cost of merchandise purchased during the period. This amount is used in preparing the income statement. The Purchases account has then served its purpose and it is closed to the Income Summary account. Since the Purchases account is closed at the end of each period, it has a zero balance at the beginning of each succeeding period.

The Inventory account

An inventory of merchandise consists of the goods on hand and available for sale to customers. In the Campus Sports Shop, the inventory consists of golf clubs, tennis rackets, and skiing equipment; in a pet shop the inventory might include puppies, fish, and parakeets. Inventories are acquired through the purchase of goods from wholesalers, manufacturers, or other suppliers. The goods on hand at the beginning of the period are referred to as the *beginning inventory;* the goods on hand at the end of the period are referred to as the *ending inventory.* Thus in our example of the September operations of Campus Sports Shop, the beginning inventory on September 1 was $4,400 and the ending inventory on September 30 was $7,500. The ending inventory of one accounting period is, of course, the beginning inventory of the following period. For the month of October, Campus Sports Shop would have a beginning inventory of $7,500—the amount determined to be on hand at the close of business on September 30.

Inventory of merchandise and cost of goods sold

The cost of the merchandise sold during the month appears in the income statement as a deduction from the sales of the month. The merchandise which is *available for sale but not sold* during the month constitutes the inventory of merchandise on hand at the end of the accounting period. It is included in the balance sheet as an asset.

How can the businessman determine, at the end of the month or year, the quantity and the cost of the goods remaining on hand? How can he determine the cost of the goods sold during the period? These amounts must be determined before either a balance sheet or an income statement can be prepared. In fact, the determination of inventory value and of the cost of goods sold may be the most important single step in measuring the profitability of a business. There are two alternative approaches to the determination of inventory and of cost of goods sold, namely, the *perpetual inventory method* and the *periodic inventory method.*

THE PERPETUAL INVENTORY METHOD Business concerns which sell merchandise of high unit value, such as automobiles or television sets, generally use a perpetual inventory system. This system requires the keeping of records showing the cost of each article in stock. Units added to inventory and units sold are recorded on a daily basis. At the end of the accounting period, the total cost of goods sold is easily determined by adding the costs recorded from day to day for the units sold. A subsidiary record (often an inventory card) is usually maintained for each of the various kinds of merchandise held for sale. To prove the accuracy of these subsidiary records, a physical count of the goods on hand should be made at least once a year. Although the inventory cards constitute a subsidiary record and are not part of the ledger, under the perpetual inventory system, the total of the costs recorded on these cards should agree with the ledger account, Inventory. In some companies the perpetual inventory records are maintained only in physical quantities of items in stock; cost data are omitted. Even without cost data on the perpetual inventory cards, a detailed current knowledge of the quantity of each item in stock may be highly useful information to business managers.

PERPETUAL INVENTORY CARD

Item ___Television Set, Model xL–220___

| Date | Quantities | | | Dollar Amounts | | |
	Purchases	Sales	Balance	Debit	Credit	Balance
19__						
May 1			8			$2,000
9		5	3		$1,250	750
11	6		9	$1,500		2,250

THE PERIODIC INVENTORY METHOD The majority of businesses, however, do not maintain perpetual inventory records; they rely instead upon a periodic inventory (a count of merchandise on hand) to determine the inventory at the end of the accounting period and the cost of goods sold during the period. The periodic inventory system may be concisely summarized as follows:

1 A physical count of merchandise on hand is made at the end of each accounting period.

2 The cost value of this inventory is computed by multiplying the quantity of each item by an appropriate unit cost. A total cost figure for the entire inventory is then determined by adding the costs of all the various types of merchandise.

3 The *cost of goods available for sale* during the period is determined by adding the amount of the inventory at the beginning of the period to the amount of the purchases during the period.

4 The **cost of goods sold** is computed by subtracting the inventory at the end of the period from the cost of goods available for sale. In other words, the difference between the cost of goods available for sale and the amount of goods remaining unsold at the end of the period is presumed to have been sold.

A simple illustration of the above procedures for determining the cost of goods sold follows:

Using the periodic inventory method

Beginning inventory (determined by count)	*$ 4,400*
Add: Purchases	*9,100*
Cost of goods available for sale	*$13,500*
Less: Ending inventory (determined by count)	*7,500*
Cost of goods sold	*$ 6,000*

The periodic inventory system is the method we shall be working with throughout most of this book. Because of the importance of the process for determining inventory and cost of goods sold, we shall now consider in more detail the essential steps in using the periodic inventory system.

Taking a physical inventory When the periodic inventory system is in use, there is no day-to-day record of the cost of goods sold. Neither is there any day-to-day record of the amount of goods unsold and still on hand. At the end of the accounting period, however, it is necessary to determine the cost of goods sold during the period and also the amount of unsold goods on hand. The figure for cost of goods sold is used in determining the net income or loss for the period, and the value of the merchandise on hand at the end of the period is included in the balance sheet as an asset.

To determine the cost of the merchandise on hand, a physical inventory is taken. The count of merchandise should be made if possible after the close of business on the last day of the accounting period. It is difficult to make an accurate count during business hours while sales are taking place; consequently, the physical inventory is often taken in the evening or on Sunday. After all goods have been counted, the proper cost price must be assigned to each article. The assignment of a cost price to each item of merchandise in stock is often described as **pricing the inventory.** Inventories of merchandise are usually valued at cost for accounting purposes. Some other aspects of accounting for inventories will be discussed in Chapter 10.

After the amount of the ending inventory has been computed by counting and pricing the goods on hand at the end of the period, this amount is entered in the records by debiting Inventory and crediting Income Summary. (This entry will be illustrated and explained more fully later in this chapter.) Entries are made in the Inventory account only at the end of the accounting period. During the period, the Inventory account shows only the cost of the merchandise which was on hand at the beginning of the current period.

Other accounts included in cost of goods sold

In the September income statement of Campus Sports Shop illustrated earlier, the cost of goods sold was derived from only three items: beginning inventory, purchases, and ending inventory. In most cases, however, some additional accounts will be involved. These include the Purchase Returns and Allowances account and the Transportation-in account.

Purchase Returns and Allowances account

When merchandise purchased from suppliers is found to be unsatisfactory, the goods may be returned, or a request may be made for an allowance on the price. A return of goods to the supplier is recorded as follows:

Journal Accounts Payable 1,200
entry for
return of   Purchase Returns and Allowances 1,200
goods to To charge Marvel Supply Co. for the cost of goods returned.
supplier

Sometimes when the purchaser of merchandise finds the goods not entirely satisfactory, he may agree to keep the goods in consideration for a reduction or allowance on the original price. The entry to record such an allowance is essentially the same as that for a return.

The use of a Purchase Returns and Allowances account rather than the recording of returns by direct credits to the Purchases account is advisable because the books then show both the total amount of the purchases and the amount of purchases which required adjustment or return. Management is interested in the percentage relationship between goods returned and goods purchased, because the returning of merchandise for credit is a time-consuming, costly process. Returning merchandise enables the purchaser to get back the price paid to the supplier, but this is only a partial recovery of the costs incurred. The time and effort spent in buying merchandise, in receiving and inspecting it, and in arranging for its return represent a costly procedure. To hold these costs to a minimum, management should be kept aware of the amount of returns and allowances. Excessive returns suggest that the purchasing department should look for more dependable sources of supply.

The Transportation-in account

The cost of merchandise acquired for resale logically includes any transportation charges necessary to place the goods in the purchaser's place of business. In some lines of business it is customary for the manufacturer to pay the cost of shipping merchandise to the retailer's store. The transportation charge may be listed as a separate charge in addition to the price of the goods or may not be shown separately. In the latter case the manufacturer tries to set the price of the goods high enough to cover the transportation charges as well as all his other costs. Consequently, the cost of merchandise to the purchaser normally includes the cost of transporting the goods, regardless of whether he pays the freight charges directly to the railroad or other carrier, or merely pays the seller a sufficiently high price to cover the cost of delivering the goods.

Transportation costs on inbound shipments *could* be debited to the Purchases account, but a more useful plan in most cases is to use a separate ledger account to accumulate the transportation charges on merchandise purchased. The journal entry to record the payment of transportation charges on inbound shipments of merchandise is as follows:

Journalizing transportation charges on purchases of merchandise

Transportation-in	*125*	
Cash (or Accounts Payable)		*125*

Air freight charges on merchandise purchased from Miller Brothers, Toronto

Since transportation charges are part of the *delivered cost* of merchandise purchased, the Transportation-in account is combined with the Purchases account in the income statement in determining the cost of goods available for sale.

One reason for using a separate ledger account for Transportation-in rather than debiting these charges directly to the Purchases account is to provide management with a clear record of the amount expended each period for inbound transportation. A knowledge of the amount and trend of each significant type of cost is a necessary first step if management is to control costs effectively. For example, detailed information concerning transportation costs would be important to management in making decisions between rail and air transportation, or in deciding whether to order in carload lots rather than in smaller quantities.

Transportation charges on inbound shipments of merchandise must not be confused with transportation charges on outbound shipments of goods to customers. Freight charges and other expenses incurred in making deliveries to customers are regarded as selling expenses; these outlays are debited to a separate account entitled Transportation-out, and are not included in the cost of goods sold.

F.O.B. shipping point and F.O.B. destination

The agreement between the buyer and seller of merchandise includes a provision as to which party shall bear the cost of transporting the goods. The term *F.O.B. shipping point* means that the seller will place the merchandise "free on board" the railroad cars or other means of transport, and that the buyer must pay transportation charges from that point. Many people in negotiating for the purchase of a new automobile have encountered the expression "F.O.B. Oshawa," meaning that the buyer must pay the freight charges from the manufacturer's location in Oshawa, in addition to the basic price of the car. In most merchandise transactions involving wholesalers or manufacturers, the buyer bears the transportation cost. Sometimes, however, as a matter of convenience, the seller prepays the freight and adds this cost to the amount billed to the buyer.

F.O.B. destination means that the seller agrees to bear the freight cost. If he prepays the truckline or other carrier, the agreed terms have been met and no action is required of the buyer other than to pay the agreed purchase price of the goods. If the seller does not prepay the freight, the buyer will pay the carrier and deduct this payment from the amount owed the seller when he makes payment for the merchandise.

Illustration of accounting cycle using periodic inventory method

The October transactions of the Campus Sports Shop will now be used to illustrate the accounting cycle for a business using the periodic inventory system of accounting for merchandise. The starting point for this illustration is an after-closing trial balance prepared on September 30. Since this trial balance was prepared after the books were closed for September, it contains balance sheet accounts only.

The amount of inventory listed below in the after-closing trial balance had been determined on September 30 by counting the merchandise on hand and pricing it at cost.

CAMPUS SPORTS SHOP
After-closing Trial Balance
September 30, 19___

Proof that Cash	$ 2,800	
the ledger Inventory	7,500	
is in Unexpired insurance	200	
balance Land	3,000	
Building	10,000	
Accumulated depreciation: building		$ 960
Accounts payable		2,600
Robert Riley, capital		19,940
	$23,500	$23,500

RECORDING SALES OF MERCHANDISE Sales of sports equipment during October amounted to $10,025. All sales were for cash, and each sales transaction was rung up on a cash register. At the close of each day's business, the total sales for the day were computed by pressing the total key on the cash register. As soon as each day's sales were computed, a journal entry was prepared and posted to the Cash account and the

Sales account in the ledger. The daily entering of cash sales in the journal is desirable in order to minimize the opportunity for errors or dishonesty by employees in handling the cash receipts. In Chapter 7 a procedure will be described which provides a daily record of sales and cash receipts yet avoids the making of an excessive number of entries in the Cash and Sales accounts.

RECORDING SALES RETURNS AND ALLOWANCES On October 27 a customer returned some unsatisfactory merchandise and was given a refund of $46. Another customer complained on October 28 of a slight defect in an article he had recently purchased and was given a refund of $10, representing half of the original price. The journal entries to record these returns and allowances were as follows:

Journal	Oct. 27	*Sales Returns and Allowances*	*46*	
entries		*Cash*		*46*
for		*Made refund for merchandise returned by customer.*		
sales				
returns	Oct. 28	*Sales Returns and Allowances*	*10*	
and allow-		*Cash*		*10*
ances		*Allowance to customer for defect in merchandise.*		

OTHER OCTOBER TRANSACTIONS Other routine transactions during October included the purchase of merchandise, the return of goods to suppliers, payment of charges for transportation-in, payment of accounts payable, and payment of operating expenses, such as salaries, telephone, and advertising. To conserve space in this illustration, these transactions will not be listed individually but are included in the ledger account balances at October 31.

WORK SHEET FOR A MERCHANDISING BUSINESS After the October transactions of the Campus Sports Shop had been posted to ledger accounts, the work sheet illustrated on page 151 was prepared. The first step in the preparation of the work sheet was, of course, the listing of the balances of the ledger accounts in the Trial Balance columns. In studying this work sheet, note that the Inventory account in the Trial Balance debit column still shows a balance of $7,500, the cost of merchandise on hand at the end of September. No entries were made in the Inventory account during October despite the various purchases and sales of merchandise. The significance of the Inventory account in the trial balance is that it shows the amount of merchandise with which the Campus Sports Shop began operations for the month of October.

Adjustments on the work sheet Only two adjustments were necessary at October 31, one to record depreciation of the building and the other to record the insurance expense for the month. The Adjustments columns were then totaled to prove the equality of the adjustment debits and credits.

Omission of Adjusted Trial Balance columns   In the work sheet previously illustrated in Chapter 4, page 119, the amounts in the Trial Balance columns were combined with the amounts listed in the Adjustments columns and then extended into the Adjusted Trial Balance columns. When there are only a few adjusting entries, many accountants prefer to omit the Adjusted Trial Balance columns and to extend the trial balance figures (as adjusted by the amounts in the Adjustments columns) directly to the Income Statement or Balance Sheet columns. This procedure is used in the work sheet for the Campus Sports Shop.

Recording the ending inventory on the work sheet   The key points to be observed in this work sheet are (1) the method of recording the ending inventory and (2) the method of handling the various accounts making up the cost of goods sold.

After the close of business on October 31, Riley and his assistants took a physical inventory of all merchandise in the store. The cost of the entire stock of goods was determined to be $9,000. This ending inventory, dated October 31, does not appear in the trial balance; it is therefore written on the first available line below the trial balance totals. The amount of $9,000 is listed in the Income Statement credit column and also in the Balance Sheet debit column. By entering the ending inventory in the Income Statement *credit* column, we are in effect deducting it from the total of the beginning inventory, the purchases, and the transportation-in, all of which are extended from the trial balance to the Income Statement *debit* column.

One of the functions of the Income Statement columns is to bring together all the accounts involved in determining the cost of goods sold. The accounts with debit balances are the beginning inventory, the purchases, and the transportation-in; these accounts total $15,800. Against this total, the two credit items of purchase returns, $600, and ending inventory, $9,000, are offset. The three merchandising accounts with debit balances exceed in total the two with credit balances by an amount of $6,200; this amount is the cost of goods sold, as shown in the income statement on page 152.

The ending inventory is also entered in the Balance Sheet debit column, because this inventory of merchandise on October 31 will appear as an asset in the balance sheet bearing this date.

Completing the work sheet   When all the accounts on the work sheet have been extended into the Income Statement or Balance Sheet columns (and the ending inventory has been entered), the final four columns should be totaled. The net income of $1,409 is computed by subtracting the Income Statement debit column from the Income Statement credit column. This same amount of $1,409 can also be obtained by subtracting the Balance Sheet credit column from the Balance Sheet debit column. To balance out the four columns, the amount of the net income is entered in the Income Statement debit column and on the same line in the Balance Sheet credit column. (The proof of accuracy afforded by the self-

CAMPUS SPORTS SHOP
Work Sheet
For the Month Ended October 31, 19___

	Trial Balance		Adjustments*		Income Statement		Balance Sheet	
	Dr	Cr	Dr	Cr	Dr	Cr	Dr	Cr
Cash	6,569						6,569	
Inventory, Sept. 30	7,500				7,500			
Unexpired insurance	200			(b) 20			180	
Land	3,000						3,000	
Building	10,000						10,000	
Accumulated depreciation: building		960		(a) 40				1,000
Accounts payable		6,700						6,700
Robert Riley, capital		19,940						19,940
Robert Riley, drawing	300						300	
Sales		10,025				10,025		
Sales returns and allowances	56				56			
Purchases	8,100				8,100			
Purchase returns and allowances		600				600		
Transportation-in	200				200			
Advertising expense	250				250			
Salaries expense	2,000				2,000			
Telephone expense	50				50			
	38,225	38,225						
Depreciation expense: building			(a) 40		40			
Insurance expense			(b) 20		20			
			60	60				
Inventory, Oct. 31						9,000	9,000	
					18,216	19,625	29,049	27,640
Net income					1,409			1,409
					19,625	19,625	29,049	29,049

Note the treatment of beginning and ending inventories

* Adjustments: (a) Depreciation of building during October.
 (b) Insurance premium expired during October.

balancing nature of the work sheet was explained in Chapter 4.) Final totals are determined for the Income Statement and Balance Sheet columns, and the work sheet is complete.

Financial statements

The work to be done at the end of the period is much the same for a merchandising business as for a service-type firm. First, the work sheet is completed; then, financial statements are prepared from the data in the work sheet; next, the adjusting and closing entries are entered in the journal and posted to the ledger accounts; and finally, an after-closing trial balance is prepared. This completes the periodic accounting cycle.

INCOME STATEMENT The income statement below was prepared from the work sheet on page 151. Note particularly the arrangement of items in the cost of goods sold section of the income statement; this portion of the income statement shows in summary form most of the essential accounting concepts covered in this chapter.

CAMPUS SPORTS SHOP
Income Statement
For the Month Ended October 31, 19___

Revenue from sales:			
Sales		$10,025	
Less: Sales returns and allowances		56	
Net sales			$9,969
Cost of goods sold:			
Inventory, Oct. 1		$ 7,500	
Purchases	$8,100		
Transportation-in	200		
Delivered cost of purchases	$8,300		
Less: Purchase returns and allowances	600		
Net purchases		7,700	
Cost of goods available for sale		$15,200	
Less: Inventory, Oct. 31		9,000	
Cost of goods sold			6,200
Gross profit on sales			$3,769
Operating expenses:			
Salaries		$ 2,000	
Advertising		250	
Telephone		50	
Depreciation		40	
Insurance		20	
Total operating expenses			2,360
Net income			$1,409

This income statement consists of three major sections

STATEMENT OF OWNER'S EQUITY The statement of owner's equity shows the increase in owner's equity from October net income and the decrease from withdrawals during the month.

CAMPUS SPORTS SHOP
Statement of Owner's Equity
For the Month Ended October 31, 19___

Which figure for owner's equity appeared on the work sheet? Robert Riley, capital, Oct. 1, 19___	$19,940
Net income for October	1,409
Subtotal	$21,349
Less: Withdrawals	300
Robert Riley, capital, Oct. 31, 19___	$21,049

BALANCE SHEET In studying the following balance sheet, note that all items are taken from the Balance Sheet columns of the work sheet, but that the amount for Robert Riley, Capital is the October 31 balance of $21,049, computed as shown in the preceding statement of owner's equity.

CAMPUS SPORTS SHOP
Balance Sheet
October 31, 19___

Assets

Cash		$ 6,569
Inventory		9,000
Unexpired insurance		180
Land		3,000
Building	$10,000	
Less: Accumulated depreciation	1,000	9,000
		$27,749

Liabilities & Owner's Equity

Liabilities:	
Accounts payable	$ 6,700
Owner's equity:	
Robert Riley, capital, Oct. 31	21,049
	$27,749

CLOSING ENTRIES The entries used in closing revenue and expense accounts have been explained in preceding chapters. The only new elements in this illustration of closing entries for a merchandising business are the entries showing the elimination of the beginning inventory and the recording of the ending inventory. The beginning inventory is cleared out of the Inventory account by a debit to Income Summary and a credit to Inventory. A separate entry could be made for this purpose, but we can save time by making one compound entry which will debit the Income Summary account with the balance of the beginning inventory and with the balances of all temporary proprietorship accounts having debit balances. The *temporary proprietorship accounts* are those which appear in the income statement. As the name suggests, the temporary proprietorship accounts are used during the period to accumulate temporarily the increases and decreases in the proprietor's equity resulting from operation of the business. The entry to close out the beginning inventory and temporary proprietorship accounts with debit balances is illustrated below.

Closing temporary proprietorship accounts with debit balances	Oct. 31	Income Summary.	*18,216*
		Inventory.	*7,500*
		Purchases	*8,100*
		Sales Returns and Allowances	*56*
		Transportation-in	*200*
		Advertising Expense.	*250*
		Salaries Expense	*2,000*
		Telephone Expense	*50*
		Depreciation Expense.	*40*
		Insurance Expense	*20*
		To close out the beginning inventory and the temporary proprietorship accounts with debit balances.	

Note that the above entry closes all the operating expense accounts as well as the accounts used to accumulate the cost of goods sold, and also the Sales Returns and Allowances account. Although the Sales Returns and Allowances account has a debit balance, it is not an expense account. In terms of account classification, it belongs in the revenue group of accounts because it serves as an offset to the Sales account and appears in the income statement as a deduction from Sales.

To bring the ending inventory on the books after the stocktaking on October 31, we could make a separate entry debiting Inventory and crediting the Income Summary account. It is more convenient, however, to combine this step with the closing of the Sales account and any other temporary proprietorship accounts having credit balances, as illustrated in the following closing entry.

Closing temporary proprietorship accounts with credit balances	Oct. 31	Inventory	*9,000*
		Sales	*10,025*
		Purchase Returns and Allowances	*600*
		Income Summary	*19,625*
		To record the ending inventory and to close all temporary proprietorship accounts with credit balances.	

The remaining closing entries serve to transfer the balance of the Income Summary account to the owner's capital account and to close the drawing account, as follows:

Closing **the Income** **Summary** **account** **and owner's** **drawing** **account**	Oct. 31	Income Summary	1,409
		Robert Riley, Capital	1,409
		To close the Income Summary account.	
	Oct. 31	Robert Riley, Capital	300
		Robert Riley, Drawing	300
		To close the drawing account.	

Summary of merchandising transactions and related accounting entries

The transactions regularly encountered in merchandising operations and the related accounting entries may be concisely summarized as follows:

Customary journal entries relating to merchandise

Transactions during the Period	Related Accounting Entries — Debit	Credit
Purchase merchandise for resale	~~Purchase~~ *Inventory* (handwritten)	Cash (or Accounts Payable)
Incur transportation charges on merchandise purchased for resale	~~Transportation-in~~ *Inventory* (handwritten)	Cash (or Accounts Payable)
Return unsatisfactory merchandise to supplier, or obtain a reduction from original price	Cash (or Accounts Payable)	~~Purchase re-~~ ~~turns and~~ *Inventory* (handwritten) ~~allowances~~
Sell merchandise to customers	Cash (or Accounts Receivable)	Sales
Permit customers to return merchandise, or grant them a reduction from original price	Sales Returns and Allowances *Or Sales* (handwritten)	Cash (or Accounts Receivable)

Inventory Procedures at End of Period

	Debit	Credit
~~Transfer the balance of the beginning in-~~ ~~ventory to the Income Summary account~~	Income Summary	Inventory
~~Take a physical inventory of goods on hand~~ ~~at the end of the period and price these~~	~~Inventory~~ Cost of goods Sold (handwritten)	~~Income Summary~~ Inventory (handwritten)

(handwritten note): Take a physical inv. & price goods at cost & adjust inventory account balance to reflect cost of goods on hand at period end

Classified financial statements

The financial statements illustrated up to this point have been rather short and simple because of the limited number of transactions and accounts used in these introductory chapters. Now let us look briefly at a more comprehensive and realistic balance sheet for a merchandising business. A full understanding of all the items on this balance sheet may not be possible until our study of accounting has progressed further, but a bird's-eye view of a fairly complete balance sheet is nevertheless useful at this point.

In the balance sheet of the Graham Company illustrated on page 157, the assets are classified into three groups: (1) current assets, (2) plant and equipment, and (3) other assets. The liabilities are classified into two types: (1) current liabilities and (2) long-term liabilities. This classification of assets and liabilities, subject to minor variations in terminology, is virtually a standard one throughout Canadian business. The inclusion of captions for the balance sheet totals is an optional step.

THE PURPOSE OF BALANCE SHEET CLASSIFICATION The purpose underlying a standard classification of assets and liabilities is to aid management, owners, creditors, and other interested persons in understanding the financial condition of the business. The banker, for example, would have a difficult time in reading the balance sheets of all the companies which apply to him for loans, if each of these companies followed its own individual whims as to the sequence and arrangement of accounts comprising its balance sheet. Standard practices as to the order and arrangement of a balance sheet are an important means of saving the time of the reader and of giving him a fuller comprehension of the company's financial position. On the other hand, these standard practices are definitely not iron-clad rules; the form and content of a well-prepared balance sheet today are different in several respects from the balance sheet of 25 years ago. No two businesses are exactly alike and a degree of variation from the conventional type of balance sheet is appropriate for the individual business in devising the most meaningful presentation of its financial position. Standardization of the form and content of financial statements is a desirable goal; but if carried to an extreme, it might prevent the introduction of new improved methods and the constructive changes necessary to reflect changes in business practices.

The analysis and interpretation of financial statements is the subject of Chapter 21. At this point our objective is merely to emphasize that classification of the items on a balance sheet aids the reader greatly in appraising the financial condition of the business. Some of the major balance sheet classifications are discussed briefly in the following section.

CURRENT ASSETS Current assets include cash, government bonds and other marketable securities, receivables, inventories, and prepaid expenses. To qualify for inclusion in the current asset category, an asset must be capable of being converted into cash within a relatively short period without interfering with the normal operation of the business. The period is usually one year, but it may be longer for those businesses having an operating cycle in excess of one year. The sequence in which current assets are listed depends upon their liquidity; the closer an asset

THE GRAHAM COMPANY
Balance Sheet
December 31, 19____

Current assets:

Cash			$24,500
Canadian government bonds			10,000
Notes receivable			2,400
Accounts receivable		$26,960	
Less: Allowance for uncollectible accounts		860	26,100
Inventory			35,200
Prepaid expenses			1,200
Total current assets			$ 93,400

Plant and equipment:

Land			$10,000
Building	$24,000		
Less: Accumulated depreciation	1,920	22,080	
Store equipment	$ 9,400		
Less: Accumulated depreciation	1,880	7,520	
Delivery equipment	$ 2,800		
Less: Accumulated depreciation	700	2,100	
Total plant and equipment			41,700

Other assets:

Land (future building site)	16,500
Total assets	$157,600

Liabilities & Owner's Equity

Current liabilities:

Notes payable	$11,500
Accounts payable	19,040
Accrued expenses payable	1,410
Deferred revenues	1,100
Total current liabilities	$ 33,050

Long-term liabilities:

Mortgage payable (due 1980)	25,000
Total liabilities	$ 58,050

Owner's equity:

George Graham, capital, Dec. 31	99,550
Total liabilities & owner's equity	$157,600

Note: A new item introduced in this balance sheet is the Allowance for Uncollectible Accounts of $860, shown as a deduction from Accounts Receivable. This is an estimate of the uncollectible portion of the accounts receivable and serves to reduce the valuation of this asset to the net amount of $26,100 that is considered collectible. Since it is assumed that an adequate allowance for uncollectible accounts has been provided, unless a statement to the contrary is made, Canadian practice does not require disclosure of the amount of the allowance.

is to becoming cash the higher is its liquidity. The total amount of a company's current assets and the relative amount of each type give some indication of the company's short-run, debt-paying ability.

The term *operating cycle* is often used in establishing the limits of the current asset classification. Operating cycle means the average time period between the purchase of merchandise and the conversion of this merchandise back into cash. The series of transactions comprising a complete cycle often runs as follows: (1) purchase of merchandise, (2) sale of the merchandise on credit, (3) collection of the account receivable from the customer. The word *cycle* suggests the circular flow of capital from cash to inventory to receivables to cash again.

In a business handling fast-moving merchandise (a supermarket, for example) the operating cycle may be completed in a few weeks; for most merchandising businesses the operating cycle requires several months but less than a year.

CURRENT LIABILITIES Liabilities that must be paid within the operating cycle or one year (whichever is longer) are called *current liabilities.* Current liabilities are paid out of current assets, and a comparison of the amount of current assets with the amount of current liabilities is an important step in appraising the ability of a company to pay its debts in the near future.

CURRENT RATIO Many bankers and other users of financial statements believe that for a business to qualify as a good credit risk, the total current assets should be at least twice as large as the total current liabilities. In studying a balance sheet, a banker or other creditor will compute the *current ratio* by dividing total current assets by total current liabilities. In the illustrated balance sheet of the Graham Company, the current assets of $99,400 are approximately three times as great as the current liabilities of $33,050; the current ratio is therefore 3 to 1, which would generally be regarded as a strong current position. The current assets could shrink by two-thirds and still be sufficient for payment of the current liabilities. Although a strong current ratio is desirable, an extremely high current ratio (such as 6 to 1 or more) may signify that a company is holding too much of its resources in cash, marketable securities, and other current assets and is not pursuing profit opportunities as aggressively as it might.

WORKING CAPITAL The excess of current assets over current liabilities is called *working capital;* the relative amount of working capital is another indication of short-term financial strength. In the illustrated balance sheet of the Graham Company, working capital is $66,350, computed by subtracting the current liabilities of $33,050 from the current assets of $99,400. The importance of solvency (ability to meet debts as they fall due) was emphasized in Chapter 1. Ample working capital permits a company to buy merchandise in large lots, to carry an adequate stock of goods, and to sell goods to customers on favorable credit terms. Many companies have been forced to suspend business because of inadequate working capital, even though total assets were much larger than total liabilities.

CLASSIFICATION IN THE INCOME STATEMENT A new feature to be noted in the illustrated income statement of the Graham Company (page 160) is the division of the operating expenses into the two categories of selling expenses and general and administrative expenses. This classification aids management in controlling expenses by emphasizing that certain expenses are the responsibililty of the executive in charge of sales, and that other types of expense relate to the business as a whole. Some expenses, such as depreciation of the building, may be divided between the two classifications according to the portion utilized by each functional division of the business. The item of Uncollectible Accounts Expense listed under the heading of General and Administrative Expenses is an expense of estimated amount. It will be discussed fully in Chapter 9.

Another feature to note in the income statement of the Graham Company is that interest earned on investments is placed after the figure showing income from operations. Other examples of such *nonoperating revenues* are dividends on shares of stock owned, and rent earned by leasing property not presently needed in the operation of the business. Any items of expense not related to selling or administrative functions may also be placed at the bottom of the income statement after the income from operations. Separate group headings of Nonoperating Revenue and Nonoperating Expenses are sometimes used.

CONDENSED INCOME STATEMENT In the published annual reports of most corporations, the income statement is usually greatly condensed because the public is presumably not interested in the details of operations. A condensed income statement usually begins with *net* sales. The details involved in computing the cost of goods sold are also often omitted and only summary figures are given for selling expenses and general and administrative expenses. A condensed income statement for the Graham Company follows:

THE GRAHAM COMPANY
Income Statement
For the Year Ended December 31, 19____

Net sales		$302,240
Cost of goods sold		208,040
Gross profit on sales		$ 94,200
Expenses:		
Selling	$53,000	
General and administrative	21,100	74,100
Income from operations		$ 20,100
Interest earned on investments		300
Net income		$ 20,400

A condensed income statement

THE GRAHAM COMPANY
Income Statement
For the Year Ended December 31, 19___

Gross sales			$310,890
Sales returns & allowances		$ 3,820	
Sales discounts		4,830	8,650
Net sales			$302,240
Cost of goods sold:			
Inventory, Jan. 1			$ 30,040
Purchases	$212,400		
Transportation-in	8,300		
Delivered cost of purchases	$220,700		
Less: Purchase returns & allowances . . . $2,400			
Purchase discounts	5,100	7,500	
Net purchases		213,200	
Cost of goods available for sale		$243,240	
Less: Inventory, Dec. 31		35,200	
Cost of goods sold			208,040
Gross profit on sales			$ 94,200
Operating expenses:			
Selling expenses:			
Sales salaries		$ 38,410	
Advertising		10,190	
Depreciation: building		840	
Depreciation: store equipment		940	
Depreciation: delivery equipment		700	
Insurance expense		1,100	
Miscellaneous selling expense		820	
Total selling expenses		$ 53,000	
General and administrative expenses:			
Office salaries		$ 19,200	
Uncollectible accounts expense		750	
Depreciation: building		120	
Insurance expense: general		100	
Miscellaneous general expense		930	
Total general and administrative expenses		21,100	
Total operating expenses			74,100
Income from operations			$ 20,100
Interest earned on investments			300
Net income			$ 20,400

QUESTIONS

1 During the current year, Green Bay Company made all sales of merchandise at prices in excess of cost. Will the business necessarily report a net income for the year? Explain.

2 Hi-Rise Company during its first year of operation had cost of goods sold of $90,000 and a gross profit equal to 40% of sales. What was the dollar amount of sales for the year?

3 During the current year, Davis Corporation Ltd. purchased merchandise costing $200,000. State the cost of goods sold under each of the following alternative assumptions:

    a No beginning inventory; ending inventory $40,000
    b Beginning inventory $60,000; no ending inventory
    c Beginning inventory $58,000; ending inventory $78,000
    d Beginning inventory $90,000; ending inventory $67,000

4 Zenith Company uses the periodic inventory method and maintains its accounting records on a calendar-year basis. Does the beginning or the ending inventory figure appear in the trial balance prepared from the ledger on December 31?

5 Compute the amount of cost of goods sold, given the following account balances: beginning inventory $25,000, purchases $84,000, purchase returns and allowances $4,500, transportation-in $500, and ending inventory $36,000.

6 Explain the terms **current assets, current liabilities,** and **current ratio.**

7 The Riblet Company has a current ratio of 3 to 1 and working capital of $60,000. What are the amounts of current assets and current liabilities?

8 Why is it advisable to use a Purchase Returns and Allowances account when the same end result may be achieved by crediting the Purchases account when goods purchased are returned to the suppliers?

9 Which party (seller or buyer) bears the transportation costs when the terms of a merchandise sale are (*a*) F.O.B. shipping point; (*b*) F.O.B. destination?

10 Where does the account Transportation-in appear in the financial statements?

11 Is the normal balance of the Sales Returns and Allowances account a debit or credit? Is the normal balance of the Purchase Returns and Allowances account a debit or credit?

12 In which columns of the work sheet for a merchandising company does the ending inventory appear?

13 In accounting for an unincorporated business, is it customary to include a salary to the owner as an expense of the business if he works full time for the business? Why or why not?

14 In appraising the adequacy of the net income of a small business in which the owner works on a full-time basis, the net income may be regarded as including three separate elements. What are these three elements?

15 State briefly the difference between the **periodic** inventory method and the **perpetual** inventory method.

16 If cost of goods sold amounts to 65% of the sales of a merchandising business and net income amounts to 5% of sales, what percentage of sales is represented by operating expenses? What percentage of gross profit is included in each dollar of sales?

17 When the periodic inventory method is in use, how is the amount of inventory determined at the end of the period?

18 What is the purpose of a closing entry consisting of a debit to the Income Summary account and a credit to the Inventory account?

19 Define a *condensed income statement* and indicate its advantages and possible shortcomings.

EXERCISES

Ex. 5-1 The Lee Company made sales of merchandise on credit during July amounting to $127,000, of which $109,000 remained uncollected at July 31. Sales for cash during July amounted to $30,000 and an additional $99,000 was received from customers in payment for goods sold to them in prior months. Also during July, the Lee Company borrowed $36,000 cash from the First Security Bank. What was the total revenue for July?

Ex. 5-2 Determine the amount of *gross* purchases for the period, given the following data:

Cost of goods sold	$126,400
Transportation-in	1,890
Beginning inventory	43,640
Purchase returns and allowances	2,150
Ending inventory	38,500
Sales	182,650

Ex. 5-3 Given the following data, determine the amount of the beginning inventory.

Ending inventory	$38,450
Purchases	65,000
Cost of goods sold	41,900
Transportation-in	2,400
Purchase returns and allowances	4,600

Ex. 5-4 Income statement data for Marvin Company for two years are shown below:

	Year 2	Year 1
Sales	$400,000	$300,000
Cost of goods sold	300,000	210,000
Selling expenses	50,000	30,000
General and administrative expenses	20,000	15,000

a The net income decreased from $_____ in Year 1 to $_____ in Year 2.
b The net income as a percentage of sales was ___% in Year 1 and decreased to ___% of sales in Year 2.
c The gross profit on sales decreased from 30% in Year 1 to ___% in Year 2.
d Selling expenses increased by $20,000 from Year 1 to Year 2, which represented an increase of ___% from the base of $30,000, while sales showed an increase of ___% from the base of $300,000.

Ex. 5-5 The following items appear on the balance sheet for the Lane Company:

Cash	$ 70,000
Accounts receivable	10,000
Inventory	80,000
Store equipment (net)	100,000
Other assets	15,000
Mortgage payable (due in 3 years)	25,000

Notes payable (due tomorrow)	$ 60,000
Accounts payable	20,000
John Lane, capital	170,000

a Total current assets for the Lane Company amount to $_____. Total current liabilities amount to $_____.
b Working capital for the Lane Company amounts to $_____.
c Current ratio for the Lane Company is _____ to 1.
d Assuming that the Lane Company pays off the notes, thus reducing cash to $10,000, the working capital would be $_____ and the current ratio would be _____ to 1.

Ex. 5-6 During its first year of operation, Yardbird Company earned net income equal to 5% of net sales. The selling expenses were twice as large as net income but only one-half as large as general and administrative expenses, which amounted to $80,000. Prepare a condensed income statement for the first year of operation, which ended on December 31, 19___.

Ex. 5-7 The following account balances are listed in random order and represent only a portion of the ledger balances of the Prairie Company at December 31.

Cash	$ 64,400
Accrued salaries payable	1,600
Accumulated depreciation: delivery equipment	1,972
Inventory	115,400
Accrued interest receivable	120
Accounts payable	37,000
Accounts receivable	56,600
Canadian government bonds	12,000
Notes payable (due in 90 days)	40,000
Advance payments from customers	3,600
Accrued interest on notes payable	640
Delivery equipment	19,720

Instructions
a Compute the amount of **working capital** by arranging the **appropriate** items in the usual balance sheet sequence. A complete balance sheet is not required.
b Compute the current ratio and state whether you regard the company as being in a strong or weak current position.

PROBLEMS

Group A

5A-1 Palms Lumber Company closes its accounts annually on December 31 and uses the periodic method of inventory. Listed below are some of the transactions for the month of August.
Aug. 1 Paid monthly rent on building, $300.
Aug. 2 Purchased merchandise on account from Grand Supply Company, $985.
Aug. 3 Cash sale of merchandise, $1,500.

Aug. 6 Purchased office equipment on account from Miner Company for use in the business, $1,543.

Aug. 8 Sold merchandise on account to Dale Construction Company, $2,200.

Aug. 9 Purchased merchandise for cash, $180.

Aug. 10 Returned defective equipment which cost $300 to Miner Company for credit.

Aug. 14 Sold merchandise on account to R. B. Green, $1,250.

Aug. 15 Granted a $50 allowance to R. B. Green on merchandise delivered on August 14, because of minor defects discovered in the merchandise.

Aug. 20 Agreed to cancel the account receivable from Dale Construction Company in exchange for their services in erecting a garage on our property. Construction completed today.

Aug. 28 Paid balance due Miner Company. (See transactions of August 6 and 10).

Instructions Prepare a separate journal entry (including an explanation) for each of the above transactions.

5A-2 An alphabetical listing of the account balances of Stylecraft Store after its second complete year of operations is shown below. All necessary adjustments as of December 31 have been recorded and posted.

Accounts receivable	$20,000	Prepaid insurance	$	390
Accounts payable	12,000	Property taxes expense		600
Accrued property taxes		Purchases		129,835
payable	580	Purchase returns and		
Accumulated depreciation:		allowances		4,280
equipment	2,275	Rent expense		7,200
Cash	8,375	Salaries and wages expense		37,565
Delivery expense	2,055	Sales		211,820
Depreciation expense	1,300	Sales returns and		
Equipment	7,960	allowances		5,820
Insurance expense	1,600	Selling commissions expense		8,000
Inventory, Jan. 1	26,780	Supplies		715
Barry Jackson, capital	41,090	Supplies expense		580
Barry Jackson, drawing	5,600	Transportation-in		4,225
Notes receivable	3,500			

The inventory, determined by count at December 31, was $19,560.

Instructions
a Prepare the income statement for the year ended December 31.
b Prepare all necessary journal entries to close the books at December 31.

5A-3 Lemon Company, a small retail store, was purchased by R. D. Maverick on July 1, 1973. After completing the first year of operations, the following trial balance was prepared from the accounts.

LEMON COMPANY
Trial Balance
June 30, 1974

Cash	$ 4,000	
Accounts receivable	17,000	
Inventory (July 1, 1973)	36,000	
Supplies	1,420	
Unexpired insurance	540	
Land	20,000	
Buildings	50,000	
Equipment	12,000	
Accounts payable		$ 28,310
R. D. Maverick, capital		85,000
R. D. Maverick, drawing	7,500	
Sales		195,250
Sales returns and allowances	4,000	
Purchases	116,000	
Purchase returns and allowances		2,840
Transportation-in	4,820	
Selling commissions	6,255	
Delivery expense	1,750	
Salaries and wages	29,615	
Property taxes	500	
	$311,400	$311,400

A physical inventory was taken at the close of business June 30,1974; this count showed merchandise on hand in the amount of $29,000.

Other data
(a) Property taxes accrued but not yet recorded, $900.
(b) A physical count showed supplies on hand of $420.
(c) The cost of insurance which had expired during the year was $280.
(d) Depreciation rates: 4% on buildings and 10% on equipment.

Instructions
a Prepare an eight-column work sheet at June 30, 1974. (Omit columns for an adjusted trial balance.)
b Prepare the necessary adjusting journal entries at June 30, 1974.
c Prepare the journal entries required to close the books as of June 30, 1974.

5A-4 The trial balance of Warner Company (on page 166) was prepared from the records of the firm on June 30, 19___, the close of its fiscal year.

WARNER COMPANY

Trial Balance

June 30, 19___

Cash	$ 18,635	
Accounts receivable	24,260	
Inventory, beginning	37,240	
Unexpired insurance	720	
Office supplies	505	
Land	10,640	
Buildings	38,000	
Accumulated depreciation: buildings		$ 9,120
Equipment	9,600	
Accumulated depreciation: equipment		1,600
Accounts payable		32,040
William Warner, capital		51,570
William Warner, drawing	5,000	
Sales		199,735
Sales returns and allowances	3,290	
Purchases	119,930	
Purchase returns and allowances		2,145
Transportation-in	2,965	
Salaries and wages expense	24,740	
Property taxes expense	685	
	$296,210	$296,210

Other data
(a) The buildings are being depreciated over a 25-year useful life and the equipment over a 12-year useful life.
(b) Accrued salaries payable as of June 30 were $3,140.
(c) Examination of policies showed $380 unexpired insurance on June 30.
(d) Supplies on hand at June 30 were estimated to amount to $235.
(e) Inventory of merchandise on June 30 was $27,910.

Instructions
a Prepare an eight-column work sheet at June 30, 19___. (Omit columns for an adjusted trial balance.)
b Prepare an income statement, a statement of owner's equity, and a classified balance sheet.
c Prepare adjusting entries.
d Prepare closing entries.

Group B

5B-1 Builders' Supply Company uses the periodic method of inventory and closes its books annually on December 31. During October the company completed the following transactions, among others.
Oct. 1 Paid rent on building for October, $850.
Oct. 2 Purchased merchandise on credit from Warner Company, $895.
Oct. 4 Sold merchandise for cash, $1,935.

Oct. 5 Purchased equipment (for use in business) on account from Daily Company, $1,670.

Oct. 6 Sold merchandise on credit to Jones Construction Company, $2,845.

Oct. 12 Returned $440 worth of defective equipment purchased on October 5 from Daily Company.

Oct. 14 Purchased merchandise for cash, $2,000.

Oct. 15 Agreed to cancel the account receivable of $2,845 from Jones Construction Company in exchange for their services in erecting a garage on the property of Builders' Supply Company. Garage completed today.

Oct. 18 Sold merchandise on credit to Lyon Brothers, $2,480.

Oct. 19 Granted an allowance of $85 to Lyon Brothers because of minor defects discovered in the merchandise sold them on October 18.

Oct. 28 Paid the balance due Daily Company. (See transactions of October 5 and 12.)

Oct. 31 Paid $935 to Miller Service Station for gasoline and oil used by our delivery trucks during the month. No prior entry had been made for these purchases which occurred on a daily basis.

Instructions Prepare a separate journal entry (including an explanation) for each of the above transactions.

5B-2 The accounting records of Miles Company are maintained on the basis of a fiscal year ending April 30. After all necessary adjustments had been made at April 30, 1974, the adjusted trial balance appeared as follows:

MILES COMPANY

Adjusted Trial Balance

April 30, 1974

Cash	$ 19,000	
Accounts receivable	34,000	
Inventory (Apr. 30, 1973)	28,900	
Unexpired insurance	700	
Supplies	1,200	
Furniture and fixtures	20,000	
Accumulated depreciation: furniture and fixtures		$ 1,200
Accounts payable		8,300
Notes payable		7,000
Eric Miles, capital		51,480
Sales		293,000
Sales returns and allowances	4,000	
Purchases	191,525	
Purchase returns and allowances		1,545
Transportation-in	10,000	
Salaries and wages expense	41,400	
Rent expense	8,400	
Depreciation expense: furniture and fixtures	1,200	
Supplies expense	1,400	
Insurance expense	800	
	$362,525	$362,525

The inventory on April 30, 1974, as determined by count, amounted to $35,880.

Instructions

a Prepare an income statement for Miles Company for the year ended April 30, 1974.

b Prepare the necessary journal entries to close the books on April 30, 1974.

5B-3 After several years of managerial experience in retailing, Alvin Hart bought a retail store on July 1, 1973. He had saved $25,000 over a period of years and had received an inheritance of $60,000, all of which he invested in the new business. Before taking this step, Hart had given considerable thought to the alternative of continuing in his present position, which paid a salary of $19,500 a year, and investing his capital in high-grade securities, which he estimated would provide an average return of 4% on the amount invested.

This trial balance was taken from the records at June 30, 1974.

HART COMPANY

Trial Balance

June 30, 1974

Cash	$ 5,000	
Accounts receivable	17,500	
Inventory (July 1, 1973)	35,650	
Supplies	1,420	
Unexpired insurance	540	
Land	20,000	
Building	50,000	
Equipment	12,000	
Accounts payable		$ 28,310
Alvin Hart, capital		85,000
Alvin Hart, drawing	7,500	
Sales		194,650
Sales returns and allowances	2,150	
Purchases	116,210	
Purchase returns and allowances		2,840
Transportation-in	4,820	
Selling commissions	6,255	
Delivery expense	1,750	
Salaries and wages	29,615	
Property taxes	390	
	$310,800	$310,800

The June 30, 1974, inventory by physical count was $29,000.

Other data

(*a*) Accrued property taxes, $870

(*b*) Supplies on hand, $570

(*c*) Insurance expired during year, $180

(*d*) Depreciation rates: 4% on buildings; $12\frac{1}{2}$% on equipment

Instructions

a Prepare an eight-column work sheet at June 30, 1974. (Omit columns for an adjusted trial balance.)

b Prepare a schedule comparing the adequacy of net income from the business for the fiscal year ended June 30, 1974, with the income Hart would have received by continuing as a salaried manager and investing his capital in securities. State your opinion based on this comparative schedule.

5B-4 Prepare a *classified* balance sheet as of December 31, 1974, from the following information applicable to the Lanham Company. The various items of prepaid expenses may be combined into a single balance sheet amount.

Cash	$ 9,000
John Lanham, capital	116,600
Accounts payable	15,980
Prepaid rent	250
Wages and salaries payable	2,350
Accumulated depreciation: buildings	14,300
Inventory	48,725
Delivery equipment	1,800
Stationery and office supplies	210
Buildings	62,800
Accounts receivable	22,100
Allowance for uncollectible accounts	400
Store equipment	17,600
Land	35,000
Advance payments by customers	375
Canadian government bonds	20,000
Bank loan (due Apr. 15, 1975)	23,000
Accumulated depreciation: store equipment	6,350
Mortgage payable (due June 30, 1980)	68,000
Notes receivable (due within six months)	3,220
Accrued interest payable	850
Unexpired insurance	600
Accumulated depreciation: delivery equipment	600
Investment in land (held as future building site)	27,500

BUSINESS DECISION PROBLEM 5

Ralph Carter, a qualified engineer, is considering buying the Westside Engineering Company from its current owner, James Aarons. Westside has been a profitable business, earning about $30,000 each year. Carter is certain he could operate the business just as profitably. Carter comes to you with the following balance sheet of Westside Engineering Company and asks your advice about buying the business.

WESTSIDE ENGINEERING COMPANY
Balance Sheet
December 31, 19___

Assets		Liabilities & Owner's Equity	
Cash	$ 20,000	Notes payable	$ 30,000
Ontario government contract		Accounts payable	9,000
receivable	50,000	Wages payable	3,000
Other contracts receivable	14,000	J. Aarons, capital	117,000
Equipment			
(net of depreciation)	45,000		
Patents	30,000		
	$159,000		$159,000

Carter immediately points out, as evidence of the firm's solvency, that the current ratio for Westside Engineering is 2 to 1. In discussing the specific items on the balance sheet, you find that the patents were recently purchased by Westside, and Carter believes them to be worth their $30,000 cost. The notes payable consists of one note to the manufacturer of the equipment owned by Westside, which Aarons had incurred five years ago to finance the purchase of the equipment. The note becomes payable, however, in February of the coming year. The accounts payable all will become due within 30 to 60 days.

Since Carter does not have enough cash to buy Aarons' equity in the business, he is considering the following terms of purchase: (1) Aarons will withdraw all the cash from the business, thus reducing his equity to $97,000; (2) Aarons will also keep the $50,000 receivable from the Ontario government, leaving his equity in the business at $47,000; and (3) by borrowing heavily, Carter thinks he can raise $47,000 in cash, which he will pay to Aarons for his remaining equity. Carter will assume the existing liabilities of the business.

Instructions
a Prepare a balance sheet for Westside Engineering Company as it would appear immediately after Carter acquired the business, assuming that the purchase is carried out immediately on the proposed terms.
b Compute the current ratio and the working capital position of Westside Engineering Company after Carter's purchase of the business.
c Write a memorandum to Carter explaining what problems he might encounter if he purchases the business as planned. (Hint: Might Carter need to come up with additional cash in the near future?)

SIX

CONTROL PROCEDURES IN A MERCHANDISING BUSINESS

Our discussion of a merchandising business in Chapter 5 emphasized the steps of the accounting cycle, especially the determination of cost of goods sold and the preparation of financial statements. In the present chapter we shall round out this discussion by considering methods by which management maintains control over purchases and sales transactions.

Internal control was defined in Chapter 1 as including all the measures taken by an organization for the purpose of (1) protecting its resources against waste, fraud, and inefficiency; (2) ensuring accuracy and reliability in accounting and operating data; (3) securing compliance with company policies; and (4) evaluating the level of performance in all divisions of the company.

Internal control as a tool of management

Procedures for controlling the purchase and sale of merchandise emphasize the subdivision of duties within the company so that no one person or department handles a transaction completely from beginning to end. When duties are divided in this manner, the work of one employee serves to verify that of another and any errors which occur tend to be detected promptly.

SUBDIVISION OF DUTIES STRENGTHENS INTERNAL CONTROL To illustrate the development of internal control through subdivision of duties, let us review the procedures for a sale of merchandise on account by a wholesaler. The sales department of the company is responsible for securing the order from the customer; the credit department must approve the customer's credit before the order is filled; the stock room assembles the goods ordered; the shipping department packs and ships the goods;

and the accounting department records the transaction. Each department receives written evidence of the action of the other departments and reviews the documents describing the transaction to see that the actions taken correspond in all details. The shipping department, for instance, does not release the merchandise until after the credit department has approved the customer as a credit risk. The accounting department does not record the sale until it has received documentary evidence that (1) the goods were ordered, (2) the extension of credit was approved, and (3) the merchandise has been shipped to the customer.

Assume for a moment, as a contrast to this procedure, that a single employee were permitted to secure the customer's order, approve the credit terms, get the merchandise from the stock room, deliver the goods to the customer, prepare the invoice, enter the transaction in the accounting records, and perhaps even collect the account receivable. If this employee made errors, such as selling to poor credit risks, forgetting to enter the sale in the accounting records, or perhaps delivering more merchandise to the customer than he was charged for, no one would know the difference. By the time such errors came to light, substantial losses would have been incurred.

PREVENTION OF FRAUD If one employee is permitted to handle all aspects of a transaction, the danger of fraud is also increased. Studies of fraud cases suggest that many individuals may be tempted into dishonest acts if given complete control of company property. Most of these persons, however, would not engage in fraud if doing so required collaboration with another employee. Losses through employee dishonesty occur in a variety of ways: merchandise may be stolen; payments by customers may be withheld; suppliers may be overpaid with a view to kickbacks to employees; and lower prices may be allowed to favored customers. The opportunities for fraud are almost endless if all aspects of a sale or purchase transaction are concentrated in the hands of one employee.

Because internal control rests so largely upon the participation of several employees in each transaction, it is apparent that strong internal control is more easily achieved in large organizations than in small ones. In a small business with only one or two office employees, such duties as the issuance of purchase orders, approval of credit, and maintenance of accounting records may necessarily have to be performed by the same employee.

SERIALLY NUMBERED DOCUMENTS—ANOTHER CONTROL DEVICE Another method of achieving internal control, in addition to the subdivision of duties, consists of having the printer include serial numbers on such documents as purchase orders, sales invoices, and cheques. The use of serial numbers makes it possible to account for all documents. In other words, if a sales invoice is misplaced or concealed, the break in the sequence of numbers will call attention to the discrepancy.

INTERNAL CONTROL IN PERSPECTIVE A description of internal control solely in terms of the prevention of fraud and the detection of errors represents too narrow a concept of this managerial technique. The building of a strong system of internal control is an accepted means of increasing operational efficiency.

In appraising the merits of various internal control procedures, the question of their cost cannot be ignored. Too elaborate a system of internal control may entail greater operating costs than are justified by the protection gained. For this reason the system of internal control must be tailored to meet the requirements of the individual business. In most organizations, however, proper subdivision of duties and careful design of accounting procedures will provide a basis for adequate internal control and at the same time will contribute to economical operation of the business.

Business papers

Carefully designed business papers and procedures for using them are necessary to ensure that all transactions are properly authorized and recorded. To illustrate this point in a somewhat exaggerated manner, let us assume that every employee in a large department store was authorized to purchase merchandise for the store and that no standard forms or procedures had been provided to keep track of these purchases. The result would undoubtedly be many unwise purchases, confusion as to what had been ordered and received, shortages of some types of merchandise, and an oversupply of other types. The opportunity for fraud by dishonest employees, as well as for accidental errors, would be unlimited under such a haphazard method of operation.

Each step in ordering, receiving, and making payment for merchandise purchases should be controlled and recorded. A similar approach is necessary to establish control over the sales function.

Purchasing procedures

In small retail businesses, the owner or manager may personally perform the purchasing function by placing orders with sales representatives of wholesalers and manufacturers. These sales representatives make regular visits to the store and may carry catalogs and samples to illustrate the products offered.

The owner-manager of a small store is sufficiently familiar with his stock of merchandise to know what items need to be replenished. He may keep a notebook record of items to be ordered, writing down each day any items which he observes to be running low. When the sales representative of a wholesaler or manufacturer visits the store, he writes up the order in his order book. A copy of the order, showing the quantities and prices of all items ordered, is left with the store owner.

PURCHASE ORDERS In many businesses and especially in large organizations, the buying company uses its own purchase order forms. A purchase order of the Zenith Company issued to Adams Manufacturing Company is illustrated below.

<table>
<tr><td colspan="2" align="center">**PURCHASE ORDER**</td><td>**Order No.**</td></tr>
<tr><td colspan="2" align="center">**ZENITH COMPANY**</td><td></td></tr>
<tr><td colspan="2" align="center">**10 Fairway Avenue**</td><td>999</td></tr>
<tr><td colspan="2" align="center">**Vancouver, British Columbia**</td><td></td></tr>
</table>

Serially numbered purchase order

To: Adams Manufacturing Company

Date Nov. 10, 1973

19 Union Street

Ship via Jones Truck Co.

Toronto, Ontario

Terms: 2/10, n/30

Please enter our order for the following:

Quantity	Description	Price	Total
15 sets	Model S irons	$60.00	$900.00
50 dozen	X3Y Shur-Par golf balls	7.00	350.00

Zenith Company

By *D. D. McCarthy*

In large companies in which the functions of placing orders, receiving merchandise, and making payment are lodged in separate departments, several copies of the purchase order are usually prepared, each on a different color paper. The original is sent to the supplier; this purchase order is his authorization to deliver the merchandise and to submit a bill based on the prices listed. Carbon copies of the purchase order are usually routed to the purchasing department, accounting department, receiving department, and finance department.

Note that the illustrated purchase order bears a serial number, 999. When purchase orders are serially numbered, there can be no doubt as to how many orders have been issued. Each department authorized to receive copies of purchase orders should account for every number in the series, thus guarding against the loss or nondelivery of any document.

When merchandise is ordered by telephone, a formal written purchase order should nevertheless be prepared and sent to the supplier to confirm the verbal instructions. Orders for office equipment, supplies, and other assets as well as merchandise should also be in writing to avoid misunderstanding and to provide a permanent record of the order.

The issuance of a purchase order does not call for any debit or credit entries in the accounting records of either the prospective buyer or seller. The company which receives an order does not consider (for accounting purposes) that a sale has been made until the merchandise is delivered. At that point ownership of the goods changes, and both buyer and seller should make accounting entries to record the transaction.

INVOICES The supplier (vendor) mails an invoice to the purchaser at the time of shipping the merchandise. An invoice contains a description of the goods being sold, the quantities, prices, credit terms, and method of shipment. The illustration below shows an invoice issued by Adams Manufacturing Company in response to the previously illustrated purchase order from Zenith Company.

ADAMS MANUFACTURING COMPANY
19 Union Street
Toronto, Ontario

Invoice is basis for accounting entry

Sold to Zenith Company	*Invoice no.* 777
10 Fairway Avenue	*Invoice date* Nov. 15, 1973
Vancouver, B.C.	*Your order no.* 999
Shipped to Same	*Date shipped* Nov. 15, 1973
Terms 2/10, n/30	*Shipped via* Jones Truck Co.

Quantity	Description	Price	Amount
15 sets	Model S irons	$60.00	$ 900.00
50 dozen	X3Y Shur-Par golf balls	7.00	350.00
			$1,250.00

From the viewpoint of the seller, an invoice is a *sales invoice;* from the buyer's viewpoint it is a *purchase invoice.* The invoice is the basis for an entry in the accounting records of both the seller and the buyer because it evidences the transfer of ownership of goods. At the time of issuing the invoice, the seller makes an entry debiting Accounts Receivable and crediting Sales. The buyer, however, does not record the invoice as a liability until he has made a careful verification of the transaction, as indicated in the following section.

Verification of invoice by purchaser Upon receipt of an invoice, the purchaser should verify the following aspects of the transaction:

1 The invoice agrees with the purchase order as to prices, quantities, and other provisions.

2 The invoice is arithmetically correct in all extensions of price times quantity and in the addition of amounts.

3 The goods covered by the invoice have been received and are in satisfactory condition.

Evidence that the merchandise has been received in good condition must be obtained from the receiving department. It is the function of the receiving department to receive all incoming goods, to inspect them as to quality and condition, and to determine the quantities received by counting, measuring, or weighing. The receiving department should prepare a serially numbered report for each shipment received; this *receiving report* is sent to the accounting department for use in verifying the invoice.

The verification of the invoice in the accounting department is accomplished by comparing the purchase order, the invoice, and the receiving report. Comparison of these documents establishes that the goods described in the invoice were actually ordered, have been received in good condition, and were billed at the prices specified in the purchase order. To ensure that this comparison of documents is made in every case and that the arithmetical accuracy of the invoice is proved, it is customary to require an invoice approval sheet such as that on page 177 to be attached to each invoice and initialed by the employees performing each step in the verification work. Some companies prefer to use a rubber stamp imprint of this form to place the verification data directly on the vendor's invoice.

When these verification procedures have been completed, the invoice is recorded as a liability by an entry debiting the Purchases account and crediting Accounts Payable.

Debit and credit memoranda

The verification procedures just described usually give the purchaser of merchandise assurance that the invoice should be paid. Sometimes, however, the verification procedures disclose irregularities which require adjustment. For example, there may be arithmetical errors in the invoice, a shortage of goods received as compared with those billed, damaged merchandise, goods received that were not ordered, or various other discrepancies. If the invoice contains an arithmetical error, the purchasing company can easily compute the correct amount. Other situations such as defects in merchandise or improper quantities may require negotiation with the seller. In all cases when the buyer makes an adjustment, he must notify the seller of the details. The buyer provides this notification by sending the seller a *debit memorandum* or a *credit memorandum.*

A debit memorandum informs the supplier that his account is being debited (reduced) on the books of the buyer and explains the circum-

Invoice Approval Form

Invoice no. ....777.. Date ....Nov. 15, 1973....

Purchase order no. ....999............................. Date ....Nov. 10, 1973....

Vendor ....Adams Manufacturing Company....

Invoice compared with purchase order as to:
Description of goods ............*L.B.a.*............

Quantities ............*L.B.a.*............

Prices ............*L.B.a.*............

Discount terms ............*L.B.a.*............

Transportation charges ............*L.B.a.*............

Receiving report compared with purchase order
and invoice as to quantities ............*D.L.W*............

Invoice verified as to:
Extensions ............*R.A.*............

Footings ............*R.A.*............

Approved for payment ............*J.R.K.*............

Paid by cheque no. ....2116............................. Date ....Nov. 25, 1973....

stances. A credit memorandum issued by the buyer has the opposite effect of informing the supplier that his account is being credited (increased) on the buyer's records. Since an error in a purchase invoice may cause the total amount to be either overstated or understated, it is clear that the purchasing company may need to issue either a debit memorandum or a credit memorandum to correct the error.

To illustrate the use of a debit memorandum, let us assume that Zenith Company receives another shipment of merchandise from Adams Manufacturing Company and a related invoice dated November 18 in the amount of $1,000. However, some of the goods with a value of $450 were badly damaged when received and cannot be accepted. Zenith Company therefore wishes to return the damaged goods and to pay only $550 of the $1,000 amount billed. One method would be to record the purchase as $550 and send a cheque for that amount to the supplier accompanied by a letter explaining the situation. To record the transaction as a $550 purchase, however, would not provide a clear and complete picture of the events. A better procedure is to record the invoice in its full amount and to make a second entry recording the return of the damaged merchandise. The debit memorandum shown below should be prepared in two or more copies and the original sent to the vendor.

The duplicate copy of the debit memorandum serves as a source document supporting an entry in the buyer's accounting records showing the return of the goods and a corresponding reduction in the liability to the vendor. The two entries to record the purchase invoice and the debit memorandum are as follows:

Entries for purchase and purchase return	Nov. 18	Purchases	*1,000*	
		Accounts Payable		*1,000*
		To record invoice from Adams Manufacturing Company.		
	Nov. 20	Accounts Payable	*450*	
		Purchase Returns and Allowances		*450*
		To record return of damaged merchandise to Adams Manufacturing Company. See our debit memo no. 42.		

ZENITH COMPANY *Debit*
10 Fairway Avenue *memorandum*
Vancouver, British Columbia *no.* ....42....

Debit memorandum reduces liability to vendor

To: Adams Manufacturing Company *Date:* Nov. 20, 1973

19 Union Street

Toronto, Ontario

We debit your account as follows:

Return of merchandise. Fifty DLX gloves arrived
badly damaged and are being returned via Jones
Truck Co. Your invoice no. 825, dated
November 18, 1973 . . . .$450.00

ADAMS MANUFACTURING COMPANY *Credit*
19 Union Street *memorandum*
Toronto, Ontario *no.* ...102...

Credit memorandum issued by seller of goods

To: Zenith Company *Date:* Nov. 22, 1973

10 Fairway Avenue

Vancouver, B.C.

We credit your account as follows:

Merchandise returned, 50 DLX gloves,
our invoice no. 825 . . . .$450.00

The supplier, upon being informed of the return of the damaged merchandise, will issue the *credit memorandum* shown on page 178 as evidence that the account receivable from the purchaser is being credited (reduced).

The entry on the part of Adams Manufacturing Company at the time of issuing this credit memorandum would be as follows:

Entry recording credit memo
Nov. 22	Sales Returns and Allowances	450	
	Accounts Receivable		450
	To record return by Zenith Company of damaged merchandise. See our credit memo no. 102.		

This credit memorandum, when received by the Zenith Company, will be filed with the original invoice and the carbon copy of the debit memorandum. These documents represent evidence supporting the entries in the accounts.

As a separate example, assume that Zenith Company, while verifying a purchase invoice, discovered an error that caused the purchase invoice to be understated by $100. To correct the error, Zenith Company would issue a *credit memorandum.* If the error were discovered before the invoice was recorded, a copy of the credit memorandum would be attached to the purchase invoice and the accounting entry debiting Purchases and crediting Accounts Payable would be for $100 more than the erroneous amount on the invoice.

Thus, a debit memorandum or a credit memorandum may be issued by either the buying or selling party in a transaction. When the buyer issues a debit memorandum, he is debiting (reducing) a liability; when he issues a credit memorandum, he is crediting (increasing) his liability to the seller. On the other hand, when the seller issues a debit memorandum, he is debiting (increasing) an account receivable from the buyer; and when he issues a credit memorandum, he is crediting (reducing) the receivable from the buyer.

Trade discounts

Manufacturers and wholesalers in many lines of industry publish annual catalogs in which their products are listed at retail prices. Substantial reductions from the *list prices* shown in the catalog are offered to dealers and other large-scale purchasers. These reductions from the list prices (often as much as 30 or 40%) are called *trade discounts.* The entire schedule of discounts may be revised as price levels and market conditions fluctuate. To publish a new catalog every time the price of one or more products changes would be an expensive practice; the issuance of a new schedule of trade discounts is much more convenient and serves just as well in revising actual selling prices.

Trade discounts may be stated as a single percentage or as a series or chain of percentages to be deducted in sequence. If the catalog or list price of merchandise is $1,000 and a single trade discount of 30% is offered, the selling price is computed as follows:

Computing
actual
selling
price

List or catalog price	$1,000
Less: Trade discount of 30%	300
Selling price	$ 700

Next, assume that the list price of merchandise is $1,000 and that a series or chain of trade discounts (20, 10, and 5%) are offered. The selling price is calculated as follows:

What
amount
should
be
recorded
by
seller
and
buyer?

List or catalog price	$1,000
Less: First trade discount of 20%	200
Remainder after first discount	$ 800
Less: Second trade discount of 10% ($800 × 10%)	80
Remainder after second discount	$ 720
Less: Third trade discount of 5% ($720 × 5%)	36
Selling price	$ 684

Assume that the selling company is a distributor of automobile parts; sales are made at wholesale and also on a retail basis. One price list or catalog is used for all customers, but the wholesale customer is allowed a discount from the list price. If his purchases exceed a specified dollar amount, he is allowed a second discount, and on still a larger volume of purchases, a third discount is available. Thus, trade discounts are merely a procedure for computing actual selling prices in various situations.

Trade discounts are not recorded in the accounting records of either the seller or the buyer. A sale of merchandise is recorded at the actual selling price and the trade discount is merely a device for computing the actual sales price. From the viewpoint of the company purchasing goods, the significant price is not the list price but the amount which must be paid, and this amount is recorded as the cost of the merchandise.

To illustrate the use of a trade discount, assume that the Martin Manufacturing Company sells goods to Austin Auto Repair at a list price of $100 with a trade discount of 30%. Martin Manufacturing Company would record the sale by the following entry:

Neither
seller . . .

Accounts Receivable	70	
Sales		70

The entry by Austin Auto Repair to record the purchase would be:

. . . nor
buyer
records
trade
discounts

Purchases	70	
Accounts Payable		70

Because trade discounts are not recorded in the accounts, they should be clearly distinguished from the cash discounts discussed later in this chapter.

Credit terms

Manufacturers and wholesalers try to increase their sales by allowing customers a considerable period of time within which to make payment for merchandise. By purchasing goods on credit, a retailer with limited capital can carry a larger inventory and increase his own sales. An ideal goal from the retailer's point of view is to buy merchandise on credit, sell it promptly, and use part of the cash received to pay the manufacturer or wholesaler.

Credit terms are precisely stated on the sales invoice issued by the manufacturer or wholesaler. If credit is allowed for a period of 30 days the invoice may bear the symbol "n/30," which is read "net 30 days" and means that the customer must make payment within 30 days from the date of the invoice. The word *net* in this expression means the list price of the merchandise less any trade discount. Credit terms of 30 to 60 days are quite common. In some industries, it is customary for invoices to become payable 10 days after the end of the month in which the sale occurs. Such invoices bear the expression "10 e.o.m." These credit terms are especially convenient for the small business in which the owner wishes to pay all the bills on a given day of the month or within a few days after the beginning of each month.

Cash discounts

Manufacturers and wholesalers generally offer a cash discount to encourage their customers to pay invoices before expiration of the credit period. For example, the credit terms may be "2% 10 days, net 30 days"; these terms mean that the authorized credit period is 30 days, but that the customer may deduct 2% of the amount of the invoice if he makes payment within 10 days. On the invoice these terms would appear in the abbreviated form "2/10, n/30"; this expression is read "2, 10, net 30." The selling company regards a cash discount as a *sales discount;* the buyer calls the discount a *purchase discount.*

To illustrate the application of a cash discount, assume that Adams Manufacturing Company sells goods to the Zenith Company and issues a sales invoice for $1,000 dated November 3 and bearing the terms 2/10, n/30. If Zenith Company mails its cheque in payment on or before November 13, it is entitled to deduct 2% of $1,000, or $20, and settle the obligation for $980. If Zenith Company decides to forego the discount, it may postpone payment for an additional 20 days until December 3 but must then pay $1,000.

REASONS FOR CASH DISCOUNTS From the viewpoint of the seller, the acceptance of $980 in cash as full settlement of a $1,000 account receivable represents a $20 reduction in the amount of revenue earned. By making this concession to induce prompt payment, the seller collects accounts receivable more quickly and is able to use the money collected to buy additional goods. A greater volume of business can be handled with a given amount of invested capital if this capital is not tied up in accounts receivable for long periods. There is also less danger of accounts receivable becoming uncollectible if they are collected promptly; in other words, the older an account receivable becomes, the greater becomes the risk of nonpayment by the customer.

Is it to the advantage of the Zenith Company to settle the $1,000 invoice within the discount period and thereby save $20? The alternative is for Zenith to conserve cash by postponing payment for an additional 20 days. The question may therefore be stated as follows: Does the amount of $20 represent a reasonable charge for the use of $980 for a period of 20 days? Definitely not; this charge is the equivalent of an annual interest rate of about 36%. (A 20-day period is approximately $\frac{1}{18}$ of a year; 18 times 2% amounts to 36%.)[1] Although interest rates vary widely, most businesses are able to borrow money from banks at an annual interest rate of 9% or less. Well-managed businesses, therefore, generally pay all invoices within the discount period even though this policy necessitates borrowing from banks in order to have the necessary cash available.

RECORDING SALES DISCOUNTS Sales of merchandise are generally recorded at the full selling price without regard for the cash discount being offered. The discount is not reflected in the seller's accounting records until payment is received. Continuing our illustration of a sale of merchandise by Adams Manufacturing Company for $1,000 with terms of 2/10, n/30, the entry to record the sale on November 3 is as shown by the following:

Sale entered at full price

Nov. 3	Accounts Receivable	1,000	
	Sales		1,000
	To record sale to Zenith Company, terms 2/10, n/30.		

Assuming that payment is made by Zenith Company on November 13, the last day of the discount period, the entry by Adams to record collection of the receivable is as follows:

Sales discounts recorded at time of collection

Nov. 13	Cash	980	
	Sales Discounts	20	
	Accounts Receivable		1,000
	To record collection from Zenith Company of invoice of November 3 less 2% cash discount.		

As previously explained, the allowing of a cash discount reduces the

[1] A more accurate estimate of interest expense on an annual basis can be obtained as follows: ($20 × 18) ÷ $980 = 36.7%.

amount received from sales. On the income statement, therefore, sales discounts appear as a deduction from sales, as shown below:

Partial Income Statement

Treatment of sales discounts on the income statement

Sales		$189,788
Less: Sales returns & allowances	$4,462	
Sales discounts	3,024	7,486
Net sales		$182,302

RECORDING PURCHASE DISCOUNTS In the accounts of the Zenith Company, the purchase of merchandise on November 3 was recorded at the gross amount of the invoice, as shown by the following entry:

Purchase entered at full price

Purchases	1,000	
Accounts Payable		1,000

To record purchase from Adams Manufacturing Company, terms 2/10, n/30.

When the invoice was paid on November 13, the last day of the discount period, the payment was recorded as follows:

Purchase discounts recorded when payment made

Accounts Payable	1,000	
Purchase Discounts		20
Cash		980

To record payment to Adams Manufacturing Company of invoice of November 3, less 2% cash discount.

The effect of the discount was to reduce the cost of the merchandise to the Zenith Company. The credit balance of the Purchase Discounts account should therefore be deducted in the income statement from the debit balance of the Purchases account.

Since the Purchase Discounts account is deducted from Purchases in the income statement, a question naturally arises as to whether the Purchase Discounts account is really necessary. Why not reduce the amount of purchases at the time of taking a discount by crediting Purchases rather than crediting Purchase Discounts? The answer is that management needs to know the amount of discounts taken. The Purchase Discounts account supplies this information. Any decrease in the proportion of purchase discounts to purchases carries the suggestion that the accounts payable department is becoming inefficient. That department has the responsibility of paying all invoices within the discount period, and management should be informed of failure by any department to follow company policies consistently. If management is to direct the business effectively, it needs to receive from the accounting system information indicating the level of performance in every department.

ALTERNATIVE METHOD: RECORDING INVOICES AT NET PRICE As previously stated, most well-managed companies have a firm policy of taking all purchase discounts offered. These companies may prefer the alternative method of recording purchase invoices at the net amount after discount rather than at the gross amount as previously described. For example, in our illustration of a $1,000 invoice bearing terms of 2/10, n/30, the entry for the purchase could be made as follows:

Entry for *purchase:* *net price* *method*	Nov. 3	Purchases	980	
		Accounts Payable		980
		To record purchase invoice from Adams Manufacturing		
		Company less 2% cash discount available.		

Assuming that the invoice is paid within 10 days, the entry for the payment is as follows:

Entry for *payment:* *net price* *method*	Nov. 13	Accounts Payable	980	
		Cash		980
		To record payment of $1,000 invoice from Adams		
		Manufacturing Company less 2% cash discount.		

Through oversight or carelessness, the purchasing company may occasionally fail to make payment of an invoice within the 10-day discount period. If such a delay occurred in paying the invoice from Adams Manufacturing Company, the full amount of the invoice would have to be paid rather than the recorded liability of $980. The journal entry to record the late payment on, say, December 3, is as follows:

Entry for *payment* *after* *discount* *period:* *net price* *method*	Dec. 3	Accounts Payable	980	
		Purchase Discounts Lost	20	
		Cash		1,000
		To record payment of invoice and loss of discount by		
		delaying payment beyond the discount period.		

Under this method the cost of goods purchased is properly recorded at $980, and the additional payment of $20 caused by failure to pay the invoice promptly is placed in a special expense account designed to attract the attention of management. The gross-price method of recording invoices previously described shows the amount of purchase discounts *taken* each period; the net price method now under discussion shows the amount of purchase discounts *lost* each period. The latter method has the advantage of drawing the attention of management to a breakdown in prescribed operating routines. The fact that a purchase discount has been taken does not require attention by management, but a discount lost because of inefficiency in processing accounts payable does call for managerial investigation.

As previously suggested, inefficiency and delay in paying invoices should not be concealed by adding the penalty of lost discount to the cost of merchandise purchased. The purchases should be stated at the net price available by taking cash discounts; the Purchase Discounts Lost account should be shown in the income statement as an operating expense.

Both the gross-price method and the net-price method are acceptable and commonly used. In working problems the student should be alert for an indication of which method is to be used.

MECHANICS OF HANDLING APPROVED INVOICES The procedures for proper verification of a purchase invoice were described earlier in this chapter. After a purchase invoice has been approved for payment, it should be filed in a manner which assures that the required payment date will not be overlooked. For example, the invoice of November 3 from Adams Manufacturing Company could be placed in a "tickler file," a file with index cards bearing dates. Since this invoice must be paid by November 13 to take advantage of the cash discount, the invoice is filed in front of the index card for November 13. On that date the invoice is removed from the tickler file and sent to the cashier. The cashier prepares a cheque for $980 payable to Adams Manufacturing Company, enters the cheque number on the invoice approval form, and forwards both documents to the treasurer. The treasurer signs the cheque , mails it, and marks the invoice "Paid." The invoice and the attached approval sheet are then returned to the accounting department and placed in an alphabetical file of paid invoices.

Sales procedures

The procedures for controlling and recording sales will necessarily vary from one business to another, depending upon the nature and size of the business. The following description of sales procedures should therefore be regarded as a generalized pattern subject to many variations.

Most orders in retail stores are received orally from customers, but in manufacturing and wholesaling companies written orders are customary. These written sales orders come through the mail from the company's staff of traveling salesmen and directly from customers. The first step in processing the order usually is to obtain the approval of the credit department as to the customer's credit rating. If credit approval is obtained, a sales invoice may be prepared in three or more copies.

The first carbon copy of the sales invoice is sent to the stock room; there the merchandise ordered is assembled and sent with this copy of the invoice to the shipping department. When the shipping department has finished packing and shipping the merchandise, the employee in charge signs the invoice, records the date of shipment, and sends the invoice to the accounting department. As an alternative, the data identifying the shipment may be placed on a separate document to accompany the invoice to the accounting department.

While this assembling, packing, and shipping of goods is taking place, a second carbon copy of the invoice is being carefully examined in the accounting department to make sure that the prices, credit terms, and all extensions and footings are correct. This copy of the invoice is also compared with the customer's order to determine that these two documents are in agreement as to quantities, prices, and other details.

When the first carbon of the sales invoice arrives from the shipping department showing that the goods have been sent to the customer, the accounting department places this invoice in a file called a *shipping record.* Now that the accounting department has written evidence that the goods have been shipped, it places its own verified copy of the invoice in a sales binder or register and makes a journal entry debiting the account receivable from the customer and crediting Sales. The original copy of the invoice is mailed to the customer promptly after the goods have been shipped. As previously mentioned, the set of procedures which has been described represents merely one of many alternative methods of processing sales orders.

Monthly statements to customers

In addition to sending an invoice to the customer for each separate sales transaction, some companies send each customer a monthly statement. The customer's statement is similar to a ledger account and is sometimes called a *statement of account.* It shows the balance receivable at the beginning of the month, the charges for sales during the month, the credits for payments received or goods returned, and the balance receivable from the customer at the end of the month. A statement sent by Zenith Company to one of its customers at the end of November appears in the illustration below.

Statement

ZENITH COMPANY
10 Fairway Avenue
Vancouver, British Columbia

Monthly statement summarizing transactions with customer

In account with:

John D. Gardner
210 Moranda Lane
Moose Jaw, Sask.

Date: Nov. 30, 1973

Date	Our Invoice No.	Charges	Credits	Balance Due
Oct. 31	Balance forwarded			125.40
Nov. 8	4127	81.00		206.40
10			125.40	81.00
21	4352	62.50		143.50

Accounts are payable on tenth of month following purchase

Upon receipt of a monthly statement from a vendor, the customer should make a detailed comparison of the purchases and payments shown on the statement with the corresponding entries in his accounts payable records. Any differences in the invoiced amounts, payments, or balance owed should be promptly investigated. Frequently the balance shown on the statement will differ from the balance of the customer's accounts payable record because shipments of merchandise and letters containing payments are in transit at month-end. These in-transit items will have been recorded by the sender but will not yet appear on the other party's records.

Cycle billing

Large department stores and other businesses with large numbers of accounts receivable may use *cycle billing* to avoid concentration of work at the end of the month. The customers' accounts are divided into alphabetical groups, and each group is billed regularly on a given day of the month. Thus, customers whose names fall in the L–M group might be billed on the seventeenth of each month, and those in the N–P block might be billed on the nineteenth. This procedure spreads the work of preparing customers' statements more evenly throughout the month. It also results in a more uniform inflow of cash from customers.

Sales taxes

Sales taxes are levied by all provinces except Alberta on certain retail sales of goods and services. Usually certain classes of sales are exempt, notably food and childrens' clothing and some commodities, such as gasoline and cigarettes, already subject to special excise taxes.

Typically a sales tax is imposed on the consumer, but the seller must collect the tax, file tax returns at times specified by law, and remit a percentage of his reported sales. The actual tax collected by the seller from his customers may be greater or less than the amount paid to the government because no tax is collected on sales under a certain amount, and due to rounding of pennies, the tax collected on a given sale may be slightly more than the specified percentage.

ACCOUNTING FOR SALES TAXES A sales tax may be collected when a cash sale is made or it may be included in the charge to the customer's account on a credit sale. The liability to the governmental unit for sales taxes may be recorded at the time the sale is made as follows:

Sales tax recorded at time of sale

Accounts Receivable (or Cash)	1,050	
Sales Tax Payable		50
Sales		1,000

To record sale of $1,000 subject to 5% sales tax.

Instead of recording the sales tax liability at the time of sale, some businesses prefer to credit the Sales account with the entire amount collected, including the sales tax, and to make an adjustment at the end of each period to reflect sales tax payable. For example, suppose that the total recorded sales for the period under this method were $315,000. Since the Sales account includes both the sale price and the sales tax (say, 5%), it is apparent that $315,000 is 105% of the actual sales figure. Actual sales are $300,000 ($315,000 ÷ 1.05) and the amount of sales tax due is $15,000. (Proof: 5% of $300,000 = $15,000.) The entry to record the liability for sales taxes would be:

Sales tax recorded as adjustment of sales

Sales	15,000	
Sales Tax Payable		15,000

To remove sales taxes of 5% on $300,000 of sales from the Sales account, and reflect as a liability.

Any discrepancy between the tax due and the amount actually collected from customers, under this method, would be automatically absorbed in the net sales figure. If certain of the products being sold (such as food) are not subject to the tax, it is necessary to keep a record of taxable and nontaxable sales.

QUESTIONS

1 State a general principle to be followed in assigning duties among employees if strong internal control is to be achieved.

2 Suggest a control device to protect a business against the loss or nondelivery of invoices, purchase orders, and other documents which are routed from one department to another.

3 Criticize the following statement: "In our company we get things done by requiring that a person who initiates a transaction follow it through in all particulars. For example, an employee who issues a purchase order is held responsible for inspecting the merchandise upon arrival, approving the invoice, and preparing the cheque in payment of the purchase. If any error is made, we know definitely whom to blame."

4 For an invoice dated October 21, what is the last day of the credit period if the credit terms are (*a*) 2/10, n/30? (*b*) 10 e.o.m.?

5 Blair Manufacturing Company sells appliances on both a wholesale and a retail basis and publishes an annual catalog listing products at retail prices. At what price should the sale be recorded when an item listed in the catalog at $400 is delivered to a wholesaler entitled to a 30% trade discount?

6 What is meant by the expressions (*a*) 2/10, n/30; (*b*) 10 e.o.m.; (*c*) n/30?

7 A company which has received a shipment of merchandise and a related invoice from the supplier sometimes finds it necessary to issue a debit memorandum. List three examples of situations that would justify such action by the purchasing company.

8 A cash discount affects both seller and buyer. What term describes a cash discount from the viewpoint of the seller? From the viewpoint of the buyer?

9 Distinguish between a trade discount and a cash discount.

10 What accounting entry, if any, is required on the part of the company issuing a purchase order? On the part of the company receiving the purchase order?

11 Under what circumstances is cycle billing of customers likely to be used? State two advantages which may be gained from cycle billing.

12 Name three documents (business papers) which are needed by the accounting department to verify that a purchase of merchandise has occurred and that payment of the related liability should be made.

EXERCISES

Ex. 6-1 James Company sold merchandise to Bay Company on credit. On the next day, James Company received a telephone call from Bay Company stating that one of the items delivered was defective. James Company immediately issued credit memorandum no. 163 for $100 to Bay Company.
   a Give the accounting entry required in James Company's records to record the issuance of the credit memorandum.
   b Give the accounting entry required on Bay Company's accounting records when the credit memorandum is received. (Assume that Bay Company had previously recorded the purchase at the full amount of the seller's invoice and had not issued a debit memorandum.)

Ex. 6-2 Taft Company received purchase invoices during July totaling $42,000, all of which carried credit terms of 2/10, n/30. It was the company's regular policy to take advantage of all available cash discounts, but because of employee vacations during July, there was confusion and delay in making payments to suppliers, and none of the July invoices were paid within the discount period.
   a Explain briefly two alternative ways in which the amount of purchases might be presented in the July income statement.
   b What method of recording purchase invoices can you suggest that would call to the attention of the Taft Company management the inefficiency of operations in July?

Ex. 6-3 Hudson Company sold merchandise to River Company for $3,000; terms 2/10, n/30. River Company paid for the merchandise within the discount period. Assume that both companies record invoices at the gross amounts.
   a Give the journal entries by Hudson Company to record the sale and the subsequent collection.
   b Give the journal entries by River Company to record the purchase and the subsequent payment.

Ex. 6-4 From the following information, determine the amount of the beginning inventory.

Ending inventory	$ 66,800	Transportation-in	$4,800
Purchases	130,000	Purchase returns & allow.	9,200
Cost of goods sold	83,800	Purchase discounts	2,200

Ex. 6-5 Malone Company purchased from Ryan Company merchandise with a list price of $2,000, subject to a chain of trade discounts of 20, 10, and 5%.
   a Give the journal entry by Malone Company to record the purchase.
   b Give the journal entry by Ryan Company to record the sale.

Ex. 6-6 The Hasagami General Store operates in an area in which a 4% sales tax is levied on all products handled by the store. On cash sales, the salesclerks include the sales tax in the amount collected from the customer and ring up the entire amount on the cash register without recording separately the tax liability. On credit sales, the customer is charged for the list price of the merchandise plus 4%, and the entire amount is debited to Accounts Receivable and credited to the Sales account. The tax collected is rounded off as follows:

Sales of 10 cents or less	no tax
Sales of 11 cents to 25 cents, inclusive	1 cent
Sales of 26 cents to 50 cents, inclusive	2 cents
Sales of 51 cents to 75 cents, inclusive	3 cents
Sales of 76 cents to $1, inclusive	4 cents

Sales tax must be remitted to the government quarterly. At March 31 the Sales account showed a balance of $152,360 for the three-month period ended March 31.

a What amount of sales tax is owed at March 31?

b Give the journal entry to record the sales tax liability on the books.

PROBLEMS

Group A

6A-1 The information listed below appeared in the income statement of Alberta Products Company for the year ended June 30, 19___ .

Purchases	$234,610	Ending inventory	$ 57,104
Sales returns &		Transportation-in	5,680
allowances	13,720	Sales discounts	4,640
Purchase returns &		Sales	368,400
allowances	10,440	Purchase discounts	3,860
Gross profit on sales	122,514	Beginning inventory	?

Instructions

a Compute the amount of net sales.

b Compute the gross profit percentage.

c What percentage of net sales represents the cost of goods sold?

d Prepare a partial income statement utilizing all the accounts listed above, including the determination of the amount of the beginning inventory.

6A-2 Milano Company carried out the following transactions relating to the purchase of merchandise during the month of June.

June   2 Purchased merchandise from Valentine Company, $6,000; terms 2/10, n/30.

June   8 Purchased merchandise from Landslide Company, $9,000; terms 2/10, n/30.

June   9 Merchandise with a list price of $900, purchased from Valentine Company on June 2, was found to be defective. It was returned to the supplier accompanied by debit memorandum no. 515.

June 18 Paid Landslide Company's invoice of June 8, less cash discount.

June 25 Purchased merchandise from Landslide Company, $5,700; terms 2/10, n/30.

June 30 Paid Valentine Company's invoice of June 2.

The inventory of merchandise on June 1 was $27,600; on June 30, $23,520.

Instructions

a Journalize the above transactions, recording invoices at the gross amount.

b Prepare the cost of goods sold section of the income statement.

c What is the amount of accounts payable at the end of June? What would the amount of accounts payable be at the end of June if Milano Company followed the policy of recording purchase invoices at the net amount?

6A-3 The following transactions were completed by Brewer Company during the month of September, 19___.

Sept. **1** Purchased merchandise from Jensen Company, $2,000; terms 2/10, n/30.

Sept. **7** Purchased merchandise from Brand-Nu Corporation Ltd., $3,000; terms 2/10, n/30.

Sept. **8** Merchandise having a list price of $300, purchased from Jensen Company, was found to be defective. It was returned to the seller, accompanied by debit memorandum no. 382.

Sept. 17 Paid Brand-Nu Corporation's invoice of September 7, less cash discount.

Sept. 24 Purchased merchandise from Brand-Nu Corporation, $1,900; terms 2/10, n/30.

Sept. 30 Paid Jensen Company's invoice of September 1, taking into consideration the return of goods on September 8.

Assume that the merchandise inventory on September 1 was $8,240; on September 30, $7,815.

Instructions

a Journalize the above transactions, recording invoices at the net amount.

b Prepare the cost of goods sold section of the income statement.

c What is the amount of accounts payable at the end of September? What would the amount of accounts payable be at the end of September if Brewer Company followed the policy of recording purchase invoices at the gross amount?

6A-4 The merchandising transactions of Wyandotte Wholesale Company for the month of March are detailed below. The company's policy is to take advantage of all cash discounts offered by suppliers; purchase invoices are recorded at the net amount. In making sales the company grants credit terms of 2/10, n/30, and strictly enforces the 10-day limitation for granting discounts. The amounts listed as cash sales are net of sales discounts.

Mar. **2** Sold merchandise to Roland Co. for cash, $54,800.

Mar. 15 Sold merchandise on account to Happy Furniture Co., $24,700.

Mar. 16 Purchased merchandise from Azle Manufacturing Co., $31,600; terms 2/10, n/30 (to be recorded at net amount).

Mar. 16 Paid transportation charges on goods received from Azle Manufacturing Co., $1,210.

Mar. 18 Issued credit memorandum no. 361 to Happy Furniture Co. for allowance on damaged goods, $700.

Mar. 24 Purchased merchandise from Dorn Manufacturing Co., $28,500; terms 1/10, n/30 (to be recorded at net amount).

Mar. 25 Returned defective goods with invoice price of $1,500 to Dorn Manufacturing Co., accompanied by debit memorandum no. 85.

Mar. 25 Received cash from Happy Furniture Co. in full payment of account.

Mar. 26 Paid Azle Manufacturing Co. account in full.

Instructions

a Record the above transactions in three-column, running balance ledger accounts. (Cash, Accounts Receivable, Accounts Payable, Sales, etc.) Journal entries are not required.

b Prepare a partial income statement for March showing sales and cost of goods sold (in detail), and gross profit on sales. Assume the inventory at February 28 to be $19,000 and at March 31 to be $23,200.

c What is the amount of accounts payable at March 31? What would be the amount of accounts payable at March 31 if the company followed a policy of recording purchase invoices at the gross amount?

Group B

6B-1 The income statement of Taylor Company contained the following items, among others, for the year ended June 30, 19___.

Sales	$546,750	Ending inventory	$?
Purchases	347,287	Sales returns &	
Transportation-in	3,860	allowances	15,450
Purchase returns &		Beginning inventory	68,600
allowances	1,750	Purchase discounts	605
Sales discounts	5,100	Gross profit on sales	178,908

Instructions
a Compute the amount of net sales.
b Compute the gross profit percentage.
c What percentage of net sales represents the cost of goods sold?
d Prepare a partial income statement utilizing all the accounts listed above, including the determination of the amount of the ending inventory.

6B-2 The following transactions were completed by Dassa Company during the month of September, 19___.

Sept. 1 Purchased merchandise from Jensen Company, $2,000; terms 2/10, n/30.

Sept. 7 Purchased merchandise from Brand-Nu Corporation Ltd., $3,000; terms 2/10, n/30.

Sept. 8 Merchandise having a list price of $300, purchased from Jensen Company, was found to be defective. It was returned to the seller, accompanied by debit memorandum no. 382.

Sept. 17 Paid Brand-Nu Corporation's invoice of September 7, less cash discount.

Sept. 24 Purchased merchandise from Brand-Nu Corporation, $1,900; terms 2/10, n/30.

Sept. 30 Paid Jensen Company's invoice of September 1.

Assume that the merchandise inventory on September 1 was $9,200; on September 30, $7,840.

Instructions
a Journalize the above transactions, recording invoices at the gross amount.
b Prepare the cost of goods sold section of the income statement.
c What is the amount of accounts payable at the end of September? What would the amount of accounts payable be at the end of September if Dassa Company followed the policy of recording purchase invoices at the net amount?

6B-3 The Lerner Company completed the following transactions relating to the purchase of merchandise during the month of September, 19___. It is the policy of the company to record all purchase invoices at the net amount and to pay invoices within the discount period.

Sept. 1 Purchased merchandise from Galt Company, $8,000; terms 2/10, n/30.

Sept. 8 Purchased merchandise from Windsor Company, $12,000; terms 2/10, n/20.

Sept. 8 Merchandise with a list price of $1,200 purchased from Galt Company on September 1 was found to be defective. It was returned to the supplier accompanied by debit memorandum no. 382.

Sept. 18 Paid Windsor Company's invoice of September 8, less cash discount.

Sept. 25 Purchased merchandise from Windsor Company, $7,600; terms 2/10, n/30.

Sept. 30 Paid Galt Company's invoice of September 1, taking into consideration the return of defective goods on September 8.

The inventory of merchandise on September 1 was $32,960; on September 30, $31,260.

Instructions

a Journalize the above transactions, recording invoices at the net amount.

b Prepare the cost of goods sold section of the income statement.

c What is the amount of accounts payable at the end of September? What would be the amount of accounts payable at the end of September if the Lerner Company followed the policy of recording purchase invoices at the gross amount?

6B-4 Greenleaf Wholesale Company completed the following merchandising transactions during August. The company's policy calls for taking advantage of all cash discounts available to it from suppliers; purchase invoices are recorded at the net amount. In making sales, the company grants credit terms of 2/10, n/30 and strictly enforces the 10-day limitation. The amounts listed as cash sales below are net of sales discounts.

Aug. 3 Sold merchandise to Rider Company for cash, $27,400.

Aug. 16 Sold merchandise on account to Burnside Company, $12,350.

Aug. 16 Purchased merchandise from Adams Supply Company, $15,800; terms 2/10, n/30 (to be recorded at the *net* amount).

Aug. 17 Paid transportation charges on goods received from Adams Supply Company, $605.

Aug. 18 Issued credit memorandum no. 102 to Burnside Company for allowance on damaged goods, $350.

Aug. 24 Purchased merchandise from Logg Manufacturing Co., $14,250; terms 1/10, n/30 (to be recorded at the net amount).

Aug. 25 Returned defective goods with invoice price of $750 to Logg Manufacturing Co., accompanied by debit memorandum no. 122.

Aug. 26 Received cash from Burnside Company in full payment of account.

Aug. 26 Paid Adams Supply Company account in full.

Instructions

a Record the above transactions in three-column running balance ledger accounts. (Cash, Accounts Receivable, Accounts Payable, Sales, etc.) Journal entries are not required.

b Prepare a partial income statement for August showing sales and cost of goods sold (in detail), and gross profit on sales. Assume the inventory at July 31 to be $9,500 and the inventory at August 31 to be $11,600.

c What is the amount of accounts payable at August 31? What would be the amount of accounts payable at August 31 if the company followed a policy of recording purchase invoices at the gross amount?

BUSINESS DECISION PROBLEM 6

Bridge Company purchased merchandise from Marble Company on five occasions during a given year. Each purchase was in the amount of $40,000 and was subject to credit terms of 2/10, n/30. Bridge Company waited the full 30 days allowable under the credit terms before making payment in any of the five cases.

At the year-end, a public accountant was retained to conduct an audit of Bridge Company. He observed that the company was in a strong cash position and maintained, in addition to its current account and payroll account, a $30,000 savings account at a local bank which paid interest at 4% yearly on savings accounts. There had been no deposits or withdrawals in the bank savings account during the year. When the public accountant asked the owner of Bridge Company why cash discounts were not taken on merchandise purchases, he was informed that the company preferred to conserve its cash and earn interest by depositing excess funds in bank savings accounts.

Instructions

a Compute the dollar amount that Bridge Company could have saved during the year by paying the five Marble Company invoices within the discount period. Also compute the interest earned during the year on the savings deposit at the bank.

b Compute the effective annual rate of interest Bridge Company incurred by not paying the Marble Company invoices within the discount period.

c Put yourself in the role of the public accountant and draft a note of suggestion and explanation to the owner concerning the company's policy on cash discounts.

SEVEN DATA PROCESSING SYSTEMS MANUAL MECHANICAL AND ELECTRONIC

In the early chapters of an introductory accounting book, basic accounting principles can most conveniently be discussed in terms of a small business with only a handful of customers and suppliers. This simplified model of a business has been used in preceding chapters to demonstrate the analysis and recording of the more common types of business transactions.

The recording procedures illustrated thus far call for recording each transaction by an entry in the journal, and then posting each debit and credit from the journal to the proper account in the ledger. We must now face the practical problem of streamlining and speeding up this recording process so that the accounting department can keep pace with the rapid flow of transactions in a modern business.

MANUAL DATA PROCESSING

In a large business there may be hundreds or even thousands of transactions every day. To handle a large volume of transactions rapidly and efficiently, it is helpful to group the transactions into like classes and to use a specialized journal for each class. This will greatly reduce the amount of detailed recording work and will also permit a division of labor, since each special-purpose journal can be handled by a different employee. The great majority of transactions (perhaps as much as 90 or 95%) usually fall into four types. These four types and the four corresponding special journals are as follows:

Type of Transaction	Name of Special Journal
Sales of merchandise on credit	Sales journal
Purchases of merchandise on credit	Purchases journal
Receipts of cash	Cash receipts journal
Payments of cash	Cash payments journal

In addition to these four special journals, a **general journal** will be used for recording transactions which do not fit into any of the above four types. The general journal is the same book of original entry illustrated in preceding chapters; the adjective "general" is added merely to distinguish it from the special journals.

Sales journal

Illustrated below is a sales journal containing entries for all sales on account made during November by the Seaside Company. Whenever merchandise is sold on credit, several copies of a sales invoice are prepared. The information listed on a sales invoice usually includes the date of the sale, the serial number of the invoice, the customer's name, the amount of the sale, and the credit terms. One copy of the sales invoice is used by the seller as the basis for an entry in the sales journal.

Sales Journal　　Page 1

	Date		Account Debited	Invoice No.	√	Amount
Entries for sales on credit during November	19__ Nov.	2	John Adams	301	√	450
		4	Harold Black	302	√	1,000
		5	Robert Cross	303	√	975
		11	H. R. Davis	304	√	620
		18	C. D. Early	305	√	900
		23	John Frost	306	√	400
		29	D. H. Gray	307	√	1,850
						6,195
						(5) (41)

Note that the illustrated sales journal contains special columns for recording each of these aspects of the sales transaction, except the credit terms. If it is the practice of the business to offer different credit terms to different customers, a column may be inserted in the sales journal to show the terms of sale. In this illustration it is assumed that all sales are made on terms of 2/10, n/30; consequently, there is no need to write the credit terms as part of each entry. **Only sales on credit are entered in the sales journal.** When merchandise is sold for cash, the transaction is recorded in a cash receipts journal, which is illustrated later in this chapter.

ADVANTAGES OF THE SALES JOURNAL Note that each of the above seven sales transactions is recorded on a single line. Each entry consists of a debit to a customer's account; the offsetting credit to the Sales account is understood without being written, because sales on account are the only transactions recorded in this special journal.

An entry in a sales journal need not include an explanation; if more information about the transaction is desired it can be obtained by referring to the file copy of the sales invoice. The invoice number is listed in the sales journal as part of each entry. The one-line entry in the sales journal requires much less writing than would be required to record a sales transaction in the general journal. Since there may be several hundred or several thousand sales transactions each month, the time saved in recording transactions in this streamlined manner becomes quite important.

Every entry in the sales journal represents a debit to a customer's account. Charges to customers' accounts should be posted daily so that each customer's account will always be up-to-date and available for use in making decisions relating to collections and to the further extension of credit. A check mark ($\sqrt{}$) is placed in the sales journal opposite each amount posted to a customer's account, to indicate that the posting has been made.

Another advantage of the special journal for sales is the great saving of time in posting credits to the Sales account. Remember that every amount entered in the sales journal represents a credit to Sales. In the illustrated sales journal above, there are seven transactions (and in practice there might be 700). Instead of posting a separate credit to the Sales account for each sales transaction, we can wait until the end of the month and make one posting to the Sales account for the total of the amounts recorded in the sales journal.

In the illustrated sales journal for November, the sales on account totaled $6,195. On November 30 this amount is posted as a credit to the Sales account, and the ledger account number for Sales (41) is entered under the total figure in the sales journal to show that the posting operation has been performed. The total sales figure is also posted as a debit to ledger account no. 5, Accounts Receivable. To make clear the reason for this posting to Accounts Receivable, an explanation of the nature of controlling accounts and subsidiary ledgers is necessary.

Controlling accounts and subsidiary ledgers

In preceding chapters all transactions involving accounts receivable from customers have been posted to a single account entitled Accounts Receivable. Under this simplified procedure, however, it is not easy to look up the amount receivable from a given customer. In practice, nearly all businesses which sell goods on credit maintain a separate account receivable with each customer. If there are 4,000 customers this would require a ledger with 4,000 accounts receivable, in addition to the accounts for other assets, and for liabilities, owner's equity, revenue, and expense. Such a ledger would be cumbersome and unwieldy. Also, the trial balance prepared from such a large ledger would be a very long one. If the trial balance showed the ledger to be out of balance, the task of locating the error or errors would be most difficult. All these factors indicate that it is not desirable to have too many accounts in one ledger. Fortunately, a simple solution is available; this solution is to divide up the ledger into several separate ledgers.

In a business which has a large number of accounts with customers and creditors, it is customary to divide the ledger into three separate ledgers. All the accounts with *customers* are placed in alphabetical order in a separate ledger, called the *accounts receivable ledger.* All the accounts with *creditors* are arranged alphabetically in another ledger called the *accounts payable ledger.* Both of these ledgers are known as *subsidiary ledgers.*

After thus segregating the accounts receivable from customers in one subsidiary ledger and placing the accounts payable to creditors in a second subsidiary ledger, we have left in the original ledger all the revenue and expense accounts and also all the balance sheet accounts except those with customers and creditors. This ledger is called the *general ledger,* to distinguish it from the subsidiary ledgers.

When the numerous individual accounts with customers are placed in a subsidiary ledger, an account entitled Accounts Receivable continues to be maintained in the general ledger. This account shows the total amount due from all customers; in other words, this single controlling account in the general ledger takes the place of the numerous customers' accounts which have been removed to form a subsidiary ledger. The general ledger is still in balance because the controlling account, Accounts Receivable, has a balance equal to the total of the customers' accounts which were removed from the general ledger. Agreement of the controlling account with the sum of the accounts receivable in the subsidiary ledger also provides assurance of accuracy in the subsidiary ledger.

A controlling account entitled Accounts Payable is also kept in the general ledger in place of the numerous accounts with creditors which have been removed to form the accounts payable subsidiary ledger. Because the two controlling accounts represent the total amounts receivable from customers and payable to creditors, a trial balance can be prepared from the general ledger alone.

POSTING TO SUBSIDIARY LEDGERS AND TO CONTROL ACCOUNTS To illustrate the posting of subsidiary ledgers and of control accounts, let us refer again to the sales journal illustrated on page 196. Each debit to a customer's account is posted currently during the month from the sales journal to the customer's account in the accounts receivable ledger. The accounts in this subsidiary ledger are usually kept in alphabetical order and are not numbered. When a posting is made to a customer's account, a check mark ($\sqrt{}$) is placed in the sales journal as evidence that the posting has been made to the subsidiary ledger.

At month-end the sales journal is totaled. The total sales for the month, $6,195, are posted as a credit to the Sales account and also as a debit to the controlling account, Accounts Receivable, in the general ledger. The controlling account will, therefore, equal the total of all the customers' accounts in the subsidiary ledger.

The diagram on this page shows the day-to-day posting of individual entries from the sales journal to the subsidiary ledger. The diagram also shows the month-end posting of the total of the sales journal to the two

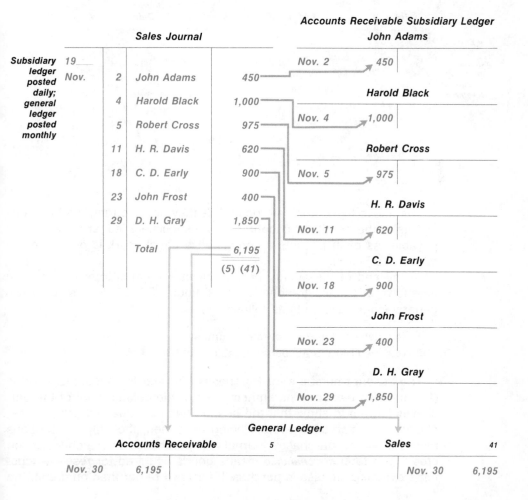

general ledger accounts affected, Accounts Receivable and Sales. Note that the amount of the monthly debit to the controlling account is equal to the sum of the debits posted to the subsidiary ledger.

Purchases journal

The handling of purchase transactions when a purchases journal is used follows a pattern quite similar to the one described for the sales journal.

Assume that the purchases journal illustrated on this page contains all purchases of merchandise on credit during the month by the Seaside Company. The invoice date is shown in a separate column because the cash discount period begins on this date.

Purchases Journal — Page 1

	Date		Account Credited	Invoice Date		√	Amount
Entries for purchases on credit during November	19__ Nov.	2	Alabama Supply Co.	19__ Nov.	2	√	3,325
		4	Barker & Bright		4	√	700
		10	Canning & Sons		9	√	500
		17	Davis Co.		15	√	900
		27	Excelsior Ltd.		25	√	1,825
							7,250
							(50) (21)

The above five entries are posted as they occur during the month as credits to the creditors' accounts in the subsidiary ledger for accounts payable. As each posting is completed a check mark is placed in the purchases journal.

At the end of the month the purchases journal is totaled and ruled as shown in the illustration. The total figure, $7,250, is posted to two general ledger accounts as follows:

1 As a debit to the Purchases account
2 As a credit to the Accounts Payable controlling account

The account numbers for Purchases (50) and for Accounts Payable (21) are then placed in parentheses below the column total of the purchases journal to show that the posting has been made.

Under the particular system being described, the only transactions recorded in the purchases journal are purchases of merchandise on credit. The term *merchandise* means goods acquired for resale to customers. If merchandise is purchased for cash rather than on credit, the transaction should be recorded in the cash payments journal, as illustrated on pages 206 and 207.

The diagram below illustrates the day-to-day posting of individual entries from the purchases journal to the accounts with creditors in the subsidiary ledger for accounts payable. The diagram also shows how the column total of the purchases journal is posted at the end of the month to the general ledger accounts, Purchases and Accounts Payable. One objective of this diagram is to emphasize that the amount of the monthly credit to the control account is equal to the sum of the credits posted to the subsidiary ledger.

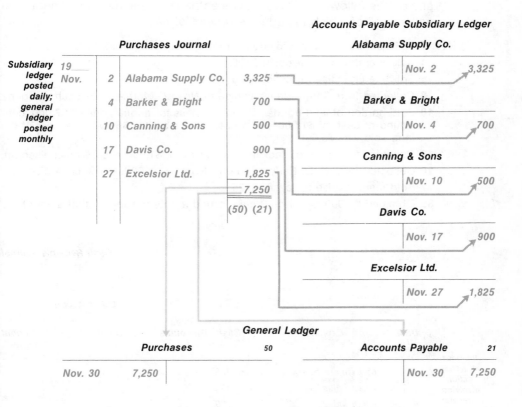

When assets other than merchandise are being acquired, as, for example, a delivery truck or an office desk for use in the business, the journal to be used depends upon whether a cash payment is made. If assets of this type are purchased for cash, the transaction should be entered in the cash payments journal; if the transaction is on credit, the general journal is used. The purchases journal is not used to record the acquisition of these assets because the total of this journal is posted to the Purchases account and this account (as explained in Chapter 5) is used in determining the cost of goods sold.

Cash receipts journal

All transactions involving the receipt of cash are recorded in the cash receipts journal. One common example is the sale of merchandise for cash. As each cash sale is made, it is rung up on a cash register. At the end of the day the total of the cash sales is computed by striking the total key on the register. This total is entered in the cash receipts journal, which therefore contains one entry for the total cash sales of the day. For other types of cash receipts, such as the collection of accounts receivable from customers, a separate journal entry may be made for each transaction. The cash receipts journal illustrated below and on the following page contains entries for selected November transactions, all of which include the receipt of cash.

Nov. 1 R. B. Jones invested $25,000 cash to establish the Seaside Company.

4 Sold merchandise for cash, $300.

5 Sold merchandise for cash, $400.

8 Collected from John Adams invoice of Nov. 2, $450 less 2% cash discount.

10 Sold portion of land not needed in business for a total price of $7,000, consisting of cash of $1,000 and a note receivable for $6,000. The cost of the land sold was $5,000.

12 Collected from Harold Black invoice of Nov. 4, $1,000 less 2% cash discount.

20 Collected from C. D. Early invoice of Nov. 18, $900 less 2% cash discount.

27 Sold merchandise for cash, $125.

30 Obtained $4,000 loan from bank. Issued a note payable in that amount.

Cash Receipts Journal

	Date		Explanation	Cash	Sales Discounts	Other Accounts Name	LP	Amount
Includes all transactions involving receipt of cash	19___ Nov.	1	Investment by owner	25,000				
		4	Cash sales	300				
		5	Cash sales	400				
		8	Invoice Nov. 2, less 2%	441	9			
		10	Sale of land	1,000		Notes Receivable	3	6,000
		12	Invoice Nov. 4, less 2%	980	20			
		20	Invoice Nov. 18, less 2%	882	18			
		27	Cash sales	125				
		30	Obtained bank loan	4,000				
				33,128	47			6,000
				(1)	(43)			(X)

Debits

Note that the cash receipts journal illustrated below has three debit columns and three credit columns as follows:

Debits:

1 Cash. This column is used for every entry, because only those transactions which include the receipt of cash are entered in this special journal.

2 Sales discounts. This column is used to accumulate the sales discounts allowed during the month. Only one line of the cash receipts book is required to record a collection from a customer who takes advantage of a cash discount.

3 Other accounts. This third debit column is used for debits to any and all accounts other than cash and sales discounts, and space is provided for writing in the name of the account. For example, the entry of November 10 in the illustrated cash receipts journal shows that cash and a note receivable were obtained when land was sold. The amount of cash received, $1,000, is entered in the Cash debit column, the account title Notes Receivable is written in the Other Accounts debit column and the amount of the debit to this account, $6,000. These two debits are offset by credit entries to Land, $5,000, and to Gain on Sale of Land, $2,000, in the Other Accounts credit column.

Credits:

1 Accounts receivable. This column is used to list the credits to customers' accounts as receivables are collected. The name of the customer is written in the space entitled Account Credited to the left of the Accounts Receivable column.

2 Sales. The existence of this column will save posting by permitting the accumulation of all sales for cash during the month and the posting of the column total at the end of the month as a credit to the Sales account (41).

Page 1

Account Credited	Credits				
	Accounts Receivable			Other Accounts	
	√	Amount	Sales	LP	Amount
R. B. Jones, Capital				30	25,000
			300		
			400		
John Adams	√	450			
Land				11	5,000 ⎱
Gain on Sale of Land				40	2,000 ⎰
Harold Black	√	1,000			
C. D. Early	√	900			
			125		
Notes Payable				20	4,000
		2,350	825		36,000
		(5)	(41)		(X)

3 Other accounts. This column is used for credits to any and all accounts other than Accounts Receivable and Sales. In some instances, a transaction may require credits to two accounts. Such cases are handled by using two lines of the special journal, as illustrated by the transaction of November 10, which required credits to both the Land account and to Gain on Sale of Land.

POSTING THE CASH RECEIPTS JOURNAL It is convenient to think of the posting of a cash receipts journal as being divided into two phases. The first phase consists of the daily posting of individual amounts throughout the month; the second phase consists of the posting of column totals at the end of the month.

Posting during the month Daily posting of the Accounts Receivable credits column is desirable. Each amount is posted to an individual customer's account in the accounts receivable subsidiary ledger. A check mark ($\sqrt{}$) is placed in the cash receipts journal alongside each item posted to a customer's account to show that the posting operation has been performed. When debits and credits to customers' accounts are posted daily, the current status of each customer's account is available for use in making decisions as to further granting of credit and as a guide to collection efforts on past-due accounts.

The debits and credits in the Other Accounts sections of the cash receipts journal may be posted daily or at convenient intervals during the month. If this portion of the posting work is done on a current basis, less detailed work will be left for the busy period at the end of the month. As the postings of individual items are made, the number of the ledger account debited or credited is entered in the LP column of the cash receipts journal opposite the item posted. Evidence is thus provided in the special journal as to which items have been posted.

Posting column totals at month-end At the end of the month, the cash receipts journal is ruled as shown on pages 202 and 203. Before posting any of the column totals, it is first important to prove that *the sum of the debit column totals is equal to the sum of the credit column totals.*

After the totals of the cash receipts journal have been crossfooted, the following column totals are posted:

1 Cash debit column. Posted as a debit to the Cash account.
2 Sales Discounts debit column. Posted as a debit to the Sales Discounts account.
3 Accounts Receivable credit column. Posted as a credit to the controlling account, Accounts Receivable.
4 Sales credit column. Posted as a credit to the Sales account.

As each column total is posted to the appropriate account in the general ledger, the ledger account number is entered in parentheses just below the column total in the special journal. This notation shows that the column total has been posted and also indicates the account to which the posting was made. The totals of the Other Accounts columns in both the debit and credit sections of the special journal are not posted, because the amounts listed in the column affect various general ledger accounts and have already been posted as individual items. The symbol (X) may be placed below the totals of these two columns to indicate that no posting is made.

Cash payments journal

Another widely used special journal is the cash payments journal, sometimes called the cash disbursements journal, in which all payments of cash are recorded. Among the more common of these transactions are payments of accounts payable to creditors, payment of operating expenses, and cash purchases of merchandise.

The cash payments journal illustrated on pages 206 and 207 contains entries for all November transactions of the Seaside Company which required the payment of cash.

Nov. 1 Paid rent on store building for November, $800.

2 Purchased merchandise for cash, $500.

8 Paid Barker & Bright for invoice of Nov. 4, $700 less 2%.

9 Bought land, $15,000, and building, $35,000, for future use in business. Paid cash of $20,000 and signed a promissory note for the balance of $30,000. (Land and building were acquired in a single transaction.)

17 Paid salesmen's salaries, $600

26 Paid Davis Co. for invoice of Nov. 17, $900 less 2%.

27 Purchased merchandise for cash, $400.

28 Purchased merchandise for cash, $650.

29 Paid for newspaper advertising, $50.

29 Paid for three-year insurance policy, $720.

Note in the illustrated cash payments journal that the three credit columns are located to the left of the three debit columns; any sequence of columns is satisfactory in a special journal as long as the column headings clearly distinguish debits from credits. The Cash column is often placed first in both the cash receipts journal and the cash payments journal because it is the column used in every transaction.

Good internal control over cash disbursements requires that all payments be made by cheque. The cheques are serially numbered and as each transaction is entered in the cash payments journal, the cheque number is listed in a special column provided just to the right of the date column. An unbroken sequence of cheque numbers in this column gives assurance that every cheque issued has been recorded in the accounting records.

The use of the six money columns in the illustrated cash payments journal parallels the procedures described for the cash receipts journal.

Cash Payments Journal

	Date	Cheque No.	Explanation	Cash	Purchase Discounts	Other Accounts Name	LP	Amount
						Credits		
Includes all trans- actions involving payment of cash	19__ Nov. 1	101	Paid November rent	800				
	2	102	Purchased merchandise	500				
	8	103	Invoice of Nov. 4, less 2%	686	14			
	9	104	Bought land and building	20,000		Notes Payable	20	30,000
	17	105	Paid salesmen	600				
	26	106	Invoice of Nov. 17, less 2%	882	18			
	27	107	Purchased merchandise	400				
	27	108	Purchased merchandise	650				
	29	109	Newspaper advertisement	50				
	29	110	Three-year ins. policy	720				
				25,288	32			30,000
				(1)	(52)			(X)

POSTING THE CASH PAYMENTS JOURNAL The posting of the cash payments journal falls into the same two phases already described for the cash receipts journal. The first phase consists of the daily posting of entries in the Accounts Payable debit column to the individual accounts of creditors in the accounts payable subsidiary ledger. Check marks (√) are entered opposite these items to show that the posting has been made. If a creditor telephones to inquire about any aspect of his account, information on all purchases and payments made to date is readily available in the accounts payable subsidiary ledger.

The individual debit and credit entries in the Other Accounts columns of the cash payments journal may be posted daily or at convenient intervals during the month. As the postings of these individual items are made, the page number of the ledger account debited or credited is entered in the LP column of the cash payments journal opposite the item posted.

The second phase of posting the cash payments journal is performed at the end of the month. When all the transactions of the month have been journalized, the cash payments journal is ruled as shown on pages 206 and 207, and the six money columns are totaled. The equality of debits and credits is then proved before posting.

After the totals of the cash payments journal have been proved to be in balance, the totals of the columns for Cash, Purchase Discounts, Accounts Payable, and Purchases are posted to the corresponding accounts in the general ledger. The numbers of the accounts to which

Account Debited	Debits				
	Accounts Payable			Other Accounts	
	√	Amount	Purchases	LP	Amount
Store Rent Expense				54	800
Purchases			500		
Barker & Bright	√	700			
Land				11	15,000⎫
Building				12	35,000⎭
Sales Salaries Expense				53	600
Davis Co.	√	900			
Purchases			400		
Purchases			650		
Advertising Expense				55	50
Unexpired Insurance				6	720
		1,600	1,550		52,170
		(21)	(50)		(X)

these postings are made are listed in parentheses just below the respective column totals in the cash payments journal. The totals of the Other Accounts columns in both the debit and credit section of this special journal are not to be posted, and the symbol (X) may be placed below the totals of these two columns to indicate that no posting is required.

The general journal

When all transactions involving cash or the purchase and sale of merchandise are recorded in special journals, only a few types of transactions remain to be entered in the general journal. Examples include the purchase or sale of plant and equipment on credit, the return of merchandise for credit to a supplier, and the return of merchandise by a customer for credit to his account. The general journal is also used for the recording of adjusting and closing entries at the end of the accounting period.

The following transactions of the Seaside Company during November could not conveniently be handled in any of the four special journals and were therefore entered in the general journal.

Nov. 25 A customer, John Frost, was permitted to return for credit $50 worth of merchandise that had been sold to him on Nov. 23.

28 The Seaside Company returned to a supplier, Excelsior, Ltd., for credit $300 worth of the merchandise purchased on Nov. 27.

29 Purchased for use in the business office equipment costing $1,225. Agreed to make payment within 30 days to XYZ Equipment Co.

General Journal   Page 1

	Date		Account Titles and Explanation	LP	Dr	Cr
	19___					
	Nov.	25	Sales Returns and Allowances	42	50	
			Accounts Receivable, John Frost . . .	5/√		50
			Allowed credit to customer for return of mer-			
			chandise from sale of Nov. 23.			
		28	Accounts Payable, Excelsior, Ltd.	21/√	300	
			Purchase Returns and Allowances . . .	51		300
			Returned to supplier for credit a portion of			
			merchandise purchased on Nov. 27.			
		29	Office Equipment.	14	1,225	
			Accounts Payable, XYZ Equipment			
			Co.	21/√		1,225
			Purchased office equipment on 30-day credit.			

Transactions which do not fit any of the four special journals

Each of the above entries includes a debit or credit to a controlling account (Accounts Receivable or Accounts Payable) and also identifies by name a particular creditor or customer. When a controlling account is debited or credited by a *general journal entry,* the debit or credit must be posted twice: one posting to the controlling account in the general ledger and another posting to a customer's account or a creditor's account in a subsidiary ledger. This double posting is necessary to keep the controlling account in agreement with the subsidiary ledger.

For example, in the illustrated entry of November 25 for the return of merchandise by a customer, the credit part of the entry is posted twice:

1 To the Accounts Receivable controlling account in the general ledger; this posting is evidenced by listing the account number (5) in the LP column of the general journal.

2 To the account of John Frost in the subsidiary ledger for accounts receivable; this posting is indicated by the check mark (√) placed in the LP column of the general journal.

Showing the source of postings in ledger accounts

When a general journal and several special journals are in use, the ledger accounts should indicate the book of original entry from which each debit and credit was posted. An identifying symbol is placed opposite each entry in the reference column of the account. The symbols used in this text are as follows:

S1   meaning page 1 of the sales journal
P1   meaning page 1 of the purchases journal
CR1   meaning page 1 of the cash receipts journal
CP1   meaning page 1 of the cash payments journal
J1   meaning page 1 of the general journal

Subsidiary ledger accounts

The following illustration shows a customer's account in a subsidiary ledger for accounts receivable.

Name of Customer

Date			Ref	Debit	Credit	Balance
19___						
July	1		S1	400		400
	20		S3	200		600
Aug.	4		CR7		400	200
	15		S6	120		320

Subsidiary ledger: account receivable

The advantage of this three-column form of account is that it shows at a glance the present balance receivable from the customer. The current amount of a customer's account is often needed as a guide to collection activities, or as a basis for granting additional credit. In studying the above illustration note also that the Reference column shows the source of each debit and credit.

Accounts appearing in the accounts receivable subsidiary ledger are assumed to have debit balances. If one of these customers' accounts should acquire a credit balance by overpayment or for any other reason, the word *credit* should be written after the amount in the Balance column.

The same three-column form of account is also generally used for creditors' accounts in an accounts payable subsidiary ledger, as indicated by the following illustration:

Name of Creditor

Date			Ref	Debit	Credit	Balance
19___						
July	10		P1		625	625
	25		P2		100	725
Aug.	8		CP4	725		0
	12		P3		250	250

Subsidiary ledger: account payable

Accounts in the accounts payable subsidiary ledger normally have credit balances. If by reason of payment in advance or accidental over-payment, one of these accounts should acquire a debit balance, the word *debit* should be written after the amount in the Balance column.

As previously stated, both the accounts receivable and accounts payable subsidiary ledgers are customarily arranged in alphabetical order and account numbers are not used. This arrangement permits unlimited expansion of the subsidiary ledgers, as accounts with new customers and creditors can be inserted in proper alphabetical sequence.

Ledger accounts

THE GENERAL LEDGER The general ledger accounts of the Seaside Company illustrated on pages 210–213 indicate the source of postings from the various books of original entry. The subsidiary ledger accounts appear on pages 213–214. To gain a clear understanding of the procedures for posting special journals, the student should trace each entry in the illustrated special journals into the general ledger accounts and also to the subsidiary ledger accounts where appropriate. The general ledger accounts are shown in T-account form in order to distinguish them more emphatically from the accounts in the subsidiary ledgers.

Note that the Cash account contains only one debit entry and one credit entry, although there were many cash transactions during the month. The one debit, $33,128, represents the total cash received during the month and was posted from the cash receipts journal on November 30. Similarly, the one credit entry of $25,288 was posted on November 30 from the cash payments journal and represents the total of all cash payments made during the month.

Cash

General ledger accounts	19					19					
	Nov.	30		CR1	33,128	Nov.	30		CP1	25,288

Notes Receivable

19									
Nov.	10		CR1	6,000					

Accounts Receivable

19					19				
Nov.	30		S1	6,195	Nov.	25		J1	50
						30		CR1	2,350

Unexpired Insurance · 6

19__										
Nov.	29		CP1	720						

Land · 11

19__					19__					
Nov.	9		CP1	15,000	Nov.	10		CR1	5,000	

Building · 12

19__										
Nov.	9		CP1	35,000						

Office Equipment · 14

19__										
Nov.	29		J1	1,225						

Notes Payable · 20

					19__					
					Nov.	9		CP1	30,000	
						30		CR1	4,000	

Accounts Payable · 21

19__					19__					
Nov.	28		J1	300	Nov.	29		J1	1,225	
	30		CP1	1,600		30		P1	7,250	

R. B. Jones, Capital · 30

					19__					
					Nov.	1		CR1	25,000	

Gain on Sale of Land · 40

					19__					
					Nov.	10		CR1	2,000	

Sales 41

				19__				
				Nov.	30		CR1	825
					30		S1	6,195

Sales Returns and Allowances 42

19__								
Nov.	25		J1	50				

Sales Discounts 43

19__								
Nov.	30		CR1	47				

Purchases 50

19__								
Nov.	30		CP1	1,550				
	30		P1	7,250				

Purchase Returns and Allowances 51

				19__				
				Nov.	28		J1	300

Purchase Discounts 52

				19__				
				Nov.	30		CP1	32

Sales Salaries Expense 53

19__								
Nov.	17		CP1	600				

Store Rent Expense 54

19__								
Nov.	1		CP1	800				

Advertising Expense   55

19__							
Nov.	29		CP1	50			

ACCOUNTS RECEIVABLE LEDGER   The subsidiary ledger for accounts receivable appears as follows after the posting of the various journals has been completed.

John Adams

Customers' accounts

19__						
Nov.	2		S1	450		450
	8		CR1		450	0

Harold Black

19__						
Nov.	4		S1	1,000		1,000
	12		CR1		1,000	0

Robert Cross

19__						
Nov.	5		S1	975		975

H. R. Davis

19__						
Nov.	11		S1	620		620

C. D. Early

19__						
Nov.	18		S1	900		900
	20		CR1		900	0

John Frost

19__						
Nov.	23		S1	400		400
	25		J1		50	350

D. H. Gray

19__						
Nov.	29		S1	1,850		1,850

ACCOUNTS PAYABLE LEDGER The accounts with creditors in the accounts payable subsidiary ledger are as follows:

Alabama Supply Co.

	19__					
Creditors' accounts	Nov.	2		P1		3,325	3,325

Barker & Bright

19__						
Nov.	4		P1		700	700
	8		CP1	700		0

Canning & Sons

19__						
Nov.	10		P1		500	500

Davis Co.

19__						
Nov.	17		P1		900	900
	26		CP1	900		0

Excelsior Ltd.

19__						
Nov.	27		P1		1,825	1,825
	28		J1	300		1,525

XYZ Equipment Co.

19__						
Nov.	29		J1		1,225	1,225

Proving the ledgers

At the end of each accounting period, proof of the equality of debits and credits in the general ledger is established by preparation of a trial balance, as illustrated in preceding chapters. When controlling accounts and subsidiary ledgers are in use, it is also necessary to prove that each subsidiary ledger is in agreement with its controlling account. This proof is accomplished by preparing a schedule of the balances of accounts in each subsidiary ledger and determining that the totals of these schedules agree with the balances of the corresponding control accounts.

SEASIDE COMPANY
Trial Balance
November 30, 19___

Cash	$ 7,840	
Notes receivable	6,000	
Accounts receivable (see schedule below)	3,795	
Unexpired insurance	720	
Land	10,000	
Building	35,000	
Office equipment	1,225	
Notes payable		$34,000
Accounts payable (see schedule below)		6,575
R. B. Jones, capital		25,000
Gain on sale of land		2,000
Sales		7,020
Sales returns and allowances	50	
Sales discounts	47	
Purchases	8,800	
Purchase returns and allowances		300
Purchase discounts		32
Sales salaries expense	600	
Store rent expense	800	
Advertising expense	50	
	$74,927	$74,927

Schedule of Accounts Receivable
November 30, 19___

Robert Cross	$ 975
H. R. Davis	620
John Frost	350
D. H. Gray	1,850
Total (per balance of controlling account)	$3,795

Schedule of Accounts Payable
November 30, 19___

Alabama Supply Co.	$3,325
Canning & Sons	500
Excelsior Ltd.	1,525
XYZ Equipment Co.	1,225
Total (per balance of controlling account)	$6,575

Variations in special journals

The number of columns to be included in each special journal and the number of special journals to be used will depend upon the nature of the particular business and especially upon the volume of the various kinds of transactions. For example, the desirability of including a Sales Discounts column in the cash receipts journal depends upon whether a business offers discounts to its customers for prompt payment and whether the customers frequently take advantage of such discounts.

A retail store may find that customers frequently return merchandise for credit. To record efficiently this large volume of sales returns, the store may establish a sales returns and allowances journal. A purchase returns and allowances journal may also be desirable if returns of goods to suppliers occur frequently.

Special journals should be regarded as labor-saving devices which may be designed with any number of columns appropriate to the needs of the particular business. A business will usually benefit by establishing a special journal for any type of transaction that occurs quite frequently.

Direct posting from invoices

In many business concerns the efficiency of data processing is increased by posting sales invoices directly to the customers' accounts in the accounts receivable ledger rather than copying sales invoices into a sales journal and then posting to accounts in the subsidiary ledger. If the sales invoices are serially numbered, a file or binder of duplicate sales invoices arranged in numerical order may take the place of a formal sales journal. By accounting for each serial number, it is possible to be certain that all sales invoices are included. At the end of the month, the invoices are totaled on an adding machine, and a general journal entry is made debiting the Accounts Receivable controlling account and crediting Sales for the total of the month's sales invoices.

Direct posting may also be used in recording purchase invoices. As soon as purchase invoices have been verified and approved, credits to the creditors' accounts in the accounts payable ledger may be posted directly from the purchase invoices.

The trend toward direct posting from invoices to subsidiary ledgers is mentioned here as further evidence that accounting records and procedures can be designed in a variety of ways to meet the individual needs of different business concerns.

MECHANICAL DATA PROCESSING

The processing of accounting data may be performed manually, mechanically, or electronically. The term *data processing* includes the preparation of source documents (such as invoices and cheques) and the flow of the data contained in these source media through the major account-ing steps of recording, classifying, and summarizing. A well-designed system produces an uninterrupted flow of all essential data needed by management for planning and controlling business operations.

Unit record for each transaction

Our discussion has thus far been limited to a manual accounting system. One of the points we have emphasized is that an immediate record should be made of every financial transaction. The *medium* used to make this record is usually a document or form, such as an invoice or a cheque. This concept of a unit record for each transaction is an important one as we consider the alternatives of processing these media by accounting machines, by punched cards, or by a computer. Regardless of whether we use mechanical or electronic equipment, the source document repre-senting a single transaction is a basic element of the accounting process.

Use of office equipment in a manual data processing system

Manually kept records are a convenient means of demonstrating ac-counting principles, and they are also used by a great many small busi-nesses. Strictly defined, a manual system of processing accounting data would call for handwritten journals, ledgers, and financial statements. Even in a small business with some handwritten records, however, the use of office machines and laborsaving devices such as cash registers, adding machines, desk calculators, and multicopy forms has become standard practice.

Simultaneous preparation of documents, journals, and ledgers

Traditionally, each business transaction was recorded, copied, and re-copied. A transaction was first evidenced by a source document such as a sales invoice, then copied into a journal (book of original entry), and later posted to a ledger. This step-by-step sequence of creating accounting records is time-consuming and leaves room for the introduc-tion of errors at each step. Whenever a figure, an account title, or an account number is copied, the danger of introducing errors exists. This is true regardless of whether the copying is done with pen and ink or by punching a machine keyboard. The copying process is subject to human errors. From this premise it follows that if several accounting records can be created by writing a transaction only once, the recording process will be not only faster but also more accurate.

Accounting machines

The development of accounting machines designed to create several accounting records with a single writing of a transaction has progressed at a fantastic rate. Machines with typewriter keyboards and computing mechanisms were early developments useful in preparing journals, invoices, payrolls, and other records requiring the typing of names and the computation of amounts. *Accounting machines* is a term usually applied to electromechanical equipment capable of performing arithmetic functions and used to produce a variety of accounting records and reports.

Punched cards and tabulating equipment

Punched cards are a widely used medium for recording accounting data. Information such as amounts, names, account numbers, and other details is recorded by punching holes in appropriate columns and rows of a standard-sized card, usually by means of a key-punch machine. The information punched on the cards can then be read and processed by machines.

Every business receives original documents such as invoices and cheques in many shapes and sizes. By punching the information on each such document into a card, we create a document of standard size which machines and computers can use in creating records and reports. For example, once the information on sales invoices has been punched into cards, these cards can be run through machines to produce a schedule of accounts receivable, an analysis of sales by product, by territory, and by each salesman, and a listing of commissions earned by salesmen.

Processing accounting data by means of punched cards may be viewed as three major steps, with specially designed machines for each step. The first step is that of recording data; a machine often used for this purpose is an electrically operated *key punch* with a keyboard similar to that of a typewriter.

The second major step is classifying or sorting the data into related groups or categories. For this step a machine called a *sorter* is used. The sorter reads the information on each punched card and then arranges the cards in a particular order, or sorts a deck of cards into groups based on the relationship of the data punched into the cards.

The third major step is summarizing the data. This step is performed by a *tabulating machine,* which has an *output* of printed information resulting from the classifying and totaling of the data on the cards.

Automated data processing

Automated data processing (ADP) is a term widely used to describe the processing of data by automatic equipment, either mechanical or electronic, with manual activities reduced to a minimum. The term *electronic data processing* (EDP) is restricted to systems which process data by use of electronic computers.

ELECTRONIC DATA PROCESSING

Although computers are vital to many complex scientific tasks such as directing the flight of space vehicles, their use is probably increasing most rapidly in the field of business. The first advantage of electronic data processing (EDP) is its incredible speed. The number of computations made by an electronic computer is measured in millions per second. In one minute an electronic printer can produce as much as the average clerk-typist in a day. A second advantage of EDP is its ability to produce more information useful in the planning and control of business activities. The use of electronic data processing usually provides information not previously available—current information which gives management better control and a better basis for making decisions.

Elements of an EDP system

An electronic data processing system includes a computer and a number of related machines, which are often called *peripheral equipment.* The computer is the heart of the system; it performs the processing function which includes the storage of information, arithmetic computations, and control. The other two major elements are (*1*) *input* devices which prepare and insert information into the computer and (*2*) *output* devices which transfer information out of the computer to the accountant or other user. Both input and output devices perform the function of *translation.* The machines used to feed information into a computer translate the data into computer language; the output devices translate the processed data back into the language of written words, or of punched cards, paper tape, or magnetic tape.

The relationship of the control unit, the arithmetic unit, the storage unit and the devices for input and output are portrayed in the diagram on page 220.

HARDWARE AND SOFTWARE The machines and related equipment used in an EDP system are called *hardware.* All the other materials utilized in selecting, installing, and operating the system (except the operating personnel) are called *software.* Software includes not only the *computer programs* (the sequence of instructions given to the computer), but also feasibility studies, training materials such as films and manuals, studies of equipment requirements, and everything about the EDP system other than the hardware.

Input devices

Among the input devices used to transfer instructions and accounting data into a computer are card readers, punched-paper-tape readers,

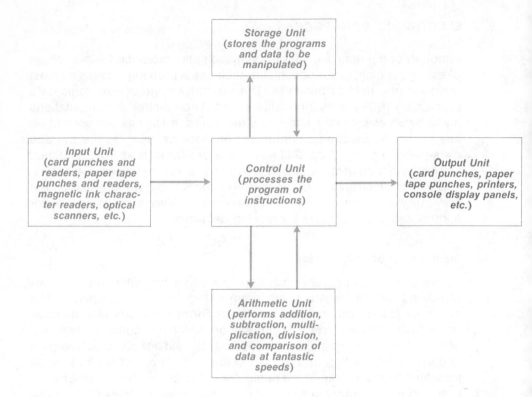

magnetic-tape readers, character readers, and keyboards. The card-reading device will either transmit information from punched cards into the memory unit of the computer or convert the information to paper or magnetic tape. Punched cards will be read by the card-reading devices at rates of several hundred or even several thousand per minute.

Punched-paper tape can be created as part of the process of recording transactions on cash registers or adding machines. This type of input medium is inexpensive to create and easy to use, but it does not permit the insertion of additional data or the making of corrections after the tape has been punched. Punched-tape readers deliver the data to the computer at high speeds. Both punched-card readers and paper-tape readers are usually connected directly to the computer and are described as part of the "on-line" system. They offer the advantage of compatibility with nonelectronic equipment utilizing punched cards or tape.

Magnetic tape is a far faster means of feeding information into a computer and has the advantage of being easily stored. Corrections are also easily made on magnetic tape. Magnetic tape reels are, however, more expensive than paper tape.

Character-reading machines are perhaps best known in the banking field. They read the account numbers printed in magnetic ink on cheques and deposit tickets and convert these data into codes acceptable to the computer. Another type of character-reading device is the optical scanner, with a photoelectric cell which can read a printed document and convert the characters into computer language. This device makes unnecessary the costly step of translating printed matter into punched-card form.

Keyboard devices make it possible to enter limited amounts of data into the EDP system without punching the information into cards or tape as a preliminary step. Keyboards are extremely slow in comparison with the operating capacity of the computer because they are manually operated. However, they may also be used separately from the computer to create punched cards or paper tape for later insertion into the computer.

MACHINE-SENSIBLE FORMS Machines have long been able to read punched cards, paper tape, and documents marked or printed with magnetic ink. Nearly all large banks provide depositors with cheque blanks on which the depositor's account number is printed in magnetic ink. When the cheque is deposited, the machine reads the account number directly from the cheque, thus reducing errors in charging the wrong account and increasing the speed of processing. Many large corporations now send their stockholders' dividend cheques in the form of punched cards. When these cheques have been deposited and returned to the company, the bank reconciliation can be quickly prepared by machine.

Output devices

The *printer* is the most important output device. It interprets the computer code and prints several hundred lines per minute, either at the computer center or at remote locations. The printer might be used to produce payroll cheques, customers' statements, and many types of accounting reports.

Card-punching machines and paper-tape-punching machines transfer data from the computer into punch cards and paper tape which later may be used as input data for subsequent analysis or processing.

Processing operations in the computer

The processing operations performed by a computer include storage of information, arithmetic manipulation of data, and control. The computer receives and stores instructions and data; it calls this information from the memory or storage unit as required by the processing routine; it goes through arithmetic operations, makes comparisons of numbers, and takes the action necessary to produce the required output of information.

The term *control* describes the ability of the computer to guide itself through the processing operations utilizing detailed lists of instructions concerning the work to be done.

PROGRAM A *program* is a series of steps planned to carry out a certain process, such as the preparation of a payroll. Each step in the program is a command or instruction to the computer. A program for payroll might be compared with a very detailed written set of instructions given to an inexperienced employee assigned to the payroll function in a manual accounting system. A most important attribute of the computer is its ability to receive and store a set of instructions which controls its behavior.

The preparation of a computer program is a complicated and costly task. A company may employ its own programmers or may rely on outside organizations which specialize in such services.

Differences between mechanical and electronic data processing systems

Mechanical data processing equipment such as electric calculators, bookkeeping machines, and key-punch machines is extremely slow when compared with electronic equipment. The processing of data in the electronic system is accomplished by electrical impulses traveling through electronic circuits. Such equipment functions hundreds of times faster than mechanical devices.

Another point of contrast is that the units of equipment comprising an EDP system are interconnected so that the processing of data is a continuous operation from the point of reading input data to the point of printing the report or other final result. On the other hand, a mechanical data processing system employs separate machines which do not communicate directly with each other. After each machine, such as a key punch, has performed its function, the output media (punched cards or paper tape) must be transported manually to another machine.

Dependability of EDP equipment

A great deal of the data going into a computer is first transferred from source documents to punched cards or paper tape. This process of key punching to create a file of punched cards is comparable to the use of a typewriter, and the making of errors is quite possible. The additional step of transferring information from invoices or cheques into the form of punched cards or tape creates new opportunities for error. The danger also exists that data may be omitted or may be processed twice. The computer program may contain errors, or the computer operator may make the mistake of using an obsolete program.

Despite these numerous possible sources of errors, electronic data processing makes possible a higher degree of accuracy and reliability than any other system of record keeping. One reason for this potential of accuracy is that the computer is extremely reliable in processing the data fed into it. If these input data are accurate and the computer program is free from error, we can have a high degree of confidence in the output of the computer. Furthermore, much progress is being made in developing techniques for detecting and correcting errors which enter the EDP system.

Earlier generations of computers were often designed to perform arithmetic operations twice and to compare the two sets of answers. This *double circuitry* has been eliminated from most later-model computers because experience has proved the reliability of electronic circuits. Many other types of controls, however, are built into the equipment. For example, the punched cards and paper tape which constitute the data being fed into the computer are read twice as they enter the equipment and any inconsistencies are automatically signaled. A similar control is the "read after write" technique in which the computer reads back the data immediately after they have been recorded. The "parity check" is another important built-in control which offers assurance as to the accuracy of data within the computer equipment.[1]

In summary, we can respect the high degree of reliability inherent in the computer yet recognize that the use of a computer entails the services of people and supporting mechanical equipment. The opportunity for error from these sources exists as it does in any type of manual or mechanical operation.

Accounting applications of the computer

The use of electronic data processing equipment is possible for virtually every phase of accounting operations. Even the CA, in conducting an annual audit, may use the computer as an audit tool. For this purpose he may employ specially written computer programs to aid in his work of sampling and analyzing data to prove the fairness of the financial statements.

The most common application of the computer, however, is to process large masses of accounting data relating to routine repetitive operations such as accounts receivable, accounts payable, inventories, and payrolls.

PAYROLLS   In a manual accounting system the preparation of payroll cheques is usually separate from the maintenance of records showing pay rates, positions, time worked, payroll deductions, and other personnel data. An EDP system, however, has the capability of maintaining all records relating to payroll as well as turning out the required paycheques. Payroll processing is usually one of the first accounting operations to be placed on the computer.

The payroll procedure consists of determining for each employee gross earnings, making deductions, computing net pay, preparing the payroll

---

[1] The computer automatically places all characters of input on a par by making binary digit totals for all characters either all odd or all even, depending on the type of computer. To achieve this parity a digit is added to any totals that deviate from the odd or even pattern. In subsequent processing any variations from this parity will indicate an error. Thus the parity check serves as a safeguard against malfunction in the processing of data by the computer.

cheque, and maintaining a record of each individual's earnings. In addition, the company needs a payroll summary for each period and usually a distribution of payroll costs by department, by product, or classified by the various productive processes. The payroll function has become increasingly complex and time-consuming in recent years because of the advent of social insurance taxes, income tax withholding, and many other payroll deductions. Each employee must receive not only a payroll cheque but a statement showing the gross earnings, deductions, and net pay. The company's records must be designed to facilitate filing with the federal and provincial governments regular payroll reports such as income tax, unemployment insurance, and workmen's compensation. The time and the expense required to prepare payrolls has risen in proportion to the need for more information. The demands by governments, labor unions, credit unions, and other outside agencies have added to the problem.

An EDP payroll system will not only maintain the necessary records, print the cheques, and print these reports, but it can also keep management informed of the costs of various functions within the business. For example, data can be produced showing the man-hours and labor costs on each job, labor cost by department for each salesclerk, or the time required by different employees to perform similar work. In other words, much current information can be developed without significant extra expense that will provide management with a detailed breakdown of labor costs.

EDP SERVICES OFFERED BY BANKS AND BY DATA PROCESSING CENTERS
A computer and related hardware are costly to buy or rent. The employment of personnel qualified to operate the equipment is also a major expense, especially for a small business. One way in which a small business can avoid investing large sums yet gain the operating efficiencies of EDP is to turn over its raw data to a bank, an accounting firm, or a computer center that offers EDP services on a fee basis.

The major banks all have modern electronic equipment, which they do not need 24 hours each day for their own work alone. In addition, some of these banks were pioneers in the field of electronic data processing and have had years of experience in developing effective systems. Similarly, some accounting firms have much experience in rendering accounting services for small businesses and have acquired EDP equipment to enable them to perform these services more effectively.

To illustrate the use of an outside EDP service by a small business, let us compare what must be done with respect to payroll if (1) the work is performed manually within the small business and (2) the work is performed by an outside agency offering EDP services.

In brief, the business which uses the EDP service offered by an outside agency is initially provided with forms on which to enter basic pay information such as employee names, pay rates, and deductions. The EDP

	Function	Payroll Prepared Manually within the Company	Payroll Handled by an Outside Agency Offering EDP Services on a Fee Basis
Payroll may be prepared within the company or by an EDP service center	1 Timekeeping	Employer fills in new set of records each period, making extensions manually.	Employer enters raw data on forms supplied by the agency.
	2 Computation of gross pay	Compute gross pay for each employee, perhaps with desk calculator, and enter manually in records.	Performed electronically.
	3 Calculation of deductions	For each employee, refer to charts and make computations; enter manually in records.	Performed electronically.
	4 Prepare cheques earnings statements, and payroll register	Write by hand or type cheques. Proofread and maintain controls.	Performed electronically.
	5 Bank reconciliation	Reconcile payroll bank account per books with monthly bank statement.	Performed electronically.
	6 Reports to government	Prepare quarterly reports showing for each employee and in total amounts earned, deducted, and paid. Reconcile individual data with controls.	Performed electronically.
	7 Managerial control data	Prepare distribution of hours and labor cost by department or by job. Other analyses may be needed.	Performed electronically.

service center incorporates these data into electronic records. Thereafter, the business need only report to the service center such variable information as hours worked and pay changes. The EDP center calculates wages and deductions, writes cheques and payroll registers, and prepares tax reports for government and for individual employees. Personnel at the computer service center can be payroll specialists conversant with current reporting requirements and with the most efficient techniques of payroll processing.

OTHER ACCOUNTING APPLICATIONS Our emphasis on electronic data processing of payrolls is not intended to minimize the potential advantages in other areas. In the area of accounts payable, for example, the computer can prepare all the various accounts payable records with one handling of the data on purchase invoices. The computer output includes a remittance advice for the vendor, an invoice register and distribution journal, the cheque to the vendor, a cheque register, and a report summarizing the distribution of charges to various accounts. Equally attractive opportunities lie in the areas of accounts receivable and inventories.

Do computers make decisions?

Computers do not make decisions in the sense of exercising judgment. A computer can choose among alternatives by following specific rules for clearly defined situations. For example, if a dollar credit limit is set for a given customer, the computer can be programmed to reject (and refer for special consideration) any sales order from that customer which would cause his account to exceed the predetermined maximum. Such an approach illustrates the principle of "management by exception"; that is, management time is reserved for problem situations.

EDP advantages other than speed

Although computers are sometimes installed simply because they are the fastest means of record keeping, management can expect more than speed of processing. As we become more skilled in developing accounting applications for the computer, we will have the opportunity to obtain currently much more information about a business than has previously been possible. We will be able, for example, to obtain answers to questions on profit margins on individual products, to forecast the profit possibilities inherent in alternative courses of action, and to determine our future financial requirements far in advance.

Information systems

The automation of an accounting system speeds up the production and transmission of information. The term *integrated data processing* (IDP) describes the current trend of providing attachments for typewriters, accounting machines, cash registers and other conventional equipment which will, as a by-product, produce perforated tape or cards acceptable to a computer. The typewriter, for example, when equipped with such attachments can be used not only to prepare conventional business documents but simultaneously to provide the same information in a form compatible with input requirements of a computer. The *integration* of processes for recording information in conventional form and concurrently providing input media for an EDP system eliminates the intermediate work of transferring information from invoices, cheques, and other documents to the tape or cards acceptable for processing by the computer.

The integration of an accounting system suggests that forms and procedures are not designed for the needs of a single department but rather as part of a complete *information system* for the entire business.

To create such an integrated system, the accounting systems specialist tries to coordinate all paper work and procedures in a manner that will provide a rapid and uninterrupted flow of all information needed in the conduct of the business as an entity.

QUESTIONS

1 What advantages are offered by the use of special journals?

2 Table Rock Company made 800 sales on credit during July. If each of these sales transactions were recorded in a two-column general journal along with all other transactions, how many times would the account title "Sales" be written as the account being credited, and how many postings to the Sales account would be required? If a sales journal were used, how many times would the word "Sales" be written, and how many postings to the Sales account would be required?

3 When accounts receivable and accounts payable are kept in subsidiary ledgers, will the general ledger continue to be a self-balancing ledger with equal debits and credits? Explain.

4 Explain how, why, and when the cash receipts journal and cash payments journal are crossfooted.

5 Pine Hill General Store makes about 500 sales on account each month, using only a two-column general journal to record these transactions. What would be the extent of the work saved by using a sales journal?

6 During November the sales on credit made by the Hardy Company actually amounted to $41,625, but an error of $1,000 was made in totaling the amount column of the sales journal. When and how will the error be discovered?

7 Considerable repetitious copying work may be entailed in the preparation of a sales invoice, a sales journal, and a receivables ledger. Is this step-by-step sequence with its attendant opportunity for errors a characteristic of all types of accounting systems? Explain.

8 Does a company with an automated data processing system (ADP) necessarily utilize an electronic computer? Explain.

9 What are the principal advantages of electronic data processing in the accounting division of a company?

10 In which phases or areas of accounting can EDP equipment be used to advantage? Which phases can most conveniently and advantageously be converted to electronic data processing?

11 What avenues are open to a small business interested in gaining the efficiencies of electronic data processing, but which lacks funds for purchase or rental of a computer and also does not have employees familiar with computer operations?

12 Evaluate the following quotation: "The computer will ultimately replace both bookkeepers and accountants and will be able to make many of the decisions now made by top management."

13 Distinguish between *hardware* and *software* as these terms are used in data processing systems.

14 Explain the meaning of the term *computer program.*

15 What are the principal elements of an electronic data processing system?

16 How does a conventional accounting system differ from an *information system?*

EXERCISES

Ex. 7-1 Flow Line Company uses a cash receipts journal, a cash payments journal, a sales journal, a purchases journal, and a general journal. Indicate which journal should be used to record each of the following transactions:

a Purchase of merchandise on account
b Purchase of delivery truck for cash
c Return of merchandise by a customer for credit to his account
d Payment of taxes
e Adjusting entry to record depreciation
f Purchase of typewriter on account
g Sale of merchandise on account
h Sale of merchandise for cash
i Refund to a customer who returned merchandise sold him for cash
j Return of merchandise to a supplier for credit

Ex. 7-2 The Island Company uses a cash receipts journal, a cash payments journal, a sales journal, a purchases journal, and a general journal.

a In which of the five journals would you expect to find the smallest number of transactions recorded?
b At the end of the accounting period, the total of the sales journal should be posted to what account or accounts? As a debit or credit?
c At the end of the accounting period, the total of the purchases journal should be posted to what account or accounts? As a debit or credit?
d Name two subsidiary ledgers which would probably be used in conjunction with the journals listed above. Identify the journals from which postings would normally be made to each of the two subsidiary ledgers.
e In which of the five journals would adjusting and closing entries be made?

Ex. 7-3 Merlin Company maintains a general journal and also four special journals for cash receipts, cash payments, sales, and purchases of merchandise. On January 31, the Accounts Receivable control account in the general ledger had a debit balance of $100,000, and the Accounts Payable control account had a credit balance of $30,000.

During February the sales journal included transactions which totaled $60,000. The purchases journal included transactions totaling $35,000. In the cash receipts journal the Accounts Receivable column showed a credit total for February of $48,000. In the cash payments journal, the Accounts Payable column showed a debit total of $42,000.

a What posting would be made of the total of the $48,000 Accounts Receivable column total in the cash receipts journal at February 28?
b What posting would be made of the $60,000 total of the sales journal at February 28?
c What posting would be made of the $35,000 total of the purchases journal at February 28?
d Based on the above information, state the balances of the Accounts Receivable control account and the Accounts Payable control account in the general ledger after completion of posting at February 28.

Ex. 7-4 A cheque for $1,470 was received from a customer within 10 days from the date of sending him a sales invoice for $1,500, with terms of 2/10, n/30. In recording the receipt of the cheque, the employee maintaining the cash receipts journal entered $1,470 in the Cash column and $1,500 in the Accounts Receivable column. He made no entry in the Sales Discounts column. What procedure should bring this error to light?

PROBLEMS

Group A

7A-1 Picket Company uses a two-column general journal, a one-column purchases journal, a one-column sales journal, a six-column cash receipts journal, and a six-column cash payments journal similar to those illustrated in this chapter. Three ledgers are used: a general ledger, an accounts receivable subsidiary ledger, and an accounts payable subsidiary ledger. The general ledger, as well as the subsidiary ledgers, is of the three-column running balance form. At October 31, the subsidiary ledger for accounts payable consisted of the following accounts with creditors.

A. Adams

Date		Explanation	Ref	Debit	Credit	Balance
19— Oct.	1		P 1		1 0 0 0 0	1 0 0 0 0
	20		P 1		8 0 0 0	1 8 0 0 0
	21	Returned mdse.	J 2	5 0 0		1 7 5 0 0
	28		CP3	9 5 0 0		8 0 0 0

B. Brown

Date		Explanation	Ref	Debit	Credit	Balance
19— Oct.	22		P 1		8 6 0 0	8 6 0 0

C. Cross

Date		Explanation	Ref	Debit	Credit	Balance
19— Sept.	30	Balance				6 0 0
Oct.	15		CP3	6 0 0		- 0 -
	16		P 1		2 4 0 0	2 4 0 0
	20		P 1		3 0 0 0	5 4 0 0

D. Davis

Date		Explanation	Ref	Debit	Credit	Balance
19— Sept.	30	Balance				2 2 0 0 0
Oct.	5	Returned mdse.	J 2	1 2 0 0		2 0 8 0 0
	20		CP3	1 5 0 0 0		5 8 0 0
	25		P 1		1 0 0 0	6 8 0 0

Instructions Prepare the general ledger controlling account, Accounts Payable, including the beginning balance at September 30, all entries during October and the running balance of the account. Show the dates and sources (journal and page number) of all items posted to the controlling account.

7A-2 Glenbar Company uses a two-column general journal, a one-column sales journal, a one-column purchases journal, a six-column cash receipts journal, and a six-column cash payments journal similar to those illustrated in this chapter. Three ledgers are used: a general ledger, an accounts receivable subsidiary ledger, and an accounts payable subsidiary ledger. The general ledger, as well as the subsidiary ledgers, is of the three-column running balance form. At December 31, the subsidiary ledger for accounts receivable consisted of the following accounts with customers.

A. Alkany

Date		Explanation	Ref	Debit	Credit	Balance
19— Nov.	30	Balance				6250
Dec.	3		J4		1200	5050
	18		CR6		5050	-0-
	28		S6	9200		9200

B. Benton

Date		Explanation	Ref	Debit	Credit	Balance
19— Dec.	2		S5	1325		1325
	27		CR6		1000	325
	27		S6	420		745

C. Crail

Date		Explanation	Ref	Debit	Credit	Balance
19— Nov.	30	Balance				4640
Dec.	5		J4		400	4240
	10		S5	1250		5490
	23		CR6		2000	3490

D. Dumfries

Date		Explanation	Ref	Debit	Credit	Balance
19— Dec.	8		S5	650		650
	12		S5	1100		1750
	31		CR6		650	1100

Instructions Prepare the general ledger controlling account, Accounts Receivable, in a three-column running balance form. Include the beginning balance at November 30, all entries during December, and the running balance of the account. Show the dates and sources (journal and page number) of all items posted to the controlling account.

7A-3 All cash transactions of Ward Company for the month of June are outlined below. The company uses multiple-column cash receipts and cash payments journals similar to those illustrated on pages 202–203 and 206–207.

June 1 The owner, R. K. Ward, invested additional cash of $10,000 in the business.

June 1 Purchased Canadian government bonds, $2,000.

June 2 Paid June rent, $650.

June 2 Cash sales of merchandise, $1,720.

June 4 Purchased fixtures, $1,600, making a down payment of $400 and issuing a 90-day, 6% note payable for the balance.

June 6 Paid Wilson Company invoice, $800 less 1%.

June 7 Cash purchase of merchandise, $2,140.

June 9 Received $300 as partial payment of Kay Co. invoice of $1,200 and 60-day, 5% note for the $900 balance.

June 10 Paid gas and oil bill, $55, for automobile belonging to Mrs. R. K. Ward. (Car is not used in the business.)

June 10 Cash sales of merchandise, $1,326.

June 12 Paid Arthur Co. invoice, $1,400 less 2%.

June 13 Sold land costing $2,800 for $2,460.

June 15 Received $588 in full settlement of Nobles Company invoice after allowing 2% discount.

June 19 Cash purchase of merchandise, $1,450.

June 20 Paid note due today, $3,000, and accrued interest amounting to $60.

June 25 Paid Strong Company invoice, $1,600 less 2%.

June 26 Paid salesmen's commissions of $790.

June 28 Paid freight charges on Grey Company invoice, $102.

June 30 Received payment in full settlement of Smith Company invoice, $1,700 less 2%.

June 30 Paid monthly salaries, $1,875.

Instructions
a Enter the above transactions in cash receipts and cash payments journals.
b Foot and rule the journals.

7A-4 All transactions of the Silver Company for the month of September are presented on page 232. The company has been using the following accounts in recording transactions:

Cash	10	Sales	60
Notes receivable	14	Sales returns and allowances	62
Accounts receivable	16	Sales discounts	64
Supplies	17	Purchases	70
Unexpired insurance	18	Purchase returns and allowances	72
Equipment	26	Purchase discounts	74
Accumulated depreciation:		Transportation-in	76
equipment	28	Salaries expense	80
Notes payable	30	Supplies expense	84
Accounts payable	32	Insurance expense	86
Mortgage payable	40	Depreciation expense: equipment	88
H. Silver, capital	50	Gain on sale of equipment	90
H. Silver, drawing	52	Interest expense	92

Sept. 2 Purchased merchandise on account from Clair Company, $7,200. Invoice was dated today with terms of 2/10, n/30.

Sept. 3 Sold merchandise to Fife Company, $4,600. Invoice no. 428; terms 2/10, n/30.

Sept. 4 Purchased supplies for cash, $175.

Sept. 5 Sold merchandise for cash, $1,120.

Sept. 7 Paid the Clair Company invoice dated September 2.

Sept. 10 Purchased merchandise from Axle Company, $6,500. Invoice dated September 9 with terms of 1/10, n/30.

Sept. 10 Collected from Fife Company for invoice no. 428.

Sept. 12 Sold merchandise to Martin Company, $4,350. Invoice no. 429; terms 2/10, n/30.

Sept. 14 Paid freight charges of $410 on goods purchased September 9 from Axle Company.

Sept. 14 Sold equipment for $1,800, receiving cash of $300 and a 30-day, 5% note receivable for the balance. Equipment cost $4,000 and accumulated depreciation was $2,600.

Sept. 15 Issued credit memorandum no. 38 in favor of Martin Company upon return of $200 of merchandise.

Sept. 18 Paid for one-year fire insurance policy, $785.

Sept. 18 Purchased merchandise for cash, $1,525.

Sept. 19 Paid the Axle Company invoice dated September 9.

Sept. 20 Sold merchandise on account to Dale Brothers, $3,930; invoice no. 430. Required customer to sign a 30-day, non-interest-bearing note. (Record this sale by a charge to Accounts Receivable, then transfer from Accounts Receivable to Notes Receivable by means of an entry in the general journal.)

Sept. 22 Purchased merchandise for cash, $810.

Sept. 22 Sold merchandise for cash, $1,000.

Sept. 22 Received payment from Martin Company for invoice no. 429. Customer made deduction for credit memorandum no. 38 issued September 15.

Sept. 25 Purchased merchandise from Davis Company, $5,300. Invoice dated September 24 with terms of 2/10, n/60.

Sept. 26 Issued debit memorandum no. 42 to Davis Company in connection with merchandise returned today amounting to $200.

Sept. 27 Purchased equipment having list price of $12,000. Paid $2,000 down and signed a promissory note for the balance of $10,000.

Sept. 30 Paid monthly salaries of $2,960 for services rendered by employees during September.

Sept. 30 Paid monthly installment on mortgage, $700, of which $204 was interest.

Instructions

a Record the September transactions in the following journals:
 General journal—2 columns
 Sales journal—1 column
 Purchases journal—1 column
 Cash receipts journal—6 columns
 Cash payments journal—6 columns

b Foot and rule all special journals.

c Show how postings would be made by placing ledger account numbers and check marks in the appropriate columns of the journals.

Group B

7B-1 Ivy Company uses a two-column general journal, a one-column sales journal, a one-column purchases journal, a six-column cash receipts journal, and a six-column cash payments journal similar to those illustrated in this chapter.

Three ledgers are used: a general ledger, an accounts receivable subsidiary ledger, and an accounts payable subsidiary ledger. The general ledger, as well as the subsidiary ledgers, is in the three-column running balance form. At November 30, the subsidiary ledger for accounts payable consisted of the following accounts with creditors.

M. Mathew

Date		Explanation	Ref	Debit	Credit	Balance
19— Oct.	31	Balance				900
Nov.	14		CP2	900		-0-
	25		P3		2500	2500
	28		P3		4000	6500

L. Lamb

Date		Explanation	Ref	Debit	Credit	Balance
19— Oct.	31	Balance				12600
Nov.	2		J1	1000		11600
	10		P3		5000	16600
	25		CP2	11600		5000

N. Naylor

Date		Explanation	Ref	Debit	Credit	Balance
19— Nov.	11		P3		1200	1200
	14		P3		2000	3200
	30		CP2	1200		2000

O. Osborne

Date		Explanation	Ref	Debit	Credit	Balance
19— Nov.	9		P3		1800	1800
	12		P3		2400	4200
	14		J1	200		4000

Instructions Prepare the general ledger controlling account, Accounts Payable, in a three-column running balance form. Include the beginning balance at October 31, all entries during November, and the running balance of the account. Show the dates and sources (journal and page number) of all items posted to the controlling account.

7B-2 Pierce Company uses a two-column general journal, a one-column sales journal, a one-column purchases journal, a six-column cash receipts journal, and a six-column cash payments journal similar to those illustrated in this chapter. Three ledgers are used: a general ledger, an accounts receivable subsidiary ledger, and an accounts payable subsidiary ledger. The general ledger, as well as the subsidiary ledgers, is in the three-column running balance form. At November 30, the subsidiary ledger for accounts receivable consisted of the following accounts with customers.

A. Arnold

Date		Explanation	Ref	Debit	Credit	Balance
19—nov.	3		S 4	1 75		1 75
	9		S 4	3 25		5 00
	27		CR 2		3 00	2 00

B. Barley

Date		Explanation	Ref	Debit	Credit	Balance
19—Oct.	31	Balance				16 20
nov.	8		CR 1		10 00	6 20
	8		J 1		2 00	4 20
	28		CR 2		4 20	- 0 -

C. Crutchfield

Date		Explanation	Ref	Debit	Credit	Balance
19—Oct.	31	Balance				11 00
nov.	10		J 1		2 50	8 50
	11		S 4	6 25		14 75
	30		CR 2		8 00	6 75

D. Dunleer

Date		Explanation	Ref	Debit	Credit	Balance
19—nov.	4		S 4	22 00		22 00
	29		S 4	6 00		28 00
	29		CR 2		22 00	6 00

Instructions Prepare the general ledger controlling account, Accounts Receivable, in a three-column running balance form. Include the beginning balance at October 31, all entries during November, and the running balance of the account. Show the dates and sources (journal and page number) of all items posted to the controlling account.

7B-3 The Mack Company uses multiple-column cash receipts and cash payments journals similar to those illustrated on pages 202–203 and 206–207. The cash transactions during the month of May were as follows:

May 1 The owner, J. L. Mack, invested additional cash of $12,000 in the business.

May 1 Purchased Canadian government bonds, $2,000.

May 2 Paid May rent, $900.

May 2 Cash sales of merchandise, $2,324.

May 4 Purchased fixtures, $3,200, making a down payment of $400 and issuing a note payable for the balance.

May 9 Received $600 as partial payment of Kay Co. invoice of $1,800 and 60-day, 5% note for the balance.

May 10 Paid gas and oil bill, $156, for automobile belonging to Mrs. Mack. (Car is not used in the business.)

May 12 Paid Archer Co. invoice, $2,500 less 2%.

May 13 Sold land costing $3,000 for $3,650.

May 15 Received $1,176 in full settlement of Waters Company invoice after allowing 2% discount.

May 19 Cash purchase of merchandise, $2,244.

May 20 Paid note due today, $2,400, and accrued interest amounting to $48.

May 21 Sold Canadian government bonds costing $1,000 for $966.

May 23 Paid installment on note payable due today, $400, of which $186 represented interest expense.

May 25 Cash sales of merchandise, $4,012.

May 25 Paid Strong Company invoice, $3,200 less 2%.

May 26 Purchased three-year fire insurance policy, $372.

May 28 Cash purchase of merchandise, $1,888.

May 30 Received payment in full settlement of Smith Company invoice, $2,400 less 2%.

May 31 Paid monthly salaries, $2,412.

Instructions

a Enter the above transactions in a six-column journal for cash receipts and a six-column journal for cash payments.

b Compute column totals and rule the journals. Determine the equality of debits and credits in column totals.

7B-4 The Mills Company began operations on July 1 using the following accounts:

Cash	10	Sales	50
Notes receivable	14	Sales returns and allowances	52
Accounts receivable	15	Sales discounts	54
Merchandise inventory	17	Purchases	60
Unexpired insurance	19	Purchase returns and allowances	62
Land	20	Purchase discounts	64
Building	21	Transportation-in	66
Furniture and fixtures	24	Rent expense	70
Notes payable	30	Salaries expense	72
Accounts payable	32	Taxes expense	74
Mortgage payable	36	Supplies expense	76
A. B. Mills, capital	40	Insurance expense	78
A. B. Mills, drawing	42	Interest earned	80
Income summary	45	Interest expense	83
		Loss on sale of property	84

The transactions for the month of July are listed below.

July 1 Mills deposited $45,000 in the bank under the name of the Mills Company.

July 4 Purchasing land and building on contract, paying $10,000 cash and signing a mortgage for the remaining balance of $15,000. Estimated value of the land was $8,000.

July 6 Sold merchandise to J. V. Thomas, $3,800. Invoice no. 1; terms 2/10, n/60.

July 7 Purchased merchandise from Drill Company, $7,100. Invoice dated today; terms 2/10, n/30.

July 7 Sold merchandise for cash, $740.

July 7 Paid $270 for a two-year fire insurance policy.

July 10 Paid freight charges of $205 on Drill Company purchase.

July 12 Sold merchandise to Everett Company, $4,900. Invoice no. 2; terms 2/10, n/60.

July 13 Purchased merchandise for cash, $1,420.

July 15 Received payment in full from J. V. Thomas. Invoice no. 1, less 2% discount.

July 15 Purchased land for $2,600, cash.

July 16 Issued credit memorandum no. 1 to Everett Company, $400, for goods returned today.

July 17 Paid Drill Company invoice of July 7, less discount.

July 18 Purchased merchandise from Wyatt Corporation Ltd. $3,700. Invoice dated today; terms 2/10, n/30.

July 20 A portion of merchandise purchased from Wyatt Corporation Ltd. was found to be substandard. After discussion with the vendor, a price reduction of $100 was agreed upon and debit memorandum no. 1 was issued in that amount.

July 22 Received payment in full from Everett Company. Invoice no. 2, less returns and discount.

July 23 Purchased merchandise from Drill Company, $4,200. Invoice dated today; terms 2/10, n/60.

July 25 Sold for $2,420 the land purchased on July 15.

July 27 Sold merchandise for cash, $515.

July 28 Borrowed $3,000 from bank, issuing a 60-day, 5% note payable as evidence of indebtedness.

July 28 Paid Wyatt Corporation Ltd. invoice of July 18, less allowance and discount.

July 30 Paid first installment on mortgage, $500. This payment included interest of $90.

July 30 Purchased merchandise for cash, $920.

July 31 Paid monthly salaries of $2,115.

July 31 Sold merchandise to B. Frank, $2,750. Invoice no. 3; terms 2/10, n/60.

Instructions

a Enter the July transactions in the following journals:
Two-column general journal
One-column sales journal
One-column purchases journal
Six-column cash receipts journal
Six-column cash payments journal

b Foot and rule all special journals.

c Show how postings would be made by placing ledger account numbers and check marks in the appropriate columns of the journals.

BUSINESS DECISION PROBLEM 7

Mail-N-Save is a mail-order clothing company which sells to the public at discount prices. Recently Mail-N-Save initiated a new policy allowing a 10-day free trial on all clothes bought from the company. At the end of the 10-day period, the customer may either pay cash for his purchase or return the goods to Mail-N-Save. The new policy caused such a large boost in sales that, even after considering the many sales returns, the policy appeared quite profitable.

The accounting system of Mail-N-Save includes a sales journal, purchases journal, cash receipts journal, cash payments journal, and a general journal. As an internal control procedure, an officer of the company reviews and initials every entry in the general journal before the amounts are posted to the ledger accounts. Since the 10-day free trial policy has been in effect, hundreds of entries recording sales returns have been entered in the general journal each week. Each of these entries has been reviewed and initialed by an officer of the firm, and the amounts have been posted to Sales Returns & Allowances and to the Accounts Receivable control account in the general ledger, and also to the customer's account in the accounts receivable subsidiary ledger.

Since these sales return entries are so numerous, it has been suggested that a special journal be designed to handle them. This could not only save time in journalizing and posting the entries, but also eliminate the time-consuming individual review of each of these repetitive entries by the officer of the company.

Instructions

a How many amounts are entered in the general journal to describe a single sales return transaction? Are these amounts the same?

b Explain why these transactions are suited to the use of a special journal. Explain in detail how many money columns the special journal should have, and what postings would have to be done either at the time of the transaction or at the end of the period.

c Assume that there were 2,000 sales returns during the month. How many postings would have to be made during the month if these transactions were entered in the general journal? How many postings would have to be made if the special journal you designed in (*b*) were used? (Assume a one-month accounting period.)

d Assume that a general journal entry requires 60 seconds to write and a special journal entry can be written in 20 seconds. Also assume that each posting requires an average of 20 seconds and that the officer of the company averages 25 seconds to review and initial a general journal entry for a sales return. The officer estimates he could review the entire sales return special journal in 10 minutes. How much time (expressed in hours, minutes, and seconds) would be required to journalize, review, and post 2,000 entries in (*1*) general journal form, and (*2*) special journal form? What is the time savings resulting from using the special journal?

e If the estimated cost of designing a sales returns journal and training employees in its use were $400, would you recommend adopting such a journal? Present a case to support your decision, assuming that the labor cost of operating either system averages $4 per hour.

EIGHT

THE CONTROL
OF CASH
TRANSACTIONS

CASH

Accountants use the word *cash* to include coin, paper money, cheques, money orders, and money on deposit with banks. However, cash does not include postage stamps, IOU's, or postdated cheques.

In deciding whether a particular item comes within the classification of cash, the following rule is a useful one: Any medium of exchange which a bank will accept for deposit and immediate credit to the depositor's account is included in cash. As an example, personal cheques and money orders are accepted by banks for deposit and are considered as cash. Postage stamps and postdated cheques are not acceptable for deposit at a bank and are not included in the accountant's definition of cash.

Balance sheet presentation

Cash is a current asset. In fact, cash is the most current and most liquid of all assets. In judging whether other types of assets qualify for inclusion in the current assets section of the balance sheet, we consider the length of time required for the asset to be converted into cash.

Some bank accounts are restricted as to their use, so that they are not available for disbursement to meet normal operating needs of the business. An example (discussed in Chapter 18) is a bond sinking fund, consisting of cash being accumulated by a corporation for the specific purpose of paying off bonded indebtedness at a future date and not available for any other disbursement. A bank account located in a foreign country may also be restricted if monetary regulations prevent the transfer of funds between the two countries. Generally, restricted bank accounts are not regarded as current assets because they are not available for use in paying current liabilities.

The banker, credit manager, or investor who studies a balance sheet critically will always be interested in the total amount of cash as compared with other balance sheet items, such as accounts payable. These outside users of a company's financial statements are not interested, however, in such details as the number of separate bank accounts, or in the distinction between cash on hand and cash in banks. A business concern that carries current accounts with several banks will maintain a separate ledger account for each bank account. On the balance sheet, however, the entire amount of cash on hand and cash on deposit with the several banks will be shown as a single amount. One objective in preparing financial statements is to keep them short, concise, and easy to read.

Management responsibilities relating to cash

Efficient management of cash includes measures that will:

1 Prevent losses from fraud or theft.
2 Provide accurate accounting for cash receipts, cash payments, and cash balances.
3 Maintain a sufficient amount of cash at all times to make necessary payments, plus a reasonable balance for emergencies.
4 Prevent unnecessarily large amounts of cash from being held idle in bank accounts which produce no revenue.

Internal control over cash is sometimes regarded merely as a means of preventing fraud or theft. A good system of internal control, however, will also aid in achieving management's other objectives of accurate accounting and the maintenance of adequate but not excessive cash balances.

Basic requirements for internal control over cash

Cash is more susceptible to theft than any other asset. Furthermore, a large portion of the total transactions of a business involve the receipt or disbursement of cash. For both these reasons, internal control over cash is of great importance to management and also to the employees of a business. If a cash shortage arises in a business in which internal controls are weak or nonexistent, every employee is under suspicion. Perhaps no one employee can be proved guilty of the theft, but neither can any employee prove his innocence.

On the other hand, if internal controls over cash are adequate, theft without detection is virtually impossible except through the collusion of two or more employees. To achieve internal control over cash or any other group of assets requires first of all that the custody of assets be clearly separated from the recording of transactions. Secondly, the recording function should be subdivided among employees, so that the work of one person is verified by that of another. This subdivision of duties discourages fraud, because collusion among employees would be necessary to conceal an irregularity. Internal control is more easily achieved in large companies than in small concerns, because extensive subdivision of duties is more feasible in the larger business.

The major steps in establishing internal control over cash include the following:

1 Separate the function of handling cash from the maintenance of accounting records. The cashier should not maintain the accounting records and should not have access to the records. Accounting personnel should not have access to cash.

2 Separate the function of receiving cash from that of disbursing cash. The same person should not handle cash receipts and also make cash disbursements.

3 Require that all cash receipts be deposited daily in the bank, and that all cash payments be made by cheque. Keep cash on hand under lock.

The application of these principles in building an adequate system of internal control over cash can best be illustrated by considering separately the topics of cash receipts and cash disbursements.

Cash receipts

Cash receipts consist of two major types: cash received over the counter at the time of a sale, and cash received through the mail as collections on accounts receivable.

USE OF CASH REGISTERS Cash received over the counter at the time of a sale should be rung up on a cash register, so located that the customer will see the amount recorded. If store operations can be so arranged that two employees must participate in each sales transaction, stronger internal control will be achieved than when one employee is permitted to handle a transaction in its entirety. In some stores this objective is accomplished by employing a central cashier who rings on a cash register the sales made by all clerks.

At the end of the day, the store manager or other supervisor should compare the cash register tape, showing the total sales for the day, with the total cash collected.

USE OF PRENUMBERED SALES TICKETS Internal control may be further strengthened by writing out a prenumbered sales ticket in duplicate at the time of each sale. The original is given to the customer and the carbon copy retained. At the end of the day an employee computes a total sales figure from these duplicate tickets, and also makes sure that no tickets are missing from the series. The total amount of sales as computed from the duplicate sales tickets is then compared with the total sales recorded on the cash register.

CASH RECEIVED THROUGH THE MAIL The procedures for handling cheques and currency received through the mail are also based on the internal control principle that two or more employees should participate in every transaction.

The employee who opens the mail should prepare a list of the amounts received. In order that this list shall represent the total receipts of the day, the totals recorded on the cash registers may be included in the list. One copy of the list is forwarded with the cash to the cashier, who will deposit the cash in the bank. Another copy of the list is sent to the accounting department, which will record the cash collections.

The total cash receipts recorded each day in the accounting records should agree with the amount of the cashier's deposit, and also with the list of total cash receipts for the day.

CASH OVER AND SHORT In handling over-the-counter cash receipts, a few errors in change making will inevitably occur. These errors will cause a cash shortage or overage at the end of the day, when the cash is counted and compared with the reading on the cash register.

For example, assume that the total cash sales for the day as recorded by the cash register amount to $500, but that the cash in the drawer when counted amounts to only $490. The following entry would be made to record the day's sales and the cash shortage of $10.

Recording cash shortage

Cash	490	
Cash Over and Short	10	
Sales		500

The account entitled Cash Over and Short is debited with shortages and credited with overages. If the cash shortages during an entire accounting period are in excess of the cash overages, the Cash Over and Short account will have a debit balance and will be shown as a miscellaneous expense in the income statement. On the other hand, if the overages exceed the shortages, the Cash Over and Short account will show a credit balance at the end of the period and should be treated as an item of miscellaneous revenue.

Cash disbursements

An adequate system of internal control requires that each day's cash receipts be deposited intact in the bank and that all disbursements be made by cheque. Cheques should be prenumbered. Any spoiled cheques should be marked "Void" and filed in sequence so that all numbers in the series can be accounted for.

The official designated to sign cheques should not be given authority to approve invoices for payment or to make entries in the accounting records. When a cheque is presented to an official for signature, it should be accompanied by the approved invoice and voucher showing that the transaction has been fully verified and that payment is justified. When the cheque is signed, the supporting invoices and vouchers should be perforated or stamped "Paid" to eliminate any possibility of their later being presented in support of another cheque. If these rules are followed, it is almost impossible for a fraudulent cash disbursement to be concealed without the collusion of two or more persons.

BANK CURRENT ACCOUNTS

Opening a bank account

When a depositor first opens a bank account, he must sign his name on a signature card, exactly as he will sign cheques. The signature card is kept on file by the bank, so that any cheque bearing a signature not familiar to bank employees may be compared with the depositor's signature card. When a corporation opens a bank account, the board of directors will pass a resolution designating the officers or employees authorized to sign cheques. A copy of this resolution is given to the bank.

Making deposits

The depositor fills out a *deposit ticket* (usually in duplicate) for each deposit. The deposit ticket includes a listing of each cheque deposited and the code number of the bank on which it is drawn. Space is also provided for listing the amounts of coin and currency deposited.

The bank statement

Each month the bank will provide the depositor with a statement of his account, accompanied by the cheques paid and charged to his account during the month. The bank statement illustrated on page 243 shows the balance on deposit at the beginning of the month, the deposits, the cheques paid, any other debits and credits during the month, and the new balance at the end of the month.

UNCOLLECTED CHEQUES Certain items in the bank statement of The Parkview Company illustrated on page 243 warrant explanation. On July 12 The Parkview Company received a cheque for $50.25 from J. B. Ball, and the cheque was included in the bank deposit made on that day. The Ball cheque was returned to the Bank of Montreal by the bank on which it was drawn marked NSF (Not Sufficient Funds), indicating that Mr. Ball did not have a sufficient balance in his account to cover the cheque. The Bank of Montreal therefore charged the NSF cheque against The Parkview Company's account as shown by the July 18 item of $50.25. (The letters RT alongside this entry stand for Returned Item).

Upon receipt of the NSF cheque returned by the bank, The Parkview Company should remove this item from the cash classification by a journal entry debiting an account receivable from J. B. Ball and crediting Cash. The NSF cheque is thus regarded as a receivable until it is collected directly from the drawer and redeposited, or is determined to be worthless.

The Parkview Company Ltd.,
19101, Parkview Road,
London, Ontario.

EXPLANATION OF CHARACTERS
C/C — Certified Item
CM — Credit Memo.
D — Loan or Discount
DM — Debit Memo.
EC — Error Corrected
IN — Interest
LT — Total of Several Cheques
OD — Overdraft
RT — Returned Item
SC — Service Charge

In Account With   **BANK OF MONTREAL**

DEBITS			CREDITS	DATE		BALANCE
Balance Brought Forward				June 30, 19--		5,029.30
			300.00	July 1		5,329.30
100.00			250.00	2		5,479.30
415.20	10.00			3		5,054.10
25.00	90.00	36.50	185.10	4		5,087.70
			60.00	7		5,147.70
96.00	400.00			10		4,651.70
500.00			147.20	12		4,298.90
425.00				15		3,873.90
50.25	RT		200.00	18		4,023.65
85.00			101.19	21		4,039.84
150.27			83.25	24		3,972.82
95.75			500.00 CM	28		4,377.07
2.00	SC		625.10	31		5,000.17

Please check this statement promptly. Any errors, irregularities or omissions found therein should be reported to the ACCOUNTANT'S DEPARTMENT within 30 days of delivery or mailing, otherwise it will be considered correct. Prompt notification of any change of address would be appreciated.

Form 182—7727
Printed in Canada

BANK SERVICE CHARGES   Under the date of July 31 on the illustrated bank statement is a debit for $2 accompanied by the symbol SC. This symbol means Service Charge, a charge made by the bank to cover the expense of handling the account. The amount of the service charge is based upon such considerations as the average balance of the account and the number of cheques and deposits. (Most banks would probably not make a service charge on The Parkview Company's account because the balance is substantial and the activity is low. However, a service charge is shown here for the purpose of illustrating its use.) When the bank sends the monthly statement and paid cheques to the depositor, it will include debit memoranda for service charges and any other charges not represented by cheques.

MISCELLANEOUS CHARGES Other charges which may appear on the bank statement include rental fees for safe deposit boxes, charges for printing cheques, collection charges on notes left with the bank for collection, and interest charges on borrowing from the bank.

Reconciling the bank account

The balance shown on the monthly statement received from the bank will usually not agree with the balance of cash shown by the depositor's books. Certain transactions recorded by the depositor will not yet have been recorded by the bank. The most common examples are:

1 Outstanding cheques. These are cheques issued and recorded by the depositor but not yet presented to the bank for payment.
2 Deposits in transit. Deposits mailed to the bank are usually not entered on the bank's books until a day or two later than the entry on the depositor's books.

Transactions which may appear on the bank statement but which have not yet been recorded by the depositor include:

1 Service charges
2 Charges for NSF cheques
3 Miscellaneous bank charges and credits

In some cases the bank reconciliation will be complete after such items as outstanding cheques, deposits in transit, and miscellaneous bank charges have been taken into account. Other cases may require the correction of errors by the bank or by the depositor to complete the reconciliation. When a company maintains accounts in several banks, one possible type of error is to record a cheque drawn on one bank as a payment from another bank account. Similar errors may occur in recording deposits.

Procedures for preparing a bank reconciliation

The term *reconciliation* means determining those items which make up the difference between the balance appearing on the bank statement and the balance of cash according to the depositor's records. By listing and studying these discrepancies, it is possible to determine the correct figure for cash to appear on the balance sheet. Specific steps to be taken in preparing a bank reconciliation are:

1 Compare the deposits listed on the bank statement with the deposits shown in the company's records. Place check marks in the company's cash records and on the bank statement beside the items which agree. Any unchecked item in the company's records of deposits will be deposits not yet recorded by the bank, and should be added to the balance reported by the bank. Determine that any deposits in transit listed in last month's bank reconciliation are included in the current month's bank statement.

2 Arrange the paid cheques in numerical order and compare each cheque with the corresponding entry in the cash payments journal. (In the case of personal bank accounts for which the only record maintained is the chequebook, compare each paid cheque with the cheque stub.) Place a check mark in the depositor's cash payments journal opposite each entry for which a paid cheque has been returned by the bank. The unchecked entries should be listed in the bank reconciliation as outstanding cheques to be deducted from the balance reported by the bank. Determine whether the cheques listed as outstanding in the bank reconciliation for the preceding month have been returned by the bank this month. If not, such cheques should be listed as outstanding in the current reconciliation.

3 Deduct from the balance per the books any debit memoranda issued by the bank which have not been recorded by the depositor. In the illustrated bank reconciliation on page 246, examples are the NSF cheque for $50.25 and the $2 service charge.

4 Add to the balance per books any credit memoranda issued by the bank which have not been recorded by the depositor. An example in the illustrated bank reconciliation on page 246 is the credit of $500 collected by the bank in behalf of The Parkview Company.

5 Prepare a bank reconciliation, reflecting the preceding steps, similar to the illustration on page 246.

6 Make journal entries for any items on the bank statement which have not yet been recorded in the depositor's accounts.

ILLUSTRATION The July bank statement prepared by the bank for The Parkview Company was illustrated on page 243. This statement shows a balance of cash on deposit at July 31 of $5,000.17. We shall assume that The Parkview Company's records at July 31 show a bank balance of $4,172.57. Our purpose in preparing the bank reconciliation is to identify the items that make up this difference and to determine the correct cash balance.

Assume that the specific steps to be taken in preparing a bank reconciliation have been carried out and that the following reconciling items have been discovered:

1 A deposit of $310.90 mailed to the bank on July 31 does not appear on the bank statement.

2 A credit memorandum issued by the bank on July 28 in the amount of $500 was returned with the July bank statement and appears in the Deposits column of that statement. This credit represents the proceeds of a note receivable left with the bank by The Parkview Company for the purpose of collection. The collection of the note has not yet been recorded by The Parkview Company.

3 Four cheques issued in July or prior months have not yet been paid by the bank. These cheques are:

Cheque No.	Date	Amount
801	June 15	$100.00
888	July 24	10.25
890	July 27	402.50
891	July 30	205.00

4 A debit memorandum issued by the bank on July 31 for a $2 service charge was enclosed with the July bank statement.

5 Cheque no. 875 was issued July 20 in the amount of $85 but was erroneously listed on the cheque stub and in the cash payments journal as $58. The cheque, in payment of telephone service, was paid by the bank, returned with the July bank statement, and correctly listed on the bank statement as an $85 charge to the account.

6 No entry has as yet been made in The Parkview Company's accounts to reflect the bank's action on July 18 of charging against the account the NSF cheque for $50.25 drawn by J. B. Ball.

The July 31 bank reconciliation for The Parkview Company follows:

THE PARKVIEW COMPANY

Bank Reconciliation

July 31, 1974

Bank statement and depositor's records must be reconciled	Balance per books, July 31		$4,172.57
	Add: Note receivable collected for us by bank		500.00
			$4,672.57
	Less: Service charge	$ 2.00	
	NSF cheque of J. B. Ball	50.25	
	Error on cheque stub No. 875	27.00	79.25
	Adjusted book balance		$4,593.32
	Balance per bank statement, July 31		$5,000.17
	Add: Deposit of July 31 not recorded by bank		310.90
			$5,311.07
	Less: Outstanding cheques		
	No. 801	$100.00	
	No. 888	10.25	
	No. 890	402.50	
	No. 891	205.00	717.75
	Adjusted bank balance (as above)		$4,593.32

The adjusted balance of $4,593.32 is the amount of cash owned by The Parkview Company and is, therefore, the amount which should appear as cash on the July 31 balance sheet.

Note that the adjusted balance of cash differs from both the bank statement and the depositor's records. This difference is explained by the fact that neither set of records is up to date as of July 31, and also by the existence of an error on The Parkview Company's records.

ADJUSTING THE RECORDS AFTER THE RECONCILIATION To make The Parkview Company's records up-to-date and accurate, entries are necessary for

1 The note receivable collected by the bank. Debit Cash $500; credit Notes Receivable $500.
2 The service charge by the bank. Debit Miscellaneous Expense $2; credit Cash $2.
3 The NSF cheque of J. B. Ball. Debit Accounts Receivable—J. B. Ball $50.25; credit Cash $50.25.
4 The error in recording the $85 cheque for telephone service as a $58 item. Debit Telephone Expense $27; credit Cash $27.

Petty cash

As previously emphasized, adequate internal control over cash requires that all receipts be deposited in the bank and all disbursements be made by cheque. However, every business finds it convenient to have a small amount of cash on hand with which to make some very small expenditures. Examples include payments for postage stamps, collect telegrams, and taxi fares. Internal control over these small cash payments can best be achieved through a petty cash fund.

ESTABLISHING THE PETTY CASH FUND To create a petty cash fund, also called an *imprest fund,* a cheque is written for a round amount such as $50 or $100, which will cover the small expenditures to be paid in cash for a period of two or three weeks. This cheque is cashed and the money kept on hand in a petty cash box or drawer in the office.

The entry for the issuance of the cheque is:

Creating the petty cash fund

Petty Cash	100	
Cash		100

To establish a petty cash fund.

MAKING DISBURSEMENTS FROM THE PETTY CASH FUND As cash payments are made out of the petty cash box, the custodian of the fund is required to fill out a *petty cash voucher* for each expenditure. A petty cash voucher shows the amount paid, the purpose of the expenditure, the date, and the signature of the person receiving the money. A petty cash voucher should be prepared for every payment made from the fund. The petty cash box should, therefore, always contain cash and/or vouchers totaling the exact amount of the fund.

The petty cash custodian should be informed that occasional surprise counts of the fund will be made and that he is personally responsible for the fund being intact at all times. Careless handling of petty cash has often been a first step toward large defalcations; consequently, misuse of petty cash funds should not be tolerated.

REPLENISHING THE PETTY CASH FUND Assume that a petty cash fund of $100 was established on June 1 and that payments totaling $89.75 were made from the fund during the next two weeks. Since the $100 originally placed in the fund is nearly exhausted, it is necessary that the fund be replenished. A cheque is drawn payable to Petty Cash for the exact amount of the expenditures, $89.75. This cheque is cashed and the money placed in the petty cash box. The vouchers totaling that amount are perforated to prevent their reuse and filed in support of the replenishment cheque. The journal entry to record the issuance of the cheque will debit the expense accounts indicated by inspection of the vouchers, as follows:

Replenishment of petty cash fund	Postage Expense	60.60
	Telephone & Telegraph Expense	4.80
	Freight-in	6.00
	Gasoline Expense	5.25
	Miscellaneous Expense	13.10
	Cash	89.75
	To replenish the petty cash fund.	

In studying the procedures for operation of a petty cash fund, emphasis should be placed on the fact that the Petty Cash account *is debited only when the fund is first established. Expense accounts will be debited each time the fund is replenished.* There will ordinarily be no further entries in the petty cash fund after it is established, unless the fund is discontinued or a decision is made to change the size of the fund from the original $100 amount.

The petty cash fund is usually replenished at the end of an accounting period, even though the fund is not running low, so that all vouchers in the fund are charged to expense accounts before these accounts are closed and financial statements prepared. If through oversight the petty cash fund were not replenished at the end of the period, expenditures from petty cash could still be reflected in the income statement for the period in which these expenditures occurred, by an entry debiting the expense accounts and crediting Petty Cash. The result would be an unintentional reduction in the Petty Cash fund, which would presumably need to be restored in the following period.

THE VOUCHER SYSTEM

Control over expenditures

Closely related to our discussion of the control of cash transactions is the problem of ensuring that expenditures are properly authorized and that payments to liquidate liabilities are legitimate. In every business, large or small, a considerable number of expenditures must be made each month for goods and services. Handling these transactions requires such steps as the following:

1 Purchase orders or other authorization for expenditures must be given.
2 Goods and services received must be inspected and approved.
3 Invoices from suppliers must be examined for correctness of prices, extensions, shipping costs, and credit terms.
4 Cheques must be issued in payment.

In a very small business it may be possible for the owner or manager to perform all these steps for every transaction. By doing this work personally, he may be assured that the business is getting what it pays for, and that funds are not being disbursed carelessly or fraudulently. As a business grows and the volume of daily transactions increases, it becomes impossible for the owner or manager to give personal attention to each expenditure. When this work is assigned to various employees, a well-designed accounting system is needed to guard against waste and fraud.

Some businesses take great pains to safeguard cash receipts and cash on hand, but quite inconsistently permit a number of employees to incur liabilities by ordering goods or services without any record being made of their actions. When an invoice is received, the absence of any record of the purchase makes it difficult to determine whether the invoice is a proper statement of an amount owed. In this confused situation, invoices are apt to be paid without adequate verification. The opportunity exists for a dishonest employee to collaborate with an outsider to arrange for duplicate payments of invoices, for payment of excessive prices, or for payment for goods and services never received.

Fraud is particularly likely when an employee has authority to incur expenses and to issue cheques in payment as well. In larger organizations, the work of placing orders, verifying invoices, recording liabilities, and issuing cheques should be divided among several employees in such a manner that the work of each person serves to prove that of the others. A chain of documentary evidence should be created for each transaction, consisting of written approvals by key employees for the phases of the transaction for which each is responsible.

One method of establishing control over the making of expenditures and the payment of liabilities is the *voucher system.* This system requires that every liability be recorded as soon as it is incurred, and that cheques be issued only in payment of approved liabilities. A written authorization called a *voucher* is prepared for each expenditure, regardless of whether the expenditure covers services, merchandise for resale, or assets for use in the business. The voucher system is widely used, and it is particularly common in large organizations which have given serious study to the problem of internal control. Perhaps the greatest single advantage of the voucher system is the assurance that every expenditure of the business is systematically reviewed and verified before payment is made.

Essential characteristics of a voucher

A voucher (as illustrated below and on page 251) is attached to each incoming invoice and given an identification number.

The voucher has spaces for listing the data from the invoice and the ledger accounts to be debited and credited in recording the transaction. Space is also provided for approval signatures for each step in the

BROADHILL CORPORATION

Sherbrooke, Quebec

Use of voucher ensures verification of invoice

Pay to..

Voucher No. ....

Date ....

Date due...............................

Date of invoice..

Gross amount $ ....

Invoice number..

Less: Cash discount...........................

Net amount $ ....

Approval

	Dates	Approved by
Extensions and footings verified		
Prices in agreement with purchase order		
Quantities in agreement with receiving report		
Credit terms in agreement with purchase order		
Account distribution & recording approved	(For Accounting Dept.)	
Approved for payment	(For Treasurer's Dept.)	

Reverse side of voucher

Date..   Voucher No. ....

Account distribution

	Amount	Date ....
Purchases	$............................	
Transportation-in	....	Date due ....
Repairs	....	
Heat, light, and power	....	Payee ....
Advertising	....	....
Delivery expense	....	....
Misc. general expense	....	Amount of invoice $................
Telephone and telegraph	....	Less: Cash discount ....
Sales salaries	....	Net amount $................
Office salaries	....	
....	....	Paid by cheque no. ....
....	....	Date of cheque ....
		Amount of cheque $................
Credit vouchers payable (total) $............		
Account distribution by................		Entered in voucher register by................

verification and approval of the liability. A completed voucher provides a description of the transaction and also of the work performed in verifying the liability and approving the cash disbursement. Regardless of the specific form of the voucher, the following features are usually present:

1 A separate voucher for every incoming invoice
2 Consecutive numbering of vouchers
3 Name and address of creditor listed on voucher
4 Description of the liability, including amount and terms of payment
5 Approval signatures for
  a Verification of invoice
  b Recording in accounts
  c Payment of liability
6 Date of cheque and cheque number listed on voucher

In preceding chapters the payment of expenses such as the monthly telephone bill was handled by an entry debiting Telephone Expense and crediting Cash. However, when a voucher system is in use the receipt and payment of the monthly telephone bill will be recorded by these entries:

1 Upon receipt of the invoice: Debit Telephone Expense; credit Vouchers Payable.

2 At time of payment: Debit Vouchers Payable; credit Cash.

These two separate entries would be made even though the bill was paid immediately upon receipt. It is fundamental to the successful operation of a voucher system that no cash payment be made except in payment of an approved and recorded voucher. Rigorous compliance with this rule gives assurance that expenditures are recorded in the proper period, and that disbursements are made only after appropriate review by the individuals responsible for the various phases in the verification of a transaction.

Preparing a voucher

To illustrate the functioning of a voucher system, let us begin with the receipt of an invoice. A voucher is prepared by filling in the appropriate blanks with information taken from the invoice, such as the invoice date, invoice number, and amount, and the creditor's name and address. The voucher with invoice (and possibly receiving report) attached is then sent to the employees responsible for verifying the extensions and footings on the invoice and for comparing prices, quantities, and terms with those

Voucher Register

Voucher No.	Date (19___)		Creditor	Payment			Vouchers Payable, Cr	Pur-chases, Dr	Transpor-tation-in, Dr
				Date (19___)		Cheque No.			
241	May	1	Black Company	May	10	632	1,000	1,000	
242		2	Midwest Freight		3	627	50		50
243		4	Ames Company		4	628	125		
244		5	Bank of Montreal		5	629	8,080		
245		5	Rathco Ltd.		6	631	1,200	1,200	
246		5	Midwest Freight		6	630	110		110
286		30	O. K. Supply Co.				70		
287		30	J. Jones		30	665	210		
288		30	Black Company				1,176	1,176	
289		31	Midwest Freight		31	666	90		90
290		31	Payroll		31	667	1,865		
							25,875	9,220	640
							(21)	(51)	(52)

specified in the purchase order and receiving report. When completion of the verification process has been evidenced by approval signatures of the persons performing these steps, the voucher and supporting documents are sent to an employee of the accounting department, who indicates on the voucher the accounts to be debited and credited.

The voucher is now reviewed by an accounting official to provide assurance that the verification procedures have been satisfactorily completed and that the liability is a proper one. After receiving this executive approval, the voucher is entered in a book of original entry called a *voucher register.*

The voucher register

The voucher register replaces the purchases journal described in Chapter 7. It may be thought of as an expanded purchases journal with additional debit columns for various types of expense and asset accounts. A typical form of voucher register is shown below and on page 252.

In comparing the voucher register with a purchases journal, it should be emphasized that the purchases journal is used *only* to record purchases of merchandise on account. Consequently, every entry in a purchases journal consists of a debit to Purchases and a credit to Accounts Payable. The voucher register, on the other hand, is used to record all types of expenditures: for plant and equipment, expenses, and payroll as well as for purchases of merchandise. Every entry in the voucher

Advertising, Dr	Supplies, Dr	Repairs, Dr	Accrued Payroll, Dr	Other General Ledger Accounts			
				Account Name	LP	Debit	Credit
		125					
				Notes Payable	25	8,000	
				Interest Expense	79	80	
	70	210					
			1,865				
510	470	335	3,800			10,900	
(61)	(14)	(74)	(24)			(x)	

register will consist of a credit to Vouchers Payable, but the debits may affect various asset and expense accounts. Occasionally the entry may require a debit to a liability account; for example, when a voucher is prepared to authorize the issuance of a cheque in payment of an existing mortgage or note payable.

A typical form of voucher register is shown on pages 252 and 253. Note that columns are provided for the voucher number, the date of entry, the name of the creditor, and the date and number of the cheque issued in payment. The first money column is a credit column and has the heading of Vouchers Payable; the amount of every voucher is entered in this column. All the other money columns in the voucher register are debit columns, with the exception of one credit column in the Other General Ledger Accounts section. Separate columns are provided for accounts frequently debited, such as Purchases and Transportation-in. At the extreme right of the register, a debit column and a credit column are provided for Other General Ledger Accounts, meaning accounts infrequently used for which special columns are not provided. In this section the account title must be written opposite the amount of each debit and credit. The entries in this section of the voucher register are posted individually and a ledger page (LP) column is provided in which the account number is listed when the individual posting is made.

Each voucher is entered in the voucher register in numerical order as soon as it is prepared and approved. When payment is made the number and date of the cheque are entered in the columns provided for this purpose. The total amount of unpaid vouchers may be determined from the register at any time merely by listing the "open" items, that is, vouchers for which no entry has yet been made in the Payment columns. The total of the unpaid vouchers appearing in the voucher register should agree with the total of the vouchers in the unpaid vouchers file at the same date.

POSTING FROM THE VOUCHER REGISTER All columns of the voucher register are totaled at the end of the month; the equality of debit and credit entries is proved by comparing the combined totals of the two credit columns with the sum of the totals of the various debit columns. After the register has been proved to be in balance, the posting to ledger accounts is begun.

The individual items listed in the Other General Ledger Accounts section are posted as debits and credits to the various accounts indicated, but the totals of these columns are not posted. The totals of the other debit columns, such as Purchases, Transportation-in, and Advertising, are posted as debits to the accounts named, and the total of the Vouchers Payable column is posted as a credit to the ledger account, Vouchers Payable. The posting of each column total is evidenced by listing the account number in parentheses just below the column total in the voucher register. In the ledger accounts the letters VR are entered to show that the posting came from the voucher register.

The balance of the general ledger account, Vouchers Payable, should be reconciled at the end of the month with the total of the unpaid vouchers shown in the voucher register and also with the total of the vouchers in the unpaid vouchers file.

PAYING THE VOUCHER WITHIN THE DISCOUNT PERIOD After the voucher has been entered in the voucher register, it is placed (with the supporting documents attached) in a tickler file according to the date of required payment. The voucher system emphasizes the required *time for payment* of liabilities rather than the identity of the creditors; for this reason, vouchers are filed by required date of payment. In computing future cash requirements of a business, the amount of a liability and the required date of payment are of basic significance; the identity of the creditor has no bearing on the problem of maintaining a proper cash position.

Cash discount periods generally run from the date of the invoice. Since a voucher is prepared for each invoice, the required date of payment is the last day on which a cheque can be prepared and mailed to the creditor in time to qualify for the discount.

When the payment date arrives, the voucher is removed from the unpaid file and sent to the cashier, who draws a cheque for signature by the treasurer. The cashier fills in the cheque number, amount, and date of payment on the voucher and presents the cheque and voucher to the treasurer. The treasurer examines the documents, especially the approval signatures, and authorizes the payment of the liability by signing the voucher in the space labeled "Approved for payment." He also signs the cheque and mails it to the creditor. (Note that the cheque does not come back into the possession of the employee who prepared it.) The voucher is forwarded to the accounting department, which will record the issuance of the cheque and also note in the voucher register the payment of the voucher.

The cheque register

A cheque register is merely a simplified version of the cash payments journal illustrated in Chapter 7. When a voucher system is in use, cheques are issued only in payment of approved and recorded vouchers. Consequently, every cheque issued is recorded by a debit to Vouchers Payable and a credit to Cash. The cheque register therefore contains a special column for debits to Vouchers Payable and a Cash credit column. The only other money column needed in this compact record is for credits to Purchase Discounts when invoices are paid within the cash discount period. Shown on page 256 is a cheque register with entries corresponding to the payments listed in the voucher register on pages 252 and 253.

To record the payment of a voucher, an entry is made in the cheque register, and a notation of the cheque number and date is placed on the appropriate line in the voucher register. At the end of the month the column totals of the cheque register are posted as for other special jour-

Cheque Register

	Cheque No.	Date (19__)		Payee	Voucher No.	Vouchers Payable, Dr	Purchase Discounts, Cr	Cash, Cr
Cheques issued only in payment of approved vouchers	627	May	3	Midwest Freight	242	50		50
	628		4	Ames Company	243	125		125
	629		5	Bank of Montreal	244	8,080		8,080
	630		6	Midwest Freight	246	110		110
	631		6	Rathco Ltd.	245	1,200		1,200
	632		10	Black Company	241	1,000	20	980
	665		30	J. Jones	287	210		210
	666		31	Midwest Freight	289	90		90
	667		31	Payroll	290	1,865		1,865
						23,660	240	23,420
						(21)	(53)	(1)

nals; this posting consists of a debit to the Vouchers Payable account for the total of the vouchers paid during the month, a credit to the Purchase Discounts account, and a credit to the Cash account. The symbol ChR is placed in the ledger accounts to indicate that a posting came from the cheque register.

ILLUSTRATION OF USE OF VOUCHER REGISTER AND CHEQUE REGISTER
The use of the voucher register and the cheque register in handling typical transactions may be further clarified by the following examples:

June 2 Paid *Morning Times* for advertising.

<table>
<tr><td colspan="2" align="center">Voucher Register</td><td colspan="2" align="center">Cheque Register</td></tr>
<tr><td>Some sample entries</td><td>Advertising Expense. . . .   xxx
    Vouchers Payable   xxx
(Also enter cheque number
and date in Payment
column.)</td><td>Vouchers Payable   xxx
    Cash . . . .   xxx</td></tr>
</table>

June 3 Received shipment of merchandise from Cross Company, terms 2/10, n/30.

<table>
<tr><td align="center">Voucher Register</td><td align="center">Cheque Register</td></tr>
<tr><td>Purchases   xxx
    Vouchers Payable   xxx</td><td>(No entry until payment is made.)</td></tr>
</table>

June 12 Paid Cross Company invoice of June 3; took discount.

Voucher Register		*Cheque Register*		
(Enter cheque number and		*Vouchers Payable*	*xxx*	
date in Payment column.)		*Purchase Discounts*		*xxx*
		Cash		*xxx*

June 13 Replenished petty cash fund.

Voucher Register		*Cheque Register*		
Various expense accounts	*xxx*	*Vouchers Payable*	*xxx*	
Vouchers Payable	*xxx*	*Cash*		*xxx*
(Enter cheque number and				
date in Payment column.)				

FILING PAID VOUCHERS   After the payment has been recorded in the cheque register and noted in the voucher register, the paid voucher is placed in numerical order in a paid vouchers file. Many companies prepare a duplicate copy of the cheque and remittance advice for filing with the paid voucher. The paid vouchers file then contains a complete set of documents describing and supporting every disbursement of cash.

Special considerations of the voucher register

AS A SUBSIDIARY LEDGER   When a voucher system is used to control liabilities and cash disbursements, there is no need to maintain an accounts payable subsidiary ledger such as the one described in Chapter 7. Since the traditional form of accounts payable ledger contains a separate account with every creditor, it requires a great deal of detailed posting and recording work. The elimination of this costly subsidiary ledger is one of the major savings to be achieved by adopting a voucher system.

Each line of the voucher register represents a liability account with an individual creditor. This liability account comes into existence when an invoice is received and a voucher is prepared and recorded, describing the amount owed under the terms of that invoice. When a voucher is paid, the cheque number and date are entered on the line for that voucher to show that the liability is ended. Inspection of the voucher register reveals which items have not been paid. A list of unpaid vouchers corresponds to a trial balance prepared from an accounts payable subsidiary ledger.

The voucher register thus serves a dual purpose; it is primarily a book of original entry, but it also serves as the equivalent of a subsidiary ledger of liability accounts. However, the voucher register does not classify invoices by creditors; it does not show the total amount owed to a given creditor with several invoices outstanding. Neither does it show the total purchases from a given supplier over a period of time.

HANDLING PURCHASE RETURNS AND ALLOWANCES The following example illustrates one of the several common methods for handling purchase returns and allowances under a voucher system.

Assume that on October 2 an invoice in the amount of $2,800 was received from a supplier, Barnard Company. Voucher no. 621 was prepared and recorded in the voucher register, as illustrated below. Shortly thereafter some of the merchandise was returned to Barnard Company, and on October 8 a credit memorandum for $800 was received.

A new voucher (no. 633) was prepared in the amount of $2,000, and the original voucher (no. 621 for $2,800) was canceled, marked with a reference to the replacement voucher, and placed in the paid vouchers file.

Voucher Register

	Voucher No.	Date (19___)		Creditor	Payment		Vouchers Payable, Cr
					Date (19___)	Cheque No.	
Note handling of purchase returns	621	Oct.	2	Barnard Co.	See vou. no. 633		2,800
	633	Oct.	8	Barnard Co.			2,000
							4,800
							(12)

Vouchers Payable (21)			Purchases (51)	
Oct. 8 2,800	Oct. 31 4,800		Oct. 31 2,800	

Purchase Returns & Allowances (53)	
	Oct. 8 800

In the voucher register the new voucher is recorded as a credit of $2,000 to Vouchers Payable in the Vouchers Payable column and as a debit of $2,800 to Vouchers Payable in the Other General Ledger Accounts section. A credit of $800 to Purchase Returns and Allowances is also recorded in the Other General Ledger Accounts section. In the Payment column of the register, a notation is entered on the line for the old voucher, "See voucher no. 633." To make this procedure clear, the illustrated voucher register on pages 258 and 259 contains only the transactions with the Barnard Company; posting to the ledger accounts is also shown.

MAKING PARTIAL PAYMENTS If it is known at the time an invoice is received that payment will be made in two or more installments, a separate voucher should be prepared for each installment. However, if the use of partial payments is decided upon after a single voucher for the entire amount of the invoice has been recorded, the original voucher should be canceled and new vouchers prepared for each expected installment payment.

CORRECTING ERRORS IN THE VOUCHER REGISTER If an error in the voucher register is discovered *before* the posting work is performed at the end of the month, the erroneous entry may be canceled by drawing a line through it and a new voucher prepared and recorded. The original

Purchases, Dr	Transpor-tation-in, Dr	Other General Ledger Accounts			
		Account Name	LP	Debit	Credit
2,800					
		Vouchers Payable	21	2,800	
		Purchase Returns			
		& Allowances	53		800
2,800				2,800	800
(51)				(x)	(x)

voucher should be marked with the word "Canceled" and a reference to the number of the replacement voucher.

If an error in the voucher register is not discovered until after the register has been posted, a general journal entry may be made to reverse the erroneous entry. A reference to the adjusting journal entry should be made in the payment column of the voucher register. A new voucher can then be prepared and recorded in the voucher register.

Presentation of liability in the balance sheet

Although the liability account title Vouchers Payable occasionally appears on a balance sheet, it is better practice to use the more widely understood term Accounts Payable.

A "voucher system" without vouchers

One interesting variation of the system described in this chapter is to use a voucher register, but not to prepare vouchers. Invoices are assigned consecutive numbers as they are received, and entered in the voucher register, which is usually given the name of invoice register. As each invoice is verified as to quantities, prices, extensions, and other aspects of the transaction, *approvals are noted on the invoice itself.* At the time of payment, the invoice is transferred from an unpaid invoices file to a paid invoices file. The invoice register is footed and posted at the end of the month in the same manner as a voucher register. The use of a cheque register follows the pattern previously described, and the review of documents by executives before approving an invoice or issuing a cheque may correspond to the control procedures described for the voucher system.

QUESTIONS

1 Mention some principles to be observed by a business in establishing strong internal control over cash receipts.

2 Explain how internal control over cash transactions is strengthened by compliance with the following rule: "Deposit each day's cash receipts intact in the bank, and make all disbursements by cheque."

3 List two items often encountered in reconciling a bank account which may cause cash per the bank statement to be larger than the balance of cash shown by the books.

4 In the reconciliation of a bank account, what reconciling items necessitate a journal entry on the depositor's books?

5 Pico Stationery Shop has for years maintained a petty cash fund of $75, which is replenished twice a month.
  a How many debit entries would you expect to find in the Petty Cash account each year?
  b When would expenditures from the petty cash fund be entered in the ledger accounts?

6 A cheque for $455 issued in payment of an account payable was erroneously listed in the cash payments journal as $545. The error was discovered early in the following month when the paid cheque was returned by the bank. What corrective action is needed?

7 It is standard accounting practice to treat as cash all cheques received from customers. When a customer's cheque is received, recorded, and deposited, but later returned by the bank marked NSF, what accounting entry or entries would be appropriate?

8 Ringo Store sells only for cash and records all sales on cash registers before delivering merchandise to the customers. On a given day the cash count at the close of business indicated $10.25 less cash than was shown by the totals on the cash register tapes. In what account would this cash shortage be recorded? Would the account be debited or credited?

9 Classify each of the numbered reconciling items listed below under one of the following headings: (*a*) an addition to the balance per books; (*b*) a deduction from the balance per books; (*c*) an addition to the balance per bank statement; (*d*) a deduction from the balance per bank statement.
  (*1*) Deposits in transit
  (*2*) Outstanding cheques
  (*3*) Customer's cheque deposited but returned by bank marked NSF.

(4) Bank service charges

(5) Collection by bank of note receivable left with bank for collection in behalf of depositor

10 Name three internal control practices relating to cash which would be practicable even in a small business having little opportunity for division of duties.

11 With respect to a *voucher system,* what is meant by the terms *voucher, voucher register,* and *cheque register?*

12 What is the greatest single advantage of the voucher system?

13 Randall Company uses a voucher system to control its cash disbursements. With respect to a purchase of merchandise, what three documents would need to be examined to verify that the voucher should be approved?

14 Assume that a company using a general journal, a cash receipts journal, a cash payments journal, a sales journal, and a purchases journal decides to adopt a voucher system. Which of the five journals would be changed or replaced? Explain.

15 In May, R Company recorded voucher no. 106 to X Company for $1,500, covering the purchase of equipment. The voucher remained unpaid at the end of May, and in June it was discovered that the invoice had been incorrectly priced; the amount should have been $1,750. Explain how this error should be straightened out in the accounting records.

16 Explain how the following would be handled in a voucher system:

a Return of merchandise to supplier in the same month as purchase but after original invoice has been entered in voucher register.

b Return of merchandise to supplier in the month following purchase.

17 The following column totals appear in a voucher register at the end of the month: transportation-in, $1,280; selling expense control, $6,020; general expense control, $4,210; vouchers payable, $61,750; accrued payroll, $15,640; purchases, $18,440; other general ledger accounts, $16,160 (notes payable, $16,000 and interest expense, $160). Prepare in general journal form an entry summarizing the voucher transactions for the month.

18 The following column totals appear in a cheque register at the end of the month: cash, $11,710; vouchers payable, $11,390; cash discounts not taken, $320. Prepare a general journal entry to summarize cash disbursements for the month. Explain how the company handles cash discounts on purchases.

EXERCISES

Ex. 8-1 Henry Able, a trusted employee of the Mannix Company, found himself in personal financial difficulties and carried out the following plan to steal $1,000 from the company and to conceal his fraud.

Able removed $1,000 in currency from the cash register. This amount represented the bulk of the cash received in over-the-counter sales during the three business days since the last bank deposit. Able then removed a $1,000 cheque from the day's incoming mail; this cheque had been mailed in by a customer, Robert Trent, in full payment of his account. Able made no entry in the cash receipts journal for the $1,000 collection from Trent, but deposited the cheque in Mannix Company's bank account in place of the $1,000 of over-the-counter cash receipts he had stolen. In order to keep Trent from protesting when his month-end statement reached him, Able made a general journal entry debiting Sales Returns and Allowances and crediting Accounts Receivable—Robert Trent. Able posted this entry to the two general ledger accounts affected and also to Trent's account in the subsidiary ledger for accounts receivable.

a Did these actions by Able cause the general ledger to be out of balance or the subsidiary ledger to disagree with the control account? Explain.

b What weaknesses in internal control apparently exist in the Mannix Company? Indicate the corrective actions needed.

Ex. 8-2 The Cash account in the ledger of Minor Company showed a balance of $10,000 at September 30. The bank statement, however, showed a balance of $12,600 at the same date. If the only reconciling items consisted of an $800 deposit in transit, a bank service charge of $4, and 30 outstanding cheques, what was the total amount of the outstanding cheques?

Ex. 8-3 Small Company received a bank statement showing a balance of $8,000 on deposit at the end of the month. Among the reconciling items were outstanding cheques totaling $1,200, bank service charges of $6, a deposit in transit of $1,000, and a memorandum showing that a $600 note receivable owned by Small Company and left with the bank for collection had been collected and credited to the company's account.

a What is the adjusted amount of cash which should appear on the Small Company's balance sheet?

b What was the balance per the books before making adjusting entries for any of the reconciling items?

Ex. 8-4 The petty cash fund of Wicker Company contained the following at December 31, 19___, the end of the fiscal year.

Cash on hand	$139.41
Expense vouchers:	
Flowers for funeral of deceased customer	10.40
Box of cigars for purchasing agent of the James Corporation	7.09
Office supplies expense	23.10
Salary advance to employee	20.00
Total	$200.00

a Since there is a substantial amount of cash in the petty cash fund, is there any reason to replenish it at December 31? Explain.

b Prepare the entry (in general journal form) to replenish the petty cash fund.

Ex. 8-5 Gray Rock Company uses a voucher system. You are to record the following transactions in **general journal form** (without explanations). Also indicate after each entry the book of original entry in which the transaction would in practice be recorded.

(a) Voucher no. 100 prepared to purchase office equipment at cost of $4,000 from Coast Furniture Co.

(b) Cheque no. 114 issued in payment of Voucher no. 100.

(c) Voucher no. 101 prepared to establish a petty cash fund of $150.

(d) Cheque no. 115 issued in payment of Voucher no. 101.

(e) Voucher no. 102 prepared to replenish the petty cash fund which contained $40 cash, and receipts for postage $38, miscellaneous expense $54, and delivery service $18.

(f) Cheque no. 116 issued in payment of Voucher no. 102. Cheque cashed and proceeds placed in petty cash fund.

PROBLEMS

Group A

8A-1 Use the information listed below to prepare a bank reconciliation for the Snipe Company at December 31, 19___:

(1) Cash per the books at December 31 amounted to $21,310; the bank statement at this date showed a balance of $18,346.

(2) The cash receipts of $3,903 on December 31 were mailed to the bank and not received by the bank during December.

(3) The paid cheques returned by the bank included a stolen cheque for $630 which had been paid in error by the bank after the Snipe Company had issued a "stop payment" order to the bank.

(4) The following memoranda accompanied the bank statement:
   (a) A debit memo for $9 for service charges for December.
   (b) A debit memo attached to a $486 cheque of a customer, Henry Wells, marked NSF.

(5) The following cheques had been issued by Snipe Company but were not included among the paid cheques returned by the bank; no. 167 for $978, no. 174 for $603, and no. 179 for $483.

8A-2 The following information summarizes the cash transactions of Bolt Company for the month of September.

(1) As of September 30, cash per books was $2,941.30; per bank statement, $2,782.78.

(2) Cash receipts of $911.26 on September 30 were not deposited until October 1.

(3) The following memoranda accompanied the bank statement:
   (a) A debit memo for service charges for the month of September, $3.15.
   (b) A debit memo attached to a cheque of P. Williams, marked NSF, for $62.45.
   (c) A credit memo for $605, representing the proceeds of a non-interest-bearing note collected by the bank for Bolt Company. The note was for $610; the bank deducted a collection fee of $5.

(4) The following cheques had been issued but were not included in the canceled cheques returned by the bank: no. 348 for $126, no. 351 for $51.80, and no. 356 for $35.54.

Instructions

a Prepare a bank reconciliation as of September 30.

b Draft in general journal form the journal entries necessary to adjust the accounts.

c State the amount of cash which should appear in the balance sheet at September 30.

8A-3 Madison Company established a petty cash fund in January of the current year and carried out the following transactions relating to the fund. (The company does not use a voucher system.)

Dec. 1 A cheque for $100 was issued and cashed to establish a petty cash fund.

Dec. 15 The fund was replenished after a count which revealed the following cash and petty cash vouchers for disbursements:

Office supplies expense	$15.70
Postage expense	26.00
Travel expense	31.25
Miscellaneous expense	8.40
Telephone and telegraph expense	12.70
Currency and coin	5.95

Dec. 31 A count of the fund at year-end disclosed the following:

Office supplies expense	$23.76
Postage expense	24.00
Travel expense	23.75
Miscellaneous expense	16.25
Currency and coin	12.24

A cheque was issued on December 31 to replenish the petty cash fund and to increase the amount of the fund to $150.

Instructions
a Prepare entries in general journal form to record the above transactions.
b Explain briefly why the petty cash fund should be replenished at the end of the accounting period even though the fund contains considerable cash.

8A-4 Mill Company uses a voucher system for all major expenditures. Selected transactions for May are presented below. As of April 30 one voucher, no H31, was outstanding.
(1) Paid a note, plus accrued interest, in favor of the Mercantile Bank.
(2) Gave a 60-day, 6% note in settlement of voucher no. H31.
(3) Drew a cheque to establish a petty cash fund.
(4) Purchased merchandise from J Company, terms 2/15, n/30.
(5) Purchased equipment, making a down payment and agreeing to pay the balance in 60 days.
(6) Received a credit memorandum from J Company for the return of a portion of the merchandise purchased from them.
(7) Made several small cash payments from the petty cash fund; all are chargeable to Office Expense.
(8) Advanced (by cheque) travel expenses to officer making a business trip
(9) Paid invoice from J Company, taking the discount.
(10) Drew cheque to reimburse petty cash fund for office expenses and delivery expense.
(11) Reimbursed officer by cheque for trip expenses incurred by him in excess of the amount advanced.

Instructions Using the form indicated in the example below, indicate how each of these transactions would be recorded by the company in the voucher register, the cheque register, and the general journal.

Example Purchased supplies from X company; paid invoice in full.

Voucher Register	Cheque Register	General Journal
Supplies on Hand xx	Vouchers Payable xx	No entry
Vouchers Payable . . xx	Cash xx	
Enter cheque number and		
date of payment.		

Group B

8B-1 From the information shown below for the Stream Company, prepare a bank reconciliation as of September 30, 19___:
(1) As of September 30, cash per books was $6,770; per bank statement, $5,782.
(2) Cash receipts of $1,301 on September 30 were not deposited until October 1.
(3) Among the paid cheques returned by the bank was a stolen cheque for $210 paid in error by the bank after Stream Company had issued a "stop payment" order to the bank.
(4) The following memoranda accompanied the bank statement:
  (a) A debit memo for service charges for the month of September, $3.
  (b) A debit memo attached to a $162 cheque of Joseph Ross, marked NSF
(5) The following cheques had been issued but were not included in the canceled cheques returned by the bank: no. 921 for $326, no. 924 for $201, and no. 925 for $161.

8B-2 Information concerning the cash operations of Pike Company for the month of December is presented below:

(1) The ledger account for Cash showed a balance at November 30 of $6,834.25.

(2) The cash receipts journal for December showed total cash received of $25,120.10.

(3) The credit to the Cash account posted from the cash disbursement journal at December 31 was $19,861.60.

(4) The cash received on December 31 amounted to $2,231.75. It was left at the bank in the night depository chute after banking hours on December 31 and was therefore not recorded by the bank on the December statement.

(5) The December bank statement showed a closing balance of $13,293.40.

(6) Also included with the December bank statement was a debit memorandum from the bank for $4.25 representing service charges for December.

(7) A credit memorandum enclosed with the December bank statement indicated that a non-interest-bearing note receivable for $2,525 from Jay Bell, left with the bank for collection, had been collected and the proceeds credited to the account of Pike Company.

(8) Comparison of the paid cheques returned by the bank with the entries in the cash payments journal revealed that cheque no. 821 for $463.90 issued December 15 in payment for office equipment had been erroneously entered in the cash payments journal as $436.90.

(9) Examination of the paid cheques also revealed that these cheques, all issued in December, had not yet been paid by the bank: no. 811 for $478.40; no. 814 for $356; no. 823 for $204.25.

(10) Included with the December bank statement was a $100 cheque drawn by William Davis, a customer of Pike Company. This cheque was marked NSF. It had been included in the deposit of December 27 but had been charged back against the company's account on December 31.

Instructions

a Prepare a bank reconciliation for the Pike Company at December 31. (*Suggestion:* As a first step compute the cash balance per the books at December 31.)

b Prepare journal entries (in general journal form) to adjust the accounts at December 31. Assume that the accounts have not been closed.

c State the amount of cash which should appear on the balance sheet at December 31.

8B-3 The following facts concern the petty cash fund of Grainhill Brewery. The company's fiscal year ends on June 30; it does not use a voucher system.

June 1 A cheque for $300 was issued and cashed to establish a petty cash fund.

June 22 A count of the fund showed petty cash vouchers and cash on hand as follows:

Office supplies expense	$ 45.65
Postage expense	33.60
Telephone and telegraph expense	10.50
Miscellaneous expense	30.20
Currency and coin	180.05

In view of the fact that the fund was less than half depleted after the first three weeks, management decided to reduce the fund permanently to the amount of $200. A cheque was issued in the amount to replenish the fund and establish it at the new authorized level.

June 30 At June 30 the fund was comprised of the following items. However, through oversight, the fund was not replenished.

Office supplies expense	*$36.00*
Postage expense	*48.00*
Telephone and telegraph expense	*12.50*
Miscellaneous expense	*34.20*
Currency and coin	*69.30*

Instructions

a Prepare entries in general journal form to record the above information. Include an entry at June 30 to record the expenditures to that date even though the fund was not replenished.

b What is the amount of the asset account, Petty Cash, at the close of business on June 30. Explain the circumstances which led to this balance, and indicate the action management will probably take early in the next fiscal year.

8B-4 **Instructions** Teal Company uses a voucher system for all cash expenditures. Following the form indicated in the example, indicate how the transactions given below would be recorded by the company.

Example Purchased supplies from X Company; paid invoice in full.

Voucher Register	*Cheque Register*	*General Journal*
Supplies on Hand . . . . . *xx*	*Vouchers Payable* . . . . . *xx*	*No entry*
Vouchers Payable . . *xx*	*Cash* . . . . *xx*	
Enter Cheque number and		
date of payment.		

(1) Purchased merchandise from R Company, terms 2/10, n/30, and paid invoice within 10 days.

(2) Received credit memorandum from R Company for the cost of merchandise returned after invoice had been paid. Teal Company will treat this as an account receivable from R Company.

(3) Purchased equipment from J Company on 30-day open account.

(4) Made a partial payment on the equipment purchase from J Company, and gave a six-month note for the balance.

(5) Paid the J Company note plus accrued interest.

(6) Drew a cheque to reimburse petty cash fund; all expenditures are chargeable to Miscellaneous Expense.

(7) Purchased merchandise from M Company, terms net 60 days.

BUSINESS DECISION PROBLEM 8

Don Stockdale inherited a highly successful business, Millstone Company, shortly after his twenty-second birthday and took over the active management of the business. A portion of the company's business consisted of over-the-counter sales for cash, but most sales were on credit and were shipped by truck. Stockdale had no knowledge of internal control practices and relied implicitly upon the bookkeeper-cashier, I. A. Green, in all matters relating to cash and accounting records. Green had been with the company for many years. He maintained the accounting records and prepared all financial statements with the help of two assistants, made bank deposits, signed cheques, and prepared bank reconciliations.

The monthly income statements submitted to Stockdale by Green showed a very satisfactory rate of net income; however, the amount of cash in the bank declined steadily during the first 18 months after Stockdale took over the business. To meet the company's weakening cash position, a bank loan was obtained and a few months later when the cash position again grew critical, the loan was increased.

On April 1, two years after Stockdale assumed the management of the company, Green suddenly left town, leaving no forwarding address. Stockdale was immediately deluged with claims of creditors who stated their accounts were several months past due and that Green had promised all debts would be paid by April 1. The bank telephoned to notify Stockdale that the company's account was overdrawn and that a number of cheques had just been presented for payment.

In an effort to get together some cash to meet this emergency, Stockdale called on two of the largest customers of the company, to whom substantial sales on account had recently been made, and asked if they could pay their accounts at once. Both customers informed him that their accounts were paid in full. They produced paid cheques to substantiate these statements and explained that Green had offered them reduced prices on merchandise if they would pay within 24 hours after delivery.

To keep the business from insolvency, Stockdale agreed to sell at a bargain price a half interest in the company. The sale was made to Brown, who had had considerable experience in the industry. One condition for the sale was that Brown should become the general manager of the business. The cash investment by Brown for his half interest was sufficient for the company to meet the demands on it and continue operations.

Immediately after Brown entered the business, he launched an investigation of Green's activities. During the course of this investigation the following irregularities were disclosed:

(1) During the last few months of Green's employment with the company, bank deposits were much smaller than the cash receipts. Green had abstracted most of the receipts and substituted for them a number of worthless cheques bearing fictitious signatures. These cheques had been accumulated in an envelope marked "Cash Receipts—For Deposit Only."

(2) Numerous legitimate sales of merchandise on account had been charged to fictitious customers. When the actual customer later made payment for the goods, Green abstracted the cheque or cash and made no entry. The account receivable with the fictitious customer remained on the books.

(3) When cheques were received from customers in payment of their accounts, Green had frequently recorded the transaction by debiting an expense account and crediting Accounts Receivable. In such cases Green had removed from the cash receipts an equivalent amount of currency, thus substituting the cheque for the currency and causing the bank deposit to agree with the recorded cash receipts.

(4) More than $3,000 a month had been stolen from petty cash. Fraudulent petty cash vouchers, mostly charged to the Purchases account, had been created to conceal these thefts and to support the cheques cashed to replenish the petty cash fund.

(5) For many sales made over the counter, Green had recorded lesser amounts on the cash register or had not rung up any amount. He had abstracted the funds received but not recorded.

(6) To produce income statements that showed profitable operations, Green had recorded many fictitious sales. The recorded accounts receivable included many from nonexistent customers.

(7) In preparing bank reconciliations, Green had omitted many outstanding cheques, thus concealing the fact that the cash in the bank was less than the amount shown by the ledger.

(8) Inventory had been recorded at inflated amounts in order to increase reported profits from the business.

Instructions

a For each of the numbered paragraphs, describe one or more internal control procedures you would recommend to prevent the occurrence of such fraud.

b Apart from specific internal controls over cash and other accounts, what general precaution could Stockdale have taken to assure himself that the accounting records were properly maintained and the company's financial statements complete and dependable? Explain fully.

NINE

RECEIVABLES AND PAYABLES

One of the key factors underlying the tremendous expansion of the Canadian economy has been the trend toward selling all types of goods and services on credit. The automobile industry has long been the classic example of the use of retail credit to achieve the efficiencies of large-scale output. Today, however, in nearly every field of retail trade it appears that sales and profits can be increased by granting customers the privilege of making payment a month or more after the date of sale. The sales of manufacturers and wholesalers are made on credit to an even greater extent than in retail trade.

ACCOUNTS RECEIVABLE

The credit department

No business concern wants to sell on credit to a customer who will prove unable or unwilling to pay his account. Consequently, most business organizations include a credit department which must reach a decision on the credit worthiness of each prospective customer. The credit department investigates the debt-paying ability and credit record of each new customer and determines the maximum amount of credit to be extended.

If the prospective customer is a business concern as, for example, a retail store, the financial statements of the store will be obtained and analyzed to determine its financial condition and the trend of operating results. The credit department will always prefer to rely upon financial statements which have been audited by independent public accountants

Regardless of whether the prospective customer is a business concern or an individual consumer, the investigation by the credit department will probably include the obtaining of a credit report from a local credit agency or from a national credit-rating institution such as Dun & Bradstreet Ltd. A credit agency compiles credit data on individuals and business concerns, and distributes this information to its clients. Most business concerns that make numerous sales on credit find it worthwhile to subscribe to the services of one or more credit agencies.

Uncollectible accounts

A business that sells its goods or services on credit will inevitably find that some of its accounts receivable are uncollectible. Regardless of how thoroughly the credit department investigates prospective customers, some uncollectible accounts will arise as a result of errors in judgment or because of unanticipated developments. As a matter of fact, a limited amount of uncollectible accounts is evidence of a sound credit policy. If the credit department should become too cautious and conservative in rating customers, it might avoid all credit losses, but in so doing, lose profitable business by rejecting many acceptable accounts.

Reflecting uncollectible accounts in the financial statements

One of the most fundamental principles of accounting is that *revenue must be matched with the expenses incurred in securing that revenue.*

Uncollectible accounts expense is caused by selling goods on credit to customers who fail to pay their bills; such expenses, therefore, are incurred in the year in which the sales are made, even though the accounts are not determined to be uncollectible until the following year. An account receivable which originates from a sale on credit in the year 1973 and is determined to be uncollectible sometime during 1974 represents an expense of the year 1973. Unless each year's uncollectible accounts expense is *estimated* and reflected in the year-end balance sheet and income statement, both of these financial statements will be seriously deficient.

To illustrate, let us assume that Arlington Distributors began business on January 1, 1973, and made most of its sales on credit throughout the year. At December 31, 1973, accounts receivable amounted to $200,000. On this date the management reviewed the status of the accounts receivable, giving particular study to accounts which were past due. This review indicated that the collectible portion of the $200,000 of accounts receivable amounted to approximately $190,000. In other words, management estimated that uncollectible accounts expense for the first year of operations amounted to $10,000. The following adjusting entry should be made at December 31, 1973:

Provision for uncollectible accounts

Uncollectible Accounts Expense	10,000	
Allowance for Uncollectible Accounts		10,000
To record the estimated uncollectible accounts expense for the year 1973.		

The Uncollectible Accounts Expense account created by the debit part of this entry is closed into the Income Summary account in the same manner as any other expense account. The Allowance for Uncollectible Accounts which was credited in the above journal entry will appear in the balance sheet as a deduction from the face amount of the accounts receivable. It serves to reduce the accounts receivable to their *realizable value* in the balance sheet, as shown by the following illustration:

ARLINGTON DISTRIBUTORS
Partial Balance Sheet
December 31, 1973
Assets

<table>
<tr><td>How much</td><td>Current assets:</td><td></td><td></td></tr>
<tr><td>is the
estimated</td><td>Cash . . . .</td><td></td><td>$ 75,000</td></tr>
<tr><td>realizable</td><td>Accounts receivable . . . .</td><td>$200,000</td><td></td></tr>
<tr><td>value of
the</td><td>Less: Allowance for uncollectible accounts . . . .</td><td>10,000</td><td>190,000</td></tr>
<tr><td>accounts</td><td>Inventory . . . .</td><td></td><td>100,000</td></tr>
<tr><td>receiv-
able?</td><td>Total current assets . . . .</td><td></td><td>$365,000</td></tr>
</table>

It is, however, also acceptable to show only the net amount of the accounts receivable without disclosing the deduction for bad debts.[1] Using the example above, it would be acceptable to present the accounts receivable in the balance sheet in the following manner:

Current assets	
Cash	$ 75,000
Accounts receivable	190,000
Inventory	100,000
Total current assets	$365,000

The allowance for uncollectible accounts

There is no way of telling in advance which accounts receivable will be collected and which ones will prove to be worthless. It is therefore not possible to credit the account of any particular customer to reflect our overall estimate of the year's credit losses. Neither is it possible to credit the Accounts Receivable control account in the general ledger. If the Accounts Receivable control account were to be credited with the estimated amount of expense from uncollectible accounts, this control account would no longer be in balance with the total of the numerous customers' accounts in the subsidiary ledger. The only practicable alternative, therefore, is to credit a separate account called Allowance for Uncollectible Accounts with the amount estimated to be uncollectible.

In the preceding chapters accounts have repeatedly been classified into five groups: (1) assets, (2) liabilities, (3) owner's equity, (4) revenue, and (5) expense. In which of these five groups of accounts does the Allowance for Uncollectible Accounts belong? The answer is indicated by the position of the Allowance for Uncollectible Accounts on the bal-

---

[1] *CICA Handbook,* Canadian Institute of Chartered Accountants, Toronto, December 1968 release. Section 3020.01

ance sheet. It appears among the assets and is used to reduce an asset (Accounts Receivable) from a gross value to a net realizable value. From the standpoint of account classification, the Allowance for Uncollectible Accounts is, therefore, included in the asset category.

The Allowance for Uncollectible Accounts is sometimes described as a *contra-asset* account, an *offset* account, an *asset reduction* account, a *negative asset* account, and most frequently of all, a *valuation* account. All these terms are derived from the fact that the Allowance for Uncollectible Accounts is an account with a credit balance, which is offset against an asset account to produce the proper balance sheet value for an asset.

Alternative titles for the Allowance for Uncollectible Accounts are Allowance for Bad Debts, or Allowance for Doubtful Accounts. Bad Debts Expense is also commonly used as an alternative title for Uncollectible Accounts Expense.

Other valuation accounts

The Allowance for Uncollectible Accounts has a good deal in common with the Accumulated Depreciation (or Allowance for Depreciation) account, which appears on the balance sheet as a deduction from depreciable asset accounts such as buildings or office equipment. Both the Allowance for Uncollectible Accounts and the Accumulated Depreciation account are created by adjusting entries and are based on estimates rather than on precisely determined amounts. In each case the debit side of the adjusting entry affects an expense account (Uncollectible Accounts Expense or Depreciation Expense).

In some respects, however, these two valuation accounts perform quite different functions. The Allowance for Uncollectible Accounts serves to reduce the accounts receivable to net realizable value. The Accumulated Depreciation account is *not* intended to reduce the building to realizable value but merely to show what portion of the original cost has expired and has been recorded as expense. Realizable value is not a significant concept in accounting for plant and equipment, because these properties are not intended to be sold but are to be used in the operation of the business.

Estimating uncollectible accounts expense

Before the accounts are closed and financial statements are prepared at the end of the accounting period, an estimate of uncollectible accounts expense must be made. This estimate will usually be based upon past experience, perhaps modified in accordance with current business conditions.

Since the allowance for uncollectible accounts is necessarily an estimate and not a precise calculation, the factor of personal judgment may play a considerable part in determining the size of this valuation account.

There is a fairly wide range of reasonableness within which the amount may be set. Most businessmen intend that the allowance shall be adequate to cover probable losses. The term *adequate,* when used in this context, suggests an amount somewhat larger than the minimum probable amount.

CONSERVATISM AS A FACTOR IN VALUING ACCOUNTS RECEIVABLE The larger the allowance established for uncollectible accounts, the lower the net valuation of accounts receivable will be. Some accountants and some businessmen tend to favor the most conservative valuation of assets that logically can be supported. Accountants necessarily make decisions under conditions of uncertainty. Conservatism in the preparation of a balance sheet implies a tendency to resolve uncertainties in the valuation of assets by reporting assets at their minimum values rather than by establishing values in a purely objective manner. From a theoretical point of view, the doctrine of balance sheet conservatism is difficult to support, but from the viewpoint of bankers and others who use financial statements as a basis for granting loans, conservatism in valuing assets has long been regarded as a desirable policy.

Assume that the balance sheet of Company A presents optimistic, exaggerated values for the assets owned. Assume also that this "unconservative" balance sheet is submitted to a banker in support of an application for a loan. The banker studies the balance sheet and makes a loan to Company A in reliance upon the values listed. Later the banker finds it impossible to collect the loan and also finds that the assets upon which he had based the loan were greatly overstated in the balance sheet. The banker will undoubtedly consider the overly optimistic character of the balance sheet as partially responsible for his loss. Experiences of this type have led bankers as a group to stress the desirability of conservatism in the valuation of assets.

In considering the argument for balance sheet conservatism, it is important to recognize that the income statement is also affected by the estimates made of uncollectible accounts expense. The act of providing a relatively large allowance for uncollectible accounts involves a correspondingly heavy charge to expense. Setting asset values at a minimum in the balance sheet has the related effect of stating the current year's net income at a minimum amount.

The provision for uncollectible accounts is an estimate of expense to be sustained. One widely used method of estimating this expense consists of adjusting the valuation account to a new balance equal to the estimated uncollectible portion of the existing accounts receivable. This method is referred to as the *balance sheet* approach and rests on an *aging of the accounts receivable.* The adjusting entry takes into consideration the existing balance in the Allowance for Uncollectible Accounts.

AGING THE ACCOUNTS RECEIVABLE A past-due account is always viewed with some suspicion. The fact that an account is past due suggests that the customer is either unable or unwilling to pay. The analysis of accounts by age is known as aging the accounts, as illustrated by the schedule below.

This analysis of accounts receivable gives management a useful picture of the status of collections and the probabilities of credit losses. Almost half of the total accounts receivable are past due. The question "How long past due?" is pertinent, and is answered by the bottom line of the aging analysis. About 29% of the total receivables are past due from 1 to 30 days; another 12% are past due from 31 to 60 days; about 3% are past due from 61 to 90 days; and 5% of the total receivables consist of accounts past due more than three months. If an analysis of

Analysis of Accounts Receivable by Age
December 31, 19___

Customer	Total	Not Yet Due	1–30 Days Past Due	31–60 Days Past Due	61–90 Days Past Due	Over 90 Days Past Due
A. B. Adams	$ 500	$ 500				
B. L. Baker	150			$ 150		
R. D. Carl	800	800				
H. V. Davis	900				$ 800	$ 100
R. M. Evans	400	400				
Others	32,250	16,300	$10,000	4,200	200	1,550
Totals	$35,000	$18,000	$10,000	$4,350	$1,000	$1,650
Percentage	100	51	29	12	3	5

If you were credit man- ager . . . ?

this type is prepared at the end of each month, management will be continuously informed of the trend of collections and can take appropriate action to ease or tighten credit policy. Moreover, a yardstick is available to measure the effectiveness of the persons responsible for collection activities.

The further past due an account receivable becomes, the greater the likelihood that it will not be collected in full. In recognition of this principle, the analysis of receivables by age groups can be used as a stepping-stone in determining a reasonable amount to add to the Allowance for Uncollectible Accounts. To make this determination it is desirable to estimate the percentage of probable expense for each age group of accounts receivable. This percentage, when applied to the dollar amount in each age group, gives a probable expense for each group. By adding together the probable expense for all the age groups, the required balance in the Allowance for Uncollectible Accounts is determined. The following schedule lists the group totals from the preceding illustration and shows how the total probable expense from uncollectible accounts is computed.

Accounts Receivable by Age Groups

	Amount	% Considered Uncollectible	Allowance for Uncollectible Accounts
Not yet due	$18,000	1	$ 180
1–30 days past due	10,000	3	300
31–60 days past due	4,350	10	435
61–90 days past due	1,000	20	200
Over 90 days past due	1,650	50	825
Totals	$35,000		$1,940

Estimate of probable uncollectible accounts expense

This summary indicates that an allowance for uncollectible accounts of $1,940 is required. Before making the adjusting entry, it is necessary to consider the existing balance in the allowance account. If the Allowance for Uncollectible Accounts presently has a credit balance of, say, $500, the adjusting entry should be for $1,440 in order to bring the account up to the required balance of $1,940. This entry is as follows:

Increasing allowance for uncollectible accounts

Uncollectible Accounts Expense	1,440	
Allowance for Uncollectible Accounts		1,440
To increase the valuation account to the estimated		
probable expense of $1,940, computed as follows:		
Present credit balance of valuation account	$ 500	
Current provision for uncollectible accounts	1,440	
New credit balance in valuation account	$1,940	

On the other hand, if the Allowance for Uncollectible Accounts contained a **debit** balance of $500 before adjustment, the adjusting entry would be made in the amount of $2,440 ($1,940 + $500) in order to create the desired credit balance of $1,940.

ESTIMATING UNCOLLECTIBLE ACCOUNTS AS A PERCENTAGE OF NET SALES An alternative approach to providing for uncollectible accounts preferred by some companies consists of computing the charge to uncollectible accounts expense as a percentage of the net sales for the year. The question to be answered is not "How large a valuation allowance is needed to show our receivables at realizable value?" Instead, the question is stated as "How much uncollectible accounts expense is associated with this year's volume of sales?" This method may be regarded as the **income statement** approach to estimating uncollectible accounts.

As an example, assume that for several years the expense of uncollectible accounts has averaged 1% of net sales (sales minus returns and allowances and sales discounts). At the end of the current year, before adjusting entries, the following account balances appear in the ledger:

	Dr	Cr
Sales		$1,060,000
Sales returns and allowances	$40,000	
Sales discounts	20,000	
Allowance for uncollectible accounts		1,500

The net sales of the current year amount to $1,000,000; 1% of this amount is $10,000. The existing balance in the Allowance for Uncollectible Accounts *should be ignored in computing the amount of the adjusting entry,* because the percentage of net sales method stresses the relationship between uncollectible accounts expense and net sales rather than the valuation of receivables at the balance sheet date. The entry is:

Provision for un-collectible accounts based on percentage of net sales

Uncollectible Accounts Expense	10,000	
Allowance for Uncollectible Accounts		10,000

To record uncollectible accounts expense of 1% of the year's net sales (.01 × $1,000,000).

If a concern makes both cash sales and credit sales, it may be desirable to exclude the cash sales from consideration and to compute the percentage relationship of uncollectible accounts expense to credit sales only.

Writing off an uncollectible account receivable

Whenever an account receivable from a customer is determined to be uncollectible, it no longer qualifies as an asset and should immediately be written off the books. To write off an account receivable is to reduce the balance of the customer's account to zero. The journal entry to accomplish this consists of a credit to the Accounts Receivable control account in the general ledger (and to the customer's account in the subsidiary ledger), and an offsetting debit to the Allowance for Uncollectible Accounts.

Referring again to the example of the Arlington Distributors as shown on page 271, the ledger accounts were as follows after the adjusting entry for estimated uncollectible accounts had been made on December 31, 1973:

Accounts receivable	$200,000
Less: Allowance for uncollectible accounts	10,000

Next let us assume that on January 27, 1974, a customer by the name of William Benton became bankrupt and the account receivable from him in the amount of $1,000 was determined to be worthless. The following entry should be made by the Arlington Distributors:

Writing off an uncol- lectible account
Allowance for Uncollectible Accounts *1,000*
        Accounts Receivable, William Benton *1,000*
To write off the receivable from William Benton as uncollectible.

The important thing to note in this entry is that the debit is made to the Allowance for Uncollectible Accounts and **not** to the Uncollectible Accounts Expense account. The estimated expense is charged to the Uncollectible Accounts Expense account at the end of each accounting period. When a particular account receivable is later ascertained to be worthless and is written off, this action does not represent an additional expense but merely confirms our previous estimate of the expense. If the Uncollectible Accounts Expense account were first charged with estimated credit losses and then later charged with proved credit losses, we would be guilty of double counting of uncollectible accounts expense.

After the entry writing off William Benton's account has been posted, the Accounts Receivable control account and the Allowance for Uncollectible Accounts appear as follows:

Accounts Receivable

Both accounts reduced by write- off of worthless receivable

1973			*1974*	
Dec. 31	*200,000*		*Jan. 27* *(Benton write-off)*	*1,000*

Allowance for Uncollectible Accounts

1974			*1973*	
Jan. 27 *(Benton write-off)*	*1,000*		*Dec. 31*	*10,000*

Note that the **net** amount of the accounts receivable was unchanged by writing off William Benton's account against the Allowance for Uncollectible Accounts.

Before the Write-off			*After the Write-off*	
Accounts receivable	*$200,000*		*Accounts receivable*	*$199,000*
Less: Allowance for un-			*Less: Allowance for un-*	
collectible accounts	*10,000*		*collectible accounts*	*9,000*
Net value of receivables ...	*$190,000*		*Net value of receivables* ...	*$190,000*

Net value of re- ceivables un- changed by write- off

The fact that writing off an uncollectible receivable against the Allowance for Uncollectible Accounts does not change the net carrying value of accounts receivable shows that no expense is entered in the books when an account is written off. This example bears out the point stressed earlier in the chapter: Credit losses belong in the period in which the sale is made, not in a later period in which the account is discovered to be uncollectible.

WRITE-OFFS SELDOM AGREE WITH PREVIOUS ESTIMATES   The total amount of accounts receivable written off in a given year will seldom, if ever, be exactly equal to the estimated amount previously credited to the Allowance for Uncollectible Accounts.

If the amounts written off as uncollectible turn out to be less than the estimated amount, the Allowance for Uncollectible Accounts will continue to show a credit balance. If the amounts written off as uncollectible are greater than the estimated amount, the Allowance for Uncollectible Accounts will acquire a debit balance, which will be eliminated by the adjustment at the end of the period.

Recovery of an account previously written off

Occasionally an account which has been written off as worthless will later be collected in full or in part. Such collections are often referred to as *recoveries* of bad debts. Collection of an account previously written off is evidence that the write-off was an error; the write-off entry should therefore be reversed.

Let us assume, for example, that a past-due account receivable in the amount of $400 from J. B. Barker was written off by the following entry:

Barker account considered uncollectible

Allowance for Uncollectible Accounts	400	
Accounts Receivable, J. B. Barker		400
To write off the receivable from J. B. Barker as uncollectible.		

At some later date the customer, J. B. Barker, pays his account in full. The entry to restore Barker's account will be:

Barker account reinstated

Accounts Receivable, J. B. Barker	400	
Allowance for Uncollectible Accounts		400
To reverse the entry writing off J. B. Barker's account.		

A separate entry will be made in the cash receipts journal to record the collection from Barker. This entry will debit Cash and credit Accounts Receivable.

Direct charge-off method of recognizing uncollectible accounts expense

Instead of making adjusting entries to record uncollectible accounts expense on the basis of estimates, some concerns merely charge uncollectible accounts to expense at the time such receivables are determined to be uncollectible. This method makes no attempt to match revenue and related expenses. Uncollectible accounts expense is recorded in the period in which the individual accounts are determined to be worthless rather than in the period in which the sales were made.

When the direct charge-off method is in use, the accounts receivable will be listed in the balance sheet at their gross amount, and no valuation allowance will be used. The receivables, therefore, are not stated at their probable realizable value.

In the determination of taxable income under present federal income tax regulations, both the direct charge-off method and the allowance method of estimating uncollectible accounts expense are acceptable. From the standpoint of accounting theory, the allowance method is much the better, for it enables expenses to be matched with related revenues and thus aids in making a logical measurement of net income.

Credit balances in accounts receivable

Customers' accounts in the accounts receivable subsidiary ledger normally have debit balances, but occasionally a customer's account will acquire a credit balance. This may occur because of overpayment, payment in advance, or the return of merchandise. Any credit balances in the accounts receivable subsidiary ledger should be accompanied by the notation "Cr" to distinguish them from accounts with normal debit balances.

Suppose that the Accounts Receivable controlling account in the general ledger has a debit balance of $9,000, representing the following individual accounts with customers in the subsidiary ledger:

49 accounts with debit balance	$10,000
1 account with a credit balance	1,000
Net debit balance of 50 customers' accounts	$ 9,000

One of the basic rules in preparing financial statements is that assets and liabilities should be shown in their gross amounts rather than being netted against each other. Accordingly, the amount which should appear as accounts receivable in the balance sheet is not the $9,000 balance of the controlling account, but the $10,000 total of the receivables with debit balances. The account with the $1,000 *credit balance is a liability* and should be shown as such rather than being concealed as an offset against an asset. The balance sheet presentation should be as follows:

Current assets:		*Current liabilities:*	
Accounts receivable	$10,000	Credit balances in customers'	
		accounts	$1,000

Analysis of accounts receivable

What dollar amount of accounts receivable would be reasonable for a business making annual credit sales of $1,200,000? Comparison of the average amount of accounts receivable with the sales made on credit during the period indicates how long it takes to convert receivables into cash. For example, if annual credit sales of $1,200,000 are made at a uniform rate throughout the year and the accounts receivable at year-end amount to $200,000, we can see at a glance that the receivables represent one-sixth of the year's sales, or about 60 days of uncollected sales. Management naturally wants to make efficient use of the available capital in the business, and therefore is interested in a rapid "turnover" of accounts receivable. If the credit terms offered by the business in the above example were, say, 30 days net, the existence of receivables equal to 60 days' sales would warrant investigation. The analysis of receivables is considered more fully in Chapter 21.

Receivables from installment sales

The importance of installment sales is emphasized by a recent annual report of Simpson-Sears Limited, which shows over $192 million of "customer installment accounts" representing over 95 per cent of total accounts receivable. Thus nearly all of the company's receivables call for collection in periodic installments.

An installment sale may or may not require a down payment; substantial interest charges are usually added to the "cash selling price" of the product in determining the total dollar amount to be collected in the series of installment payments. The seller usually has the right to repossess the merchandise if installments are not collected according to the terms of the installment contract. Repossessed merchandise is recorded at its current value rather than at its original cost or at the uncollected portion of the installment receivable.

Although the collection period for an installment sale often runs as long as 24 to 36 months, such installment receivables are regarded as current assets if they correspond to customary terms of the industry. For installment receivables maturing beyond one year, the amounts and maturity dates should be disclosed.[2]

NOTES RECEIVABLE

Definition of a promissory note

A promissory note is an unconditional promise in writing to pay on demand or at a future date a definite sum of money.

The person who signs the note and thereby promises to pay is called the *maker* of the note. The person to whom payment is to be made is called the *payee* of the note. In the illustration below G. L. Smith is the maker of the note and A. B. Davis is the payee.

Simplified form of promissory note

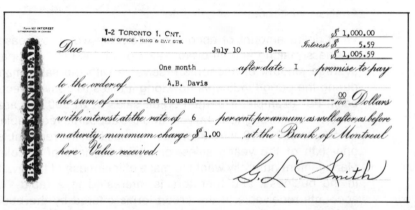

---

[2] *Ibid*, Section 3020.2

From the viewpoint of the maker, G. L. Smith, the illustrated note is a liability and is recorded by crediting the Notes Payable account. However, from the viewpoint of the payee, A. B. Davis, this same note is an asset and is recorded by debiting the Notes Receivable account. The maker of a note expects to pay cash at the maturity date; the payee expects to receive cash at that date.

Maturity dates

Days of grace In determining the legal due date of all notes or bills, except notes payable on demand, three days of grace are added to the time of payment fixed by the note. The date when payment of a note is required may be indicated in several different ways, as for example:

1 The maturity date may be named in the note: "I promise to pay $1,000 on September 30." The legal due date of the note would be October 3, allowing for the three days of grace.

2 The note may be payable after the expiration of a stated period of time. The time period may be stated in years, months, or days, as follows:

a. Time period stated in years: "Five years after date I promise to pay $1,000." If this note were dated September 30, 1960, the legal due date would be October 3, 1965 (that is, September 30, 1965, plus three days of grace).

b. Time period stated in months: "Six months after date I promise to pay $1,000." If this note were dated January 15 it would mature on July 18 (July 15, plus three days of grace), regardless of the fact that some of the intervening months had more or less than 30 days. In other words, it is not necessary to count days to determine the legal due date of a note drawn in terms of months or years.

c. Time period stated in days: "Ninety days after date I promise to pay $1,000." If this note were dated March 15, the legal due date would be June 16, computed as follows:

Days remaining in March (31 minus 15)	*16*
Days in April	*30*
Days in May	*31*
	77
Days in June (including 3 days of grace)	*16*
	93

Note that the day on which the note is issued is not counted as part of the 90-day period but that the date on which payment must be made (June 16) is included as one of the 90 days.

3 The note may be payable on demand: "On demand, I promise to pay $1,000." The note is legally due at the time when the payee demands payment. No days of grace are allowed.

4 The note may mature in installments. For example, a note dated June 10, 1961, in the amount of $1,000, might provide for a series of payments by the following wording of the maturity clause. "I promise to pay the principal sum of $1,000 in ten equal successive installments of $100 each, commencing on July 10, 1961, and continuing on the same date of each month thereafter until fully paid." Three days of grace are allowed on each installment. The legal due date of the first installment would be July 13, 1961, and the legal due dates for the nine remaining installments would be on the 13th of each successive month.

When the legal due date of a note falls on a legal holiday or a non-juridical day, the note is payable on the first business day following. Legal holidays and non-juridical days are defined by the Bills of Exchange Act.[3]

Nature of interest

Interest is a charge made for the use of money. To the borrower (maker of a note) interest is an expense; to the lender (payee of a note) interest is revenue.

COMPUTING INTEREST A formula used in computing interest is as follows:

Principal × rate of interest × time = interest

In computing interest, the exact number of days must be used. Interest rates are usually stated on an annual basis. For example, the interest on a $1,000, 6% note for 70 days is computed as follows:

Principal—$1,000
Rate of interest—6% per annum or 365 days (366 days in a leap year)
Time—73 days (70 days plus three days of grace)

$1,000 × 0.06 × $\frac{73}{365}$ = $12.00

If the term of $1,000, 6% note, issued on September 14, 1963, were two months instead of 70 days, the interest charge would be computed as follows

Principal—$1,000
Rate of interest—6% per annum
Time—

Days remaining in September (30-14)	16
Days in October	31
Days in November to legal due date (November 17)	17
Total number of days (including three days of grace)	64

$1,000 × 0.06 × $\frac{64}{365}$ = $10.52

INTEREST TABLES To simplify the interest computation, interest tables are used. The table given in this text indicates the interest earned, at selected rates of interest, on $100 for varying periods of time. When calculating the interest for a given note, the interest indicated in the appropriate column of the interest table is multiplied by the principal of the note and divided by 100. The steps in calculating interest by the use of interest tables are illustrated in the following examples.

---

[3] The following days are observed, under the Bills of Exchange Act, as legal holidays or non-juridical days: Saturdays, Sundays, New Year's Day, Good Friday, Easter Monday, Victoria Day, Dominion Day, Labour Day, Remembrance Day, Christmas Day, the birthday of the reigning sovereign, Thanksgiving Day, a provincial holiday proclaimed by the Lieutenant-Governor (observed only in that province), and civic holiday proclaimed by resolution of the municipal authority (observed only in that city or region). There are four additional legal holidays observed, under the Bills of Exchange Act in the province of Quebec; namely, the Epiphany, the Ascension, All Saints Day and Conception Day.

Example 1.

Compute the interest on a $1,000, 5% note dated June 10, due thirty days after issue date.

Steps in using the interest table at the end of this chapter:

a Set out the principal of the note ($1,000), the rate of interest (5% per annum) and the term of the note (33 days).

b Refer to the 5% column in the interest table.

c Move down the 5% column until you reach the 33 day line.

d Multiply the indicated figure (.45205) by the principal of the note ($1,000) and divide the answer ($452.05) by 100 to determine the interest ($4.52).

Example 2.

Compute the interest on a $1,200, 7% note due 90 days after issue.

a Principal is $1,200; rate of interest is 7% per annum; and the term of the note is 93 days.

b Refer to the 7% column in the interest table.

c Since the table does not go beyond 50 days, it is necessary to add two figures in order to determine the interest on $100 for 93 days.

Interest for 50 days	.95890
Interest for 43 days	.82466
Interest for 93 days	1.78356

d Multiply $1.78356 \times \frac{1200}{100}$ to compute the interest on $1,200 for 93 days. The interest amounts to $21.40.

Example 3.

Compute the interest on a $1,000, $4\frac{1}{2}$% note due 45 days after issue.

a Principal is $1,000; rate of interest is $4\frac{1}{2}$% per annum; and the term of the note is 48 days.

b Since the interest table does not have a column for $4\frac{1}{2}$%, it is necessary to interpolate as follows:

Interest at 4% for 48 days	.52603
Interest $\frac{1}{10}$ of 5% for 48 days ($\frac{1}{10}$ of .65753)	.06575
Interest at $4\frac{1}{2}$% for 48 days	.59178

c Interest on $1,000 for 48 days is $.59178 \times \frac{1,000}{100} = 5.92

Accounting for notes receivable

In some lines of business, notes receivable are seldom encountered; in other fields they occur frequently and may constitute an important part of total assets. Business concerns that sell high-priced durable goods such as automobiles and farm machinery often accept notes receivable from their customers. Many companies obtain notes receivable in settlement of past-due accounts.

All notes receivable are usually posted to a single account in the general ledger. A subsidiary ledger is not essential because the notes themselves, when filed by due dates, are the equivalent of a subsidiary ledger and provide any necessary information as to maturity, interest rates, collateral pledged, and other details. The amount debited to Notes Receivable is always the face amount of the note, regardless of whether or not the note bears interest. When an interest-bearing note is collected, the amount of cash received will be larger than the face amount of the note. The interest collected is credited to an Interest Earned account, and only the face amount of the note is credited to the Notes Receivable account.

ILLUSTRATIVE ENTRIES Assume that a 6%, 70-day note receivable is acquired from a customer, Marvin White, in settlement of an existing account receivable of $2,000. The entry for acquisition of the note is as follows:

Note received to replace account receivable	Notes Receivable 2,000	
	Accounts Receivable, Marvin White	2,000
	Accepted 6%, 70-day note in settlement of account receivable.	

The entry 73 days later to record collection of the note will be:

Collection of principal and interest	Cash 2,024	
	Notes Receivable	2,000
	Interest Earned	24
	Collected 6%, 90-day note from Marvin White.	

When a note is received from a customer at the time of making a sale of merchandise on account, two entries should be made, as follows:

Sale may be run through accounts receivable when note is received from customer	Accounts Receivable, F. H. Russ 1,500	
	Sales	1,500
	To record sale of merchandise on account.	
	Notes Receivable 1,500	
	Accounts Receivable, F. H. Russ	1,500
	To record receipt of note from customer.	

When this procedure is employed, the customer's account in the subsidiary ledger for accounts receivable provides a complete record of all transactions with him, regardless of the fact that some sales may have been made on open account and others may have involved a note receivable. Having a complete history of all transactions with a customer on a single ledger card may be helpful in reaching decisions as to collection efforts or further extensions of credit.

WHEN THE MAKER OF A NOTE DEFAULTS A note receivable which cannot be collected at maturity is said to have been *dishonored* by the maker.

Failure by the maker to pay interest or principal of a note at the due date is also known as *defaulting* on the note. Immediately after the dishonor or default of a note, an entry should be made by the holder to transfer the amount due from the Notes Receivable account to an account receivable from the debtor.

Assuming that a 60-day, 6% note receivable from Robert Jones is not collected at maturity, the following entry would be made:

Default *of note* *receivable*	Accounts Receivable, Robert Jones 1,010.36	
	Notes Receivable	1000.00
	Interest Earned	10.36

To record dishonor by Robert Jones of a 6%, 60-day note.

The interest earned on the note is recorded as a credit to Interest Earned and is also included in the account receivable from the maker. The interest receivable on a defaulted note is just as valid a claim against the maker as is the principal of the note; if the principal is collectible, then presumably the interest too can be collected.

By transferring past-due notes receivable into Accounts Receivable, two things are accomplished. First, the Notes Receivable account is limited to current notes not yet matured and is, therefore, regarded as a highly liquid type of asset. Secondly, the account receivable ledger card will show that a note has been dishonored and will present a complete picture of all transactions with the customer.

RENEWAL OF A NOTE RECEIVABLE Sometimes the two parties to a note agree that the note shall be renewed rather than paid at the maturity date. If the old note does not bear interest, the entry could be made as follows:

Renewal *of note* *should be* *recorded*	Notes Receivable 1,000	
	Notes Receivable	1,000
	A 60-day, non-interest-bearing note from Ray Bell renewed today with new 60-day, 6% note.	

Since the above entry causes no change in the balance of the Notes Receivable account, a question may arise as to whether the entry is necessary. The renewal of a note is an important transaction requiring managerial attention; a general journal entry is needed to record the action taken by management and to provide a permanent record of the transaction. If journal entries were not made to record the renewal of notes, confusion might arise as to whether some of the notes included in the balance of the Notes Receivable account were current or dishonored.

ADJUSTMENTS FOR INTEREST AT END OF PERIOD Notes receivable acquired in one accounting period often do not mature until a following period. Interest is being earned throughout the life of the note, and this revenue should be apportioned between the two accounting periods on a time basis. At the end of the accounting period, interest earned to date on notes receivable should be accrued by an adjusting entry debiting the asset account, Accrued Interest Receivable, and crediting the revenue account, Interest Earned. When the note matures and the interest is received in the following period, the entry to be made consists of a debit to Cash, a credit to Accrued Interest Receivable for the amount of the accrual, and a credit to Interest Earned for the remainder of the interest collected.

Discounting notes receivable

Many business concerns which obtain notes receivable and drafts from their customers prefer to sell the notes to a bank for cash rather than to hold them until maturity. Selling a note receivable to a bank or finance company is often called *discounting* a note receivable. The holder of the note signs his name on the back of the note (as in endorsing a cheque) and delivers the note to the bank. The bank expects to collect the *maturity value* (principal plus interest) from the maker of the note at the maturity date, but if the maker fails to pay, the bank can demand payment from the endorser.

When a businessman endorses a note and turns it over to a bank for cash, he is promising to pay the note if the maker fails to do so. The endorser is therefore contingently liable to the bank. A *contingent liability* may be regarded as a potential liability which either will develop into a full-fledged liability or will be eliminated entirely by a subsequent event. The subsequent event in the case of a discounted note receivable is the payment (or dishonoring) of the note by the maker. If the maker pays, the contingent liability of the endorser is thereby ended. If the maker fails to pay, the contingent liability of the endorser becomes a real liability. In either case the period of contingent liability ends at the maturity date of the note.

The discounting of notes receivable with a bank may be regarded by the businessman as an alternative to borrowing by issuing his own note payable. To issue his own note payable to the bank, would, of course, mean the creation of a liability; to obtain cash by discounting a note receivable creates only a contingent liability.

COMPUTING THE PROCEEDS The amount of cash obtained by discounting a note receivable is called the *proceeds* of the note. In some instances the bank may compute the proceeds merely by applying an interest rate to the face amount of the note for the period of time remaining before the note matures. This approach is logical when a non-interest-bearing note is discounted, because the face amount of the note and the maturity value are identical. If the note bears interest, however, the banker will surely give consideration to the rate of interest specified in the note and to any interest accrued as of the date of discounting. After considering these factors, the bank may set its own interest charge (discount) by applying to the face of the note a lower rate than it would require to discount a non-interest-bearing note. A more precise method of computing the discount charge to be made by the bank consists of the following steps:

1 Determine the maturity value of the note. The maturity value is the amount (including interest) which the holder of the note will be entitled to collect when the note matures. For a non-interest-bearing note, the maturity value is the face amount. For an interest-bearing note, the maturity value is the face amount plus the interest.

2 Determine the length of the discount period by counting the exact number of days from the date of discount to the date of maturity. In counting the number of days, exclude the date of discount but include the maturity date. The discount period is usually shorter than the life of the note; occasionally it equals the life of the note, but obviously, it can never exceed the life of the note.

3 Compute the discount by applying the discount rate (interest rate) charged by the bank to the maturity value of the note for the discount period.

4 Deduct the discount from the maturity value. The resulting amount represents the cash received from the bank, or the proceeds of the note.

To illustrate the application of the above steps, assume that on July 2 Roger Barnes receives a 70-day, 6% note for $8,000 from Raymond Kelly. The note will mature on September 13 (29 days in July, 31 days in August, and 13 days in September). On July 16, Roger Barnes discounts this note receivable with his bank, which charges a discount rate of 6% a year. How much cash does Barnes receive? The computation is as follows:

Face of the note	*$8000.00*
Add: Interest from date of note to maturity	*96.00*
Maturity value . . . . '	*8,096.00*
Less: Bank discount at 6% for the discount period of 59 days	
(July 16 to Sept. 13)	*78.53*
Proceeds (cash received from bank)	*8017.47*

The entry made by Barnes to record his discounting of the Kelly note would be as follows:

Cash	*8017.47*	
Notes Receivable		*8000.00*
Interest Earned		*17.47*
Discounted Raymond Kelly note at bank for 6%		

In this illustration, the cash of $8017.47 received from the bank was greater than the $8,000 face amount of the note. The proceeds received from discounting a note may be either more or less than the face amount of the note, depending upon the interest rates and time periods involved. The difference between the face amount of the note being discounted and the cash proceeds is usually recorded as either Interest Earned or Interest Expense. If the proceeds exceed the face value, the difference is credited to Interest Earned. However, if the proceeds are less than the face value of the note, the difference is debited to Interest Expense.

DISCOUNTED NOTE RECEIVABLE PAID BY MAKER Before the maturity date of the discounted note, the bank will notify the maker, Raymond Kelly, that it is holding the note. Kelly will therefore make payment directly to the bank.

DISCOUNTED NOTE RECEIVABLE DISHONORED BY MAKER If Kelly should be unable to pay the note at maturity, the bank will give notice of the default to the endorser, Roger Barnes. Barnes immediately becomes obligated to pay, and will make the following entry:

Accounts Receivable, Raymond Kelly *8,096*
    Cash *8,096*
To record payment to bank of discounted Kelly note, dishonored by
maker.

Under these assumptions Barnes's contingent liability to the bank has become a real liability and has been discharged by a cash payment. Barnes now has an account receivable from the maker of the defaulted note for the amount which he was compelled to pay to the bank.

Classification of receivables in the balance sheet

Accounts receivable from customers will ordinarily be collected within the operating cycle; they are therefore listed among the current assets on the balance sheet. Receivables may also arise from miscellaneous transactions other than the sale of goods and services. These miscellaneous receivables, such as advances to officers and employees, and claims against insurance companies for losses sustained, should be listed separately on the balance sheet and should not be merged with trade accounts receivable. If an account receivable from an officer or employee originates as a favor to the officer or employee, efforts at collection may await the convenience of the debtor. Consequently, it is customary to exclude receivables of this type from the current asset category.

Notes receivable usually appear among the current assets; however, if the maturity date of a note is more than a year distant and beyond the operating cycle of the business, it should be listed as noncurrent under a heading such as Investments. Any accrued interest receivable at the balance sheet date is a current asset but may be combined on the balance sheet with other accrued items such as accrued rents receivable or royalties receivable.

Contingent liabilities should be reflected in the balance sheet, because they have a considerable bearing on the credit rating of the person or firm contingently liable. A business concern with large contingent liabilities may encounter greater difficulties in obtaining bank loans than would otherwise be the case. The contingent liability arising from the discounting of notes receivable is usually disclosed by a *footnote* to the balance sheet. The following footnote is typical: "Note: At December 31, 19___, the company was contingently liable for notes receivable discounted in the amount of $250,000."

CURRENT LIABILITIES

Current liabilities are obligations that must be paid within the operating cycle or one year (whichever is longer). Comparison of the amount of current liabilities with the amount of current assets is one means of appraising the financial position of a business. In other words, a comparison of the amount of current liabilities with the amount of current assets available for paying these debts helps us in judging a company's short-run debt-paying ability.

In accounting for current liabilities, we are especially interested in making certain that all such obligations are included in the balance sheet. Fraud may be concealed by deliberate understatement of a liability. The omission or understatement of a liability will usually be accompanied by an overstatement of owner's equity or else by an understatement of assets. Depending on the nature of the error, the net income of the business may also be overstated.

Among the more common current liabilities are notes payable, accounts payable, and accrued or estimated liabilities, such as wages, interest, and taxes. An *estimated* liability is an obligation known to exist but for which the dollar amount is uncertain. In this chapter we shall consider the accounting problems relating to notes payable; the liabilities arising from payrolls will be considered in Chapter 13.

NOTES PAYABLE

Notes payable are issued whenever bank loans are obtained. Other transactions which may give rise to notes payable include the purchase of real estate or costly equipment, the purchase of merchandise, and the substitution of a note for a past-due open account. The use of notes payable in each of these situations is illustrated in the following pages.

Notes payable issued to banks

Assume that John Caldwell, the sole proprietor of a retail business, applies to his bank for a 90-day, unsecured loan of $7,300. In support of the loan application Caldwell submits a balance sheet and income statement.

After studying the financial statements, reading the auditor's report, and making inquiries about Caldwell's credit rating, the bank indicates its willingness to lend the $7,300 requested, at an interest rate of 10% The note which Caldwell signs will read as shown below, if we omit some of the minor details.

Interest stated separately

Vancouver, B.C.   June 15, 19—

....

Ninety days .... after date I promise to pay to Bank of British

Columbia the sum of $ .... 7,300 .... with interest at the rate of 10% per

annum.

John Caldwell

The journal entry on Caldwell's books to record this borrowing from the bank is:

Face amount of note

Cash   7,300
    Notes Payable   7,300
Borrowed $7,300 for 90 days at 10%

No interest expense is recorded at the time of issuing the note. When the note is paid on September 16, the entry to be made is:

Payment of principal and interest

Notes Payable   7,300
Interest Expense   186
    Cash   7,486
Paid bank at maturity date of loan.

ALTERNATIVE FORM OF NOTES FOR BANK LOANS   Instead of stating the interest separately as in the preceding illustration, the note payable to the bank could have been so drawn as to include the interest charge in the *face amount* of the note, as shown below:

Interest included in face amount of note

Vancouver, B.C.   June 15, 19—

....

On .... September 16, 19— .... the undersigned promises to pay to

Bank of British Columbia or order the sum of $7,486

John Caldwell

When the note is drawn in this manner the entry on Caldwell's books is:

Notes payable credited for face amount of note	Cash	7,300
	Discount on Notes Payable	186
	Notes Payable	7,486
	Borrowed $7,300 for 90 days at 10%	

Note that the amount of money borrowed ($7,300) was less than the face amount of the note ($7,486). However, as in all previous illustrations, the amount of the credit to the Notes Payable account was the face amount of the note. The liability to the bank at this time is equal to the amount of money borrowed, or $7,300. In order to show the proper measurement of the liability on the balance sheet, the Discount on Notes Payable account should be listed as a deduction from the Notes Payable account. The result is $7,486–186, or a net liability of $7,300.

On September 16, the maturity date of the note, Caldwell will hand the bank a cheque for $7,486 in payment of the note and will make the following journal entries:

Payment of note and interest expense	Notes Payable	7,486
	Cash	7,486
	Paid bank at maturity date of loan.	
	Interest Expense	186
	Discount on Notes Payable	186
	To record interest expense on matured note.	

Adjustments for interest at end of period

When a note is issued in one accounting period and matures in a later period, the interest expense must be apportioned. Adjusting entries for interest-bearing notes were illustrated in Chapter 4.

A different type of adjustment is necessary at the end of the period for notes payable to banks in which the interest has been included in the face amount of the note. For example, assume that Baker Company borrows $36,500 from its bank on November 1 on a 6%, 180 day note with interest of $1,098 included in the face of the note. The entry for the borrowing on November 1 would be:

Interest included in face of note and . . .	Cash	36,500
	Discount on Notes Payable	1,098
	Notes Payable	37,598
	Issued to bank a 6%, six-month note payable with interest included in face amount of note.	

At December 31, the adjusting entry required is:

. . . related
adjusting
entry

Interest Expense 360
    Discount on Notes Payable . . . . · 360
To record interest expense incurred to end of year on 6%, 180 day
note dated Nov. 1 (60/183 × 1,098)

On May 3, when the six-month note matures and the Baker Company pays the bank, the entry is as follows:

*Interest
applicable
to second
year*

Notes Payable 37,598
Interest Expense 738
    Cash 37,598
    Discount on Notes Payable 738
To record payment to bank of 6%, six-month note dated
Nov. 1, with interest included in face of note.

Discount on Notes Payable should be classified as a *contra-liability* account and deducted from the face value of notes payable in the current liability section of the balance sheet. This treatment results in showing as a liability at statement date the principal of the debt plus the accrued interest payable at that time.

Prepaid interest

Discount on notes payable is sometimes called *prepaid interest* and classified as a current asset, a practice which has little theoretical justification. To prepay interest on a loan has the effect of reducing the amount of money borrowed and increasing the effective rate of interest. Assume that on July 1 you borrow $1,000 from a bank for a period of $1\frac{1}{2}$ years at an annual interest rate of 8%. Assume also that you pay the bank the full 18 months' interest ($1,000 × 8% × 1.5) of $120 (ignoring days of grace) at the date of borrowing the $1,000. Under this procedure you have increased your cash position by only $880. A more realistic view of the transaction is to say you have incurred a liability of $880 which will increase to $1,000 during the next year and one-half.

Other transactions involving notes payable

Notes payable are often issued for the acquisition of real estate or expensive equipment. In recording such a transaction, the debit to the asset account (such as Land or Office Equipment) should be for the amount which would be paid if the asset were being purchased for cash. Any additional charge because of the delay in payment is interest, and is an expense applicable to the period of credit extension. In other words, we do not conceal interest expense by inflating the cost of assets acquired through issuance of notes payable.

If an account payable becomes past due, the debtor may be asked to sign a note payable to replace the open account. The issuance of the note payable is recorded by a debit to Accounts Payable and a credit to Notes Payable. When the debtor pays the note at maturity, his accounting entry will be a debit to Notes Payable and to Interest Expense, offset by a credit to Cash.

Next, let us assume the issuance of a note in payment for a $2,000 purchase of merchandise from National Supply Co. A note issued for the purchase of merchandise could be recorded by debiting Purchases and crediting Notes Payable. However, a more informative record will be available if the following pair of entries is made at the time of the purchase. (In practice, the first of these two entries would be made in the purchases journal.)

Purchase may be run through accounts payable when note is issued to supplier

Purchases	*2,000*	
* Accounts Payable, National Supply Co. . . . .*		*2,000*
To record purchase of merchandise.		
Accounts Payable, National Supply Co.	*2,000*	
* Notes Payable . . . .*		*2,000*
Issued a 60-day, 8% note to National Supply Co. for merchandise.		

Under this method, information on the total volume of purchases from a particular supplier will be readily available by reference to the supplier's account in the subsidiary ledger for accounts payable.

DEMONSTRATION PROBLEM FOR YOUR REVIEW

Among the receivables of the Bart Corporation Ltd. on January 1, 1974, were the following items:

Accounts receivable:

A. B. Cole	$ 5,040
M. E. White	7,600
I. J. Wall	17,200
Total	$29,840

Notes receivable:

R. K. Rogers, 6%, 45-day note, due Jan. 20, 1974	$20,000
P. J. King, 4½%, 60-day note, due Feb. 21, 1974	8,000
Total	$28,000

Installment contracts receivable:

L. D. Harris *(monthly payment $1,590)*	$11,130

Other data The installment contract receivable represents the unpaid balance of a 6%, one-year contract dated August 1, 1973. During the month of January, 1974, the following additional transactions took place.

Jan. 3 Received a 30-day, 5% note from A. B. Cole in full settlement of his account.

Jan. 14 M. E. White paid $3,000 on his account and gave a 60-day, 4% note to cover the balance.

Jan. 23 R. K. Rogers wrote that he would be unable to pay his note due today. He included a cheque to cover the interest due and a new 30-day, 6% note renewing the old note.

Jan. 27 Discounted the A. B. Cole note at the bank. The discount rate charged by the bank was 7%, applied to the maturity value of the note.

Jan. 30 Received the monthly payment on the L. D. Harris contract.

Instructions

a Prepare journal entries (in general journal form) for January, including any adjusting entries relating to accrued interest at January 31.

b Show how the accounts relating to notes receivable, accounts receivable, installment contracts receivable, and interest would appear on the balance sheet as of January 31. Show the actual balances.

Bills of exchange or drafts

A bill of exchange, commonly referred to as a draft in business practice, is an order in writing by one person on another person to pay on demand or at a future date a definite sum of money.[4] A draft is subject to acceptance by the person to whom it is addressed (the drawee). Although the draft is an order to the drawee to pay a sum of money, he is not under any obligation to accept the draft unless he has agreed in advance to do so. Generally, a business firm will not draw a draft on a customer unless it has reasonable assurance that the draft will be accepted. Once it is accepted, a draft is similar to a promissory note.

There are always three parties to a draft, namely:

The drawer—the person who draws and signs the draft.

The drawee—the person to whom the draft is addressed and who is ordered to make the payment.

The payee—the person to whom the payment is made.

Form of draft

[4]A more precise definition taken from the Bills of Exchange Act is as follows: "A bill of exchange is an unconditional order in writing, addressed by one person to another, signed by the person giving it, requiring the person to whom it is addressed to pay, on demand or at a fixed or determinable future time, a sum certain in money to or to the order of a specified person or to a bearer." (Section 17(1))

TABLE OF SIMPLE INTEREST

$$100 \times \text{Per Annum Rate} \times \frac{\text{Days effective}}{365}$$

| Days | PER ANNUM RATES | | | | | | | | | |
	1%	2%	3%	4%	5%	6%	7%	8%	9%	10%
1	.00274	.00548	.00822	.01096	.01370	.01644	.01918	.02192	.02466	.02740
2	.00548	.01096	.01644	.02192	.02740	.03288	.03836	.04384	.04932	.05479
3	.00822	.01644	.02466	.03288	.04110	.04932	.05753	.06575	.07397	.08219
4	.01096	.02192	.03288	.04384	.05479	.06575	.07671	.08767	.09863	.10959
5	.01370	.02740	.04110	.05479	.06849	.08219	.09589	.10959	.12329	.13699
6	.01644	.03288	.04932	.06575	.08219	.09863	.11507	.13151	.14795	.16438
7	.01918	.03836	.05753	.07671	.09589	.11507	.13425	.15342	.17260	.19178
8	.02192	.04384	.06575	.08767	.10959	.13151	.15342	17534	.19726	.21918
9	.02466	.04932	.07397	.09863	.12329	.14795	.17260	.19726	.22192	.24658
10	.02740	.05479	.08219	.10959	.13699	.16438	.19178	.21918	.24658	.27397
11	.03014	.06027	.09041	.12055	.15068	.18082	.21096	.24110	.27123	.30137
12	.03288	.06575	.09863	.13151	.16438	.19726	.23014	.26301	.29589	.32877
13	.03562	.07123	.10685	.14247	.17808	.21370	.24932	.28493	.32055	.35616
14	.03836	.07671	.11507	.15342	.19178	.23014	.26849	.30685	.34521	.38356
15	.04110	.08219	.12329	.16438	.20548	.24658	.28767	.32877	.36986	.41096
16	.04384	.08767	.13151	.17534	.21918	.26301	.30685	.35068	.39452	.43836
17	.04658	.09315	.13973	.18630	.23288	.27945	.32603	.37260	.41918	.46575
18	.04932	.09863	.14795	.19726	.24658	.29589	.34521	.39452	.44384	.49315
19	.05205	.10411	.15616	.20822	.26027	.31233	.36438	.41644	.46849	.52055
20	.05479	.10959	.16438	.21918	.27397	.32877	.38356	.43836	.49315	.54795
21	.05753	.11507	.17260	.23014	.28767	.34521	.40274	.46027	.51781	.57534
22	.06027	.12055	.18082	.24110	.30137	.36164	.42192	.48219	.54247	.60274
23	.06301	.12603	.18904	.25205	.31507	.37808	.44110	.50411	.56712	.63014
24	.06575	.13151	.19726	.26301	.32877	.39452	.46027	.52603	.59178	.65753
25	.06849	.13699	.20548	.27397	.34247	.41096	.47945	.54795	.61644	.68493
26	.07123	.14247	.21370	.28493	.35616	.42740	.49863	.56986	.64110	.71233
27	.07397	.14795	.22192	.29589	.36986	.44384	.51781	.59178	.66575	.73973
28	.07671	.15342	.23014	.30685	.38356	.46027	.53699	.61370	.69041	.76712
29	.07945	.15890	.23836	.31781	.39726	.47671	.55616	.63562	.71507	.79452
30	.08219	.16438	.24658	.32877	.41096	.49315	.57534	.65753	.73973	.82192
31	.08493	.16986	.25479	.33973	.42466	.50959	.59452	.67945	.76438	.84932
32	.08767	.17534	.26301	.35068	.43836	.52603	.61370	.70137	.78904	.87671
33	.09041	.18082	.27123	.36164	.45205	.54247	.63288	.72329	.81370	.90411
34	.09315	.18630	.27945	.37260	.46575	.55890	.65205	.74521	.83836	.93151
35	.09589	.19178	.28767	.38356	.47945	.57534	.67123	.76712	.86301	.95890
36	.09863	.19726	.29589	.39452	.49315	.59178	.69041	.78904	.88767	.98630
37	.10137	.20274	.30411	.40548	.50685	.60822	.70959	.81096	.91233	1.01370
38	.10411	.20822	.31233	.41644	.52055	.62466	.72877	.83288	.93699	1.04110
39	.10685	.21370	.32055	.42740	.53425	.64110	.74795	.85479	.96164	1.06849
40	.10959	.21918	.32877	.43836	.54795	.65753	.76712	.87671	.98630	1.09589
41	.11233	.22466	.33699	.44932	.56164	.67397	.78630	.89863	1.01096	1.12329
42	.11507	.23014	.34521	.46027	.57534	.69041	.80548	.92055	1.03562	1.15068
43	.11781	.23562	.35342	.47123	.58904	.70685	.82466	.94247	1.06027	1.17808
44	.12055	.24110	.36164	.48219	.60274	.72329	.84384	.96438	1.08493	1.20548
45	.12329	.24658	.36986	.49315	.61644	.73973	.86301	.98630	1.10959	1.23288
46	.12603	.25205	.37808	.50411	.63014	.75616	.88219	1.00822	1.13425	1.26027
47	.12877	.25753	.38630	.51507	.64384	.77260	.90137	1.03014	1.15890	1.28767
48	.13151	.26301	.39452	.52603	.65753	.78904	.92055	1.05205	1.18356	1.31507
49	.13425	.26849	.40274	.53699	.67123	.80548	.93973	1.07397	1.20822	1.34247
50	.13699	.27397	.41096	.54795	.68493	.82192	.95890	1.09589	1.23288	1.36986

The payee and the drawer of the draft may be the same person. Thus, while there are always three parties to a draft, only two persons may be involved.

Drafts are commonly used as collection devices and in connection with the sales of goods. The seller may require the purchaser to accept a time draft for the amount of the invoice covering the merchandise shipped to him. This practice is followed by the seller because the amount owing by the debtor is put in writing with a definite due date; and secondly, the draft may be discounted providing the seller with immediate funds.

MATURITY DATES OF DRAFTS Drafts may be required to be paid as follows:

(a) On demand: the bill of exchange or demand draft is payable immediately upon presentation to and acceptance by the debtor (drawee).

(b) On sight: a sight draft is payable three days after it has been accepted by the debtor (drawee).

(c) At a specified future date: a time draft or trade acceptance is payable upon the expiration of the specified period. Three days of grace are allowed on time drafts.

RECORDING DRAFTS As previously stated, an accepted draft is similar to a promissory note. Accounting for drafts is essentially the same as accounting for notes except that the creditor (drawer) usually makes no entry until the draft has been accepted.

QUESTIONS

1 Adams Company determines at year-end that its Allowance for Uncollectible Accounts should be increased by $6,500. Give the adjusting entry to carry out this decision.

2 In making the annual adjusting entry for uncollectible accounts, a company may utilize a *balance sheet approach* to make the estimate or it may use an *income statement approach.* Explain these two alternative approaches.

3 At the end of its first year in business, Baxter Laboratories had accounts receivable totaling $148,500. After careful analysis of the individual accounts, the credit manager estimated that $146,100 would ultimately be collected. Give the journal entry required to reflect this estimate in the accounts.

4 In February of its second year of operations, Baxter Laboratories (Question 3 above) learned of the failure of a customer, Sterling Corporation Ltd., which owed Baxter $800. Nothing could be collected. Give the journal entry to recognize the uncollectibility of the receivable from Sterling Corporation.

5 What is the *direct charge-off method* of handling credit losses as opposed to the *allowance method?* What is its principal shortcoming?

6 Morgan Corporation Ltd. has decided to write off the account receivable from Brill Company because the latter has entered bankruptcy. What general ledger accounts should be debited and credited, assuming that the allowance method is in use? What general ledger accounts should be debited and credited if the direct charge-off method is in use?

7 Mill Company, which has accounts receivable of $309,600 and an allowance for uncollectible accounts of $3,600, decides to write off as worthless a past-due account receivable for $1,500 from J. D. North. What effect will the write-off have upon total current assets? Upon net income for the period? Explain.

8 Describe a procedure by which management could be informed each month of the status of collections and the overall quality of the accounts receivable on hand.

9 The A Corporation Ltd. has in its ledger an account entitled Allowance for Bad Debts; B Corporation Ltd. uses an account entitled Allowance for Doubtful Accounts; and C Corporation Ltd. maintains an account called Reserve for Uncollectible Accounts. Does this information indicate that the three companies follow different methods of accounting for the expense arising from uncollectible accounts? Into which of the five major groups of accounts would you classify the three accounts listed?

10 Magnum Corporation Ltd. had accounts receivable of $100,000 and an Allowance for Uncollectible Accounts of $3,500 just prior to writing off as worthless an account receivable from Standard Company in the amount of $1,000. State the net realizable value of the accounts receivable before and after the write-off of this receivable from Standard Company.

11 Determine the maturity date of the following notes:
a A three-month note dated March 10
b A 30-day note dated August 15
c A 90-day note dated July 2

12 X Company acquires a 6%, 60-day note receivable from a customer, Robert Waters, in settlement of an existing account receivable of $4,000. Give the journal entry to record acquisition of the note and the journal entry to record its collection at maturity.

13 Jonas Company issues a 90 day, 6% note payable to replace an account payable to Smith Supply Company in the amount of $8,000. Draft the journal entries (in general journal form) to record the issuance of the note payable and the payment of the note at the maturity date.

14 Distinguish between
a Current and long-term liabilities
b Estimated and contingent liabilities

15 Howard Benson applied to the Royal Bank for a loan of $20,000 for a period of 91 days. The loan was granted at an annual interest rate of 8%. Show how the note would be drawn if
a Interest is stated separately in the note.
b Interest is included in the face amount of the note.

16 With reference to Question 15 above, give the journal entry required on the books of Howard Benson for issuance of each of the two types of notes.

EXERCISES

Ex. 9-1 Milo Company has accounts receivable from 100 customers; the controlling account shows a debit balance of $400,000. The subsidiary ledger shows that 99 customers' accounts have debit balances and 1 has a credit balance of $15,000. How should these facts be shown in the balance sheet? Give the reason for the treatment you recommend.

Ex. 9-2 The general ledger control account for accounts receivable shows a balance of $40,000 at the end of the year. An aging and analysis of the individual customers' accounts indicates doubtful accounts totaling $3,400. Draft the year-end adjusting entry for uncollectible accounts under each of the following independent assumptions:

a The allowance for uncollectible accounts has a credit balance of $1,100.
b The allowance for uncollectible accounts has a debit balance of $370.

Ex. 9-3 Using the simple interest table, compute interest on the following notes:
a $2,200 at 6% for 60 days
b $4,000 at 6% for 90 days
c $7,000 at 6% for 30 days
d $8,400 at 4% for 60 days
e $12,000 at 7% for 120 days
f $4,500 at 5% for 90 days

Ex. 9-4 Three notes receivable, each in the amount of $5,000, were discounted by a businessman at his bank on May 10. The bank charged a discount rate of 6%, applied to the maturity value. From the following data compute the proceeds of each note.

	Date of Note	Interest Rate, %	Life of Note
a	Apr. 10	6	3 months
b	Mar. 31	5	60 days
c	Mar. 11	8	90 days

Ex. 9-5 Fallon Company on October 31 borrowed $50,000 by issuing its note for six months, with interest at 6% on this sum included in the face amount of the note. Assuming that proper adjusting entries were made at year-end, what information relating to the borrowing would appear in the December 31 balance sheet? Where in the balance sheet would this information be placed?

PROBLEMS

Group A

9A-1 The balance sheet of Harvey Company at December 31 of last year showed $210,000 in accounts receivable and a credit balance of $11,000 in the allowance for uncollectible accounts. The following summary shows the totals of certain types of transactions occurring during January of the current year.

(1) Sales on account		$150,000
(2) Sales returns & allowances		3,000
(3) Cash payments by customers (no cash discounts)		148,000
(4) Account receivable from Rex Wiley written off as worthless following		
the failure of his business		3,200

At January 31, after a careful aging and analysis of all customers' accounts, the company decided that the allowance for uncollectible accounts should be adjusted to the amount of $12,200 in order to reflect accounts receivable at net realizable value in the January 31 balance sheet.

Instructions
a Give the appropriate entry in general journal form for each of the four numbered items above and the adjusting entry at January 31 to provide for uncollectible accounts.
b Show the amounts of accounts receivable and the allowance for uncollectible accounts as they would appear in a partial balance sheet at January 31.
c Assume that six months after the receivable from Rex Wiley had been written off as worthless, he won $100,000 in a lottery and immediately paid the $3,200 owed to Harvey Company. Give the journal entry or entries to reflect this collection in Harvey Company's accounts. (Use general journal form.)

9A-2 The credit policy of the Orange Company calls for all sales to be made on 30-day open account but requires customers who fail to pay invoices as agreed to substitute 6% promissory notes for their past-due accounts. No sales discounts are offered. A partial list of recent transactions follows:

Apr. 16 Sold merchandise to G. H. Blair on account, $30,000, terms n/30.

May 16 Received a 60-day, 6% note from G. H. Blair in settlement of his open account of $30,000.

June 25 Discounted the Blair note at bank. The bank discount rate was 6% applied to the maturity value of the note for the 23 days remaining to maturity.

July 18 Received notice from the bank that the Blair note due today was in default. Paid the bank the maturity value of the note. Since Blair owns a large amount of real estate in the area it is believed that Orange Company will not sustain any loss with respect to this account.

July 21 Loaned $15,000 to J. D. Black on a 60-day, 6% note.

Instructions

a Prepare in general journal form the entries necessary to record the above transactions.

b Prepare any adjusting journal entries needed at July 31, the end of the company's fiscal year, to record interest accrued on notes receivable. (Include interest at 6% from date of default on the maturity value of the Blair note.)

9A-3 Frame Corporation Ltd. engaged in the following transactions involving promissory notes during the fiscal year ended October 31.

June 6 Borrowed $8,000 from E. J. Davis, issuing to him a 45-day, 6% note payable.

July 13 Purchased office equipment from Daily Company. This invoice amount was $12,000 and the Daily Company agreed to accept as full payment a 6%, three-month note for the invoiced amount.

July 24 Paid the Davis note plus accrued interest.

Sept. 1 Borrowed $168,000 from Bank of Montreal at an interest rate of 6% per annum; signed a 90-day note with interest included in the face amount of the note.

Oct. 1 Purchased merchandise in the amount of $1,800 from Camp Co. Gave in settlement a 90-day note bearing interest at 4%.

Oct. 16 The $12,000 note payable to Daily Company matured today. Paid the interest accrued and issued a new 30-day, 6% note to replace the maturing note.

Instructions

a Prepare journal entries (in general journal form) to record the above transactions.

b Prepare the adjusting entries needed at October 31, prior to closing the books.

9A-4 Monaco Company has been expanding rapidly and finds itself short of working capital. The company therefore decides to obtain notes receivable from customers whenever feasible and to speed up the inflow of cash by discounting these notes receivable at the bank. The bank applies a discount rate to the maturity value of the notes, which varies with the quality of the note and the general level of interest rates. The company makes some sales on 30-day open account, but any customer who does not pay in full within 30 days is asked to substitute an interest-bearing note for the past-due account. Some customers are required to sign promissory notes at the time of sale.

The company uses the allowance method in accounting for uncollectible accounts.

A partial list of transactions for the six months ended December 31, 19____, is given below.

July 1 Sale of merchandise to P. Linn on account, $1,545. It was agreed that Linn would submit a 70-day, 8% note upon receipt of the merchandise, and should deduct any freight he paid on the goods.

July 3 Received from Linn a letter stating that he had paid $45 freight on the shipment of July 1. He enclosed a 70-day, 8% note dated July 3 for $1,500.

July 18 Sold merchandise on account, $2,200, to Baxter Company; terms 2/10, n/30.

July 27 Discounted Linn note at bank and received $1,508 in cash.

July 28 Baxter Company paid account in full.

Aug. 8 Sold merchandise to E. Jones on account, $1,200; terms 2/10, n/30

Sept. 14 Received notice from the bank that Linn had dishonored this note due today. The bank charged the company's account for $1,524, the maturity value of the note.

Sept. 7 Received a 70-day, 7% note from E. Jones in settlement of open account.

Sept. 10 It was ascertained that an account receivable from K. L. Treff amounting to $120 could not be collected and it was written off.

Oct. 15 An account receivable of $300 from Allen Blaine had been written off in June; full payment was unexpectedly received from Blaine.

Oct. 25 Received cash from P. Linn in full settlement of his account due today, including interest of 8% on $1,524 from September 1, maturity date of note.

Nov. 19 E. Jones paid his note due today.

Dec. 31 As a result of substantial write-offs, the Allowance for Uncollectible Accounts has a *debit* balance of $200. Aging of the accounts receivable (which amount to $80,000) indicates that a credit balance of $1,200 in the Allowance for Uncollectible Accounts is required.

Instructions Prepare journal entries (in general journal form) to record the transactions and adjustments listed above.

Group B

9B-1 The balance sheet prepared by Fernando Romero and Associates at December 31 last year included $315,000 in accounts receivable and an allowance for uncollectible accounts of $16,500. During January of the current year selected transactions are summarized as follows:

(1) *Sales on account*	*$230,000*
(2) *Sales returns & allowances*	*4,600*
(3) *Cash payments by customers (no cash discounts)*	*228,000*
(4) *Account receivable from Tyler Company written off as worthless*	*5,800*

After a careful aging and analysis of all customers' accounts at January 31, it was decided that the allowance for uncollectible accounts should be adjusted to a balance of $18,300 in order to reflect accounts receivable at net realizable value in the January 31 balance sheet.

Instructions

a Give the appropriate entry in general journal form for each of the four numbered items above and the adjusting entry at January 31 to provide for uncollectible accounts.

b Show the amounts of accounts receivable and the allowance for uncollectible accounts as they would appear in a partial balance sheet at January 31.

c Assume that three months after the receivable from Tyler Company had been written off as worthless, Tyler Company won a large award in the settlement of patent litigation and immediately paid the $5,800 debt to Fernando Romero and Associates. Give the journal entry or entries (in general journal form) to reflect this recovery of a receivable previously written off.

9B-2 Tile Company makes all its sales on 30-day open account, but requires customers who fail to pay invoices within 30 days to substitute promissory notes for their past-due accounts. No sales discount is offered. Among recent transactions were the following:

May 17 Sold merchandise to R. Scott on account, $60,000, terms n/30.

June 16 Received a 60-day, 9% note from Scott dated today in settlement of his open account of $60,000.

July 29 Discounted the Scott note at bank. The bank discount rate was 6% applied to the maturity value of the note for the 20 days remaining to maturity.

Aug. 18 Received notice from the bank that the Scott note due today was in default. Paid the bank the maturity value of the note. Since Scott has extensive business interests, the management of Tile Company is confident that no loss will be incurred on the defaulted note.

Aug. 25 Made a $40,000 loan to J. Reynolds on a 30-day, 9% note.

Instructions

a Prepare in general journal form the entries necessary to record the above transactions.

b Prepare the adjusting journal entry needed at August 31, the end of the company's fiscal year, to record interest accrued on the two notes receivable. (Accrue interest at 9% per annum from date of default on the maturity value of the Scott note.)

9B-3 The following transactions relating to notes payable occurred during the fiscal year ending September 30 in the Ivy Company:

May 6 Borrowed $4,000 from A. B. Clawson and issued a 45-day, 8% note payable as evidence of the debt.

June 12 Purchased office equipment from G-D Company. The invoice amount was $6,000 and the G-D Company agreed to accept as full payment a 6%, three-month note for the invoiced amount.

June 23 Paid the note made out to A. B. Clawson plus accrued interest.

Aug. 1 Borrowed $80,000 from Bank of Montreal at an interest rate of 7% per annum; signed a 90-day note with interest included in the face amount of the note.

Aug. 31 Purchased merchandise in the amount of $3,000 from Erdmore Company. Gave in settlement a 90-day note bearing interest at 8%.

Sept. 15 The $6,000 note payable to G-D Company matured today. Paid in cash the interest accrued and issued a new 30-day note bearing interest at 7% to replace the maturing note.

Instructions

a Prepare journal entries (in general journal form) to record the above transactions.

b Prepare the adjusting entries needed at September 30, prior to closing the books.

9B-4 Beach Company is short of working capital and attempts to minimize the funds tied up in receivables by discounting at the bank the notes receivable obtained from customers. The bank applies a discount rate of 6% to the maturity value of the notes on these transactions. The company makes some sales on 30-day open account, but any customer who does not pay in full within 30 days is asked to substitute an interest-bearing note for the past-due account. Some customers are required to sign promissory notes at the time of sale. When a note receivable is discounted, the company's policy calls for crediting the Notes Receivable account. A memorandum record of contingent liabilities is maintained.

A partial list of transactions for the six months ended December 31 is given below.

July 3 Sale of merchandise to E. Edwards on account, $20,075. It was agreed that Edwards would submit a 70-day, 6% note upon receipt of the merchandise, and should deduct any freight he paid on the goods.

July 5 Received from Edwards a letter stating that he had paid $75 freight on the shipment of July 3. He enclosed a 70-day, 6% note dated July 5 for $20,000, the net amount owed.

Aug.   4 Discounted Edwards note at bank. (Bank discount rate 6%.)

Aug. 23 Sold merchandise to D. E. Baker on account, $1,500; terms 2/10, n/30.

Sept. 16 Received notice from the bank that Edwards had dishonored his note due today. Made payment to bank for maturity value of note.

Sept. 22 Received a 70-day, 6% note from D. E. Baker in settlement of open account.

Oct.   2 Sold merchandise on account, $1,800, to Smithers Company; terms 2/10, n/30.

Nov.   1 Received a 90-day, 6% note as settlement of the $1,800 account receivable from Smithers Company.

Nov.   2 Received cash from E. Edwards in full settlement of his account due today, including interest of 6% from September 16 on maturity value of the note.

Dec.   4 D. E. Baker was unable to pay his note due today. Received a new 70-day, 6% note in settlement of old note and interest.

Instructions

a Prepare journal entries (in general journal form) to record the transactions listed above.

b Prepare any necessary adjusting entries for interest at December 31.

c Prepare a partial balance sheet at December 31 showing the notes and interest resulting from the above transactions.

BUSINESS DECISION PROBLEM 9

Roger Cannon, a friend of yours who owns Cannon Supply Company, comes to you for advice concerning his policy of accounting for uncollectible accounts. "My primary goal," he explains, "is that the balance sheet should show accounts receivable at the nearest possible carrying value to the amount we will actually collect. Our present policy doesn't seem to do this very well, and some of my relatives who have been lending money to my company have been very critical of this aspect of our balance sheet."

Upon investigation you find that the company has followed the policy of providing for uncollectible accounts at the rate of $\frac{1}{2}$ of 1% of net sales. However, it appears that this provision has been inadequate, because the Allowance for Uncollectible Accounts had a debit balance of $1,224.50 at December 31 prior to making the annual provision. At December 31, the accounts receivable totaled $81,280; this total amount included past-due accounts in the amount of $16,810. None of these past-due accounts was considered hopeless; all accounts receivable regarded as worthless had been written off the books as rapidly as they were determined to be uncollectible. These write-offs had totaled $2,324.50 during the year. After discussions with the credit manager, you conclude that the probable uncollectible portion of the past-due accounts on the books at December 31 is 10%, and that in addition the company should anticipate a loss of 1% of the current accounts receivable.

Instructions

a Explain to Roger Cannon the method of estimating uncollectible accounts receivable you would recommend in order to achieve his stated goal of showing receivables in the balance sheet as closely as possible to their realizable value.

b Compute the probable uncollectible portion of the accounts receivable at December 31.

c Prepare the journal entry to carry out the change in company policy which you have recommended with respect to providing for uncollectible accounts receivable.

INVENTORIES

TEN

Some basic questions relating to inventory

In earlier sections of this book the procedures for recording inventory at the end of the accounting period have been illustrated. The use of the inventory figure in both the balance sheet and the income statement has been demonstrated, and particular emphasis has been placed on the procedure for computing the cost of goods sold by deducting the ending inventory from the cost of goods available for sale during the period.

In all the previous illustrations, the dollar amount of the ending inventory has been given with only a brief explanation as to how this amount was determined. The valuation of inventory, as for most other types of assets, has been stated to be at cost, but the concept of cost as applied to inventories of merchandise has not been explored or defined.

In this chapter we shall consider some of the fundamental questions involved in accounting for inventories. Among the questions to be considered are these:

1 What goods are to be included in inventory?
2 How is the amount of the ending inventory determined?
3 What are the arguments for and against each of several alternative methods of inventory valuation?

Inventory defined

One of the largest assets in a retail store or in a wholesale business is the inventory of merchandise, and the sale of this merchandise at prices in excess of cost is the major source of revenue. The inventory of a merchandising concern consists of all goods owned and held for sale in the regular course of business. Merchandise held for sale will normally be converted into cash within less than a year's time and is therefore regarded as a current asset. In the balance sheet, inventory is listed immediately after accounts receivable, because it is just one step further removed from conversion into cash than are the accounts receivable.

In manufacturing businesses there are three major types of inventories: *raw materials, goods in process of manufacture,* and *finished goods.* All three classes of inventories are included in the current asset section of the balance sheet.

The term *inventory* has been defined by the Canadian Institute of Chartered Accountants to mean "items of tangible personal property which are held for sale in the ordinary course of business, or are in process of production for such sale, or are to be currently consumed in the production of goods or services to be available for sale."[1]

Inventory valuation and the measurement of income

In measuring the gross profit on sales earned during an accounting period, we subtract the *cost of goods sold* from the total *sales* of the period. The figure for sales is easily accumulated from the daily record of sales transactions, but in many businesses no day-to-day record is maintained showing the cost of goods sold.[2] The figure representing the cost of goods sold during an entire accounting period is computed at the end of the period by separating the cost of goods available for sale into two elements:

1 The cost of the goods sold
2 The cost of the goods not sold, which therefore comprise the ending inventory

This idea, with which you are already quite familiar, may be concisely stated in the form of an equation as follows:

Finding cost of goods sold

$$\text{Cost of Goods Available for Sale} - \text{Ending Inventory} = \text{Cost of Goods Sold}$$

Determining the amount of the ending inventory is the key step in establishing the cost of goods sold. In separating the *cost of goods available for sale* into its components of *goods sold* and *goods not sold,* we are just as much interested in establishing the proper amount for cost of goods sold as in determining a proper figure for inventory. Throughout this chapter you should bear in mind that the procedures for determining the amount of the ending inventory are also the means for determining the cost of goods sold. The valuation of inventory and the determination of the cost of goods sold are in effect the two sides of a single coin.

The Canadian Institute of Chartered Accountants has summarized this relationship between inventory valuation and the measurement of income in the following words: ". . . the most suitable method for determining cost (of inventory) is that which results in charging against operations costs which most fairly match the sales revenue for the period."[3] The expression "matching costs against revenues" means determining what portion of the cost of goods available for sale should be deducted from the revenues of the current period and what portion should be carried forward (as inventory) to be matched against the revenues of the following period.

[1] Canadian Institute of Chartered Accountants, *Terminology for Accountants*, revised edition (Toronto, 1962), page 39.
[2] As explained in Chap. 5, a company that maintains perpetual inventory records will have a day-to-day record of the cost of goods sold and of goods in inventory. Our present discussion, however, is based on the assumption that the periodic method of inventory is being used.
[3] *CICA Handbook*, Section 3030.08

Importance of an accurate valuation of inventory

The most important current assets in the balance sheets of most companies are cash, accounts receivable, and inventory. Of these three, the inventory of merchandise is usually much the largest. Because of the relatively large size of this asset, an error in the valuation of inventory may cause a material misstatement of financial condition. An error of 20% in valuing the inventory may have as much effect on the financial statements as would the complete omission of the asset cash.

An error in inventory will of course lead to other erroneous figures in the balance sheet, such as the total current assets, total assets, owner's equity, and the total of liabilities and owner's equity. The error will also affect key figures in the income statement, such as the cost of goods sold, the gross profit on sales, and the net income for the period. Finally, it is important to recognize that the ending inventory of one year is also the beginning inventory of the following year. Consequently, the income statement of the second year will also be in error by the full amount of the original error in inventory valuation.

ILLUSTRATION OF THE EFFECTS OF AN ERROR IN VALUING INVENTORY
Assume that on December 31, 1973, the inventory of the Hillside Company is actually $100,000 but, through an accidental error, it is recorded as $90,000. The effects of this $10,000 error on the income statement for the year 1973 are indicated in the first illustration on page 304, showing two income statements side by side. The left-hand set of figures shows the inventory of December 31, 1973, at the proper value of $100,000 and represents a correct income statement for the year 1973. The right-hand set of figures represents an incorrect income statement, because the ending inventory is erroneously listed as $90,000. Note the differences between the two income statements with respect to net income, gross profit on sales, and cost of goods sold.

This illustration shows that an understatement of $10,000 in the ending inventory for the year 1973 caused an understatement of $10,000 in the net income for 1973. Next, consider the effect of this error on the income statement of the following year. The ending inventory of 1973 is, of course, the beginning inventory of 1974. The preceding illustration is now continued to show side by side a correct statement and an incorrect statement for 1974. The ending inventory of $120,000 for the year 1974 is the same in both statements and is to be considered correct. Note that the $10,000 error in the beginning inventory of the right-hand statement causes an error in the cost of goods sold, in gross profit, and in net income for the year 1974.

COUNTERBALANCING ERRORS The illustrated income statements for the years 1973 and 1974 show that an understatement of the ending inventory in 1973 caused an understatement of net income in that year and an

HILLSIDE COMPANY

Income Statement

For the Year Ended December 31, 1973

<table>
<tr><td></td><td></td><td colspan="2">**With Correct
Ending Inventory**</td><td colspan="2">**With Incorrect
Ending Inventory**</td></tr>
<tr><td>*Effect of
error in
inventory*</td><td>Sales . . . .</td><td></td><td>$240,000</td><td></td><td>$240,000</td></tr>
<tr><td></td><td>Cost of goods sold:</td><td></td><td></td><td></td><td></td></tr>
<tr><td></td><td>Beginning inventory, Dec. 31, 1972 . . .</td><td>$ 75,000</td><td></td><td>$ 75,000</td><td></td></tr>
<tr><td></td><td>Purchases. . . . .</td><td>210,000</td><td></td><td>210,000</td><td></td></tr>
<tr><td></td><td>Cost of goods available for sale. . . .</td><td>$285,000</td><td></td><td>$285,000</td><td></td></tr>
<tr><td></td><td>Less: Ending inventory, Dec. 31, 1973 .</td><td>100,000</td><td></td><td>90,000</td><td></td></tr>
<tr><td></td><td>Cost of goods sold . . . .</td><td></td><td>185,000</td><td></td><td>195,000</td></tr>
<tr><td></td><td>Gross profit on sales . . . .</td><td></td><td>$ 55,000</td><td></td><td>$ 45,000</td></tr>
<tr><td></td><td>Operating expenses . . . .</td><td></td><td>30,000</td><td></td><td>30,000</td></tr>
<tr><td></td><td>Net income . . . .</td><td></td><td>$ 25,000</td><td></td><td>$ 15,000</td></tr>
</table>

HILLSIDE COMPANY

Income Statement

For the Year Ended December 31, 1974

<table>
<tr><td></td><td></td><td colspan="2">**With Correct
Beginning Inventory**</td><td colspan="2">**With Incorrect
Beginning Inventory**</td></tr>
<tr><td>*Effect on
succeeding
year*</td><td>Sales . . . .</td><td></td><td>$265,000</td><td></td><td>$265,000</td></tr>
<tr><td></td><td>Cost of goods sold:</td><td></td><td></td><td></td><td></td></tr>
<tr><td></td><td>Beginning inventory, Dec. 31, 1973 . . .</td><td>$100,000</td><td></td><td>$ 90,000</td><td></td></tr>
<tr><td></td><td>Purchases. . . . .</td><td>230,000</td><td></td><td>230,000</td><td></td></tr>
<tr><td></td><td>Cost of goods available for sale. . . .</td><td>$330,000</td><td></td><td>$320,000</td><td></td></tr>
<tr><td></td><td>Less: Ending inventory, Dec. 31, 1974 .</td><td>120,000</td><td></td><td>120,000</td><td></td></tr>
<tr><td></td><td>Cost of goods sold . . . .</td><td></td><td>210,000</td><td></td><td>200,000</td></tr>
<tr><td></td><td>Gross profit on sales . . . .</td><td></td><td>$ 55,000</td><td></td><td>$ 65,000</td></tr>
<tr><td></td><td>Operating expenses . . . .</td><td></td><td>33,000</td><td></td><td>33,000</td></tr>
<tr><td></td><td>Net ncome . . . .</td><td></td><td>$ 22,000</td><td></td><td>$ 32,000</td></tr>
</table>

offsetting overstatement of net income for 1974. Over a period of two years the effects of an inventory error on net income will counterbalance, and the total net income for the two years together is the same as if the error had not occurred. Since the error in reported net income for the first year is exactly offset by the error in reported net income for the second year, it might be argued that an inventory error has no serious consequences. Such an argument is not sound, for it disregards the fact that accurate yearly figures for net income are a primary objective of the accounting process. Moreover, many actions by management and many decisions by creditors and owners are based directly on the annual financial statements. To produce dependable annual statements, inventory must be accurately determined at the end of each accounting period. The counterbalancing effect of an inventory error is illustrated below:

	With Inventory Correctly Stated	With Inventory at Dec. 31, 1973, Understated	
		Reported Net Income Will Be	Reported Net Income Will Be Overstated (Understated)
Counter- Net income for 1973.	$25,000	$15,000	($10,000)
balancing *effect* Net income for 1974.	22,000	32,000	10,000
on net *income* Total net income for two years	$47,000	$47,000	–0–

RELATION OF INVENTORY ERRORS TO NET INCOME The effects of errors in inventory upon net income may be summarized as follows:

1 When the *ending* inventory is understated, the net income for the period will be understated.

2 When the *ending* inventory is overstated, the net income for the period will be overstated.

3 When the *beginning* inventory is understated, the net income for the period will be overstated.

4 When the *beginning* inventory is overstated, the net income for the period will be understated.

Taking a physical inventory

At the end of each accounting period up-to-date balances for most of the assets will be shown in the ledger accounts. For inventory, however, the balance in the ledger account represents the *beginning* inventory, because no entry has been made in the Inventory account since the end of the preceding period. All purchases of merchandise during the present period have been recorded in the Purchases account. The ending inventory does not appear anywhere in the ledger accounts; it must be determined by a physical count of merchandise.

Establishing a balance sheet valuation for the ending inventory requires two steps: (*1*) determining the quantity of each kind of merchandise on hand, and (2) multiplying the quantity by the cost per unit. The first step is called *taking the inventory;* the second is called *pricing the inventory.* Taking inventory, or more precisely, taking a physical inventory, means making a systematic count of all merchandise on hand.

In most merchandising businesses the taking of a physical inventory is a year-end event. In some lines of business an inventory may be taken at the close of each month. It is common practice to take inventory after regular business hours or on Sunday. By taking the inventory while business operations are suspended, a more accurate count is possible than if goods were being sold or received while the count was in process.

PLANNING THE PHYSICAL INVENTORY Unless the taking of a physical inventory is carefully planned and supervised, serious errors are apt to occur which will invalidate the results of the count. To prevent such errors as the double counting of items, the omission of goods from the count, and other quantitative errors, it is desirable to plan the inventory so that the work of one person serves as a check on the accuracy of another.

There are various methods of counting merchandise. One of the simplest procedures is carried out by the use of two-man teams. One member of the team counts and calls the description and quantity of each item. The other person lists the descriptions and quantities on an inventory sheet. (In some situations, a tape recorder is useful in recording quantities counted.) When all goods have been counted and listed, the items on the inventory sheet are priced at cost, and the unit prices are multiplied by the quantities to determine the valuation of the inventory.

To assure the accuracy of the recorded counts, a representative number of items should be recounted by supervisors. Some businesses make a practice of counting all merchandise a second time and comparing the quantities established by the different teams. The initials of the persons making both the first and the second counts should be placed on an inventory tag attached to each lot of merchandise counted. Once it is known that all merchandise has been tagged and that the counts are accurate, the tags are gathered and sent to the accounting office for completion of the inventory.

INCLUDING ALL GOODS OWNED All goods to which the company has title should be included in the inventory, regardless of their location. Title to merchandise ordinarily passes from seller to buyer at the time the goods are delivered. No question arises as to the ownership of merchandise on the shelves, in stock rooms, or in warehouses. A question of ownership does arise, however, for merchandise en route from suppliers but not yet received on the last day of the year. A similar question of ownership concerns goods in the process of shipment to customers at year-end.

Goods in transit Do goods in transit belong in the inventory of the seller or of the buyer? If the seller makes delivery of the merchandise in his own trucks, the merchandise remains his property while in transit. If the goods are shipped by rail, air, or other public carrier, the question of ownership of the goods while in transit depends upon whether the public carrier is acting as the agent of the seller or of the buyer. If the terms of the shipment are *F.O.B.* (free on board) *shipping point,* title passes at the point of shipment and the goods are the property of the buyer while in transit. If the terms of the shipment are *F.O.B. destination,* title does not pass until the shipment reaches the destination, and the goods belong to the seller while in transit. In deciding whether goods in transit at year-end should be included in inventory, it is therefore necessary to refer to the terms of the agreements with vendors (suppliers) and customers.

At the end of the year a company may have received numerous orders from customers, for which goods have been segregated and packed but not yet shipped. These goods should generally be included in inventory. An exception to this rule is found occasionally when the goods have been prepared for shipment but are being held for later delivery at the request of the customer.

Passage of title to merchandise The debit to the customer's account and the offsetting credit to the Sales account should be made when title to the goods passes to the customer. It would obviously be improper to set up an account receivable and at the same time to include the goods in question in inventory. Great care is necessary at year-end to ensure that all last-minute shipments to customers are recorded as sales of the current year and, on the other hand, that no customer's order is recorded as a sale until the date when the goods are shipped. Sometimes, in an effort to meet sales quotas, companies have recorded sales on the last day of the accounting period, when in fact the merchandise was not shipped until early in the next period. Such practices lead to an over-statement of the year's earnings and are not in accordance with generally accepted principles of accounting.

Merchandise in inventory is valued at *cost,* whereas accounts receivable are stated at the *sales price* of the merchandise sold. Consequently, the recording of a sale prior to delivery of the goods results in an un-justified increase in the total assets of the company. The increase will equal the difference between the cost and the selling price of the goods in question. The amount of the increase will also be reflected in the income statement, where it will show up as additional earnings. An unscrupulous company, which wanted to make its financial statements present a more favorable picture than actually existed, might do so by treating year-end orders from customers as sales even though the goods were not yet shipped.

Pricing the inventory

One of the most interesting and widely discussed problems in accounting is the pricing of inventory. Even those business men who have little knowledge of accounting are usually interested in the various methods of pricing inventory, because inventory valuation has a direct effect upon reported net income. Income taxes are based on income, and the choice of inventory method may have a considerable effect upon the amount of income taxes payable. The Income Tax department will accept any of the commonly used methods for determining the cost or fair market value of inventory except the last-in, first-out method. However, once the taxpayer has selected a particular method, he must continue to follow that method.

In approaching our study of inventory valuation, however, it is impor-tant that we do not overemphasize the income tax aspects of the problem.

It is true that in selected cases one method of inventory valuation may lead to a substantially lower income tax liability than would another method, but there are other important considerations in pricing inventory apart from the objective of minimizing the current income tax burden.

Proper valuation of inventory is one part of a larger undertaking, that is, to measure net income accurately and to provide all those persons interested in the financial condition and operating results of a business with accounting data which are dependable and of maximum usefulness as a basis for business decisions.

Although several acceptable methods are used in pricing the inventory, the most significant basis of accounting for inventories is *cost.* Another important method, which is acceptable for income tax purposes and is widely used, is known as the *lower of cost or market.* First we shall consider the cost basis of accounting for inventories, for an understanding of the meaning of the term *cost* as applied to inventories is a first essential in appreciating the complexity of the overall problem of inventory valuation.

Cost basis of inventory valuation

"The primary basis of accounting for inventory is cost, which has been defined generally as the price paid or consideration given to acquire an asset. As applied to inventories, cost means in principle the sum of the applicable expenditures and charges directly or indirectly incurred in bringing an article to its existing condition and location."[4]

TRANSPORTATION-IN AS AN ELEMENT OF COST The starting point in determining the cost of an article of merchandise is the price paid, as shown by the vendor's invoice. To this acquisition cost should be added the cost of transportation incurred in bringing the merchandise to the location where it is to be offered for sale.

The logic of treating transportation-in as part of the cost of goods purchased is indicated by the following example. A Calgary appliance dealer orders 10 refrigerators from a Hamilton manufacturer. The manufacturer pays the cost of shipping the refrigerators to Calgary and submits an invoice in the amount of $2,000. This is the total amount to be paid by the Calgary merchant, so the cost of the goods is clearly $2,000. Now assume that the appliance dealer places a second order for another 10 identical refrigerators. On this second order the invoice from the Hamilton manufacturer is for only $1,800; under the terms of this purchase, however, the Calgary merchant is required to pay the railroad for the freight charges of $200 applicable to the shipment. On both of these identical shipments the total cash paid by the Calgary merchant was $2,000, so clearly the charge for transportation is part of the cost of merchandise purchased.

---

[4] American Institute of Certified Public Accountant, *Accounting Research and Terminology Bulletins,* Final Edition, (New York, 1961), page 28. (The *CICA Handbook, ibid,* on page 1081 makes essentially the same recommendation.)

At the end of the year when a physical inventory is taken, the cost of each kind of merchandise is multiplied by the quantity on hand to determine the dollar amount of the ending inventory. The price paid for an article may readily be found by referring to the invoice from the supplier, but often there is no convenient method of determining how much transportation cost may have been incurred on specific types of merchandise. This is particularly true when certain shipments have included various kinds of merchandise and the freight charge was for the shipment as a whole. For reasons of convenience and economy, therefore, a merchandising business may choose to determine inventory cost at year-end by listing each item in stock at the purchase invoice price, and then adding to the inventory as a whole a reasonable proportion of the transportation charges incurred on inbound shipments during the year.

In many lines of business it is customary to price the year-end inventory without giving any consideration to transportation charges. This practice may be justified by the factors of convenience and economy, even though it is not theoretically sound. If freight charges are not material in amount, it may be advisable in terms of operating convenience to treat the entire amount as part of the cost of goods sold during the year. Accounting textbooks stress theoretical concepts of cost and of income determination; the student of accounting should be aware, however, that in many business situations an approximation of cost will serve the purpose at hand. In other words, the extra work involved in computing more precise cost data must be weighed against the benefits to be obtained.

OTHER CHARGES RELATING TO ACQUISITION OF MERCHANDISE If transportation-in is part of the cost of merchandise purchased, what about the other incidental charges relating to the acquisition of merchandise, such as the salary of the purchasing agent, insurance of goods in transit, cost of receiving and inspecting the merchandise, etc.? Although in theory these incidental charges should be identified and apportioned among the various items of merchandise purchased, the expense of computing cost on such a precise basis would usually outweigh the benefits to be derived. The costs of operating the purchasing department and the receiving department are customarily treated as expense of the period in which incurred, rather than being carried forward to another period by inclusion in the balance sheet amount for inventory.

PURCHASE DISCOUNTS AS A FACTOR IN INVENTORY VALUATION When a merchant purchases goods he often has the opportunity of saving 1 to 2% of the invoiced amount by making payment within a specified period, usually 10 days. Since purchase discounts are shown as a deduction from purchases in the income statement, they should logically be deducted from the invoice price of the items comprising the year-end inventory. Often, however, it is impracticable to compute the precise amount of discount applicable to each item in inventory. One reasonable alternative is to deduct from the invoice cost of the entire ending inventory an amount representing the estimated purchase discounts applicable to these goods. If purchase discounts are not significant in amount, they may be ignored for the purpose of inventory pricing.

Determining cost of inventory when purchase prices vary

The prices of many kinds of merchandise are subject to frequent change. When identical lots of merchandise are purchased at various dates during the year, each lot may be acquired at a different cost price.

To illustrate the several alternative methods in common use for determining which purchase prices apply to the units remaining in inventory at the end of the period, assume the data shown below.

	Number of Units	Cost per Unit	Total Cost
Beginning inventory	10	$ 8	$ 80
First purchase (Mar. 1)	5	9	45
Second purchase (July 1)	5	10	50
Third purchase (Oct. 1)	5	12	60
Fourth purchase (Dec. 1)	5	13	65
Available for sale	30		$300
Units sold	18		
Units in ending inventory	12		

This schedule shows that 18 units were sold during the year and that 12 units are on hand at year-end to make up the ending inventory. In order to establish a dollar amount for cost of goods sold and for the ending inventory, we must make an assumption as to which units were sold and which units remain on hand at the end of the year. There are several acceptable assumptions on this point; four of the most common will be considered. Each assumption made as to the cost of the units in the ending inventory leads to a different method of pricing inventory and to different amounts in the financial statements. The four assumptions (and inventory valuation methods) to be considered are known as: (1) specific identification, (2) average cost, (3) first-in, first-out, and (4) last-in, first-out.

Although each of these four methods will produce a different answer as to the cost of goods sold and the cost of the ending inventory, the valuation of inventory in each case is said to be at "cost." In other words, *these methods represent alternative definitions of inventory cost.*

SPECIFIC IDENTIFICATION METHOD If the units in the ending inventory can be identified as coming from specific purchases, they **may** be priced at the amounts listed on the purchase invoices. Continuing the example already presented, if the ending inventory of 12 units can be identified as, say, five units from the purchase of March 1, four units from the purchase of July 1, and three units from the purchase of December 1, the cost of the ending inventory may be computed as follows:

Specific identifica-tion method and . . .	Five units from the purchase of Mar. 1 @ $9	$ 45
	Four units from the purchase of July 1 @ $10	40
	Three units from the purchase of Dec. 1 @ $13	39
	Ending inventory (specific identification)	$124

The cost of goods sold during the period is determined by subtracting the ending inventory from the cost of goods available for sale.

. . . cost of goods sold com-putation	Cost of goods available for sale	$300
	Less: Ending inventory	124
	Cost of goods sold	$176

A business may prefer not to use the specific identification method even though the cost of each unit sold could be identified with a specific purchase. The flow of cost factors may be more significant than the flow of specific physical units in measuring the net income of the period.

As a simple example, assume that a coal dealer purchased 100 tons of coal at $18 a ton and a short time later made a second purchase of 100 tons of the same grade coal at $20 a ton. The two purchases are in separate piles and it is a matter of indifference as to which pile is used in making sales to customers. Assume that the dealer makes a retail sale of one ton of coal at a price of $25. In measuring the gross profit on the sale, which cost figure should be used, $18 or $20? To insist that the cost depended on which of the two identical piles of coal was used in filling the delivery truck is an argument of questionable logic.

A situation in which the specific identification method is more likely to give meaningful results is in the purchase and sale of such high-priced articles as boats, automobiles, and jewelry.

AVERAGE-COST METHOD Average cost is computed by dividing the total cost of goods available for sale by the number of units available for sale. This computation gives a **weighted average unit cost,** which is then applied to the units in the ending inventory.

Average-cost method and . . .	Cost of goods available for sale	$300
	Number of units available for sale	30
	Average unit cost	$ 10
	Ending inventory (at average cost, 12 units @ $10)	$120

Note that this method, when compared with the actual invoice price method, leads to a different amount for cost of goods sold as well as a different amount for the ending inventory.

Cost of goods available for sale	$300
Less: Ending inventory	120
Cost of goods sold	$180

When the average-cost method is used, the cost figure determined for the ending inventory is influenced by all the various prices paid during the year. The price paid early in the year may carry as much weight in pricing the ending inventory as a price paid at the end of the year. A common criticism of the average-cost method of pricing inventory is that it attaches no more significance to current prices than to prices which prevailed several months earlier.

FIRST-IN, FIRST-OUT METHOD The first-in, first-out method, which is often referred to as *fifo,* is based on the assumption that the first merchandise acquired is the first merchandise sold. In other words, each sale is made out of the oldest goods in stock; the ending inventory therefore consists of the most recently acquired goods. The fifo method of determining inventory cost may be adopted by any business, regardless of whether or not the physical flow of merchandise actually corresponds to this assumption of selling the oldest units in stock. Using the same data as in the preceding illustrations, the 12 units in the ending inventory would be regarded as consisting of the most recently acquired goods, as follows:

First-in, first-out method and . . .

Five units from the Dec. 1 purchase @ $13	$ 65
Five units from the Oct. 1 purchase @ $12	60
Two units from the July 1 purchase @ $10	20
Ending inventory, 12 units (at fifo cost)	$145

During a period of rising prices the first-in, first-out method will result in a larger amount being assigned as the cost of the ending inventory than would be assigned under the average-cost method. When a relatively large amount is allocated as cost of the ending inventory, a relatively small amount will remain as cost of goods sold, as indicated by the following calculation:

. . . cost of goods sold com- putation

Cost of goods available for sale	$300
Less: Ending inventory	145
Cost of goods sold	$155

It may be argued in support of the first-in, first-out method that the inventory valuation reflects recent costs and is therefore a realistic value in the light of conditions prevailing at the balance sheet date.

LAST-IN, FIRST-OUT METHOD The title of this method of pricing suggests that the most recently acquired goods are sold first, and that the ending inventory consists of "old" merchandise acquired in the earliest purchases. Such an assumption is, of course, not in accord with the actual physical movement of goods in most businesses, but there is nevertheless a strong logical argument to support this method. As merchandise is sold, more goods must be purchased to replenish the stock on hand. Since the making of a sale necessitates a replacement purchase of goods, the cost of replacement should be offset against the sales price to determine the gross profit realized.

The supporters of last-in, first-out, or *lifo,* as it is commonly known, contend that the accurate determination of income requires that primary emphasis be placed on the matching of current costs of merchandise against current sales prices, regardless of which physical units of merchandise are being delivered to customers. Keeping in mind the point that the *flow of costs* may be more significant than the *physical movement* of merchandise, we can say that, under the lifo method, the cost of goods sold consists of the cost of the most recently acquired goods, and the ending inventory consists of the cost of the oldest goods which were available for sale during the period.

Using the same data as in the preceding illustrations, the 12 units in the ending inventory would be priced as if they were the oldest goods available for sale during the period, as follows:

Last-in,	*Ten units from the beginning inventory @ $8*	*$80*
first-out	*Two units from the purchase of Mar. 1 @ $9*	*18*
method		
and . . .	*Ending inventory, 12 units (at lifo cost)*	*$98*

Note that the lifo cost of the ending inventory ($98) is very much lower than the fifo cost ($145) of ending inventory in the preceding example. Since a relatively small part of the cost of goods available for sale is assigned to ending inventory, it follows that a relatively large portion must have been assigned to cost of goods sold, as shown by the following computation:

. . . cost	*Cost of goods available for sale*	*$300*
of goods	*Less: Ending inventory*	*98*
sold com-		
putation	*Cost of goods sold*	*$202*

COMPARISON OF THE ALTERNATIVE METHODS OF PRICING INVENTORY We have now illustrated four common methods of pricing inventory at cost; the specific identification method, the average-cost method, first-in, first-out method, and the last-in, first-out method. By way of contrasting the results obtained from the four methods illustrated, especially during a period of rapid price increases, let us summarize the amounts computed for ending inventory, cost of goods sold, and gross profit on sales under each of the four methods. Assume that sales for the period amounted to $275.

<table>
<tr><td></td><td>Specific Identifi-cation Method</td><td>Average-cost Method</td><td>First-in, First-out Method</td><td>Last-in, First-out Method</td></tr>
<tr><td>Sales . . . .</td><td>$275</td><td>$275</td><td>$275</td><td>$275</td></tr>
<tr><td>Cost of goods sold:</td><td></td><td></td><td></td><td></td></tr>
<tr><td>Beginning inventory . . . .</td><td>$ 80</td><td>$ 80</td><td>$ 80</td><td>$ 80</td></tr>
<tr><td>Purchases . . . .</td><td>220</td><td>220</td><td>220</td><td>220</td></tr>
<tr><td>Cost of goods available for sale . . .</td><td>$300</td><td>$300</td><td>$300</td><td>$300</td></tr>
<tr><td>Less: Ending inventory . . . .</td><td>124</td><td>120</td><td>145</td><td>98</td></tr>
<tr><td>Cost of goods sold . . . .</td><td>$176</td><td>$180</td><td>$155</td><td>$202</td></tr>
<tr><td>Gross profit on sales . . . .</td><td>$ 99</td><td>$ 95</td><td>$120</td><td>$ 73</td></tr>
</table>

Four methods of deter-mining inventory cost compared

This comparison of the four methods makes it apparent that during periods of *rising prices,* the use of lifo will result in lower profits being reported than would be the case under the other methods of inventory valuation. Perhaps for this reason many businesses have adopted lifo.

During a period of *declining prices,* the use of lifo will cause the reporting of relatively large profits as compared with fifo, which will hold reported profits to a minimum. Obviously, the choice of inventory method becomes of greatest significance during prolonged periods of drastic changes in price levels.

WHICH METHOD OF INVENTORY VALUATION IS BEST? All four of the inventory methods described are regarded as acceptable accounting practices and all methods, except lifo, are acceptable in the determination of taxable income. No one method of inventory valuation can be considered as the "correct" or the "best" method. In the selection of a method, consideration should be given to the probable effect upon the balance sheet, upon the income statement, upon the amount of taxable income, and upon such business decisions as the establishment of selling prices for goods.

When prices are changing drastically, the most significant cost data to use as a guide to sales policies are probably the current replacement costs of the goods being sold. The lifo method of inventory valuation comes closer than any of the other methods described to measuring net income in the light of current selling prices and current replacement costs.

On the other hand, the use of lifo during a period of rising prices is apt to produce a balance sheet figure for inventory which is far below the current replacement cost of the goods on hand. The fifo method of inventory valuation will lead to a balance sheet valuation of inventory more in line with current replacement costs.

Some business concerns which adopted lifo more than 30 years ago now show a balance sheet figure for inventory which is less than half the present replacement cost of the goods in stock. An inventory valuation method which gives significant figures for the income statement may thus produce misleading amounts for the balance sheet, whereas a method which produces a realistic figure for inventory on the balance sheet may provide less realistic data for the income statement.

The search for the "best" method of inventory valuation is rendered difficult because the inventory figure is used in both the balance sheet and the income statement, and these two statements are intended for different purposes. In the income statement the function of the inventory figure is to permit a matching of costs and revenues. In the balance sheet the inventory and the other current assets are regarded as a measure of the company's ability to meet its current debts. For this purpose a valuation of inventory in line with current replacement cost would appear to be most significant.

Where the method of determining cost, such as lifo, results in a figure on the balance sheet significantly different from recent cost, "the method of determining cost should be disclosed."[5]

The lower-of-cost-or-replacement-cost rule

Although cost is the primary basis for valuation of inventories, circumstances may arise under which inventory may properly be valued at less than its cost. If the utility of the inventory has fallen below cost by reason of physical deterioration, obsolescence, or decline in the price level, a loss has occurred. This loss may appropriately be recognized as a loss of the current period by reducing the accounting value of the inventory from cost to a lower level designated as market. The word *market* as used in this context *means current replacement cost.* For a merchandising concern, *market* is the amount which the concern would have to pay at the present time for the goods in question, purchased in the customary quantities through the usual sources of supply and including transportation-in. To avoid misunderstanding, the rule might better read "lower of cost or replacement cost." In accordance with the CICA recommendation,[6] replacement cost will be used instead of market in the remainder of this discussion.

In the early days of accounting when the principal users of financial statements were creditors and attention was concentrated upon the balance sheet, conservatism was a dominant consideration in asset valuation. The lower-of-cost-or-replacement cost rule was then consid-

[5] CICA Handbook, op., cit., Section 3030.11
[6] *Ibid.*

ered justifiable because it tended to produce a "safe" or minimum value for inventory. The rule was widely applied for a time without regard for the possibility that although replacement costs had declined, there might be no corresponding and immediate decline in selling prices.

As the significance of the income statement has increased, considerable dissatisfaction with the lower-of-cost-or-replacement cost rule has developed. If ending inventory is written down from cost to a lower replacement cost figure but the merchandise is sold during the next period at the usual selling prices, the effect of the write-down will have been to reflect a fictitious loss in the first period and an exaggerated profit in the second period. Arbitrary application of the lower-of-cost-or-replacement cost rule ignores the historical fact that selling prices do not always drop when replacement prices decline. Even if selling prices do follow replacement prices downward, they may not decline by a proportionate amount.

Because of these objections, the lower-of-cost-or-replacement cost rule has undergone some modification and is now qualified in the following respects. If the inventory can probably be sold at prices which will yield a *normal profit,* the inventory should be carried at cost even though current replacement cost is lower. Assume, for example, that merchandise is purchased for $1,000 with the intention of reselling it to customers for $1,500. The replacement cost then declines from $1,000 to $800, but it is believed that the merchandise can still be sold to customers for $1,450. In other words, the normal anticipated profit has shrunk by $50. The carrying value of the inventory could then be written down from $1,000 to $950. There is no justification for reducing the inventory to the replacement cost of $800 under these circumstances.

Another qualification of the lower-of-cost-or-replacement cost rule is that inventory should never be carried at an amount greater than *net realizable value* which may be defined as prospective selling price minus anticipated selling expenses. Assume, for example, that because of unstable market conditions, it is believed that goods acquired at a cost of $500 and having a current replacement cost of $450 will probably have to be sold for no more than $520 and that the selling expenses involved will amount to $120. The inventory should then be reduced to a carrying value (net realizable value) of $400, which is less than current replacement cost.

APPLICATION OF THE LOWER-OF-COST-OR-REPLACEMENT COST RULE
The lower of cost or replacement cost for an inventory is most commonly computed by determining the cost and the replacement cost figures for each item in inventory and using the lower of the two amounts in every case. If, for example, item A cost $100 and replacement cost is $90, the item should be priced at $90. If item B cost $200 and replacement cost is $225, this item should be priced at $200. The total cost of the two items is $300 and total replacement cost is $315, but the total inventory value

determined by applying the lower-of-cost-or-replacement cost rule to each item in inventory is only $290. This application of the lower-of-cost-or-replacement cost rule is illustrated by the tabulation shown below.

Application of Lower-of-cost-or-replacement cost Rule, Item-by-item Method

	Item	Quantity	Unit Price		Lower of Cost or Replacement Cost
			Cost	Replacement Cost	
Pricing	A	10	$100	$ 90	$ 900
inventory at lower	B	8	200	225	1,600
of cost or	C	50	50	60	2,500
replacement cost	D	80	90	70	5,600
	Total				$10,600

If the lower-of-cost-or-replacement cost rule is applied item by item, the carrying value of the above inventory would be $10,600. However, an alternative and less rigorous version of the lower-of-cost-or-replacement cost rule calls for applying it to the total of the entire inventory rather than to the individual items. If the above inventory is to be valued by applying the lower-of-cost-or-replacement cost rule to the total of the inventory, the balance sheet amount for inventory is determined merely by comparing the total cost of $12,300 with the total replacement cost of $11,300 and using the lower of the two figures. Still another alternative method of using the lower-of-cost-or-replacement cost concept is to apply it to categories of the inventory rather than item by item. These alternative methods of applying the lower-of-cost-or-replacement cost rule are appropriate when no loss of income is anticipated, because the decline in replacement costs of certain goods is fully offset by higher replacement costs for other items.

Gross profit method of estimating inventories

The taking of a physical inventory is a time-consuming and costly job in many lines of business; consequently, a physical inventory may be taken only once a year. Monthly financial statements are needed, however, for intelligent administration of the business, and the preparation of monthly statements requires a determination of the amount of inventory at the end of each month. In many cases this dilemma may be solved satisfactorily by estimating the inventory each month by using the **gross profit method.**

The gross profit method of estimating the inventory is based on the assumption that the rate of gross profit remains approximately the same from year to year. This assumption is a realistic one in many fields of business. The first step in using the gross profit method is to obtain from the ledger the figures for beginning inventory, net purchases, and net sales. Cost of goods sold is then computed by reducing the sales figure by the usual gross profit rate. The difference between the cost of goods available for sale and the cost of goods sold represents the estimated ending inventory.

To illustrate, let us assume that the beginning inventory is $25,000, the net purchases of the period $70,000, and the net sales $100,000. The gross profit rate is assumed to have approximated 40% of net sales for the past several years. This information is now assembled in the customary form of an income statement as follows:

Gross profit method . . . **Net sales**		$100,000 (100%)
Beginning inventory	$25,000	
Net purchases	70,000	
Cost of goods available for sale	$95,000	
Less: Ending inventory	?	
Cost of goods sold		60,000 (60%)
Gross profit on sales (40% × $100,000)		$ 40,000 (40%)

Customarily, in preparing an income statement, the ending inventory is deducted from the cost of goods available for sale to determine the cost of goods sold. In this case our calculation to determine the ending inventory consists of deducting the estimated cost of goods sold from the cost of goods available for sale.

. . . to estimate ending inventory **Cost of goods available for sale**		$95,000
Less: Cost of goods sold (60% of $100,000)		60,000
Ending inventory (estimate)		$35,000

The gross profit method of estimating inventory has several uses apart from the preparation of monthly financial statements. This calculation may be used after the taking of a physical inventory to confirm the overall reasonableness of the amount determined by the counting and pricing process. In the event of a fire which destroys the inventory, the approximate amount of goods on hand at the date of the fire may also be computed by the gross profit method.

The retail method of inventory valuation

The retail method of estimating an ending inventory is somewhat similar to the gross profit method. It is widely used by chain stores, department stores, and other types of retail business. Goods on sale in retail stores are marked at the retail prices; it is therefore more convenient to take inventory at current retail prices than to look up invoices to find the unit cost of each item in stock. After first determining the value of the inventory at retail price, the next step is to convert the inventory to cost price by applying the ratio prevailing between cost and selling price during the current period. This method of approximating an inventory may also be carried out by using data from the accounts without taking any physical count of the goods on hand. The underlying basis for the retail method of inventory valuation is the percentage of markup for the current period, whereas the gross profit method of estimating inventory rests on the rate of gross profit experienced in preceding periods.

When the retail method of inventory is to be used, it is necessary to maintain records of the beginning inventory and of all purchases during the period in terms of selling price as well as at cost. Goods available for sale during the period can then be stated both at cost and at selling price. By deducting the sales for the period from the sales value of the goods available for sale, the ending inventory at selling price may be determined without the need for a physical count. The ending inventory at selling price is then converted to a cost basis by using the percentage of cost to selling price for the current period.

In practice, the application of this method may be complicated because the originally established sales prices are modified by frequent price markups and markdowns. These frequent changes in retail price present some difficulties in determining the correct rate to use in reducing the inventory from selling price to cost. The following illustration shows the calculation of inventory by the retail method, without going into the complications which would arise from markups and markdowns in the original retail selling price.

	Cost Price	Selling Price
Beginning inventory	*$20,000*	*$30,000*
Net purchases during the month	*11,950*	*15,000*
Cost of goods available for sale	*$31,950*	*$45,000*
Less: Net sales for the month		*20,000*
Ending inventory at selling price		*$25,000*
Cost ratio ($31,950 ÷ $45,000)		*71%*
Ending inventory at cost (71% × $25,000)	*$17,750*	

Used by many department stores

Consistency in the valuation of inventory

A business has considerable latitude in selecting a method of inventory valuation best suited to its needs; once a method has been selected, however, that method should be followed consistently from year to year. A change from one inventory method to another will ordinarily cause reported income to vary considerably in the year in which the change occurs. Frequent switching of methods would therefore make the income statements quite undependable as a means of portraying operating results.

The need for consistency in the valuation of inventory does not mean that a business should *never* make a change in inventory method. However, when a change is made, full disclosure of the nature of the change and of its effect upon the year's net income should be included in the financial statements or in a footnote to the statements.

Perpetual inventory method

Many businesses, especially those handling products of high unit cost, prefer to use a perpetual inventory system which provides a continuous running record of the inventory. Under the perpetual inventory system, a purchase of merchandise is debited to the Inventory account rather than to a Purchases account. A sale of merchandise requires two entries: (1) a debit to Cash or Accounts Receivable and a credit to Sales for an amount equal to the sales price of the merchandise, and (2) a debit to a Cost of Goods Sold account and a credit to the Inventory account for an amount equal to the cost of the merchandise sold. The balance in the Cost of Goods Sold account at any time during the accounting period shows the total cost of the merchandise sold to date and the Inventory account shows the cost of merchandise on hand.

The use of a perpetual inventory system does not eliminate the need for taking a physical inventory. When the physical count indicates a disagreement with the book record (perhaps because of theft of goods or from accounting errors), the Inventory account and the Cost of Goods Sold account are adjusted to agree with the results of the physical count.

QUESTIONS

1 Is the establishment of an appropriate valuation for the merchandise inventory at the end of the year more important in producing a dependable income statement, or in producing a dependable balance sheet?

2 Explain the meaning of the term *physical inventory.*

3 Through an accidental error in counting of merchandise at December 31, 1973, the Trophy Company overstated the amount of goods on hand by $8,000. Assuming that the error was not discovered, what was the effect upon net income for 1973? Upon the owner's equity at December 31, 1973? Upon the net income for 1974? Upon the owner's equity at December 31, 1974?

4 Near the end of December, Hadley Company received a large order from a major customer. The work of packing the goods for shipment was begun at once but could not be completed before the close of business on December 31. Since a written order from the customer was on hand and the goods were

nearly all packed and ready for shipment, Hadley felt that this merchandise should not be included in the physical inventory taken on December 31. Do you agree? What is probably the reason behind Hadley's opinion?

5 During a prolonged period of rising prices, will the fifo or lifo method of inventory valuation result in higher reported profits?

6 Throughout several years of strongly rising prices, Company A used the lifo method of inventory valuation and Company B used the fifo method. In which company would the balance sheet figure for inventory be closer to current replacement cost of the merchandise on hand? Why?

7 Explain the usefulness of the **gross profit method** of estimating inventories.

8 Estimate the ending inventory by the gross profit method, given the following data: beginning inventory $40,000; purchases $100,000; net sales $106,667; average gross profit rate 25% of net sales.

9 One of the items in the inventory of Grayline Stores is marked for sale at $125. The purchase invoice shows the item cost $95, but a newly issued price list from the manufacturer shows the present replacement cost to be $90. What inventory valuation should be assigned this item if Grayline Stores follows the lower-of-cost-or-replacement-cost rule?

10 You are making a detailed analysis of the financial statements and accounting records of two companies in the same industry, Adams Corporation Ltd. and Bar Corporation Ltd. Price levels have been rising steadily for several years. In the course of your investigation, you observe that the inventory value shown on the Adams Corporation balance sheet is quite close to the current replacement cost of the merchandise on hand. However, for Bar Corporation, the carrying value of the inventory is far below current replacement cost. What method of inventory valuation is probably used by Adams Corporation? By Bar Corporation? If we assume that the two companies are identical except for the inventory valuation method used, which company has probably been reporting higher net income in recent years?

11 Explain the meaning of the term **market** as used in the expression "lower of cost or market."

12 Summarize the difference between the **periodic system** and the **perpetual system** of accounting for inventory. Which system would usually cost more to maintain? Which system would be most practicable for a restaurant, a retail drugstore, a new car dealer?

13 A store using the **retail inventory method** takes its physical inventory by applying current retail prices as marked on the merchandise to the quantities counted. Does this procedure indicate that the inventory will appear in the financial statements at retail selling price? Explain.

EXERCISES

Ex. 10-1 Condensed income statements for Storm Company for two years are shown below:

	Year 2	Year 1
Sales	$131,000	$120,000
Cost of goods sold	76,000	96,000
Gross profit on sales	$ 55,000	$ 24,000
Operating expenses	20,000	20,000
Net income	$ 35,000	$ 4,000

The inventory at the end of Year 1 was understated by $12,000, but the error was not discovered until after the accounts had been closed and financial statements prepared at the end of Year 2. The balance sheets for the two years showed owner's equity of $51,000 at the end of Year 1 and $62,000 at the end of Year 2.

Compute the correct net income figure for Year 1 and Year 2 and the gross profit percentage for each year based on corrected data. What correction, if any, should be made in owner's equity at the end of Year 1 and at the end of Year 2?

Ex. 10-2 The following information has been compiled by Ling Company concerning items in its inventory at December 31:

		Unit Price	
Item	Quantity	Cost (fifo)	Replacement Cost
A	100	$ 80	$ 82
B	60	150	140
C	80	40	48
D	70	200	201

Determine the total inventory value to appear on Ling Company's balance sheet under the lower-of-cost-or-replacement-cost rule, assuming (*a*) that the rule is applied to inventory as a whole, and (*b*) that the rule is applied on an item-by-item basis.

Ex. 10-3 When James Flagg arrived at his store on the morning of May 29, he found empty shelves and display racks; thieves had broken in during the night and stolen the entire inventory. Flagg's accounting records showed that he had $30,000 inventory on May 1 (cost value). From May 1 to May 29, he had made sales of $120,000 and purchases of $94,500. The gross profit during the past several years had consistently averaged 30% of sales. Flagg wishes to file an insurance claim for the theft loss. What is the estimated cost of his inventory at the time of the theft? Show computations.

Ex. 10-4 The beginning inventory balance of Item Y on July 1 and the purchases of this item during July were as follows:

July 1 Beginning inventory	300 units @ $1.00	$ 300
July 7 Purchase	1,200 units @ $1.10	1,320
July 14 Purchase	600 units @ $1.12	672
July 22 Purchase	600 units @ $1.16	696
July 28 Purchase	300 units @ $1.25	375
Totals	3,000	$3,363

At July 31 the ending inventory consisted of 450 units. Determine the cost of the ending inventory, based on each of the following methods of inventory valuation:
a Average cost
b First-in, first-out
c Last-in, first-out

Ex. 10-5 Zeeman's Dress Shop wishes to determine the approximate month-end inventory using data from the accounting records without taking a physical count of merchandise on hand. From the following information, estimate the cost of the September 30 inventory by the retail method of inventory valuation.

	Cost Price	Selling Price
Inventory of merchandise, Aug. 31	$165,500	$250,000
Purchases (net) during September	106,500	150,000
Sales (net) during September		172,000

PROBLEMS

Group A

10A-1 The president of Star Company is particularly pleased over the rising trend of the gross profit percentage in recent years. Selected information from the income statements of Star Company for a three-year period are listed below:

	Year 3	Year 2	Year 1
Net sales	$600,000	$375,000	$300,000
Cost of goods sold	402,000	255,000	210,000
Gross profit on sales	$198,000	$120,000	$ 90,000
Gross profit percentage	33%	32%	30%

An audit of the company's affairs performed after the books had been closed at the end of Year 3 disclosed the following errors: (1) an arithmetical error in the computation of inventory at the end of Year 1 had caused a $7,500 under-statement in that inventory; and (2) a duplication of figures in the computation of inventory at the end of Year 3 had caused an overstatement of $24,000 in that inventory.

Instructions
a Prepare a three-year schedule in the form illustrated above, using figures that reflect correction of the erroneous inventory amounts. Include the revised gross profit percentage for each year. (Round any fractions to the nearest full percentage point.)
b Is the president of Star Company justified in his enthusiasm for the trend of the gross profit percentage of the company? Explain.

10A-2 The Air Filter Company deals in a single product of relatively low cost. The volume of sales in 1974 was $420,000, at a unit price of $6. The inventory at January 1, 1974, amounted to 8,000 units valued at cost of $24,000; purchases for the year were as follows: 21,000 units @ $3.10; 33,000 units @ $3.25; 23,000 units @ $3.40; and 9,600 units @ $3.50.

Instructions
a Compute the December 31, 1974, inventory using (1) the first-in, first-out method; and (2) the last-in, first-out method.
b Prepare comparative income statement data for each of the above two methods of pricing inventory. The income statements are to be carried only to the determination of gross profit on sales.
c Comment on the significance of the inventory figure under the method you recommend with respect to current replacement cost.

10A-3 For the years 1973 and 1974, Coast Company reported the following operating results:

	1974	1973
Net sales	$350,000	$330,000
Cost of goods sold:		
Beginning inventory	$126,520	$120,000
Net purchases	213,480	204,663
Cost of goods available for sale	$340,000	$324,663
Ending inventory	130,000	126,520
Cost of goods sold	$210,000	$198,143
Gross profit on sales	$140,000	$131,857
Expenses	50,000	45,000
Net income	$ 90,000	$ 86,857

The owner's equity as shown in the company's balance sheets was as follows: December 31, 1972, $100,000; December 31, 1973, $186,857; and December 31, 1974, $276,857.

Early in 1975, Mike Carl, accountant for the Coast Company, made a review of the documents and procedures used in taking the physical inventory at December 31, 1973 and 1974. His investigation disclosed the two questionable items listed below:

(1) Merchandise shipped to a customer on December 31, 1973, F.O.B. shipping point, was included in the physical inventory taken that date. The cost of the merchandise was $1,450 and the sales price was $1,800. Because of the press of year-end work, the sales invoice was not prepared until January 6, 1974. On that date the sale was recorded as a January transaction by entry in the sales journal, and the sales invoice was mailed to the customer.

(2) Merchandise costing $3,420, which had been received on December 31, 1973, had been included in the inventory taken on that date, although the purchase was not recorded until January 8 when the vendor's invoice arrived. The invoice was then recorded in the purchases journal.

Instructions

a Prepare corrected income statements for the years ended December 31, 1973 and 1974. (You may find it helpful to set up T accounts for Sales, 1973 and Sales, 1974; Purchases, 1973 and Purchases, 1974; and Inventory, December 31, 1973.)

b Compute corrected amounts for owner's equity at December 31, 1973 and 1974.

10A-4 Inland Company suffered the loss of its entire inventory by fire on May 25, 1974. The periodic method of inventory is in use and a physical inventory was last taken on December 31, 1973. In order to advise the insurance adjuster of the amount of the inventory loss, it is necessary to estimate the cost of the merchandise on hand at the date of the fire. The last income statement of the company was prepared for the year ended December 31, 1973, and appears as follows:

Net sales		$800,000
Cost of goods sold:		
Inventory, Jan. 1, 1973	$160,000	
Purchases	740,000	
Cost of goods available for sale	$900,000	
Less: Inventory, Dec. 31, 1973	260,000	640,000
Gross profit on sales		$160,000

Included in the purchases figure shown above was $25,000 of office equipment which the company had acquired late in December of 1973 for its own use from a competing concern which was quitting business. The bookkeeper had not understood the nature of this transaction and had recorded it by debiting the Purchases account. The office equipment, however, was not included in the inventory as of December 31, 1973.

The sales figure of $800,000 for 1973 did not include $20,000 of merchandise packaged and ready for shipment to a customer on December 31, 1973. This lot of merchandise was being held by Inland Company merely as an accommodation to the customer. The customer had originally ordered this merchandise for delivery on December 10; just prior to that date he had requested, because of overcrowded warehouses, that the goods be held by the Inland Company until January 10. It was agreed that the regular 30-day credit terms should run from December 10 per the original agreement. This merchandise had not been included in the Inland Company's year-end inventory; the goods were delivered to the customer on January 10, 1974, and payment of $20,000 was received the same day.

Records salvaged from the fire revealed the merchandise transactions from January 1, 1974, to the date of the fire to be: sales, $360,000; sales returns and allowances, $3,000; transportation-in, $2,000; purchases, $220,000; purchase returns and allowances, $4,000. The sales figure for 1974 includes the $20,000 described above.

Instructions
a Prepare a report addressed to the insurance adjuster summarizing your findings. Include an estimate of the inventory value as of the date of the fire and a computation of the applicable gross profit rate, after making appropriate corrections to the 1973 income statement.

b Explain how the gross profit method of estimating inventories may be used other than in case of a fire loss.

10A-5 Lexington Center is a retail store carrying a wide range of merchandise, mostly articles of low unit price. The selling price of each item is marked on the merchandise. At each year-end, the company has taken a physical count of goods on hand and has priced these goods at cost by looking up individual purchase invoices to determine the unit cost of each item in stock. Thomas, the store manager, is anxious to find a more economical method of assigning dollar values to the year-end inventory. He explains that it takes much more time to price the inventory than to count the merchandise on hand.

Through analysis of the accounting records, you find that the sales of the year just ended amounted to $1,590,000. During the year, net purchases of merchandise aggregated $1,200,000; the retail selling price of this merchandise was $1,680,000. At the end of the year, a physical inventory showed goods on hand *priced to sell* at $330,000. This amount represented a substantial increase over the inventory of a year earlier. At December 31 of the prior year, the inventory on hand had appeared in the balance sheet at a cost of $144,000, although it had a retail value of $240,000.

Instructions

a Outline a plan whereby the inventory can be computed without the necessity of looking up individual purchase invoices. List step by step the procedures to be followed. Ignore the possibility of markups and markdowns in the original retail price of merchandise.

b Compute the cost of the inventory for the year just ended using the method described in *a*.

c Explain how the adoption of the inventory method you have described would facilitate the preparation of monthly financial statements.

Group B

10B-1 The income statements prepared by the Spiral Company for a three-year period included the following information:

	Year 3	Year 2	Year 1
Net sales	$200,000	$125,000	$100,000
Cost of goods sold	134,000	85,000	70,000
Gross profit on sales	$ 66,000	$ 40,000	$ 30,000
Gross profit percentage	33%	32%	30%

The company was being offered for sale and the owner emphasized the rising trend of the gross profit percentage as a very favorable factor. Assume that you are retained by a prospective purchaser of the business to make an investigation of the fairness and reliability of the Spiral Company's accounting records and financial statements. You find everything in order except for the following: (1) The inventory was understated by $2,500 at the end of Year 1 and (2) it was overstated by $8,000 at the end of Year 3. The company uses the periodic inventory system and these errors had not been brought to light prior to your investigation.

Instructions

a Prepare a revised three-year schedule along the lines of the one illustrated above.

b Comment on the trend of gross profit percentages before and after the revision.

10B-2 The Shore Line Corporation Ltd. deals in a single product of relatively low cost. The volume of sales in 1973 was $480,000 at a unit price of $6. The inventory at January 1, 1973, amounted to 14,500 units valued at cost of $43,500; purchases for the year were as follows: 20,500 units @ $3.10; 33,000 units @ $3.25; 23,000 units @ $3.40; and 9,000 units @ $3.50.

Instructions

a Compute the December 31, 1973, inventory using

(1) The weighted average method (Compute average unit cost to the nearest cent.)

(2) The first-in, first-out method

(3) The last-in, first-out method

b Prepare income statement data for each of the above three methods of pricing inventory. The income statements are to be carried only to the determination of gross profit on sales.

c Comment on the significance of the inventory figure under the method you recommend with respect to current replacement cost.

10B-3 Mandalay Company presented the following income statements for the years 1973 and 1974.

	1974	1973
Net sales	$1,050,000	$990,000
Cost of goods sold:		
Beginning inventory	$ 379,560	$360,000
Net purchases	640,440	613,989
Cost of goods available for sale	$1,020,000	$973,989
Ending inventory	390,000	379,560
Cost of goods sold	$ 630,000	$594,429
Gross profit on sales	$ 420,000	$395,571
Expenses	150,000	135,000
Net income	$ 270,000	$260,571

The owner's equity as shown in the company's balance sheets was as follows: December 31, 1972, $300,000; December 31, 1973, $560,571; and December 31, 1974, $830,571.

Grant Higuchi, accountant for the Mandalay Company, decided early in 1975 to make a review of the documents and procedures used in taking the physical inventory at December 31, 1973 and 1974. His investigation revealed two questionable items as indicated below:

(1) Merchandise with a cost of $10,260 which had been received on December 31, 1973, had been included in the inventory taken on that date, although the purchase was not recorded until January 8, when the vendor's invoice arrived. The invoice was then recorded in the purchases journal as a January transaction.

(2) Merchandise shipped to a customer on December 31, 1973, F.O.B. shipping point, was included in the physical inventory at December 31, 1973. The cost of the merchandise was $4,350 and the sales price was $5,400. Because of the press of year-end work, the sales invoice was not prepared until January 8, 1974. On that date the sale was recorded as a January, 1974 transaction in the sales journal, and the invoice was mailed to the customer.

Instructions

a Prepare corrected income statements for the years ended December 31, 1973 and 1974. (You may find it helpful to set up T accounts for Sales, 1973 and Sales, 1974; Purchases, 1973 and Purchases, 1974; and Inventory, December 31, 1973.)

b Compute corrected amounts for owner's equity at December 31, 1973 and 1974.

10B-4 The entire inventory of Wilson Company was destroyed by fire on May 15, 1973, and an estimate of the inventory value must be prepared in order to file an insurance claim. The following income statement for the year 1973 is available to aid you in estimating the amount of inventory at the date of the fire.

WILSON COMPANY

Income Statement

For the Year Ended December 31, 1973

Net Sales		$400,000
Cost of goods sold:		
Inventory, Jan. 1	$ 80,000	
Purchases	370,000	
Cost of goods available for sale	$450,000	
Less: Inventory, Dec. 31	130,000	320,000
Gross profit on sales		$ 80,000
Expenses		30,000
Net income		$ 50,000

Other data Included in the purchases figure shown in the income statement was $12,500 of office equipment which the Wilson Company had acquired late in December for its own use from a competing concern which was quitting business. The bookkeeper of the Wilson Company had not understood the nature of this transaction and had recorded it by debiting the Purchases account. The office equipment, however, was not included in the inventory at December 31, 1973.

Records salvaged from the fire revealed the merchandise transactions from December 31, 1973, to the date of the fire to be: sales, $170,000; sales returns and allowances, $1,500; transportation-in, $1,000; purchases, $109,000; purchase returns and allowances, $2,000.

Instructions

a Prepare a report directed to the insurance adjuster summarizing your findings. Include an estimate of the inventory value as of the date of the fire and a computation of the applicable gross profit rate.

b Explain how the gross profit method of estimating inventories may be used other than in case of a fire loss.

c Is the rate of gross profit customarily computed as a percentage of the cost of merchandise or as a percentage of sales? Show how the gross profit rate in this problem would vary if based on cost of goods sold rather than on sales.

10B-5 Ajax Limited, a retail store, carries a wide range of merchandise consisting mostly of articles of low unit price. The selling price of each item is plainly marked on the merchandise. At each year-end, the company has taken a physical count of goods on hand and has priced these goods at cost by looking up individual purchase invoices to determine the unit cost of each item in stock. Anthony, the store manager, is anxious to find a more economical method of assigning dollar values to the year-end inventory. He explains that it takes much more time to price the inventory than to count the merchandise on hand.

By analyzing the accounting records you are able to determine that the sales of the current year, 1974, amounted to $650,000. During the year, net purchases of merchandise totaled $500,000; the retail selling price of this merchandise was $700,000. At the end of 1974, a physical inventory showed goods on hand priced to sell at $150,000. This represented a considerable increase over the inventory of a year earlier. At December 31, 1973, the inventory on hand had appeared in the balance sheet at cost of $60,000, although it had a retail value of $100,000.

Instructions

a Outline a plan whereby the inventory can be computed without the necessity of looking up individual purchase invoices. List step by step the procedures to be followed. Ignore the possibility of markups and markdowns in the original retail price of merchandise.

b Compute the cost of the inventory at December 31, 1974, using the method described in *a*.

c Explain how the adoption of the inventory method you have described would facilitate the preparation of monthly financial statements.

BUSINESS DECISION PROBLEM 10

You are the sales manager of Import Motors, an automobile dealership specializing in European imports. Among the automobiles on Import Motors' showroom are two Italian sports cars, which are identical in every respect except for color; one is red and the other white. The red car had been ordered last February, at a cost of $4,200 Canadian dollars. The white car had been ordered early last March, but because of a revaluation of the Italian lira relative to the dollar, the white car had cost only $3,900 Canadian dollars. Both cars arrived in Canada on the same boat and had just been delivered to your showroom. Since the cars were identical except for color and both colors were equally popular, you had listed both cars at the same suggested retail price, $6,000.

Smiley Jones, one of your best salesmen, comes into your office with a proposal. He has a customer in the showroom who wants to buy the red car for $6,000. However, when Smiley pulled the inventory card on the red car to see what options were included, he happened to notice the inventory card of the white car. Import Motors, like most automobile dealerships, uses the specific identification method to value inventory. Consequently, Smiley noticed that the red car had cost $4,200, while the white one had cost Import Motors only $3,900. This gave Smiley the idea for the following proposal.

"If I sell the red car for $6,000, Import Motors makes a gross profit of $1,800. But if you'll let me discount that white car $100, I think I can get my customer to buy that one instead. If I sell the white car for $5,900, the gross profit will be $2,000, so Import Motors is $200 better off than if I sell the red car for $6,000. Since I came up with this plan, I feel I should get part of the benefit, so Import Motors should split that extra $200 with me. That way, I'll get an extra $100 commission, and the company still makes $100 more than if I sell the red car."

Instructions

a Prepare a schedule which shows the total revenue, cost of goods sold, and gross profit to Import Motors if *both* cars are sold for $6,000 each.

b Prepare a schedule showing the revenue, cost of goods sold, and gross profit to Import Motors if both cars are sold but Smiley's plan is adopted and the white car is sold for $5,900. Assume the red car is still sold for $6,000. To simplify comparison of this schedule to the one prepared in part *a*, include the extra $100 commission to Smiley in the cost of goods sold of the part *b* schedule.

c Write out your decision whether or not to accept Smiley's proposal, and explain to Smiley why the proposal either would or would not be to the advantage of Import Motors. (*Hint:* Refer to your schedules prepared in parts *a* and *b* in your explanation.)

PLANT AND EQUIPMENT DEPRECIATION

Nature of plant and equipment

The term *plant and equipment* is used to describe long-lived assets acquired for use in the operation of the business and not intended for resale to customers. Among the more common examples are land, buildings, machinery, furniture and fixtures, office equipment, and automobiles. A delivery truck in the showroom of an automobile dealer is inventory; when this same truck is sold to a drugstore for use in making deliveries to customers it becomes a unit of plant and equipment.

Although land used in the business is classified under plant and equipment, a tract of land acquired as a future building site and not presently being used in the business is classified under the balance sheet caption of Investments or under Other Assets. Similar reasoning indicates that a building formerly used in the business, but now idle and not required for operating purposes, should be excluded from the plant and equipment category.

The term *fixed assets* has long been used in accounting literature to describe all types of plant and equipment. This term, however, has virtually disappeared from the published financial statements of large corporations. *Plant and equipment* appears to be a more descriptive term. Another alternative title used on many corporation balance sheets is *property, plant, and equipment.*

Plant and equipment represent bundles of services to be received

It is convenient to think of a plant asset as a bundle of services to be received by the owner over a period of years. Ownership of a delivery truck, for example, may provide about 100,000 miles of transportation. The cost of the delivery truck is customarily entered in a plant and equipment account entitled Delivery Truck, which in essence represents payment in advance for several years of transportation service. Similarly, a building may be regarded as payment in advance for several years' supply of housing services. As the years go by, these services are utilized by the business and the cost of the plant asset is gradually transferred into depreciation expense.

An awareness of the similarity between plant assets and prepaid expenses is essential to an understanding of the accounting process by which the cost of plant assets is allocated to the years in which the benefits of ownership are received.

Major categories of plant and equipment

Plant and equipment items are often classified into one of the following groups:

1 Tangible plant assets. The term *tangible* denotes bodily substance, as exemplified by land, a building, or a machine. This category may be subdivided into two distinct classifications:
   a Plant property subject to depreciation; included are plant assets of limited useful life such as buildings and office equipment.
   b Land. The only plant asset not subject to depreciation is land, which has an unlimited term of existence.
2 Intangible assets. Examples are patents, copyrights, trademarks, franchises, organization costs, leaseholds, leasehold improvements, and goodwill. Current assets such as accounts receivable or prepaid rent are not included in the intangible classification, even though they are lacking in physical substance. The term *intangible assets* is used to describe a noncurrent asset which is lacking in physical substance.

Natural resources

Natural resources are subject to depletion rather than to depreciation. Examples are mines, oil and gas wells, and tracts of timber. The term *depletion* means the exhaustion of a natural resource through mining, pumping, cutting, or otherwise using up the deposit or growth.

Accounting problems relating to plant and equipment

Some major accounting problems relating to plant and equipment are indicated by the following questions:

1 How is the cost of plant and equipment determined?
2 How should the costs of plant and equipment be allocated against revenues?
3 How should charges for repairs, maintenance, and replacements be treated?
4 How should disposals of plant assets be recorded?

We are presently concerned with answering the first of these questions; an understanding of how the cost of plant and equipment is determined will be helpful in subsequent study of the problem of depreciation.

DETERMINING THE COST OF PLANT AND EQUIPMENT The cost of plant and equipment includes all expenditures reasonable and necessary in acquiring the asset and placing it in a position and condition for use in the operations of the business. Only *reasonable* and *necessary* expenditures should be included. For example, if the company's truck driver receives a traffic ticket while hauling a new machine to the plant, the traffic fine is *not* part of the cost of the new machine. If the machine is dropped and damaged while being unloaded, the expense of repairing the damage should *not* be added to the cost of the asset.

Cost is most easily determined when an asset is purchased for cash. The cost of the asset is then equal to the cash outlay necessary in acquiring the asset plus any expenditures for freight, insurance while in transit, installation, trial runs, and any other costs necessary to make the asset ready for use. If plant assets are purchased on the installment plan or by issuance of notes payable, the interest element or carrying charge should be recorded as interest expense and not as part of the cost of the plant assets.

This principle of including in the cost of a plant asset all the incidental charges necessary to put the asset in use is illustrated by the following example. A factory in Hamilton orders a machine from a Windsor tool manufacturer at a list price of $10,000, with terms of 2/10, n/30. A sales tax of 5% must be paid, also freight charges of $1,250. Transportation from the railroad station to the factory costs $150 and installation labor amounts to $400. The cost of the machine and the amount to be entered in the Machinery account are computed as follows:

Items	*List price of machine*	*$10,000*
included		
in cost of	*Less: Cash discount (2% × $10,000)*	*200*
machine	*Net cash price*	*$ 9,800*
	Sales tax (5% × $9,800)	*490*
	Freight	*1,250*
	Transportation from railroad station to factory	*150*
	Installation labor	*400*
	Cost of machine	*$12,090*

Why should all the incidental charges relating to the acquisition of a machine be included in its cost? Why not treat these incidental charges as expenses of the period in which the machine is acquired?

The answer is to be found in the basic accounting principle of *matching costs and revenues.* The benefits of owning the machine will be received over a span of years, 10 years, for example. During those 10 years the operation of the machine will contribute to revenues. Consequently, the total costs of the machine should be recorded in the accounts as an asset and allocated against the revenues of the 10 years. All costs incurred in acquiring the machine are costs of the services to be received from using the machine.

Land When land is purchased, various incidental charges are generally incurred, in addition to the purchase price. These additional costs may include commissions to real estate brokers, legal fees for examining the title, accrued taxes paid by the purchaser, and fees for surveying, draining, clearing, grading, and landscaping the property. All these expenditures are part of the cost of the land. Special assessments for local improvements, such as the paving of a street or the installation of sewers, may also be charged to the Land account, for the reason that a more or less permanent value is being added to the land.

Separate ledger accounts are necessary for land and buildings, because buildings are subject to depreciation and land is not. The treatment of land as a nondepreciable asset is based on the premise that land used as a building site has an unlimited life. When land and building are purchased for a lump sum, the purchase price must be apportioned between the land and the building. An appraisal may be necessary for this purpose. Assume, for example, that land and a building are purchased for a bargain price of $100,000. The apportionment of this cost on the basis of an appraisal may be made as follows:

	Value per Appraisal	Percentage of Total	Apportionment of Cost
Land	$ 48,000	40%	$ 40,000
Building	72,000	60%	60,000
Total	$120,000	100%	$100,000

Apportioning cost between land and building

Sometimes a tract of land purchased as a building site has on it an old building which is not suitable for the buyer's use. The Land account should be charged with the entire purchase price plus any costs incurred in tearing down or removing the building. Salvage proceeds received from sale of the building are recorded as a credit in the Land account.

Land acquired as a future building site should be reported under Other Assets, rather than as part of Plant and Equipment, since it is not currently used in operations.

Land improvements Improvements to real estate such as driveways, fences, parking lots, and sprinkler systems have a limited life and are therefore subject to depreciation. For this reason they should be recorded not in the Land account but in a separate account entitled Land Improvements. On the other hand, any improvements which will last indefinitely and are not to be depreciated are entered in the Land account.

Buildings Old buildings are sometimes purchased with the intention of repairing them prior to placing them in use. Repairs made under these circumstances are charged to the Building account. After the building has been placed in use, ordinary repairs are considered as maintenance expense when incurred.

When a building is constructed by the business itself, rather than being purchased, cost includes the materials and labor used plus an equitable portion of overhead or other indirect costs, such as executive salaries. Any other outlays specifically relating to the construction such as architectural fees, insurance during the construction period, and building permits should also be included in the cost of the building. A building or machine constructed by a company for its own use should be recorded in the accounts at cost, not at the price which might have been paid to outsiders if the asset had been acquired through purchase.

Depreciation

ALLOCATING THE COST OF PLANT AND EQUIPMENT Plant assets, with the exception of land, are of use to a company for only a limited number of years, and the cost of each plant asset is allocated as an expense of the years in which it is used. Accountants use the term *depreciation* to describe this gradual conversion of the cost of a plant asset into expense.

Depreciation, as the term is used in accounting, does not mean the physical deterioration of an asset. Neither does depreciation mean the decrease in market value of a plant asset over a period of time. *Depreciation means the allocation of the cost of a plant asset to the periods in which services are received from the asset.*

When a delivery truck is purchased, its cost is first recorded as an asset. This cost becomes expense over a period of years through the accounting process of depreciation. When gasoline is purchased for the truck, the price paid for each tankful is immediately recorded as expense. In theory, both outlays (for the truck and for a tank of gas) represent the acquisition of assets, but since it is reasonable to assume that a tankful of gasoline will be consumed in the accounting period in which it is purchased, we record the outlay for gasoline as an expense immediately. It is important to recognize, however, that both the outlay for the truck and the payment for the gasoline become expense in the period or periods in which each is assumed to render services.

A separate Depreciation Expense account and a separate Accumulated Depreciation account are generally maintained for each group of depreciable assets such as factory buildings, delivery equipment, and office equipment so that a proper allocation of depreciation expense can be made between functional areas of activity such as sales and manufacturing. Depreciation on manufacturing facilities is not necessarily an expense of the period in which it is recorded; the depreciation charge is first embodied in the inventory of goods manufactured, and the cost of this inventory is later deducted from revenue as an expense of the period when the goods are sold.

Because of the noncash nature of depreciation expense and because the dollar amount is materially affected by the depreciation method selected, it is generally desirable that the total amount of depreciation be disclosed in the income statement.

DEPRECIATION NOT A PROCESS OF VALUATION Accounting records and financial statements do not purport to show the constantly fluctuating market values of plant and equipment. Occasionally the market value of a building may rise substantially over a period of years because of a change in the price level, or for other reasons. Depreciation is continued, however, regardless of the increase in market value. The accountant recognizes that the building will render useful services for only a limited number of years, and that its full cost must be allocated as expense of those years regardless of fluctuations in market value.

CAUSES OF DEPRECIATION There are two major causes of depreciation, physical deterioration and obsolescence.

Physical deterioration Physical deterioration of a plant asset results from use, and also from exposure to sun, wind, and other climatic factors. When a plant asset has been carefully maintained, it is not uncommon for the owner to claim that the asset is as "good as new." Such statements are not literally true. Although a good repair policy may greatly lengthen the useful life of a machine, every machine eventually reaches the point at which it must be discarded. In brief, the making of repairs does not lessen the need for recognition of depreciation.

Obsolescence The term *obsolescence* means the process of becoming out of date or obsolete. An airplane, for example, may become obsolete even though it is in excellent physical condition; it becomes obsolete because better planes of superior design and performance have become available. Obsolescence relates to the capacity of a plant asset to render services to a particular company for a particular purpose.

The usefulness of plant assets may also be reduced because the rapid growth of a company renders such assets inadequate. Inadequacy of a plant asset may necessitate replacement with a larger unit even though the asset is in good physical condition and is not obsolete. Obsolescence and inadequacy are often closely associated; both relate to the opportunity for economical and efficient use of an asset rather than to its physical condition. Obsolescence is probably a more significant factor than physical deterioration in putting an end to the usefulness of most depreciable assets. Current accounting practice, however, does not usually attempt to separate the effects of physical deterioration and obsolescence.

Methods of computing depreciation

A business need not use the same method of depreciation for all its various assets. Management also has the option of using different methods of depreciation in the accounting records and financial statements than are employed in the determination of taxable income. The most widely used methods (straight-line, units-of-output, fixed percentage on declining balance, and sum-of-the-years'-digits) are explained and illustrated in the following sections.

STRAIGHT-LINE METHOD   The simplest and most widely used method of computing depreciation is the straight-line method. This method was described in Chapter 3 and has been used repeatedly in problems throughout this book. Under the straight-line method, an equal portion of the cost of the asset is allocated to each period of use; consequently, this method is most appropriate when usage of an asset is fairly uniform from year to year.

In theory, the computation of the periodic charge for depreciation is made by deducting the estimated residual or salvage value from the cost of the asset and dividing the remaining *depreciable cost* by the years of estimated useful life, as shown in the following example:

Computing Cost of the depreciable asset	*$5,200*
deprecia- Less: Estimated residual value (amount to be realized by sale of	
tion by	
straight- asset when it is retired from use)	*400*
line	
method Total amount to be depreciated (depreciable cost)	*$4,800*
Estimated useful life	*4 years*
Depreciation expense each year ($4,800 ÷ 4)	*$1,200*

The following schedule summarizes the accumulation of depreciation over the useful life of the asset. The amount to be depreciated is $4,800 (cost of $5,200 minus estimated residual value of $400).

Depreciation Schedule: Straight-line Method

	Year	Computation	Depreciation Expense	Accumulated Depreciation	Book Value
					$5,200
Constant	First	($\frac{1}{4}$ × $4,800)	$1,200	$1,200	4,000
annual	Second	($\frac{1}{4}$ × $4,800)	1,200	2,400	2,800
depreciation					
expense	Third	($\frac{1}{4}$ × $4,800)	1,200	3,600	1,600
	Fourth	($\frac{1}{4}$ × $4,800)	1,200	4,800	400
			$4,800		

In practice, the possibility of residual value is often ignored and the annual depreciation charge computed by dividing the total cost of the asset by the number of years of estimated useful life. This practice is justified in many cases in which residual value is not material and is difficult to estimate accurately. Under this approach the yearly depreciation expense in the above example would be $5,200 ÷ 4, or $1,300.

UNITS-OF-OUTPUT METHOD A more equitable allocation of the cost of some plant assets can be obtained by dividing the cost (minus salvage value, if significant) by the estimated units of output rather than by the estimated years of useful life. A truck line or bus company, for example, might compute depreciation on its vehicles by a mileage basis. If a truck costs $10,000 and is estimated to have a useful life of 200,000 miles, the depreciation rate per mile of operation is 5 cents ($10,000 ÷ 200,000). At the end of each year, the amount of depreciation to be recorded would be determined by multiplying the 5-cent rate by the number of miles the truck had operated during the year. This method is not suitable to situations in which obsolescence is an important factor.

ACCELERATED DEPRECIATION METHODS The term *accelerated depreciation* means recognition of relatively large amounts of depreciation in the early years of use and reduced amounts in the later years. Many types of plant and equipment are most efficient when new, and therefore provide more and better services in the early years of useful life. If we assume that the benefits derived from owning an asset are greatest in the early years when the asset is relatively new, then the amount of the asset's cost which we allocate as depreciation expense should be greatest in these same years. This is consistent with the basic accounting concept of matching costs with related benefits.

One reason for adoption of accelerated methods of depreciation is that the increasingly rapid pace of invention of new products is making obsolescence a factor of greater significance than physical deterioration. When an industry is in a period of rapid technological change, plant and equipment may have to be replaced within shorter periods than would be necessary in a less dynamic economy. Businessmen may, therefore, reason that the acquisition of a new plant facility is justified only if most of the cost can be recovered within a comparatively short period of years. Also significant is the pleasing prospect of reducing the current year's income tax burden by recognizing a relatively large amount of depreciation expense.

Another argument for allocating a comparatively large share of the cost of a depreciable asset to the early years of use is that repair expenses tend to increase as assets grow older. The combined expense of depreciation and repairs may be more uniform from year to year under an accelerated method of depreciation than when straight-line depreciation is followed. Whether a uniform total amount of depreciation expense plus repairs expense from year to year is realistic accounting, however, depends upon whether the benefits received from owning the asset are relatively constant from year to year.

Fixed-percentage-on-declining-balance method For income tax purposes the only acceptable method of writing-off certain depreciable assets consists of doubling the normal rate of depreciation and applying this doubled rate each year to the undepreciated cost (book value) of the asset.[1]

Assume, for example, that an automobile is acquired for business use at a cost of $4,000. Estimated useful life is four years; therefore, the depreciation rate under the straight-line method would be 25%. To depreciate the automobile by the fixed-percentage-on-declining-balance method, we double the straight-line rate of 25% and apply the doubled rate of 50% to the book value. Depreciation expense in the first year would then amount to $2,000. In the second year the depreciation expense would drop to $1,000, computed at 50% of the remaining book value of $2,000. In the third year depreciation would be $500, and in the fourth year only $250. The following table shows the allocation of cost under this method of depreciation:

Depreciation Schedule: Fixed-percentage-on-declining-balance Method

	Year	Computation	Depreciation Expense	Accumulated Depreciation	Book Value
Accelerated depreciation: fixed percentage on declining balance					*$4,000*
	First	(50% × $4,000)	$2,000	$2,000	2,000
	Second	(50% × $2,000)	1,000	3,000	1,000
	Third	(50% × $1,000)	500	3,500	500
	Fourth	(50% × $500)	250	3,750	250

If the automobile is continued in use beyond the estimated life of four years, depreciation will be continued at the 50% rate on the book value. In the fifth year, for example, the depreciation expense will be $125 (50% × $250), and in the sixth year $62.50 (50% × $125). When the fixed-percentage-on-declining-balance method is used, the cost of a depreciable asset will never be entirely written off as long as the asset continues in use. Because of the existence of this undepreciated balance of original cost, no deduction from original cost for salvage value is required when this method of depreciation is used.

Sum-of-the-years'-digits method This is another method of allocating a large portion of the cost of an asset to the early years of its use. The depreciation rate to be used is a fraction, of which the numerator is the remaining years of useful life (as of the beginning of the year) and the denominator is the sum of the years of useful life. Consider again the example of an automobile costing $4,000 and having an estimated life of four years, but in this instance assume an estimated residual value of $400. Since the automobile has an estimated life of four years,

[1] Canadian income tax regulations require all taxpayers, except farmers and fishermen, to use a fixed-percentage-on-declining-balance method of depreciation for tax purposes. Assets are grouped into classes and depreciation (more accurately described as capital cost allowance when referring to income tax practice) is taken on the net book value at rates not exceeding those prescribed by the Income Tax Regulations. A more detailed discussion of tax practice will be found in Chapter 20.

the denominator of the fraction will be 10, computed as follows $(1 + 2 + 3 + 4 = 10)$. For the first year, the depreciation will be $\frac{4}{10} \times$ $3,600$, or $1,440$. For the second year, the depreciation will be $\frac{3}{10} \times$ $3,600$, or $1,080$; in the third year $\frac{2}{10} \times$ $3,600$, or 720; and in the fourth year, $\frac{1}{10} \times$ $3,600$, or 360. In tabular form this depreciation program will appear as follows:

Depreciation Schedule: Sum-of-the-years'-digits Method

	Year	Computation	Depreciation Expense	Accumulated Depreciation	Book Value
					$4,000
Accelerated depreciation: sum-of-the-years'-digits	First	($\frac{4}{10} \times \$3,600$)	$1,440	$1,440	2,560
	Second	($\frac{3}{10} \times \$3,600$)	1,080	2,520	1,480
	Third	($\frac{2}{10} \times \$3,600$)	720	3,240	760
	Fourth	($\frac{1}{10} \times \$3,600$)	360	3,600	400

DEPRECIATION FOR FRACTIONAL PERIODS In the case of depreciable assets acquired sometime during the year, it is customary to figure depreciation to the nearest month. For example, if an asset is acquired on July 12, depreciation would be computed from July 1; if the asset had been acquired on July 18 (or any other date in the latter half of July), depreciation would be recorded for only five months (August through December) for the current calendar year.

Some businesses prefer to begin depreciation on the first of the month following the acquisition of a depreciable asset. This method, or any one of many similar variations, is acceptable so long as it is followed consistently by the business.

Revision of depreciation rates

Depreciation rates are based on estimates of the useful life of assets. These estimates of useful life are seldom precisely correct and sometimes are grossly in error. Consequently, the annual depreciation expense based on the estimated useful life may be either excessive or inadequate. What action should be taken when, after a few years of using a plant asset, it is decided that the asset is actually going to last for a considerably longer or shorter period than was originally estimated? When either of these situations arises, a revised estimate of useful life should be made and the periodic depreciation expense decreased or increased accordingly.

The procedure for correcting the depreciation program may be stated in a very few words: *Spread the undepreciated cost of the asset over the years of remaining useful life.* The annual depreciation expense is increased or decreased sufficiently so that the depreciation program will be completed in accordance with the revised estimate of remaining useful life. The following data illustrate a revision which increases the estimate of useful life and thereby decreases the annual depreciation expense.

Data Cost of asset	*$10,000*
prior to *Estimated useful life (no residual value)*	*10 years*
revision ***of depre-*** *Annual depreciation expense (prior to revision)*	*$ 1,000*
ciation ***rate*** *Accumulated depreciation at end of six years ($1,000 × 6)*	*$ 6,000*

At the beginning of the seventh year, it is decided that the asset will last for eight more years. The revised estimate of useful life is, therefore, a total of 14 years. The depreciation expense to be recognized for the seventh year and for each of the remaining years is $500, computed as follows:

Revision *Undepreciated cost at end of sixth year ($10,000 − $6,000)*	*$4,000*
of depre- ***ciation*** *Revised estimate of remaining years of useful life*	*8 years*
program *Revised amount of annual depreciation expense ($4,000 ÷ 8)*	*$ 500*

The method described above for the revision of a depreciation program is generally used and is supported by the CICA Accounting and Auditing Research Committee for financial reporting purposes.[2]

Depreciation and income taxes

Accelerated methods of depreciation have received increased attention in recent years because the federal and provincial governments have required their use for income tax purposes. By offering businessmen the opportunity of writing off as depreciation expense a large portion of the cost of a new asset during its early years of use, governments have provided a powerful incentive for investment in new productive facilities. Since an increased charge for depreciation expense will reduce taxable income, the businessman may feel that by purchasing new assets and writing off a large part of the cost in the early years of use, he is in effect paying for the new assets with dollars that otherwise would have been used to pay income taxes.

In theory, the ideal depreciation policy is one that allocates the cost of a depreciable asset to the several periods of its use in proportion to the services received each period. Accelerated methods of depreciation sometimes fail to allocate the cost of an asset in proportion to the flow of services from the property and therefore prevent the determination of annual net income on a realistic basis. If annual net income figures are misleading, stockholders, creditors, management, and others who use

---

[2]*CICA Handbook*, Section 3600.04. The Committee does not consider "adjustments arising from . . . changes in the estimated useful life of fixed assets" as a prior period adjustment.

financial statements as a basis for business decisions may be seriously injured. For income tax purposes, however, accelerated methods of depreciation may be effective in encouraging businessmen to invest in new productive facilities and thereby to raise the level of business activity.

It should be noted that depreciation (called capital cost allowance in the Income Tax Act) taken for tax purposes need not be the same as depreciation recorded on the books and financial statements. Therefore, depreciation may be recorded on the books on the straight-line basis even though the fixed-percentage-on-declining-balance method must be used for income tax purposes.

Depreciation and inflation

The valuation of plant and equipment on a cost basis and the computation of depreciation in terms of cost work very well during periods of stable price levels. However, the substantial rise in the price level in recent years has led many businessmen to suggest that a more realistic measurement of net income could be achieved by basing depreciation on the estimated replacement cost of plant assets rather than on the original cost of the assets presently in use. An alternative proposal is to adjust each year's depreciation expense by a price index measuring changes in the purchasing power of the dollar. This price-level adjustment would cause depreciation expense to be stated in *current dollars,* as are such expenses as wages and taxes.

As a specific illustration, assume that a manufacturing company purchased machinery in 1960 at a cost of $100,000. Estimated useful life was 15 years and straight-line depreciation was used. Throughout this 15-year period the price level rose sharply. By 1975 the machinery purchased in 1960 was fully depreciated; it was scrapped and replaced by new machinery in 1975. Although the new machines were not significantly different from the old, they cost $300,000, or three times as much as the depreciation expense which has been recorded during the life of the old machinery. Many businessmen would argue that the depreciation expense for the 15 years was in reality $300,000, because this was the outlay required for new machinery if the company was merely to "stay even" in its productive facilities. It is also argued that reported profits will be overstated during a period of rising prices if depreciation is based on the lower plant costs of some years ago. An overstatement of profits may cause larger demands for wage increases than are justified by the company's financial position and earnings.

As yet there has been no general acceptance of the suggestion for basing depreciation on replacement cost. Replacement cost is difficult to determine on any objective basis. Who can say how much it will cost to buy a new machine 15 years from now? The proposal to use a general price index to adjust each year's depreciation expense appears more promising.

Depreciation and the problem of asset replacement

Many readers of financial statements who have not studied accounting mistakenly believe that accumulated depreciation accounts (depreciation reserves) represent funds accumulated for the purpose of buying new equipment when the present equipment wears out. Perhaps the best way to combat such mistaken notions is to emphasize that the credit balance in an accumulated depreciation account represents the expired cost of assets acquired in the past. The amounts credited to the accumulated depreciation account could, as an alternative, have been credited directly to the plant and equipment account. An accumulated depreciation account has a *credit* balance; it does not represent an asset; and it cannot be used in any way to pay for new equipment. To buy a new plant asset requires cash; the total amount of cash owned by a company is shown by the asset account for cash.

Capital expenditures and revenue expenditures

The term *expenditure* means making a payment or incurring an obligation to make a future payment for an asset or service received. The acquisition of an asset (such as an automobile) or of a service (such as repairs to the automobile) may be for cash or on credit. In either situation the transaction is properly referred to as an expenditure.

Expenditures for the purchase or expansion of plant assets are called *capital expenditures* and are recorded in asset accounts. Expenditures for repairs, maintenance, fuel, and other items necessary to the ownership and use of plant and equipment are called *revenue expenditures* and are recorded by debits to expense accounts. The charge to an expense account is based on the assumption that the benefits from the expenditure will be used up in the current period, and the payment should therefore be deducted from the revenues of the current period in determining the net income. In brief, *any expenditure that will benefit several accounting periods is considered a capital expenditure; any expenditure that will benefit only the current accounting period is referred to as a revenue expenditure.*

Careful distinction between capital and revenue expenditures is important in the determination of net income. If the cost of constructing a new building, for example, is recorded as ordinary repairs expense (a revenue expenditure), the net income of the current period will be understated. The net income of future periods will be overstated because of the absence of depreciation expenses applicable to the unrecorded asset.

Examples We have already stressed the basic point that a careful distinction between capital expenditures and revenue expenditures is essential to a proper measurement of net income and to an accurate accounting for plant and equipment. Many companies develop formal policy statements defining capital and revenue expenditures as a guide toward consistent accounting practice in all branches and divisions and from year to year. These policy statements often set a minimum dollar limit for a capital expenditure (such as $50 or $100). Such limits are reasonable because a small expenditure will require much less time and paper work if charged to expense at the time of the transaction than if it were entered in an asset account and depreciated over a period of years. For example, the acquisition of a pencil sharpener at a cost of, say, $4 is reasonably charged to expense, despite the fact that it will probably have a useful life extending beyond the current accounting period.

Among the more common types of *capital expenditures* are:

1 Acquisition cost of plant and equipment, including freight, sales tax, and installation charges. When secondhand property is purchased, the cost of any repairs made to put the property in good operating condition before placing it in use is also considered as a capital expenditure and is charged to the asset account.

2 Additions. If a building is enlarged by adding a new wing or a mezzanine floor, the benefits from the expenditure will be received over a period of years, and the outlay should be debited to the asset account.

3 Betterments. The replacement of a stairway with an escalator is an example of an expenditure for a betterment or improvement which will yield benefits over a period of years and should therefore be charged to the asset account.

Among the more common types of *revenue expenditures* relating to plant and equipment are the repairs, maintenance, lubrication, cleaning, and inspection necessary to keep an asset in good working condition. The term *ordinary repairs* is often used to include all expenditures of this type. The cost of replacing small component parts of an asset (such as window panes in a building or tires and battery in an automobile) are also included in ordinary repairs.

Any expenditure made for the purpose of maintaining a plant asset in normally efficient working condition is an expense and will appear on the income statement as a deduction from the revenues of the current period. The treatment of an expenditure as a deduction from the revenues of the current period is the reason for the term revenue expenditure.

EFFECT OF ERRORS IN DISTINGUISHING BETWEEN CAPITAL AND REVENUE EXPENDITURES Because a capital expenditure is recorded by debiting an asset account, the transaction has no immediate effect upon net income. However, the depreciation of the amount entered in the asset account will be reflected as an expense in future periods. A revenue expenditure, on the other hand, is recorded by debiting an expense account and therefore represents an immediate deduction from earnings in the current period.

If a capital expenditure is erroneously recorded as a revenue expenditure, as, for example, the cost of a new typewriter charged to the Office Expense account, the result will be an understatement of the current year's net income. If the error is not corrected, the net income of subsequent years will be overstated because no depreciation expense will be recognized during the years in which the typewriter is used.

If a revenue expenditure is erroneously treated as a capital expenditure, as, for example, the outlay for truck repairs charged to the asset account, Delivery Truck, the result will be an overstatement of the current year's net income. If the error is not corrected, the net income of future years will be understated because of excessive depreciation charges based on the inflated amount of the Delivery Truck account.

These examples indicate that a careful distinction between capital and revenue expenditures is essential to attainment of one of the most fundamental objectives of accounting—the determination of net income for each year of operation of the business.

Extraordinary repairs

The term *extraordinary repairs* has a specific meaning in accounting terminology; it means a reconditioning or major overhaul that will extend the useful life of a plant asset beyond the original estimate. For example, a new automobile may be depreciated on the basis of an estimated useful life of four years. Assume that after three years of use, a decision is made to install a new engine in the automobile and thereby to extend its overall useful life from the original estimate of four years to a total of six years.

An extraordinary repair of this type may be recorded by debiting the Accumulated Depreciation account. This entry is sometimes explained by the argument that the extraordinary repair cancels out some of the depreciation previously recorded. The effect of this reduction (debit entry) in the Accumulated Depreciation account is to *increase* the book value of the asset by the cost of the extraordinary repair. Since an extraordinary repair causes an increase in the book value of the asset and has no immediate direct effect upon net income, it may be regarded as a form of capital expenditure.

To expand the above example of an extraordinary repair to an automobile, assume the following data: on January 1, 1972, a new automobile was acquired at a cost of $4,000, estimated useful life, four years; salvage value, zero; annual depreciation expense, $1,000. Three years later on December 31, 1974, extraordinary repairs (a new engine) were made at a cost of $1,100. Estimated useful life of the automobile beyond this date was thereby increased from the original estimate of one year to a revised estimate of three more years. The ledger accounts will appear as follows after recording these events.

Automobile		Accumulated Depreciation	
Jan. 1, 1972 4,000		Dec. 31, 1974 1,100	Dec. 31, 1972 1,000
			Dec. 31, 1973 1,000
			Dec. 31, 1974 1,000

Extraordi-
nary
repair
charged to
Accumu-
lated De-
preciation

The book value of the automobile is now $2,100, and the balance sheet presentation will be as follows on December 31, 1974.

Increased
book value
for depre-
ciable
asset

Plant and equipment:

Automobile	$4,000	
Less: Accumulated depreciation	1,900	$2,100

In the remaining three years of estimated life for the automobile, the annual depreciation expense will be $700 (book value $2,100 ÷ 3). Three years later at the end of 1977, the automobile will be fully depreciated, and the Accumulated Depreciation account (illustrated below) will show a credit balance of $4,000 (credits of $5,100 less debits of $1,100).

Accumulated Depreciation

Total de-
preciation
equals
total cost
incurred

Dec. 31, 1974	1,100	Dec. 31, 1972	1,000
		Dec. 31, 1973	1,000
		Dec. 31, 1974	1,000
		Dec. 31, 1975	700
		Dec. 31, 1976	700
		Dec. 31, 1977	700

The valuation account, Accumulated Depreciation, now exactly offsets the asset account and no more depreciation can be taken. Observe that the total depreciation recorded during the six years the automobile was in use amounts to $5,100; this agrees exactly with the total expended for the automobile and for the extraordinary repair. In other words, these two capital expenditures have been transformed into expense over a period of six years, during which the business was receiving the benefits from the expenditures.

QUESTIONS

1 Which of the following items should be included in the balance sheet category of "plant and equipment"?
  a A machine in good physical condition which has been used in operations in the past, but is now idle and awaiting disposal by sale or scrapping. No future use of the machine is contemplated by the company.
  b A typewriter acquired by an office supply firm for the purpose of resale to customers.

    c An item capable of use in operations of the business over several years which has recently been acquired and placed in use but has not yet been paid for. Cost is substantial and payment will probably be made in installments.

    d Cost of paving a parking lot, $10,000. Expected life of the paving five years.

    e Advertising designed to make the public aware of the air pollution control features of a new steel mill.

    f Installation of waste disposal equipment which will avoid the dumping of waste products in a river, but which will not reduce the cost of production or increase the efficiency of the manufacturing process.

2 The following expenditures were incurred in connection with a large new machine acquired by a metals manufacturing company. Identify those which should be included in the cost of the asset. (*a*) Freight charges, (*b*) sales tax on the machine, (*c*) payment to a passing motorist whose car was damaged by the equipment used in unloading the machine, (*d*) wages of employees for time spent in installing and testing the machine before it was placed in service, (*e*) wages of employees assigned to lubrication and minor adjustments of machine one year after it was placed in service.

3 Which of the following statements best describes the nature of depreciation?

    a Regular reduction of asset value to correspond to changes in market value as the asset ages. _book value._

    b A process of correlating the carrying value of an asset with its gradual decline in physical efficiency.

    c Allocation of cost in a manner that will ensure that plant and equipment items are not carried on the balance sheet at amounts in excess of net realizable value.

    d Allocation of the cost of a plant asset to the periods in which services are received from the asset.

4 Should depreciation continue to be recorded on a building when ample evidence exists that the current market value is greater than original cost and that the rising trend of market values is continuing? Explain.

5 Which of the following characteristics would prevent an item from being included in the classification of plant and equipment? (*a*) Intangible, (*b*) limited life, (*c*) unlimited life, (*d*) held for sale in the regular course of business, (*e*) not capable of rendering benefits to the business in the future.

6 What is the distinction between *capital expenditures* and *revenue expenditures?*

7 What connection exists between the choice of a depreciation method for expensive new machinery and the amount of income taxes payable in the near future?

8 What is an *extraordinary repair* and how is it recorded in the accounts?

9 Company A's balance sheet shows accumulated depreciation on machinery and equipment of $100,000 and Company B shows accumulated depreciation of $50,000. Both companies are considering the acquisition of new equipment costing $60,000. From the information given, can you determine which company is in a better position to purchase the new equipment for cash? Explain.

10 Criticize the following quotation:

    "We shall have no difficulty in paying for new plant assets needed during the coming year because our estimated outlays for new equipment amount to only $20,000, and we have more than twice that amount in our depreciation reserves at present."

11 A factory machine acquired at a cost of $93,600 was to be depreciated by the sum-of-the-years'-digits method over an estimated life of eight years. Residual salvage value was estimated to be $1,600. State the amount of depreciation during the first year and during the eighth year.

12 After four years of using a machine acquired at a cost of $15,000, Kral

Construction Company determined that the original estimated life of 10 years had been too short and that a total useful life of 12 years was a more reasonable estimate. Explain briefly the method that should be used to revise the depreciation program, assuming that straight-line depreciation has been used.

13 *a* Give some reasons why a company may change its depreciation policy for financial reporting purposes from an accelerated-depreciation method to the straight-line method.

   b Is it possible for a corporation to use accelerated depreciation for income tax purposes and straight-line depreciation for financial reporting purposes?

EXERCISES

Ex. 11-1 New office equipment was purchased by the Carlsbad Company at a list price of $72,000 with credit terms of 2/10, n/30. Payment of the invoice was made within the discount period; it included 5% sales tax on the net price. Transportation charges of $2,400 on the new equipment were paid by Carlsbad Company as well as labor cost of $4,800 for installing the equipment in the appropriate locations. During the unloading and installation work, some of the equipment fell from a loading platform and was damaged. Repair of the damaged parts cost $3,600. After the equipment had been in use for three months, it was thoroughly cleaned and lubricated at a cost of $800. Prepare a list of the items which should be capitalized by debit to the Office Equipment account and state the total cost of the new equipment.

Ex. 11-2 McIntyre Company is presently using factory machinery acquired two years ago and considered at that time to be physically capable of rendering 15 years of service. However, at the time of acquisition, management of McIntyre Company was convinced that the development of new, more efficient types of machines would make it necessary to replace the equipment within 10 years.

   After using the machines for two years, the company changed from its customary one work shift of eight hours per day to the use of three shifts maintaining continuous operation day and night. The new three-shift operation was expected to continue for about one year to meet a temporary increase in demand resulting from a strike affecting competing plants. Operations would then return to the original one shift per day.

   Assuming that the company employs straight-line depreciation, what period of useful life should be used? Should the company increase its depreciation charges proportionately during the year when operations were increased from one to three shifts daily?

Ex. 11-3 Identify the following expenditures as capital expenditures or revenue expenditures:

   a Purchased new spark plugs at a cost of $10 for two-year-old delivery truck.
   b Installed an escalator at a cost of $9,800 in a three-story building which had previously been used for some years without elevators or escalators.
   c Purchased a pencil sharpener at a cost of $3.25.
   d Immediately after acquiring new delivery truck at a cost of $4,800, paid $75 to have the name of the store and other advertising material painted on the truck.
   e Painted delivery truck at a cost of $100 after two years of use.
   f Original life of the delivery truck had been estimated as four years and straight-line depreciation of 25% yearly had been recognized. After three years' use, however, it was decided to recondition the truck thoroughly, including a new engine and transmission, at a cost of $1,600. By making this expenditure it was believed that the useful life of the truck would be extended from the original estimate of four years to a total of six years.

Ex. 11-4 Two businessmen were discussing the accounting issues involved in distin-guishing between capital expenditures and revenue expenditures. A made the following statement: "A good example of a revenue expenditure is the cost of painting our factory building and of replacing broken window glass all the time. Certainly all costs of this nature should always be charged to expense."

B replied as follows: "Your examples are good but on the other hand we recently had a rather special situation in which we capitalized the cost of re-painting a building and of replacing a large number of window panes."

"You were way off base," said A. "The Income Tax Department won't allow it and your CA won't approve your financial statements."

Evaluate these statements. What kind of special situation might B be referring to?

Ex. 11-5 Campbell River Company bought three machines at an auction for $22,600. A cost of $1,400 was incurred to have the machines delivered to the company's plant and $1,600 interest was paid in advance on a bank loan to finance the purchase of the machines. Estimated fair market value of the machines and the cost of preparing the machines for use are approximately as follows:

	Machine No. 1	Machine No. 2	Machine No. 3
Fair market value	$10,000	$16,000	$4,000
Installation costs	600	1,300	300
Costs of trial runs	200	240	None

You are to compute the cost of each machine for accounting purposes (the amount to be capitalized), assuming that the auction and delivery cost is appor-tioned to the three machines on the basis of fair market value.

PROBLEMS

Group A

11A-1 The following entries are contained in an account entitled Property in the ledger of the Orient Trading Company at the end of 1974:

Debit entries:

4/3 Amount paid to acquire building site	$ 25,000
4/15 Cost of removing old unusable building from site	2,000
9/30 Contract price for new building completed Sept. 30	80,000
9/30 Insurance, inspection fees, and other costs directly related to con-	
struction of new building	4,000
Total debits	$111,000

Credit entries:

4/15 Proceeds from sale of old lumber and other material from		
demolition of old building	$3,000	
12/31 Depreciation for 1974, computed at 5% of balance in		
Property account ($108,000). Debit was to Deprecia-		
tion Expense	5,400	
Total credits		8,400
12/31 Balance in Property account at year-end		$102,600

Instructions

a List the errors made in the application of accounting principles or practices by Orient Trading Company.

b Prepare a compound correcting journal entry at December 31, 1974, assuming that the estimated life of the new building is 20 years and that depreciation is to be recognized for three months of 1974 using the straight-line method. The accounts have not been closed for 1974.

11A-2 Columbia Company acquired new machinery at a cost of $183,200 with residual salvage value estimated to be $3,200, and an estimated useful life of five years.

Instructions Compute the annual depreciation expense throughout the five-year life of the machinery under each of the following methods of depreciation:
a Straight-line
b Sum-of-the-years'-digits
c Double-declining-balance

11A-3 The Mint Corporation Ltd. has acquired four machines in recent years, but management has given little consideration to depreciation policies. At the time of acquisition of each machine, a different bookkeeper was employed; consequently, various methods of depreciation have been adopted for the several machines. Information concerning the four machines appears below:

Machine	Date Acquired	Cost	Estimated Useful Life, Years	Estimated Residual Value	Method of Depreciation
A	Jan. 1, 1972	$ 81,000	6	None	Fixed-percentage-on-declining-balance
B	June 30, 1972	168,000	8	10%	Straight-line
C	Jan. 1, 1973	56,000	10	$1,000	Sum-of-the-years'-digits
D	Jan. 1, 1974	66,000	12	None	Fixed-percentage-on-declining-balance

Instructions

a Compute the amount of accumulated depreciation, if any, on each machine at December 31, 1973. For machines A and D, assume that the depreciation rate was double the rate which would be applicable under the straight-line method.

b Prepare a depreciation schedule for use in the computation of the 1974 depreciation expense. Use the following column headings:

Machine	Method of Depreciation	Date of Acquisition	Cost	Estimated Residual Value	Amount to Be Depreciated	Useful Life, Years	Accumulated Depreciation, Dec. 31, 1973	Depreciation Expense, 1974

c Prepare a journal entry to record the depreciation expense for 1974.

11A-4 On July 1, 1973, Southern Milling Company purchased a new machine at the advertised price of $36,000. The terms of payment were 2/10, n/30 and payment was made immediately, including a 4% provincial sales tax. On July 3, the machine was delivered; Southern Milling Company paid freight charges of $788.80 and assigned its own employees to the task of installation. The labor costs for installing the machine amounted to $2,520. During the process of installation, carelessness by a workman caused damage to an adjacent machine, with resulting repairs of $320.

On November 10, 1973, after more than four months of satisfactory operations, the machine was thoroughly inspected, cleaned, and oiled at a cost of $420.

The useful life of the machine was estimated to be 10 years and the residual scrap value zero. The policy of the Southern Milling Company is to use straight-line depreciation and to begin depreciation as of the first of the month in which a plant asset is acquired. During 1973 and 1974, however, numerous changes in the company's accounting personnel were responsible for a number of errors and deviations from policy.

At December 31, 1974, the unaudited financial statements of the Southern Milling Company showed the machine to be carried at a cost of $35,280 and the accumulated depreciation as $5,292. Net income reported for 1973 was $99,200 and for 1974 it was $110,600.

Instructions
a Prepare correct journal entries for all the above transactions from July 1 to December 31, 1973. Include the year-end entry for depreciation and the related closing entry. The sales tax was $1,411.20.
b Compute the correct balances for the Machinery account and for the Accumulated Depreciation: Machinery account at December 31, 1974.
c Compute revised figures for net income for 1973 and 1974. Disregard income taxes.

11A-5 Among the plant assets used by Quebec Company is a large machine which was acquired new on March 31, 1971, at a cost of $88,000. Depreciation has been computed by the straight-line method based on an estimated life of five years and residual scrap value of $8,000.

On January 2, 1974, extraordinary repairs (which were almost equivalent to a rebuilding of the machine) were performed at a cost of $19,000. Because of the thoroughgoing nature of these repairs, the normal life of the machine was extended materially. The revised estimate of useful life was four years from January 1, 1974.

Instructions Prepare journal entries to record the original purchase of the machine; the provision for depreciation on December 31, 1971, 1972, and 1973; the expenditure for the extraordinary repairs in January, 1974; and the provision for depreciation on December 31, 1974. Assume payment in cash for the machine and for the extraordinary repairs.

Group B

11B-1 During 1974 the Santa Cruz Company purchased some hilly land with old abandoned buildings. The old buildings were removed, the land was leveled, and a new building was constructed. The company moved from its former rented quarters into the new building on October 1. Transactions relating these events were recorded in an account entitled Property which contained the following entries at the end of 1974.

Debit entries:

3/9 Purchase for cash of building site	$ 27,500
4/28 Payment for demolition of old building......................	3,000
5/15 Payment for leveling of land	10,000
9/28 Payment for insurance of building during construction...........	6,000
9/28 Payment for new building completed today	120,000
10/7 Payment to caterer for office party for employees, customers, and friends to celebrate the move to new building	1,500
Total debits	$168,000

Credit entries:

4/28 Cash received from sale of materials from
      demolished building $4,500

12/31 Depreciation for 1974, computed at 4% of balance
      in Property account ($163,500). Debit was
      to Depreciation Expense.   6,540

      Total credits   11,040

12/31 Balance in Property account at year-end. $156,960

Instructions

a List the errors made in the application of accounting principles or practices by Santa Cruz Company.

b Prepare a compound correcting journal entry at December 31, 1974, assuming that the estimated life of the new building is 25 years and that depreciation is to be recognized for the three months the building was in use during 1974, using the straight-line method. The accounts have not been closed for 1974.

11B-2 Klamath Company purchased new equipment at a cost of $45,800, with residual salvage value estimated to be $800 and estimated useful life five years.

Instructions Compute the annual depreciation expense throughout the five-year life of the equipment under each of the following methods of depreciation:

a Straight-line

b Sum-of-the-years'-digits

c Double-declining-balance.

11B-3 The Stocker Company has acquired four costly machines in recent years, but management has given little consideration to depreciation policies. At the time of acquisition of each machine, a different bookkeeper was employed; consequently, various methods of depreciation have been adopted for the several machines. Information concerning the four machines may be summarized as follows:

Machine	Date Acquired	Cost	Estimated Useful Life, Years	Estimated Residual Value	Method of Depreciation
A	Jan. 1, 1972	$54,000	6	None	Fixed-percentage-on-declining-balance
B	June 30, 1972	84,000	8	10%	Straight-line
C	Jan. 1, 1973	56,000	10	$1,000	Sum-of-the-years'-digits
D	Jan. 1, 1974	66,000	12	None	Fixed-percentage-on-declining-balance

Instructions

a Compute the amount of accumulated depreciation, if any, on each machine at December 31, 1973. For machines A and D, assume that the depreciation rate was double the rate which would be applicable under the straight-line method.

b Prepare a depreciation schedule for use in the computation of the 1974 depreciation expense. Use the following column headings:

Machine	Method of Depreciation	Date of Acquisition	Cost	Estimated Residual Value	Amount to Be Depreciated	Useful Life, Years	Accumulated Depreciation, Dec. 31, 1973	Depreciation Expense, 1974

c Prepare a journal entry to record the 1974 depreciation expense.

11B-4 On July 1, 1973, Cabot Company purchased a new machine at the advertised price of $9,000. The terms of payment were 2/10, n/30 and payment was made immediately, including a 4% provincial sales tax. On July 3, the machine was delivered; Cabot Company paid freight charges of $197.20 and assigned its own employees to the task of installation. The labor costs for installing the machine amounted to $630. During the process of installation, carelessness by a workman caused damage to an adjacent machine, with resulting repairs of $80.

On October 15, after more than three months of satisfactory operation, the machine was thoroughly inspected, cleaned, and oiled at a cost of $105.

The useful life of the machine was estimated to be 10 years and the residual scrap value to be zero. The policy of the Cabot Company is to use straight-line depreciation and to begin depreciation as of the first of the month in which a plant asset is acquired. During 1973 and 1974, however, numerous changes in the company's accounting personnel were responsible for a number of errors and deviations from policy.

At December 31, 1974, the unaudited financial statements of the Cabot Company showed the machine to be carried at a cost of $8,820 and the accumulated depreciation as $1,323. Net income reported for 1973 was $24,800 and for 1974 $27,650.

Instructions

a Prepare entries in general journal form for all the above transactions from July 1 to December 31, 1973. Include the year-end entry for depreciation and the related closing entry.

b Compute the correct balances for the Machinery account and for accumulated depreciation at December 31, 1974.

c Compute revised figures for net income for 1973 and 1974.

11B-5 On April 1, 1970, Big Sky Ltd., acquired a new large machine at a cost of $440,000. The company has used the straight-line method of depreciation based on an estimated life of five years and a residual scrap value of $40,000.

After three years of use, on January 2, 1973, extraordinary repairs were made on the machine at a cost $95,000. The repairs were virtually the equivalent of rebuilding the machine, and management believed that this thorough reconditioning would extend the normal life of the machine substantially. The revised estimate of useful life was four years from January 1, 1973.

Instructions Prepare journal entries to record the original purchase of the machine; the provision for depreciation on December 31, 1970, 1971, and 1972; the expenditure for the extraordinary repairs in January, 1973; and the provision for depreciation on December 31, 1973. Assume payment in cash for the machine and for the extraordinary repairs.

BUSINESS DECISION PROBLEM 11

Randolph Hayes is interested in buying a manufacturing business and has located two similar companies being offered for sale. Both companies began operations three years ago, each with invested capital of $300,000. A considerable part of the assets in each company is represented by a building with an original cost of $100,000 and an estimated life of 40 years, and by machinery with an original cost of $100,000 and an estimated life of 20 years. Residual scrap value is negligible.

Company A uses straight-line depreciation and Company B uses fixed-per-centage-on-declining-balance depreciation. In all other respects the accounting policies of the two companies are quite similar. Neither company has borrowed from banks or incurred any indebtedness other than normal trade payables. The nature of products and other characteristics of operations are much the same for the two companies.

Audited financial statements for the three years show net income as follows:

Year	Company A	Company B
1	$21,000	$20,000
2	23,100	22,100
3	25,400	24,300

Hayes asks your advice as to which company he should buy. They are offered for sale at approximately the same price, and he is inclined to choose Company A because of its consistently higher earnings. On the other hand, he is impressed with the fact that Company B has more cash and a stronger working capital position. The audited financial statements show that withdrawals by the two owners have been approximately equal during the three-year life of the two companies.

Instructions

a Compute the depreciation recorded by each company in the first three years. Round off depreciation expense for each year to the nearest dollar.

b Write a memorandum to Hayes advising him as to which company in your judgment represents the more promising purchase. Give specific reasons to support your recommendation.

TWELVE

PLANT AND EQUIPMENT NATURAL RESOURCES AND INTANGIBLES

Disposal of plant and equipment[1]

When units of plant and equipment wear out or become obsolete, they must be discarded, sold, or traded in on new equipment. Upon the disposal or retirement of a depreciable asset, the cost of the property is removed from the asset account, and the accumulated depreciation is removed from the related valuation account. Assume, for example, that office equipment purchased 10 years ago at a cost of $500 has been fully depreciated and is no longer useful. The entry to record the discarding of the worthless equipment is as follows:

Scrapping fully depreciated asset

Accumulated Depreciation: Office Equipment	500	
Office Equipment.		500

To remove from the accounts the cost and the accumulated depreciation on fully depreciated office equipment now being discarded. No salvage value.

Some plant assets last much longer than the original estimate of useful life; others may be discarded earlier than indicated by the estimate of useful life. When an asset has been fully depreciated, no more depreciation should be recorded on it, even though the property is in good condition and is continued in use. The objective of depreciation is to spread the *cost* of an asset over the periods of its usefulness; in no case can total depreciation expense be greater than the amount paid for the asset. When a fully depreciated asset is continued in use beyond the original estimate of useful life, the asset account and the Accumulated

---

[1] The income tax regulations dealing with disposal of fixed assets are discussed in Chapter 20.

Depreciation account may be permitted to remain on the books without further entries until the asset is discarded.

GAINS AND LOSSES ON DISPOSAL OF PLANT AND EQUIPMENT When depreciable assets are disposed of at any date other than the end of the year, an entry should be made to record depreciation for the fraction of the year ending with the date of disposal. In the following illustrations of the disposal of items of plant and equipment, it is assumed that any necessary entries for fractional-period depreciation have been recorded. The *book value* of a plant asset is its cost minus the total recorded depreciation, as shown by the Accumulated Depreciation account. For a fully depreciated asset, the book value is zero, since the credit balance in the Accumulated Depreciation account exactly offsets the debit balance in the asset account. If a depreciable asset is discarded before it is fully depreciated, and there is no salvage value, a loss results in an amount equal to the book value of the asset. When a depreciable asset is sold, the loss or gain on the disposal is computed by comparing the book value with the amount received from the sale. A sales price in excess of the book value produces a gain; a sales price below the book value produces a loss. If these gains or losses are material in amount, they should be shown separately in the income statement under Extraordinary Items, a category placed near the bottom of the income statement after the income from operations has been shown.

Disposal at a price above book value Assume that a machine which cost $10,000 and has a book value of $2,000 is sold for $3,000. The journal entry to record this disposal is as follows:

Gain on *plant asset* *disposed of*	*Cash*	*3,000*	
	Accumulated Depreciation: Machinery	*8,000*	
	Machinery		*10,000*
	Gain on Disposal of Plant Assets		*1,000*
	To record sale of machinery at a price above book value.		

Disposal at a price below book value Now assume that the same machine were sold for $500. The journal entry in this case would be as follows:

Loss on *plant asset* *disposed of*	*Cash*	*500*	
	Accumulated Depreciation: Machinery	*8,000*	
	Loss on Disposal of Plant Assets	*1,500*	
	Machinery		*10,000*
	To record sale of machinery at a price below book value.		

The disposal of a depreciable asset at a price equal to book value would result in neither a gain nor a loss. The entry for such a transaction would consist of a debit to Cash for the amount received, a debit to Accumulated Depreciation for the balance accumulated, and a credit to the asset account for the original cost.

DEPRECIATION FOR FRACTIONAL PERIOD PRECEDING DISPOSAL When depreciable assets are disposed of at any date other than the end of the year, it is customary to record depreciation for the fraction of the year ending with the date of disposal. Assume that the accounts showed the following balances as of December 31.

Office equipment.	$2,000
Accumulated depreciation: office equipment	1,600

The balance of $1,600 in the Accumulated Depreciation account was the result of eight annual credits of $200 each. On the following March 31, the office equipment was sold for $100. No depreciation had been recorded since the books were adjusted and closed on December 31. Two entries are necessary at the time of disposing of the office equipment: one to record depreciation for the three months ending with the date of disposal, and a second to record the sale of the equipment.

Record de-	Depreciation Expense: Office Equipment	50	
preciation	Accumulated Depreciation: Office Equipment		50
to date of			
disposal	To record depreciation for the three months prior to disposal of office		
	equipment ($200 × $\frac{1}{4}$).		

	Cash	100	
	Accumulated Depreciation: Office Equipment	1,650	
	Loss on Disposal of Plant Assets	250	
	Office Equipment.		2,000
	To record sale of office equipment at less than book value.		

Trading in used assets on new

Certain types of depreciable assets, such as automobiles and office equipment, are customarily traded in on new assets of the same kind. The trade-in allowance granted by the dealer may differ materially from the book value of the old asset. If the dealer grants a trade-in allowance in excess of the book value of the asset being traded in, there is the suggestion of a profit being realized on the exchange. The evidence of a gain is not conclusive, however, because the list price of the new asset may purposely have been set higher than a realistic cash price to permit the offering of inflated trade-in allowances.

To illustrate the handling of an exchange transaction in the manner followed by most companies, assume that a delivery truck is acquired at a cost of $3,200. The truck is depreciated on the straight-line basis with the assumption of a four-year life. After three years of use, the truck is traded in on a new model having a list price of $4,000. The truck dealer grants a trade-in allowance of $1,200 for the old truck; the additional amount to be paid to acquire the new truck is, therefore, $2,800 ($4,000 list price minus $1,200 trade-in allowance). The **cost basis** of the new truck is computed as follows:

(c)

Trade-in:	Cost of old truck	$3,200
cost of new equipment	Less: Accumulated depreciation ($800 × 3)	2,400
	Book value of old truck	$ 800
	Add: Cash payment for new truck (list price, $4,000 − $1,200 trade-in	
	allowance)	2,800
	Cost basis of new truck	$3,600

The trade-in allowance and the list price of the new truck are not recorded in the accounts; their only function lies in determining the amount which the purchaser must pay in addition to turning in the old truck. The journal entry for this exchange transaction is as follows:

Entry for trade-in	Delivery Truck (new)	3,600	
	Accumulated Depreciation: Delivery Truck (old)	2,400	
	Delivery Truck (old)		3,200
	Cash		2,800

To remove from the accounts the cost of old truck and accumulated depreciation thereon, and to record new truck at cost equal to book value of old truck traded in plus cash paid.

An alternate method of recording trade-ins, having strong theoretical support, calls for recognizing a gain or loss on the exchange in an amount equal to the difference between the book value of the old asset and its estimated fair market value at the time of the trade-in. The validity of this alternative method rests upon the assumption that the trade-in allowance is generally composed of two elements: (1) the actual current market value or the amount that could be obtained from the sale of the old asset, and (2) the discount given on the new asset being purchased. The discount equals the difference between the list price, or quoted selling price, and the market price at which the new asset would be sold if no trade-in had been included in the transaction. If we make the assumption for the preceding example, that the fair market value of the trade-in was $1,000, the journal entry would be as follows:

Trade-in: alternative method	Delivery Truck (new)	3,800	
	Accumulated Depreciation: Delivery Truck (old)	2,400	
	Delivery Truck (old)		3,200
	Cash		2,800
	Gain on Disposal of Plant Assets		200

To remove from the accounts the cost of the old truck and accumulated depreciation thereon, and to record the new truck at its fair market value (List price $4000 less overallowance on trade-in of $200)

Maintaining control over plant and equipment: subsidiary ledgers

Unless internal controls over plant and equipment are carefully designed, many units of equipment are likely to be broken, discarded, or stolen without any entry being made in the accounting records for their disposal.

The asset accounts will then be overstated, and depreciation programs for such missing units of equipment will presumably continue. Consequently, net income will be misstated because of the omission of losses on retirement of plant assets and because of erroneous depreciation charges.

One important control device which guards against failure to record the retirement of assets is the use of control accounts and subsidiary ledgers for plant and equipment. The general ledger ordinarily contains a separate asset account and related depreciation accounts for each major classification of plant assets, such as land, buildings, office equipment, and delivery equipment. For example, the general ledger will contain the account Office Equipment, and also, the related accounts Depreciation Expense: Office Equipment, and Accumulated Depreciation: Office Equipment. The general ledger account for office equipment contains entries for a variety of items: typewriters, filing cabinets, dictaphones, desks, etc. It is not possible in this one general ledger account to maintain adequate information concerning the cost of each item, its estimated useful life, book value, insured value, and other data which may be needed by management as a basis for decisions on such issues as replacement, insurance, and taxation.

A subsidiary ledger should therefore be established for office equipment, and for each of the other general ledger accounts which represents many separate units of plant property. The subsidiary ledger usually consists of a card file, with a separate card for each unit of property, such as a typewriter or desk. Each card shows the name of the asset, identification number, and such details as date of acquisition, cost, useful life, depreciation, accumulated depreciation, insurance coverage, repairs, and gain or loss on disposal. The general ledger account, Office Equipment, serves as a control; the balance of this control account is equal to the total cost of the items in the subsidiary ledger for office equipment. The general ledger account, Accumulated Depreciation: Office Equipment, is also a control account; its balance is equal to the total of the accumulated depreciation shown on all the cards in the office equipment ledger. Every acquisition of office equipment is entered in the control account and also on a card in the subsidiary ledger. Similarly, every disposal of an item of office equipment is entered in both the control account and the subsidiary ledger.

Each card in a subsidiary ledger for plant and equipment shows an identification number which should also appear in the form of a metal tag attached to the asset itself. Consequently, a physical inventory of plant and equipment is easily taken and will prove whether all units of equipment shown by the records are actually on hand and being used in operations.

Other advantages afforded by a plant and equipment ledger are the ready availability of information for the periodic computation of depreciation, and for entries to record the disposal of individual items of property.

A better basis is also available for supporting the data in tax returns, for obtaining proper insurance coverage, and for supporting claims for losses sustained on insured property. In well-managed companies, it is standard practice to control expenditures for plant and equipment by preparing a budget of all planned acquisitions for at least a year in advance. A first essential to the preparation of such a budget is a detailed record showing the assets presently owned, their cost, age, and remaining useful life.

NATURAL RESOURCES

Accounting for natural resources

Mining properties, oil and gas wells, and tracts of standing timber are leading examples of natural resources or "wasting assets." The distinguishing characteristics of these assets are that they are physically consumed and converted into inventory. In a theoretical sense, a coal mine might even be regarded as an "underground inventory of coal"; however, such an inventory is certainly not a current asset. In the balance sheet, mining property and other natural resources are usually listed as a separate group of tangible assets.

Natural resources should be recorded in the accounts at cost. As the resource is removed through the process of mining, cutting, or drilling, the asset account must be proportionately reduced. The carrying value (book value) of a coal mine, for example, is reduced by a small amount for each ton of coal mined. The original cost of the mine is thus gradually transferred out of the asset account and becomes part of the cost of the coal mined and sold.

DEPLETION The term *depletion* is used to describe the pro rata allocation of cost of a natural resource to the units removed. Depletion is computed by dividing the cost of the natural resource by the estimated available number of units, such as barrels of oil or tons of coal. The depletion charge per unit is then multiplied by the number of units actually removed during the year to determine the total depletion charge for that period.

To illustrate the computation of depletion expense, assume that the sum of $500,000 is paid for a coal mine believed to contain 1 million tons of coal. The depletion charge per unit is $500,000 ÷ 1,000,000, or 50 cents a ton. If we assume that 200,000 tons of coal were mined and sold during the first year of operation, the depletion charge for the year would be 50 cents × 200,000, or $100,000. The journal entry necessary at the end of the year to record depletion of the mine would be as follows:

Recording Depletion Expense *100,000*
depletion   Accumulated Depletion: Coal Mine *100,000*
            To record depletion expense for the year; 200,000 tons mined
            @ 50 cents per ton.

In reporting natural resources in the balance sheet, accumulated depletion should be deducted from the cost of the property. A recent balance sheet of Central-Del Rio Oils Limited, for example, reports its natural resources as follows:

Natural resources in the balance sheet

Petroleum, natural gas and mineral properties	*$189,021,019*
Less accumulated depletion	*41,055,630*

Depletion expense in a mining business might be compared with the Purchases account in the ledger of a retail store. The Purchases account represents part of the cost to the store of the goods available for sale; the Depletion Expense account in a mining company represents a part of the cost of the coal or other product available for sale. To the extent that coal produced during the year is not sold but is carried forward as inventory for sale in the following year, **the depletion charge will also be carried forward as part of the inventory value.** In other words, depletion is recorded in the year in which extraction of the product occurs but becomes a deduction from revenue in the period in which the product is sold. Of course, the cost of the inventory of coal or other extracted product on hand at the end of the year includes not only the depletion charge but also the labor cost and other expenditures incurred in bringing the coal to the surface.

INV COST included DEPLETION!

PERCENTAGE DEPLETION VERSUS COST DEPLETION Depletion for income tax purposes has been widely publicized in the news media. For the determination of taxable income, the Income Tax Act permits a deduction for depletion expense equal to a specified percentage of the revenue from production. Consequently, **percentage depletion** can exceed the cost of the natural resource, which could never happen when depletion is based on cost. Currently, the percentage depletion rate for oil and gas wells is $33\frac{1}{3}$% of the net income from the property during the year.

Percentage depletion is used **only for income tax purposes, not for financial statements.** The topic is mentioned here because nearly everyone is exposed to political arguments over the merits of percentage depletion. The usual argument advanced in its favor is that it encourages the risk-taking inherent in the search for and development of oil, gas, and other natural resources.

DEVELOPMENT COSTS The cost of a natural resource may include not only the purchase price of the property, but also expenditures for recording fees, surveying, and a variety of exploratory and developmental activities.

Some exploratory and developmental expenditures will prove to be unproductive; these expenditures should be recognized as losses or expenses of the current period and not carried forward as assets. The dividing line between productive and nonproductive expenditures for exploration and development is not always easy to draw. The drilling of a dry hole in a new oil field might be regarded as a loss, or, on the other hand, as an integral step in an overall successful development of the area.

There is a noticeable trend for companies engaged in the extraction of natural resources to plan for continuity of existence, rather than to end their operations with the exhaustion of a single property. These companies maintain their productive capacity by carrying on a continuous program of exploration and development of new areas. Since outlays for exploration and development thus become normal and continuous, these expenditures are commonly charged to expense in the year in which the exploration or development is performed. Such practices have been condoned by accountants more on the grounds of expediency than on theoretical considerations.

DEPRECIATION OF BUILDINGS AND EQUIPMENT CLOSELY RELATED TO NATURAL RESOURCES Assume that a building costing $20,500 and having a normal useful life of 20 years is erected at the site of a mine estimated to contain 100,000 tons of ore. Once the mine is exhausted, the building will have only scrap value, say, $500. Production of ore is being carried on at a rate which will probably exhaust the mine within four to six years. During the first year after construction of the building, ore is mined in the amount of 25,000 tons. How much depreciation should be recognized on the building?

In this situation, depreciation of the building should be based on the life of the mine, and computed in the same manner as depletion. Cost, $20,500, minus scrap value, $500, times 25,000/100,000 equals $5,000 depreciation for the first year. The formula may be concisely stated as

$$\text{Depreciation per Year} = (\text{Cost} - \text{Scrap}) \times \frac{\text{Units Produced}}{\text{Estimated Total Units}}$$

INTANGIBLE ASSETS

Characteristics

As the word *intangible* suggests, assets in this classification have no physical substance. Leading examples are goodwill, leaseholds, copyrights, franchises, licenses, and trademarks. Intangible assets are classified on the balance sheet as a subgroup of plant assets. However, not all assets which lack physical substance are regarded as intangible assets; an account receivable, for example, or a prepaid expense, is of nonphysical nature but is classified as a current asset and is not regarded as an intangible. In brief, intangible assets are noncurrent and nonphysical.

The basis of valuation for intangible assets is cost. In some companies, certain intangible assets such as trademarks may be of great importance but may have been acquired without the incurring of any cost. An intangible asset should appear on the balance sheet *only* if a cost of acquisition or development has been incurred.

In *Opinion No. 17* of the Accounting Principles Board of the AICPA, the Board points out that a business may acquire intangible assets by purchase from others or may develop them itself.[2] This Opinion stresses that many intangible assets may be identified and given descriptive names such as patents and franchises. Other intangibles, notably goodwill, cannot be readily identified and cannot be purchased or sold except as part of an entire enterprise. The Accounting Principles Board emphasizes that accounting for intangible assets involves the same kinds of problems as accounting for other long-lived assets, that is:

1 Determining an initial carrying amount
2 Accounting for the carrying amount under normal circumstances, that is, systematic write-off or amortization (similar to depreciation)
3 Accounting for the carrying amount of the asset if the value declines substantially and permanently

However, accounting for an intangible asset is rendered somewhat difficult because the lack of physical substance makes evidence of its existence more elusive, may make its value more debatable, and may make the length of its useful life more questionable. These characteristics of intangible assets suggest that realizable value may be undeterminable or even nonexistent. Perhaps because of the lack of clear support for precise valuation of intangibles, many companies choose to carry their intangible assets on the balance sheet at a nominal valuation of $1; Hiram Walker—Gooderham & Worts Ltd., the well known distillery, is one prominent example.

There is little doubt, however, that in some companies the intangible assets, such as goodwill or trademarks, may be vitally important to profitable operations. The carrying of intangible assets on the balance sheet is justified only when there is good evidence that future earnings will be derived from these assets.

Classification

The traditional classification of intangible assets has merely separated those with limited lives (such as patents) from those with unlimited terms of existence (such as a perpetual franchise granted to a public utility). An unlimited legal life is of course no assurance of an unending economic usefulness.

[2] Accounting Principles Board, *Opinion No. 17*, "Intangible Assets," AICPA (New York: 1970), p. 332.

A more recent and informative classification of intangibles uses several bases of classification as follows:[3]

1 Identifiability—separately identifiable or lacking specific identification. Manner of acquisition—acquired singly, in groups, or in business combinations or developed internally.

2 Expected period of benefit—limited by law or contract, related to human or economic factors, or indefinite or indeterminate duration.

3 Separability from an entire enterprise—rights transferable without title, salable, or inseparable from the enterprise or a substantial part of it.

Operating expenses versus intangible assets

Many types of expenditures offer at least a half promise of yielding benefits in subsequent years, but the evidence is so nebulous and the period of usefulness so hard to define that it is expedient to treat these expenditures as expense when incurred. Another reason for charging these outlays to expense is the practical difficulty of separating them from the recurring expenses of current operations.

Examples are the expenditures for intensive advertising campaigns to introduce new products, and the expense of training employees to work with new types of machinery or office equipment. There is little doubt that some benefits from these outlays continue beyond the current period, but because of the indeterminable duration of the benefits, it is almost universal practice to treat expenditures of this nature as expense of the current period.[4] Although the dividing line between expenditures to be expensed and those to be charged to intangible asset accounts is admittedly somewhat arbitrary, the establishment of a universal rule has the merit of narrowing the range of acceptable accounting alternatives and thereby contributing to more comparability in financial statements.

For income tax purposes, a business has an option to deduct its outlays for research and similar expenditures as current expense or to capitalize them for later amortization.

Amortization

The term *amortization* is used to describe the systematic write-off to expense of the cost of an intangible asset over the periods of its economic usefulness. The usual accounting entry for amortization consists of a debit to an expense account and a credit to the intangible asset account. There is no theoretical objection to crediting an accumulated amortization account rather than the intangible asset, but this method is seldom encountered in current practice.

[3] *Ibid.*, p. 334.

[4] In the words of the Accounting Principles Board: "A company should record as expenses the costs to develop intangible assets which are not specifically identifiable." *Ibid.*, p. 334.

Although it is difficult to estimate the useful life of an intangible such as goodwill, it is highly probable that such an asset will not contribute to future earnings on a permanent basis. The cost of the intangible asset should, therefore, be deducted from revenues during the years in which it may be expected to aid in producing revenues.[5] The Accounting Principles Board has ruled, however, that the period of amortization should not exceed 40 years.[6]

ARBITRARY WRITE-OFF OF INTANGIBLES Arbitrary, lump-sum write-off of intangibles (leaving a nominal balance of $1 in the accounts) is a practice sometimes found in companies which have not adopted a systematic amortization program. Arguments for this practice emphasize the element of conservatism, the practical difficulty of estimating an appropriate period for amortization, and the absence of any realizable value for intangibles. Accountants generally agree that whenever any event occurs which indicates that an intangible has lost all value, immediate write-off of the entire cost is warranted regardless of whether an amortization program has previously been followed. Lump-sum write-offs of intangible assets should be reported as extraordinary items in the income statement.

On the other hand, arbitrary write-offs of valuable, revenue-producing intangible assets are no more in accordance with accounting theory than would be the arbitrary write-off of land or buildings.

Goodwill

Businessmen and lawyers used the term *goodwill* in a variety of meanings before it became a part of accounting terminology. One of the more common meanings of goodwill in a nonaccounting sense concerns the benefits derived from a favorable reputation among customers. To accountants, however, goodwill has a very specific meaning not necessarily limited to customer relationships. It means the *present value of future earnings in excess of the earnings normally realized in the industry.* Above-average earnings may arise not only from favorable customer relations but also from such factors as location, monopoly, manufacturing efficiency, and superior management.

The existence of the intangible asset of goodwill is indicated when an entire business is sold for a price in excess of the fair market value of the other assets. The willingness of the purchaser of a going business to pay a price greater than the sum of the values of the tangible assets indicates that he is paying for intangible assets as well. If the business does not include such specific intangibles as patents or franchises, the extra amount paid is presumably for goodwill. Superior earnings in past years are of significance to a prospective purchaser of an enterprise only

---

[5] Present tax regulations permit the amortization of goodwill, acquired after December 31, 1971, in computing taxable income. The CICA Accounting and Auditing Research Committee does not require the amortization of goodwill.
[6] Accounting Principles Board, *op. cit.,* p. 334.

to the extent that he believes such earnings may continue after he acquires the business. If the prospective purchaser believes that, by purchasing a particular company with a record of superior earnings in the past, he will earn these above-average earnings in the future, he may reasonably be expected to pay a premium price for the business. The premium which he pays represents the cost of purchased goodwill and may properly be recorded in the accounting records of the new owner in a Goodwill account.

Assume that two businesses in the same line of trade are for sale and that the normal rate of earnings on capital invested in this industry is 10% a year. The relative earning power of the two companies during the past five years is indicated by the following schedule.

	Company X	Company Y
Measuring superior earning power Net assets other than goodwill	$1,000,000	$1,000,000
Normal rate of earnings on invested capital	10%	10%
Average net income for past five years	$ 100,000	$ 140,000
Net income computed at normal rate (10%) on net assets other than goodwill	100,000	100,000
Annual earnings in excess of average for the industry . . .	$ -0-	$ 40,000

A prospective investor would be willing to pay more for Company Y than for Company X because Y has a record of superior earnings which will presumably continue for some time in the future. Company Y has goodwill; Company X does not. Very few concerns are able to maintain above-average earnings for more than a few years. Consequently, the purchaser of a business will usually limit his payment for goodwill to not more than four or five times the excess annual earnings.

ESTIMATING THE AMOUNT OF GOODWILL   Goodwill is to be recorded in the accounts only when paid for; this situation usually occurs only when a going business is purchased in its entirety. When ownership of a business changes hands, any amount paid for goodwill rests on the assumption that earnings in excess of normal will continue under the new ownership. The following are methods of estimating a value for goodwill:

1 Arbitrary agreement between buyer and seller of the business may be reached on the amount of goodwill. For example, it might be agreed that the fair market value of the net tangible assets is $1,000,000 and that the total purchase price for the business will be $1,100,000, thus providing a $100,000 payment for goodwill. (We are assuming in this example that the business has no identifiable intangible assets such as patents.) The term *net tangible assets* may require explanation. *Net assets* means assets minus liabilities; *net tangible assets* therefore means all assets (except the intangibles) minus liabilities. Another way of computing the amount of net tangible assets is merely to deduct the intangible assets from the owner's equity.

2 Goodwill may be determined as a multiple of the average net income of past years. For example, assume that a business has earned an average annual net income of $25,000 during the past five years. The business is sold for the book value of the net tangible assets, plus two years' average net income. The payment for goodwill is, therefore, $50,000. This method may be criticized because it ignores completely the concept of *excess earnings* as a basis for estimating goodwill.

3 Goodwill may be determined as a multiple of the amount by which the average annual earnings exceed normal earnings. To illustrate, assume the following data:

Goodwill as multiple of excess earnings · *Average investment in the business*	*$100,000*
Average annual earnings (rate of 14%)	*$ 14,000*
Normal earnings for this industry (rate of 10%)	*10,000*
Average earnings in excess of normal	*$ 4,000*
Multiple of excess annual earnings	*4*
Goodwill	*$ 16,000*

The multiple applied to the excess annual earnings may vary widely from perhaps 1 to 10, depending on the nature of the industry and the reliance placed on the earnings projections. This method is more in accord with the concept of goodwill as earning power in *excess* of normal, whereas method 2 relates goodwill to the *total* profits.

4 Goodwill may be determined as the capitalized value of excess earning power, using a capitalization rate considered normal in the industry. Assume that the normal rate of earnings in a given line of business is 10% and that a particular company presents the following picture:

Goodwill based on capitalization of excess earnings · *Average investment in the business*	*$100,000*
Average annual earnings (rate of 14%)	*$ 14,000*
Normal earnings for this industry (rate of 10%)	*10,000*
Average earnings in excess of normal	*$ 4,000*
Goodwill, computed by capitalizing excess earnings of 10% ($4,000 ÷ .10)	*$ 40,000*

Leaseholds

In discussing the leasing of business property, it is convenient to refer to the owner as the "lessor" and to the tenant as the "lessee." The signing of a long-term lease of business property does not necessarily call for the use of a leasehold account. A leasehold account is needed only when the lease requires a substantial advance payment applicable to future years. Some leases merely provide for regular monthly payments of rent; in these cases the lease is not recorded in the accounts. The monthly payments to the lessor are recorded as rent expense by the lessee when they are paid.

Sometimes a lease is so drawn as to require the payment in advance of only the final year's rent. Rent payments for all but the final year may be made on a month-to-month basis. In this case the Leasehold account will be debited with the advance payment of the final year's rent at the time the lease is signed, and this amount will remain in the account until the final year of the lease, at which time the advance payment will be transferred to the Rent Expense account.

During periods of rising property values, a long-term lease may become extremely valuable because the agreed rental is much less than would be charged under current market conditions. Such a development is particularly likely for leases that run for 20 or 30 years or more. No entry is usually made in the accounts to reflect the increased value of the lease attributable to rising property values, because assets are accounted for on the basis of cost, not on the basis of estimated market values. However, if the lessee should sell his rights under the lease to someone else, the new tenant would record the cost to him of the lease.

Assume, for example, that A Company owns a new building which it leases to B Company for 15 years at an annual rental of $12,000. After five years, during which property values and rental rates have increased sharply, B Company sells its rights under the lease to C Company for a cash payment of $10,000. The new tenant, C Company, also assumes the obligation of making the required yearly payments of $12,000 to A Company during the remaining 10 years of the lease. The annual rent expense to C Company will be $13,000, consisting of $12,000 payable in cash each year plus $1,000 in amortization of the cost incurred in acquiring the lease. By transferring $1,000 a year from the Leasehold account to the Rent Expense account, C Company will spread the cost of this favorable lease uniformly over the 10 years during which it occupies the property. The journal entry on C Company's books will be as follows:

Leasehold	10,000	
Cash		10,000

To record purchase of a lease with 10 years life remaining.
Annual cash payments of $12,000 to owner are required.

The Leasehold account will be written off to Rent Expense by the following entry in each of the next 10 years.

Rent Expense	1,000	
Leasehold		1,000

To transfer to expense one-tenth of the cost of a lease having 10 years to run from date of acquisition.

Leasehold improvements

When buildings or other improvements are constructed on leased property by the lessee, the costs should be recorded in a Leasehold Improvements account, and written off as expense during the remaining life of the lease or of the estimated useful life of the building, whichever is shorter. This procedure is usually followed even though the lessee has an option to renew the lease, because there is no assurance in advance that conditions will warrant the exercise of the renewal clause.

Patents

A patent is an exclusive right granted by the federal government for manufacture, use, and sale of a particular product. Patents, like other intangible assets, should be recorded in the accounts at cost. Since patents may be acquired by purchase or may be obtained directly from the government by the inventor, the cost may consist of the purchase price or of the expenditures for research and development leading to the application for the patent. In addition, cost may include legal fees for obtaining the patent and for infringement suits. Companies which carry on extensive research and development programs on a permanent basis often treat the costs of such work as expense when incurred, on the grounds that constant research is necessary merely to maintain a competitive position in the industry. Often it is difficult to determine what portion of research expenditures is related to a given patent, and what earnings may be derived from the patented device. For these reasons, it is common to find that patents developed within the organization are carried on the books at a nominal valuation, such as $1.

Patents are granted for a period of 17 years, and the period of amortization must not exceed that period. However, if the patent is likely to lose its usefulness in less than 17 years, amortization should be based on the shorter period of estimated useful life. Assume that a patent is purchased from the inventor at a cost of $30,000, after five years of the legal life have expired. The remaining *legal* life is, therefore, 12 years, but if the estimated *useful* life is only five years, amortization should be based on this shorter period. The entry to be made to record the annual amortization expense would be:

Entry for amortization of patent

Amortization Expense: Patents	6,000	
Patents		6,000

To amortize cost of patent on a straight-line basis and estimated life of five years.

If new information becomes available indicating a different useful life for a patent than was originally estimated, the revising of the amortization rate should be carried out in the same manner described in Chapter 11 for revising depreciation rates. In brief, spread the unamortized cost over the remaining life indicated by the new estimate, but in no case beyond the legal life of the patent.

Copyrights

A copyright is an exclusive right granted to protect the production and sale of literary or artistic materials for a period consisting of the life of the author plus fifty years after his death, except in certain special cases. The cost of obtaining a copyright is minor and therefore is chargeable to expense when paid. Only when a copyright is purchased will the expenditure be material enough to warrant capitalization and spreading over the useful life. The revenues from copyrights are usually limited to only a few years, and the purchase cost should, of course, be amortized over the years in which the revenues are expected.

Trademarks

A permanent exclusive right to the use of a trademark, brand name, or commercial symbol may be obtained by registering it. Because of the unlimited legal life, a trademark may be carried without amortization at the original cost. If the use of the trademark is abandoned or if its contribution to earnings becomes doubtful, immediate write-off of the cost is called for. The outlay for securing a trademark is often not consequential, and it is common practice to treat such outlays as expense when incurred.

Other intangibles and deferred charges

Many other types of intangible assets are found in the published balance sheets of large corporations. Some examples are oil exploration costs, formulas, processes, designs, research and development costs, franchises, name lists, and film rights.[7]

Intangibles, particularly those with limited lives, are sometimes classified as "deferred charges" in the balance sheet. A *deferred charge* is an expenditure that is expected to yield benefits for several accounting periods, and should be amortized over its estimated useful life. Included in this category are such items as bond issuance costs, plant rearrangement and moving costs, start-up costs, and organization costs. The distinction between intangibles and deferred charges is not an important one; both represent "bundles of services" in the form of long-term prepayments awaiting allocation to those accounting periods in which the services will be consumed.

QUESTIONS

1 Describe briefly three situations in which debit entries may properly be made in accumulated depreciation accounts.
2 Student A asserts that when a depreciable plant asset is to be sold a first step is to record depreciation for the fractional period to the date of sale. Student B argues that an entry for depreciation at the date of disposing of the asset is inefficient because in his opinion it is more convenient to make

[7] In a recent survey of the financial statements of 325 leading corporations, 141 reportedly carried one or more types of intangible assets on their balance sheets. Canadian Institute of Chartered Accountants, *Financial Reporting In Canada,* ninth edition (Toronto, 1971), page 57.

all depreciation entries at the end of the year. At that time he would take into consideration that certain depreciable assets had been in use for only a portion of the year prior to their disposal. Evaluate these arguments.

3 If gains or losses from disposal of plant and equipment items are material in amount, where should they be shown in the income statement and under what group heading?

4 Topeka Corporation Ltd. maintains a general ledger control account for office equipment. This controlling account is supported by a subsidiary ledger in the form of a card file with a card for each unit of equipment. On 30 of these cards, the accumulated depreciation is equal to the cost of the asset. Assuming that the 30 items represented by the cards are still in regular use, should additional depreciation be recorded on them? When should these 30 cards be removed from the subsidiary ledger, and the cost and accumulated depreciation be removed from the general ledger accounts?

5 What is the term used to describe the pro rata allocation of the cost of a mine or other natural resource to the units removed during the year?

6 Lead Hill Corporation Ltd. recognizes $1 of depletion for each ton of ore mined. During the current year the company mined 600,000 tons but sold only 500,000 tons, as it was attempting to build up inventories in anticipation of a possible strike by employees. How much depletion should be deducted from revenues of the current year?

7 Under what circumstances does good accounting call for a mining company to depreciate a plant asset over a period shorter than the normal useful life?

8 Define *intangible asset.* Would an account receivable arising from a sale of merchandise under terms of 2/10, n/30 qualify as an intangible asset under your definition?

9 The James Electric Shop obtained its store building under a 10-year lease at $400 a month. The lease agreement required payment of rent for the tenth year at the time of signing the lease. All other payments were on a monthly basis. Give the journal entry required at the date of signing the lease when James wrote a cheque for $5,200, representing payment of the current month's rent and the $4,800 applicable to the tenth year of the lease. What entries, if any, are indicated for the tenth year of the lease?

10 The Accounting Principles Board of the AICPA has drawn a distinction between *identifiable* intangible assets and intangibles which cannot readily be identified. Give an example of each type. Can both types be purchased or sold separately from the business?

11 Under what circumstances should goodwill be recorded in the accounts?

12 In reviewing the financial statements of Digital Products Co. with a view to investing in the company's stock, you notice that net tangible assets total $1 million, that goodwill is listed as $100,000, and that average earnings for the past five years have been $20,000 a year. How would these relationships influence your thinking about the company?

13 Space Research Company paid $500,000 cash to acquire the entire business of Saturn Company, a strong competitor. In negotiating this lump-sum price for the business, a valuation of $60,000 was assigned to goodwill, representing four times the amount by which Saturn Company's annual earnings had exceeded normal earnings in the industry. Assuming that the goodwill is recorded on the books of Space Research Company, should it remain there permanently or be amortized? What basis of amortization might be used?

14 The Accounting Principles Board has expressed the view that accounting for intangibles involves the same kinds of problems as accounting for other long-lived assets. What are three of the problems the APB was considering?

15 The Accounting Principles Board has concluded that the cost of various types of intangible asset should be amortized by regular charges against income over what period of time? (Your answer should be in the form of a principle or guideline rather than a specific number of years.)

EXERCISES

Ex. 12-1 A tractor which cost $4,800 had an estimated useful life of five years and an estimated salvage value of $800. Straight-line depreciation was used. Give the entry required by each of the following alternative assumptions:
a The tractor was sold for cash of $3,000 after two years' use.
b The tractor was traded in after three years on another tractor with a list price of $6,000. Trade-in allowance was $2,700. Fair market value was $2,500.
c The tractor was scrapped after four years' use. Since scrap dealers were unwilling to pay anything for the tractor, it was given to a scrap dealer for his services in removing it.

Ex. 12-2 A truck with a book value (cost minus accumulated depreciation) of $1,600 is traded in on a new truck with a list price of $16,000. The trade-in allowance (not necessarily the fair market price) on the old truck is $2,400.
a How much cash must be paid for the new truck?
b How much depreciation should be recorded on the new truck for the first year of use, assuming a four-year life, a residual value of $1,000, and the use of straight-line depreciation?

Ex. 12-3 Lincoln Company on April 1 purchased machinery priced at $90,000, but received a trade-in allowance of $8,000 for used machinery. Cash of $20,000 was paid and a 6%, one-year note payable given for the balance. The machinery traded in had an original cost of $60,000 and had been depreciated at the rate of $6,000 a year. Residual value had been ignored on the grounds of not being material. Accumulated depreciation amounted to $48,000 at December 31 prior to the year of the acquisition. No depreciation had been recorded between the closing of the books on December 31 and the exchange for the new machinery on April 1.
In general journal form, give the entries to record:
a Depreciation for the fraction of a year prior to the April 1 transaction
b The acquisition of the new machinery on April 1 under the rules generally followed in practice.
c The acquisition of the new machinery on April 1 under the assumption that gain or loss is to be recognized and that the trade-in allowance represents the fair market value of the old machinery being traded in.

Ex. 12-4 Platt River Mining Company started mining activities early in 1974. At the end of the year its accountant prepared the following summary of its mining costs:

Labor	$1,700,000
Materials	175,000
Miscellaneous	385,200

These costs do not include any charges for depletion or depreciation. Data relating to assets used in mining the ore follow:

Cost of mine (estimated deposit, 10 million tons; residual value of the mine estimated at $300,000)	$1,500,000
Buildings (estimated life, 15 years; no residual value)	132,000
Equipment (useful life, six years regardless of number of tons mined; residual value $30,000)	240,000

During the year 800,000 tons (8%) of ore were mined, of which 600,000 tons were sold. It is estimated that it will take at least 15 years to extract the ore.

Determine the cost that should be assigned to the inventory of unsold ore at the end of 1974.

Ex. 12-5 The Fremont Company has net assets (total assets less all liabilities) of $200,000 and has earned an average return of 5% on average sales of $650,000 per year for the past several years. An investor is negotiating to purchase the company. He offers to pay an amount equal to the book value for the net assets (assets minus liabilities) and to assume all liabilities. In addition, he is willing to pay for goodwill an amount equal to net earnings in excess of 12% on net assets, capitalized at a rate of 20%.

On the basis of this agreement, what price should the investor offer for the Fremont Company?

PROBLEMS

Group A

12A-1 The Machinery account on the books of the Sundown Corporation Ltd. contained the following information for the current year:

Jan. 2 Acquired four identical machines @ $3,000 each	*$12,000*
Jan. 4 Installation costs	*400*
Total debits	*$12,400*
Dec. 31 Less: Credit for proceeds from sale of one machine	*(2,300)*
31 Balance in Machinery account	*$10,100*

The corporation's policy for depreciating the machines is to use the straight-line method with an estimated useful life of five years and an estimated residual value of $350 per machine. The December 31 transaction for the sale of one machine was recorded by a debit to Cash for the full sales price of $2,300 and a credit to Machinery for $2,300.

Instructions
a Prepare one journal entry at December 31 to record depreciation expense for the year on all four machines.
b What was the amount of the gain or loss on the sale of the machine on December 31? Show computations.
c Prepare one journal entry to **correct the accounts** at December 31. In drafting your correcting entry, give consideration to the debit and credit already entered in the accounts on December 31 to record the sale of one of the machines. Your entry should reduce the Machinery account and the Accumulated Depreciation account and should record the gain or loss on the disposal of the machine which was not recognized in the entry made at the time of the sale.

12A-2 Straight-line depreciation is used by Ecology Services on all of its plant and equipment. The company adjusts and closes its accounts at the end of each calendar year. On January 2, 1971, machinery was purchased for cash at a cost of $305,250. Useful life was estimated to be 10 years and residual value $5,250.

Three years later in December, 1973, after steady use of the machinery, the company decided that because of rapid technological change, the estimated total useful life should be revised from 10 years to 6 years. No change was made in the estimate of residual value. The revised estimate of useful life was decided upon prior to recording depreciation for the year ended December 31, 1973.

On June 30, 1974, Ecology Services decided to lease new, more efficient machinery; consequently the machinery described above was sold on this date for $75,000 cash.

Instructions Prepare journal entries to record the purchase of the machinery, the recording of depreciation for each of the four years, and the disposal of the machinery on June 30, 1974. Do not prepare closing entries.

12A-3 Hiawatha Company purchased for $80,000 a new patent from an inventor immediately after its issuance on January 2, 1972. The patented device was promptly put to use in Hiawatha's production operations. Although the legal life of the patent was 17 years, the company estimated that technological changes in its industry would limit the economic usefulness of the patent to 10 years.

On March 1, 1972, the company paid $45,000 in legal fees for the services of lawyers who successfully defended an infringement suit against the patent.

In December of 1974, Hiawatha Company decided that the *total* useful life of the patent would be limited to 6 years rather than the original estimate of 10 years. This decision was reached before amortization was recorded for the year 1974.

Instructions Prepare journal entries to record the above events relating to the acquisition and amortization of the patent from January 2, 1972, through December 31, 1974.

12A-4 On January 1, 1973, Dell Oil Company, an established concern, borrowed $1.5 million from the National Canadian Bank, issuing a note payable in five years with interest at 6% payable annually, on December 31. Also on January 1, the company purchased for $800,000 an undeveloped oil field estimated to contain at least 2 million barrels of oil. Movable equipment having an estimated useful life of five years and no scrap value was also acquired at a cost of $26,000.

During January the company spent $125,000 in developing the field, and several shallow wells were brought into production. The established accounting policy of the company was to treat drilling and development charges of this type as expense of the period in which the work was done.

Construction of a pipeline was completed on May 1, 1973, at a cost of $240,000. Although this pipeline was physically capable of being used for 10 years or more, its economic usefulness was limited to the productive life of the wells; therefore, the depreciation method employed was based on the estimated number of barrels of oil to be produced.

Operating costs incurred during 1973 (other than depreciation and depletion) amounted to $160,000, and 230,000 barrels of oil were produced and sold.

In January, 1974, further drilling expense was incurred in the amount of $100,000, and the estimated total capacity of the field was raised from the original 2,000,000 barrels to 2,590,000 barrels, including oil produced to date.

Cash operating costs for 1974 amounted to $250,000, in addition to the $100,000 of drilling expense mentioned above. Oil production totaled 800,000 barrels, of which all but 80,000 barrels were sold during the year.

Instructions Prepare journal entries to record the transactions of 1973 and 1974, including the setting up of the inventory at December 31, 1974. Do not prepare entries for sales. The inventory valuation should include an appropriate portion of the operating costs of the year, including depreciation and depletion.

12A-5 After several years of managerial experience in the retailing of sporting goods, Paul Bell decided to buy an established business in this field. He is now attempting to make a choice among three similar concerns which are available for purchase. All three companies have been in business for five years. The balance sheets presented by the three companies may be summarized as follows:

Assets	Company A	Company B	Company C
Cash	$ 15,000	$ 15,000	$ 25,000
Accounts receivable	116,000	119,000	136,000
Inventory	220,000	180,000	180,000
Plant assets (net)	69,000	80,000	50,000
Goodwill		3,000	
	$420,000	$397,000	$391,000
Liabilities & Owner's Equity			
Current liabilities	$178,000	$185,000	$200,000
Owner's equity	242,000	212,000	191,000
	$420,000	$397,000	$391,000

The average net earnings of the three businesses during the past five years had been as follows: Company A, $37,000; Company B, $32,000; and Company C, $34,000.

With the permission of the owners of the three businesses, Bell arranged for a chartered accountant to examine the accounting records of the companies. This investigation disclosed the following information:

Accounts receivable In Company A, no provision for uncollectible accounts had been made at any time, and no accounts receivable had been written off. Numerous past-due receivables were on the books, and the estimated uncollectible items which had accumulated during the past five years amounted to $10,000. In both Company B and Company C, the receivables appeared to be carried at net realizable value.

Inventories Company B had adopted the first-in, first-out method of inventory valuation when first organized but had changed to the last-in, first-out method after one year. As a result of this change in method of accounting for inventories, the present balance sheet figure for inventories was approximately $20,000 less than replacement cost. The other two companies had used the first-in, first-out method continuously, and their present inventories were approximately equal to replacement cost.

Plant and equipment In each of the three companies, the plant assets included a building which had cost $50,000 and had an estimated useful life of 25 years with no residual scrap value. Company A had taken no depreciation on its building; Company B had used straight-line depreciation at 4% annually; and Company C had depreciated its building by applying a constant rate of 4% to the undepreciated balance. All plant assets other than buildings had been depreciated on a straight-line basis in all companies. Bell believed that the book value of the plant assets of all three companies would approximate fair market value if depreciation were uniformly computed on a straight-line basis.

Goodwill The item of goodwill, $3,000, on the balance sheet of Company B represented the cost of a nonrecurring advertising campaign conducted during the first year of operation.

Bell is willing to pay for net tangible assets (except cash) at book value, plus an amount for goodwill equal to three times the average annual net earnings in excess of 10% on the net tangible assets. Cash will not be included in the transfer of assets.

Instructions
a Prepare a revised summary of balance sheet data after correcting all errors made by the companies. In addition to correcting errors, make the necessary changes to apply straight-line depreciation and first-in, first-out inventory methods in all three companies.
b Determine revised amounts for average net earnings of the three companies after taking into consideration the correction of errors and changes of method called for in *a* above.
c Determine the price which Bell should offer for each of the businesses.

Group B

12B-1 The following summary schedule shows the entries made in the Office Equipment account during the current year by Village Data Center.

Debits:

Jan. 2 Acquired four identical data processing machines @ $7,500 each . . .	$30,000
Jan. 5 Installation costs	1,000
Total debits	$31,000

Credits:

Dec. 31 Proceeds from sale of one data processing machine	(5,750)
Dec. 31 Balance in Office Equipment account	$25,250

The company depreciates the data processing machines on a straight-line basis with an estimated useful life of five years and an estimated residual value of $875 per machine. The December 31 transaction for the sale of one machine was recorded by a debit to Cash for the full sales price of $5,750 and a credit to Office Equipment for $5,750.

Instructions
a Prepare one journal entry at December 31 to record depreciation for the year on all four machines.
b What was the amount of gain or loss on the sale of the machine on December 31? Show computations.
c Prepare one journal entry to *correct the accounts* at December 31. In drafting your correcting entry, give consideration to the debit and credit already entered in the accounts on December 31 to record the sale of one of the machines. Your entry should reduce the Office Equipment account and the Accumulated Depreciation account and should record the gain or loss on the disposal of the machine which was not recognized in the entry made at the time of the sale.

12B-2 Munroe Company uses straight-line depreciation on all of its plant and equipment. The accounts are adjusted and closed at the end of each calendar year. On January 2, 1971, the company purchased machinery for cash at a cost of $203,500. Useful life was estimated to be 10 years and scrap value $3,500.

After almost three years of using the machinery the company decided in December, 1973, that because of rapid technological change, it should revise the estimated total life from 10 years to 6 years. The estimate of scrap value was not changed. The revised estimate of useful life was decided upon prior to recording depreciation for the year ended December 31, 1973.

On June 30, 1974, the company decided to lease new, more efficient machinery and the machinery described above was sold for $50,000 cash.

Instructions Prepare journal entries to record the purchase of the machinery, depreciation for years 1971 to 1974, and the disposal. Do not prepare closing entries.

12B-3 On July 1, the first day of its fiscal year, Ozark Company leased a store building from National Corporation for a period of 10 years at a total price of $240,000. The terms of the lease called for an immediate cash payment of $24,000, representing rent for the final year of the 10-year lease period. Also on July 1, Ozark (the lessee) paid $2,000 for the current month's rent and agreed to pay rent monthly in advance during the first nine years of the lease. The lease also provided that Ozark must pay for any repairs or improvements it wished to make.

An escalator was immediately installed by the lessee at a cost of $16,000, paid in cash. The normal life of the escalator was stated by the manufacturer to be 20 years. Some lighting fixtures were also installed at a cost of $2,000 paid in cash, for which the estimated life was five years.

Instructions Prepare journal entries to record:
a Payment of $26,000, representing $2,000 rent for July and $24,000 for the final year's rent under the 10-year lease contract.
b Payment for the escalator and lighting fixtures.
c First annual amortization of the cost of the escalator.
d First annual amortization of the cost of the lighting fixtures.
e Final disposition of the $24,000 advance payment of rent applicable to the tenth year of the lease.

12B-4 The Martin Mining Company acquired a coal mine on January 1, 1971, for a cash price of $340,000. Estimates by the company's engineers indicated that the mine contained 1,700,000 tons of coal. The equipment required to extract the coal from the mine was purchased January 2, 1971, for $116,000 cash. The useful life of this equipment was estimated to be five years, with a residual scrap value of $11,000. The straight-line method of depreciation was used by the company on this equipment and on all its depreciable assets.

On July 1, 1971, three trucks intended for use around the mine were purchased for $29,000 cash. Depreciation was to be computed on the basis of an estimated useful life of four years, with a residual scrap value of $3,000.

Construction of a frame building to be used as a mine office was completed on July 1, 1971, at a cost of $23,000 cash. Estimated life of this building was 10 years; the residual scrap value was estimated as no more than enough to cover the cost of demolition.

An assortment of secondhand office equipment approximately five years old was purchased on July 1, 1971, for $2,700 cash. The remaining useful life of this used equipment was estimated at five years, and the residual scrap value was estimated at $700.

During 1971, a total of 120,000 tons of coal was mined and sold. In 1972, production increased to 190,000 tons, and again the entire output was sold. On March 31, 1973, after 70,000 tons of coal had been extracted and sold, the mine and all related property were sold for $417,000 cash. The contract covering the sale of the mine specified the following prices for the various assets being transferred: mine, $310,000; equipment, $77,000; trucks, $13,000; building, $16,000; and office equipment, $1,000.

Instructions
a Prepare general journal entries to record all transactions and necessary adjustments from January, 1971, through March 31, 1973. Include depreciation entries using the straight-line method. Record depreciation for the fraction of 1973 prior to the sale.
b Prepare a schedule showing the gain or loss on the disposal of each of the five items of plant and equipment.

12B-5 The Gilmore Company is considering purchase of the assets of Oxford Company, exclusive of cash, on January 2, 1974. The Oxford Company has been in business for six years and has had average net earnings of $16,300 during this period.

The purchase plan calls for a cash payment of $50,000 and a 6% note payable, due January 2, 1976, with interest payable annually, as payment for the assets including goodwill after any necessary adjustments have been made. The goodwill is to be determined as four times the average excess earnings over a normal rate of return of 8% on the present net tangible assets.

The balance sheet of Oxford Company on December 31, 1973, follows:

Cash			$ 15,000
Other current assets			25,000
Plant and equipment:			
Land			$30,000
Buildings	$122,000		
Less: Accumulated depreciation	31,500	90,500	
Machinery	$ 95,000		
Less: Accumulated depreciation	64,500	30,500	
Equipment	$ 60,000		
Less: Accumulated depreciation	33,500	26,500	177,500
Patents			13,125
Goodwill			5,000
			$235,625

Liabilities & Owner's Equity

Current liabilities	$ 37,000
Long-term liabilities:	
Notes payable, 5%, due Jan. 2, 1976	89,500
Andrew Oxford, capital	109,125
	$235,625

Other data

(1) Goodwill was written on the books three years ago when Oxford decided that the increasing profitability of the company should be recognized.

(2) The patent appears at original cost. It was acquired by purchase six years ago from a competitor who had recorded amortization for two years on the basis of its legal life. The patent is highly useful to the business, and its usefulness is expected to continue.

Instructions

a Prepare any adjusting entries needed on the books of Oxford Company as a preliminary step toward carrying out the sale agreement.

b Determine the amount to be paid by Gilmore Company for goodwill after considering the effects of the entries in *a*.

c Prepare the entry on Oxford Company's books to record the sale to Gilmore Company. The notes payable are not transferred to Gilmore Company.

d Prepare a revised balance sheet for the Oxford Company as of January 2, 1974, after the journal entries in *c* are posted.

BUSINESS DECISION PROBLEM 12

James Finley, president of Finley Home Products Ltd., states that his company has spent nearly a half million dollars during the current year on special advertising campaigns to introduce new products. "The campaigns were begun and completed during the current year," he explains, "but I believe we will be selling these new products for many years in the future. Consequently, I wanted to show the cost of this advertising as an intangible asset on the balance sheet and amortize it over, maybe, 10 years. However, the CA firm that audits our company insisted on treating this advertising as a charge against this year's operations."

a Is Mr. Finley's argument that benefits will be received in future years from the advertising this year to introduce new products a logical and valid one? Explain.
b What is the position of the Accounting Principles Board with respect to expenditures for developing intangible assets which are not specifically identifiable?
c On balance, what is your conclusion as to whether the advertising expenditures should be an expense of the current year or listed as intangible assets on the balance sheet?

THIRTEEN

PAYROLL ACCOUNTING

Labor costs and related payroll taxes constitute a large and constantly increasing portion of the total costs of operating most business organizations. In the commercial airlines, for example, labor costs represent over 50% of total operating costs.

The task of accounting for payroll costs would be an important one simply because of the large amounts involved; however, it is further complicated by the many federal and provincial laws which require employers to maintain certain specific information in their payroll records not only for the business as a whole but also for each individual employee. Regular reports of total wages and amounts withheld must be filed with government agencies, accompanied by payments of the amounts withheld from employees and payroll taxes levied on the employer.

A basic rule in most business organizations is that every employee must be paid on time, and the payment must be accompanied by a detailed explanation of the computations involved in determining the net amount received by the employee. The payroll system must therefore be capable of processing the input data (such as employee names, social insurance numbers, regular hours worked, pay rates, overtime, and taxes) and producing a prompt and accurate output of paycheques, payroll records, withholding statements, and reports to government agencies. In addition, the payroll system must have built-in safeguards against overpayments to employees, the issuance of duplicate paycheques, payments to fictitious employees, and the continuance on the payroll of persons who have been terminated as employees.

Internal control over payrolls

The requirements for a payroll system as enumerated in the preceding section indicate the need for strong internal control over payrolls. The large dollar amounts involved, the need for fast, accurate processing of data, the requirement of prompt, regular distribution of payroll cheques, the required reports to government—all these factors point to the need for strong internal controls, regardless of whether the business entity is a small one with a manual accounting system or a very large organization with an electronic data processing system.

Some specific characteristics of present-day payroll accounting reduce the likelihood of payroll frauds, which in the past were common and often substantial. These helpful factors include the required frequent filing of payroll data with the government, and the universal use of employer identification numbers and employees' social insurance numbers. For example, "padding" a payroll with fictitious names is more difficult when social insurance numbers must be on file for every employee, individual earnings records must be created, and annual reports must be submitted showing for every employee the gross earnings, social insurance taxes, and income tax withheld.

The repetitive nature of payroll preparation also encourages careful system design, extensive subdivision of duties relating to payroll, and automation of the processes for computation and record preparation. The records must be retained for extended periods and must be available for inspection by government agencies.

The widespread use of computers for processing payroll should not be taken as assurance that payroll fraud is no longer a threat. The separation and subdivision of duties is still essential, although the nature of the skills involved is quite different from those required for the manual preparation of payrolls. For the company with an EDP system, adequate internal control over payrolls demands clear separation of the functions of systems analysts, programmers, key-punch operators, computer operators, librarians, and control group personnel. If this segregation of duties is not maintained, the opportunity exists for payroll fraud on a gigantic scale. The fact that virtually all phases of payroll accounting can be handled rapidly by a computer may have induced some companies to place less emphasis on the separation of duties essential to strong internal control. One recent payroll fraud case in a huge company was linked with a well-publicized change in income tax rates. Knowing that employees expected a change in the amount of tax withheld on the officially scheduled date, a computer operator with wide latitude of duties purposely overstated each employee's tax by a few cents and diverted to himself the aggregate of these amounts. Since a very large labor force was involved, the dollar amount of the fraud was quite substantial. This irregularity would not have been possible if reasonable standards for subdivision of duties had been maintained.

In most organizations the payroll activities include the functions of (1) employing workers, (2) timekeeping, (3) payroll preparation and record keeping, and (4) the distribution of pay to employees. Internal control will be strengthened if each of these functions is handled by a separate department of the company.

THE EMPLOYMENT FUNCTION For each new employee hired, the personnel department should create a record showing the date of employment, the authorized rate of pay, and payroll deductions. Subsequent changes in pay rates and the termination of employees will also be entered in personnel department records. The performance of these steps by the personnel department does not prevent job applicants from being interviewed in various departments of the company, but these steps do ensure that names and rates which appear on the payroll will be properly authorized prior to any payment.

TIMEKEEPING For employees paid by the hour, it is desirable that the hours of arrival and departure be punched on time clocks. Procedures should be designed to ensure that each employee punch his own time card and no other. For salaried personnel, a weekly or monthly time report may replace the time card. The timekeeping function should be lodged in a separate department which will control the time cards and transmit these source documents to the payroll department.

THE PAYROLL DEPARTMENT The input of information to the payroll department consists of hours reported by the timekeeping department, and authorized names, pay rates, and payroll deductions received from the personnel department. The output of the payroll department includes (*1*) payroll cheques, (*2*) individual employee records of earnings and deductions, and (*3*) regular reports to the government showing the earnings of employees and taxes withheld.

DISTRIBUTION OF PAYCHEQUES The paycheques prepared in the payroll department may be transmitted to a paymaster (usually in the treasurer's office) for signature and distribution to employees. Paycheques for absent employees should never be turned over to other employees or to supervisors for delivery. Instead, the absent employee should pick up the paycheque at the paymaster's office after properly identifying himself and signing a receipt.

Other uses of payroll records

We have already stressed that federal and provincial laws require the maintenance and retention of detailed payroll records. In addition, good payroll records are often useful to personnel specialists in dealing with employee grievances, authorizing vacations and sick leaves, and determining eligibility for retirement pensions. In negotiations with labor unions, the development from the records of complete information concerning total labor costs and trends in wage rates is a necessary preliminary step.

Distinction between employees and independent contractors

Every business obtains personal services from *employees* and also from *independent contractors.* The distinction between the two groups is important because payroll systems, taxes, reports, and records cover *employees* only. The employer-employee relationship exists when the business or individual paying for the services has a right to direct and supervise the performance of the person rendering the services.

A chartered accountant performing an annual audit for a company must determine independently the scope and character of his investigation; he is not controlled or supervised by the client company. Consequently, the CA is an independent contractor and not an employee. However, if the CA should leave the practice of public accounting and accept a position as controller of a company, he would become an employee. Another example of an independent contractor is a typist who types term papers for college students, using her own typewriter and supplies and working in her own office or home. The *fees* paid to independent contractors are distinct from *salaries* and *wages;* they are not included in payroll records and are not subject to withholding.

Compensation to employees on an hourly rate or on a piecework basis is usually called *wages.* Compensation on a monthly or yearly basis is usually referred to as *salary.* The *hourly payroll* for wages is often prepared separately from the *monthly salary payroll* as a matter of convenience in computation, but both are subject to the same tax rules. In practice, one often finds the terms *wages* and *salaries* used interchangeably.

Deductions from earnings of employees

The take-home pay of most employees is considerably less than the gross earnings. Major factors explaining this difference between the amount earned and the amount received are unemployment insurance and Canada Pension Plan contributions, federal income taxes withheld, and other deductions discussed below.

UNEMPLOYMENT INSURANCE Under the Unemployment Insurance Act (1940), a federal statute, all employment in Canada is insurable unless it is specifically exempt by the Act. The new 1971 Unemployment Insurance Act greatly expanded coverage, making it almost universal. Classifications of employment which were not insurable have been reduced and now include the following major groups: (1) employees in agriculture, forestry and lumbering with annual cash earnings each of less than $250 or who were employed by an employer for less than 25 days in a year; (2) employees over 70 years of age or over 65 years of age who are entitled to a retirement pension under the Canada or Quebec Pension Plans; (3) casual employment; (4) employees who are dependents of the employer; (5) a spouse (husband or wife) of the employer; (6) clergymen; (7) a shareholder employed by the corporation which he controls; and (8) employees whose weekly earnings are less than a certain minimum (in 1976 this minimum will be $40).

The purpose of the Act is to provide some relief from the hardships of unemployment. An insured person who is unemployed while willing and able to work is entitled to receive certain benefits. The amount of weekly benefits received by an unemployed person is two-thirds of his average insurable earnings over his last eight weeks of employment. Benefits will be paid for a period of eight to fifty-one weeks depending upon the length of the employee's insurable employment and the national rate of unemployment.[1]

Both the employer and employee are required to contribute to the unemployment insurance fund. The employee's contribution, which is withheld by the employer from his salary or wages, is 1.65 per cent of his insurable earnings. Insurable earnings is the gross value of the employee's remuneration from his employment. In addition to the regular salary or wages, insurable earnings will include bonuses, gratuities (tips), vacation pay, and the value of free board and room. The maximum weekly insurable earnings is $200 and the minimum is $40. That is, no deduction is made for unemployment insurance if the employee's weekly remuneration is less than $40 and the maximum deduction is computed on a weekly remuneration of $200. The employer contributes 1.4 times the amount deducted from his employees' salaries. The total contributions, including the amounts deducted from employees, must be remitted by the employer to the Department of National Revenue by the 15th of the month following the month in which deductions were made.

CANADA PENSION PLAN[2] The Canada Pension Plan Act provides for disability, death and survivors' benefits for qualified employees and members of their families. To finance the payment of benefits under the Act, both employers and employees are taxed at the same rate. Each employee is required to contribute 1.8 per cent of his annual salary or wages between $800 and $8,300.[3] His employer must match this contribution. For example, if an employee earns a salary of $8,500 in 1976, the employee contributes 1.8 per cent of $7,500 or $135.00 to the pension plan. His employer must also contribute $135.00. Under the Act, the employer is responsible for deducting the employee's contribution from his salary. The amount of both the employer's and employee's tax must be remitted monthly by the employer to the Department of National Revenue.

The employer must deduct 1.8 per cent of each employee's salary less the pro-rated exemption of $800 per year on each pay period. These deductions continue until the maximum contribution of $135.00 has been reached. For example, assume that Smith, an employee is paid on a

---

[1] The benefit period is extended by four weeks if the national rate of unemployment is more than four per cent and eight weeks if the rate is more than five per cent.
[2] The Canada Pension Plan applies in all provinces except Quebec which has enacted its own legislation. The provisions of the Quebec Pension Plan Act are analogous to the Federal Act.
[3] The range of salary ($801 - $8,300 in 1976) which is subject to the 1.8 per cent tax will be adjusted in succeeding years by using a special earnings index defined by the Act.

monthly basis and receives an annual salary of $9,000. The Canada Pension Plan deduction from Smith's cheque in January 1976 would be computed as follows:

Salary	$750
Less: ¹⁄₁₂ of $800 exemption	67
Amount subject to Canada Pension Plan deduction of 1.8%	$683

The employer would be required to make a similar contribution. The $12.30 monthly deduction would be made until a total of $135.00 has been deducted and then no further deductions would be made until the next calendar year. Thus, in this example, deductions of $12.30 would be made for eleven months. Deductions would resume in January, 1977.

With limited exceptions, the Canada Pension Plan taxes apply to all employers of one or more persons. Employees of these firms are also subject to the tax. The main types of employment which are excepted from the provisions of the Act are similar to those exempt under the Unemployment Insurance Act.[4]

FEDERAL AND PROVINCIAL INCOME TAXES Our pay-as-you-go system of income taxes requires employers to withhold a portion of the earnings of their employees. The amount withheld depends upon the amount of the earnings and upon the number of exemptions allowed the employee. The employee is entitled to one exemption for himself, and an additional exemption for each person qualifying as a dependent.

Tax deductions are made from employees' earnings on the basis of taxable income. Taxable income is determined by deducting allowable exemptions from the employee's gross earnings. Gross earnings include salaries, free board and lodging and other compensation received from the employer. Every taxpayer is permitted to deduct from his gross income certain expenses incurred to earn that income and exemptions based on his marital status. The following exemptions may be deducted in computing taxable income:[5]

Basic exemption for single person	$1,878
Additional exemption, if married	1,644
Exemption for each dependent child Under 16	352
Over 16	646

More extensive consideration of exemptions and of other aspects of income taxes will be found in Chapter 20.

---

[4]Self-employed persons who have an annual income in excess of $800 are also covered by the Canada Pension Plan. These persons are required to pay a tax of 3.6 per cent on yearly income between $800 and $8,300.

[5]Personal exemptions are now being indexed to reflect changes in the cost of living and will thus vary from year to year. The exemptions shown are for 1975.

A tax deduction declaration (Form TD-1) must be prepared by each employee, stating the number of exemptions to which he is entitled; this declaration is given to the employer so that he will be able to compute the proper amount of tax to be withheld. As a matter of convenience to employers, the government provides withholding tax tables which indicate the amount of tax to be withheld for any amount of earnings and any number of exemptions.

Employers must submit the taxes deducted from employees in a given month to the Federal government by the fifteenth of the following month.

In addition to collecting its own income taxes, the Federal government has entered into agreements with all provinces, except Quebec, to collect the income taxes which these provinces levy. In Quebec employers must make separate deductions for the Federal and Quebec income taxes.

OTHER DEDUCTIONS FROM EMPLOYEES' EARNINGS   In addition to the compulsory deductions for income taxes, Canada (or Quebec) Pension Plan and unemployment insurance, many other deductions are voluntarily authorized by employees. Union dues, insurance premiums and savings bond purchases have already been mentioned as examples of payroll deductions. Others include charitable contributions, supplementary retirement programs and pension plans, and repayments of payroll advances or other loans.

EMPLOYER'S RESPONSIBILITY FOR AMOUNTS WITHHELD   When an employer withholds a portion of an employee's earnings for any reason, he must maintain accounting records which will enable him to file required reports and make designated payments of the funds withheld. From the employer's viewpoint, most amounts withheld from employees' earnings represent current liabilities. In other words, the employer must pay to the government or some other agency the amounts which he withholds from the employee's earnings. An exception would be the deductions made from an employee's pay to liquidate a previous loan to the employee. A statement of earnings and deductions is usually prepared by the employer and presented to the employee with each paycheque or pay envelope to explain how the net pay was determined.

Illustration: computation of employee's net pay

This illustration shows the deductions which typically may explain the difference between *gross earnings* for a pay period and the "take-home" pay, or net amount received by an employee. The deductions are in part based upon the two exemptions indicated in Ralph Miller's Employee's Tax Deduction Exemption Certificate (Form TDI) discussed previously. The pay period is for the month of May.

<table>
<tr><td rowspan="9">Computing the take-home pay</td><td>Gross earnings for the month . . . .</td><td></td><td>$800.00</td></tr>
<tr><td>Deductions:</td><td></td><td></td></tr>
<tr><td> CPP deduction . . . .</td><td>$ 13.20</td><td></td></tr>
<tr><td> Federal income tax . . . .</td><td>123.25</td><td></td></tr>
<tr><td> Retirement plan (assume 4%) . . . .</td><td>32.00</td><td></td></tr>
<tr><td> Group insurance . . . .</td><td>17.15</td><td></td></tr>
<tr><td> UI deduction . . . .</td><td>13.20</td><td></td></tr>
<tr><td>   Total deductions . . . .</td><td></td><td>198.80</td></tr>
<tr><td>Net pay . . . .</td><td></td><td>$601.20</td></tr>
</table>

In the preceding illustration, the inclusion of the CPP deduction shows that Ralph Miller's earnings thus far in the calendar year had not reached the $8,300 maximum earnings assumed to be subject to Canada Pension Plan deductions. The Unemployment Insurance deduction is based on a maximum monthly remuneration of $867. Since Miller earns $800 a month, his take-home pay of $601.20 can be expected to rise by $13.20 after November when his gross earnings will have reached the $8,300 limitation.

The amount of federal and provincial (Ontario) income tax withheld, $123.25, was determined by reference to the wage bracket for a married taxpayer with exemptions of $3,000 as shown in the withholding schedules published each year by the Department of National Revenue. The other two deductions from gross earnings (for a retirement plan and for group insurance) were voluntary and had been authorized in writing by Ralph Miller.

WAGES AND HOURS   The federal government, for industries under its control,[6] and all provinces have enacted maximum hours of work and minimum wage rates. Details of the legislation vary in each jurisdiction; but, in general, the legislation provides for payment of an overtime premium of at least one-half of the regular rate for time worked in excess of 8 hours per day and 40 hours in any week. Many companies also pay overtime premium rates for night shifts and for work on Sundays and holidays. Union contracts often provide better working conditions than the minimum levels specified by legislation. Since wages earned are now commonly based on hours worked at various rates, the function of time-keeping has become of increased importance. Time clocks and time cards are widely used in compiling the detailed information required for payroll purposes.

Payroll records and procedures

Although payroll records and procedures vary greatly according to the number of employees and the extent of automation in processing payroll

[6]The Federal government, as a result of court decisions, has a very small sphere of authority in labor matters. Most industries fall under provincial jurisdiction. Federal jurisdiction covers the following industries: navigation and shipping, interprovincial railways, telegraphs, air transportation, broadcasting, banks and works declared by Parliament to be for the general advantage of Canada or two or more provinces.

data, there are a few fundamental steps common to payroll work in most organizations. One of these steps taken at the end of each pay period is the preparation of a payroll showing the names and earnings of all employees. The information entered in this payroll record will include the authorized rate of pay for each employee and the number of hours worked, taken from time cards or similar documents. After separating the regular hours from overtime hours and applying appropriate pay rates for each category, the total taxable earnings are determined. Federal and provincial income tax, CPP and UI taxes, and any items authorized by the employee are then deducted to arrive at the net amount payable. When the computation of the payroll sheet has been completed, the next step is to reflect the expense and the related liabilities in the ledger accounts. A general journal entry such as shown below may be made to bring into the accounts the payroll and the deductions from employees' earnings. Assume that there are six employees, and therefore, $400 ($66.67 x 6) of the earnings are not subject to the CPP deduction. This entry does not include payroll taxes on the employer.

Entry to record payroll

Sales Salaries Expense	2,200	
Office Salaries Expense	1,800	
CPP Taxes Payable		65
U.I.Taxes Payable		66
Liability for Income Tax Withheld		830
Group Insurance Payments Withheld		100
Accrued Payroll		2,939

To record the payroll and related deductions for the pay period ended Jan. 15.

The two debits to expense accounts indicate that the business has incurred a total salary expense of $4,000; however, only $2,939 of this amount will be paid to the employees. The remaining $1,061 (consisting of deductions for taxes and insurance premiums withheld) is lodged in liability accounts. Payment of these liabilities will be made at various later dates.

PAYMENT OF EMPLOYEES The preceding section illustrated the recording of the payroll and showed the sum of $2,939 in a current liability account entitled Accrued Payroll. The procedures for the actual payment to employees to discharge this liability will depend upon whether the company pays salaries by cheques on the regular bank account, by cheques drawn on a special bank account, or in cash. These payment procedures also depend on whether a voucher system is in use.

The advantages of establishing a separate payroll bank account were discussed in Chapter 8. At the close of each pay period, a cheque is drawn on the general bank account for the entire amount of the payroll and deposited in the payroll bank account. Paycheques to individual employees are then drawn on the payroll bank account, which is immediately reduced to zero. If the voucher system is in use, a voucher for the payroll would be prepared and recorded in the voucher register as a debit to

Payroll Bank Account and a credit to Vouchers Payable in the amount of $2,939.[7] The transfer of the funds would then be carried out by issuing a cheque on the general bank account and recording this disbursement in the cheque register by a debit to Vouchers Payable and a credit to Cash.

PAYMENT OF EMPLOYEES IN CASH Payment of salaries in cash affords less internal control than the use of cheques, but it is preferred by some companies in locations where banks or other cheque-cashing facilities are not readily available. The recording procedures do not differ significantly from those previously described; a voucher is prepared for the amount of the payroll, and a single cheque drawn and cashed to obtain the cash to fill the individual pay envelopes. As previously mentioned, a statement of earnings and deductions is usually furnished to the employee each payday. When payment is made by cheque, this information may be printed on a stub attached to the paycheque. When wages are paid in cash, the information is usually printed on the pay envelope.

WITHHOLDING STATEMENT By February 28 each year, employers are required to furnish every employee with a withholding statement (Form T-4), illustrated on page 391. This form shows the gross earnings for the preceding calendar year and the amounts withheld for CPP and U.I. taxes and income tax. The employer sends one copy of this form to the Department of National Revenue and also gives two copies to the employee. When the employee files his income tax return he must attach a copy of the withholding statement.

INDIVIDUAL EARNINGS RECORDS FOR EMPLOYEES At the end of each payroll period, it is essential to have available the cumulative amount of each employee's earnings for the year to date. Otherwise, the employer would not know whether CPP and UI taxes should be withheld from the earnings by the employee during the current week or month.

This detailed record also shows for each employee the gross earnings for each pay period, the portion, if any, not subject to CPP and UI taxes, the deduction for CPP and UI taxes, the income tax withheld, other deductions authorized by the employee, and the amount of net pay. These employee earnings records are also used by the employer in preparing the annual reports which he must file with federal and provincial authorities. A variety of other uses may occur such as calculating bonuses or proving compliance with the Federal and Provincial labor codes relating to wages and hours of work.

Payroll taxes on the employer

The discussion of payroll taxes up to this point has dealt primarily with taxes levied on the employee and withheld from his pay. From the view-

---

[7]No vouchers need be prepared at this time for the $1,061 of liabilities resulting from deductions. Vouchers will be prepared prior to the time for payment of these liabilities.

20977270

DEPARTMENT OF NATIONAL REVENUE, TAXATION
MINISTÈRE DU REVENU NATIONAL, IMPÔT

STATEMENT OF REMUNERATION PAID
ÉTAT DE LA RÉMUNÉRATION PAYÉE

• For District Taxation Office
• Pour le bureau de district d'impôt

CANADA
T4-1972
Supplementary — Supplémentaire

EMPLOYEE: SURNAME FIRST, AND FULL ADDRESS
EMPLOYÉ: NOM DE FAMILLE D'ABORD, ET ADRESSE COMPLÈTE

NAME AND ADDRESS OF EMPLOYER — NOM ET ADRESSE DE L'EMPLOYEUR

(A) PROVINCE OF EMPLOYMENT
PROVINCE D'EMPLOI

(B) SOCIAL INSURANCE NUMBER
N° D'ASSURANCE SOCIALE

(K) EMPLOYEE NO.
N° DE L'EMPLOYÉ

(C) TOTAL EARNINGS
BEFORE DEDUCTIONS
GAINS TOTAUX
AVANT DÉDUCTIONS

BOX (C) AMOUNT INCLUDES
ANY AMOUNTS IN BOXES
(H), (J), (L) AND (M).
LE MONTANT DE LA CASE (C)
COMPREND TOUS MONTANTS
FIGURANT AUX CASES
(H), (J), (L) ET (M).

(D) EMPLOYEE'S PENSION CONTRIBUTION
QUEBEC PLAN
CANADA PLAN
DU CANADA   DU QUÉBEC
COTISATION DE PENSION (EMPLOYÉ)

(E) U.I.
PREMIUM
PRIME
D'A.-C.

(F) REGISTERED PENSION
PLAN CONTRIBUTION
CONTRIBUTIONS: RÉGIME
ENREGISTRÉ DE PENSIONS

(G) INCOME TAX
DEDUCTED
IMPÔT SUR LE
REVENU DÉDUIT

(H) U.I. INSURABLE
EARNINGS
GAINS ASSURABLES
A.-C.

(I) U.I. PREM.
RATE
%
TAUX DE
PRIME D'A.-C.

(J) C.P.P. CONTRIBUTORY
EARNINGS
GAINS COTISABLES
POUR R.P.C.

If different from Box (C)
★ S'ils sont différents de la Case (C)

(L) TAXABLE ALLOWANCES
AND BENEFITS
ALLOCATIONS ET PRESTA-
TIONS IMPOSABLES

(M) COMMISSIONS
COMMISSIONS

(N) PENSION PLAN
REGISTRATION NUMBER
N° D'ENREGISTREMENT DU
RÉGIME DE PENSIONS

point of the employer, such taxes are significant because he must account for and remit the amounts withheld to the appropriate government offices. Payroll taxes are also levied on the *employer;* these taxes are expenses of the business and are recorded by debits to expense accounts, just as in the case of property taxes or license fees for doing business. The major payroll tax levied on employers, in addition to unemployment insurance and Canada Pension Plan, is workmen's compensation.

WORKMEN'S COMPENSATION All provinces have enacted legislation which pays the hospital and medical expenses of a worker injured by an accident "arising out of and in the course of employment" and also pays him a certain percentage (usually 75%) of his salary while he is unable to work as a result of an injury suffered on the job. To finance the benefits provided under this legislation, all provinces require the employer to contribute to a workmen's compensation fund with the amount of the contribution based on the assessable annual payroll of the business. The rate levied on the employer varies with the type of industry and the safety record of the business. Payment is made by the employer to the Workmen's Compensation Board usually in semi-annual equal installments. There is *no* deduction made from the employee's salary for workmen's compensation.

The employer is required to estimate his assessable annual payroll at the beginning of each calendar year. By January 31 of each year, the employer submits a return to the Workmen's Compensation Board containing this estimate and the actual annual assessable payroll for the previous year. The amount of his workmen's compensation is then computed for the current year by applying the rate for the industry as shown by the following example:

Estimated assessable payroll for 1974	*$ 990,000*
Adjustment of 1973 actual assessable payroll (Difference	
between 1973 actual assessable payroll of $980,000 and	
1973 estimated assessable payroll of $970,000)	*10,000*
	$1,000,000
Workmen's compensation premium for 1974 is 4% of	
$1,000,000	*$ 40,000*

One-half of this premium must usually be paid when the return is submitted in January; and the remainder must be paid by July 31.

While each provincial statute has its own definition of assessable annual payroll, the amount of annual assessable payroll is, in general, equal to the firm's total annual salaries except that a maximum amount is included in the total assessable annual payroll for each employee whose salary exceeds that amount.

The journal entry to record the 1974 workmen's compensation liability when the return is submitted in January is as follows:

| Prepaid Workmen's Compensation. | $40,000 | |
| Workmen's Compensation Payable | | $40,000 |

As indicated in our previous discussion on unemployment insurance and Canada Pension Plan, a tax is levied on the employer for these two items as follows:

Unemployment insurance—the employer's contribution is 1.4 times the amount deducted from employees.

Canada Pension Plan—the employer contributes an amount equal to the amount deducted from employees.

ACCOUNTING ENTRY FOR EMPLOYER'S PAYROLL TAXES The entry to record the employer's payroll taxes is usually made at the same time the payroll is recorded. To illustrate, let us use again the $4,000 payroll first used on page 389 in the discussion of amounts withheld from employees; this time, however, we are illustrating taxes levied on the *employer,* as follows:

Entry for payroll taxes on employer

Payroll Taxes Expense	157	
CPP Taxes Payable ($3,600 x 1.8)		65
Unemployment Insurance Taxes Payable (1.4 x $66)		92

To record payroll taxes on employer for pay period ended January 15.

Since this payroll is for the period ended January 15, we may assume that none of the employees has as yet reached the $8,300 level of cumulative earnings constituting the maximum amount for the CPP deduction or the $10,400 earnings constituting the maximum amount for the UI deduction. Consequently, the illustrated entry shows UI taxes being applied to the full $4,000 of the company's payroll and $3,600 ($4,000 less the exemption of $400 for the six employees) being applied to CPP taxes for this period early in the year.

Combined entry for payroll and all related taxes and deductions

The preceding illustration shows the recording of taxes on the *employer,* whereas the entry illustrated on page 389 showed the recording of the payroll (wages earned) and the amounts withheld as taxes and other deductions from employees. Let us now combine these two illustrative entries into one entry which will record the $4,000 total payroll and all taxes and deductions applicable to both the employer and the employees.

Sales Salaries Expense	2,200	
Office Salaries Expense	1,800	
Payroll Taxes Expense	157	
CPP Taxes Payable		130
Unemployment Insurance Taxes Payable		158
Liability for Income Tax Withheld		830
Group Insurance Payments Withheld		100
Accrued Payroll		2,939

To record payroll, payroll taxes expense, and amounts withheld from employees for pay period ended Jan. 15

In studying this illustrated entry, note that the employer's basic payroll expense of $2,200 in sales salaries and $1,800 in office salaries, or $4,000 in total salaries, is increased by $157 to a total payroll expense of $4,157.

Accrual of payroll taxes at year-end

The payroll taxes levied against an employer become a legal liability when wages are actually paid, rather than at the time the services by employees are rendered. If the wages earned in a given accounting period are paid in the same period, the payroll tax expense is clearly applicable to that period. However, at year-end, most businesses make an adjusting entry to accrue wages earned by employees but not payable until the following period. Should the related payroll taxes on the employer also be accrued? Logically, both wages and taxes on such wages are an expense of the period in which the wages are earned and should therefore be accrued. However, as a practical matter, many businesses do not accrue the payroll tax expense because legally the liability does not come into being untii the following year when the wages are paid. In determining income subject to income tax, the legal concept prevails, and payroll tax cannot be deducted until the period in which paid. As a matter of convenience, many companies want their accounting records and their income tax returns to agree as closely as possible; therefore such companies prefer *not to accrue* payroll tax on employers. This conflict between the logic of accounting principles and the administrative conveniences built into income tax laws appears in many other areas of accounting apart from payroll taxes.

Presentation of payroll taxes in the financial statements

The payroll taxes levied on the employer and the taxes withheld from employees are current liabilities of the business until payment to the government is made. The following accounts are, therefore, classified in the balance sheet as current liabilities: CPP and UI Taxes Payable, and Liability for Income Tax Withheld.

Payroll Taxes Expense appears in the income statement: it may be apportioned between selling expenses and general expenses on the basis of the amount of payroll originating in each functional division. Thus, payroll tax on salaries of salesmen is classified as a selling expense, and payroll tax on office salaries is classified as a general expense.

Payment of payroll taxes

A business must use the calendar year in accounting for payroll taxes, even though it uses a fiscal year for its financial statements and its income tax returns. Each year, the employer is required to report to the government the amounts withheld from employees' pay for income taxes and

CPP and UI taxes. The amounts withheld from employees plus payroll taxes on the employer must be remitted monthly to the Department of National Revenue. These payments must be made by the fifteenth of the month following that in which the income and payroll taxes were deducted from the earnings of employees.

The employer must file a summary of annual wages paid and income taxes deducted each year with the Federal government by February 28 of the following year.

QUESTIONS

1 Name the federal taxes that most employers are required to withhold from employees. What account or accounts would be credited with the amounts withheld?

2 Distinguish between an employee and an independent contractor. Why is this distinction important with respect to payroll accounting?

3 Explain which of the following taxes relating to an employee's wages are borne by the employee, and which by both parties.
  a Canada Pension Plan
  b Unemployment Insurance
  c Workmen's Compensation
  d Federal Income taxes

4 List four kinds of information which constitute input to the payroll accounting system and four kinds of information included in the output of the payroll system.

5 That type of payroll fraud known as "padding" a payroll is a more difficult maneuver under today's payroll accounting practices than it was a generation or more ago. What present-day factors make the padding of payrolls a complex and more difficult type of fraud?

6 Is Salary Expense equal to "take-home" pay or to gross earnings? Why?

7 When and for what purpose is an Employee's Tax Deduction Form obtained?

8 What purposes are served by maintaining a detailed earnings record for each employee?

9 Are the payroll taxes levied against employers considered a legal liability and a deductible expense in the period the wages are earned by the employees or in the period the wages are paid?

EXERCISES

Ex. 13-1 Hale earns a salary of $12,000 a year from Bix Corporation Ltd. CPP taxes are 1.8% of wages up to $8,300 a year. Unemployment Insurance taxes are 1.65% of wages up to $10,400 a year. Federal and Provincial income taxes of $2,400 were withheld from Hale's paycheques during the year.
  a Prepare in general journal form a compound entry summarizing the payroll transactions for employee Hale for the full year. (In drafting this entry, ignore any payments of tax during the year and let the liability accounts show the totals for the year.)
  b What is the total yearly cost (including taxes) to Bix Corporation Ltd. of having Hale on the payroll at an annual salary of $12,000?

Ex. 13-2 During the current year, the payroll of Pico Company may be summarized as follows:

Gross earnings of employees	$100,000
Employee earnings not subject to CPP tax	20,000
Employee earnings not subject to UI tax	16,000

Assuming that the payroll is subject to CPP tax rate of 1.8%, a UI tax rate of 2.31%, compute the amount of the Pico Company's payroll tax expense for the year, showing separately the amount of each of the three taxes. (Note: taxes on employees are not involved in this exercise.)

Ex. 13-3 Milo Milling Company had 100 employees throughout the current year. The lowest-paid employee had gross earnings of $12,000. Assume that the 1976 Unemployment Insurance Act specifies a rate of 1.65% on the first $10,400 of gross earnings. Compute the following:

a The Unemployment Insurance deducted from employees for the year.

b The total unemployment insurance tax paid by the employer.

Ex. 13-4 John Peterson works for a company which is subject to the provisions of the Federal labor legislation. The company has just adopted a 4-day, 40-hour week in response to the desire of employees to spend less time commuting and have longer weekends.

Peterson's base rate of pay is $5.50 an hour, but since the change to the four-day week his hours have been somewhat irregular. During the past week his working hours were as follows: Monday, 13 hours; Tuesday, 11 hours; Wednesday, 12 hours; and Thursday, 7 hours. Compute the amount of his gross earnings for the week. Show computations.

PROBLEMS

Group A

13A-1 Mrs. Ann Watson, owner of five drive-in hamburger stands, known as A-W Drive-Ins, asks you to review the internal controls relating to payrolls. Mrs. Watson is semiretired and employs a manager for each of the five business units. However, she devotes some time to personal review of the operations of the business.

Approximately eight employees work at each location. Each week the managers prepare payroll sheets showing hours worked as reported by the employees on time cards which are approved by the managers. Each manager's salary is also listed on his weekly payroll. Upon completion of the payroll, the manager pays all employees and himself in cash. Each employee acknowledges receipt of payment by signing the payroll sheet.

Employees at each branch are employed and terminated by the local managers, who also set wage rates. The salaries of the managers are authorized by Mrs. Watson.

Each week the payroll sheets are mailed by the managers to Mrs. Watson, whose secretary prepares individual earnings records for each employee and compiles federal tax returns from the weekly payroll sheets.

Instructions

a What is your general evaluation of the adequacy of internal control over payrolls?

b List four specific ways in which payroll fraud could be carried on by the manager of any of the five drive-ins.

13A-2 Mid-City Wholesalers has 50 employees. The following is a list of the payroll taxes and fringe benefits included in the company's compensation plans:

Type	Rate Paid by Employee	Rate Paid by Employer	When Payable by Employer
Canada Pension Plan	1.8% of salary of wages between $800 and $8,300	1.8% on all wages between $800 and $8,300	Monthly
Unemployment Insurance	1.65% on earnings to a maximum of $867 monthly	1.4 times the amount deducted from employees	Monthly
Workmen's Compensation	Nil	4% of assessable payroll (includes maximum of $6,000 for each employee)	Semi-annually (Jan 31 & July 31)
Medical and Hospital Plans	$4.00 per month for single persons and $10.00 per month for married persons	An amount equal to employee contributions	Monthly
Vacation Pay		2 weeks for employees with two years or more of service, Accrue	Annually (when employee takes his vacation)

The total payroll for July covering the 50 employees amounted to $30,000 of which a total of $850 is not subject to workmen's compensation. Workman's Compensation was estimated at $13,800 for the year. All employees earned less than $650 per month with the exception of the following (monthly salaries shown in brackets): Jones ($1,400); Bull ($900); Smith ($967); and Campbell ($1,500). Ten employees, who earned a total of $3,500 in July, have been employed for less than two years. Forty of the employees are married. Income tax deductions of $600 have been deducted for July.

Instructions
Prepare a journal entry to record the July payroll. Mid-City pays all liabilities arising from the July payroll on August 5. Prepare the journal entry to record the payment of the payroll liabilities.

13A-3 Eureka Company has six employees; two are employed on a monthly salary, and four are paid an hourly rate with provision for time and one-half for overtime. The basic data for the July 31 payroll are given below:

Employee	Hours Reg.	OT	Pay Rate	Compensation to June 30	Gross Pay Due for July	Federal Income Tax Withheld
Ames	160	14	$ 4.50 hr	$4,650.00	$ 814.50	$ 85.00
Barker	160		8.00 hr	7,600.00	1,280.00	89.50
Cross	160	21	3.00 hr	2,450.00	574.50	35.10
Davis	Salary		1,200.00 mo	7,200.00	1,200.00	130.00
Elliot	160		4.00 hr	720.00	640.00	49.40
Farmer	Salary		1,500.00 mo	9,000.00	1,500.00	118.00

Other data Compensation of Davis and Farmer is considered an administrative expense; the balance of the earnings is chargeable to Shop Wages. Payroll taxes apply as follows: CPP, 1.8% up to maximum of $8,300; Unemployment Insurance, 1.65% up to maximum of $867 per month. Eureka Company has group insurance and a supplementary retirement plan under which each employee contributes 6% of his gross pay, and the company matches this contribution. Both employees' and employer's contributions are deposited with the Midwest Insurance Company at the end of each month.

Instructions
a Prepare a payroll record for July, using the following columns:

		Amount Subject to		Income	CPP	UI	Retire-	
				Tax	Tax	Tax	ment	Net
	Gross	Unemploy-	CPP	With-	With-	With-	Deduc-	Pay
Employee	Pay	ment Taxes	Taxes	held	held	held	tion	Due

b Explain how the gross pay for Cross was computed for the month of July.
c Explain why the federal income taxes withheld for Farmer are less than those withheld for Davis despite the fact that Farmer received a higher gross compensation.
d Prepare in general journal form the entry to record the payroll for the month of July and the amounts withheld from employees.
e Prepare in general journal form the entry to record the employer's payroll taxes and insurance plan contributions for the month of July.

Group B

13B-1 The Ace Loan Company has 100 branch loan offices. Each office has a manager and four or five subordinates who are employed by the manager. Branch managers prepare the weekly payroll, including their own salaries, and pay employees from cash on hand. The employee signs the payroll sheet signifying receipt of his salary. Hours worked by hourly personnel are inserted in the payroll sheet from time cards prepared by the employees and approved by the manager.

The weekly payroll sheets are sent to the home office along with other accounting statements and reports. The home office compiles employee earnings records and prepares all federal and provincial salary reports from the payroll sheets.

Salaries are established by home office job-evaluation schedules. Salary adjustments, promotions, and transfers of full-time employees are approved by a home office salary committee based upon the recommendations of branch managers and area supervisers. Branch managers advise the salary committee of new full-time employees and terminations. Part-time and temporary employees are hired without referral to the salary committee.

Instructions After evaluation of the company's payroll system, especially the internal control features, suggest five ways in which the branch managers might carry out payroll fraud. (AICPA adapted.)

13B-2 Norcal Vendors Limited prepares its payroll on a monthly basis for its 20 employees. For the month of July, the payroll figures were:

Salaries   **$10,000**
All employees, except Mills whose monthly salary is $1,200 and Clarke whose monthly salary is $1,500, earn less than $450 per month.

Vacation Pay   **Accrue 4% per month**
Three employees, who took their vacations in July, had salaries during their vacation period of $600.

Income Tax
$220 was withheld from employees in July.

Workmen's Compensation   **4% on assessable payroll**
Assessable payroll includes the salary of an individual employee up to a maximum of $6,000. The total estimated Workmen's Compensation expense for 1976 is $3,500 payable in equal amounts on January 31 and July 31.

Unemployment Insurance	*1.65% of each employee's earnings is deducted to a maximum of $867 monthly. Employer pays 1.4 times the employees' contributions.*
Canada Pension Plan	*1.8% of each employee's earnings is deducted on all annual wages between $800 and $8,300. Employer makes an equal contribution*
Medical Plan	*$6.00 per month per employee paid by the employer.*

All payroll liabilities are paid by Norcal on July 31.

Instructions
Prepare the journal entries to record the July payroll and its payment on July 31.

13B-3 Mill Run Company has six employees; two are employed on a monthly salary, and four are paid an hourly rate with provision for time and one-half for overtime. The basic data for the July 31 payroll are given below:

Employee	Hours Reg.	OT	Pay Rate	Compensation to June 30	Gross Pay Due for July	Income Tax Withheld
Allen	160	14	$ 3.00 hr	$3,100	$ 543.00	$53.70
Brown	160		3.50 hr	3,400	560.00	61.40
Carter	160	21	2.00 hr	2,450	383.00	22.10
Dean	Salary		1,000.00 mo	6,000	1,000.00	120.00
Evans	160		2.25 hr	720	360.00	35.40
Folger	Salary		1,600.00 mo	9,600	1,600.00	113.30

Other data Compensation of Dean and Folger is considered an administrative expense; the balance of the earnings is chargeable to Shop Wages. Payroll taxes apply as follows: CPP, 1.8% up to maximum of $8,300; Unemployment Insurance 1.65% up to maximum of $867 per month. Mill Run Company has group insurance and a supplementary retirement plan under which each employee contributes 6% of his gross pay, and the company matches this contribution. Both employees' and employer's contributions are deposited with the Standard Insurance Company at the end of each month.

Instructions
a Prepare a payroll record for July, using the following columns:

Employee	Gross Pay	Amount Subject to Unemployment Taxes	CPP Taxes	Federal Income Tax Withheld	CPP Tax Withheld	UI Withheld	Retirement Deduction	Net Pay Due

b Explain how the gross pay for Carter was computed for the month of July.

c Explain why the federal income taxes withheld for Folger are less than those withheld for Dean despite the fact that Folger received a higher gross compensation.

d Prepare in general journal form the entry to record the payroll for the month of July and the amounts withheld from employees.

e Prepare in general journal form the entry to record the employer's payroll taxes and insurance plan contributions for the month of July.

BUSINESS DECISION PROBLEM 13

The payroll procedures of Marlon Company, a manufacturing concern with 80 factory employees, may be summarized as follows:

1 Applicants are interviewed and hired by the factory foreman. He obtains an Employee's Tax Deduction Certificate (a TD-1 form) from each new employee and writes on it the hourly rate of pay to be used. The foreman gives this certificate to a payroll clerk as notice that a new employee has been added.

2 When hourly pay rate changes are made, the foreman advises the payroll clerk verbally of the new rate for the employee(s) affected.

3 Blank time cards are kept in a box at the factory entrance. On Mondays each employee takes a time card, writes in his name, and makes pencil notations during the week of his hours of arrival and departure. At the end of the week, he returns the card to the box.

4 The completed cards are taken from the box on Monday mornings. Two payroll clerks divide the cards alphabetically between them; compute the gross pay, deductions, and net pay; post the information to the employees' individual earning records; and prepare and number the payroll cheques.

5 The payroll cheques are signed by the chief accountant and given to the foreman, who distributes them to employees and holds those for any absent employees.

6 The payroll bank account is reconciled by the chief accountant, who also prepares the quarterly and annual payroll tax reports.

Instructions You are to recommend any new equipment, forms, and positions (perhaps personnel transfers or new employees) needed as basic changes. Then list specific hiring practices and payroll procedures which you believe should be instituted.

FOURTEEN

ACCOUNTING PRINCIPLES

Throughout this book we try to explain the theoretical roots of each new accounting procedure as it comes under consideration. Anyone who travels through new territory, however, finds it useful to pause at some intermediate stage in his trip to consider what he has seen and to sort out his observations into some meaningful overall impression. This seems an appropriate point in our discussion of accounting for such a pause. You now have an overview of the accounting process and should be better prepared to understand how accounting procedures are shaped by theoretical concepts.

The need for accounting principles

The need for medicine arrived with the first sickness and for engineering when man first tried to transport an object too heavy for him to lift. The roots of accounting do not lie in such primitive soil. Society had to develop a number system, the use of money as a medium of exchange, and commercial organizations before the need for accounting could be recognized.

The art of accounting developed rapidly during and after the Industrial Revolution. Early accounting records were used primarily by the owner-managers as an aid in running their businesses. Creditors were interested in financial reports, but they often knew the business owner well and relied more heavily on their personal knowledge of his financial status and business ability than on accounting information.

The emergence of the publicly owned corporation transformed accounting from a system of historical record keeping into an art based on a cohesive set of measurement principles. Large amounts of economic resources were gathered under the corporate wing, which focused attention on the corporation's financial position and operating results.

Corporate managers needed more sophisticated information systems in order to cope effectively with the resources under their control. More important to the development of accounting theory, outsiders—large credit grantors, stockholders, potential investors, and government agencies—demanded reliable information about the financial affairs of corporations. The need for accepted standards and a body of principles to govern accounting measurements reported to the public by corporations was apparent. A new profession, public accounting, emerged in the latter half of the 1800s. The independent public accountant filled the need for an outside expert to review the accounting records and financial statements of corporations for the benefit of management, stockholders, and creditors.

THE NEEDS OF MANAGEMENT Managers are interested in having information that will aid them in making business decisions. This phase of accounting is primarily concerned with generating reports and summaries for internal use by management and is known as *management accounting.*

In management accounting, theory is not a major issue, since any information that aids in making rational choices among alternative courses of action is relevant and useful. One measurement method may be used for one managerial purpose and another for a different purpose. Accounting measurements of past operating results and current financial position are useful to management, but it is not necessary that all internal information be developed in accordance with any particular set of accounting principles.

THE NEEDS OF STOCKHOLDERS AND CREDITORS While management accounting provides information for internal purposes, *financial accounting* deals primarily with reporting of financial information to outsiders. Measurement of periodic net income and financial position and the reporting of the results to stockholders and creditors are the key objectives of financial accounting.

In reporting to stockholders and creditors, different considerations come into play. Corporate managers, even in small companies, have always been accountable to the owners who employ them. But the responsibility for managing a large corporation carries with it a great deal of economic and social power and requires a more extensive accountability. In most large corporations, stock ownership is widely scattered. The owner of even several thousand of the nearly 300 million shares of General Motors common stock can scarcely expect to exert much influence on managerial policy. As stockholder power has diminished, managerial power and responsibility have broadened.

Modern corporate managers are accountable not only to stockholders and creditors but also to employees, customers, potential investors, and the public at large. Financial statements are the primary means by which management reports on its accountability. Such statements are used to evaluate management's performance, to measure borrowing power, to guide investment decisions, and to support arguments on public policy issues. It is necessary to the functioning of our economy that financial information be widely used and clearly understood. It is also important that there be general confidence in the reliability of financial statements. In short, we need *standards of disclosure* and a well-defined body of accounting principles to govern managers in preparing financial statements and to guide the public accountant in attesting to their fairness.

The accounting environment

The principles of accounting are to a large extent shaped by the environment in which business operates. Accounting is a subsystem of society; it is concerned with economic activity, that is, the ownership and exchange of goods and services. Accountants as well as business executives are now belatedly recognizing that the cost to society of maintaining an economic activity, such as a manufacturing plant, includes the pollution of air and water and other damage to the environment. The identification and measurement of these "social costs" is a newly recognized responsibility of the professional accountant.

Accounting systems developed in response to the need for information about business activity as an aid both to management and outsiders in making rational economic decisions. Since money is a common denominator in which the value of goods and services is measured, the accounting process is implemented in terms of a monetary unit. Most goods and services produced in our economy are distributed through exchange rather than being directly consumed by producers. It is logical, therefore, to base accounting measurements on exchange (market) prices generated by *past, present,* and *future* transactions and events.

For example, when the accountant reports the original cost of a plant site acquired some years ago, he is reflecting a past exchange. When he states inventory at market under the lower-of-cost-or-market rule, he is using a present exchange price (market value) as the basis for his measurement. When he records a liability for income taxes, he is measuring the present effect of a future cash outflow to the government.

Since present decisions can affect only current and future outcomes, current and future exchange prices are in general more relevant for decision making than past exchange prices. We live in a world of uncertainty, however, and estimates of future, and even current, exchange prices are often subject to wide margins of error. Where to draw the line of acceptability in the trade-off between *reliability* and *relevance* is one of the crucial issues in accounting theory. The need for reliable and verifiable data is an important constraint, particularly with respect to information reported to outsiders. This factor has led the accountant to rely heavily on past exchange prices as the basis for his measurements.

In the remaining sections of this chapter we shall summarize briefly the major assumptions and principles that govern the accounting process, and comment on some areas of controversy. We have noted the need for accepted principles to foster confidence in the published statements of widely held corporations. Most accounting principles are equally applicable to profit-making organizations of any size or form.

ASSUMPTIONS AND PRINCIPLES UNDERLYING
THE ACCOUNTING PROCESS

Financial statements are prepared using a body of accounting theory as a guide. Accounting theory consists of a collection of principles which have been developed in order to measure and report the financial activities of business units. These principles rest on a foundation of *assumptions* which establish the boundaries of the accounting process and serve as a cohesive force in preparing financial statements.

Accounting entities

One of the basic assumptions of accounting is that information is compiled for a clearly defined accounting entity. Most economic activity is carried on through entities. An individual person is an accounting entity. So is a business enterprise, whether conducted as a single proprietorship, partnership, or corporation. The estate of a deceased person is an accounting entity, as are nonprofit clubs and organizations. The basic accounting equation, Assets = Liabilities + Owner's Equity, reflects the *accounting entity concept,* since the elements of the equation relate to the particular entity whose economic activity is being metered in accounting statements.

We should distinguish between accounting and legal entities. In some cases the two coincide. For example, corporations, estates, trusts, and governmental agencies are both accounting and legal entities. In other cases, accounting entities differ from legal entities. For example, the *proprietorship* is an *accounting* entity, as indicated by the fact that only the assets and liabilities of the business unit are included in its financial statements. The proprietorship is not a legal entity; the *proprietor* is a *legal* entity. He is legally liable both for his personal obligations and for those incurred in his business. For accounting purposes, the proprietor as an individual and his business enterprise are separate entities. Furthermore, a proprietor may own several businesses, each of which is treated as a separate entity for accounting purposes.

The choice of an accounting entity is somewhat flexible and is based on informational needs. As a general rule, we can say that any legal or economic unit which controls economic resources and is accountable for these resources is an accounting entity.

Going-concern concept

An underlying assumption in accounting is that an accounting entity will continue in operation for an indefinite period of time sufficient to carry out its existing commitments. This assumption is sometimes called the *going-concern concept.* Since most accounting entities have indefinite lives, the assumption of continuity is in accord with experience in our economic system. In general, the going-concern assumption justifies ignoring immediate liquidating values in presenting assets and liabilities in the balance sheet.

For example, suppose that a company has just purchased a five-year insurance policy for $5,000. If we assume that the business will continue in operations for five years or more, we will consider the $5,000 payment for the insurance as an asset whose services (freedom from risk) will be enjoyed by the business over a five-year period. On the other hand, if we assume that the business is likely to terminate in the near future, the insurance policy should be recorded at its cancellation value—the amount of cash which can be obtained from the insurance company as a refund on immediate cancellation of the policy, which may be, say, $4,800.

In summary, the going-concern assumption may be dropped when it is not in accord with the facts. Accountants are sometimes asked to prepare a statement of financial position for an enterprise that is about to liquidate. In this case the assumption of continuity is no longer valid and the accountant drops the going-concern assumption and reports assets at their current liquidating value and liabilities at the amount required to settle the debts immediately.

Periodic financial reports

We assume an indefinite life for most accounting entities. But accountants are asked to measure operating progress and changes in economic position at relatively short time intervals during this indefinite life. Users of financial statements want periodic measurements for decision-making purposes. The selection of a *fiscal period,* such as a quarter of a year or a full year, facilitates periodic reporting by business units.

Dividing the life of an enterprise into time segments and measuring changes in financial position periodically is a difficult process. A precise measurement of net income and financial position can be made only when a business has been liquidated and its resources have been fully converted into cash. At any time prior to liquidation, the worth of some assets and the amount of some liabilities are matters of speculation. Thus periodic measures of net income and financial position are at best only informed estimates.

Periodic measurements of net income are generally *tentative.* This fact should be clearly understood by those who rely on periodic accounting information. The need for periodic measurements creates many of accounting's most serious problems. For example, the attempt to measure income over short time periods requires the selection of inventory-flow assumptions and depreciation methods. The end-of-period adjustments discussed in Chapter 4 stem directly from the need to update accounting information to a particular point in time.

Objectivity and exchange prices

A basic principle of accounting is that changes in the valuations assigned to assets and liabilities, and their resultant effect on net income and owner's equity, should not be recognized until they can be measured objectively in terms of an *exchange price (cost).*

The term *objective* refers to measurements that are unbiased and subject to verification by independent experts. For example, the price established in an arm's-length transaction is an objective measure of exchange value at the time of the transaction. It is not surprising, therefore, that exchange prices established in business transactions constitute much of the raw material from which accounting information is generated.

If a measurement is objective, 10 competent investigators who make the same measurement will come up with substantially identical results. It is probably true, however, that 10 competent accountants who set out independently to measure the net income of a given business would not arrive at an identical result. In the light of the objectivity principle, why is this so? The variation would probably arise because of the existence of alternative accounting measurement methods, rather than the lack of objectivity in any given measurement method. To illustrate, in measuring the cost of goods sold one accountant might use the lifo method, and another the weighted-average method for valuing inventory. These choices could produce significant variations in net income.

The accountant relies on various kinds of evidence to support his financial measurements, but he seeks always the most objective evidence he can get. Invoices, contracts, canceled cheques, physical counts of inventory are examples of objective evidence used by accountants.

Despite the goal of objectivity, it is not possible to insulate accounting information from opinion and personal judgment. The cost of a depreciable asset can be objectively determined but not the periodic depreciation expense. To measure the cost of the asset services that have expired during a given period requires estimates of the salvage value and service life of the asset and judgment as to the depreciation method that should be used.

Furthermore, objectivity is a relative term which allows for some reasonable latitude in the quality of the evidence. A past exchange price (historical cost) is more objective than a current market price because the accountant can observe an actual exchange transaction. Both are more objective than an estimated future exchange price. All three, however, may be independently verified within a range of accuracy that permits their use as accounting inputs.

Objectivity in accounting has its roots in the quest for reliability. The accountant wants to make his economic measurements reliable and at the same time as relevant to decision makers as possible. The accountant is constantly faced with the necessity of compromising between what users of financial information would like to know and what it is possible to measure with a reasonable degree of reliability. Some authorities believe that the accountant is too conservative and waits too long to measure and recognize changes in assets and liabilities, and that he could measure some changes sooner than he does. Those who support present measurement principles argue that it is important that users have confidence in financial statements, and that this confidence can best be maintained if the accountant recognizes changes in assets and liabilities only on the basis of objective evidence.

Stability of the measuring unit

Money is the common denominator in which accounting measurements are made and summarized. The dollar, or any other monetary unit, represents a unit of value; that is, it reflects the ability to command goods and services. Implicit in the use of money as a measuring unit is the *assumption that the dollar is a stable unit of value,* just as the mile is a stable unit of distance, and an acre is a stable unit of area.

Having accepted money as his measuring unit, the accountant freely combines dollar measures of economic transactions that occur at various times during the life of an accounting entity. He combines, for example, a $5,000 cost of equipment purchased in 1965 and the $10,000 cost of equipment purchased in 1975 and reports the total as a $15,000 investment in equipment.

Unlike the mile and the acre, which are stable units of distance and area, respectively, unfortunately the dollar *is not a stable unit of value.* The prices of goods and services in our economy change over time. When the *general price level* (a phrase used to describe the average of all prices) increases, the value of money (that is, its ability to command goods and services) decreases.

Despite the steady erosion in the purchasing power of the dollar in Canada for over 25 years, accountants continue to assume that the value of the dollar is stable. This somewhat unrealistic assumption is one of the reasons why accounting statements are viewed by some users as misleading. Restatement of accounting information for the changing value of the dollar and the preparation of supplementary statements in terms of constant dollars have received much attention in recent years. Such *common dollar statements* will be discussed in a subsequent section of this chapter.

Consistency

The assumption of *consistency* implies that a particular accounting method, once adopted, will not be changed from period to period. This assumption is important because it enables users of financial statements to interpret intelligently the changes in financial position and the amount of net income.

As a practical matter, management (with approval from its accountants) *can* change an accounting method when in its judgment a different method would better serve the needs of users of financial statements. It would hardly be a virtue to employ an improper accounting method consistently year after year. When a significant change in accounting occurs, however, the independent public accountant is obliged to report both the fact that a change in method has been made and the dollar effect of the change. In published financial statements, this disclosure is incorporated in the auditor's opinion. A typical disclosure might be as follows: "During the current year the company changed from the lifo to the fifo method of accounting for inventory. This change in method had the effect of increasing the ending inventories by $400,000 and net income (after taxes) by $210,000."

If income statements for previous years are included alongside the current statement for comparison purposes, particulars should be disclosed of any change in accounting principals or practice which materially affects the comparability of the current statements and those of the corresponding preceding period. The effect of any such change on the current statements should be reported. The figures for the preceding year should be restated unless the change in accounting principle or practice has not been applied retroactively.[1]

Consistency applies to a single accounting entity and promotes the comparability of financial statements from period to period. Different companies, even those in the same industry, may follow different accounting methods. For this reason, it is important to determine the accounting methods used by companies whose financial results are being compared.

Disclosure of relevant information

One of the most important objectives of financial reporting is to make certain that all *material* and *relevant facts* concerning financial position and the results of operations *are communicated to users.* This can be accomplished either in the financial statements or in the notes accompanying the statements. Such disclosure should make the statements more useful and less subject to misinterpretation.

Naturally, there are practical limits to the amount of disclosure that can be made in financial statements or the accompanying notes. As a minimum, the following information would generally be disclosed:

1 Terms of major borrowing arrangements and existence of large contingent liabilities
2 Contractural provisions relating to leasing arrangements, employee pension and bonus plans, and major proposed asset acquisitions

[1] *CICA Handbook,* Canadian Institute of Chartered Accountants, Toronto, 1969, Section 1500.09.

3 Accounting methods used in preparing the financial statements

4 Changes in accounting methods effected during the latest period

5 Other significant events affecting financial position, including major new contracts for sale of goods or services, labor strikes, shortages of raw materials, and pending legislation which may significantly affect operations

Supplementary disclosure through footnotes, however, should not take the place of sound accounting practices in preparing financial reports. The primary information made available to readers of financial statements is derived from the accounting records, but it is not necessarily limited to such information. The key point to keep in mind is that the supplementary information should be *relevant to the user.* Even significant events which occur *after* the end of the accounting period but before the financial statements are released should be disclosed.

Materiality

The term *materiality* refers to the *relative importance* of an item or event. Disclosure of relevant information is closely related to the concept of materiality; what is material is likely to be relevant. For practical reasons, accountants are primarily concerned with significant information and are not overly concerned with those items which have little effect on financial statements. For example, should the cost of a pencil sharpener, a wastepaper basket, or a stapler be set up as assets and depreciated over their useful lives? Even though more than one period will benefit from the use of these assets, the concept of materiality permits the immediate recognition of the cost of these items as an expense on grounds that it would be too expensive to undertake depreciation accounting for such low-cost assets and that the results would not differ significantly.

We must recognize that the materiality of an item is a relative thing; what is material for one business unit may not be material for another. Materiality of an item may depend not only on its *amount* but also on its *nature.* In summary, we can state the following rule: *An item is material if there is a reasonable expectation that knowledge of it would influence the decisions of prudent users of financial statements.*

Conservatism as a guide in resolving uncertainties

We have previously referred to the use of *conservatism* in connection with the measurement of net income and the reporting of accounts receivable and inventories in the balance sheet. Although the concept of conservatism may not qualify as an accounting principle, it has long been a powerful influence upon asset valuation and income determination. Conservatism is most useful when matters of judgment or estimates are involved. Ideally, the accountant should base his estimates on sound logic and select those acceptable accounting procedures which neither overstate nor understate the facts. When some doubt exists in the accountant's mind, however, he traditionally leans in the direction of caution and selects the accounting option which produces a lower net income for the current period and a less favorable financial position. Conservatism, however, may be viewed as a double-edged sword. If an asset is prematurely recognized as an expense in Year 1, for example, the balance sheet and net income for Year 1 will be conservatively stated but the net income for Year 2 will be overstated.

An example of conservatism is the traditional practice of pricing inventory at the lower of cost or market (replacement cost). Decreases in the market value of the inventory are recognized as a part of the cost of goods sold in the current period, but increases in market value of inventory are ignored. A judicious application of conservatism to the accounting process should produce more useful information; in contrast, the excessive use of conservatism or failure to apply conservatism may produce misleading information and result in losses to creditors and stockholders.

What are "generally accepted accounting principles"?

The phrase "generally accepted accounting principles" as used in practice encompasses a broad set of basic assumptions, measurement methods, and reporting procedures followed by accountants. For many years accounting theorists have been arguing about the precise nature of accounting principles. Even today the subject generates heated controversy, and precise terminology has yet to be established. There is a growing consensus that *accounting principles consist of the major objectives sought by accountants and the guidelines to be followed in making accounting measurements.* There is also agreement that these principles rest on certain assumptions which establish the boundaries of the accounting process.

The *basic principles* of accounting have remained relatively unchanged for a long time; the *procedures* of accounting (such as different ways of computing depreciation) are subject to more frequent changes. Procedures are modified in response to improvements in the art of accounting, in response to changes in the laws governing business operations and income taxation, and at times in response to pressures from various groups who want to shape financial results to attain particular ends.

Authoritative support for accounting principles

To qualify as "generally accepted," an accounting principle must usually receive "substantial authoritative support." The most influential authoritative groups in this country are: (1) the Canadian Institute of Chartered Accountants and (2) the Society of Industrial Accountants of Canada.

The CICA has long been concerned with stating and defining accounting principles because its members face the problem of making decisions every day about generally accepted principles in their professional work. In 1946, the CICA established the Accounting and Auditing

Research Committee, comprising practitioners, educators, and industry representatives. This Board was authorized to issue *Pronouncements* which would improve financial reporting and narrow areas of differences and inconsistencies in accounting practices and which would be regarded as expressions of generally accepted accounting principles. At the same time, the CICA expanded its research efforts and sponsored a series of Accounting Research Studies to aid the Research Committee in its work.

The Accounting and Auditing Research Committee has issued a number of pronouncements, now forming part of the *CICA Handbook,* on specific accounting problems and continues its efforts to improve the quality of financial reporting and the comparability of financial reports among companies.

The Society has sponsored a number of research studies and monographs by individual authors and Society committees dealing primarily with areas of management accounting.

Governments influence financial reporting through minimum standards contained in legislation dealing with incorporation of limited companies and the establishment of reporting requirements by regulatory agencies.

In addition to the foregoing, "substantial authoritative support" may include accounting practices commonly found in certain industries and in the literature of accounting, including books, journal articles, and expert testimony offered in court.

Opinions and research studies of the American Institute of Certified Public Accountants are important to Canadian accountants because of their quality and the tremendous American involvement in Canadian commercial activity. Another important source of accounting thought is the American Accounting Association, an academic organization comprised primarily of American and Canadian accounting professors.

Accounting: a measurement process

Accounting is basically a measurement process in terms of a monetary unit. Within the framework of the assumptions and principles previously discussed, the accountant attempts to:

1 Measure the *assets* owned by the accounting entity
2 Measure the *liabilities* (creditors' claims) against the assets and the resultant *owners' equity* in the accounting entity
3 Measure the *changes* that occur in the assets, liabilities, and owners' equity
4 Assign the changes in owners' equity to specific periods of time and thus measure the *net income* of the accounting entity

Financial measurements are expressed in the basic accounting equation:

Owners' equity is also called net assets. Why?

Assets = Liabilities + Owners' Equity (or Net Assets)

If we examine the components of this equation, we see that assets and liabilities are the independent variables. The owners' equity in any accounting entity is a residual amount (the dependent variable) which can be determined only when the assets and liabilities have been measured.

Assets are expected future economic benefits, the rights to which have been acquired by the entity. For measurement purposes, assets may be classified in two categories: (1) cash and claims to cash, and (2) all other assets. The first category (*monetary assets*) includes cash, investments in marketable securities, notes receivable, and accounts receivable. These assets represent present holdings of cash or cash equivalents and future claims against cash. They are measured (with the exception of marketable securities) at their present monetary value. Cash is automatically stated at its monetary value. Receivables are stated at the present value of the future expected cash inflow, taking into account estimates of uncollectible amounts. Many accountants are presently arguing that investments in marketable securities should also be measured at their current market value.

Assets other than cash and claims to cash are service potentials to be converted into cash through operations. The major classes of assets falling into this category are inventories, prepaid expenses, plant and equipment, and intangibles. At the date of acquisition, these assets are stated at the cost of acquiring them.

Liabilities, the claims against assets, are obligations to convey assets or perform services and require settlement in the future. Liabilities are typically measured in terms of the value of the assets or services that will be given up by the accounting entity to pay the obligations.

Measuring changes in assets and liabilities

A primary objective of the accounting process is the measurement of changes in assets and liabilities. Transactions involving an equal increase in assets and liabilities (for example, the acquisition of an asset on credit) create few accounting problems. Similarly, transactions involving an identical decrease in both assets and liabilities (for example, the payment of a debt) cause little difficulty. The central problem is to determine *when a change in net assets* has occurred, and to *measure this change.*

INCREASES IN NET ASSETS Changes which increase net assets (owners' equity) are of three basic types:

1 Additional investments of capital by owners
2 Revenues—the gross increase in net assets resulting from the production or delivery of goods and the rendering of services to customers
3 Gains—any increase in net assets other than those resulting from revenues or additional investments of capital by owners

DECREASES IN NET ASSETS Changes which decrease net assets (owners' equity) may also be divided into three classes:

1 Distributions to owners, for example, drawings by proprietors or dividends paid to stockholders by a corporation

2 Expenses—decreases in net assets resulting from the use of economic goods and services to produce revenues or from the imposition of taxes by governmental bodies

3 Losses—decreases in net assets other than those resulting from operating expenses or distributions to owners

If we ignore the cases of increased investments and distributions to owners, the resultant of increases and decreases in net assets is what accountants call **net income.** This is illustrated below:

How precise is this measurement?

Revenues and Gains — Expenses and Losses = Net Income (or Net Loss)

It is clear that the accountant's measurement of periodic net income is the direct result of his measurement of the changes in assets and liabilities as a result of the day-to-day operations. But keep in mind that estimates and professional judgment on the part of the accountant play an important role in this measurement process.

Recognizing revenues

Revenues measure the firm's **output** of goods and services; expenses measure the **input** of goods and services required to produce the revenue; losses measure the destruction of asset values (as from fire and theft) without any contribution to the firm's output. Net income results when the value of output exceeds the cost of input. The process of recording revenue in the accounting records as earned is known as revenue **realization.** Revenue may be realized at a number of different points in time: (*1*) When sale or delivery of the product is made or the services are rendered (sales basis); (*2*) when cash is collected from customers (cash basis); (*3*) during production; (*4*) when production is completed and the product is ready for sale.

In most cases the accountant chooses to recognize revenue **at the time of the sale of goods or the rendering of services.** Recognizing revenue at this point is logical because the firm has essentially completed the earning process and the realized value of the goods or services sold can be objectively measured in terms of the price billed to customers. At any time prior to sale, the ultimate realizable value of the goods or services sold can only be estimated. After the sale, the only step that remains is to collect from the customer, and this is usually a relatively certain event.

An accounting procedure also exists for delaying the measurement of revenues until **cash is collected.** In Chapter 3, we have described a complete **cash basis** of income measurement whereby revenues are considered realized only when cash is collected from customers and expenses are recorded when cash is actually paid out. Farmers and fishermen, for example, generally use the cash basis of accounting in computing their taxable income. In computing realized revenue on the cash basis, receivables from clients or customers are ignored; only the actual cash collections are recorded as revenue.

Companies selling goods on the installment plan sometimes use the *installment method* of accounting. This method would be considered appropriate when collections extend over relatively long periods of time and there is a strong possibility that full collection will not be made. As customers make installment payments, the seller recognizes the gross profit on sales in proportion to the cash collected. Thus, if the gross profit on installment sales is 30%, out of every dollar collected on installment accounts receivable 30 cents represents *realized gross profit.* For example, assume that a retailer sells a television set in Year 1 for $400 which cost him $280, or 70% of sales price. The collections (revenue) and the profit earned would be recognized over a three-year period as follows:

	Year	Cash Collected	−	Cost Recovery, 70%	=	Profit Earned, 30%
Installment	1	$150		$105		$ 45
method	2	200		140		60
illustrated	3	50		35		15
	Totals	$400		$280		$120

From an accounting viewpoint, there is little theoretical justification for delaying the recognition of revenues beyond the point of sales, because few if any cases exist where the realizable value of the receivable cannot be measured at that time through the establishment of an adequate allowance for uncollectible accounts.

There are some circumstances in which the accountant finds it appropriate to recognize revenue as realized *during production* or when production is completed. An example arises in the case of *long-term construction contracts,* such as the building of a dam over a three-year period. In this case the revenue (contract price) is known when the construction job is begun, and it would be unreasonable to assume that the entire revenue is realized in the accounting period in which the project is completed. The accountant therefore estimates the portion of the dam completed during each accounting period, and recognizes revenues and profits in proportion to the work completed. This is known as the *percentage-of-completion method* of accounting for long-term contracts.

Assume, for example, that the costs to be incurred over a three-year period on a $500,000 contract are estimated at $400,000. Using the percentage-of-completion method of accounting, the profits on the contract would be recognized over the three-year period as follows:

	Year	Actual Cost Incurred	Estimated Total Cost, %	Portion of Contract Price Realized	Profit Considered Realized
Profit	1	$ 60,000	15	$ 75,000	$15,000
recognized	2	200,000	50	250,000	50,000
as work	3	145,200	*	175,000 balance	29,800 balance
progresses	Totals	$405,200		$500,000	$94,800

*Balance required to complete the contract.

The portion of the contract price realized in Years 1 and 2 is determined by taking the percentage of estimated total cost incurred in each year and applying it to the contract price of $500,000. Because 15% ($60,000/$400,000) of the total estimated cost was incurred in Year 1, 15% of the total estimated profit of $100,000 ($500,000 − $400,000) was considered realized; in Year 2, 50% ($200,000/$400,000) of the cost was incurred, and therefore 50% of the estimated profit was considered realized. In Year 3, however, the total actual cost is known and the final profit is determined to be $94,800 (500,000 − $405,200). Since profits of $65,000 ($15,000 + $50,000) were previously recognized in Years 1 and 2, the rest of the profit, $29,800, must be recognized in Year 3. If at the end of any accounting period it appears that a loss will be incurred on a contract in progress, *the loss should be recognized at once.*

If it is difficult to estimate the degree of contract completion or if there are extreme uncertainties involved in measuring the ultimate profit on a contract in progress, revenue may be recognized when the *production is completed.* This approach is often referred to as the *completed-contract method* and is supported by many accountants because it is conservative and requires little subjective judgment. If the completed-contract method of accounting for long-term construction contracts had been used in the preceding example, no profit would have been recognized in Years 1 and 2; the entire profit of $94,800 would be recorded in Year 3 when the contract was completed and actual costs known.

Measuring expenses: the concept of matching costs and revenues

Revenues, the gross increase in net assets resulting from the production or sale of goods and services, are offset by expenses incurred in bringing the firm's output to the point of sale. The cost of merchandise sold, the expiration of asset services, and out-of-pocket expenditures for operating costs are examples of expenses relating to revenues. The measurement of expenses occurs in two stages: (1) measuring the *cost* of goods and services that constitute the firm's input in generating revenues, and (2) determining when the goods and services acquired have contributed to revenues and their cost thus *becomes an expense.* The second aspect of the measurement process is often referred to as *matching costs and revenues* and is fundamental to the *accrual method* of accounting.

Costs are associated with revenues (and thus become expenses) in two major ways:

1 In relation to the product sold or service rendered If a good or service can be related to the product or service which constitutes the output of the enterprise, its cost becomes an expense when the product is sold or the service rendered to customers. The cost of goods sold in a merchandising firm is a good example of this type of expense. Similarly, a commission paid to a real estate salesman by a real estate brokerage office is an expense directly related to the revenues generated by the salesman.

2 In relation to the time period during which revenues are earned Some costs incurred by businesses cannot be directly related to the product or service output of the firm. Expired fire insurance, property taxes, depreciation on a building, the salary of the president of the company—all are examples of costs incurred in generating revenues which cannot be related to specific transactions. The accountant refers to this class of costs as *period costs,* and charges them to expense by associating them with the period of time during which they are incurred and presumably contribute to revenues, rather than by associating them with specific revenue-producing transactions.

Recognition of gains and losses

The same standards applied in recognizing revenues are applicable to the measurement of gains and losses on assets other than inventories. In general, an increase in the value of a productive asset, such as machinery or buildings, is not recognized until the asset in question is sold, in which case the amount of the gain is objectively determinable.

If a productive asset increases in value while it is in service, the accountant ordinarily does not record this gain because it has not been realized. "Not realized" means that the gain in value has not been substantiated by a transaction in which an exchange price has been established.

For many years accounting theorists have debated the question whether it would be desirable to attempt to recognize gains in the value of productive assets prior to their sale or disposal. This debate becomes particularly heated during periods of rising prices when it is likely that assets carried at cost less accumulated depreciation will be stated at figures considerably less than their current market value. The majority of accountants have rejected proposals for reporting assets at a figure in excess of undepreciated cost because of the difficulty of obtaining objective measures of the current market value of assets and because realization of the gain has not taken place.

Accountants are not so insistent on following the rules of *realization* in measuring losses. We have seen in Chapter 10, for example, that the lower-of-cost-or-market valuation of inventories results in the recognition of losses in inventory investment prior to the sale of the goods in question. Recognizing losses when inventories appear to be worth less than their cost but refusing to recognize gains when inventories appear to be worth more than their cost is logically inconsistent. This inconsistency is justified by an accounting presumption that assets should not be reported in the balance sheet in excess of the amount which can be expected to be recovered through revenues.

Realized gains and losses, net of income taxes, are reported in the income statements of corporations as *extraordinary items.* These extraordinary items, plus the income from operations (after taxes), produce the net income for the period.[2]

Opinion on financial statements rendered by independent public accountants

After independent public accountants have audited the financial statements and accounting records of a business, they attest to the reasonableness of the financial statements by issuing an *audit opinion* (sometimes called a *certificate*). This opinion is published as part of the company's annual report to stockholders. Because of its importance, the wording of the audit opinion has been carefully considered and a standard form has been developed. Considering the extensive investigation that precedes it, the audit opinion is surprisingly short. It usually consists of two brief paragraphs unless the public accountants comment on unusual features of the financial picture. The first paragraph describes the *scope* of the auditors' examination; the second states their *opinion* of the financial statements. A report of independent accountants[3] might read as follows:

AUDITOR'S REPORT

To the Shareholders of . . . .

We have examined the balance sheet of . . . . as at . . . ., 19. . . . . . and the statements of income, retained earnings and source and application of funds for the year then ended. Our examination included a general review of the accounting procedures and such tests of accounting records and other supporting evidence as we considered necessary in the circumstances.

In our opinion these financial statements present fairly the financial position of the company as at . . . ., 19. . . . . . and the results of its operations and the source and application of its funds for the year then ended, in accordance with generally accepted accounting principles applied on a basis consistent with that of the preceding year.

(signed) . . . .

CHARTERED ACCOUNTANTS

City
Date

Observe that CAs *do not guarantee* the accuracy of the financial statements. The financial statements are issued by management of the business; the CAs render a professional opinion as to the "fairness" of the presentation. The important point to keep in mind is that the *primary responsibility for the accuracy of the financial statements rests with the management* of the business entity issuing the statements.

---

[2] Certain extraordinary items recognized in the current period may relate directly to a prior year. The special accounting treatment of such *prior period adjustments* is discussed in Chapter 17.

[3] *CICA Handbook*, op. cit., Section 2500.10

The phrase "in conformity with generally accepted accounting principles" in the second paragraph of the audit opinion is particularly relevant to our discussion in this chapter. *An authoritative exhaustive list of generally accepted accounting principles does not exist.* Yet the widespread reliance upon this phrase implies that there is general consensus as to what these accounting principles are.

THE SEARCH FOR BETTER FINANCIAL REPORTING

Accounting is a man-made information system. It is an imperfect system, and constant efforts are being made to improve the precision and relevance of accounting measurements and the usefulness of the end products of the accounting process—financial statements. Because economic conditions are full of uncertainty and business transactions are often complex, the end products of the accounting process must be accepted for what they are—tentative in nature and subject to certain limitations. Accordingly, we should not expect financial statements to attain a higher level of certainty than the business transactions which they summarize.

While accounting may never become a precise science, no one can argue that further improvements are not possible in measuring and communicating financial information. Should accountants, for example, continue to adhere to the assumption that the monetary unit is stable and that historical costs are the most relevant measures of "value" for financial reporting purposes? In the remaining pages of this chapter, we shall examine the implications of this important question.

Financial statements adjusted for changes in the value of the dollar

As stated earlier, the general price level[4] in Canada has been going up for many years, yet accountants continue to assume that the value of the dollar is stable. What effect do material changes in general price levels, and thus changes in the value of money, have on accounting measurements? By combining transactions measured in dollars of varying years, the accountant in effect ignores changes in the size of his measuring unit. For example, suppose that a company purchased land early in Year 1 for $50,000 and sold this land for $100,000 late in Year 10. If prices roughly doubled during that 10-year period and the value of money was cut in half, we might say that the company was no better off as a result of these two transactions; the $100,000 received for the land in Year 10 represented approximately the same command over goods and

---

[4] The general price level is the weighted average of the prices of goods and services within the economy. Generally, it is measured by an index with a base year assigned a value of 100. The reciprocal of the price index represents the purchasing power of the dollar. Thus, if Year 1 = 100 and Year 5 = 125, prices have risen 25% and purchasing power has decreased by 20% [100 − (100 ÷ 125)]. The most common measures of the general price level are the consumer price index, the wholesale price index, and the Gross National Product Implicit Price Deflator. The GNP Deflator is the most comprehensive index and is widely accepted as the best measure of the general price level.

services as $50,000 did when invested in the land in Year 1. In terms of the *dollar* as a measuring unit, however, the accountant would record a gain of $50,000 ($100,000 − $50,000) at the time the land was sold in Year 10. Thus, by combining the Year 1 and Year 10 transactions in dollar terms to measure gains and losses, *the accountant assumes that a firm is as well off when it has recovered its original dollar investment, and that it is better off whenever it recovers more than the original number of dollars invested in any given asset.*

The assumption that the dollar is a stable measuring unit can hardly be defended on factual grounds. The issue is not whether money *is* a stable measuring unit; we know it is not. The question is whether financial statements prepared using historical dollars as the measuring unit are more useful than financial statements prepared on some other basis. Years ago methods were devised for making accounting measurements and presenting financial statements in terms of current dollars rather than historical dollars. Such statements have come to be known as *common dollar financial statements,* because all historical dollar amounts are restated in terms of the current value of the dollar.

An extended discussion of the procedures used to prepare common dollar statements is beyond the scope of this book, but the process may be visualized through a brief discussion of a few key ideas.

MONETARY ITEMS AND COMMON DOLLAR FINANCIAL STATEMENTS In discussing the changing value of the dollar, we must identify the balance sheet accounts which are affected by such changes and those which are not. In general, cash, notes receivable, accounts receivable, and all liabilities are *monetary items* because they represent claims to purchasing power or obligations to pay out cash. Monetary items are already stated in terms of current dollars and need not be restated. All other balance sheet accounts (inventories, investments in stock of other companies, plant and equipment, intangibles, and owners' equity accounts) are *nonmonetary items* and must be restated to current dollars in preparing common dollar financial statements.

Changes in price levels give rise to gains and losses as a result of holding monetary items. Owning cash or claims to cash (such as accounts or notes receivable) results in a loss of purchasing power when the general price level is rising; owing money during a period of rising price levels, on the other hand, gives rise to a purchasing power gain because fixed-dollar liabilities can now be paid off with dollars having less purchasing power. We can summarize this point as follows: *In a period of inflation (increasing price levels), it is better to be in debt and hold a minimum of monetary assets; in a period of deflation (decreasing price levels), it is better to hold monetary assets and avoid taking on debts.* To illustrate, assume the following condensed balance sheets, stated in terms of historical costs, for two companies:

	Company A	Company B
Cash and receivables	$500	$200
Merchandise and plant	300	600
Total assets	$800	$800
Liabilities	$150	$700
Owners' equity	650	100
Total liabilities & owners' equity	$800	$800

What effect will inflation have on each company?

If we assume that the general price level had increased by 50% since the merchandise and plant were acquired by companies A and B, their balance sheets restated to current dollars would appear as follows:

	Company A	Company B
Cash and receivables	$500	$ 200
Merchandise and plant	450 ($300 × 1.5)	900 ($600 × 1.5)
Total assets	$950	$1,100
Liabilities	$150	$ 700
Owners' equity	975 ($650 × 1.5)	150 ($100 × 1.5)
Net purchasing power (loss) or gain	(175)*	250†
Total liabilities & owners' equity	$950	$1,100

High debt and small amount of monetary assets result in a purchasing power gain for Company B

* Loss from holding cash and receivables $250 ($500 × 50%), plus the gain on holding liabilities $75 ($150 × 50%) = $175 net purchasing power loss.

† Gain from holding liabilities $350 ($700 × 50%), reduced by the loss from holding cash and receivables $100 ($200 × 50%) = $250 net purchasing power gain.

Holding monetary assets during a period of rising prices results in a loss of purchasing power because the value of money is falling. This is illustrated by the $250 loss experienced by Company A as a result of carrying $500 in monetary assets during a period when prices increased by 50%. In contrast, the purchasing power loss for Company B as a result of holding monetary assets during the same period was only $100 (50% of $200).

Owing money during a period of rising prices results in a purchasing power gain. This gain results because the debtor company can settle its liabilities in a fixed number of dollars which have a lesser value than the dollars which represented the original amount borrowed. This is illustrated by the purchasing power gain of $75 realized by Company A as a result of owing $150 while prices were rising by 50%. In contrast, the purchasing power gain for Company B is $350 because it owed a much larger sum, $700, while prices increased by 50%. Thus, Company A shows a net purchasing power loss of $175 ($250 − $75) while Company B shows a net purchasing power gain of $250 ($350 − $100).

INCOME MEASUREMENT UNDER COMMON DOLLAR REPORTING As stated earlier, a business entity is assumed to be better off (that is, to have earned income) only after it has recovered the equivalent general purchasing power represented by the dollars originally invested in assets. Depreciation expense, for example, should be restated in terms of the general price index at the end of the accounting period. If a building with a useful life of 20 years was acquired for $100,000 when the general price level stood at 100, depreciation expense for the latest year when the price level stood at 170 would be $8,500 ($5,000 × 1.70). Other expense and revenue items would be similarly adjusted in terms of current general purchasing power in preparing a common dollar income statement.

COMMON DOLLAR STATEMENTS IN PRACTICE Common dollar financial statements are *not* generally accepted as primary reports to stockholders. A few companies have published some version of common dollar financial statements in supplementary schedules included in their annual reports.[5]

The conversion of accounting data into common dollars is not widely used in Canada because thus far the business community is apparently not convinced of the increased usefulness of this information.

The effort required to make accounting measurements in common dollar terms and to prepare financial statements on this basis is considerable. In an age of electronic computers, however, this additional data-processing effort is not a practical barrier to the preparation of common dollar statements.

Replacement costs distinguished from common dollar accounting

We have used the expression *common dollar accounting* to describe financial statements in which historical costs were adjusted to reflect changes in the general price level. Common dollar accounting *does not abandon historical cost* as the basis of measurement but simply expresses cost in terms of the current value of money. Also, common dollar accounting does not mean that *replacement costs* (which may be assumed to approximate fair market value) are used in the preparation of financial statements. For example, a tract of land which cost $100,000 many years ago would be stated at $150,000 in common dollars if the general price level had risen by 50%. However, the replacement cost of the land might be $400,000 because land prices might have risen much more than the general price level.

If accountants were to use current replacement costs in financial statements, the unit of measurement would be current dollars since replacement costs are stated in these terms. But the use of replacement costs in preparing financial statements *would be a departure from the historical cost concept,* and would require that accountants develop reli-

[5]For further discussion, see: Accounting Research Study No. 6, *Reporting the Financial Effects of Price-Level Changes,* AICPA (New York: 1963). pp. 169–219; Accounting Principles Board Statement No. 3, *Financial Statements Restated for General Price-Level Changes,* AICPA (New York: 1969); L. S. Rosen, *Current Value Accounting and Price-Level Restatements,* CICA (Toronto, 1972).

able techniques for measuring the current cost of replacing various types of assets.

Some accountants have recommended that supplementary financial statements showing appraisal values of assets be prepared and submitted along with conventional statements. Accountants for the most part are not in favor of this, because such appraised values lack the objectivity desired by most users of financial statements. When assets show a significant increase in value, it is difficult to argue that historical costs continue to provide investors with useful information, even though the estimates of replacement costs are subject to some lack of precision and objectivity. In dealing with this problem, accountants are faced with a fundamental issue: Can the usefulness of accounting reports be improved by providing more relevant information while sacrificing some objectivity? Accountants continue to seek a satisfactory answer to this question.

QUESTIONS

1 What developments were primarily responsible for the transformation of double-entry bookkeeping into the measurement process we now know as accounting?

2 What is the primary informational need of managers? How do the needs of creditors and owners differ from those of management?

3 Accounting measurements are based on past, present, and future exchange transactions. Give an example of accounting measurement based on each kind of transaction.

4 Explain what is meant by the expression "trade-off between *reliability* and *relevance*" in connection with the preparation of financial statements.

5 Barker Company has at the end of the current period an inventory of merchandise which cost $500,000. It would cost $600,000 to replace this inventory, and it is estimated that the goods will probably be sold for a total of $700,000. If the firm were to terminate operations immediately, the inventory could probably be sold for $480,000. Discuss the relative reliability and relevance of each of these dollar measurements of the ending inventory.

6 Differentiate between *assumptions* of accounting and *accounting principles.*

7 Why is it necessary for accountants to assume the existence of a clearly defined accounting entity?

8 If the going-concern assumption were dropped, there would be no point in having current asset and current liability classifications in the balance sheet. Explain.

9 "The matching of costs and revenues is the natural extension of the fiscal period assumption." Evaluate this statement.

10 Define *objectivity, consistency, materiality,* and *conservatism.*

11 Is the assumption that the dollar is a stable unit of measure realistic? What alternative procedure would you suggest?

12 a Why is it important that any change in accounting procedures from one period to the next be disclosed?
   b Does the concept of consistency mean that all companies in a given industry follow similar accounting procedures?

13 Briefly define the concept of *disclosure.* List five examples of information that should be disclosed in financial statements or in notes accompanying the statements.

14 In the phrase "generally accepted accounting principles," what determines general acceptability? Name three authoritative bodies that exercise influence over the development of accounting principles.

15 List four stages of the productive process which might become the accountant's basis for recognizing changes in the value of a firm's output. Which stage is most commonly used as a basis for revenue recognition? Why?

16 The CAs standard audit opinion consists of two major paragraphs. Describe the essential content of each paragraph.

17 Define *monetary assets* and indicate whether a gain or loss results from the holding of such assets during a period of rising prices.

18 Why is it advantageous to be in debt during an inflationary period?

19 Evaluate the following statement: "During a period of rising prices, the conventional income statement overstates net income because the amount of depreciation recorded is less than the value of the service potential of assets consumed."

20 In presenting financial information to their stockholders and the public, it is not generally acceptable practice for corporations to report in *common dollar* terms, although such statements are occasionally presented in addition to regular financial statements as supplementary information. Why has the use of common dollars in financial reporting not gained general acceptance?

21 An increasing number of companies include in their annual report a description of the accounting principles followed in the preparation of their financial statements. What advantages do you see in this practice?

EXERCISES

Ex. 14-1 For each situation described below, indicate the concept (or concepts) of accounting that is violated, if any. You may choose among the following concepts: Conservatism, consistency, disclosure, entity, going concern, matching, materiality, objectivity.

Situations
a The assets of a partnership are combined with the separate assets of the partners in preparing a balance sheet.
b The estimated salvage value of equipment is reported in the balance sheet; book value exceeds salvage value.
c The cost of merchandise purchased is recognized as expense before it is sold in order to report a less favorable financial position.
d Plans to dispose of a major segment of the business are not communicated to readers of the balance sheet.
e A portion of the cost of a major television promotional campaign in the month of May is deferred and arbitrarily allocated to revenue over a five-year period.
f The method of depreciation is changed every two years and the change is disclosed in financial statements.

Ex. 14-2 The Pittman Corporation Ltd. recognizes the profit on a long-term construction project as work progresses. From the information given below, compute the profit that should be recognized each year, assuming that the original cost estimate on the contract was $500,000 and that the contract price is $600,000:

Year	Costs Incurred	Profit Considered Realized
1	$120,000	$?
2	300,000	?
3	76,190	?
Totals	$496,190	$103,810

Ex. 14-3 On September 15, Year 1, Robert Hamilton sold a piece of property which cost him $24,000 for $40,000, net of commissions and other selling expenses. The terms of sale were as follows: Down payment, $4,000; balance, $1,500 on the fifteenth day of each month for 24 months, starting October 15, Year 1. Compute the gross profit to be recognized by Hamilton in Year 1, Year 2, and Year 3 (*a*) on the *accrual basis* of accounting and (*b*) on the *installment basis* of accounting.

Ex. 14-4 Three companies started business with $100,000 at the beginning of the current year when the general price index stood at 120. The First Company invested the money in a note receivable due in four years; the Second Company invested its cash in land; and the Third Company purchased a building for $500,000, assuming a liability for the unpaid balance of $300,000. The price level stood at 130 at the end of the year. Compute the purchasing power gain or loss for each company during the year.

Ex. 14-5 In Year 1, the New Company Ltd. was started with a total capitalization of $5 million in order to acquire land for long-term investment. At this time, the general price index was 100. In Year 5, the general price index stands at 140 but the price of all land in the area in which the New Company invested has doubled in value. Rental receipts for grazing and farming during the five-year period were sufficient to pay all carrying charges on the land.

    a What is the purchasing power gain or loss for the New Company Ltd. during the five-year period?

    b What is the "economic" gain or loss during this period?

Ex. 14-6 The following information relating to the latest fiscal year is available for Joe's Twine Shop, a single proprietorship:

	Balance, Jan. 1	Cash Receipts or (Payments)	Balance, Dec. 31
Accounts receivable—sale of merchandise . . .	$15,500	$200,000	$20,500
Accounts payable	9,750	(88,200)	10,200
Prepaid supplies balance (or paid)	1,360	(4,900)	800
Merchandise inventories	20,000		23,600
Operating expenses, excluding supplies, accrued (or paid)	2,500	(39,000)	4,000

Compute the net income for the year:

a On a *cash basis,* showing only cash receipts and disbursements.

b On an *accrual basis,* as required by generally accepted accounting principles.

PROBLEMS

Group A

14A-1 In each of the situations described below, the question is whether generally accepted accounting principles have been violated. In each case state the accounting principle or concept, if any, that has been violated and explain briefly the nature of the violation. If you believe the treatment *is in accord with generally accepted accounting principles,* state this as your position and briefly defend it.

    a Merchandise inventory which cost $2 million is reported in the balance sheet at $3 million, the expected sales price less estimated direct selling expenses.

b New Mining Company Ltd. reports net income for the current year of $1,300,010. In the audit report the auditors stated: "We certify that the results of operations shown in the income statement are a true and accurate portrayal of the company's operations for the current year."

c The Mundie Company has purchased a computer for $1.5 million. The company expects to use the computer for five years, at which time it will acquire a larger and faster computer. The new computer is expected to cost $3.5 million. During the current year the company debited $700,000 to the Depreciation Expense account to "provide for one-fifth of the estimated cost of the new computer."

d John Lucky operates a mine as a single proprietorship. During the current year, geologists and engineers revised upward the estimated value of ore deposits on his property. Lucky instructed his accountant to record goodwill of $2 million, the estimated value of unmined ore in excess of previous estimates. The offsetting credit was made to John Lucky, Capital.

e The Rex Oil Company reported on its balance sheet the total of all wages, supplies, depreciation on equipment, and other costs related to the drilling of a producing oil well as an intangible asset, and then amortized this asset as oil was produced from the well.

14A-2 Community Market sells its product on open account due 90 days after the date of sale. The company pays a commission of 10% of selling price to its salesmen as soon as the customers pay their accounts.

During the first three years of operations, the company reported sales on a cash basis; that is, it did not record the sale until the cash was collected. Commissions to salesmen were recorded only when cash was collected from customers. Net income figures computed on this basis were:

Year 1	$20,000
Year 2	30,000
Year 3	45,000

An accountant, called in at the end of Year 3 to review the store's accounting system, suggested that a better picture of earnings would be obtained if both sales and commissions were recorded on the accrual basis. After analyzing the company's records, he reported that accounts receivable at the end of each year were as follows:

Year 1	$15,000
Year 2	24,000
Year 3	11,000

Sales commissions should be accrued at the rate of 10% of accounts receivable.

Instructions

a On the basis of this information, prepare a schedule showing the amount of net income Community Market would have reported in each of the three years if it had followed accrual accounting for its sales and sales commissions.

b Comment on the differences in net income under the two methods and the significance of the trend in the net income figures as revised.

14A-3 James R. Early had substantial income from many sources. He instructed his accountant to prepare the income statement for his business, the Early Construction & Sales Company, on the most conservative basis possible in order to minimize demands from his wife that he increase his drawings from the business. Following his instruction, the accountant prepared the following income statement:

EARLY CONSTRUCTION & SALES COMPANY
Income Statement
First Year of Operations

Revenues:

Sales—regular	$105,000	
Collections on installment sales	150,000	
Construction work completed.	45,000	
Total revenues.		$300,000

Costs and expenses:

Cost of goods sold—regular	$ 84,000	
Cost of goods sold—installment basis, 80% of collections . .	120,000	
Cost of construction work completed.	36,500	
Operating expenses.	60,000	
Interest expense.	24,500	
Total costs and expenses.		325,000
Loss for first year of operations		$(25,000)

Early was pleased to know that he will be able to reduce his other taxable income as a result of the loss from his business. He was, however, concerned because his banker refused to lend him $50,000 for use in his business because, as the banker put it, "You've lost too much money in your first year of operations and I have a policy against lending money to unprofitable businesses." At this point, Early comes to you for advice and gives you additional information relating to the items appearing in the income statement. After reviewing this information, you suggest that the following changes be made:

(1) Installment sales amounted to $325,000; the cost of the goods was $260,000, or 80% of sales. The accountant reported only the cash collections as revenue and deducted a proportional amount as the cost of the goods sold on the installment basis. You recommend that the entire income on installment sales be included in the income statement.

(2) The revenue and cost of construction work include three contracts started and completed in the first year. In addition, the following data relate to the six contracts started in the first year which will be completed in the following year:

Total contract price	$540,000
Total estimated cost of contracts	450,000
Actual costs incurred in first year.	150,000

You suggest that profit on these contracts be recognized on the percentage-of-completion basis.

(3) The ending inventory of goods to be sold on the regular basis was valued on the lifo basis at $25,500; this inventory on a fifo basis would have been $28,000. You propose that the first-in, first-out method be used in preparing the income statement to be resubmitted to the banker.

(4) Included in operating expense is depreciation of $8,000, computed by using an accelerated method. You recommend the use of the straight-line depreciation method, which would result in depreciation of only $6,000.

(5) Also included in operating expenses is $15,000 of expenditures which are applicable to future periods. You suggest that these items be deferred and reported in the balance sheet as assets.

Instructions
Prepare a revised income statement for the Early Construction & Sales Company, giving effect to the changes in accounting you suggested to Early. (Ignore income taxes.)

14A-4 Edward Bilder began business early in Year 1 with $25 million in cash. He was the successful bidder on the construction of a section of highway. The bid price of the construction was $30 million. The construction will begin in Year 1 and will take two years to complete; the deadline for completion is near the end of Year 2.

The contract calls for payments of $6 million per year to Edward Bilder at the end of Year 1 and at the end of each of the next four years. Bilder expects that construction costs will total $25 million, of which $10 million will be incurred in Year 1 and $15 million in Year 2.

Bilder's accountant recognizes that there are a number of ways he might account for this contract. He might recognize income at the time the contract is completed (sales method), near the end of Year 2. Alternatively, he might recognize income during construction (production method), in proportion to the percentage of the total cost incurred in each of Years 1 and 2. Finally, he might recognize income in proportion to the percentage of the total contract price collected in installment receipts during the five-year period (installment method).

Instructions
a Assuming that the timing and cost of construction are exactly according to plan and that this contract is Bilder's sole activity during the five-year period beginning with Year 1, prepare a comparative five-year statement (in millions of dollars) showing the amount of annual net income that would be reported each year and the balance in Bilder's capital account (net assets) at the end of each year under each of the accounting methods considered by Bilder's accountant. (Ignore income taxes.)
b Prepare comparative balance sheets (in millions of dollars) for Edward Bilder as of the end of Year 1 and Year 2, under each of the three accounting methods.
c Explain how the measurement of Bilder's capital (net assets) and the recognition of net income are related under each of the three accounting methods.

Group B

14B-1 In each of the situations described below, the question is whether generally accepted accounting principles have been properly observed. In each case state the accounting principle or concept, if any, that has been violated and explain briefly the nature of the violation. If you believe the treatment *is in accord with generally accepted accounting principles,* state this as your position and defend it.
a For a number of years the Ice Maid Company used the declining-balance method of depreciation both on its financial accounting records and in its income tax returns. During the current year the company decided to employ the straight-line method of depreciation in its accounting records but to continue to use the declining-balance method for income tax purposes.
b During the current year the Beamer Company adopted a policy of charging purchases of small tools (unit cost less than $100) to expense as soon as they were acquired. In prior years the company had carried an asset account Small Tools which it had depreciated at the rate of 10% of the book value at the beginning of each year. The balance in the Small Tools account represented about 1% of the company's total plant and equipment, and depreciation on small tools was 0.4% of sales revenues. It is expected that purchases of small tools each year will run about the same as the depreciation that would be taken on these small tools.

c Idaho Company printed a large mail-order catalog in July of each year, at a cost of $1.8 million. Customers ordered from this catalog throughout the year and the company agreed to maintain the catalog prices for 12 months after the date of issue. The controller charged the entire cost of the catalog to Advertising Expense in August when it was issued. The Idaho Company's fiscal year ends on January 31 of each year. In defending his policy, the controller stated, "Once those catalogs are mailed they are gone. We could never get a nickel out of them."

14B-2 The Health Spa opened for business early in Year 1 in a large eastern city. Its program of weight reduction and body building was received with great enthusiasm and by June of Year 1 it was selling franchises to independent businessmen (franchisees) throughout Canada.

A franchise contract is sold for $10,000, payable $1,000 down and $3,000 per year, commencing one year after the contract is sold, assuming that the franchisee is still in business and servicing his customers. Even though the Health Spa must provide considerable services to the franchisees for at least three years, its management records the sale of a franchise as follows:

Cash	1,000
Accounts Receivable from Franchise Sales	9,000
Revenue from Franchise Sales	10,000

Information relating to franchise sales during the first three years of operations is given below:

	Year 1	Year 2	Year 3
Number of franchises sold	50	80	40
Number of franchises going out of business	5	10	20
Cash collected from franchisees	$ 50,000	$215,000	$385,000
Revenue recorded as realized	500,000	800,000	400,000
Accounts written off as uncollectible	45,000	69,000*	102,000†
Operating expenses related directly to franchise sales	15,000	31,000	48,000

* Three @ $9,000 and 7 @ $6,000 = $69,000.
† Four @ $9,000, 6 @ $6,000, and 10 @ $3,000 = $102,000.

All franchisees still in business make payments to the Health Spa shortly after the payments become due.

Instructions
a Prepare a schedule summarizing the Health Spa's income from franchise sales as reported by the company (before income taxes) for the first three years of operations. Comment briefly on the propriety of the company's accounting policy.
b Prepare a schedule summarizing the Health Spa's income from the franchise sales (before income taxes), assuming that the revenue from franchise sales is reported on a cash basis, as would be required under generally accepted accounting procedures because the Health Spa "must provide considerable services to the franchisees for at least three years." Comment briefly on the propriety of this accounting procedure.

14B-3 The information below is given to you by the owner of the Hobby Shop (a single proprietorship) for the current year:

Sales (net of returns and allowances).	$400,000
Cost of goods purchased for resale (net)	270,000
Inventory at Jan. 1 (at selling price).	50,000
Inventory at Dec. 31 (at selling price), replacement cost $58,000.	100,000
Cash payments for operating expenses, including prepayments	60,000
Estimated profit on sales orders for goods not yet delivered to customers . .	12,100
Depreciation expense based on actual cost	10,000
Depreciation expense based on current replacement cost	15,000
Increase in prepaid expenses during the year	300
Estimated uncollectible accounts receivable at end of year	1,100
Increase in accrued expenses during the year	1,500
Increase in goodwill (value of the business) during the year.	25,000
Net purchasing power gain resulting from increase in	
general price level during the year	4,200

The gross profit on sales is constant on all items normally included in inventory.

Instructions
a Prepare a schedule computing the relationship between the sales value and the cost of the merchandise handled by the Hobby Shop during the current year.
b Prepare an income statement for the current year in accordance with generally accepted accounting principles. Ending inventory is to be valued at the lower of cost or market. Indicate the proper disposition of any item not used in preparing the income statement.

14B-4 On January 2, Year 1, Joseph Logan started a consulting practice using the business name of Research Associates. He rented a small building for $1,000 per month and invested $50,000 of his savings in the business. At the end of Year 1, having kept only cash receipts and disbursements records during the year, Logan prepared the following financial statements:

RESEARCH ASSOCIATES

Income Statement

Year 1

Cash received for consulting services		$195,000
Salaries and payroll taxes	$126,200	
Rent expense	13,000	
Travel expense	28,500	
Office expense	27,000	
Miscellaneous expense.	15,300	210,000
Net loss for the year		$(15,000)

RESEARCH ASSOCIATES

Balance Sheet

December 31, Year 1

Assets

Cash	$ 8,000
Office equipment.	27,000
Total assets	$35,000

Capital

Joseph Logan, capital [$50,000 − $15,000 (net loss for the year)]	$35,000

Logan was understandably discouraged by his first year's results. Before deciding whether to disband his operations, he asks you to go over his records and review the situation with him. You make the following notes as a result of your investigation:

(1) Office equipment was purchased on January 2, Year 1. Logan paid cash of $27,000 and signed a $20,000, 8% note. The note, along with interest of $2,400, is payable on July 2, Year 2. The equipment has an average service life of 10 years and a salvage value of $3,000 (straight-line depreciation).

(2) Accounts receivable from clients at the end of Year 1 total $30,000, of which $600 is in dispute and is probably not collectible.

(3) Three research projects are in progress at the end of Year 1, on which no billings have yet been made to clients. Memorandum records indicate that the following direct charges relate to these projects and should be deferred: Salaries and payroll taxes, $12,000; travel, $2,800; miscellaneous, $2,200.

(4) Rent on the building for one month ($1,000) has been prepaid at December 31.

(5) At December 31, Logan owed $1,500 to the Ace Travel Bureau and $500 to various creditors who furnished office supplies.

(6) Office supplies on hand at December 31, $3,500. Insurance premiums paid during Year 1 amounted to $2,400, of which $900 is applicable to Year 2. Premiums paid were recorded in the Miscellaneous Expense account.

(7) Accrued but unpaid salaries and payroll taxes at December 31, $12,500.

Instructions

a On the basis of your notes, prepare a revised balance sheet as of the end of Year 1 and an income statement for the year in accordance with generally accepted accounting principles. Use an eight-column work sheet to revise Logan's figures and compile the necessary account balances for the statements. The following column headings are suggested: Unadjusted Balances, Adjustments, Income Statement, and Balance Sheet.

b Write a letter to Logan commenting on the results of his first year of operations as restated, including the rate of earnings (if any) on his investment of $50,000.

BUSINESS DECISION PROBLEM 14

For many years, John Lee used the lifo method of inventory valuation and a declining-balance method of depreciation in measuring the net income of his mail order business. In addition, he charged off all costs of catalogs as incurred. In Year 10, he changed his inventory pricing method to fifo, adopted the straight-line method of depreciation, and decided to charge off catalog costs only as catalogs are distributed to potential customers.

The following information for the last three years is taken from Lee's records:

	Year 10	Year 9	Year 8
Sales (net).............................	$500,000	$400,000	$350,000
Purchases (net)	300,000	220,000	200,000
Ending inventory—fifo.................	50,000	45,000	40,000
Ending inventory—lifo.................	30,000	28,000	25,000
Depreciation—declining-balance method	27,500	30,000	35,000
Depreciation—straight-line method	20,000	20,000	20,000
Operating expenses other than depreciation....	120,500	93,000	80,000
Catalog costs included in operating expenses but considered applicable to future revenues ..	18,500	8,000	5,000
Net income as computed by Lee	100,000	60,000	37,000

At the end of Year 10, Lee prepared the following comparative income statement and presented it to his banker:

JOHN LEE
Comparative Income Statement
For Years Ended December 31

	Year 10	Year 9
Sales (net).....................................	$500,000	$400,000
Cost of goods sold*.............................	278,000	217,000
Gross profit on sales	$222,000	$183,000
Operating expenses	122,000	123,000
Net income	$100,000	$ 60,000

* Based on lifo inventory method in Year 9; inventory at end of Year 10 was valued on fifo basis.

The loan officer for the Unity Bank of Canada, where Lee has applied for a loan, asks you to help him decide whether to lend the money to Lee.

Instructions
a Prepare a detailed explanation of the way Lee computed the income statement for Year 10, and briefly evaluate his approach.
b Determine whether Lee's net income has, in fact, increased in Year 10, and recommend whether the comparative income statement for Years 9 and 10 should be prepared (1) on the same accounting basis as in prior years, or (2) on the revised accounting basis. You should prepare a comparative income statement both ways and indicate which approach is more appropriate.

FIFTEEN

PARTNERSHIPS

Three types of business organization are common to Canadian business: the single proprietorship, the partnership, and the corporation. In this chapter we shall concentrate on the accounting problems peculiar to a partnership. A partnership is defined as "an association of two or more persons to carry on, as co-owners, a business for profit."[1]

Reasons for formation of partnerships

In the professions and in businesses which stress the factor of personal service, the partnership form of organization is widely used. The rules of professional conduct may even deny the incorporation privilege to persons engaged in such professions as medicine, law, and public accounting, because the personal responsibility of the professional practitioner to his client might be lost behind the impersonal legal entity of the corporation. However, in recent years some provinces have had under consideration legislation extending the privilege of incorporation to professional firms. In the fields of manufacturing, wholesaling, and retail trade, partnerships are also popular, because they afford a means of combining the capital and abilities of two or more persons. Perhaps the most common factor which impels a businessman to seek a partner is the lack of sufficient capital of his own to carry on a business. A partnership is customarily referred to as a *firm;* the name of the firm often includes the word "company" as, for example, "Adams, Barnes, and Company."

Significant features of a partnership

Before taking up the accounting problems peculiar to partnerships, it will be helpful to consider briefly some of the distinctive characteristics of the partnership form of organization. These characteristics (such as

[1] A more precise definition taken from the Partnership Act (British Columbia) is as follows: "(1) Partnership is the relation which subsists between persons carrying on business in common with a view of profit. (2) But the relation between members of any company or association which is—(a) Incorporated under the provisions of any Act of the Legislature . . . relating to the incorporation of joint-stock companies, or licensed or registered under the provision of any such Act relating to the licensing or registration of extra-provincial companies; or (b) Formed or incorporated by or in pursuance of any other Statute or Letters Patent or Royal Charter,—is not a partnership within the meaning of this Act." The definition of partnership is similar in the Partnership Act of each of the other provinces. (Quebec does not have a Partnership Act. Partnerships in that province are governed by the Civil Code which, in respect to partnership law, is based largely on Common Law.)

limited life and unlimited liability) all stem from the basic point that a partnership is not a separate legal entity in itself but merely a voluntary association of individuals.

EASE OF FORMATION A partnership can be created with few legal formalities. When two persons agree to become partners, a partnership is automatically created. The voluntary aspect of a partnership agreement means that no one can be forced into a partnership or forced to continue as a partner.

LIMITED LIFE A partnership may be ended at any time by the death or withdrawal of any member of the firm. Other factors which may bring an end to a partnership include the bankruptcy or incapacity of a partner, the expiration of the period specified in the partnership contract, or the completion of the project for which the partnership was formed. The admission of a new partner or the retirement of an existing member means an end to the old partnership, although the business may be continued by the formation of a new partnership.

MUTUAL AGENCY Each partner acts as an agent of the partnership, with authority to enter into contracts for the purchase and sale of goods and services. The partnership is bound by the acts of any partner as long as these acts are within the scope of normal operations. The factor of mutual agency suggests the need for exercising great caution in the selection of a partner. To be in partnership with an irresponsible person or one lacking in integrity is an intolerable situation.

UNLIMITED LIABILITY Each partner is personally responsible for all the debts of the firm. The lack of any ceiling on the liability of a partner may deter a wealthy person from entering a partnership.

When a new member joins an existing partnership, he may or may not assume liability for debts incurred by the firm prior to his admission. When a partner withdraws from membership, he must give adequate public notice of his withdrawal; otherwise, he may be held liable for partnership debts incurred subsequent to his withdrawal. The retiring partner remains liable for partnership debts existing at the time of his withdrawal unless the creditors agree to release him.

CO-OWNERSHIP OF PARTNERSHIP PROPERTY AND PROFITS When a partner invests a building, inventory, or other property in a partnership, he does not retain any personal right to the assets contributed. The property becomes jointly owned by all partners. Each member of a partnership also has an ownership right in the profits.

Sometimes a store manager or other supervisory employee is allowed a certain percentage of the profits as a bonus, or in lieu of a fixed salary. This arrangement is merely a device for computing the bonus or salary;

it does *not* give the employee an ownership right in the profits and does not make him a partner. Some retail stores rent their buildings under an agreement calling for a yearly rental computed as a percentage of profits. This type of rental agreement does not make the landlord a partner. To be a partner one must have an *ownership* right in the profits.

Advantages and disadvantages of a partnership

Perhaps the most important advantage and the principal reason for the formation of most partnerships is the opportunity to bring together sufficient capital to carry on a business. The opportunity to combine special skills, as, for example, the specialized talents of an engineer and an accountant, may also induce individuals to join forces in a partnership. The formation of a partnership is much easier and less expensive than the organization of a corporation. Operating as a partnership may produce income tax advantages. The partnership itself is not a legal entity and does not have to pay income taxes as does a corporation, although the individual partners pay taxes on their respective shares of the firm's income. Members of a partnership enjoy more freedom and flexibility of action than do the owners of a corporation; the partners may withdraw funds and make business decisions of all types without the necessity of formal meetings or legalistic procedures.

Offsetting these advantages of a partnership are such serious disadvantages as limited life, unlimited liability, and mutual agency. Furthermore, if a business is to require a large amount of capital, the partnership is a less effective device for raising funds than is a corporation.

The partnership contract

Although a partnership can generally be formed without any written agreement, it is highly desirable that a written contract of partnership be prepared by a lawyer, setting forth the understanding between the partners on such points as the following:

1 The name, location, and nature of the business.
2 Names of the partners, and the duties and rights of each.
3 Amount to be invested by each partner. Procedure for valuing any noncash assets invested or withdrawn by partners.
4 Procedure for sharing profits and losses.
5 Withdrawals to be allowed each partner.
6 Provision for insurance on the lives of partners, with the partnership or the surviving partners named as beneficiaries.
7 The accounting period to be used.
8 Provision for periodic audit by public accountants.
9 Provision for arbitration of disputes.
10 Provision for dissolution. This part of the agreement may specify a method for computing the equity of a retiring or deceased partner and a method of settlement which will not disrupt the business.

Partnership accounting

An adequate accounting system and an accurate measurement of income are needed by every business, but they are especially important in a partnership because the net income is divided among two or more owners. Each partner needs current, accurate information on profits so that he can make intelligent decisions on such questions as additional investments, expansion of the business, or sale of his interest.

Partnership accounting requires the maintenance of a separate capital account for each partner; a separate drawing account for each partner is also desirable. The other distinctive feature of partnership accounting is the division of each year's net profit or loss among the partners in the proportions specified by the partnership agreement. In the study of partnership accounting, the new concepts lie almost entirely in the owners' equity section; accounting for partnership assets and liabilities follows the same principles as for other forms of business organization.

Opening the books

When a partner contributes assets other than cash, a question always arises as to the value of such assets; the valuations assigned to noncash assets should be their *fair market values* at the date of transfer to the partnership. The valuations assigned must be agreed to by all the partners.

To illustrate the opening entries for a newly formed partnership, assume that on January 1 John Blair and Richard Cross, who operate competing retail stores, decide to form a partnership by consolidating their two businesses. A capital account will be opened for each partner and credited with the agreed valuation of the *net assets* (total assets less total liabilities) he contributes. The journal entries to open the books of the partnership of Blair and Cross are as follows:

Entries for
formation of
partnership

Cash	20,000	
Accounts Receivable	30,000	
Inventory	45,000	
Accounts Payable		15,000
John Blair, Capital		80,000
To record the investment by John Blair in the partnership of Blair and Cross.		

Cash	5,000	
Land	30,000	
Building	50,000	
Inventory	30,000	
Accounts Payable		35,000
Richard Cross, Capital		80,000
To record the investment by Richard Cross in the partnership of Blair and Cross.		

The values assigned to assets on the books of the new partnership may be quite different from the amounts at which these assets were carried on the books of their previous owners. For example, the land contributed by Cross and valued at $30,000 might have appeared on his books at a cost of $10,000. The building which he contributed was valued at $50,000 by the partnership, but it might have cost Cross only $40,000 some years ago and might have been depreciated on his records to a net value of $30,000. Assuming that market values of land and buildings had risen sharply while Cross owned this property, it is no more than fair to recognize the present market value of these assets at the time he transfers them to the partnership and to credit his capital account accordingly. Depreciation of the building will begin anew on the partnership books and will be based on the assigned value of $50,000 at date of acquisition by the partnership.

Additional investments

Assume that after six months of operation the firm is in need of more cash, and the partners make an additional investment of $5,000 each on July 1. These additional investments are credited to the capital accounts as shown below:

Entry for additional investment

Cash	10,000	
John Blair, Capital		5,000
Richard Cross, Capital		5,000
To record additional investments.		

Drawing accounts

The drawing account maintained for each partner serves the same purpose as the drawing account of the owner of a single proprietorship. The transactions calling for debits to the drawing accounts of partners may be summarized as follows:

1 Cash or other assets withdrawn by a partner
2 Payments from partnership funds of the personal debts of a partner
3 Partnership cash collected on behalf of the firm by a partner but retained by him personally

Credits to the drawing accounts are seldom encountered; one rather unusual transaction requiring such an entry consists of the payment of a partnership liability by a partner out of his personal funds.

Loans from partners

Ordinarily any funds furnished to the firm by a partner are recorded by crediting his capital account. Occasionally, however, a partnership may be in need of funds but the partners do not wish to increase their permanent investment in the business, or perhaps one partner is willing to advance funds when the others are not. Under these circumstances, the advance of funds may be designated as a loan from the partner and credited to a partner's loan account. Partnership liabilities to outsiders always take precedence over any claims of partners.

Admission of a new partner

A partner may gain admission to the firm in either of two ways: (*1*) by buying an interest from one or more of the present partners, or (*2*) by making an investment in the partnership. When an incoming partner purchases his equity from a present member of the firm, his payment goes personally to the old partner, and there is no change in the assets or liabilities of the partnership. On the other hand, if the incoming partner acquires his equity by making an investment in the partnership, the assets of the firm are increased by the amount paid in by the new partner.

BY PURCHASE OF AN INTEREST When a new partner buys an interest from a present member of a partnership, the only change in the accounts will be a transfer from the capital account of the selling partner to the capital account of the incoming partner.

Assume, for example, that L has a $25,000 equity in the partnership of L, M, and N. Partner L arranges to sell his entire interest to X for $40,000 cash. Partners M and N agree to the admission of X, and the transaction is recorded on the partnership books by the following entry:

Incoming partner buys interest from present partner

L, Capital	25,000	
X, Capital		25,000
To record the transfer of L's equity to the incoming partner, X.		

Note that the entry on the partnership books was for $25,000, the recorded amount of Partner L's equity. *The amount of this entry was not influenced by the price paid the retiring partner by the new member.* The payment of $40,000 from X to L was a personal transaction between the two men; it did not affect the assets or liabilities of the partnership and is therefore not entered on the partnership books.

As a separate but related example, assume that X is to gain admission to the firm of L, M, and N by purchasing one-fourth of the equity of each partner. The present capital accounts are as follows: Partner L, $40,000; Partner M, $40,000; and Partner N, $40,000. The payments by the incoming partner X are to go to the old partners personally and not to the partnership. The only entry required is the following:

No change in total capital

L, Capital	10,000	
M, Capital	10,000	
N, Capital	10,000	
X, Capital		30,000
To record admission of X to a one-fourth interest in the firm by purchase of one-fourth of the equity of each of the old partners.		

BY AN INVESTMENT IN THE FIRM When an incoming partner acquires his equity by making an investment in the firm, his payment increases the partnership assets and also the total owners' equity of the firm. As an example, assume that D. E. Phillips and J. K. Ryan are partners, each having a capital account of $50,000. They agree to admit B. C. Smith to a one-half interest in the business upon his investment of $100,000 in cash. The entry to record the admission of Smith would be as follows:

Investment	*Cash*	*100,000*	
in business	*B. C. Smith, Capital*		*100,000*
by new		
partner	*To record the admission of B. C. Smith to a one-half interest in*	
	the firm.	

Although Smith has a one-half equity in the net assets of the new firm of Phillips, Ryan, and Smith, he is not necessarily entitled to receive one-half of the profits. Profit sharing is a matter for agreement among the partners; if the new partnership contract contains no mention of profit sharing, the assumption is that the three partners intended to share profits and losses equally.

ALLOWANCE OF A BONUS TO FORMER PARTNERS If an existing partnership has exceptionally high earnings year after year, the present partners may demand a *bonus* as a condition for admission of a new partner. In other words, to acquire an interest of, say, $40,000, the incoming partner may be required to invest $60,000 in the partnership. The excess investment of $20,000 may be regarded as a bonus to the old partners and credited to their capital accounts in the established ratio for profit sharing.

To illustrate the recording of a bonus to the old partners, let us assume that James Rogers and Richard Steel are members of a highly successful partnership. As a result of profitable operations, the partners' capital accounts have doubled within a few years and presently stand at $50,000 each. David Taylor desires to join the firm and offers to invest $50,000 for a one-third interest. Rogers and Steel refuse this offer but extend a counteroffer to Taylor of $60,000 for a one-fourth interest in the capital of the firm and a one-fourth interest in profits. Taylor accepts these terms because of his desire to share in the unusually large profits of the business. The recording of Taylor's admission to partnership is based on the following calculations:

Calculation	*Net assets (owners' equity) of old partnership*	*$100,000*
of bonus to	*Cash investment by Taylor*	*60,000*
old partners	*Net assets (owners' equity) of new partnership*	*$160,000*
	Taylor's one-fourth interest	*$ 40,000*

To acquire an interest of $40,000 in the net assets of $160,000, Taylor has invested $60,000. His excess investment or bonus of $20,000 will be divided equally between Rogers and Steel, since their partnership agreement called for equal sharing of profits and losses.

The entry to record Taylor's admission to partnership is as follows:

Recording	*Cash*	*60,000*	
bonus to old partners	*David Taylor, Capital*		*40,000*
	James Rogers, Capital		*10,000*
	Richard Steel, Capital		*10,000*
	To record admission of David Taylor as a partner with a one-fourth interest in capital and profits.		

RECORDING GOODWILL OF THE OLD PARTNERSHIP An alternative method of handling Taylor's investment in the partnership is to say that the old partnership possesses *goodwill* and to record goodwill in the accounts at a value based on the investment by Taylor of $60,000 for a one-fourth interest in the business.

To illustrate the recording of goodwill upon the admission of a partner, let us refer to the Rogers and Steel partnership example. Rogers and Steel are partners each having a capital of $50,000. They agree to admit Taylor as a partner with a one-fourth interest in capital and profits upon his investing $60,000. If a one-fourth interest in the business is worth $60,000, the entire business must be worth four times as much, or $240,000. The amount of goodwill to be recognized may be computed as follows:

Goodwill in-	*Investment by Taylor for a one-fourth interest in capital*		*$ 60,000*
dicated by price to new	*Indicated value of the net assets of the business ($60,000 × 4)*		*$240,000*
partner	*Net assets of the business before recording goodwill:*		
	Capital of old partners ($50,000 each)	*$100,000*	
	Investment by new partner	*60,000*	*160,000*
	Goodwill		*$ 80,000*

The sale of a one-fourth interest to Taylor for $60,000 indicated that the net assets of the entire business were worth $240,000. Since the tangible net assets (including Taylor's cash investment of $60,000) total only $160,000, the difference of $80,000 must be the intangible asset of goodwill. The journal entries to record Taylor's admission with goodwill being recognized are as follows:

Entries for	*Cash*	*60,000*	
investment and	*David Taylor, Capital*		*60,000*
indicated	*Investment by new partner for a one-fourth interest in the firm.*		
goodwill	*Goodwill*	*80,000*	
	James Rogers, Capital		*40,000*
	Richard Steel, Capital		*40,000*
	To bring on the books the goodwill indicated to exist by new partner's investment of $60,000 for a one-fourth interest.		

Using the goodwill method of handling the excess investment by the new partner causes the capital accounts of all three partners to be larger than if the bonus method had been used. The capital accounts are larger because the recorded assets have been increased by entering goodwill on the books. The recording of a journal entry to bring goodwill on the books as an asset does not make the business any more valuable. It is the existence of goodwill, and not the act of recording it on the books, that gives value to a business. The price that Taylor was willing to pay is evidence that unrecorded goodwill existed in the business at that time.

Many businessmen prefer to use the bonus method, because the presence of a large amount of goodwill on the balance sheet may create a skeptical attitude on the part of some readers of the financial statements. Bankers, financial analysts, and other informed users of financial statements know that many highly successful companies possess goodwill even though it is not listed on their balance sheets. Consequently, the company that does include a large amount of goodwill among the assets on its balance sheet may arouse an unfavorable reaction; readers of the statement may feel that the company is trying to exaggerate its size and financial strength.

The following schedule affords a comparison of the results from the two alternative methods of recording a new partner's investment when he pays a premium to gain admission to the firm:

	Bonus Method		Goodwill Method	
	Amount	Fractional Interest	Amount	Fractional Interest
James Rogers, Capital	$ 60,000	$\frac{3}{8}$	$ 90,000	$\frac{3}{8}$
Richard Steel, Capital	60,000	$\frac{3}{8}$	90,000	$\frac{3}{8}$
David Taylor, Capital	40,000	$\frac{2}{8}$	60,000	$\frac{2}{8}$
Totals	$160,000	$\frac{8}{8}$	$240,000	$\frac{8}{8}$

Bonus method versus goodwill method

ALLOWING GOODWILL TO NEW PARTNER A new partner may be the owner of a profitable business of his own which he contributes to the partnership rather than investing cash. Assume, for example, that William Jones and Robert Brown are partners, each having a capital account of $40,000. In order to induce Henry Smith, the owner of a very profitable competing business, to enter partnership with them, they agree to allow Smith goodwill of $10,000. The tangible assets of Smith's business which will be brought into the partnership are valued at $30,000. This amount represents the present fair market value of Smith's assets, not necessarily the carrying value on his books. All three partners in the new firm of Jones, Brown, and Smith are to have equal interests in the business. The entry to record Smith's admission to the firm would be as follows:

<table>
<tr><td>*New partner*
may con-
tribute
goodwill</td><td>Goodwill ....</td><td>10,000</td><td></td></tr>
</table>

New partner may con- tribute goodwill	Goodwill	10,000	
	Various Tangible Assets	30,000	
	Henry Smith, Capital		40,000

To record admission of Smith to a one-third interest upon contribution of various tangible assets and goodwill.

ALLOWING A BONUS TO NEW PARTNER An existing partnership may sometimes be very anxious to bring in a new partner who can bring needed cash to the firm. In other instances the new partner may be a man of extraordinary ability or possessed of advantageous business contacts that will presumably add to the profitability of the partnership. Under either of these sets of circumstances, the old partners may offer the new member a bonus in the form of a capital account larger than the amount of his investment.

Assume, for example, that A. M. Bryan and R. G. Davis are equal partners, each having a capital account of $18,000. Since the firm is in desperate need of cash, they offer to admit K. L. Grant to a one-third interest in the firm upon his investment of only $12,000 in cash. The amounts of the capital accounts for the three members of the new firm are computed as follows:

Total capital of old partnership:
A. M. Bryan, capital .	$18,000	
R. G. Davis, capital .	18,000	$36,000
Cash invested by K. L. Grant .		12,000
Total capital of new three-man partnership .		$48,000

Capital of each partner in the new firm:
A. M. Bryan ($48,000 × $\frac{1}{3}$) .	$16,000	
R. G. Davis ($48,000 × $\frac{1}{3}$) .	16,000	
K. L. Grant ($48,000 × $\frac{1}{3}$) .	16,000	48,000

The following journal entry records the admission of Grant to a one-third interest in the business and also adjusts each capital account to the required level of $16,000.

Entry for bonus to new partner	Cash	12,000	
	A. M. Bryan, Capital .	2,000	
	R. G. Davis, Capital .	2,000	
	K. L. Grant, Capital .		16,000

To record admission of Grant to a one-third interest, and the allowance of a bonus to him.

In this illustration, the bonus to the new partner is more appropriate than allowing him goodwill, because no evidence of superior earning power exists. In fact, the firm's desperate need of cash and the willingness of the old partners to sell a one-third investment in the business at less than book value suggest that the total value of the old partnership may be less than indicated on the books.

Closing the books of a partnership

At the end of the accounting period, the balance in the Income Summary account is closed to the partners' capital accounts, in accordance with the profit-sharing provisions of the partnership contract. If there is no agreement to the contrary, the law assumes that the intention of the partners was for an equal division of profits and losses. If the partnership agreement specifies a method of dividing profits but does not mention the possibility of losses, any losses are divided in the proportions provided for sharing profits.

In the previous illustration of the firm of Blair and Cross, an equal sharing of profits was agreed upon. Assuming that a profit of $30,000 was realized during the first year of operations, the entry to close the Income Summary account would be as follows:

Closing Income Summary: profits shared equally

Income Summary	30,000	
John Blair, Capital		15,000
Richard Cross, Capital		15,000

To divide net income for 19___ in accordance with partnership agreement to share profits equally.

The next step in closing the books is to transfer the balance of each partner's drawing account to his capital account. Assuming that withdrawals during the year amounted to $6,000 for Blair and $4,000 for Cross, the entry at December 31 to close the drawing accounts is as follows:

Closing the drawing accounts to capital accounts

John Blair, Capital	6,000	
Richard Cross, Capital	4,000	
John Blair, Drawing		6,000
Richard Cross, Drawing		4,000

To transfer debit balances in partners' drawing accounts to their respective capital accounts.

WORKING PAPERS The working papers for a partnership may include a pair of columns for each partner. These columns are placed between the Income Statement columns and the Balance Sheet columns of the work sheet. The net income or loss as shown in the Income Statement columns is also carried to the partners' capital columns and allocated between them as provided in the partnership agreement. In all other aspects, the working papers for a partnership are identical to those for a single proprietorship as illustrated in Chapters 4 and 5.

INCOME STATEMENT FOR A PARTNERSHIP The income statement for a partnership differs from that of a single proprietorship in only one respect:

a final section may be added to show the division of the net income between the partners, as illustrated on this page for the firm of Blair and Cross.

BLAIR AND CROSS

Income Statement

For the Year Ended December 31, 19___

Note distri-	Sales		$300,000
bution of	Cost of goods sold:		
net income	Inventory, Jan. 1	$ 75,000	
	Purchases	155,000	
	Cost of goods available for sale	$230,000	
	Less: Inventory, Dec. 31	100,000	
	Cost of goods sold		130,000
	Gross profit on sales		$170,000
	Operating expenses:		
	Selling expenses	$100,000	
	General & administrative expenses	40,000	140,000
	Net income		$ 30,000
	Distribution of net income:		
	To John Blair (50%)	$ 15,000	
	To Richard Cross (50%)	15,000	$ 30,000

STATEMENT OF PARTNERS' CAPITALS   The partners will usually want an explanation of the change in their capital accounts from one year-end to the next. A supplementary schedule called a *statement of partners' capitals* is prepared to show this information.

BLAIR AND CROSS

Statement of Partners' Capitals

For the Year Ended December 31, 19___

		Blair	Cross	Total
Changes in	Investment, Jan. 1, 19___	$ 80,000	$ 80,000	$160,000
capital ac-	Add: Additional investment	5,000	5,000	10,000
counts dur-	Net income for the year	15,000	15,000	30,000
ing the year	Subtotals	$100,000	$100,000	$200,000
	Less: Drawings	6,000	4,000	10,000
	Balances, Dec. 31, 19___	$ 94,000	$ 96,000	$190,000

The balance sheet for Blair and Cross would show the capital balance for each partner, as well as the total of $190,000.

Partnership profits and income taxes

Partnerships are not required to pay income taxes. Each partner must include his share of the partnership profit on his individual income tax return. Partnership net income is thus taxable to the partners individually in the year in which it is earned. In the partnership of Blair and Cross illustrated above, each would report and pay tax on $15,000 of partnership net income.

Note that partners report and pay tax on their respective shares of the profits earned by the partnership during the year and not on the amount which they have drawn out of the business during the year. The entire net income of the partnership is taxable to the partners each year, even though there may have been no withdrawals. This treatment is consistent with that accorded a single proprietorship.

The nature of partnership profits

The profit earned by a partnership, like that of a single proprietorship, may be regarded as consisting of three distinct elements: (1) compensation for the personal services rendered by the partners, (2) compensation (interest) for the use of invested capital, and (3) a "pure" profit or reward for the entrepreneurial functions of risk taking and policy making. Recognition of these three elements of partnership profits will be helpful in formulating an equitable plan for the division of profits.

If one partner devotes full time to the business while another does not participate actively, the profit-sharing plan should give weight to this disparity in contributions of services. Any salaries authorized for partners *are regarded as a preliminary step in the division of profits, not as an expense of the business.* The partner is considered an owner, not an employee. The services which he renders to the firm are, therefore, considered to be rendered in anticipation of a share in profits, not in contemplation of a salary. Another reason for not treating salaries of partners as an expense of the business is that the amounts are often set arbitrarily without the arm's-length bargaining typical of employer-employee contracts. Consequently, the salary of a partner may not be closely related to the fair market value of the personal services he renders to the business. The net profit reported by a partnership cannot be compared directly with the profit earned by a corporation of similar size, because the corporation treats as expense any payments to owner-managers for personal services rendered.

In the solution of problems in this book, the student should record all withdrawals of assets by partners as debits to the partners' drawing accounts, regardless of whether or not the withdrawals are described as salaries. Some alternative treatments of salaries of partners can be more effectively explored in advanced accounting courses.

In the preceding illustrations of the partnership of Blair and Cross, we assumed that the partners invested equal amounts of capital, rendered equal services, and divided profits equally. We are now ready to consider cases in which the partners invest unequal amounts of capital and services.

Alternative methods of dividing profits and losses

The following alternative methods of dividing profits and losses place varying degrees of emphasis on the three elements (interest, salaries, and "pure" profit) comprising partnership profits.

1 A fixed ratio

2 A capital ratio

3 Interest on capital, salaries to partners, and remaining profits in a fixed ratio

FIXED RATIO   The fixed-ratio method has already been illustrated in the example of the Blair and Cross partnership in which profits were divided equally. Partners may agree upon any fixed ratio, such as 60% and 40%, or 70% and 30%. In demonstrating the various other methods of profit sharing, the following capital accounts will be used:

	A. B. Adams, Capital			B. C. Barnes, Capital	
Capital accounts used in illustration	*19___*			*19___*	
	Jan. 1	*40,000*		*Jan. 1*	*10,000*
	July 1	*5,000*		*July 1*	*5,000*

During the first year of operations, Adams withdrew a total of $6,000 in cash and merchandise; Barnes made withdrawals of $12,000. These withdrawals were recorded by debits in the partners' drawing accounts. At year-end, the Income Summary account showed a credit balance of $24,000, representing the net income for the year, before any salaries or interest to partners.

CAPITAL RATIO   The division of profits on the basis of relative capital investments may be appropriate in a merchandising or manufacturing business if invested capital is regarded as the most important factor in the production of income. The capital ratio would generally not be a satisfactory basis for sharing profits in a partnership of professional men, such as a law firm or public accounting firm. The technical skill and professional reputations of lawyers and accountants are usually much more significant in achieving profitable operations than is the small amount of capital required to establish a professional firm. When partners agree to base their profit-sharing plan on the factor of capital invested, the question of whether to use beginning capital balances or average capital must be decided.

Ratio of beginning capitals The beginning capitals for the firm of Adams and Barnes were as follows: A. B. Adams, $40,000, and B. C. Barnes, $10,000. Adams's beginning capital constitutes 80% ($40,000/$50,000) of the total beginning capital, and Barnes's beginning capital constitutes the other 20% ($10,000/$50,000). If the partners agreed to share profits in the ratio of their beginning capitals, the division of the first year's net income of $24,000 would be computed as follows:

	Division of Profit
Profit sharing; beginning capitals as basis A. B. Adams ($24,000 × .80)	$19,200
B. C. Barnes ($24,000 × .20)	4,800
Total	$24,000

The entry to close the Income Summary account is as follows:

Income Summary	24,000	
A. B. Adams, Capital		19,200
B. C. Barnes, Capital		4,800

To close the Income Summary account by dividing the year's
net income in the ratio of the beginning capitals.

The capital accounts of Adams and Barnes in this illustration will not remain in the original 80:20 proportion for two reasons: neither the additional investments made by the partners on July 1 nor the withdrawals of cash and merchandise during the year were in the proportion of the original investments. When profits are to be divided in the ratio of "beginning capitals," the partnership agreement may provide that the ratio will be set at the first of each year on the basis of the *new capital balances,* or the agreement may provide for the original ratio to remain in force regardless of subsequent changes in capital accounts.

Ratio of average capital investments If the balances in the capital accounts change significantly during the course of a year, the partners may prefer to use the *average* capitals rather than the beginning balances as the basis for dividing profits. To compute the average capital for a partner during the year, the first step is to multiply the capital balance at the beginning of the year by the number of months until the date of a change in the capital account. Multiply the new balance in the capital account by the number of months until the next change in the account. After carrying out this procedure for the entire year, add together the amounts thus obtained. The total represents the *dollar-months* of capital invested. Each partner's share of profits is equal to the ratio of his dollar-months to the total dollar-months for all the capital accounts.

In the partnership of Adams and Barnes the beginning capitals were $40,000 and $10,000, respectively. The only change in the capital accounts occurred on July 1 when each partner invested an additional

$5,000. If we ignore the periodic withdrawals by the partners, the division of the year's profit of $24,000 would be computed as follows:

		Dollar-months
Profit sharing; average capitals as basis	*A. B. Adams:*	
	Jan. 1 to June 30 ($40,000 × 6 months)	*$240,000*
	July 1 to Dec. 31 ($45,000 × 6 months)	*270,000*
	Total	*$510,000*
	B. C. Barnes:	
	Jan. 1 to June 30 ($10,000 × 6 months)	*$ 60,000*
	July 1 to Dec. 31 ($15,000 × 6 months)	*90,000*
	Total	*$150,000*
	Total dollar-months for both partners	*$660,000*

	Division of Profit
A. B. Adams $\left(\dfrac{510,000}{660,000} \times \$24,000 \; profit\right)$	*$ 18,545*
B. C. Barnes $\left(\dfrac{150,000}{660,000} \times \$24,000 \; profit\right)$	*5,455*
Total profit divided	*$ 24,000*

The entry to close the Income Summary account is:

Income Summary	*24,000*	
A. B. Adams, Capital		*18,545*
B. C. Barnes, Capital		*5,455*

To divide the year's net income between the partners in the ratio of average capital investments.

SALARIES, INTEREST, AND REMAINDER IN A FIXED RATIO Since partners often contribute varying amounts of personal services as well as different amounts of capital, partnership agreements often provide for partners' salaries as a factor in the division of profits.

As a first example, assume that Adams and Barnes agree that Adams will be allowed an annual salary of $6,000 and Barnes an annual salary of $12,000. Any remaining profits will be divided equally. It is agreed that the salaries will be withdrawn in cash each month and recorded by debits to the drawing accounts.[2] The authorized salaries total $18,000 a year; this amount represents a first step in the division of the year's profit and is therefore subtracted from the net income of $24,000. The remaining profit of $6,000 will be divided equally.

---

[2] Salaries may be used as a device for dividing partnership net income, even though the partners do not wish to make any withdrawals of cash whatsoever. In this illustration, however, it is assumed that cash is withdrawn by each partner in an amount equal to his authorized salary.

Distribution of Net Income

Profit sharing; salaries and fixed ratio as basis	Net income to be divided.		$24,000
	Salaries to partners:		
	A. B. Adams	$ 6,000	
	B. C. Barnes	12,000	18,000
	Remaining profit, to be divided equally		$ 6,000
	A. B. Adams	$ 3,000	
	B. C. Barnes	3,000	6,000

Under this agreement, Adams's share of the $24,000 net income amounts to $9,000 ($6,000 + $3,000) and Barnes's share amounts to $15,000 ($12,000 + $3,000). The entry to close the Income Summary account would be:

Income Summary	24,000	
A. B. Adams, Capital		9,000
B. C. Barnes, Capital		15,000
To close the Income Summary account by crediting each		
partner with his authorized salary and dividing the remaining		
profits equally.		

The preceding example took into consideration the difference in the value of personal services contributed by Adams and Barnes but ignored the disparity in capital contributions. In the next example, we shall assume that the partners agree to a profit-sharing plan providing for interest on beginning capitals as well as salaries. Salaries, as before, are authorized at $6,000 for Adams and $12,000 for Barnes. Each partner is to be allowed interest at 6% on his beginning capital balance, and any remaining profit is to be divided equally.

Distribution of Net Income

Profit sharing; salaries, interest, and fixed ratio as basis	Net income to be divided.			$24,000
	Salaries to partners:			
	A. B. Adams	$ 6,000		
	B. C. Barnes	12,000	$18,000	
	Interest on invested capital:			
	A. B. Adams ($40,000 × .06)	$ 2,400		
	B. C. Barnes ($10,000 × .06)	600	3,000	21,000
	Remaining profit to be divided equally			$ 3,000
	A. B. Adams	$ 1,500		
	B. C. Barnes	1,500	3,000	

This three-step division of the year's profit of $24,000 has resulted in giving Adams a total of $9,900 and Barnes a total of $14,100. The amounts credited to each partner may be summarized as follows:

	Adams	Barnes	Together
Salaries	$6,000	$12,000	$18,000
Interest on beginning capitals	2,400	600	3,000
Remaining profit divided equally	1,500	1,500	3,000
Totals	$9,900	$14,100	$24,000

The entry to close the Income Summary account will be:

Income Summary	24,000	
A. B. Adams, Capital		9,900
B. C. Barnes, Capital		14,100

To close the Income Summary account by crediting each partner
with his authorized salary and with interest on his beginning
capital at 6%, and by dividing the remaining profits equally.

AUTHORIZED SALARIES AND INTEREST IN EXCESS OF NET INCOME In the
preceding example the total of the authorized salaries and interest was
$21,000 and the net income to be divided was $24,000. Suppose that
the net income had been only $15,000; how should the division have been
made?

If the partnership contract provides for salaries and interest on invested
capital, these provisions are to be followed even though the net income
for the year is less than the total of the authorized salaries and interest.
If the net income of the firm of Adams and Barnes amounted to only
$15,000, this amount would be distributed as follows:

Distribution of Net Income

Authorized	Net income to be divided			$15,000
salaries and	Salaries to partners:			
interest may	A. B. Adams	$ 6,000		
exceed net	B. C. Barnes	12,000	$18,000	
income	Interest on invested capital:			
	A. B. Adams ($40,000 × .06)	$ 2,400		
	B. C. Barnes ($10,000 × .06)	600	3,000	21,000
	Residual loss to be divided equally			$ 6,000
	A. B. Adams	$ 3,000		
	B. C. Barnes	3,000	6,000	

The residual loss of $6,000 must be divided equally because the part-
nership contract states that profits and losses are to be divided equally
after providing for salaries and interest.

The result of this distribution of the net income of $15,000 has been
to give Adams a total of $5,400 and Barnes a total of $9,600. The entry
to close the Income Summary account will be as follows:

Income Summary	15,000	
A. B. Adams, Capital		5,400
B. C. Barnes, Capital		9,600

*To close the Income Summary account by crediting each partner
with his authorized salary and with interest on his beginning capital
at 6% and by dividing the residual loss equally.*

Retirement of a partner

A partner interested in retirement may, with the consent of his partners, sell his interest to an outsider. In this case the payment by the incoming partner goes directly to the retiring partner, and there is no change in the assets or liabilities of the partnership. The only entry required is to transfer the capital account of the retiring partner to an account with the new partner. This transaction is virtually the same as the one described on page 435 for the admission of a partner by purchase of an interest.

Next, let us change our assumptions slightly and say that C, the retiring partner, has a $50,000 interest which he sells to his fellow partners, A and B, in equal amounts. A and B make the agreed payment to C from their personal funds, so again the partnership assets and liabilities are not changed. Regardless of the price agreed to for C's interest, the transaction can be handled on the partnership books merely by transferring the $50,000 balance in C's capital account to the capital accounts of the other two partners.

No change in total capital

C, Capital	50,000	
A, Capital		25,000
B, Capital		25,000

To record the sale of C's interest in equal portions to A and B.

There are other acceptable methods of handling this transaction. For example, if A and B agree to pay C an amount greater than the balance of his capital account, the reason for the excess payment may be that the present market values of the partnership assets are greater than the amounts shown by the books. Under these circumstances a revaluation of the assets may be decided upon.

PAYMENT TO RETIRING PARTNER FROM PARTNERSHIP ASSETS A retiring partner may be paid from partnership funds an amount equal to his capital account or a larger or smaller amount. The present market values of the partnership assets may be quite different from the book figures and goodwill may have been developed although not recorded in the accounts. One solution is to adjust the asset accounts to current appraised values and to place goodwill on the books. A corresponding increase or decrease would be made in the partners' capital accounts in the agreed ratio for sharing profits and losses.

As an alternative, any excess payment to the retiring partner may be treated as a bonus to him which must be charged against the capital accounts of the continuing partners in the agreed ratio for sharing profits and losses, as shown below:

Bonus paid to retiring partner	C, Capital	*50,000*	
	A, Capital	*10,000*	
	B, Capital	*10,000*	
	Cash		*70,000*

To record the retirement of partner C, and payment of his capital account plus a bonus of $20,000.

As a separate example, assume that C is to receive a settlement smaller than his capital account balance, because certain assets are believed to be worth less than book value or because he agrees to take a loss in order to expedite the settlement. If C surrenders his $50,000 interest for $40,000, the entry will be:

Payment to retiring partner of less than book equity	C, Capital	*50,000*	
	Cash		*40,000*
	A, Capital		*5,000*
	B, Capital		*5,000*

To record the retirement of C, and settlement in full for $10,000 less than the balance of his capital account.

Death of a partner

A partnership is dissolved by the death of any member. To determine the amount owing to the estate of the deceased partner, it is usually necessary to close the books and prepare financial statements. This serves to credit each partner with his share of the net income earned during the fractional accounting period ending with the date of *dissolution.*

The partnership agreement may prescribe procedures for making settlement with the estate of a deceased partner. Such procedures often include an audit by independent public accountants, appraisal of assets, and computation of goodwill. If payment to the estate must be delayed, the amount owed should be carried in a liability account replacing the deceased partner's capital account.

INSURANCE ON LIVES OF PARTNERS Members of a partnership often obtain life insurance policies which name the partnership as the beneficiary. Upon the death of a partner, the cash collected from the insurance company is used to pay the estate of the deceased partner. An alternative plan is to have each partner named as the beneficiary of an insurance policy covering the lives of his partners. In the absence of insurance on the lives of partners, there might be insufficient cash available to pay the deceased partner's estate without disrupting the operation of the business.

Liquidation of a partnership

A partnership is terminated or dissolved whenever a new partner is added or an old partner withdraws. The termination or dissolution of a partnership, however, does not necessarily indicate that the business is to be discontinued. Often the business continues with scarcely any outward evidence of the change in membership of the firm. Termination of a partnership indicates a change in the membership of the firm, which may or may not be followed by liquidation.

The process of breaking up and discontinuing a partnership business is called *liquidation.* Liquidation of a partnership spells an end to the business. If the business is to be discontinued, the assets will be sold, the liabilities paid, and the remaining cash distributed to the partners.

SALE OF THE BUSINESS The partnership of X, Y, and Z sells its business to the North Corporation Ltd. The balance sheet appears as follows:

X, Y, AND Z
Balance Sheet
December 31, 19___

Partnership at time of sale

Cash	$ 25,000	Accounts payable	$ 50,000
Inventory	100,000	X, capital	70,000
Other assets	75,000	Y, capital	60,000
		Z, capital	20,000
	$200,000		$200,000

The terms of sale provide that the partnership will retain the cash of $25,000 and will pay the liabilities of $50,000. The inventory and other assets will be sold to the North Corporation for a consideration of $115,000. The entry to record the sale of the inventory and other assets is as follows:

Entries for sale of business

Accounts Receivable, North Corporation	115,000	
Loss on Sale of Business	60,000	
Inventory		100,000
Other Assets		75,000
To record the sale of all assets other than cash to North Corporation.		
Cash	115,000	
Accounts Receivable, North Corporation		115,000
Collected the receivable from sale of assets.		

Division of the gain or loss from sale of the business The gain or loss from the sale of the business must be divided among the partners in the agreed profit- and loss-sharing ratio *before* any cash is distributed to them. The amount of cash to which each partner is entitled in liquidation cannot be determined until his capital account has been increased or decreased by his share of the gain or loss on disposal of the assets. Assuming that X, Y, and Z share profits and losses equally, the entry to allocate the $60,000 loss on the sale of the business will be as follows:

Entry to
divide loss
on sale

X, Capital	20,000
Y, Capital	20,000
Z, Capital	20,000
Loss on Sale of Business	60,000

To divide the loss on the sale of the business among the partners
in the established ratio for sharing profits and losses.

Distribution of cash   The balance sheet of X, Y, and Z appears as follows after the loss on the sale of the assets has been entered in the partners' capital accounts:

X, Y, AND Z

Balance Sheet

(After the Sale of All Assets Except Cash)

Balance
sheet after
sale of
assets

Assets		Liabilities & Partners' Equity	
Cash	$140,000	Accounts payable	$ 50,000
		X, capital	50,000
		Y, capital	40,000
		Z, capital	-0-
	$140,000		$140,000

The creditors must be paid in full before cash is distributed to the partners. The sequence of entries is, therefore, as follows:

(1) Pay
creditors

Accounts Payable	50,000
Cash	50,000

To pay the creditors in full.

(2) Pay
partners

X, Capital	50,000
Y, Capital	40,000
Cash	90,000

To complete liquidation of the business by distributing the
remaining cash to the partners according to the balances in
their capital accounts.

Note that the equal division of the $60,000 loss on the sale of the business reduced the capital account of Partner Z to zero; therefore, he received nothing when the cash was distributed to the partners. This action is consistent with the original agreement of the partners to share profits and losses equally. In working partnership liquidation problems, accounting students sometimes make the error of dividing the cash among the partners in the profit- and loss-sharing ratio. A profit- and loss-sharing ratio means just what the name indicates; it is a ratio for sharing profits and losses, **not a ratio for sharing cash or any other asset.** The amount of cash which a partner should receive in liquidation will be indicated by the balance in his capital account after the gain or loss from the disposal of assets has been divided among the partners in the agreed ratio for sharing profits and losses.

Treatment of debit balance in a capital account To illustrate this situation, let us change our assumptions concerning the sale of the assets by the firm of X, Y, and Z, and say that the loss incurred on the sale of assets was $72,000 rather than the $60,000 previously illustrated. Z's one-third share of a $72,000 loss would be $24,000, which would wipe out the $20,000 credit balance in his capital account and create a $4,000 debit balance. After the liabilities had been paid, a balance sheet for the partnership would appear as follows:

X, Y, AND Z
Balance Sheet
(After the Sale of All Assets Except Cash)

Z now owes	Cash	$78,000	X, capital.............	$46,000
$4,000 to	Z, capital..............	4,000	Y, capital.............	36,000
the partner-		$82,000		$82,000
ship				

To eliminate the debit balance in his capital account, Z should pay in $4,000 cash. If he does so, his capital balance will become zero, and the cash on hand will be increased to $82,000, which is just enough to pay X and Y the balances shown by their capital accounts.

If Z is unable to pay the $4,000 due to the firm, how should the $78,000 of cash on hand be divided between X and Y, whose capital accounts stand at $46,000 and $36,000, respectively? Failure of Z to pay in his debit balance means an additional loss to X and Y; according to the original partnership agreement, X and Y are to share profits and losses equally. Therefore, each must absorb $2,000 of the $4,000 additional loss thrown on them by Z's inability to meet his obligations. The $78,000 of cash on hand should be divided between X and Y in such a manner that the capital account of each will be paid down to $2,000, his share of the additional loss. The journal entry to record this distribution of cash to X and Y is as follows:

Entry to re-	X, Capital	44,000	
cord distri-	Y, Capital	34,000	
bution of	Cash		78,000
cash on			
hand	*To divide the remaining cash by paying down the capital accounts*		
	of X and Y to a balance of $2,000 each, representing the		
	division of Z's loss between them.		

After this entry has been posted the only accounts still open in the partnership books will be the capital accounts of the three partners. A trial balance of the ledger will appear as follows:

X, Y, AND Z
Trial Balance
(After Distribution of Cash)

<table>
<tr><td rowspan="4">*Trial balance after cash distribution*</td><td>X, capital...</td><td></td><td>$2,000</td></tr>
<tr><td>Y, capital...</td><td></td><td>2,000</td></tr>
<tr><td>Z, capital...</td><td>$4,000</td><td></td></tr>
<tr><td></td><td>$4,000</td><td>$4,000</td></tr>
</table>

If Z is able later to pay in his $4,000 debit balance, X and Y will then receive the additional $2,000 each indicated by the credit balances in their accounts. If Z is not able to make good his debit balance, the distribution of cash to X and Y will have been equitable under the circumstances.

An early English court case, *Garner v. Murray,* decided that a debit balance created in a partner's capital account as a result of the liquidation of the partnership must be borne by the other solvent partners in the ratio of their capital accounts immediately prior to liquidation. While the *Garner v. Murray* decision still appears to be good law, many accountants and businessmen consider the rule inequitable. Since the rule applies only when the partnership agreement does not cover this situation, it is common business practice to provide in the partnership agreement that a debit balance in one partner's account be assumed by the other partners in their profit- and loss-sharing ratio. In completing problems on liquidation of partnerships in the text, students should, therefore, ignore the *Garner v. Murray* rule.

DEMONSTRATION PROBLEM FOR YOUR REVIEW

The accounts shown below appear on the books of the Bison Company after all revenue and expense accounts have been closed at the end of the first year of operations:

Partner B, Capital

	Jan. 1	Bal.	54,000
	Nov. 1	Investment	27,000

Partner B, Drawing

Dec. 31	Bal.	9,000		

Partner S, Capital

July 31	Excess withdrawal	12,000	Jan. 1	Bal.	54,000

Partner S, Drawing

Dec. 31 Bal.		*10,800*	

Income Summary

		Dec. 31 Bal.	*38,000*

The partnership agreement (drawn up by B's uncle) contains the following provision relative to the division of income: "Partner B shall be allowed a salary of $750 per month; Partner S shall be allowed a salary of $900 per month. Each partner shall be allowed 20% per annum on his invested capital. Any excess or deficiency shall be divided equally. Withdrawals in excess of above salary allowances in any month shall be charged against capital."

At the end of the year, the partners find they cannot agree on the division of income. Partner S maintains that 20% interest on capital as of the beginning of the year should be credited to each partner. Partner B maintains that the 20% should be applied to capital as of the end of the year and that he should be credited with $16,200 and S with $8,400 as interest. When it is apparent that agreement is impossible, the partners consent to submit their controversy to arbitration.

Instructions
a As an arbitrator, how would you settle this disagreement? How might the partnership agreement be amended to avoid this difficulty in future years?
b Assuming that your decision in (*a*) is adopted, make the journal entries necessary to complete the closing of the partnership books at December 31.

QUESTIONS

1 Explain the difference between being admitted to a partnership by buying an interest from an existing partner and by making an investment in the partnership.

2 Is it possible that a partnership agreement containing interest and salary allowances as a step toward distributing income could cause a partnership net loss to be distributed so that one partner's capital account would be decreased by more than the amount of the entire partnership net loss?

3 Miller is the proprietor of a small manufacturing business. He is considering the possibility of joining in partnership with Bracken, whom he considers to be thoroughly competent and congenial. Prepare a brief statement outlining the advantages and disadvantages of the potential partnership to Miller.

4 Scott has land having a book value of $5,000 and a fair market value of $8,000, and a building having a book value of $50,000 and a fair market value of $40,000. The land and building become Scott's sole capital contribution to a partnership. What is Scott's capital balance in the new partnership? Why?

5 Allen and Baker are considering forming a partnership. What do you think are the two most important factors for them to include in their partnership agreement?

6 Partner X withdraws $25,000 from a partnership during the year. When the statements are made at the end of the year, X's share of the partnership income is $15,000. Which amount must he report on his income tax return?

7 Partner Y has a choice to make. He has been offered by his partners a choice between no salary allowance and a one-third share in the partnership income or a salary of $6,000 per year and a one-quarter share of residual profits. Write a brief memorandum explaining the factors he should consider in reaching a decision.

8 What factors should be considered in drawing up an agreement as to the way in which income shall be shared by two or more partners?

9 Bray and Carter are partners who share profits and losses equally. The current balances in their capital accounts are: Bray, $20,000; Carter, $15,000. If Carter sells his interest in the firm to Deacon for $20,000 and Bray consents to the sale, what entry should be made on the partnership books?

10 What is meant by the term *mutual agency?*

11 If C is going to be admitted to the partnership of A and B, why is it first necessary to determine the current fair market value of the assets of the partnership of A and B?

12 Describe how a *dissolution* of a partnership may differ from a *liquidation* of a partnership.

13 What measure can you suggest to prevent a partnership from having insufficient cash available to pay the estate of a deceased partner without disrupting the operation of the business?

14 What factors should be considered when comparing the net income figure of a partnership to that of a corporation of similar size?

EXERCISES

Ex. 15-1 State the effect of each of the transactions given below on a partner's capital and drawing accounts:

a Partner borrows funds from the business.

b Partner collects a partnership account receivable while on vacation and uses the funds for personal purposes.

c Partner receives in cash the salary allowance provided in the partnership agreement.

d Partner takes home merchandise (cost $40; selling price $65) for his personal use.

e Partner has loaned money to the partnership. The principal together with interest at 6% is now repaid in cash.

Ex. 15-2 X and Y are partners having capital balances of $20,000 and $10,000, respectively, and sharing profits equally. They agree to admit Z to a one-third interest in the partnership for an investment of $18,000. Describe two different approaches that might be used in recording the admission of Z.

Ex. 15-3 The capital accounts of the CDE partnership are as follows: C, $24,000; D, $12,000; E, $18,000. Profits are shared equally. Partner D is withdrawing from the partnership and it is agreed that he shall be paid $15,000 for his interest because the business is worth more than the book value of its net assets. Assuming that the increase in asset value indicated by D's withdrawal is to be recorded as goodwill, give the entries to record D's retirement.

Ex. 15-4 The LMN partnership is being liquidated. After all liabilities have been paid and all assets sold, the balances of the partners' capital accounts are as follows: L, $6,000 credit balance; M, $4,000 debit balance; N, $9,000 credit balance. The partners share profits equally.

a How should the available cash be distributed if it is impossible to determine at this date whether M will be able to pay the $4,000 he owes the firm?

b Draft the journal entries to record a partial payment of $3,000 to the firm by M, and the subsequent distribution of this cash.

Ex. 15-5 Reed and Smith open a TV repair business on January 2, 19___, and agree to share net income as follows:

(*1*) Interest at 8% of beginning capital balances. Reed invested $15,000 in cash, and Smith invested $9,500 in merchandise.

(*2*) Salary allowances of $8,000 to Reed and $6,000 to Smith.

(3) Any partnership earnings in excess of the amount required to cover the interest and salary allowances to be divided 45% to Reed and 55% to Smith. The partnership net income for the first year of operations amounted to $20,000 before interest and salary allowances. Show how this $20,000 should be divided between the two partners.

PROBLEMS

Group A

15A-1 John Barr and Howard Carey form a partnership on July 1, agreeing to invest equal amounts and to share profits equally. The investment by Barr consists of $12,000 cash and an inventory of merchandise valued at $18,000. Carey also is to contribute a total of $30,000. However, it is agreed that his contribution will consist of the following assets of his business along with the transfer to the partnership of his business liabilities. The agreed values of the various items as well as their carrying values on Carey's books are listed below. Carey also contributes enough cash to bring his capital account to $30,000.

	Investment by Carey	
	Balances on Carey's Books	*Agreed Value*
Accounts receivable	$28,000	$28,000
Allowance for uncollectible accounts	1,200	2,500
Inventory	3,000	4,000
Office equipment (net)	4,000	2,500
Accounts payable	9,000	9,000

Instructions
a Draft entries (in general journal form) to record the investments of Barr and Carey in the new partnership.
b Prepare the beginning balance sheet of the partnership (in report form) at the close of business July 1, reflecting the above transfers to the firm.
c On the following June 30 after one year of operation, the Income Summary account showed a credit balance of $40,000 and the Drawing account for each partner showed a debit balance of $10,000. Prepare journal entries to close the Income Summary account and the drawing accounts at June 30.

15A-2 X, Y, and Z are partners of the XYZ Company. During the current year their average capital balances were as follows: X, $70,000; Y, $50,000; and Z, $30,000. The partnership agreement provides that partners shall receive an annual allowance of 6% of their average capital balance and a salary allowance as follows: X, none; Y, $12,000; and Z, $10,000. Partner Y, who manages the business, is to receive a bonus of 25% of the income in excess of $18,000 after partners' interest and salary allowances. Residual profits are to be divided: X, $\frac{1}{2}$; Y, $\frac{1}{3}$; and Z, $\frac{1}{6}$.

Instructions Prepare separate schedules showing how income will be divided among the three partners in each of the following cases. The figure given is the annual income available for distribution among the partners.
a Loss of $11,000
b Income of $19,000
c Income of $65,000

15A-3 The statement on page 459 shows the position of a partnership on June 30, on which date it was agreed to admit a new partner, Ford. North and Lewis share income in a ratio of 3:2 and will continue this relationship after Ford's admission.

NORTH-LEWIS COMPANY
Balance Sheet, June 30

Current assets	$ 45,000	Liabilities	$ 40,000
Plant & equipment (net) . . .	105,000	North, capital	70,000
		Lewis, capital	40,000
	$150,000		$150,000

Instructions Described below are four different situations under which Ford might be admitted to partnership. Considering each independently, prepare the journal entries necessary to record the admission of Ford to the firm.
a Ford purchases a one-half interest (50% of the entire ownership equity) in the partnership from North for $65,000.
b Ford purchases one-half of North's interest and one-half of Lewis's interest, paying North $42,000 and Lewis $24,000.
c Ford invests $75,000 in the partnership and receives a one-half interest in capital and income. It is agreed that there will be no change in the valuation of the present net assets.
d Ford invests $140,000 in the partnership and receives a one-half interest in capital and income. It is agreed that the allowance for uncollectible accounts is currently overstated by $5,000. Assets are carried at amounts approximating current fair value; therefore, any further revaluation necessary to record Ford's investment is to be recorded as goodwill.

15A-4 The following account balances appear on the records of the L-M Company as of December 31, the close of the current year, after all revenue and expense accounts have been closed to Income Summary:

	December 31 Balance	
	Debit	Credit
Partner L, capital		$48,320
Partner L, drawing	$11,690	
Partner M, capital		37,250
Partner M, drawing	9,860	
Income summary		12,410

Other data
(1) During the year Partner M took out of stock for his personal use merchandise which cost the company $690 and had a retail value of $1,150. The bookkeeper credited Sales and charged Miscellaneous Expense for the retail value of all merchandise taken by M.
(2) Partner L paid $600 from his personal funds on November 18 to a lawyer for legal services. Of this amount $250, which was for services relating to partnership business, should be treated as an additional investment by L.
(3) Partner M borrowed $5,400 from the partnership on September 1 of the current year, giving a six-month note with interest at 5%. The only record made of this transaction was a charge to M's drawing account for $5,400 at the time of the loan. M intends to repay the loan with interest at maturity.
(4) Partner L had the full-time use of a company-owned car. All operating expenses were paid by the partnership. It was agreed that L's drawing account would be charged 5 cents per mile for all miles driven for personal use. At the end of the year L reported that he had driven 6,000 miles for personal reasons, but the bookkeeper filed this information and made no entry.

(5) On March 31 Partner L invested an additional $10,000 in the business. Other than this, no changes in partners' capital accounts have been recorded during the year.

Instructions

a On the basis of the above information, make any adjusting or correcting entries necessary at December 31. The portion of any entry affecting revenue or expense accounts may be charged or credited directly to Income Summary.

b Prepare a schedule showing how the adjusted partnership income would be divided between the partners. The partnership agreement calls for salary allowances of $500 per month to L and $800 per month to M. The balance of profits is to be shared in a 3:2 ratio.

c What effect did the adjustments have on L's share of the partnership income for the year? Determine the amount and explain briefly.

d Prepare a statement of changes in partners' capitals for the year.

Group B

15B-1 George Davis and William Glenn form a partnership on July 1, 19___, agreeing to invest equal amounts and to share profits equally. The investment by Davis consists of $36,000 cash and an inventory of merchandise valued at $54,000. Glenn is also to contribute a total of $90,000. However, it is agreed that his contribution will consist of the following assets of his business along with the transfer to the partnership of his business liabilities. The agreed values of the various items as well as their carrying values on Glenn's books are listed below:

	Investment by Glenn	
	Balances on Glenn's Books	Agreed Value
Accounts receivable	$84,000	$84,000
Allowance for uncollectible accounts	3,600	7,500
Inventory	9,000	12,000
Office equipment (net)	12,000	7,500
Accounts payable	27,000	27,000

Glenn also contributes enough cash to bring his capital account to $90,000.

Instructions

a Draft general journal entries to record the investments of Davis and Glenn in the new partnership.

b Prepare the beginning balance sheet of the partnership (in report form) at the close of business July 1, reflecting the above transfers to the firm.

c On the following June 30 after one year of operations, the Income Summary account had a credit balance of $120,000 and the Drawing account for each partner showed a debit balance of $30,000. Prepare journal entries to close the Income Summary account and the drawing accounts at June 30.

15B-2 The capital accounts and profit- and loss-sharing ratios of the partners of the Northwest Company at the close of the current year are given below. At this date it is agreed that a new partner, Tom Jones, is to be admitted to the firm.

	Capital	Profit-sharing Ratio
Richard Scott	$40,000	$\frac{5}{8}$
Bob Hill	32,000	$\frac{1}{4}$
Dan Nolan	24,000	$\frac{1}{8}$

Instructions For each of the following situations involving the admission of Jones to the partnership, give the necessary journal entry to record his admission.
a Jones purchases one-half of Hill's interest in the firm, paying Hill $19,000.
b Jones buys a one-quarter interest in the firm for $28,000 by purchasing one-fourth of the present interest of each of the three partners.
c Jones invests $46,000 and receives a one-quarter interest in the capital and profits of the business. Give the necessary journal entries to record Jones' admission under two alternative interpretations, and write a brief paragraph explaining the circumstances under which each method of recording his admission would be appropriate.

15B-3 Mills, Nutter, and Olsen decided some time ago to liquidate their partnership. All the assets have been sold, but the accounts receivable remain uncollected. The balances in the general ledger at the present time are:

Cash	$17,000	
Accounts receivable.	73,000	
Allowance for uncollectible accounts		$ 4,000
Liabilities		23,000
Mills, capital (profit share 30%)		27,000
Nutter, capital (profit share 50%).		21,000
Olsen, capital (profit share 20%).		15,000

Instructions Present in general journal form the entries necessary to record the liquidation of the partnership and the distribution of all cash under each of the circumstances shown below. Support all entries with adequate explanations showing how amounts were determined.
a Collections of $42,000 are made on receivables, and the remainder are deemed uncollectible.
b Receivables are sold to a collection agency; the partnership receives in cash as a final settlement 30% of the gross amount of its receivables. The personal financial status of the partners is uncertain, but all available cash is to be distributed at this time.

15B-4 Jules Kievits owns a fashion shop. Because he needs additional working capital in the business and has an immediate personal need for $15,000 in cash, Kievits agreed on July 31, 19___, to join in partnership with Leon Abrams. It is agreed that Kievits will contribute all noncash assets of his fashion shop to the partnership and will withdraw (from funds supplied by Abrams) $15,000 in cash. Abrams will invest $40,000 in the business. The partnership contract provides that income shall be divided 55% to Kievits and 45% to Abrams.

Information as to the assets and liabilities of Kievits' business on July 31, 19___, and their agreed valuation is shown below. None of the receivables has been identified as definitely uncollectible.

	Per Kievits' Books	Agreed Valuation
Accounts receivable.	$34,000	
Allowance for uncollectible accounts	3,200	$28,400
Merchandise	66,400	54,000
Store equipment	12,400	
Accumulated depreciation	4,200	9,000
7% note payable (dated May 1, 19___, due Apr. 30, next year) .	24,000	24,420
Accounts payable	14,000	14,000

It is agreed that the new partnership (to be called Mod Fashion Shop) will assume all present debts of Kievits' business.

Instructions

a Make the necessary journal entries to record the formation of the Mod Fashion Shop partnership at July 31, 19___. (Credit Allowance for Uncollectible Accounts $5,600.)

b At the end of August, after all adjusting entries, the Income Summary account of the Mod Fashion Shop shows a credit balance of $4,500. The partners' drawing accounts have debit balances as follows: Kievits, $2,000; Abrams, $1,000. Make the journal entries necessary to complete the closing of the partnership books at the end of August.

c Prepare a statement of partners' capitals for the month of August.

BUSINESS DECISION PROBLEM 15

Les and Ray are considering the formation of a partnership to engage in the business of aerial photography. Les is a licensed pilot, is currently employed at a salary of $15,000 a year, and has $40,000 to invest. Ray is a recent university graduate who has been earning $7,000 a year working in a photographic shop; he has just inherited $100,000 which he plans to put into the business. The partners, after a careful study of their requirements, conclude that $60,000 additional funds will be required, and they have been assured by a local investor, R. J. Chambers, that he will lend them this amount on a five-year, 6% note.

Both partners will devote full time to the business. They have prepared a careful estimate of their prospects and expect that revenues during the first year will just cover expenses, with the exception of the interest expense on the $60,000 loan from Chambers. During the second year the estimates indicate that revenues should exceed expenses (other than the interest expense on the loan) by $20,000. For the third year it is believed that revenues will exceed expenses (other than the interest expense on the loan) by $45,000.

Instructions

a On the basis of the above information, draw up a brief statement of the income-sharing agreement you would recommend that the partners adopt, explaining the basis for your proposal.

b Assuming that the income expectations of the partners are reasonable, draw up a schedule for each of the three years showing how the partners will share in income under the arrangement you have proposed in (*a*). No significant change has occurred in capitals of partners. (This simplifying assumption makes it possible to ignore the possibility of capital account changes resulting from the division of profits or losses, or from drawings and investments. Any such influences are assumed to counterbalance. In other words, it is arbitrarily assumed that the original capital balances for both partners remained unchanged throughout the first three years of operations.) Write a brief statement defending the results of the profit-sharing plan you have devised.

CORPORATIONS ORGANIZATION AND OPERATION

SIXTEEN

The corporation has become the dominant form of business organization on the Canadian economic scene, probably because it gathers together large amounts of capital more readily than single proprietorships or partnerships. Because of its efficiency as a device for pooling the savings of many individuals, the corporation is an ideal means of obtaining the capital necessary for large-scale production and its inherent economies. Virtually all large businesses are corporations.

There are still many more single proprietorships and partnerships than corporations, but in terms of dollar volume of output, the corporations hold an impressive lead. In the field of manufacturing, more than three-quarters of the total value of goods produced comes from corporations. Corporations account for over 90% of the goods and services supplied in such industries as public utilities, banking, transportation, and mining. The rise of the corporation to this commanding position has been inseparably linked with the trend toward larger factories and stores, organized research and development of new products, nationwide marketing areas, and the professionalization of business management.

Definition of corporation

The corporation was defined by Chief Justice Marshall in these words: "A corporation is an artificial being, invisible, intangible, and existing only in contemplation of the law." This definition indicates that one of the most significant characteristics of the corporation is its separate legal entity. The corporation is regarded as a legal person, having a continuous existence apart from that of its owners. By way of contrast, a partnership is a relatively unstable type of organization which is dissolved by the death or retirement of any one of its members, whereas the continuous existence of a corporation is in no way threatened by the death of a stockholder.

Ownership in a corporation is evidenced by transferable shares of stock, and the owners are called *stockholders* or *shareholders.* To administer the affairs of the corporation, the stockholders elect a *board of directors.* The directors in turn select a president and other corporate officers to carry on active management of the business.

Advantages of the corporate form of organization

The corporation offers a number of advantages not available in other forms of organization. Among these advantages are the following:

1 *Greater amounts of capital can be gathered together.* Some corporations have a half million or more stockholders. The sale of stock is a means of obtaining funds from the general public; both small and large investors find stock ownership a convenient means of participating in ownership of business enterprise.

2 *Limited liability.* Creditors of a corporation have a claim against the assets of the corporation only, not against the personal property of the owners of the corporation. Since a stockholder has no personal liability for the debts of the corporation, he can never lose more than the amount of his investment.

3 *Shares of stock in a corporation are readily transferable.* The ease of disposing of all or part of one's stockholdings in a corporation makes this form of investment particularly attractive.

4 *Continuous existence.* A corporation is a separate legal entity with a perpetual existence. The continuous life of the corporation despite changes in ownership is made possible by the issuance of transferable shares of stock.

5 *Centralized authority.* The power to make all kinds of operating decisions is lodged in the president of a corporation. He may delegate to others limited authority for various phases of operations, but he retains final authority over the entire business.

6 *Professional management.* The person who owns a few shares of stock in a large corporation usually has neither the time nor the knowledge of the business necessary for intelligent participation in operating problems. Because of this the functions of management and of ownership are sharply separated in the corporate form of organization, and the corporation is free to employ as executives the best managerial talent available.

Disadvantages of the corporate form of organization

Among the disadvantages of the corporation are:

1 *Heavy taxation.* A corporation must pay a high rate of taxation on its income. If part of its net income is distributed to the owners in the form of dividends, the dividends are considered to be personal income to the stockholders and are subject to personal income tax. This practice of first taxing corporate income to the corporation and then dividends to the stockholder is referred to as *double taxation.* Canadian stockholders are entitled to a dividend tax credit which minimizes the impact of "double taxation."

2 *Greater regulation.* Corporations come into existence under the terms of federal or provincial laws and these same laws may provide for considerable regulation of the corporation's activities. For example, the withdrawal of funds from a corporation is subject to certain limits set by law. Large corporations, especially those with securities listed on stock exchanges, have gradually come to accept the necessity for extensive public disclosure of their affairs. Private corporations, which may be incorporated in most Canadian jurisdictions, are exempt from many of the regulations applied to public companies.

3 **Separation of ownership and control.** The separation of the functions of ownership and management may be an advantage in some cases but a disadvantage in others. On the whole, the excellent record of growth and earnings in most large corporations indicates that the separation of ownership and control has benefited rather than injured stockholders. In a few instances, however, a management group has chosen to operate a corporation for the benefit of insiders (for example, paying excessive executive salaries and bonuses). The stockholders may find it difficult in such cases to take the concerted action necessary to oust the officers. The management group has the privilege of using company funds to solicit proxies from shareholders. Most shareholders who become dissatisfied with existing management policies are inclined to sell their shares rather than to try to influence management policies.

4 **Type of business restricted.** A limited company can conduct only the kind of business permitted in its charter. If it wishes to expand the nature of its activities, it must obtain an amendment to its charter. This restriction is overcome to a great extent in practice by stating in very broad terms the nature of the business to be conducted.

Formation of a corporation

A corporation or limited company may be incorporated under the Canada Business Corporations Act, a federal statute, or under the legislation of one of the provinces, such as the Business Corporations Act (Ontario) or the Companies Act (British Columbia). Corporations which intend to carry on operations in several provinces or in foreign countries usually find it advisable to obtain incorporation under the federal legislation. There are certain disadvantages, however, to federal incorporation and it should be used only as an exception. Provincial incorporation is less expensive and it is more convenient to deal with local officials than with the Department of Consumer and Corporate Affairs, the federal department concerned with company legislation.

It should be noted that a corporation incorporated under the laws of a particular province can operate in other provinces by registering in those provinces in which it desires to carry on business. A province cannot refuse to register a federally-incorporated company since it has the right and capacity to do business in any province. A provincially-incorporated company can be denied the right to carry on operations in another province. Ordinarily, however, no difficulty is encountered, in practice, by a provincially-incorporated company in registering as an extra-provincial company in another province with the right to carry on activities in that province.

Certain types of businesses, such as railroads, interprovincial pipelines, banks, insurance companies and trust companies, must seek incorporation under special legislation and are specifically excluded from the provisions of the general companies acts.

Private companies may be formed under the provisions of most provincial acts. A private company has essentially the same characteristics as a public company except that (a) the number of its shareholders is limited to fifty exclusive of employees and former employees, (b) the right to transfer its shares is restricted, and (c) it is not permitted to offer its shares or debentures to the public. As previously stated, private companies are subject to less rigid regulations than public companies.

While the new Canada Business Corporations Act does not provide for the concept of private companies, its provisions remove much of the red tape and many onerous burdens from closely held corporations. For example, a corporation need not make its financial statements accessible to the general public if (1) it has no securities outstanding in the hands of the public, (2) its gross revenues do not exceed ten million dollars, and (3) the book value of its assets does not exceed five million dollars. Also, formal meetings of shareholders and directors can be dispensed with altogether by a resolution receiving unanimous consent from the shareholders or directors. Corporations with less than fifteen share-holders are not required to solicit proxies.

The methods and procedures required to incorporate a company will vary somewhat in the different jurisdictions. Our discussion will deal with the formation of a limited company under the Canada Business Corporations Act, which was proclaimed on December 31, 1975.

The application to form a corporation need be signed by only one incorporator. This application contains such information as the following:

1 Proposed name of the company, the last word of which, either in full or abbreviated form, usually must be Limited (Ltd.), or Incorporated (Inc.).
2 The number of directors, or where applicable, the minimum and maximum number of directors.
3 Any restrictions on the business that the corporation may carry on.
4 The classes and any maximum number of shares that the corporation is authorized to issue; and, where two or more classes are to be permitted, the rights, privileges, restrictions and conditions attaching to each class.
5 The restriction, if any, on the right to transfer shares of the corporation, including the nature of the restriction.

After the payment of the incorporation fee and approval of the application by the Department of Consumer and Corporate Affairs, the limited company comes into existence. A charter, which may be merely the approved application, is issued as evidence of the company's corporate status. A meeting is held to elect directors and to pass bylaws as a guide to the conduct of the company's affairs. The directors in turn hold a meeting at which officers of the corporation are appointed to serve as active managers of the business; share certificates are issued to the subscribers; and the formation of the corporation is complete.

ORGANIZATION COSTS The formation of a corporation is a much more costly step than the organization of a partnership. The necessary costs include the payment of an incorporation fee to the applicable government, the payment of fees to lawyers for their services in drawing up the articles of incorporation, payments to promoters, and a variety of other outlays necessary to bring the corporation into existence. These costs are charged to an asset account called Organization Costs.

The result of organization costs is the existence of the corporate entity;

consequently, the benefits derived from these costs may be regarded as extending over the entire life of the corporation. Since the life of a corporation is indefinite, organization costs may be carried at the full amount until the corporation is liquidated. Because present income tax law permits a portion of organization costs to be written off over a period of years[1], many companies elect to write off organization costs over this same period. Accountants have been willing to condone this practice, despite the lack of theoretical support, on the grounds that such costs are relatively immaterial in relation to other assets. Unnecessary detail on the balance sheet is always to be avoided, and there seems to be little reason for carrying indefinitely organization costs of modest amount.

THE RIGHTS OF STOCKHOLDERS The ownership of stock in a corporation usually carries the following basic rights:

1 To vote for directors, and thereby to be represented in the management of the business. The approval of a majority of stockholders is usually also required for such important corporate actions as mergers and acquisitions, the incurring of long-term debts, establishment of stock option plans, or the splitting of capital stock into a larger number of shares.

2 Election of auditors.

3 To share in profits by receiving dividends declared by the board of directors.

4 To share in the distribution of assets if the corporation is liquidated. When a corporation ends its existence, the creditors of the corporation must first be paid in full; any remaining assets are divided among stockholders in proportion to the number of shares owned.

5 To subscribe for additional shares in the event that the corporation decides to increase the amount of stock outstanding. This *preemptive right* entitles each stockholder to maintain his percentage of ownership in the company by subscribing, in proportion to his present stockholdings, to any additional shares issued. (The pre-emptive right is not a legal requirement of the Canada Business Corporations Act.)[2]

The ownership of stock does not give a stockholder the right to intervene in the management of a corporation or to transact business in its behalf. Although the stockholders as a group own the corporation, they do not personally own the assets of the corporation; neither do they personally owe the debts of the corporation. The stockholders have no direct claim on income earned; income earned by a corporation does not become income to the stockholders unless the board of directors orders the distribution of the income to stockholders in the form of a dividend.

Stockholders' meetings are usually held once a year. Each share of stock is entitled to one vote. In large corporations, these annual meetings are usually attended by relatively few persons, often by less than 1% of the stockholders. Prior to the meeting, the management group will request stockholders who do not plan to attend in person to send in *proxy statements* assigning their votes to the existing management. Through this use

---

[1]One-half of the cost of Organization Costs can be amortized, for income tax purposes, at the annual rate of 10 per cent using the declining balance method.

[2]The Canada Business Corporations Act does not require that a corporation recognize the pre-emptive right but permits a corporation, if it wishes to do so, to provide, in its articles of incorporation, for the pre-emptive right.

of the proxy system, management may secure the right to vote as much as, perhaps, 90% or more of the total outstanding shares.

THE ROLE OF THE BOARD OF DIRECTORS The board of directors is elected by the stockholders; the primary functions of the board are to manage the corporation and to protect the interests of the stockholders. At this level, management may consist principally of formulating policies and reviewing acts of the officers. Specific duties of the directors include declaring dividends, setting the salaries of officers, authorizing officers to arrange loans from banks, and authorizing important contracts of various kinds.

The extent of active participation in management by the board of directors varies widely from one company to another. In some corporations the officers also serve as directors and a meeting of directors may differ only in form from a conference of operating executives. In other corporations the board may consist of outsiders who devote little time to the corporation's affairs and merely meet occasionally to review and approve policies which have been formed and administered by the officers.

The official actions of the board are recorded in minutes of their meetings. The *minutes book* is the source of many of the accounting entries affecting the owners' equity accounts.

THE RESPONSIBILITIES OF CORPORATE OFFICERS Corporate officers usually include a president, one or more vice-presidents, a controller, a treasurer, and a secretary. A vice-president is often made responsible for the sales function; other vice-presidents may be given responsibility for such important functions as personnel, finance, production, and research and development.

The responsibilities of the controller, treasurer, and secretary are most directly related to the accounting phase of business operation. The *controller* is the chief accounting officer. He is responsible for the maintenance of adequate internal control and for the preparation of accounting records and financial statements. Such specialized activities as budgeting, tax planning, and preparation of tax returns are usually placed under his jurisdiction. The *treasurer* has custody of the company's funds and is generally responsible for planning and controlling the company's cash position. The *secretary* maintains minutes of the meetings of directors and stockholders and represents the corporation in many contractual and legal matters. Another of his responsibilities is to coordinate the preparation of the *annual report,* which includes the financial statements and other information relating to corporate activities. In small corporations, one officer frequently acts as both secretary and treasurer. The organization chart below indicates lines of authority extending from stockholders to the directors to the president and other officers.

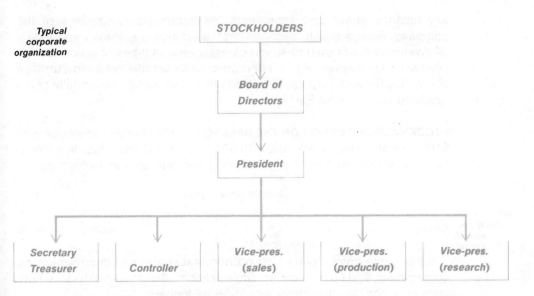

Typical corporate organization

SOURCES OF CORPORATE CAPITAL The sections of a balance sheet showing assets and liabilities will be much the same for a corporation as for a single proprietorship or partnership. The owners' equity section is the principal point of contrast. In a corporation the term *stockholders' equity* is synonymous with owners' equity. The capital of a corporation, as for other types of business organizations, is equal to the excess of the assets over the liabilities. However, the capital of a corporation may be divided into several segments. In succeeding chapters, these various classifications of corporate capital will be considered in some detail, but at this point we are concerned with a simplified model in which the capital of a corporation is carried in only two ledger accounts and shown on the balance sheet in two separate portions. These two classifications are (*1*) the capital contributed by the stockholders, and (2) the capital accumulated through profitable operations.

The capital contributed by stockholders is regarded as permanent capital not ordinarily subject to withdrawal. The unit of corporate ownership is a *share of stock,* and the balance of the Capital Stock account, for companies incorporated under the Canada Business Corporations Act, is always equal to the total number of shares of stock issued, multiplied by the consideration received per share.

The second major type of corporate capital is retained earnings. At the end of each accounting period, the balance of the Income Summary account is closed into the Retained Earnings account. Any dividends distributed to stockholders serve to reduce the Retained Earnings account. Consequently, the balance of the Retained Earnings account at any balance sheet date represents the accumulated earnings of the company since the date of incorporation, minus any losses and minus all dividends distributed to stockholders. (Various types of dividends are discussed in Chapter 17.) An alternative name for the Retained Earnings account is Earned Surplus. This is an older term which is gradually being replaced by Retained Earnings.

STOCKHOLDERS' EQUITY ON THE BALANCE SHEET For a corporation with $100,000 of capital stock and $40,000 of retained earnings, the stockholders' equity section of the balance sheet will appear as follows:

Stockholders' Equity

Stockholders Capital stock	*$100,000*	
equity and Retained earnings	*40,000*	*$140,000*
earned		
capital		

If this same company had been unprofitable and had incurred losses aggregating $30,000 since its organization, the stockholders' equity section of the balance sheet would be as follows:

Stockholders' Equity

Stockholders		
equity		
reduced by Capital stock	*$100,000*	
losses Less: Deficit	*30,000*	*$70,000*
incurred		

This second illustration tells us that $30,000 of the original $100,000 invested by stockholders has been lost. Note that the capital stock in both illustrations remains at the fixed amount of $100,000, the stockholders' original investment. The accumulated profits or losses since the organization of the corporation are shown as *retained earnings* or as a *deficit* and are not intermingled with the capital stock.

INCOME TAXES IN CORPORATE FINANCIAL STATEMENTS A corporation is a legal entity subject to corporation income tax; consequently, the ledger of a corporation should include accounts for recording income taxes. No such accounts are needed for a business organized as a single proprietorship or partnership.

Income taxes are based on a corporation's earnings. At year-end, before preparing financial statements, income taxes are recorded by an adjusting entry such as the following:

Recording Income Taxes	*45,650*	
corporate Income Taxes Payable		*45,650*
income		
taxes *To record the income taxes payable for the year ended*		
Dec. 31, 19____ .		

The account debited in this entry, Income Taxes, is an expense account and usually appears as the very last deduction in the income statement as follows:

Final step in income statement

Income before income taxes	$100,000
Income taxes	45,650
Net income	$ 54,350
Earnings per share	$2.17

The liability account, Income Taxes Payable, will ordinarily be paid within a few months and should, therefore, appear in the current liability section of the balance sheet. More detailed discussion of corporation taxes is presented in Chapter 20.

AUTHORIZATION AND ISSUANCE OF CAPITAL STOCK

The articles of incorporation specify the classes and the maximum number of shares of capital stock which a corporation is authorized[3] to issue. The corporation may choose not to issue immediately all of the authorized shares; in fact, it is customary to secure authorization for a larger number of shares than presently needed. In future years, if more capital is needed, the previously authorized shares will be readily available for issue; otherwise, the corporation would be forced to apply to Department of Consumer and Corporate Affairs for permission to alter its charter by increasing the number of authorized shares.

Capital stock outstanding

The unit of stock ownership is the share, but the corporation may issue stock certificates in denominations of 10 shares, 100 shares, or any other number. The total capital stock outstanding at any given time represents 100% ownership of the corporation. Outstanding shares are those in the hands of stockholders. Assume, for example, that the Draper Corporation Ltd. is organized with authorization to issue 100,000 shares of stock. However, only 50,000 shares are issued, because this amount of stock provides all the capital presently needed. The holders of the 50,000 shares of stock own the corporation in its entirety.

If we assume further that Thomas Draper acquires 5,000 shares of the 50,000 shares outstanding, we may say that he has a 10% interest in the corporation. Suppose that Draper now sells 2,000 shares to Evans. The total number of shares outstanding remains unchanged at 50,000, although Draper's percentage of ownership has declined to 6% and a new stockholder, Evans, has acquired a 4% interest in the corporation. The transfer of 2,000 shares from Draper to Evans had no effect upon the corporation's assets, liabilities, or amount of stock outstanding. The only way in which this transfer of stock affects the corporation is that the list of stockholders must be revised to show the number of shares held by each owner.

Preferred and common stock

The Canada Business Corporations Act permits shares of different classes

---

[3]There is no requirement in the Canada Business Corporations Act for a ceiling on the number of shares which may be issued. However, if the articles of incorporation place a ceiling on the number of shares that may be issued, such a ceiling may be referred to as authorized share capital. Many provincial acts require that the amount of authorized share capital be established.

to be issued but requires the issue of one "residual" class of shares that may vote at meetings of shareholders and may receive the remaining property of the corporation upon dissolution. Although the Act speaks of shares in general and does not use the terms, common and preferred, it is likely that this terminology will continue to be used.

In order to appeal to as many investors as possible, a corporation may issue more than one kind of stock, just as an automobile manufacturer may make sedans, convertibles, and station wagons in order to appeal to various groups of car buyers. When only one type of stock is issued, it is called **common stock.** Common stock has the four basic rights previously mentioned. Whenever these rights are modified, the term **preferred stock** (or sometimes Class B Common) is used to describe this second type of stock. A few corporations issue two or three classes of preferred stock, each class having certain distinctive features designed to interest a particular type of investor. In summary, we may say that every business corporation has common stock; a good many corporations also issue preferred stock; and some companies have two or more types of preferred stock.

Common stock may be regarded as the basic, residual element of ownership. It carries voting rights and, therefore, is the means of exercising control over the business. Common stock has unlimited possibilities of increase in value; during the last decade the market prices of common stocks of many leading corporations rose to three or four times their former values. On the other hand, common stocks lose value more rapidly than other types of securities when corporations encounter periods of unprofitable business or of unfavorable external economic conditions.

The following stockholders' equity section illustrates the balance sheet presentation for a corporation having both preferred and common stock; note that the item of retained earnings is not apportioned between the two groups of stockholders.

Balance sheet presentation	Stockholders' equity:	
	Preferred stock, $5 cumulative, no par value, authorized and issued	
	100,000 shares	$10,000,000
	Common stock, no par value, authorized and issued 1 million shares .	5,000,000
	Retained earnings	3,500,000
	Total stockholders' equity	$18,500,000

CHARACTERISTICS OF PREFERRED STOCK Most preferred stocks have the following distinctive features:

1 Preferred as to dividends
2 Preferred as to assets in event of the liquidation of the company
3 Redeemable at the option of the corporation
4 No voting power

Another very important but less common feature is a clause permitting the **conversion** of preferred stock into common at the option of the holder.

Preferred stocks vary widely with respect to the special rights and privileges granted. Careful study of the terms of the individual preferred stock contract is a necessary step in the evaluation of any preferred stock.

Shares preferred as to dividends Shares preferred as to dividends are entitled to receive each year a dividend of specified amount before any dividend is paid on the common shares. The dividend may be stated as a dollar amount per share. For example, the balance sheet of Domtar Limited indicates preferred shares outstanding with an annual dividend as follows:

Dividend stated as dollar amount

Capital stock:
$1 cumulative redeemable preference shares
par value $23.50, redeemable at $25.00
Authorized—600,000 shares
Outstanding—592,746 shares $13,929,531

Some preferred shares state the dividend preference as a percentage of par value. For example, 5% preferred share capital with a par value of $100 per share would mean that $5 must be paid yearly on each share of preferred share capital before any dividends are paid to the common. An example of the percentage method of stating the dividend on preferred shares is found in the balance sheet of B.C. Sugar Refinery Ltd.:

Dividend stated as percentage

Capital stock:
5% cumulative redeemable preferred
shares of a par value of $20.
Authorized—300,000 shares
Issued—170,000 shares . . . . $ 3,400,000

Corporations incorporated under the Canada Business Corporations Act must state the dividend in dollar terms since the Act does not permit the issue of par value shares. However, par value shares will continue to exist for companies incorporated under a number of provincial acts and for as long as five years (until December 31, 1980) for corporations incorporated under the old Canada Corporations Act.

The holder of a preferred stock has no assurance that he will always receive the indicated dividend. A corporation is obligated to pay dividends to stockholders only when the board of directors declares a dividend. Dividends must be paid on preferred stock before anything is paid to the common stockholders, but if the corporation is not prospering, it may decide not to pay dividends on either preferred or common stock. For a corporation to pay dividends, profits must be earned and cash must be available. However, preferred stocks in general offer more assurance of regular dividend payments than do common stocks.

Cumulative preferred stock The dividend preference carried by most preferred stocks is a *cumulative* one. If all or any part of the regular dividend on the preferred stock is omitted in a given year, the amount in arrears must be paid in a subsequent year before any dividend can be paid on the common stock. Assume that a corporation was organized

January 1, 1973, with 1,000 shares of $4 cumulative preferred stock and 1,000 shares of common stock. Dividends paid in 1973 were at the rate of $4 per share of preferred stock and $3 per share of common. In 1974, earnings declined sharply and the only dividend paid was $1 per share on the preferred stock. No dividends were paid in 1975. What is the status of the preferred stock as of December 31, 1975? Dividends are in arrears in the amount of $7 a share ($3 omitted during 1974 and $4 omitted in 1975). On the entire issue of 1,000 shares of preferred stock, the dividends in arrears amount to $7,000.

In 1976, we shall assume that the company earned large profits and wished to pay dividends on both the preferred and common stocks. Before paying a dividend on the common, the corporation must pay the $7,000 in arrears on the cumulative preferred stock plus the regular $4 a share applicable to the current year. The preferred stockholders would, therefore, receive a total of $11,000 in dividends in 1976; the board of directors would then be free to declare dividends on the common stock.

Dividends in arrears *are not listed among the liabilities of a corporation,* because no liability exists until a dividend is declared by the board of directors. Nevertheless, the amount of any dividends in arrears on preferred stock is an important factor to investors and should always be disclosed. This disclosure is usually made by a note accompanying the balance sheet such as the following:

"As of December 31, 1975, dividends on the $4 cumulative preferred stock were in arrears to the extent of $7 per share, and amounted in total to $7,000."

For a *noncumulative preferred stock,* any unpaid or omitted dividend is lost forever. Because of this factor, investors view the noncumulative feature as an unfavorable element, and very few noncumulative preferred stocks are issued.

Participating clauses in preferred stock Since participating preferred stocks are very seldom issued, discussion of them will be brief. A fully participating preferred stock is one which, in addition to the regular specified dividend, is entitled to participate in some manner with the common stock in any additional dividends paid. For example, a $5 participating preferred stock would be entitled to receive $5 a share before the common stock received anything. After $5 a share had been paid to the preferred stockholders, a $5 dividend could be paid on the common stock. If the company desired to pay an additional dividend to the common, say, an extra $3 per share, the preferred stock would also be entitled to receive an extra $3 dividend. In brief, a fully participating preferred stock participates dollar for dollar with the common stock in any dividends paid in excess of the stated rate on the preferred stock.

Stock preferred as to assets Most preferred stocks carry a preference as to assets in the event of liquidation of the corporation. If the business is terminated, the preferred stock is entitled to payment in full of a stated liquidation value (or par value) before any payment is made on the common stock. This priority also includes any dividends in arrears.

Redeemable preferred stock Most preferred stocks are redeemable at the option of the corporation at a stipulated price, usually slightly above the issuance price. The *redemption price* for a $100 par value preferred stock is often $103 or $104 per share.

In the financing of a new or expanding corporation, the organizers usually hold common stock, which assures them control of the company. However, it is often necessary to obtain outside capital. One way of doing this, without the loss of control or any serious reduction in possible future earnings on the common stock, is to issue redeemable preferred stock.

It may be argued that the position of the holder of redeemable preferred stock is more like that of a creditor than that of an owner. He supplies capital to the company for an agreed rate of return, has no voice in management, and may find his relationship with the company terminated at any time through the calling in of his certificate. If a company is so fortunate as to enter upon a period of unusually high earnings, It will probably increase the dividend payments on its common stock, but it will not consider increasing the income of the preferred stockholder. On the contrary, the corporation may decide that this era of prosperity is a good time to eliminate the preferred stock through exercise of the redemption provision.

Regardless of the fact that preferred stock lacks many of the traditional aspects of ownership, it is universal practice to include all types of preferred stock in the stockholders' equity section of the balance sheet.[4]

Convertible preferred stock In order to add to the attractiveness of preferred stock as an investment, corporations sometimes offer a conversion privilege which entitles the preferred stockholder to exchange his shares for common stock in a stipulated ratio. If the corporation prospers, its common stock will probably rise in market value, and dividends on the common stock will probably be increased. The investor who buys a convertible preferred stock rather than common stock has greater assurance of regular dividends. In addition, through the conversion privilege, he is assured of sharing in any substantial increase in value of the company's common stock.

As an example, assume that the Remington Corporation Ltd. issued a $5, no par, convertible preferred stock on January 1, at a price of $100 a share. Each share was convertible into four shares of the company's no-par value common stock at any time. The common stock had a market price of $20 a share on January 1, and an annual dividend of 60 cents a share was being paid. The yield on the preferred stock was 5% ($5 ÷ $100); the yield on the common stock was only 3% ($0.60 ÷ $20).

During the next few years, the Remington Corporation's earnings increased, the dividend on the common stock was raised to an annual rate of $1.50, and the market price of the common stock rose to $40 a

[4]The legal requirements and procedures for recording the redemption of preferred shares are discussed in *Intermediate Accounting*, the second book in this series by Meigs, Johnson, Keller and Blazouske.

share. At this point the preferred stock would have a market value of at least $160, since it could be converted at any time into four shares of common stock with a market value of $40 each. In other words, the market value of a convertible preferred stock will tend to move in accordance with the price of the common. When the dividend rate is increased on the common stock, some holders of the preferred stock may convert their holdings into common stock in order to obtain a higher return on their investments.

If the holder of 100 shares of the preferred stock presented these shares for conversion, the Remington Corporation Ltd. would make the following entry:

Conversion of preferred stock into common

$5 Convertible Preferred Stock, no par value *10,000*
   Common Stock *10,000*
To record the conversion of 100 shares of preferred stock, no par value, into 400 shares of no-par value common stock.

The preceding illustration was based on the assumption that the Remington Corporation Ltd. enjoyed larger earnings after the issuance of its convertible preferred. Let us now make a contrary assumption and say that shortly after issuance of the convertible preferred stock, the company's profits declined and the directors deemed it necessary to cut the annual dividend on the common stock from 60 cents a share to 20 cents a share. A stockholder who acquired common stock at a cost of $20 a share now finds that his dividend income has dropped to a rate of 1% ($0.20 ÷ $20 cost). The dividend on the preferred stock remains at $5 a share.

These two illustrations indicate that the convertible preferred stock has two important advantages from the viewpoint of the investor: It increases in value along with the common stock when the company prospers, and it offers greater assurance of steady dividend income during a period of poor earnings.

Par value and no-par value stock

An understanding of no-par stock can best be gained by reviewing the reasons why par value was originally required in an earlier period of Canadian corporate history. The use of the par value concept in federal and provincial laws was intended for the protection of creditors and of public stockholders. Shares could not be issued at less than par value. A corporation was thus discouraged from selling its stock to the public at, say, $100 a share and concurrently to insiders or promoters at, say, $50 a share.

Protection was also afforded to creditors by laws prohibiting a corporation from paying any dividend which would "impair its capital" (reduce its capital to an amount less than the par value of the outstanding shares). Because of these statutes concerning par value, a creditor of a corporation could tell by inspection of the balance sheet the amount which owners had invested permanently in the corporation. This permanent investment of ownership capital (par value times the number of outstanding shares) represented a buffer which protected the corporation creditor from the impact of any losses sustained by the corporation. Such protection for creditors was considered necessary because stockholders have no personal liability for the debts of the corporation.

The par value device proved rather ineffective in achieving its avowed objective of protecting creditors and public shareholders. Although limited companies were prohibited from selling their shares at less than par, the law could easily be circumvented by issuing shares in exchange for property other than cash. In some cases large amounts of shares were issued for worthless mining claims, patents, and other assets of unproved value. The assets acquired in this manner were recorded at the par value of the shares issued in payment, resulting in a serious overstatement of asset values and invested capital on the balance sheet. Such abuses of the par value concept paved the way for legislation permitting the issuance of shares with no-par value.

Because par value is relatively meaningless, the Canada Business Corporations Act has abolished the concept of par value. All shares issued by corporations incorporated – or continued – by this Act must be no-par value shares.

No-par value shares Creditors of a limited company can look only to the company for payment of their claims and not to the shareholders personally. Consequently, creditors want assurance that the capital invested in a limited company by shareholders will not be withdrawn in the event the company encounters financial difficulties.

No-par value shares may be sold at any price determined by the directors acting in the best interests of the company. While all no-par value shares issued at a given time must be sold at the same price by the issuing company, the sale price of no-par value shares can change on subsequent issues of the same class of shares. There is no effective minimum price at which no-par value shares must be issued.

When all shares were of the par value type, the par value of the shares issued represented the stated capital or legal capital not available for dividends or withdrawal by shareholders. With the advent of no-par shares, federal or provincial governments attempted to continue the protection of creditors by designating all or part of the amount received by the corporation for its no-par shares as share capital not subject to withdrawal.

Recording the issuance of no-par shares Assume that a share of no-par share capital is issued at a price of $25. How much of the $25 of contributed capital is to be recorded by a credit to the Capital Stock account? In some jurisdictions the law requires that the entire amount received from issuance of no-par shares be credited to the Capital Stock account. Under the provisions of the Canada Business Corporations Act, the entire proceeds received from the sale of no-par value shares must be credited to the Capital Stock account. Therefore, the entire $25 received from the issue of each no-par value share in the above example must be recorded as a credit to Capital Stock.

Other jurisdictions permit the board of directors of the issuing company to decide upon the stated value per share at the time of each issue. Once the stated value has been established, it applies to all shares issued at that given time. The remaining portion of the amount received from the shareholders is credited to an account called "distributable" surplus. "Distributable" surplus should be classified as part of contributed surplus.[5] Under the provisions of the old Companies Act (Canada), the board of directors was permitted to allocate to a contributed surplus account, called "distributable" surplus, a maximum of 25% of the proceeds received from the issue of no-par shares. Where no-par shares were issued to acquire a going concern, the board of directors could apportion to distributable surplus an amount equal to the unappropriated earned surplus of the going concern immediately prior to its acquisition. The resolution of the board of directors determined the amount of the proceeds to be credited to the Capital Stock account and the amount to be credited to distributable surplus. If no resolution was passed by the directors, the entire proceeds had to be credited to the Capital Stock account. While it is no longer possible to create or increase distributable surplus under the provisions of the Canada Business Corporations Act since the entire proceeds from the issue of no-par value shares must be credited to capital stock, the distributable surplus account is still important because it will appear on many balance sheets. Distributable surplus which was set up previous to the new legislation, may be continued and, therefore, may appear on corporate balance sheets for many years in the future. Also, many provincial companies' acts still permit corporations incorporated under their jurisdictions to create distributable surplus on the issue of no-par value shares.

Illustrative entries for issuance of no-par shares Assume that a corporation is organized under the Canada Business Corporations Act, which requires the entire proceeds from issuance of no-par shares to be treated as share capital. The company obtains authorization to issue 10,000 no-par shares, and makes a memorandum notation in the Capital Stock account to record this authorization. Six thousand shares are issued at a price of $12 each. The entry is as follows:

Note preceding assumption as to law

Cash	72,000	
Capital Stock		72,000
Issued 6,000 no-par value shares at $12 each.		

After this entry has been posted, the ledger account for Capital Stock will appear as follows:

[5]This classification is recommended by the Canadian Institute of Chartered Accountants in the *CICA Handbook*, Section 3250, 1955. The nature of surplus is further discussed in Chapter 17.

Entire proceeds in capital stock account

Capital Stock

(Authorized for issuance 10,000 no-par value shares)

Date (issued 6,000 shares) 72,000

Par value   In an earlier period of the history of Canadian corporations, all capital stock had par value, but since 1909 limited companies incorporated under federal legislation were permitted to choose between par value stock and no-par value stock. The corporate charter always states the par value, if any, of the shares to be issued.

Par value may be $1 per share, $5, $100, or any other amount decided upon by the corporation. The par value of the stock is no indication of its market value; the par value merely indicates the amount per share to be entered in the Capital Stock account. The par value of most common stocks is relatively low. Canadian Pacific Ltd. common stock, for example, has a par value of $5; Royal Bank of Canada common stock has a par of $2; Maritime Telegraph and Telephone Ltd. stock has a par value of 10 cents per share. The market value of all these securities is far above their par value.

As stated previously, the Canada Business Corporations Act does not permit the issuance of par value shares. Furthermore, the shares of all corporations continued under this Act will be deemed to be no-par value shares. Existing corporations have five years (that is, to December 31, 1980) in which to apply for continuance under this new Act. During that period, therefore, a number of federally incorporated companies will still have par value shares outstanding. Also, par value shares may still be issued by corporations incorporated under many of the provincial acts. Thus, a knowledge of the provisions relating to par value shares is not yet obsolete.

The chief significance of par value is that it represents the *legal capital* per share, that is, the amount below which stockholders' equity cannot be reduced except by (1) losses from business operations, or (2) legal action taken by a majority vote of stockholders. A dividend cannot be declared by a corporation if such action would cause the stockholders' equity to fall below the par value of the outstanding shares. Par value, therefore, may be regarded as a minimum cushion of capital existing for the protection of creditors.

Issuance of par value stock   Mere authorization of a stock issue does not bring an asset into existence, nor does it give the corporation any capital. The obtaining of authorization from the federal or a provincial government for a stock issue merely affords a legal opportunity to obtain assets through sale of stock.

When par value stock is issued, the Capital Stock account is credited with the par value of the shares issued, regardless of whether the issuance price is more or less than par. Assuming that 6,000 of the authorized 10,000 shares of $10 par value stock are issued at a price of

$10 each, Cash would be debited and Capital Stock would be credited for $60,000. When stock is sold for more than par value, the Capital Stock account is credited with the par value of the shares issued, and a separate account, Premium on Capital Stock, is credited for the excess of selling price over par. If, for example, the issuance price is $15, the entry is as follows:

Stockholders' investment in excess of par value

Cash	90,000	
Capital Stock, $10 par		60,000
Premium on Capital Stock		30,000
Issued 6,000 shares of $10 par value stock at a price of $15		
a share.		

The premium or amount received in excess of par value does not represent a profit to the corporation. It is part of the invested capital and it will be included in the stockholders' equity of the balance sheet. The stockholders' equity section of the balance sheet would be as follows (the existence of $10,000 in retained earnings is assumed in order to have a complete illustration):

Corporation's capital classified by source

Stockholders' equity:

Capital stock, $10 par value, authorized 10,000 shares, issued and	
outstanding 6,000 shares	$ 60,000
Premium on Capital Stock[6]	30,000
Retained earnings	10,000
Total stockholders' equity	$100,000

Shares issued at a price below par As a general rule, it is illegal for companies in Canada to issue shares at a discount. However, companies incorporated in New Brunswick and mining companies incorporated in a number of other provinces are permitted to issue shares at a discount provided the prescribed statutory procedures are followed. In this illustration the issuance price of the $10 par value shares is assumed to be $8 a share. The entry for the issuance of 6,000 shares at $8 is as follows:

Shares issued at discount

Cash	48,000	
Discount on Common Shares . . . :	12,000	
Common Share Capital		60,000
Issued 6,000 shares of $10 par value at a price		
of $8 each.		

In the balance sheet the discount account would appear as a deduction from the common share capital, as follows:

[6] Premium on Capital Stock is part of contributed surplus. See Chapter 17 for a discussion of surplus accounts.

Stockholders' equity:

Common share capital, $10 par value, authorized 10,000 shares,	
issued and outstanding 6,000 shares	*$60,000*
Less: discount an common shares	*12,000*
	48,000
Retained earnings	*10,000*
	$58,000

Nature of discount on share capital In planning the issuance of share capital, the limited company is free to set the par value of the shares as low as it pleases, and a par value of $1 a share is not uncommon. Since par value is usually set at an amount considerably below the offering price, the question of discount on share capital is of little practical importance. Once shares have been issued, they may be sold by one investor to another at more or less than par without any effect on the limited company's accounts. In other words, discount on shares refers only to the original issuance of shares by a limited company at a price below par.

The underwriting of stock issues

When a large amount of stock is to be issued, the corporation will probably utilize the services of an investment dealer, frequently referred to as an *underwriter.* The underwriter guarantees the issuing corporation a specific price for the stock and makes a profit by selling the stock to the investing public at a higher price. For example, an issue of 1,270,000 shares of $1 par value common stock might be sold to the public at a price of $47 a share, of which $2.35 a share is retained by the underwriter and $44.65 represents the net proceeds to the issuing corporation.[7] The corporation would enter on its books only the net amount received from the underwriter ($44.65) for each share issued.[8] The use of an underwriter assures the corporation that the entire stock issue will be sold without

---

[7] These figures are taken from a recent prospectus issued by Levi Strauss & Co. covering issuance of 1,070,000 shares by the corporation and 200,000 shares by stockholders in an initial public offering by the corporation. Figures taken from the face of the prospectus follow:

	Price to Public	Underwriting Discounts and Commissions*	Proceeds to the Company†	Proceeds to Selling Stockholders
Per Share	$47.00	$2.35	$44.65	$44.65
Total	$59,690,000	$2,984,500	$47,775,500	$8,930,000

* The Company has agreed to indemnify the Underwriters against certain liabilities under the Securities Act of 1933.
† Before deducting expenses payable by the Company estimated at $200,000.

[8] Par value shares may be sold to the public at par with the underwriter receiving a commission. Payment of a commission for the sale of shares is allowed by most Canadian jurisdictions. The commission, in the situation where sale price to the public is at par, is recorded in a manner similar to the sale of shares at a discount.

delay, and the entire amount of funds to be raised will be available on a specific date.

Market price of common stock

The preceding sections concerning the issuance of stock at prices above and below par raise a question as to how the market price of stock is determined. The price which the corporation sets on a new issue of stock is based on several factors including (1) an appraisal of the company's expected future earnings, (2) the probable dividend rate per share, (3) the present financial condition of the company, and (4) the current state of the investment market.

After the stock has been issued, the price at which it will be traded among investors will tend to reflect the progress of the company, with primary emphasis being placed on earnings and dividends per share. *Earnings per share* of common stock, for example, is computed by dividing the annual net income available to the common stock by the number of shares outstanding. At this point in our discussion, the significant fact to emphasize is that market price is not related to par value, and that it tends to reflect current and future earnings and dividends. (Earnings per share is discussed in some detail in Chapter 17.)

Stock issued for assets other than cash

Corporations generally sell their capital stock for cash and use the cash obtained in this way to buy the various types of assets needed in the business. Sometimes, however, a corporation may issue shares of its capital stock in a direct exchange for land, buildings, or other assets. Stock may also be issued in payment for services rendered by lawyers and promoters.

When a corporation issues capital stock in exchange for services or for assets other than cash, a question arises as to the proper valuation of the property or services received. For example, assume that a corporation issues 1,000 shares of its $1 par value common stock in exchange for a tract of land. A problem may exist in determining the fair market value of the land, and consequently in determining the amount of paid-in capital. If there is no direct evidence of the value of the land, we may value it by using indirect evidence as to the alternative amount of cash for which the shares might have been sold. Assume that the company's stock is listed on a stock exchange and is presently selling at $90 a share. The 1,000 shares which the corporation exchanged for the land could have been sold for $90,000 cash, and the cash could have been used to pay for the land. The direct exchange of stock for land may be considered as the equivalent of selling the stock for cash and using the cash to buy the land. It is therefore logical to say that the cost of the land to the company was $90,000, the market value of the stock given in exchange for the land. *Note that the par value of the stock is not any indication of the fair value of the stock or of the land.*

Once the valuation question has been decided, the entry to record the issuance of stock in exchange for noncash assets can be made as follows:[9]

How were dollar amounts determined?

Land	90,000	
Common Stock, $1 par value		1,000
Premium on Common Shares		89,000

To record the issuance of 1,000 shares of $1 par value common stock in exchange for land. Current market value of stock ($90 a share) used as basis for valuing the land.

Subscriptions to capital stock

Corporations sometimes sell stock on a subscription plan, in which the investor agrees to pay the subscription price at a future date or in a series of installments. For example, Subscriptions Receivable: Common would be debited and Common Stock Subscribed would be credited when the subscription contract was signed. Collections would be credited to Subscriptions Receivable: Common; when the entire subscription price had been collected and the stock issued, Common Stock Subscribed would be debited and Common Stock would be credited. The following illustration demonstrates the accounting procedures for stock subscriptions.

In this example, 10,000 shares of no par value stock are subscribed at a price of $15. Subscriptions for 6,000 shares are collected in full. A partial payment is received on the other 4,000 shares.

Subscription price above par

Subscriptions Receivable: Common	150,000	
Common Stock Subscribed		150,000

Received subscriptions for 10,000 shares of no par value stock at price of $15 a share.

When the subscriptions for 6,000 shares are collected in full, certificates for 6,000 shares will be issued. The following entries are made:

Certificates issued for fully paid shares

Cash	90,000	
Subscriptions Receivable: Common		90,000

Collected subscriptions in full for 6,000 shares at $15 each.

Common Stock Subscribed	90,000	
Common Stock		90,000

Issued certificates for 6,000 fully paid $10 par value shares.

The subscriber to the remaining 4,000 shares paid only half of the amount of his subscription but promised to pay the remainder within a month. Stock certificates will not be issued to him until his subscription

[9] If no par value shares were issued for the land, the entire $90,000 would be credited to the Common Stock, no par value, account.

is collected in full, but the partial collection is recorded by the following entry:

Cash 30,000
    Subscriptions Receivable: Common 30,000
Collected partial payment on subscription for 4,000 shares.

Shares may be sold, under the Canada Business Corporations Act, for payments on an installment basis. But the shares cannot be issued until they have been fully paid for; and the purchaser will have no rights as a shareholder until full payment has been made.

From the corporation's point of view, Subscriptions Receivable is a current asset, which ordinarily will be collected within a short time.[10] If financial statements are prepared between the date of obtaining subscriptions and the date of issuing the stock, the Common Stock Subscribed account will appear in the stockholders' equity section of the balance sheet.

Special records of corporations

The financial page of today's newspaper reports that the most actively traded stocks on the Toronto Stock Exchange during the current week were the following:

	Number of Shares sold	*Closing Price*
Canadian Pacific Ltd.	*231,000*	*$19*
Massey-Ferguson Ltd.	*158,300*	*20½*
Canadian Industrial Gas & Oil Co.	*156,400*	*8½*

Several significant facts concerning capital stock transactions are implicit in this brief news item. In the first place, the three corporations listed did not necessarily sell any shares of their stock today. The quantities of shares listed above were probably sold by existing stockholders to other investors. When a corporation first issues its stock, the transaction is between the corporation and the investor; once the stock is outstanding, most further stock transactions are between individuals and do not affect the corporation which issued the stock. However, the corporation must be informed of each such stock transaction so that it can correct its records of stock ownership by eliminating the name of the former owner and adding the name of the new owner.

A second observation which might be made from the above news item is that a great volume of trading occurs each business day in the stocks of large corporations listed on the nation's stock exchanges. The availability of a ready market which permits the individual investor to convert his stockholdings into cash at any time is one of the principal rea-

---

[10]When the corporation does not intend to ask subscribers to pay in the near future the amounts which they owe, the subscriptions receivable may be shown on the balance sheet as a non-current asset or be deducted from the Common Stock account.

sons that corporations have become the dominant form of business organization.

STOCK CERTIFICATES Ownership of a corporation is evidenced by stock certificates. A large corporation with stock listed on an organized stock exchange usually has many millions of shares outstanding and may have several hundred thousand stockholders. The number of shares changing hands on a typical business day may be as many as 10,000 shares. Alcan Aluminum Ltd., for example, has almost 33 million shares of stock outstanding. These shares are owned by approximately 63,000 investors. (The term *investor* as used in this discussion is meant to include investment groups or entities such as pension funds, investment clubs, and similar organizations, as well as individual investors.)

Even a small corporation is apt to have a considerable number of stock certificates to account for. It is essential, therefore, that detailed records be maintained showing exactly how many shares are outstanding and the names and addresses of the shareholders. These capital stock records are in a process of continual change to reflect the purchase and sale of shares among the army of public investors.

A small corporation may order blank stock certificates from a printer, usually in a bound book with stubs similar to a chequebook. The certificates and the stubs are serially numbered by the printer, which aids the corporation in maintaining control over both the outstanding and the unissued certificates. At the time of issuance, a certificate is signed by the president and the secretary of the corporation, the number of shares represented by the certificate is filled in, and the certificate is delivered to a stockholder.

A stock certificate and the related stub are shown on page 486. This certificate is ready to be detached from the stub and delivered to the shareholder, Richard Warren. Note that the certificate has been signed by the officers of the company and that the following information is listed on both the certificate and the stub:

1 Certificate number. 901
2 Name of shareholder . . . . Richard Warren
3 Number of shares 100
4 Date issued . . . . January 10, 1974
5 Type of stock . . . . Common

The certificate is now detached from the stub and delivered to Richard Warren. The open stubs in the certificate book (stubs without any certificates attached) represent outstanding certificates. If a stockholder sells his shares, his certificate is returned to the company, canceled, and attached to the corresponding stub in the stock certificate book. The total number of shares of stock outstanding at any time can be determined by adding up the number of shares listed on all the open stubs.

Certificate No. .... 901 ....

For .... −100− .... Common Shares
The Gold Cup Company Ltd.

ISSUED TO:
.... Richard Warren ....

Date ...... January 10, 1974 ....

FROM WHOM TRANSFERRED:

.... −−Original issue−− ....

No. of Original Certificate	No. of Original Shares	No. of Shares Transferred

---

Certificate No. .... 901 ....   −100− ..... Shares

THE GOLD CUP COMPANY LIMITED

Incorporated under the Laws of Canada

Authorized Capital Stock

10,000 Common Shares of $10.00 par value each

THIS IS TO CERTIFY that .... Richard Warren ....
is the owner of ...... −one hundred− ...... fully paid and non-assessable Common Shares of the Gold Cup Company Ltd., transferable only on the books of this company by the said owner hereof in person or by agent, upon surrender of this certificate properly endorsed.

In Witness Whereof the seal of the company and the signatures of its duly authorized officers on this . 10th . day of January 1974 .

Murray Whitehall
President

Byron Bannock
Secretary

STOCKHOLDERS' LEDGER For a company with a large number of stockholders, it is not practicable to include in the general ledger an account with each stockholder. Instead a single controlling account entitled Common Stock is carried in the general ledger and a subsidiary stockholders' ledger with individual stockholders is maintained. (A ledger is usually in the form of a file of cards rather than a book, when a great many separate accounts must be maintained.) In this stockholders' ledger, each stockholder's account shows the number of shares which he owns, the certificate numbers, and the dates of acquisition and sale. Entries are not made in dollars but in number of shares.

The stockholders' ledger contains essentially the same information as the stock certificate book, but the arrangement of the information is in an alphabetical listing of stockholders rather than in the sequence of stock certificate numbers. One stockholder may own a number of certificates, acquired at various dates. His entire holdings would be summarized in his account in the stockholders' ledger.

STOCK TRANSFER AGENT AND STOCK REGISTRAR The large corporation with thousands of stockholders and a steady flow of stock transfers usually turns over the function of maintaining capital stock records to an independent stock transfer agent and a stock registrar. A trust company serves as stock transfer agent and another trust company acts as the stock registrar. When certificates are to be transferred from one owner to another, the certificates are sent to the transfer agent, who cancels them, makes the necessary entries in the stockholders' ledger, and signs new certificates which are forwarded to the stock registrar. The function of the registrar is to prevent any improper issuance of stock certificates. To accomplish this objective, the trust company acting as registrar maintains records showing the total number of shares outstanding at all times. The use of an independent stock transfer agent and a stock registrar is an excellent control device, which eliminates the possibility that a dishonest officer or employee of a corporation might issue stock certificates for cash without making any entry in the records.

MINUTES BOOK A corporate minutes book consists of a narrative record of all actions taken at official meetings of the corporation's board of directors and of its stockholders. Typical of the actions described in the minutes book are the declaration of dividends by the board of directors, the authorization of important transactions such as the obtaining of bank loans or the purchase of plant and equipment, the setting of officers' salaries, and the adoption of retirement plans or pension agreements.

Illustration of corporation balance sheet

In this chapter, sections of balance sheets have been shown in several illustrations. A complete and fairly detailed balance sheet of the Crenshaw Corporation Ltd. is presented on pages 488 and 489 to bring together many of the individual features which have been discussed in this chapter or will be discussed in Chapters 17 and 18. In studying this corporation balance sheet, however, the student should bear in mind that current practice includes many variations and alternatives in the choice of terminology and the arrangement of items in the statements.

Statement of financial condition

A variation from the account form and report form of balance sheet previously illustrated is the *statement of financial condition.* In this variation, emphasis is placed on the working capital position of the company by deducting the current liabilities from the current assets and showing the working capital as a separate figure. Noncurrent assets are then added to working capital and long-term liabilities deducted to arrive at the total net assets, which represent the stockholders' equity. One disadvantage of the statement of financial condition (or statement of financial position, as it is sometimes called) is the absence of a figure for total assets. For an example of the statement of financial condition, see the statements of the Hudson Bay Mining and Smelting Co. Ltd. in the Appendix.

Detailed balance sheet for corporation

CRENSHAW CORPORATION LTD.
Balance Sheet
December 31, 1976

Assets

Current assets:

Cash			$ 355,612
Canadian government securities, at cost (market value $812,800)			810,000
Accounts receivable		$1,180,200	
Less: Allowance for uncollectible accounts		15,000	1,165,200
Inventories			1,300,800
Prepaid expenses			125,900
Total current assets			$3,757,512
Investments:			
Bond sinking fund		$ 364,938	
Real estate not used in business		80,000	444,938
Plant and equipment (at cost):			
Land		$ 500,000	
Buildings	$3,482,100		
Less: Accumulated depreciation	400,000	3,082,100	3,582,100
Other assets:			
Organization costs		$ 60,000	
Long-term deposit on lease		50,000	110,000
Total assets			$7,894,550

QUESTIONS

1 Distinguish between corporations and partnerships in terms of the following characteristics:
  a Owners' liability
  b Transferability of ownership interest
  c Continuity of existence
  d Federal taxation on income

2 The corporate form of organization is usually considered advantageous for large enterprises. Why do you suppose large firms of chartered accountants, lawyers, or architects do not incorporate?

3 Describe three kinds of expenses that may be incurred in the process of organizing a corporation. How are such expenditures treated for accounting purposes? Why?

4 What are the basic rights of the owner of a share of corporate stock? In what way are these basic rights commonly modified with respect to the owner of a share of preferred stock?

5 Describe the usual nature of the following features as they apply to a share of preferred stock: (*a*) cumulative, (*b*) participating, (*c*) convertible, and (*d*) redeemable.

Liabilities & Stockholders' Equity

Current liabilities:

Accounts payable		$1,065,840
Estimated income taxes payable		384,310
Dividends payable		10,000
Bond interest payable		10,000
Total current liabilities		$1,470,150

Long-term liabilities:

Bonds payable, 4%, due Oct. 1, 1984	$1,000,000	
Less: Discount on bonds payable	18,000	982,000
Total liabilities		$2,452,150

Stockholders' equity:[11]

Capital stock

$5 Cumulative preferred stock, no par value, 8,000 shares issued	$ 800,000	
Common stock, no par value, authorized 1,000,000 shares, issued 600,000 shares	3,000,000	
	3,800,000	

Retained earnings

Reserve for contingencies	$ 400,000		
Unappropriated – per schedule[12]	1,242,400	1,642,400	
Total stockholders' equity			5,442,400
Total liabilities & stockholders' equity			$7,894,550

---

6 Why is noncumulative preferred stock considered a very unattractive form of investment opportunity?

7 Smith owns 200 of the 8,000 shares of common stock issued and outstanding in X Company. The company issued 2,000 additional shares of stock. What is Smith's position with respect to the new issue if he is entitled to preemptive rights?

8 What are the advantages and disadvantages of the use of no-par capital stock?

9 When stock is issued by a corporation in exchange for assets other than cash, the accountant faces the problem of determining the dollar amount at which to record the transaction. Discuss the factors he should consider and explain their significance.

10 State the classification (asset, liability, stockholders' equity, or expense) of each of the following accounts:

[11]While contributed surplus is not included in this illustrated balance sheet, it will continue to be part of many balance sheets. Corporations which were incorporated under the old Canada Corporations Act may elect to include in stated capital the premium on shares existing at the date of continuance under the Canada Business Corporations Act. Also, many provincial Acts still permit the issue of par value shares.

[12]See Chapter 17, page 506 for an example of a Statement of Retained Earnings.

  a Subscriptions receivable: *e* Capital stock subscribed:
    common   preferred
  b Organization costs   *f* Premium on common stock
  c Capital stock, common   *g* Federal and provincial income taxes
  d Retained earnings

  11 Explain the following terms:
    a Stock transfer agent   *d* Minutes book
    b Stockholders' ledger   *e* Stock registrar
    c Underwriter

EXERCISES

Ex. 16-1 The stockholders' equity section of the balance sheet appeared as follows in a recent annual report of North Corporation Ltd. incorporated under the Ontario Business Corporations Act:

Capital stock:

$5.50 dividend cumulative preferred stock without par value 10°

   Authorized—274,425 shares

   Outstanding—128,000 shares . . . . $ 12,800,000

Common stock, $2.50 par value

   Authorized—6,000,000 shares

   Issued—4,298,140 shares   10,745,350

                                                23,545,350

Premium on common stock   27,209,890

Retained earnings   72,748,347

   Total stockholders' equity $123,503,587

From this information compute answers to the following:

a What is the amount of the annual dividend requirement on the preferred stock issue?

b Total dividends of $4,983,817 were declared on the preferred and common stock during the year, and the balance in retained earnings at the beginning of the year amounted to $63,770,512. What was the amount of net income for the year?

c What is the stated value per share of the preferred stock?

d What was the average issuance price of a share of common stock?

Ex. 16-2 Heritage Corporation Ltd. was incorporated under the Canada Business Corporations Act on July 1, 1976. The corporation was authorized to issue 10,000 shares of no par value, $8 cumulative preferred stock, and 100,000 shares of no-par common stock.

    All the preferred stock was issued at $100 and 80,000 shares of the common stock were sold for $22 per share. Prepare a statement of stockholders' equity for Heritage Corporation Ltd. immediately after the sale of the securities but prior to any operation of the company.

Ex. 16-3 Atlas Mineral Company Ltd. has outstanding two classes of $100 par value stock: 1,000 shares of 6% cumulative preferred and 5,000 shares of common. The company had a $10,000 deficit at the beginning of the current year, and preferred dividends had not been paid for two years. During the current year, the company earns $50,000. What will be the balance in retained earnings at the end of the current year, if the company pays a dividend of $2 per share on common stock?

Ex. 16-4 A portion of the stockholders' equity section for the McCall Corporation Ltd. is shown below:

Stockholders' equity:

Preferred stock, $3 cumulative, no par value, authorized and issued

  100,000 shares . . . . $ 5,000,000

Preferred stock, $9 noncumulative, no par value, authorized and
  issued 20,000 shares   2,000,000
Common stock, no par value, authorized and issued 1 million shares   5,000,000
                                                                                $12,000,000

Assume that all the stock was issued on January 1, 19___, and that no dividends were paid during the first two years of operations. During the third year, McCall Corporation Ltd. paid total cash dividends of $1,280,000.

a Compute the amount of cash dividends paid during the third year to each of the three classes of stock.

b Compute the dividends paid *per share* during the third year for each of the three classes of stock.

Ex. 16-5 Clayton Tidyman owns 1,000 shares of convertible preferred stock of North Oil Company Ltd., each of which is convertible into 1.5 shares of North's common stock. The preferred stock is currently selling at $80 per share and pays a dividend of $2.50 per year. The common stock sells for $50 and pays an annual dividend of $2 per share. Tidyman wants to convert the preferred stock in order to increase his total dividend income, but an accounting student suggests that he sell his preferred stock and then buy 1,500 shares of common on the open market. Tidyman objects to the student's suggestion on the grounds that he would have to pay income taxes at the rate of 50% on one-half of the gain from sale of preferred stock, which he had acquired at $68 per share a year ago. Prepare a schedule showing the results under the two alternatives.

PROBLEMS

Group A

16A-1 Case A The Greer Corporation Ltd. has agreed to issue 20,000 shares of common stock in exchange for a manufacturing plant having an agreed valuation of $500,000.

Instructions Give the journal entry that should be made to record this transaction under each of the following assumptions:

a The stock has a $25 par value.
b The stock has a $2 par value.
c The stock is no par.

Case B Several years later the Greer Corporation Ltd. issued 2,000 shares of its $25 par value common in exchange for certain patent rights. The patent rights were entered on the books at $50,000. At the time Greer common stock was quoted on the over-the-counter market at "35 bid and 37 asked"; that is, sellers were offering a given quantity of the stock at $37 per share, and buyers were offering to buy certain quantities at $35 per share.

Instructions Comment on the company's treatment of this transaction. Write a brief statement explaining whether you agree or disagree, and why. What is the essential difference between the evidence available to the accountant as a basis for his record in Case A and the evidence available in Case B?

16A-2 The three partners of Diller & Company agreed on December 31, 1975, to incorporate their business. The balance sheet of the partnership on this date is shown below:

Assets	$500,000	Accounts payable	$125,000
		Kleeman, capital	188,000
		Lewis, capital	112,000
		Mars, capital	75,000
	$500,000		$500,000

The partners applied for and received a charter authorizing 100,000 shares of no par value common stock and 10,000 shares of no par value $6 cumulative preferred stock. Organization costs amounted to $8,200. On January 1, 1976, the corporation was formed, and each partner was issued, no par, common stock for one-half of his capital interest and preferred stock for the remaining half. The preferred stock is to be issued at $100 per share and the common stock at $10. The organization costs were paid on January 1 and were not amortized during the year.

During 1976, the corporation earned $125,000 before income taxes. Accounts payable increased by $24,800 during 1976; the only other liability at year-end was income taxes payable. Income taxes are 40% of taxable income. (Assume net income and taxable income are the same amount.) Regular quarterly dividends were paid on preferred stock, and a dividend of $1.50 per share was paid on common stock.

Instructions Prepare the balance sheet of Diller Corporation, as of December 31, 1976. Show in two separate supporting schedules how you arrive at:
a The amounts of stock issued
b The amount of retained earnings at December 31, 1976

16A-3 Dixon Corporation Ltd. had net assets of $900,000 as of January 1, 1973, represented by 90,000 shares of $5 par value common and 1,200 shares of 6%, $100 par value, cumulative preferred stock. All shares had been issued at par. The preferred stock is convertible into common at any time on the basis of one share of preferred for 20 shares of common. Income before income taxes is expected to be 20% of net assets during 1973. The company is subject to income taxes at an average rate of 40%.

Instructions Assuming that earnings are as forecast,
a Compute the amount of net income in 1973 that is allocable to common stock, assuming that none of the preferred shares is converted during the year.
b Compute the 1973 net income available per share of common stock, assuming that all preferred shares are converted at the beginning of 1973. Round off to the nearest cent.
c Determine the maximum legal dividend per share of common that could be paid at the end of 1973, assuming that all shares of preferred were converted at the beginning of 1973.

16A-4 The stockholders' equity section of the Manning Corporation's balance sheet at the close of the current year is given below.

MANNING CORPORATION LTD.
Stockholders' Equity
December 31, Current Year

$2.75 preferred stock, $50 par value, authorized 10,000 shares:		
Issued	$180,000	
Subscribed	90,000	$270,000
Common stock, no par value, authorized 80,000 shares:		
Issued		$171,000
Contributed surplus		
Premium on preferred stock	$ 27,000	
Distributable surplus	57,000	84,000
Retained earnings (deficit)...........................		(75,000)
Total stockholders' equity		$450,000

Manning Corporation Ltd. was incorporated under the Companies Act (Canada) in 1964. All the common stock was issued in 1964 and 25% of all the proceeds (equal to $1.25 per share) was credited to distributable surplus.

Among the assets of the corporation appears the following item: Subscriptions Receivable: Preferred, $45,000.

Instructions On the basis of this information, write a brief answer to the following questions, showing any necessary supporting computations.

a How many shares of preferred and common have been issued?

b How many shares of preferred have been subscribed?

c What was the average price per share received by the corporation on its preferred stock including preferred stock subscribed?

d What is the average amount per share that subscribers of preferred stock have yet to pay on their subscriptions?

e What is the total legal value of its capital stock?

16A-5 Each of the cases described below is independent of the others. (All corporations were incorporated or continued under the Canada Business Corporations Act.)

Case A Corporation X was organized in 1974 and was authorized to issue 100,000 common shares without par value. The stock was issued at $5, and the corporation reported a net loss of $30,000 for 1974 and a net loss of $70,000 in 1975. In 1976 net income was $2.10 per share.

Case B Corporation Y was organized in 1972. The company was authorized to issue 125,000 shares of no par value common and 10,000 shares of $6 cumulative preferred stock. All of the preferred and 120,000 shares of common were issued at $100 and $10 each respectively. The preferred stock was redeemable at $105. During the first five years of its existence, the corporation earned a total of $720,000 and paid dividends of 25 cents per share each year on the common stock.

Case C Corporation Z was organized in 1973, issuing at $20 one-half of the 100,000 shares of common stock authorized. On January 1, 1974, the company sold at $100 the entire 5,000 authorized shares of $5, cumulative preferred. On January 1, 1975 the company issued 8,000 shares of an authorized 10,000 shares of $6 no-par cumulative preferred, for $815,000. The $6 preferred cumulative provided that after common stockholders had received $3 per share, it participated in all additional dividends on a share-for-share basis up to $6 per share. The company suffered losses in 1973 and 1974, reporting a deficit of $150,000 at the end of 1974. Dividends of $1 per share of common were paid in 1975 and $4.25 in 1976. The company earned a total of $752,600 during 1975 and 1976.

Instructions For each of the independent situations described, prepare in good form the stockholders' equity section of the balance sheet as of December 31, 1976. Include a supporting schedule for each case showing your determination of the balance of retained earnings that should appear in the balance sheet.

16A-6 At the end of the current year, the bookkeeper has prepared the following statement of stockholders' equity for the Jayde Products Corporation Ltd.:

JAYDE PRODUCTS CORPORATION LTD.
Capital
December 31, Current Year

Preferred stock, 5,000 shares	$317,300
Preferred stock, $75 par value, issued 2,400 shares	180,000
Common stock, par value $25	300,000
Surplus	161,500
	$958,800

The company has two classes of preferred shares. It is authorized to issue 5,000 shares of 5½%, $100 par value, preferred, and 8,000 shares of $4 preferred, par value $75. To date 2,000 shares of the 5½% preferred have been sold for cash at 102 per share, and 2,200 shares have been subscribed at 103 per share. One-half of the subscription price has thus far been received by the company. The $4 preferred was issued in exchange for property. At the date of acquisition the board of directors, after careful investigation, estimated that the fair market value of the property was $200,000.

Common share capital authorization is 20,000 shares, of which 12,000 shares were sold for cash and 400 shares were given to promoters in settlement of a charge for $10,000 covering legal costs and services in organizing the company. The bookkeeper states that the corporation realized a gain by issuing 4,000 common shares at a price that was $6 per share in excess of par value, and that this gain is included in the surplus balance. The company has had a net income during its lifetime of $225,000 and has paid $87,500 in dividends.

Instructions

a Prepare in good form a revised version of the stockholders' equity section of the balance sheet.

b Some of the changes you should make in the bookkeeper's figures will increase or decrease the net assets reported by this company. Prepare a schedule showing the amount of the increase or decrease resulting from your corrections and the source of the change, that is, the asset or liability accounts and amounts involved.

Group B

16B-1 Instructions For each of the independent situations described below, prepare in good form the stockholders' equity section of the balance sheet as of December 31, 1978. Include a supporting schedule for each case showing your determination of the balance of retained earnings that should appear in the balance sheet. Both corporations were incorporated or continued under the Canada Business Corporations Act.

(1) Corporation A was organized in 1976 and was authorized to issue 20,000 shares of no par value common. The stock was issued at $5, and the corporation reported a net loss of $5,000 for 1976 and a net loss of $13,000 in 1977. In 1978 net income was $1.60 per share.

(2) Corporation B was organized in 1974. The company was authorized to issue 25,000 shares of no par value common and 1,000 shares of cumulative preferred stock. All of the preferred was issued at $100 and 20,000 shares of common were issued at $10. The preferred stock was redeemable at $105 and was entitled to dividends of $6 before any dividends were paid to common. During the first five years of its existence, the corporation earned a total of $140,000 and paid dividends of 20 cents per share each year on common stock.

16B-2 The three partners of the Signal Company agreed on December 31, 1976, to incorporate their business. The balance sheet of the partnership is shown below.

SIGNAL COMPANY
Balance Sheet
December 31, 1976

Various assets	$300,000	Accounts payable	$ 50,000
		Duncan, capital	130,000
		Latham, capital	70,000
		Wallace, capital	50,000
	$300,000		$300,000

Other data The partners applied for and received a charter authorizing 25,000 shares of no par value common stock and 2,000 shares of no par value, $6 cumulative preferred stock. Organization costs were $3,000. On January 1, 1977, the corporation was formed, and each partner was issued, at $10, common stock for one-half of his capital interest and preferred stock at $100 for the remaining half. The organization costs were paid on January 1 and were not amortized during the year.

During 1977 the corporation earned $120,000 before income taxes. Accounts payable increased by $20,000 during 1977; the only other liability at year-end was income taxes payable. The provision for income taxes was 25% of the first $100,000 of net income and 46% of net income in excess of $100,000. Dividends were paid on preferred stock, and dividends of $1 per share were paid on common stock.

Instructions Prepare the balance sheet of the Signal Company Ltd. as of December 31, 1977. Show in two separate supporting schedules how you arrive at (*a*) the amounts of stock issued and (*b*) the amount of retained earnings at December 31, 1977.

16B-3 Troon Corporation was organized on July 1, 1976, with authorized stock of 100,000 shares of no par value common and 5,000 shares of no par value, $6 preferred stock. Troon was given 100 shares of preferred and 1,000 shares of common for his work and expenses in organizing and promoting the corporation. The value of Troon's services was $20,000 with ½ of this amount being assigned to the common shares. Lawyers' fees of $900 in connection with the formation of the corporation have been billed but not paid.

Near the end of July, 40,000 shares of common were sold for cash at $10 each, $60,000 of which was used to buy land and $300,000 applied to the price of a building. The building cost $670,000; the balance was represented by a 6% mortgage due in 10 years.

Troon transferred assets from a previous business in exchange for 3,000 shares of preferred. The current fair value of these assets was as follows: notes receivable, $180,000; inventories, $30,000; equipment, $90,000.

The business did not begin operation until after July 31, but interest of $750 accrued on the notes receivable between the time they were turned over to the corporation and July 31. Interest on the mortgage payable did not begin until August 1. (Ignore income taxes.)

Instructions Prepare in good form the balance sheet of the Troon Corporation Ltd. as of July 31, 1976.

16B-4 The stockholders' equity section of the Balboa Corporation's balance sheet at the close of the current year is given below:

Stockholders' equity:

$1.50 preferred stock, $25 par value, authorized 500,000 shares:		
Issued	$3,600,000	
Subscribed	1,800,000	$ 5,400,000
Common stock no par value, authorized		
2,000,000 shares		4,050,000
Contributed surplus		
Premium on preferred stock		270,000
Retained earnings (deficit)		(200,000)
Total stockholders' equity		$ 9,520,000

The common stock was sold at two different times. The first issue, representing one-half of the common shares now outstanding, was sold at $8. Remaining shares were sold for $10.

Among the assets of the corporation appears the following item: Subscriptions Receivable: Preferred, $374,400.

Instructions On the basis of this information, write a brief answer to the following questions, showing any necessary supporting computations.
a How many shares of preferred and common stock have been issued?
b How many shares of preferred stock have been subscribed?
c What was the average price per share received (including stock subscribed) by the corporation on its preferred stock?
d What was the average price per share received by the corporation on its common stock?
e What is the average amount per share that subscribers of preferred stock have yet to pay on their subscriptions?
f What is the total amount paid-in by stockholders?
g What is the total legal value of the capital stock including stock subscribed?

16B-5 The cases described below are independent of one another.

Case A On May 31, 1976, the B.C. Corporation Ltd. had outstanding 175,000 of 300,000 authorized shares of $20 par value common stock, and 15,000 of 50,000 authorized shares of $7 preferred stock, cumulative, par value $100. The preferred was entitled to liquidation preference of par, plus any dividends in arrears. The company had been in existence for three years and had lost money in each year, accumulating a deficit of $148,000 as of May 31, 1976. On that date all assets, other than cash on hand of $92,000, were sold for 80% of their book value, and the liabilities of $800,000 were paid in full.

Instructions Prepare a schedule showing the amount of assets available for distribution to stockholders, and the amount per share that would be received in liquidation on each of the two kinds of stock as of May 31, 1976.

Case B Ontario Corporation Ltd. was organized on January 1, 1975, and authorized to issue 200,000 shares of $10 par value common stock and 25,000 shares of $2 cumulative preferred stock, par value $40 per share. Promoters and lawyers were given 10,000 shares of common stock for their services in organizing the corporation, and 85,000 shares were sold at $12 in cash. During 1975, the company lost $100,000. At the beginning of 1976, the company needed funds, and in order to sell its preferred at par, the preferred stock was made convertible into four shares of common stock. On this basis, 12,000 shares of preferred were sold at par early in 1976. During 1976, Ontario Corporation Ltd. earned $380,000 and declared a dividend of $1.50 per share on common stock after 10,000 of the preferred shares were converted into common stock. A $1 dividend was declared on these shares and was paid before they were converted. All of the 135,000 common shares outstanding on December 31, 1976, received the $1.50 dividend.

Instructions Prepare in good form the stockholders' equity section of the balance sheet as of December 31, 1976. Show in a separate schedule how you arrived at the balance of retained earnings at that date.

16B-6 The Wilson Corporation Ltd. was organized under the Ontario Business Corporations Act on March 1 of the current year. The company is legally authorized to issue 10,000 $3 preferred shares, par value $50 per share, and 30,000 no-par common shares. The transactions given below took place during March and April:

Mar. 1 Issued for cash 2,000 shares of preferred for $52 per share.
Mar. 10 Received subscriptions for 4,000 shares of preferred at $54 per share, and one-half the subscription price in cash.
Mar. 12 Issued for cash 3,000 common shares at $28 each.

Mar. 15 Received subscriptions for 10,000 common shares at $30 each. 25 per cent of the subscription price was paid in cash.

Apr. 10 Subscribers to 2,400 shares of preferred paid the balance of their subscriptions in cash and shares were issued.

Apr. 18 Received from lawyers a bill for $3,200 covering legal services in connection with the organization of the limited company. In lieu of payment, they agreed to accept 100 common shares.

Apr. 19 Issued 12,000 shares of common in full payment for land building appraised at $375,000 of which 10% applies to the land.

Apr. 25 Received an additional 25% of the subscription price from March 15 subscribers.

Instructions
a Record the above transactions in general journal form.
b Post entries to T accounts.
c Prepare a balance sheet for the Wilson Corporation Ltd. as of April 30.

BUSINESS DECISION PROBLEM 16

Upstate Electric and Downstate Power are two utility companies with very stable earnings. Upstate Electric consistently has a net income of approximately $16,000,000 per year, and Downstate Power's net income consistently approximates $14,000,000 per year. Upstate Electric has 1,800,000 shares of $3 preferred stock, no par value, and 2,650,000 shares of no par value common stock outstanding. Downstate Power has 800,000 shares of $6 preferred stock, no par value, and 1,840,000 shares of no par value common stock outstanding. Assume that both companies distribute all net income as dividends every year, and will continue to do so. Neither company plans to issue any more stock.

Instructions
a Compute the annual dividend which would be paid on the common stock issue of each company, assuming that Upstate Electric has a net income of $16,000,000 and Downstate Power has a net income of $14,000,000.
b Which company's common stock would you expect to have the higher *market price per share?* Support your answer with information provided in the problem.

SEVENTEEN

CORPORATIONS EARNINGS PER SHARE RETAINED EARNINGS AND DIVIDENDS

REPORTING THE RESULTS OF OPERATIONS

The most important aspect of corporate financial reporting, in the view of most stockholders, is the determination of periodic net income. The level of dividends and the market price of common stock depend heavily on the company's operating performance. For this reason, the *earnings per share* figure is of particular interest to stockholders.

Extraordinary gains and losses

From time to time, most businesses will realize gains and incur losses which are not a part of the main activities of the business. Examples of such items include (*1*) gains and losses on the sale of plant assets; (*2*) uninsured losses from fires, theft, floods, and earthquakes; (*3*) gains and losses from the sale of investments; and (*4*) damages awarded in lawsuits. These gains and losses are shown in the income statement, usually under a separate caption such as Extraordinary Gains and Losses, Nonrecurring Gains and Losses, or Nonoperating Gains and Losses. To warrant this separate reporting in the income statement, the item must be *material* in amount and *significantly different* from the regular activities of the business.

Extraordinary items should include only gains and losses which are not typical of the normal business activities of the enterprise and are not expected to occur regularly over a period of years.[1]

The Accounting and Auditing Research Committee of the CICA has taken the position that extraordinary items, as distinct from prior period adjustments and capital transactions, should be included in the determination of net income for the period.[2] The CICA requires that extraordinary gains and losses be reported separately (net of tax) in arriving at net income. Not all gains or losses, however large, should be treated as extraordinary items, because they "result from occurrences the underlying nature of which is typical of the customary business activities of the enterprise."[3] and therefore should be included in the determination of income *before* extraordinary items. These items should be disclosed separately or by way of footnote.

As an illustration of an item *which should be taken into account in arriving at income before extraordinary items,* consider the situation in which the amount of accounts receivable determined to be uncollectible is much larger than the balance in Allowance for Uncollectible Accounts. The recognition of this large collection loss should be shown as part of the current year's operations and not as an extraordinary loss.

What if a business discovers that the remaining useful life of its depreciable assets will be less than previously estimated? The increased amount of depreciation expense to be recognized during the remaining useful life of the asset should be treated as an element in the determination of operating income for the current and future periods, and not as a prior period adjustment or as an extraordinary loss.

Still another example of a correction which does not qualify either as a prior period adjustment or as an extraordinary item is a write-off to recognize inventory obsolescence. In other words, the normal recurring errors which inevitably come to light in any business are not to be treated as extraordinary items or as corrections to retained earnings, but should be treated as revenue or deductions from revenue *in arriving at income from operations.*

The use of estimates to deal with uncertainties is a necessary part of the accounting process. Since these estimates are seldom, if ever, entirely accurate, a number of inaccuracies will come to light which relate to some extent to prior fiscal periods. We have mentioned as examples the noncollectibility of receivables, the change in the estimated life of a depreciable asset, and inventory obsolescence. Financial reporting would not be improved by giving all these corrections special treatment in the income statement. Because of the inevitability of these corrections, the user of financial statements should be aware that the operating results reported each year may include the effects of some inaccurate estimates made in prior periods.

[1] Canadian Institute of Chartered Accountants, *CICA Handbook,* paragraph 3480.05.
[2] *Ibid.,* paragraph 3480.07
[3] *Ibid.,* paragraph 3480.11

Income statement for a corporation illustrated

To illustrate the preparation of an income statement for a corporation with extraordinary items, assume that the Thunder Corporation Ltd. had a net gain of $1,300,000 after applicable income taxes from sale of plant assets in 1974 and a net loss of $800,000 from disposal of long-term investments in 1973. In 1974, the corporation paid $1,950,000 of additional income taxes applicable to fiscal year 1972 and also wrote off $600,000 of obsolete inventory. A condensed income statement as it might appear in the annual report of the Thunder Corporation Ltd. is shown below:

THUNDER CORPORATION LTD.
Income Statement
For Years Ended June 30, 1974, and June 30, 1973

	1974	1973
Net sales and other revenues	$42,200,000	$37,200,000
Costs and expenses:		
Costs of goods sold (includes write-off of $600,000 of		
obsolete inventory in 1974)	$28,000,000	$25,300,000
Operating expenses	6,000,000	5,200,000
Other miscellaneous deductions	300,000	250,000
Income taxes, excluding tax on extraordinary items		
shown below	3,700,000	3,300,000
Total costs and expenses	$38,000,000	$34,050,000
Income before extraordinary items	$ 4,200,000	$ 3,150,000
Extraordinary items, net of tax*	1,300,000	(800,000)
Net income	$ 5,500,000	$ 2,350,000
Per share of common stock:		
Income before extraordinary items	$4.20	$3.15
Extraordinary items, net of tax*	1.30	(.80)
Net income	$5.50	$2.35

How is this company doing?

*Gain on sale of plant assets in 1974 and loss on disposal of long-term investments in 1973.

Note that the income tax assessment of $1,950,000 applicable to fiscal year 1972 is not shown in the income statement; this item is a "prior period adjustment" and will appear on the statement of retained earnings, which is illustrated on page 506. The write-off of obsolete inventory is included in the cost of goods sold for 1974 and is disclosed parenthetically. The extraordinary gain or loss is added to income before extraordinary items in arriving at net income and the earnings per share.

Companies whose stock is widely held or is listed on the major stock exchanges provide to their stockholders *interim* income statements (usually quarterly) in order to provide them with current earnings progress.

Earnings per share

The most widely used of all accounting statistics is probably *earnings per share* of common stock. The amount of annual earnings per share is used especially in making investment decisions. Since a purchase or sale of common stock is executed on the basis of the market price *per share,* it is helpful to know the amount of earnings applicable to a single share.

Both management and investors use earnings per share in evaluating the past performance of a business and in forming an opinion as to its potential for future performance. Because of the wide publicity given to earnings per share data in newspapers and business journals, it is important that these data be computed in a consistent and meaningful manner. The CICA Accounting Research Committee has concluded that *earnings per share data should be shown on the face of the income statement or in a note to the financial statements cross-referenced to the income statement.*[4] Such data customarily appear immediately following the figure for total net income. This type of presentation was illustrated on page 500 in showing the earnings per share for the Thunder Corporation Ltd. both before and after considering the effect of extraordinary items.

The computation of earnings per share is easily done for companies with common stock only: that is, companies not having convertible securities, stock options, warrants, or other rights capable of being converted into additional common shares. Such conversion would increase the number of common shares and therefore *dilute* (reduce) the earnings per common share. In the simplest situation, earnings per share is computed merely by dividing the net income for the period by the number of shares outstanding.

Many corporations have complex capital structures including various securities convertible into common stock. In this situation, a dual presentation is necessary: *basic earnings per share* based on the common shares actually outstanding, and *fully diluted earnings per share* based on the potential number of shares outstanding.[5] The fully diluted earnings per share of common stock is computed by assuming that all securities having the potential for conversion into common stock had actually been converted into common at the beginning of the current period. To illustrate, let us assume that a company has issued stock options to some of its officers entitling them to purchase common stock of the company at any time in the next several years at the market price which existed at the time the options were granted. The dual presentation of earnings per share data on the income statement would consist of (*1*) the basic earnings per share computed by dividing net income by the shares actually outstanding, and (2) the fully diluted earnings per share computed by dividing the net income figure, adjusted for the imputed income on the proceeds received from the exercise of the stock option, by a

[4] *Ibid.,* paragraph 3500.09.
[5] *Ibid.,* paragraph 3500.30.

number of shares equal to those presently outstanding plus those additional shares that would be outstanding if the stock options were exercised.

The work involved in making this dual presentation of earnings per share is often quite complex; therefore consideration of the implications of "fully diluted earnings per share" is more appropriately treated in the *Intermediate Accounting* volume of this series.

Retained earnings

In Chapter 16 the term *retained earnings* was used to describe that portion of stockholders' equity derived from profitable operations. An older term for this part of stockholders' equity is *earned surplus.* Because of the misleading connotations of the word "surplus," accountants have recommended that use of the term be discontinued. In accordance with this recommendation, a strong trend has developed to use "retained earnings" or "accumulated earnings" in place of "earned surplus" in corporate balance sheets.

The following table[6] indicates the increasing acceptance of the term, retained earnings, by Canadian companies.

		Number of Companies			Percentage		
	Term Used	1974	1973	1972	1974	1973	1972
Use of retained earnings in published statements	Earned surplus	4	6	9	1	2	3
	Retained earnings	292	290	280	90	89	86
	Other	29	29	36	9	9	11
		325	325	325	100	100	100

Retained earnings is a historical concept, representing the accumulated earnings (including prior period adjustments) minus dividends declared from the date of incorporation to the present. Each year the Income Summary account is closed by transferring the net income or net loss into the Retained Earnings account. If we assume that all extraordinary gains and losses are cleared through the Income Summary account and that there are no prior period adjustments, the only entries in the Retained Earnings account will be (1) the periodic transfer of net income (or loss) from the Income Summary account, (2) the debit entries for dividend declarations, and (3) transfers to or from reserve accounts representing appropriations of accumulated earnings.

In successful corporations the Retained Earnings account normally has a credit balance; but if total losses should exceed total net income, the Retained Earnings account will have a debit balance. This debit amount is listed in the balance sheet under the title Deficit, and is deducted from the total of the paid-in capital, as previously illustrated on page 470.

[6]Source: Canadian Institute of Chartered Accountants, *Financial Reporting in Canada,* Eleventh edition, Toronto, 1975 page 117.

Prior period adjustments to Retained Earnings account

Earlier in this chapter, it was suggested that extraordinary items of gain or loss should be included in the income statement, and that prior period adjustments be reported as debits or credits directly to the Retained Earnings account. Such adjustments are rare since they must be material items which are directly related to the activities of a prior period and which were not susceptible to a reasonably accurate measurement in the prior period. Furthermore, such adjustments must not be attributable, in any sense, to an economic event of the current year and must depend primarily on determinations by persons other than management (governmental agencies, for example).[7] Examples of adjustments which should be recorded directly in the Retained Earnings account include (1) additional tax assessments for prior years and (2) settlement of litigation based on events of earlier periods. Two other types of adjustments are treated as prior period adjustments even though they do not have all the four characteristics normally required for prior period adjustments. These two other types of prior period adjustments are a retroactive change in accounting principles and adjustments required to correct errors made in prior period.[8]

Going back to the Thunder Corporation Ltd. example described on page 500, the income tax assessment of $1,950,000 assessed in 1974 applicable to the fiscal year 1972 would be recorded in 1974 as follows:

Recording a prior period adjustment

Retained Earnings	*1,950,000*	
Income Tax Assessment Payable—Prior Period		*1,950,000*
To record income tax assessment applicable to the fiscal year		
1972 as a prior period adjustment.		

The presentation of this prior period adjustment in the statement of retained earnings for the Thunder Corporation Ltd. is illustrated on page 506.

Appropriations from retained earnings

Some corporations subdivide their retained earnings into two or more accounts. This subdivision is accomplished by journal entries which transfer a portion of the Retained Earnings account into various "reserve" accounts. A reserve account established in this manner is referred to as an *appropriation of retained earnings.*

Assume, for example, that a corporation is engaged in a highly speculative business in which operations may result in either large profits or large losses from one year to the next. The corporation has accumulated a balance of $1 million in the Retained Earnings account, and the board of directors decides to make a portion of this amount unavailable for

[7] *CICA Handbook,* paragraph 3400.01.
[8] *Ibid.,* paragraphs 3600.11 and 3600.12.

dividends by transferring $250,000 from the Retained Earnings account to a Reserve for Contingencies. The journal entry to carry out the decision of the directors is as follows:

Establishing a reserve for contin- gencies

Retained Earnings	*250,000*	
Reserve for Contingencies		*250,000*
To establish a reserve for contingencies.		

The point of this action is to make clear to readers of the financial statements that $250,000 of the retained earnings is not available for dividends. The Reserve for Contingencies appears in the stockholders' equity section of the balance sheet; the corporation still has a total of $1 million of retained earnings, but it shows this $1 million as two separate items, as follows:

No change in total retained earnings

Retained Earnings:		
Free and available for declaration of dividends	*$750,000*	
Reserve for contingencies	*250,000*	*$1,000,000*

Both the total stockholders' equity and the equity of each stockholder would be unchanged by this subdivision of retained earnings.

Contractual and voluntary appropriations of retained earnings

The reserve for contingencies described in the preceding section was created voluntarily by the board of directors. The board may bring an end to the existence of the reserve at any time merely by ordering it to be transferred back into the Retained Earnings account. The entry to dispose of the reserve would be as follows:

Reserve eliminated

Reserve for Contingencies	*250,000*	
Retained Earnings		*250,000*
To eliminate the reserve for contingencies.		

Not all appropriations of retained earnings are voluntary. When a corporation borrows money through the issuance of long-term notes or bonds, the borrowing contract may place a limit on the cash dividends which the corporation can pay during the life of the indebtedness. One means of limiting cash dividends is to transfer a portion of the retained earnings into a reserve account with a title such as Reserve for Retirement of Long-term Debt.

Reserves do not consist of assets

Some readers of financial statements erroneously assume that a Reserve for Contingencies consists of cash set aside for emergencies. This is completely untrue. A Reserve for Contingencies has a credit balance; it does not consist of cash or any other assets; it is merely a subdivision of retained earnings. This comment applies not only to Reserve for

Contingencies but to all reserves created from retained earnings. If management wishes to set aside a fund of cash for a specific future use, this is done by transferring cash to a special bank account. This special bank account would be a *fund* and not a reserve. It would have a debit balance and would appear on the asset side of the balance sheet.

Are appropriations of retained earnings necessary?

The only purpose of appropriating retained earnings is to inform readers of the financial statements that a portion of the retained earnings is "reserved" for a specific purpose and is not available for dividends. This information could be conveyed more directly, with less danger of misunderstanding, by a note accompanying the balance sheet. Only the board of directors has the authority to declare dividends. If the board wishes to retain the earnings in the business for plant expansion or other purposes, it is free to do so without going through the procedure of dividing the Retained Earnings account into two or more portions. Similarly, creditors can limit the payment of dividends by requiring that dividend payments shall not exceed a specified percentage of net income during the period of indebtedness, or that dividends can be paid only if the current ratio and the amount of working capital are above specified levels.

Misuse of the term "reserve"

In present-day terminology, the term *reserve* is properly used in only one sense, that is, to describe appropriations of retained earnings. Therefore, "reserves" should appear only in the stockholders' equity section of the balance sheet. In past years, the word *reserve* was often applied to asset valuation accounts, such as Reserve for Doubtful Accounts and Reserve for Depreciation. It was also used to describe liabilities of estimated amount, such as Reserve for Income Taxes. Such overworking of the term caused confusion and misunderstanding among readers of financial statements. Some companies aggravated the situation by including in their balance sheets a separate section for reserves, located between the liabilities and the stockholders' equity sections. Some of these undesirable practices persist today in published balance sheets, although considerable progress has been made in improving the terminology used in financial statements.

Statement of retained earnings

In addition to the balance sheet and the income statement, most corporations include a statement of retained earnings and a statement of changes in financial position in their annual reports to stockholders. (The latter statement will be discussed in Chapter 22.) The typical format of the statement of retained earnings is illustrated below for the Thunder Corporation Ltd., based on data given earlier in this chapter:

THUNDER CORPORATION LTD.
Statement of Retained Earnings
For Years Ended June 30, 1974, and June 30, 1973

	1974	1973
Retained earnings at beginning of year:		
As originally reported.	$15,400,000	$14,850,000
Prior period adjustment—additional income taxes,		
applicable to fiscal year ended June 30, 1972	(1,950,000)	(1,950,000)
As restated	$13,450,000	$12,900,000
Net income	5,500,000	2,350,000
Subtotal.	$18,950,000	$15,250,000
Less: Cash dividends on common stock:		
$2.40 per share in 1974	(2,400,000)	
$1.80 per share in 1973		(1,800,000)
Retained earnings at end of year	$16,550,000	$13,450,000

(Margin note: Statement of retained earnings shows prior period adjustments, net income, and dividends)

The additional income tax assessment for 1972 is shown as a correction to the balance in retained earnings for both years, since both beginning figures are overstated as originally reported. The statement of retained earnings thus provides a useful vehicle for the disclosure of prior period adjustments and for the reconciliation of changes in the Retained Earnings account resulting from net income (or net loss) and dividends declared.

An alternative presentation of net income and retained earnings is used by many companies. The reconciliation of retained earnings is shown in the body of the **combined statement of income and retained earnings,** as illustrated below for Aztec Corporation Ltd.:

AZTEC CORPORATION LTD.
Consolidated Statement of Operations
and Accumulated Earnings

	52 Weeks Ended	
	Oct. 26, 1974	Oct. 28, 1973
Revenues	$2,832,022,624	$2,924,449,385
Cost and expenses	2,805,300,329	2,872,228,093
Earnings before income taxes and extraordinary		
items	$ 26,722,295	$ 52,221,292
Income taxes	11,289,562	22,108,317
Earnings before extraordinary items	$ 15,432,733	$ 30,112,975
Extraordinary credit (charge)	(57,000,000)	827,240
Net earnings (loss)	$ (41,567,267)	$ 30,940,215
Accumulated earnings at beginning of year	220,452,931	202,855,837
	$ 178,885,664	$ 233,796,052

(Margin note: Combined statement of income and retained earnings)

Dividends on common stock:		
$0.90 per share ($1.10 per share in 1973)	11,016,755	13,343,121
Accumulated earnings at end of year	$ 167,868,909	$ 220,452,931
Earnings (loss) per common share:		
Earnings before extraordinary items	$ 1.12	$2.32
Extraordinary credit (charge)	$(4.66)	$0.07
Net earnings (loss)	$(3.54)	$2.39

The Aztec statement emphasizes the close relationship of operating results and accumulated earnings. Some readers of financial statements, however, object to the fact that net income (or loss) is "buried" in the body of the statement rather than being prominently displayed as the final figure before earnings per share are computed.

DIVIDENDS AND STOCK SPLITS

The term *dividend,* when used by itself, is generally understood to mean a distribution of cash by a corporation to its stockholders. Dividends are stated as a specific amount per share as, for example, a dividend of $1 per share. It follows that the amount received by each stockholder is in proportion to the number of shares owned.

Dividends are paid only through action by the board of directors. The board has full discretion to declare a dividend or to refrain from doing so. Once the declaration of a dividend has been announced, the obligation to pay the dividend is a current liability of the corporation and cannot be rescinded.

Dividends are occasionally paid in assets other than cash. When a corporation goes out of existence (particularly a small corporation with only a few stockholders), it may choose to distribute noncash assets to its owners rather than to convert all assets into cash.

A dividend may also be paid in the form of additional shares of a company's own stock. This type of distribution is called a *stock dividend.* Stock dividends are of great practical importance and also of much theoretical interest. They will be discussed at length later in this chapter.

A *liquidating* dividend occurs when a corporation returns to stockholders all or part of their paid-in capital investment. Liquidating dividends are usually paid only when a corporation is going out of existence or is making a permanent reduction in the size of its operations. Normally dividends are paid from the profits of a corporation, and the recipient of a dividend is entitled to assume that the dividend represents a distribution of profits unless he is specifically notified that the dividend is a return of invested capital.

Cash dividends

The prospect of receiving cash dividends is a principal reason for investing in the stocks of corporations. An increase or decrease in the established rate of dividends will usually cause an immediate rise or fall in the market price of the company's stock. Stockholders are keenly interested in prospects for future dividends and as a group are generally strongly in favor of more generous dividend payments. The board of directors, on the other hand, is primarily concerned with the long-run growth and financial strength of the corporation; it may prefer to restrict dividends to a minimum in order to conserve cash for purchase of plant and equipment or for other needs of the company. The so-called "growth companies" generally plow back into the business most of their earnings and pay little or nothing in cash dividends.

The preceding discussion suggests three requirements for the payment of a cash dividend. These are:

1 **Retained earnings.** Since dividends represent a distribution of earnings to stockholders, the theoretical maximum for dividends is the total net income (after income taxes) of the company. As a practical matter, most corporations limit dividends to somewhere near 50% of earnings, in the belief that a major portion of the profits must be retained in the business if the company is to grow and to keep pace with its competitors.

2 **An adequate cash position.** The fact that the company reports large earnings does not mean that it has a large amount of cash in the bank. Earnings may have been invested in new plant and equipment, or in paying off debts, or in stocking a larger inventory. There is no necessary relationship between the balance in the Retained Earnings account and the balance in the Cash account. The traditional expression of "paying dividends out of retained earnings" is misleading. Cash dividends can be paid only "out of" cash.

3 **Dividend action by the board of directors.** Even though the company's profits are substantial and its cash position seemingly satisfactory, dividends are not paid automatically. A positive action by the directors is necessary to declare a dividend.

Regular and special dividends

Many corporations establish a regular quarterly or annual dividend rate and pay this same amount for a period of years regardless of the year-to-year changes in earnings. Such a policy gives a higher investment quality to a company's stock. A strong cash position is necessary if a company is to be prepared to make regular dividend payments in the face of irregular earnings.

If earnings increase but the increase is regarded as a temporary condition, the corporation may decide to pay a *special dividend* in addition to the *regular dividend.* The implication of a special dividend is that the company is making no commitments as to a permanent increase in the amount of dividends to be paid. Of course, even a "regular" dividend may be reduced or discontinued at any time, but well-financed companies which have long-established regular dividend rates are not likely to omit or reduce dividend payments except in extreme emergencies.

Dividends on preferred stock

As indicated in Chapter 16, a preferred stock carries a stated annual dividend rate, such as $5 per share, or 5% of par value. Under no circumstances does a corporation pay more than the required dividend on preferred stock. This policy of not permitting the preferred stockholder to share in any unusually large profits suggests that the corporation views the preferred stockholder only as a supplier of capital rather than as a full-fledged owner in the traditional sense of the word.

Dividends on preferred stocks are not paid unless declared by the board of directors. Since most preferred stocks are of the cumulative variety, any omitted dividend must be made up before any payment can be made to the common. Dividends in arrears on preferred stock do not constitute a liability of the corporation but should be disclosed by a footnote to the balance sheet. Separate accounts are used to record the declaration of preferred and common dividends.

Dividend dates

Four significant dates are involved in the distribution of a dividend. These dates are:

1 **Date of declaration.** On the day on which the dividend is declared by the board of directors, a liability to make the payment comes into existence. A Dividends account is debited and a liability account, Dividends Payable, is credited.

2 **Date of record.** The date of record always follows the date of declaration, usually by a period of two or three weeks, and is always stated in the dividend declaration. In order to be eligible to receive the dividend, a person must be listed as the owner of the stock on the date of record.

3 **Ex-dividend date.** The ex-dividend date is significant for investors in companies with stocks traded on the stock exchanges. To permit the compilation of the list of stockholders as of the record date, it is customary for the stock to go "ex-dividend" three business days before the date of record. A stock is said to be selling ex-dividend on the day that it loses the right to receive the latest declared dividend. A person who buys the stock before the ex-dividend date is entitled to receive the dividend; conversely, a stockholder who sells his shares in the period between the date of declaration and the ex-dividend date does not receive the dividend.

4 **Date of payment.** The declaration of a dividend always includes announcement of the date of payment as well as the date of record. Usually the date of payment comes from two to four weeks after the date of record.

Stock dividends

Stock dividend is an important but confusing term which requires close attention. It is confusing because all dividends are distributions to stockholders and "stock dividend" may suggest to some people merely a dividend on capital stock. *A stock dividend is a pro rata distribution of additional shares to a company's stockholders;* in brief, the dividend consists of shares of stock rather than cash. Perhaps a better term for a stock dividend would be a "dividend payable in capital stock," but the expression "stock dividend" is too firmly entrenched to be easily replaced. Most stock dividends consist of common stock distributed to holders of common stock, and our discussion will be limited to this type of stock dividend.

What is the effect of a stock dividend on the company's financial position? Why does a corporation choose to pay a dividend in shares of stock rather than in cash? Would you as an investor prefer to receive a stock dividend or a cash dividend? These questions are closely related, and a careful analysis of the nature of a stock dividend should provide a basis for answering them.

A cash dividend reduces the assets of a corporation and reduces the stockholders' equity by the same amount. A stock dividend, on the other hand, causes no change in assets and no change in the *total* amount of the stockholders' equity. The only effect of a stock dividend on the accounts is to transfer a portion of the retained earnings into the Capital Stock and Contributed Surplus accounts. In other words, a stock dividend merely "reshuffles" the stockholders' equity accounts, increasing the permanent capital accounts and Contributed Surplus and decreasing the Retained Earnings account. A stockholder who receives a stock dividend will possess an increased number of shares, but his equity in the company will be no larger than before.

An example may make this fundamental point clear. Assume that a corporation with 800 shares of stock is owned equally by James Davis and Frank Miller, each owning 400 shares of stock. The corporation pays a stock dividend of 25% and distributes 200 additional shares (25% of 800 shares), with 100 shares going to each of the two stockholders. Davis and Miller now hold 500 shares apiece, but each still owns one-half of the business. The corporation has not changed; its assets and liabilities and its total capital are exactly the same as before the dividend. From the stockholder's viewpoint, the ownership of 500 shares out of a total of 1,000 outstanding shares represents no more than did the ownership of 400 shares out of a total of 800 shares previously outstanding.

Assume that the market value of this stock was $10 per share prior to the stock dividend. Total market value of all the outstanding shares was, therefore, 800 times $10, or $8,000. What would be the market value per share and in total after the additional 200 dividend shares were issued? The 1,000 shares now outstanding should have the same total market value as the previously outstanding 800 shares, because the "pie" has merely been divided into more but smaller pieces. The price per share should have dropped from $10 to $8, and the aggregate market value of outstanding shares would consequently be computed as 1,000 shares times $8, or $8,000. Whether the market price per share will, in actuality, decrease in proportion to the change in number of outstanding shares is another matter, for market prices are subject to many conflicting influences, some as unpredictable as the state of mind of investors.

REASONS FOR DISTRIBUTION OF STOCK DIVIDENDS Many reasons have been given for the popularity of stock dividends, for example:

1 To conserve cash. When the trend of profits is favorable but cash is needed for expansion, a stock dividend may be an appropriate device for "passing along the profits" to stockholders without weakening the corporation's cash position.[9]

2 To reduce the market price of a corporation's stock to a more convenient trading range by increasing the number of shares outstanding. This objective is usually present in large stock dividends (25 to 100% or more).

Some critics of stock dividends argue that a stock dividend is not really a dividend at all. These critics say that a company which cannot afford to pay a cash dividend should pay no dividends, rather than trying to deceive stockholders by increasing the number of outstanding shares. The popularity of stock dividends, according to such critics, is based on a lack of understanding on the part of stockholders.

Regardless of the merit of the arguments for and against stock dividends, most stockholders welcome these distributions. In many cases a small stock dividend has not caused the market price per share to decline appreciably; consequently, the increase in the number of shares in the hands of each stockholder has, regardless of logic, resulted in an increase in the total market value of his holdings.

ENTRIES TO RECORD STOCK DIVIDENDS Assume that a corporation had the following stockholders' equity accounts on December 15, 1975, just prior to declaring a 10% stock dividend:

Stockholders' equity before stock dividend

Stockholders' Equity

Common stock, no par value, authorized 30,000 shares, issued and outstanding 10,000 shares	$150,000
Retained earnings	200,000
Total stockholders' equity	$350,000

Assume also that the closing market price of the stock on December 15, 1975, was $30 a share. The company declares and issues a 10% stock dividend, consisting of 1,000 shares (10% × 10,000 = 1,000). The entry to record the *declaration* of the dividend is as follows:

[9] For example, the Standard Oil Company of California, in a letter to its stockholders, gave the following reason for the "payment" of a 5% stock dividend: "Payment of this stock dividend recognizes the continuing increase in your stockholder's equity in the Company's assets, resulting from reinvestment of part of the Company's earnings. Reinvestment of earnings has helped to sustain the Company's long-range program of capital and exploratory expenditures and investments aimed to increase future income and enhance further the value of your shareholding."

Stock divi-
dend de-
clared; note
use of mar-
ket price

1975

Dec. 15   Retained Earnings   30,000

          Stock Dividends to Be Distributed[10]   30,000

          To record declaration of a 10% stock dividend consisting

          of 1,000 shares of no par value common stock. To be

          distributed on February 9, 1976, to stockholders of

          record on January 15, 1976. Amount of retained earnings

          transferred is based on market price of $30 a share

          on December 15, 1975.

The entry to record *distribution* of the dividend shares is as follows:

Stock divi-
dend dis-
tributed

1976

Feb. 9   Stock Dividends to Be Distributed   30,000

          Common Stock   30,000

          To record distribution of stock dividend of 1,000 shares.

Note that the amount of retained earnings transferred to the Capital Stock account by the above entries is not the stated value of the new shares, but the *fair market value,*[11] as indicated by the market price prevailing at the date of declaration. The reasoning behind this practice is simple: Since stockholders tend to measure the "worth" of a small stock dividend (say, 20 to 25% or less) in terms of the market value of the additional shares issued, then Retained Earnings should be reduced by this amount. *Stock dividends in excess of 20 to 25% should be recorded by transferring only the par or stated value of the dividend shares from the Retained Earnings account to the Common Stock account.*

The Stock Dividends to Be Distributed account is not a liability, because there is no obligation to distribute cash or any other asset. If a balance sheet is prepared between the date of declaration of a stock dividend and the date of distribution of the shares, this account should be presented in the stockholders' equity section of the balance sheet.

Stock splits

Most large corporations are interested in as wide as possible a distribution of their securities among the investing public. If the market price reaches very high levels as, for example, $150 per share, the corporation may feel that, by splitting the stock 5 to 1 and thereby reducing the price to $30 per share, the number of shareholders may be increased. The bulk of trading in securities occurs in 100-share lots and an extra commission is charged on smaller transactions. Many investors with limited funds prefer to make their investments in 100-share lots of lower-priced stocks.

Many leading Canadian corporations have split their stock; some have done so several times. Generally the number of shareholders has increased noticeably after the stock has been split.

A stock split consists of increasing the number of outstanding shares and reducing the par or stated value per share in proportion. For example, assume that a corporation has outstanding 1 million shares of $10 par value stock. The market value is $90 per share. The corporation now reduces the par value from $10 to $5 per share and increases the number of shares from 1 million to 2 million. This action would be called a 2 for 1 stock split. A stockholder who formerly owned 100 shares of the $10 par old stock would now own 200 shares of the $5 par new stock. Since the number of outstanding shares has been doubled without any change in the affairs of the corporation, the market price will probably drop from $90 to approximately $45 a share.

A stock split does not change the balance of any ledger account; consequently, the transaction may be recorded merely by a memorandum notation in the general journal and in the Common Stock account.

DISTINCTION BETWEEN STOCK SPLITS AND LARGE STOCK DIVIDENDS What is the difference between a 2 for 1 stock split and a 100% stock dividend? Both will double the number of outstanding shares without changing total stockholders' equity, and both will serve to cut the market price of the stock in half. The stock dividend, however, will cause a transfer from the Retained Earnings account to the Common Stock account equal to the par or stated value of the dividend shares, whereas the stock split does not change the dollar balance of any account. After an increase in the number of shares as a result of a stock split or stock dividend, earnings per share are of course computed in terms of the increased number of shares. In presenting five- or ten-year summaries, the earnings per share for earlier years are revised to reflect the increased number of shares and thus make the trend of earnings per share from year to year a valid and meaningful basis for comparison.

Contributed surplus as a basis for dividends

Among the several sources of contributed surplus are: (1) premiums on par value stock, (2) excess of issuance price over stated value of no-par stock,[12] (3) purchase and retirement of shares at a cost less than the issuance price, (4) conversion of preferred stock and bonds into common stock, and (5) donations of property to a corporation by local governments seeking to attract new industries.

A separate ledger account may be used for each specific type of contributed surplus. Examples of the appropriate ledger titles are Premium on Capital Stock, Distributable Surplus, Paid-in Surplus from Retirement of Stock, Paid-in Surplus from Conversion of Preferred Stock, and Donated Surplus. In a condensed balance sheet, two or more of these ledger accounts

may be combined into a single amount and labeled as Contributed Surplus.

Is Contributed Surplus available for dividends? Although the law makes it legally possible to declare dividends from contributed surplus, this is rarely done. Whenever a corporation does declare a dividend from any source other than retained earnings, it is obligated to disclose to stockholders that the dividend represents a return of contributed surplus rather than a distribution of earnings.

REACQUISITION OF SHARES[13]

Corporations have traditionally been prohibited, under Canadian law, from acquiring their own shares except for redeemable preferred shares. This long-time situation has been drastically changed. The Ontario (which led the way in 1971) and British Columbia corporation acts and the Canada Business Corporations Act now permit corporations under their jurisdiction to acquire their own shares. There is one fundamental restriction on this right. A corporation cannot acquire its own shares if it is (a) unable to pay its liabilities as they become due, or (b) the realizable value of its assets, after the purchase of its own shares, would be less than the aggregate of its liabilities and total stated capital.

Corporations, where permitted by law, frequently reacquire shares of their own capital stock by purchase in the open market. The effect of reacquiring shares is to reduce the assets of the corporation and to reduce the stockholders' equity by the same amount. The right to purchase its own shares permits a corporation to adjust its financial structure to the needs of the business. Other reasons for a corporation to purchase its own shares include a desire to support the market value of the shares, to increase reported earnings per share, and to have shares available for acquisition of other companies or for re-issue to employees under some type of bonus plan.

Recording purchases of a corporation's own shares under the Canada Business Corporations Act

The Canada Business Corporations Act permits a corporation to purchase its own

---

[12]As indicated previously, only no par value shares may be issued under the Canada Business Corporations Act and the entire proceeds from the issue of these shares must be credited to the capital stock account.

[13]Shares may be reacquired through purchase or redemption. Redemption of redeemable preferred shares, which has always been permitted under Canadian law, is discussed in the *Intermediate Accounting* volume of this series.

shares but requires that these shares be cancelled upon their purchase. Reacquired shares lose their existence, and thus, there is no such thing as treasury shares[14] as would exist under the Ontario or British Columbia acts. The reacquired shares, as such, cannot be re-issued; and any new issue is like an original issue.

Upon the purchase of its own shares, a corporation shall deduct from the stated capital, an amount equal to the result obtained by multiplying the stated capital by the following fraction:

$$\frac{\textit{Number of shares purchased}}{\textit{Total number of shares outstanding}}$$

For example assume the following:

Common stock issued and outstanding

20,000 shares $100,000

100 shares are purchased on the open market

by the corporation at a cost of $800

The reduction in stated capital would be

$$\$100,000 \times \frac{100}{20,000} = \$500$$

The entry to record purchase of the 100 shares is as follows:

Cancellation of reacquired shares

Common stock	500	
Retained earnings*	300	
Cash		800

*or Contributed Surplus.

Purchased 100 shares of the corporation's

own common stock at a cost of $800.

When the difference between the cost of the reacquired shares is less than the amount that must be deducted from stated capital, it is credited to a contributed surplus account. On the other hand, if the cost of the reacquired shares is greater than the amount that must be deducted from stated capital, this excess is debited to a contributed surplus account to the extent that there were accumulated gains from previous reacquisitions and cancellations of shares with any remainder being debited to retained earnings.

Treasury stock

Under both the Ontario and British Columbia acts, reacquired shares, purchased on the open market, need not be cancelled. Therefore, treasury stock (or treasury shares) will result from the purchase of its own shares by a corporation in one of these jurisdictions.

Treasury stock may be defined as a corporation's own stock which has been issued, fully paid and reacquired but not cancelled. Treasury stock may be held indefinitely or may be issued again at any time. Treasury stock is not entitled to share in cash dividends.[15] It has no voting rights, no pre-emptive right to share in new issues, and no right to share in assets in event of dissolution of the corporation.

Recording purchases and sales of treasury stock

Purchase of treasury stock is customarily recorded **at cost** regardless of whether it is par value or no par stock, and regardless of the price paid or of the price at which the shares were originally issued. In short, it is current practice to record all treasury stock at cost.

Further, the purchase and resale of treasury stock is viewed as a single transaction. No adjustment would be made to share capital and related accounts until the shares are resold.[16] When the treasury shares are reissued, the Treasury Stock account would be credited for **the cost** of the shares sold, and a surplus account would be debited or credited for the difference between cost and resale price. The Paid-in Surplus from Treasury Stock Transactions, a part of contributed surplus, would be credited for any gain on the resale of treasury shares. As long as the losses on the resale of treasury shares did not exceed the credit balance of the Paid-in Surplus from Treasury Stock Transactions, they would be charged to that account; however, if losses on the resale of treasury shares exceeded accumulated gains, the excess would be charged to the Retained Earnings Account.

Assume that X Corporation Ltd. acquired 1,000 shares of its common stock in May, 1975, at a cost of $8,000. It resold 600

---

[14]Treasury stock is discussed below.

[15]Some authorities argue that stock dividends should be computed on the total number of shares *issued*, including treasury stock, rather than on the number outstanding. The issuance of stock dividends on treasury stock is theoretically sound because it maintains the percentage relationship of treasury stock to total shares issued. A similar position should be taken with respect to stock splits.

[16]This single transaction method for recording treasury stock transactions is recommended by the *CICA Handbook*, paragraphs 3240.09 and 3240.10.

of these treasury shares in September, 1975, for $5,400 and 200 shares in December, 1975, for $1,500. The entries to record these transactions are as below.

The loss on the resale of treasury shares in December, 1975, is debited to the Paid-in Surplus from Treasury Stock Transactions because accumulated gains exceeded the loss. If the loss had been greater than accumulated gains, the excess would have been debited to the Retained Earnings account. The balance sheet treatment of the treasury stock transactions above is shown in the illustration of the Stockholders' Equity section of the balance sheet on page 517.

Treasury stock recorded at cost	*Treasury Stock*	*8,000*	
	Cash		*8,000*
	Purchased 1,000 of the corporation's common stock at a cost of $8 per share		
Reissue of treasury shares above cost	*Cash*	*5,400*	
	Treasury Stock		*4,800*
	Paid-in Surplus from Treasury Stock Transactions		*600*
	Resale of 600 treasury shares at $9 per share		
Reissue of treasury shares below cost	*Cash*	*1,500*	
	Paid-in Surplus from Treasury Stock Transactions	*100*	
	Treasury Stock		*1,600*
	Resale of 200 treasury shares at $7.50 per share		

BOOK VALUE PER SHARE OF CAPITAL STOCK

The word *value* is applied with various meanings to a share of stock. Par value, stated value, and market value per share have previously been discussed. Since there are several other types of value for a share of stock, to avoid confusion "value" should be used only with a qualifying adjective, as for example, book value, liquidation value, and redemption value.

The *book value* of a share of stock, as the name suggests, is determined by referring to the books of account, or more specifically to a balance sheet prepared from the books. Book value is equal to the net assets per share of stock. It is computed by dividing the capital stock, contributed surplus and retained earnings applicable to a class of stock by the number of outstanding shares of that class.

For example, assume that a corporation has 4,000 shares of capital stock outstanding and the stockholders' equity section of the balance sheet is as follows:

How much is book value per share?	*Capital stock, no par value*	*$44,000*
	Retained earnings	*76,000*
	Total stockholders' equity	*$120,000*

The book value per share is $30; it is computed by dividing the stockholders' equity of $120,000 by the 4,000 shares of outstanding stock. In computing book value, we are not concerned with the number of authorized shares but merely with the outstanding shares, because the total of the outstanding shares represents 100% of the stockholders' equity.

What is the significance of book value per share of stock? The stockholders' equity in total is equal to the book value of the assets minus the liabilities. Therefore, the stockholders' equity is equal to the *net assets* (assets minus liabilities), and the book value of each share of stock may be thought of as the net assets represented by a single share.

Book value does *not* indicate the amount which the holder of a share of stock would receive if the corporation were to be dissolved. In liquidation, the assets would probably be sold at prices quite different from their carrying values on the books, and the stockholders' equity would go up or down accordingly.

The concept of book value is of vital importance in many contracts. For example, a majority stockholder might obtain an option to purchase the shares of the minority stockholders at book value at a specified future date. Many court cases have hinged on definitions of book value.

Book value is occasionally used in judging the reasonableness of the market price of a stock. However, it must be used with great caution; the fact that a stock is selling at less than its book value does not necessarily indicate a bargain. Earnings per share, dividends per share, and prospects for future earnings are usually more important factors affecting market price than is book value.

Book value when company has both preferred and common stock

When a company has two or more issues of stock outstanding, the book value for each class of stock may be computed by dividing the capital stock, contributed surplus and retained earnings applicable to that class of stock by the number of shares outstanding. Book value is generally computed for common stock only, so the practical aspect of the question may be stated as follows: How is book value per common share computed when a company has both preferred and common stock?

Assuming that there are no dividends in arrears on the preferred stock, book value per common share is equal to the total stockholders' equity (exclusive of the redemption value of the preferred stock) divided by the number of common shares outstanding.

To illustrate, assume that the stockholders' equity is as follows:

Two classes of stock — 5% preferred stock, no par, redeemable at $110	$1,000,000
Common stock no par value; authorized 100,000 shares issued and	
outstanding 80,000 shares	1,200,000
Retained earnings	900,000
Total stockholders' equity	$3,100,000

All the capital belongs to the common stockholders, except the $1.1 million applicable to the preferred stock (and any dividends in arrears on the preferred stock). This reasoning is supported by the general practice of making the preferred stock redeemable at or near its issuance price, so that the eventual elimination of the preferred stock is not at all improbable. The calculation of book value per share of common stock can therefore be made as follows:

Compute book value per share of common stock

Total stockholders' equity	$3,100,000
Less: Preferred stock (at redemption price of $110 per share)	1,100,000
Equity of common stockholders	$2,000,000
Number of shares of common stock outstanding	80,000
Book value per share of common stock $\dfrac{\$2,000,000}{80,000}$	$25

The computation of book value is made in the same way for par value and no-par value stock. The basic concept is the net assets per share.

Illustration of stockholders' equity section

The following illustration of a stockholders' equity section of a balance sheet shows a fairly detailed classification by source of the various elements of corporate capital:

Stockholders' Equity

Share capital:			
6% preferred shares, $100 par value, authorized and issued 1000 shares		$100,000	
Common shares, no par, authorized 100,000 shares, issued 60,000 shares of which 200 are held in treasury		365,000	$465,000
Surplus:			
Contributed surplus			
Premium on preferred shares		10,000	
Paid-in surplus from treasury stock transaction		500	
		10,500	
Retained earnings			
Appropriated			
Reserve for contingencies	$30,000		
Reserve for building expansion	50,000		
	80,000		
Unappropriated	110,000	190,000	200,500
			665,500
Less: Cost of 200 shares of treasury stock			1,600
Shareholders' equity			$663,900

The above illustration assumes that the corporation was incorporated under a jurisdiction (such as British Columbia or Ontario) which permits a corporation to have treasury stock and to issue shares with a par value. Neither of these practices is permitted under the Canada Business Corporations Act.

The published financial statements of leading corporations indicate that there is no one standard arrangement for the various items making up the stockholders' equity section. Variations occur in the selection of titles, in the sequence of items, and in the extent of detailed classification. Many companies, in an effort to avoid excessive detail in the balance sheet, will combine several related ledger accounts into a single balance sheet item. Several examples of published financial statements appear in the Appendix.

DEMONSTRATION PROBLEM FOR YOUR REVIEW

The stockholders' equity of the Mathewson Corporation Ltd. on December 31, 1975, appears below.

Common stock, $30 par, 24,000 shares issued and outstanding	*$ 720,000*
Premium on common stock	*134,000*
Retained earnings	*240,000*
Total stockholders' equity	*$1,094,000*

Other data On the basis of the number of shares outstanding at the end of each year, the book value of the common stock was $85 per share on December 31, 1974, and $100 per share on December 31, 1973. Early in 1975, the company split its shares 2 for 1. A 20% stock dividend was declared in 1974, at a time when the market value of the stock was $77 per share.

The balance of retained earnings on January 1, 1973, was $280,000, and the changes in retained earnings throughout the three-year period resulted solely from net income and dividends.

Sydney, a stockholder of Mathewson, owned 200 shares of stock on December 31, 1973, and has neither sold any shares nor purchased additional shares. He received cash dividends at the end of each year as follows: 1973, $280; 1974, $360; 1975, $480.

Instructions On the basis of the above information:
a Prepare a statement of stockholders' equity at December 31, 1974.
b Prepare a statement of stockholders' equity at December 31, 1973.
c Determine the net income of the Mathewson Corporation Ltd. for each of the three years 1973, 1974, and 1975.

QUESTIONS

1 Name two essential characteristics a gain or loss must have to qualify for treatment as an *extraordinary item,* as defined by the Accounting Research Committee of the CICA.

2 Identify each of the following as (*a*) extraordinary items or (*b*) a part of operating results before extraordinary items:
   (*1*) Write-off of a large account receivable from a bankrupt customer
   (*2*) Large loss from sale of a factory constituting a major segment of the business
   (*3*) Large gain from sale of an investment held for 20 years
   (*4*) Large write-off of inventory which has become obsolete
   (*5*) Large uninsured loss from earthquake
   (*6*) Large damages payable as result of unfavorable settlement of a lawsuit applicable to the current year in which company was defendant

3 In preparing an income statement, what is the recommendation of the CICA Research Committee as to the treatment of extraordinary items related to the current period?

4 Distinguish between *extraordinary items* and *prior period adjustments.*

5 The accountant of W Company Ltd. discovers during the current year that the Dept. of National Revenue has determined that an additional $100,000 of income tax applicable to last year's operations is due. W Company Ltd. agrees with this reassessment. How should this tax deficiency be recorded in the accounts? How should it be shown in the financial statements? The amount is regarded as material.

6 Define *retained earnings.*

7 If the Retained Earnings account has a debit balance, how is it presented in the balance sheet and what is it called?

8 Favorable settlement of a lawsuit relating to events which occurred several years ago brought the Pine Woods Company Ltd. a court award of very large revenue during the current year. What special accounting term is used to describe transactions of this type? What account should be credited to record receipt of the large cash settlement?

9 What is the purpose of an appropriation of retained earnings? What are the arguments for and against the use of such appropriations?

10 Explain the nature of the following items appearing on a corporate balance sheet: Reserve for Depreciation, Reserve for Income Taxes Payable, and Reserve for Future Plant Expansion. What better titles can you suggest?

11 What type of transaction most frequently appears as a deduction in a statement of retained earnings?

12 Explain the significance of the following dates relating to dividends: date of declaration, date of record, date of payment, ex-dividend date.

13 Distinguish between a *stock split* and a *stock dividend.* Is there any reason for the difference in accounting treatment of these two events?

14 How would the *book value* of a share of common stock be computed, assuming that preferred stock with dividends in arrears is also outstanding? List three events which increase the book value of a share of common stock, and three events which decrease the book value of a share of common stock.

15 Why do corporations purchase their own shares? How does a corporation incorporated under the Canada Business Corporations Act record the purchase of its own shares?

16 What is *treasury stock?* Is treasury stock an asset? How should it be reported on the balance sheet?

EXERCISES

Ex. 17-1 Jones purchased 100 shares of stock in X Corporation Ltd. at the time it was organized. At the end of the first year's operations, the corporation reported earnings (after taxes) of $5 per share, and declared a dividend of $2.50 per share. Jones complains that he is entitled to the full distribution of the amount earned on his investment. Is there any reason why a corporation that earns $5 per share may not be able to pay a dividend of this amount? Are there any advantages to Jones in the retention by the company of one-half of its earnings?

Ex. 17-2 Precision Corporation Ltd. has a total of 10,000 shares of common stock outstanding and no preferred stock. The net assets of the Precision Corporation Ltd. at the end of the current year are $200,000, and the market value of the stock is $24 per share. At year-end, the company declares a stock dividend of one share for each five shares held. If all parties concerned clearly recognized the nature of the stock dividend, what would you expect the market value per share of Precision's common stock to be on the ex-dividend date?

Ex. 17-3 International Machinery Corporation Ltd. sold to the public 125,000 shares of common stock (*$1 par value*) at $21 per share (*issuance price*). The *book value* of the 750,000 shares previously outstanding was approximately $4.50 per share and the *market price* a few weeks after this initial public offering was over $30 per share. The *earnings per share* of the company in the preceding four years had increased steadily and had averaged $0.90. Define each italicized per-share value mentioned above and suggest some factors which may have been important in determining the initial public offering price of $21 per share.

Ex. 17-4 The Forbes Corporation Ltd. has 1 million shares of $1 par value capital stock outstanding. You are to prepare the journal entries to record the following transactions.

Feb. 4 Declared a cash dividend of 5 cents per share.
Mar. 1 Paid the 5-cent cash dividend to stockholders.

June 14 Declared 2% stock dividend. Market value of stock was $18 per share.
July   6 Issued 20,000 shares pursuant to 2% stock dividend.
Dec. 20 Declared 50% stock dividend. Market value of stock was $30 per share.

Ex. 17-5 K owns 1,000 out of a total of 20,000 outstanding common shares of Javo Corporation Ltd. The Javo Corporation Ltd. reports total assets of $340,000 and total liabilities of $120,000 at the end of the current year, and at that time the board declares a stock dividend of one share for each 10 shares held. Compute the book value *per share* of K's stock and the total book value of K's investment in the corporation: (**a**) before the stock dividend; (**b**) after the stock dividend.

Ex. 17-6 Barron's Mining Company Ltd. has 100,000 shares of $10 par value stock outstanding at the end of 1974. During 1974, the stock was split 2 for 1 and the company earned $320,000 from mining activities and $210,000 (net of taxes) from the sale of timberlands surrounding an abandoned mine. In 1973, the company had earned $4.10 per share from mining activities (based on the 50,000 shares then outstanding), and reported an extraordinary loss of $40,000 (net of taxes). How should the foregoing information be presented on a per-share basis in reporting the company's earnings for the last two years in terms of the 100,000 shares now outstanding?

Ex. 17-7 Company Y has 100,000 shares of $10 par common stock. Net income for the current year is $330,000. The officers of the company were given stock options two years ago which entitle them to purchase a total of 10,000 shares of common stock at any time within four years at the price which prevailed when the options were granted. What data should appear at the bottom of the current year's income statement? (Compute basic and fully diluted earnings per share.)

PROBLEMS

Group A

17A-1 The Chronicle Company Ltd. has 10,000 shares of capital stock outstanding. The stock was originally issued at the par value of $10 per share. The book value per share of stock on January 1, 1973, is $30. During 1973, the following transactions were completed by the company:

Jan.   4 An additional 2,000 shares of stock were sold to investors at $45 per share.
Nov. 30 A cash dividend of 60 cents per share was declared by the board of directors.
Dec. 31 A net income of $38,400 was reported for 1973.

Instructions Compute the successive book values per share of Chronicle Company Ltd. stock after each transaction.

17A-2 The Alberta Company Ltd. prepared the following income statement for the current year. (The statement was not prepared in conformity with generally accepted accounting principles.)

Net sales		$1,500,000
Gain on sale of securities		30,000
Issuance of capital stock at a premium		160,000
Total revenues		$1,690,000
Less:		
Cost of goods sold	$ 825,000	
Operating expenses	340,000	
Dividends declared on capital stock	120,000	
Addition to reserve for contingencies	100,000	
Income taxes (estimated)	80,000	1,465,000
Net income		$ 225,000

At the beginning of the current year, the audited financial statements of the company show unappropriated retained earnings of $322,000 and a balance in the Reserve for Contingencies account of $150,000. One-half of the gain on the sale of securities is included in computing taxable income. Income taxes should be estimated at 50% of *income from operations,* and the gain on the sale of securities should be reported *net of income taxes.*

Instructions
a Prepare a revised income statement, assuming that the extraordinary gains and losses are reported in the income statement as recommended by the CICA Research Committee. The company has 100,000 shares of capital stock outstanding. Show data for earnings per share at the end of the income statement.
b Prepare a statement of retained earnings. The statement should have three columns as follows: Reserve for Contingencies, Unappropriated, and Total Retained Earnings.

17A-3 The information given below is related to the stockholders' equity of the Echo Corporation Ltd.:

(1) The company has received a total of $126,000 in exchange for the 2,000 shares of $3 preferred stock, no par value, that are currently outstanding (authorized: 6,000 shares).
(2) The company has received from stockholders $275,000 in exchange for 10,000 outstanding shares of no-par value common stock (authorized 50,000 shares).
(3) Total net income since the date of organization has been $191,000.
(4) Cash dividends paid since the date of organization, $78,000.
(5) Stock dividend declared (but not yet distributed to stockholders) amounts to 1,000 shares of common. The market value of the common at the date of record was $40 per share.
(6) Certain land having an assessed valuation of $10,000 was donated to the corporation by the city as a site for a manufacturing plant. The fair market value of the land at the time of the gift was $32,000.
(7) The amount of $20,000 was recently authorized by the board of directors as a reserve for contingencies.

Instructions On the basis of this information, prepare in good form the stockholders' equity section of the Echo Corporation Ltd. balance sheet.

17A-4 The accounts listed alphabetically below appear in the general ledger of the Hunter Corporation Ltd. at December 31, 1974, after the books have been closed.

Accounts payable	$ 39,640
Accounts receivable	98,730
Accrued liabilities	27,590
Accumulated depreciation: buildings	180,000
Accumulated depreciation: equipment	159,600
Allowance for uncollectible accounts	8,000
Buildings	510,000
Cash	34,830
Common stock, no par, issued at, $25	320,000
Distributable surplus	32,000
Dividends payable	15,000
Equipment	506,300
Income taxes payable	34,000
Inventories (fifo cost)	145,000
Land	60,000
Long-term notes payable, due July 1, 1982	250,000
Notes receivable	48,400

Organization costs.	29,000
Preferred stock, 6%, par value, $100	200,000
Premium on preferred stock.	10,000
Prepaid expenses	6,500
Reserve for future plant expansion.	85,000
Retained earnings, as of Dec. 31.	77,930

The company is authorized to issue 20,000 shares of 6%, $100 par value, preferred stock and 40,000 shares of no-par common, maximum consideration of $30. The company was incorporated on January 1, 1964.

17A-5 Instructions Prepare the December 31, 19___, balance sheet for the Hunter Corporation in a form suitable for publication.

Tastee Bakeries Company Ltd. is incorporated under the Canada Business Corporations Act. On January 1 of the current year it had retained earnings of $5,920,000. On July 31, the company declared and paid a cash dividend of 50 cents per share.

At November 30 of the current year, the stockholders' equity was as follows:

Capital stock, no par value, authorized 1,000,000 shares, issued and	
outstanding 700,000 shares	$11,200,000
Retained earnings	6,790,000
Total stockholders' equity	$17,990,000

During December the company earned net income of $132,540, and on December 30 the board of directors declared a cash dividend of 60 cents per share. Early in December, the company reacquired 10,000 shares of its own capital stock for $295,000.

Instructions

a Prepare the stockholders' equity section of the balance sheet at December 31.

b Prepare a statement of retained earnings for the year.

c Compute book value per share at November 30 and at December 31.

Group B

17B-1 The following data are taken from the records of the Sentinel Corporation:

7% preferred stock, cumulative (liquidation value, $105,000)	$100,000
Common stock, no par, 51,500 shares issued.	640,000
Dividends in arrears on preferred stock	21,000
Deficit	110,000
Organization costs.	10,000
Total liabilities	370,000

Instructions

a Compute the amount of net assets (stockholders' equity).

b If all assets are sold for 80% of book value, how much would each share of common stock receive as a liquidating dividend?

17B-2 The Inca Company Ltd. prepared the following income statement for the current year:

Net sales		$4,500,000
Gain on sale of land		100,000
Issuance of capital stock at a premium		480,000
Total revenues		$5,080,000
Less:		
Cost of goods sold	$2,475,000	
Operating expenses	1,020,000	
Loss on disposal of franchise	10,000	
Dividends declared on capital stock	150,000	
Addition to reserve for contingencies	300,000	
Income taxes (estimated)	240,000	4,195,000
Net income		$ 885,000

At the beginning of the current year, the audited financial statements of the company show unappropriated retained earnings of $966,000 and a balance in the Reserve for Contingencies account of $450,000. One-half of the gain on the sale of land is taxable and one-half of the loss on the disposal of franchise is deductible in computing the net capital gain. Income taxes should be estimated at 40% of *income from operations* and the net capital gain should be reported as an extraordinary item *net of income taxes.*

Instructions

a Prepare a revised income statement, assuming that the extraordinary gains and losses are reported in the income statement as recommended by the CICA Research Committee. The company has 100,000 shares of capital stock outstanding. Show data for earnings per share at the end of the income statement.

b Prepare a statement of retained earnings. The statement should have three columns as follows: Reserve for Contingencies, Unappropriated, and Total Retained Earnings.

17B-3

The Wyatt Corporation Ltd. was organized early in 1976 and was authorized to issue 70,000 shares of no par value common stock and 25,000 shares of no par value $3.50 preferred stock. During 1976 the company sold 35,000 shares of common, at an average price of $32 per share, and issued 10,000 shares in exchange for certain patents worth $310,000. The company earned a net income of $91,250 and paid dividends of 75 cents per share during 1976.

On January 1, 1977, the company issued 12,000 shares of preferred stock in exchange for timber property valued at $625,000. Quarterly dividends were declared and paid on preferred shares in April, July, and October of 1977. On December 28, 1977, the company declared the fourth quarterly dividend on preferred stock and a 10% stock dividend to be distributed to common stockholders. Net income for 1977 was $137,000. The market value of common stock at the end of 1977 was 31½ per share.

Instructions Prepare the stockholders' equity section of the Wyatt Corporation Ltd. balance sheet at

a December 31, 1976

b December 31, 1977

17B-4

Naylor Company Ltd., incorporated under the Ontario Business Corporations Act, is authorized to issue 25,000 shares of 6%, $100 par value preferred stock and 50,000 shares of no-par common, maximum value $20. At December 31, 1976, the company reported earnings of $199,650.

During 1977, the company declared and paid quarterly dividends on its 6% preferred stock and on December 30 declared a total dividend of $36,000 on outstanding common shares, payable January 30, 1978. Net sales for 1977 were $2,500,000; gross profit on sales was 30% of net sales; and corporate income taxes amounted to $120,000, or 40% of taxable income.

The accounts listed alphabetically on top of page 524 appeared in the general ledger of the Naylor Company Ltd. at December 31, 1977, after the books had been closed.

Instructions

a Prepare a combined statement of income and retained earnings for the Naylor Company similar to the statement illustrated for Aztec Corporation on page 506.

b Prepare a balance sheet suitable for publication for the Naylor Company as of December 31, 1977. (Use the illustrated balance sheet on pages 488 and 489 and the illustration of the Stockholders' Equity section on page 517 as a guide.)

Accounts payable	$ 56,340
Accounts receivable	101,000
Accrued liabilities	25,320
Accumulated depreciation: buildings	180,000
Accumulated depreciation: equipment	159,600
Allowance for uncollectible accounts	8,000
Buildings	597,070
Cash	120,340
Common stock, no par, issued at $10	320,000
Dividends payable	36,000
Equipment	506,300
Income taxes payable (balance due on 1974 income)	34,000
Inventories	145,000
Land	60,000
Long-term note payable, due July 1, 1980	239,000
Notes receivable	48,400
Organization costs	15,300
Preferred stock, 6%, par value, $100	200,000
Premium on preferred stock	10,000
Prepaid expenses	6,500
Retained earnings, as of Dec. 31	331,650

17B-5 The stockholders' equity of the Riley Corporation Ltd. on January 1 of the current year is as follows:

Capital stock:		
$6 preferred stock, no par value, 50,000 authorized, 7,500		
shares issued		$ 825,000
Common stock, no par value, 500,000 shares authorized, 240,000		
shares issued		2,160,000
		2,985,000
Retained earnings:		
Reserve for plant expansion	$ 600,000	
Unappropriated	1,350,000	
		1,950,000
Total stockholders' equity		$4,935,000

The transactions relating to the stockholders' equity accounts during the current year are shown below:

Feb. 1 Paid regular semiannual dividend on preferred stock, and 80 cents per share cash dividend on common. Both these dividends were declared in December of the past year and properly recorded at that time.

June 20 Declared semiannual dividend on preferred stock to stockholders of record on July 15, payable on July 28 (debit Dividends on Preferred Stock).

July 28 Paid preferred dividend.

Oct. 10 Declared a 5% stock dividend on common to stockholders of re-

buted November 15; market value $12 a share.

Nov. 15 Distributed 5% stock dividend.

Nov. 18 Sold 20,000 shares of common stock for $13.50 per share.

Nov. 20 The board of directors authorized the addition of $100,000 to the Reserve for Plant Expansion.

Dec. 20 Declared regular semiannual dividend on preferred stock and a dividend of 80 cents per share on common shares of record at January 4, payable on January 20.

Dec. 31 Net income for the current year amounted to $525,000 (debit Income Summary and credit Retained Earnings). (Other closing entries may be omitted.)

Instructions

a Prepare in general journal form the entries necessary to record these transactions on the books of the Riley Corporation Ltd. during the current year.

b Did Riley Corporation Ltd. increase or decrease the total amount of cash dividend *declared* on common shares during the current year in comparison with the dividends declared in the past year? Explain.

c Prepare a balance sheet for the Riley Corporation Ltd. at the end of the current year, assuming that total assets amount to $7,500,000.

17B-6 Upper Canada Wholesale Limited is incorporated under the Ontario Business Corporations Act. Its stockholders' equity at January 1, 1976, was as follows:

Common stock, $50 par value, 20,000

shares authorized, 12,000 shares

issued and outstanding $600,000

Retained earnings 320,000

$920,000

During 1976, the following transactions took place:

1 Purchase by the company in January of 1,000 of its own common shares for $80 per share.

2 Dividends declared and paid in June of $2.00 per share.

3 Sale of 200 treasury shares in September for $90 per share.

4 Dividends declared and paid in December of $2.00 per share.

5 Net income for 1976 was $94,000.

Instructions

a Prepare journal entries, with narratives, to record the above transactions.

b Prepare in good form the stockholders' equity section of the Upper Canada Wholesale Limited balance sheet.

BUSINESS DECISION PROBLEM 17

Near the end of the current year, the board of directors of the Trojan Corporation Ltd. is presented with the following statement of the company's capital position:

Common stock (15,000 shares issued) $300,000

Premium on common stock 180,000

Retained earnings 240,000

Total stockholders' equity $720,000

Trojan Corporation Ltd. has paid dividends of $3.60 per share in each of the last five years. After careful consideration of the company's cash needs, the board of directors declared a stock dividend of 3,000 shares of common stock. Shortly after the stock dividend had been distributed and before the end of the year, the company declared a cash dividend of $3 per share.

James Pratt owned 3,600 shares of Trojan common stock which he acquired several years ago. The market price of this stock before any dividend action was $60 per share.

Instructions On the basis of the above information, answer each of the following questions, showing computations where pertinent.

a What is Pratt's share (in dollars) of the net assets as reported in the financial statement of the Trojan Corporation Ltd. before the stock dividend action? What is his share after the stock dividend action? Explain why there is or is not any change as a result of the stock dividend.

b What are the probable reasons why the market value of Pratt's stock differs from the amount of net assets per share shown on the books?

c Compare the amount of cash dividends that Pratt receives this year with dividends received in prior years.

d On the day the common stock went ex-dividend (with respect to the stock dividend), its quoted market value fell from $60 to $50 per share. Did this represent a loss to Pratt? Explain.

e If the Trojan Corporation Ltd. had announced that it would continue its regular cash dividend of $3.60 per share on the increased number of shares outstanding after the stock dividend, would you expect the market value of the common stock to react in any way different from the change described in (**d**)? Why?

EIGHTEEN CORPORATIONS BONDS PAYABLE AND INVESTMENTS IN CORPORATE SECURITIES

BONDS PAYABLE

A corporation may obtain funds for a long-term purpose, such as construction of a new plant, by issuing a long-term mortgage note payable or by issuing bonds payable. Usually the amount of money needed is greater than any single lender can supply. In this case the corporation may sell bonds to the investing public, thus splitting the loan into a great many units, usually of $1,000 each. An example of corporation bonds is the 8% first mortgage bonds of Westcoast Transmission Company Limited due 1991 by which Westcoast borrowed $90 million. These bonds may be bought and sold by investors daily from investment dealers.

Characteristics of a bond

A bondholder is a creditor of the corporation; a stockholder is an owner. From the viewpoint of the issuing corporation, bonds payable constitute a long-term liability. Throughout the life of this liability the corporation makes semiannual payments of interest to the bondholder for the use of his money. These interest payments constitute an expense to the corporation and are deducted from each year's revenues in arriving at net income for the year.

Formal approval of the board of directors and of the stockholders is usually required before bonds can be issued. The contract between the corporation and the trustee representing the bondholders may place some limitation on the payment of dividends to stockholders during the life of the bonds. For example, dividends may be permitted only when cash or total current assets are above specified amounts. This type of restriction protects the bondholder more effectively than does the creation of a reserve by appropriation of retained earnings.

Of course, in the event that the corporation encounters financial difficulties and is unable to make the required payments of interest or principal, the bondholders may foreclose on the pledged assets, but this is a slow and complicated procedure which bondholders look upon only as a last-ditch alternative. When investing in a bond, the bondholder hopes and expects to receive all payments promptly without the need for taking any legal action.

Not all bonds are secured by the pledge of specific assets. An unsecured bond is called a *debenture bond;* its value rests upon the general credit of the corporation. A debenture bond issued by a very large and strong corporation may have a higher investment rating than a secured bond issued by a corporation in less satisfactory financial condition.

Some bonds have a single fixed maturity date for the entire issue. Other bond issues, called *serial bonds,* provide for varying maturity dates to lessen the problem of accumulating cash for payment. For example, serial bonds in the amount of $10 million issued in 1972 might call for $1 million of bonds to mature in 1982, and an additional $1 million to become due in each of the succeeding nine years. Almost all bonds are *callable,* which means that the corporation reserves the right to pay off the bonds in advance of the scheduled maturity date. The call price is usually somewhat higher than the face value of the bonds.

As an additional attraction to investors, corporations sometimes include a conversion privilege in the bond contract. A *convertible bond* is one which may be exchanged for common stock at the option of the bondholder. The advantages to the investor of the conversion feature in the event of increased earnings for the company have already been described in Chapter 16 with regard to convertible preferred stock.

REGISTERED BONDS AND COUPON BONDS Nearly all corporation bonds issued in recent years have been *registered* bonds; that is, the name of the owner is registered with the issuing corporation. Payment of interest is made by semiannual cheques mailed to the registered owner.

Coupon bonds were popular some years ago and many are still outstanding. Coupon bonds have interest coupons attached; each six months during the life of the bond one of these coupons becomes due. The bondholder detaches the coupon and deposits it with his bank for collection.

TRANSFERABILITY OF BONDS Bonds, unlike common and preferred shares are not listed on organized security exchanges. However they may be readily purchased and sold through investment dealers. The holder of a 25-year bond need not wait 25 years to convert his investment into cash. By placing a telephone call to a broker, he may sell his bond within a matter of minutes at the going market price. This quality of liquidity is one of the most attractive features of an investment in corporation bonds.

QUOTATIONS FOR BONDS Corporate bond prices are quoted at a given amount per $100 of face value. For example, assume that a bond of $1,000 face amount (par value) is quoted at 106. The total price for the bond is 10 times 106, or $1,060. Market quotations for corporate bonds use an eighth of a dollar as the minimum variation. The following line from the financial page of a daily newspaper illustrates the manner in which bond prices are quoted:

Bonds	Bid	Ask
Simpsons 9.5/89	*106*	*108*

This line of condensed information indicates that certain holders of Simpsons Ltd. 9.5% bonds maturing in 1989 were willing to sell these bonds at 108 or $1,080 for a bond with a face value of $1,000, and that there were potential purchasers of the bonds willing to buy them at 106 or $1,060. Transactions in these bonds will usually take place at a price between the bid and asked quotations. Accrued interest since the last interest payment date is added to the quoted price for the bonds.

Effect of bond financing on holders of common stock

Interest payments on bonds payable are deductible as an expense in determining the income subject to corporation income tax, but dividends paid on common and preferred stock are not. High tax rates on corporate earnings thus encourage the use of bonds to obtain long-term capital.

Assume that a growing and profitable corporation with 100,000 shares of common stock outstanding is in need of $10 million cash to finance a new plant. The management is considering whether to issue $6\frac{1}{2}$% preferred stock, issue an additional 100,000 shares of common stock, or sell 6% bonds. Assume also that after acquisition of the new plant, the annual earnings of the corporation, before deducting interest expense or income taxes, will amount to $2 million. From the viewpoint of the common stockholders, which financing plan is preferable? The following schedule shows the net earnings per share of common stock under the three alternative methods of financing:

Which financing plan is best?

	If 6½% Preferred Stock Is Issued	*If Common Stock Is Issued*	*If 6% Bonds Are Issued*
Annual earnings before bond interest or income taxes	$2,000,000	$2,000,000	$2,000,000
Less: Interest on bonds, 6% of $10,000,000			600,000
Earnings before income taxes	$2,000,000	$2,000,000	$1,400,000
Less: Income taxes (assume 50% rate)	1,000,000	1,000,000	700,000
Net income	$1,000,000	$1,000,000	$ 700,000
Less: Preferred stock dividends	650,000		
Net income available for common stock	$ 350,000	$1,000,000	$ 700,000
Number of shares of common stock outstanding	100,000	200,000	100,000
Net income per share of common stock	$3.50	$5.00	$7.00

The use of 6% bonds rather than 6½% preferred stock under these circumstances offers a yearly saving to common stockholders of $350,000, or $3.50 per share of common stock. The saving arises from two factors: (*1*) the deductibility of bond interest for income tax purposes and (*2*) the fact that the bonds were marketed at an interest rate lower than the dividend rate on the preferred stock. Financing through issuance of additional common stock rather than sale of bonds saves $300,000 (after taxes) but results in ***lower earnings per share*** because of the ***dilution*** caused by doubling the number of common shares outstanding.

The principal argument for the 6½% preferred stock as opposed to the 6% bond issue is that if the company's earnings should fall drastically, the operation of the business might be disrupted by inability to meet the fixed bond interest payments, whereas a preferred dividend could be postponed for a year or longer without serious repercussions.

The use of stockholders' equity as a basis for borrowing is referred to as ***trading on the equity;*** this is discussed further in Chapter 21.

Management planning of the bond issue

A corporation wishing to borrow money by issuing bonds faces months of preliminary work. Decisions must be made on such points as the amount to be borrowed, the interest rate to be offered, the conversion privilege, if any, the maturity date, and the property to be pledged, if any. Answers must be found for such questions as the following: How much debt can the company safely handle in the event of adverse business conditions? What volume of sales will be necessary for the company to "break even" in the future after the fixed expenses have been increased by agreeing to make regular interest payments?

In forecasting the company's cash position for future periods, consideration must be given to the new requirement of semiannual bond interest payments as well as to the long-range problem of accumulating the cash required to pay the bonds at maturity. If the borrowed funds are to be invested in new plant facilities, will this expansion produce an increase in the cash inflow sufficient to meet the interest payments? Perhaps the bond issue should be of the convertible variety; this feature might attract investors even though the interest rate were set at a relatively low level. In addition, if the bonds are convertible, the company may not have to accumulate cash for repayment of the entire issue. Effective long-range planning of the company's financial needs will greatly reduce the cost of securing capital and will leave the door open to issuing additional securities in the future on advantageous terms.

AUTHORIZATION OF A BOND ISSUE   After the board of directors has decided upon the details of a bond issue, the proposal is presented to stockholders for their approval. Once this approval has been gained, the *deed of trust* is drawn and the bonds are printed. If the company's present financial requirements are for less than the amount of bonds authorized, only a portion of the bonds may be issued at this time. As each bond is issued it must be signed or "authenticated" by the trustee.

No formal entry in the accounts is required for the act of authorization; however, a memorandum notation may be made in the Bonds Payable ledger account indicating the total amount of bonds authorized. The total authorized amount of a bond issue should always be disclosed in the balance sheet.

RECORDING THE ISSUANCE OF BONDS   To illustrate the entries for issuance of bonds, assume that Bidwell Corporation Ltd. was authorized on June 1, 1973, to issue $1 million of 20-year, 8% debenture bonds. All the bonds in the issue bear the June 1, 1973, date, and interest is computed from this date. On June 1, 80% of the bonds were issued at face value, and the following entry was made:

Issuance of bonds

Cash	800,000	
8% Debenture Bonds Payable		800,000
To record sale of 800 8%, 20-year bonds at par.		

The balance sheet should disclose all significant features of each bond issue, including exact title, interest rate, maturity date, and amounts authorized and issued. Thus, in our example, the fact that only 80% of the authorized bonds have been issued is significant; issuance of the remaining 20% would materially change the ratio of debt to stockholders' equity and also the relationship between bond interest expense and the company's earnings.

RECORDING THE ISSUANCE OF BONDS BETWEEN INTEREST DATES   The semiannual interest dates (such as January 15 and July 15, or April 1 and October 1) are printed on the bond certificates. However, bonds are often issued between the specified interest dates. The investor is then required to pay the interest accrued to date of issuance in addition to the stated price of the bond. This practice enables the corporation to pay a full six months' interest on all bonds outstanding at the semiannual interest payment date. The accrued interest collected from an investor purchasing a bond between interest payment dates is thus returned to him on the next interest payment date. To illustrate, let us modify our previous example of Bidwell Corporation Ltd. and assume that the $800,000 face value of 8% bonds were issued at par and accrued interest, *three months after the interest date printed on the bonds.* The entry will be:

Bonds issued between interest dates

Cash	816,000
8% Debenture Bonds Payable	800,000
Bond Interest Payable	16,000

Issued $800,000 face value of 8%, 20-year bonds at 100 plus accrued interest for three months.

Three months later on the regular semiannual interest payment date, a full six months' interest ($40 per bond) will be paid to all bondholders, regardless of when they purchased their bonds. The entry for the semiannual interest payment is illustrated below.

How much net interest expense?

Bond Interest Payable	16,000
Bond Interest Expense	16,000
Cash	32,000

Paid semiannual interest on $800,000 face value of 8% bonds.

Now consider these interest transactions from the standpoint of the investor. He paid for three months' accrued interest at the time of purchasing the bonds, and he received a cheque for six months' interest after holding the bonds for only three months. He has, therefore, been reimbursed properly for the use of his money for three months.

Bond discount

A corporation wishing to borrow money by issuing bonds must pay the going market rate of interest. On any given date, the going market rate of interest is in reality a whole schedule of rates corresponding to the financial strength of different borrowers. Since market rates of interest are constantly fluctuating, it must be expected that the contract rate of interest printed on the bonds will seldom agree with the market rate of interest at the date the bonds are issued.

If the interest rate carried by an issue of bonds is lower than the market rate for bonds of this grade, the bonds can be sold only at a discount. For example, assume that a corporation issues $1 million face value of 7%, 10-year bonds. Each bond will pay the holder $70 interest (7% × $1,000) each year, consisting of two semiannual payments of $35 each. If the market rate of interest were exactly 7%, the bonds would sell at par, but if the market rate of interest is higher than 7%, no one will be willing to pay $1,000 for a bond which will return only $70 a year. The price at which the bonds can be sold will, therefore, be less than par. Assume that the best price obtainable is 98 ($980 for each $1,000 bond). The issuance of the bonds will be recorded by the following entry:

Issuing bonds at discount

Cash	980,000	
Discount on Bonds Payable	20,000	
Bonds Payable		1,000,000

Issued $1,000,000 face value of 7%, 10-year bonds at 98.

BOND DISCOUNT AS PART OF THE COST OF BORROWING Whenever bonds are issued at a discount, *the total interest cost over the life of the issue is equal to the amount of the discount plus the regular cash interest payments.* For the $1 million bond issue in our example, the total interest cost over the 10-year life of the bonds is $720,000, of which $700,000 represents 20 semiannual cash payments of interest and $20,000 represents the discount on the issue. On a yearly basis, total interest expense is $72,000, consisting of $70,000 paid in cash and $2,000 of the bond discount. This analysis is illustrated by the following tabulation of the total amounts of cash received and paid out by the corporation in connection with the bond issue.

Cash received and paid over life of bond issue

Cash to be paid by the borrowing corporation:

Face value of bonds at maturity	$1,000,000
Interest ($70,000 a year for 10 years)	700,000
Total cash to be paid	$1,700,000
Cash received:	
From issuance of bonds at a discount	980,000
Excess of cash to be paid over cash received (total interest expense)	$ 720,000
Yearly interest expense ($720,000 ÷ 10)	$ 72,000

In our example the Discount on Bonds Payable account has an initial debit balance of $20,000; each year one-tenth of this amount, or $2,000, will be amortized or written off to Bond Interest Expense. Amortizing bond discount means transferring a portion of the discount to Bond Interest Expense each accounting period during the life of the bonds. Assuming that the interest payment dates are June 30 and December 31, the entries to be made each six months to record bond interest expense are as follows:

Payment of bond interest and amortization of bond discount

Bond Interest Expense	35,000	
Cash		35,000

Paid semiannual interest on $1,000,000 of 7% 10-year bonds.

Bond Interest Expense	1,000	
Discount on Bonds Payable		1,000

Amortized $\frac{1}{20}$ of discount on 10-year bond issue.

The above entries serve to charge Bond Interest Expense with $36,000 each six months, or a total of $72,000 a year. Bond interest expense will be uniform throughout the 10-year life of the bond issue, and the Discount on Bonds Payable account will be completely written off by the end of the tenth year. As an alternative, some companies choose to record amortization of bond discount or premium only at the end of the year rather than at each interest payment date.

Bond premium

Bonds will sell above par if the contract rate of interest specified on the bonds is higher than the current market rate for bonds of this grade. Let us now change our basic illustration by assuming that the $1 million issue of 7%, 10-year bonds is sold at a price of 102 ($1,020 for each $1,000 bond). The entry is shown below.

Issuing *Cash*	*1,020,000*	
bonds at *Bonds Payable*		*1,000,000*
premium *Premium on Bonds Payable*		*20,000*
Issued $1,000,000 face value of 7% 10-year bonds at price		
of 102.		

The amount received from issuance of the bonds is $20,000 greater than the amount which must be repaid at maturity. This $20,000 premium is not a gain but is to be offset against the regular cash interest payments in determining the net cost of borrowing. Whenever bonds are issued at a premium, *the total interest cost over the life of the issue is equal to the regular cash interest payments minus the amount of the premium.* In our example, the total interest cost over the life of the bonds is computed as $700,000 of cash interest payments minus $20,000 of premium amortized, or a net borrowing cost of $680,000. The annual interest expense will be $68,000, consisting of $70,000 paid in cash less an offsetting $2,000 transferred from the Premium on Bonds Payable account to the credit side of the Bond Interest Expense account. The semiannual entries on June 30 and December 31 to record payment of bond interest and amortization of bond premium are as follows:

Payment *Bond Interest Expense*	*35,000*	
of bond *Cash*		*35,000*
interest and *Paid semiannual bond interest on $1,000,000 of 7%,*		
amortization *10-year bonds.*		
of bond		
premium *Premium on Bonds Payable*	*1,000*	
Bond Interest Expense		*1,000*
Amortized $\frac{1}{20}$ of premium on 10-year bond issue.		

Year-end adjustments for bond interest expense

In the preceding illustration, it was assumed that one of the semiannual dates for payment of bond interest coincided with the end of the company's accounting year. In most cases, however, the semiannual interest payment dates will fall during an accounting period rather than on the last day of the year.

For purposes of illustration, assume that $1 million of 8%, 10-year bonds are issued at a price of 98 on October 1, 1973. Interest payment dates are April 1 and October 1. The total discount to be amortized amounts to $20,000, or $1,000 in each six-month interest period. The company keeps its accounts on a calendar-year basis; consequently, adjusting entries will be necessary as of December 31 for the accrued interest and the amortization of discount applicable to the three-month period since the bonds were issued.

The effect of these year-end adjusting entries is to make the Bond Interest Expense account show the proper interest expense ($20,500) for the three months that the bonds were outstanding (October 1 to December 31) during 1973. The Bond Interest Expense account will be closed to the Income Summary account; the Bond Interest Payable account will remain on the books as a liability until the next regular interest payment date, at which time $20,000 of the interest payment will be charged to Bond Interest Payable and the other $20,000 to Bond Interest Expense.

Adjusting bond interest expense at year-end	*Bond Interest Expense* *20,000*	
	Bond Interest Payable.	*20,000*
	To record bond interest accrued for three-month period from Oct. 1 to Dec. 31 ($1,000,000 × .08 × $\frac{3}{12}$).	
	Bond Interest Expense *500*	
	Discount on Bonds Payable	*500*
	To record amortization of bond discount for three-month period from Oct. 1 to Dec. 31 ($20,000 × $\frac{3}{120}$).	

If the above bonds had been issued at a premium, similar entries would be made at the end of the period for any accrued interest and for amortization of premium for the fractional period from October 1 to December 31.

Bond discount and bond premium in the balance sheet

In the preceding example, an 8%, 10-year bond issue of $1 million was issued for $980,000, and bond discount of $20,000 was recorded. One year later, on October 1, 1974, the bond discount would have been amortized to the extent of $2,000 and the *net liability* would have risen to $982,000 as illustrated on page 535.

Bond	*Long-term liabilities:*		
discount on balance sheet	*8% bonds payable, due Oct. 1, 1983*	*$1,000,000*	
	Less: Discount on bonds payable	*18,000*	*$982,000*

At the maturity of the bond issue 10 years after issuance, the corporation must pay $1 million, but at the time of issuing bonds, the "present value" of this debt is $980,000. As the bond discount is amortized, the **net amount** of the liability shown on each succeeding balance sheet will be $2,000 greater than for the preceding year. At the maturity date of the bonds, the valuation account, Discount on Bonds Payable, will have been reduced to zero and the liability will have risen to $1 million.

Parallel reasoning applies to bond premium, which is logically shown on the balance sheet as an addition to bonds payable. As the premium is amortized, the net amount of the liability is reduced year by year, until, at the maturity date of the bonds, the premium will have been completely written off and the liability will stand at the face amount of the bond issue.

The role of the underwriter in marketing a bond issue

An investment dealer or underwriter is usually employed to market a bond issue, just as in the case of capital stock. The corporation turns the entire bond issue over to the underwriter at a specified price (say, 98); the underwriter sells the bonds to the public at a slightly higher price (say, 100). By this arrangement the corporation is assured of receiving the entire amount of funds on a specified date. The calculation of the bond discount or bond premium is based on the net amount which the issuing corporation receives from the underwriter, not on the price paid by the public for the bonds.

Retirement of bonds before maturity

Bonds are sometimes retired before the scheduled maturity date. Most bond issues contain a call provision, permitting the corporation to redeem the bonds by paying a specified price, usually a few points above par. Even without a call provision, the corporation may retire its bonds before maturity by purchasing them in the open market. If the bonds can be purchased by the issuing corporation at less than their book value, a gain is realized on the retirement of the debt. By **book value** is meant the face value of the bonds plus any unamortized premium or minus any unamortized discount.

For example, assume that the Pico Corporation Ltd. has outstanding a $1 million bond issue and there is unamortized premium on the books in the amount of $20,000. The bonds are callable at 105 and the company exercises the call provision on 100 of the bonds, or 10% of the issue. The entry would be as follows:

Bonds	Bonds Payable	100,000	
called at	Premium on Bonds Payable	2,000	
price above			
book value	Loss on Retirement of Bonds	3,000	
	Cash		105,000
	To record retirement of $100,000 face value of bonds called		
	at 105.		

The book value of each of the 100 called bonds was $1,020, whereas the call price was $1,050. For each bond called the company incurred a loss of $30, a total loss of $3,000 on the bonds retired. Note that when 10% of the total issue was called, 10% of the unamortized premium was written off.

Retirement of bonds at maturity

On the maturity date of the bonds, the discount or premium will be completely amortized and the accounting entry to retire the bonds (assuming that interest is paid separately) will consist of a debit to Bonds Payable and a credit to Cash.

One year before the maturity date, the bonds payable may be reclassified from long-term debt to a current liability in the balance sheet if payment is to be made from current assets rather than from a sinking fund.

Bond sinking fund

To make a bond issue attractive to investors, the corporation may agree in the bond contract to create a sinking fund, exclusively for use in paying the bonds at maturity. A bond sinking fund is created by depositing cash at regular intervals with a trustee, who invests it in conservative securities and adds the interest earned on these securities to the amount of the sinking fund. The periodic deposits of cash plus the interest earned on the sinking fund securities should cause the fund to approximately equal the amount of the bond issue by the maturity date. When the bond issue approaches maturity, the trustee sells all the securities in the fund and uses the cash proceeds to pay the holders of the bonds. Any excess cash remaining in the fund will be returned to the corporation.

A bond sinking fund is not included in current assets because it is not available for payment of current liabilities. The cash and securities comprising the fund are usually shown as a single amount under the group heading Investments, placed just below the current asset section. Interest earned on sinking fund securities constitutes earnings of the corporation.

Mortgages and other long-term liabilities

Mortgages are usually payable in equal monthly installments. A portion of each payment represents interest on the unpaid balance of the loan and the remainder of the payment reduces the amount of the unpaid balance (principal). This process is illustrated by the following schedule of payments for a three-month period on a 6.6% mortgage note with an unpaid balance of $100,000 at September 11, 19___.

	Monthly Payment	Interest for One Month at 6.6% on Unpaid Balance	Reduction in Principal	Unpaid Principal Balance
Sept. 11				$100,000.00
Oct. 11	$1,000.00	$550.00	$450.00	99,550.00
Nov. 11	1,000.00	547.53	452.47	99,097.53
Dec. 11	1,000.00	545.04	454.96	98,642.57

Monthly payments on a mortgage

On December 31, 19___, the portion of the unpaid principal of $98,642.57, due within one year, should be classified as a current liability and the remainder as a long-term liability. In addition, accrued interest for 20 days amounting to $356.69 ($98,642.57 × 6.6% × 20/365) should be shown as a current liability.

Other long-term liabilities often appearing in published balance sheets of corporations include pension obligations, amounts payable under deferred compensation plans, deferred income taxes,[1] leases, and deferred credits.

INVESTMENTS IN CORPORATE SECURITIES

Security transactions from the viewpoint of investors

In the preceding section, the issuance of securities and such related transactions as the payment of dividends and interest have been considered primarily from the viewpoint of the issuing corporation. Now we shall consider these transactions from the viewpoint of the investor.

The capital stocks of most large corporations are listed on the Toronto Stock Exchange or on other organized security exchanges. Among the investors in these securities are trust funds, pension funds, universities, banks, insurance companies, industrial corporations, and great numbers of individuals. The stocks of many smaller companies are not listed on an organized exchange but are bought and sold *over the counter.* At the time of issuance of bonds or stocks, the transaction is between the investor and the issuing corporation (or its underwriting agent). The great daily volume of security transactions, however, consists of the sale of stocks and bonds by investors to other investors. Virtually all these

[1] See chap. 20.

security transactions are made through a stockbroker acting as intermediary.

LISTED CORPORATIONS REPORT TO A MILLION OWNERS   When a corporation invites the public to purchase its stocks and bonds, it accepts an obligation to keep the public informed on its financial condition and the profitability of operations. This obligation of disclosure includes public distribution of financial statements. The Ontario Securities Commission, and similar bodies in other provinces, are government agencies responsible for seeing that corporations make full and fair disclosure of their affairs so that investors have a basis for intelligent investment decisions. The flow of corporate accounting data distributed through newspapers and financial advisory services to millions of investors is a vital force in the functioning of our economy; in fact, the successful working of a profit-motivated economy rests upon the quality and dependability of the accounting information being reported.

LISTED CORPORATIONS ARE AUDITED BY INDEPENDENT PUBLIC ACCOUNTANTS   Corporations with securities listed on organized stock exchanges are required to have regular audits of their accounts by independent public accountants. The financial statements distributed each year to stockholders are accompanied by a report by a firm of chartered accountants indicating that an audit has been made and expressing an opinion as to the fairness of the company's financial statements. It is the independent status of the auditing firm that enables investors to place confidence in audited financial statements.

Government bonds as current assets

A recent balance sheet of Simpsons-Sears Limited shows the following items listed first in the current asset section:

Current assets:
Cash *$4,530,877*
Government of Canada bonds *112,669*

The action of Simpsons-Sears in investing in Canadian government bonds is in no way unusual. The published balance sheets of a great many corporations show holdings of such securities. The government bonds owned by corporations differ from the Canada Savings Bonds owned by many individuals, in that they cannot be resold at any time before maturity at par to the government. Government bonds are just as safe[2] and almost as liquid as cash itself. In the event that cash is needed for any operating purpose, the bonds can be quickly converted into cash; in the meantime, bonds are preferable to cash because of the interest income which they produce.

---

[2] There may be a gain or loss on the sale of government bonds on the securities market prior to their maturity date because of a change in the market rate of interest.

From the viewpoint of creditors as well as that of management, it is often said in appraising a company's financial strength that "cash and marketable securities" amount to so many dollars. This practice of lumping together cash and marketable securities reflects the general attitude that these two assets are essentially similar.

A security investment consisting of Canadian government bonds or high-grade corporate bonds is a current asset, regardless of the maturity date of the bonds and regardless of how long the bonds have been held or how long the company expects to hold them. The important point is that these securities *can be converted into cash at any time without interfering with the normal operation of the business.* A principal purpose of the balance sheet classification of current assets and current liabilities is to aid in portraying short-run debt-paying ability. For this purpose government bonds and other high-grade securities deserve to be listed immediately after cash because they are even more liquid than accounts receivable or inventory. To a loan officer in a bank reviewing an application for a loan, there is no more impressive or reassuring asset on the balance sheet of a prospective borrower than a large amount of high-quality bonds.

Investments in other marketable securities

Some corporations choose to invest in bonds and stocks of other corporations as well as in Canadian government bonds. If these industrial securities are listed on a securities exchange and are not held for the purpose of exercising control over the issuing corporation, they should be classified as current assets. Some accounting writers have attempted to distinguish between "temporary" and "permanent" investments in marketable securities with the objective of excluding the latter type from current assets. In the opinion of the authors, such a distinction cannot be made consistently in practice and, furthermore, is quite unnecessary. For example, assume that a department store owns 500 shares of the common stock of British Columbia Telephone Company. The store has owned the stock for several years and has no intention of selling it in the near future, so this investment could reasonably be called a permanent one. Of course these shares are not held for the purpose of exercising control over the telephone company, or for any business reason other than that of sound investment. This security investment is a current asset of the highest quality; any analysis of the store's balance sheet for credit purposes would be facilitated by having the B.C. Telephone stock listed immediately after cash in the current asset action.

In summary, if security investments are limited to securities of unquestioned marketability (and are not owned for the purpose of bolstering business relations with the issuing corporation), these stocks and bonds may be converted into cash at any time without interfering with normal operations. An expressed *intention* by management as to near-term sale of the securities is *not* a requisite for classification as a current asset.

INVESTMENTS FOR PURPOSE OF CONTROL Some corporations buy stocks of other corporations in sufficient quantity that a degree of control may be exercised over the issuing corporation. Sometimes a substantial investment in stock of a customer company may be helpful in maintaining good business relations. Investments of this type cannot be sold without disturbing established policies; therefore, such investments are not current assets. On the balance sheet, they should be listed below the current asset section under a heading such as Investments.[3]

Valuation of marketable securities

VALUATION AT COST Investments in securities have traditionally been carried at cost, and no gain or loss recognized until the securities were sold. One of the basic concepts in accounting is that gains shall not be recognized until they are realized, and the usual test of realization is the sale of the asset in question. In current practice the market value of securities is often disclosed in a parenthetical note on the balance sheet.

VALUATION AT THE LOWER OF COST OR MARKET The valuation of investment securities at cost is generally accepted, but accounting theory also treats as acceptable the lower-of-cost-or-market method. The objective of this method of valuation is to give effect to market declines without recognizing market increases, and the result is a most conservative statement of investments in the balance sheet.

One argument against market price as a valuation basis is that in a rising market the writing up of the Investments account would involve the recording of an unrealized profit. However, accountants often recognize losses on the basis of objective evidence, even though the amount of the loss has not been established through sale of the property. Consequently, when the current value of marketable securities declines below cost, some accountants would favor writing down the Investment account and debiting an account such as Loss from Decline in Market Value of Securities.

The lower-of-cost-or-market concept has two alternative interpretations. It may be applied by (1) taking the lower of cost or market for each security owned, or (2) comparing the cost of the total holdings of securities with the market value of the securities as a group. Application of the lower-of-cost-or-market rule to each security individually will produce the lowest possible balance sheet amount for security investments, as shown by the following example:

		Cost	Present Market Price	Lower of Cost or Market
Lower of cost or market: alternative methods	Adams Limited stock	$10,000	$ 9,000	$ 9,000
	Zenith Limited stock.	15,000	17,000	15,000
	Totals	$25,000	$26,000	$24,000

---

[3]See Chap. 19 for a more detailed discussion of investments for the purpose of controlling other corporations.

If the lower-of-cost-or-market rule is applied to these two securities individually, the amount to appear in the balance sheet for Investments would be $24,000, which represents the present *market price* of the Adams stock plus the *cost* of the Zenith stock. In other words, the decrease in value of the Adams stock would be recognized but the increase in value of the Zenith stock would be ignored. The alternative application of the lower-of-cost-or-market rule would be made as follows: The cost of the two securities together amounted to $25,000; the present market value of the two stocks is $26,000; the lower of these two totals is the amount to be used in the balance sheet and would be labeled as follows in the current assets section:

Marketable securities, at cost (market value, $26,000) *$25,000*

Once the carrying value of an investment in securities has been written down to reflect a decline in market price, it is not considered acceptable to restore the amount written off even though the market price afterward recovers to as much as or more than the original cost. To do so would be regarded as recording an unrealized profit. When the security is sold, the gain or loss to be recorded is the difference between the sale price and the adjusted carrying value of the security on the books.

In terms of the usefulness of the balance sheet to creditors and other readers, it seems probable that the lower-of-cost-or-market rule should be applied to the securities holdings as a group rather than on an individual basis. Assume, for example, that a company owned a dozen securities and 11 of them advanced strongly in price during the year while the price of the twelfth security declined below its cost. If the lower-of-cost-or-market rule were applied on an individual basis, the company's balance sheet at the end of the year would show a reduction in the carrying value of securities and the income statement would show a loss from decline in market value of securities. Such reporting seems to have no justification other than conservatism, and *conservatism is surely not a virtue when it results in misleading financial statements.*

VALUATION AT MARKET   An increasing number of accountants argue that investments in marketable securities *should* be valued in the balance sheet at *current market price* regardless of whether this price is above or below cost.

There appear to be at least three strong arguments for showing security investments at current market value: (*1*) the keen interest of creditors in the present market value of security holdings, (*2*) the availability of current market quotations, which definitely establish market value for this type of asset, and (*3*) the fact that the securities can be sold without interfering with the normal operation of the business.

The CICA Accounting and Auditing Research Committee recommends that temporary investments be carried at market value where market value has declined significantly from cost; but, in other cases, accepts valuation at cost requiring disclosure of quoted market value in addition to cost only where holdings of marketable securities are significant.[4]

DISCLOSING THE BASIS OF VALUATION IN THE BALANCE SHEET Because of the variety of methods possible for valuation of investments in securities, the balance sheet should contain a notation as to the valuation method being used. It is also important that the method selected be used consistently from year to year. To illustrate the balance sheet presentation of marketable securities, the following excerpts are taken from published statements of leading corporations:

Reporting marketable securities in the balance sheet

Loblaw Companies Limited

Marketable securities, at cost (approximately quoted market value) . . . . $ 897,000

Imperial Oil Limited

Government securities, at lower of cost or market $18,000,000

Toronto Star Limited

Marketable securities at amortized cost (market value $4,368,000)   4,438,000

Distillers Corporation-Seagrams Limited

Short-term investments and other marketable securities, at cost   10,017,000

In all these examples, marketable securities appeared immediately after Cash in the current asset group.

The Canadian Institute of Chartered Accountants in its analysis of financial statement presentation[5] reports the following classification of marketable securities in the balance sheets of Canadian companies:

	Marketable Securities					
	Number of Companies			Percentage		
Classification						
	1970	*1969*	*1968*	*1970*	*1969*	*1968*
Included in current assets	121	125	137	99%	99%	99.5%
Basis of Valuation						
Cost	82	92	103	67	73	75
Lower of cost and market	13	6	8	11	5	6
Miscellaneous	5	5	4	4	4	3
Basis not disclosed	22	23	23	18	18	16
	122	126	138	100	100	100
Disclosure of Market Value						
Market disclosed	95	102	109	78	81	79
Market not disclosed	27	24	29	22	19	21
	122	126	138	100	100	100

[4] Canadian Institute of Chartered Accountants, *CICA Handbook,* (Toronto, 1968) Section 3010.

[5] Canadian Institute of Chartered Accountants, *Financial Reporting in Canada,* Ninth Edition, (Toronto, 1971) page 25 and 26.

EFFECT OF INCOME TAX REGULATIONS UPON SECURITY VALUATION For tax purposes, no gain or loss is recognized on an investment in securities until the time of sale. Many businesses which invest in securities prefer to follow this policy for general accounting purposes as well and therefore carry their security investments at cost, unless there is a substantial and apparently permanent decrease in the market value of securities owned.

Determining the cost of investments in stocks and bonds

The par value or face value of the security is not used in recording an investment; only the cost is entered in the Investments account. Cost includes any commission paid to a broker.

The principal distinction between the recording of an investment in bonds and an investment in stocks is that interest on bonds accrues from day to day. The interest accrued since the last semiannual interest payment date is paid for by the purchaser and should be recorded separately from the cost of the bond itself. Dividends on stock, however, do not accrue and the entire purchase price paid by the investor in stocks is recorded in the Investments account.

INCOME ON INVESTMENTS IN STOCKS Dividends are seldom recorded as income until received. The entry upon receipt of a dividend cheque consists of a debit to Cash and a credit to Dividends Earned.

Dividends in the form of additional shares of stock are not income to the stockholder, and only a memorandum entry needs to be made to record the increase in number of shares owned. The *cost basis per share* is decreased, however, because of the larger number of shares comprising the investment after distribution of a stock dividend. As an example, assume that an investor paid $72 a share for 100 shares of stock, a total cost of $7,200. Later he received 20 additional shares as a stock dividend. His cost per share is thereby reduced to $60 a share, computed by dividing his total cost of $7,200 by the 120 shares owned after the 20% stock dividend.

PURCHASE OF BONDS BETWEEN INTEREST DATES When bonds are purchased between interest dates, the purchaser pays the agreed price for the bond plus the interest accrued since the last interest payment date. By this arrangement the new owner becomes entitled to receive in full the next semiannual interest payment. An account entitled Accrued Bond Interest Receivable should be debited for the amount of interest purchased. For example, assume the purchase of a 9%, $1,000 bond at a price of 100 (100% of par value) and two months' accrued interest of $15. The entry is as follows:

Separate	Investment in Bonds.................................	1,000	
account for	Accrued Bond Interest Receivable........................	15	
accrued			
bond	Cash...		1,015
interest			
purchased	Purchased 9% bond of XYZ Co. at 100 and accrued interest.		

Four months later at the next semiannual interest payment date, the investor will receive an interest cheque for $45, which will be recorded as follows:

<table>
<tr><td>*Note portion*</td><td>Cash</td><td>. . . . .</td><td>45</td><td></td></tr>
<tr><td>*of interest*</td><td></td><td></td><td></td><td></td></tr>
<tr><td>*cheque*</td><td>Accrued Bond Interest Receivable</td><td>. . . . .</td><td></td><td>15</td></tr>
<tr><td>*earned*</td><td>Bond Interest Earned</td><td>. . . . .</td><td></td><td>30</td></tr>
<tr><td></td><td colspan="4">*Received semiannual interest on XYZ Co. bond.*</td></tr>
</table>

This $30 credit to Bond Interest Earned represents the amount actually earned during the four months the bond was owned.

ENTRIES TO RECORD BOND INTEREST EARNED EACH PERIOD If the investor in bonds is to determine bond interest earned each year on an accrual basis, an adjusting entry will be necessary at the balance sheet date for any interest earned but not yet received. This procedure is similar to that used in accounting for interest on notes receivable. The following series of entries illustrates the accounting for bond interest earned by a company on a calendar-year basis of accounting. The investment consists of $100,000 face value of 6% bonds (purchased at par) with interest dates of February 28 and August 31.

Allocating **Year 1**
bond
interest Dec. 31 Accrued Bond Interest Receivable 2,000
earned   Bond Interest Earned. 2,000
by years   *To accrue four months' interest earned on $100,000 face*
                     value of 6% bonds.

Year 2
Feb. 28 Cash. 3,000
             Accrued Bond Interest Receivable 2,000
             Bond Interest Earned. 1,000
             Received semiannual bond interest.

Aug. 31 Cash. 3,000
             Bond Interest Earned. 3,000
             Received semiannual bond interest.

Dec. 31 Accrued Bond Interest Receivable 2,000
             Bond Interest Earned. 2,000
             To accrue four months' interest earned on $100,000 face
             value of 6% bonds.

Acquisition of bonds at premium or discount

In the discussion of bonds payable from the viewpoint of the issuing corporation, emphasis was placed on the point that the issuing company *must* amortize the premium or discount over the life of the bonds. The position of the *investor in bonds,* however, is very different with respect to the significance of premium or discount. Many investors purchasing bonds above or below par do *not* amortize the premium or discount on these investments, because they do not expect to hold the bonds until maturity. Since bond issues often run for 25 years or more, it is the exception rather than the rule for an individual investor to hold the bond until it matures. If the investor sells the bond before it matures, the price he receives may be either above or below his cost, according to the current state of the bond market. Under these circumstances there is no assurance that amortization of premium or discount would give any more accurate measurement of investment income than would be obtained by carrying the bonds at cost.

AMORTIZATION OF PREMIUM ON BONDS OWNED Some investors such as insurance companies are required by law to follow a policy of amortizing or writing off the premium or discount over the remaining life of the bonds. When a bond reaches maturity, only the face value of $1,000 will be paid by the issuing corporation. The value of a bond purchased at a premium will, therefore, tend to decrease toward par as the maturity date approaches, and the carrying value of the bond in the balance sheet can logically be reduced in each successive year.

The income to an investor from a bond purchased at a premium and held until maturity *equals the total interest received minus the premium paid;* consequently, the interest earned in each year should be reduced by deducting a portion of the premium paid for the bond. As an example, assume that on January 1, 1973, an investor purchased $100,000 of 8% bonds of the Fox Corporation Ltd. payable January 1, 1983. Interest is payable on July 1 and January 1. The purchase price was 105, making a total cost of $105,000. The $5,000 excess of cost over maturity value is to be written off against the interest received during the 10 years the bonds will be held. Since there are 20 interest periods of six months each, the premium to be amortized each six months is $5,000 ÷ 20, or $250. A cheque for $4,000 bond interest will be received each six months; of this amount $250 may be regarded as recovery of the premium paid and the remaining $3,750 as interest earned. The journal entries for the first year the bonds are owned will be as follows:

Investor's 1973
entries
showing
amortization
of premium

Jan.	1	Investment in Bonds	105,000	
		Cash		105,000
		Purchased 100 8% bonds of Fox Corporation Ltd. at 105 plus commission of $500. Bonds mature Jan. 1, 1983.		
July	1	Cash	4,000	
		Bond Interest Earned		4,000
		Received semiannual bond interest payment.		

```
July  1 Bond Interest Earned. . . . . . . . . . . . . . . . . . . . . . . .      250
          Investment in Bonds . . . . . . . . . . . . . . . . . .                    250
       To amortize 1⁄20 of $5,000 premium.

Dec. 31 Accrued Bond Interest Receivable  . . . . . . . . . . . . .    4,000
          Bond Interest Earned. . . . . . . . . . . . . . . . . .                  4,000
       To accrue bond interest earned to end of year.

Dec. 31 Bond Interest Earned. . . . . . . . . . . . . . . . . . . . . .      250
          Investment in Bonds . . . . . . . . . . . . . . . . . .                    250
       To amortize 1⁄20 of $5,000 premium.

Dec. 31 Bond Interest Earned. . . . . . . . . . . . . . . . . . . . . .    7,500
          Income Summary . . . . . . . . . . . . . . . . . . . .                  7,500
       To close Bond Interest Earned account.
```

The accrued bond interest receivable of $4,000 at December 31 will appear in the balance sheet as a current asset, which will be collected January 1 upon receipt of the bond interest cheque. The bonds will also appear in the current asset section at $104,500, which represents the cost of $105,000 minus the $500 of premium amortized during the year.

The two essential ideas portrayed by this series of entries may be stated as follows: (1) The carrying value of the bonds is gradually being reduced to par by amortizing the premium; and (2) the net interest earned each year is equal to the interest received minus the amount of premium amortized.

AMORTIZATION OF DISCOUNT ON BONDS OWNED The value of a bond purchased for *less than its face value* will tend to increase to par as the maturity date approaches. Amortization of the discount on an investment in bonds means writing up the carrying value of the bonds each year with an offsetting credit to the Bond Interest Earned account. The income from a bond purchased at a discount and held until maturity is equal to the total of the interest payments received plus the amount of the discount.

As an example of the periodic entries for amortization of discount on bond investments, assume that on January 1, 1973, an investor purchased $200,000 face value of 7% bonds of the Bay Corporation Ltd. payable January 1, 1983. Interest is payable July 1 and January 1. The purchase price was 95, making a cost of $190,000. Since there are 20 interest periods of six months each, the discount to be amortized each six months is $10,000 ÷ 20, or $500. A cheque for $7,000 bond interest will be received each six months; in addition, the bond interest earned will be increased $500 by writing up the carrying value of the investment.

The journal entries for the first year the bonds are owned will be as follows:

Investor's entries showing amortization of discount

1973

Jan. 1 Investment in Bonds   190,000
        Cash   190,000
      Purchased 200 7% bonds of Bay Corporation Ltd. at 95
      plus commission of $1,000. Bonds mature Jan. 1, 1983.

July 1 Cash   7,000
        Bond Interest Earned   7,000
      Received semiannual bond interest payment.

July 1 Investment in Bonds   500
        Bond Interest Earned   500
      To amortize $\frac{1}{20}$ of $10,000 discount.

Dec. 31 Accrued Bond Interest Receivable   7,000
        Bond Interest Earned   7,000
      To accrue bond interest earned to end of year.

Dec. 31 Investment in Bonds   500
        Bond Interest Earned   500
      To amortize $\frac{1}{20}$ of $10,000 discount.

Dec. 31 Bond Interest Earned   15,000
        Income Summary   15,000
      To close Bond Interest Earned account.

The fact that a bond will be paid at par at a distant maturity date does not ensure that its price will move closer to par during each year of its life; bond prices fluctuate with changes in market rates of interest, business activity, and other elements of the economic environment.

Gains and losses from sale of investments in securities

The sale of an investment in stocks is recorded by debiting Cash for the amount received and crediting the Investment account for the carrying value of the stocks sold. Any difference between the proceeds of sale and the carrying value of the investment is recorded by a debit to Loss on Sale of Investments or by a credit to Gain on Sale of Investments.

At the date of sale of an investment in bonds, any interest accrued since the last interest payment date should be recorded. For example, assume that 10 bonds of the Elk Corporation Ltd. carried on the books of an investor at $9,600 are sold at a price of 94 and accrued interest of $90. The following entry should be made:

Investment in bonds sold at a loss

Cash   9,490
Loss on Sale of Investments   200
    Investment in Bonds   9,600
    Bond Interest Earned   90
Sold 10 bonds of Elk Corporation Ltd. at 94 and accrued interest of $90.

Gains and losses on the sale of investments are extraordinary items and, if material, should be presented in the income statement (net of income taxes) below the figure representing "income before extraordinary items."

Investments in mortgages and long-term notes

Mortgages are often acquired at less than face value. As an example, an investor purchases for $18,000 a mortgage of $20,000 face amount maturing in five years and paying interest quarterly at the rate of 6% a year. Two alternatives are open with regard to the recognition of income: (1) The mortgage may be carried at cost and only cash interest payments credited to income; or (2) the mortgage investment account may be written up by one-fifth of the discount in each of the five years and this amount credited to Interest Earned, in addition to the cash interest received. Under the first method, the yearly interest earned will be $1,200 (6% × $20,000), but when the mortgage is collected at the end of the fifth year an additional $2,000 of income (the excess of the face amount over cost) must be recognized. Under the second method calling for the yearly amortization of discount, the annual interest earned would be $1,600, consisting of $1,200 received in cash plus a $400 increase in the carrying value of the investment. The second method will usually give a more meaningful picture of periodic income and is preferable from the viewpoint of accounting theory. Both methods, however, are acceptable in the determination of taxable income.

QUESTIONS

1 Distinguish between the two terms in each of the following pairs:
   a Long-term notes; bonds
   b Mortgage bonds; debenture bonds
   c Fixed-maturity bonds; serial bonds
   d Coupon bonds; registered bonds

2 K Company Ltd. has decided to finance expansion by issuing $10 million of 20-year debenture bonds and will ask a number of underwriters to bid on the bond issue. Discuss the factors that will determine the amount bid by the underwriters for these bonds.

3 What are *convertible bonds?* Discuss the advantages and disadvantages of convertible bonds from the standpoint of (a) the investor and (b) the issuing corporation.

4 The Computer Sharing Co. Ltd. has paid-in capital of $10 million and retained earnings of $3 million. The company has just issued $1 million in 20-year, 8% bonds. It is proposed that a policy be established of appropriating $50,000 of retained earnings each year to enable the company to retire the bonds at maturity. Evaluate the merits of this proposal in accomplishing the desired result.

5 The following excerpt is taken from an article in a leading business periodical: "In the bond market high interest rates mean low prices. Bonds pay out a

fixed percentage of their face value, usually $1,000; a 5% bond, for instance, will pay $50 a year. In order for its yield to rise to $6\frac{1}{4}$%, its price would have to drop to $800." Give a critical evaluation of this quotation.

6 A recent annual report of Lear Siegler, Ltd., contained the following note accompanying the financial statements: "The loan agreements . . . contain provisions as to working capital requirements and payment of cash dividends. At June 30, retained earnings of approximately $13,400,000 were available for payment of cash dividends." What is the meaning of this note and why is it considered necessary to attach such a note to financial statements? (The total retained earnings of Lear Siegler, Ltd., at this date amounted to $77.5 million; working capital amounted to $100 million; and total liabilities amounted to $142 million.)

7 Discuss the advantages and disadvantages of a call provision in a bond contract from the viewpoint of (*a*) the bondholder and (*b*) the issuing corporation.

8 Why are government securities commonly called *secondary cash reserves?*

9 To what extent should the maturity date or the intention of management as to the holding period of an investment in marketable securities influence its classification on the balance sheet?

10 Writing down securities to market value when market is below cost, but refusing to recognize an increase in valuation when market is above cost, is inconsistent procedure. What arguments may be given in favor of this treatment?

11 "To substitute present market value for cost as a basis for valuing marketable securities would represent a departure from traditional accounting practice." Discuss the case for and against using market value consistently as the basis of valuation in accounting for marketable securities.

12 An investor buys a $1,000, 9%, 10-year bond at 110 and a $1,000, 7%, 10-year bond at 90, both on the date of issue. Compute the average annual interest income that will be earned on these bonds if they are held to maturity.

13 If an investor buys a bond between interest dates he pays, as a part of the purchase price, the accrued interest since the last interest date. On the other hand, if he buys a share of common or preferred stock, no "accrued dividend" is added to the quoted price. Explain why this difference exists.

14 Z buys a $1,000, 8% bond for 106, five years from the maturity date. After holding the bond for four years, he sells it for 102. Z claims that he has a loss of $40 on the sale. A friend argues that Z has made a gain of $8 on the sale. Explain the difference in viewpoint. With whom do you agree? Why?

EXERCISES

Ex. 18-1 Companies X and Y have the same amount of operating income. Determine the amount earned per share of common stock for each of the two companies and explain the source of any difference.

	Company X	Company Y
5% debenture bonds payable	$500,000	$ 200,000
6% cumulative preferred stock, $100 par	500,000	300,000
Common stock, $25 par value	500,000	1,000,000
Retained earnings	250,000	250,000
Operating income, before interest and income taxes (assume a 40% tax rate)	300,000	300,000

Ex. 18-2 The following liability appears on the balance sheet of the Smiddy Company Ltd. on December 31, 1973:

Bonds payable, 6%, due 12/ 31/ 87	$1,000,000	
Premium on bonds payable.	42,000	$1,042,000

On January 1, 1974, 20% of the bonds are retired at 98. Interest was paid on December 31, 1973.
a Record the retirement of $200,000 of bonds on January 1, 1974.
b Record the interest payment for the six months ending December 31, 1974, and the amortization of the premium on December 31, 1974, assuming that amortization is recorded only at the end of each year.

Ex. 18-3 Determine the average annual interest cost of the following bond issues:

	Company C	Company D
Maturity value of bonds	$1,000,000	$4,000,000
Contract interest rate	5%	4%
Price received for bonds on issue date	103	96
Length of time from issue date to maturity	10 years	10 years

Ex. 18-4 Peter Ellery acquires $10,000 par value 6% bonds of the Evers Co. Ltd. on May 1, 1973, for a total cost of $9,700, including accrued interest of $200 from January 1, 1973. The bonds mature on June 30, 1977. Interest on the bonds is paid by the Evers Co. on June 30 and December 31 of each year. The discount on the bonds is amortized only at the end of Ellery's fiscal period, which ends on December 31.

Prepare all entries (including the closing entry) required on the books of Peter Ellery for 1973 relating to the investment in Evers Co. Ltd. bonds.

PROBLEMS

Group A

18A-1 Ex-Mar Company Ltd. issued $100,000 par value 6% bonds on July 1, 1973, at $97\frac{1}{2}$. Interest is due on June 30 and December 31 of each year and the discount is amortized only at the end of the fiscal year, which is the calendar year. The bonds mature on June 30, 1983.

Instructions Prepare the required journal entries on
a July 1, 1973, to record the sale of the bonds.
b December 31, 1973, to pay interest and to amortize the discount.
c June 30, 1983, to pay interest, amortize the discount, and retire the bonds.

18A-2 First Company Ltd. issued $5 million of 7%, 10-year bonds on January 1, 1973. Interest is payable semiannually on June 30 and December 31. The bonds were sold to an underwriting group at 110.

Second Company Ltd. issued $5 million of 5%, 10-year bonds on January 1, 1973. Interest is payable semiannually on June 30 and December 31. The bonds were sold to an underwriting group at 90% of par value.

Instructions
a Prepare journal entries, omitting explanations, to record all transactions relating to the bond issues of these two companies during the year 1973.
b Explain why the average bond interest cost per year is the same for the two companies, despite the difference in the terms of the two bond contracts.

18A-3 The items shown below appear on the Reese Company Ltd. balance sheet as of December 31, 1973.

Current liabilities:

Bond interest payable (3 months)		$ 50,000
Long-term liabilities:		
Bonds payable, 5%, due Apr. 1, 1983	$4,000,000	
Discount on bonds payable	295,200	3,704,800

The bonds are callable on any interest date; on October 1, 1973, the Reese Company Ltd. called $1 million of its bonds at 102.

Instructions

a Prepare journal entries to record the semiannual interest payment on April 1, 1973. Discount is amortized at each interest payment date.

b Prepare journal entries to record the call of the bonds and payment of interest on October 1, 1973.

c Prepare a journal entry to record the accrual of interest expense as of December 31, 1973. Include the amortization of bond discount to the year-end.

18A-4 Rex Corporation Ltd. purchased $300,000 of 4%, 10-year provincial bonds at 94. The bonds mature eight years from the date of purchase. The bonds were sold by Rex Corporation Ltd. for 96½ four years after the date of purchase.

Instructions

a Assuming that Rex Corporation Ltd. had no intention of holding the bonds to maturity at the time of purchase, determine the total interest revenue during the four-year period and the gain or loss on disposal.

b Assuming that Rex Corporation Ltd. intended to hold the bonds until maturity at the time of purchase, determine the total interest revenue during the four-year period and the gain or loss on disposal.

18A-5 John Herman purchased 500 shares of Mason Company Ltd. common stock at 42 plus brokerage fees of $200 on March 31. The company had declared a cash dividend of 60 cents per share on March 20, payable on April 15 to stockholders of record on April 6. On June 30 the company declared a 20% stock dividend. On December 15 the shares were split 2 for 1. On December 20 the company declared a cash dividend of 50 cents per share to stockholders of record on December 30, payable on January 10. On December 31, Herman sold 300 shares of the stock at $30 per share, net of commission.

Instructions Prepare journal entries to account for this investment on Herman's books. Since Herman keeps accrual records, an entry to Dividends Receivable should be made on December 30.

18A-6 The investment portfolio of the Royce Corporation Ltd. on January 1, 1973, consists of the following three securities:

$100,000 par value Bay Resorts Corp. Ltd. 6% bonds due Dec. 31, 1980.	
Interest is payable on June 30 and Dec. 31 of each year	$97,600
$50,000 par value Copper Products Co. Ltd. 7½% bonds due Apr. 30, 1984.	
Interest is payable on Apr. 30 and Oct. 31 of each year	52,720
1,000 shares of no-par $4.50 cumulative preferred stock of Donner-Pass, Ltd.	80,000

Transactions relating to investments that were completed during the first six months of 1973 follow.

Jan. 10 Acquired 500 shares of Evans Co. Ltd. common stock at 72. Brokerage commissions paid amounted to $231.

Jan. 21 Received quarterly dividend of 1.12\frac{1}{2}$ per share on 1,000 shares of Donner-Pass, Ltd., preferred stock.

Mar. 5 Sold 200 shares of Donner-Pass, Ltd., preferred stock at 84$\frac{1}{2}$, less commissions amounting to $105.

Apr. 1 Received additional 1,000 shares of Evans Co. Ltd. common stock as a result of a 3 for 1 split.

Apr. 20 Received quarterly dividend of 1.12\frac{1}{2}$ per share on 800 shares of Donner-Pass, Ltd., preferred stock.

Apr. 30 Received semiannual interest on Copper Products Co. Ltd. 7$\frac{1}{2}$% bonds and amortized premium on these bonds from January 1 to April 30. Accrued interest of $625 had been recorded on December 31, 1972, in the Accrued Bond Interest Receivable account.

May 1 Sold entire holdings of Copper Products Co. Ltd. 7$\frac{1}{2}$% bonds at 102$\frac{1}{2}$.

June 4 Received a cash dividend of 70 cents per share on Evans Co. Ltd. common stock.

June 30 Received semiannual interest on Bay Resorts Corp. Ltd. 6% bonds. Amortized the discount on the Bay Resorts Corp. Ltd. bonds for six months.

Instructions
a Prepare journal entries to record the foregoing transactions.
b Prepare a schedule of the investment portfolio for the Royce Corporation Ltd. as of June 30, 1973. Show the name of the security, the number of shares (or par value), and the cost basis for financial reporting purposes.

Group B

18B-1 The Oreville Mine Company Ltd. issued, on September 1, 1972, $600,000 in 9% debenture bonds. Interest is payable semiannually and the bonds mature in 10 years.

Instructions Make the necessary adjusting entries as of December 31, 1972, and the journal entry to record the payment of bond interest on March 1, 1973, under each of the following assumptions:
a The bonds were issued at 96.
b The bonds were issued at 103.

18B-2 Company D issued $600,000 of 6%, 10-year bonds on January 2, 19___. Interest is payable semiannually on June 30 and December 31. The bonds were sold to an underwriting group at 110.
Company E issued $600,000 of 4%, 10-year bonds on January 2, 19___. Interest is payable semiannually on June 30 and December 31. The bonds were sold to an underwriting group at 90.

Instructions
a Prepare journal entries, omitting explanations, to record all transactions relating to the bond issues of these two companies during the year.
b Explain why the average bond interest cost per year is the same for Company D and Company E, despite the difference in the terms of the two bond contracts.

18B-3 Mavis Company Ltd. is authorized to issue $700,000 in 6%, 12-year debenture bonds dated January 1, 1973. Interest is to be paid semiannually on June 30 and December 31. The bonds were sold to an underwriter at 91, plus accrued interest, on May 1, 1973.

Instructions
a Prepare all journal entries necessary to record the bond issue and the bond interest cost during the year 1973. (Note that the bonds will be outstanding for a period of 11 years and 8 months.)

b Prepare a schedule showing the total amount of bond interest cost incurred by the Mavis Company Ltd. during 1973 and 1974.

18B-4 Bengal Corporation Ltd. purchased $500,000 of 7%, 10-year provincial bonds at 94. The bonds mature eight years from the date of purchase. The bonds were sold for 96½ four years after the date of purchase.

Instructions
a Assuming that at the time of purchase the corporation had no intention of holding the bonds to maturity, determine the total interest revenue during the four-year period and the gain or loss on disposal.
b Assuming that at the time of purchase the corporation intended to hold the bonds until maturity, determine the total interest revenue recorded during the four-year period and the gain or loss on disposal.

18B-5 The items shown below appear on the balance sheet of the Peckham Corporation Ltd. as of December 31, 1973.

Current liabilities:		
Bond interest payable (3 months)		$ 121,875
Long-term debt:		
Bonds payable, 6½% due Apr. 1, 1984.	$7,500,000	
Discount on bonds payable	147,600	7,352,400

The bonds are callable on any interest date; on October 1, 1974, the Peckham Corporation Ltd. called $1 million of its bonds at 103½.

Instructions
a Prepare journal entries to record the semiannual interest payment on April 1, 1974. Discount was amortized to December 31, 1973, and is amortized at each interest payment date. Base the amortization on the 123-month period from December 31, 1973, to April 1, 1984.
b Prepare journal entries to record the amortization of bond discount and payment of bond interest at October 1, 1974, and also to record the calling of the bonds at this date.
c Make a journal entry to record the accrual of interest expense as of December 31, 1974. Include the amortization of bond discount to the year-end.

18B-6 James Ross keeps a detailed record of his investments and amortizes discounts and premiums in determining his investment earnings. He held the portfolio shown below throughout the current year:

1,000 shares of Davis Corporation Ltd. common stock; cost $170 per share, market value at December 31 $290 per share. Received dividends of $5 per share on March 1, 10% stock dividend on June 1, and $4 per share on December 1 of current year.

$60,000 in 4% Yarbrought County school bonds, maturing eight years from the date of purchase. Purchased for $56,120, market value on December 31, 94½. Received two regular semiannual interest payments during the current year.

$100,000 in 5% Greene Corporation Ltd. debenture bonds, due four years and two months from date of purchase. Purchased for $102,500; market value at end of current year, 101⅞. Received two regular semiannual interest payments during current year.

1,600 shares of Zeder Corporation Ltd. $6 convertible preferred stock, no par value. Purchased for $159,800, current market value at end of year, 102⅜. Received regular dividends on March 1 and September 1 of current year.

Instructions
a Prepare a schedule showing the amount earned during the current year on each of these investments and the rate of return as a percentage of cost and

of market value at the end of the year. This schedule may be in columnar form with the following column headings:

Name of Security	Original Cost	End-of-year Market Value	Earnings This Year	Rate Earned on Cost, %	Rate Earned on Market Value, %

b In a friendly discussion with a business associate, Ross commented on his average return for the year on the total cost of his investment. His friend retorted that return on market value was a better measure of earning performance. Discuss the merits of the percentage earned on cost and the percentage earned on market value as measures of investment success.

BUSINESS DECISION PROBLEM 18

Ecology Industries Ltd., reported the balances given below at the end of the current year:

Total assets	$7,000,000
Current liabilities	1,400,000
Stockholders' equity:	
Common stock, par $20	2,000,000
Premium on common stock	1,500,000
Retained earnings	1,900,000

The company is planning an expansion of its plant facilities, and a study shows that $6 million of new funds will be required to finance the expansion. Two proposals are under consideration:

Proposal A Issue 120,000 shares of common stock at a price of $50 per share.

Proposal B Borrow $6 million on a 20-year bond issue, with interest at 7%.

The assets and liabilities of Ecology Industries, Ltd. have remained relatively constant over the past five years, and during this period the earnings *after* income taxes have averaged 10% of the stockholders' equity as reported at the end of the current year. The company expects that its earnings *before* income taxes will increase by an amount equal to 12% of the new investment in plant facilities.

Past and future income taxes for the company may be estimated at 40% of taxable income.

Instructions
a Prove that the company's average income *before* income taxes during the past five years was $900,000.
b Prepare a schedule showing the expected net income per share of common stock during the first year of operations following the completion of the $6 million expansion, under each of the two proposed means of financing.
c Evaluate the two methods of financing from the viewpoint of a major stockholder of Ecology Industries, Ltd.

NINETEEN CORPORATIONS CONSOLIDATED STATEMENTS

Since corporations are usually granted the power to hold title to any form of property, one corporation may own shares of stock in another. When one corporation controls another corporation through the ownership of a majority of its capital stock, the controlling corporation is called a *parent* company, and the company whose stock is owned is called a *subsidiary* company. Because both the parent and subsidiary companies are legal entities, separate financial statements may be prepared for each company. However, it may also be useful to prepare financial statements for the *affiliated* companies (the parent company and its subsidiaries) as if they were a single unified business. Such statements are called *consolidated financial statements.*

In a *consolidated balance sheet,* the assets and liabilities of the affiliated companies are combined and reported as though only a single entity existed. Similarly, in a *consolidated income statement,* the revenues and expenses of the affiliated companies are combined, on the assumption that the results of operations for a single economic entity are being measured.

There are a number of economic, financial, and legal, advantages which encourage businessmen to operate through subsidiaries rather than through a single business entity. As a result corporate affiliations are common in Canada. A majority of the companies whose stock is listed on the Toronto Stock Exchange and the Montreal Stock Exchange have one or more subsidiaries and include *consolidated* financial statements in their annual reports. Thus anyone using financial statements to make business decisions will find it useful to know something about the basic principles used in preparing consolidated financial statements for the parent company and its subsidiaries.

Nature of business combinations

There are several ways in which a corporation can acquire or control another corporation. Two or more corporations may, for example, transfer their assets and liabilities to a newly organized corporation and conduct business as a single unit; this type of transaction is called a *consolidation.* If a parent owns all the stock of a subsidiary, it can liquidate the subsidiary and simply take over its assets and liabilities. The capital stock of the subsidiary would be canceled and the combined resources of the two companies would then be able to operate as a single legal and economic entity; this type of transaction is called a *merger.* Mergers and consolidations are frequently referred to as *business combinations.*

If a parent company acquires less than 100% of the stock in a subsidiary, the subsidiary must be maintained as a separate legal entity unless outside stockholders in the subsidiary are willing to sell their stock to the parent company. This form of business combination is also called a merger.

When subsidiaries are operated as separate legal entities, each subsidiary keeps a set of records and prepares separate financial statements. But the parent company and its subsidiaries are in effect an integrated business unit controlled by the board of directors of the parent company, and consolidated statements for such a unit are needed. Only consolidated statements can give a fair presentation of the overall financial position and results of operations of a group of affiliated companies.

An ownership of a majority of the voting shares in a subsidiary gives the parent company a *controlling* interest in the subsidiary's net assets. If the parent company owns less than 100% of the subsidiary's stock, outside stockholders would own a *minority interest* in the subsidiary's net assets. For example, if a parent owns 80% of the stock in a subsidiary, the minority interest would be 20%. This relationship is illustrated below:

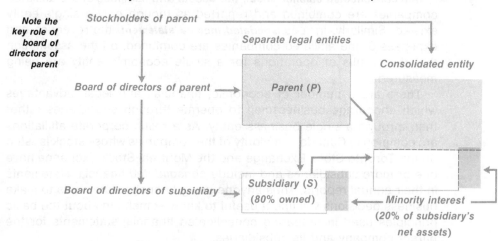

Note the key role of board of directors of parent

The stockholders of the parent (P) company elect the board of directors of P, who in turn appoint the corporate officers of P. The officers of P manage and control all assets owned by P. Included in P's assets is 80% of the capital stock of the subsidiary (S). Therefore when the time comes to vote these shares, directors of P can determine how these votes should be cast and can elect the board of directors of S. Through the board of directors of S, the parent company controls the resources and actions of S. In effect, P and S are operating under the unified control of the board of directors of the parent company, control which is exercised through stock ownership.

Consolidation at date of acquisition

A consolidated balance sheet is prepared by combining the accounts that appear in the separate balance sheets of the parent and subsidiary companies. In the combining process, certain adjustments are made to eliminate the duplication of accounts and to reflect the assets, liabilities, and stockholders' equity from the viewpoint of a *single economic entity.*

To illustrate the process of consolidation, we shall start with a very simple case involving P Company Ltd. A highly condensed balance sheet for P Company Ltd. at the beginning of Year 1 is given below:

P Company Ltd.
Balance Sheet
At Beginning of Year 1

Cash	$200,000	Liabilities	$150,000
Other assets	300,000	Capital stock, $5 par value .	300,000
		Retained earnings	50,000
	$500,000		$500,000

Balance sheet for P Company Ltd.

At this time, P Company Ltd. organizes a fully owned subsidiary, S Company Ltd., which issues all its capital stock (12,000 shares, with a par value of $10 per share) to P Company Ltd. for $120,000 in cash. The journal entries to record this transaction for each company are:

S Company Ltd. issues stock to P Company Ltd.

P Company's Books		*S Company's Books*	
Investment in		Cash 120,000	
S Company Ltd. 120,000		Capital Stock . . .	120,000
Cash	120,000	Sold 12,000 shares	
Acquired 12,000 shares		of stock to	
of stock issued by		P Company Ltd.	
S Company Ltd.			

This transaction has not changed the total assets of P Company Ltd.; cash in the amount of $120,000 has simply been replaced by the investment in S Company Ltd. The cash invested in S Company Ltd., however, is now legally owned by S Company Ltd. Since S Company Ltd. is 100% owned by P Company Ltd., we can conclude that the amount of economic resources controlled by P Company Ltd. has not changed. If we combine the balance sheets of the two companies at the beginning of Year 1 into a single balance sheet, we would expect that the resulting consolidated balance sheet would be identical to the balance sheet of P Company Ltd. before the investment in S Company Ltd. was made. A set of working papers is often helpful in visualizing the "consolidating" process:

P COMPANY LTD.
Working Papers—Consolidated Balance Sheet
At Beginning of Year 1 (Date of Acquisition)

	P Company Ltd.	S Company Ltd.	Intercompany Eliminations		Consolidated Balance Sheet
			Debit	Credit	
Cash	80,000	120,000			200,000
Other assets	300,000				300,000
Investment in S Company Ltd.	120,000			(1) 120,000	
Totals	500,000	120,000			500,000
Liabilities	150,000				150,000
Capital stock—P Company Ltd.	300,000				300,000
Capital stock—S Company Ltd.		120,000	(1) 120,000		
Retained earnings— P Company Ltd.	50,000				50,000
Totals.	500,000	120,000	120,000	120,000	500,000

Explanation of elimination:
(1) To eliminate the Investment in S Company Ltd. account against the subsidiary's Capital Stock account. These are reciprocal accounts without significance when the two companies are viewed as a single economic entity. This elimination entry appears only in the working papers; it is not recorded in the accounts of either the parent or the subsidiary.

Note that the Consolidated Balance Sheet column shows the same amounts found in the separate balance sheet of P Company Ltd. before it organized S Company Ltd. as a 100% owned subsidiary. One of the important points to keep in mind at this stage of our discussion is that *the stockholders' equity of the parent company is also the stockholders' equity which appears in the consolidated balance sheet.*

The Investment in S Company Ltd. and the Capital Stock of S Company Ltd. are eliminated because these accounts were set up by transferring cash of $120,000 from P Company Ltd. to S Company Ltd., which is fully owned by P Company Ltd. To include both of these accounts (the Investment in S Company Ltd., $120,000, and S Company's Cash, $120,000) in the consolidated balance sheet would mean that the same asset would be included twice. Similarly, there would be a double counting of stockholders' equity. From the consolidated viewpoint, the $120,000 capital stock of S Company Ltd. is already included in the stockholders' equity of P Company Ltd. because P Company's stockholders own 100% of P Company's assets, which include the shares of S Company Ltd. By eliminating the investment account on the books of P Company Ltd. against the Capital Stock account of S Company Ltd., *we have a consolidated statement of assets, liabilities, and stockholders' equity* as shown below:

P COMPANY LTD.
and its wholly owned subsidiary
Consolidated Balance Sheet
At Beginning of Year 1 (Date of Acquisition)

Cash	*$200,000*	*Liabilities*	*$150,000*
Other assets	*300,000*	*Capital stock, $5 par value*	*300,000*
		Retained earnings	*50,000*
	$500,000		*$500,000*

This is the same as the separate balance sheet for P Company Ltd shown on page 557

Consolidation after date of acquisition

If the parent company and a 100%-owned subsidiary operate profitably after affiliation, the stockholders' equity (net assets) of both companies will increase. The parent company carries its investment in the subsidiary on the *equity method.* Under the equity method, the earnings of the subsidiary are debited to the investment account and credited to the earnings of the parent; cash dividends received from the subsidiary are recorded by a debit to Cash and a credit to the investment account. A loss reported by a subsidiary is recorded by the parent as a reduction in earnings and a credit to the investment account.

To illustrate this procedure, let us assume that P Company Ltd. and S Company Ltd., discussed in the preceding section, reported net income and paid cash dividends for Year 1 as follows:

	P Company Ltd.	*S Company Ltd.*
Net income (P's net income does not include any earnings of S Company Ltd.)	*$60,000*	*$20,000*
Cash dividends paid	*none*	*5,000*

Net income and cash dividends for Year 1

For the sake of simplicity, let us assume that the net income for each company results in an increase in Other Assets and in the Retained Earnings accounts. Using the equity method, the entries to record the activities for Year 1 on the books of each company would be:

Events	P Company's Books		S Company's Books	
Recording changes in net assets for both companies for Year 1	Net income reported by P Co. Ltd.	Other Assets .... 60,000 Retained Earnings 60,000	None	
	Net income reported by S Co. Ltd.	Investment in S Co. Ltd. .... 20,000 Retained Earnings 20,000	Other Assets .... 20,000 Retained Earnings ... 20,000	
	Dividends paid by S Co.	Cash .... 5,000 Investment in S Co. Ltd. 5,000	Retained Earnings ..... 5,000 Cash 5,000	

When these entries are combined with the information appearing on the separate balance sheets for each company at the date of acquisition, we have the balance sheets for each company as shown in the first two columns of the working papers shown below. For example, P Company's cash balance of $85,000 now consists of the beginning balance on its separate balance sheet, $80,000, plus dividends received from S Company, $5,000; the Investment in S Company, $135,000, now consists of the beginning balance, $120,000, plus the earnings of S Company for Year 1 not distributed in the form of cash dividends, $15,000 ($20,000 − $5,000). These working papers also show the elimination entry required to arrive at the consolidated balance sheet figures shown in the last column:

P COMPANY LTD.
Working Papers—Consolidated Balance Sheet
At End of Year 1 (One Year after Acquisition)

	P Company Ltd.	S Company Ltd.	Intercompany Eliminations		Consolidated Balance Sheet
			Debit	Credit	
Cash	85,000	115,000			200,000
Other assets	360,000	20,000			380,000
Investment in S Company Ltd.	135,000			(1) 135,000	
Totals	580,000	135,000			580,000
Liabilities	150,000				150,000
Capital stock—P Company Ltd.	300,000				300,000
Capital stock—S Company Ltd.		120,000	(1) 120,000		
Retained earnings— P Company Ltd.	130,000				130,000
Retained earnings— S Company Ltd.		15,000	(1) 15,000		
Totals	580,000	135,000	135,000	135,000	580,000

Explanation of elimination:
(1) To eliminate the investment in S Company Ltd. against the subsidiary's stockholders' equity accounts one year after acquisition of 100% of S Company's capital stock by P Company Ltd.

In preparing a consolidated balance sheet after the date of acquisition, the assets (other than the Investment in S Company Ltd. account) and the liabilities of the parent and subsidiary *at statement date* are combined and the investment account is eliminated against the stockholders' equity of S Company Ltd. Since the parent company has already recorded the net income and dividends of the subsidiary in the investment account, this account increased by $15,000 during the year (net income of the subsidiary, $20,000, less dividends paid by the subsidiary, $5,000), an amount equal to the total increase in the stockholders' equity of S Company Ltd. In other words, the balance in the Investment in S Company Ltd. account, $135,000, is equal to the total stockholders' equity of S Company Ltd. consisting of capital stock, $120,000, and retained earnings, $15,000. After these "reciprocal" balances are eliminated, the remaining accounts are extended to the Consolidated Balance Sheet column and are used to prepare a formal balance sheet for the two affiliated companies. Note that the consolidated stockholders' equity consists of P Company's capital stock, $300,000, and P Company's retained earnings, $130,000, as adjusted for P Company's share of S Company's earnings for Year 1.

Less than 100% ownership in subsidiary

If a parent company owns a controlling interest in a subsidiary but less than 100% of the outstanding shares, a new kind of account known as the *minority interest* will appear in the consolidated balance sheet. Minority interest represents that part of the subsidiary's net assets, or subsidiary's stockholders' equity, which is not owned by the parent company. The consolidated balance sheet will include all the assets and liabilities of the affiliated companies (other than the parent's investment in subsidiary, which is eliminated). Only a portion of the ownership equity in these net assets is represented by the equity of the parent company stockholders because some of the equity interest in the subsidiary's net assets is held by the minority stockholders of the subsidiary. We might conceivably prepare a consolidated balance sheet which included only the parent company's share of the assets of the subsidiary. A more complete and useful financial picture of the consolidated entity results, however, if we include all of the subsidiary's assets and allocate the ownership equity in these assets between the controlling and minority interests.

To illustrate, assume that at the end of Year 4 the Park Company Ltd. *purchased* 75% of the outstanding capital stock of Sims Company Ltd. for $150,000 in cash, *an amount equal to the book value of the stock acquired.* The working papers to prepare a consolidated balance sheet on the date that control of Sims Company Ltd. is acquired appear on page 562.

In the eliminating entry on the working papers, the stockholders' equity of Sims Company Ltd. (capital stock, $125,000, and retained earnings, $75,000) is eliminated. Of this stockholders' equity, $50,000 (25% of $200,000) is shown as minority interest, and the remaining 75% is offset against the $150,000 investment account which appears on Park Com-

PARK COMPANY LTD.
Working Papers—Consolidated Balance Sheet
At End of Year 4 (Date of Acquisition)

	Park Company Ltd.	Sims Company Ltd.	Intercompany Eliminations Debit	Intercompany Eliminations Credit	Consolidated Balance Sheet
Cash	200,000	50,000			250,000
Other assets	500,000	210,000			710,000
Investment in Sims Company Ltd.	150,000			(1) 150,000	
Totals	850,000	260,000			960,000
Liabilities	250,000	60,000			310,000
Capital stock—Park Company Ltd.	500,000				500,000
Capital stock—Sims Company Ltd.		125,000	(1) 125,000		
Retained earnings—Park Company Ltd.	100,000				100,000
Retained earnings—Sims Company Ltd.		75,000	(1) 75,000		
Minority interest (25% of $200,000)				(1) 50,000	50,000 M
Totals	850,000	260,000	200,000	200,000	960,000

Explanation of elimination:
(1) To eliminate Park Company's investment in Sims Company's stockholders' equity, and to establish the 25% minority interest in Sims Company (25% of total stockholders' equity of Sims Company Ltd.).

pany's books. As an alternative, we might have eliminated only 75% of Sims Company's capital stock and retained earnings, leaving 25% of each to be carried into the consolidated balance sheet column to reflect the $50,000 minority interest. The reader of consolidated financial statements is primarily concerned with the total amount of the minority interest and not with its composition. Therefore no significant information is lost if we eliminate completely the stockholders' equity accounts of the subsidiary and establish the minority interest in consolidated net assets as a single amount.

On the consolidated balance sheet for Park Company Ltd., the minority interest would appear separately on the consolidated balance sheet between the liabilities and stockholders' equity sections as illustrated below:

Minority interest: an element of stockholders' equity				
Cash	*$250,000*	*Liabilities*		*$310,000*
Other assets	*710,000*	*Minority Interest*		*50,000*
		Stockholders' equity:		
		Capital stock	*$500,000*	
		Retained earnings	*100,000*	*600,000*
	$960,000			*$960,000*

The minority interest amounts to $50,000 (25% of the $200,000 total stockholders' equity in Sims Company Ltd.) and represents the ownership in consolidated net assets held by the stockholders of Sims Company Ltd. Minority interest should be reported "as a separate item on the balance sheet outside of stockholders' equity."[1] This method of reporting minority interest conforms with the concept that consolidated financial statements are prepared primarily from the viewpoint of the parent company's stockholders. The following is a summary of the disclosure of minority interest by Canadian companies[2]:

	Number of Companies		
	1974	*1973*	*1972*
Total number of companies	*99*	*104*	*93*
Minority interest set out separately outside the stockholders' equity section of the balance sheet	*98*	*102*	*91*

Acquisition of subsidiary stock at more (or less) than book value

When a parent corporation purchases a controlling interest in a subsidiary it will probably pay a price for the shares that differs from their underlying book value. In consolidating the financial statements of two affiliated corporations, we cannot ignore a discrepancy between the cost of the parent company's investment in subsidiary shares and the book

[1] Canadian Institute of Chartered Accountants, *CICA Handbook,* paragraphs 1600.66 - 1600.68
[2] Source: *Financial Reporting in Canada,* Eleventh edition 1975, Canadian Institute of Chartered Accountants, Toronto page 106.

value of these shares on the statements of the subsidiary company. In consolidation, the parent's investment is offset against the appropriate stockholders' equity accounts of the subsidiary, and if the two amounts are not equal, we must determine what the difference between them represents.

To illustrate, suppose that at the end of the current year, C Company Ltd. purchased *all* the outstanding shares of D Company Ltd. for $120,000. At the date of acquisition, D Company Ltd. reported on its balance sheet total stockholders' equity of $95,000, consisting of capital stock of $50,000 and retained earnings of $45,000. In preparing the elimination entry on the working papers for a consolidated balance sheet at the date of acquisition, we must determine what to do with the $25,000 discrepancy between the price paid, $120,000, and the stockholders' equity of D Company Ltd., $95,000.

If we ask ourselves why C Company Ltd. paid $120,000 for the stock of D Company Ltd., the answer must be that the management of C Company considered the net assets of D Company Ltd. to be worth $120,000 rather than their book value of $95,000. C's management may believe that the fair market value of certain specific assets of D Company Ltd. is in excess of book value, or they may believe that D Company's future earnings prospects are so favorable as to justify paying $25,000 for D Company's unrecorded goodwill. Since C Company Ltd. paid $120,000 for a 100% interest in D Company Ltd. in an arm's-length market transaction, the accountant has objective evidence that certain assets of D Company Ltd. are undervalued, or that unrecorded goodwill of $25,000 exists. Where possible, the excess of purchase price over book value of net assets should be assigned to specific identifiable assets. Only that portion of the excess which cannot be attributed to identifiable assets should be allocated to goodwill.[3] This evidence provides a basis for making the following eliminating entry *on the working papers* for a consolidated balance sheet on date of acquisition:

D. Company's Ltd.	*Capital Stock—D Company Ltd.*	*50,000*	
assets are	*Retained Earnings—D Company Ltd.*	*45,000*	
understated	**Specific Assets (or Goodwill) of D Company Ltd.**	**25,000**	
	Investment in D Company Ltd. (on C's books)		*120,000*

To eliminate the cost of C Company's 100% interest in D Company Ltd. against the appropriate stockholders' equity accounts and to restate undervalued assets of D Company Ltd. (or establish unrecorded goodwill of D Company Ltd.).

The $25,000 in increased valuation assigned to specific assets (or goodwill) of D Company Ltd. will be carried over as assets in the consolidated balance sheet. The amount reflected as goodwill at the date of acquisition should be amortized as a charge against income by the

[3]*CICA Handbook, op.cit.,* paragraph 1580.44.

straight-line method over the estimated life of the goodwill. The amortization period should not exceed forty years.[4]

If the parent company *pays less than book* value for its interest in a subsidiary, a similar problem of interpretation exists. For example, suppose in the previous case that C Company Ltd. had paid only $85,000 for all the outstanding shares of D Company Ltd., which have a book value of $95,000. In this case we may assume that the management of C Company Ltd. considered that D Company's assets were overvalued by $10,000. The eliminating entry on the working papers to consolidate the financial statements of the two companies on the date of acquisition would be:

D Company's Ltd. assets are overstated

Capital Stock—D Company Ltd.	*50,000*	
Retained Earnings—D Company Ltd.	*45,000*	
Investment in D Company Ltd. (on C's books)		*85,000*
Specific Assets of D Company Ltd.		*10,000*

To eliminate investment in D Company Ltd. against appropriate stockholder's equity accounts, and to record the indicated reduction in D Company's assets.

The credit excess of $10,000 should be reported in the consolidated balance sheet as a reduction in the book value of specific assets of D Company Ltd. The amounts assigned to identifiable non-monetary assets should be reduced such that the excess is eliminated.[5]

Intercompany receivables and payables

If one affiliated company (either a parent or subsidiary) owes money to another there will be an asset (receivable) on the individual balance sheet of the creditor firm and a liability (payable) on the statement of the debtor company. When the financial statements of the two companies are consolidated, however, *both the asset and liability should be eliminated.* Neither a receivable nor a liability exists from the viewpoint of the consolidated entity. The situation is analogous to that of a student who has saved $500 to pay his fall semester tuition and who then borrows $10 from this fund for a date. In his internal financial thinking the student will consider that he owes $10 from his recreational fund to his tuition fund, but if he were to prepare a personal balance sheet he would not show this $10 receivable and payable as an asset and liability.

---

[4]*Ibid*, paragraph 1580.58.

The following example of a footnote on the amortization of goodwill is from the 1974 annual report of Silverwood Industries Ltd.:

Goodwill representing the excess of the purchase price of subsidiaries over the net book value of the underlying assets, and purchased goodwill prior to December 31, 1973 is carried at cost less any disposals.

In accordance with the recommendations of the Canadian Institute of Chartered Accountants, goodwill purchased subsequent to December 31, 1973 is being amortized on a straight-line basis. The goodwill purchased in 1974 is being amortized over a period of five to ten years.

[5]*Ibid*, paragraph 1580.44.

On consolidating working papers an eliminating entry is made to cancel out any intercompany debt between affiliated companies. Suppose, for example, that a parent company has borrowed $10,000 from its subsidiary and at the balance sheet date owes this amount plus $500 accrued interest. On consolidating working papers for a consolidated balance sheet the following elimination entry would be made:

<table>
<tr><td rowspan="5">*To cancel intercom-pany debt on working papers*</td><td>*Notes Payable—(Parent's balance sheet)* . . . .</td><td>*10,000*</td><td></td></tr>
<tr><td>*Interest Payable—(Parent's balance sheet)* . . . .</td><td>*500*</td><td></td></tr>
<tr><td>   *Notes Receivable—(Subsidiary's balance sheet)* . . . .</td><td></td><td>*10,000*</td></tr>
<tr><td>   *Interest Receivable—(Subsidiary's balance sheet)* . . . .</td><td></td><td>*500*</td></tr>
<tr><td>*To eliminate intercompany payables and receivables.*</td><td></td><td></td></tr>
</table>

The elimination entry shown above appears *only* on consolidating working papers; it would *not appear on the accounting records* of either the parent company or the subsidiary.

Consolidated income statement

A consolidated income statement is prepared by combining the revenue and expense accounts of the parent and subsidiary. Revenues and expenses arising from *intercompany transactions* are eliminated because they reflect transfers of assets from one affiliated company to another and do not change the net assets from a consolidated viewpoint. Some of the more common examples of intercompany items that should be eliminated in preparing a consolidated income statement are:

1 Sales to affiliated companies
2 Purchases from affiliated companies
3 Interest paid on loans from affiliated companies
4 Interest received on loans made to affiliated companies
5 Rent or other revenues received for services rendered to affiliated companies
6 Rent or other expenses paid for services received from affiliated companies

To illustrate the procedure, consider the following income statement data for X Company Ltd. and its 90%-owned subsidiary, Y Company Ltd., several years after control was achieved. X Company Ltd. has not yet recorded its share of Y Company's earnings for Year 10.

X COMPANY LTD.
and its subsidiary company
Year 10 Income Statements

	X Company	Y Company	Total
Sales	$600,000	$300,000	**$900,000**
Other revenues	50,000	25,000	75,000
Total revenues	$650,000	$325,000	**$975,000**
Cost of goods sold	$400,000	$225,000	**$625,000**
Expenses (including income taxes)	190,000	60,000	250,000
Total expenses	$590,000	$285,000	**$875,000**
Net income	$ 60,000	$ 40,000	**$100,000**

Does the total reflect consoli-dated results?

The Total column would represent the consolidated income statement *only if there were no intercompany transactions and if X Company Ltd. owned 100% of the stock in Y Company Ltd.* Any revenues and expenses arising from transactions between the two companies must be eliminated, however, when the affiliated companies are viewed as a single economic entity. Assume, for example, that the following intercompany transactions had taken place during Year 10 between X Company Ltd. and Y Company Ltd.:

1 All the goods sold by Y Company Ltd. were acquired from X Company Ltd. for $225,000. Y Company Ltd. has no inventory at the end of the year.

2 Other revenues of X Company Ltd. include rental revenue of $45,000 received from Y Company Ltd.

Keep in mind that X Company Ltd. has not recorded its share of Y Company's net income. The intercompany eliminations necessary to arrive at a consolidated income statement for Year 10 are shown in the working papers below:

X COMPANY LTD.
Working Papers—Consolidated Income Statement
Year 10

	X Company Ltd.	Y Company Ltd.	Intercompany Eliminations Debit	Intercompany Eliminations Credit	Consolidated Income Statement
Sales (credit)	600,000	300,000	(1) 225,000		675,000
Other revenues (credit) . . .	50,000	25,000	(2) 45,000		30,000
Total revenues	650,000	325,000			705,000
Cost of goods sold (debit) .	400,000	225,000		(1) 225,000	400,000
Expenses, including income taxes (debit)	190,000	60 000		(2) 45,000	205,000
Net income (credit)	60,000	**40,000**	(3) 4,000		96,000
Minority interest in net income of Y Company Ltd. (10% of $40,000) . . .				(3) 4,000	4,000 M
Totals	650,000	325,000	274,000	274,000	705,000

Explanations of eliminations:
(1) To eliminate intercompany sales and purchases, included in the cost of goods sold.
(2) To eliminate rental revenue and rental expense.
(3) To recognize minority interest in net income of Y Company, 10% of $40,000.

COMMENTS ON WORKING PAPER ELIMINATIONS **Entry (1)** This entry eliminated the intercompany sales and purchases. In other words, the sale recorded by X Company Ltd. was recorded as a purchase by Y Company Ltd. at the same dollar amount, $225,000. In preparing a consolidated income statement, this transaction (sale and purchase) is viewed as an *internal transfer* between affiliated units of a single entity and is considered irrelevant in preparing a consolidated income statement.

Entry (2) This entry eliminates the intercompany rental revenue and rent expense accounts. Rent paid by Y Company Ltd. to X Company Ltd. is included in X Company's revenue and Y Company's expenses. The debit portion of the eliminating entry cancels the revenue recorded by X Company Ltd. and the credit portion cancels the expense recorded by Y Company Ltd. This eliminating entry has no effect on consolidated net income, because we are simply offsetting an item recorded as revenue by one company in the affiliated structure against the expense recorded by the other affiliated company.

Entry (3) The purpose of this eliminating entry in the working papers is to recognize the share of the net income of Y Company Ltd. accruing to the minority stockholders of Y Company Ltd. Since the net income of Y Company Ltd. amounts to $40,000 and X Company Ltd. owns 90% of the stock of Y Company Ltd., $36,000 (90% × $40,000) of Y Company's net income accrues to X Company Ltd. and becomes a part of **consolidated net income;** the other $4,000 (10% × $40,000) of Y Company's net income accrues to the minority interest. This is recognized in the working papers by debiting (reducing) net income of Y Company Ltd. (a credit balance) and crediting Minority Interest in Net Income for $4,000. This minority interest in net income is generally shown as a deduction from "income before minority interest" in arriving at "net income" in the consolidated income statement.

When the various income statement items are combined, after the effect of the eliminating entries on the working papers has been taken into account, the figures in the last column of the working papers provide the basis for the preparation of a consolidated income statement. A condensed consolidated income statement of X Company Ltd. for Year 10 is shown below:

X COMPANY LTD.
and its subsidiary company
Consolidated Income Statement
For Year 10

Sales and other revenues			*$705,000*
Less:			
Cost of goods sold		*$400,000*	
Expenses (including income taxes)		*205,000*	*605,000*
Income before minority interest			*$100,000*
Less: Minority interest in net income of subsidiary			***4,000***
Net income			*$ 96,000*

Minority stockholders' equity in earnings of subsidiary is deducted in computing net income

Observe that the net income of the consolidated entity for Year 10 actually amounts to $100,000, of which $96,000 is allocated to the controlling interest and $4,000 is allocated to the minority interest. The income accruing to the controlling interest is usually labeled "net income," although it is sometimes referred to as "consolidated net income." Instead of showing "income before minority interest" as illustrated above, some companies include the minority interest in net income under the Expenses caption in the income statement.[6]

Consolidated statement of retained earnings

The net income reported in the consolidated income statement also appears in the consolidated statement of retained earnings. Assume, for example, that the retained earnings appearing in the consolidated balance sheet at the end of Year 9 for X and Y Companies in the previous illustration amounted to $345,000 and that X Company Ltd. declared cash dividends of $47,500 in Year 10. The consolidated statement of retained earnings would appear as follows:

Only dividends declared by parent company appear in consolidated statement of retained earnings

X COMPANY LTD.
and its subsidiary company
Consolidated Statement of Retained Earnings
For Year 10

Retained earnings, beginning of year	$345,000
Add: Net income for year.	96,000
Total	$441,000
Less: Cash dividends declared (by parent company)	**47,500**
Retained earnings, end of year	$393,500

It is important to remember that the consolidated statement of retained earnings includes only the net income accruing to the controlling interest and the dividends declared by the parent company. Any dividends received by the parent from the subsidiary would be eliminated in preparing a consolidated income statement; dividends paid to minority stockholders by the subsidiary simply reduce the amount of minority interest reported in the consolidated balance sheet.

Unrealized profits on intercompany sales

Assume that a subsidiary company sells to its parent for $1,000 goods which cost the subsidiary $700. From the viewpoint of the subsidiary as a legal entity, a gross profit of $300 has been realized on this transaction. From the viewpoint of a single entity, however, goods have been trans-

[6]In a recent study of 325 annual reports by the CICA, 99 companies reported minority interests in their consolidated statements. Of these, 15 companies listed the minority interest in earnings among expenses. 62 companies listed the minority interest as a deduction from income after income taxes and 11 companies listed the minority interest elsewhere on the consolidated income statement. The remaining 11 companies did not disclose the minority stockholders' share of income.

ferred from one division of the economic entity to another, and no gain will be realized until the goods have been sold to someone outside the consolidated entity. If these goods are in the parent company's inventory at the time a consolidated balance sheet is prepared, the goods should be valued at $700, the cost to the consolidated entity. Therefore, in the process of consolidation, it would be necessary to remove $300 from the inventory account of the parent company and $300 from the retained earnings account of the subsidiary company.

The problem of eliminating unrealized increases in inventory valuation as a result of intercompany sales should be distinguished from that of eliminating the dollar amount of intercompany sales and purchases. When one affiliated company sells goods to another, and the second affiliate in turn sells these goods to outsiders, there is no *unrealized* intercompany profit. The profit recognized by each affiliate on the sale of these goods has been realized by the sale of the goods to outsiders. For example, suppose that a subsidiary sells goods which cost $40,000 to the parent for $50,000, and the parent in turn sells these goods to outsiders for $65,000. Both the $10,000 gross profit recognized by the subsidiary and the $15,000 gross profit recognized by the parent are fully realized, since none of the goods remain in inventory within the consolidated entity. In preparing a consolidated income statement for these companies, how-ever, it would be necessary to eliminate $50,000 from the sales of the subsidiary and $50,000 from the purchases (or cost of goods sold) of the parent. This elimination would have no effect on consolidated assets or net income, since its purpose is simply to remove the *double counting* of revenues and expenses resulting from the transfer of goods from one affiliate to another.

The procedures necessary to remove unrealized profits in transactions between affiliates are somewhat complicated. However, familiarity with the technical procedure is not necessary to understand consolidated financial statements; the reader of such statements may assume that unrealized profits on transfers of assets between affiliates have been eliminated.

Consolidated statements on a pooling-of-interests basis

In recent years the acquisition of a subsidiary corporation has often been carried out by an *exchange of stock,* and the preparation of consolidated statements has followed a "pooling-of-interests" method. A key aspect of such acquisitions is that the stockholders of the subsidiary company being acquired become stockholders of the parent corporation. The stockholders of the two companies are said to have *pooled their interests,* rather than one ownership group having sold its equity to the other.[7]

---

[7]For a more complete discussion of the methods of accounting for business combinations, see Section 1580 of the *CICA Handbook.*

If we accept the view that no ownership interests have been severed (in other words no purchase or sale occurred), then there is no reason to revalue the assets of the acquired company, regardless of the market value of the securities exchanged. When the acquisition is treated as a pooling of interests, the investment account on the books of the parent can be established at the par or stated value of the shares issued by the parent regardless of the current market price of the stock issued. Furthermore, if the parent acquired 100% of the stock of the subsidiary late in the year, the earnings (revenue and expenses) of the subsidiary *for the entire year* can be included in consolidated earnings.

To illustrate, let us assume that P Company Ltd. acquired 100% of S Company Ltd. stock on November 1, Year 1, and that each company earned $60,000 during Year 1. The consolidated net income for the two companies on a pooling basis would be $120,000, even though $50,000 (10/12 of $60,000) of the earnings of S Company Ltd. were earned before the two companies became affiliated on November 1.

The following brief summary emphasizes some of the points of contrast between treating a corporate acquisition as a *purchase* or as a *pooling of interests.*

Purchase Method	*Pooling-of-interests Method*
1 *Parent records its investment in subsidiary at amount of cash paid or at market value of shares issued by parent in exchange for shares of subsidiary. Excess of cost over book value (or book value over cost) may result.*	*Parent records its investment in subsidiary at par (or stated) value of shares issued; the market value of shares issued (or assets acquired) is ignored.*
2 *Retained earnings of subsidiary at date of acquisition do not become part of consolidated retained earnings.*	*Retained earnings of subsidiary at date of acquisition generally become part of consolidated retained earnings.*
3 *Earnings of subsidiary are combined with the earnings of the parent only from the date of the affiliation.*	*Earnings of subsidiary for the entire year in which the affiliation occurs are included in the consolidated income statement.*

The popularity of the pooling concept in recent years can be attributed largely to two factors. The first is the opportunity for the parent company to acquire valuable assets and to record these assets at relatively low values as shown on the books of the subsidiary company. As a result the consolidated earnings will not be penalized through amortization of higher (current) asset values against revenues. A second reason for the popularity of the pooling concept is that it permits a company whose stock sells at a high price-earnings multiple to show an *instant increase* in its earnings per share by issuing additional stock to acquire companies whose stock customarily sells at a low price-earnings multiple. A "growth" company may thus be able to maintain its reputation for reporting higher per-share earnings each year by continually acquiring other companies and accounting for such acquisitions on a pooling-of-interests basis.

A great many abuses were perpetuated in using the pooling-of-interests basis to record business combinations. In Canada, use of the pooling-of-interests method is now severely curtailed. The **CICA Handbook**[8] takes the position that all corporate combinations should be accounted for as a purchase except for those rare cases where it is not possible to identify an acquirer. Thus, the pooling-of-interests method may now be used in Canada to account for a business combination only in those cases, which will be rare, where it is impossible to identify one of the parties as an acquirer.

The preparation of a consolidated balance sheet using the pooling-of-interests approach will be illustrated for the Parent and Sub companies. Assume that at the end of Year 1, the Parent Company Ltd. issues 10,000 shares of its stock ($10 par) in exchange for the 12,500 shares of Sub Company Ltd. stock. The market value of Parent Company's stock at this time is $35 per share. The Parent Company Ltd. records the shares issued at par value, $100,000; the market value of Parent Company's stock, $350,000, is not considered relevant and is ignored for accounting purposes under the pooling concept. The working papers to develop a consolidated balance sheet on a pooling basis are shown below:

PARENT AND SUB COMPANIES
Working Papers—Consolidated Balance Sheet (Pooling Basis)
End of Year 1 (Date of Acquisition)

	Parent Company Ltd.	Sub Company Ltd.	Intercompany Eliminations		Consolidated Balance Sheet
			Debit	Credit	
Other assets	700,000	400,000			1,100,000
Investment in Sub Company Ltd......	100,000			(1) 100,000	
Totals	800,000	400,000			1,100,000
Liabilities	200,000	75,000			275,000
Capital stock, $10 par	390,000	125,000	(1) 125,000		390,000
Retained earnings ...	200,000	200,000			400,000
Contributed surplus—Premium on shares	10,000			(1) 25,000	35,000
Totals	800,000	400,000	125,000	125,000	1,100,000

A pooling combines retained earnings of both companies on date of acquisition

Explanation of elimination:
(1) To eliminate investment in subsidiary account. $100,000, and subsidiary's capital stock, $125,000; the excess, $25,000 is recognized as premium on shares.

The eliminating entry on the working papers cancels the balance in the investment account, $100,000 (par value of stock issued to acquire control of Sub Company Ltd.), and the capital stock of the Sub Company Ltd., $125,000. Since the par value of the stock issued, $100,000, is less

[8]Op.cit., paragraphs 1580.18 and 1580.21.

than the par value of the acquired company's stock, $125,000, the excess of $25,000 is recorded as Premium on Shares. Note that the retained earnings balances of the two companies ($200,000 for each company), are combined in the consolidated balance sheet even though the retained earnings of Sub Company Ltd were earned *before* Parent Company Ltd. acquired control of Sub Company Ltd. The consolidated balance sheet on a pooling basis is shown below:

PARENT COMPANY LTD.

and Its Subsidiary Company

Consolidated Balance Sheet (Pooling Basis)

End of Year 1 (Date of Acquisition)

A pooling may increase the paid-in capital in excess of par	*Other assets*	$1,100,000	*Liabilities*	$ 275,000
			Capital stock, $10 par	390,000
			Contributed Surplus—	
			Premium on shares	35,000
			Retained earnings	400,000
		$1,100,000		$1,100,000

If the Parent Company Ltd. had issued 13,500 shares of $10 par value stock in exchange for all the capital stock of Sub Company Ltd., the excess of the $135,000 par value of stock issued over the $125,000 par value of Sub Company Ltd. stock acquired would be debited to Premium on Shares. If the Parent Company Ltd. had no premium on shares, the $10,000 charge could be made against retained earnings.

When should consolidated statements be prepared?

Accounts of some subsidiary companies may not be included in consolidated statements. Consolidation of accounts is deemed appropriate only when effective control over the subsidiary is *present* and *continuing* and when the consolidated statements *give a meaningful picture of financial position and results of operations.* For example, a subsidiary's accounts should not be consolidated with those of the parent if control is likely to be temporary or if the subsidiary is facing bankruptcy. Similarly, if the assets of a foreign subsidiary cannot be withdrawn by the parent because of restrictions placed on such assets by foreign governments, consolidation of accounts should be avoided.

When the parent company controls a subsidiary but consolidation is not considered appropriate, the question arises as to how the investment in the *unconsolidated subsidiary* should be reported in the separate financial statements of the parent. For many years, both the *cost* and the *equity* method of accounting for the investment were widely used. The equity method *is now required.*[9] Under the *equity method,* the parent company "accrues" its share of the subsidiary's net income by debiting the

[9]*Ibid,* Section 3050.

Investment in Subsidiary account and crediting Earnings of Unconsolidated Subsidiary; losses are debited to Loss of Unconsolidated Subsidiary and credited to the Investment in Subsidiary account. Dividends received are debited to Cash and credited to the Investment in Subsidiary account. Under the *cost method*, earnings of the subsidiary would be recognized only to the extent of cash dividends received from the subsidiary; earnings not distributed in the form of dividends and losses incurred by the subsidiary would be ignored.

The application of the equity method in financial statements is illustrated below for Southam Press Limited (newspaper and magazine publisher):

Consolidated Balance Sheet	*Dec. 31, 1974*	*Dec. 31, 1973*
Investments		
Companies 50% owned	*$7,743,000*	*$7,366,000*
Note to financial statements		
Companies 50% Owned		

The equity in the earnings of companies 50 per cent owned is included in income and the investment in such companies is carried at the book value of their underlying net tangible assets.

Consolidated Statement of Income		
Revenue item added to operating income		
Equity in net income of companies 50 per cent owned	*$2,957,000*	*$2,847,000*

The *CICA Handbook* recommends that the equity method of accounting for an investment in common stock be followed by companies whose investment enables them to exercise effective control over the operating and financial decisions of the investee even though the investor does not hold more than 50% of its voting stock.[10] This recommendation is made because: (1) the investor has a degree of responsibility for the return on its investment, and (2) the equity method meets the objectives of the accrual principle of accounting.

Effective control is not defined by the *CICA Handbook* but is a matter to be determined in the particular circumstances. In *Opinion No. 18,* the AICPA Accounting Principles Board considered that holding 20% or more of the voting stock was sufficient to exercise "significant influence" over the investee.

The accounting requirements for investments in subsidiaries and significant investments in other corporations are summarized below:

---

[10]*Ibid,* paragraphs 3050.18 to 3050.25.

Situation	*General Practice*
1 Controlled subsidiary (more than 50% owned)	Consolidate, *except in situations where activities of subsidiary are significantly different from those of the parent or where assets of a foreign subsidiary cannot be withdrawn by the parent company. The equity method of accounting for uncon-solidated subsidiaries would generally be used.*
2 Effective control with ownership of less than 50% of voting stock	*The use of the equity method by investor corporation is generally required.*
3 Portfolio investments	Cost method must be used; *only cash dividends received on stock owned is in-cluded in net income of investor corpora-tion.*

More complex corporate affiliations

Throughout this chapter we have assumed relatively simple corporate affiliations—the direct ownership of a controlling interest of one company in another. Many extremely complex corporate affiliations are found among Canadian corporations. Some corporations control a large number of subsidiaries which may in turn control subsidiaries of their own. In other cases, one company may own only 40% of the stock of another but it may exercise control over that company because one of its other subsidiaries owns, say, 45% of the stock. This type of corporate affiliation is illustrated in the diagram below:

Does P Company control S Company?

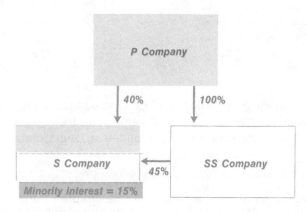

In this case, P Company Ltd. in effect controls 85% of the stock of S Company Ltd. and the preparation of consolidated statements for the three companies would be appropriate.

Product-line reporting by diversified companies

We have seen that consolidated statements for two or more affiliated companies engaged in similar activities may be more informative than the separate statements for each company. But this may not be true if the affiliated companies are engaged in *significantly different lines of business.* Assume, for example, that Do-All Corporation Ltd. controls subsidiaries which own copper mines, manufacture appliances, and operate shipyards. Would you, as a prudent investor, like to know the proportion of sales and income that is generated from each of these diverse lines of business before investing in the common stock of this company?

A consolidated income statement for this *diversified* or *conglomerate* company does not report the sales volume or the net income by product lines. Users of financial statements are interested in a breakdown of the aggregate data included in the consolidated statements of such companies in order to see where a company's strengths and weaknesses lie and thus be able to make better business decisions. Such a breakdown may include: (*1*) revenues by industry activity or type of customer, (*2*) segment margins, (*3*) segment balance sheet data.[7] An example of product-line reporting found in an annual report of a well-known company is shown below:

Operating Results by Product Lines during 19___

		Net Sales		Segment Income	
		Amount (millions)	%	Amount (millions)	%
Sales and operating income by product lines	Tobacco products:				
	Domestic	$1,100.6	58.0	$167.1	74.6
	International	358.8	18.9	27.7	12.4
	Distilled beverages	126.5	6.7	16.6	7.4
	Food products	289.1	15.2	9.8	4.4
	Other	22.9	1.2	2.9	1.2
	Total	$1,897.9	100.0	$224.1	100.0

Financial reporting by diversified companies has been receiving a great deal of attention in recent years. The trend toward more extensive disclosures by diversified companies appears certain to continue.

Who uses consolidated statements?

As noted at the beginning of this chapter, consolidated statements are designed to set aside the legal boundaries between affiliated companies and present a financial picture of the resources and operations of an economic entity. Persons looking to their *legal* rights will not find pertinent information in consolidated statements.

[7] *Ibid,* Section 1700.

Consolidated statements are not significant to the minority stockholders or creditors of the subsidiary company. A strong financial position shown in a consolidated balance sheet may conceal a very weak situation in the particular subsidiary company in which a creditor or minority stockholder has a legal interest. These groups should rely on the individual financial statements of the affiliate in which they have a legal claim.

Long-term creditors of the parent company may find consolidated statements useful in assessing the general strength or weakness of the economic entity. In the long run, earning power is the primary source of creditor safety. The operating performance of the affiliated group may be a significant safety index for creditors of the parent company.

The stockholders, managers, and members of the board of directors of the parent company have the primary interest in consolidated statements. The managers and directors are responsible for the entire resources under their control and for managing these resources profitably. Similarly, the stockholders of the parent company will prosper as the consolidated entity prospers. Their ownership interest is controlling, and they thus stand to benefit from strength anywhere in the entity and to suffer from weakness.

Additional uses of consolidated financial statements and more complex problems encountered in preparing them are discussed in the *Advanced Accounting* volume of this series.

QUESTIONS

1 Define each of the following: (a) merger, (b) consolidation, (c) consolidated balance sheet, and (d) consolidated income statement.

2 Alexander Corporation Ltd. owns 80% of the outstanding common stock of Benton Company. Explain the basis for the assumption that these two companies constitute a single economic entity operating under unified control.

3 The following item appears on a consolidated balance sheet: "Minority interest in subsidiary . . . $620,000." Explain the nature of this item, and where you would expect to find it on the consolidated balance sheet.

4 The annual report of the Standard Oil Company (Indiana) and Subsidiaries included the following note: "Accounts of all subsidiaries in which the Company directly or indirectly owns more than 50 per cent of the voting stock are included in the consolidated financial statements, with three exceptions: Imperial Casualty and Indemnity Company and Amoco Credit Corporation, which are accounted for on an equity basis, and Amoco Argentina Oil Company, which is accounted for on a cost basis."

Explain what is meant by the *equity basis* and the *cost basis* and give a possible reason for not consolidating the three subsidiaries.

5 The Excelsior Corporation Ltd. "purchased" 80% of the stock of the Acme Co. Ltd. on July 1, 1970, when the retained earnings of the Acme Co. Ltd. amounted to $100,000. The retained earnings of the Acme Co. Ltd. now amount to $750,000. Show how much of the retained earnings of the Acme Co. Ltd. would be reported on the latest consolidated balance sheet and what disposition would be made of any portion of Acme's retained earnings not reported on the consolidated balance sheet.

6 Explain why the price paid to acquire a controlling interest in a subsidiary company may be different from the book value of the equity acquired.

7 Explain why intercompany sales, rents, interest, etc., should be eliminated in preparing consolidated income statements in order to avoid double counting of revenues and expenses. Do these eliminations have any effect on consolidated net income? Why?

8 Indiana Company Ltd. owns an 85% interest in Jin Company Ltd. During Year 1, Jin Company Ltd. sold to Indiana Company Ltd. for $300,000 merchandise which cost Jin Company Ltd. $210,000. At the end of Year 1, Indiana Company Ltd. has in its ending inventory goods purchased from Jin Company Ltd. at a cost of $75,000. What amount of intercompany profit should be eliminated in preparing consolidated statements? When will this profit be realized by the consolidated entity?

9 Briefly explain the differences found in consolidated financial statements when the merger of two companies is viewed as a *pooling of interests* rather than as a *purchase.*

10 The 19___ annual report of the Fedders Corporation Ltd. stated that its consolidated statement of income for the year ended August 31, 19___, included sales of $19,500,000 and net income of $120,000 from the Norge Division purchased on July 1, 19___. The Division was acquired for approximately $45 million in cash, notes, and common stock. The balance sheet reported total assets of $129 million compared to only $61 million for the previous year. Would any of the foregoing amounts be reported differently if only common stock was issued in acquiring the Norge Division and the transaction was treated as a pooling of interests?

11 As a general rule, when should consolidated financial statements be prepared?

12 a How should the investment in an unconsolidated subsidiary be reported on the balance sheet of the parent company?
b Explain the generally accepted accounting procedures for an investment representing effective control of the voting stock held in another corporation.

13 What type of information should be provided by diversified companies in order for users of financial statements to make better business decisions?

14 What classes of persons are likely to be primarily interested in consolidated financial statements? Why?

15 A creditor of Great Mining Company Ltd. is concerned because the company is in financial difficulty and has reported increasingly large losses in the past three years. Great Mining Company Ltd. is a 75%-owned subsidiary of Hannah Company Ltd. When the creditor examines the consolidated statements of the two companies he finds that the earnings are satisfactory and that the consolidated entity is in sound financial condition. To what extent should the creditor be reassured by the consolidated statements, assuming that the information contained in them fairly presents the financial condition of the consolidated entity?

EXERCISES

Ex. 19-1 Heller Company Ltd. paid $380,000 for all the capital stock of Lewis Company Ltd. At the date of acquisition, Heller Company's total stockholders' equity of $1 million is composed of $800,000 in capital stock and $200,000 of retained earnings. Lewis Company Ltd. has $400,000 in capital stock and a deficit of $20,000 at the date of acquisition. What is the total amount of stockholders' equity that will appear on a consolidated balance sheet prepared for these two affiliated companies at date of acquisition?

Ex. 19-2 Q Company Ltd. has purchased all the outstanding shares of X Company Ltd. for $900,000. At the date of acquisition, an X Company Ltd. balance sheet showed total assets of $1,300,000 and total liabilities of $500,000. Assuming that X

Company's retained earnings at date of acquisition are one-third the amount of its capital stock, prepare the eliminating entry necessary on the working papers to consolidate the balance sheets of these two companies.

Ex. 19-3 On June 30 of Year 1, P Company Ltd. *purchased* 80% of the stock of S Company Ltd. for $120,000 in cash. The separate condensed balance sheets immediately after the purchase are shown below:

	P Company Ltd.	S Company Ltd.
Other assets	$580,000	$200,000
Investment in S Company Ltd. (80%)	120,000	—
	$700,000	$200,000
Liabilities	$150,000	$ 50,000
Capital stock, $5 par value	300,000	120,000
Retained earnings	250,000	30,000
	$700,000	$200,000

Prepare a consolidated balance sheet immediately after P Company Ltd. acquired control of S Company Ltd.

Ex. 19-4 The separate balance sheets of Large Co. Ltd. and its 80%-owned Sub Corp. Ltd. show the following account balances.

	Large Co. Ltd.	Sub Corp. Ltd.	Consolidated
Accounts receivable	$100,000	$ 40,000	$
Interest receivable—bonds of Large Co. Ltd.		1,000	
Investment in stock of Sub Corp. Ltd. 80%	310,000		
Investment in bonds of Large Co. Ltd.			
(at par)	.	50,000	
Accounts payable	80,000	30,000	
Interest payable—bonds	4,000		
Bonds payable	200,000		
Capital stock	500,000	250,000	

Large Co. Ltd. owes Sub Corp. Ltd. $10,000 for purchase of merchandise and Sub Corp. Ltd. owes Large Co. Ltd. $5,000 for services. In the Consolidated column, show the amounts that should appear in the consolidated balance sheet for each account.

Ex. 19-5 The Paren Co. Ltd. acquired all the stock of Subb Co. Ltd. at the beginning of Year 1. The acquisition is treated as a *purchase* for accounting purposes. Relevant information for Year 1 is given below:

	Paren Co. Ltd.	Subb Co. Ltd.
Retained earnings, beginning of Year 1	$100,000	$50,000
Net income for Year 1 (including dividends from Subb Co. Ltd.)	40,000	20,000
Dividends declared during Year 1	30,000	10,000

Prepare a statement of consolidated retained earnings for the two companies covering the activities of Year 1. (The equity method was not used.)

Ex. 19-6 Given below are selected accounts appearing on the balance sheets of the Parent and its 100%-owned Subsidiary shortly after affiliation:

	Parent	Subsidiary
Investment in Subsidiary (at par value of Parent stock issued		
to former stockholders of Subsidiary)	$200,000	
Capital stock	500,000	$200,000
Premium on capital stock	150,000	10,000
Retained earnings	600,000	195,000

Prepare the stockholders' equity section of the consolidated balance sheet on a ***pooling-of-interests*** basis.

PROBLEMS

Group A

19A-1 Condensed balance sheets of Paper and Sanders Companies at the end of Year 1 are shown below:

Assets	Paper Company Ltd.	Sanders Company Ltd.
Current assets	$1,400,000	$200,000
Other assets	1,600,000	550,000
Total assets	$3,000,000	$750,000

Liabilities & Stockholders' Equity

Current liabilities	$ 700,000	$100,000
Long-term debt	500,000	70,000
Capital stock	1,000,000	300,000
Retained earnings	800,000	280,000
Total liabilities & stockholders' equity	$3,000,000	$750,000

Instructions Assume that, at the end of Year 1, the Paper Company Ltd. purchased (using current assets) all the outstanding capital stock of the Sanders Company Ltd. for $640,000. Prepare a consolidated balance sheet for Paper and Sanders Companies at the date of acquisition.

19A-2 The following information is given to you relating to Owner Company and its subsidiary, the Worker Company:

Assets	Owner Company Ltd.	Worker Company Ltd.	Consolidated
Cash	$ 40,000	$ 25,000	$ 65,000
Accounts receivable	60,000	30,000	50,000
Merchandise inventory	120,000	80,000	200,000
Investment in Worker Company Ltd. (at			
equity)	300,000		
Other assets	400,000	200,000	600,000
Excess of cost over book value of			
investment in subsidiary			10,000
Total assets	$920,000	$335,000	$925,000

Liabilities & Stockholders' Equity

Accounts payable	$ 55,000	$ 30,000	$ 45,000
Accrued liabilities	10,000	15,000	25,000
Capital stock	500,000	100,000	500,000
Premium on capital stock	105,000	40,000	105,000
Retained earnings	250,000	150,000	250,000
Total liabilities & stockholders' equity	$920,000	$335,000	$925,000

The excess of cost over book value of investment in subsidiary has not been amortized since Owner Company Ltd. acquired control of Worker Company Ltd. The Owner Company Ltd. issued notes valued at $220,000 for the stock of Worker Company Ltd.

Instructions

a What percentage of the outstanding stock of Worker Company Ltd. is held by Owner Company Ltd.?

b What is the amount of intercompany accounts receivable and accounts payable?

c Was the consolidation of the accounts of the two companies effected as a purchase or as a pooling of interests? Why?

d How much of the retained earnings of Worker Company Ltd. are included in the consolidated retained earnings figure of $250,000?

e What was the amount of retained earnings reported by Worker Company Ltd. on the date Owner Company Ltd. acquired control of Worker Company Ltd.?

19A-3 Given below are the balance sheet accounts for the James Company Ltd. and the Kane Company Ltd. at the end of Year 1:

Assets	James Company Ltd.	Kane Company Ltd.
Cash	$ 50,000	$ 20,000
Accounts receivable	85,000	30,000
Inventories	60,000	40,000
Investment in Kane Company stock (equity method)	162,000	
Plant and equipment	250,000	180,000
Accumulated depreciation	(50,000)	(40,000)
Total assets	$557,000	$230,000

Liabilities & Stockholders' Equity		
Accounts payable	$ 40,000	$ 40,000
Accrued liabilities	25,000	10,000
Capital stock, $1 par	300,000	100,000
Retained earnings	192,000	80,000
Total liabilities & stockholders' equity	$557,000	$230,000

Additional information

(1) The entries in Investment in Kane Company Ltd. Stock account on the books of James Company Ltd. are given below.

Cost of 90,000 shares (90%) acquired on Jan. 2, Year 1	$135,000
Add: 90% of net income of Kane Company Ltd.	36,000
Less: 90% of dividend paid by Kane Company Ltd.	(9,000)
Balance, end of Year 1	$162,000

(2) On January 2, Year 1, the Kane Company Ltd. had 100,000 shares of capital stock outstanding and retained earnings of $50,000.

(3) Kane Company Ltd. owes James Company Ltd. $25,000 for merchandising purchases. All of the merchandise purchased by Kane Company Ltd. from James Company Ltd. has been sold.

Instructions Prepare working papers for a consolidated balance sheet at the end of Year 1. Use the form illustrated on page 562.

19A-4 The Pandora Company Ltd. owns 70% of the capital stock of Sesame Company Ltd. The income statements for each company for Year 1 are presented below:

	Pandora Company Ltd.	Sesame Company Ltd.
Sales	$1,500,000	$800,000
Cost of goods sold	1,000,000	650,000
Gross profit on sales	$ 500,000	$150,000
Operating expenses	(200,000)	(60,000)
Interest expense	(20,000)	(10,000)
Interest earned	10,000	
Income taxes	(140,000)	(32,000)
Net income	$ 150,000	$ 48,000

Pandora Company Ltd. sold merchandise costing $300,000 to the Sesame Company Ltd. for $420,000. All this merchandise was sold by Sesame Company Ltd. to its customers during Year 1. The interest expense incurred by Sesame Company Ltd. represents interest at 8% on a $125,000 note payable to Pandora Company Ltd. Pandora Company Ltd. has not recorded its share of Sesame Company's net income.

Instructions

a Prepare working papers for a consolidated income statement for Pandora Company Ltd. and its subsidiary. Use the format illustrated on page 567.

b Prepare a consolidated income statement for Year 1.

19A-5 Kent Company Ltd. and Littler Company Ltd. are planning to **pool** their activities into a single company. Data relating to the two companies follow:

	Kent Company Ltd.	Littler Company Ltd.
Total assets, net of accumulated depreciation	$1,500,000	$2,800,000
Total liabilities	500,000	800,000
Capital stock, $5 par (80,000 shares)	400,000	400,000
Retained earnings	600,000	1,600,000
Annual earnings per share	$3.00	$3.00
Price per share of stock	$60	$30
Price-earnings ratio	20 times	10 times

Instructions

a Assuming that Kent Company Ltd. issues 40,000 additional shares of its capital stock in exchange for all the stock of Littler Company Ltd., prepare a consolidated balance sheet on a **pooling-of-interest** basis. You need not use working papers.

  b If Kent Company Ltd. issues 40,000 additional shares in exchange for all the stock of Littler Company Ltd. and the earnings for the two companies remain unchanged, compute the earnings per share on Kent Company Ltd. stock after the *pooling* of the two companies.

  c Assuming that Kent Company Ltd. stock continues to sell at 20 times earnings, what would be the price of its stock after the *pooling* of the two companies?

Group B

19B-1 Below are the liabilities and stockholders' equity sections of the balance sheets of Peat Company Ltd. and Sea Company Ltd. at the end of the current year:

Liabilities & Stockholders' Equity	Peat Company Ltd.	Sea Company Ltd.
Liabilities	$ 500,000	$ 300,000
Capital stock, $10 par value	1,500,000	800,000
Retained earnings	700,000	250,000
Total liabilities & stockholders' equity	$2,700,000	$1,350,000

Instructions For each of the following independent fact situations, prepare the liabilities and stockholders' equity section of the consolidated balance sheet as of the end of the current year:

  a Peat Company Ltd. acquired all the outstanding capital stock of Sea Company Ltd. just prior to the date of the above statements, in exchange for 70,000 shares of Peat Company Ltd. capital stock. The consolidated statements are prepared on a *pooling-of-interests* basis.

  b Peat Company Ltd *purchased* for cash all the outstanding capital stock of Sea Company Ltd., at the time of the latter's organization. The Peat Company Ltd. carries its investment in Sea Company Ltd. on the equity method.

19B-2 The following data relate to P Company Ltd. and S Company Ltd., several years after P Company Ltd. acquired control of S Company Ltd. for $390,000 in cash:

Assets	P Company Ltd.	S Company Ltd.	Consolidated
Investment in S Company Ltd. stock (at equity)	$ 570,000		
Other assets	1,700,000	$1,030,000	$2,500,000
Total assets	$2,270,000	$1,030,000	$2,500,000
Liabilities & Stockholders' Equity			
Bonds payable	$ 500,000		$ 350,000
Other liabilities	280,000	$ 330,000	530,000
Capital stock, no par	600,000	200,000	600,000
Retained earnings	890,000	500,000	890,000
Minority interest			70,000
Excess of book value over cost of investment in subsidiary			60,000
Total liabilities & stockholders' equity	$2,270,000	$1,030,000	$2,500,000

The excess of book value over cost of investment in subsidiary has not been amortized since acquisition. Additional stock has not been issued by either company.

Instructions

a Compute the percentage of stock in S Company Ltd. owned by P Company Ltd.

b Compute the par value of bonds issued by P Company Ltd. now held by S Company Ltd.

c If S Company Ltd. owes P Company Ltd. $70,000 on open account, how much does P Company apparently owe to S Company Ltd.?

d How much of the retained earnings of $500,000 currently reported by S Company Ltd. is included in the $890,000 retained earnings figure appearing on the consolidated balance sheet?

e Compute S Company's retained earnings balance on the date that P Company Ltd. acquired control of S Company Ltd.

19B-3 At the beginning of Year 10, the Mann Corporation Ltd. acquired all the capital stock of the Neal Corporation Ltd. for $365,000 in cash and $160,000 in notes, payable at the rate of $20,000 per month. The balance sheets of the two companies at the end of Year 10 are given below:

Assets	Mann Corporation Ltd.	Neal Corporation Ltd.
Cash	$ 35,000	$ 18,000
Note receivable from Neal Corporation Ltd.	50,000	
Accounts receivable	90,000	50,000
Inventories	100,000	45,000
Investment in Neal Corporation Ltd. stock (equity method)	475,000	
Plant and equipment	350,000	550,000
Accumulated depreciation	(140,000)	(83,000)
Total assets	$960,000	$580,000

Liabilities & Stockholders' Equity		
Notes payable	$100,000	$ 50,000
Accounts payable	120,000	60,000
Accrued liabilities	30,000	20,000
Capital stock, $5 par	400,000	200,000
Retained earnings	310,000	250,000
Total liabilities & stockholders' equity	$960,000	$580,000

Additional information

(1) A summary of the Investment in Neal Corporation Ltd. Stock account for Year 10 on the records of Mann Corporation Ltd. follows:

Cost of 40,000 shares (100%), beginning of Year 10	$525,000
Less: 100% of net loss incurred by Neal Corporation Ltd. during Year 10	50,000
Balance, end of Year 10	$475,000

(2) At the beginning of Year 10, the Neal Corporation Ltd. had $200,000 in capital stock and $300,000 in retained earnings.

(3) The excess of cost over book value of investment in Neal Corporation Ltd. cannot be allocated to any specific asset and should be reported at "Excess of Cost over Book Value of Investment in Subsidiary" in the consolidated balance sheet.

(4) Late in Year 10, the Neal Corporation Ltd. borrowed $50,000 from Kane Corporation Ltd. for a one-year period.

Instructions Prepare working papers for a consolidated balance sheet at the end of Year 10. Use the form illustrated on page 560.

19B-4 E Company Ltd. owns 100% of the stock of F Company Ltd. The income statements for each company for Year 1 appear below.

	E Company Ltd.	F Company Ltd.
Sales	$600,000	$300,000
Cost of goods sold	400,000	210,000
Gross profit on sales	$200,000	$ 90,000
Operating expenses	(83,000)	(30,000)
Interest expense	(5,000)	(8,000)
Interest earned	8,000	
Income taxes	(50,000)	(18,500)
Net income	$ 70,000	$ 33,500

F Company Ltd. sold merchandise to E Company Ltd. for $30,000 which cost $24,000. One-half of this merchandise has not been sold by E Company Ltd. to its customers and is included in its ending inventory at $15,000. F Company Ltd. paid $8,000 interest to E Company Ltd. in Year 1 on a long-term loan. E Company Ltd. has not recorded its share of F Company's net income.

Instructions
a Prepare a consolidated income statement for Year 1 for E Company Ltd. and its subsidiary, F Company Ltd. You need not use working papers.
b Prepare a consolidated income statement for the two companies, assuming the same facts as above except that E Company Ltd. owns only 80% of the stock of F Company Ltd. and that all the merchandise acquired by E Company Ltd. from F Company Ltd. has been sold by E Company Ltd. You need not use working papers.

19B-5 The Bider Corporation Ltd. plans to acquire the Levin Corporation Ltd. on a *pooling-of-interests* basis by issuing 100,000 shares of its $1 par value capital stock for the 50,000 shares of stock of Levin Corporation Ltd. outstanding. Given below are selected figures taken from the financial statements of the two corporations for Year 1:

	Bider Corporation Ltd.	Levin Corporation Ltd.
Total assets, net of accumulated depreciation	$3,350,000	$1,500,000
Total liabilities	1,000,000	650,000
Capital stock, $1 par	500,000	50,000
Retained earnings	1,850,000	800,000
Net income for latest year	600,000	300,000
Market price per share of stock	$30	$60
Earnings per share	$1.20	$6.00

Instructions

a Prepare a consolidated sheet for the two companies on a *pooling-of-interests* basis, after Bider Corporation Ltd. issues 100,000 additional shares of its capital stock in exchange for the 50,000 shares of Levin Corporation's capital stock.

b What would be the amount of net income for the two corporations on a consolidated basis if the *pooling-of-interests* is completed on the last day of Year 1? What would be the earnings per share of Bider Corporation's stock after the pooling?

c Assuming that the stock of Bider Corporation Ltd. continues to sell at 25 times earnings ($1.20 × 25 = $30), at what price should its stock sell shortly after the *pooling* is effected?

BUSINESS DECISION PROBLEM 19

On March 1, Year 1, Patten Paper Company Ltd. invested $1,590,000 cash in the capital stock of Secoy Book Company Ltd. This represents 58% (58,000 shares) of the outstanding capital stock of Secoy Book Company Ltd. The balance sheets of Secoy Book Company Ltd. at date of acquisition and at the end of Year 10 include the following:

	December 31 Year 10	March 1 Year 1
Current assets	$4,500,000	$2,500,000
Current liabilities	3,000,000	1,300,000
Other assets	5,000,000	3,000,000
Long-term liabilities	800,000	1,500,000
Capital stock, $5 par value	1,000,000	1,000,000
Retained earnings	4,700,000	1,700,000

The balance sheet of the Patten Paper Company Ltd. at December 31, Year 10, is shown below:

PATTEN PAPER COMPANY LTD.
Balance Sheet
December 31, Year 10

Assets

Current assets	$ 7,500,000
Investment in capital stock of Secoy Book Company Ltd. (58%, at cost)	1,590,000
Other assets	5,910,000
Total assets	$15,000,000

Liabilities & Stockholders' Equity

Current liabilities		$ 4,000,000
Bonds payable		3,000,000
Total liabilities		$ 7,000,000
Stockholders' equity:		
Capital stock, no par	$2,500,000	
Retained earnings	5,500,000	
Total stockholders' equity		8,000,000
Total liabilities & stockholders' equity		$15,000,000

The accounts receivable of Patten Paper Company Ltd. include $2,500,000 due from Secoy Book Company Ltd. The accounts of the two companies have never been consolidated because one manufactures a variety of paper products while the other publishes children's books. However, if a consolidated balance sheet were prepared at December 31, Year 10, the current assets would be $9,500,000 and the current liabilities would be $4,500,000.

Abner Adams, a director of Patten Paper Company Ltd. suggests that a consolidated balance sheet be prepared for the two companies in order to show a more meaningful financial position. He also suggests that the increase in the net assets of the Secoy Book Company Ltd. since acquisition, $1,740,000, [58% × ($4,700,000−$1,700,000)], be included in the separate balance sheet of Patten Paper Company Ltd.

Bernie Barnes, another director, objects to Adams' suggestion in view of the poor working capital position of Secoy Book Company Ltd. and the low percentage of stock held in Secoy Book Company Ltd. "Why should we hide our strong working capital position in consolidated statements? We only own 58% of the stock in Secoy and I hate to see us show a liability to minority stockholders of $2,394,000 on our balance sheet. Besides, Secoy is not in our kind of business, and I don't even want us to take up the profits of Secoy earned since we made our investment because we haven't realized that profit and it violates the accounting principle of conservatism."

Instructions Carefully evaluate the points made by Bernie Barnes and give your recommendation whether or not the preparation of consolidated statements for the two companies would be appropriate.

TWENTY

INCOME TAXES
AND BUSINESS
DECISIONS

The critical importance of income taxes

Taxes levied by Federal, provincial, and local governments are a significant part of the cost of operating a typical household, as well as a business enterprise. The knowledge required to be expert in taxation has made it a field of specialty among professional accountants. However, every manager who makes business decisions, and every individual who makes personal investments, urgently needs some knowledge of income taxes to make him aware of the tax implications of his decisions. A general knowledge of income taxes will help any businessman to benefit more fully from the advice of the professional tax accountant.

Some understanding of income taxes will also aid the individual citizen in voting intelligently, because a great many of the issues decided in every election have tax implications. Such issues as pollution, inflation, foreign policy, and employment are inextricably linked with income taxes. For example, the offering of special tax incentives to encourage businesses to launch massive programs to reduce pollution is one approach to protection of the environment.

In terms of revenue, the three most important taxes in Canada are income taxes, sales taxes and property taxes. The income tax and sales taxes, including custom duties, are the major sources of revenue for the Federal government. Most provinces rely heavily on sales taxes. At the time of writing, only Alberta did not have a direct sales tax. The property tax is the mainstay of local government units such as counties, municipalities, and school districts.

Sources of revenue of the Federal, provincial and municipal governments in the 1968–9 fiscal year can be summarized as follows:

Sources of Revenue	Federal Government	Provincial and Municipal Governments
Tax Revenue		
Income taxes (1)	56.2%	17.7%
Sales taxes (2)	17.4	18.9
Custom duties and excise taxes	13.6	—
Real and personal property taxes	—	18.4
Tax equalization payments and subsidies from the federal government	—	17.8
Other	1.0	8.0
	88.2	80.8
Non-tax Revenue	11.8	19.2
	100.0%	100.0%

Sources of revenue of Federal Provincial and Municipal Governments

Notes: (1) Over ⅔ of income taxes are collected from individuals

(2) Over ⅓ of provincial sales taxes are derived from motor fuel sales

Income taxes provide almost one-half of total tax revenue raised by Canadian governments and also exert a pervasive influence on all types of business decisions. For this reason we shall limit our discussion to the Federal income tax.

Income taxes are usually determined from information contained in accounting records. The amount of income tax is computed by applying the appropriate tax rates (as set by federal and provincial governments) to *taxable income.* As explained more fully later in this chapter, taxable income is not necessarily the same as accounting income even though both are derived from the accounting records. Although taxes are involuntary and often unrelated to benefits received, some degree of control over the amount of tax is usually attainable. Businessmen may legally alter the amount of taxes they pay by their choice of form of business organization, methods of financing, and alternative accounting methods. Thus income taxes are inevitably an important factor in arriving at business decisions.

THE FEDERAL INCOME TAX

The British North America Act, Canada's constitution, permits the federal government to levy both direct and indirect taxes while the provinces are permitted to levy only direct taxes. A direct tax is one which is collected from the persons upon whom it is levied, while an indirect tax is initially collected from persons who are able to shift ultimate payment of the tax to others. For example, a manufacturer whose products are subject to the Federal sales tax includes this tax in the selling price of his products; and consequently, the tax forms part of the price which is charged to the wholesale or retail customer of the manufacturer. The final consumer of the product ultimately pays the tax. As the provinces, on the other hand, cannot levy indirect taxes, provincial sales taxes are collected directly from the consumer when he purchases goods subject to these taxes. A province is required to have all the retailers in the province act as collection agents for its sales tax while the Federal government, with its powers to levy indirect taxes, is able to collect its sales taxes at the manufacturer's level.

The first Federal income tax act was passed in 1917. At present, income tax acts have been enacted by the Federal government and all provincial governments. The Federal government collects the personal income taxes for all provinces except Quebec; and it collects the corporate income taxes for all provinces except Ontario and Quebec.

There was a redrafting of the Canadian income tax structure in 1948 and 1952. In 1962, the Carter Royal Commission was appointed to make a critical review of the federal tax system. The Commission issued its Report in 1967 after a comprehensive study of federal tax legislation. While the Report was highly controversial, it was widely acclaimed as a milestone in tax reform. The Federal government made its position on the Carter Report clear in a White Paper published in 1969. Many of the Carter recommendations were found unacceptable by the Federal government but a number of key recommendations were adopted with modifications. Following extensive public debate, the government further modified its position, and introduced its "tax reform bill" in the House of Commons in 1971 and it became law effective January 1, 1972.

Originally the purpose of the Federal income tax was simply to obtain revenue for the government. And at first, the tax rates were quite low—by today's standards. In 1917 a married man with an income of $13,000 would have been subject to a tax of $240. Today, a married man with a $13,000 income (worth far less in purchasing power) would pay over $1,800 in federal income tax.

The purpose of federal income tax today includes a number of goals in addition to raising revenue. Among these other goals are to combat inflation or deflation, to influence the rate of economic growth, to encourage full employment, to favor small businesses, and to redistribute national income on a more equal basis.

The administration and enforcement of the income tax laws are the duties of the Taxation Division of the Department of National Revenue which maintains district offices in all the major cities of Canada.

The Income Tax Act sets out who is liable to pay income tax and the principles of determining the tax, but it contains only part of the detailed law. Details of the application of a number of sections of the Act are set out in the Income Tax Regulations which are issued by the Federal

Cabinet by orders-in-council and do not require approval of Parliament. The Income Tax Act itself authorizes the issue of detailed regulations by orders-in-council. Administrative rules can thus be established without the necessity of separate approval by Parliament for each rule. Another element of income tax law is derived from the actual decisions of the courts. While the courts do not issue any new tax policies, they interpret and clarify the meaning of certain sections of the Act. These legal decisions must be given consideration in determining the answer to any income tax problem.

Tax planning

To minimize income taxes is the goal of tax planning. Almost every business decision is a choice among alternative courses of action. For example, should we lease or buy business automobiles; should we obtain needed capital by issuing bonds or preferred stock; should we use straight-line depreciation or an accelerated method? Some of these alternatives will lead to much lower income taxes than others. Tax planning, therefore, means *determining in advance the income tax effect* of every proposed business action and then making business decisions which will minimize the income tax burden. Tax practice is an important element of the services furnished to clients by public accounting firms. This service includes not only the computing of taxes and preparing of tax returns, but also tax planning.

Classes of taxpayers

In the eyes of the income tax law, there are four major classes of taxpayers: individuals, corporations (limited companies), estates and trusts. Proprietorships and partnerships are not taxed as business units; their income is taxed directly to the individual proprietor or partners, whether or not actually withdrawn from the business. A proprietor reports his business income on a separate schedule and attaches it to his personal tax return. A partner includes on his personal return his share of partnership income.

A corporation is a separate taxable entity; it must file a tax return and pay a tax on its annual taxable income. In addition, individual shareholders must report dividends received as part of their personal taxable income. This has led to the charge that there is "double taxation" of corporate income—once to the limited company and again when it is distributed to shareholders. The validity of this charge depends on whether the corporations are able to pass on the income tax to their customers through higher prices, and the evidence as well as opinion on this point is conflicting. The impact of any double taxation which may exist is reduced by the dividend tax credit allowed to individual taxpayers.

Accounting methods for tax returns

The student who has progressed this far in his study of accounting is well aware that business income is not a precise calculation. Various accounting procedures result in different net income figures, and matters of judgment that allow for varying results are always present. This lack of precision carries over into the determination of taxable income. The tax law and regulations specify certain procedures that must be followed and set rules governing the adoption of optional accounting procedures. In general, individuals who obtain their income from employment, property or investments, compute their income on a cash basis.

Taxpayers engaged in farming are permitted to compute their income on a cash basis. Most other businesses and taxpayers carrying on a professional practice must report income on an accrual basis.

Cash Basis Strictly speaking, the cash basis of measuring income is just what the title implies: income is recognized when cash is received, and expenses are recorded when they are paid. This method does not reflect income in the accounting sense, but with some modifications it is allowed for income tax purposes because it is simple, requires a minimum of records, and produces reasonably satisfactory results for individuals not engaged in business and for simple businesses in which receivables, payables, and inventories are not a major factor.[1]

The cash basis allowed for tax purposes varies in two important ways from a simple compilation of cash receipts and disbursements. On the expenditure side, the taxpayer who buys property having a service life of more than one year is not allowed to deduct the entire cost in the year of purchase but must treat it as an asset and deduct depreciation each year.

On the revenue side, a cash basis taxpayer must report revenue when it has been *constructively* received, even though the cash is not yet in his possession. Constructive receipt means that the revenue is so much within the control of the taxpayer as to be equivalent to receipt. For example, if a taxpayer has a savings account, the interest on that account is constructively received for income tax purposes, even though he does not actually draw it out. Similarly a salary cheque received on December 31 is constructively received even though it is not cashed until January 2.

From the taxpayer's viewpoint, choosing between the cash and accrual methods is not entirely a matter of deciding which provides the best measure of income. There is a tendency for taxpayers to elect the cash

---

[1] It is believed that the Taxation Division will permit individuals who carry on a business in which receivables, payables and inventories are comparatively unimportant, to report on a cash basis even though Section 28 of the Act extends this privilege only to income from a farming business.

basis wherever possible in order to postpone the recognition of taxable income and payment of the tax. In this way they have the interest-free use of funds that would otherwise be paid in taxes. To prevent the undue use of the cash basis for this reason, the Act limits the taxpayers who are entitled to use the cash basis of computing income.

Tax rates

All taxes may be characterized as proportional, regressive, or progressive with respect to any given base. A *proportional* tax remains a constant percentage of the base no matter how that base changes. For example, a 4% sales tax remains a constant percentage of sales regardless of changes in the sales figure. A *regressive* tax becomes a smaller percentage of the base as the base increases. A business licence tax of $500, for example, is regressive with respect to income, since the larger the income the smaller the licence tax as a percentage of income. A *progressive* tax becomes a larger portion of the base as that base increases. Federal income taxes are *progressive* with respect to income, since a higher tax rate applies as the amount of taxable income increases.

INDIVIDUAL TAX RATES Few generalizations can be made about individual income tax rates since they are frequently changed by legislation. In computing the amount of the tax, the tax rates are applied to taxable income, the computation of which is discussed in a later section of this chapter. The rate schedules below show the personal income tax rates in effect at the time this was written. These rates are frequently changed by Parliament.

Taxable Income	Amount of Tax
$0 - $587	9%
587 - 1,174	$53 plus 18% of the amount over $587
1,174 - 2,348	158 plus 19% of the amount over 1,174
2,348 - 3,522	382 plus 20% of the amount over 2,348
3,522 - 5,870	616 plus 21% of the amount over 3,522
5,870 - 8,218	1,109 plus 23% of the amount over 5,870
8,218 - 10,566	1,649 plus 25% of the amount over 8,218
10,566 - 12,914	2,236 plus 27% of the amount over 10,566
12,914 - 16,436	2,870 plus 31% of the amount over 12,914
16,436 - 28,176	3,962 plus 35% of the amount over 16,436
28,176 - 45,786	8,071 plus 39% of the amount over 28,176
45,786 - 70,440	14,939 plus 43% of the amount over 45,786
Over 70,440	25,540 plus 47% of the amount over 70,440

Provincial Tax Rates for Individuals

The Federal government collects the personal income taxes for the following provinces. At the time of writing, the provincial tax rates were the following percentages of the federal tax payable:

Newfoundland	*40%*
Nova Scotia	*38.5%*
Prince Edward Island	*36%*
New Brunswick	*41.5%*
Ontario	*30.5%*
Manitoba	*42.5%*
Saskatchewan	*36%*
Alberta	*26%*
British Columbia	*30.5%*

Quebec collects its own personal income taxes. Quebec rates work out overall to approximately 58% of the federal rate scale.

CORPORATION TAX RATES The corporate tax rate schedule is much simpler than the schedule for individuals. The rate for a corporation in effect at the time this was written (1975) was 47%.

The corporate tax rate will drop by 1% in 1976 when it becomes 46%. For a Canadian-controlled private corporation, the rate is reduced to 25% on the first $100,000 of taxable income earned in a year so long as its accumulated retained earnings, since 1971, do not exceed $500,000. This small business deduction is designed to offset the difficulties faced by small businesses in raising capital to finance expansion.

For corporations engaged in manufacturing and processing, there is a further reduction in tax. The tax rate on taxable income derived from manufacturing and processing activities is 40%; that is a reduction in the maximum rate of 7% in 1975 and 6% in 1976. For taxable income which is subject to the small business deduction, the tax rate on that portion of manufacturing profits is 20% which is a 5% reduction in the rate.

MARGINAL VERSUS AVERAGE TAX RATES In any analysis of tax costs, it is important to distinguish the *marginal* rate of tax from the *average* rate. This distinction may be illustrated as follows: If a Canadian-controlled private corporation has a taxable income of $150,000, its federal income tax[2] will be $48,500 ($150,000 × 47% − $100,000 × 22%), an average tax rate of approximately 32% of taxable income. On the last dollar of income, however, the tax is 47 cents, since the corporation is subject to a marginal tax rate of 47% on all income over $100,000.

Note from the tax table on page 593 that an even wider discrepancy between marginal and average tax rates may exist in the case of individual taxpayers. To illustrate, assume that Boris Clark, a resident of Ontario

[2]The provinces levy an income tax on corporations. The Federal Act permits a 10% provincial tax abatement. The three Maritime provinces levy a 10% tax on corporations, and for these provinces, the above analysis applies. All other provinces levy higher rates (ranging from 11% to 13%) and in these cases the marginal corporate rate would be somewhat higher.

having a taxable income of $46,000, is considering a change to a job that pays $6,000 more per year in salary. Using the illustrative tax rates, Clark now pays federal and provincial income taxes of $19,215, an average of 42% of his taxable income. His marginal tax rate on $6,000 salary increase, however, is 56%. His decision with respect to the new position may well be affected by the fact that he will be able to keep less than half of the $6,000 increase in his salary.

INCOME AVERAGING FOR INDIVIDUAL TAXPAYERS Because of the progressive nature of the tax rates, taxpayers whose incomes fluctuate widely from year to year are taxed more heavily than those who receive the same total income in a relatively stable pattern. To illustrate, suppose that two single taxpayers, Jones and Smith, each receive $36,000 in taxable income during a two-year period. Jones receives $4,000 the first year and $32,000 the second, while Smith receives $18,000 in each year. Over the two-year period, Jones would pay $14,081 in Federal and provincial income taxes while Smith would pay only $12,541. To alleviate this inequity the Act includes a complex formula designed to relieve the effect of an abnormal portion of extra income being included in taxable income in one year.

Liability for tax

Every person resident in Canada is required to pay income tax on his taxable income for the taxation year. A person who lives in Canada for 183 days or more in a calendar year is deemed to be a resident of Canada. Residents of Canada pay income tax on their world income while non-residents are subject to Canadian income tax only on that portion of income earned in Canada. For individuals, the taxation year is the calendar year; for corporations it is the fiscal year. An individual who derives income from a *non-incorporated* business must include in his income reported for the calendar year his share of the business profits for the fiscal year of that business ending in the calendar year. For example, Mr. Jones is the proprietor of the Corner Grocery and is also employed by XYZ Wholesale Ltd. In 1975, Mr. Jones earned a salary of $7,000 and had interest income from Government of Canada bonds of $80. The Corner Grocery's net profit for its fiscal year ended May 31, 1975 was $1,600. Mr. Jones reports the following income in his income tax return for the calendar year, 1975:

Salary income	*$7,000*
Interest income	*80*
Net profit of Corner Grocery	*1,600*
	$8,680

The income tax for individuals

An individual pays income tax on his taxable income for the taxation year. The formula for computation of taxable income is as follows:

Taxable income

Income for the year		*$xxx*
Minus: *Personal exemptions*	*$xxx*	
Charitable donations	*xxx*	
Medical expenses	*xxx*	
Non-capital losses	*xxx*	
Net capital losses	*xxx*	
Interest and dividend deduction	*xxx*	*xxx*
Taxable Income		*$xxx*

Income   The income of a taxpayer is his world income from all sources and includes income for the year from all (a) businesses, (b) properties (c) offices and employment and (d) capital gains. It should be noted that income for tax purposes is not restricted to these four sources but may also flow from other sources.

To determine whether any given item is included in income, two tests may be applied: (1) Is it income (as distinguished, for example, from a return of capital)? (2) Is there a provision in the law excluding this item from taxation? If the answer to the first question is yes, and to the second no, the item must be included in gross income.

In practice it is often necessary to refer to the act, regulations, and court decisions to determine whether a particular item is or is not included in gross income. Some idea of the major items that are included or excluded, however, may be gained from the following tabulation, which is illustrative only and does not represent a complete enumeration.

Examples of Items Included in and Excluded from Income

Included in Income	Excluded from Income
Compensation for services in all forms; wages, salaries, bonuses, commissions, tips, gratuities; fair market value of noncash compensation	*Gifts, inheritances, and bequests*
	Life insurance proceeds received because of the death of the insured
Rents and royalties	*Amounts received from workmen's compensation insurance*
Taxpayer's share of income from business or profession, conducted as a proprietorship or partnership	*The portion of receipts from annuities that represent return of cost*
Taxpayer's share of income from estates or trusts	*Interest on War Savings Certificates*
All pensions except a Service pension received under such statutes as the War Veterans' Allowance Act	
Unemployment insurance	
Old age security pension	

What does income include?

Examples of Items Included in and Excluded from Income

Included in Income

Periodic alimony payments received by
 taxpayer
Dividends and interest income
Capital gains
Income from illegal activities

Capital Gains and Losses Beginning in 1972, capital gains are subject to tax in Canada. However, special treatment is given to capital gains or losses since only one-half of the capital gain or loss is included in net income subject to income tax. A capital gain is a "gain made on the realization of an investment rather than in the carrying on of a business or an adventure in the nature of trade." While it may be difficult, in borderline cases, to determine whether a gain represents ordinary income or a capital gain, the question to be answered is whether the gain is a "mere enhancement of value by realizing an investment or is it a gain made in an operation of a business in carrying out a scheme for profit-making?"

An example may help to clarify the distinction between a capital gain and a taxable receipt. If an individual sells his residence, the profit realized on the sale would be a capital gain. On the other hand, the profit realized by a real estate company on the disposal of any houses which they owned would be ordinary income from a business. Similarly, an individual would be taxed on the gains realized on the sale of securities as a capital gain while such profits made by an investment dealer would be ordinary income with the entire amount subject to tax.

Criteria for determining capital gains. The factors which are considered in determining whether or not a receipt is a capital gain are the following:

1 The nature of the property on which the gain is realized. Gains realized on any form of property may be capital gains. However, gains from property which is normally the subject of trading (for example, inventory of raw materials) or which does not yield income to its owner solely by virtue of its ownership (for example, speculative securities) often may not qualify as capital gains.

2 The length of the period of ownership. Property held for a long time before it is realized is more likely to result in a capital gain than property which was owned only for a short time before its disposal.

3 The number and frequency of similar transactions by the same person. If a taxpayer engages in a number of similar transactions in succession over a period of years, the gains realized would be taxed as ordinary income. However, it should be noted that profit made from an isolated transaction also may be taxable as ordinary income if the transaction is a venture in the nature of trade.

4 The circumstances that were responsible for the realization. An exceptional circumstance, such as expropriation by a governmental body or an emergency need for money, would indicate that the transaction is not a venture in the nature of trade.

5 Supplementary efforts in connection with the realization of the property. If there is an organized effort to obtain profit, such as large-scale advertising or subdivision of land into lots, the gain would probably be ordinary income.

6 Intention. The circumstances surrounding the transaction should clearly indicate that the initial purpose of acquiring the property was for investment and not for resale.

For a given transaction, it is a question of fact whether the resultant profit is or is not a capital gain. The basic consideration is the taxpayer's whole course of conduct as evidenced by the six factors discussed in the preceding paragraphs.

Taxable Capital Gains and Losses A capital gain or loss is the difference between the proceeds received on disposal of a capital asset and its cost.[3] Capital assets include tangible and intangible fixed assets, securities (bonds and shares), interest in a partnership, mortgages receivable, and personal property. Disposal of capital assets arises as a result of such events as: (1) a sale (2) destruction or damage of the property (3) expropriation (4) gift (5) death of the taxpayer and (6) termination of the taxpayer's residence in Canada.

Capital losses on personal use property are not deductible, although capital gains are taxable. Personal use property is property acquired primarily for personal use and enjoyment such as furniture, recreational equipment and clothing. There is a special category of personal use property called listed personal property. It includes such items as jewellery, paintings, stamp and coin collections. Capital losses on listed personal property are deductible but only against capital gains on listed personal property.

Certain capital gains are not taxable. The capital gain on the disposal of a house ordinarily inhabited by the taxpayer, called the taxpayer's principal residence, is not normally subject to tax. Similarly, capital gains resulting from gambling winnings, such as the Olympic Lottery, are not taxable.

One-half of the capital gain must be included in net income for tax purposes in the year in which the gain is realized. Similarly, one-half of the capital losses are deductible. Allowable capital losses must first be deducted in the year incurred from taxable capital gains. Individuals may deduct, in addition, any unused portion, up to a maximum of $1,000, in arriving at net income for the year for tax purposes. Allowable capital losses which are not absorbed in the current year may be carried back one year and forward indefinitely to be offset against taxable gains in those years plus, in the case of individuals, a maximum of $1,000 each year against other income.

For example, assume that Mr. Jones who earns an annual salary of $20,000 sold the following capital assets: land (cost $10,000) for $16,000 in 1973 and securities (cost $26,000) for $8,000 in 1973 and securities (cost $4,000) for $7,000 in 1974. Mr. Jones would report the following on his tax returns:

[3] Because capital gains and losses were not taxable in Canada prior to 1972, special transitional rules have been enunciated to value capital assets on hand on December 31, 1971. Basically, the taxpayer can use the greater of fair market value on valuation day or original cost to value capital assets on hand at December 31, 1971 which were sold in 1972 or subsequent years at a gain. For such capital assets sold at a loss, the lower of fair market value or original cost can be used.

		1972		1973		1974
Income						
Salary		$20,000		$20,000		$20,000
Taxable capital gains		(Land) $3,000		(Securities) $1,500		
Capital losses (allowable amt.)		3,000(1)		∅		1,500
		20,000		20,000		21,500
Allowable capital loss				1,000(1)		
Net income		$20,000		$19,000		$21,500
Personal exemptions	$1,600		$1,700		$1,806	
Net capital losses	1,000(2)	2,600		1,700	2,500(3)	4,306
Taxable income		$17,400		$17,300		$17,194

(1) One-half of the capital loss on securities in 1973 amounting to $9,000 is deductible first to the extent of taxable capital gains realized in 1973. An additional $1,000 is deductible in computing net income in 1973. The net capital losses not absorbed ($5,000) in 1973 are deductible in 1972 and subsequent years.

(2) Since there were no capital gains in 1972, only $1,000 of the 1973 unabsorbed capital loss can be carried back to 1972. An amended tax return will be filed for 1972.

(3) In 1974, the amount of the unabsorbed loss that can be carried forward is 2,500 ($1,500 to offset the capital gains realized in 1974 and the additional $1,000 deduction permitted to individuals). The net capital loss that is still remaining ($1,500) can be carried forward indefinitely until it has been absorbed.

Income from employment. The income of an individual from an office or employment is the aggregate of the following:

1 Salary, wages, gratuities and other remuneration received.

2 The value of any benefits (such as board, lodging, and use of an employer-owned automobile for personal services) received or enjoyed except those benefits specifically exempted by the Act.

3 The amount received as an allowance for any purpose except those allowances specifically exempted by the Act.

The Canadian Income Tax Act permits very few deductions in calculating income from employment. Because of this severe restriction on permissible deductions, the definition of the term "employee" is important. There must be a master-servant relationship for the recipient to be regarded as an employee. The form of remuneration is irrelevant. As long as the master-servant relationship exists, the individual may be paid on a piece-work, hourly or monthly basis and still be classified as an employee.

A distinction must be made between a member of a profession or a tradesman who is operating his own practice or business and one who is receiving salaried income as an employee. If the professional man or tradesman is "self-employed", he is entitled to deductions in computing his income similar to those permitted to a business.

Benefits, allowances and expenses which are not included in or may be deducted from income from employment are:

1 Contributions to a registered pension plan or fund, and Canada Pension Plan contributions.
2 Travelling expenses of salesmen, transport employees, and other employees required to work away from their employer's place of business (travel expenses include transportation fare, meals, lodging and automobile expenses).
3 Legal expenses incurred to collect salary or wages due.
4 Professional or union dues required under the terms of employment and unemployment insurance premiums.
5 The cost of supplies that were used directly in the performance of his employment and that the employee was required to provide and pay for.
6 Office rent or salary to an assistant which the employee was required to pay under the terms of his employment.
7 Tuition fees paid by a student taking a recognized course of studies may be deducted from the Student's income.
8 Moving expenses when the employee moves his residence as a result of changing his job.
9 Child care expenses.
10 Employment expense deduction equal to 3% of income from employment up to a maximum of $150.

Income from business or property. Income from a business or property is defined by the Act as "the profit therefrom for the year." Expenses may be deducted in computing the profit of the business for income tax purposes provided that they are incurred in order to produce income, are not a capital outlay and are reasonable. It should be noted that profit from a business, for income tax purposes, is the profit determined in accordance with generally accepted accounting principles and practices unless the Act specifically provides otherwise. One of the most important departures from generally accepted accounting principles are the provisions relating to capital cost allowances.

Capital Cost Allowances   Taxpayers cannot depreciate their tangible fixed assets on a straight-line basis but must write-off the cost of these assets in accordance with the capital cost allowance regulations. These regulations, in many instances, may be entirely different from the accountant's concept of depreciation. To the accountant, depreciation is the systematic allocation of the cost of a fixed asset over its estimated useful life. While the capital cost regulations recognize that fixed assets do wear out, the deductions permitted by these regulations more closely reflect government policy than the decline in the useful life of the asset. (One purpose of permitting the rapid write-off of fixed assets is to encourage new investment in plant and equipment.)

Depreciable fixed assets of a similar nature are grouped into separate pools or classes. Depreciable assets are fixed assets other than land. Capital cost allowance is taken on the balance remaining in the pool at the fiscal year-end. Assets are treated on a pool, not an individual, basis. There are twenty-nine classes or pools of assets established by the

Regulations with each class being given a maximum capital cost allowance rate. The taxpayer is not required to claim each year the maximum rate allowed. He cannot take more than the maximum rate in any year but he may take less than the maximum, or if he wishes, he may claim no capital cost allowance in a particular year. The more important classes of assets with their maximum rates of capital cost allowance are as follows:

Asset classes	Class	Maximum Rate
3	Brick buildings	5%
6	Frame buildings	10%
8	Machinery and equipment, furniture and fixtures	20%
10	Automotive equipment	30%

Fixed assets are added to their respective pools or classes at their capital cost. Generally, the capital cost of an asset is the invoice price of the asset plus the costs of installation. An asset is added to the pool in the year when it is acquired.

When assets are disposed of, they are deducted from the pool. A disposal of an asset occurs when it is sold, traded, destroyed, or scrapped. The amount deducted from the pool is the proceeds received from the disposal of the asset except when these proceeds exceed the capital cost. In such a case, the amount deducted is the capital cost of the disposed asset.

Capital cost allowance is claimed on the balance, called the undepreciated capital cost, in the pool at the end of the fiscal year. Generally, there is no pro-rating of capital cost allowance for assets acquired or disposed of during the year. If the asset is acquired during the year and is on hand at the end of the year, a full year's capital cost allowance may be claimed on it. Similarly, if the asset is disposed of during the year, it will not be included in the year-end balance of the pool and no capital cost allowance can be claimed on this asset in the year of disposal. Finally, it should be noted that capital cost allowance is somewhat similar to the reducing-balance methods of depreciation since capital cost allowance is taken on the remaining balance in the class at year-end and not on the total capital cost of the assets in the class.

To illustrate, assume the following: X Co. Ltd. decides to perform its own delivery service and purchases two trucks at a cost of $5,000 each on February 11, 1974. On May 3, 1975 an additional truck is purchased for $5,200. Truck No. 2 is sold for $2,540 on July 15, 1976. The company's fiscal year ends on December 31 and it claims maximum capital cost allowance each year. The capital cost schedule for the company appears at the top of page 602.

The capital cost allowance regulations are designed to allow the taxpayer to recover the actual cost to him of depreciable fixed assets.

February 11, 1974	Capital cost (Class 10):	
	Truck No. 1	$ 5,000
	Truck No. 2	5,000
		10,000
December 31, 1974	Capital cost allowance (30%)	3,000
	Undepreciated capital cost	7,000
May 3, 1975	Addition at capital cost:	
	Truck No. 3	5,200
		12,200
December 31, 1975	Capital cost allowance (30%)	3,660
	Undepreciated capital cost	8,540
July 15, 1976	Disposal—proceeds received	2,540
		6,000
December 31, 1976	Capital cost allowance (30%)	1,800
	Undepreciated capital cost	4,200

Therefore, profits and losses on the disposal of such assets are to be taken into account in calculating income for tax purposes. If disposals of fixed assets result in a credit balance in the asset pool at the end of the fiscal year, this credit balance, called a recapture of depreciation, must be included in income. The recapture of depreciation arises from "excessive depreciation" previously claimed which cannot be absorbed by assets remaining in the class.

An example will illustrate this provision. Assume that Y Co. Ltd. opened four branch warehouses in the western provinces. Frame buildings were constructed in 1971 in Calgary, Regina, Vancouver and Winnipeg at a cost of $70,000, $50,000, $60,000 and $60,000 respectively. In May, 1975, the company decided to service British Columbia, Alberta and Saskatchewan from the Winnipeg warehouse and accordingly sold the buildings as follows: Calgary $80,000; Regina $45,000; and Vancouver $55,000. The fair market value of the Calgary building on December 31, 1971 was $75,000. Y Company's year-end is November 30, and maximum capital cost allowance is claimed each year.

1971

	Capital cost (Class 6):	
	Buildings at: Vancouver	$ 60,000
	Calgary	70,000
	Regina	50,000
	Winnipeg	60,000
		240,000
November 30, 1971	Capital cost allowance (10%)	24,000
	Undepreciated capital cost	216,000
November 30, 1972	Capital cost allowance (10%)	21,600
	Undepreciated capital cost	194,400
November 30, 1973	Capital cost allowance (10%)	19,440
	Undepreciated capital cost	174,960
November 30, 1974	Capital cost allowance (10%)	17,496
	Undepreciated capital cost	157,464

May, 1975	Proceeds from disposal	
	Buildings at:	
	Calgary $70,000 (cannot exceed the capital cost);	
	Vancouver $55,000; Regina $45,000	170,000
	Recapture of depreciation	
	(Credit balance)	($12,536)

The recapture of depreciation of $12,536 must be added to the 1975 income.

There is a capital gain on the sale of the Calgary building of $5,000.[4] On-half of this capital gain (i.e. $2,500) must be added to 1975 income.

Even though one building (the Winnipeg warehouse) still remains in the pool or class, no capital cost allowance may be claimed on Class 6 assets in 1975 since there will be a nil balance remaining in the class after the recapture is transferred to income.

Should a debit balance remain in an asset pool after disposal of *all* the assets in the pool, this debit balance, or terminal loss, must be deducted from income of the current year.

The following example will illustrate the terminal loss provision. F. Clark, a grocer, purchased two delivery trucks in 1973 at a cost of $3,000 each. In 1975, these trucks were sold to the drivers for $1,200 each and Clark then contracted with these drivers to handle his deliveries. Clark's year-end is December 31 and he claims maximum capital cost allowance each year.

Schedule showing terminal loss

1973	Capital cost (Class 10):	
	Trucks (2)	$6,000
December 31, 1973	Capital cost allowance	1,800
	Undepreciated capital cost	4,200
December 31, 1974	Capital cost allowance	1,260
	Undepreciated capital cost	2,940
1975	Proceeds from disposal	2,400
	Terminal loss	$ 540

A terminal loss can only be claimed if there are no assets remaining in an asset class or pool. The terminal loss of $540 must be deducted from Clark's 1975 income.

It should be noted that a recapture of capital cost allowance does *not* arise on the disposal of a depreciable asset but *only* when there is a credit balance in the class at the end of the taxation year. Similarly, there is a terminal loss only when there are *no* assets at the end of the taxation year in an asset class with a debit balance.

Asset Classes Subject to Straight-Line Basis of Computation   There are a number of classes for which capital cost allowances are computed on a straight-line basis. In many cases, these classes have been introduced to reflect the government's economic and social objectives. Capital cost

[4] Transitional rules govern the determination of a capital gain on the scale of a depreciable asset which was on hand at December 31, 1971. Essentially, for such assets, the capital gain is the difference between the proceeds received (in our example, $80,000) and the fair market value at December 31, 1971 (in our example, $75,000).

allowance has been accelerated or restricted in order to spur or dampen economic activity. At the present time, Class 29 is the most important example of the use of the capital cost allowance system to encourage investment. It permits the write-off in two years of expenditures incurred to acquire manufacturing and processing machinery and equipment. It became effective for machinery and equipment acquired after May 8, 1972. There is no expiry date. Accelerated capital cost allowance is also available on pollution equipment acquired within a prescribed time period.

The following is a table of the more important classes for which capital cost allowance is computed on a straight-line basis:

Class	Types of Assets Included	Maximum Rate	Effective Date	Expiry Date
13	Leasehold improvements	20% (Note 1)	1949	None
14	Franchises, patents, concessions	Write-off over life of asset	1949	None
24	Water pollution control equipment	50%	1965	Dec. 31, 1976
27	Air pollution control equipment	50%	1970	Dec. 31, 1976
29	Manufacturing and processing machinery and equipment	50%	1972	None

Note 1: *Classes 13 and 14 have been straight-line classes since the inception of the capital cost allowance system. The leasehold improvements can be written off over the greater of (1) 5 years or (2) the life of the lease.*

Taxable Income As explained previously, an individual is permitted four general deductions from income in computing his taxable income, namely: (1) personal exemptions, (2) charitable donations, (3) medical expenses, (4) non-capital losses, and (5) allowable net capital losses.

Personal exemptions. By permitting an individual to deduct certain personal exemptions, the Act ensures that a minimum level of income will not be subject to tax. These exemptions, coupled with the graduated rates of income tax, are designed to provide a certain degree of social equity. The following are the more important personal exemptions which are allowed:[5]

(1) Basic exemption $1,878
(2) Additional exemption if taxpayer is married 1,644
*(3) Exemption for each child entitled to receive Family
    Allowances* 352
*(4) Exception for each child not entitled to receive
    Family Allowances* 646

The exemption for married status is reduced by the wife's income in excess of $334. For example, if the wife's income is $900, the husband's

---

[5]The personal exemptions listed are for 1975. Personal exemptions are now being indexed to offset the effects of inflation and may thus change every year.

exemption for married status is $1,644 – ($900 – $334) or $1,078.

No exemption is allowed for a child over the age of 21 unless the child is a student in full-time attendance at a school or university or is mentally or physically infirm. The exemption for a child is reduced for a child under 16 years of age by one-half of his income over $1,274 and for a child 16 years old and over by his income over $1,332. In both categories, the exemption for the child is completely lost when his income reaches $1,978.

Charitable donations. An individual may deduct from income gifts made to charitable, religious, amateur athletic or educational organizations. The deduction in any one year cannot exceed 20 per cent of net income.

Medical expenses. Medical expenses in excess of 3 per cent of the taxpayer's income may be deducted in computing taxable income.

Non-Capital losses. To provide some relief for the fluctuations in income that frequently occur, a taxpayer is permitted to deduct a non-capital loss of the current year from the income of the previous year. If the income of the preceding year is not sufficient to absorb the current year's loss, the loss not previously absorbed may be deducted from the incomes of the five succeeding years. Thus the taxpayer has a total of six years in which to average non-capital losses against income.

Capital losses. Capital losses are deductible as previously discussed on pages 598–599.

Standard deduction. If the taxpayer does not claim any charitable donations or medical expenses, he may make a standard deduction of $100 in computing taxable income. While receipts are required to support the claims for charitable donations and medical expenses, no receipts are required to claim the standard deduction.

Computation of an Individual's Tax The gross tax liability is computed by applying the rates of tax (see Table on page 593) to the taxable income. Certain tax credits are allowed against this gross tax liability. The most common tax credits are:

1 Dividend tax credit. A tax credit is allowed of 20% of the grossed-up dividends received from taxable Canadian corporations.[6]
2 Foreign tax credit. A tax credit is allowed to offset income taxes paid to a foreign country on foreign income.

Tax Returns and Payment of the Tax Every individual who has taxable income must file an income tax return by April 30 for the previous calendar year.

The payment of Federal income taxes is on a "pay as you go" basis. The procedure by which employers withhold income taxes from the wages of employees has been discussed in a previous chapter. To equalize the treatment of employees and self-employed persons, the tax law requires persons who have income in excess of a given amount, from which no withholdings have been made, to file an Income Tax Remittance Form and to pay estimated taxes in quarterly installments[7]. An under- or overpayment is adjusted when the tax return is filed at the regular time. This provision also applies to employees whose income from employment is

[6]Dividends received from Canadian taxable corporations must be grossed-up by one-third. Thus, a dividend of $600 will be included in an individual's income as $800. The dividend tax credit is ⅘ of the gross-up (i.e., ⅘ of $200) or 20% of the grossed-up dividend (20% of $800).

less than 25 per cent of their total income. Persons who do not comply with these requirements are subject to a penalty equivalent to an interest charge on the tax not paid at the proper time, with allowances made for reasonable errors in forecasting income.

Illustrative Individual Income Tax Computation The following demonstration, based on assumed data for a hypothetical taxpayer, illustrates the main features of the individual income tax computation:

Statement of facts. Mr. M. J. Bricker is married and has two children. The son, aged twenty, is a full-time student (8-month academic year) at the University of Alberta, and earned $1,700 in part-time work during the current year. He paid tuition fees of $300 for the academic year. The daughter is fifteen years of age and had income of $200 from babysitting. Neither Mr. nor Mrs. Bricker is sixty-five years of age or over, or blind. Mr. Bricker is a practising lawyer. Mrs. Bricker works part time as a secretary for an insurance company. This information is from the business and personal records of the family:

Gross fees from law practice	$40,000
Operating expenses of law practice	
Salaries to staff	8,400
Rent of office	3,600
Automobile expenses (not including depreciation or capital cost allowance)	1,750
Telephone, postage and stationery	2,290
Convention expenses—Canadian Bar Association	460
Professional dues	100
Miscellaneous (Law Reports, etc.)	539
Mrs. Bricker's salary	860
Interest on provincial bonds	250
Interest credited to savings accounts	220
Dividends received (on shares owned by Mr. Bricker)	1,200
Gain on sale of securities (shares purchased by Mr. Bricker for $1,600; sold for $2,400, net of brokerage fees)	800

Expenditures:

Contributions to church and university	$ 1,500
Other contributions to recognized charitable organizations	800
Interest paid on mortgage on residence	912
Property taxes paid on residence	480
Purchase of a new automobile. A trade-in allowance of $1,700 was received on the old automobile which had cost $3,000. At the time of trade-in the old automobile had an undepreciated capital cost of $1,470. The net cost of the new automobile was ($4,000 less $1,700). The automobile is used entirely for business purposes	2,300
Family medical expenses:	
Doctor's fees	800
Drugs	300
Tax installment payments during the year	4,000

The computation of Mr. Bricker's income tax might appear as follows,

MR. M. J. BRICKER
Illustrative Income Tax Computation
(See Schedules A to G for details)

Schedule				
	Gross income from practice			$40,000
A-B	Operating expenses			18,270
	Net income from practice			21,730
C	Investment income			2,070
	Capital gain on sale of securities			
	(one-half of $800)			400
	Net income			24,200
	Exemptions			
D	Personal exemptions		$3,663	
E	Charitable donations		2,300	
	Living allowance for son while			
	at university (8 months at $50			
	per month) – Entire amount may			
	be claimed by father since son			
	has no taxable income		400	
F	Medical expenses		374	
G	Interest and dividend deduction		1,000	7,737
	Taxable income			16,463
H	Amount of Tax			$3,971
	Dividend tax credit (20% of 1,600)			320
	Basic Tax			3,651
	Special reduction (8% of basic			
	tax; $200 minimum; $500 maximum)			292
	Federal tax payable			3,359
	Provincial tax (Alberta, 26% of $3,651)			949
	Total Tax			4,308
	Deduct: Installment Payments			4,000
	Income Tax Due			$ 308

Detailed Schedules Supporting
Computation of Mr. M. J. Bricker's Income Tax

Schedule A:

Operating expenses of law practice

Salaries to staff	$ 8,400
Rent of office	3,600
Automobile expenses (automobile is entirely for business purposes) ...	1,750
Capital cost allowance on automobile (see Schedule B below)	1,131
Telephone, postage and stationery	2,290
Convention expenses (attendance at not more than two professional conventions is allowed)	460
Professional fees	100
Miscellaneous	539
	$18,270

Schedule B:

December 31, previous year

Undepreciated capital cost . . . . $ 1,470

Current year

Addition (new automobile) 4,000

5,470

Proceeds from disposal 1,700

3,770

Capital cost allowance 1,131

Undepreciated capital cost . . . . $ 2,639

Schedule C

Investment income

Interest on provincial bonds . . . . $ 250

Interest on savings accounts 220

Dividends received from taxable

Canadian corporations $1,200

Add: $\frac{1}{3}$ gross-up 400   1,600

$ 2,070

Schedule D

Personal exemptions

Basic exemption $1,878

Married status ($1,644 minus wife's net income in

excess of $334) (Note 1) 804

Son

Income of son $1,700

Deduct: Employment deduction . . . . $ 51

Tuition fees paid 300   351

Net income for tax purposes (Note 2) $1,349

Income limit permitted 1,332

Deduction from exemption of $646 . . . . $ 17   629

Daughter (qualifies for family allowance as she

is under 16) 352

$3,663

Note 1: Wife's net income is salary of $1,200 less employment deduction of $36 or $1,174

Note 2: The son's taxable income is nil. (Net income $1,349 less personal exemption of

$1,878)

Schedule E

Charitable donations

Contribution to church and university . . . . $ 1,500

Other contributions to recognized charities 800

$ 2,300

All charitable donations are deductible since the total is within the limit of 20% *of net income.*

Schedule F

Medical expenses

Doctor's fees		$ 800
Drugs		300
		$ 1,100
Deduct 3% of net income		726
		$ 374

Schedule G

Interest and Dividends Deductible

The lesser of

a) Interest income		$ 470
Grossed-up dividend income		1,600
		$2,070

or b) $1,000

Schedule H

Tax computation (See Table on page 593)

Tax on first $16,436 is		$3,962
Tax on remaining $27 at 35% is		9
		$3,971

Partnerships

The Federal income tax law generally follows a "conduit" theory of partnership income; that is, partnerships are treated as a conduit through which taxable income flows to the partners. Under the conduit philosophy, the income of each partner for income tax purposes is his share of the partnership income whether or not he withdraws it from the business. Salaries and interest paid to partners are a method of distributing or allocating partnership income and are not deductions in calculating that income.

Corporations

The ordinary business corporation (limited company) is a taxable entity and is subject to a tax at special rates on its net taxable income. Corporate taxable income in general is computed in the same manner as for individuals, with the following major differences:

1 Corporations are not entitled to certain deductions of a personal nature allowed to individuals. Examples are medical expenses, the standard deduction, and personal exemptions.

2 Dividends received by a corporation from other taxable Canadian corporations are not included in the corporation's taxable income. Since intercorporate dividends are not taxable, a corporation is not entitled to the dividend tax credit. (Private corporations pay a special refundable tax of 33⅓% on dividend income. This tax is refunded to the private corporation when it pays dividends to its shareholders.)

3 Corporations may deduct capital losses only to the extent of capital gains. If capital losses exceed capital gains, the net capital loss may be carried back against net capital gains of the preceding year and be offset against net capital gains of future years indefinitely.

Corporate tax returns must be filed within 6 months after the end of the fiscal year. A corporation must pay its income tax in monthly installments beginning with the first month of its fiscal year with the final payment due three months after the end of its fiscal year. That is, a corporation will have paid its income taxes in full three months before it is required to file its tax return.

To illustrate some of the features of the income tax law as it applies to corporations, the federal tax computation for a hypothetical Canadian-controlled private corporation is as follows:

ONTARIO WHOLESALE CO. LTD.
Illustrative Tax Computation

Revenues		
Sales revenues		$200,000
Dividends received from other Canadian corporations		12,000
		212,000
Expenses		
Cost of goods sold	$114,000	
Other operating expenses	30,000	144,000
		68,000
Deduct:		
Charitable donations	2,800	
Dividends received	12,000	14,800
Taxable income		$ 53,200
Tax computation		
Tax of 47% on Taxable income		25,004
Small business deduction (22% of $53,200)		11,704
		13,300
Refundable tax on dividend income ⅓ of $9,000		3,000
		16,300
Provincial tax (Ontario) – 13% of 53,200		$ 6,916
Total tax payable		$17,896
Provincial tax (Ontario) – 13% of 53,200		$ 6,916
Total tax payable		$17,896

The small business deduction is 22% of the lesser of (1) active business income ($56,000), or (2) taxable income ($53,200) or (3) business limit ($100,000). (It is assumed that the total business limit of $500,000 has not been reached. Total business limit is essentially the total active business income in 1972 and subsequent taxation years minus the dividends paid in the same period which represent distribution of active business income.)

Accounting income versus taxable income

The accountant's objective in determining accounting income is to measure business operating results as accurately as possible, in accordance with the generally accepted accounting principles summarized in Chapter 14. Taxable income, on the other hand, is a legal concept governed by statute. In setting the rules for determining taxable income, Parliament is interested not only in meeting the revenue needs of government but in achieving certain public policy objectives. Since accounting and taxable income are determined with different purposes in mind, it is not surprising that they often differ by material amounts.

CASH VERSUS ACCRUAL BASIS OF INCOME MEASUREMENT   The *accrual basis* of measuring income has been discussed throughout the preceding chapters of this book, because it is the method used by most business enterprises. Revenue is recognized when it is realized, and expenses are recorded when they are incurred, without regard to the timing of receipt or payment. Any taxpayer who maintains a set of accounting records may elect to use the accrual basis for tax purposes. When the production, purchase, or sale of merchandise is a significant factor in a business, the accrual method is mandatory.

The *cash basis* of measuring income does not reflect income in the accounting sense. Revenues are recognized when cash is received, and expenses are recorded when they are paid. This method is allowed for tax purposes because it is simple, requires a minimum of records, and produces reasonably satisfactory results for individuals not engaged in business or professional practices. Farmers are also allowed to use the cash basis for tax purposes.

SPECIAL TAX TREATMENT OF REVENUES AND EXPENSES   Differences between taxable and accounting income may occur. Some differences result from special tax rules which are unrelated to accounting principles.

1 Some items included in accounting income are not taxable. For example, most dividends received by Canadian corporations are excluded from taxable income.

2 Some business expenses are not deductible. For example, donations to political parties are not totally deductible.

3 Special deductions in excess of actual business expenses are allowed some taxpayers. For example, depletion deductions in excess of actual cost are allowed taxpayers in the oil industry. This "statutory depletion" allowance is one-third of the income derived from oil and gas operations.

4 Some business expenses must be treated as capital expenditures for tax purposes. For example, goodwill may be amortized for accounting purposes; for tax purposes only one-half of goodwill may be amortized.

In addition, the *timing* of the recognition of certain revenues and expenses under tax rules differs from that under accounting principles. Some items of income received in advance may be taxed in the year of receipt while certain accrued expenses may not be deductible for tax purposes until the cost is actually paid in cash. For example accountants usually estimate future warranty costs applicable to sales of the current year and deduct this estimated amount in computing the net income for the current year. However, these estimated costs are not deductible in calculating income for the purposes. Warranty costs are allowed for tax purposes in the year in which they become known and are actually payable.

ALTERNATIVE ACCOUNTING METHODS Various accounting methods result in different net income figures, largely because of difference in the timing of revenue and expense recognition. The tax law permits taxpayers, in some cases, to adopt for income tax purposes accounting methods which differ from those used for financial reporting. Businessmen are therefore faced with the option of choosing an accounting method for tax purposes that will result in minimizing their tax burdens— usually by postponing the tax.

The choice of inventory pricing methods will affect the timing of net income recognition, as we have seen in Chapter 10. One of the reasons for the popularity of the lifo pricing method is that it results in lower net income during periods of rising prices. While the last-in, first-out method of inventory valuation is acceptable for many situations by Canadian accountants, this method is not acceptable in computing income for tax purposes.

The tax law requires the use of a form of the reducing balance method of depreciation in computing taxable income. For accounting purposes, other methods may be more suitable in computing net income.

There are a number of other less common examples of elective methods which postpone taxes. Taxpayers who sell merchandise on the *installment basis* may elect to report income in proportion to the cash received on the installment contract, rather than at the time of sale. The cost of drilling oil wells and preparing wells for production may be charged off as incurred, rather than capitalized and depreciated. Most research and development expenditures are accorded similar treatment.

TAXES AND FINANCIAL REPORTING; INCOME TAX ALLOCATION When there are differences between accounting principles and tax rules, many businesses choose to keep their accounting records on a tax basis as a matter of bookkeeping convenience. In other words, accounting principles give way to tax laws. If the differences are not material, there is no objection to this practice as a means of simplifying the keeping of tax records. Where the differences between tax rules and accounting principles are material, however, the result of following the tax law is to distort financial statements. It is clearly preferable to maintain accounting records to meet the need for relevant information about business operations, and to adjust such data to arrive at taxable income.

When a corporation follows different accounting methods for book and tax purposes, a financial reporting problem arises. The difference in method will usually have the effect of postponing the recognition of income (either because an expense deduction is accelerated or because revenue recognition is postponed). The question is whether the income tax expense should be accrued when the income is recognized on the accounting records, or when it is actually subject to taxation.

To illustrate the problem, let us consider a very simple case. Suppose the Pryor Company Ltd. has before-tax accounting income of $200,000 in each of two years. However, the company takes as a tax deduction in Year 1 an expense of $80,000 which is reported for accounting purposes in Year 2. The company's accounting and taxable income, and the actual income taxes due (assuming a tax rate of 50%) are shown below:

	Year 1	Year 2
Accounting income (before income taxes)	$200,000	$200,000
Taxable income	120,000	280,000
Actual income taxes due each year, at assumed rate of 50%		
of taxable income	60,000	140,000

Following one approach, the Pryor Company Ltd. might simply report in its income statement in each year the amount of income taxes due for that year as computed on the company's tax returns. The effect on reported net income would be as follows:

	Year 1	Year 2
Company Accounting income (before income taxes)	$200,000	$200,000
reports Income taxes	60,000	140,000
actual taxes Net Income	$140,000	$ 60,000

The reader of the Pryor Company's income statement might well wonder why the same accounting income before taxes in the two years produced such widely variant tax expense and net income figures.

To deal with this distortion between pre- and after-tax income, an accounting policy known as *income tax allocation* has been devised, which is required for financial reporting purposes.[8] Briefly, the objective of the tax allocation procedure is to accrue income taxes in relation to accounting income, whenever differences between accounting and taxable income are caused by differences in the *timing* of revenues or expenses. In the Pryor Company Ltd. example, this means we would report on the Year 1 income statement a tax on the $80,000 ($200,000 − $120,000) of income which was reported for accounting purposes in Year 1 but which will be taxed in Year 2. The effect of this accounting procedure is demonstrated by the journal entries that would be made to record the income tax expense in each of the two years:

Entries to record income tax allocation

Year 1   Income taxes 100,000
        Current Income tax liability 60,000
        Deferred Income tax credit 40,000
        To record current and deferred income taxes at 50% of accounting income of $200,000.

Year 2   Income taxes 80,000
        Deferred income tax credit 40,000
        Current income tax liability 120,000
        To record income taxes at 50% of accounting income of $200,000

---

[8]For a more complete discussion of tax allocation procedures, see *CICA Handbook*, issued by the Canadian Institute of Chartered Accountants Accounting Research Committee.

Using tax allocation procedures, the Pryor Company Ltd. would report its net income during the two-year period as follows:

	Year 1	Year 2
Income before income taxes	*$200,000*	*$200,000*
Income taxes (tax allocation basis)	*100,000*	*100,000*
Income	*100,000*	*100,000*

Company uses tax allocation procedure

In this simple example, the difference between taxable and accounting income (caused by the accelerated deduction of an expense) was fully offset in a period of two years. In practice, differences between accounting and taxable income may persist over extended time periods and deferred tax credits may accumulate to significant amounts. For example, in a recent balance sheet of Simpsons-Sears Limited, deferred taxes of over $12 million were reported as a result of the use of capital cost allowance for tax purposes while reporting net income in financial statements on the basis of straight-line depreciation.

In contrast to the example for the Pryor Company Ltd. in which income taxes were deferred, income taxes *may be prepaid* when taxable income exceeds accounting income because of timing differences. The portion of taxes paid on income deferred for accounting purposes would be reported as prepaid taxes in the balance sheet; when the income is reported as earned for accounting purposes in a later period, the *prepaid taxes are recognized as tax expense* applicable to the income currently reported in financial statements but which *was taxed in an earlier period.*[9]

ALLOCATION OF INCOME TAXES BETWEEN OPERATING INCOME AND EXTRAORDINARY ITEMS In Chapter 17 we stated that extraordinary gains and losses should be separately reported *net of taxes* in the income statement. This means that the amount of taxes deducted from operating income would be the amount of taxes due *if there were no extraordinary gains or losses.* The tax on any gain would be netted against the gain and any tax reduction attributed to a loss would be offset against the loss.

To illustrate, assume that the Queen Company Ltd. has an operating income of $150,000 taxable at 50%, and a capital gain of $250,000, taxable at 25%.[10] The total tax liability of $137,500 ($62,500 + $75,000) would be reported in the income statement as follows:

An extraordinary gain is reported net of taxes

Operating Income	$150,000
Income taxes (actual taxes are $137,500, of which $75,000 is applicable to ordinary gain)	75,000
Income before extraordinary gain	$ 75,000
Extraordinary gain, net of taxes ($250,000 − $62,500)	187,500
Net income	$262,500

[9]A good example of this treatment is the deduction on the books of estimated warranty expense from revenue in the period in which the product is sold; for income tax purposes, this expense is deductible only when it is actually incurred.
[10]The effective tax rate on capital gains is 25% since only one-half of the capital gains is taxable.

If the entire tax of $137,500 was deducted from operating income, both the income before extraordinary gain and the extraordinary gain would be distorted as illustrated below:

Failure to allocate taxes gives a distorted picture

Operating income	$150,000
Income taxes	137,500
Income before extraordinary gain	$ 12,500
Extraordinary gain (before taxes)	250,000
Net Income	$262,500

Assume now that instead of a capital gain, the Queen Company Ltd. had an operating income of $150,000 and a fully deductible fire loss of $120,000. The proper way to report this follows:

A loss of $120,000 is reduced to $60,000 after tax effect

Operating income	$150,000
Income taxes (actual taxes are $15,000 as a result of fire loss)	75,000
Income before extraordinary loss	$ 75,000
Extraordinary loss, net of taxes (120,000 − $60,000)	60,000
Net Income	$ 15,000

If tax allocation procedures were not followed, the net income of $15,000 would be improperly reported as consisting of income before extraordinary loss of $135,000 ($150,000 − $15,000), less the pre-tax extraordinary loss of $120,000.

Tax considerations in launching and operating a business

Federal income tax laws have become so complex that detailed tax planning has become a way of life for most business firms. Almost all businesses today engage professional tax specialists to review the tax aspects of major business decisions and to develop plans for legally minimizing income taxes. Because it is important for even the non-specialist to recognize areas in which tax factors may be of consequence, a few of the major opportunities for tax planning are discussed briefly below.

EFFECT OF TAXES ON FORM OF BUSINESS ORGANIZATION Tax factors should be carefully considered at the time a business is organized. As a single proprietor or partner, a business man will pay federal and pro-vincial taxes[11] at individual rates, ranging currently from 18% to 61% on his share of the business income earned in any year whether or not he withdraws it from the business. Corporations, on the other hand, are taxed on earnings at a dual rate of 25% on the first $100,000 of income and 47% on income in excess of $100,000.[12] Corporations may deduct salaries paid to owners and to owners' spouses for services but may not deduct dividends paid to stockholders. Both salaries and dividends are taxed to their recipients.

These factors must be weighed in deciding in any given situation whether the corporate or noncorporate form of business organization is preferable. There is no simple rule of thumb, even considering only these

[11]Provincial taxes have been included at the approximate rate imposed by Ontario. Most other provinces impose higher rates.

[12]The dual rate applies only for Canadian controlled private corporations who are eligible for the small business deduction. It is not, however, likely that other corporations could have considered other forms of organization.

basic differences. To illustrate, suppose that Able, a married man, starts a business which he expects will produce, before any compensation to himself and before income taxes, an average annual income of $50,000. If he incorporates the business, Able plans to pay himself a salary of $20,000 which is the fair value of his services. In Case 1, he plans to withdraw the entire after-tax profits of $22,500 (30,000 — taxes of $7,500) in the form of dividends. In Case 2, it is assumed that no dividends are withdrawn. The combined corporate and individual taxes under the corporate and single proprietorship form of business organization are summarized below:

	Form of Organization		
	Corporate (Case 1)	Corporate (Case 2)	Single Proprietorship
Dividends paid	$22,500	Nil	
Business income before salary to Able . . .	50,000	50,000	50,000
Salary to Able.	20,000	20,000	—
Net income before income taxes	$30,000	30,000	50,000
Combined corporate and individual tax			
Individual tax			
Income			
Dividends received	22,500		
Gross-up-1/3	7,500		
	30,000		
Salary.	20,000	20,000	
Individual taxable income	$50,000	20,000	50,000
Federal tax before dividend credit			
(Assume personal exemptions of $1,600)	16,797	4,945	16,797
Dividend tax credit (4/5 of $7,500).	6,000		
Federal tax	10,797	4,945	16,797
Provincial tax (30.5% of Federal tax)	3,293	1,508	5,123
	14,090	6,453	21,920
Corporation tax[13]	7,500	7,500	
	$21,590	$13,953	$21,920

At first glance this comparison suggests that, from a tax viewpoint, there is little to choose between the various forms of business organizations if all profits are distributed to the shareholders; but if profits are retained in the business, the corporate form is distinctly advantageous. In Case 2, where all profits are not withdrawn, the net tax deferment of approximately 8,000 dollars ($21,920 — 13,953) can be used by the business interest free. It must be noted, however, that the $22,500 ($30,000 — $7,500) of earnings retained in the corporation will be taxed to Able as ordinary income (subject to the dividend tax credit) when and if they are distributed as dividends. On the other hand, if Able later sells his business and realizes these earnings in the form of the increased

[13]Provincial corporation tax has been ignored because of its immaterial effect, after the provincial tax abatement, on this analysis.

value of his capital stock, one-half of any gain will be taxed as ordinary income or an effective maximum rate of about 30%. In either case Able can postpone the payment of tax on retained earnings so long as they remain reinvested in the business.

It is clear that both the marginal rate of tax to which individual business owners are subject and the extent to which profits are to be withdrawn from the business must be considered in assessing the relative advantages of one form of business organization over another.

PLANNING TRANSACTIONS TO MINIMIZE TAXES Business transactions may often be arranged in such a way as to produce favorable tax treatment. Capital cost allowance regulations have been changed from time to time to further the government's economic policies. In the past, the government has allowed accelerated capital cost allowance on certain capital additions and has, at other times, disallowed or permitted only reduced capital cost allowances to be taken in designated cases. Currently, a fast write-off per annum of 50% of capital cost may be claimed on equipment acquired for producing income from Canadian manufacturing operations. Timing of investment in depreciable assets has a significant impact on the payment of tax in any one year since capital cost allowance is computed on the balance in a class at the end of the taxation year. Effective investment policies requires cognizance of these regulations.

Sometimes a seller tries to arrange a transaction one way to his tax benefit and the buyer tries to shape it another way to produce tax savings for him. Income tax effects thus become a part of price negotiations. For example, in buying business property, the purchaser will try to allocate as much of the cost of the property to the building and as little to the land as possible, since building costs can be depreciated for tax purposes. Similarly, in selling a business the seller will try to allocate as much of the selling price as possible to goodwill. The buyer of the business, however, will want the purchase price to be attributable to the purchase of inventories or depreciable assets, which are deductible against ordinary income, since only one-half of goodwill can be amortized for tax purposes. The point is, *the failure to consider the tax consequences of major business transactions can be costly.*

TAXES AND FINANCIAL PLANNING Different forms of business financing produce different tax expense. Interest on debt, for example, is fully deductible while dividends on preferred or common stocks are not. This factor operates as a strong incentive to finance expansion by borrowing.

Suppose that a company needs $100,000 to invest in productive assets on which it can expect to earn a 12% annual return. If the company issues $100,000 in 6% preferred stock, it will earn after taxes, assuming a 47% marginal tax rate, $6,360 ($12,000 less taxes at 47% of $12,000). This is barely enough to cover the $6,000 preferred dividend. If, on the other hand, the company borrowed the $100,000 at 6% interest, its taxable income would be $6,000 ($12,000 earnings less $6,000 interest expense). The tax on this amount at 47% would be $2,820, leaving income of $3,180 available for common stockholders or for reinvestment in the business. A similar analysis should be made in choosing between debt and common stock financing.

Taxable income computed on the accrual basis is not necessarily matched by an inflow of cash. A healthy profit picture accompanied by a tight cash position is not unusual for a rapidly growing company. Income taxes are a substantial cash drain and an important factor in preparing cash budgets, as described in Chapter 26.

QUESTIONS

1 List several ways in which businessmen may legally alter the amount of taxes they pay.

2 What is meant by the expression "tax planning"?

3 What are the three major classes of taxpayers under the federal income tax law?

4 It has been claimed that corporate income is subject to "double taxation." Explain the meaning of this expression.

5 Taxes are characterized as *proportional, progressive,* or *regressive* with respect to any given base. Describe an income tax rate structure that would fit each of these characterizations.

6 List and discuss briefly the criteria used in determining whether or not a receipt is a capital gain.

7 Outline concisely the tax treatment of non-capital losses.

8 In computing income taxes, why does it make any difference whether a given deduction may be taken before or after net income for tax purposes?

9 List some differences in the tax rules for corporations in contrast to those for individuals.

10 Jacobs files his income tax return on a cash basis. During the current year $300 of interest was credited to him on his savings account; he withdrew this interest on January 18 of the following year. Jacobs purchased a piece of business equipment having an estimated service life of five years in December of the current year. He also paid a year's rent in advance on certain business property on December 29 of the current year. Explain how these items would be treated on Jacobs' current year's income tax return.

11 Even when a taxpayer uses the accrual method of accounting, his taxable income may differ from his accounting income. Give three examples of differences between the tax and accounting treatment of items that are included in the determination of income.

12 Under what circumstances is the accounting procedure known as *income tax allocation* appropriate? Explain the purpose of this procedure.

13 List some tax factors to be considered in deciding whether to organize a new business as a corporation or as a partnership.

14 Explain how the corporate income tax makes debt financing in general more attractive than financing through the issuance of preferred stock.

EXERCISES

Ex. 20-1 From the tax table on page 593, compute the federal tax for each of the following:

	Taxable Income
a Unmarried individual	$ 7,500
b Unmarried individual	150,000
c Married individual	7,500
d Married individual	150,000

Ex. 20-2 The General Trading Corporation Ltd., a Canadian controlled private corporation reports the following income during Year 1:

Operating income (*income before extraordinary items and income taxes*) . .	$110,000
Extraordinary items:	
Gain on sale of Z Ltd. Company stock	50,000
Loss from flood (*fully deductible*)	10,000

Assume that corporate tax rate is 47%. General Trading Corporation is eligible for the Small Business Deduction (22%).

a Compute the federal tax liability for the General Trading Corporation Ltd. for Year 1.

b Prepare the lower section of the income statement for the General Trading Corporation Ltd., showing income before extraordinary items, extraordinary items net of taxes, and net income.

Ex. 20-3 From the following information for Paul Grosch, compute his taxable income for 1975:

Salary	$20,000
Gain on sale of land	4,000
Dividends from Canadian corporations	3,000

Mr. Grosch is married and has two children under 16.

Ex. 20-4 For each year 1973, 1974 and 1975 determine the amount of capital gain and loss included in net income for tax purposes or the capital loss deducted in arriving at taxable income for an individual taxpayer in the trucking business.

	1973	1974	1975
Gain on sale of securities	$8,000	$3,000	
Loss on sale of truck			$500
Loss on sale of equipment		8,000	

Ex. 20-5 The Barryman Company Ltd. uses accelerated depreciation and charges off currently all the exploration costs for income tax purposes. On its financial statements it uses straight-line depreciation and amortizes exploration costs over a 5-year period. Its taxable and accounting income for the last five years are shown below:

	Year 5	Year 4	Year 3	Year 2	Year 1
Taxable income . . .	$350,000	$300,000	$200,000	$150,000	$100,000
Accounting income .	200,000	250,000	300,000	280,000	250,000

Assuming that corporate income is taxable at a flat rate of 45%, compute the net income for the company for each of the five years.

a Based on actual taxes paid.

b Based on taxes that would be paid on the net income reported for accounting purposes.

Comment on the differences in results obtained in (**a**) and (**b**).

PROBLEMS

Group A

20A-1 You are to consider the income tax status of each of the items listed below. List the numbers 1 to 15 on your answer sheet. For each item state whether it is

included in net income or *excluded from net income* for federal income tax purposes.
(1) Cash dividends received on stock of Dow Chemical Company, Ltd.
(2) Value of a color TV set won as a prize in a quiz contest.
(3) Gain on the sale of an original painting.
(4) Inheritance received on death of a rich uncle.
(5) Interest received on City of Calgary municipal bonds.
(6) Proceeds of life insurance policy received on death of husband.
(7) Tips received by a waitress.
(8) Value of Canada Savings Bonds received as a gift from aunt.
(9) Rent received on personal residence while on extended vacation trip.
(10) Share of income from partnership which exceeds the drawings from the partnership.
(11) Amount received as damages for injury in automobile accident.
(12) Salary received from a corporation by a stockholder who owns directly or indirectly all the shares of the company's outstanding stock.
(13) Gain on sale of Avon Corporation Ltd. capital stock, held for five months.
(14) Taxpayer owed $1,000 on a note payable. During the current year the taxpayer painted a building owned by the creditor, and in return the creditor canceled the note.
(15) Trip to Tahiti given by employer as reward for performance to a top salesman.

20A-2 Elmer Rollins is an engineer with a wife and four children under 16. His income and expenses for the latest year are as follows:

Salary from City Design Company Ltd.	$25,000
Consulting fees (net of applicable expenses)	3,000
Dividends from Canadian corporations	3,600
Interest on bonds of Province of Quebec	600
Gain on sale of painting.	
(Selling price $2,400; cost $800)	1,600
Capital loss on sale of securities in previous year. Loss	
in previous year was $9,000. $1,000 was carried back to the year	
prior to year of loss and $1,000 was deducted in year of loss	7,000
Gain on sale of bonds	500
Proceeds on insurance policy on life of uncle	5,000
General expenses (see below)	15,100
Details of general expense	
Theft of furniture on July 20 while on vacation	$ 1,500
Interest paid on loans to buy stock	1,800
Medical expenses	800
Insurance on home	180
Income taxes withheld from salary	4,500
Clothes, food, and other living expenses	5,290
Investment counsellor fees	1,000
Safety deposit box rental	30
	$15,100

Instructions Compute the taxable income and the income tax for Mr. Rollins.

20A-3 A is a married man, 67 years old, with three children aged 14, 16 and 22. The oldest child is attending a Canadian university and paid $600 tuition fees for the 1975 academic year (8 months). During the summer vacation, he earns $1,500 in salary. Mrs. A receives $400 annually as secretary of a rural mutual telephone association.

A is employed at a yearly rate of $12,000. His employer withheld $1,100 in respect of taxes and $600 as contributions to the pension plan during 1975. A's income from investments during 1975 was as follows:

Interest on Government of Canada bonds	$ 320
Dividends on shares of Canadian corporations	1,800
Mortgage interest	1,200

A is also a partner in A, B & C Co. After paying salaries to the partners, A, B and C, of $2,000, $8,000 and $8,000 respectively each year, the net profit of the partnership for the year ended February 28, 1975 was $3,000 and for the year ended February 28, 1976 was $5,000.

During 1975 A sold for $6,700 land that he had acquired in 1964 for $4,000. The fair market value of the land at December 31, 1971 was $5,000.

During 1975, as a result of an automobile accident, A paid medical, nursing and hospital expenses amounting to $1,200 for himself and $1,800 for his wife. Medical expenses for his children amounted to $180 for the year.

On March 31, June 30, September 30, and December 31, 1975, A made installment payments totalling $500 on his 1975 taxes.

Required. Statement showing your computation of the balance of taxes on income owing by A for 1975.

20A-4 James and Doris White have three dependent children aged 13, 16 and 19. You obtain the following information in preparing James' income tax return for 1975:

Gross receipts received during the year

Salary of James White (including year-end bonus of $500)	$17,500
Dividends from Canadian corporations	3,900
Proceeds on life insurance policy upon death of brother	11,000
Interest on municipal bonds	200
Interest on savings accounts	2,450
Received on sale of securities (cost $2,000)	4,000
Received on sale of furniture (cost $4,000)	3,000
Salary of Mrs. White	900
	$42,950

The securities and furniture had been purchased by the Whites in 1973.

Personal expenses paid during the year:

Income tax withheld by employer	$2,800
Registered and Canada Pension Plan contributions withheld by employer	300
Grocery bills	3,240
Sales taxes	320
Contributions to church and other charities	450
Property taxes on residence and vacant lot	860
Gifts to needy friends	280
Interest on home mortgage	2,100
School tuition for child attending university	600
Child care fees	280
Medical expenses	700
Legal fees in connection with personal injury case	250
	$12,180

Instructions Compute the tax payable by Mr. White in 1975. White lived in Alberta.

20B-1 **a** State for each of the following items whether, for Federal income tax purposes, it should be included in income or excluded from income, on a return filed by an individual who is not in business.
(1) Tips received by a waiter
(2) Value of trip to Bermuda, given as a prize in a sales contest by an employer
(3) Proceeds of life insurance policy received on death of a parent
(4) Inheritance received on death of rich uncle
(5) Dividends on shares of Atlanta Paper Company Ltd.
(6) Value of automobile won as a prize in a television quiz contest
(7) Value of Canada Savings Bonds received as a gift from an aunt
(8) Gain on the sale of personal residence
b State for each of the following items whether, for Federal income tax purposes, it should be deducted to arrive at income of an individual who is not in business.
(1) Interest paid on mortgage covering rental property
(2) Expenses incurred by employee in connection with his job, for which he is reimbursed by employer
(3) Rent expense paid on personal residence
(4) Interest paid on mortgage covering personal residence
(5) Damage in storm to motorboat used for pleasure
(6) Loss on the sale of corporation bonds, by owner
(7) Fee paid for assistance in contesting additional income taxes assessed by Department of National Revenue.

20B-2 The information given below has been taken from the records of the Xena Corporation Ltd., a public corporation:

Sales	$836,000
Sales returns and allowances	8,670
Cost of goods sold	573,290
Officer's salaries expense	42,000
Dividends declared	25,000
Dividends received (on shares of taxable Canadian subsidiary)	18,000
Other administrative expenses	62,180
Selling expenses	78,300
Gain on sale of marketable securities	12,420
Net operating loss in previous year, first year of operations	4,180

Instructions On the basis of this information, prepare an income statement for the Xena Corporation Ltd.

In a separate schedule, show your computation of the provision for Federal income taxes for the year (rounding the provision to the nearest dollar). Xena takes depreciation on its books in accordance with the tax regulations.

20B-3 **a** At the beginning of its taxation year 19A, a company purchased a wooden building at a cost of $100,000. This building is the only item in its prescribed class. It is resold during the year 19D, for the sum of
(i) $150,000
(ii) $ 85,000
(iii) $ 40,000

Instructions Determine the amount of profit or loss on the disposition of the building in each of the three cases, assuming that the maximum capital cost allowance was taken for each year. State also how this profit or loss is to be treated from a tax viewpoint.

b A taxpayer bought a first truck on December 1, 19A, at a cost of $3,000 and a second one on September 1, 19B at a cost of $4,500. On October 1, 19D, he sold the first truck for $3,200.

Instructions Calculate the maximum cost allowance for the year 19D.

20B-4 Dr. Smith, who lives in Toronto, Ont., gives you his cash book for 19C.

Receipts:

Cash on hand and in bank on January 1, 19C	$ 3,000
Fees	20,000
Interest on bonds	5,000
Dividends	6,300
Rents	2,440
Gain on sale of securities	2,000
	$38,740

Disbursements:

Drugs purchased		$ 2,500
Nurse's salary		4,300
Telephone and electricity—office		175
Paid to wife for housekeeping		5,000
Down-payment on a property		6,000
Charitable donations		2,000
Books, magazines, contributions to medical associations		275
Postage and stationery		125
Disbursements made with respect to property:		
Municipal and school taxes	$250	
Maintenance and repairs	660	
Insurance	100	
Heating	225	
Payment on mortgage	720	1,955
19B income tax		2,400
Automobile expenses		1,500
Net cost of an automobile		2,000
Purchase of bonds		2,050
Cash on hand and in bank on December 31, 19C		8,460
		$38,740

You are also given the following information:
(1) During 19A, Dr. Smith bought a property for $18,000. The land is worth $3,000 and the building is a brick one. The building is rented and part is used by Dr. Smith for his office.
(2) Dr. Smith was married during the year.
(3) The payment on mortgage includes $350 as interest.
(4) Dr. Smith, who uses his automobile about 100 per cent of the time for business purposes, traded in his old automobile which had cost him $2,400 when purchased in 19A on a new automobile. Dr. Smith had claimed maximum capital cost allowance for tax purposes on the old automobile. He received a trade-in allowance of $1,000 on the old automobile.
(5) Dr. Smith has no receivables or payables at the beginning or end of 19C.

Instructions Compute the Federal and provincial income taxes payable by Dr. Smith.

BUSINESS DECISION PROBLEM 20

Bill Hartman is in the process of organizing a business which he expects will produce, before any compensation to himself and before income taxes, an income of $60,000 per year. In deciding whether to operate as a single proprietorship or as a corporation, Hartman is willing to make the choice on the basis of the relative income tax advantage under either form of organization.

Hartman is married, and has 2 children aged 13 and 15.

If the business is operated as a single proprietorship, Hartman expects to withdraw the entire income of $60,000 each year including a salary to Mrs. Hartman of $4,000.

If the business is operated as a corporation, Hartman and his wife will own all the shares; he will pay himself a salary of $35,000 and his wife a salary of $4,000 and will withdraw as dividends the entire amount of the corporation's net income after income taxes.

It may be assumed that the accounting income and the taxable income for the corporation would be the same. Mr. and Mrs. Hartman have only minor amounts of nonbusiness income, which may be ignored.

Instructions

a Determine the relative income tax advantage to Bill Hartman of operating either as a single proprietorship or as a corporation, and make a recommendation as to the form of organization he should adopt. Hartman lives in Alberta.

b Suppose that Bill Hartman planned to withdraw only $35,000 per year from his business, as drawings from a single proprietorship or as salary from a corporation. Would this affect your recommendation? Explain.

TWENTY-ONE
ANALYSIS AND INTERPRETATION OF FINANCIAL STATEMENTS

Financial statements are the instrument panel of a business enterprise. They constitute a report on managerial performance, attesting to managerial success or failure and flashing warning signals of impending difficulties. In reading a complex instrument panel, one must understand the gauges and their calibration to make sense out of the array of data they convey. Similarly, one must understand the inner workings of the accounting system and the significance of various financial relationships to interpret the data appearing in financial statements. To an astute reader, a set of financial statements tells a great deal about a business enterprise.

The financial affairs of any business are of interest to a number of different groups: management, creditors, investors, union officials, and government agencies. Each of these groups has somewhat different needs, and accordingly each tends to concentrate on particular aspects of a company's financial picture.

Sources of financial information

For the most part, the discussion in this chapter will be limited to the kind of analysis that can be made by "outsiders" who do not have access to internal accounting records. Investors must rely to a considerable extent on financial statements in published annual and quarterly reports. In the case of large publicly owned corporations, certain statements that must be filed with public agencies, such as the Ontario Securities Commission;[1] are available. Financial information for most corporations is also published by Moody's *Manual of Investments* and the Financial Post's Corporation Service.

Bankers are usually able to secure more detailed information by requesting it as a condition for granting a loan. Trade creditors may obtain

---

[1] Large private corporations, incorporated under the Canadian Corporations Act, must file certain financial information with the Federal Department of Consumer and Corporate Affairs.

financial information for businesses of almost any size from credit-rating agencies such as Dun & Bradstreet, Ltd.

Tools of analysis

Few figures in a financial statement are highly significant in and of themselves. It is their relationship to other quantities, or the amount and direction of change since a previous date, that is important. Analysis is largely a matter of establishing significant relationships and pointing up changes and trends. There are three widely used analytical techniques: (1) dollar and percentage changes, (2) component percentages, and (3) ratios.

DOLLAR AND PERCENTAGE CHANGES The change in financial data over time is best exhibited in statements showing data for a series of years in adjacent columns. Such statements are called *comparative financial statements.* A highly condensed comparative balance sheet is shown below:

BENSON CORPORATION LTD.
Comparative Balance Sheet
As of December 31
(*in thousands of dollars*)

	Year 3	Year 2	Year 1
Assets:			
Current assets	$180	$150	$120
Plant and equipment (net).	450	300	345
Total assets	$630	$450	$465
Liabilities & Stockholders' Equity:			
Current liabilities	$ 60	$ 80	$120
Long-term liabilities	200	100	
Capital stock	300	300	300
Retained earnings (deficit)	70	(30)	45
Total liabilities & stockholders' equity	$630	$450	$465

Condensed three-year balance sheet

The usefulness of comparative financial statements covering two or more years is well recognized. Published annual reports often contain comparative financial statements covering a period as long as 10 years. By observing the change in various items period by period, the analyst may gain valuable clues as to growth and other important trends affecting the business.

The dollar amount of change from year to year is of some interest; reducing this to percentage terms adds perspective. For example, if sales this year have increased by $100,000, the fact that this is an increase of 10% over last year's sales of $1 million puts it in a different perspective than if it represented a 1% increase over sales of $10 million for the prior year.

The dollar amount of any change is the difference between the amount for a *base* year and for a *comparison* year. The percentage change is computed by dividing the amount of the change between years by the amount for the base year. This is illustrated in the tabulation below, using data from the comparative balance sheet on page 626.

| | In Thousands | | | Increase or (Decrease) | | | |
| | | | | Year 3 over Year 2 | | Year 2 over Year 1 | |
	Year 3	Year 2	Year 1	Amount	%	Amount	%
Current assets	$180	$150	$120	$30	20%	$30	25%
Current liabilities	$ 60	$ 80	$120	($20)	(25%)	($40)	(33.3%)

Dollar and percentage changes

Although current assets increased $30,000 in both Year 2 and Year 3, the percentage of change differs because of the shift in the base year from Year 1 to Year 2.

COMPONENT PERCENTAGES The phrase "a piece of pie" is subject to varying interpretations until it is known whether the piece represents one-sixth or one-half of the total pie. The percentage relationship between any particular financial item and a significant total that includes this item is known as a *component percentage;* this is often a useful means of showing relationships or the relative importance of the item in question. Thus if inventories are 50% of total current assets, they are a far more significant factor in the current position of a company than if they are only 10% of total current assets.

One application of component percentages is to express each asset group on the balance sheet as a percentage of total assets. This shows quickly the relative importance of current and noncurrent assets, and the relative amount of financing obtained from current creditors, long-term creditors, and stockholders.

Another application is to express all items on an income statement as a percentage of net sales. Such a statement is sometimes called a *common size* income statement. A highly condensed income statement in dollars and in common size form is illustrated on page 628.

Looking only at the component percentages, we see that the decline in the gross profit rate from 40 to 30% was only partially offset by the decrease in expenses as a percentage of net sales, causing net income to decrease from 15 to 10% of net sales. The dollar amounts in the first pair of columns, however, present an entirely different picture. It is true that net sales increased faster than net income, but net income improved significantly in Year 2, a fact not apparent from a review of component percentages alone. This points up an important limitation in the use of

Income Statement

	Dollars		Component Percentages	
	Year 2	Year 1	Year 2	Year 1
Net sales.	$500,000	$200,000	100.0%	100.0%
Cost of goods sold	350,000	120,000	70.0	60.0
Gross profit on sales	$150,000	$ 80,000	30.0%	40.0%
Expenses (including income taxes) .	100,000	50,000	20.0	25.0
Net income	$ 50,000	$ 30,000	10.0%	15.0%

How suc-
cessful was
Year 2?

component percentages. Changes in the component percentage may result from a change in the component, in the total, or in both. Reverting to our previous analogy, it is important to know not only the relative size of a piece of pie, but also the size of the pie; 10% of a large pie may be a bigger piece than 15% of a smaller pie.

RATIOS A ratio is a simple mathematical expression of the relationship of one item to another. Ratios may be expressed in a number of ways. For example, if we wish to clarify the relationship between sales of $800,000 and net income of $40,000, we may state: (1) The ratio of sales to net income is 20 to 1 (or 20:1); (2) for every $1 of sales, the company has an average net income of 5 cents; (3) net income is $\frac{1}{20}$ of sales. In each case the ratio is merely a means of describing the relationship between sales and net income in a simple form.

In order to compute a meaningful ratio, there must be a significant relationship between the two figures. A ratio focuses attention on a relationship which is significant, but a full interpretation of the ratio usually requires further investigation of the underlying data. Ratios are an aid to analysis and interpretation; they are not a substitute for sound thinking in the analytical process.

Standards of comparison

In using dollar and percentage changes, component percentages, and ratios, the analyst constantly seeks some standard of comparison against which to judge whether the relationships that he has found are favorable or unfavorable. Two such standards are (1) the past performance of the company and (2) the performance of other companies in the same industry.

PAST PERFORMANCE OF THE COMPANY Comparing analytical data for a current period with similar computations for prior years affords some basis for judging whether the position of the business is improving or worsening. This comparison of data over time is sometimes called *horizontal* or *dynamic* analysis, to express the idea of reviewing data for a number of periods. It is distinguished from *vertical* or *static* analysis, which refers to the review of the financial information for only one accounting period.

In addition to determining whether the situation is improving or becoming worse, horizontal analysis may aid in making estimates of future prospects. Since changes may reverse their direction at any time, however, projecting past trends into the future is always a somewhat risky statistical pastime.

A weakness of horizontal analysis is that comparison with the past does not afford any basis for evaluation in absolute terms. The fact that net income was 2% of sales last year and is 3% of sales this year indicates improvement, but if there is evidence that net income *should be* 5% of sales, the record for both years is unfavorable.

INDUSTRY STANDARDS   The limitations of horizontal analysis may be overcome to some extent by finding some other standard of performance as a yardstick against which to measure the record of any particular firm.[2] The yardstick may be a comparable company, the average record of several companies in the same industry, or some predetermined standard based upon the past experience of the analyst.

Suppose that Y Company Ltd. suffers a 5% drop in its sales during the current year. The discovery that the sales of all companies in the same industry fell an average of 20% would indicate that this was a favorable rather than an unfavorable performance. Assume further that Y Company's net income is 2% of net sales. Based on comparison with other companies in the industry, this would be grossly substandard performance if Y Company Ltd. were an automobile manufacturer; but it would be a satisfactory record if Y Company Ltd. were a grocery chain.

When we compare a given company with its competitors or with industry averages, our conclusions will be valid only if the companies in question are reasonably comparable. Because of the large number of *conglomerate* companies formed in recent years, the term *industry* is difficult to define, and companies that fall roughly within the same industry may not be comparable in many respects. One company may engage only in the marketing of oil products; another may be a fully integrated producer from the well to the gas pump, yet both are said to be in the "oil industry."

Differences in accounting procedures may lessen the comparability of financial data for two companies. For example, the understatement of inventories on the balance sheet of a company using lifo may be so serious as to destroy the significance of comparisons with companies whose inventories are valued on a fifo basis. Similarly, companies may employ different depreciation methods or estimates of the useful life of

[2] For example, Dun & Bradstreet, Ltd. annually publishes *Key Business Ratios* in 125 lines of business divided by retailing, wholesaling, manufacturing, and construction. A total of 14 ratios are presented for each of the 125 industry groups. Similarly, Statistics Canada publishes a wide range of ratios for many industries.

substantially similar assets; research and development costs may be charged off to expense by one company and deferred by another; and the timing of revenue recognition may differ significantly among companies engaged in certain industries. Despite these limitations, studying comparative performances is a useful method of analysis if carefully and intelligently done.

Objectives of financial analysis

Business decisions are made on the basis of the best available estimates of the outcome of such decisions. The purpose of financial analysis is to provide information about a business unit for decision-making purposes, and such information need not be limited to accounting data. While ratios and other relationships based on *past performance* may be helpful in predicting the future earnings performance and financial health of a company, we must be cognizant of the inherent limitations of such data. Financial statements are essentially summary records of the past, and we must go beyond the financial statements and look into the nature of the company's industry, its competitive position, its product lines, its research expenditures, and, above all, the quality of its management.

In many respects the key objectives of financial analysis are to determine the company's earnings performance and the soundness of its financial position. We are essentially interested in financial analysis as a predictive tool; accordingly, we want to examine both quantitative and qualitative data in order to ascertain the *quality of earnings* and the *quality and protection of assets*.

QUALITY OF EARNINGS   The main objective of a business firm is to earn a profit. Profits are the lifeblood of a business entity. No entity can survive for long and accomplish its other goals unless it is profitable. Continuous losses drain assets from the business, consume owners' equity, and leave the company at the mercy of creditors. For this reason, we are interested not only in the total *amount* of earnings but also in the *rate* of earnings on sales, on total assets, and on owners' equity. In addition, we must look to the *stability* and *source* of earnings. An erratic earnings performance over a period of years, for example, is less desirable than a steady level of earnings. A history of increasing earnings is preferable to a "flat" earnings record.

A breakdown of sales and earnings by major product lines is useful in evaluating the future performance of a company. In recent years many publicly owned companies have broadened their reporting to include sales and profits by product lines, and the *CICA Handbook*[3] now requires such reporting from diversified companies.

---

[3] CICA Handbook, Section 1700.

The accounting procedures used in measuring earnings are an important consideration in evaluating the quality of earnings. The careful analyst should raise questions such as: Are the accounting options selected by management conservative or do they tend to inflate current earnings by deferring certain costs or anticipating certain revenues? What has been the effect on earnings of any accounting changes? How much of the net income or loss is attributable to extraordinary gains and losses? Because a wide variety of accounting procedures are considered "generally acceptable," the analyst must ask these questions and evaluate to the fullest extent possible the impact of accounting practices on the earnings reported by a business unit.

QUALITY AND PROTECTION OF ASSETS Protecting the company's assets from loss is probably the most important task of management. Although a satisfactory level of earnings may be a good indication of the company's long-run ability to pay its debts and dividends, we must also look at the composition of assets, their condition and liquidity, the relationship between current assets and current liabilities, and the total amount of debt outstanding. A company may be profitable and yet be unable to pay its liabilities on time; sales and earnings may be satisfactory but plant and equipment may be deteriorating because of poor maintenance policies; valuable patents may be expiring; and substantial losses may be buried in slow-moving inventories and past-due receivables. Extensive use of credit and a liberal dividend policy may result in a low owners' equity and thus expose stockholders to substantial risks in case of a downturn in business.

Illustrative analysis for Weaver Company Ltd.

Keep in mind the above discussion of analytical principles as you study the illustrative financial analysis which follows. The basic information for our discussion is contained in a set of condensed two-year comparative financial statements for the Weaver Company Ltd. shown on the following pages. Summarized statement data, together with computations of dollar increases and decreases, and component percentages where applicable, have been compiled.

Using the information in these statements, let us consider the kind of analysis that might be of particular interest to: (1) common stockholders, (2) long-term creditors, (3) preferred stockholders, and (4) short-term creditors. Organizing our discussion in this way emphasizes the differences in the viewpoint of these groups; all of them have, of course, a considerable common interest in the performance of the company as a whole. This approach should be viewed as only one of many that may be used in analyzing financial statements. Furthermore, the ratios and other measurements illustrated here are not exhaustive; the number of

WEAVER COMPANY LTD.
Condensed Comparative Balance Sheet*
December 31

	Year 2	Year 1	Increase or (Decrease) Dollars	%	Percentage of Total Assets Year 2	Year 1
Assets						
Current assets	$390,000	$288,000	$102,000	35.4	41.1	33.5
Plant and equipment (net)	500,000	467,000	33,000	7.1	52.6	54.3
Other assets (loans to officers)	60,000	105,000	(45,000)	(42.8)	6.3	12.2
Total assets	$950,000	$860,000	$ 90,000	10.5	100.0	100.0
Liabilities & Stock- **holders' Equity**						
Liabilities:						
Current liabilities	$147,400	$ 94,000	$ 53,400	56.8	15.5	10.9
Long-term liabilities	200,000	250,000	(50,000)	(20.0)	21.1	29.1
Total liabilities	$347,400	$344,000	$ 3,400	1.0	36.6	40.0
Stockholders' equity:						
6% preferred stock	$100,000	$100,000			10.5	11.6
Common stock ($50 par)	250,000	200,000	$ 50,000	25.0	26.3	23.2
Premium on common stock	70,000	40,000	30,000	75.0	7.4	4.7
Retained earnings	182,600	176,000	6,600	3.8	19.2	20.5
Total stockholders' equity	$602,600	$516,000	$ 86,600	16.8	63.4	60.0
Total liabilities & stockholders' equity .	$950,000	$860,000	$ 90,000	10.5	100.0	100.0

* In order to focus attention on important subtotals, this statement is highly condensed and does not show individual asset and liability items. These details will be introduced as needed in the text discussion. For example, a list of the Weaver Company's current assets and current liabilities appears on page 642.

measurements that may be developed for various analytical purposes is almost without limit.

Analysis by common stockholders

Common stockholders and potential investors in common stock look first at a company's earnings record. Their investment is in shares of stock, so *earnings per share and dividends per share* are of particular interest.

EARNINGS PER SHARE OF COMMON STOCK As indicated in Chapter 17, earnings per share of common stock are computed by dividing the income available to common stockholders by the number of shares of common stock outstanding. Any preferred dividend requirements must be sub-

WEAVER COMPANY LTD.
Comparative Income Statement
Years Ended December 31

	Year 2	Year 1	Increase or (Decrease) Dollars	%	Percentage of Net Sales Year 2	Year 1
Net sales	$900,000	$750,000	$150,000	20.0	100.0	100.0
Cost of goods sold	585,000	468,800	116,200	24.9	65.0	62.5
Gross profit on sales	$315,000	$281,200	$ 33,800	12.0	35.0	37.5
Operating expenses:						
Selling expenses	$117,000	$ 75,000	$ 42,000	56.0	13.0	10.0
Administrative expenses	126,000	94,500	31,500	33.3	14.0	12.6
Total operating expenses	$243,000	$169,500	$ 73,500	43.4	27.0	22.6
Operating income	$ 72,000	$111,700	$ (39,700)	(35.6)	8.0	14.9
Interest expense	12,000	15,000	(3,000)	(20.0)	1.3	2.0
Income before income taxes	$ 60,000	$ 96,700	$ (36,700)	(38.0)	6.7	12.9
Income taxes	23,400	44,200	(20,800)	(47.1)	2.6	5.9
Net income	$ 36,600	$ 52,500	$ (15,900)	(30.3)	4.1	7.0
Earnings per share of common stock	$6.12	$11.63	$5.51	(47.4)		

WEAVER COMPANY LTD.
Statement of Retained Earnings
Years Ended December 31

	Year 2	Year 1	Increase or (Decrease) Dollars	%
Balance, beginning of year	$176,000	$149,500	$26,500	14.0
Net income	36,600	52,500	(15,900)	(30.3)
	$212,600	$202,000	$10,600	4.4
Less: Dividends on common stock	$ 24,000	$ 20,000	$ 4,000	20.0
Dividends on preferred stock	6,000	6,000		
	$ 30,000	$ 26,000	$ 4,000	15.4
Balance, end of year	$182,600	$176,000	$ 6,600	3.0

tracted from net income to determine income available for common stock, as shown in the following computations for Weaver Company Ltd.:

Earnings per Share of Common Stock

		Year 2	Year 1
Net income		$36,600	$52,500
Less: Preferred dividend requirements		6,000	6,000
Net income available for common stock	(a)	$30,600	$46,500
Shares of common outstanding, end of year	(b)	5,000	4,000
Earnings per share of common stock (a ÷ b)		$6.12	$11.63

Earnings related to number of common shares outstanding

Earnings per share of common stock are shown in the income statement below the net income figure. When the income statement includes extraordinary items, the earnings per share of common stock are reported in the income statement in three amounts as follows: (1) before extraordinary items, (2) extraordinary gain (or loss), and (3) net income. The Weaver Company Ltd. had no extraordinary items and thus the amount earned per share is computed by dividing the net income available for common by the number of shares of common stock outstanding at the end of each year.[4]

DIVIDEND YIELD AND PRICE-EARNINGS RATIO The importance of dividends varies among stockholders. Earnings reinvested in the business should produce an increase in the net income of the firm and thus tend to make each share of stock more valuable. Because the federal income tax rates applicable to dividend income are often much higher than the rate of tax on capital gains from the sale of shares of stock, some stockholders may prefer that the company reinvest most of its earnings. Others may be more interested in dividend income despite the tax disadvantage.

If we compare the merits of alternative investment opportunities, we should relate earnings and dividends per share to market value of stock. Dividends per share divided by market price per share determines the *yield* rate of a company's stock. Net income per share divided by market price per share determines the *earnings rate* of a company's stock. In financial circles earnings performance of common stock is often expressed as a *price-earnings ratio* by dividing the price per share by the net income per share. Thus, a stock selling for $60 per share and earning $3 per share may be said to have a price-earnings ratio of 20 times earnings ($60 ÷ $3).

Assume that the 1,000 additional shares of common stock issued by Weaver Company Ltd. early in Year 2 received the full dividend of $4.80

[4]When shares of stock are issued or retired during the period or when convertible bonds, convertible preferred stock, or options to purchase stock are outstanding, the computation and reporting of earnings per share are much more complicated. In such cases, earnings per share are based on the *weighted average* number of shares actually outstanding during the period; in addition, *fully diluted* earnings per share are presented on the assumption that all convertible securities are exchanged for common stock and that all options to acquire common stock are exercised. For a complete discussion of the complex procedures required under such circumstances, see *CICA Handbook,* Section 3500.

paid in Year 2. When these new shares were issued, Weaver Company Ltd. announced that it planned to continue indefinitely the $4.80 dividend per common share currently being paid. With this assumption and the use of assumed market prices of the common stock at December 31, Year 1 and Year 2, the earnings per share and dividend yield may be summarized as follows:

Earnings and dividends related to market price of common stock

Earnings and Dividends per Share of Common Stock

Date	Assumed Market Value per Share	Earnings per Share	Price- Earnings Ratio	Dividends per Share	Dividend Yield, %
Dec. 31, Year 1	$125	$11.63	11	$5.00	4.0
Dec. 31, Year 2	$100	$ 6.12	16	$4.80	4.8

The decline in market value during Year 2 presumably reflects the decrease in earnings per share. An investor appraising this stock at December 31, Year 2, would consider whether a price-earnings ratio of 16 and a dividend yield of 4.8% represented a satisfactory situation in the light of alternative investment opportunities open to him. Obviously he would also place considerable weight on his estimates of the company's prospective future earnings and their probable effect on the future market value of the stock.

BOOK VALUE PER SHARE OF COMMON STOCK   The procedures for computing book value per share were fully described in Chapter 17 and will not be repeated here. We will, however, determine the book value per share of common stock for the Weaver Company Ltd.

Book Value per Share of Common Stock

	Year 2	Year 1
Why did book value per share decrease? Common stockholders' equity:		
Common stock	$250,000	$200,000
Premium on common stock	70,000	40,000
Retained earnings	182,600	176,000
Total common stockholders' equity . . . .(a)	$502,600	$416,000
Shares of common stock outstanding . . . .(b)	5,000	4,000
Book value per share of common stock (a ÷ b)	$100.52	$104.00

During Year 2, book value of common stock was increased as a result of earnings: book value was reduced as a result of dividend payments and the sale of 1,000 additional shares of stock at $80 per share, a figure significantly below per-share book value.

REVENUE AND EXPENSE ANALYSIS   The trend of earnings of the Weaver Company Ltd. is unfavorable and stockholders would want to know the reasons for the decline in net income. The comparative income statement on page 633 shows that despite a 20% increase in net sales, net income fell from $52,500 in Year 1 to $36,600 in Year 2, a decline of 30.3%. The *net income as a percentage of net sales* went from 7.0% to only 4.1%. The primary causes of this decline were the increases in selling expenses (56.0%), in administrative expenses (33.3%), and in the cost of goods sold (24.9%), all exceeding the 20% increase in net sales.

These observations suggest the need for further investigation. Suppose we find that the Weaver Company Ltd. cut its selling prices in Year 2. This fact would explain the decrease in *gross profit rate* from 37.5 to 35% and would also show that sales volume in physical units rose more than 20%, since it takes proportionally more sales at lower prices to produce a given increase in dollar sales. If reduced sales prices and increased volume had been accomplished with little change in expenses, the effect on net income would have been favorable. Operating expenses, however, rose by $73,500, resulting in a $39,700 decrease in operating income.

The next step would be to find which expenses increased and why. An investor may be handicapped here, because detailed operating expenses are not usually shown in published statements. Some conclusions, however, can be reached on the basis of even the condensed information available in the comparative income statement for the Weaver Company Ltd. shown on page 633.

The $42,000 increase in selling expenses presumably reflects greater selling effort during Year 2 in an attempt to improve sales volume. However, the growth in selling expenses from 10 to 13% of net sales indicates that the cost of this increased sales effort was not justified in terms of results. Even more disturbing is the change in administrative expenses. Some growth in administrative expenses might be expected to accompany increased sales volume, but because some of the expenses are fixed, the growth should be less than proportional to any increase in sales. The increase in administrative expenses from 12.6 to 14% of sales would be of serious concern to astute investors.

Management generally has greater control over operating expenses than over revenues. The *operating expense ratio* is often used as a measure of management's ability to control its operating expenses. The unfavorable trend in this ratio for the Weaver Company Ltd. is shown below:

Operating Expense Ratio

Does a higher operating expense ratio indicate higher net income?

		Year 2	Year 1
Operating expenses . . . .(a)		$243,000	$169,500
Net sales. . . . .(b)		$900,000	$750,000
Operating expense ratio (a ÷ b)		27.0%	22.6%

If management were able to increase the sales volume while at the same time increasing the gross profit rate and decreasing the operating expense ratio, the effect on net income could be quite dramatic. For example, if the Weaver Company Ltd. increased its sales in Year 3 by

11% to $1,000,000, increased its gross profit rate from 35 to 38%, and reduced the operating expense ratio from 27 to 24%, its operating income would increase from $72,000 to $140,000 ($1,000,000 – $620,000 – $240,000), an increase of over 94%.

RETURN ON TOTAL ASSETS An important test of management's ability to earn a return on funds supplied from all sources is the rate of return on total assets.

The income figure used in computing this ratio should be ***income before deducting interest expense,*** since interest is a payment to creditors for money used to ***acquire assets.*** Net income before interest reflects earnings throughout the year and therefore should be related to the average investment in assets during the year. The computation of this ratio for the Weaver Company Ltd. is shown below:

Percentage Return on Total Assets

Earnings related to investment in assets

		Year 2	*Year 1*
Net income		*$ 36,600*	*$ 52,500*
Add back: Interest expense		*12,000*	*15,000*
Income before interest expense	*(a)*	*$ 48,600*	*$ 67,500*
Total assets, beginning of year		*$860,000*	*$820,000*
Total assets, end of year		*950,000*	*860,000*
Average investment in assets	*(b)*	*$905,000*	*$840,000*
Return on total assets (a ÷ b)		*5.4%*	*8.0%*

This ratio shows that earnings per dollar of assets invested have fallen off in Year 2. If the same ratios were available for other companies of similar kind and size, the significance of this decline could be better appraised.

Management's effectiveness in employing assets can be measured by dividing sales for the year by the average assets used in producing these sales. In computing this ***asset turnover*** rate, those assets not contributing directly to sales (such as long-term investments and loans to officers) should be excluded. A higher asset turnover suggests that management is making better use of assets, and if the earnings rate on sales remains relatively constant, a higher rate of return on total assets will result.[5]

[5] In order to show that the return on total assets is dependent on both the asset turnover rate and the earnings rate on sales, we can develop the following formula:

$$\frac{\text{Sales}}{\text{Assets}} \times \frac{\text{Net Income}}{\text{Sales}} = \text{Return on Assets}$$

If we assume sales of $100, assets of $50, and net income of $10, the formula yields the following result:

$$\frac{\$100}{\$50} \times \frac{\$10}{\$100} = 20\%$$

The asset turnover (2 times) multiplied by earnings rate on sales (10%) results in a 20% return on assets. Assume that management is able to improve the asset turnover by increasing sales to $200 without increasing total assets and that the earnings rate on sales actually declines to 8%. Then the formula yields:

$$\frac{\$200}{\$50} \times \frac{\$16}{\$200} = 32\%$$

Despite a lower earnings rate on sales (8%), the return on total assets increased dramatically because assets were more effectively utilized, as indicated by the higher asset turnover rate of 4 times ($200 ÷ $50).

RETURN ON COMMON STOCKHOLDERS' EQUITY Because interest and dividends paid to creditors and preferred stockholders are fixed in amount, a company may earn a greater or smaller return on the common stockholders' equity than on its total assets. The computation of return on stockholders' equity for the Weaver Company Ltd. is shown below:

Return on Common Stockholders' Equity

			Year 2	Year 1
Net income			$ 36,600	$ 52,500
Less: Preferred dividend requirements			6,000	6,000
Net income available for common stock		(a)	$ 30,600	$ 46,500
Common stockholders' equity, beginning of year			$416,000	$389,500
Common stockholders' equity, end of year			502,600	416,000
Average common stockholders' equity		(b)	$459,300	$402,750
Return on common stockholders' equity (a ÷ b)			6.7%	11.6%

Does trading on the equity benefit common stockholders?

In both years the rate of return to common stockholders was higher than the return on total assets, because the average combined rate of interest paid to creditors and dividends to preferred stockholders was less than the rate earned on each dollar of assets used in the business.

Financing with fixed-return securities is often called *trading on the equity.* Results may be favorable or unfavorable to holders of common stock:

1 If the rate of return on total assets is *greater* than the average rate of payment to creditors and preferred stockholders, the common stockholders will *gain* from trading on the equity. This was the case in the Weaver Company Ltd.

2 If the rate of return on total assets is *smaller* than the average rate of payments to creditors and preferred stockholders, the common stockholders will *lose* from trading on the equity.

EQUITY RATIO The equity ratio measures the proportion of the total assets financed by stockholders, as distinguished from creditors. It is computed by dividing total stockholders' equity by total assets (or the sum of liabilities and stockholders' equity, which is the same). The equity ratio for the Weaver Company Ltd. is determined as follows:

Equity Ratio

			Year 2	Year 1
Total assets		(a)	$950,000	$860,000
Total stockholders' equity		(b)	$602,600	$516,000
Equity ratio (b ÷ a)			63.4%	60.0%

Proportion of assets financed by stockholders

The Weaver Company Ltd. has a higher equity ratio in Year 2 than in Year 1. Is this favorable or unfavorable?

From the common stockholder's viewpoint, a low equity ratio (that is, a large proportion of financing supplied by creditors) will produce maximum benefits from trading on the equity if management is able to earn a rate of return on assets greater than the rate of interest paid to creditors. However, a low equity ratio can be very unfavorable if the rate of return on total assets falls below the rate of interest paid to creditors. Furthermore, if a business incurs so much debt that it is unable to meet the required interest or principal payments, creditors may force liquidation or reorganization of the business, to the detriment of stockholders.

Because of these factors, the equity ratio is usually judged by stockholders in the light of the probable stability of the company's earnings, as well as the rate of earnings in relation to the rate of interest paid to creditors.

As we saw earlier in our analysis, trading on the equity from the common stockholder's viewpoint can also be accomplished through the issuance of preferred stock. Since preferred stock dividends are not deductible for income tax purposes, however, the advantage gained in this respect will usually be much smaller than in the case of debt financing.

Analysis by long-term creditors

Bondholders and other long-term creditors are primarily interested in three factors: (*1*) the rate of return on their investment, (*2*) the firm's ability to meet its interest requirements, and (*3*) the firm's ability to repay the principal of the debt when it falls due.

YIELD RATE ON BONDS The yield rate on bonds or other long-term indebtedness cannot be computed in the same manner as the yield rate on shares of stock, because bonds, unlike stocks, have a definite maturity date and amount. The ownership of a 6%, 10-year bond represents the right to receive $1,000 at the end of 10 years and the right to receive $60 per year during each of the next 10 years. If the market price of this bond is $950, the yield rate on an investment in the bond is the rate of interest that will make the present value of these two contractual rights equal to $950. Determining the effective interest rate on such an investment requires the use of compound interest tables, a discussion of which is reserved to a more advanced coverage of this subject. We can, however, generalize the relation between yield rate and bond price as follows: *The yield rate varies inversely with changes in the market price of the bond.* If the price of a bond is above maturity value, the yield rate is less than the bond interest rate; if the price of a bond is below maturity value, the yield rate is higher than the bond interest rate.

NUMBER OF TIMES INTEREST EARNED Long-term creditors have learned from experience that one of the best indications of the safety of their investment is the fact that, over the life of the debt, the company has sufficient income to cover its interest requirements by a wide margin. A failure to cover interest requirements may have serious repercussions on the stability and solvency of the firm.

A common measure of debt safety is the ratio of income available for the payment of interest to the annual interest expense, called *times interest earned.* This computation for the Weaver Company Ltd. would be:

Number of Times Interest Earned

		Year 2	Year 1
Operating income (before interest and income taxes) . . . . . *(a)*		*$72,000*	*$111,700*
Annual interest expense . . . . *(b)*		*$12,000*	*$ 15,000*
Times interest earned (a ÷ b)		*6.0*	*7.4*

Long-term creditors watch this ratio

The decline in the ratio during Year 2 is unfavorable, but a ratio of 6.0 times interest earned for that year would still be considered quite adequate.

Since businessmen and investors are strongly conditioned to an after-tax view of corporate affairs, the times interest earned ratio is often computed by a more conservative method of taking net income (after taxes) plus interest expense and dividing this total by the annual interest expense.

DEBT RATIO Long-term creditors are interested in the amount of debt outstanding in relation to the amount of capital contributed by stockholders. The *debt ratio* is computed by dividing total liabilities by total assets, shown below for the Weaver Company Ltd.

Debt Ratio

		Year 2	Year 1
Total liabilities . . . . *(a)*		*$347,400*	*$344,000*
Total assets (or total liabilities & stockholders' equity) . . . *(b)*		*$950,000*	*$860,000*
Debt ratio (a ÷ b)		*36.6%*	*40.0*

What portion of total assets is financed by debt?

From a creditor's viewpoint, the lower the debt ratio (or the higher the equity ratio) the better, since this means that stockholders have contributed the bulk of the funds to the business, and therefore the margin of protection to creditors against a shrinkage of the assets is high. When large amounts of debt fall due, repayment in some form must be made. On the other hand, dividend payments to preferred and common stockholders are contingent upon the profitability of the business. Furthermore, the amounts invested by stockholders do not fall due on a certain date as do liabilities.

Analysis by preferred stockholders

If preferred stock is convertible, the interests of preferred stockholders are similar to those of common stockholders, previously discussed. If preferred stock is not convertible, the interests of preferred stockholders are more closely comparable to those of long-term creditors. (In this discussion we shall ignore participating preferred stock because such issues are extremely rare.)

Preferred stockholders are interested in the yield on their investment. The yield is computed by dividing the dividend per share by the market value per share. The dividend per share of Weaver Company Ltd. preferred stock is $6. If we assume that the market value at December 31, Year 2, is $80 per share, the yield rate at that time would be 7.5% ($6 ÷ $80).

The primary measurement of the safety of an investment in preferred stock is the ability of the firm to meet its preferred dividend requirements. The best test of this ability is the ratio of the net income available to pay the preferred dividend to the amount of the annual dividend, as shown below.

Times Preferred Dividends Earned

		Year 2	Year 1
Net income available to pay preferred dividends . . . .(a)		$36,600	$52,500
Annual preferred dividend requirements . . . .(b)		$ 6,000	$ 6,000
Times dividends earned (a ÷ b)		6.1	8.8

Is the preferred dividend safe? (marginal note)

Although the margin of protection declined in Year 2, the annual preferred dividend requirement appears well-protected.

Analysis by short-term creditors

Bankers and other short-term creditors share the interest of stockholders and bondholders in the profitability and long-run stability of a business. Their primary interest, however, is in the current position of the firm—its ability to generate sufficient funds (working capital) to meet current operating needs and to pay current debts promptly. Thus the analysis of financial statements by a banker considering a short-term loan, or by a trade creditor investigating the credit position of a customer, is likely to center on the working capital position of the prospective debtor.

AMOUNT OF WORKING CAPITAL The amount of working capital is measured by the *excess of current assets over current liabilities.* The details of the working capital of the Weaver Company Ltd. are shown on page 642. This schedule shows that current assets increased $102,000, while current liabilities rose by only $53,400, with the result that working capital increased $48,600. There was a shift in the composition of the current assets and current liabilities; cash dropped from 13.9 to 9.8% of current assets, and inventories rose from 41.6 to 46.1%. The increase in notes and accounts payable is significant both in amount and in percentage terms. We may surmise that the decline in accrued liabilities was caused primarily by a reduction in income tax liabilities in Year 2, as a result of the fall in net income previously noted.

WEAVER COMPANY LTD.
Comparative Schedule of Working Capital
As of December 31

	Year 2	Year 1	Increase or (Decrease) Dollars	%	Percentage of Total Current Items Year 2	Year 1
Current assets:						
Cash	$ 38,000	$ 40,000	$ (2,000)	(5.0)	9.8	13.9
Receivables (net)	117,000	86,000	31,000	36.0	30.0	29.9
Inventories	180,000	120,000	60,000	50.0	46.1	41.6
Prepaid expenses	55,000	42,000	13,000	31.0	14.1	14.6
Total current assets	$390,000	$288,000	$102,000	35.4	100.0	100.0
Current liabilities:						
Notes payable to creditors	$ 50,000	$ 10,000	$ 40,000	400.0	33.9	10.7
Accounts payable	66,000	30,000	36,000	120.0	44.8	31.9
Accrued liabilities	31,400	54,000	(22,600)	(42.0)	21.3	57.4
Total current liabilities	$147,400	$ 94,000	$ 53,400	56.8	100.0	100.0
Working capital	$242,600	$194,000	$ 48,600	25.0		

THE CURRENT RATIO One means of further evaluating these changes in working capital is to observe the relationship between current assets and current liabilities, a test known as the *current ratio.* The current ratio for the Weaver Company Ltd. is computed below:

Current Ratio

		Year 2	Year 1
Does this indicate satisfactory debt-paying ability?	Total current assets ... (a)	$390,000	$288,000
	Total current liabilities ... (b)	$147,400	$ 94,000
	Current ratio (a ÷ b)	2.6	3.1

Despite the increase of $48,600 in the amount of working capital in Year 2, current assets per dollar of current liabilities declined. The margin of safety (current ratio), however, still appears satisfactory.

In interpreting the current ratio, a number of factors should be kept in mind:

1 Creditors tend to feel that the larger the current ratio the better; however, from a managerial view there is an upper limit. Too high a current ratio may indicate that capital is not productively used in the business.

2 Because creditors tend to stress the current ratio as an indication of short-term solvency, some firms may take conscious steps to improve this ratio just before statements are prepared at the end of a fiscal period for sub-mission to bankers or other creditors. This may be done by postponing purchases, allowing inventories to fall, pressing collections on accounts receivable, and using all available cash to pay off current liabilities.

3 The current ratio computed at the end of a fiscal year may not be repre-sentative of the current position of the company throughout the year. Since many firms arrange their fiscal year to end during an ebb in the seasonal swing of business activity, the current ratio at year-end is likely to be more favorable than at any other time during the year.

Use of both the current ratio and the amount of working capital helps to place debt-paying ability in its proper perspective. For example, if Company X has current assets of $20,000 and current liabilities of $10,000 and Company Y has current assets of $2,000,000 and current liabilities of $1,990,000, both companies would have $10,000 of working capital, but the current position of Company X is clearly superior to that of Company Y. If the current ratio were computed for both companies, the difference would be clearly revealed.

As another example, assume that Company A and Company B both have current ratios of 3 to 1. However, Company A has working capital of $20,000 and Company B has working capital of $200,000. Although both companies appear to be good credit risks, Company B would no doubt be able to qualify for a much *larger* bank loan than would Company A.

A widely used rule of thumb is that a current ratio of 2 to 1 or better is satisfactory. Like all rules of thumb this is an arbitrary standard, subject to numerous exceptions and qualifications.

QUICK RATIO Because inventories and prepaid expenses are further removed from conversion into cash than other current assets, a ratio known as the *quick ratio* or *acid-test ratio* is sometimes computed as a supplement to the current ratio. This ratio compares the highly liquid current assets (cash, marketable securities, and receivables) with current liabilities. The Weaver Company Ltd. has no marketable securities; its quick ratio is computed as follows:

Quick Ratio

		Year 2	Year 1
A measure of liquidity	Quick assets (cash and receivables) . . . .(a)	$155,000	$126,000
	Current liabilities. . . . .(b)	$147,400	$ 94,000
	Quick ratio (a ÷ b).	1.1	1.3

Here again the analysis reveals an unfavorable trend. Whether the quick ratio is adequate depends on the amount of receivables included among quick assets and the average time required to collect receivables as compared to the credit period extended by suppliers. If the credit periods extended to customers and granted by creditors are roughly equal, a quick ratio of 1.0 or better would be considered satisfactory.

In recent years, many analysts have made reference to a *liquidity ratio* of corporations as a useful measure of immediate ability to pay short-term debts. This ratio is computed by dividing the total of cash and government securities owned by the total current liabilities outstanding.

INVENTORY TURNOVER The cost of goods sold figure on the income statement represents the total cost of all goods that have been transferred out of inventories during any given period. Therefore the relationship between cost of goods sold and the average balance of inventories maintained throughout the year indicates the number of times that inventories "turn over" and are replaced each year.

Ideally we should total the inventories at the end of each month and divide by 12 to obtain an average inventory. This information is not always available, however, and the nearest substitute is a simple average of the inventory at the beginning and at the end of the year. This tends to overstate the turnover rate, since many companies choose an accounting year that ends when inventories are at a minimum.

Assuming that only beginning and ending inventories are available, the computation of inventory turnover for the Weaver Company Ltd. may be illustrated as follows:

Inventory Turnover

		Year 2	Year 1
Cost of goods sold	(a)	$585,000	$468,800
Inventory, beginning of year		$120,000	$100,000
Inventory, end of year		180,000	120,000
Average inventory	(b)	$150,000	$110,000
Average inventory turnover per year (a ÷ b)		3.9 times	4.3 times
Average days to turn over (divide 365 days by inventory turnover)		94 days	85 days

What does inventory turnover mean?

The trend indicated by this analysis is unfavorable, since the average investment in inventories in relation to the cost of goods sold is rising. Stating this another way, the company required on the average 9 days more during Year 2 to turn over its inventories than during Year 1. Furthermore, the inventory status *at the end of the year* has changed even more: At the end of Year 1 there were 94 days' sales in the ending inventory ($120,000/$468,800 × 365 days) compared to 112 days' sales in the ending inventory at the end of Year 2 ($180,000/$585,000 × 365 days).

The relation between inventory turnover and gross profits per dollar of sales may be significant. A high inventory turnover and a low gross profit rate frequently go hand in hand. This, however, is merely another way of saying that if the gross profit rate is low, a high volume of business is necessary to produce a satisfactory return on total assets. Although a high inventory turnover is usually regarded as a good sign, a rate that is high in relation to that of similar firms may indicate that the company is losing sales by a failure to maintain an adequate stock of goods to serve its customers promptly.

ACCOUNTS RECEIVABLE TURNOVER The turnover of accounts receivable is computed in a manner comparable to that just described for inventories. The ratio between the net sales for the period and the average balance in accounts receivable is a rough indication of the average time required to convert receivables into cash. Ideally, a monthly average of receivables should be used, and only *sales on credit* should be included in the sales figure. For illustrative purposes, we shall assume that Weaver Company Ltd. sells entirely on credit and that only the beginning and ending balances of receivables are available:

Accounts Receivable Turnover

		Year 2	Year 1
Are Net sales on credit	(a)	$900,000	$750,000
customers Receivables, beginning of year		$ 86,000	$ 80,000
paying Receivables, end of year		117,000	86,000
promptly? Average receivables	(b)	$101,500	$ 83,000
Receivable turnover per year (a ÷ b)		8.9 times	9.0 times
Average age of receivables (*divide 365 days by receivable*			
turnover)		41 days	41 days

There has been no significant change in the average time required to collect receivables. The interpretation of the average age of receivables would depend upon the company's credit terms and the seasonal activity immediately before year-end. If the company grants 30-day credit terms to its customers, for example, the above analysis indicates that accounts receivable collections are lagging. If the terms were for 60 days, however, there is evidence that collections are being made ahead of schedule. On the other hand, if the sales in the last month of the year were unusually large, the average age of receivables as computed above can be misleading.

The *operating cycle* in Year 2 was approximately 135 days (computed by adding the 94 days required to turn over inventory and the average 41 days required to collect receivables). This compares to an operating cycle of only 126 days in Year 1. The operating cycle measures the time interval required to convert inventory to accounts receivable and then accounts receivable to cash. A trend toward a longer operating cycle suggests that inventory and receivables are increasing relative to sales and that profits may be hurt because of lower sales volume and an increasing investment in current assets.

Summary of analytical measurements

The basic ratios and other measurements discussed in this chapter and their significance are summarized below:

Ratio or Other Measurement	Method of Computation	Significance
1 Earnings per share on common stock	$$\frac{\text{Net income} - \text{preferred dividends}}{\text{Shares of common outstanding}}$$	Gives the amount of earnings applicable to a share of common stock.
2 Dividend yield	$$\frac{\text{Dividend per share}}{\text{Market price per share}}$$	Shows the rate earned by stockholders based on current price for a share of stock.
3 Price-earnings ratio	$$\frac{\text{Market price per share}}{\text{Earnings per share}}$$	Indicates whether price of stock is in line with earnings.
4 Book value per share of common stock	$$\frac{\text{Common stockholders' equity}}{\text{Shares of common outstanding}}$$	Measures net assets as reported on books behind each share of stock.
5 Operating expense ratio	$$\frac{\text{Operating expenses}}{\text{Net sales}}$$	Indicates management's ability to control expenses.
6 Return on total assets	$$\frac{\text{Net income} + \text{interest expense}}{\text{Average investment in assets}}$$	Measures the productivity of assets regardless of capital structures.
7 Return on common stockholders' equity	$$\frac{\text{Net income} - \text{preferred dividends}}{\text{Average common stockholders' equity}}$$	Indicates the earning power on common stockholders' equity.
8 Equity ratio	$$\frac{\text{Total stockholders' equity}}{\text{Total assets}}$$	Shows the protection to creditors and the extent of trading on the equity.
9 Number of times interest earned	$$\frac{\text{Operating income}}{\text{Annual interest expense}}$$	Measures the coverage of interest requirements, particularly on long-term debt.
10 Debt ratio	$$\frac{\text{Total liabilities}}{\text{Total assets}}$$	Indicates the percentage of assets financed through borrowing; it shows the extent of trading on the equity.
11 Times preferred dividends earned	$$\frac{\text{Net income}}{\text{Annual preferred dividends}}$$	Shows the adequacy of current earnings to pay dividends on preferred stock.
12 Current ratio	$$\frac{\text{Current assets}}{\text{Current liabilities}}$$	Measures short-run debt-paying ability.
13 Quick (acid-test) ratio	$$\frac{\text{Quick assets}}{\text{Current liabilities}}$$	Measures the short-term liquidity of a firm.

14 Inventory turnover	$\dfrac{\text{Cost of goods sold}}{\text{Average inventory}}$	Indicates management's ability to control the investment in inventory.
15 Accounts receivable turnover	$\dfrac{\text{Net sales on credit}}{\text{Average receivables}}$	Indicates reasonableness of accounts receivable balance and effectiveness of collections.

The student should keep in mind the fact that the full significance of any of the foregoing ratios or other measurements depends on the *direction of its trend* and on its *relationship to some predetermined standard* or industry average.

DEMONSTRATION PROBLEM FOR YOUR REVIEW

Given below are the financial statements for the Knight Company Ltd. for Year 2 and Year 1, accompanied by miscellaneous additional information. From these statements and additional information, certain ratios and other measurements can be computed in the process of evaluating the financial position and results of operations for the company.

	Year 2	Year 1
Cash	$ 35,000	$ 25,000
Accounts receivable (net)	91,000	90,000
Merchandise inventory	160,000	140,000
Prepaid expenses	4,000	5,000
Investments in real estate	90,000	100,000
Equipment	880,000	640,000
Less: Accumulated depreciation	(260,000)	(200,000)
	$1,000,000	$ 800,000
Accounts payable	$ 105,000	$ 46,000
Taxes payable and other accrued liabilities	40,000	25,000
Bonds payable—8%	280,000	280,000
Premium on bonds payable	3,600	4,000
Common stock, $5 par	165,000	110,000
Retained earnings	406,400	335,000
	$1,000,000	$ 800,000
Sales (net of discounts and allowances)	$2,200,000	$1,600,000
Cost of goods sold	1,606,000	1,120,000
Gross profit on sales	$ 594,000	$ 480,000
Operating expenses	(330,000)	(352,000)
Income taxes	(110,000)	(48,000)
Gain on sale of real estate	12,400	-0-
Net income	$ 166,400	$ 80,000

Cash dividends of $40,000 were paid and a 50% stock dividend was distributed early in Year 2. All sales were made on credit at a relatively uniform rate during the year. Inventories and receivables did not fluctuate materially. The market value of the company's stock on December 31, Year 2, was $86 per share; on December 31, Year 1, it was $43.50 (before the 50% stock dividend) distributed in Year 2.

Instructions
Compute the following for Year 2 and Year 1:
 (1) Quick ratio
 (2) Current ratio
 (3) Equity ratio
 (4) Debt ratio
 (5) Book value per share of stock (based on shares outstanding after 50% stock dividend in Year 2)
 (6) Earnings per share (including extraordinary item) based on number of shares outstanding at end of Year 2.
 (7) Price-earnings ratio
 (8) Gross profit percentage
 (9) Operating expense ratio
 (10) Income before extraordinary item as a percentage of net sales
 (11) Inventory turnover (Assume an average inventory of $150,000 for both years.)
 (12) Accounts receivable turnover (Assume average accounts receivable of $90,000 for Year 1.)
 (13) Times bond interest earned (based on net income plus interest expense)

QUESTIONS

1 a What groups are interested in the financial affairs of a publicly owned corporation?
  b List some of the more important sources of financial information for investors.

2 In financial statement analysis, what is the basic objective of observing trends in data and ratios? What is an alternative standard of comparison?

3 In financial analysis, what information is produced by computing a ratio that is not available in a simple observation of the underlying data?

4 Explain the distinction between *percentage change* and *component percentages.*

5 "Although net income declined this year as compared with last year, it increased from 6 to 10% of net sales." Are sales increasing or decreasing?

6 Differentiate between *horizontal* and *vertical* analysis.

7 Assume that the Chemco Corporation Ltd. is engaged in the manufacture and distribution of a variety of chemicals. In analyzing the financial statements of this corporation, why would you want to refer to the ratios and other measurements of companies in the chemical industry? In comparing the financial results of the Chemco Corporation Ltd. with another chemical company, why would you be interested in the accounting procedures used by the two companies?

8 What are the key objectives of financial analysis? What types of nonaccounting information may be relevant in evaluating the future profitability of a company?

9 What single ratio do you think should be of greatest interest to:
  a a banker considering a short-term loan?
  b a common stockholder?
  c an insurance company considering a long-term mortgage loan?

10 Modern Company Ltd. earned (after taxes) an 8% return on its total assets. Current liabilities are 10% of total assets and long-term bonds carrying a $6\frac{1}{2}\%$ coupon rate are equal to 30% of total assets. There is no preferred stock. Would you expect the rate of return on stockholders' equity to be greater or less than 8%? Explain.

11 In deciding whether a company's equity ratio is favorable or unfavorable, creditors and stockholders may have different views. Why?

12 Company A has a current ratio of 5 to 1. Company B has a current ratio of 3 to 1. Does this mean that A's operating cycle is longer than B's? Why?

13 An investor states, "I bought this stock for $50 several years ago and it now sells for $100. It paid $5 per share in dividends last year so I'm earning 10% on my investment." Criticize this statement.

14 Company C experiences a considerable seasonal variation in its business. The high point in the year's activities comes in November, the low point in July. During which month would you expect the company's current ratio to be higher? If the company were choosing a fiscal year for accounting purposes, how would you advise them?

15 Both the inventory turnover and accounts receivable turnover increased from 10 times to 15 times from Year 1 to Year 2, but net income decreased. Can you offer some possible reasons for this?

EXERCISES

Ex. 21-1 Given below is a condensed balance sheet for the Miller Company Ltd.

Assets		Liabilities & Stockholders' Equity	
Cash	$ 10,000	Current liabilities	$ 25,000
Accounts receivable	20,000	Long-term liabilities	50,000
Inventory	45,000	Capital stock, $10 par	100,000
Prepaid expense	15,000	Retained earnings	25,000
Plant assets (net)	100,000		
Other assets	10,000	Total liabilities &	
Total assets	$200,000	stockholders' equity	$200,000

During the latest year, the company earned a gross profit of $160,000 on sales of $400,000. Accounts receivable, inventory, and plant assets remained relatively constant during the year. From this information, compute the following:
a Current ratio
b Acid-test ratio
c Equity ratio
d Asset turnover
e Accounts receivable turnover (all sales are on credit)
f Inventory turnover
g Book value per share of capital stock

Ex. 21-2 The information below relates to the activities of a hardware store:

	Year 2	Year 1
Sales (terms 2/10, n/30)	$400,000	$300,000
Cost of goods sold	260,000	210,000
Inventory at end of year	47,500	52,500
Accounts receivable at end of year	80,000	25,000

Complete the following for Year 2:
a Gross profit percentage
b Inventory turnover
c Accounts receivable turnover

Ex. 21-3 The following information is available for the Adams Company Ltd.

	Year 2	Year 1
Total assets (40% of which are current)	$800,000	$650,000
Current liabilities.	$160,000	$200,000
Bonds payable, 7%	200,000	100,000
Capital stock, $10 par value	300,000	300,000
Retained earnings	140,000	50,000
Total liabilities & stockholders' equity.	$800,000	$650,000

The income tax rate is 50% and dividends of $12,000 were declared in Year 2.
Compute the following:
a Current ratio for Year 2 _____ and Year 1 _____
b Debt ratio for Year 2 _____ and Year 1 _____
c Earnings per share for Year 2 _____

Ex. 21-4 Figures for two companies engaged in the same line of business are presented below for the latest year:

	A Company	B Company
Sales (all on credit)	$1,600,000	$1,200,000
Total assets	800,000	400,000
Total liabilities	100,000	100,000
Average receivables.	200,000	100,000
Average inventory	240,000	140,000
Gross profit as a percentage of sales	40%	30%
Operating expenses as a percentage of sales	30%	18%
Net income as a percentage of sales	6%	8%

Compute the following for each company:
a Net income
b Net income as a percentage of total assets
c Net income as a percentage of stockholders' equity
d Accounts receivable turnover
e Inventory turnover

Ex. 21-5 Given below is the stockholders' equity for Thomas Lynch Ltd.

Nonparticipating and nonredeemable cumulative preferred stock, 5%,	
(dividends two years in arrears)	$ 200,000
Common stock, $1 par.	300,000
Retained earnings.	2,620,000
Total stockholders' equity.	$3,120,000

a Compute the book value per share of common stock.
b If the debt ratio for Thomas Lynch Ltd., is 40%, what is the amount of its total assets?

Ex. 21-6 The following information relates to the operations of the Senn Corporation Ltd.

Sales (60% on credit)	$2,500,000
Beginning inventory, Year 1	350,000
Purchases	2,100,000
Ending inventory, Year 1	?
Ending accounts receivable, Year 1	150,000

Sales are made at 25% above cost. Compute:
a The inventory turnover for Year 1.
b The number of days credit sales in accounts receivable at the end of Year 1. A year equals 365 days.

PROBLEMS

Group A

21A-1 The Universal Company Ltd. manufactures and distributes a full line of farm machinery. Given below for Year 1 is the income statement for the company and a common size summary for the industry in which the company operates:

	Universal Company	Industry Average
Sales (net)	$2,000,000	100%
Cost of goods sold	1,440,000	68
Gross profit on sales	$ 560,000	32%
Operating expenses:		
Selling	$ 160,000	7%
General and administrative	180,000	10
Total operating expenses	$ 340,000	17%
Operating income	$ 220,000	15%
Income taxes	100,000	6
Net income	$ 120,000	9%

Instructions
a Prepare a common size income statement comparing the results for the Universal Company Ltd. for Year 1 with the average for the farm machinery industry.
b Briefly mention the significance of the results obtained in the comparative income statement prepared in part (*a*).

21A-2 Listed below is the working capital information for the Rossmoor Corporation Ltd. at the end of Year 1:

Cash	$ 75,000
Temporary investments in marketable securities	40,000
Notes receivable—current	60,000
Accounts receivable	100,000
Allowance for uncollectible accounts	5,000

Inventory	80,000
Prepaid expenses	10,000
Notes payable within one year	30,000
Accounts payable	82,500
Accrued liabilities	7,500

The following transactions are completed early in Year 2:
 (0) Sold inventory costing $12,000 for $10,000.
 (1) Declared a cash dividend, $40,000.
 (2) Declared a 10% stock dividend.
 (3) Paid accounts payable, $20,000.
 (4) Purchased goods on account, $15,000.
 (5) Collected cash on accounts receivable, $30,000.
 (6) Borrowed cash on short-term note, $50,000.
 (7) Issued additional shares of capital stock for cash, $150,000.
 (8) Sold temporary investments costing $10,000 for $9,000.
 (9) Acquired temporary investments, $17,500.
 (10) Wrote off uncollectible accounts, $3,000.
 (11) Sold inventory costing $12,500 for $16,000.
 (12) Acquired plant and equipment for cash, $80,000.

Instructions
a Compute the following at the end of Year 1: (1) Current ratio, (2) acid-test ratio, and (3) working capital.
b Indicate the effect (increase, decrease, none) of each transaction listed above for Year 2 on the current ratio, acid-test ratio, and working capital. Use the following four-column format (Item 0 is given as an example):

	Effect on		
Item	**Current Ratio**	**Acid-test Ratio**	**Working Capital**
0	*Decrease*	*Increase*	*Decrease*

21A-3 The following information is taken from the records of the Young Corporation Ltd. at the end of Year 1:

Sales (all on credit)	$200,000
Cost of goods sold	120,000
Average inventory (fifo method)	30,000
Average accounts receivable	40,000
Net income for Year 1	20,000
Total assets at end of Year 1	250,000
Total liabilities at end of Year 1	140,000

The corporation did not declare dividends during the year and capital stock was neither issued nor retired. The liabilities consisted of accounts payable and accrued items; no interest expense was incurred.

Instructions From the information given, compute the following for Year 1:
a Inventory turnover
b Accounts receivable turnover
c Total operating expenses, assuming that income taxes amounted to $7,500
d Gross profit percentage
e Rate earned on average stockholders' equity
f Rate earned on total assets (Use end-of-year total.)
g Asset turnover rate (Assume that average total assets were $250,000.)

21A-4 Given below are selected balance sheet items and ratios for the Prospect Corporation Ltd. at June 30, 1973:

Total stockholders' equity (includes 100,000 shares of no-par value capital stock issued at $6 per share)	$1,000,000
Plant and equipment (net)	$ 470,000
Asset turnover rate per year (sales ÷ total assets)	3 times
Inventory turnover rate per year.	6 times
Average accounts receivable collection period (assuming a 360-day year) .	30 days
Gross profit percentage	30%
Ratio of current liabilities to stockholders' equity (there is no long-term debt)	1.2 to 1
Acid-test ratio (quick ratio)	0.8 to 1

Assume that balance sheet figures represent average amounts and that all sales are made on account.

Instructions From the foregoing information, construct a balance sheet for the Prospect Corporation Ltd. as of June 30, 1973, in as much detail as the data permit.

21A-5 East Co. Ltd. and West Co. Ltd. operate in the same industry and are generally comparable in terms of product lines, scope of operations, and the accounting methods used in preparing financial statements. The financial information given below for these two companies (except market price per share of stock) is stated in thousands of dollars and figures are as of the end of the current year:

Assets	East Co. Ltd.	West Co. Ltd.
Current assets	$ 97,450	$132,320
Plant and equipment	397,550	495,680
Less: Accumulated depreciation	(55,000)	(78,000)
Total assets	$440,000	$550,000

Liabilities & Stockholders' Equity	East Co. Ltd.	West Co. Ltd.
Current liabilities.	$ 34,000	$ 65,000
Bonds payable, 8%, due in 15 years	120,000	100,000
Capital stock, no par*	150,000	200,000
Retained earnings	136,000	185,000
Total liabilities & stockholders' equity	$440,000	$550,000

Analysis of retained earnings:	East Co. Ltd.	West Co. Ltd.
Balance, beginning of year	$125,200	$167,200
Net income for the year	19,800	37,400
Dividends	(9,000)	(19,600)
Balance, end of year	$136,000	$185,000

	East Co. Ltd.	West Co. Ltd.
Market price of capital stock, per share	$30	$61
*Number of shares of capital stock outstanding	6 million	8 million

Instructions
a Although market prices for the bonds are not stated, which company's bonds do you think will sell at the higher price per $1,000 bond? Which company's

bonds will probably yield the higher rate of return? (You may assume that the safer the bonds, according to your analysis, the lower the yield rate.)

b What are the dividend yield, the price-earnings ratio, and book value per share for the stock of each company? Which company's stock is a better investment?

Group B

21B-1 In the schedule below, certain items taken from the income statements of the Chavez Company Ltd. for two fiscal years ending January 31 have been expressed as a percentage of net sales:

	Percentage of Net Sales	
	Year 2	Year 1
Net sales.	100%	100%
Beginning inventory	10	16
Net purchases	68	60
Ending inventory	8	12
Selling expenses	13	15
Administrative expenses	8	9
Income taxes	4	5

Net sales were $1 million in Year 1 and increased by 20% in Year 2.

Instructions Did the net income increase or decrease in Year 2 as compared with Year 1? By how much? Prepare a comparative income statement to support your answer.

21B-2 Listed in the left-hand column below is a series of business transactions and events relating to the activities of the Plunkett Corporation Ltd. Opposite each transaction is listed a particular ratio used in financial analysis:

Transaction	Ratio
(1) Purchased inventory on open account.	Quick ratio
(2) A larger physical volume of goods was sold at smaller unit prices.	Gross profit percentage
(3) Corporation declared a cash dividend.	Current ratio
(4) An uncollectible account receivable was written off against the allowance account.	Current ratio
(5) Issued additional shares of common stock and used proceeds to retire long-term debt.	Rate of earnings on total assets
(6) Paid stock dividend on common stock, in common stock.	Earnings per share
(7) Operating income increased 25%; interest expense increased 10%.	Times interest charges earned
(8) Appropriated retained earnings.	Rate of return on stockholders' equity

(9) *During period of rising prices, company changed from fifo to lifo method of inventory pricing.*　　　*Inventory turnover*

(10) *Paid previously declared cash dividend.*　　　*Debt ratio*

(11) *Purchased factory supplies on open account.*　　　*Current ratio (assume that ratio is greater than 1:1)*

(12) *Issued shares of capital stock in exchange for patents.*　　　*Equity ratio*

Instructions What effect would each transaction or event have on the ratio listed opposite to it; that is, as a result of this event would the ratio increase, decrease, or remain unchanged? Why?

21B-3 The data below are taken from the records of the Woodcraft Company Ltd. at the close of the current year:

Accounts and notes payable.	$ 49,300
Accrued liabilities (including income taxes payable).	30,700
Cash	54,000
Inventories, beginning of year. . . . . . . :	42,300
Inventories, end of year.	66,900
Marketable securities	21,000
Operating expenses	107,000
Prepaid expenses	7,500
Income taxes expense (portion has already been paid)	39,400
Purchases (net)	351,600
Receivables, beginning of year (net of allowance)	85,400
Receivables, end of year (net of allowance)	70,600
Sales (net).	526,000

Instructions On the basis of this information, determine the following:
a Amount of working capital
b Current ratio
c Quick ratio
d Inventory turnover and days' sales in inventory
e Accounts receivable turnover and days' sales in accounts receivable
f Rate of gross profit on net sales
g Rate of net income on net sales

21B-4 The accountant for the Mobile Corporation Ltd. prepared the financial statements for Year 1, including all ratios, and agreed to bring them along on a hunting trip with the executives of the corporation. To his embarrassment, he found that he had only placed certain fragmentary information in his briefcase and had left the completed statements in his office. One hour before he was to present the financial statements to the executives, he was able to come up with the following information:

MOBILE CORPORATION LTD.
Balance Sheet
End of Year 1
(in thousands of dollars)

Assets			Liabilities & Stockholders' Equity		
Current assets:			Current liabilities	$	?
Cash	$	?	Long-term debt, 8% interest		?
Accounts receivable (net)		?	Total liabilities	$	?
Inventory		?	Stockholders' equity:		
Total current assets	$	?	Capital stock, $5 par . . . $300		
Plant assets:			Retained earnings 100		
Machinery and equipment $580			Total stockholders' equity . . .		400
Less: Accumulated					
depreciation 80		500	Total liabilities &		
Total assets	$	?	stockholders' equity	$	?

MOBILE CORPORATION LTD.
Income Statement
For Year 1
(in thousands of dollars)

Net sales.	$?
Cost of goods sold	?
Gross profit on sales (25% of net sales)	$?
Operating expenses	?
Operating income (10% of net sales)	$?
Interest expense	28
Income before income taxes	$?
Income taxes—40% of income before income taxes	?
Net income	$60

Additional information
(1) The equity ratio was 40%; the debt ratio was 60%.
(2) The only interest expense paid was on the long-term debt.
(3) The beginning inventory was $150,000; the average inventory turnover was 4.8 times. (Inventory turnover = cost of goods sold ÷ average inventory.)
(4) The current ratio was 2 to 1; the acid-test ratio was 1 to 1.
(5) The beginning balance in accounts receivable was $80,000; the average accounts receivable turnover for Year 1 was 12.8 times. All sales were made on account. (Average receivable turnover = net sales ÷ average accounts receivable.)

Instructions Using only the information available, the accountant asks you to help him complete the financial statements for the Mobile Corporation Ltd. Present supporting computations and explanations for all amounts appearing in the balance sheet and the income statement. *Hint:* In completing the income statement, start with the net income figure (60% of income before income taxes) and work up.

21B-5 Certain financial information relating to two companies, Lee Company Ltd. and Moe Company Ltd. as of the end of the current year, is shown below. All figures (except market price per share of stock) are in *thousands of dollars.*

Assets	Lee Company Ltd.	Moe Company Ltd.
Cash	$ 126.0	$ 180.0
Marketable securities, at cost	129.0	453.0
Accounts receivable, net	145.0	167.0
Inventories	755.6	384.3
Prepaid expenses	24.4	15.7
Plant and equipment, net	1,680.0	1,570.0
Intangibles and other assets	140.0	30.0
Total assets	$3,000.0	$2,800.0

Liabilities & Stockholders' Equity		
Accounts payable	$ 344.6	$ 304.1
Accrued liabilities, including income taxes	155.4	95.9
Bonds payable, 7%, due in 10 years	200.0	500.0
Capital stock ($10 par)	1,000.0	600.0
Premium on common stock	450.0	750.0
Retained earnings	850.0	550.0
Total liabilities & stockholders' equity	$3,000.0	$2,800.0

Analysis of retained earnings:		
Balance, beginning of year	$ 652.0	$ 430.0
Add: Net income	297.0	240.0
Less: Dividends	(99.0)	(120.0)
Balance, end of year	$ 850.0	$ 550.0
Market price per share of stock, end of year	$50	$40

Instructions Lee Company Ltd. and Moe Company Ltd. are in the same industry and are generally comparable in the nature of their operations and accounting procedures used. Write a short answer to each of the following questions, using whatever analytical computations you feel will best support your answer. Show the amounts used in calculating all ratios and percentages. Carry per-share computations to the nearest cent and percentages one place beyond the decimal point, for example, 9.8%.
a What is the book value per share of stock for each company?
b From the viewpoint of creditors, which company has a more conservative capital structure? Determine the percentage of total assets financed by each group.
c What are the price-earnings ratios and the dividend yield on the stock of each company?
d Which company is covering its bond interest by the greater margin?
e Which company has a more liquid financial position?

BUSINESS DECISION PROBLEM 21

Condensed comparative financial statements for Old Rivers Ltd., appear below:

OLD RIVERS LTD.
Comparative Balance Sheets
As of May 31
(in thousands of dollars)

Assets	Year 3	Year 2	Year 1
Current assets	$ 1,320	$ 870	$ 1,200
Plant and equipment (net of depreciation)	7,080	6,630	4,800
Total assets	$ 8,400	$ 7,500	$ 6,000

Liabilities & Stockholders' Equity

	Year 3	Year 2	Year 1
Current liabilities.	$ 738	$ 684	$ 600
Long-term liabilities	1,572	1,236	1,200
Capital stock ($10 par)	4,200	4,200	2,700
Retained earnings	1,890	1,380	1,500
Total liabilities & stockholders' equity	$ 8,400	$ 7,500	$ 6,000

OLD RIVERS LTD.
Comparative Income Statements
For Years Ended May 31
(in thousands of dollars)

	Year 3	Year 2	Year 1
Net sales.	$30,000	$25,000	$20,000
Cost of goods sold	19,500	15,500	12,000
Gross profit on sales	$10,500	$ 9,500	$ 8,000
Operating expenses	9,390	8,425	7,080
Income before income taxes	$ 1,110	$ 1,075	$ 920
Income taxes	510	500	420
Net income	$ 600	$ 575	$ 500
Cash dividends paid (plus 20% in stock in Year 2)	$90	$155	$135
Cash dividends per share	$0.21	$0.37	$0.50

Instructions

a Prepare a three-year comparative balance sheet in percentages rather than dollars, using Year 1 as the base year.

b Prepare common size comparative income statements for the three-year period, expressing all items as percentage components of net sales for each year.

c Comment on the significant trends and relationships revealed by the analytical computations in (*a*) and (*b*).

d Would you consider buying this company's stock if it is now selling for $11.50 per share? Why?

TWENTY-TWO

STATEMENT OF CHANGES IN FINANCIAL POSITION FUNDS FLOW ANALYSIS

The heartbeat of any profit-making enterprise is reflected in the pulsing rhythm of its operating cycle. The business obtains capital from various sources and invests it in revenue-producing assets. These investments are in turn converted into goods and services which are sold to customers. When customers pay their accounts, the company again has resources to apply against its debts and begin the operating cycle anew.

The balance sheet represents an attempt to reflect the overall financial position of the business at any given time in this recurring cycle of investment, recovery of investment, and reinvestment. The income statement shows the growth in the amount of resources as a result of operations. In a sense, the fate of any given business investment is read in the income statement, since it tells whether revenues are larger or smaller during any period than the cost of the resources used up in generating these revenues. In this chapter we introduce a third major financial statement generally prepared for a business unit, the **statement of changes in financial position**[1] and a related summary of cash movements, the **cash flow statement.**

---

[1] In *Opinion No. 19*, "Reporting Changes in Financial Position," issued in 1971, the Accounting Principles Board of the AICPA concluded (p. 373) that "information concerning the financing and investing activities of a business enterprise and the changes in its financial position for a period is essential for financial statement users, particularly owners and creditors, in making economic decisions. When financial statements purporting to present both financial position (balance sheet) and results of operations (statement of income and retained earnings) are issued, a statement summarizing changes in financial position should also be presented as a basic financial statement for each period for which an income statement is presented." Section 1540 of the *CICA Handbook* supports this view.

STATEMENT OF CHANGES IN FINANCIAL POSITION

A statement of changes in financial position shows the sources and uses of working capital during an accounting period. It also reports the financing and investing activities not directly affecting working capital. For example, the issuance of capital stock or bonds in exchange for equipment is both a financing and an investing transaction which does not affect working capital. However, in order to meet its objectives, the statement of changes in financial position should include such a transaction in order to give the reader a complete picture of the inflow and outflow of "financial resources" during an accounting period.

In published annual reports of corporations, the funds flow statement has often been labeled as *a statement of source and application of funds.*[2] A statement of changes in financial position is useful to management, creditors, investors, and financial analysts because it can help answer questions such as: What use was made of net income? Why have current assets declined even though net income has increased? How was new construction of plant and equipment financed? What became of the proceeds of the stock (or bond) issue? How much long-term debt or preferred stock was converted into common stock?

Working capital viewed as a fund of liquid resources

In ordinary usage, the term *funds* usually means cash. Businessmen and financial analysts, however, think of "funds" in a broader sense. Short-term credit is often used as a substitute for cash; notes and accounts payable as well as accrued liabilities are used to meet the short-term financing needs of a business. Current assets are constantly being converted into cash, which is used to pay current liabilities. The net amount of short-term liquid resources available to a firm at any given time, therefore, is represented by its working capital—the difference between current assets and current liabilities. This explains why it is natural to think of working capital as a fund of liquid resources on hand at any given time.

If working capital increases during a given fiscal period, this means that more working capital was generated than was used for various business purposes; if a decrease in working capital occurs, the reverse is true. One of the key purposes of the statement of changes in financial position is to explain fully the increase or decrease in working capital during a fiscal period. This is done by showing where working capital originated and how it was used.

[2] In 1970, 70% of the annual reports of major Canadian corporations used this title. Source: *Financial Reporting in Canada,* 1971, CICA, Toronto.

Sources and uses of working capital

Any transaction that increases the amount of working capital is a *source of working capital.* For example, the sale of merchandise for an amount greater than its cost is a source of working capital, because the increase in cash or receivables is greater than the decrease in inventories.

Any transaction that decreases working capital is a *use of working capital.* For example, either incurring a current liability to acquire a non-current asset or paying expenses in cash represents a decrease in working capital.

On the other hand, any transaction that affects current assets or current liabilities but does not result in a change in working capital is not a source or use of liquid funds (working capital). For example, the collection of an account receivable (which increases cash and decreases an account receivable by an equal amount) is not a source of liquid funds. Similarly, the payment of an account payable (which decreases cash and decreases an account payable by an equal amount) does not change the amount of working capital.

The principal sources and uses of working capital are listed below:

Sources of working capital:

Operations (revenues minus expenses that require the use of funds)
Sale of noncurrent assets
Borrowing through the use of long-term debt contracts
Issuing additional shares of capital stock

Uses of working capital:

Declaration of cash dividends
Repayment of long-term debt
Purchase of noncurrent assets

The relationship between working capital and other balance sheet accounts is illustrated in the diagram on page 662.

The shaded area in the diagram represents working capital, that is, current assets less current liabilities. The arrows flowing into the shaded area represent sources of working capital; the arrows flowing out of the shaded area represent uses of working capital. You may find it useful to refer to this diagram as you study the effect of transactions on working capital in the discussion and illustrations which follow.

Simple illustration

Let us begin with a very simple set of facts. Suppose that John Claire started a business as a single proprietorship on April 30 by investing $30,000 in cash; he rented a building on May 1 and completed the transactions shown on page 662 during the month of May.

Balance Sheet
End of Year 1

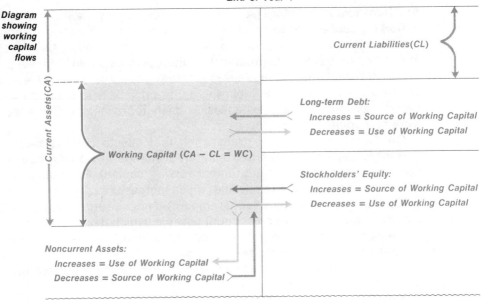

Diagram showing working capital flows

(1) Invested an additional $10,000 in the business.

(2) Purchased merchandise costing $40,000 on credit and sold three-fourths of this, also on credit, for $58,000.

(3) Collected $45,000 on receivables; paid $32,000 on accounts payable.

(4) Paid $15,500 in cash for operating expenses.

(5) Purchased land for the construction of a store. Gave $15,000 in cash and a six-month note for $12,000 in payment for the land.

(6) Withdrew $2,000 from the business for personal use.

Claire's financial statements at the end of May are shown below:

JOHN CLAIRE
Income Statement
Month of May

Statements covering one month's operations of single proprietorship Sales			*$58,000*
Cost of goods sold:			
Purchases.		*$40,000*	
Less: Ending inventory (one-fourth of purchases)		*10,000*	*30,000*
Gross profit on sales			*$28,000*
Operating expenses			*15,500*
Net income for the month of May			*$12,500*

JOHN CLAIRE
Comparative Balance Sheet

Assets		May 31	May 1
Cash		$20,500	$30,000
Accounts receivable		13,000	
Merchandise inventory		10,000	
Land		27,000	
Total assets		$70,500	$30,000

Liabilities & Owner's Equity

Note payable		$12,000	
Accounts payable		8,000	
John Claire, capital		50,500	$30,000
Total liabilities & owner's equity		$70,500	$30,000

The working capital amounted to $30,000 (consisting entirely of cash) on May 1 but was only $23,500 ($43,500 − $20,000) on May 31, a decrease of $6,500. In analyzing the six transactions completed during the month of May, we see that working capital was increased and decreased as follows:

Effect of Transactions on Working Capital

Land and the owner's capital accounts were increased as a result of these transactions

Increases:			
Additional investment by owner			$10,000
Sale of merchandise for more than cost ($58,000 − $30,000)			28,000
Total increases			$38,000
Decreases:			
Payment of operating expenses		$15,500	
Payment of cash for purchase of land		15,000	
Issuance of current note payable for purchase of land		12,000	
Withdrawal by owner		2,000	44,500
Net decrease in working capital during May			$ 6,500

A complete list of transactions for a fiscal period may not be readily available, and even if it were, analysis of such a list would be a laborious process. In practice, the statement of changes in financial position is generally prepared in summary form by analyzing the changes that occurred in the noncurrent accounts during a fiscal period. An analysis of the comparative balance sheet for John Claire indicates that the Land account increased by $27,000 (a use of working capital) and that Claire's capital account increased by $20,500 as a result of (*1*) additional investment of $10,000 (a source of working capital), (*2*) net income of $12,500 (a source of working capital), and (*3*) a withdrawal of $2,000 (a use of working capital). We can therefore prepare the following statement of changes in financial position for the month of May:

JOHN CLAIRE
Statement of Changes in Financial Position
For Month of May

<table>
<tr><td rowspan="8">*A simple statement of changes in financial position*</td><td>Sources of working capital:</td><td></td><td></td></tr>
<tr><td>Operations (net income) . . . .</td><td></td><td>$12,500</td></tr>
<tr><td>Additional investment by owner . . . .</td><td></td><td>10,000</td></tr>
<tr><td>Total sources of working capital . . . .</td><td></td><td>$22,500</td></tr>
<tr><td>Uses of working capital:</td><td></td><td></td></tr>
<tr><td>Purchase of land . . . .</td><td>$27,000</td><td></td></tr>
<tr><td>Withdrawal by owner . . . .</td><td>2,000</td><td></td></tr>
<tr><td>Total uses of working capital . . . .</td><td></td><td>29,000</td></tr>
<tr><td></td><td>Decrease in working capital ($30,000 − $23,500) . . . .</td><td></td><td>$ 6,500</td></tr>
</table>

Effect of transactions on working capital

In preparing a statement of changes in financial position, it is convenient to view all business transactions as falling into three categories:

1 Transactions which affect *only current asset or current liability accounts* but which do not change the amount of working capital. These transactions produce changes in individual working capital accounts but are not a factor in explaining any change in the amount of working capital. For example, the purchase of merchandise increases inventories and accounts payable but has no effect on working capital; it may therefore be ignored in preparing a statement of changes in financial position.

2 Transactions which affect a *current asset or current liability account and a nonworking capital account.* These transactions bring about either an increase or a decrease in the amount of working capital. The issuance of long-term bonds, for example, increases current assets and increases bonds payable, a non-working capital account; therefore, the issuance of bonds payable is a source of working capital. Similarly, when the bonds approach maturity they are transferred to the current liability classification on the balance sheet. This causes a reduction (a use) of working capital. If changes in non-working capital accounts are analyzed, these events are brought to light, and their effect on working capital will be reported in the statement of changes in financial position.

3 Transactions which affect *only noncurrent accounts* and therefore have no direct effect on the amount of working capital. The entry to record depreciation and the entry to record a stock dividend are examples of such transactions. Other transactions in this category, such as the issuance of bonds payable in exchange for plant assets, are viewed as both a source and use of working capital, but do not change the net amount of working capital.

TRANSACTIONS AFFECTING ONLY NONCURRENT ACCOUNTS Transactions of this type will be brought to light by an analysis of the changes in noncurrent accounts, but they may not be relevant in preparing the statement of changes in financial position. To illustrate the procedures for handling such items, consider the following two examples: (*1*) issuing bonds payable in exchange for a building and (*2*) recording depreciation expense.

Suppose that a building worth $105,000 is acquired in exchange for $100,000 par value of bonds payable. The entry to record this purchase would be:

An
exchange
transaction

Building	*105,000*
Bonds Payable	*100,000*
Premium on Bonds Payable	*5,000*

Exchange of $100,000 par value of bonds payable for building worth $105,000.

It is quite clear that this transaction did not increase or decrease any current asset or current liability and for that reason had no direct effect on working capital. An exchange transaction of this type, however, should be viewed as consisting of two transactions: (*1*) the sale of bonds for $105,000, and (*2*) the application of the proceeds to purchase a building for $105,000. Instead of ignoring an exchange transaction of this type in analyzing the flow of working capital, it is possible for us to view the exchange both as a source of working capital (the sale of bonds), and a use of working capital (the purchase of the building). This treatment, it is argued, is more informative since it shows more completely the movement of the company's financial resources during the year.

Similarly, the conversion of bonds payable or preferred stock into common stock results only in changes in noncurrent accounts but should be reported as both an increase and a decrease in working capital. On the other hand, the declaration of a stock dividend or the retirement of a fully depreciated asset are not exchange transactions and need not be reported in the statement of changes in financial position.

EFFECT OF DEPRECIATION ON WORKING CAPITAL PROVIDED BY OPERATIONS Some expenses, such as depreciation, deferred income tax expense (which will not be paid within one year), amortization of intangibles, and amortization of discount on bonds payable, reduce net income but have no immediate effect on the amount of working capital provided by operations. Such expenses *should be added back to net income in measuring the increase in working capital as a result of current operations.*

To illustrate the reason for this, assume the following: Paul Rey starts a delivery service on January 2, with a truck that cost $10,000; he has no other assets or liabilities at this time. He does business on a cash basis and during the year collects $12,500 in revenue and pays out $4,500 in expenses, thus showing an $8,000 increase in cash, which is his only working capital account. Rey then records depreciation expense of $3,000 on the truck, resulting in a net income of $5,000 for the year. The recording of depreciation expense did not change any current account for Paul Rey, and his increase in working capital remains at $8,000. Thus, in order to measure this increase in working capital from current operations, we can either take the income figure *before depreciation expense,* $8,000, or take the net income of $5,000 and add back depreciation expense of $3,000.

Obviously, the depreciation expense itself is not a source of working capital. The net income figure, however, understates the amount of working capital provided by operations. The *depreciation expense recorded during the period is therefore shown as an addition to net income in measuring the working capital actually provided by operations.*

We have seen that some expenses do not reduce working capital. Similarly, some items in the income statement increase net income without increasing working capital and should be deducted from net income in arriving at the liquid resources provided by operations. An example of such an item is the amortization of premium on bonds payable, which causes annual interest expense to be less than the cash payments of interest to bondholders.[3]

Extraordinary gains and losses, if material in amount, should be eliminated from net income in order to show the working capital generated from recurring activities (operations). For example, if land costing $100,000 is sold at a net gain of $50,000, the net proceeds received on the sale, $150,000, should be reported as "working capital provided through sale of land," and the gain should be deducted from net income. As a separate example, assume that the same land is sold for $70,000; then the loss of $30,000 should be added to net income in arriving at the income from operations, and the working capital provided through sale of land should be reported at $70,000. The foregoing discussion relating to the measurement of working capital provided by operations can be summarized as follows:

Computation of Working Capital Provided by Operations

Impact of net income on working capital					
	Net income +	Depreciation Deferred income tax expense Amortization of intangibles Amortization of discount on bonds payable Extraordinary losses (net)	−	Amortization of premium on bonds payable Extraordinary gains (net)	= Working capital provided by operations

[3]The treatment of this item in working papers and in the statement of changes in financial position is illustrated in the Demonstration Problem for Your Review on page 678.

Preparation of more complex statement of changes in financial position illustrated

To illustrate the points just discussed, we shall prepare a statement of changes in financial position for the Allison Corporation Ltd. from the comparative balance sheet and the condensed income statement shown below. Note that the balance sheet is not classified, except for current assets and current liabilities.

ALLISON CORPORATION LTD.
Comparative Balance Sheet
At December 31

Assets	1974	1973
Current assets:		
Cash	$ 15,000	$ 35,000
Accounts receivable (net)	105,000	85,000
Inventory	200,000	120,000
Prepaid expenses	25,000	12,000
Total current assets	$345,000	$252,000
Land	40,000	50,000
Equipment	290,000	230,000
Less: Accumulated depreciation	(107,500)	(80,000)
Total assets	$567,500	$452,000

Can you give the reasons for the increase of $57,500 in working capital?

Liabilities & Stockholders' Equity	1974	1973
Current liabilities:		
Notes payable to merchandise creditors	$ 60,000	$ 40,000
Accounts payable	85,000	50,000
Accrued liabilities	22,500	42,000
Total current liabilities	$167,500	$132,000
Notes payable, due 1/1/87	15,000	10,000
Bonds payable, due 6/30/90	60,000	100,000
Capital stock, $5 par	215,000	110,000
Premium on capital stock	50,000	30,000
Retained earnings	60,000	70,000
Total liabilities & stockholders' equity	$567,500	$452,000

ALLISON CORPORATION LTD.
Condensed Income Statement
For Year Ended December 31, 1974

Sales (net)	$900,000
Cost of goods sold	585,000
Gross profit on sales	$315,000
Operating expenses and income taxes	255,000
Income before extraordinary item	$ 60,000
Extraordinary item—gain on sale of land (net of taxes)	20,000
Net income	$ 80,000

A summary of the transactions completed by the Allison Corporation Ltd. which resulted in changes in *noncurrent accounts* during 1974 follows:

1 Changes in noncurrent assets:
  a Land costing $10,000 was sold for $30,000, net of income taxes on the gain.
  b Equipment was purchased for $60,000; the invoice was paid within ten days.
  c Depreciation of $27,500 was recorded.

2 Changes in noncurrent liabilities:
  a An additional $5,000 was borrowed on long-term notes due in 1987.
  b Bonds payable of $40,000 were retired at a price equal to par value.

3 Changes in stockholders' equity accounts:
  a A 50% stock dividend was declared in January, requiring a transfer of $55,000 from the Retained Earnings account to the Capital Stock account.
  b In February, 10,000 shares of $5 par value stock were sold at $7 per share, thus increasing Capital Stock by $50,000 and Premium on Capital Stock by $20,000.
  c In addition to the $55,000 reduction in retained earnings as a result of the 50% stock dividend, cash dividends of $35,000 were declared.
  d The net income for the year, $80,000 (including the extraordinary gain of $20,000), was transferred to the Retained Earnings account.

From the comparative balance sheets, the income statement, and the summary of the transactions during the year affecting noncurrent accounts, we can prepare a statement of changes in financial position by completing the following three steps:

Follow these steps **1** Compute the change in working capital during the period.

2 Prepare working papers for analysis of changes in noncurrent accounts.

3 Prepare the formal statement of changes in financial position.

COMPUTATION OF CHANGE IN WORKING CAPITAL DURING THE PERIOD
The first step in preparing a statement of changes in financial position is to determine the net increase or decrease in working capital during the period covered by the statement.

The working capital of the Allison Corporation Ltd. increased by $57,500 during 1974, determined as follows:

Computation of Increase in Working Capital

	12/31/74	12/31/73
Current assets	$345,000	$252,000
Less: Current liabilities	167,500	132,000
Working capital	$177,500	$120,000
Increase in working capital during 1974		57,500
	$177,500	$177,500

Sources of working capital exceed uses by $57,500

The purpose of the statement of changes in financial position is to explain the reasons for the change in working capital. This is accomplished by listing the specific sources and uses of working capital during the period. Since the working capital for the Allison Corporation Ltd. increased by $57,500, the sources of working capital during 1974 exceeded the uses by this amount. But before a formal statement of changes in financial position can be prepared, it is generally useful to analyze the changes in noncurrent accounts which took place during the year by preparing a set of working papers.

PREPARATION OF WORKING PAPERS FOR ANALYSIS OF CHANGES IN NON-CURRENT ACCOUNTS Working papers showing the analysis of changes in noncurrent accounts for the Allison Corporation Ltd. are illustrated on page 670. The amount of working capital and the balances in noncurrent accounts at the beginning of the period are listed in the first column of the working papers. Transactions for the period (in summary form) are then recorded in the next pair of columns. Here the impact of each transaction on noncurrent accounts is recorded as a debit or a credit and the effect on working capital (funds) is listed either as a *source* of working capital or as a *use* of working capital in the lower section of the working papers.

EXPLANATION OF TRANSACTIONS ON WORKING PAPERS By studying the changes in the noncurrent accounts during 1974, we are able to find the specific reasons for the $57,500 increase in working capital. As previously stated, only changes in the noncurrent accounts represent sources and uses of working capital. The analyses of the transactions completed by the Allison Corporation Ltd. during 1974 are explained below:

(*1*) The net income of $80,000 is closed to the Retained Earnings account and is shown under "sources of working capital: operations." Net income represents an increase in stockholders' equity and is one of the major sources of working capital for most business units. Net income, however, is only a tentative measure of the increase in working capital from operations because not all revenue and expense items represent sources and uses of working capital (depreciation, for example). Furthermore, any extraordinary items are eliminated from net income because the transactions giving rise to extraordinary gains and losses included in net income are reported separately if they generate or use working capital.

(2) Since depreciation expense does not reduce a current asset or increase a current liability, it has no effect on working capital. Therefore, the depreciation expense of $27,500 for the year is shown as an increase to net income in the working papers and is credited to Accumulated Depreciation. The net income, $80,000, plus depreciation expense, $27,500, or a total of $107,500, represents a *tentative* increase in working capital as a result of profitable operations. This $107,500 figure is viewed as tentative because it will be reduced in adjustment (3) by the amount of the extraordinary gain (net of taxes) from the sale of land ($20,000) which was included in the net income of $80,000; this gain will be listed as part of the $30,000 source of working capital from the sale of land.

Working Papers for Statement of Changes in Financial Position
For Year Ended December 31, 1974

	Account Balances 1/1/74	Analysis of Transactions for 1974		Account Balances 12/31/74
		Debit	Credit	
Debits				
Working capital	120,000	(x) 57,500		177,500
Land	50,000		(3) 10,000	40,000
Equipment	230,000	(6) 60,000		290,000
Total debits	400,000			507,500
Credits				
Accumulated depreciation	80,000		(2) 27,500	107,500
Notes payable, due 1/1/87	10,000		(5) 5,000	15,000
Bonds payable, due 6/30/90	100,000	(7) 40,000		60,000
Capital stock, $5 par	110,000		(4) 50,000 ⎫ (9) 55,000 ⎭	215,000
Premium on capital stock	30,000		(4) 20,000	50,000
Retained earnings	70,000	(8) 35,000 (9) 55,000	(1) 80,000 ⎫ ⎭	60,000
Total credits	400,000			507,500
Sources of working capital:				
Operations—net income		(1) 80,000 ⎫		
Add: Depreciation		(2) 27,500 ⎪		(From operations,
Less: Gain on sale of land		⎬	(3) 20,000 ⎭	$87,500)
Sale of land		(3) 30,000		
Sale of capital stock		(4) 70,000		
Borrowed on notes payable, due				
1/1/87		(5) 5,000		
Uses of working capital:				
Purchase of equipment			(6) 60,000	
Retirement of bonds payable			(7) 40,000	
Cash dividends declared			(8) 35,000	
Total sources and uses of working capital		212,500	155,000	
Increase in working capital during 1974			(x) 57,500	
		212,500	212,500	

Explanation of transactions for 1974:

(1) Net income $80,000 (including extraordinary gain of $20,000) is transferred to Retained Earnings. This is a tentative source of working capital to be adjusted in (2) and (3) below.

(2) Depreciation for the year, $27,500, is added to net income in arriving at the working capital provided by operations because it did not reduce a current asset or increase a current liability.

(3) Sale of land for $30,000; the gain of $20,000 is deducted from net income in order that entire proceeds (net of taxes) can be reported separately as a source of working capital.

(4) Sale of capital stock, providing working capital of $70,000.

(5) Working capital was provided by borrowing $5,000 on long-term notes.

(6) Working capital was reduced through purchase of equipment, $60,000.

(7) Working capital of $40,000 was used to retire bonds payable.

(8) Cash dividends declared, $35,000; this is a use of working capital.

(9) Board of directors declared a 50% stock dividend; this transaction had no effect on working capital.

(x) Balancing figure—increase in working capital during 1974.

(3) The sale of land is recorded as a source of working capital of $30,000 because cash was generated when the land was sold. The cost of the land, $10,000, is credited to the Land account and the gain, $20,000, is shown as a reduction to the net income in order that the net proceeds on the sale of the land ($30,000) can be listed as a source of working capital. This adjustment gives us net "working capital provided by operations," $87,500, consisting of income *before the extraordinary item,* $60,000, plus depreciation, $27,500.

(4) The sale of capital stock in February for $70,000 is recorded in the working papers as a source of working capital (debit entry); the credits are made to Capital Stock, $50,000 (10,000 shares with a $5 par value), and to Premium on Capital Stock, $20,000. This transaction results in an increase to stockholders' equity, and such an increase is a source of working capital.

(5) An increase in a long-term debt as a result of borrowing is a source of liquid assets (cash). Therefore, the borrowing of $5,000 on long-term notes payable is recorded in the working papers as a source of working capital (debit entry) and a credit to Notes Payable, due January 1, 1987.

(6) Equipment was purchased for $60,000, causing a reduction in working capital. This is recorded in the working papers as a debit to Equipment and a credit to Purchase of Equipment.

(7) A reduction in long-term debt represents a use of liquid assets (cash). During 1974, the Allison Corporation Ltd. retired $40,000 of bonds payable at par. This is recorded in the working papers as a debit to Bonds Payable and a credit to Retirement of Bonds Payable. If a retirement of bonds payable results in a material loss or gain, the loss or gain would be reported as an extraordinary item in the income statement and would be treated in the same manner as the gain on sale of land in transaction (3) above.

(8) Cash dividends declared on capital stock outstanding reduce both working capital and stockholders' equity and should be listed on a statement of changes in financial position as a use of working capital. The required working paper entry is a debit to Retained Earnings and a credit to Cash Dividends Declared for $35,000. A cash dividend need not be paid in order to represent a reduction in working capital. It is the *declaration* of the cash dividend that establishes a current liability and thus reduces working capital. The actual payment of the cash dividend has no effect on working capital because this transaction merely reduces a current liability (Dividends Payable) and a current asset (Cash) by the same amount; *a transaction which changes only current accounts cannot be a source or use of working capital.*

(9) The declaration of a stock dividend is merely a transfer from retained earnings to paid-in capital; a stock dividend has no effect on working capital because no working capital account is affected. The working paper entry to recognize the 50% stock dividend distributed by the Allison Corporation Ltd. in January is a debit to Retained Earnings for $55,000 and a credit to Capital Stock for the same amount.

(x) After all changes in noncurrent accounts are analyzed in the working papers, the sources, $212,500, and uses, $155,000 of working capital should be totaled. At this point, the increase in working capital during the year, $57,500, should be entered as a debit to Working Capital on the first line of the second column in the working papers and also as a balancing figure on the next to the last line of the third column in the working papers. The account balances at December 31, 1974, can now be determined and totals obtained for the debits and credits. If the total of the debits and the total of the credits agree ($507,500 in the Allison Corporation Ltd. example), we know that our analysis is correct, at least so far as the mechanics are concerned.

PREPARATION OF FORMAL STATEMENT OF CHANGES IN FINANCIAL POSITION The foregoing working paper entries explained all changes in noncurrent accounts that took place during 1974. In making these entries, we listed the individual sources and uses of working capital below the broken line in the lower section of the working papers on page 670. The increase of $57,500 in working capital has been confirmed and a formal statement of changes in financial position can now be prepared as follows:

ALLISON CORPORATION LTD.

Statement of Changes in Financial Position

For Year Ended December 31, 1974

Sources of working capital:		
Operations:		
Income before extraordinary gain		$ 60,000
Add: Expense not requiring the use of current funds—depreciation		27,500
Total working capital provided by operations		$ 87,500
Sale of land		30,000
Sale of capital stock		70,000
Borrowed on long-term notes payable, due 1/1/87		5,000
Total sources of working capital		$192,500
Uses of working capital:		
Purchase of equipment	$60,000	
Retirement of bonds payable, due 6/30/90	40,000	
Declaration of cash dividends	35,000	
Total uses of working capital		135,000
Increase in working capital		$ 57,500

Statement of changes in financial position shows sources and uses of working capital

We can see that the $87,500 of working capital provided by operations exceeds the net income before extraordinary gain because depreciation expense was added to net income; another $105,000 of working capital came from nonoperating sources (sale of land, sale of additional capital stock, and long-term borrowing). Working capital totaling $135,000 was used to purchase equipment, retire bonds payable, and declare cash dividends. These sources and uses resulted in a net increase of $57,500 in working capital. The statement of changes in financial position thus provides a concise view of the way in which the Allison Corporation Ltd. generated and used its working capital during the year.

Investors and creditors find the statement of changes in financial position helpful not only in evaluating the past performance of a company but also in projecting future movements of working capital and in evaluating the probable *liquidity* (the ability to pay debts as they become payable) of a business unit.

CASH FLOW STATEMENT

While the statement of changes in financial position reports the inflow and outflow of liquid resources (working capital) during an accounting period, management is often more concerned with having enough cash to meet its operating needs and to pay maturing liabilities. Cash is the most liquid asset, and the efficient use of cash is one of the most important tasks of management. A *cash flow statement* is often prepared in order to give a full and complete picture of historical cash receipts and disbursements for an accounting period. Such a cash flow statement may also be useful in preparing a projected cash budget, as discussed in Chapter 26.

In recent years such terms as *cash earnings* or *cash generated per share* have appeared with increasing frequency in financial magazines and annual reports of corporations. The cash earnings referred to in these reports are usually computed by adding back to net income expenses such as depreciation and amortization of intangibles, which do not reduce working capital. The term *cash earnings* used in this context is ambiguous, and the implication that the resulting figure reflects the cash flow from operations is erroneous. To interpret such statements, it is important to understand the relation between net income and cash flows from operations.

Income statements, as we have shown in prior chapters, are prepared on an accrual basis. Accrual accounting was developed to overcome the limitations of cash movements as indicators of business performance. Cash outlays simply represent investments which may or may not prove sound. Cash receipts represent disinvestment and, taken by themselves, tell nothing about whether the inflow is beneficial or not. The accountant's measurement of net income is designed to tell something about the fate of a company's overall investment and disinvestment activities during a given period of time. Granting its imperfections, the income statement is still the best means we have for reporting operating performance of business enterprises.

However, there are occasions when one may wish to reverse the accrual process and determine the amount of cash generated by operations. Reports of past cash flow may reveal a good deal about the financial problems and policies of a company. Forecasts of cash flows and cash budgets are useful managerial planning tools. The measurement of past and future cash flows from all sources, including operations, provides valuable information. But cash flow data are in no way a substitute for an income statement nor is the "cash earnings" figure in any sense a better indication of a company's operating performance.

Cash flow from operations

Suppose we wished to convert a company's income statement into a report of its cash flow from operations. How should we go about adjusting the data on the income statement to convert it into cash flow information?

To answer this question, we must consider the relationship between accrual basis income statement amounts and cash movements within the firm. For illustrative purposes, consider the income statement of the Allison Corporation Ltd. for 1974, which was presented earlier in this chapter.

ALLISON CORPORATION LTD.
Condensed Income Statement
For Year Ended December 31, 1974

Sales (net)	*$900,000*
Cost of goods sold	*585,000*
Gross profit on sales	*$315,000*
Operating expenses and income taxes	*255,000*
Income before extraordinary item	*$ 60,000*
Extraordinary item—gain on sale of land (net of taxes)	*20,000*
Net income	*$ 80,000*

Condensed income statement: accrual basis

From the statement of changes in financial position presented on page 672, we already know that cash was received from the sale of land ($30,000), from the sale of capital stock ($70,000), and from borrowing on long-term notes ($5,000). We also know that cash was paid to acquire equipment ($60,000), to retire bonds payable ($40,000), and to pay cash dividends ($35,000). The remaining cash movements must consist of cash collected from customers and cash payments for merchandise purchases and expenses, including income taxes.

CASH RECEIPTS FROM CUSTOMERS Sales on account are an important factor in most companies. The relationship between the amount of cash collected from customers and the net sales reported on the income statement depends on the change in accounts receivable between the beginning and end of any period. The relationship may be stated as follows:

Converting sales to cash basis

$$\text{Net sales} \left\{ \begin{array}{c} - \text{ increase in accounts receivable} \\ \text{or} \\ + \text{ decrease in accounts receivable} \end{array} \right\} = \begin{array}{l} \text{cash receipts from} \\ \text{customers} \end{array}$$

In the Allison Corporation Ltd. example, a glance at the comparative balance sheet on page 667 tells us that net accounts receivable increased from $85,000 to $105,000 during 1974, an increase of $20,000. Therefore, the amount of cash received from customers during 1974 can be determined as follows:

Net sales on cash basis

Net sales	*$900,000*
Less: Increase in accounts receivable during the year	*20,000*
Cash receipts from customers	*$880,000*

CASH PAYMENTS FOR MERCHANDISE PURCHASES The relationship between the cost of goods sold for a period and the cash payments for
the purchase of merchandise depends both on the change in inventories
and the change in notes and accounts payable to merchandise creditors
during the period. The relationship may be stated, in two stages, as
follows:

*Converting
cost of
goods sold
to cash
basis*

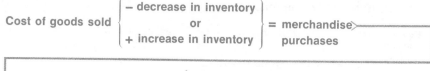

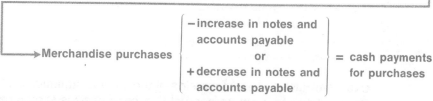

Again referring to the Allison Corporation Ltd. example, we can see
that the company increased its inventory by $80,000 and that notes and
accounts payable to merchandise creditors increased by $55,000 during
the year. The cash payments for the merchandise purchases during 1974
would be computed as follows:

*Cost of
goods sold
on cash
basis*

Cost of goods sold	$585,000
Add: Increase in inventory	80,000
Merchandise purchases (accrual basis)	$665,000
Less: Increase in notes and accounts payable to creditors.	55,000
Cash payments for merchandise purchases	$610,000

The result of this computation makes sense. If a company is increasing
its inventory, it will be buying more merchandise than it sells during the
period; furthermore, if the company is increasing its notes and accounts
payable to merchandise creditors, it is not paying for all of its current
purchases.

CASH PAYMENTS FOR EXPENSES Expenses on the income statement
arise from three major sources: cash expenditures, the write-off of prepayments, and incurring obligations for accrued expenses. The relationship between operating expenses and cash payments, therefore,
depends on changes in asset accounts representing the prepayment of
expenses, and on changes in accrued liability accounts. These relationships may be stated as follows:

*Converting
an expense
on accrual
basis to
cash basis*

$$\text{Expense} \begin{cases} - \text{ increase in related accrued liability} \\ \text{or} \\ + \text{ decrease in related accrued liability} \\ - \text{ decrease in related prepayment} \\ \text{or} \\ + \text{ increase in related prepayment} \end{cases} = \begin{array}{l} \text{cash payments for} \\ \text{expense} \end{array}$$

In the case of a nonfund expense such as depreciation, the decrease in the book value of a depreciable asset is exactly equal to the expense recorded, and the resultant cash payment is zero.

Using the information for the Allison Corporation Ltd., we can summarize the relationship between the operating expenses and income taxes reported in the income statement and cash payments for these expenses during 1974 as follows:

Expenses on cash basis	*Total operating expenses and income taxes reported in the income statement*	*$255,000*
	Add: Decrease in accrued liabilities	*19,500*
	Increase in prepaid expenses	*13,000*
	Less: Depreciation, a noncash expense	*(27,500)*
	Cash payments for operating expenses and income taxes	*$260,000*

CASH EARNINGS The conversion of the income statement of the Allison Corporation Ltd. from an accrual to a cash basis is summarized below. Note that this schedule incorporates the adjustments discussed in the preceding paragraphs.

ALLISON CORPORATION LTD.
Conversion of Income Statement from Accrual to Cash Basis
For Year Ended December 31, 1974

	Income Statement (Accrual Basis)	*Add (Deduct)*	*Cash Basis*
How much is "cash flow" for 1974? *Net sales*	*$900,000*		
Less: Increase in accounts receivable		*$(20,000)*	*$880,000*
Cost of goods sold	*585,000*		
Add: Increase in inventory		*80,000*	
Less: Increase in notes and accounts payable to merchandise creditors		*(55,000)*	*610,000*
Gross profit on sales	*$315,000*		*$270,000*
Operating expenses and income taxes	*255,000*		
Add: Decrease in accrued liabilities		*$ 19,500*	
Increase in prepaid expenses		*13,000*	
Less: Depreciation expense		*(27,500)*	*260,000*
Income before extraordinary item (accrual basis)	*$ 60,000*		
Cash flow from operations			*$ 10,000*

The cash flow from operations for the Allison Corporation Ltd., $10,000, is lower than the amount of net income, $60,000, during 1974. This difference is caused by a series of variations between revenues and expense transactions on the accrual basis and cash inflows and outflows during the year.

In the past, some financial analysts added back depreciation to net income and referred to the total as "cash flow from operations." In our example, such an approach would lead to the figure of $107,500, that is, $80,000 net income plus depreciation of $27,500. However, the actual cash flow from operations for the Allison Corporation Ltd. is only $10,000, and not $107,500. It would be misleading to say that the *cash earnings* of the Allison Corporation Ltd. for 1974 were $2.50 per share of capital stock ($107,500 divided by 43,000 shares of capital stock outstanding at year-end), and to suggest that this is a better measure of the company's performance than the *earnings per share* figure of $1.86 (net income, $80,000, divided by 43,000 shares of capital stock outstanding at year-end). In *Opinion No. 19,* the Accounting Principles Board made the following recommendation:

> The amount of working capital or cash provided from operations is not a substitute for or an improvement upon properly determined net income as a measure of results of operations and the consequent effect on financial position. . . . The Board strongly recommends that isolated statistics of working capital or cash provided from operations, especially per-share amounts, not be presented in annual reports to shareholders.[4]

COMPLETE CASH FLOW STATEMENT The cash flow from operations shown on page 676 for Allison Corporation Ltd. does not tell the complete story of cash movements during the period. Let us now combine the $10,000 cash flow from operations with the information on cash receipts and payments gleaned from the comparative balance sheet by way of the statement of changes in financial position. The result will be a statement that explains in full the $20,000 decrease in the cash balance during 1974. Such a statement of cash flows for the Allison Corporation Ltd. is shown below:

ALLISON CORPORATION LTD.
Cash Flow Statement
For Year Ended December 31, 1974

Complete summary of cash movements for 1974

Cash payments:		
Purchase of equipment		$ 60,000
Retirement of bonds payable		40,000
Payment of cash dividends		35,000
Total cash payments		$135,000
Cash receipts:		
Cash generated from operations (see schedule on page 676)	$10,000	
Sale of land	30,000	
Sale of capital stock	70,000	
Borrowing on long-term notes	5,000	
Total cash receipts		115,000
Decrease in cash during the year ($35,000 − $15,000)		$ 20,000

[4] *Op. cit.,* p. 377.

The Allison Corporation Ltd. example was sufficiently simple that we could develop cash flow information from a direct inspection of the income statement and comparative balance sheets. In more complex situations, the accountant will usually use some form of working papers to convert the income statement from an accrual to a cash basis and to develop cash flow information in a systematic fashion. Familiarity with these working paper procedures is not necessary in order to be able to understand and interpret cash flow information; therefore, discussion of this process is reserved for the *Intermediate Accounting* volume in this series.

DEMONSTRATION PROBLEM FOR YOUR REVIEW

The comparative financial data for the Liquid Gas Company Ltd. for the last two years are shown below:

	December 31	
Debits	**Year 2**	**Year 1**
Cash	$ 39,220	$ 15,800
Receivables (net of allowance for uncollectible accounts)	41,400	24,000
Inventories, lower of cost or market	27,600	36,800
Prepaid expenses	4,180	4,400
Land	9,000	19,000
Buildings	270,000	250,000
Equipment	478,600	450,000
Total debits	$870,000	$800,000
Credits		
Accumulated depreciation: buildings	$ 95,000	$ 77,000
Accumulated depreciation: equipment	153,000	120,000
Accounts payable	59,200	30,000
Accrued liabilities	20,000	10,000
Bonds payable	90,000	90,000
Premium on bonds payable	2,800	3,000
Preferred stock ($100 par)	70,000	100,000
Common stock ($25 par)	260,000	250,000
Premium on Common stock	45,000	40,000
Retained earnings	75,000	80,000
Total credits	$870,000	$800,000

Other data

(1) During Year 2 the board of directors of the company authorized a transfer of $15,000 from retained earnings to reflect a 4% stock dividend on the common stock.

(2) Cash dividends of $6,000 were paid on the preferred stock, and cash dividends of $50,000 were paid on the common stock.

(3) During Year 2, 300 shares of preferred stock were redeemed at par value. (The preferred shares are redeemable "out of capital.")

(4) The only entries recorded in the Retained Earnings account were for divi-

dends and to close the Income Summary account, which had a credit balance of $66,000.

(5) There were no sales or retirements of buildings and equipment during the year; land was sold for $8,000.

Instructions

a Compute the change in working capital during Year 2. You may use totals for current assets and current liabilities.

b Prepare working papers for a statement of changes in financial position for Year 2.

c Prepare a formal statement of changes in financial position for Year 2.

d Prepare a cash flow statement, with a supporting schedule converting the net income from the accrual basis to a cash basis.

QUESTIONS

1 Why is working capital viewed as a "fund of liquid resources"?

2 What are the primary ways in which a firm generates working capital and the primary ways in which a firm uses working capital?

3 What information can a reader gain from a statement of changes in financial position that is not apparent from reading an income statement?

4 In preparing a statement of changes in financial position, business transactions may be classified into three categories. List these categories and indicate which category results in changes in working capital.

5 Give examples of expenses, other than depreciation expense, which reduce net income but which do not result in the use of working capital during the period.

6 Give an example of an increase in net income which does not result in an increase in working capital during the period.

7 The following quotation appeared in a report issued by a major investment banking firm: "Depreciation, depletion, and amortization charges, etc., which supply the funds for the new facilities that sustain the competitive competence of our leading companies, are increasing at a faster rate than is net income." Evaluate this quotation.

8 Although extraordinary gains and losses may be included in net income in measuring the working capital generated by operations, can you give a reason for excluding such gains and losses from net income? Use the following facts to illustrate your point: Net income including gain on sale of land, $100,000; sale of land, with a book value of $70,000, for $150,000.

9 What is the major difference between the statement of changes in financial position and a cash flow statement?

10 Criticize the following statement: "Although earnings fell from $3.40 per share in the previous year to $2.50 per share in the current year, cash earnings increased from $4.00 to $4.80 per share, a 20% increase that testifies to the continuing strength in the company's profitability."

11 The president of a small corporation was puzzled by the following statement made by his accountant: "Our cash flow, net income plus depreciation, amounted to $85,000 last year but our cash generated from operations was only $10,000 because of the increases in our inventory and receivables and the decrease in our accounts payable." Explain what the accountant meant.

12 An outside member of the board of directors of a small corporation made the following comment after studying the comparative financial statements for the past two years: "I have trouble understanding why our cash has increased steadily during the past two years, yet our profits have been negligible: we have paid no dividends; and inventories, receivables, payables,

cost of plant and equipment, long-term debt, and capital stock have remained essentially unchanged.'' Write a brief statement to the director explaining how this situation might occur.

EXERCISES

Ex. 22-1 Indicate the amount of the increase or decrease (if any) in working capital as a result of each of the following events:
  a Purchase and retirement of bonds payable, $1,000,000, at 96. The unamortized premium on bonds payable at the time of the retirement is $50,000.
  b Declaration of a 25% stock dividend on $600,000 of par value capital stock outstanding.
  c Purchase of equipment costing $400,000 for $100,000 in cash and $75,000 (plus interest) payable every six months over the next two years.
  d A $40,000 write-down of inventory to a market value below cost.

Ex. 22-2 The Bridge Company Ltd. reports a net loss of $20,000 on its income statement. In arriving at this figure, the following items among others were included:

Amortization of patents	$ 4,000
Amortization of premium on bonds payable	2,500
Gain on sale of land for cash	10,000
Depreciation expense	12,500
Uninsured fire loss: building	22,100

What was the working capital increase or decrease as a result of *operations?*

Ex. 22-3 The information below is taken from comparative financial statements for the Rudd Corporation Ltd.

	Year 10	Year 9
Income before extraordinary items	$60,000	$37,000
Depreciation expense	42,500	31,800
Inventory at end of year	15,000	28,000
Accounts receivable at end of year	9,000	12,000
Accounts payable at end of year	8,000	6,000
Cash dividends declared in December of each year payable Jan. 15 of following year	22,500	15,000

From the data above, determine the following:
  a The working capital provided by operations in Year 10.
  b The cash generated by operations in Year 10.
  c Working capital used in Year 10 for dividends.

Ex. 22-4 The data below are taken from the records of the Rose Company Ltd.

	End of Year	Beginning of Year
Accounts receivable	$ 20,200	$10,200
Inventories	32,000	40,000
Prepaid expenses	2,300	1,500
Accounts payable (merchandise creditors)	28,000	25,000
Miscellaneous liabilities (accrued expenses)	1,000	1,200
Net sales	300,000	
Cost of goods sold	180,000	
Operating expenses (includes depreciation of $10,000)	80,000	

From the foregoing information, compute the following for the current year:
a Cash collected from customers during the year.
b Cash paid to merchandise creditors during the year.
c Cash paid for operating expenses during the year.

PROBLEMS

Group A

22A-1 Below are described a number of business transactions and adjustments. In each instance you are to determine whether the result of the transaction or adjustment is to increase working capital (current assets less current liabilities), to decrease working capital, or to effect no change in working capital:
(1) Sale of capital stock for cash
(2) Payment of an account payable
(3) Declaration of a cash dividend on common stock
(4) Payment of a previously declared cash dividend
(5) Purchase of land for cash and a long-term mortgage note
(6) Recognition of accrued income tax liability for current year
(7) Purchase of merchandise on open account
(8) Sale of merchandise on open account at normal markup
(9) Depreciation recorded for the period
(10) Purchase of patent, giving 100 shares of the company's common stock in exchange

Instructions List the numbers 1 to 10 on your answer sheet. Opposite each number state whether working capital is increased, decreased, or not affected (no change), and write a brief explanation of your reasoning.

22A-2 Given below are the changes in account balances for Edna Corporation Ltd. during Year 4:

	Change during Year 4	
	Debit	Credit
Current assets	$ 50,000	
Plant and equipment	100,000	
Accumulated depreciation		$ 25,000
Current liabilities	30,000	
Capital stock, $10 par		80,000
Premium on capital stock		20,000
Retained earnings		55,000
	$180,000	$180,000

During Year 4 the company issued 8,000 shares of capital stock and applied the proceeds to the purchase of equipment. There were no retirements of plant and equipment items in Year 4. Dividends of $40,000 were paid during Year 4.

Instructions Prepare a statement of changes in financial position for Year 4, without using working papers.

22A-3 The account balances of Pollution Control Ltd., at the end of Years 1 and 2 are shown on page 682.

The following additional information for Year 2 is available for your consideration:
(1) The net loss for Year 2 amounted to $8,000.
(2) Cash dividends of $2,000 were declared.
(3) Land for future expansion was acquired.

	Year 2	Year 1
Cash	$ 12,000	$ 20,000
Accounts receivable (net)	30,000	35,000
Merchandise inventory	65,000	50,000
Land for future expansion	15,000	
Plant and equipment (see accumulated depreciation below) . . .	160,000	125,000
Patents (net of amortization)	18,000	20,000
	$300,000	$250,000
Accumulated depreciation	$ 52,500	$ 40,000
Accounts payable	30,500	15,000
Dividends payable	2,000	
Notes payable due in Year 5	5,000	
Capital stock, $10 par	200,000	175,000
Retained earnings	10,000	20,000
	$300,000	$250,000

(4) Equipment costing $35,000 was purchased for cash; $5,000 was borrowed for three years in order to pay for this equipment.
(5) Additional shares of capital stock were sold at par value.
(6) Other changes in noncurrent accounts resulted from the usual transactions recorded in such accounts.

Instructions
a Prepare a schedule computing the change in working capital during Year 2.
b Prepare working papers for a statement of changes in financial position for Year 2.
c Prepare a formal statement of changes in financial position for Year 2.

22A-4 The account balances for the Stanford Company Ltd. at the end of Year 2 and Year 1 are shown below:

	Year 2	Year 1
Cash	$ 31,000	$ 40,000
Accounts receivable	55,000	35,000
Merchandise inventory	95,000	150,000
Long-term investments	15,000	
Equipment	390,000	225,000
Accumulated depreciation	(80,000)	(60,000)
Land	80,000	35,000
	$586,000	$425,000
Accounts payable	$ 45,000	$ 20,000
Notes payable (current)	5,000	30,000
Bonds payable, due in Year 10	100,000	80,000
Unamortized premium on bonds payable	1,800	1,900
Capital stock, $1 par	200,000	150,000
Premium on capital stock	80,000	50,000
Retained earnings	154,200	93,100
	$586,000	$425,000

Net income for Year 2 amounted to $86,000. Cash dividends of $24,900 were paid during Year 2. Additional purchases of investments, equipment, and land were completed during Year 2, financed in part through the sale of bonds at par and 50,000 shares of capital stock. Equipment costing $25,000 was sold at a price equal to its book value of $10,000.

Instructions
a Prepare a schedule of changes in working capital during Year 2.
b Prepare working papers for a statement of changes in financial position for Year 2. See the solution to the demonstration problem in this chapter for proper handling of the premium on bonds payable.
c Prepare a formal statement of changes in financial position for Year 2.

22A-5 The following information is presented to you by Emily Chang, owner of Emily's Fabric Shop:

Assets	Year 2	Year 1
Cash	$ 15,000	$ 40,000
Marketable securities	10,000	20,000
Accounts receivable (net)	100,000	35,000
Merchandise inventory	75,000	60,000
Equipment (net of accumulated depreciation)	30,000	45,000
	$230,000	$200,000

Liabilities & Stockholders' Equity		
Accounts payable	$ 27,000	$ 40,000
Accrued expenses	8,000	2,500
Note payable to bank, due early in Year 2		12,500
Emily Chang, capital	195,000	145,000
	$230,000	$200,000

Income Statement, Year 2	
Sales (net).	$400,000
Cost of goods sold	300,000
Gross profit on sales	$100,000
Operating expenses (including $15,000 depreciation)	60,000
Income before extraordinary loss.	$ 40,000
Loss on sale of marketable securities.	2,500
Net income	$ 37,500
Drawings by owner	22,500
Increase in owner's capital as a result of operations	$ 15,000

Miss Chang is concerned over the decrease in her cash position during Year 2, particularly in view of the fact that she invested an additional $35,000 in the business and had a net income of $37,500 during the year. She asks you to prepare a statement which will explain the decrease in the Cash account. You point out that while cash decreased by $25,000, the working capital increased by $65,000. You conclude that a statement of cash receipts and cash disbursements, showing cash collected from customers, cash paid to merchandise creditors, cash paid for operating expenses, etc., would give her the information she needs.

Instructions

a Prepare a schedule showing the conversion of the income statement from an accrual to a cash basis, thus determining the cash outflow from operations.

b Prepare a cash flow statement which explains the decrease of $25,000 in cash during Year 2.

c Prepare a statement of changes in financial position, without using working papers.

22A-6 When the controller of the J & K Company Ltd. presented the following condensed comparative financial statements to the board of directors at the close of Year 2, the reaction of the board members was very favorable.

J & K COMPANY LTD.
Comparative Income Statements
(in thousands of dollars)

	Year 2	Year 1
Net sales.	$ 985	$700
Cost of goods sold	610	480
Gross profit on sales	$ 375	$220
Operating expenses, including depreciation	(190)	(160)
Income taxes	(80)	(25)
Net income	$ 105	$ 35

J & K COMPANY LTD.
Comparative Financial Position
As of December 31
(in thousands of dollars)

Current assets	$ 380	$365
Less: Current liabilities	200	225
Working capital	$ 180	$140
Plant and equipment (net)	995	680
Total assets minus current liabilities	$1,175	$820
Financed by following sources of long-term capital:		
Long-term liabilities	$ 250	
Capital stock ($50 par value)	500	$500
Retained earnings	425	320
Total sources of long-term capital	$1,175	$820

Noting that net income rose from $3.50 per share of capital stock to $10.50 per share, one member of the board proposed that a substantial cash dividend be paid. "Our working capital is up by $40,000; we should be able to make a distribution to stockholders," he commented. To which the controller replied that the company's cash position was precarious and pointed out that at the end of Year 2, a cash balance of only $15,000 was on hand, a decline from $145,000 at the end of Year 1. He also reminded the board that the company bought $400,000 of new equipment during Year 2. When a board member asked for an explanation of the increase of $40,000 in working capital, the controller presented the following schedule (in thousands of dollars):

	Effect on Working Capital
Increase in working capital:	
Accounts receivable increased by	$ 83
Inventories increased by	45
Prepaid expenses increased by	17
Accounts payable were reduced by	52
Accrued expenses were reduced by	28
Total increases in working capital	$225
Decreases in working capital:	
Cash decreased by $130	
Income tax liability increased by 55	185
Increase in working capital during Year 2	$ 40

After examining this schedule, the board member shook his head and said, "I still don't understand how our cash position can be so tight in the face of a tripling of net income and a substantial increase in working capital!"

Instructions
a Prepare a statement converting J & K Company's income statement to a cash basis, determining the cash generated by operations during Year 2.
b From the information in (*a*) and an inspection of the comparative balance sheet, prepare a cash flow statement for Year 2, explaining the $130,000 decrease in the cash balance.
c Prepare a statement accounting for the increase in working capital (statement of changes in financial position) for J & K Company Ltd. in a more acceptable form.
d Write a brief note of explanation to the board member.

Group B

22B-1 Below is given a list of business transactions and adjustments. For each item you are to indicate the effect first on net working capital, and second on cash. In each case the possible effects are an increase, a decrease, or no change.
    (*1*) Sale of long-term investment at a loss
    (*2*) Payment of the current year's income tax liability, previously recorded on the accounting records
    (*3*) Convertible bonds converted into a company's common stock
    (*4*) An uncollectible account receivable written off against the Allowance for Uncollectible Accounts
    (*5*) Machinery sold for cash in excess of its book value
    (*6*) Warehouse destroyed by fire; one-half of its book value covered by insurance and recorded as a receivable from the insurance company
    (*7*) Amortization of discount on bonds payable
    (*8*) Premium on a one-year insurance policy paid
    (*9*) Payment of previously declared cash dividend on common stock
    (*10*) Sale of merchandise for cash at a price below cost

Instructions List the numbers 1 to 10 on your answer sheet, and set up two columns headed "working capital effect" and "cash effect." For each transaction, write the words *increase, decrease,* or *no change* in the appropriate column to indicate the effect of the transaction on working capital and on cash.

22B-2 The following information is taken from the annual report of the Lin Company Ltd.

	Year 2	Year 1
Current assets	$200,000	$135,000
Equipment	300,000	210,000
Less: Accumulated depreciation	(100,000)	(60,000)
Investments	40,000	50,000
Current liabilities	115,000	40,000
Capital stock	100,000	100,000
Retained earnings	225,000	195,000

Cash dividends declared amounted to $35,000; no equipment items were sold; investments were sold at a gain of $5,000; and net income (including extraordinary gain) for Year 2 was $65,000.

Instructions From the information given, prepare a statement of changes in financial position for Year 2, without using working papers.

22B-3 The following changes in working capital and noncurrent accounts for Year 1 were obtained from the books and records of the Clark Corporation Ltd.

Accounts	Net Change during Year 1	
	Debit	Credit
Current assets	$ 76,500	
Plant and equipment (net)	25,000	
Goodwill		$ 30,000
Current liabilities		70,000
Bonds payable, 7%		100,000
Discount on bonds payable	3,800	
Preferred stock, $10 par	100,000	
Common stock, no par		50,000
Retained earnings	44,700	
Total changes in accounts	$250,000	$250,000

Analysis of the Retained Earnings account for the Clark Corporation Ltd. is shown below:

Beginning balance		$ 60,000
Add: Net income (including extraordinary items)		53,800
		$113,800
Less: Stock dividend of 25% on common stock	$50,000	
Cash dividends paid	13,500	
Premium paid on redemption of preferred stock	5,000	
Goodwill written off	30,000	98,500
Ending balance		$ 15,300

Bonds payable were issued on July 1 at 96, proceeds being used for the redemption of preferred stock. Land costing $45,000 was sold for $65,000. The cash proceeds from the sale were applied to the construction of a new building costing $85,000. Depreciation recorded for the year was $15,000 and amortization of discount on bonds payable was $200; both of these adjustments reduced net income but had no effect on working capital.

Instructions

a Prepare a statement of changes in financial position in good form which would explain the increase of $6,500 in working capital.

b Prepare a working paper analysis of changes in noncurrent accounts, using the following headings and sample analyses:

Accounts	Changes in Account Balances		Analysis of Transactions for Year 1	
	Debit	*Credit*	*Debit*	*Credit*
Increase in working				
capital ($76,500 − $70,000)	*6,500*		*(x) 6,500*	
Plant and equipment (net)	*25,000*		*(?) 85,000*	*(?) 15,000*
				(?) 45,000

22B-4 Comparative post-closing trial balances for the Winter Heating Company Ltd. are shown below:

Debits	*Year 2*	*Year 1*
Cash	*$ 63,000*	*$ 65,000*
Marketable securities		*80,000*
Accounts receivable	*100,000*	*190,000*
Inventories	*110,000*	*150,000*
Prepaid expenses	*27,000*	*20,000*
Land	*100,000*	
Buildings	*500,000*	
	$900,000	*$505,000*

Credits	*Year 2*	*Year 1*
Allowance for uncollectible accounts	*$ 5,000*	*$ 10,000*
Accounts payable	*115,000*	*85,000*
Accrued liabilities	*85,000*	*65,000*
Long-term notes payable	*250,000*	*50,000*
Capital stock, $10 par	*330,000*	*205,000*
Retained earnings	*115,000*	*90,000*
	$900,000	*$505,000*

During Year 1 the Winter Heating Company Ltd. operated in rented space. Early in Year 2 the company acquired suitable land and made arrangements to borrow funds from a local bank on long-term notes to finance the construction of new buildings. The company also sold additional stock at par and all its marketable securities at book value. Construction of the buildings was completed near the end of Year 2. The only entries in the company's Retained Earnings account during the two-year period were the closing of the annual net income and the payment of cash dividends of $30,000 in Year 1 and $40,000 in Year 2.

Instructions

a Prepare a schedule of changes in working capital during Year 2. The schedule should show the balances of each current account at the beginning and at the end of Year 2 and the effect of the change in the account balance on working capital.

b Prepare working papers for a statement of changes in financial position, as illustrated on page 670.

c Prepare a formal statement of changes in financial position for Year 2, showing first the uses of working capital followed by sources of working capital.

22B-5 Below is given a comparative statement of the Valley Feed Company's working capital as of the end of two recent years and a condensed income statement for the second of the two years:

VALLEY FEED COMPANY LTD.

Comparative Statement of Working Capital

As of December 31

	Year 2	Year 1
Current assets:		
Cash	$ 56,600	$ 20,000
Receivables (net)	78,000	85,000
Inventories	161,000	150,000
Prepaid expenses	10,400	15,000
Total current assets	$306,000	$270,000
Current liabilities:		
Notes payable to bank	$ 64,000	$ 70,000
Accounts payable to merchandise creditors.	44,000	32,000
Accrued liabilities	14,500	17,500
Income taxes payable	32,000	20,500
Total current liabilities.	$154,500	$140,000
Working capital at end of year	$151,500	$130,000

VALLEY FEED COMPANY LTD.

Income Statement

Year 2

Net sales.		$910,000
Cost of goods sold		670,000
Gross profit on sales		$240,000
Various expenses (detail omitted)	$123,500	
Depreciation expense	21,000	
Interest expense	3,500	
Income taxes	32,000	
Total expenses.		180,000
Net income		$ 60,000

During Year 2 the company paid $9,500, including the interest of $3,500 listed above, on a note payable issued in connection with a bank loan of $70,000 at the beginning of Year 1. The bank loan was due six months after issue, and has been repeatedly renewed since then.

Instructions

a Prepare a schedule showing the conversion of the income statement from an accrual to a cash basis, and determining the cash flow generated by operations for Year 2.

b Assume that Valley Feed Company Ltd. paid dividends of $39,000 during Year 2, purchased new equipment for $40,500, and sold investments for $20,000. There were no other changes in noncurrent accounts. Prepare a statement explaining the increase in the cash balance during Year 2.

c Without preparing a formal statement of changes in financial position, give an explanation of the $21,500 increase in working capital during Year 2.

22B-6 The account balances given below in alphabetical order are from the ledger of the Olympic Products Company Ltd.

	June 30, 1973		June 30, 1972	
	Debit	Credit	Debit	Credit
Accounts payable		$ 43,500		$ 24,500
Accounts receivable	$ 63,500		$ 48,000	
Accrued miscellaneous current				
liabilities		18,600		28,400
Accumulated depreciation: buildings		52,100		45,700
Accumulated depreciation: equipment		48,600		31,900
Allowance for doubtful accounts . . .		5,000		4,600
Buildings	186,700		156,300	
Cash	43,400		30,200	
Common stock, $50 par		220,000		200,000
Convertible bonds payable		20,000		50,000
Equipment	190,500		198,500	
Inventories	58,400		49,400	
Land	21,000		30,000	
Premium on common stock		30,000		20,000
Notes payable (short-term)		22,500		15,000
Prepaid expenses	6,200		7,600	
Retained earnings		109,400		99,900
Totals	$569,700	$569,700	$520,000	$520,000

The analysis of the Retained Earnings account for the year ended June 30, 1973, is given below:

Balance, June 30, 1972	$ 99,900
Net income for year ended June 30, 1973	24,500
Gain on sale of land	5,000
Dividends declared	(20,000)
Balance, June 30, 1973	$109,400

Additional information available for your consideration follows:
(1) Land was sold on March 10, 1973, for $14,000. The gain was erroneously credited directly to Retained Earnings.

(2) Owners of $30,000 of the convertible bonds exchanged their bonds for 400 shares of common stock on July 20, 1972.
(3) In August, 1972, fully depreciated equipment costing $8,000 was abandoned and written off.
(4) Other changes in noncurrent accounts resulted from the usual transactions affecting these accounts.
(5) The notes payable represent bank loans. The balance payable on June 30, 1972, was paid in December, 1972 and a new loan was negotiated early in 1973.

Instructions
a Compute the change in working capital for the year ended June 30, 1973.
b Prepare working papers for a statement of changes in financial position for the year ended June 30, 1973. You need not prepare a formal statement.
c Prepare a schedule converting the net income of $24,500 to a cash basis, and prepare a cash flow statement explaining the $13,200 increase in cash.

BUSINESS DECISION PROBLEM 22

Gilles Company Ltd. has working capital of $2,050,000 at the beginning of Year 10. Restrictions contained in bank loans require that working capital not fall below $2,000,000. The following projected information is available for Year 10:
(1) Budgeted net income (including extraordinary items) is $2,500,000. In addition to the extraordinary items described below, the following items were included in estimating net income: Depreciation, $700,000; amortization of premium on bonds payable, $50,000; uncollectible accounts expense, $60,000; and income taxes, $2,100,000.
(2) Cash dividends of $1,500,000 have been paid in recent years. The company would like to maintain dividends at this level.
(3) Sale of plant assets with a book value of $400,000 is expected to bring $500,000 net of income taxes.
(4) Additional plant assets costing $5,000,000 will be acquired. Payment will be as follows: 20% cash, 20% short-term note, and 60% through issuance of capital stock.
(5) Long-term investment will be sold at cost, $200,000.
(6) Bonds payable in the amount of $500,000, bearing interest at 11%, will be redeemed at 105 approximately 10 years prior to maturity in order to eliminate the high interest expense of $55,000 per year. The elimination of this interest was taken into account in estimating net income for Year 10. These bonds had been issued at par.

Instructions
a Consider all the information given above and prepare a projected statement of changes in financial position in order to determine the estimated increase or decrease in working capital for Year 10. Some of the information given may be irrelevant.
b Does it appear likely that the past dividend policy can be maintained in Year 10? What factors other than working capital position should be considered in determining the level of cash dividends declared by the board of directors?

TWENTY-
THREE

RESPONSIBILITY ACCOUNTING DEPARTMENTS AND BRANCHES

In most of our discussion thus far, we have viewed accounting as a system for information processing and measurement of assets, liabilities, and net income for a business unit as a whole. Considerable attention has been given to meeting the informational needs of outsiders, such as investors and creditors. In this and succeeding chapters, we shall focus closer attention on the *uses of accounting information by management* in planning and controlling the activities of a business unit.

Planning and control involve the formulation of plans, the taking of action, reporting the results of the action, and finally the evaluation of the action. This process can be illustrated as follows:

Managers need information to plan, act, report, and evaluate performance

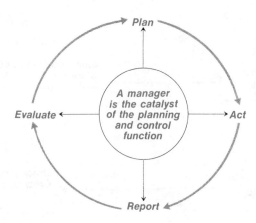

The key to this process is the manager, because each step requires decisions to be made based on relevant information. The outcome of management decisions must then be measured, reported, and evaluated on a regular basis. To be useful to management, an effective accounting system should yield information which is useful not only in arriving at decisions, but also in evaluating decisions and in making managers more accountable for their actions.

Responsibility accounting

Operating a business unit is a complex undertaking. Even in a single proprietorship it would be desirable for the owner to establish goals and measure performance so that he may know if he is attaining these goals and meeting his responsibilities to his business. In larger enterprises, with perhaps hundreds of managers and thousands of employees, it is necessary to assign specific organizational responsibilities to different managers. An information system designed to measure the performance of that segment of a business for which a given manager is responsible is often referred to as a *responsibility accounting system.*

A responsibility accounting system attempts to fit the functions of information gathering and internal reporting to the organizational structure of the business. In this way, the effectiveness of a manager can be judged on the basis of expenses incurred (or revenues earned) which are *directly under his control.* To illustrate, assume that a grocery chain operates stores at six different locations and that each store is divided into four departments. A diagram depicting a *partial* responsibility accounting system for sales salaries incurred by this grocery chain might appear as follows:

Who is responsible for total sales salaries of $810,000?

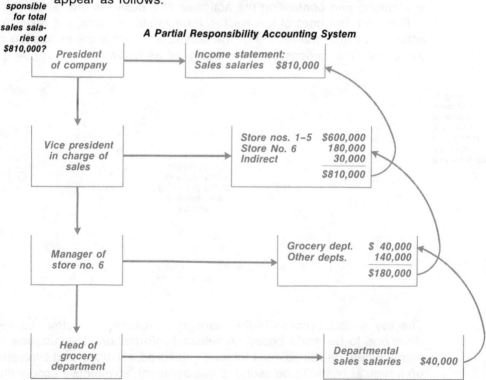

A Partial Responsibility Accounting System

| President of company | → | Income statement: Sales salaries $810,000 |

| Vice president in charge of sales | → | Store nos. 1–5 $600,000 / Store No. 6 180,000 / Indirect 30,000 / $810,000 |

| Manager of store no. 6 | → | Grocery dept. $ 40,000 / Other depts. 140,000 / $180,000 |

| Head of grocery department | → | Departmental sales salaries $40,000 |

This diagram indicates that the head of the grocery department is responsible for only the sales salaries incurred in his department; the manager of Store No. 6 is accountable for all salaries paid within his store; and the vice-president in charge of sales has responsibility for all sales salaries for the company. In a responsibility accounting system all expenses and contributions to net income can be similarly traced from the income statement down through the various levels of responsibility.

A responsibility accounting system should reflect the plans and performance of each segment or activity of a business organization. It is designed to provide timely information for decision making and for the evaluation of performance. In addition to being timely, such information should be understandable and should highlight deviations from plans so that appropriate corrective action can be taken.

All items of expense are the responsibility of some individual and should be charged to that individual at the *point of origin.* In other words, expenses should be viewed as the responsibility of the manager of the organizational unit where costs originate. The manager at this level is authorized to incur expenses and is in a position to exercise direct control over them. A department head, for example, is generally in the best position to exercise control over the expenses incurred in his department. When a responsibility accounting system is used, the amount of expenses the department head incurred in generating sales or in providing services to other segments of the business would be clearly reported. In this way the department head is held accountable for his area of responsibility without being able to pass the blame for poor overall company performance to "the other guys."

Responsibility accounting systems may be developed at all levels of an organization where specific areas of authority and responsibility can be reasonably identified. Top management has the ultimate responsibility for overall profitability of a business enterprise; vice-presidents and different levels of "middle management" are responsible for generating revenues from various products or territories and for controlling costs incurred in generating such revenues; at lower levels, managers are charged with the responsibility of reaching the revenue goals and controlling costs incurred within the units which they supervise. In the remaining pages of this chapter we shall direct our attention to two types of accountability units—departments and branches.

THE NEED FOR DEPARTMENTAL INFORMATION

If a business entity includes two or more segments, each providing a different service or handling different classes of merchandise, organization along departmental lines is a natural development. For example, a company consisting of a car rental service and an automobile repair shop could reasonably be operated as a two-department business. Departments are found in businesses of all sizes but are more likely to be found in larger companies; they are useful to service, merchandising, and manufacturing firms. A manager is usually put in charge of each department, and resources are assigned to enable him to carry out his responsibility. In addition, he may draw upon the general resources and staff talent of the entity for such services as accounting, financing, hiring, legal advice, advertising, transportation, and storage.

This kind of organizational subdivision creates a need for internal information about the operating results of each department. Top management can then determine the relative profitability of the various departments and evaluate the performance of department heads. Departmental accounting information also provides a basis for intelligent planning and control, as well as for assessing the effect of new ideas and procedures. To serve these managerial needs, the accountant has to refine his measurement process. In addition to determining the revenues and expenses of the business as a whole, he faces the problem of measuring the revenues and expenses attributable to each subdivision of the business.

Departments may be cost centers or profit centers

For information processing and control purposes, subdivisions of a business may be organized as either cost centers or profit centers. A *cost center* is a unit of a business which incurs expenses (or costs) but which does not directly generate revenues. Examples of cost centers include such *service departments* as personnel, accounting, and public relations, which provide services to other departments. A *profit center,* on the other hand, is a segment of a business which not only incurs expenses (or costs) but also produces revenues that can be identified with such a segment. A profit center is expected to make a profit contribution to the business by earning a fair rate of return on the assets it employs. Examples of profit centers include a furniture department of a large retail store, a branch of a large bank, and the Chevrolet Motor Division of General Motors Corporation.

Cost and profit centers represent control or responsibility units and are extensively used in business. Managers of cost centers are typically evaluated in terms of their ability to keep costs and expenses within budgeted allowances; managers of profit centers are most frequently judged on their ability to generate earnings. In this chapter we are primarily concerned with units of a retail business (departments and branches) which are organized as profit centers for accounting purposes.

The managerial viewpoint

The details of departmental revenues and expenses are not usually made available to the public, on the grounds that such information would be of considerable aid to competitors. Departmental accounting information, therefore, is designed to serve the needs of internal management, and we might ask, what use is made of such information?

1 *As a basis for planning and allocating resources.* Management wants to know how various departments are doing in order to have a guide in planning future activities and in allocating the resources and talent of the firm to those areas that have the greatest profit potential. If one department is producing larger profits than another, this may indicate that greater effort should be made to expand and develop the activities in the more profitable department.

2 *As a basis for corrective action.* A well-designed accounting system will throw a spotlight on troubled areas. A manager who is not doing a good job should be replaced; costs that are out of line should be more closely controlled; an unsuccessful department should be revamped or perhaps dropped altogether. Pointing up the areas that need managerial attention is an important function of responsibility accounting.

3 *As a basis for pricing decisions.* The idea that product prices are determined by finding costs and adding a required margin of profit contains only a grain of truth. For the average firm, prices are set by the market; and management's ability to exercise control over prices is severely limited by the prices of substitute products and by the actions of competitors. Nevertheless, over the long run, a firm must either set its prices high enough to cover all operating expenses plus a reasonable return on its investment or face extinction. If we are careful not to attribute too much to the statement, it may be said that departmental cost information is useful in making pricing decisions.

This is not a complete list of the uses that might be made by management of departmental accounting information. It serves to indicate, however, that we must keep the decision-making objective in mind in allocating revenues and expenses among departments.

Collecting information on departmental revenues and expenses

Two basic approaches may be used in developing departmental information for a business engaged in merchandising activities:

1 *Establish separate departmental accounts for each item of revenue and expense and identify each item with a particular department.* This method is easily adapted for accounts such as sales, purchases, and inventories. For example, a business having three departments would use a sales account, a purchase account, and an inventory account for each department. In large companies most of this data gathering would be computerized. Department stores, for example, may use *punched tags* such as the one illustrated below:

Punched tag used by department store

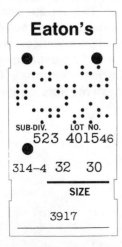

When the item is sold, the tag is removed and is mechanically processed in order to generate departmental sales and inventory information.

2 *Maintain only one general ledger account for a particular item of revenue or expense, and distribute the total amount among the various departments at the end of the accounting period.* When this procedure is used, distribution by departments is made on a work sheet at the end of the accounting period rather than in the ledger accounts. For example, rent might be recorded in a single expense account and the total allocated among departments. A simple departmental expense allocation sheet is illustrated on page 691.

Some companies carry departmentalization of operating results only as far as gross profit on sales; others extend the process to include certain direct operating expenses such as wages; a few go so far as to apportion *all* expenses among departments and compute net income on a departmental basis.

Departmental gross profit on sales

In a merchandising business a figure of extreme interest to management is the total gross profit realized over and above the cost of merchandise sold in any department. Gross profit on sales is a function of two variables: (*1*) the volume of goods sold and (*2*) the gross profit earned on each dollar of sales. The same total gross profit may be realized from a large volume of sales made at a low rate of gross profit, or from a smaller volume of sales made at a higher rate of gross profit.

Within any given business, department managers are constantly making decisions that affect the gross profit rate, in the hope of maintaining a sales volume that will maximize the total dollar gross profit realized by their departments. This is not to say that operating expenses may be ignored; obviously the ultimate objective is to earn a satisfactory level of net income.

DEPARTMENTAL REVENUES The first step in arriving at departmental gross profit is to departmentalize revenues. To illustrate, assume that the Mod Corporation Ltd. maintains in its general ledger separate departmental accounts for sales, sales returns and allowances, and sales discounts. As a convenient means of accumulating departmental revenue data, special columns may be added to the various journals. For example, the Mod Corporation's sales journal and cash receipts journal for a typical month might appear as shown on page 697.

Sales Journal

	Date	Invoice No.	Account Debited	LP	Accounts Receivable Dr	Cash Dr	Sales Dept. A Cr	Sales Dept. B Cr
Recording departmental revenue data	19___ Aug.	1	100	Abar Co. Ltd.	√		700		700	
				Cash sales			1,180	470	710
	31		Totals		50,200	4,900	32,600	22,500
					(5)	(√)	(200)	(300)

Cash Receipts Journal

Date		Account Credited	LP	Other Accounts Cr	Cash Sales Cr	Accounts Receivable Cr	Sales Discounts Dept. A Dr	Sales Discounts Dept. B Dr	Cash Dr
19___ Aug.	1	Cash sales			1,180				1,180
		High Co. Ltd.	√			1,000	15	5	980
	2	Sale of equipment at cost	206	800					800
	31	Totals		8,600	4,900	34,800	520	270	47,510
				(√)	(5)	(201)	(301)	(1)

The amount of credit sales applicable to each department may be computed from the original sales invoices. If cash registers are used, the division of cash sales by departments may be made at the time each sale is rung up; daily totals by departments will thus be available on the cash register tapes.

In the illustrative journals, cash sales have been recorded in both the sales and cash receipts journals. This procedure makes it possible to omit departmental sales columns in the cash receipts journal, since the distribution of sales by departments is made in the sales journal. The totals of the Cash debit column in the sales journal ($4,900) and the Cash Sales credit column in the cash receipts journal ($4,900) exactly offset and need not be posted.

If there is a large number of departments in a business, using a separate journal column for each departmental account would result in journals of unmanageable size. In such cases it is more efficient to analyze duplicate copies of sales invoices by departments, posting the totals directly to the departmental accounts in the ledger. The trend in modern accounting systems is to avoid journals with numerous columns by using various machine methods of sorting, classifying, and summarizing original data prior to recording in journals.

Regardless of the system used, the basic procedures are: (1) See that data by departments are entered on original invoices, credit memorandums, cash register tapes, etc.; (2) sort and accumulate these individual transaction figures to arrive at subtotals for each departmental account; (3) enter this information in ledger accounts.

Since separate departmental accounts for sales, sales returns and allowances, and sales discounts are used by the Mod Corporation Ltd., the net sales (as reported in the income statement on page 699) can be determined directly from the balances in these accounts.

DEPARTMENTAL COST OF GOODS SOLD We shall assume that the Mod Corporation Ltd. keeps separate departmental accounts for each element of cost of goods sold. Inventories, purchases, and purchase returns are readily identified by department. Purchase discounts and transportation-in must also be classified by department to determine the cost of goods sold by each department. This classification may be made at the time of each transaction or the total purchase discounts and total transportation-in may be allocated to individual departments at the end of the accounting period. The cost of goods sold by departments for the current year is shown in the income statement illustrated in the following section.

INCOME STATEMENT: GROSS PROFIT BY DEPARTMENTS An income statement for the Mod Corporation Ltd., departmentalized only through the gross profit on sales, is shown on page 699. Note that the gross profit as a percentage of net sales is given for the business as a whole and by departments.

If the number of departments were large, a horizontal expansion of the income statement in this fashion might become unwieldy, in which case separate statements of gross profit on sales for each department might be prepared and attached to the income statement for the business as a whole.

It is evident that Department A contributes a much higher rate of gross profit than Department B. By studying the reasons for this difference, management may be led to make changes in buying policies, selling prices, or the personnel of Department B in an effort to improve its performance. Whether Department A contributes more than B to the net income of the business, however, depends on the amount of operating expenses attributable to each department.

MOD CORPORATION LTD.
Income Statement
Current Year

	Total	Dept. A	Dept. B
Sales	$500,000	$320,000	$180,000
Less: Sales returns and allowances	(5,000)	(2,300)	(2,700)
Sales discounts	(8,000)	(6,000)	(2,000)
Net sales	$487,000	$311,700	$175,300
Cost of goods sold:			
Beginning inventory	$ 70,000	$ 28,000	$ 42,000
Purchases	360,000	205,200	154,800
Transportation-in	17,000	4,800	12,200
Purchase returns	(10,000)	(5,700)	(4,300)
Purchase discounts	(6,100)	(3,000)	(3,100)
Merchandise available for sale	$430,900	$229,300	$201,600
Less: Ending inventory	90,000	36,000	54,000
Cost of goods sold	$340,900	$193,300	$147,600
Gross profit on sales	$146,100	$118,400	$ 27,700
Gross profit as percentage of net sales (30% combined)		38%	16%
Operating expenses (details omitted)	125,500		
Operating income	$ 20,600		
Income taxes, 22%	4,532		
Net income	$ 16,068		
Net income per share	$0.12		

Allocating operating expenses to departments

An analysis of expenses by departments provides information about the cost of departmental operations and makes it possible to prepare an income statement showing departmental net income. Two steps are generally involved in allocating operating expenses to departments: First, identify the expenses which are considered *direct* expenses of certain departments, and second, identify the expenses which are considered *indirect* departmental expenses and allocate these to the respective departments on some basis which would properly recognize the benefits received by each department.

Direct expenses are those which may be identified by department, in the sense that if the department did not exist, the expense would not be incurred. *Indirect expenses* are incurred for the benefit of the business as a whole; they cannot be identified readily with the activities of a given department. These would, for the most part, continue even though a particular department were discontinued.

Some direct expenses may be charged to separate departmental expense accounts at the time they are incurred. Other expenses, even though they are direct in nature, may be more conveniently charged to a single account and allocated to departments at the end of the accounting period.

Indirect expenses, by their very nature, can be assigned to departments only by a process of allocation. For example, the salary of the president of the company is an expense not directly related to the activities of any particular department. If it is to be divided among the departments, some method of allocation is necessary which would charge each department with the approximate cost of the benefits it received.

Operating expenses may be allocated to departments through the use of a *departmental expense allocation sheet* similar to the one illustrated below for the Mod Corporation Ltd.:

MOD CORPORATION LTD.
Departmental Expense Allocation Sheet
Current Year

		Total Operating Expenses	Department A		Department B	
			Direct	Indirect	Direct	Indirect
Sales force expense	(1)*	$ 27,000	$16,900		$10,100	
Advertising expense	(2)	18,000	5,000	$ 6,250	3,000	$ 3,750
Building expense	(3)	16,000		9,600		6,400
Buying expense	(4)	26,800	14,000	2,850	7,800	2,150
Delivery expense	(5)	12,000		3,000	2,000	7,000
Administrative expense	(6)	25,700	3,100	12,800	2,600	7,200
Totals—direct and indirect		$125,500	$39,000	$34,500	$25,500	$26,500
Total for each department			$73,500		$52,000	

* See explanations below.

In order to keep this example short and simple, we have assumed that the Mod Corporation Ltd. grouped its operating expenses into various functions or activities performed. For example, sales force expense includes all compensation and payroll-related costs of salesmen and sales executives; delivery expense includes all costs of operating delivery trucks, wages of drivers, and all other costs relating to shipping merchandise to customers. The allocation of operating expenses in the departmental expense allocation sheet prepared by the Mod Corporation Ltd. is explained in the following sections.

1 Sales force expense. Mod Corporation's salespeople work exclusively in either Department A or Department B. This is an example of a direct expense clearly identified with the departments involved and thus charged to departments on the basis of the personnel involved. The expense allocation sheet shows that direct sales force expense incurred was $16,900 for Department A and $10,100 for Department B.

2 Advertising expense. The Mod Corporation Ltd. advertises primarily through newspapers, with occasional spot advertisements on radio and television. Direct advertising expense amounts to $8,000 and represents the cost of newspaper space and time purchased to advertise specific products identified with each department. Indirect advertising expense amounts to $10,000 and includes the cost of administering the advertising program, plus advertising applicable to the business as a whole. Indirect advertising expense is allocated in proportion to the direct advertising expense:

	Direct Advertising Expense	% of Total	Indirect Advertising Expense	Total Direct and Indirect
Department A	$5,000	62.5	$ 6,250	$11,250
Department B	3,000	37.5	3,750	6,750
Total	$8,000	100.0	$10,000	$18,000

3 Building expense. This includes all costs relating to the occupancy of the building. The Mod Corporation Ltd. allocates the building expense on the basis of square feet occupied by each department, 60% by Department A and 40% by Department B. Thus $9,600 (60% of $16,000) was allocated to Department A and $6,400 (40% of $16,000) was allocated to Department B. If the value of the floor space varies (as, for example, between the first floor and the second floor) then the allocation would be made on the basis of *value of space* rather than square footage.

4 Buying expense. The compensation of departmental buyers, their travel expenses, and certain merchandise handling costs, a total of $21,800, were considered direct expenses and assigned to the two departments on the basis of the personnel involved. Department A was charged with $14,000 of this direct expense and Department B absorbed $7,800. The indirect buying expense of $5,000 was allocated on the basis of total departmental purchases of $360,000 as follows: Department A, $205,200/$360,000 × $5,000, or $2,850; Department B, $154,800/$360,000 × $5,000, or $2,150. The possible defects of purchases as an allocation basis are obvious; there is no necessary reason why the cost of buying or handling an item of large dollar value is significantly greater than for a less costly item.

5 Delivery expense. Department B shipped certain merchandise by common carrier at a cost of $2,000, a direct expense of this department. The $10,000 balance of the cost of maintaining a delivery service applies to both departments. A study covering several months of typical operation showed that on the average 70% of all delivery requests originated in Department B; therefore 30% ($3,000) of the indirect delivery expense was charged to Department A, and 70% ($7,000) to Department B.

6 Administrative expense. Two direct expenses were included in the administrative expense category; the remainder were indirect:

	Total	Department A	Department B
Direct administrative expense:			
Uncollectible accounts expense	$ 3,700	$ 2,300	$1,400
Insurance on inventories	2,000	800	1,200
Total direct expenses	$ 5,700	$ 3,100	$2,600
Indirect administrative expense (allocated on basis of net sales)	20,000	12,800	7,200
Total administrative expense	$25,700	$15,900	$9,800

The division of the $3,700 uncollectible accounts expense was made on the basis of an analysis of accounts charged off during the period.

If this had not been feasible, allocation on the basis of credit sales in each department would have been reasonable. Insurance on inventories of $2,000 was charged to the departments on the basis of the average inventory in each department ($32,000 and $48,000, respectively), or a 40:60 ratio. Indirect administrative expense of $20,000 was allocated on the basis of net sales, for want of a more reasonable basis.

Department A, $311,700/$487,000 × $20,000	$12,800
Department B, $175,300/$487,000 × $20,000	7,200
Total	$20,000

The following summary of operating expenses for the Mod Corporation Ltd. will be useful to us in discussing the possibility of discontinuing Department B, which appears to be losing money:

	Total	Department A	Department B
Operating expenses:			
Direct	$ 64,500	$39,000	$25,500
Indirect	**61,000**	**34,500**	**26,500**
Total	$125,500	$73,500	$52,000

Departmental income statement

On the basis of departmental data developed thus far, we can now prepare a statement showing the net income of the business and of each department.

MOD CORPORATION LTD.
Departmental Income Statement
Current Year

	Total	Department A	Department B
Net sales.....................	$487,000	$311,700	$175,300
Cost of goods sold	340,900	193,300	147,600
Gross profit on sales	$146,100	$118,400	$ 27,700
Operating expenses (see departmental expense allocation sheet on page 700):			
Sales force expense	$ 27,000	$ 16,900	$ 10,100
Advertising expense	18,000	11,250	6,750
Building expense	16,000	9,600	6,400
Buying expense	26,800	16,850	9,950
Delivery expense	12,000	3,000	9,000
Administrative expense	25,700	15,900	9,800
Total operating expenses	$125,500	$ 73,500	$ 52,000
Income (or loss) before income taxes	$ 20,600	$ 44,900	$(24,300)
Income taxes (or credit), 22%.....	4,532	9,878	(5,346)
Net income (or loss)	$ 16,068	$ 35,022	$(18,954)
Net income per share...........	$0.12		

Should Department B be closed?

For the sake of simplicity, we are assuming that income taxes are paid by the Mod Corporation Ltd. at the flat rate of 22%. To reflect clearly the relationship between income taxes and operating results, the income tax expense charged to Department A is 22% of the income before income taxes of that department, and this is offset by a credit of $5,346 equal to 22% of the loss before income taxes of $24,300 reported in Department B.

WHEN IS A DEPARTMENT UNPROFITABLE?   The first reaction of management, confronted with the departmental income statement shown above, might be that the corporation would be better off if Department B were dropped. The income statement appears to indicate that net income would have been $35,022 rather than $16,068 were it not for the existence of Department B. Is this true?

If we could, with a wave of the hand, blot Department B out of existence, the income statement of the Mod Corporation Ltd. for the current year would probably appear as follows:

MOD CORPORATION LTD.
Income Statement Reflecting Elimination of Department B
Current Year

Effect of eliminating Department B	*Net sales.*		*$311,700*
	Cost of goods sold		*193,300*
	Gross profit on sales		*$118,400*
	Operating expenses:		
	Direct expenses of Department A (see departmental allocation sheet on page 700)	*$39,000*	
	Indirect expenses (total originally allocated to both departments, $34,500 + $26,500)	*61,000*	*100,000*
	Income before income taxes		*$ 18,400*
	Income taxes (22%)		*4,048*
	Net income		*$ 14,352*
	Net income per share.		*$0.11*

Instead of improving the company's showing, the result is a *decrease* in income of $1,716 ($16,068 − $14,352). Apparently the information in the departmental income statement is misleading. The answer to this paradox is that *the elimination of Department B would eliminate the entire gross profit on sales earned in that department but not any of the indirect expenses that were allocated to Department B.* An explanation of the estimated decline in net income of $1,716 shown above ($16,068 − $14,352), is summarized on page 704.

It is apparent from this summary that reducing direct expenses by $25,500 and eliminating $484 in income taxes are not sufficient to offset the decrease in gross profit on sales of $27,700 that would follow from

MOD CORPORATION LTD.
Estimated Effect of Elimination of Department B
Current Year

	Depart-ment B's share	Not Eliminated (Indirect)	Eliminated (Direct)	Effect on Net Income
Gross profit on sales	$27,700		$27,700	$(27,700)
Operating expenses	52,000	$26,500	25,500	25,500
Effect on income before income taxes				$ (2,200)
Reduction in income taxes (22% of $2,200)				484
Reduction in net income if Department B is eliminated				$ (1,716)

Is Depart-ment B un-profitable? (Assuming Elimination of Department B)

the elimination of Department B. If we compare the effect on expenses shown on this summary with the expenses allocated to Department B as shown on page 700, we see that only direct expenses of $25,500 were assumed to be eliminated as a result of the elimination of this department. This is no coincidence, since direct expenses were defined as those relating to the activities of a particular department that would be eliminated if the department did not exist. Thus compensation of sales and buying personnel, cost of direct advertising space, outbound transportation paid to carriers, uncollectible accounts expense, and insurance on inventories would presumably disappear along with Department B.

The $26,500 of operating expenses that would *not* be eliminated is the amount of indirect expenses assigned to Department B. The assumption that indirect expenses are inescapable (fixed) and that they would remain unchanged is a convenient assumption but, realistically, some reduction in indirect expenses would probably occur if Department B were eliminated. The change in indirect expenses that follows from departmental changes will depend to some extent on the alternatives that are being considered. For example, the indirect expense, building expense, would continue largely unchanged whether Department B existed or not, since the Mod Corporation Ltd. owns the entire building. However, if the Mod Corporation Ltd. were to drop Department B and reduce the scale of its activities, it might rent the surplus space to outsiders and thus reduce building expense. On the other hand, if the question were whether Department B should be reorganized or a new kind of operation substituted for it, building expenses and other indirect expenses would probably not change by an amount large enough to influence the decision.

There is considerable wisdom in the phrase "different costs for different purposes." The allocation of costs for one purpose may not produce results that are significant for a different kind of decision; special cost studies are often necessary to answer particular questions. Some of these will be discussed in subsequent chapters.

Departmental contribution to indirect expenses (overhead)

We have seen that the gross profit on sales by departments can be determined with good assurance that the results are meaningful and useful. We have seen also that the division of direct expenses among departments is a fairly straightforward process. Sales revenues, cost of goods sold, and direct expenses are all operating elements that, in general, relate clearly to the existence of a given department and its activities.

On the other hand, most indirect expenses (*overhead*) are costs associated with the business as a whole, and in general they lie outside the control of department managers. Because of their indirect relationship to departmental activities, any basis of allocation used is somewhat arbitrary and the proper interpretation of the results is often in doubt.

Some accountants argue that the important benefits of departmental accounting can be gained by stopping short of a full allocation of all expenses to departments. They urge that each department be credited with revenues and charged with expenses that, in the opinion of management, would disappear if the department did not exist. This approach leads to a departmental income statement showing the **contribution of each department to the indirect expenses of the business.** Such a statement, using figures previously developed for the Mod Corporation Ltd., is illustrated below:

MOD CORPORATION LTD.
Departmental Income Statement Showing Contribution to Indirect Expenses
Current Year

	Total	Department A	Department B
Net sales	$487,000	$311,700	$175,300
Cost of goods sold	340,900	193,300	147,600
Gross profit on sales	$146,100(30%)	$118,400(38%)	$ 27,700(16%)
Direct departmental expenses (see page 700):			
Sales force expense	$ 27,000	$ 16,900	$ 10,100
Advertising expense	8,000	5,000	3,000
Buying expense	21,800	14,000	7,800
Delivery expense	2,000		2,000
Administrative expense	5,700	3,100	2,600
Total direct expenses	$ 64,500	$ 39,000	$ 25,500
Contribution to indirect expenses	$ 81,600	$ 79,400	$ 2,200

Indirect expenses

(see page 691):

Advertising	
expense......	*$10,000*
Building	
expense......	*16,000*
Buying	
expense......	*5,000*
Delivery	
expense......	*10,000*
Administrative	
expense......	*20,000*
Total indirect expenses	*61,000*
Income before income taxes	*$ 20,600*
Income taxes, 22%........	*4,532*
Net income	*$ 16,068*
Net income per share	*$0.12*

In contrast to the departmental net income statement on page 702, which shows that Department B suffered a net loss of $18,954, this statement shows that Department B contributed $2,200 (before income taxes) to the indirect expenses of the business. This figure agrees with the estimated reduction in net income *before income taxes* (see page 704) if Department B were discontinued.

The performance of department managers can be better judged by their contribution to indirect expenses than by the *net income* or *loss* for a department, since to a large extent indirect expenses are outside the control of department managers. Furthermore, so long as a department is covering its direct expenses, it is probably contributing to the profitability of the business as a whole.

WORKING PAPERS FOR DEPARTMENTAL OPERATIONS A work sheet, similar to the one illustrated in Chapter 5, may still be used when operating expenses are allocated among departments. Each revenue and expense item is extended into the proper departmental columns, as illustrated in the solution to the Demonstration Problem for Your Review at the end of this chapter. The difference between the departmental Debit and Credit columns in the income statement section is the contribution to indirect expenses for each department.

A separate departmental expense allocation sheet, similar to the one illustrated on page 700, is usually prepared to support the amount of each departmental expense item shown on the work sheet and the departmental income statement.

ACCOUNTING SYSTEMS FOR BRANCH OPERATIONS

Merchandising companies often do business in more than one location by opening *branch stores.* As a business grows it may open branches in order to market its products over a larger territory and thus increase its profits. A branch is typically located at some distance from the *home office* and generally carries a stock of merchandise, sells the merchandise, makes collection on receivables, and pays some of its operating expenses. It should be emphasized that a branch is not a separate legal entity; it is simply a segment of a business which may be a single proprietorship, a partnership, or a corporation. From an accounting standpoint, a branch is a clearly identifiable *profit center* and offers an opportunity to implement the principles of responsibility accounting discussed earlier in this chapter.

An accounting system for a branch should generate information needed to measure the profitability of the branch and to ensure strong control over branch assets. Management needs information to answer questions such as: Is the branch yielding a satisfactory rate of return on the capital invested in it? Should the branch be expanded or closed? Are prices on merchandise sold by the branch too low? How much of a bonus should the branch manager receive? How much merchandise does the branch have in stock?

The home office may provide the branch with a cash *working fund* to be used for the payment of branch expenses. The merchandise handled by a branch may be obtained solely from the home office or a portion may be purchased from outside suppliers. Bills for merchandise purchases and certain operating expenses, such as wages and insurance, may be paid by the home office, depending on the size of the branch working fund. Cash receipts of the branch may be deposited either in a branch or a home office bank account. When a branch is authorized to have its own bank account, it will also generally pay its bills and remit any surplus cash to the home office. The amount of operating independence given to a branch varies among companies and even among branches within the same company.

The accounting system designed for a branch also varies among companies and among branches of the same company. Although many variations exist, branch accounting systems are either *centralized* in the home office or *decentralized* at the branch.

Branch records centralized in home office

In a *centralized* accounting system, the branch is provided with a small working fund (similar to a petty cash fund which is replenished periodically) to pay for small items of expense. The home office keeps most of the accounting records relating to the branch. Records of branch assets, liabilities, revenues, payrolls, and other expenses are maintained in the home office which processes the business documents (sales slips, deposit slips, invoices, etc.) received from the branch. The branch keeps very few accounting records and is generally instructed to deposit cash receipts in a home office account with a local bank. A centralized system is particularly appropriate when data processing equipment is located in the home office or when the branch is too small to hire a full-time accountant.

Separate records of revenues and expenses for each branch are maintained in the journals and ledgers of the home office. In this way the operating results for each branch can be readily ascertained. Thus the three important features of a centralized accounting system for a branch are: (1) A working fund for the branch is established and is replenished as needed; (2) all business documents originating at the branch are transmitted to the home office; and (3) a separate record of branch assets, liabilities, revenues, and expenses is maintained by the home office.

Records decentralized at the branch

In contrast to the accounting system which is centralized in the home office, a branch may keep a complete self-balancing set of books with journals, ledgers, and a chart of accounts. Such a *decentralized* accounting system enables the branch accountant to prepare a complete set of financial statements for the branch. These statements are then submitted to the home office. The number and type of accounts, the internal control procedures, the form and content of financial statements, and the accounting policies are generally prescribed by the home office. As a minimum, the transactions recorded by the branch generally include the expenses under the control of the branch manager and the revenues generated at the branch. At the end of the accounting period, the home office may notify the branch that certain expenses incurred at the home office have been allocated to the branch. Records of certain assets purchased by the home office and assigned to the branch, such as furniture and equipment and the related depreciation accounts, are often kept at the home office. Bank loans may be negotiated and recorded by the home office; the proceeds on such loans are advanced to the branch, or simply deposited in the branch bank account.

TYPICAL BRANCH TRANSACTIONS ILLUSTRATED In order to illustrate the basic features of a decentralized branch accounting system, assume that on March 1st, Homer & Company (a single proprietorship) opens a branch in the city of Brady. The company rents a fully equipped store and transfers cash of $10,000 and store supplies of $1,500 to the branch. The entries on the books of the Brady Branch and the home office to record this transfer, along with other *branch* transactions during March, are shown in summary form on page 709.

Summary of Transactions for March

	Branch Books			Home Office Books		
(1) Home office opened Brady Branch and transferred cash and store supplies to the branch.	Cash	10,000		Brady Branch	11,500	
	Store Supplies	1,500		Cash		10,000
	Home Office		11,500	Store Supplies		1,500
(2) Merchandise purchased by branch. Branch uses a perpetual inventory system.[1]	Inventory	18,000		No entry		
	Accounts Payable		18,000			
(3) Expenses incurred by branch.	Selling Expense	2,500		No entry		
	General Expense	1,900				
	Cash		3,200			
	Accounts Payable		1,000			
	Store Supplies		200			
(4) General expense incurred by home office allocated to branch.	General Expense	100		Brady Branch	100	
	Home Office		100	General Expense		100
(5) Sales made by branch.	Cash	3,000		No entry		
	Accounts Receivable	17,000				
	Sales		20,000			
(6) Collections by branch on accounts receivable.	Cash	13,000		No entry		
	Accounts Receivable		13,000			
(7) Payments by branch to merchandise creditors.	Accounts Payable	14,500		No entry		
	Cash		14,500			
(8) Branch remits cash to home office at end of month.	Home Office	5,000		Cash	5,000	
	Cash		5,000	Brady Branch		5,000
(9) To record the cost of goods sold by branch during the month.	Cost of Goods Sold	12,000		No entry		
	Inventory		12,000			

[1] See p. 322 for a description of a perpetual inventory system.

Only transactions (*1*), (*4*), and (*8*) are recorded on the home office books, because these three transactions involve both the branch and the home office and thus require the use of the *reciprocal* accounts as follows:

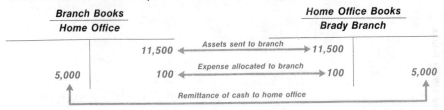

Branch Books		Home Office Books	
Home Office		Brady Branch	
	11,500 ← Assets sent to branch → 11,500		
5,000	100 ← Expense allocated to branch → 100		5,000
↑	Remittance of cash to home office		↑

Note that the debit balance in the Home Office account, $6,600, is equal to the credit balance in the Brady Branch account, $6,600.

The Home Office account on the branch books may be viewed as a "proprietorship" account which shows the net investment in the branch made by the home office. It is credited for assets transferred to the branch and for expenses allocated to the branch by the home office; it is debited when cash or other assets are remitted to the home office by the branch. At the end of the accounting period when the branch closes its books, the branch income or loss is closed into the Home Office account. A branch income is debited to the Income Summary account and credited to the Home Office account; a loss reported by the branch would be debited to the Home Office account and credited to Income Summary.

The net investment in the branch is recorded in the Brady Branch account on the books of the home office. This account is debited when assets are transferred to the branch or when expenses incurred at the home office are allocated to the branch; it is credited when cash or other assets are received from the branch. Income reported by the branch is debited to the Brady Branch account and credited to Income—Brady Branch; branch losses would be debited to Loss—Brady Branch and credited to the Brady Branch account.

STATEMENTS FOR THE BRANCH After the transactions illustrated above are recorded and summarized, the accountant for the Brady Branch submits the following statements to the home office:

BRADY BRANCH		
Income Statement		
For Month of March		
Sales		$20,000
Cost of goods sold		12,000
Gross profit on sales		$ 8,000
Less: Selling expense	$2,500	
General expense	2,000	4,500
Net income		$ 3,500

BRADY BRANCH	
Balance Sheet	
March 31	
Cash	$ 3,300
Accounts receivable	4,000
Inventory	6,000
Store supplies	1,300
	$14,600
Accounts payable	$ 4,500
Home office	6,600
Net income	3,500
	$14,600

WORKING PAPERS FOR COMBINED STATEMENTS FOR HOME OFFICE AND BRANCH When the accountant for the home office receives the branch statements for March, he can prepare *combined statements* through the use of working papers similar to those illustrated below. The branch figures are taken from the statements submitted by the branch and the home office figures are assumed.

HOMER & COMPANY

Working Papers for Combined Statements

For Month Ended March 31

	Adjusted Trial Balances		Eliminations		
	Home Office	Branch	Debit	Credit	Combined
Debit balances:					
Cash	9,100	3,300			12,400
Accounts receivable	26,000	4,000			30,000
Inventory	34,000	6,000			40,000
Store supplies	3,000	1,300			4,300
Land	25,000				25,000
Buildings and equipment	60,000				60,000
Brady Branch	6,600			(1) 6,600	
Cost of goods sold	50,000	12,000			62,000
Selling expense	6,500	2,500			9,000
General expense	5,800	2,000			7,800
Interest expense	300				300
Total debits	226,300	31,100			250,800
Credit balances:					
Notes payable	40,000				40,000
Accounts payable	22,500	4,500			27,000
Accrued liabilities	2,800				2,800
Home office		6,600	(1) 6,600		
John Homer, capital	75,000				75,000
Sales	85,000	20,000			105,000
Purchase discounts	1,000				1,000
Total credits	226,300	31,100	6,600	6,600	250,800

Explanation of elimination:
(1) Reciprocal accounts on books of home office and branch are eliminated. These accounts have no significance since the home office and the branch are a single entity. This elimination entry is made only on the working papers; it is not recorded on the books of either the home office or the branch.

The figures in the Combined column are used to prepare the income statement and the balance sheet for Homer & Company, and since there is nothing unusual about these statements, they will not be illustrated.

CLOSING ENTRIES FOR BRANCH At the end of the accounting period, the revenue and expense accounts on the books of the branch are closed and the income of $3,500 is transferred to the Home Office account. The home office records the branch income in the Income—Brady Branch account; the balance in this account is then closed to Income Summary when the home office books are closed. These entries are illustrated below:

Branch Books			Home Office Books		
Sales	20,000		Brady Branch	3,500	
Cost of Goods Sold .		12,000	Income—Brady Branch		3,500
Selling Expense . . .		2,500	To record branch income.		
General Expense . . .		2,000	Income—Brady Branch . .	3,500	
Income Summary . .		3,500	Income Summary . . .		3,500
To close revenue and			To close branch income		
expense accounts.			to Income Summary.		
Income Summary	3,500				
Home Office		3,500			
To transfer balance in					
Income Summary ac-					
count to Home Office					
account.					

Interdepartmental and interbranch pricing policies

In order to obtain a better measure of departmental or branch profit performance, some companies bill the merchandise transferred to departments or branches at prices above cost. Of course, a company does not "make a profit" by simply transferring merchandise to one of its departments or branches; a profit on such transfers can only be realized when the merchandise is sold to customers. When end-of-period statements for the company as a whole are prepared, the *unrealized profits* on intracompany transfers of merchandise are eliminated. The *actual* cost of merchandise sold is deducted from revenue and the actual cost of merchandise on hand is included among the current assets in the balance sheet.

DEMONSTRATION PROBLEM FOR YOUR REVIEW

The summarized adjusted trial balance of the Suburb Outlet Company Ltd. for the fiscal year ending on September 30 is shown on page 713. (Note that the items are listed in alphabetical order for the objectives of this problem.)

SUBURB OUTLET COMPANY LTD.
Adjusted Trial Balance
September 30, Current Year

Administrative expense	$ 43,600	
Advertising expense	40,600	
Accumulated depreciation		$ 72,000
Buildings and equipment	167,000	
Building occupancy expense	18,000	
Buying expense	25,600	
Capital stock		50,000
Cost of goods sold	368,500	
Current assets	166,000	
Current liabilities		84,400
Goodwill	25,000	
Interest expense	5,500	
Interest earned		1,200
Land	42,000	
Long-term notes payable		80,000
Net sales		578,600
Retained earnings		70,600
Sales salaries	35,000	
	$936,800	$936,800

Revenues and expenses are analyzed below:

	Total	Direct Expenses		Indirect Expenses
		Dept. A	Dept. B	
Net sales	$578,600	$360,000	$218,600	
Interest earned	1,200	500	700	
Administrative expense	43,600	12,300	5,900	$25,400
Advertising expense	40,600	12,400	12,200	16,000
Building occupancy expense . . .	18,000	2,800	4,000	11,200
Buying expense	25,600	10,300	5,600	9,700
Cost of goods sold	368,500	218,500	150,000	
Sales salaries	35,000	18,000	9,000	8,000

No provision has been made for corporate income taxes, which are 25% on the first $50,000 of income and 49% on income in excess of $50,000.

Instructions Prepare year-end working papers (10-column) from which a departmental income statement and a balance sheet could be prepared. The Suburb Outlet Company Ltd. is interested in knowing the contribution that each department makes toward the indirect expenses of the business.

Since all adjustments other than for income taxes have been made, the working papers may start with the adjusted trial balance. Allow two columns each for the following: Income Statement, Department A; Income Statement, Department B; Unallocated (for indirect expenses and total departmental contribution to indirect expenses); and Balance Sheet.

QUESTIONS

1 What is a *responsibility accounting* system?

2 Distinguish between a *cost center* and a *profit center.*

3 What are some uses that management may make of departmental accounting information?

4 The College Bookstore has hired a new manager. In the past the income statement of the bookstore has shown only total revenues and operating expenses. The new manager wants to introduce procedures for measuring gross profits for each of three departmental areas: textbooks, general books, and merchandise. Explain what changes in the accounting system will be required and what benefits the new manager may expect to gain from the departmental information.

5 The manager of a retail store states that the selling prices in his business are established by adding 50% to merchandise cost.
  a If this statement is factual, what rate of gross profit per dollar of gross sales should the company realize?
  b Assuming that the actual gross profit for one department of this firm for a given period is 28% of *net* sales, what reasons can you give to explain this?

6 What two steps are generally involved in allocating operating expenses to departments?

7 Explain the distinction between direct expenses and indirect expenses as these terms are used in relation to expense allocation among departments.

8 Atwood Hardware has three operating departments. In its departmental income statement, building occupancy expenses are allocated among departments on the basis of sales. Explain why you do or do not agree that this procedure will produce useful information for management.

9 After examining an income statement showing net income by departments, the manager of one department complains that the amount of income taxes allocated to his department is greater than the amount the business as a whole will have to pay, and he feels this is entirely unreasonable. Explain how this could happen, and whether or not you agree with the department manager's view.

10 What is meant by the term *contribution to indirect expenses?* Explain why management may find information about the contribution to overhead of each department more useful than departmental net income figures.

11 Briefly describe the type of information that managers should obtain from a branch accounting system.

12 Differentiate between a *centralized* and a *decentralized* accounting system for branch operations.

13 Describe the nature of the Home Office account which appears on the books of the branch and the Branch account which appears on the books of the home office. Why are these two accounts referred to as *reciprocal* accounts?

14 What is the reason for preparing working papers for combined statements of the home office and branch?

EXERCISES

Ex. 23-1 The floor space on the first floor is twice as valuable as the floor space on the second floor. Each of the two floors has 12,000 square feet and total monthly rental paid on the building is $1,500. How much of the monthly rental expense should be allocated to a department which occupies 4,800 square feet on the second floor?

Ex. 23-2 The Feltham Company Ltd. allocates indirect operating expenses to its two departments on the basis of sales. In Year 1, the following allocation was made:

	Total	Dept. A	Dept. B
Sales	$500,000	$300,000	$200,000
Indirect operating expenses	140,000	84,000	56,000

Assume that the sales price of the products sold in Department B are increased by 100% in Year 2 resulting in total sales of $400,000 for Department B. Assume also that indirect operating expenses remain unchanged at $140,000. How much of these expenses will be allocated to each department in Year 2? Is the result logical?

Ex. 23-3 The president of Beaver Company Ltd. wants to eliminate Department B "because it's losing money." The operating results for the latest year appear below:

	Total	Dept. A	Dept. B
Sales	$150,000	$100,000	$ 50,000
Operating expenses (40% of which remain			
constant at all levels of sales)	135,000	60,000	75,000
Operating income	$ 15,000	$ 40,000	$(25,000)

What advice would you give the president, assuming that the indirect operating expenses of $54,000 would remain unchanged if Department B is eliminated?

Ex. 23-4 A given department shows an annual operating loss of $12,000 after deducting $18,000 of operating expenses. If $8,000 of the operating expenses allocated to this department are fixed and cannot be avoided, what would be the effect on the company's operating income if this particular department is closed?

Ex. 23-5 Given below are the reciprocal interbranch accounts at the end of Year 1:

Branch Books

Home Office

Date	Transaction	Dr	Cr	Balance
12/1	Balance			91,600
12/10	Cash remitted	14,000		77,600
12/20	Merchandise received		10,000	87,600
12/31	Net income		6,500	94,100

Home Office Books

Jersey Branch

Date	Transaction	Dr	Cr	Balance
12/1	Balance			91,600
12/12	Cash received		14,000	77,600
12/19	Merchandise shipped	10,000		87,600
12/29	Equipment sent	2,000		89,600

Prepare the entries required to bring each set of books up to date at the end of Year 1.

Ex. 23-6 Refer to Ex. 23-5 above.

 a What is the *correct* balance in each account at the end of Year 1?

 b Give the elimination entry that would be required on the working papers at end of Year 1 in preparing combined statements for the home office and the branch.

PROBLEMS

Group A

23A-1 Given below are the results for the two departments operated by Sally's Smart Shop during Year 1:

	Dept. X	Dept. Y
Sales	$311,000	$175,000
Sales returns and allowances	6,000	10,000
Direct departmental expenses	60,000	40,000
Indirect departmental expenses (not allocated), $45,000		
Interest earned (not allocated), $5,000		
Gross profit percentage (on net sales)	40%	30%

Instructions Prepare a departmental income statement for Year 1 showing contribution to indirect expenses. Use three columns as follows: Total, Dept. X, and Dept. Y. Disregard income taxes.

23A-2 The Winnipeg Company Ltd. operates a retail business in a three-story building. Each floor has usable space of 20,000 square feet. The occupancy cost for the building per year averages $128,400. There are a number of separate departments in the store, and departmental income statements are prepared each year. Department no. 4 occupies 10,000 square feet of space on the first floor. Department no. 8 occupies 12,500 square feet of space on the third floor.

In allocating occupancy cost among the various departments, the accountant has determined that the average annual occupancy cost per square foot is $2.14 ($128,400 ÷ 60,000); therefore he has charged Department no. 4 with $21,400 of occupancy cost and Department no. 8 with $26,750, on the basis of space occupied.

Hank Mays, the manager of Department no. 8, feels that this allocation is unreasonable. He has made a study of rental prices being charged for similar property in the area and finds the following:

	Average Yearly Rental per Square Foot
First-floor space	$5.00
Second-floor space	3.00
Third-floor space	2.00

On the basis of this evidence, Mays argues that the charge to his department should be made on the *relative value* of space on each floor.

Instructions
a Comment on the validity of Mays' position.
b On the basis of Mays' findings, how much occupancy cost per year should be charged to Department no. 4 and to Department no. 8? Show computations.

23A-3 Elmer Young owns an apple orchard, from which he harvested and sold during the current year 200,000 pounds of apples. The price received varied in accordance with the grade of apple, as shown in the table below:

Grade of Apple	Pounds	Price per Pound	Receipts
Superior	40,000	$0.24	$ 9,600
Medium	100,000	0.108	10,800
Cooking	60,000	0.06	3,600
	200,000		$24,000

Young's expenses for the year, as taken from his accounting records, are given below:

		Dollars	Per Pound
Growing expenses		$ 6,000	$0.03
Harvesting expenses		4,000	0.02
Packing and shipping:			
Superior (40,000 pounds)	$2,000		0.05
Medium (100,000 pounds)	4,000		0.04
Cooking (60,000 pounds)	1,800	7,800	0.03
Total expenses		$17,800	

Young asked a friend, who was taking an accounting course at a nearby university, to determine his income from each grade of apple. The friend gave him the following statement:

	Total	Superior	Medium	Cooking
Sales	$24,000	$9,600	$10,800	$ 3,600
Expenses:				
Growing	$ 6,000	$1,200	$ 3,000	$ 1,800
Harvesting	4,000	800	2,000	1,200
Packing and shipping	7,800	2,000	4,000	1,800
Total expenses	$17,800	$4,000	$ 9,000	$ 4,800
Net income (or loss)	$ 6,200	$5,600	$ 1,800	$(1,200)

After studying this statement, Young remarked to a neighbor, "I made a lot of money on my superiors and a little bit on the mediums, but I should have dumped the cooking apples in the river; they cost me more than I got for them!"

Instructions Do you agree with Young's remark to his neighbor? Discuss. What kind of statement of income per grade of apple would you have prepared for Young? Illustrate the results that would be obtained, assuming that the indirect expenses (growing and harvesting) are allocated on the basis of total sales value of the different grades of apples.

23A-4 The summarized adjusted trial balance shown below was prepared from the records of Hewitt & O'Rourke, a retailing partnership, at the end of July of the current year. The partnership keeps separate departmental accounts for sales and cost of goods sold.

	Debit	Credit
Administrative expense	$ 23,300	
Advertising expense	17,600	
Accumulated depreciation		$149,300
Buildings and equipment	338,100	
Buying expense	20,000	
Cost of goods sold: Dept. A	99,000	
Cost of goods sold: Dept. B	81,000	
Current assets	107,000	
Current liabilities		42,700
Hewitt, capital, June 30		86,000
Interest expense	600	
Land	25,000	
Mortgage payable		120,000
Net sales: Dept. A		180,000
Net sales: Dept. B		120,000
Occupancy expense	22,000	
O'Rourke, capital, June 30		64,000
Selling expense	28,400	
	$762,000	$762,000

An analysis of operating expenses during July indicates that the following amounts in each class of expense are directly chargeable to the departments. (The allocation basis of the indirect portion of each class of expense is shown in brackets.)

	Direct Expenses		Indirect
	Dept. A	Dept. B	Expenses
Administrative expense (8 to 5 ratio)	$ 6,000	$3,000	$14,300
Advertising expense (on basis of net sales)	7,000	5,000	5,600
Buying expense (on basis of cost of goods sold)	7,300	5,500	7,200
Occupancy expense (equally)	500	1,000	20,500
Selling expense (on basis of net sales)	11,800	7,200	9,400

The partnership agreement provides that net income shall be divided as follows: Hewitt, 60%; O'Rourke, 40%. The partners made no withdrawals during July.

Instructions

a Prepare a departmental expense allocation sheet for the month of July. Use the form illustrated on page 700.

b Prepare a departmental income statement for July showing contribution to indirect expenses. Use the form illustrated on page 705. Show the division of net income among the partners below the net income figure in the income statement.

c Prepare a condensed income statement for July, assuming that both direct and indirect expenses are allocated to the departments. Show a single figure for operating expenses. Does this statement suggest that Department B should be eliminated?

23A-5 For many years the Colonial Furniture Company Ltd. has operated a store near downtown Vancouver. Early in Year 10, the company decided to open a branch store in Surrey and to use a decentralized accounting system for the branch. Both the branch and the home office use a perpetual inventory system. During the month of February the following transactions (given in summary form) were completed by the branch:

Feb. 1 The home office sent $5,000 cash to the branch to be used as a working fund and authorized the branch manager to sign a lease on a store.

Feb. 2 The branch manager signed the lease and paid rent for February, $1,000 (debit Operating Expense on branch books).

Feb. 3 Received merchandise from home office, $7,200 (debit Inventory on branch books; credit Inventory on home office books).

Feb. 5 Purchased merchandise on credit from local factory, $6,800 (debit Inventory on branch books).

Feb. 10 Received office equipment from home office, $1,500. The Office Equipment account is carried on the books of the home office.

Feb. 12 Borrowed $3,000 from local bank and deposited balance in bank current account.

Feb. 28 Sales during February: cash, $4,200; credit, $12,100.

Feb. 28 Payments to merchandise creditors, $4,000.

Feb. 28 Collections on accounts receivable, $5,750.

Feb. 28 Paid operating expenses, $1,650.

Feb. 28 Sent cash of $4,500 to home office. Returned to home office damaged sofa, which had been billed to the branch at $175.

Feb. 28 Home office notified branch that operating expenses allocated to the branch for the month of February amounted to $420. This included depreciation on office equipment and other expenses (such as advertising) paid by the home office. These expenses were originally recorded by the home office in the Operating Expense account.

Feb. 28 Cost of goods sold by the Surrey Branch during February amounted to $11,200.

Instructions

a Record the foregoing transactions in journal entry form on the books of the branch. Also prepare closing entries. Compute the balance at February 28 in the Home Office account which appears in the books of the branch.

b Select the transactions which should be recorded on the books of the home office (including entry to record branch net income) and prepare entries to record them. Ignore closing entries. Compute the balance in the Surrey Branch account at February 28 which appears in the books of the home office.

Group B

23B-1 A preliminary summary of the operating results for the Balboa Company Ltd. for the Year 1 follows:

	Total	Department C	Department D
Net sales.	$800,000	$320,000	$480,000
Operating income	80,000	45,000	35,000
Advertising expense (allocated on			
basis of net sales)	100,000	40,000	60,000

Advertising expense consists of $60,000 in direct product advertising (70% of which was applicable to Department C and 30% to Department D) and $40,000 in general advertising which promoted the image of the company. The manager of Department D thinks that his department was actually more profitable than Department C and argued that he was charged with an unreasonable amount of advertising expense. He maintains that the direct product advertising should be assigned to the departments on the basis of actual expenditures and that only the $40,000 of general (indirect) advertising should be allocated in proportion to net sales.

Instructions Prepare a departmental income statement for Year 1, following the expense allocation procedure suggested by the manager of Department D. Which department was more profitable? Why?

23B-2 Maternity Shop offers its customers a 2% cash discount on all cash sales and adds a financing charge of 1% per month to all account balances that are not paid within 30 days of the invoice date. Cash discounts are allocated directly to its three operating departments at the time of sale. Revenues from financing charges are allocated to the departments on the basis of net credit sales.

These data are taken from the Maternity Shop accounts for the current year:

	Total	Department X	Department Y	Department Z
Sales	$618,000	$183,600	$326,000	$108,400
Revenues from financing				
charges	37,500			
Sales returns (all from				
credit sales)	(18,000)	(3,600)	(6,000)	(8,400)
Cash discounts on				
sales	(4,500)	(1,000)	(2,900)	(600)
Net revenues from				
sales	$633,000			

Instructions
a Determine the amount of net credit sales for each of the three departments.
b Determine the amount of financing charges that will be allocated to each department by the accountant of the Maternity Shop.
c Comment on the validity of the method used by this company in allocating financing charges to departments. Explain why you think it will or will not produce accurate results.

23B-3 DeLange Company Ltd. has four operating departments. At the end of the current year the controller has computed departmental results in three ways, showing net income by departments, the departmental contribution to indirect expenses, and the gross profit on sales for each department as shown on page 721.

	Total	Dept. One	Dept. Two	Dept. Three	Dept. Four
Departmental net income.	$ 21,200	$ 68,300	$(4,000)	$(13,100)	$(30,000)
Departmental contribution to indirect expenses ..	88,800	98,000	14,000	(2,000)	(21,200)
Departmental gross profit on sales	184,000	128,000	36,000	22,000	(2,000)
Gross profit as a percentage of sales	23%	40%	20%	10%	$(2\frac{1}{2}\%)$

Note: Parentheses indicate a loss.

Instructions

a On the basis of the above information, prepare a departmental income statement for the DeLange Company Ltd. It will be necessary to compute the following amounts: net sales, cost of goods sold, direct expenses, and indirect expenses. (*Hint:* Gross profit on sales is given for the company as a whole and for each department. Net sales can be computed from this information.)

b What conclusions would you reach about the operations of Departments Two, Three, and Four on the basis of the statement prepared in (*a*)? Should any of these departments be discontinued? Explain your reasoning.

23B-4 Dale Taylor operates a retail business having three departments. Departmental expense accounts are maintained for some expenses, with the rest being allocated to the departments at the end of each accounting period. The operating expenses and other departmental data for the current year are shown below:

	Dept. K	Dept. L	Dept. M	Indirect Expenses
Departmental operating expenses:				
Sales salaries (direct)	$ 30,000	$ 25,750	$19,250	
Indirect salaries				$25,000
Building rental				9,600
Advertising (direct and indirect)	1,800	1,200	600	1,500
Supplies used (direct)	600	700	500	
Payroll taxes (5% of salaries)				5,000
Insurance expense				900
Depreciation on equipment (direct)	375	530	695	
Miscellaneous expense (direct and indirect) .	300	200	100	2,400
Other departmental data:				
Net sales	$212,500	$127,500	$85,000	
Cost of goods sold	158,500	82,950	48,550	
Equipment (original cost)	3,640	3,900	5,460	
Average inventory	15,860	19,500	29,640	
Value of floor space	50%	30%	20%	
Floor space (square feet)	1,600	1,600	800	

Indirect expenses are allocated among the departments on the bases given on page 722.

Indirect Expense	Basis of Allocation
Indirect salaries	Amount of gross profit
Building rental	Value of floor space occupied
Advertising	Direct departmental advertising
Payroll taxes	Salaries, both direct and indirect
Insurance expense	Sum of equipment (original cost) and average inventory
Miscellaneous expense	Net sales

Instructions

a Prepare a schedule showing the allocation of operating expenses among the three departments. Use four money columns headed: Total, Department K, Department L, and Department M. Give schedules for each expense item in support of the amounts allocated to departments. Round all expense allocations to the nearest dollar.

b Prepare a summarized departmental income statement for Dale Taylor's business, using the same column headings as in part (*a*). Show summary figures for both total and departmental operating expenses, using totals from the schedule in (*a*). Disregard income taxes.

23B-5 Muffler King, Ltd., operates several sales and service outlets (branches) throughout the metropolitan area of a large city. A decentralized accounting system is used by each branch. At the end of October, the following reciprocal accounts appear on the books of the Central branch and the home office:

Branch Books	Home Office Books
Home Office (credit balance). . . $17,970	Central Branch (debit balance) . . $17,210

The reason for the discrepancy in the amounts shown in the two accounts is that the branch net income for October, $1,800, and a cash deposit made by the branch to the account of the home office, $1,040, have not been recorded by the home office. Both the branch and the home office use a perpetual inventory system.

During November, the following transactions affected the two accounts:

Nov. 6 Home office shipped merchandise to branch, $7,250. Debit Inventory account on branch books; credit Inventory account on home office books.

Nov. 12 Branch transferred $4,950 from its bank account to the bank account of the home office.

Nov. 19 Branch returned shop supplies costing $610 to the home office. Shop supplies are carried in the Shop Supplies account on both sets of books.

Nov. 30 Home office notified branch that operating expenses of $1,100 which had been recorded on the books of the home office in the Operating Expense account were chargeable to the Central branch.

Nov. 30 The Income Summary account on the books of the branch showed a debit balance of $590 at the end of November.

Instructions

a Record the transactions listed above in the books of the Central branch.

b Record the two transactions relating to the month of October and all transactions for November in the books of the home office.

c Determine the balances in the Home Office account and the Central Branch account at the end of November.

BUSINESS DECISION PROBLEM 23

The owner of Harper Drug Company Ltd. is considering the advisability of dropping all services in his store that are not pharmaceutical in nature and concentrating on the drug business. At the present time, in addition to drugs, James C. Harper has a fountain and handles various general merchandise such as magazines, candy, toys, and cosmetics. During the past year, the sales and cost of goods sold for his store were as follows:

	Total	Drugs	Fountain	General Merchandise
Sales (net).	$318,600	$240,000	$27,000	$51,600
Cost of goods sold	180,300	120,000	21,600	38,700

Harper has studied trade association studies summarizing the reports of other store owners who have made similar decisions. They report that after dropping fountain operations, drug sales declined an average of 10% and sales of general merchandise fell 8%. Reports from store owners who discontinued general merchandise operation, but continued to operate a fountain, indicate that drug sales fell by an average of 4% and fountain sales declined by $7\frac{1}{2}$%. If Harper Drug Company Ltd. discontinued general merchandise operation it could lease the surplus floor space for $1,500 per month to another business which would use it as a storage facility.

At the present time Harper employs three pharmacists at combined annual salaries of $45,000, and a fountain man at $6,000 per year. It is a rule of the trade that one pharmacist is required for every $80,000 of annual drug sales. The fountain man spends about 40% of his time stocking shelves and selling general merchandise items. If he were not there, a pharmacist would have to do this work and Harper estimates that drug sales would decline an additional 2% (of present sales) as a result of inconvenience to customers.

The pharmacists have stated they would not be willing to take over the fountain operation, but Harper believes that he could employ student help at a cost of $3,000 per year if the general merchandise sales were dropped. Harper estimates that if the fountain were discontinued he might realize about $2,400 from the sale of fountain equipment, but he would have to spend about this amount in remodeling. He also considers that the effect on indirect operating expenses as a result of dropping either department would be negligible.

Instructions
a Determine the departmental contribution to indirect expenses during the past year.
b Prepare an analysis of the estimated dollar benefit or loss that might be expected to result if Harper discontinued the fountain. Prepare a similar analysis assuming discontinuance of the general merchandise operation. What would be your advice to Harper?

TWENTY-FOUR ACCOUNTING FOR MANUFACTURING OPERATIONS

In preceding chapters we have considered accounting principles and procedures applicable to nonmanufacturing businesses—firms engaged in buying and selling merchandise, or in furnishing services. Another large and important category of business operation is *manufacturing.* All of the accounting principles and most of the accounting procedures we have discussed are equally applicable to manufacturers. Firms engaged in manufacturing, however, face some special accounting problems and require additional accounting procedures to measure, control, and report factory production costs.

Accounting problems of manufacturers

A typical manufacturing firm buys raw materials and parts and converts them into a finished product. The raw materials and parts purchased by an aircraft manufacturer, for example, include sheet aluminum, jet engines, and a variety of electronic gear and control instruments. The completed airplanes assembled from these components are the *finished goods* of the aircraft manufacturer. The terms *raw materials* and *finished goods,* as used in accounting, are defined from the viewpoint of each manufacturing firm. Sheet aluminum, for example, is a raw material from the viewpoint of an aircraft company, but it is a finished product of an aluminum company.

In converting raw materials into finished goods, the manufacturer employs factory labor, uses machinery, and incurs many other manufacturing costs, such as heat, light, and power, machinery repairs, and supervisory salaries. These production costs are added to the cost of raw materials to determine the cost of the finished goods manufactured during any given period. The accounting records of a manufacturing firm must be expanded to include ledger accounts for these various types of factory costs. Financial statements must also be changed to reflect the costs of manufacturing and several new classes of inventories. At any given moment, a manufacturer will have on hand a stock of raw materials, finished goods awaiting shipment and sale, and partially completed products in various stages of manufacture. Inventories of each of these classes of items must be taken at the end of each accounting period in order to measure the cost of goods that have been completed and sold during the period.

The accounting records of a manufacturer are more complex than those of the merchandising or service business because an additional function is involved. The merchandising firm is engaged in distributing goods or services. The manufacturer has two major functions: the production of finished goods and the sale of the goods produced. Many of the accounting problems of a manufacturer relate to the production function; however, manufacturing firms also incur selling and administrative expenses comparable to those of merchandising concerns.

DETERMINING THE COST OF GOODS SOLD The principal difference in accounting for a merchandising business and for a manufacturing business is found in computing the cost of goods sold. In a merchandising business the cost of goods sold is computed as follows:

$$\begin{array}{c} \text{Beginning Inventory} \\ \text{of Merchandise} \end{array} + \begin{array}{c} \text{Purchases of} \\ \text{Merchandise} \end{array} - \begin{array}{c} \text{Ending Inventory} \\ \text{of Merchandise} \end{array} = \begin{array}{c} \text{Cost of} \\ \text{Goods Sold} \end{array}$$

In a manufacturing business the cost of goods sold is determined by a parallel computation, as follows:

$$\begin{array}{c} \text{Beginning inventory} \\ \text{of Finished Goods} \end{array} + \begin{array}{c} \text{Cost of Goods} \\ \text{Manufactured} \end{array} - \begin{array}{c} \text{Ending Inventory} \\ \text{of Finished Goods} \end{array} = \begin{array}{c} \text{Cost of} \\ \text{Goods Sold} \end{array}$$

Comparison of these two similar computations shows that the *cost of goods manufactured* in a manufacturing company is in a sense the equivalent of *purchases of merchandise* in a merchandising business. This point is further emphasized by comparing the income statements of a merchandising company and a manufacturing company.

COMPARISON OF INCOME STATEMENTS FOR MANUFACTURING AND MERCHANDISING COMPANIES The treatment of sales, selling expenses, general administrative expenses, and income taxes is the same on the income statement of a manufacturing company as for a merchandising company. The only difference in the two partial income statements on page 726 lies in the cost of goods sold section. In the income statement of the manufacturing company, Cost of Goods Manufactured replaces the item labeled Purchases in the income statement of the merchandising company.

STATEMENT OF COST OF GOODS MANUFACTURED The principal new item in the illustrated income statement for a manufacturing company is the item: "Cost of goods manufactured . . . $600,000." This amount was determined from the Statement of Cost of Goods Manufactured, a statement prepared to accompany and support the income statement. This statement is illustrated in condensed form on page 726.

A MERCHANDISING COMPANY
Partial Income Statement
For the Current Year

Sales		$1,000,000
Cost of goods sold:		
Beginning inventory of merchandise	$300,000	
Purchases	600,000	
Cost of goods available for sale	$900,000	
Less: Ending inventory of merchandise	250,00	
Cost of goods sold		650,000
Gross profit on sales		$ 350,000

A MANUFACTURING COMPANY
Partial Income Statement
For the Current Year

Sales		$1,000,000
Cost of goods sold:		
Beginning inventory of finished goods	$300,000	
Cost of goods manufactured (Exhibit A)	600,000	
Cost of goods available for sale	$900,000	
Less: Ending inventory of finished goods	250,000	
Cost of goods sold		650,000
Gross profit on sales		$ 350,000

Observe that the final amount of $600,000 on the statement of cost of goods manufactured shown below is carried forward to the income statement and is used in determining the cost of goods sold, as illustrated in the income statement for the manufacturing company above.

A MANUFACTURING COMPANY   *Exhibit A*
Statement of Cost of Goods Manufactured
For the Current Year

Goods in process inventory, beginning of year			$ 70,000
Raw materials used:			
Beginning raw materials inventory		$ 50,000	
Purchases of raw materials	$100,000		
Less: Purchase returns and allowances	3,000	97,000	
Transportation-in		5,000	
Cost of raw materials available for use		$152,000	
Less: Ending raw materials inventory		42,000	
Cost of raw materials used		$110,000	
Direct labor		230,000	
Factory overhead (detail omitted)		250,000	
Total manufacturing costs			590,000
Total cost of goods in process during the year			$660,000
Less: Goods in process inventory, end of year			60,000
Cost of goods manufactured			$600,000

Manufacturing costs

To gain a better understanding of how the cost of goods manufactured is determined, we must now examine the nature of the costs incurred in a manufacturing plant. To paint a clear picture of the major elements of manufacturing costs and to distinguish clearly between manufacturing costs on the one hand and administrative and selling expenses on the other, assume that our hypothetical manufacturing company owns five separate buildings, each used exclusively for a single function of the business. These five buildings, as shown in the sketch below, consist of (1) a raw materials warehouse, (2) a factory building, (3) a finished goods warehouse, (4) a general office building, and (5) a building housing the sales division of the company.

   The raw materials received from suppliers are first placed in the raw materials warehouse; as these raw materials are needed in the production process they are moved into the factory, as shown by the arrow connecting these two buildings. In the factory building the raw materials are converted (cut up, processed, and assembled) into finished goods. Each unit of finished product is moved immediately upon completion out of the factory into the finished goods warehouse. As sales orders are obtained from customers, shipments are made from the finished goods warehouse.

   Each unit of finished goods leaving the factory includes these elements of manufacturing cost. Each of the three cost elements will now be discussed in some detail.[1]

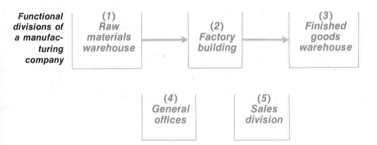

Functional divisions of a manufacturing company

(1) Raw materials warehouse	(2) Factory building	(3) Finished goods warehouse
(4) General offices	(5) Sales division	

   Now let us concentrate our attention upon the factory building, for it is here that all manufacturing costs are incurred. These costs are classified into three groups:

1 Raw materials used

2 Direct labor

3 Factory overhead

---

[1] The Committee on Terminology of the American Institute of Certified Public Accountants has recommended that "... items entering into the computation of cost of manufacturing, such as material, labor, and overhead, should be described as *costs* and not as *expenses.*"

RAW MATERIALS The cost of raw materials (also called *direct materials*) represents the delivered cost of materials and parts which enter into and become part of the finished product. In thinking about the elements of manufacturing cost during a given period, we are interested in the cost of raw materials *used* rather than the amount of raw materials purchased. Purchases of raw materials flow into the raw materials warehouse, but the consumption or use of raw materials consists of the materials moved from the raw materials warehouse into the factory to be processed. The computation of the cost of raw materials used was illustrated in the statement of cost of goods manufactured on page 726. The raw materials section of that statement is presented again at this point to emphasize the flow of cost for materials.

Computing the cost of raw materials used	*Raw materials used:*		
	Beginning raw materials inventory		$ 50,000
	Purchases of raw materials	$100,000	
	Less: Purchase returns and allowances	3,000	97,000
	Transportation-in		5,000
	Cost of raw materials available for use		$152,000
	Less: Ending raw materials inventory		42,000
	Cost of raw materials used		$110,000

Since the cost of raw materials used is computed by subtracting the amount of raw materials on hand at the end of the period from the total of the beginning inventory plus the purchases of raw materials during the period, any raw materials which were stolen, spoiled, or lost will be included in the residual amount labeled "cost of raw materials used." Inability to spotlight shortages or wastage of materials is one of the weaknesses inherent in the periodic inventory method.

In order to have the information for computing the cost of raw materials used readily available in the accounting records, the following ledger accounts are maintained:

	Raw Materials Inventory		**Transportation-in**
Ledger accounts for raw materials	50,000		5,000
	Purchases of Raw Materials		**Raw Materials Returns and Allowances**
	100,000		3,000

The Raw Materials Inventory account is used only at the end of the year, when a physical count of raw materials on hand is made, and the cost of these materials on hand is recorded by a debit to the Raw Materials Inventory account. The offsetting credit is made to the Manufacturing account, which will be explained later in this chapter. The other three accounts illustrated are used throughout the year to accumulate (1) the purchases of raw materials, (2) the transportation charges on inbound shipments of raw materials, and (3) the returns to suppliers of unsatis-factory or excessive raw materials.

DIRECT LABOR COST   The second major element of manufacturing costs is called *direct labor* and consists of the wages paid to factory employees who work directly on the product being manufactured. Direct labor costs include the payroll costs of machine operators, assemblers, and those who work on the product by hand or with tools, but not the wages of indirect workers such as plant watchmen, janitors, timekeepers, and supervisors.

What is the reason for separating the costs of direct labor and indirect labor? Direct labor is expended in converting raw materials into finished goods. If factory output is to be increased, it will be necessary to employ more direct workers and direct labor costs will rise. If factory output is to be reduced, any existing hours of overtime will be reduced and workers may be discharged. Direct labor costs vary directly with changes in the level of output; consequently, in planning operations for future periods, management can estimate the direct labor cost required for any desired volume of production.

Indirect labor, on the other hand, is much less inclined to rise and fall with changes in factory output. An increase or decrease of 10%, for example, in the number of units being produced will ordinarily not cause any change in the salary of the factory superintendent or in the number of janitors or guards. A large change in the volume of production will, of course, have some impact upon indirect labor costs.

FACTORY OVERHEAD   *Factory overhead* includes all costs incurred in the factory other than the costs of raw material and direct labor. Included in factory overhead are such costs as the following:

1 *Indirect labor*
   a Supervision
   b Timekeeping
   c Janitorial and maintenance
   d Production scheduling and quality control
   e Plant security service

2 *Occupancy cost*
   a Depreciation of buildings
   b Insurance on buildings
   c Property taxes on land and buildings
   d Repairs and maintenance of buildings
   e Heat, light, and power

3 *Machinery and equipment costs*
   a Depreciation of machinery and equipment
   b Insurance on machinery and equipment
   c Property taxes on machinery and equipment
   d Repairs and maintenance of machinery and equipment
   e Small tools used in the factory

This is not a complete list of factory overhead costs; in fact, it is the impossibility of preparing a complete list that leads accountants to define factory overhead as *all costs incurred in the factory other than raw material and direct labor.* A significant characteristic of factory overhead is that these costs cannot be directly related to units of product as can the costs of direct labor and direct material. In a factory producing two different products such as radios and television sets, it is possible to measure fairly accurately the costs of raw material and direct labor applied to each product, but the nature of factory overhead costs (such as insurance and repairs to buildings) is such that they cannot be associated directly with the particular articles being produced. For this reason, raw materials and direct labor are sometimes referred to as the *direct costs* or *prime costs* of manufacturing in contrast to factory overhead, which may be regarded as an *indirect cost.* Alternative titles for factory overhead include *indirect manufacturing cost, factory burden, manufacturing burden,* and *manufacturing overhead.* The total of direct labor and factory overhead costs is frequently referred to as *processing costs* or *conversion costs.*

Certain costs such as insurance, property taxes, telephone, and salaries of executives may be applicable in part to factory operations and in part to administrative and selling functions of the company. In such cases the costs may be apportioned among factory overhead, general administrative expense, and selling expense accounts at the time incurred; or as an alternative, the costs may be recorded in a single ledger account and the apportionment made through the use of working papers.

The flow of costs in manufacturing business

The sketch shown below emphasizes the flow of costs in a manufacturing business and some of the principal concepts appearing in the financial statements.

Raw materials warehouse	The cost of raw materials used consists of:
	    Beginning inventory of raw materials
	    Plus the delivered cost of net purchases
	    Minus the ending inventory of raw materials

Factory	Manufacturing costs consist of:
	    Cost of raw materials used
	    Direct labor
	    Factory overhead

	The cost of goods manufactured, which refers to the cost of units completed and moved out of the factory, consists of:
	    Beginning inventory of goods in process
	    Plus manufacturing costs
	    Minus ending inventory of goods in process

Finished goods warehouse	The cost of goods sold consists of:
	    Beginning inventory of finished goods
	    Plus cost of goods manufactured
	    Minus ending inventory of finished goods

	Shipments of finished goods to customers are made from the finished goods warehouse.

PRODUCT AND PERIOD COSTS   Costs that become a part of goods in process and finished goods inventories are called *product costs.* In theory, product costs include all costs associated with the production and flow of manufactured goods up to the point where the goods are completed and ready for sale. Product costs become a part of the asset valuations assigned to inventories at the end of each accounting period. They are charged against revenues as the cost of goods sold in the period when the goods to which they attach are sold.

Costs that are charged to expense in the period in which they are incurred are called *period costs.* Such costs are not related to the production and flow of product but are charged against revenues immediately, on the assumption that the associated benefits expire in the same period as the expenditures are made.

The exact dividing line between product and period costs is not always clear. Traditionally, expenditures relating to the manufacturing function are considered product costs, and those relating to the selling and administrative functions are considered period costs. In some cases it is difficult to determine whether a particular cost relates to manufacturing or administrative functions. For example, the cost of maintaining a cost accounting department, or a personnel department, or a plant guard service may be treated by some companies as factory overhead (product costs) and by other firms as administrative expense (period cost). These variations in accounting practice, however, stem more from differences of interpretation than from lack of agreement as to theoretical distinctions.

FULL (ABSORPTION) COSTING AND VARIABLE (DIRECT) COSTING   The process of treating as product costs all costs relating to the manufacturing function of a business is known as *full* or *absorption costing.* In recent years an alternative concept, called *variable,* or *direct, costing,* has received considerable attention and some support. Under this procedure product costs are limited to raw material, direct labor, and that portion of factory overhead that *varies directly* with changes in the volume of products manufactured. The *fixed* portion of factory overhead, that is, manufacturing costs that continue regardless of changes in the volume of output, are not included in inventories but are deducted from revenue in the period in which they are incurred. It is apparent that when variable costing is used inventory valuations will be lower, and reported net income will differ period by period, since many costs normally converted into inventory values will be charged to expense immediately. We shall discuss variable costing and its implications in more detail in Chapter 28. Throughout this chapter the full costing concept is used; that is, all elements of factory overhead are included as a part of the cost of goods manufactured, and thus are included in the valuation assigned to inventories of goods in process and finished goods.

Additional accounts needed by a manufacturing firm

A considerable expansion in the number of ledger accounts is required by a manufacturing firm in order to measure and report costs of production. Accounts relating to sales, selling expenses, administrative expenses, ownership equity, and many common kinds of assets and liabilities are handled in the same manner as in a merchandising or service business. However, manufacturing involves some additional asset accounts, and a number of new income statement accounts.

CURRENT ASSET ACCOUNTS In place of the single inventory account found on the balance sheet of a retail or wholesale business, a manufacturing firm has three separate inventory accounts:

1 *Raw materials inventory.* This account represents the unused portion of the raw materials purchased. The amount is determined at year-end by taking a physical count of the raw materials which have not yet been placed in production. In our earlier example of the company with five buildings, this inventory would be located in the raw materials warehouse. As a matter of convenience, *factory supplies* on hand (oil, grease, sweeping compounds) acquired for use in maintaining and servicing the factory building and machinery are often merged with raw materials.

2 *Goods in process inventory.* This inventory consists of the partially completed goods on hand in the factory at year-end, determined by a physical count. The cost of these partially manufactured goods is determined by estimating the costs of the raw materials, direct labor, and factory overhead associated with these units. The goods in process inventory appears on the balance sheet as a current asset and also appears on the statement of cost of goods manufactured (page 726).

3 *Finished goods inventory.* This account shows the cost of finished goods on hand and awaiting sale to customers as of the end of the year. The cost of these finished units is composed of the costs of raw material used, direct labor, and factory overhead. The method of pricing finished goods will be discussed later in this chapter. In the balance sheet, the finished goods inventory appears as a current asset; it is also used in computing the cost of goods sold in the income statement.

PLANT AND EQUIPMENT ACCOUNTS Manufacturing companies generally invest a large part of their total capital in plant and equipment, including tools, dies, conveyors, etc. In recent years the trend toward automation of production has led to particularly heavy investment in manufacturing facilities. Depreciation of the plant and equipment is one of the costs included in factory overhead; the cost of the plant and equipment is thereby gradually transformed into the cost of goods manufactured. If a company rents or leases its plant and equipment, the monthly rentals paid would be included in factory overhead.

Because of the great variety of items of manufacturing equipment, it is customary to maintain a subsidiary plant ledger as described in Chapter 12. On the balance sheet the caption of Plant and Equipment, or Machinery and Equipment, is often used to summarize all types of productive facilities.

RESEARCH AND DEVELOPMENT COSTS   Intangible assets (see Chapter 12), such as patents and deferred costs of research and development, are also commonly found on the balance sheets of manufacturing concerns. In recent years success in the field of manufacturing seems to have been closely related to leadership in research and development of new products. In many organizations, the heavy cost of maintaining large research departments has been treated as current expense deducted from revenues in the period in which incurred. Other companies have charged research and development costs to asset accounts such as Deferred Research and Development Costs. Assets of this type are amortized over the years in which they contribute to revenues; through the process of amortization these costs become part of the cost of goods manufactured.

A policy of capitalizing research and development costs is entirely acceptable in terms of accounting theory. However, many manufacturing companies find that continuous operation of a research program is necessary merely to maintain a competitive position in the industry; as a consequence, these companies regard research expenditures as period costs to be deducted from revenue in the year incurred. This procedure is also acceptable for income tax purposes.

RAW MATERIAL, DIRECT LABOR, AND FACTORY OVERHEAD   The accounts required for recording the three major elements of production cost have already been discussed. In recording factory overhead a separate account must be created for each type of indirect manufacturing cost (Depreciation of Machinery, Repairs, Timekeeping, etc.) as indicated on page 729. If there are a great many of these factory overhead accounts, it is convenient to transfer them to a subsidiary ledger which will be controlled by a general ledger account entitled Factory Overhead.

THE MANUFACTURING ACCOUNT   Last in our list of ledger accounts peculiar to a manufacturing business is a summary account called *Manufacturing,* which is used at the end of each period to summarize the various elements of factory cost and to determine the cost of goods manufactured. The balance of this account represents the cost of goods manufactured during the period. The Manufacturing account is closed by transferring its $600,000 debit balance to the Income Summary account, as shown in the illustration on page 734. This $600,000 is the cost of the units completed during the year. It is entered as a debit in the Income Summary account so that we can compare the costs and revenues for the year.

Manufacturing

Note kinds
of costs
summarized
in Manufac-
turing
account

19___			19___		
Dec. 31	Beginning goods in process inventory	70,000	Dec. 31	Ending goods in process inventory	60,000
31	Beginning raw materials inventory	50,000	31	Ending raw materials inventory	42,000
31	Purchases of raw materials	100,000	31	Raw materials purchase returns and allowances	3,000
31	Transportation-in	5,000	31	Cost of goods manufactured, to Income Summary	600,000
31	Direct labor	230,000			
31	Factory overhead (total)	250,000			
		705,000			705,000

Income Summary

19___			19___		
Dec. 31	Beginning finished goods inventory	300,000	Dec. 31	Ending finished goods inventory	250,000
31	Cost of goods manufactured	600,000			

It is important to distinguish between the terms *cost of goods manufactured* and *total manufacturing costs.* Cost of goods manufactured means the cost of the units of finished product completed during the period and transferred from the factory to the warehouse for finished goods. Total manufacturing costs, on the other hand, include the cost of raw materials used, direct labor, and factory overhead for the period, whether the units worked on have been completed or are still in process at the end of the period. As an extreme example, consider a manufacturing plant engaged in the construction of a single huge airplane. During the first year of work on the plane the manufacturing costs are as follows:

Compare
"total man-
ufacturing
costs" with
"cost of
goods man-
ufactured"

Cost of raw materials used	$ 300,000
Direct labor	700,000
Factory overhead	1,000,000
Total manufacturing costs	$2,000,000
Less: Goods in process inventory, ending	2,000,000
Cost of goods manufactured	$ —0—

The cost of goods manufactured is zero in the above illustration because no products (airplanes) were completed during the year, and we have defined the term *cost of goods manufactured* to mean the manufacturing cost of units that have been *completed and moved out* of the factory during the year.

Working papers for a manufacturing business

The work sheet for a merchandising business illustrated in Chapter 5 can be adapted for use in a manufacturing company merely by adding a pair of columns for the data which will appear in the statement of cost of goods manufactured. Illustrative working papers for the Chemical Manufacturing Corporation Ltd. are presented on the following page. As a means of simplifying the illustration, it is assumed that all adjusting entries were made before the trial balance was entered on the work sheet and that numerous factory overhead and operating expense accounts have been combined. The Adjustments columns are, therefore, omitted and the illustration begins with an Adjusted Trial Balance. Adjusting entries for a manufacturing business do not differ significantly from those previously described for a merchandising business.

TREATMENT OF INVENTORIES IN THE WORKING PAPERS   Since the Manufacturing columns are the distinctive feature of this work sheet, they require close study, especially the handling of the inventory accounts.

1 The beginning inventory of raw materials and the beginning inventory of goods in process have become part of the cost of goods manufactured and are, therefore, carried from the Adjusted Trial Balance debit column to the Manufacturing debit column.

2 The ending inventories of raw materials and of goods in process must be recorded as assets and must be shown as a deduction in determining the cost of goods manufactured. This step requires the listing of the two inventories as debits in the Balance Sheet columns and as credits in the Manufacturing columns.

The nature of the Manufacturing columns may be clarified by a brief summary of the items placed in each column. The debit column includes the beginning inventories of raw materials and goods in process, plus all the manufacturing costs of the period. The credit column contains credits for the ending inventories of raw materials and goods in process. The total of the amounts in the debit column exceeds the total of the credit column by $371,800. This debit balance represents the cost of goods manufactured and is extended as a debit to the Income Statement columns.

Note that the beginning and ending inventories of finished goods appear in the Income Statement columns but not in the Manufacturing columns. The illustration earlier in this chapter (A Manufacturing Company), involving separate buildings for factory operations and for the storage of finished goods was designed to emphasize that changes in the finished goods inventory are not a factor in computing the cost of goods that are manufactured in the factory.

Financial statements

Four statements for the Chemical Manufacturing Corporation Ltd. prepared from the illustrated work sheet on page 736 are presented on pages

CHEMICAL MANUFACTURING CORPORATION LTD.
Working Papers
For the Year Ended December 31, Year 1

	Adjusted Trial Balance		Manufacturing		Income Statement		Retained Earnings		Balance Sheet	
	Dr	Cr	Dr	Cr	Dr	Cr	Dr	Cr	Dr	Cr
Cash	20,600								20,600	
Accounts receivable	40,000								40,000	
Allowance for uncollectible accounts		1,000								1,000
Inventories, beginning:										
Finished goods	55,000				55,000					
Goods in process	18,000		18,000							
Raw materials	10,000		10,000							
Machinery and equipment	136,000								136,000	
Accum. depr.: mach. and equip.		40,000								40,000
Furniture and fixtures	14,000								14,000	
Accum. depr.: furn. and fix.		4,200								4,200
Patents	8,000								8,000	
Deferred research and develop. costs	12,000								12,000	
Accounts payable		40,200								40,200
Accrued factory payroll		800								800
Income taxes payable		6,460								6,460
Notes payable, 6½%, due Year 5		80,000								80,000
Capital stock, $10 par value		100,000								100,000
Retained earnings, beginning		48,200						48,200		
Dividends	16,000						16,000			
Sales (net)		500,000				500,000				
Purchases of raw materials (net)	101,000		101,000							
Direct labor	171,750		171,750							
Indirect labor	67,250		67,250							
Rent on plant facilities	12,000		12,000							
Other factory overhead costs	23,800		23,800							
Advertising	14,000				14,000					
Sales salaries	32,000				32,000					
Other selling expenses	3,400				3,400					
Administrative salaries	40,000				40,000					
Uncollectible accounts expense	2,700				2,700					
Other general and adm. expenses	11,900				11,900					
Interest expense	5,000				5,000					
Income taxes	6,460				6,460					
	820,860	820,860								
Inventories, ending:										
Finished goods						62,800			62,800	
Goods in process				20,000					20,000	
Raw materials				12,000					12,000	
Cost of goods manufactured				371,800	371,800					
			403,800	403,800						
Net income					20,540			20,540		
					562,800	562,800				
Retained earnings, ending							52,740			52,740
							68,740	68,740	325,400	325,400

739 to 741. These statements are the balance sheet (Exhibit A, page 739), statement of retained earnings (Exhibit B, page 740), income statement (Exhibit C, page 740), and statement of cost of goods manufactured (Exhibit D, page 741).

Closing the books

The entries to close the books of a manufacturing company can be taken directly from the work sheet. A Manufacturing account is opened by debiting it with the total of all the amounts listed in the Manufacturing debit column of the work sheet. A second entry is made crediting the Manufacturing account with the total of all the accounts listed in the Manufacturing credit column. These two entries serve to close out all the operating accounts used in computing the cost of goods manufactured. The next step in the closing procedure is to transfer the balance of the Manufacturing account to the Income Summary. Note that this balance is the cost of goods manufactured. Inventories of finished goods and all expenses are closed to the Income Summary account. Finally, the balances in the Income Summary and Dividends accounts are closed to Retained Earnings. The closing entries at December 31, Year 1, for the Chemical Manufacturing Corporation Ltd. are illustrated below:

Closing entries for a manufacturing firm

Manufacturing		*403,800*
Goods in Process Inventory (beginning)		*18,000*
Raw Materials Inventory (beginning)		*10,000*
Purchases of Raw Materials (net)		*101,000*
Direct Labor		*171,750*
Indirect Labor		*67,250*
Rent on Plant Facilities		*12,000*
Other Factory Overhead Costs		*23,800*
To close manufacturing accounts having debit balances.		
Goods in Process Inventory (ending)	*20,000*	
Raw Materials Inventory (ending)	*12,000*	
Manufacturing		*32,000*
To record ending inventories of goods in process and raw materials.		
Income Summary	*542,260*	
Finished Goods Inventory (beginning)		*55,000*
Advertising		*14,000*
Sales Salaries		*32,000*
Other Selling Expenses		*3,400*
Administrative Salaries		*40,000*
Uncollectible Accounts Expense		*2,700*
Other General and Administrative Expenses		*11,900*

Interest Expense	*5,000*	
Income Taxes	*6,460*	
Manufacturing	***371,800***	

To close beginning inventory of finished goods, all expense
accounts, and Manufacturing account to Income Summary.

Sales (net)	*500,000*	
Finished Goods Inventory (ending)	*62,800*	
Income Summary		*562,800*

To close Sales account and to record ending finished goods
inventory.

Income Summary	*20,540*	
Dividends		*16,000*
Retained Earnings		*4,540*

To transfer balance in Income Summary (net income) to retained
earnings and to close Dividends account.

Valuation of inventories in a manufacturing business

Under the periodic inventory method described in this chapter, a manufacturing business determines inventory amounts on the basis of a physical count of raw materials, goods in process, and finished goods at the end of each accounting period. When the physical quantity of raw materials on hand has been established, the cost of the raw materials inventory is determined in the same manner as an inventory of merchandise in a trading company. Cost is readily determinable by reference to purchase invoices. If the raw materials inventory is to be priced at the lower of cost or market, the "market" prices to be used are the current replacement costs for the materials on hand.

Determining the cost of an inventory of goods in process and an inventory of finished goods is usually a more difficult process. Cost cannot be derived merely by pulling a purchase invoice out of the files. If a manufacturing plant produces only a single product, the cost per unit for the finished goods inventory can be computed by dividing the cost of goods manufactured by the number of units produced. For example, if the cost of goods manufactured were $100,000 in a given year, during which the factory turned out 1,000 identical units, the cost per unit would be $100. Most factories, however, produce more than one product, and the unit cost of each product must be determined by deriving from the accounting records the approximate amount of raw material, direct labor, and factory overhead applicable to each unit. In this situation the determination of cost of a unit of the work in process at the year-end requires the following steps:

1 Estimate the cost of the raw materials in the partially completed units.

2 Add the estimated direct labor cost incurred.

3 Add an appropriate amount of factory overhead.

CHEMICAL MANUFACTURING CORPORATION LTD.   *Exhibit A*
Balance Sheet
December 31, Year 1

Assets

Current assets:

Cash		$ 20,600
Accounts receivable	$40,000	
Less: Allowance for uncollectible accounts	1,000	39,000
Inventories:		
Finished goods	$62,800	
Goods in process	20,000	
Raw materials	12,000	94,800
Total current assets		$154,400

Plant and equipment:

	Cost	Accumulated Depreciation	Book Value	
Machinery and equipment	$136,000	$40,000	$96,000	
Furniture and fixtures	14,000	4,200	9,800	
	$150,000	$44,200		105,800

Intangible assets:

Patents	$ 8,000	
Deferred research and development costs	12,000	20,000
Total assets		$280,200

Liabilities & Stockholders' Equity

Current liabilities:

Accounts payable		$ 40,200
Accrued factory payroll		800
Income taxes payable		6,460
Total current liabilities		$ 47,460
Notes payable, $6\frac{1}{4}$%, due Year 5		80,000
Total liabilities		$127,460

Stockholders equity:

Capital stock, $10 par value; authorized and issued 10,000 shares	$100,000	
Retained earnings (Exhibit B)	52,740	152,740
Total liabilities & stockholders' equity		$280,200

CHEMICAL MANUFACTURING CORPORATION LTD. *Exhibit B*
Statement of Retained Earnings
For the Year Ended December 31, Year 1

Retained earnings, beginning of year	$48,200
Net income for the year (Exhibit C)	20,540
Subtotal	$68,740
Less: Dividends	16,000
Retained earnings, end of year	$52,740

CHEMICAL MANUFACTURING CORPORATION LTD. *Exhibit C*
Income Statement
For the Year Ended December 31, Year 1

Net sales		$500,000
Cost of goods sold:		
Beginning finished goods inventory	$ 55,000	
Cost of goods manufactured (Exhibit D)	371,800	
Total cost of finished goods available for sale	$426,800	
Less: Ending finished goods inventory	62,800	
Cost of goods sold		364,000
Gross profit on sales		$136,000
Operating expenses:		
Selling expenses:		
Advertising	$14,000	
Sales salaries	32,000	
Other selling expenses	3,400	
Total selling expenses	$ 49,400	
General and administrative expenses:		
Administrative salaries	$40,000	
Uncollectible accounts expense	2,700	
Other general and administrative expenses	11,900	
Total general and administrative expenses	54,600	
Total operating expenses		104,000
Income from operations		$ 32,000
Less: Interest expense		5,000
Income before income taxes		$ 27,000
Income taxes		6,460
Net income		$ 20,540
Earnings per share of capital stock		$ 2.05

CHEMICAL MANUFACTURING CORPORATION LTD. **Exhibit D**
Statement of Cost of Goods Manufactured
For the Year Ended December 31, Year 1

Goods in process inventory, beginning of year			$ 18,000
Raw materials used:			
Beginning raw materials inventory.	$ 10,000		
Purchases of raw materials (net)	101,000		
Cost of raw materials available for use.	$111,000		
Less: Ending raw materials inventory	12,000		
Cost of raw materials used.	$ 99,000		
Direct labor	171,750		
Factory overhead:			
Indirect labor.	$67,250		
Rent on plant facilities	12,000		
Other factory overhead costs	23,800		
Total factory overhead		103,050	
Total manufacturing costs			373,800
Total cost of goods in process during the year			$391,800
Less: Goods in process inventory, end of year			20,000
Cost of goods manufactured			$371,800

This same procedure of computing a total cost by combining the three elements of manufacturing cost is followed in pricing the finished goods inventory.

The raw material cost included in a unit of goods in process or a unit of finished goods may be established by reference to the engineering specification for the article. The cost of the direct labor embodied in each unit may be estimated on the basis of tests and observations by supervisors of the direct labor time required per unit of output. In other words, both raw material cost and direct labor cost *are directly associated* with units of product.

The third element of manufacturing cost to be included in pricing the inventory of goods in process is factory overhead, and this cost element *is not directly related* to units of output. Factory overhead, however, is usually related to the amount of direct labor. A factory overhead rate may, therefore, be computed by dividing the total factory overhead for the period by the total direct labor cost for the same period. The resulting factory overhead rate is then applied to the direct labor cost of the goods in process to determine the amount of factory overhead to be included in the inventory cost. In the illustrated statement of cost of goods manufactured of the Chemical Manufacturing Corporation Ltd. shown above, *direct labor cost* is *$171,750* and *factory overhead* is *$103,050.*

The *factory overhead rate* is $103,050 ÷ $171,750, or 60% of direct labor cost. This 60% rate was used in determining the factory overhead cost in the ending inventories of goods in process and of finished goods, as shown on page 742.

CHEMICAL MANUFACTURING CORPORATION LTD.
Valuation of Ending Inventories
December 31, Year 1

	Prime Costs per Unit		Factory Overhead, 60% of Direct Labor Cost	Total Unit Cost	Units in Inventory	Total Cost of Inventory
Inventory	Raw Materials	Direct Labor				
Goods in process:						
Product D-3 . . .	$8	$10	$ 6	$24	500	$12,000
Product D-4 . . .	2	5	3	10	800	8,000
Total						$20,000
Finished goods:						
Product D-3 . . .	$8	$20	$12	$40	820	$32,800
Product D-4 . . .	6	15	9	30	1,000	30,000
Total						$62,800

Note the three cost elements in ending inventories

Cost accounting and perpetual inventories

The periodic method of inventory and the related accounting procedures described in this chapter are used by many small manufacturing companies, but these procedures have serious deficiencies and **they do not constitute a cost accounting system.** The shortcomings inherent in the use of periodic inventories by a manufacturing company include the following:

1 The estimates used in computing the inventories of goods in process and finished goods are rough and inexact. Any inaccuracy in pricing the inventories causes a corresponding error in net income for the period.

2 Taking and pricing inventories is so time-consuming that it usually is done only once a year; consequently, operating statements are not available to management at sufficiently frequent intervals.

3 Cost data available to management are not sufficiently detailed to afford a sound basis for control of operations.

The greater the number of products being manufactured, the more critical these deficiencies become. Management needs detailed day-to-day information on the costs of each product being manufactured. Decision making with respect to possible discontinuance of certain products or increases in the output of other articles requires current detailed reporting of cost data. An accurate determination of costs for individual products is also very useful in setting selling prices. Many progressive manufacturing companies achieve control of costs and operations by the preparation of budgets which indicate far in advance what the outlays for material, labor, and factory overhead **should** be.[2] The accounting records and procedures are so designed as to provide a steady flow of reports summarizing actual cost results for comparison with the budgeted figures. A key step in providing the cost information needed by management for planning and controlling manufacturing

[2] See Chap. 26 for a more detailed discussion of budgeting.

operations with optimum efficiency is the maintenance of perpetual inventories.

Cost accounting is a specialized field of accounting, with the objective of providing management with means of planning and controlling manufacturing operations. A cost accounting system is characterized by the maintenance of perpetual inventories and by the development of cost figures for each unit of product manufactured. An introduction to the subject of cost accounting is presented in the following chapter.

QUESTIONS

1 What are the three major components of the cost of manufactured goods?

2 A manufacturing firm has four inventory control accounts. Name each of the accounts, and describe briefly what the balance in each at the end of any accounting period represents.

3 Into which of the three elements of manufacturing cost would each of the following be classified?
 a Wages of the factory payroll clerk
 b Briar used in the manufacture of pipes
 c Wages paid to employees who test-drive completed automobiles
 d Cost of making duplicate copies of blueprints in engineering department
 e Cost of glue used to bind layers of plywood
 f Property taxes on machinery
 g Small tools used in the factory

4 Explain the distinction between *product* and *period costs* under the full costing concept. Why is this distinction important?

5 During a given period the cost of raw material used by a manufacturing firm was $22,000. The raw material inventory decreased by $4,500 during the period, and purchase returns amounted to $1,200. What was the delivered cost of raw materials purchased?

6 Distinguish between *total manufacturing costs* and the *cost of goods manufactured.*

7 What does the balance in the Manufacturing account represent, before the account is closed?

8 What is meant by the term *factory overhead rate?*

9 Explain how the cost of the ending inventory of goods in process is determined under the physical inventory system at the end of the period.

10 What are the major shortcomings of the periodic inventory method when used by a manufacturing company?

EXERCISES

Ex. 24-1 The information below is taken from the financial statements of Kronos Buchwald, Ltd., at the end of Year 1:

Goods in process inventory, ending	$ 25,000
Cost of raw materials used	130,000
Cost of goods manufactured	310,000
Factory overhead, 75% of direct labor cost	75,000

Compute the cost of the goods in process inventory at January 1.

Ex. 24-2 Factory overhead is 30% of cost of goods manufactured. Direct labor is 20% of sales and 40% of cost of goods manufactured. Ending raw materials inventory is $4,000 more than beginning raw materials inventory. Sales totaled $100,000 for the year. Compute the net cost of raw materials purchased during the year.

Ex. 24-3 From the following account balances, prepare the entries required to close the manufacturing accounts at the end of Year 1. Include an entry to close the Manufacturing account to the Income Summary account:

	End of Year	Beginning of Year
Raw materials inventory	$15,000	$17,500
Goods in process inventory	23,500	19,200
Purchases of raw materials (net)	80,000	
Direct labor	72,000	
Factory overhead (detail omitted)	39,800	

Ex. 24-4 From the following account balances for the Acme Products Corporation Ltd., determine the factory overhead rate based on direct labor cost:

Raw materials used	$240,000
Direct labor	200,000
Indirect labor	49,000
Factory maintenance	26,000
Depreciation on factory plant and machinery	19,500
Other factory overhead costs	25,500
Selling expenses (balance in controlling account)	40,000
General expenses (balance in controlling account)	60,000
Interest expense	10,000

Ex. 24-5 The City Mfg. Company Ltd. produces a single product. At the end of the current year, the inventories of goods in process and finished goods are summarized below:

	Units	Raw Materials per Unit	Direct Labor per Unit
Goods in process (75% finished)	500	$6	$3
Finished goods	600	8	4

Factory overhead is applied to units produced at the rate of 110% of direct labor cost. Compute the cost of the ending inventory of goods in process and finished goods.

Ex. 24-6 From the following information determine the cost which would be assigned to the ending inventory of finished goods, assuming that variable (direct) costing is used to value inventories:

			Costs per Unit	
			Factory Overhead	
	Units	Prime Costs*	Variable	Fixed
Finished goods inventory:				
Item X	200	$10.00	$5.00	$2.00
Item Y	600	6.00	3.50	1.50
Item Z	500	8.00	4.50	2.50

*Raw materials and direct labor.

PROBLEMS

Group A

24A-1 The following information was taken from the adjusted trial balance and other records of Pride Manufacturing Company Ltd. for the month of June, Year 1:

	June 30	June 1
Inventories:		
Raw materials	$19,600	$25,300
Finished goods	27,000	20,700
Goods in process	20,000	15,700

	Month of June
Purchases of raw materials	$229,200
Transportation-in on raw materials	27,800
Factory overhead (control account)	84,500
Direct labor	101,800
Selling expense (control account)	38,600
Raw material purchase discounts	2,300
Raw material purchase returns	2,400
General expense (control account)	76,800

Instructions
a Prepare a statement of cost of goods manufactured for the month of June.
b Compute the cost of goods sold for the month of June.

24A-2 The president of Soporific Mattress Company Ltd., is unhappy because his accountant left the office on July 10 before completing the financial statements for the year ended June 30, Year 1. He goes to the accountant's desk and finds a Statement of Cost of Goods Manufactured which shows that the cost of products completed during the year was $500,000. He also finds the following account balances on working papers prepared by the accountant:

Raw materials used in production	$180,000
Direct labor	225,000
Indirect labor	68,400
Heat, light, and power	7,200
Depreciation: factory building and machinery	19,600
Miscellaneous factory costs	22,900
Sales	710,000
Sales returns and allowances	5,000
Finished goods inventory, ending	52,000
Goods in process inventory, ending	50,600
Selling expenses (control account)	43,000
General and administrative expenses (control account)	74,000
Income taxes: 25% on income up to $25,000 and 48% on any additional income	?

The beginning inventories consisted of the following:

Raw materials	$42,000
Goods in process	27,500
Finished goods	40,000

Instructions Prepare an income statement in good form for the year ended June 30, Year 1. You may assume that the accountant's determination of cost of goods manufactured is correct, although you may wish to check his work. In computing earnings per share, assume that 10,000 shares of capital stock are outstanding.

24A-3 The following information was taken from the books of Clay Manufacturing Company Ltd.

Inventories, July 1, 1974:

Raw materials	$44,000
Goods in process	32,400
Finished goods	48,200

Inventories at December 31, 1974:

	Raw Materials	Goods in Process	Finished Goods
Raw materials	$48,000	$12,900	$43,500
Direct labor		8,000	30,000
Factory overhead		? 6,400	24,000
Totals	$48,000	$ 27300	$97,500

Data for the six months ended December 31, 1974:

Cost of goods manufactured	$810,000
Factory overhead, 80% of direct labor	178,400

The company also paid transportation costs of $30,000 on materials purchased; it received credit of $16,300 for materials returned to suppliers.

Instructions On the basis of the above information and missing data which can be derived from it, prepare a statement of cost of goods manufactured for the six months ended December 31, 1974.

24A-4 The Quiet Washer Company Ltd. manufactures dishwashers in three models. The unit cost information for these products during the month of January is as follows:

Product	Raw Material Cost	Direct Labor Cost
Model 100	$ 9	$15
Model 200	13	20
Model 300	16	25

Manufacturing costs for the month are listed below:

Raw materials used	$509,100
Direct labor	532,000
Factory overhead	425,600

The inventories of Quiet Washer Company Ltd. at the beginning and end of January were as follows:

Raw materials, Jan. 1	$45,900
Raw materials, Jan. 31	42,600
Goods in process, Jan. 1	13,100
Goods in process, Jan. 31 (fully complete as to materials, and 50% complete as to direct labor and factory overhead):	
Model 100	200 units
Model 200	150 units
Model 300	100 units
Finished goods, Jan. 1	$83,800
Finished goods, Jan. 31:	
Model 100	500 units
Model 200	600 units
Model 300	400 units

Factory overhead is allocated to products on the basis of its relation to direct labor cost.

Instructions
a Determine the cost of the inventories of goods in process and finished goods at January 31.
b Compute the cost of goods manufactured for January.
c Compute the cost of goods sold for January.

24A-5 The adjusted trial balance for the Greer Company Ltd. on September 30, 1974, the end of its fiscal year, is given below and on page 748.

GREER COMPANY LTD.
Adjusted Trial Balance
September 30, 1974

Cash	$ 23,000	
Accounts receivable	59,200	
Allowance for uncollectible accounts		$ 2,900
Raw materials inventory, Oct. 1, 1973	15,300	
Goods in process inventory, Oct. 1, 1973	13,800	
Finished goods inventory, Oct. 1, 1973	7,500	
Prepaid expenses	3,200	
Factory machinery	243,000	
Accumulated depreciation: factory machinery		72,800
Sales and office equipment	142,300	
Accumulated depreciation: sales and office equipment . . .		47,400
Deferred research and development costs	14,200	
Accounts payable		30,600
Miscellaneous current payables		23,500
Income taxes payable		27,400
Capital stock, $2 par value		200,000
Premium on capital stock		50,000

Retained earnings, Oct. 1, 1973		44,700
Dividends	22,000	
Sales (net)		751,200
Purchases of raw materials	166,700	
Purchase returns		8,300
Transportation-in	27,800	
Direct labor	235,400	
Factory overhead (control)	121,500	
Selling expenses (control)	72,400	
Administrative expenses (control)	64,100	
Income taxes	27,400	
	$1,258,800	$1,258,800

Inventories at September 30, 1974, are shown below:

Raw materials inventory	$16,100
Goods in process inventory	14,500
Finished goods inventory	6,700

Instructions   Prepare:
a Working papers (10 columns including a pair of columns for retained earnings)
b Statement of cost of goods manufactured
c Income statement
d Balance sheet in report form

Group B

24B-1   The following closing entries appear on the books of Ontario Metals Corporation Ltd. at the end of the current year:

Manufacturing		203,400
Raw Materials Inventory (beginning)	20,600	
Goods in Process Inventory (beginning)	10,900	
Purchases of Raw Materials	90,200	
Transportation-in	2,300	
Direct Labor	38,600	
Indirect Labor	21,400	
Factory Lease Rental	4,300	
Occupancy Cost	3,200	
Machinery Repairs and Maintenance	4,500	
Taxes and Insurance	1,900	
Depreciation: Machinery	3,500	
Tools Used in Factory	2,000	
Purchase Returns and Allowances	3,000	
Purchase Discounts	2,700	
Raw Materials Inventory (ending)	22,500	
Goods in Process Inventory (ending)	9,800	
Manufacturing		38,000

Instructions Prepare a statement of cost of goods manufactured for the year.

24B-2 The inexperienced accountant for the Serendipity Manufacturing Company Ltd. prepared the income statement for the first year of operations as follows:

SERENDIPITY MANUFACTURING COMPANY LTD.
Income Statement
For First Year of Operations

Sales (net)		$650,000
Cost of goods sold:		
Purchases of raw materials	$175,000	
Transportation-in	8,000	
Direct labor	250,000	
Indirect labor	60,000	
Depreciation on machinery—factory	20,000	
Rent	18,000	
Insurance	4,000	
Utilities	12,000	
Miscellaneous factory overhead	32,000	
Other operating expenses	87,500	
Dividends declared on capital stock	25,000	
Cost of goods sold		691,500
Loss for year		$(41,500)

You are asked to help management prepare a corrected income statement for the first year of operations. Management informs you that 60% of rent, insurance, and utilities is applicable to the factory and that correct ending inventories consist of the following: Raw materials, $25,000; finished goods, $40,000; goods in process, none. The company has 25,000 shares of capital stock outstanding.

Instructions
a Prepare a statement of cost of goods manufactured.
b Prepare a corrected income statement. Assume that income taxes are 25% on the first $25,000 of taxable income and 48% on taxable income in excess of $25,000.

24B-3 The amounts shown below and on page 750 were taken from the adjusted trial balance of the Terzian Manufacturing Company Ltd. at the end of May:

Goods in process inventory, May 1	$ 46,000
Direct labor	425,000
Indirect labor	158,750
Raw materials inventory, May 1	165,500
Raw materials inventory, May 31	148,000
Raw materials purchases	621,800
Maintenance and repairs	15,000
Heat, light, and power	21,500
Property taxes: factory buildings and equipment	19,000

Depreciation: factory buildings and equipment	47,700
Insurance on manufacturing operations	6,000
Amortization of patents on products manufactured	12,300
Other factory overhead costs	17,250

The factory superintendent reports that raw materials costing $30,000 and direct labor of $50,000 are applicable to uncompleted product in process at the close of business on May 31.

Instructions
a Compute the factory overhead rate for the month of May based on direct labor cost.
b Determine the cost of the May 31 inventory of goods in process.
c Prepare a statement of cost of goods manufactured for May.

24B-4 At the end of March the accountant of the Stardust Manufacturing Company Ltd. reported the results shown below for the month of March.

Cost of goods manufactured	$174,800
Cost of goods sold	171,900
Net income	44,600

The company auditor, after reviewing the records, reports that he has discovered the following errors:
(1) The inventory of raw materials on hand at March 31 did not include materials costing $800 which were on hand but were inadvertently missed in taking the inventory.
(2) The following expenses incurred in March, which apply in part to selling and administrative functions, were charged entirely to factory overhead:

	Total	Manufacturing	Selling	Administrative
Building occupancy	$37,200	$27,900	$2,100	$7,200
Taxes and insurance	5,300	3,900	300	1,100

(3) Sales returns of $2,300 were treated as a part of factory overhead for the month of March.
(4) Research and development costs of $5,000, charged to factory overhead during the month of March, are applicable to future production.
(5) As the result of the above errors, the goods in process inventory at March 31 was overstated by $2,700, and the finished goods inventory was overstated by $3,300.

Instructions
a Determine the proper amount of the cost of goods manufactured, the cost of goods sold, and the net income for the month of March. Set up a schedule with three columns headed: Cost of Goods Manufactured, Cost of Goods Sold, and Net Income, and enter the amounts of each as determined by the accountant. In the space below, explain the effect of each of the above errors, and show the amount that should be added to or subtracted from the accountant's figures to arrive at the corrected totals.
b Did the company's finished goods inventory, as corrected, increase or decrease during March, and by what amount?

24B-5 The adjusted trial balance taken from the records of Genstar Mfg. Corporation Ltd. on April 30, 1974, the end of its fiscal year, is given on page 751.

GENSTAR MFG. CORPORATION LTD.
Adjusted Trial Balance
April 30, 1974

Cash	$ 40,700	
Accounts receivable	59,200	
Allowance for uncollectible accounts		$ 2,900
Raw materials inventory, May 1, 1973	15,300	
Goods in process inventory, May 1, 1973	13,800	
Finished goods inventory, May 1, 1973	7,500	
Prepaid expenses	3,200	
Factory machinery	243,000	
Accumulated depreciation: factory machinery		72,800
Sales and office equipment	142,300	
Accumulated depreciation: sales and office equipment		47,400
Deferred research and development costs	14,200	
Accounts payable		30,600
Miscellaneous current payables		5,700
Income taxes payable		45,200
Capital stock, $5 par value		200,000
Premium on common stock		50,000
Retained earnings, May 1, 1973		44,700
Dividends	22,000	
Sales		792,400
Sales returns	5,700	
Purchases of raw materials	166,700	
Purchase returns		8,300
Transportation-in	27,800	
Direct labor	235,400	
Factory overhead (control)	121,500	
Selling expenses (control)	72,400	
Administrative expenses (control)	64,100	
Income taxes	45,200	
	$1,300,000	$1,300,000

Inventories at April 30, 1974 are as follows:

Raw materials inventory	$16,100
Goods in process inventory	14,500
Finished goods inventory	6,700

Instructions Prepare:
a Working papers (10 columns including a pair of columns for retained earnings)
b Statement of cost of goods manufactured
c Income statement
d Balance sheet in report form

BUSINESS DECISION PROBLEM 24

Susan Specialty Shops Ltd., has its main manufacturing plant in an industrial park of a large Eastern city. It also operates two satellite plants in nearby cities of Oakville and Trenton which produce different lines of products. Each of the three plants has a complete set of books and each determines its own cost of goods manufactured. For several years, however, certain factory overhead costs were incurred in the main plant which were not allocated to the Oakville and Trenton plants. These costs included, for example, property taxes and insurance paid by the main plant, and a certain percentage of the production manager's salary, who made frequent trips to Oakville and Trenton to help solve certain production problems.

Joe College is hired as the assistant to the controller of Susan Specialty Shops, Ltd., and he recommends that the accounting for that portion of the factory overhead costs incurred in the main plant which are applicable to the Oakville and Trenton plants should be changed. He points out that the ending inventories of all three plants are incorrectly stated at the end of the current year (as was the case in prior years).

The controller disagrees with Joe College, taking the following position: "We have been doing it this way for fifteen years, and we could not possibly be wrong for that long a period. All overhead costs have been charged to one plant or another; it all ends up in cost of goods sold eventually anyway. Furthermore, for control purposes we want to record the indirect costs where the responsibility for their control lies, and the responsibility for the costs in question rests in the main plant."

In presenting his recommendation to the controller, Joe College accumulated the following information:

Factory overhead costs for current year incurred in main plant which are
allocable equally to Oakville and Trenton plants $50,000
Percentage of current year's output included in ending inventories of
finished goods and goods in process:

Main plant	30%
Oakville plant	10%
Trenton plant	5%

Instructions
a What would be the effect on total ending inventories if Joe College's recommendation is implemented?
b Briefly evaluate the positions of Joe College and the controller and suggest a possible solution to the dispute.

TWENTY-FIVE

COST
ACCOUNTING
SYSTEMS

In Chapter 24 the financial statements for a manufacturing business were introduced. Among the matters emphasized were the cost of goods manufactured schedule and the several asset and factory cost accounts not found in the ledger of a merchandising business. In this chapter we are concerned with the more complex task of determining the *cost of activities and products* through the use of cost accounting systems.

Cost accounting systems

A cost accounting system is a method of developing cost information within the framework of general ledger accounts. Because cost accounting systems are more widely used in manufacturing industries, we shall focus our attention on manufacturing costs. The need for cost information, however, is much broader than this. Many of the procedures used to obtain manufacturing costs are applicable to a variety of business situations and have been used by retailers, wholesalers, governmental agencies, and such service organizations as hospitals, public utilities, banks, and accounting firms to determine the cost of performing various service functions.

Cost accounting serves two important managerial objectives: (*1*) to determine product costs, and (*2*) to control the cost of business operations. *Product costs* are determined by relating prices paid for materials, labor, and factory overhead costs to some unit of output such as tons of steel produced. Product cost information has some influence on pricing decisions; it also provides a basis for inventory valuation needed to measure periodic net income and for bidding on contracts. *Control of costs* is a part of management's general responsibility for carrying on the functions of a business efficiently and economically. Knowing the cost of making a product, performing a manufacturing operation, or carrying on some other function of a business is a starting point in control. By comparing actual costs with budgets, standards, or other yardsticks, management finds a basis for controlling costs and planning future operations.

Problems of cost determination

A common misconception about accounting figures is that the cost of any product or unit of output can be measured with precision.

There are two reasons for the difficulty in measuring accurately *the cost* of anything: First, the relationship between the costs incurred and the output produced is often difficult to establish. Secondly, a number of different relationships may be found, each useful for different purposes, but none of which can really claim to be *the cost.* Let us consider these two problems briefly.

RELATING COSTS TO OUTPUT Costs are related to units of output in two stages. The first stage, common to all phases of accounting, is to measure the cost of resources used up in the total productive effort of a given accounting period. Dividing the cost of assets or services among accounting periods is more a matter of judgment than arithmetic. For example, raw materials are purchased at different unit prices. Determining which prices are applicable to materials used and which to materials and supplies on hand for future use requires some rather arbitrary assumptions (such as fifo, lifo, or weighted average). The services of long-lived assets, such as plant and equipment, are purchased in "bundles" and used up over a number of accounting periods. Both the total service life of such assets and the relative amount and value of services withdrawn from the bundle each period are uncertain. The portion of the total cost of the asset to be charged against the production of any given accounting period is therefore, at best, an educated guess.

The second stage in cost accounting is to relate total manufacturing cost to the output of any given accounting period. This, also, is a process fraught with difficulties. Almost all total cost figures include some joint costs which cannot be traced directly to any given unit of output. These costs must therefore be assigned or allocated on some reasonable, but necessarily arbitrary, basis. For example, a part of the cost of a barrel of crude oil is clearly a part of the cost of each product (gasoline, fuel oil, lubricating oil) that emerges from the refinery, but no one can determine exactly how the cost of crude oil should be divided among these products. Similarly, some part of the salary of the plant manager is a cost of operating each department within the plant, but the precise portion cannot be determined for any particular department. Is the cost of training a new employee chargeable to his production during the training period, or to production after he is fully trained? Resolving these issues and assigning such costs to products or processes is the distinguishing feature of cost accounting.

DIFFERENT COSTS FOR DIFFERENT PURPOSES The second reason it is meaningless to talk about *the cost* of anything is that *for different purposes different costs may be useful.* In reporting on the overall position and progress of a business, cost information is needed primarily to determine the valuation of raw materials, goods in process, and finished goods inventories in the balance sheet, and the cost of goods sold figure in the income statement. For these purposes total manufacturing costs are usually associated with the flow of products through the factory to determine the "full" cost of products sold and those on hand at the end of the accounting period.

Cost information is also used, however, as a *basis for managerial decisions.* For these purposes certain portions of the total cost figure may not be relevant. For example, consider the cost of heating a factory building. In arriving at inventory valuation and cost of goods sold, some portion of the total heating cost should be allocated to the various operations and in turn to the production of the period. If the decision is whether or not to shut down the plant, only the cost of standby heating is a significant factor. In a study of the operating efficiency of factory foremen, the cost of heating the building is largely outside their control and should be ignored. If we are planning the addition of a wing to the building, the *change* in the heating cost as a result of the addition is the relevant cost figure. Thus for some purposes the entire heating cost is useful, for some only a part of the heating cost is relevant, and for still other purposes this cost may be omitted altogether.

If cost information is to be used intelligently, the user must understand that any cost figure has inherent limitations and that no single method of arriving at cost will serve equally well all the varied purposes for which such information is needed. Most cost systems are designed to meet the general purpose of income determination and to develop in the accounts the basic information from which cost studies for special purposes can be derived. In the balance of this chapter two basic cost systems will be briefly described.

Flow of costs through inventory accounts in cost systems

In Chapter 24 we saw that even when periodic inventories are used, certain overall cost information can be obtained. Under the periodic inventory system, however, much potentially useful information is buried in totals; cost data are available only at infrequent intervals; and the details of product or departmental costs are not available. The first step in setting up a cost system, therefore, is to establish *perpetual* inventories.

The cost elements that enter into the valuation of inventories are called *product costs;* costs that are charged against revenues in the period in which they are incurred are called *period costs.*

Product costs typically consist of manufacturing costs, as distinguished from selling and general administrative expenses. The flow of costs through perpetual inventories is therefore usually limited to direct materials, direct labor, and factory overhead.

Three perpetual inventory accounts are used to trace the flow of costs through the manufacturing operations and to associate costs with output:

1 Materials Inventory (raw materials and factory supplies)
2 Goods In Process Inventory (product in the process of manufacture)
3 Finished Goods Inventory (completed product)

To visualize basic cost flows, look at the diagram shown below. The arrows show the flow of costs through the perpetual inventory accounts; arrows connecting two items indicate the two sides of an accounting entry. Thus the use of raw materials reduces the Materials Inventory account and increases the Goods in Process Inventory. Some items are not connected with arrows because the accounts appearing in the diagram are not complete. For example, the debit to Materials Inventory for *Arrows show flow* raw materials and supplies purchased is offset by a credit to Accounts *of costs* Payable, which is not shown on the diagram.

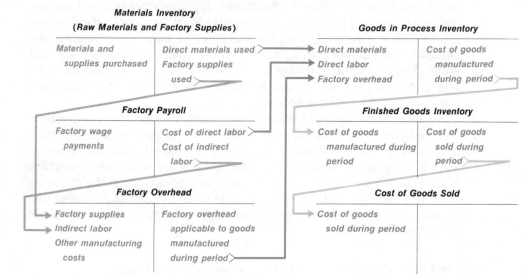

Note that when all the indicated entries have been made, the balance in the Materials Inventory, Goods in Process Inventory, and Finished Goods Inventory accounts represents the dollar valuation of these inventories. When a perpetual inventory system is used, the cost of goods sold can be taken directly from the ledger and placed in the income statement.

Even under a perpetual inventory system it will be advisable to take a physical inventory at various times to verify the accuracy of the book figure and to disclose losses due to waste, theft, or breakage that for one reason or another were not recorded in the accounts.

Two basic types of cost accounting systems

There are two distinct types of formal cost accounting systems; an end product of each is the average unit cost of physical output.

Under a *job order cost system,* the focal point of costing is a particular quantity of finished product known as a *job* or *lot.* The cost of raw materials, direct labor, and factory overhead applicable to each job is compiled and divided by the number of finished units in the job to arrive at average unit cost.

A job order cost sheet for a completed job is illustrated below:

Job Order Cost Sheet

Cost sheet for one job

Job Number: __1101__

Product: __Model P Hand Drill__

Units Completed: __2,000__

Date Started: __3/10/—__

Date Completed: __4/15/—__

Raw materials used	$ 7,500
Direct labor cost applicable to this job	10,000
Factory overhead applicable to this job, 125% of direct labor cost	12,500
Total cost of job no. 1101	$30,000
Average cost per unit ($30,000 ÷ 2,000)	$15

Under a *process cost system,* the focal points in costing are the various departments or processes in the production cycle. First the cost of raw materials, direct labor, and factory overhead applicable to each department or process for *a given period of time* is compiled. Then the average cost of running a unit of product through each department is determined by dividing the total departmental cost by the number of units processed in that department during the period.

Buildup of costs in two departments (processes)

When a product moves through two or more departments, the total unit cost of finished product is accumulated by tracing the costs incurred in each department to the product as it moves from process to process. The following process cost accounts for two departments illustrate how this is done:

Goods in Process, Mixing Department

Raw material	4,000	Transferred to Packing Dept.	
Direct labor	5,000	1,000 units @ $12	
Factory overhead applicable		($12,000 ÷ 1,000)	
to mixing process	3,000		12,000

Goods in Process, Packing Department

From Mixing Dept. (1,000 units		Transferred to finished goods	
@ $12)	12,000	inventory, 1,000 units @	
Materials added	2,000	$28 ($28,000 ÷ 1,000)	28,000
Direct labor	6,000		
Factory overhead applicable			
to packing process	8,000		

Each kind of cost accounting system (job order and process) has advantages in particular manufacturing situations. Both are widely used; sometimes a combination of the two systems is found within the same company. In the sections that follow we shall examine briefly the basic structure of the two cost accounting systems.

JOB ORDER COST SYSTEM

In general, a job order cost system is applicable when each product or batch of product is significantly different. It is the only system possible in the construction industry, for example, since each construction project is to some extent unique. Job order cost systems are also used in the aerospace, machine tool, job printing, motion picture, and shipbuilding industries for similar reasons.

An essential requirement of a job order cost system is that each product or batch of product can be identified in each step of the manufacturing operation. Through the use of various subsidiary detailed cost records, the cost of raw materials, direct labor, and factory overhead applicable to each job is recorded on a *job cost sheet,* so that when the job is finished the total and the average unit cost of the job can be computed.

Job order cost flow chart

A flow chart showing the accounts used in a simple job order cost system, together with lines indicating the flow of costs from one account to another, appears on pages 762 and 763. We shall use the figures in this illustration to outline the essential features of job order costing.

The flow chart contains figures representing one month's operations for the Job Manufacturing Company Ltd. The company makes three products, identified as product A, product B, and product C. Two kinds of raw materials (materials Y and Z) are used. Each of the three perpetual inventory accounts (Materials Inventory, Goods in Process Inventory, and Finished Goods Inventory) is supported by subsidiary ledger records in which the details of the flow of costs are recorded.

MATERIALS Accounting for the purchase and use of raw materials and factory supplies is a straightforward application of the use of perpetual inventories. The summary entries in the Materials Inventory control account are matched by detailed entries in the subsidiary ledger accounts as follows:

1 The $17,000 beginning balance in the Materials Inventory control account is equal to the beginning balances in the subsidiary ledger accounts for Factory Supplies, $4,000, Material Y, $6,000, and Material Z, $7,000.

2 The record in the subsidiary ledger accounts for the quantity and cost of materials purchased is made from information on suppliers' invoices. The cost

of materials purchased, $58,000, was posted in total from the cash payments journal (or the voucher register if one is used).

3 Materials and factory supplies are issued on the basis of *requisitions,* which show the quantity needed and the identity of the job on which raw materials are to be used or the Factory Overhead account to which supplies should be charged. The *direct materials cost* is the cost of raw materials identified with specific jobs; *indirect materials* refers to materials or supplies charged to the Factory Overhead account.

4 The materials clerk refers to individual materials ledger cards to get the cost of each item requisitioned, and enters this on the requisition form. Since purchases are at different prices, the costing of materials used requires some systematic cost flow assumption such as lifo, fifo, or weighted average. A summary of the materials requisitions for the month becomes the basis for the entries crediting Materials Inventory ($56,500) and debiting Goods in Process Inventory ($50,000) for the cost of direct materials used and Factory Overhead ($6,500) with the cost of factory supplies used.

In the flow chart on pages 762 and 763, subsidiary materials ledger accounts are shown in T-account form only as a matter of convenience; in practice they would contain more detailed unit cost information and dates of entries. An illustrative materials ledger card, showing the record for material Y during the month, appears below:

Materials Ledger Card

Material Y

		Received			Issued			Balance	
	Ref*	Quan-tity, lb	Unit Cost	Amount	Quan-tity, lb	Unit Cost†	Amount	Quan-tity, lb	Balance
Subsidiary ledger record for material Y	*Balance at beginning of month*							6,000	$ 6,000
	Inv. no. 47	7,500	$1.20	$9,000				13,500	15,000
	Req. no. 3				6,000	$1.00	$6,000		
					4,000	1.20	4,800	3,500	4,200
	Inv. no. 98	3,000	1.30	3,900				6,500	8,100
	Req. no. 6				3,500	1.20	4,200		
					1,000	1.30	1,300	2,000	2,600

* Identifying number of invoice or requisition from which data were taken.
† fifo basis.

FACTORY LABOR Payment of factory employees usually occurs after the services have been performed. During the pay period, detailed records of time, rates of pay, and the jobs on which employees worked must be kept in order to compile the necessary cost information. The wages earned by employees who work directly on job production are referred to as *direct labor* and are charged to each job. The wages earned by employees whose work is not directly associated with any particular job, known as *indirect labor,* are charged to Factory Overhead.

A number of mechanical and computerized means have been devised for compiling payroll information. A common system, which is illustrative, is to prepare *time tickets* for each employee, showing the time worked on each job, the rates of pay, and the total cost chargeable to each job. These tickets, summarized periodically, become the basis for preparing the payroll and paying factory employees. They also become the basis for entries on various job cost sheets showing the direct labor cost incurred.

In the flow chart on pages 762 and 763, $60,000 of direct labor was charged to the three jobs in process and $18,000 of indirect labor was charged to Factory Overhead. Of the total wage cost of $78,000, only $70,000 was actually paid during the month. The balance of $8,000 in the Factory Payroll account represents the liability for unpaid wages at the end of the month.

FACTORY OVERHEAD Included in factory overhead are all manufacturing costs other than *prime costs* (direct materials and direct labor). Direct labor and factory overhead costs are often referred to as *processing* or *conversion costs.* The Factory Overhead account is usually a control account; details of individual factory overhead costs are kept in a subsidiary ledger or cost analysis records. The source of individual overhead charges varies: Indirect labor charges are summarized from payroll records; factory supplies used are summarized from materials requisitions; charges for such current services as electricity and water are posted from the cash payments journal (or the voucher register); depreciation on plant assets, the expiration of prepaid expenses, and overhead costs resulting from accrued liabilities (for example, property taxes) are recorded as adjusting entries at the end of the period.

Determining the total factory overhead cost for a given accounting period is relatively easy. The major problem is to relate overhead cost to physical output. The nature of factory overhead is such that the direct relation between cost and output, which exists in the case of direct labor and materials, is lacking. We might determine an average overhead cost per unit by dividing the total overhead for a given period by the units of output produced in that period. Most manufacturing firms, however, produce several different products (or different models of the same product). A meaningful average factory overhead cost figure is not possible where the units of output are significantly different.

This problem is usually solved by relating factory overhead costs to some other cost factor which *can* be directly identified with units or lots of output. Many factory overhead costs either are a function of the passage of time (for example, building rent, foreman's salary) or tend to vary with the amount of labor or machine time involved in manufacture. For these reasons, charging factory overhead against units of output in proportion to the amount of *direct labor cost, direct labor hours,* or *machine-hours* involved in production is a reasonable and widely used procedure.

PREDETERMINED OVERHEAD RATES There is another problem in overhead cost allocation. Since many overhead costs tend to remain relatively fixed (constant) from month to month, total monthly overhead does not vary in proportion to seasonal or cyclical variations in factory output. Examples of *fixed costs* are property taxes and insurance on plant assets, straight-line depreciation on plant assets, and the monthly salary of the plant superintendent. *Variable costs* are those which change in direct proportion to output. If we allocate actual overhead costs incurred each month to the output of that month, the unit cost of production is likely to vary widely month by month. In months of high output, unit overhead costs would be low; in months of low output, unit overhead costs would be high. We can illustrate this for a company with a capacity to produce 10,000 units per month:

Overhead Costs per Unit at Different Levels of Output

	Level of Output			
	100% of Capacity*	75% of Capacity	50% of Capacity	25% of Capacity
Overhead unit costs increase as volume decreases Fixed overhead costs (constant at all levels)	$ 60,000	$ 60,000	$ 60,000	$60,000
Variable overhead costs	100,000	75,000	50,000	25,000
Total overhead costs	$160,000	$135,000	$110,000	$85,000
Number of units produced	10,000	7,500	5,000	2,500
Overhead cost per unit	$16	$18	$22	$34

*100% = normal level of output.

Note that the *fixed cost per unit increases as the level of output decreases* and that the variable cost remains constant at $10 per unit. For most business purposes, it is more confusing than helpful to have product cost figures that vary widely in response to short-run variations in the volume of output. Management needs product cost information for long-range product pricing decisions, income determination, and inventory valuation. For these purposes it is more useful to use what might be called "normal" costs than to have unit cost figures that reflect short-run variations in volume. For example, if we were determining the cost of two identical units of product in the finished goods inventory, it would not seem reasonable to say that one unit cost $30 because it was produced in a low-volume month and the other cost $20 because it was produced in a high-volume month.

The solution to this problem is to predetermine overhead application rates for an entire year in advance. To do this we first make an estimate

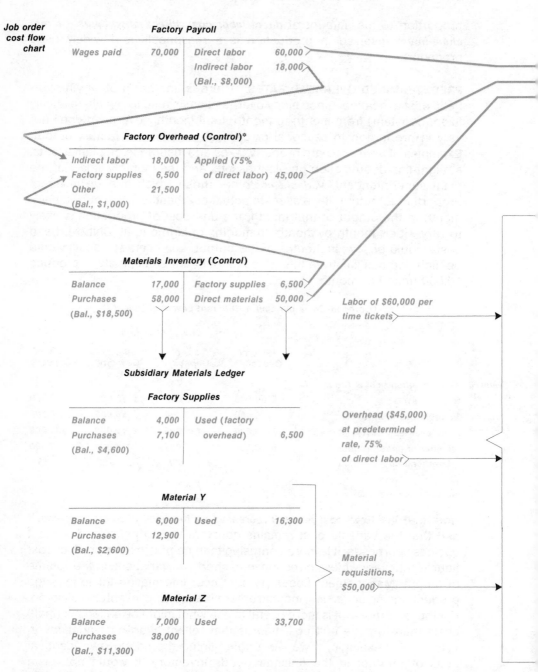

Factory Payroll

Wages paid	70,000	Direct labor	60,000
		Indirect labor	18,000
		(Bal., $8,000)	

Factory Overhead (Control)*

Indirect labor	18,000	Applied (75%	
Factory supplies	6,500	of direct labor)	45,000
Other	21,500		
(Bal., $1,000)			

Materials Inventory (Control)

Balance	17,000	Factory supplies	6,500
Purchases	58,000	Direct materials	50,000
(Bal., $18,500)			

Labor of $60,000 per time tickets

Subsidiary Materials Ledger

Factory Supplies

Balance	4,000	Used (factory	
Purchases	7,100	overhead)	6,500
(Bal., $4,600)			

Overhead ($45,000) at predetermined rate, 75% of direct labor

Material Y

Balance	6,000	Used	16,300
Purchases	12,900		
(Bal., $2,600)			

Material requisitions, $50,000

Material Z

Balance	7,000	Used	33,700
Purchases	38,000		
(Bal., $11,300)			

* Debit balance of $1,000 in this account represents underapplied factory overhead for the month.

Job order cost flow chart

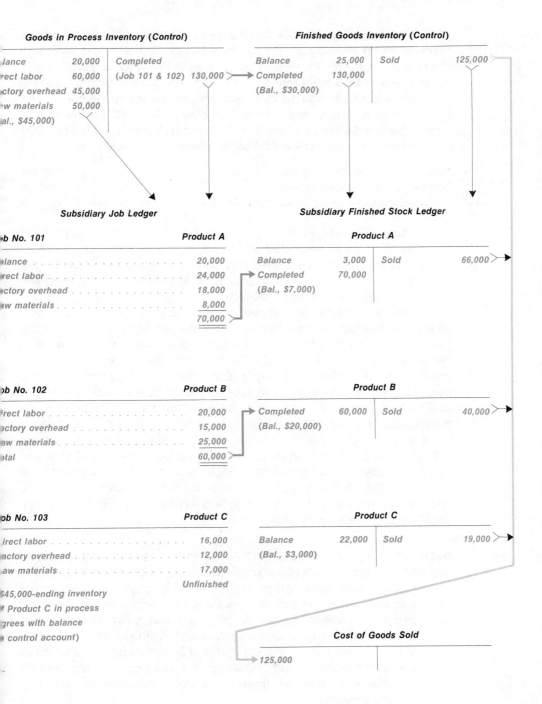

Goods in Process Inventory (Control)

...lance	20,000	Completed	
...rect labor	60,000	(Job 101 & 102)	130,000
...ctory overhead	45,000		
...w materials	50,000		
(...al., $45,000)			

Finished Goods Inventory (Control)

Balance	25,000	Sold	125,000
Completed	130,000		
(Bal., $30,000)			

Subsidiary Job Ledger

...b No. 101   **Product A**

...lance	20,000
...rect labor	24,000
...ctory overhead	18,000
...w materials	8,000
	70,000

Subsidiary Finished Stock Ledger

Product A

Balance	3,000	Sold	66,000
Completed	70,000		
(Bal., $7,000)			

...b No. 102   **Product B**

...rect labor	20,000
...ctory overhead	15,000
...w materials	25,000
...tal	60,000

Product B

Completed	60,000	Sold	40,000
(Bal., $20,000)			

...b No. 103   **Product C**

...irect labor	16,000
...actory overhead	12,000
...aw materials	17,000
	Unfinished

...$45,000-ending inventory
...f Product C in process
...grees with balance
...n control account)

Product C

Balance	22,000	Sold	19,000
(Bal., $3,000)			

Cost of Goods Sold

125,000	

of the total overhead costs for the year. This is called the **budgeted overhead.** Then we estimate the machine-hours, or direct labor hours, or direct labor cost, whichever is to be used as the **overhead application base** for the year. The predetermined overhead rate used in costing units of production is the budgeted overhead divided by the application base. For example, if factory overhead is budgeted at $600,000 for the coming year and it is estimated that the direct labor cost will amount to $500,000, the factory overhead rate would be determined as follows:

Pre-	*Budgeted factory overhead for year*	*$600,000*
determined	*Budgeted direct labor cost for year*	*500,000*
factory		
overhead	*Predetermined factory overhead rate ($600,000 ÷ $500,000)*	*120%*
rate		

The use of predetermined overhead rate has another advantage. Because the rate is estimated at the beginning of the year, "normal" product costs can be determined as various jobs are completed. It is not necessary to wait until the end of any period to know the factory overhead chargeable against goods produced.

Assume, for illustrative purposes, that we are using direct labor cost as the overhead application base and that the predetermined application rate is 75% of direct labor cost. The actual overhead cost for any given period will be accumulated in the Factory Overhead control account. As production takes place and direct labor cost is charged against jobs, overhead will also be applied to jobs at the predetermined rate of 75% of direct labor cost. As soon as a job is completed, we can determine the total cost and the unit cost of that job order. In the general accounting records, the total amount of overhead applied to jobs during the period will be debited to Goods in Process and credited to Factory Overhead.[1] In the flow chart on pages 762 and 763, for example, the total direct labor charged against the three jobs worked on during the month was $60,000 and 75% of this amount, or $45,000, was applied as the overhead cost applicable to these three jobs.

OVER- OR UNDERAPPLIED OVERHEAD We should not expect that applied overhead will ever exactly equal actual overhead, since the predetermined overhead rate was based on estimates. A debit balance in the Factory Overhead account at the end of a period indicates that actual overhead exceeded the overhead applied to jobs; a credit balance shows that overhead applied was greater than the actual overhead costs incurred.

What is the significance of the amount of over- or underapplied overhead at the end of any period? How should this amount be reported on financial statements? Basically there are two interpretations, each leading to a different procedure:

---

[1] Some accountants feel that actual overhead charges and applied overhead credits should not be mixed in the same account. Therefore, they credit applied overhead to a special account called Applied Factory Overhead, which has a credit balance until closed at the end of an accounting period.

1 There has been an error in allocating actual overhead against the production of the period This interpretation suggests that the error (in computing the overhead rate, for example) should be corrected by apportioning over- or underapplied overhead among the Goods in Process Inventory, the Finished Goods Inventory, and Cost of Goods Sold on some reasonable basis to restate them at "actual" cost. Often the entire amount is charged to Cost of Goods Sold, on the ground that most of the error applied to goods sold during the period.

2 Actual overhead incurred during the period differs from the normal overhead absorbed by the production of the period Under this interpretation, inventories are priced on the basis of predetermined overhead rates, and any balance of over- or underapplied overhead is added to or deducted from revenue, reflecting an unexpected volume of production or some other abnormal conditions of that period.

Since the bases used in applying overhead (direct labor, machine-hours) vary with production and many elements of overhead do not, overhead will tend to be *underapplied* during months of low production and *overapplied* during months of high production. The difference between actual and applied overhead is usually carried forward from month to month, and the overapplied overhead of one month is offset against the underapplied overhead of another. At the end of the year, any net balance of over- or underapplied overhead is then handled in accordance with one of the two basic interpretations described above.

GOODS IN PROCESS INVENTORY The Goods in Process Inventory account is charged with the cost of direct materials, direct labor, and an estimate of the factory overhead costs applicable to all jobs. The supporting subsidiary ledger records for this control account are the job cost sheets relating to each job in process during the period. In the flow chart on pages 762 and 763, note that the balance in the goods in process inventory at the beginning of the month, $20,000, represents the cost incurred on job no. 101 during the previous month. During the current month additional costs of $155,000 were incurred. The flow of costs through subsidiary cost sheets and the Goods in Process Inventory control account is illustrated on page 763.

Note that the only job in process at the end of the month is job 103, and the cost of this job to date, $45,000, is equal to the balance in the control account, Goods in Process Inventory. The Goods in Process Inventory account includes all the information needed to prepare a statement of cost of goods manufactured at the end of an accounting period.

FINISHED GOODS INVENTORY When a job is completed, the information on the job cost sheet is summarized and the total cost of that job becomes the basis for an entry crediting Goods in Process Inventory and debiting

Subsidiary Job Order Cost Sheets

	Job 101	Job 102	Job 103	Total (Control Account)
Flow of costs through job order cost sheets and control account **Goods in process inventory,** beginning of month	$20,000			$ 20,000
Direct labor	24,000	$20,000	$16,000	60,000
Raw materials.	8,000	25,000	17,000	50,000
Factory overhead	18,000	15,000	12,000	45,000
Total costs incurred	$70,000	$60,000	$45,000	$175,000
Less: Cost of jobs completed— transferred to Finished Goods Inventory account	(70,000)	(60,000)		(130,000)
Goods in process inventory, end of month (job 103)				$ 45,000

Finished Goods Inventory. Stock ledger cards are maintained as subsidiary ledger records for each type of finished product. When finished product is sold, Cash (or Accounts Receivable) is debited and Sales is credited. In addition, information on the stock ledger cards becomes the basis for removing the cost of these products from the Finished Goods Inventory account and charging the Cost of Goods Sold account. Once more some flow assumption (such as fifo or lifo) is required.

The relation between entries in the Finished Goods Inventory control account and the subsidiary finished stock ledger, as shown on the flow chart on pages 762 and 763, is summarized in the following schedule:

	Finished Goods Inventory, Control Account		**Subsidiary Finished Stock Ledger**		
Stock ledger supports entries in control account Beginning balance	$ 25,000	{	Product A Balance	$ 5,000	
			Product C Balance.	20,000	
		{	Product A (job 101)	70,000	
Completed during period . . .	130,000		Product B (job 102)	60,000	
Total goods available for sale	$155,000			$155,000	
Less: Cost of goods sold		{	Product A	$66,000	
during the period	(125,000)	{	Product B	40,000	
		{	Product C	19,000	(125,000)
			Product A	$ 7,000	
Balance on hand at end of		{	Product B	20,000	
period	$ 30,000	{	Product C	3,000	$ 30,000

PROCESS COST SYSTEM

In many industries the production of a large volume of standard products on a relatively continuous basis is the typical situation. The natural focus of cost measurement in such situations is a ***cost center*** such as a manufacturing operation, a department, or a process. A process cost system is a method of accumulating cost information in the accounts for such cost centers.

Process costs are particularly suitable for mass-production operations of all types. They are used in such industries as appliances, cement, chemicals, dairy products, lumber, and petroleum. The process cost approach also may be used in the analysis of nonmanufacturing costs. Distribution activities, for example, may be divided into such functions as sales visitations, receipt of orders, filling orders, packing and shipping, and the cost per unit sold computed for any given period of time.

Characteristics of a process cost system

In a process cost system, no attempt is made to determine the cost of particular lots of product as they move through the factory. Instead the costs of materials, labor, and factory overhead during any given time period (such as a month) are traced to various manufacturing processes (or departments). The costs incurred in each process are accumulated in separate goods in process accounts, and a record is kept of the units produced in that process in each period. The *cost report* of each process shows the average per unit cost of processing output during the period, and this figure becomes the basis for tracing the flow of costs through the various goods in process accounts and finally to Finished Goods Inventory and to Cost of Goods Sold.

In a very simple situation, only one product is processed in each department. Process costs can be used, however, when more than one product is involved. In such cases, charges for materials and direct labor are identified with individual products or models and accumulated separately in each department's cost reports. Since all products utilize departmental machinery and other indirect services, these costs may be divided among various products on the basis of their relative usage of departmental facilities. To simplify our illustrations, we shall assume that only a single product is manufactured.

Direct and indirect process costs

Whether a given process cost is direct or indirect depends, not on its relation to particular units of output, but on its relation to the operations of a process. *Direct process costs* are those associated with the operations of a particular process; *indirect process costs* are common to several processes and are treated as a part of factory overhead.

MATERIALS AND LABOR The cost of materials and supplies used, and the wages of production line workers can usually be traced directly to the operations of each process; if not, they are recorded as factory overhead. Note that direct departmental or process costs are not necessarily variable in relation to output. For example, a department foreman's salary is a direct cost of the department in which he works, but his salary is a fixed cost in relation to variations in the output of that department.

FACTORY OVERHEAD   The simplest method of handling factory overhead in a process cost system is to allocate *actual* overhead costs among the various processes at the end of each period. If this is done, goods produced during any given period are charged with the actual overhead costs incurred and there is no balance in the factory overhead account at the end of the period.

Alternatively, factory overhead rates may be predetermined by setting up a factory overhead budget for each department or process at the beginning of the period. Overhead is then charged to the department or process in proportion to labor cost, labor hours, machine hours, or some other basis. When predetermined rates are used in applying factory overhead, a balance of under- or overapplied factory overhead will usually appear in the Factory Overhead account at the end of the period. This represents the difference between actual factory overhead costs incurred and factory overhead allocated to the units produced during the period. The problem of disposing of this balance was discussed earlier in connection with the job order cost system; the same concepts apply for a process cost system.

A refinement in overhead accounting is to set up special overhead cost accounts for one or more *service departments,* that is, departments that do not actually process raw materials or otherwise work directly on the units produced. For example, a power department might be established, and all costs of producing power for the factory would be charged to this department. A maintenance department is another example of a service department. The cost of operating a service department would in turn be charged to *productive departments* in proportion to their relative use of the service.

To illustrate, suppose that a maintenance department is set up, a record is kept of maintenance work done for three productive departments (A, B, and C), and an hourly charge is made to each productive department. The Maintenance Department account for a month might appear as follows:

Maintenance Department (a Service Department)

Use of	Wages	2,000	*Allocated to productive departments:*	
service	Supplies	900	*Dept. A, 250 hr @ $8*	2,000
department				
to allocate	Portion of various factory costs		*Dept. B, 150 hr @ $8*	1,200
costs to	applicable to maintenance		*Dept. C, 100 hr @ $8*	800
productive				
departments	department	1,100		
		4,000		4,000

A total of 500 hours of maintenance work was done during the month for three productive departments (A, B, and C) at a total cost of $4,000. Each productive department is therefore charged with an average hourly cost of $8 per hour ($4,000 ÷ 500 hours). Alternatively, a predetermined hourly rate for maintenance work might have been set and used to charge the productive departments as maintenance services were performed.

Flow of costs in a process cost system illustrated

To illustrate the main features of a process cost system, let us assume a very simple manufacturing situation. The Process Manufacturing Company Ltd. makes a standard-size steel container. The company has two processing departments: In the Cutting Department, the metal is cut and shaped to required uniform specifications; in the Assembly Department, the metal parts are welded, ground, and sprayed with a chemical coating. Finished containers are stored in the warehouse and shipped to customers as orders are received.

The cost flow diagram on page 770 shows the basic process cost accounts and a summary of the journal entries for the month of July. A careful study of the diagram will show that the Goods in Process account for each department contains the information needed to prepare a statement of cost of goods manufactured. When perpetual inventories are used, it is unnecessary to show the beginning and ending inventories and the purchases of materials in the statement of cost of goods manufactured; only the cost of materials transferred to production need be shown. Each major step in the process will now be examined briefly to demonstrate the process cost accounting under these relatively simple conditions.

MATERIALS There was a $4,000 balance in the Materials Inventory control account at the beginning of July. During the month of July purchases of materials were charged to the Materials Inventory account in the amount of $34,000. All material needed to complete a unit in each department is placed in process at the beginning of production. At the end of July a summary of direct materials requisitioned by each department and factory supplies used by all departments became the basis for the following entry:

End-of-	Goods in Process: Cutting Department	29,400
month *entry:*	Goods in Process: Assembly Department	3,460
materials	Factory Overhead	2,000
used	Materials Inventory	34,860
	To record materials used in July.	

FACTORY LABOR On the basis of departmental payroll records, the total cost of direct labor used in each department during July was determined.

The wages of personnel (such as the factory superintendent, cost accountant, general maintenance employees) whose work is applicable to all departments were charged to Factory Overhead. The entry summarizing the payroll (ignoring various withholdings from wages) would be:

<table>
<tr><td rowspan="5">End-of-month entry: factory payroll</td><td>Goods in Process: Cutting Department . . . .</td><td>24,600</td><td></td></tr>
<tr><td>Goods in Process: Assembly Department . . . .</td><td>12,000</td><td></td></tr>
<tr><td>Factory Overhead . . . .</td><td>5,100</td><td></td></tr>
<tr><td>　　　Factory Payroll . . . .</td><td></td><td>41,700</td></tr>
<tr><td>To record factory labor used in July.</td><td></td><td></td></tr>
</table>

Cost flow diagram for process costing— compare with job order flow chart on pages 762 and 763

Total factory labor cost incurred amounted to $41,700 and payments to employees during the month amounted to $37,800, leaving a credit balance of $3,900 in the Factory Payroll account, which represents wages payable at the end of July.

FACTORY OVERHEAD The Process Manufacturing Company Ltd. prepares a departmental factory overhead budget at the beginning of each

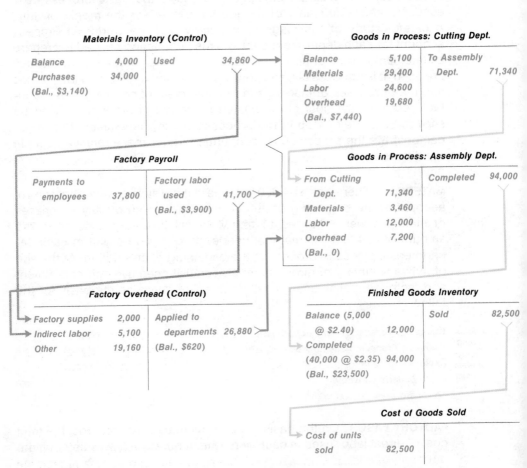

year, and factory overhead is applied to departmental goods in process accounts on the basis of departmental direct labor cost at the following rates:

Pre-determined overhead rates for our example

Cutting Department . . . . *80% of direct labor cost*
Assembly Department . . . . *60% of direct labor cost*

The entry charging the departmental goods in process accounts for their share of factory overhead, at these predetermined rates, may be summarized as follows:

End-of-month entry: factory overhead applied

Goods in Process: Cutting Department (80% of $24,600)	*19,680*	
Goods in Process: Assembly Department (60% of $12,000)	*7,200*	
Factory Overhead		*26,880*

To record factory overhead applied to production on basis of direct labor cost.

Actual overhead for July totaled $26,260, leaving a credit balance of $620 in the Factory Overhead account, representing overapplied overhead for the month. This amount would be carried forward month to month, and any balance at the end of the year would be apportioned between ending inventories of goods in process and finished goods and the cost of goods sold during the year, or simply closed out to the Cost of Goods Sold account.

Determining unit costs for inventory valuation and control

If all units of product in any particular department are completely processed during the period, computing unit costs is a simple matter of dividing departmental costs by the number of units processed. In some cases, however, there may be unfinished units of product on hand at the beginning as well as at the end of an accounting period. The total costs incurred in each department during the period, plus the cost of any partially completed units at the beginning of the period, must then be allocated between the units that have been completed and the units that are left in various stages of completion at the end of the period. Obviously, total costs cannot be divided by the total number of units worked on during the period, some of which are complete and some of which are only partly finished, to obtain a meaningful unit cost. If completed and partly completed units of product are expressed in *equivalent full units* of completed product, however, this difficulty is overcome and a meaningful unit cost can be determined by dividing total costs by the equivalent full units produced. For example, this can be illustrated for materials as follows:

A key step in process cost accounting

$$\text{Cost per unit of materials} = \frac{\text{total cost of materials for current month}}{\text{equivalent full units produced in current month}}$$

Equivalent full units is a measure of the productive effort for a given accounting period. This measure of unit output is used to obtain separate unit costs for material, labor, and factory overhead; the unit cost of goods produced can then be used to assign a value to ending inventories and to units sold. Unit costs are also useful for other management purposes.

When materials and processing costs (direct labor and factory overhead) are applied uniformly to the units being produced, the equivalent full units of work done will be identical for all three cost elements. If the materials are placed in process at various stages (such as 100% at the beginning, or 60% at the beginning and 40% when most of the processing has been completed), the equivalent unit figure for material will differ from that for processing costs. In such situations, the equivalent-unit computation must be determined separately for each cost element.

The computation of equivalent full units for a hypothetical company for the month of March is illustrated below:

Computation of Equivalent Full Units

	Units	×	Portion Completed during March	=	Equivalent Full Units Completed (All Costs)
Beginning inventory in process (3/1), 80% completed in February but finished in March	20,000	×	20%	=	4,000
Units started and completed in March	50,000	×	100%	=	50,000
Units completed and transferred to storage	70,000				
Ending inventory in process (3/31), 40% completed in March	25,000	×	40%	=	10,000
Output in March in terms of equivalent full units					64,000

Equivalent full units— an index of productive effort for a period

Equivalent full units should be viewed as a physical measure of production activity for a period. Although 70,000 units were completed and transferred to storage in our example, the actual measure of work accomplished during March was only 64,000 units. These units consist of 54,000 equivalent full units of work (4,000 + 50,000) on the 70,000 units transferred to storage and 10,000 equivalent full units (40% of 25,000) on the 25,000 units still in process at the end of March.

The computation of unit cost and the assignment of departmental costs to goods completed and goods in process at the end of the period will now be illustrated using the information for the Cutting Department and the Assembly Department for the Process Manufacturing Company Ltd. which appears on the cost flow chart on page 770. The costs incurred in the two processing departments during July appear in the departmental goods in process accounts. A **production report** for the Process Manufacturing Company Ltd. shows the units of product processed in each department for July:

Production Report for July

	Cutting Dept.	Assembly Dept.
Units in process on July 1	4,000	None
Add: Units placed in production during July	42,000	40,000
Total units worked on during July	46,000	40,000
Less: Units in process on July 31	6,000	none
Units completed during July	40,000	40,000

Production report shows units only

Using this information, we can now determine unit costs in each of the two departments.

CUTTING DEPARTMENT   In the Cutting Department, we have both beginning and ending inventories in process which are 100% completed as to material and 50% completed as to labor and overhead. On the basis of cost information and the production report above, a *cost report* for the Cutting Department for July may be prepared as illustrated on page 774.

The total cost inputs in the Cutting Department during July amounted to $78,780, including the cost of $5,100 applicable to the beginning goods in process inventory carried forward from June. This total cost of $78,780 was incurred on the 46,000 units worked on during the month. We could not, however, divide the total cost by 46,000 to determine the cost per unit. Not all of these units were entirely produced in July: 4,000 units were carried forward from June with all material cost and 50% of processing costs (labor and overhead) included, while another 6,000 units in process at the end of July were 100% complete as to material cost but only 50% completed as to processing costs. We first had to compute the equivalent full units of work for material and for processing costs.

The reasoning behind the computation of equivalent full units in the Cutting Department may be stated as follows: The equivalent full units of work in the beginning inventory of goods in process must be subtracted from units completed during the period, because the cost of these goods is included in the $5,100 carried forward from the previous month. The equivalent finished units in the ending inventory must then be added, because the cost of this productive effort is included in the costs for the current period. The result is the equivalent production in terms of finished units during July, and this is divided into the costs incurred during July to derive a unit production cost for July. Applying this procedure, it was determined that 42,000 equivalent full units of material and 41,000 equivalent full units of labor and overhead were completed during July. Dividing the cost of material, $29,400, by the equivalent full units of material used, 42,000, gives us a unit cost for material of $0.70; dividing the direct labor cost, $24,600, by the equivalent full units of direct labor, 41,000, gives us a unit cost for direct labor of $0.60; dividing factory overhead, $19,680, by the equivalent full units of factory overhead, 41,000, gives us a unit

CUTTING DEPARTMENT
Cost Report for July

	Total Units	Total Costs ÷	Equivalent Full Units* =	Unit Cost
Inputs:				
Units in process at beginning of month (100% complete as to materials and 50% as to processing)	4,000	$ 5,100		
Materials requisitions	42,000	29,400	42,000	**$0.70**
Direct labor		24,600	41,000	**0.60**
Factory overhead		19,680	41,000	**0.48**
Total inputs—units and costs	46,000	$78,780		
Unit cost for July				**$1.78**
Outputs (see Exhibit A on page 775 for supporting computations):				
Transferred to Assembly Department, $1.7835 per unit	40,000	$71,340		
Units in process at end of month (100% complete as to materials and 50% as to processing)	6,000	7,440		
Total outputs—units and costs	46,000	$78,780		

Cost report for July. Note how unit costs were computed and then used to assign value to the outputs

*Computation of equivalent full units:

	Materials	Labor and Overhead
Units completed during July	40,000	40,000
Less: Units in process at start of month (4,000):		
Material equivalent (4,000 × 100%)	(4,000)	
Labor and overhead equivalent (4,000 × 50%)		(2,000)
Add: Units in process at end of month (6,000):		
Material equivalent (6,000 × 100%)	6,000	
Labor and overhead equivalent (6,000 × 50%)		3,000
Equivalent full units (expressed in finished units)	42,000	41,000

cost for factory overhead of $0.48.[2] The total of these three cost elements gives a unit cost per container of $1.78 in the Cutting Department for the month of July.

Once unit costs for materials, direct labor, and factory overhead are determined, the total cost inputs of $78,780 can be assigned to units completed and transferred to the Assembly Department and to the units still in process in the Cutting Department at the end of July as follows:

[2] The unit cost of factory overhead can also be computed by taking 80% of $0.60, the direct labor cost per unit, because factory overhead is applied at the rate of 80% of direct labor cost. See top of page 771.

CUTTING DEPARTMENT
Exhibit A

Assignment of Cost Inputs—Month of July

Total cost inputs assigned to units completed and to units in process

Beginning inventory in process (4,000 units):		
Cost brought forward from previous month	$5,100	
Cost to complete during July:		
Materials	—	
Labor (4,000 × 50% × $0.60)	1,200	
Overhead (4,000 × 50% × $0.48)	960	
Total cost of first 4,000 units finished		$ 7,260
Goods started and finished during July (36,000 units):		
Materials, labor, and overhead (36,000 × $1.78)		64,080
Cost of goods transferred to Assembly Department (40,000 units @ $1.7835) .		$71,340
Cost of units in process at end of month (6,000 units):		
Materials (6,000 × 100% × $0.70)	$4,200	
Labor (6,000 × 50% × $0.60)	1,800	
Overhead (6,000 × 50% × $0.48)	1,440	
Cost of ending goods in process inventory (6,000 units)		$ 7,440

In computing the cost of the 40,000 units transferred to the Assembly Department, it is necessary to make some assumption as to which units are involved. A *first-in, first-out* assumption has been used in this illustration. This means that the 40,000 units transferred out consist of 4,000 units which were in process at the beginning of the period, and 36,000 units which were **started and finished** during the period. The cost allocated to these 40,000 units is $71,340, or $1.7835 each,[3] and the cost allocated to the 6,000 units in process at the end of July is $7,440. Thus, the total cost inputs of $78,780 have been assigned to goods completed and transferred to the Assembly Department and to the ending goods in process inventory. The entry to transfer the cost of the units completed in the Cutting Department to the Assembly Department is illustrated below:

Transfer of cost to next department

Goods in Process: Assembly Department	71,340	
Goods in Process: Cutting Department		71,340
To transfer cost of 40,000 units completed in July from Cutting Department to Assembly Department.		

ASSEMBLY DEPARTMENT There was neither a beginning nor an ending inventory of goods in process in the Assembly Department. Therefore, the unit cost in this department may be determined by dividing each cost element by the 40,000 units started, completed, and transferred to Finished Goods Inventory during July. The cost report for the Assembly Department follows:

---

[3] Actually the first 4,000 units cost $7,260, or $1.815 per unit, and the other 36,000 units cost $64,080, or $1.78 per unit. It would be possible to carry these slightly different unit costs forward to the Assembly Department, but such refinement is generally considered unnecessary.

ASSEMBLY DEPARTMENT

Cost Report for July

	Total Units	Total Costs	÷	Equivalent Full Units	=	Unit Cost
Inputs:						
Transferred from Cutting Department	40,000	$71,340		40,000		**$1.7835**
Materials added in Assembly						
Department		3,460		40,000		**0.0865**
Direct labor		12,000		40,000		**0.3000**
Factory overhead		7,200		40,000		**0.1800**
Total inputs—units and costs	40,000	$94,000				
Unit cost for July.						**$2.3500**
Outputs:						
Transferred to Finished Goods						
Inventory, $2.35 per unit	40,000	$94,000				

Cost report—no goods in process inventories

The $2.35 unit cost of the steel container completed in the Assembly Department includes $1.7835 incurred in the Cutting Department and $0.5665 incurred in the Assembly Department. It is important to keep in mind that this is an *average cost* and that it includes both variable costs (direct materials, direct labor, and variable factory overhead) and fixed costs (fixed portion of factory overhead). If the variable cost per unit amounted to only $2, for example, the Process Manufacturing Company Ltd. might accept a special order for 1,000 units at $2.25 per unit and thereby recover all variable cost assigned to these units and have $250 available to help defray the total fixed costs for the period.

Given below is the entry to transfer the cost of goods completed in the Assembly Department during July to the Finished Goods Inventory account:

Transfer of cost to finished goods inventory

Finished Goods Inventory	94,000	
Goods in Process: Assembly Department		94,000
To transfer cost of 40,000 units completed in Assembly		
Department during July to Finished Goods Inventory.		

The entries to record the sale of goods by the Process Manufacturing Company Ltd. during July appear below:

Entries to record sales and cost of goods sold

Accounts Receivable	120,000	
Sales		120,000
To record sales on account during July.		
Cost of Goods Sold	82,500	
Finished Goods Inventory		82,500
To record the cost of containers sold in July.		

Summary of job order and process cost systems

Several simplifying assumptions have been made in developing the illustrations of job order and process cost systems; nevertheless, the essential features of the two types of cost systems were included. Both the job order and the process cost systems are essentially devices for collecting cost information. A job order cost system produces information about the cost of manufacturing a particular product or a batch of a given product; a process cost system produces information about the *average cost* of putting a homogeneous unit of product through various manufacturing operations for a given time period. A job order cost system usually involves more detailed cost accounting work and in return gives more specific cost information. A process cost system involves less detailed accounting work and accumulates costs in terms of major production sequences (processes) or departmental cost centers. Both systems provide the information required to prepare a statement of cost of goods manufactured, to arrive at unit costs, and to formulate business decisions.

DEMONSTRATION PROBLEM FOR YOUR REVIEW

The Diversified Mfg. Company Ltd. started operations early in January with two production departments, Foundry and Blending. The Foundry produces special castings to customer specifications and the Blending Department produces an industrial compound which is sold by the pound. The company uses a job order cost system in the Foundry and a process cost system in the Blending Department.

The following schedule summarizes the operations for January:

	Total Costs Incurred	Foundry	Blending	Inventory at Jan. 31
Materials	$40,000	$13,000	$23,000	$4,000
Direct labor	56,800	20,000	36,800	
Factory overhead	43,600	16,000	27,600	

Shown below is the schedule of the jobs in process in the Foundry at January 31:

	Materials	Direct Labor
Job no. 9	$600	$400
Job no. 10	580	500

All other jobs were shipped to customers at a billed price of $60,000. The factory overhead in the Foundry is applied on the basis of direct labor cost.

The January production report for the Blending Department shows the following:

	Pounds
Placed in production	95,000
Completed	80,000
In process at Jan. 31, 80% complete as to materials and conversion costs . .	15,000

Of the units completed, 70,000 were sold for $92,500 and the other 10,000 are stored in the warehouse. Selling expenses for January amounted to $14,250 and general and administrative expenses amounted to $12,500.

Instructions

a Prepare the journal entries to record (*1*) materials purchases and the requisitions for the Foundry and Blending departments and (*2*) the labor and overhead costs (including allocation to the two departments).

b Determine the cost of the jobs in process in the Foundry at the end of January and prepare journal entries (*1*) to transfer the cost of jobs completed to Finished Goods Inventory and (*2*) to record the sales and cost of goods sold for the month.

c Prepare a cost report for the Blending Department and prepare journal entries (*1*) to transfer the cost of the finished product to the Finished Goods Inventory account and (*2*) to record the sales and cost of goods sold for the month.

d Prepare a condensed income statement for January. (Ignore income taxes.)

QUESTIONS

1 What is a cost accounting system?

2 What are the two major objectives of cost accounting?

3 Why is it difficult to measure the precise cost of a product or a service produced by a business enterprise?

4 What is meant by the phrase, "different costs for different purposes"? Illustrate by explaining how factory superintendent's salary might be treated differently, as a cost, for different purposes.

5 Differentiate between *product costs* and *period costs.*

6 What factors should be taken into account in deciding whether to use a job order cost system or a process cost system in any given manufacturing situation?

7 Describe the three kinds of charges on a job cost sheet. For what general ledger control account do job cost sheets constitute supporting detail?

8 Explain why it is advantageous to use predetermined overhead rates in associating factory overhead with output.

9 Define each of the following: *Prime costs, conversion costs, fixed costs,* and *variable costs.*

10 Gerox Company Ltd. applies factory overhead on the basis of machine-hours, using a predetermined overhead rate. At the end of the current year the factory overhead account has a credit balance. What are the possible explanations for this? What disposition should be made of this balance?

11 What are the characteristics of a process cost system?

12 Define *direct* and *indirect* process or departmental costs.

13 What is the purpose of service department cost accounts? Give some examples of service departments in a factory.

14 What is meant by the term *equivalent full units?* How is this concept used in computing average unit costs?

15 Briefly describe a *cost report* as it might be prepared for a department using a process cost system.

EXERCISES

Ex. 25-1 The Patio Floorings Company Ltd. uses a process cost accounting system but does not use a predetermined overhead rate. Its records show the following information for the month of June:

Inventories:	June 30	June 1
Raw materials	$ 8,000	$10,000
Goods in process	7,500	4,000
Finished goods	13,000	12,000
Purchases of raw materials	30,000	
Direct labor	40,000	
Factory overhead	25,000	

Compute the following:
a Overhead rate based on direct labor cost _____%
b Cost of goods manufactured in June $_____
c Cost of goods sold in June $_____

Ex. 25-2 The information below is taken from the job order cost system used by the East Furniture Company Ltd.

Job Number	Balance, July 1	Production Costs in July
101	$1,400	
102	1,080	
103	300	$ 650
104	750	1,300
105		1,900
106		1,210

Jobs no. 103 and 104 were completed and Jobs no. 101, 102, and 103 were delivered to customers in July. From the foregoing information, compute the following:
a The goods in process inventory at July 1 $_____
b The finished goods inventory at July 1 $_____
c The cost of goods sold during July $_____
d The goods in process inventory at July 31 $_____
e The finished goods inventory at July 31 $_____

Ex. 25-3 The following information appears in the Goods in Process account of Garson Enterprises for the month of January:

Debits to account:	
Raw materials	$12,000
Direct labor	20,000
Factory overhead (applied to jobs at 120% of direct labor cost)	24,000
Total debits to account	$56,000
Credits to account:	
Transferred to Finished Goods Inventory account	48,000
Balance in account, end of January	$ 8,000

If the cost of raw materials relating to the jobs in process on January 31 amounts to $3,600, determine the amount of direct labor and factory overhead which has been charged to the jobs still in process at January 31.

Ex. 25-4 The Expo Corporation Ltd. which used a job order cost system, completed the following transactions during the month of November.
  a Direct labor, $15,000, and indirect labor, $5,000, are transferred from the Factory Payroll account to other appropriate accounts.
  b Other factory overhead costs of $11,500 are incurred (credit Miscellaneous Accounts).
  c Factory overhead costs are applied to goods in process at the rate of 80% of direct labor cost.
  d Raw materials identified with specific jobs amount to $8,200.
  e Jobs with total accumulated costs of $30,000 are finished.
  f The cost of units sold during the month amounts to $28,800; the sales price of units sold is $40,000.

Prepare entries in journal form to record the foregoing transactions.

Ex. 25-5 The following relates to the Assembly Department which manufactures product Y:

Units in process at beginning of period (60% completed) 2,000
Additional units placed in production during the period 20,000
Units in process at end of period (80% completed) 5,000

Determine the equivalent full units of production during the period, assuming that all costs are incurred uniformly as the units move through the production line.

Ex. 25-6 Given below are the production data for Department no. 1 for the first month of operation:

Inputs to department:
  Material, 1,000 units $10,000
  Direct labor   19,000
  Factory overhead   14,250

   During the first month, 800 units were completed and the remaining 200 units are 100% completed as to material and 75% completed as to direct labor and factory overhead.
   You are to determine:
  a Unit cost of material used: $_____ per unit
  b Equivalent full units of production for direct labor and factory overhead: _____ units
  c Cost of direct labor: $_____ per unit
  d Cost of factory overhead: $_____ per unit
  e Total cost of 800 units completed: $_____
  f Total cost of 200 units in process at end of month $_____

PROBLEMS

Group A

25A-1 Bunyon Cabinet Shop applies a predetermined overhead rate to production on the basis of direct labor hours in Department One and on the basis of machine-hours in Department Two. The budget estimates for the current year are:

	Department One	Department Two
Direct labor cost	$200,000	$150,000
Direct labor hours	40,000	37,500

Shop overhead (fixed and variable)	$120,000	$ 60,000
Machine-hours	10,000	15,000

Production of a batch of custom furniture ordered by the City Furniture Chain (job no. 58) was started early in the year and completed three weeks later on January 29. The records for this job show the following cost information:

	Department One	Department Two
Job order for City Furniture Chain (job no. 58):		
Direct materials cost	$10,100	$ 4,600
Direct labor cost	$16,000	$10,200
Direct labor hours	3,100	2,600
Machine-hours	750	880

Selected additional information for January is given below:

	Department One	Department Two
Direct labor hours—month of January	3,700	3,000
Machine-hours—month of January	1,000	1,400
Shop overhead incurred in January	$10,800	$6,100

Instructions
a Compute the predetermined overhead rate for each department.
b What is the total cost of the furniture produced for the City Furniture Chain?
c Prepare the entries required to record the shipment of the furniture to the City Furniture Chain. The sales price of the order was "cost plus 20%."
d Determine the over- or underapplied overhead for each department at the end of January.

25A-2 The owner of Specialty Products Company Ltd. has requested your assistance in preparing a summary of operations during June for a job order cost system. Inventories at June 1, 1973, are shown below:

Raw materials inventory	$30,000
Factory supplies inventory	1,000
Goods in process (Foundry, $8,000; Machine Shop, $12,000)	20,000
Finished goods inventory	15,000

Purchases and factory requisitions of raw materials and factory supplies during June are summarized as follows:

	Purchases	Requisitions
Raw materials	$20,000	$39,500
Factory supplies	2,150	2,500

After reviewing the work done up to June 1, you accumulate the following cost information for the month of June:

Costs	Total	Service Depts.		Productive Depts.	
		Power Plant	General Plant	Foundry	Machine Shop
Direct departmental					
labor	$26,150	$2,300	$1,350	$12,500	$10,000
Raw materials	39,500	500	1,000	23,500	14,500
Depreciation	1,100	140	80	350	530
Property taxes	250	40	20	70	120
Insurance	500	100	25	150	225
Repairs	200	200			
Miscellaneous factory					
costs	2,800	130	205	630	1,835
Factory supplies	2,500	150	1,100	500	750
Totals	$73,000	$3,560	$3,780	$37,700	$27,960

The overhead costs in the Foundry and the Machine Shop are allocated to individual jobs on the basis of direct labor costs. The following direct costs have been incurred on the four production orders in process at the end of June:

	Foundry	Machine Shop
Raw materials	$3,000	$1,200
Direct departmental labor	1,800	900

Instructions
a Prepare a work sheet showing the distribution of factory overhead costs to the departments for the month of June. Power Plant costs are allocated equally to the two productive departments and the costs of the General Plant are allocated to the Foundry and Machine Shop in a 2:1 ratio. Determine the factory overhead rate for the Foundry and the Machine Shop.
b Determine the total cost to be assigned to the four production orders in process at the end of June.
c Determine the cost of goods completed in June in each of the two departments. You need not prepare a formal statement of cost of goods manufactured.

25A-3 The information below relates to a production department operated by the Processo Corporation Ltd.

Units in process at beginning of May—40% complete as to materials and 60% complete as to conversion costs	2,000
Cost of units in process at beginning of May	$20,000
Units placed in production during May	11,000
Cost of materials placed in production	$91,600
Direct labor cost incurred	56,000
Factory overhead costs incurred (applied at 120% of direct labor cost) . . .	67,950
Units in process at end of May—75% complete as to materials and 80% complete as to conversion costs	3,000

Underapplied factory overhead amounts to $750 at the end of May.

Instructions
a Compute the equivalent full units completed during May. Use one column for materials and one for conversion costs.

b Prepare a cost report for May. Prepare a separate schedule (Exhibit A) showing the assignment of cost inputs to the units completed during May and to the units in process at the end of May.

c Prepare journal entries to record the costs allocated to production and the cost of goods completed during May.

25A-4 The Industrial Processing Company manufactures a chemical XPO-2 in four sequential processes. The Fourth Process is the last step before the chemical is transferred to the warehouse as finished inventory.

All material needed to complete XPO-2 is added at the beginning of the Fourth Process. The company accumulated the following cost information for the Fourth Process during the month of April:

Costs assigned to the 40,000 units in process on April 1:

Costs from Third Process transferred to Fourth Process in March	$ 76,000
Costs added in Fourth Process in March:	
Materials (100% of total requirement)	43,000
Direct labor (75% of total requirement)	78,000
Factory overhead (75% of total requirement)	84,000
Cost of goods in process inventory, April 1	$ 281,000

Cost inputs in the Fourth Process during April:

From Third Process (140,000 units)	$ 280,000
Materials requisitions	140,000
Direct labor added	312,500
Factory overhead costs incurred	375,000
Total inputs during April	$1,107,500

During April, 130,000 units of XPO-2 were completed and transferred to the warehouse. The 50,000 units in process at the end of April were 50% completed as to direct labor and factory overhead and 100% completed as to materials.

Instructions

a Compute the equivalent full units completed during April. Use one column for materials and one for labor and overhead.

b Prepare a cost report for the month of April. Prepare a separate Exhibit A showing the assignment of cost inputs to units completed and goods in process.

c Prepare journal entries to record:

(1) Costs incurred in the Fourth Process during April.

(2) Transfer of the 130,000 units completed from the Fourth Process to the Finished Goods Inventory account.

25A-5 Office King, Ltd., produces a line of metal filing cabinets. The company has been divided into a number of departments, one of which is the Lock Assembly Department. The company uses a process cost system. The following information pertains to the goods in process in the Lock Assembly Department during the month of April:

Beginning inventory	$ 22,000
Materials used	79,000
Direct labor	155,000
Applied factory overhead (80% of direct labor cost)	124,000
Total cost inputs	$380,000

Production Report for April

Units in process April 1 (100% complete as to materials, 75% complete as to labor and factory overhead)	3,000
Units put into process during April	40,000
Total units to account for	43,000
Units transferred to the Painting Department	38,000
Units in process April 30 (90% complete as to materials; 60% complete as to labor and factory overhead)	5,000
Total units accounted for	43,000

Instructions

a Compute the unit costs for materials, direct labor, and factory overhead for the Lock Assembly Department for the month of April. You should first compute the equivalent full units of work completed.

b Make the journal entry necessary to transfer the product from the Lock Assembly Department to the Painting Department for the month of April. Show how you determined the cost of the units transferred. (You may use the first-in, first-out assumption.)

c Prepare a schedule showing the computation of the cost of the ending inventory of goods in process in the Lock Assembly Department.

Group B

25B-1 Brand Grinding Company Ltd. uses a predetermined rate in applying factory overhead to individual production orders. Overhead is applied in Department C on the basis of machine-hours, and in Department D on the basis of direct labor hours. At the beginning of the current year, management made the following budget estimates:

	Department C	Department D
Direct labor	$ 55,000	$192,000
Factory overhead	$108,000	$120,000
Machine-hours	72,000	900
Direct labor hours	25,000	100,000

Production order no. 399 for 2,000 units was started in the middle of January and completed two weeks later. The cost records for this job show the following information:

	Department C	Department D
Job no. 399 (2,000 units of product):		
Cost of materials used on job	$3,000	$7,090
Direct labor cost	$4,000	$8,000
Direct labor hours	1,000	1,800
Machine-hours	2,500	100

Instructions

a Determine the overhead rate that should be used for each department in applying overhead costs to job no. 399.

b What is the total cost of job no. 399, and the unit cost of the product manufactured on this production order?

c Assume that actual overhead costs for the year were $107,500 in Department C and $118,200 in Department D. Actual machine-hours in Department C were 75,000, and actual direct labor hours in Department D were 90,000 during the year. On the basis of this information, determine the over- or underapplied overhead in each department for the year.

25B-2 Below is a summary of the cost flow relating to production orders in process in the Micromil Corporation Ltd. during the month of June:

	Production Order 22	Production Order 23	Production Order 24	Production Order 25	Production Order 26
In process on June 1 . . .	$11,400	$2,920			
Costs in June:					
Direct Materials	1,200	8,600	$12,500	$15,800	$4,700
Direct labor	3,300	9,700	15,800	20,300	6,400
Overhead applied, 110%	3,630	10,670	17,380	22,330	7,040
Total cost.	$19,530	$31,890	$45,680	$58,430	$18,140

Other data At the beginning of June, the following inventories appeared on the records of the company: materials $24,100, goods in process $14,320, finished goods $24,600. During June production orders numbered 22, 23, and 24 were completed and production was transferred to finished goods inventory. All finished product in the beginning inventory was sold, and 90% of June's production was sold, for $200,000. All sales were on open account. Below is a summary of other transactions during June:

(*1*) In addition to direct labor, the accrued payroll for indirect labor during the month was $28,200, and for selling and administrative salaries was $40,000. Credit Accrued Payroll for $123,700.

(*2*) Raw materials and supplies purchased on open account during June amounted to $49,000.

(*3*) Depreciation on buildings and equipment was $6,000 (75% related to manufacturing and 25% to selling and administrative functions).

(*4*) Additional factory costs amounting to $27,700 were incurred. Credit Materials Inventory, $18,850 and Accounts Payable, $8,850.

(*5*) Other selling and administrative expenses incurred totaled $7,040. Credit Prepaid Expenses, $3,240, and Accounts Payable, $3,800.

Instructions

a Prepare general journal entries summarizing the transactions of the Micromil Corporation Ltd. for the month of June. Use a single control account for factory overhead and for selling and administrative expenses.

b Set up ledger control accounts in three-column form for Materials Inventory, Goods in Process Inventory, and Finished Goods Inventory accounts, and for the Factory Overhead account, and enter the June 1 balances and transactions relating to these accounts for the month of June.

c Prepare in condensed form an income statement for the month of June. Assume that over- or underapplied overhead is closed to the Cost of Goods Sold account at the end of each month.

25B-3 The Sporting Goods Mfg. Company Ltd. uses a process cost accounting system for all three of its departments. The following information was prepared by the company's cost accountant, summarizing the activities of the Finishing Department for the current month:

Cost inputs—Finishing Department:

Beginning goods in process inventory, 200 units, all materials included,	
80% completed as to processing costs	$ 2,606
Direct materials placed in production, sufficient to produce 8,000 units	
(includes costs transferred from preceding department).	80,400
Direct labor and factory overhead incurred during the month	38,808
Total cost inputs	$121,814

Cost inputs assigned to:	
Units completed, 7,700 @ $15.82	$121,814
Ending goods in process inventory, 500 units, all materials included,	
60% completed as to processing costs	none
Total cost inputs assigned.	$121,814

The beginning inventory of finished goods consisted of 2,000 units costing $24,000 (on a fifo basis). A total of 6,700 units were sold during the current month. The company's cost accountant computed the cost of goods sold and the ending inventory of finished goods as follows:

Cost of goods sold:	
2,000 units @ $12.00	$24,000
4,700 units @ $15.82	74,354
Total cost of goods sold	$98,354
Finished goods inventory, 3,000 units @ $15.82	47,460

No value was assigned to ending goods in process.

Instructions
a Compute the equivalent full units of work done during the month relating to direct materials and processing costs and determine the cost per unit. Do not prepare a formal cost report.
b Prepare a schedule showing the assignment of the cost inputs to the 7,700 units completed during the month and to the 500 units in process at the end of the month.
c Assuming that the books are still open, prepare a correcting entry to restate the Cost of Goods Sold and the Finished Goods Inventory accounts and to establish the appropriate balance in the Goods in Process account. The inventory of finished goods should be valued at the average manufacturing cost for the current month ($15).

25B-4 Systems Structures Corporation Ltd. manufactures a standard subassembly which it sells to another division of the company at $50 per unit. The plant manager has prepared a budget for the current year which calls for the production and delivery of 32,000 units at an average unit cost of $38 per unit; this is composed of material cost $12, direct labor cost $15, and factory overhead $11. The manager estimates that income before taxes will be $6.50 per unit delivered, after allowing for operating expenses.

The plant had no inventory of goods in process at the beginning of the year. During the current year 42,000 units of product were put into production, and 30,000 units were completely finished. The 12,000 units in process at the end of the year were fully complete as to materials but were only 50% complete, on the average, as to labor and factory overhead.

The cost data shown below were taken from the accounting records at the close of the current year:

Materials used	$483,000
Direct labor	576,000
Factory overhead	270,000
Operating expenses	160,000

The plant had beginning finished goods inventory of 4,000 units carried at a cost of $152,000. During the current year 32,000 finished units were delivered and billed at $50 each to the sister division of the company.

Instructions

a Compute the per-unit material, labor, and overhead cost of production during the year. (Hint: First determine equivalent full units produced.)

b Determine the cost of the ending inventories of goods in process and finished goods. (Assume fifo flow of costs.)

c Prepare a comparative statement showing the actual income (before income taxes) and the income which was anticipated by the manager on the basis of his budget estimates. Comment on the differences between the two income figures.

25B-5 One of the primary products of Photocision Ltd., is Photorex, a product which is processed successively in Department A and Department B, and then transferred to the company's sales warehouse. After having been shut down for three weeks as a result of a material shortage, the company resumed production of Photorex on May 1. The flow of product through the departments during May is shown below.

Department A		Department B	
Goods in Process		**Goods in Process**	
Input—	To Dept. B—	From Dept. A—	To warehouse—
30,000 units	25,000 units	25,000 units	21,000 units

Departmental manufacturing costs applicable to Photorex production for the month of May were as follows:

	Department A	Department B
Raw materials	$11,200	$ 4,680
Direct labor	9,800	7,020
Factory overhead	7,000	14,040
Total manufacturing costs	$28,000	$25,740

Unfinished goods in each department at the end of May were on the average 60% complete, with respect to both raw materials and processing costs.

Instructions

a Determine the present status of the 30,000 units put into production in Department A during May.

b Determine the equivalent full units of production in each department during May.

c Compute unit production costs in each department during May.

d Prepare the necessary journal entries to record the transfer of product out of Departments A and B during May.

BUSINESS DECISION PROBLEM 25

The demand for the product made by Reid Manufacturing Company Ltd. fluctuates seasonally. Units costs are computed quarterly on the basis of actual material, labor, and factory overhead costs charged to goods in process at the end of each quarter. At the close of the current year, Reid received the following cost report, by quarters, for the year. (Fixed factory overhead represents items of manufacturing costs that remain relatively constant month by month; variable factory overhead includes those costs that tend to move up and down in proportion to changes in the volume of production.)

	First Quarter	Second Quarter	Third Quarter	Fourth Quarter
Direct materials	$ 9,200	$ 37,200	$ 26,500	$ 19,900
Direct labor	21,000	80,000	60,000	39,000
Fixed factory overhead	25,000	25,000	25,000	25,000
Variable factory overhead	14,800	47,000	38,500	25,700
Total manufacturing cost	$70,000	$189,200	$150,000	$109,600
Units produced	10,000	40,000	30,000	20,000
Unit costs	$ 7.00	$ 4.73	$ 5.00	$ 5.48

Reid is concerned about the wide variation in quarterly unit costs. He notes that his unit product cost was $7.00 in the first quarter of the year but only $4.73 in the second quarter. He asks you to study the problem and see whether the method of computing unit costs could be improved.

You point out that the primary reason for the quarterly variation in unit costs is the seasonal fluctuation in volume of production and suggest that the company change its costing system.

Instructions
a What change in the company's costing procedure would you recommend? Redetermine the unit cost for each quarter using the procedure you recommend.
b At the end of the first quarter of the year, the company had received an offer from an exporter to buy 8,000 units at a special price of $4.70 per unit. The company's normal selling price is $8 per unit. Since the company's total unit costs had never been as low as $4.70, and amounted to $7.00 in the first quarter, Reid refused the offer. On the basis of the information that you have, would you have made the same decision? Why?

TWENTY-SIX

MANAGERIAL CONTROL STANDARD COSTS AND BUDGETING

One of the primary functions of management is to control the operations of the organization for which it is responsible. In a broad sense, managerial control includes: (1) *planning*—setting organizational objectives, standards of performance, and choosing among alternative courses of action; (2) *action*—seeing that plans are put into effect and that policies are followed; (3) *reporting*—measuring the results of actions taken; and (4) *evaluation*—assessing the quality of performance and taking necessary steps to correct deviations from plans. In a nutshell, the function of managerial control is to see that what is intended to be done is in fact done.

Management needs information to implement control

Accounting information is useful in all four areas of managerial control. However, the information needed by management frequently differs materially from the data collected in the accounting records. The primary purpose of most accounting systems is to provide information for the preparation of financial statements. Management's internal needs for information, however, extend beyond the data contained in financial statements. To exercise effective control, management must estimate future costs and revenues, measure the effect of alternative actions, and compare past performance with predetermined standards. In developing information for its own internal use, management is not tied to generally accepted accounting principles. Estimates may be incorporated freely into the data and whatever measurement rules prove most useful and relevant may be adopted.

An accounting system that serves all possible external and internal informational needs is a dream that will probably never become a reality. Too many different ways of measuring and relating costs and benefits can be devised that are useful and relevant in making business decisions. Therefore, anyone who depends on accounting data for control purposes should know how to rearrange and modify the informational output of an accounting system to meet varying decision-making needs.

In this chapter we discuss two important concepts that have proved useful to managers in planning and controlling operations—standard costs and budgeting.

STANDARD COSTS FOR PRODUCT COSTING AND CONTROL

In the preceding chapter it was stated that one of the objectives of cost accounting is to determine the unit cost of production. We saw that *actual* costs are determined through *process cost* or *job order cost* systems, and that such actual costs are used to compute the cost of goods sold, to value ending inventories, and to control factory operations.

If a process or job order cost system is to be of maximum value to management, however, *predetermined* cost estimates for material, labor, and factory overhead should be introduced into such a system in order to have a bench mark against which actual costs can be compared. These predetermined costs are called *standard costs.* A standard cost is the cost that *should be* incurred to produce a given product or to perform a particular operation under relatively ideal conditions. The use of such costs in the accounting records is known as a *standard cost system.*

As stated previously, an effective managerial control system calls for the setting of standards of performance, measuring actual performance, and taking corrective action when necessary. Standard costs can be used to establish cost goals and to direct management's attention to areas requiring corrective action. This is known as *management by exception* because managers should not spend time on areas of activity which are running according to plans. Effective managers focus attention on those activities which are "off target," that is, those not meeting the established standards of performance. For example, if a standard cost to produce a given product is set at $10 per unit and the actual cost is $12.50 per unit, management would want to know why actual cost exceeded standard cost by such a large margin and would strive to attain tighter control over production costs.

Establishing and revising standard costs

In establishing a standard cost for a manufactured product, for example, factory conditions and prices for materials, labor, and factory overhead must be studied. The most efficient methods for the use of materials, men, and machinery should be selected before cost standards for each operation or product can be established.

Once cost standards are set, they should be periodically reviewed and changed only when production methods change, when products are redesigned, or when prices paid for materials, labor, and factory overhead change. Standard costs should not be changed simply because actual costs are excessive. If standard costs are too low and actual costs regularly exceed standard costs by a large margin, the standards should be revised upward; if standard costs are too high, they may be easily achieved and much of the potential benefit of using a standard cost system as a control instrument may be lost.

A standard cost for materials, for example, would not be changed if 10% of material placed in production has been spoiled because of carelessness by employees; the standard cost for material would be changed, however, if the price for materials is reduced by suppliers. Similarly, the standard cost for labor would not be changed if too many hours of labor are wasted; but the standard cost for labor would be changed if labor-saving equipment is installed or if new contracts with labor unions call for increased wage rates.

Cost variances

Even though standard costs may be carefully set and revised as conditions change, actual costs will still vary from standard costs. The differences between standard costs and actual costs are known as *cost variances.* Cost variances for materials, direct labor, and factory overhead result from a wide variety of causes which must be carefully measured and analyzed. As might be expected, different individuals within an organization are responsible for different cost variances.

It is possible to use standard costs only for cost control purposes and for the preparation of various internal reports for management's use. In most cases, however, standard costs and cost variances are recorded in the accounts. Under standard cost procedures, the costs charged to Goods in Process, Finished Goods, and Cost of Goods Sold are the standard costs of materials, direct labor, and factory overhead, not the actual costs. Any differences between the actual costs and the standard costs of goods produced are accumulated in a number of *variance accounts.*

In order to illustrate the application of standard cost procedures, assume that the Standard Manufacturing Company Ltd. has a normal monthly capacity to work 10,000 direct labor hours and to produce 10,000 units of product M. The standard cost for a unit of product M follows:

Standard cost for a unit of product M

Materials, one pound at $5 per pound.	*$ 5*
Direct labor, one hour at $4 per hour	*4*
Factory overhead, based on direct labor hours:	
Fixed ($20,000 ÷ 10,000 labor hours of monthly capacity)	*$2*
Variable ($10,000 ÷ 10,000 labor hours of monthly capacity)	*1 3*
Standard cost per unit of product M	*$12*

During the month of March, the following actual costs were incurred in producing 9,500 units of product M. There was no work in process either at the beginning or at the end of March.

Were standard cost targets achieved?

Materials, 9,400 pounds at $5.20 per pound		$ 48,880
Direct labor, 9,600 hours at $4.10 per hour		39,360
Factory overhead:		
Fixed	$20,000	
Variable, 9,600 hours at $1.30 per hour	12,480	32,480
Total actual costs incurred in March		$120,720

Even though the company "saved" 100 pounds of materials, (9,500 − 9,400), its total actual costs were $6,720 in excess of costs that *should have been incurred* in producing 9,500 units of product M. This is the *total cost variance,* determined as follows:

Who is responsible for the apparent waste of $6,720?

Total actual costs (see above)	$120,720
Total standard costs for units produced, 9,500 units at $12 per unit	114,000
Total cost variance (excess of actual over standard costs)	$ 6,720

MATERIAL PRICE AND MATERIAL QUANTITY VARIANCES In establishing the standard material cost for each unit of product, two factors were considered: (1) the quantity of material that should have been used in making a unit of finished product, and (2) the prices that should have been paid in acquiring this quantity of material. Therefore, the total material cost variance may result from differences between standard and actual material usage, or between standard and actual prices paid for materials, or from a combination of these two factors. This can be illustrated by the following diagram:

Material variances illustrated

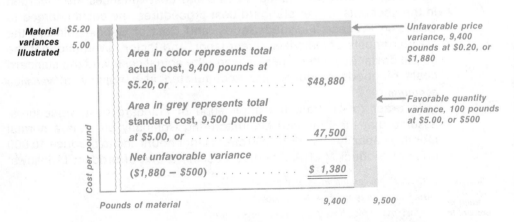

The variances for materials and the journal entry required to record the cost of material incurred by the Standard Manufacturing Company Ltd. in the month of March may be summarized as follows:

Material Price and Quantity Variances

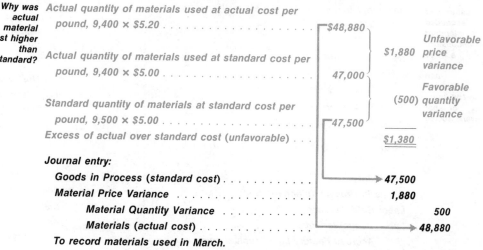

Why was
actual
material
cost higher
than
standard?

Actual quantity of materials used at actual cost per
pound, 9,400 × $5.20 . . . . $48,880

Actual quantity of materials used at standard cost per
pound, 9,400 × $5.00 47,000

Standard quantity of materials at standard cost per
pound, 9,500 × $5.00 47,500

Excess of actual over standard cost (unfavorable) . . . $1,380

Unfavorable
$1,880 price
variance

Favorable
(500) quantity
variance

Journal entry:

Goods in Process (standard cost)   47,500
Material Price Variance   1,880
Material Quantity Variance   500
Materials (actual cost)   48,880

To record materials used in March.

The excess of actual cost of materials over standard cost was caused by two factors: The unfavorable *material price variance* of $1,880 resulted from the fact that each pound of material used cost 20 cents more than the standard price of $5; this portion of the total material variance is the responsibility of the person placing orders for materials. The favorable *material quantity variance* of $500 resulted from using 100 fewer pounds of materials than the standard allowed; this variance indicates that the shop foreman is doing a good job because he is responsible for seeing that materials are not wasted or spoiled.

Note that in the example above the Goods in Process account is debited for the standard cost of materials used and that the Materials account is reduced by an amount equal to the actual cost of materials used. An alternative procedure would be to record materials purchased in the Materials account at standard cost, thus recording the price variance at the time of purchase. The unfavorable material price variance is recorded as a debit (a loss) and the favorable material quantity variance is recorded as a credit (a gain).

LABOR RATE AND LABOR USAGE VARIANCES Labor cost standards are also a product of two factors: (1) the hours of labor that should be used in making a unit of product, and (2) the wage rate that should be paid for that labor. An analysis of the total labor variance will indicate whether the variance was due to the fact that more (or less) than standard time was required in production, or that more (or less) than standard wage rates were paid, or some combination of these two factors. The computation of the labor variances for the Standard Manufacturing Company Ltd. and the journal entry required to record the direct labor cost for March are illustrated on page 794.

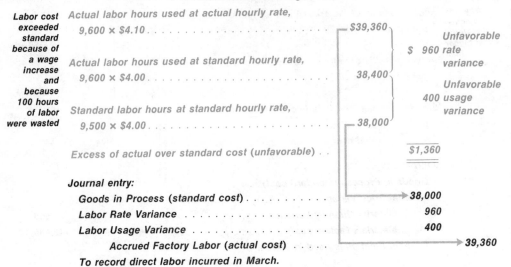

Labor Rate and Usage Variances

Labor cost exceeded standard because of a wage increase and because 100 hours of labor were wasted

Actual labor hours used at actual hourly rate,
9,600 × $4.10 . . . . $39,360 ⎫
                                                                  ⎬ Unfavorable $ 960 rate variance
Actual labor hours used at standard hourly rate,   ⎭
9,600 × $4.00 . . . .   38,400 ⎫
                                                                  ⎬ Unfavorable 400 usage variance
Standard labor hours at standard hourly rate,   ⎭
9,500 × $4.00   38,000

Excess of actual over standard cost (*unfavorable*) . . $1,360

Journal entry:
   Goods in Process (standard cost)   38,000
   Labor Rate Variance   960
   Labor Usage Variance   400
      Accrued Factory Labor (actual cost)   39,360
To record direct labor incurred in March.

The foregoing tabulation indicates that both the *labor rate variance* and the *labor usage variance* are unfavorable. The causes of these variances should be carefully investigated. If the rate increase of 10 cents per labor hour resulted from a new union contract, nothing much can be done; however, if the increase resulted from using higher-rated employees on the production line or from unnecessary overtime work, corrective action on the part of the shop foreman may be in order. The foreman should also be asked to explain the reason why 100 hours of labor in excess of standard were used during the month.

FACTORY OVERHEAD VARIANCES The difference between actual factory overhead costs incurred and the standard factory overhead costs charged to the units produced during the period is called the *overhead variance.* The standard factory overhead cost is applied to goods in process by the Standard Manufacturing Company Ltd. on the basis of a predetermined factory overhead rate of $3 per direct labor hour.

The association of factory overhead with production depends on estimates of factory overhead costs for the normal volume of production. *Normal volume* is the expected average utilization of plant capacity over many years. The presence of fixed costs in factory overhead means that the amount of factory overhead per unit of output will differ depending on the *actual* production volume attained. It is not surprising, therefore, that the analysis of the factory overhead variance is a complicated undertaking.

One possible approach is to take the difference between actual factory overhead incurred and standard factory overhead and divide it into two variances: (1) the difference between actual factory overhead and the factory overhead budgeted for the level of output attained (called the **controllable factory overhead variance**), and (2) the difference between factory overhead budgeted for the level of output attained and the standard factory overhead for the volume of output attained (called the **volume variance**). The computation of these two variances for the Standard Manufacturing Company Ltd. and the journal entry required to record factory overhead for March follow:

Factory Overhead Variances

Actual factory overhead exceeded standard. Can you explain why this happened?

Actual factory overhead incurred (see page 792)	$32,480	
Factory overhead budgeted for level of production attained, 9,500 units:		Unfavorable
Fixed $20,000		$2,980 controllable variance
Variable, 9,500 × $1.00 9,500	29,500	Unfavorable 1,000 volume variance
Standard factory overhead, 9,500 × $3.00	28,500	
Excess of actual over standard cost (unfavorable) . . .		$3,980

Journal entry:

Goods in Process (standard cost)	28,500
Controllable Factory Overhead Variance	2,980
Volume Variance	1,000
Factory Overhead (actual overhead incurred)	32,480

To transfer factory overhead incurred in March to goods in process and variance accounts.

The major reason for the large unfavorable factory overhead variance is that variable factory overhead incurred amounted to $1.30 per hour compared to the standard variable factory overhead of $1.00 per hour. This increase accounted for $2,880 (9,600 hours × $0.30) of the **controllable factory overhead variance.** The excess of hours worked (9,600) over standard hours (9,500) accounted for the other $100 of the controllable factory overhead variance. This is determined by multiplying the 100 excess hours worked by the standard variable factory overhead rate of $1.00. The reason this variance is "controllable" is that the two factors which are responsible for it, variable factory overhead costs incurred and the actual hours worked, can both be heavily influenced by an effective cost control system.

The unfavorable **volume variance** of $1,000 is the portion of the total fixed factory overhead not applied to production, 500 units not produced × $2.00 (fixed factory overhead rate per unit). Since the Standard Manufacturing Company Ltd. produced only 9,500 units of product M, it fell 5% short of its monthly capacity of 10,000 units. Therefore, 5% of the total capacity (fixed) costs of $20,000, or $1,000, was **not applied** to units produced. In other words, this was the *idle capacity loss* for the month of March.

TRANSFER OF COST OF UNITS COMPLETED TO FINISHED GOODS INVENTORY At the end of March, the entry to record the transfer of cost of goods completed from the Goods in Process account to the Finished Goods Inventory account is shown below:

Entry to record goods completed	*Finished Goods Inventory (at standard cost)*............ 114,000	
	Goods in Process (at standard cost)..............	114,000
	To transfer cost of units completed to finished goods inventory.	

Disposition of variance accounts

Under a standard cost system, monthly inventories of goods in process and finished goods may be priced at standard cost. Cost variances are allowed to accumulate from month to month; hopefully, only a small total variance will remain because unfavorable variances in one month are offset by favorable variances in other months. At the end of the fiscal year, however, a net unfavorable cost variance would be added to Cost of Goods Sold, as illustrated below:

RAQUEL MFG. COMPANY LTD.

Partial Income Statement

Year 1

Unfavorable cost variance is added to cost of goods sold	*Sales (net)*.................................		$450,000
	Cost of goods sold, at standard...............	$300,000	
	Add: Net unfavorable cost variance.............	3,000	
	Cost of goods sold and net unfavorable cost variance..........		303,000
	Gross profit on sales...........................		$147,000

A net favorable cost variance would be deducted from Cost of Goods Sold at the end of the fiscal year.

However, if the total cost variance (either favorable or unfavorable) for the year is large, it would be more appropriate to prorate the total cost variance between Goods in Process, Finished Goods, and Cost of Goods Sold in order to restate these accounts to *actual cost*. This would be particularly appropriate when the cost variance is caused by unrealistic standards rather than from outright waste or idle capacity losses. A large cost variance representing both inefficiency and idle capacity losses generally would be charged off in the period in which it was incurred.

Summary of advantages of standard cost system

Among the advantages accruing to management from the use of a standard cost system are the following:

1 The setting of standards requires a thorough analysis of operations; this tends to uncover inefficiencies and helps management maximize profits.

2 A standard cost system assists in the establishment of clearly defined organizational lines of authority and responsibility; this may result in less day-to-day confusion and higher employee morale.

3 Analysis of variances from standard costs helps management control costs in future periods.

4 Standard cost information is often useful in formulating pricing decisions concerning products and services.

5 Standard costs are useful in designing an effective system of responsibility accounting and budgetary controls throughout the organization.

BUDGETING AS AN AID TO PLANNING AND CONTROL

A *budget* is a summary statement of plans expressed in quantitative terms; it guides individuals or an accounting entity in reaching financial or operational goals. If standard costs are used in the accounting system for a company engaged in manufacturing activities, such costs are also used in the preparation of budgets.

Most college students have at one time or another drawn up plans for the effective use of their time to secure a balance between academic and extracurricular activities. This is a *time budget* expressed in days or hours. Similarly, a student with limited financial resources finds it helpful to write down a plan for spending his money which will see him through a semester or year of schooling. This is an *expenditure budget* expressed in monetary terms.

The problem that plagues college students—planning the efficient use of limited resources—also faces managers of organizations of every type. Businessmen must plan to attain profit objectives and meet their financial obligations as they become due. Administrators of nonprofit organizations and government agencies must plan to accomplish objectives of programs with the resources available to them. Budgets are as universal as the concept of planning; as a matter of fact, a budget is often viewed as a comprehensive *financial plan*—a kind of compass designed to guide managers through the turbulent waters of business activity.

The purpose of budgeting

Every budget is a forecast of future events. Business budgets show anticipated revenues, expenses, and the financial position of the company at some future point in time, assuming that the budget estimates are met. Systematic forecasting serves the control function in two major ways:

First, by showing what results will be if present plans are put into effect, a budget discloses areas that require attention or *corrective action.* For example, the college student whose budget shows potential expenditures of $3,000 for the year and who has only $2,000 in financial resources is forewarned. By knowing this in advance, he may be able to find ways of augmenting his resources or reducing his expenses. If he waits until his funds are gone in midyear, effective action may no longer be possible. Similarly, a business budget showing that profit objectives will not be met or that working capital will not be sufficient may enable management to act in advance to alter the revenue and cost picture or to obtain additional financing.

The second use of budgets for control purposes is in *evaluating performance.* Organizational plans are carried out by people. Control is thus exercised not over operations, revenues, and costs, but over the persons responsible for various business functions and the revenue and expense results attained. Budgets provide a yardstick against which a manager's actual performance may be compared.

It is this latter feature—performance evaluation—that accounts for the general unpopularity of budgets. Managers are human, and few of us are overjoyed about techniques which enable our boss to check our performance. Furthermore, budgets often restrict freedom of action, since they are designed to motivate personnel to follow a plan. Unbridled freedom is generally more fun than following an orderly plan of action. Therefore, budgets are often regarded by business managers as penny-pinching, restrictive devices designed to harass them and prevent them from doing their job as they would like to do it.

The largest part of effective budgeting is the delicate task of dealing with its *human relations* aspects. Budgets themselves are inanimate and mechanical. They will be effective only if those who are responsible for carrying out plans and whose performance will be measured against planned results participate fully in the development of the budget. The greater the participation in the planning process, the greater the awareness of a company's objectives and problems throughout the organization. Meaningful participation in the preparation of a budget by managers at all levels of the organization is an important prerequisite to successful budgeting.

The budget period

As a general rule, the period covered by a budget should be long enough to show the effect of managerial policies but short enough so that estimates can be made with reasonable accuracy. This suggests that different types of budgets should be made for different time spans.

A *master budget* is an overall financial and operating plan for a forthcoming fiscal period and the coordinated program for achieving the plan. It is usually prepared on a quarterly or an annual basis. Long-range budgets, called *capital budgets,* which incorporate plans for major expenditures for plant and equipment or the addition of product lines, might be prepared to cover plans for as long as 5 to 10 years. *Responsibility budgets,* which are segments of the master budget relating to the aspect of the business that is the responsibility of a particular manager, are often prepared monthly. *Cash budgets* may be prepared on a day-to-day basis. Some companies follow a *continuous budgeting* plan whereby budgets are constantly reviewed and updated. The updating is accomplished, for example, by extending the annual budget one additional month at the end of each month. A review of the budget may also suggest that the budget be changed as a result of changing business and operating conditions.

Preparing a master budget

The major steps in developing a master budget may be outlined as follows:

1 Establish basic goals and long-range plans for the company.

2 Prepare a sales forecast for the budget period. The sales forecast, of course, will be based on the forecast of general business and economic conditions anticipated during the budget period. This is a starting point because to a significant extent production or purchases, inventory levels, cash requirements, and operating expenses are governed by the expected volume of sales.

3 Estimate the cost of goods sold and operating expenses. These estimates will depend directly on the sales budget and a thorough knowledge of the relation between costs and volume of activity. Production costs used to estimate cost of goods sold are often based on standard costs for the products manufactured.

4 Determine the effect of budgeted operating results on asset, liability, and ownership equity accounts. The cash budget is the largest part of this step, since changes in many asset and liability accounts will depend on cash flow forecasts.

5 Summarize the estimated data in the form of a projected income statement for the budget period and a projected (sometimes called a *pro forma*) balance sheet as of the end of the budget period.

Master budget illustrated

Master budgets are the culmination of the entire planning process throughout an organization. The detailed mechanics of a master budget may become quite complex. To illustrate master budgeting in an introductory fashion, it is necessary to assume a very simple budgeting situation and to condense detail as much as possible.

We shall assume a manufacturing company that makes and sells a single product. The balance sheet for the Berg Company Ltd. as of January 1 is shown on page 800. Management has asked for a master

BERG COMPANY LTD.
Actual Balance Sheet
January 1, Current Year

Assets

Current assets:

Cash		$ 75,000
Receivables		82,000
Inventories:		
Materials	$ 25,000	
Finished goods *(fifo method)*	52,000	77,000
Prepayments		21,000
Total current assets		$255,000
Plant and equipment:		
Buildings and equipment	$970,000	
Less: Accumulated depreciation	420,000	
Total plant and equipment		550,000
Total assets		$805,000

Liabilities & Stockholders' Equity

Current liabilities:

Notes payable, 8% ($40,000 payable quarterly)		$160,000
Other current payables		78,000
Income taxes payable		50,000
Total current liabilities		$288,000
Stockholders' equity:		
Capital stock, no par, 100,000 shares	$350,000	
Retained earnings	167,000	517,000
Total liabilities & stockholders' equity		$805,000

budget that will provide an estimate of net income for the first and second quarters of the coming year and a projected balance sheet at the end of each of the first two quarters. The company has notes payable of $160,000 due in quarterly installments of $40,000, starting on March 31 of the current year. Sales of the company's product are seasonal; sales during the second quarter are expected to exceed first-quarter sales by 50%. However, the economy of stabilizing production and a very tight labor supply have led management to plan for stable production of 120,000 units during the first and second quarters. This will require an increase in inventory during the first quarter to meet second-quarter sales demand. Management is concerned about its ability to finance the inventory buildup during the first quarter and meet the quarterly payments on the bank loan.

OPERATING BUDGET ESTIMATES The operating data estimates needed to prepare a budgeted income statement for each of the first two quarters are shown on page 802.

Estimates of unit sales and sales price per unit (Schedule A1) are based on marketing plans and pricing policy in the light of past experience. The production budget (Schedule A2) reflects not only the decision to stabilize production, but the decision to reduce the inventory of finished goods from its January 1 level of 30,000 units to 20,000 units at the end of June to minimize funds tied up in finished goods and thus help meet the second-quarter loan repayment. The cost estimates (Schedule A3) provide the basis for attaching dollars to production and for budgeting operating expenses. Details of operating expenses are omitted. *Note that variable factory overhead is stated in terms of units manufactured, and variable selling and administrative expenses in terms of units sold.* Schedules A4 and A6 show the determination of budgeted costs of goods manufactured and operating expenses. The ending finished goods inventory is computed in Schedule A5.

PROJECTED INCOME STATEMENT   The projected income statement on page 803 is based on the operating budget estimates in Schedules A1 to A6. Schedule numbers are indicated parenthetically on the statement. Two items need further comment:

Interest on the $160,000 bank loan is estimated on the assumption that the $40,000 installment will be paid at the end of the first quarter. Interest at 8% per year, or 2% per quarter, is computed on the outstanding balance of $160,000 during the first quarter and on $120,000 during the second quarter.

Income tax expense is budgeted on the assumption that combined federal and provincial income taxes will amount to 50% of income before income taxes. We shall assume that last year's tax liability of $50,000 will be paid in two equal installments in the first two quarters of the current year.

FINANCIAL BUDGET ESTIMATES   The estimates and data necessary to prepare a cash budget and projected balance sheet for each quarter are shown on pages 804 and 805. A forecast of the Berg Company's financial position at the end of each quarter requires that the account balances on the January 1 balance sheet be adjusted to reflect projected revenues and expenses and the resulting changes in assets and liabilities. Since cash is the most active financial account in a business, the key to preparing a financial budget is a forecast of cash flows, leading to a cash budget by quarters.

The starting point in this process is to convert the operating budget data into cash flows and changes in financial accounts. We begin by scheduling the source of budgeting operating costs (Schedule B2). It is first necessary to convert the materials used figure in the cost of goods manufactured statement into materials purchased, which requires an estimate of the materials inventories at the end of each quarter. The production manager feels that the January 1 materials inventory of

BERG COMPANY LTD.
Operating Budget Estimates
First and Second Quarters of Current Year

Schedule		1st Quarter	2d Quarter
A1	Sales budget:		
	Selling price per unit	$ 3.00	$ 3.00
	Sales forecast in units	100,000	150,000
	Budgeted sales	$300,000	$450,000
A2	Production budget (in units):		
	Planned production	120,000	120,000
	.Inventory at beginning of quarter	30,000	50,000
	Units available for sale.	150,000	170,000
	Estimated sales (A1)	100,000	150,000
	Inventory at end of quarter	50,000	20,000

		Both 1st and 2d quarters (120,000 units each quarter)
A3	Cost estimates:	
	Variable costs:	
	Per unit manufactured:	
	Materials	$ 0.50
	Direct labor	0.60
	Variable factory overhead	0.30
	Per unit sold:	
	Selling and administrative expense.	0.30
	Fixed costs (per quarter):	
	Factory overhead	$ 42,000
	Selling and administrative expense	70,000
A4	Budgeted cost of goods manufactured (120,000 units):	
	Materials used ($0.50 per unit).	$ 60,000
	Direct labor ($0.60 per unit)	72,000
	Variable factory overhead ($0.30 per unit).	36,000
	Fixed factory overhead.	42,000
	Total cost of goods manufactured	$210,000
	Cost per unit ($210,000 ÷ 120,000 units)	$1.75

Schedule		1st Quarter	2d Quarter
A5	Ending finished goods inventory:		
	50,000 units at $1.75	$ 87,500	
	20,000 units at $1.75		$ 35,000
A6	Selling and administrative expense budget:		
	Variable expenses ($0.30 × units sold).	$ 30,000	$ 45,000
	Fixed expenses	70,000	70,000
	Total selling and administrative expense.	$100,000	$115,000

BERG COMPANY LTD.
Projected Income Statement
First Two Quarters of Current Year

	1st Quarter	2d Quarter
Sales	$300,000	$450,000
Cost of goods sold:		
Finished goods, beginning inventory	$ 52,000	$ 87,500
Cost of goods manufactured (A4)	210,000	210,000
Cost of goods available for sale	$262,000	$297,500
Less: Finished goods, ending inventory (A5)	87,500	35,000
Cost of goods sold	$174,500	$262,500
Gross profit on sales	$125,500	$187,500
Expenses:		
Selling and administrative expense (A6)	$100,000	$115,000
Interest expense	3,200	2,400
Total expenses	$103,200	$117,400
Income before income taxes	$ 22,300	$ 70,100
Income taxes (50% of income before income taxes)	11,150	35,050
Net income	$ 11,150	$ 35,050
Earnings per share	$0.11	$0.35

Here is what quarterly income should be

$25,000 is too low. To meet the production schedule, he would like to have on hand at the end of the first quarter and throughout the second quarter about two-thirds of the materials usage for the second quarter. The desired ending inventory in Schedule B1 is therefore set at $40,000, which is two-thirds of the $60,000 projected materials usage in the second quarter.

The three primary sources of operating costs are current payables (accounts payable and accrued liabilities), the write-off of prepaid expenses, and depreciation of plant and equipment. The analysis of the source of manufacturing, selling, and administrative costs in Schedule B2 provides the key to estimates of the required outlays for current payables in Schedule B3. The estimate of the ending balance of current payables ($98,500 at the end of the first quarter and $85,500 at the end of the second quarter) has been made by the company treasurer on the basis of past experience and his knowledge of suppliers' credit terms and the wage payment policies of the company.

The Berg Company Ltd. sells to customers entirely on account. Therefore, the sole source of cash receipts for this company during the two quarters is the collection of accounts receivable. Losses from uncollectible accounts and cash discounts are ignored in this example. The credit manager estimates that two-thirds of the sales in any quarter will be collected in that quarter, and the remaining one-third of the quarter's

BERG COMPANY LTD.
Financial Budget Estimates
First and Second Quarters of Current Year

Schedule		1st Quarter	2d Quarter
B1	Budgeted materials purchases and inventory:		
	Materials used (A4)...............	$ 60,000	$ 60,000
	Desired ending inventory	40,000	40,000
	Materials available for use	$100,000	$100,000
	Less: Inventory at beginning of quarter.....	25,000	40,000
	Budgeted material purchases...........	$ 75,000	$ 60,000

B2   Source of budgeted operating costs:

	Total	Current Payables	Prepayment Write-off	Depre-ciation
First quarter:				
Material purchases (B1)	$ 75,000	$ 75,000		
Direct labor (A4).....	72,000	72,000		
Factory overhead (A4) .	78,000	64,000	$ 4,400	$ 9,600
Selling and administra-				
tive expense (A6)...	100,000	94,600	3,000	2,400
Total	$325,000	$305,600	$ 7,400	$ 12,000
Second quarter:				
Material purchases (B1)	$ 60,000	$ 60,000		
Direct labor (A4).....	72,000	72,000		
Factory overhead (A4) .	78,000	64,400	$ 4,000	$ 9,600
Selling and administra-				
tive expense (A6)...	115,000	109,500	3,100	2,400
Total	$325,000	$305,900	$ 7,100	$ 12,000

		1st Quarter	2d Quarter
B3	Payments on current payables:		
	Balance at beginning of quarter	$ 78,000	$ 98,500
	Increase in payables during quarter (B2) ...	305,600	305,900
	Total payables during quarter	$383,600	$404,400
	Estimated balance at end of quarter (given)..	98,500	85,500
	Payments on current payables during quarter	$285,100	$318,900

sales will be collected in the following quarter. The forecast of cash collections (B6) and estimated balance of receivables (B7) are based on these estimates.

CASH BUDGET The information derived in the financial budget schedules forms the basis for the quarterly cash budget for the Berg Company Ltd. which appears on page 806.

Schedule		1st Quarter	2d Quarter
B4	Prepayments budget:		
	Balance at beginning of quarter	$ 21,000	$ 15,600
	Estimated cash expenditure during quarter . . .	2,000	5,000
	Total prepayments	$ 23,000	$ 20,600
	Write-off of prepayments (B2)	7,400	7,100
	Prepayments at end of quarter	$ 15,600	$ 13,500
B5	Budgeted income taxes:		
	Income tax liability at beginning of quarter . . .	$ 50,000	$ 36,150
	Estimated income taxes for the quarter		
	(income statement)	11,150	35,050
	Total accrued income tax liability	$ 61,150	$ 71,200
	Cash outlay (one-half of last year's tax liability)	25,000	25,000
	Income tax liability at end of quarter	$ 36,150	$ 46,200
B6	Estimated cash collections on receivables:		
	Balance of receivables at beginning of year . .	$ 82,000	
	Collections on first-quarter sales of $300,000		
	($\frac{2}{3}$ in first quarter and $\frac{1}{3}$ in second)	200,000	$100,000
	Collections on second-quarter sales of		
	$450,000 ($\frac{2}{3}$ in second quarter)		300,000
	Total cash collections by quarter	$282,000	$400,000
B7	Budgeted accounts receivable:		
	Balance at the beginning of the quarter	$ 82,000	$100,000
	Sales on open account during quarter (A1) . .	300,000	450,000
	Total accounts receivable	$382,000	$550,000
	Less: Estimated collections on accounts		
	receivable (B6)	282,000	400,000
	Estimated accounts receivable balance at end		
	of quarter	$100,000	$150,000

Note that the quarterly payments of $40,000 on the bank loan, plus $3,200 interest in the first quarter and $2,400 interest in the second quarter, are included in the cash budget. In many cases a cash budget becomes the basis for determining a company's short-term borrowing needs and in establishing a reasonable repayment schedule for loans. In this example the loan was already in existence and only the scheduled repayments are included in the budget.

PROJECTED BALANCE SHEET We now have the necessary information to forecast the financial position of the Berg Company Ltd. at the end of each of the next two quarters. The projected balance sheets are shown on page 807. Budget schedules from which various figures on the balance sheet have been derived are indicated parenthetically on the statement.

BERG COMPANY LTD.

Cash Budget

First Two Quarters of Current Year

	1st Quarter	2d Quarter
Cash balance at beginning of quarter	$ 75,000	$ 1,700
Receipts:		
Collections on receivables (B6)	282,000	400,000
Total cash available	$357,000	$401,700
Disbursements:		
Payment of current payables (B3)	$285,100	$318,900
Income tax payments (B5)	25,000	25,000
Prepayments (B4)	2,000	5,000
Payments on notes (interest included)	43,200	42,400
Total disbursements	$355,300	$391,300
Cash balance at end of the quarter	$ 1,700	$ 10,400

Projected cash flow and ending cash balance

In this simple budget example, the balance sheets may be prepared directly from the budget schedules. In a more complex budgeting case, it might be desirable to set up the beginning balance sheet amounts on a work sheet and trace through the budgeted transactions for each quarter.

Using budgets effectively

The process of systematic planning would probably be of some value even if a budget, once prepared, were promptly filed away and forgotten. In preparing a budget managers are forced to look into all aspects of a company's activity, and this in itself will often enable them to do a better job of managing. The primary benefits of budgeting, however, stem from uses made of budgeted information after it is prepared. We have noted three ways in which budgets serve management: (1) as a plan or blueprint for accomplishing a set of objectives, (2) as a warning system for anticipating conditions that require advanced remedial action, and (3) as a means of evaluating the performance of company personnel.

Let us consider briefly how the master budget we have just demonstrated might serve these three functions.

A PLAN FOR ACCOMPLISHING OBJECTIVES   A number of operating objectives were incorporated in the budget estimates of the Berg Company Ltd. A primary objective was to achieve management's profit goals. Secondary objectives were to stabilize production throughout the first two quarters and to reduce the inventory of finished goods by the end of the second quarter. The operating budget is a set of plans for doing these things.

The budgeted income statement (page 803) shows an improved net income during the second quarter, reflecting the favorable effect of

BERG COMPANY LTD.
Projected Balance Sheet
As of the End of First Two Quarters of Current Year

	1st Quarter	2d Quarter
Assets		
Current assets:		
Cash (per cash budget)	$ 1,700	$ 10,400
Receivables (B7)	100,000	150,000
Inventories:		
Materials (B1)	40,000	40,000
Finished goods (A5)	87,500	35,000
Prepayments (B4)	15,600	13,500
Total current assets	$244,800	$248,900
Plant and equipment:		
Buildings and equipment	$970,000	$970,000
Less: Accumulated depreciation (B2)	(432,000)	(444,000)
Total plant and equipment	$538,000	$526,000
Total assets	$782,800	$774,900
Liabilities & Stockholders' Equity		
Current liabilities:		
Notes payable (8%, $40,000 due quarterly)	$120,000	$ 80,000
Other current payables (B3)	98,500	85,500
Income taxes payable (B5)	36,150	46,200
Total current liabilities	$254,650	$211,700
Stockholders' equity:		
Capital stock, no par, 100,000 shares issued and		
outstanding	$350,000	$350,000
Retained earnings, beginning of quarter	167,000	178,150
Net income for the quarter	11,150	35,050
Total stockholders' equity	$528,150	$563,200
Total liabilities & stockholders' equity	$782,800	$774,900

Projected quarterly balance sheet

increased sales volume in relation to the existence of certain fixed costs. The responsibility for securing the volume of sales revenues budgeted in each quarter rests with the sales department. The problem of scheduling the production of 120,000 units each quarter and of seeing that production costs do not exceed budget estimates is the responsibility of the manufacturing department. General management is charged with maintaining control over administrative expenses.

In order to relate budgeted information to these various responsibilities, it is desirable to rearrange the overall master budget figures in terms of responsibility centers. In broad outline, such a rearrangement might be accomplished by preparing quarterly budget estimates for major centers of responsibility, such as sales by territories, factory overhead costs, cash receipts and disbursements, manpower requirements, research expenditures, etc.

Dividing the total budget plan into responsibility segments ensures that each executive knows the goals and his part in achieving them. The use of responsibility budgets requires a carefully designed system of *responsibility accounting* in order that the results of a given responsibility center can be compared with the budget plan.

AN ADVANCE WARNING OF POTENTIAL TROUBLE   One of the major concerns of the management of the Berg Company Ltd. was the ability of the company to meet the quarterly payments on its loan obligation. The cash budget for the first two quarters of the year indicates that the cash position of the company at the end of each quarter will be precariously low. A cash balance of $1,700 is forecast at the end of the first quarter, and a balance of $10,400 at the end of the second quarter (see page 806). This indicates that if all goes well the payments *can* be met, but there is little margin for error in the estimates.

Management, when confronted with such a forecast, should take steps in advance to prevent the cash balance from dropping as low as the budgeted amounts. It may be possible to obtain longer credit terms from suppliers and thus reduce payments on accounts payable during the first two quarters. The company may decide to let inventories fall below scheduled levels in order to postpone cash outlays. An extension of the terms of the note payable might be sought, or the possibility of long-term financing might be considered. If any or all of these steps were taken, it would be necessary to revise the budget estimates accordingly. The fact that management is *forewarned* of this condition several months before it happens, however, illustrates one of the prime values of budgeting.

A YARDSTICK FOR APPRAISING PERFORMANCE   The effective use of budgets in gauging performance is not an easy task. It is not feasible to discuss all facets of this problem here, but let us consider briefly two points:

1 The heart of successful responsibility budgeting is to hold each supervisor accountable for the costs and revenues over which he can exercise significant control, and for which he is responsible.[1]

For example, the foreman of a manufacturing department can influence labor costs in his department through his control over idle time, overtime hours, and the number of employees to be hired. He may also exert some control over such overhead costs as equipment maintenance, supplies used, and power expenses. On the other hand, he probably has no influence on either the salary of the plant superintendent or the amount of building depreciation, some portion of which might be charged to his department.

The view that a manager should not be charged with costs over which

[1] See Chap. 23 for a discussion of responsibility accounting, which serves as a basis for the preparation of responsibility budgets.

he has no control is widely used in modern budgeting practice, with the result that responsibility budgets commonly include only **controllable costs.** An alternative is to segregate noncontrollable costs in a separate section of a manager's budget and to use only the figures that are in the "controllable" section of the budget in appraising his performance.

2 The problem does not end here, however. Even controllable costs may be affected by factors over which a manager has little influence. A primary example is the effect of significant differences between the volume of sales or production budgeted and the volume actually attained. The fact that attainment varied from budgeted volume will, of course, show up in comparisons with the overall budget. However, the effect of volume variations may lead to confusion when actual and budgeted results are compared for various responsibility centers. This confusion can be avoided through the use of a flexible budget.

Flexible budget—a more effective control tool

Suppose, for example, that the production manager of the Berg Company Ltd. is presented with the following schedule of budgeted and actual results at the end of the first quarter's operations:

BERG COMPANY LTD.
Production Costs—Budgeted and Actual for First Quarter
(Master Budget)

		Budgeted	Actual	Over or (under) Budget
Is this a good or a bad performance?	Production costs			
	Materials used	$ 60,000	$ 63,800	$ 3,800
	Direct labor	72,000	76,500	4,500
	Variable factory overhead	36,000	38,000	2,000
	Fixed factory overhead	42,000	42,400	400
	Total production costs	$210,000	$220,700	$10,700

At first glance it appears that the production manager's cost control performance is bad, since his production costs are $10,700 in excess of budget. But can we charge the production manager with a bad performance until we know the actual production volume for the quarter? One piece of information has been deliberately omitted from the above schedule. *Instead of the 120,000 units of production planned for the first quarter, 130,000 units were actually manufactured.*

Under these circumstances, the above comparison of budgeted and actual costs becomes meaningless as a measure of the production manager's performance. There is no point in comparing actual and budgeted cost performance at two different volume levels.

One solution to this problem is to base performance evaluation on a **flexible budget** which reflects projected production costs for the **actual** volume of operations during the period. On a flexible budgeting basis, a comparison of the production manager's budgeted and actual performance might be made as follows:

BERG COMPANY LTD.
Production Costs—Budgeted and Actual for First Quarter
(Flexible Budget)

	Originally Budgeted	Flexible Budget	Actual Costs	Actual Costs over or (under) Flexible Budget
Units of production	120,000	130,000	130,000	
Production costs:				
Materials used	$ 60,000	$ 65,000	$ 63,800	$(1,200)
Direct labor	72,000	78,000	76,500	(1,500)
Variable factory overhead	36,000	39,000	38,000	(1,000)
Fixed factory overhead	42,000	42,000	42,400	400
Total production costs	$210,000	$224,000	$220,700	$(3,300)

Flexible budget shows a different picture

This comparison gives quite a different picture of the production manager's cost performance. On the basis of actual volume, he has done better than budgeted costs in all categories except fixed factory overhead, most of which is probably outside his control.

Many well-managed companies prepare a flexible budget for different levels of production and sales. A flexible budget is in reality a series of budgets for **different levels of activity.** The preparation of a flexible budget rests on the ability to predict the probable cost behavior at different activity levels. The installation of a standard cost system is generally quite useful for this purpose.

DEMONSTRATION PROBLEM FOR YOUR REVIEW

The budget committee of Modern Toy Company Ltd. made a sales forecast for Year 5 (its first year of operations) of 180,000 toy rockets, each selling for $2.40. An additional 20,000 rockets will be produced for stock. The committee estimates that 80,000 pounds of sheet metal at $0.20 per pound, and 700 gallons of paint at $5.00 per gallon are required to produce the 200,000 rockets. Estimated wage rates for direct labor and labor hours required to produce 200,000 rockets are:

Machine operators, 20,000 hours @ $4.00	$ 80,000
Painters, 10,000 hours @ $4.50	45,000
Total, 30,000 hours	$125,000

Budgeted factory overhead for the production of 200,000 rockets is shown below:

Fixed factory overhead:

Depreciation: building	$ 4,600
Depreciation: machinery	9,500
Salary of plant manager	11,500
Insurance and property taxes	2,900

Variable factory overhead:

Indirect labor	*$1.50 per direct labor hour*
Indirect materials and supplies	*0.15 per rocket produced*
Miscellaneous factory costs	*0.22 per direct labor hour*

Operating expenses are budgeted as follows:

Fixed	*$15,500*
Variable	*$0.30 per rocket sold*

Assume that the corporate income tax rate is 40% of taxable income.

Instructions

a Prepare a projected income statement for Year 5, supported by a projected statement of cost of goods manufactured (Schedule A). Compute the estimated cost of each rocket.

b Calculate the planned factory overhead rate for Year 5, based on direct labor hours.

QUESTIONS

1 What are the four primary elements of the managerial control function?

2 To what extent may generally accepted accounting principles be ignored in developing information for managerial control and decision-making purposes?

3 Define **standard costs** and briefly indicate how they may be used by management in planning and control.

4 What is meant by the expression **management by exception?**

5 What is wrong with the following statement: "There are three basic kinds of cost systems: job order, process, and standard."

6 Once standard costs are established, what conditions would require that standards be revised?

7 List the variances from standard cost that are generally computed for materials, direct labor, and factory overhead.

8 Define each of the following terms: **normal volume, fixed costs,** and **idle capacity loss.**

9 "The cost of waste and inefficiency cannot be regarded as an asset." Explain how this statement supports the use of standard costs in the valuation of goods in process and finished goods inventories.

10 Briefly list some of the advantages of using a standard cost system.

11 What would be the purposes of preparing a budget for a business of any size?

12 An article in **Business Week** stated that approximately one-third of the total American federal budget (which exceeds $200 billion dollars by a substantial margin) is considered "controllable." What is meant by a budgeted expenditure being controllable? Give two examples of government expenditures that may be considered "noncontrollable."

13 Describe the five major steps in the preparation of a master budget.

14 Describe three ways in which budgets serve management.

15 What is a **flexible budget?** Explain how a flexible budget increases the usefulness of budgeting as a means of evaluating performance.

EXERCISES

Ex. 26-1 The standard for materials in manufacturing item Z is one pound at $1.00. During the current month, 5,000 units of Item Z were produced and 5,100 pounds of materials costing $5,355 were used. Analyze the $355 variance between actual cost and standard cost in such a way as to show how much of it was attributable to price change and how much to excess quantity of materials used. Indicate whether the variances are favorable or unfavorable.

Ex. 26-2 The standard costs and variances for direct materials, direct labor, and factory overhead for the month of April are given below:

	Standard Cost	Variances Unfavorable	Variances Favorable
Direct materials	$10,000		
Price variance			$500
Quantity variance			300
Direct labor	20,000		
Rate variance.		$200	
Usage variance			900
Factory overhead.	30,000		
Controllable variance		400	
Volume variance.		600	

Determine the actual costs incurred during the month of April for direct materials, direct labor, and factory overhead.

Ex. 26-3 From the following information for the J. Bowman Corporation Ltd. compute the controllable factory overhead variance and the volume variance and indicate whether the variances are favorable or unfavorable.

Standard factory overhead based on direct labor hours at normal capacity:

Fixed ($40,000 ÷ 10,000 hours)	$4.00	
Variable ($60,000 ÷ 10,000 hours)	6.00	$10.00
Direct labor hours actually worked		9,000 hours
Actual factory overhead costs incurred (including $40,000 fixed)		$92,200

Ex. 26-4 The flexible budget at the 70 and 80% levels of activity is shown below:

	At 70%	At 80%	At 90%
Sales	$105,000	$120,000	$
Cost of goods sold	77,000	88,000	
Gross profit on sales	$ 28,000	$ 32,000	$
Operating expenses ($12,000 fixed)	26,000	28,000	
Operating income	$ 2,000	$ 4,000	$
Income taxes, 30%.	600	1,200	
Net income	$ 1,400	$ 2,800	$

Complete the flexible budget at the 90% level of activity.

Ex. 26-5 Sales on account for the first quarter are budgeted as follows:

January	$40,000
February	50,000
March	60,000

All sales are made on terms of 2/10, n/30; collections on accounts receivable are typically made as follows:

In month of sale:	
Within discount period	50%
After discount period	20%
In month following sale:	
Within discount period	15%
After discount period	10%
Returns, allowances, and uncollectibles	5%
Total	100%

Compute the estimated cash collections on accounts receivable for the month of March.

Ex. 26-6 The cost accountant for the Kane Casting Co. Ltd. prepared the following monthly report relating to the Grinding Department:

	Budget (10,000 hours)	Actual (11,000 hours)	Variances Unfavorable	Favorable
Direct materials	$30,000	$32,000	$2,000	
Direct labor	20,000	21,500	1,500	
Variable factory overhead . .	25,000	27,850	2,850	
Fixed factory overhead	15,000	14,950		$50

Prepare a revised report of production costs in which the variances are computed by comparing the actual costs incurred with estimated costs *using a flexible budget* for 11,000 hours. Assume that direct materials, direct labor, and variable factory overhead would all be 10% higher when 11,000 hours are worked than when only 10,000 hours are worked.

PROBLEMS

Group A

26A-1 The Anna Company Ltd. produces a machine part. Each part must move through Department X and Department Y and factory overhead is applied on the basis of machine-hours. The number of machine-hours required to produce a unit and the factory overhead rate per machine-hour are shown below:

Department	Standard Machine-hours	Factory Overhead Rate per Machine-hour
X	5	$2.10
Y	3	1.80

The factory overhead rate is based on a normal volume of production of 1,000 units per month; the rate for each department includes $0.60 of fixed costs. The variable factory overhead cost per unit for January is expected to be 5% above standard. The company plans to produce 800 units during January.

Instructions Prepare a budget for factory overhead costs for January. Use column heading as follows: Total, Department X, and Department Y.

26A-2 The standard cost and the actual cost per unit of a product manufactured by the Plastics Design Company Ltd. last month are summarized below:

	Standard Cost	Actual Cost
Materials:		
Standard: 10 ounces at $0.15 per ounce	$1.50	
Actual: 11 ounces at $0.16 per ounce		$1.76
Direct labor:		
Standard: .50 hour at $4.00 per hour	2.00	
Actual: .45 hour at $4.20 per hour		1.89
Factory overhead:		
Standard: $5,000 fixed cost and $5,000 variable cost for 10,000		
units budgeted to be produced	1.00	
Actual: $5,000 fixed cost and $4,600 variable cost for 8,000		
units actually produced		1.20
Total unit cost	$4.50	$4.85

The normal capacity level is 10,000 units per month. Last month 8,000 units were manufactured.

Instructions Compute the following cost variances for last month and indicate whether each variance is favorable or unfavorable:
a Material price variance and material quantity variance
b Labor rate variance and labor usage variance
c Controllable factory overhead variance and volume variance.

26A-3 On November 1, Year 1, the Karen Supply Company Ltd. wants a projection of cash receipts and disbursements for the month of November. On November 28, a note will be payable in the amount of $40,400, including interest. The cash balance on November 1 is $13,700. Accounts payable to merchandise creditors at the end of October were $77,500.
The company's experience indicates that 60% of sales will be collected during the month of sale, 30% in the month following the sale, and 8% in the second month following the sale; 2% will be uncollectible. The company sells various products at an average price of $8 per unit. Selected sales figures are shown below:

	Units
September—actual	20,000
October—actual	30,000
November—estimated	40,000
December—estimated	25,000
Total estimated for Year 1	400,000

Because purchases are payable within 15 days, approximately 50% of the purchases in a given month are paid in the following month. The average cost of units purchased is $5 per unit. Inventories at the end of each month are maintained at a level of 1,000 units plus 10% of the number of units that will be sold in the following month. The inventory on October 1 amounted to 4,000 units.
Budgeted operating expenses for November are $85,000. Of this amount, $30,000 is considered fixed (including depreciation of $12,000). All operating

expenses, other than depreciation, are paid in the month in which they are incurred.

The company expects to sell fully depreciated equipment in November for $9,500 cash.

Instructions Prepare a cash budget for the month of November, supported by schedules of cash collections on accounts receivable and cash disbursements for purchases of merchandise.

26A-4 Gen-Tronics Ltd., uses standard costs in its Assembly Department. At the end of the current month, the following information is prepared by the company's cost accountant:

	Materials	Direct Labor	Factory Overhead
Actual costs incurred	$32,000	$27,500	$41,080
Standard costs	30,000	28,000	38,500
Material price variance	800		
Material quantity variance	2,800		
Labor rate variance		1,000	
Labor usage variance		500	
Controllable factory overhead variance			1,080
Volume variance			1,500

The total standard cost per unit of finished product is $10. During the current month, 9,000 units were completed and transferred to the finished goods inventory and 8,800 units were sold. The inventory of goods in process at the end of the month consists of 1,000 units which are 65% completed. There was no inventory in process at the beginning of the month.

Instructions
a Prepare journal entries to record all variances and the costs incurred (at standard) in the Goods in Process account. Prepare separate compound entries for (1) materials, (2) direct labor, and (3) factory overhead.
b Prepare journal entries to record (1) the transfer of units finished to the Finished Goods Inventory account and (2) the cost of goods sold (at standard) for the month.
c Assuming that the company operated at 90% of its normal capacity during the current month, what is the amount of the fixed factory overhead per month?

26A-5 The Excello Lamp Corporation Ltd. employs departmental budgets and performance reports in planning and controlling its manufacturing operations. The budget for Year 1 called for the production of 15,000 lamps.

The following performance report for the production department for Year 1 was presented to the president of the company:

	Budgeted Costs	Actual Costs	Over or (under)
Variable manufacturing costs:			
Direct materials	$ 30,000	$ 32,300	$ 2,300
Direct labor	48,000	51,000	3,000
Indirect labor	15,000	18,500	3,500
Indirect materials, supplies, etc.	9,000	8,700	(300)
Total variable manufacturing costs	$102,000	$110,500	$ 8,500

Fixed manufacturing costs:

Lease rental	$ 9,000	$ 9,000	*None*
Salaries of foremen	24,000	25,000	$ 1,000
Depreciation and other	15,000	15,500	500
Total fixed manufacturing costs	$ 48,000	$ 49,500	$ 1,500
Total manufacturing costs	$150,000	$160,000	$10,000

The production and shipping count for Year 1 is shown below:

	Units
Lamps completed and transferred to warehouse	*17,000*
Lamps shipped to customers	*15,000*
Lamps in process of production	*None*

The corporation does not close its books on a monthly basis. In preparing monthly financial statements, however, a predetermined factory overhead rate based on direct labor cost is used. This rate for Year 1 was 150% ($72,000 ÷ $48,000).

After a quick glance at the performance report showing an unfavorable manufacturing cost variance of $10,000, the president said to the accountant: "Fix this thing so it makes sense. It looks as though our production people really blew the budget. Remember that we exceeded our budgeted production schedule by a significant margin. I want this performance report to show a better picture of our ability to control costs."

Instructions

a Prepare a revised performance report on a flexible budget basis for Year 1. Show the budgeted costs for 15,000 lamps in the first column, the budgeted figures for the actual level of production (17,000 lamps) in the second column, and the actual costs incurred in the third column. In the fourth column show the difference between amounts in columns 2 and 3, and indicate whether the differences are favorable or unfavorable.

b In a few sentences compare the original performance report with the revised report.

c What is the amount of over- or underapplied factory overhead for Year 1? (Note that a standard cost system is not used.)

26A-6 At the end of each calendar quarter, the accountant for Shoppers Center, Ltd., prepares a budget for the coming three-month period. At the end of March of the current year, the balance sheet includes the following accounts:

Cash	$ 60,000	Accounts payable (gross)	$150,000
Receivables	200,000	Income taxes payable	50,000
Inventories	100,000	Capital stock	350,000
Plant and equipment (net)	400,000	Retained earnings	210,000

Operations during the quarter ending June 30 are budgeted as follows:
(1) Estimated sales by month are: April, $300,000; May, $350,000; June, $420,000.
(2) The cost of goods purchased (before purchase discounts) is 70% of sales; inventories at June 30 will be $150,000. Purchases are estimated as follows: April, $200,000; May, $260,000; June, $339,000.

(3) Operating expenses:

Fixed expenses per month:

Salaries	*$40,000*
Depreciation.	*4,000*
Other	*5,000*

Variable expenses:

10% of sales

(4) All sales are made on credit and are collected in full in the following month. Payments on purchases are made in the month following purchase. A 2% discount is taken on all purchases.

(5) Operating expenses (other than depreciation) are paid in the month in which such expenses are incurred. Federal and provincial income taxes are expected to average 40% of taxable income; the income taxes payable on March 31 will be paid during the second quarter.

Instructions Prepare the budgeted income statement for the quarter ending June 30 of the current year and the budgeted balance sheet at June 30. Give supporting schedules for (1) sales, (2) purchases, (3) operating expenses, and (4) cash receipts and disbursements.

Group B

26B-1 Jeffrey Chemco, Ltd., manufactures a compound which is first refined and then packed for shipment to customers. The standard direct labor cost per 100 pounds in each process follows:

Process	Direct Labor Hours per 100 Pounds	Standard Direct Labor Cost per Hour
Refining	2	*$5.00*
Packing	1	*4.00*

The budget for October calls for the production of 100,000 pounds of compound. The expected labor cost in the refinery is expected to be 8% above standard for the month of October as a result of higher wage rates and inefficiencies in the scheduling of work. The expected cost of labor in the packing room is expected to be 5% below standard because of a new arrangement of equipment.

Instruction Prepare a budget for direct labor costs for October. Use column headings as follows: Total, Refining, and Packing.

26B-2 The Oak Furniture Company Ltd. uses a standard cost system in accounting for its production costs. The standard cost for a certain product for the normal volume of 1,000 units is as follows:

Lumber, 100 feet @ $150 per 1,000 feet.		*$15.00*
Direct labor, 5 hours at $4.00 per hour		*20.00*
Factory overhead (applied at $11.00 per unit produced):		
Fixed ($5,000 ÷ 1,000 units)	*$5.00*	
Variable	*6.00*	*11.00*
Total standard unit cost.		*$46.00*

The actual unit cost for a given month in which 800 units were produced is shown on page 818.

Lumber, 110 feet at $140 per 1,000 feet $15.40
Direct labor 5½ hours at $3.90 per hour 21.45
Factory overhead, $9,000 ÷ 800 units 11.25
    Total actual unit cost $48.10

At the end of the month, the company's accountant submitted the following cost report to management relating to the 800 units produced:

	Total	Per Unit
Excess lumber used in production	$ 320	$0.40
Excess labor cost incurred	1,160	1.45
Actual factory overhead in excess of standard:		
$9,000 − (800 × $11.00)	200	0.25
Actual cost in excess of standard	$1,680	$2.10

Instructions Prepare a schedule which would give management a better understanding of the reasons for the $1,680 excess cost incurred. This schedule should include the following:
a Material price variance and material quantity variance
b Labor rate variance and labor usage variance
c Controllable factory overhead variance and volume variance

Indicate whether each variance is favorable or unfavorable.

26B-3 Joseph Reed, owner of the Reed Equipment Company, is negotiating with his bank for a $100,000, 6%, 90-day loan effective July 1 of the current year. If the bank grants the loan, the proceeds will be $98,500, which Reed intends to use on July 1 as follows: pay accounts payable, $75,000; purchase equipment, $8,000; add to bank balance, $15,500.

The current position of the Reed Equipment Company, according to financial statements as of June 30, is as follows:

Cash in bank . . . . $ 5,500
Receivables (net of allowance for uncollectible accounts) 80,000
Merchandise inventory 45,000
Total current assets $130,500
Accounts payable (including accrued operating expenses) 75,000
Working capital . . . . $ 55,500

The bank loan officer asks Reed to prepare a forecast of his cash receipts and disbursements for the next three months, to demonstrate that the loan can be repaid at the end of September.

Reed has made the following estimates, which are to be used in preparing a three-month cash budget: Sales (all on open account) for July, $150,000; August, $180,000; September, $135,000; and October, $100,000. Past experience indicates that 80% of the receivables generated in any month will be collected in the month following the sale, 19% in the second month following the sale, and 1% will prove uncollectible. Reed expects to collect $60,000 of the June 30 receivables in July, and the remaining $20,000 in August.

Cost of goods sold has averaged consistently about 65% of sales. Operating expenses are budgeted at $18,000 per month plus 8% of sales. With the exception of $2,200 per month depreciation expense, all operating expenses and purchases are on open account and are paid in the month following their incurrence.

Merchandise inventory at the end of each month should be sufficient to cover the following month's sales.

Instructions

a Prepare a monthly cash budget showing estimated cash receipts and disbursements for July, August, and September, and the cash balance at the end of each month. Supporting schedules should be prepared for estimated collections on receivables, estimated merchandise purchases, and estimated payments of accounts payable for merchandise purchases and operating expenses.

b On the basis of this cash forecast, write a brief report to Reed explaining whether he will be able to meet his $100,000 loan at the bank at the end of September.

26B-4 All-Together Chemical Company Ltd. processes a product known as REN and uses a standard cost accounting system. The process requires preparation and blending of materials in 400-pound batches. You are engaged to explain any differences between standard and actual costs incurred in producing 100 batches during the first month of operation. The following additional information is available:

(*1*) The standard costs for a 400-pound batch are as follows:

	Quantity	Price	Total Cost
Materials:			
Different grades of chemicals	*400 pounds*	*$0.30*	*$120*
Direct labor:			
Preparation, blending, etc.	*20 hours*	*5.00*	*100*
Factory overhead:			
Variable costs	*20 hours*	*3.00*	*60*
Fixed costs	*20 hours*	*1.00*	*20*
Total standard cost per 400-pound batch			*$300*

(*2*) During the first month, 41,000 pounds of chemicals were purchased for $11,480, an average cost of $0.28 cents per pound. All the chemical was used during the month, resulting in a price variance of $820 and a quantity variance of $300.

(*3*) Average wage paid for 1,900 hours of direct labor was $4.80 per hour and amounted to $9,120. The labor rate variance was $380 and the labor usage variance was $500.

(*4*) The standards were established for a normal production volume of 125 batches per month. At this level of production, variable factory overhead was budgeted at $7,500 per month and fixed factory overhead was budgeted at $2,500 per month. During the first month, actual factory overhead amounted to $8,800, including $2,500 fixed costs. The controllable factory overhead variance was $300 and the volume variance was $500.

Instructions

a Prepare schedules showing how the variances from standard for materials, labor, and factory overhead were computed. Indicate whether the variances are favorable or unfavorable.

b Prepare journal entries to record the variances and costs incurred (at standard) in the Goods in Process account for (*1*) materials, (*2*) labor, and (*3*) factory overhead.

26B-5 Buyers Delight Ltd., has suffered losses in recent years. A new management, brought in to put the company on a profitable basis, prepared the following flexible budget for the current year:

	Yearly Fixed Expenses	Variable Expenses per Sales Dollar
Cost of merchandise sold		$0.700
Selling and promotion expense	$ 70,000	0.082
Building occupancy expense	62,000	0.022
Buying expense	50,000	0.052
Delivery expense	37,000	0.034
Credit and collection expense	24,000	0.002
Administrative expense	49,000	0.003
Totals	$292,000	$0.895

The new management expected to attain a sales level of $4 million during the current year. At the end of the year the actual results achieved by the firm were as follows:

Net sales	$3,500,000
Cost of goods sold	2,380,000
Selling and promotion expense	340,000
Building occupancy expense	140,000
Buying expense	240,000
Delivery expense	145,000
Credit and collection expense	30,000
Administrative expense	60,000

Instructions

a Prepare a statement comparing the actual and budgeted revenues and expenses for the current year, showing variations between actual and budgeted amounts. Use a flexible budget procedure to determine budgeted revenues and expenses.

b Write a brief statement evaluating the company's performance in relation to planning as reflected in the flexible budget.

26B-6 The condensed balance sheet for River Supply Company Ltd. on March 31, Year 1, is shown below:

Assets

Cash	$ 20,000
Receivables from customers (to be collected in April)	40,000
Inventory	25,000
Plant assets, net of accumulated depreciation	90,000
Total assets	$175,000

Liabilities & Stockholders' Equity

Dividends payable	$ 5,000
Accounts payable, merchandise creditors	50,000
Capital stock, $10 par value	100,000
Retained earnings	20,000
Total liabilities & stockholders' equity	$175,000

Budgeted information relating to the operations for the following month (April) follows:

(1) Cash sales for April are expected to be $50,000 and credit sales $60,000. Collections on credit sales are 50% in the month of sale, and the remainder in the month following the month in which the sale is made.

(2) Cash purchases for April are expected to be $32,000; credit purchases are estimated at $55,000. Payments on credit purchases are made in full in the month following the purchase.

(3) Inventory is expected to be $42,500 at the end of April.

(4) Operating expenses for April include wages and other (all paid in cash), $28,000; and depreciation, $4,000.

(5) Dividends of $5,000 declared in March will be paid in April.

(6) The owner of the company wishes to have a cash balance of at least $17,500 on hand at the end of April. He has made arrangements with a local bank for a temporary loan if necessary. You are to indicate on the cash budget for April the amount, if any, that he may have to borrow.

Instructions

a Prepare a cash budget for April of Year 1.

b Prepare a projected income statement for April, Year 1. Disregard income taxes.

c Prepare a projected balance sheet at April 30, Year 1.

BUSINESS DECISION PROBLEM 26

Shown below is the long-established standard cost per unit of product 21, scheduled to be manufactured by the Forge Appliance Company Ltd. during Year 1:

	Prime Cost	Factory Overhead	Cumulative Cost
Material X-1, one component	$13		$13
Material X-2, one pound	6		19
Direct labor:			
Shaping and Assembly Department	12	$6	37
Packing Department	2	1	40
Totals	$33	$7	40

There were no inventories at the beginning of Year 1. During Year 1, 1,000 units of product 21 were produced and 600 units were sold. The factory overhead rate was determined by dividing budgeted factory overhead for Year 1 by the 1,000 units scheduled to be produced in Year 1.

Actual costs incurred during Year 1 are:

Material X-1 purchased, 1,200 components @ $9		$10,800
Material X-2 purchased, 1,150 pounds @ $6		6,900
Direct labor:		
Shaping and Assembly Department	$13,200	
Packing Department	2,200	15,400
Factory overhead		7,000
Total production costs incurred in Year 1		$40,100

At the end of Year 1, the following variance accounts appear on the accounting records of the Forge Appliance Company Ltd.

Favorable price variance on all material X-1 purchased,	
1,200 components (credit)	*$(4,800)*
Unfavorable material quantity variance, 50 pounds of material	
X-2 spoiled in production (debit)	*300*
Unfavorable direct labor rate variance because of 10% wage	
increase early in Year 1 (debit)	*1,400*
Net favorable variance	*$ 3,100*

The total inventory at end of Year 1, at standard cost, consists of the following:

Materials:		
Material X-1, 200 components @ $13 per component	*$2,600*	
Material X-2, 100 pounds @ $6 per pound	*600*	*$ 3,200*
Finished goods:		
Product 21 shaped and packed, 400 units @ $40		*16,000*
Total inventory at end of Year 1 at standard cost		*$19,200*

The independent chartered accountant, who has been engaged to audit the company's financial statements, wants to adjust this inventory to "a revised standard cost" which would take into account the favorable price variance on material X-1 ($4 per component) and the 10% wage increase at the beginning of Year 1. The president of the company objects on the following grounds: "Such a revision is not necessary because the cost of material X-1 already shows signs of going up and the wage increase was not warranted because the productivity of workers did not increase one bit. Furthermore, if we revise our inventory figure of $19,200, our operating income will be reduced from the current level of $10,000." You are called in by the president to help resolve the controversy.

Instructions Do you agree with the president? Assuming that you conclude that the standards for July should be revised, what value should be assigned to the inventory at the end of Year 1?

TWENTY-SEVEN

COST-REVENUE
ANALYSIS
FOR DECISION
MAKING

In addition to standard costs and budgeting discussed in Chapter 26, management uses many other aids to plan and control the activities of a business. One of the more important analytical tools used by management and others interested in the affairs of a business unit is cost-revenue analysis. *Cost-revenue analysis* is a means of learning how revenues and costs behave in response to changes in the level of business activity. It is a *predictive* rather than a historical concept and is primarily concerned with the possible outcomes of various business decisions (or conditions) contemplated by management.

Uses of cost-revenue analysis

Cost-revenue analysis may be used by management to answer questions such as the following:

1 What level of sales must be reached to cover all expenses, that is, to break even?

2 How many units of a product must be sold to earn a given net income per year?

3 What will happen to our net income if we expand capacity and add $50,000 to our annual fixed costs?

4 What will be the effect of change in salesmen's compensation from a fixed monthly salary to a straight commission of 10% on sales?

5 If we spend $100,000 per month on advertising, what increase in sales volume will be required to maintain our current level of net income?

Cost and revenue relationships are useful not only to management but also to creditors and investors. The ability of a business to pay its debts and to increase dividend payments, for example, depends largely on its ability to generate earnings. Thus the level of earnings is important to creditors and investors, and earnings depend on selling prices, number of units sold, the amount of variable and fixed costs, and the mix of different products sold. All these variables are used in analyzing cost and revenue relationships and in predicting the profitability of a business under various assumptions and management strategies.

To illustrate one possible use of cost-revenue analysis by an investor, assume that the shares of each of two companies (A and B) are selling at $10 a share. The earnings for each company amount to $1 per share, resulting in a price-earnings ratio of 10 times earnings. Company A has large fixed costs and is operating near full capacity, while Company B has low fixed costs and is operating at less than 50% of capacity. At full capacity, Company B is capable of earning over $8 per share. The demand for the products sold by both companies is strong and should increase. Which stock would you buy?

Obviously, the prospects for an increase in the earnings per share for Company A (with existing facilities) are rather dim, and the price of its stock is not likely to increase. On the other hand, the earnings of Company B "have room to grow" without additional investment in plant and equipment (which would increase fixed costs). For example, if the sales for Company B should double, the earnings could reach $8 per share and the price of its stock might increase spectacularly. Without knowledge of the cost and revenue structure for the two companies, you would not be able to make an intelligent decision.

We should point out that cost-revenue analysis may be used not only for the business as a whole, but also for a segment of a business such as a division, a branch, a department, or a given product line.

A nonbusiness example—operating a personal automobile

An important first step in cost-revenue analysis is to know how costs behave in response to changes in the level of activity. Understanding cost behavior is particularly important in planning to meet objectives, in evaluating past performance, and in taking corrective action to control costs. To illustrate this point we shall first consider cost behavior in a simple and familiar setting, the cost of operating a personal automobile.

THE VOLUME INDEX Suppose that someone told you it cost $1,900 a year to own and operate an automobile. If you thought about this statement a bit, you would soon conclude that it was too ambiguous to be very enlightening. One reason is that a year's automobile ownership is not an operational description of the quantity of service provided by this asset during a year. Ignoring psychological and status benefits, an automobile provides transportation measured in miles. The cost of x miles of automobile transportation during a year would be a more useful cost concept for analytical purposes.

In studying cost behavior, we first look for some measurable concept of volume or activity that is meaningful to the person responsible for controlling the cost, and then try to find out how the cost changes with changes in volume. The volume index may be measured in terms of cost *inputs,* such as tons of raw peaches processed, hours of labor used, or machine-hours worked; or volume may be measured in terms of *outputs,* such as units of services rendered, units of physical products produced, or the dollar value of sales revenue generated. Student credit hours is a significant volume index in analyzing educational costs; seat miles flown is a useful volume index in airline operations; dollar sales is an important volume measure for a department store.

In our example, we shall use *miles driven* as the volume index of operating a personal automobile. Once an appropriate volume index has been found, we can classify all costs into three general categories:

VARIABLE COSTS A *variable* cost increases and decreases directly and proportionately with changes in volume. If, for example, volume increases 10%, a variable cost will also increase by approximately 10%. Gasoline is an example of a variable automobile cost, since fuel consumption is directly related to miles driven.

SEMIVARIABLE (OR MIXED) COSTS Costs which change in response to changes in volume but by less than a proportionate amount are called *semivariable* or *mixed* costs. A 10% increase in volume, for example, may result in a 6% increase in a semivariable cost. Automobile maintenance and repair costs rise as miles driven increase, but a certain amount of such costs will be incurred without regard to mileage. For example, tire and battery deterioration occurs in response to both miles driven and the passage of time.

FIXED (OR NONVARIABLE) COSTS Costs which remain unchanged despite changes in volume are called *fixed* or *nonvariable.* Usually such costs are incurred as a function of some other factor such as time. For example, the annual insurance premium and license fee on an automobile are fixed costs since they are independent of the number of miles driven.

Automobile costs—graphic analysis To illustrate automobile cost-volume behavior, we shall assume the following somewhat simplified data to describe the cost of owning and operating a typical full-sized automobile:

Type of Cost	Amount
Three classes of automobile costs *Variable costs:*	
Gasoline, oil, and servicing	*3 cents per mile*
Semivariable costs:	
Maintenance and repairs	*$100 per year plus 1 cent per mile*
Depreciation	*$500 per year plus 1 cent per mile*
Fixed costs:	
Insurance	*$260 per year*
License fee	*$40 per year*

We can express these cost-volume relationships graphically. The relation between volume (miles driven per year) and the three types of cost both separately and combined is shown in the diagrams below:

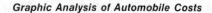

Graphic Analysis of Automobile Costs

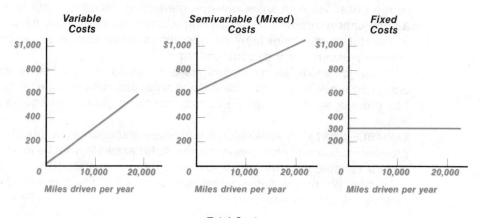

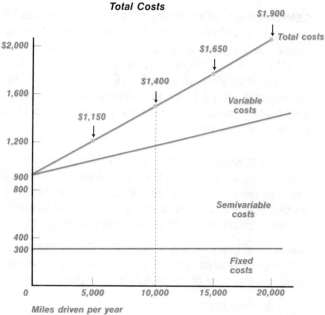

We can read from the total costs graph the estimated annual automobile cost for any assumed mileage. For example, an owner who expects to drive 10,000 miles in a given year may estimate his total cost at $1,400, or 14.0 cents per mile. By combining all the fixed and variable elements of cost, we can generalize the cost-volume relationship and state simply that the cost of owning an automobile is $900 per year plus 5 cents per mile driven during the year.

The effect of volume on unit (per-mile) costs can be observed by converting total cost figures to average unit costs as follows:

Cost per Mile of Owning and Using an Automobile

<table>
<tr><td>Miles driven</td><td>5,000</td><td>10,000</td><td>15,000</td><td>20,000</td></tr>
<tr><td>Costs:</td><td></td><td></td><td></td><td></td></tr>
<tr><td>Fully variable</td><td>$ 150</td><td>$ 300</td><td>$ 450</td><td>$ 600</td></tr>
<tr><td>Semivariable:</td><td></td><td></td><td></td><td></td></tr>
<tr><td>Variable portion</td><td>100</td><td>200</td><td>300</td><td>400</td></tr>
<tr><td>Fixed portion</td><td>600</td><td>600</td><td>600</td><td>600</td></tr>
<tr><td>Completely fixed</td><td>300</td><td>300</td><td>300</td><td>300</td></tr>
<tr><td>Total costs</td><td>$1,150</td><td>$1,400</td><td>$1,650</td><td>$1,900</td></tr>
<tr><td>Cost per mile</td><td>$ 0.23</td><td>$ 0.14</td><td>$ 0.11</td><td>$0.095</td></tr>
</table>

Note rapid decrease in cost per mile as use increases

It should be noted that the variable portion of the costs incurred in operating an automobile increases in total as miles driven increase but *remains constant on a per-mile basis* (5 cents per mile). In contrast, total fixed costs remain the same regardless of the number of miles driven but *decrease on a per-mile basis* as miles driven increase. The average unit-cost behavior of operating an automobile may be presented graphically as follows:

Unit cost behavior

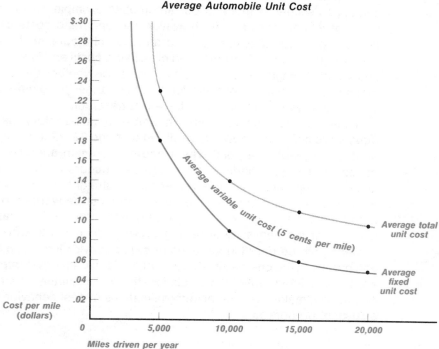

Average Automobile Unit Cost

Average variable unit cost (5 cents per mile)

Average total unit cost

Average fixed unit cost

Cost per mile (dollars)

Miles driven per year

Measuring capacity of a business unit

In analyzing cost-revenue relationships of a business, reference is often made to the *capacity* of a plant, a store, or a company as a whole. For example, a refinery may be able to process a maximum of 50,000 barrels of crude oil per month, or a factory may be capable of assembling 1,000 cars per day. These measures of capacity represent the number of units of input or the units of output that may be processed under ideal conditions, that is, *theoretical capacity.* Under ideal conditions there would be no curtailment in production for any reason, such as holidays, material shortages, strikes, machine breakdowns, etc. Deducting from theoretical capacity the losses in output because of these factors gives us *practical capacity,* which is the maximum level of output if all goods produced can be sold. Needless to say, such a blissful condition is seldom encountered, and a more realistic measure of capacity for cost accounting purposes is based on existing factory conditions and the level of demand expected over a relatively long period of time; we shall refer to such a realistic measure of capacity as *normal capacity* or *normal volume.*

Cost behavior in businesses

As pointed out in earlier chapters, cost relationships in a business are seldom as simple as those in our automobile example. Given a suitable index of volume (or activity), however, the operating costs of all businesses exhibit variable, semivariable, and fixed characteristics. Admittedly there are many difficult problems in classifying costs and identifying fixed and variable elements. We must also consider whether the assumption that costs vary in a straight-line relation to changes in volume is reasonable in analyzing cost behavior for a business unit.

Some business costs increase in lump-sum steps rather than continuous increments, as shown in graph (*a*) on page 829. For example, when production reaches a point where another foreman and crew must be added, a lump-sum addition to labor costs occurs at this point. Other costs may vary along a curve rather than a straight line, as in graph (*b*) on page 829. For example, when overtime must be worked to increase production, the labor cost per unit may rise more rapidly than volume because of the necessity of paying overtime premium to workers.

Taking all the possible vagaries of cost behavior into account would add greatly to the complexity of cost-volume analysis. How far from reality are the assumed straight-line relationships? Fortunately, there are two factors that make straight-line approximations of cost behavior useful for analytical purposes.

"Stairstep" and curvilinear costs

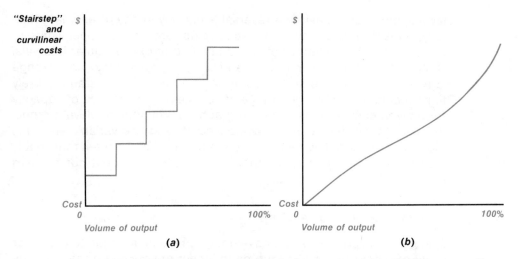

(a)   (b)

First, unusual patterns of cost behavior tend to offset one another. If we were to plot actual total costs incurred by a business over a time period in which volume changes occurred, the result might appear as in the cost-volume graph (*a*) below:

Are straight-line cost patterns realistic?

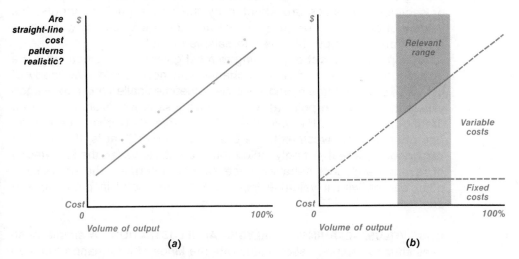

(a)   (b)

Total cost often moves in close approximation to a straight-line pattern when the various "stair-step" and curvilinear cost patterns of individual costs are combined.

Second, and more important, is the fact that the relevant range of volume variation is usually quite narrow. *Relevant range* is the span of output over which the assumptions made about cost behavior are generally valid. In making decisions, management may consider the effect of fairly wide swings in volume, but the range from zero to maximum capacity shown on the cost-volume graph is seldom realistic. An extreme decline in volume might involve shutting down plants and extensive layoffs, but such an extreme reversal is unlikely in any given year. Similarly, variable costs may curve sharply upward at the upper limits of capacity, but full-capacity volume is attained at only irregular intervals. In short, the probability that volume will vary outside a fairly narrow range is usually remote. The significant area of a cost-volume graph is likely to be the normal or relevant range of volume (say, 45 to 75% of capacity for a given company) as shown in graph (**b**). Within this relevant range, the assumption that costs are composed of fixed and variable elements that vary in straight-line relation to changes in volume is often reasonably realistic. Exceptions to this general rule, however, would not be hard to find.

Cost-volume-earnings analysis

In our discussion thus far we have not given much attention to the dollar value of output (volume) or the direct effect of volume on the earnings of a business. Managers continually study the effect of internal decisions and external conditions on revenues, expenses, and ultimately on net income. Revenues are affected by the actions of competitors, a firm's pricing policies, and changes in the market demand for a firm's products or services. Expenses are affected by the prices paid for inputs, the volume of production or business activity, and the efficiency with which a firm translates input factors into salable output.

An important aspect of planning to meet given profit objectives is the analysis of the effect of volume changes on net income. The study of business profit-volume relationships is sometimes called **break-even** analysis, in honor of the point at which a business moves from a loss to a profit position. Since the objective of business endeavor is to earn a fair rate of return on investment, the break-even point (that is, the point of zero income) is really of only incidental interest. However, the knowledge of revenue and cost behavior necessary to determine the break-even point carries with it valuable insights that are useful in planning and control.

COST-VOLUME-EARNINGS ANALYSIS—AN ILLUSTRATION A simple business situation will be used to illustrate the kinds of information that can be derived from cost-volume-earnings analysis. The Percy Ice Cream Company (a single proprietorship) has a chain of stores located throughout a large city, selling ice cream in various flavors. Although the company sells to customers in packages of different size, we shall assume that volume of business is measured in gallons of ice cream sold. The company buys its ice cream from a dairy at a price of $1.10 per gallon. Retail sales prices vary depending on the quantity purchased by a customer, but revenue per gallon of ice cream sold *averages* $2 per gallon and does not vary significantly from store to store or from period to period. Monthly operating statistics for a typical store are shown on page 831.

PERCY ICE CREAM COMPANY
Monthly Operating Data—
Typical Retail Store

		Variable Expenses per Gallon	Variable Expenses as Percentage of Sales Price
Note variable and fixed expense elements	Average selling price	*$2.00*	*100%*
	Cost of ice cream (including delivery)	*$1.10*	*55.0%*

	Fixed Expenses		
Monthly operating expenses:			
Manager's salary	$1,100		
Wages	2,100 +	.07	3.5
Store rent	800		
Utilities	90 +	.02	1.0
Miscellaneous	410 +	.01	.5
Total expenses	$4,500 +	$1.20	60.0%
Contribution to fixed expenses	$ .80	40.0%	

GRAPHIC ANALYSIS A *profit-volume* (or *break-even*) graph for the typical retail store of the Percy Ice Cream Company, based on the above data, is shown on page 832. The horizontal scale represents volume in thousands of gallons of ice cream per month. Since none of the company's stores sells more than 10,000 gallons per month, this is assumed to be the upper limit of the relevant volume range. The vertical scale is in dollars of revenues or expenses. The steps in plotting this profit-volume graph are as follows:

1 First the revenue line is plotted, running from $0 at zero volume of sales to $20,000, representing 10,000 gallons of sales per month at $2 per gallon.

2 The fixed (nonvariable) monthly operating expenses are plotted as a horizontal line at the level of $4,500 per month.

3 Starting at the $4,500 fixed expense line, the variable expense of $1.20 per gallon is plotted. Note that this line also becomes the total expense line since it is added on top of the fixed expense line.

The monthly profit or loss that may be expected at any sales volume level per store may be read from the profit-volume graph. For example, the break-even point (zero profit) is 5,625 gallons per month, or $11,250 of sales per month. Sales below 5,625 gallons per month will result in a net loss, and sales above 5,625 gallons per month will result in net income. Income taxes are not relevant in our example because the Percy Ice Cream Company is a single proprietorship.

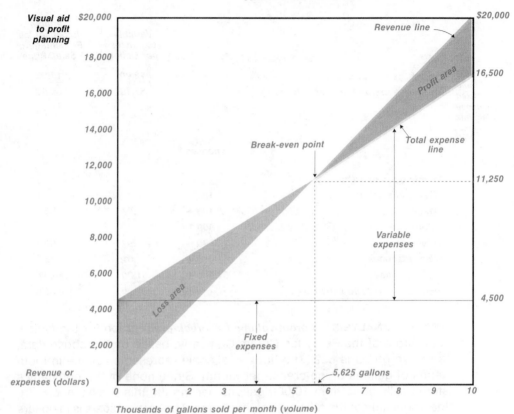

PERCY ICE CREAM COMPANY
Monthly Profit—Volume Graph
Typical Retail Store

Visual aid to profit planning

Revenue or expenses (dollars)

Thousands of gallons sold per month (volume)

PROFIT-VOLUME FORMULA A formula may be developed for general use in analyzing profit-volume behavior. The formula is based on the factors that make up the computation of net income.

Sales (*S*) = Variable Expense (*V*) + Fixed Expense (*F*) + Net Income (*I*)

We are usually looking for a "target volume" in profit-volume analysis. For example, we want to know the volume necessary to break even, or the volume necessary to earn a given net income, or the effect of a change in variable or fixed expenses on the volume necessary to produce a given net income. The target volume in any given case is represented by sales (*S*).

To illustrate, in computing the break-even point for a Percy Ice Cream Company store, we want to know the sales volume (either dollars or gallons) at which net income will be zero. Fixed expenses (*F*) and net income (*I*) are given in dollars, and variable expenses (*V*) can be expressed as a function of sales (S). Thus we have one unknown, S, and can solve our equation, expressed either in dollars or gallons, as follows:

Break-even Sales Volume (in dollars)	Break-even Sales Volume (in gallons)

Two ways of computing break-even sales volume

$S = V + F + I$

$S = .60S + \$4,500 + \$0$

$.40S = \$4,500$

$S = \$11,250$ to break even

$S = V + F + I$

$\$2S = \$1.20S + \$4,500 + \$0$

$\$.80S = \$4,500$

$S = 5,625$ gallons to break even

Determining the break-even volume in dollars is a more practical approach, because volume is most often expressed in terms of revenue dollars rather than physical units. This is particularly true in the usual situation where a company sells more than one product. We shall therefore express volume in sales dollars in subsequent illustrations.

CONTRIBUTION MARGIN APPROACH The *contribution margin,* in profit-volume analysis, is the excess of sales (in dollars) over variable expenses. The *contribution margin ratio* is the percentage of sales (in dollars) available to cover fixed expenses and yield a net income. The contribution margin ratio is computed as follows:

A key to profit-volume analysis

$$\text{Contribution Margin Ratio} = \frac{\text{Sales (in dollars)} - \text{Variable Expenses}}{\text{Sales (in dollars)}}$$

The contribution margin ratio does not vary with changes in sales volume; it represents the average contribution that each dollar of sales makes to the recovery of fixed expenses and toward generating a net income. Therefore, we can simplify our profit-volume formula by expressing dollar volume (S) in terms of the contribution margin ratio as follows:

Simplified profit-volume formula

$$\text{Dollar Sales Volume } (S) = \frac{\text{Fixed Expenses} + \text{Net Income}}{\text{Contribution Margin Ratio}}$$

To illustrate, in terms of our ice cream store example, suppose that we want to know the sales volume per store necessary to produce a monthly net income of $700. The contribution margin ratio is 40% ($\$.80 \div \$2.00$), as shown in the operating data on page 831. Therefore, the sales volume necessary to produce $700 in monthly net income may be computed as follows:

$$\text{Dollar Sales Volume } (S) = \frac{\$4,500 + \$700}{.40} = \$13,000 \text{ per month}$$

(or 6,500 gallons
@ $2 per gallon)

PROFIT-VOLUME PLANNING Once profit-volume relationships have been established, it is possible to provide planning information that is useful in arriving at a variety of decisions. To illustrate the process, consider a number of different questions that might be raised by the management of the Percy Ice Cream Company:

1 Question. To increase volume, management is considering a policy of giving greater discounts on gallon and half-gallon packages of ice cream. It is estimated that the effect of this pricing policy would be to reduce the average selling price per gallon by 8 cents (that is, from $2 per gallon to $1.92). Management is interested in knowing the effect of such a price reduction on the monthly break-even volume per store.

Analysis. The proposed change in average sales price changes the contribution margin from .40 to .375 as shown below:

$$\frac{\$1.92 - \$1.20}{\$1.92} = .375 \text{ (or } 37\tfrac{1}{2}\%)$$

The cost of ice cream and fixed operating expenses remain unchanged by this pricing decision. Therefore, the target monthly sales volume to break even under the new pricing situation would be:

$$\text{Dollar Sales Volume } (S) = \frac{\$4,500 + \$0}{.375} = \$12,000 \text{ per month}$$

In terms of gallons sold per month, the break-even volume would be $12,000 ÷ $1.92 = 6,250 gallons, or more than 11% higher than the present 5,625 gallon break-even volume. Thus management should be advised that the proposed pricing policy is desirable only if the unit sales volume per store can be expected to increase more than 11% per month as a result of the lower sales prices on gallon and half-gallon packages.

2 Question. Management is considering a change in the method of compensating store managers. Instead of a fixed salary of $1,100 per month, it is proposed that managers be put on a salary of $330 per month plus a commission of 12 cents per gallon of sales. The present average monthly net income per store is $1,200 on sales of $14,250 ($14,250 × 40% − $4,500 = $1,200). What sales volume per store will be necessary to produce the same monthly net income under the proposed incentive compensation arrangement?

Analysis. This proposal involves a change in both the contribution margin ratio and the fixed monthly operating expenses. Adding 12 cents per gallon to variable costs raises the total variable cost to $1.32 per gallon, and reduces the contribution margin ratio to 34% as computed below:

$$\frac{\$2.00 - \$1.32}{\$2.00} = 34\%$$

Cutting the manager's salary from $1,100 to $330 per month will reduce monthly fixed expenses from $4,500 to $3,730. The sales volume required to produce a monthly net income of $1,200 may be computed as follows:

$$\text{Required Sales Volume } (S) = \frac{\$3,730 + \$1,200}{.34} = \$14,500 \text{ per month}$$

To produce the same $1,200 per month net income under the new compensation plan, sales volume per store would have to be increased by $250 (or 125 gallons) over the current monthly sales volume of $14,250. The issue thus boils down to whether the incentive compensation arrangement will induce store managers to increase volume by more than 125 gallons per month. Profit-volume analysis does not answer this question, but it provides the information which enables management to exercise its judgment intelligently.

3 Question. The Percy Ice Cream Company stores are now open 12 hours each day (from 9 A.M. to 9 P.M.). Management is considering a proposal to decrease store hours by opening two hours later each morning. It is estimated that this policy would reduce sales volume by an average of 500 gallons per month and would cut fixed expenses (utilities and wages) by $500 per month. Assuming a present average net income of $1,200 per store, would it pay the company to change its store hours?

Analysis. The loss of 500 gallons of sales per month would decrease revenues by $1,000 (500 × $2). This would result in the loss of contribution margin of $400 ($1,000 × 40%). Therefore, whether the reduction in store hours would increase net income per store may be determined by direct *incremental analysis* as follows:

Reduction in fixed operating expenses	$500
Less: Loss of contribution margin ($1,000 × 40%)	400
Prospective increase in monthly net income per store	$100

Note that the present average monthly net income of $1,200 per store is not considered relevant in making this analysis. Incremental analysis indicates that reducing store hours will decrease any net loss by $100 or add $100 to any net income figure. The incremental approach to cost and revenue analysis is discussed in more detail in Chapter 28.

Other uses of profit-volume graph

The profit-volume graph is a flexible planning and control tool; its form can be changed to meet various decision-making needs of management. Two examples are presented below.

SALES VOLUME REQUIRED TO RECOVER CASH EXPENDITURES Management may wish to determine a cash (or funds) break-even point by excluding depreciation and other noncash expense items from total expenses.[1] For example, if total fixed expenses for accounting purposes amount to $10,000 per month and the contribution margin ratio is 40%, the monthly sales volume necessary to break even would be $25,000 ($10,000 ÷ .40). However, if $3,000 of the monthly fixed expenses consists of depreciation (a noncash expense) computed on the straight-line basis, the sales volume required to recover all variable expenses and the "out-of-pocket" fixed expenses would be only $17,500 ($7,000 ÷ .40). *Out-of-pocket* expenses are those requiring the use of current funds. When a sales volume of $17,500 is reached, the loss from operations would be $3,000 (the unrecovered portion of fixed expenses), and the funds provided by operations would be zero, as illustrated on page 836.

---

[1] See Chap. 22 for a complete discussion of funds flow as reported in a statement of changes in financial position.

Sales volume required to recover cash outlays

Sales		$17,500
Less: Fixed expenses, including depreciation of $3,000	$10,000	
Variable expenses ($17,500 × 60%)	10,500	20,500
Loss from operations		$(3,000)
Add: Depreciation, a noncash expense		3,000
Funds provided by operations		$ –0–

PROFIT-VOLUME GRAPH SHOWING TOTAL CONTRIBUTION MARGIN AND MARGIN OF SAFETY A profit-volume graph may be prepared in such a way that it shows the total contribution margin at any level of activity (sales volume) and the margin of safety sales volume. For example, assume that Safeco Company Ltd. has total fixed expenses of $180,000 per year, that the contribution margin ratio is 45%, and that sales at full capacity would be $800,000 per year. A profit-volume graph may be prepared as follows:

SAFECO COMPANY LTD.
Annual Profit–Volume Graph

Profit-volume graph, showing contribution margin and margin of safety sales volume

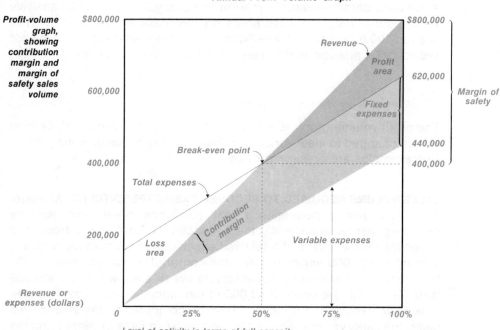

When the profit-volume graph is prepared in this form, it is easy to determine the total contribution margin (the difference between total revenue and variable expenses) at any level of activity. We can see that at the break-even point the total contribution margin is equal to total fixed expenses ($180,000); at any level beyond the break-even point, the profit area is equal to the difference between the total contribution margin and total fixed expenses. For example, at full capacity the profit is equal to $180,000, which is the excess of the contribution margin, $360,000 ($800,000 − $440,000), over total fixed expenses, $180,000.

The *margin of safety* is the dollar amount by which actual sales exceed break-even sales volume. It measures the amount by which sales can decrease (assuming that expense relationships remain unchanged) without producing a loss. In the graph illustrated above, the margin of safety sales volume at 100% level of activity is $400,000; at the 75% level, the margin of safety sales volume is $200,000 ($600,000 − $400,000). If you study the graph carefully, you will see that the net income may be determined as follows:

Margin of Safety Sales Volume × Contribution Margin Ratio = Net Income

This relationship gives us a quick tool in projecting net income at various levels of sales. For example, if sales are expected to be $500,000 and the break-even point is $400,000, the net income will be $45,000 when the contribution margin ratio is 45%. This is determined by simply multiplying the margin of safety sales volume, $100,000 ($500,000 − $400,000), by the contribution margin ratio, 45%.

Assumptions underlying profit-volume analysis

In preparing a profit-volume graph, accountants assume the following:

1 Sales price per unit remains constant.
2 If more than one product is sold, the proportion of the various products sold (sales mix) is assumed to be constant.
3 Fixed expenses remain constant at all levels of sales within the assumed relevant range of activity.
4 Variable expenses remain constant as a percentage of sales revenue.
5 For a business engaged in manufacturing, the number of units produced is assumed to be equal to the number of units sold.

These assumptions greatly simplify profit-volume analysis. In actual practice, however, none of these assumptions may hold true. But this does not necessarily lead to the conclusion that profit-volume analysis is not a useful planning and control tool for management. As changes take place in selling prices, sales mix, expenses, and production levels, management should incorporate such changes into profit-volume analysis and revise any previous estimates of probable results. A careful study of the assumptions underlying profit-volume analysis suggests that this management tool should be continuously monitored and revised as conditions change.

Importance of sales mix in profit-volume analysis and management decisions

In our example for the Percy Ice Cream Company, we have assumed that the contribution margin ratio *averaged* 40% of sales expressed in dollars and that the *average* selling price was $2 per gallon of ice cream sold. Let us now change our example and assume that a detailed analysis indicates that ice cream is actually sold in three packages as follows:

	Quart	Half-gallon	Gallon
Sales price per package	$0.60	$1.00	$1.80
Less: Variable expense per package	0.42	0.55	0.90
Contribution margin per package	$0.18	$0.45	$0.90
Contribution margin ratio (contribution margin ÷ sales price)	30%	45%	50%
Break-even sales volume, assuming that only the one size package was sold (fixed expenses, $4,500, divided by contribution margin ratio)	$15,000	$10,000	$9,000

Why would you prefer to sell only the gallon size?

Earlier in this chapter we stated that the Percy Ice Cream Company is now selling a certain *mix* of the three sizes and that a sales volume of $11,250 is required to break even ($4,500 ÷ .40). If ice cream were sold exclusively in quarts, sales of $15,000 would be required to break even; if only half-gallon packages were sold, the break-even sales volume would be $10,000; if only gallon packages were sold, the break-even sales volume would be $9,000. The reason the break-even sales volume differs for each size is because each size yields a different contribution margin per dollar of sales (contribution margin ratio). *The larger the contribution margin ratio, the lower the sales volume that is required to cover a given amount of fixed expenses.*

The amount of net income earned by a business unit depends not only on the volume of sales and the ability to control expenses, but also on the quality of sales. Sales yielding a high contribution margin are more profitable than sales yielding a low contribution margin. Thus, sales with a high contribution margin percentage are said to be *high-quality sales.* A shift from low-margin sales to high-margin sales can materially increase net income even though total sales decrease; on the other hand, a shift from high-margin to low-margin sales can turn a net income into a loss despite an increase in total sales.

Contribution margin per unit of scarce resource

The contribution margin approach is useful to management in deciding what products to manufacture (or purchase for resale) and what products to eliminate when certain factors of production are available only in limited quantity. One of the important functions of management is to develop the most profitable uses of such scarce resources as raw materials, skilled labor, high-cost equipment, and factory floor space.

Assume that you are offered two equally satisfactory jobs, one paying $3 per hour and one paying $5 per hour. Which would you choose? Since your time is scarce and you wish to maximize the pay that you receive for an hour of your time, you would naturally choose the job paying $5 per hour. For the same reason, if a company has a plant capacity of only 100,000 direct labor hours, management would want to use this capacity in such a way as *to produce the maximum contribution margin per hour of direct labor.* To illustrate this concept, assume that the Maximus Corporation Ltd. is considering the production of three products. The contribution margin per direct labor hour required to produce each of the three products is estimated as follows:

MAXIMUS CORPORATION LTD.
Contribution Margin per Hour of Direct Labor

Product	Sales Price per Unit	− Variable Costs per Unit	= Contribution Margin per Unit	÷ Direct Labor Hours Required to Produce One Unit	= Contribution Margin per Hour of Direct Labor
A . . .	$100	$60	$40	10	$ 4
B . . .	80	50	30	5	6
C . . .	60	40	20	2	10

Should production of product C be expanded?

Even though a unit of product A yields the highest contribution margin ($40) and the highest contribution margin ratio (40%), it is *the least profitable product in terms of contribution margin per hour of direct labor.* If sales of products B and C do not depend on the sales of product A and there are no operational problems involved in varying the production mix of the three products, the production of product A should be kept to a minimum. This would be particularly appropriate if the Maximus Corporation Ltd. could not meet the demand for all three products because of inability to expand plant capacity beyond 100,000 direct labor hours.

We can see that a unit of product A requires 10 hours of direct labor and generates $40 in contribution margin; a unit of product B requires only 5 hours of direct labor and yields $30 in contribution margin; and a unit of product C requires only 2 hours of direct labor and yields $20 in contribution margin. In summary, 10 hours of effort on product A yields $40 in contribution margin while 10 hours of effort on product B yields $60 in contribution margin, and 10 hours of effort on product C generates a whopping $100 in contribution margin. If the entire capacity of 100,000 direct labor hours were used to produce *only a single product,* the following total contribution margin would result:

Product	Total Capacity (hours)	× Contribution Margin per Hour of Direct Labor	= Total Contribution Margin if Only One Product Is Manufactured
A	100,000	$ 4	$ 400,000
B	100,000	6	600,000
C	100,000	10	1,000,000

Why should we continue to produce product A?

This schedule does not mean that the production of product A can be discontinued. While product C is clearly the most profitable, perhaps the demand for it is not enough to keep the plant working at full capacity; or the sales of product C may to some extent depend on sales of products A and B. In most cases, a company is not in a position to manufacture only the product which yields the highest contribution margin and let other less astute businessmen manufacture the low-margin products. A company should, however, try to sell as much of the high-margin products as possible in order to maximize its net income.

One of the key functions of business organizations is to employ scarce economic resources in ways which will best serve the needs of society. The net income earned by a business is, in a way, a reward for producing the goods needed by a society at the lowest possible cost. Sales mix and contribution margin analyses are useful in realizing the twin goals of producing goods at low cost and at the same time earning a satisfactory net income in order for a business unit to survive and thus to continue to meet social needs.

Summary of cost-revenue analysis

In this chapter we limited our discussion to a few key ideas which will be further developed in Chapter 28. For example, cost behavior patterns, the contribution margin concept, sales mix data, and the amount of idle plant capacity are often useful in developing quantitative information in arriving at answers to some puzzling problems facing management.

The important point to keep in mind is that cost-revenue analysis rests on many rather static assumptions which give management useful, but rough, estimates of *probable* results of future courses of action.

DEMONSTRATION PROBLEM FOR YOUR REVIEW

The management of the Fresno Processing Company Ltd. has engaged you to assist in the development of information to be used for managerial decisions.

The company has the capacity to process 20,000 tons of cottonseed per year. The yield from a ton of cottonseed is as shown below. (There is a 10% shrinkage and waste.)

Product	Average Yield per Ton* of Cottonseed	Average Selling Price	Total Revenue
Oil.	300 pounds	$ 0.19 per pound	$57
Meal	600 pounds	60.00 per ton	18
Hulls	800 pounds	30.00 per ton	12
Lint	100 pounds	0.03 per pound	3
Totals	1,800 pounds		$90

*There are 2,000 pounds in a ton.

A special marketing study revealed that the company can expect to sell its entire output for the coming year at the average selling prices listed above.

You have determined the company's cost structure to be as follows:

Processing costs:
  Variable: *$13 per ton of cottonseed placed into process.*
  Fixed: *$120,000 per year at all levels of production.*
Marketing costs: *All variable, $30 per ton of all products sold. (Note that only 90%*
                    of the input results in marketable products.)
Administrative costs: All fixed, $70,000 per year at all levels of production and sales
                    activity.

Instructions

a Compute the average maximum amount that the company can afford to pay for a ton of raw material (cottonseed). The average maximum amount that the company can afford to pay for a ton of cottonseed is the amount that would result in the company having losses no greater when operating than when closed down under the existing cost and revenue structure.

b Assuming that the company pays $30 per ton of cottonseed, how many tons of raw cottonseed must be processed and sold if the company is to break even?

c Assuming that the company has 10,000 shares of stock and that the income tax rate is 50%, how many tons of raw cottonseed must the company process and sell, if it pays $30 per ton of cottonseed, in order to report earnings of $8 per share?

QUESTIONS

1 Why is it important for management to focus attention on cost-revenue relationships?

2 What is a *volume index* and why is it important in analyzing cost behavior?

3 List and briefly explain two general ways in which the capacity of a business unit may be measured.

4 Explain what is meant by the *normal volume* of operations.

5 A is a variable cost; B is a fixed (nonvariable) cost; and C is a semivariable cost. How would you expect each of these total dollar costs to vary with changes in production volume? How would they vary with changes in production if they were expressed in *dollars per unit* of production?

6 The simplifying assumption that costs and volume vary in straight-line relationships makes the analysis of cost behavior much easier. What factors make this a reasonable and useful assumption in many cases?

7 What important relationships are shown on a profit-volume (break-even) graph?

8 Kris Company Ltd. has an average contribution margin of 35%. What target sales volume per month is necessary to produce a monthly operating income of $22,000, if fixed (nonvariable) expenses are $118,000 per month?

9 Why is the profit-volume formula a more flexible analytical tool than a profit-volume graph?

10 Define *margin of safety* and *relevant range* of activity.

11 A top executive of a major steel company was recently quoted as follows: "The industry finds itself at the highest break-even point in our history. In the past we could make a profit at a 50% operating rate, but now that has gone up 20 points." List some reasons why the break-even point probably increased to 70% of capacity for the steel industry.

12 An executive of the Manitoba Steel Corporation Ltd. put the blame for lower net income for a recent fiscal period on the "shift in product mix to higher proportion of export sales." Sales for the period increased slightly while net income declined by 28%. Explain how a change in product (sales) mix to a higher proportion in export sales would result in a lower level of net income.

13 Why is it helpful to know the approximate amount of contribution margin generated from the use of a scarce resource such as a machine-hour or an hour of direct labor?

14 A few years ago the president of a major airline blamed a profit squeeze on "unwise and unjustifiable promotional fares." He pointed out that 50% of his company's revenue came from "discount fares." Explain why discount fares tend to reduce net income and point out circumstances in which a discount from the regular price of a plane fare could possibly increase net income.

15 An economist writing in the *Financial Post* stated that inflation is caused by a shortage of supply in relation to demand. He suggested that businessmen should try to maintain profits by increasing sales and reducing prices rather than by increasing prices. Evaluate his argument.

16 In a recent report to stockholders, the management of a large corporation stated that lower sales volume, coupled with higher material and labor costs, resulted in a first-quarter loss of $131,292, compared with a profit of $506,258 in the first quarter of the preceding year. In order to keep costs and expenses in line with anticipated volume, budgeted fixed costs and expenses for the current year were reduced from $28.3 million to $25 million, thus reducing the break-even sales level from $80.4 million to "a more comfortable $76 million." According to the report, variable costs and expenses amounted to 64% of each sales dollar in the original budget.

List some ways that fixed costs and expenses can be reduced and mention several other actions which were probably taken by management to attain a lower break-even point.

EXERCISES

Ex. 27-1 The following information relates to the single product manufactured by the Relevance Mfg. Company Ltd.:

Selling price per unit		*$10.00*
Variable cost per unit:		
Direct materials	*$2.00*	
Direct labor	*2.00*	
Factory overhead and selling expenses	*1.00*	*5.00*
Contribution margin per unit		*$ 5.00*

a Assuming that the sales volume at the break-even point stands at $20,000 per month, what are total fixed costs for the year?

b What increase in selling price is necessary to cover a 15% increase in direct labor cost per unit and still maintain the current contribution margin ratio at 50%?

Ex. 27-2 Data relating to product X-12 manufactured by the Nutter Corporation Ltd. appear below:

Sales price per unit	*$10.00*
Variable cost per unit	*6.00*
Total fixed production and operating costs	*$40,000*
Maximum capacity with present facilities	*20,000 units*

Determine the following for product X-12:
a The contribution margin per unit
b The number of units that must be sold to break even
c The sales level that must be reached in order to earn $32,000 before income taxes

Ex. 27-3 The break-even sales volume for the Leslye Bragg Corporation Ltd. is $60,000 per month. Because of an increase of $5,000 in fixed expenses, the sales volume required to break even increased to $80,000. The sales price and the variable expenses of the single product produced did not change. Based on the foregoing information, compute:
a Variable expenses as a percentage of sales.
b Total fixed expenses before the $5,000 increase.
c From the facts given in this exercise, we can conclude that a ___% increase in total fixed expenses increases the break-even sales volume by ___%.

Ex. 27-4 The Susan Corporation Ltd. has fixed expenses of $12,000 per month. It sells two products as follows:

	Sales Price	Variable Expense	Contribution Margin
Product no. 1	$10	$4	$6
Product no. 2	10	7	3

a What sales volume is required to break even if two units of product no. 1 are sold with one unit of product no. 2?
b What sales volume is required to break even if one unit of product no. 1 is sold with two units of product no. 2?

Ex. 27-5 You recently leased manufacturing facilities which are sufficient to produce 10,000 units per year of a new product. The following information is available to you:

	Amount	Total per Unit	Variable per Unit
Estimated costs and expenses (except selling):			
Direct materials	$30,000	$3.00	$3.00
Direct labor	10,000	1.00	1.00
Factory overhead (60% of total is fixed)	20,000	2.00	0.80
Administrative expense (all fixed)	15,000	1.50	
Total	$75,000	$7.50	$4.80

Selling expenses are expected to be 12% of sales and profit before income taxes is projected at $1.30 per unit at the current sales level of 10,000 units.
a Compute the selling price per unit.
b What is the margin of safety in terms of sales dollars?

Ex. 27-6 Maxi-Tech Products Ltd., produces two models of laboratory equipment. Information for each model is shown below:

	Model 100	Model 101
Sales price per unit	$60	$40
Costs and expenses per unit:		
Direct materials	$17	$11
Direct labor	11	10

Factory overhead (applied at the rate of $6 per machine-hour)	$12	$6
Variable selling expenses	10	5
Total costs and expenses per unit	$50	$32
Profit per unit	$10	$ 8

Total factory overhead amounts to $60,000 per month, one-third of which is fixed. The demand for either product is sufficient to keep the plant operating at full capacity of 10,000 machine-hours per month. Assuming that *only one product is to be produced,* prepare a schedule showing which of the two products should be discontinued. Explain your recommendation.

Ex. 27-7 For each of the six independent situations below, compute the missing amounts:
a Only one product is manufactured:

	Sales	Variable Expenses	Contribution Margin per Unit	Fixed Expenses	Income (before taxes)	Units Sold
(1)	$_____	$40,000	$ 6	$_____	$ 8,000	4,000
(2)	60,000	_____	_____	15,000	10,000	5,000
(3)	200,000	_____	10	50,000	30,000	_____

b Many products are manufactured:

	Sales	Variable Expenses	Contribution Margin, %	Fixed Expenses	Income (before taxes)
(1)	$300,000	$240,000	___%	$_____	$26,000
(2)	200,000	_____	40%	_____	15,000
(3)	_____	_____	30%	35,000	10,000

PROBLEMS

Group A

27A-1 Kwik Service Ltd., is an independent gasoline retailer operating three gasoline stations in a medium-sized metropolitan area. The stations sell one grade of gasoline purchased from one of the major oil companies. No mechanical or other major services are offered. Miscellaneous revenues from vending machine sales and other sources are so negligible that for planning purposes they are treated as an offset against fixed expenses.

The president is studying the advisability of opening another station. His estimate of monthly expenses for the proposed location are:

Fixed expenses:	
Rent	$1,500
Wages	3,500
Other (net of miscellaneous revenues)	1,300
Variable expense	$0.27 per gallon

The planned sales price of gasoline is 36 cents per gallon.

Instructions
a What is the break-even point for the proposed station, in dollars of sales volume per month, and in gallons?

b Draw a monthly profit-volume graph for the proposed station, assuming 120,000 gallons per month as the maximum sales potential. Show fixed expenses on the bottom of the graph.

c The president thinks that the monthly volume at 36 cents per gallon will average 90,000 gallons and that, if the price of gasoline is reduced to 34 cents per gallon, the monthly volume will average 110,000 gallons. How much income (before taxes) would be earned per month at each sales volume?

27A-2 The Shaver Corporation Ltd. which has been operating at full capacity, shows the following results for 1973:

Sales (200,000 units at $4.00 per unit)		$800,000
Fixed manufacturing costs	$200,000	
Variable manufacturing costs	350,000	
Selling and administrative expenses ($50,000 fixed and		
$50,000 variable)	100,000	650,000
Income before income taxes		$150,000

Sales volume can be increased by 40% by improving and enlarging plant facilities. It is estimated that this expansion and modernization will increase fixed manufacturing costs by 51%; however, variable manufacturing costs are expected to decrease from $1.75 to $1.55 per unit. Fixed selling and administrative expenses will not change; however, the variable selling and administrative expenses will remain at $0.25 per unit, but the total will increase in proportion to the increase in volume (40%). The selling price will remain at $4.00 per unit.

Instructions
a Determine the break-even point in terms of dollars (*1*) before the expansion and (*2*) after the expansion.
b Draw a profit-volume graph similar to the one illustrated on page 836, which shows the total contribution margin and the margin of safety after the expansion.
c Compute the total dollar volume in sales required after the expansion to earn a pretax income of $165,000.
d What is the maximum pretax income that the Shaver Corporation Ltd. can earn after the expansion?

27A-3 The Elite Hand Tool Company Ltd. budgeted the following costs for the production and sale of 40,000 units of a certain product:

	Total Annual Costs	Unit Costs and Expenses	Percentage of Total Annual Costs and Expenses That Are Variable
Direct materials	$200,000	$ 5	100%
Direct labor	160,000	4	100
Factory overhead (fixed and			
variable)	80,000	2	40
Administrative expenses	40,000	1	20
Totals	$480,000	$12	

The unit will be sold by manufacturer's representatives who will receive a commission of 10% of the gross sales price. Management wants to price the product to realize a 15% profit (before income taxes) on gross sales price.

Instructions

a Compute the gross sales price per unit that would result in a pretax profit of 15% on sales if sales amount to 40,000 units.

b Assuming that the gross sales price per unit is set at $20, compute the number of units that must be sold annually in order to break even.

27A-4 The Fort Frances Company Ltd. manufactures two products from a single raw material. The company's plant has a capacity to process 150,000 pounds of raw material per month. The cost inputs and the outputs from the various processing operations are summarized below:

Inputs	*Outputs*
1 100 pounds of raw material at 40 cents per pound	*1 60 pounds of product X, which sells for $1.60 per pound*
2 Variable processing costs, 60 cents per pound	*2 40 pounds of product Y, which sells for $2.60 per pound*
3 Fixed processing costs per month, $16,000	

The finished product is shipped from the plant daily; therefore, ending inventories of goods in process and finished product are negligible. Fixed selling and administrative expenses are estimated at $32,000 per month. Variable selling and administrative expenses are budgeted at 18% of dollar sales.

Instructions

a Compute the contribution margin ratio and the monthly sales volume (in pounds) which must be sold in order to break even.

b Prepare a budgeted income statement for the month of June, Year 1, showing the operating income that should be forecast if the plant operated at 80% of capacity. Ignore income taxes.

27A-5 Playtime Products Company Ltd. manufactures four products in four different departments. The estimated demand for the products for Year 4 is such that production will not be able to keep pace with incoming orders. Some pertinent data for each product are listed below:

Product	Estimated Sales for Year 4, Units	Sales Price	Direct Material Cost	Direct Labor Cost	Variable Factory Overhead
A	8,000	$11.00	$3.00	$4.00	$1.00
B	1,200	9.00	2.00	4.00	1.00
C	4,000	6.50	1.00	2.00	1.00
D	6,000	4.25	0.25	1.00	1.20

Direct labor costs an average of $4.00 per hour.

Instructions

a Prepare a schedule showing the contribution margin per one unit of each product and also the contribution margin per one hour of direct labor applied to the production of each class of product.

b If you were to reduce the production of one of the products in order to meet the demand for the others, what would that product be? Why? Assume that direct labor hours represent the scarce resource.

c Assume that the 8,000 hours of direct labor hours now used to produce Product A are used to produce additional units of Product C. What would be the effect on total contribution margin?

Group B

27B-1 Ed's Car Rest operates a downtown parking lot containing 800 parking spaces. The lot is open 2,500 hours per year. The parking charge per car is 40 cents per hour; the average customer parks two hours. Ed's Car Rest rents the lot for $6,250 per month. The lot supervisor is paid $12,000 per year. Five employees who handle the parking of cars are paid $150 per week for 50 weeks, plus $300 each for the two-week vacation period. Employees rotate vacations during the slow months when four men can handle the reduced load of traffic. Lot maintenance, payroll taxes, and other fixed expenses amount to $3,000 per month, plus 4 cents per parking hour sold.

Instructions
a Draw a profit-volume graph for Ed's Car Rest on an annual basis. Use parking-space hours as the measure of volume of activity and show fixed expenses on the bottom of the graph.
b What is the contribution margin ratio? What is the annual break-even point in dollars of parking revenues?
c Suppose that the five employees were taken off the hourly wage basis and paid 12 cents per car parked, with the same vacation pay as before. (1) How would this change the contribution margin per parking-space hour sold and total fixed expenses? (2) What annual sales revenues would be necessary to produce $25,500 per year income before taxes under these circumstances?

27B-2 George Slater, an engineer, has been offered an opportunity to invest in a vending machine operation involving 50 vending machines located in various plants around the city. The machine manufacturer reports that similar vending machine routes have produced a sales volume ranging from 500 to 1,000 units per machine per month. The following information is made available to Slater in evaluating the possible profitability of the operation.
(1) An investment of $25,000 will be required, $7,000 for merchandise and $18,000 for the 50 machines.
(2) The machines have a service life of five years and no salvage value at the end of that period. Depreciation will be computed on the straight-line basis.
(3) The merchandise (candy and soft drinks) retails for an average of 15 cents per unit and will cost Slater an average of 6 cents per unit.
(4) Owners of the buildings in which the machines are located are paid a commission of 3 cents per unit of candy and soft drinks sold.
(5) One man will be hired to service the machines. He will be paid $700 per month.
(6) Other expenses are estimated at $200 per month. These expenses do not vary with the number of units sold.

Instructions
a Determine the break-even volume in dollars and in units per month.
b Draw a monthly profit-volume graph for sales volume up to 1,000 units per machine per month. The graph should be similar to the one illustrated on page 836 which shows the total contribution margin and the margin of safety.
c What sales volume per month will be necessary to produce a return of 12% (before taxes) on Slater's investment during his *first year* of operation?
d Slater is considering offering the building owners a flat rental of $15 per machine per month in lieu of the commission of 3 cents per unit sold. What effect would this change in commission arrangement have on his *monthly* break-even volume in terms of units?

27B-3 Right-On Industries operates its production department only when orders are received for its one product, a metal disc. The manufacturing process begins with the cutting of "rings" from strips of sheet metal; these rings are then pressed into discs. The sheets of metal, each 4 feet long and weighing 33.2 ounces (2.075 pounds), are purchased for $6.32 each.

The following information is available for the first year of operations:

(1) Five thousand 4-foot pieces of metal were used to produce 30,000 discs, each weighing 5 ounces and selling for $3.10 each.

(2) The company has been operating at 50% of capacity and has had no spoilage in the cutting step of the process. The skeletons remaining after the rings have been cut are sold for scrap at $1.60 per pound. The proceeds on the sale of scrap have been improperly credited to Sales.

(3) The variable conversion cost of each disc is 130% of the direct material cost (metal), after deducting the proceeds from the sale of scrap. Variable conversion cost is the sum of direct labor and variable factory overhead.

(4) Fixed costs amount to $40,000 per year.

Instructions

a Prepare schedules computing the following for the first year of operations: (1) Cost of metal per disc (after deducting the proceeds from the sale of scrap), (2) variable conversion cost per disc, (3) contribution margin on each disc, and (4) total contribution margin for all units sold.

b Compute the number of discs that must be sold per year to break even.

c Management of Right-On Industries thinks that they could sell 50,000 discs if the price were reduced to $2.60 per disc. Would you advise them to reduce the price? Why?

27B-4 Fidelity Sound, Ltd., manufactures tape decks and currently sells 9,250 units annually to producers of sound reproduction systems. The owner anticipates a 15% increase in the cost per unit of direct labor on January 1 of next year. He expects all other costs and expenses to remain unchanged. The owner has asked you to assist him in developing the information he needs to formulate a reasonable product strategy for next year.

You are satisfied that volume is the primary factor affecting costs and expenses and have separated the semivariable costs and expenses into their fixed and variable segments. Beginning and ending inventories generally remain at a level of 1,000 units.

Below are the current-year data assembled for your analysis:

Selling price per unit		$ 100.00
Variable costs and expenses per unit:		
Materials	$30.00	
Direct labor	20.00	
Factory overhead and selling and administrative expenses	10.00	60.00
Contribution margin per unit (40%)		$ 40.00

Fixed costs and expenses (factory and other), $200,000

Instructions

a What increase in the selling price is necessary to cover the 15% increase in direct labor cost and still maintain the current contribution margin ratio of 40%?

b How many tape decks must be sold to maintain the current operating income of $170,000 if the sales price remains at $100 and the 15% wage increase goes into effect? Disregard income taxes.

c The owner believes that an additional $300,000 of machinery (to be depreciated at 20% annually) will increase present capacity (10,000 units) by 40%. If all tape decks produced can be sold at the present price of $100 per unit and the wage increase goes into effect, how would the estimated operating income before capacity is increased compare with the estimated operating income after capacity is increased? Prepare schedules of estimated operating income at full capacity *before* and *after* the expansion. Disregard income taxes.

27B-5 The owner of Executive Desk Company Ltd. has asked for your assistance in determining an economical sales and production mix of his product line for next year (Year 10). The company's sales department provides the following estimates for Year 10:

Desk Model	Estimated Sales for Year 10, Units	Price Per Unit
Elite	1,000	$318.00
Presidente	1,200	270.00
Secretare	1,500	200.00
Populare	2,000	155.00

You gather the following information from the company's accounting records: (1) The cost standards per unit for direct materials and direct labor are:

Desk Model	Cost of Direct Materials	Hours of Direct Labor	Total Direct Labor Cost
Elite	$62.40	18	$72.00
Presidente	57.00	15	60.00
Secretare	53.60	12	48.00
Populare	40.70	9	36.00

(2) The rate paid by the company for direct labor is $4.00 per hour, including payroll taxes and other fringe benefits. The plant has a capacity of only 54,000 labor hours per year on a single-shift basis. Present equipment is capable of producing all the desk models.

(3) The total fixed factory overhead for Year 10 is budgeted at $88,000. Variable factory overhead is estimated at 80% of direct labor cost.

Instructions

a Prepare a schedule computing the total direct labor hours required to produce the estimated sales volume for Year 10. Indicate whether capacity is sufficient to meet the demand or whether demand exceeds the available capacity.

b Prepare a schedule computing the estimated contribution margin on each desk model and the **contribution margin per hour of direct labor** needed to manufacture each desk model.

c Management does not wish to expand capacity, work overtime, or start another shift. Instead, it wants to discontinue the production of one of the models. What model should be discontinued? Why?

BUSINESS DECISION PROBLEM 27

The Campus Ice Cream Company Ltd. operates a chain of drive-ins selling only ice cream products. The following information is taken from the records of a typical drive-in now operated by the company:

Average selling price of ice cream per gallon	$	1.60
Number of gallons sold per month		15,000
Variable expenses per gallon:		
Ice cream	$0.90	
Supplies (cups, cones, toppings, etc.)	0.30	
Total variable expenses per gallon	$	1.20

Fixed expenses per month:

Rent on building and parking lot	$ 600.00
Utilities and upkeep	380.00
Wages, including payroll taxes	2,270.00
Manager's salary, including payroll taxes but excluding any bonus	900.00
Other fixed expenses	350.00
Total fixed expenses per month	$4,500.00

Based on these data, the monthly break-even point sales volume is determined as follows:

$$\frac{\$4,500 \text{ (Fixed Expenses)}}{\$0.40 \text{ (Contribution Margin per Unit)}} = 11,250 \text{ Gallons (or \$18,000)}$$

Instructions

a Assuming that the manager has a contract calling for a bonus of 5 cents per gallon for each gallon sold beyond the break-even point, compute the number of gallons of ice cream that must be sold per month in order to earn $1,400 per month. Disregard income taxes.

b In order to increase monthly income, the company is considering the following two alternatives:

(1) Reduce the selling price to $1.50 per gallon. This action is expected to increase the number of gallons sold by 40%. The manager would be paid a salary of $900 per month without a bonus.

(2) Spend $500 per month on advertising without any change in selling price. This action is expected to increase the number of gallons sold by 20%. The manager would be paid a salary of $900 per month without a bonus.

Which of these two alternatives would be more profitable for a typical drive-in store now selling 15,000 units? How many gallons must be sold per month under each alternative in order to break even? Give complete schedules in support of your answers and indicate to management which of the two alternatives it should adopt.

OTHER USES BY MANAGEMENT OF ACCOUNTING INFORMATION

TWENTY-
EIGHT

A business organization is affected by external as well as internal forces. Management needs information relating to economic trends, government fiscal and monetary policies, changes in consumer preferences, actions of competitors, changes in regulatory laws, and technological developments. Internal data must be developed in the key functional areas of finance, production, and marketing, as well as in service areas such as personnel, administration, accounting, research, and training. Management makes decisions in each of these areas, and the quality of the decisions depends to a large extent on the quality of the information that is available to management.

In earlier chapters we have made extensive reference to management's use of accounting information. Additional uses of such information are discussed in this chapter.

Special reports for management

Accounting is a process of measuring and communicating business and economic information to decision makers. Management, as the primary consumer of accounting data, needs a wide variety of reports and other information. To be effective in arriving at timely decisions, special reports prepared for the various levels of management should be *relevant, timely, concise,* and *understandable.*

Reports intended to be used as a basis for action should deal with the critical variables of the proposed decision or activity under review. Decision making by management deals with the future and actions should be taken in time to produce the best possible results. It follows, then, that the information used as a basis for action should be as current and predictive as possible. To be of maximum use to management, information and reports of all types should be prepared in summary form, should be flexible, and should highlight deviations from previously established performance standards.

Controlling day-to-day operations

An efficient business organization generally has a comprehensive reporting system designed to assist management in determining the actions to be taken. Businesses operate in a dynamic and competitive environment. Effective managers continuously monitor the results within their areas of responsibility and look for exceptions which may be impeding the attainment of established goals.

One of the most useful management tools in controlling daily activities is a strong system of internal control. Such a system consists of procedures established to safeguard assets, to provide accurate accounting data, to promote efficient operations, and to encourage adherence to policies established by management.

Many types of reports may be prepared to assist management in planning and controlling daily activities. These may include, for example, reports on daily material spoilage, new orders received, or sales by territories. Periodic performance reports for cost and profit centers, showing actual and budgeted figures, are probably the most widely used control devices in many businesses.[1]

Using accounting information intelligently

The broad *functions of management* may be described as organizing, staffing, directing, and planning and controlling the activities of a business enterprise. Few of the problems that arise in performing these managerial functions can be solved *solely* by collecting and analyzing numerical data. Business is an activity involving humans, and in dealing with human behavior there are always factors that cannot be reduced to quantitative terms. To illustrate, the manager of a baseball team probably has more numerical information about his players than the manager of any business organization. Statistics are kept on almost every significant action of each player in every game. Yet, in deciding in a crucial spot whether to use player X or player Y, a manager of a baseball team considers a number of unmeasurable factors such as mental attitude, relations with other players, and ability to play under pressure. The ability to use quantitative information intelligently in planning and controlling complex activities is therefore an important but not the sole element of managerial skill.

Quantitative information is useful in three areas of managerial activity: (1) deciding what should be done, (2) getting it done, and (3) checking up to see what was done and how well it was done. Planning is a matter

---

[1] See Chaps. 23 and 26 for a more extensive discussion on this subject.

of looking ahead at prospective events; supervising current operations requires attention to present events; measuring performance involves looking back at past activities.

Management is obviously more interested in the meaning and interpretation of information than in the systems and procedures used in its accumulation. The accountant, however, is responsible for providing useful data and must concern himself with the details of deciding what figures are relevant, how they can be determined or estimated, what conclusions can be derived from them, and how the analysis can be reported in the most concise and meaningful way.

An accounting system has not yet been devised that will accumulate and classify cost and revenue information in all the different ways that will be useful to the decision maker. Different costs are needed for different purposes because a wide variety of relationships exists between costs incurred and results obtained. The results obtained are most frequently expressed in terms of revenues generated from the sale of different products or services. It is the breakdown of costs and revenues, not aggregate totals, which serves as a basis for decisions. Information about net income and financial position is useful to management as well as outsiders, but it is not enough. For managerial purposes the accounting system must provide costs classified by organization. Management needs to know the quality of current performance of individuals who have been assigned responsibility. Finally, management needs to know what costs are expected to be, and how they are likely to vary under alternative courses of action.

Cost concepts and terminology

In preceding chapters we described several different costs in terms of their controllability and behavior patterns. A brief review of some of these is in order at this point. *Direct costs* can be readily identified with departments, products, or activities; *indirect costs,* on the other hand, are incurred for the benefit of the business as a whole and are allocated to departments, products, or activities. *Fixed costs* are those which do not vary despite changes over relatively wide ranges in the volume of activity; strictly *variable costs* change directly and proportionately with changes in volume; *semivariable costs* are those whose pattern of variation with changes in volume is neither strictly fixed nor variable. Other cost concepts relevant to our discussion in this chapter are considered below.

MARGINAL AND INCREMENTAL COSTS *Marginal cost* may be defined as the cost of the last small increase in output (in units or other variables) under consideration. The concept of marginal cost was developed by economists to arrive at theoretically optimal price and volume decisions in situations where changes in both price and volume were assumed to occur in very small increments or over a continuous range of activity.

Marginal costs are very difficult to measure in many practical situations, and in many cases it is virtually impossible to determine the change in total cost that would result from adding one more unit of output. Fortunately the relevant factor in most business decisions is the *difference* in costs incurred under two or more alternative courses of action. For this purpose a knowledge of *incremental* (or *differential*) *costs* may be sufficient. Any cost that changes as a result of a proposed action or decision is an incremental cost in relation to that action or decision. Incremental costs are an important piece of information for management since, in choosing between alternative A and B, any costs that are the same under either alternative may safely be ignored.

We should point out that variable and incremental costs are not the same. Variable costs vary in proportion with change in volume of output; incremental costs vary in relation to the specific alternatives under study. If we are analyzing a change in volume over the relevant range of output, variable costs and incremental costs are often assumed to be the same. If the decision is whether to manufacture or buy a certain item, however, incremental costs relevant to this decision may consist of both variable and fixed costs.

SUNK AND OUT-OF-POCKET COSTS A cost that has been irrevocably incurred at some time in the past is a *sunk* cost. An *out-of-pocket* cost involves the expenditure of current funds. Out-of-pocket costs may be fixed (for example, the salary of an additional shop foreman) or variable (commissions paid to salesmen). Sunk costs are usually fixed (for example, rent paid in advance and not subject to refund), but in certain cases they may have the characteristics usually attributed to variable costs (such as a year's supply of raw materials purchased in advance, which do not have much resale value if not used). It is important to recognize the distinction between sunk and out-of-pocket costs in making decisions. *Sunk costs are irrelevant to future decisions because they cannot be changed no matter what decision is made.*

AVOIDABLE AND UNAVOIDABLE COSTS Knowing that a cost is fixed or variable, or that it is either sunk or out-of-pocket does not tell us whether it can be avoided. A manager's salary is a fixed cost that can be avoided if it is possible to cancel his contract. The fuel consumed on an airplane flight is a variable cost that is unavoidable unless a different means of powering planes is developed. Sunk costs are unavoidable unless we can recover them through resale, but not all unavoidable costs are sunk. The next month's salary of a railroad fireman is unavoidable if the train must run and the union contract specifies that a fireman must be hired, but it is an out-of-pocket cost rather than a sunk cost.

OPPORTUNITY COSTS If a building can be used in our production activities *or* rented to another company, there is an opportunity cost of continuing to use the building in our own production work. An *opportunity cost* is the measurable sacrifice of foregoing some alternative course of action. Opportunity costs are not recorded in accounting records, but they are an important factor in arriving at many decisions. *Ignoring opportunity costs is a common source of error in making cost analyses.*

To illustrate, suppose we are considering whether to manufacture product X or product Y in a certain department. Product X is estimated to yield an annual income of $10,000 while product Y will yield only $8,000 per year. The decision to produce product X results in an opportunity cost of $8,000 because that is what we forego when we decide not to produce product Y. On the other hand, a decision to produce product Y would result in an opportunity cost of $10,000, the income on product X we would lose by producing product Y.

In certain situations opportunity costs may be zero or very small. For example, suppose we use our own equipment to haul a product from point A to point B and return with an empty truck. If we are considering whether it would be profitable to pick up a return load, the opportunity cost of the truck and driver is zero, since they must return in any event. Only the slight incremental costs of fuel and wear and tear on the truck due to a load need be taken into account in deciding whether the proposed price for the return haul will be profitable.

An important example of an opportunity cost that should be considered in investment decisions is the *time value of money.* Suppose we are faced with two alternative actions producing equal gross revenues. One involves the investment of $10,000 immediately; the other requires an expenditure of $10,000 at the end of one year. Obviously, the second alternative is preferable because we can invest the $10,000, at 8% for example, and earn $800 for the year on this capital. In any decision where the timing of costs to be incurred or revenues to be realized varies, the opportunity cost of spending or receiving funds at an earlier or later date is an important factor. The easiest method of incorporating the time value of money into the decision involves the use of *present value* formulas and compound interest tables. For example, the present cost of an expenditure of $10,000 one year from now if the interest rate is 8% would be $9,259.26 ($10,000 ÷ 1.08). In other words, a sum of $9,259.26 invested at 8% would earn $740.74 for one year and would give us a sum of $10,000 at the end of the year. This topic is considered in detail in *Advanced Accounting;* in this chapter we shall generally ignore the opportunity cost of money.

Deciding among alternatives

All business decisions involve a choice among alternative courses of action. The criteria for such choices may be subjective (attitudes of employees, inconvenience, lack of qualified talent), objective (dollars of cost or revenue), or what is more likely, a combination of both. In most situations it is possible to analyze some of the consequences of alternative actions in quantitative terms and to use the results of this analysis in making a decision.

If two alternative actions are under consideration, quantitative analysis will generally show which action will lead to the higher profit, or if an investment is involved, to the higher return on investment. *Return on investment* may be expressed as the ratio of income per period to the average investment for the period. Since income is influenced by both revenues and costs (expenses), any expected change either in revenues or in costs (expenses) is relevant to the decision.

If a decision involves a new investment that will be recovered through increased net revenues or cost savings over a period of several years, we are involved in an analysis of cash flows over time, an analysis which requires the use of present value computations. We shall not bring present value computations into our discussion, however, in order to avoid making this introduction to decision analysis overly complex. The focal point of our study will be the impact of proposed actions on cost and revenue flows.

OUTLINE OF AN ALTERNATIVE-CHOICE PROBLEM An organized approach is an important element in solving any problem. The solution to most alternative-choice problems is formulated through the following steps:

1 Define the problem and identify the alternative solutions to be considered.
2 Measure and compare the consequences of each alternative, insofar as these consequences can be expressed quantitatively.
3 Evaluate the subjective factors and determine their merit and the extent to which they offset quantitative considerations.
4 Arrive at a decision.

Recognizing that a problem exists and being able to define the alternatives is the most important step in the analysis. Often the existence of a problem comes to light through a proposal to change what is now being done. Once the issue is raised, however, the alternatives to consider may be more numerous than simply making a choice between what is now being done and the specific proposed change. For example, suppose that the installation of a certain computer for data processing has been proposed. If we are seriously considering this computer, the alternatives may be to: (*1*) continue our present data processing system; (*2*) buy the computer in question; (*3*) buy some other type of computer; (*4*) lease the computer selected; and (*5*) improve the present data processing system by eliminating unnecessary steps. If too many alternatives are considered the analysis becomes hopelessly complex. Fortunately, it is usually possible to rule out certain choices on the basis of a rough analysis, leaving only a few alternatives for serious consideration.

Measuring the outcome or consequences of alternative courses of action involves a forecast of the future, and some degree of error is always present. We may decide to estimate what will probably happen and proceed with our analysis on the assumption that our expectations will be fully realized. On the other hand, we may formulate two or more possible outcomes, assess the **probability** of each and arrive at an expected outcome which is a weighted average of the probability of a number of outcomes. It is clearly advantageous to express as many consequences of a decision in quantitative terms as possible because it is easy to find the net effect of quantitative factors. **Costs** and **cost additions** can be subtracted from **revenues** and **cost savings** to produce a net numerical representation of the advantage or disadvantage associated with a given course of action.

A few of the more common applications of alternative-choice decisions are discussed in the following sections.

Illustration of an alternative-choice decision: unprofitable product line

The Elixer Company Ltd. manufactures household mixers in three models: Deluxe, Standard, and Economy. The overall profit margins for the last few years have been unsatisfactory, and the issue has been raised whether one or more of the models should be dropped from production. An income statement showing product results for last year is shown below:

ELIXER COMPANY LTD.

Income Statement—Last Year

	Total	Deluxe Model	Standard Model	Economy Model
Sales (units)	34,000	4,000	20,000	10,000
Sales revenues	$960,000	$160,000	$600,000	$200,000
Manufacturing costs	730,000	138,000	412,000	180,000
Gross profit on sales	$230,000	$ 22,000	$188,000	$ 20,000
Operating expenses	223,200	38,200	125,000	60,000
Income or (loss) before taxes	$ 6,800	$(16,200)	$ 63,000	$(40,000)
Income or (loss) per unit	$0.20	$(4.05)	$3.15	$(4.00)

Should the Deluxe and Economy models be dropped?

This information suggests that if the company were to drop both the Deluxe and Economy models and produce only the Standard model it might expect earnings of around $63,000 per year—a striking improvement. On the other hand, it might be argued that the Deluxe model contributes $22,000 of gross profit and the Economy model $20,000, and that they should be continued since this is a positive contribution to operating expenses. The trouble with both these conclusions is that they are based on irrelevant information. The fact that a given expense is allocated to a particular product, for example, does not mean that this cost would disappear if the product were dropped.

A first step in obtaining information more useful for decision purposes would be to determine the contribution margin of each product. ***Contribution margin*** per unit is the difference between unit sales price and all variable costs per unit. The contribution margin per unit, based on the Elixer Company Ltd. data, is shown below:

ELIXER COMPANY LTD.
Per-unit Contribution Margin by Models—Last Year

All models are covering their variable costs

	Deluxe Model	Standard Model	Economy Model
Selling price per unit	*$40*	*$30*	*$20*
Variable costs per unit:			
Variable manufacturing costs	*$30*	*$18*	*$15*
Variable operating expenses	*6*	*4*	*4*
Total variable costs per unit	*$36*	*$22*	*$19*
Contribution margin per unit	*$ 4*	*$ 8*	*$ 1*

This per-unit data may be reconciled with the income statement figures as follows:

ELIXER COMPANY LTD.
Income Statement—Last Year

Total contribution margin by products

	Total	Deluxe Model	Standard Model	Economy Model
Number of units sold (a)	*34,000*	*4,000*	*20,000*	*10,000*
Contribution margin per unit (b)		*$4*	*$8*	*$1*
Total contribution margin (a × b)	***$186,000***	***$ 16,000***	***$160,000***	***$ 10,000***
Less: All fixed costs	*179,200*	*32,200*	*97,000*	*50,000*
Income or (loss) before taxes	*$ 6,800*	*$(16,200)*	*$ 63,000*	*$ (40,000)*

The contribution margin analysis begins to sharpen the picture. Apparently each of the three models makes some contribution to fixed costs. Dropping the Deluxe model would reduce income by $16,000 and dropping the Economy model would reduce income by $10,000. Before accepting this conclusion, however, we should ask ourselves whether the assumptions used in dividing costs into their fixed and variable components are sound.

Two assumptions, inherent in the fixed and variable cost data, are important to our tentative conclusions. First, we have assumed that the variable and fixed relationship of cost to volume holds for variations in output all the way down to zero for a particular model. In our discussion of cost-volume relationships in Chapter 27, we noted that the division of costs into fixed and variable components may be quite meaningful for variations in output somewhat above and below the normal scale of production, but the actual discontinuance of production entirely often results in a change in the nature of operations so that ***some fixed costs can be eliminated*** if production is discontinued altogether.

Secondly, the use of contribution margin data rests on the assumption that the sales of any particular model are independent of the sales of the other two models. It is entirely possible that dropping either the Deluxe or Economy model *will result in an increase in sales of the other models;* it is also possible that dropping one model *may adversely affect the sale of the other models.*

Let us see how these two factors might affect our analysis. In view of its low contribution margin, the Economy model seems the most likely candidate for elimination. A careful study of fixed costs indicates that the elimination of this model would enable the Elixer Company Ltd. to reduce certain fixed costs by $7,000.

It seems likely that some buyers of the Economy model might shift to the Standard model if the Economy model were no longer offered. When asked for an estimate of this factor, the sales manager presented the following report:

	Number of Economy Model Sales That Might Shift to Standard Model (per Year)	x	My Estimate of the Probability That This Many Would Shift	=	Expected Shift in Sales
Sales manager's estimate of shift in sales	1,000		.05		50
	2,000		.10		200
	3,000		.30		900
	4,000		.40		1,600
	5,000 or more		.15		750
					3,500 units

Note: The fact that we did not maintain a full line of mixers may be expected to result in the loss of the entire business of some dealers, especially those who put special emphasis on the low-priced Economy model. *I would expect a reduction of 10% in our present sales of Deluxe and Standard models due to this factor.*

By incorporating the expected reduction in fixed costs and shift in sales into our analysis, we can prepare the schedule shown on the following page.

We have now finally isolated the data relevant to the decision. If our assumptions and estimates are realized, dropping the Economy model from the line will increase the annual income of the Elixer Company Ltd. to $14,200 ($6,800 + $7,400).

Replacement of old equipment

A problem often facing management is whether it should buy new and more efficient equipment or whether it should continue to use existing equipment. Assume, for example, that the Ardmore Company Ltd. is meeting increasing competition in the sale of product Q. The sales manager believes the source of the trouble is that competitors have installed more efficient equipment and are therefore able to reduce prices. The issue raised therefore is whether Ardmore Company Ltd. should: (1) buy new equipment at a cost of $80,000, or (2) continue using its present equipment. Both the new and present equipment have a remaining useful

ELIXER COMPANY LTD.

Estimate of Annual Change in Income from Dropping Economy Model

<table>
<tr><td rowspan="16">Complete analysis of decision variables</td><td colspan="3">Increase in annual income from dropping Economy model:</td></tr>
<tr><td>Estimated reduction in costs presently classified as fixed . . . .</td><td></td><td>$ 7,000</td></tr>
<tr><td>Gain in contribution margin because of shift in sales from</td><td></td><td></td></tr>
<tr><td>Economy model to Standard model:</td><td></td><td></td></tr>
<tr><td>Sales manager's expected sales shift to Standard model . . . .</td><td>3,500</td><td></td></tr>
<tr><td>Contribution margin per unit of Standard model . . . .</td><td>×$8</td><td>28,000</td></tr>
<tr><td>Total increase in annual income . . . .</td><td></td><td>$35,000</td></tr>
<tr><td>Less: Reduction in annual income from dropping Economy model:</td><td></td><td></td></tr>
<tr><td>Contribution margin on Economy models now sold: 10,000</td><td></td><td></td></tr>
<tr><td>units × $1 contribution margin per unit . . . .</td><td>$10,000</td><td></td></tr>
<tr><td>Contribution margin on 10% reduction in sales of Standard and</td><td></td><td></td></tr>
<tr><td>Deluxe models as a result of elimination of Economy model:</td><td></td><td></td></tr>
<tr><td>2,000 units of Standard model × $8 contribution margin per</td><td></td><td></td></tr>
<tr><td>unit . . . .</td><td>16,000</td><td></td></tr>
<tr><td>400 units of Deluxe models × $4 contribution margin per</td><td></td><td></td></tr>
<tr><td>unit . . . .</td><td>1,600</td><td></td></tr>
<tr><td></td><td>Total reduction in annual income . . . .</td><td></td><td>27,600</td></tr>
<tr><td></td><td colspan="2">Estimated net increase in annual income if Economy model is dropped . . . .</td><td>$ 7,400</td></tr>
</table>

life of five years and neither will have any residual value. The new equipment will produce substantial savings in direct labor, direct materials, and factory overhead costs. The company does not believe the use of new equipment will have any effect on sales volume, so the decision rests entirely on whether cost savings are possible.

An analysis prepared by the assistant controller shows the following expected cost savings over the next five years if the new equipment is purchased:

<table>
<tr><td rowspan="5">Do you see anything wrong with this analysis?</td><td>Savings in variable manufacturing costs ($18,000 per year)</em> . . . .</td><td></td><td><em>$ 90,000</td></tr>
<tr><td>Less: Cost of new equipment . . . .</td><td>$80,000</td><td></td></tr>
<tr><td>Loss on sale of old equipment, which can be sold now</td><td></td><td></td></tr>
<tr><td>for $5,000 and has a present book value of $45,000 . . . . .</td><td>40,000</td><td>120,000</td></tr>
<tr><td>Estimated five-year disadvantage if new equipment is purchased .</td><td></td><td>$(30,000)</td></tr>
</table>

On the basis of this information the assistant controller feels the company should continue using the old equipment. In addition to the above factors, he points out that a reduction of direct production workers is likely to increase unemployment compensation rates for the company and have a bad effect on employee morale.

The primary error in this analysis is the failure to recognize the ***irrelevance of sunk costs.*** The investment in old equipment is already made and cannot be changed by the present decision, except for the $5,000 estimated current residual value of the old equipment. A better analysis would be as follows:

		If New Equipment Is Purchased
Better analysis: differential cost basis	Estimated savings in variable manufacturing costs ($18,000 per year)	$90,000
	Add: Proceeds from sale of old equipment	5,000
	Total savings	$95,000
	Less: Cost of new equipment (assuming no residual value)	80,000
	Estimated five-year advantage if new equipment is purchased . . .	$15,000

We can substantiate the validity of this analysis by projecting the income from the sale of product Q over the next five years as follows:

		If Old Equipment Is Retained	If New Equipment Is Purchased
Five-year summary of projected income	Assumed sales of product Q over five-year period	$ 500,000	$ 500,000
	Manufacturing costs:		
	Variable (estimated savings, $90,000) . . .	(300,000)	(210,000)
	Fixed factory overhead (other than depreciation on equipment)	(50,000)	(50,000)
	Depreciation on equipment:		
	Old (no residual value in five years) . . .	(45,000)	
	New (no residual value in five years) . .		(80,000)
	Loss on sale of old equipment if new equipment is purchased ($45,000 − $5,000)		(40,000)
	Projected income over five-year period	$ 105,000	$ 120,000

This projection indicates an improvement of $15,000 in the income over a five-year period, rather than the $30,000 loss shown by the assistant controller's figures. The "other factors" suggested by the assistant controller (possible increase in unemployment taxes and relations with employees) remain to be considered.

In this analysis we have ignored the fact that the new equipment requires an immediate net cash investment of $75,000 ($80,000 − $5,000 residual value of old equipment) while the savings in variable manufacturing costs of $90,000 will be realized gradually over the next five years if the new equipment is purchased. Obviously the present value of the cost savings is less than $90,000, because of the time value of money. Also we have omitted income tax considerations. If the old equipment were continued in use, the $45,000 in unrecovered cost would be depreciated for tax purposes at the rate of 20 per cent per year using the reducing-balance method of depreciation. On the other hand, larger income tax benefits would result from the purchase of the new equipment because $120,000 (the cost of the new equipment plus the loss on the disposal of the old equipment) would be depreciated for income tax purposes.

Sell or lease surplus equipment

Equipment is generally acquired by a business to meet current and anticipated future needs. As the requirements of the business change because of technological developments, consumer preferences, or other reasons, the equipment may no longer meet the needs of the business. Management must then decide what to do with the surplus equipment. The choice may be to sell the equipment, probably at a loss, or to lease it for a certain number of years at a fixed monthly rental. If the equipment is leased, the owner may continue to pay taxes, insurance, and repair costs. These costs can be avoided if the equipment is sold.

Consider the case of High-Tech Corporation Ltd., which bought a machine only three years ago for $200,000 and at the time of purchase estimated a ten-year productive life for it. Present technology has made the machine inefficient for the company's use, although only $60,000 of depreciation has been recorded on it. The Agar Company Ltd. offers to lease the machine for seven years for an annual rental of $15,000, if the High-Tech Corporation Ltd. agrees to pay for all repairs, taxes, and insurance, which are estimated to be $5,000 per year. The machine would have no residual value at the end of seven years. The Sharp Salvage Co. Ltd. offers to buy the machine outright for $40,000 in cash. An analysis of the two alternatives (sell or lease) is shown below:

	Alternatives Evaluated		Incremental (or Differential) Analysis
	Sell	Lease	
Proceeds from sale	$ 40,000		
Revenue from lease ($15,000 × 7) . . .		$105,000	$ 65,000
Book value of machine	(140,000)		
Depreciation expense		(140,000)	
Repairs, taxes, and insurance		(35,000)	(35,000)
Total (loss) or gain	$(100,000)	$(70,000)	$ 30,000

Can an alternative resulting in a loss be the more attractive one?

This analysis illustrates that the book value of the equipment is a *sunk cost* because it cannot be changed as to its effect on the future. Although both alternatives result in a reported loss, leasing will result in the smaller loss and is therefore the more attractive alternative.

There are three other factors that should be considered in arriving at a decision of this type: (1) other alternative actions available, such as use of the machine to produce a different product; (2) the effects of income taxes on the analysis; and (3) the effect of the earnings on the funds received if the equipment is sold. For example, assuming that the High-Tech Corporation pays taxes at the marginal rate of 48%, it would save $48,000 ($100,000 loss × .48) in income taxes in the year of sale provided it had no other assets of this class.[2] This, combined with the

---

[2] If High-Tech Corporation Ltd. had other assets of the same class, its depreciation expense (capital cost allowance) for tax purposes would be increased annually by 20 per cent of the loss using the reducing-balance method of depreciation.

$40,000 proceeds on sale, would give the company $88,000 to invest. If the equipment is leased, however, its net annual cash flow is $10,000 ($15,000 − $5,000) plus annual tax savings of $4,800 (48% of annual loss of $10,000 after depreciation of $20,000 per year), or only $14,800 per year for seven years. The company's annual cash flow from leasing could be increased in the earlier years if it claimed maximum capital cost allowance. For example, by claiming maximum capital cost allowance, the tax saving in the first year would be $18,640 rather than $14,800. Tax savings in the later years would, of course, be correspondingly reduced. Assuming that the company is able to invest money at 8%, for example, it would appear that company would be better off selling the equipment rather than leasing it. It should be noted that the tax savings would have much less impact on the decision whether to sell or lease if High-Tech Corporation Ltd. had other assets of the same class as the disposed machine. In such an instance, $40,000 would be available for investment in the first year as a result of the sale of the machine; and there would be an annual tax saving based on the annual capital cost allowance claimed on the $100,000 loss which would remain as part of the amount in the assets class.

Make or buy decisions

In many manufacturing situations, companies are often faced with decisions whether (1) to produce a certain component part required in the assembly of its finished products or (2) to buy the part from outside suppliers. If a company produces a part which can be purchased at a lower cost, it may be more profitable for the company to buy the part and utilize its productive resources for other purposes.

For example, if a company can buy a part for $5 per unit which costs the company $6 per unit to produce, the choice seems to be clearly in favor of buying. But the astute reader will quickly raise the question, "What is included in the cost of $6 per unit?" Assume that the $6 unit cost of producing 10,000 units was determined as follows:

		Cost of Part
What is the variable cost per unit for this company?	*Direct materials*	*$ 8,000*
	Direct labor	*12,500*
	Variable factory overhead	*10,000*
	Fixed factory overhead	*29,500*
	Total costs	*$60,000*
	Cost per unit ($60,000 ÷ 10,000 units)	*$6*

A careful review of operations indicates that if the production of this part were discontinued, all the cost of direct materials and direct labor and $9,000 of the variable factory overhead would be eliminated. In addition, $2,500 of the fixed factory overhead can be eliminated. These, then, are the relevant costs in producing the 10,000 parts, and we can summarize them as follows:

<table>
<tr><td rowspan="2" style="text-align:left;">*Incremental costs ($32,000) exceed the variable cost ($30,500); however, it would cost $50,000 to buy the part from outside suppliers*</td><td></td><td>**Make the Part**</td><td>**Buy the Part**</td><td>**Incremental (or Differential) Analysis**</td></tr>
<tr><td>*Manufacturing costs for 10,000 units:*</td><td></td><td></td><td></td></tr>
<tr><td></td><td>Direct materials . . . .</td><td>$ 8,000</td><td></td><td>$ 8,000</td></tr>
<tr><td></td><td>Direct labor . . . .</td><td>12,500</td><td></td><td>12,500</td></tr>
<tr><td></td><td>Variable factory overhead . . . .</td><td>10,000</td><td>$ 1,000</td><td>9,000</td></tr>
<tr><td></td><td>Fixed factory overhead . . . .</td><td>29,500</td><td>27,000</td><td>2,500</td></tr>
<tr><td></td><td>Purchase price of part, $5 per unit . . . .</td><td></td><td>50,000</td><td>(50,000)</td></tr>
<tr><td></td><td>Totals . . . .</td><td>$60,000</td><td>$78,000</td><td>$(18,000)</td></tr>
</table>

It appears that the company should continue to produce this part. The incremental cost per unit is only $3.20 [($8,000 + $12,500 + $9,000 + $2,500) ÷ 10,000 units], and it would cost the company $1.80 per unit (or $18,000) more to buy the part than it is costing to produce. If, however, in place of this particular part, the company had an opportunity to manufacture another product which would produce a contribution margin greater than $18,000, then the part should be purchased.

Note that, in the foregoing analysis, not all the variable factory overhead costs incurred in producing the part would be eliminated if the part were not produced and only $2,500 of fixed factory costs would be eliminated. We have assumed these facts in order to illustrate that not all variable costs are necessarily incremental and that *some fixed costs may be incremental* in a given situation.

Special order for a product

If a company is operating below its plant capacity, it should carefully evaluate special orders for its product. Acceptance of special orders will improve net income if the revenue from the special orders exceeds the incremental costs incurred in connection with the orders.

For example, the Sports Supply Company Ltd. estimates its production of golf balls for the coming year at 400,000 dozen, although its plant capacity is approximately 525,000 dozen golf balls per year. The company receives an order from a foreign company for 100,000 dozen golf balls to be used for sales promotion efforts. The foreign company would pay all shipping costs and wants a special imprint on the ball. The company normally sells golf balls for $6 per dozen and the foreign company's offer is for $4 per dozen. If the order is accepted, the company will have to spend $15,000 in cash to design and set up the special imprint on the golf balls. A summary of estimated results for the coming year is presented below:

	Planned Output (400,000 Dozen)	With Special Order (500,000 Dozen)	Incremental (or Differential) Analysis
Sales: $6 per dozen	$2,400,000	$2,400,000	
$4 per dozen		400,000	$400,000
Variable costs:			
$3 per dozen	(1,200,000)	(1,500,000)	(300,000)
Fixed costs	(900,000)	(900,000)	
Special imprint costs		(15,000)	(15,000)
Estimated income	$ 300,000	$ 385,000	$ 85,000

A special order is profitable if revenue from it exceeds incremental costs

The incremental (or differential) analysis illustrated above indicates that fixed costs will not change and that variable costs will remain at $3 per dozen. The special order should be accepted because it would increase income by $85,000. The **regular sales price** of $6 per dozen and the **average cost** of $5.25 per dozen without the special order [($1,200,000 + $900,000) ÷ 400,000 dozen] are both irrelevant for purposes of arriving at this decision. The price offered on the special order of $4 per dozen, the variable cost of $3 per dozen, and the out-of-pocket cost of $15,000 for the special imprint are the relevant figures.

In evaluating the merits of a special order such as the one received by the Sports Supply Company Ltd., we must give particular attention to the effect that such an order may have on the company's regular sales volume and selling prices. Obviously, it would not be wise for the Sports Supply Company Ltd. to sell 100,000 dozen golf balls to a domestic company which might try to sell the golf balls to the regular customers of Sports Supply Company Ltd. for, say, $5 per dozen.

Scrap or rebuild defective units

When units are spoiled in production, management has to decide what to do with them. Assume, for example, that 1,000 television sets which cost $40,000 to manufacture are found to be defective because of numerous faulty parts and sloppy assembly. These sets can be sold for $15,000 "as is" or they can be rebuilt and placed in good condition at an additional out-of-pocket cost of $20,000. If the sets are rebuilt, they can be sold for $52,500. Should the sets be sold or rebuilt?

If we ignore the cost already incurred in producing the sets, $40,000, the answer is readily apparent: By rebuilding the sets the company will realize $32,500 ($52,500 sales price less $20,000 cost to rebuild); if it sells the defective sets as is, it will realize only $15,000. Thus, the company would be better off by $17,500 ($32,500 − $15,000) if it rebuilt the sets, unless it can earn a greater profit by using its production facilities to manufacture other television sets. In other words, the company may find it more profitable not to waste time and effort on rebuilding defective sets when this same time and effort might generate greater profits by concentrating on regular production schedules.

The original $40,000 cost of manufacturing the sets is irrelevant; this cost is a sunk cost because it has already been incurred and cannot be changed.

VARIABLE (DIRECT) COSTING AS AN AID TO MANAGEMENT

The discussion in Chapter 25 dealing with job order and process cost systems was based on the assumption that the actual manufacturing costs incurred in any given period are assigned to the units produced of that period. Manufacturing costs (fixed and variable) were ultimately associated with the goods in process inventory, the finished goods inventory, and the goods sold. This procedure is known as **full costing** or **absorption costing.** An alternative costing assumption which can be useful to management, **variable costing** (or **direct costing**), was briefly described on page 731.

The three basic features of variable costing are:

1 All manufacturing costs are first divided into those which are variable and those which are fixed.

2 Variable manufacturing costs are treated as **product costs** and are assigned to the goods produced. Some of the goods produced are found in ending inventories (goods in process and finished goods) and the rest become a part of cost of goods sold during the current period.

3 Fixed manufacturing costs, along with all selling and administrative expenses, are treated as **period costs** and are charged to revenue of the period in which they are incurred.

The flow of costs under variable and full costing is illustrated in the diagram below:

Flow of Costs under Variable and Full Costing

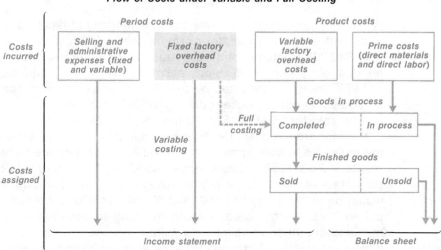

The diagram shows that selling and administrative expenses and fixed factory overhead costs are charged to revenue of the current period when variable costing is used. As a result, the Goods in Process account is charged only with variable manufacturing costs and the ending inventories of goods in process and finished goods include only variable manufacturing costs. When full costing is used, fixed factory overhead costs are treated as product costs, a portion of which is assigned to the ending inventories of goods in process and finished goods.

Illustration of variable costing

The differences between variable costing and full costing may be illustrated by preparing an income statement under each method, using the following information for the Hamilton Corporation Ltd.:

Data for Year 1

Production—Year 1 (assume no goods in process)	40,000 units
Sales—Year 1	30,000 units
Sales price per unit	$10
Variable manufacturing costs per unit	$4
Variable selling and administrative expenses per unit	$1
Fixed costs:	
Manufacturing	$40,000
Selling and administrative expenses	$30,000

A partial[3] income statement based on this information, using the variable cost assumption, appears below:

HAMILTON CORPORATION LTD.
Partial Income Statement—Variable Costing
Year 1

Fixed factory overhead costs excluded from inventory— Year 1

Sales (30,000 units @ $10).		$300,000
Cost of goods sold (30,000 units @ $4 variable manufacturing costs).		120,000
Manufacturing margin.		$180,000
Variable selling and administrative expenses (30,000 units @ $1).		30,000
Contribution margin		$150,000
Fixed costs:		
Manufacturing	$40,000	
Selling and administrative expenses	30,000	70,000
Income from operations		$ 80,000

(Ending inventory of finished goods, 10,000 units @ $4 = $40,000)

In the partial income statement using variable costing, the variable manufacturing costs of the units sold are deducted from sales in arriving at the *manufacturing margin.* When variable selling and administrative expenses are deducted from the manufacturing margin we have the *contribution margin* which is available to cover all fixed (or period) costs. Income from operations is then determined by subtracting all fixed costs from the contribution margin.

A partial income statement using the same information but following the traditional full cost assumption is presented on page 868.

[3] The income statements illustrated here are not complete because they do not include income taxes and earnings per share.

HAMILTON CORPORATION LTD.
Partial Income Statement—Full Costing
Year 1

Fixed factory overhead costs included in inventory— Year 1

Sales (30,000 units @ $10)...................................	$300,000
Cost of goods sold*.......................................	150,000
Gross profit on sales	$150,000
Selling and administrative expenses (fixed and variable).............	60,000
Income from operations	$ 90,000

* Computation of cost of goods sold:

Variable manufacturing costs (40,000 units @ $4).................	$160,000
Fixed manufacturing costs	40,000
Full cost of production (40,000 units @ $5).....................	$200,000
Less: Ending inventory of finished goods (10,000 units @ $5)...........	50,000
Cost of goods sold (30,000 units)	$150,000

Effect of variable costing on income and inventory

Comparing the partial income statements on page 867 and above shows that the income from operations using full costing exceeds by $10,000 the income using variable costing. This difference is explained by analyzing the disposition of fixed manufacturing costs under the two costing methods. Under variable costing the fixed manufacturing costs, $40,000, are recognized as expenses in the current period; under full costing, fixed manufacturing costs are apportioned between the ending inventory of finished goods and the cost of goods sold. Since only 75% of units produced were sold, only $30,000 of the fixed manufacturing costs were included in the cost of goods sold figure.

When *inventories are increasing* (that is, units produced exceed units sold), the use of variable costing will result in a smaller net income than when full costing is used because under variable costing fixed manufacturing costs are charged immediately to expense. Under full costing, fixed manufacturing costs are included in inventories. As inventories increase, some fixed costs expensed under variable costing will remain in inventories under full costing. When *inventories are decreasing* (that is, units sold exceed units produced), the income under variable costing will be larger than the income under full costing, because the decrease in inventory will be charged against revenue at less than full cost.

To illustrate one possible case (an increase in inventories), assume that the sales volume for the Hamilton Corporation Ltd. in Year 2 remained unchanged at 30,000 units at $10 per unit, and that the level of production increased to 50,000, thus increasing the ending inventory of finished goods from 10,000 units to 30,000 units. The following information is available in Year 2. *(Note that unit variable costs and total fixed costs are exactly the same as in Year 1.)*

Data for Year 2	Production—Year 2 (assume no goods in process).............	50,000 units
	Sales—Year 2.......................	30,000 units
	Sales price per unit......................	$10
	Variable manufacturing costs per unit................	$4
	Variable selling and administrative expenses per unit...........	$1
	Fixed costs:	
	Manufacturing	$40,000
	Selling and administrative expenses	$30,000

A partial income statement for Year 2, using the variable cost assumption, is illustrated below:

HAMILTON CORPORATION LTD.
Partial Income Statement—Variable Costing
Year 2

Fixed factory overhead costs excluded from inventory— Year 2	Sales (30,000 @ $10)........................		$300,000
	Cost of goods sold (30,000 units @ $4 variable manufacturing costs).....		120,000
	Manufacturing margin......................		$180,000
	Variable selling and administrative expenses (30,000 units @ $1)........		30,000
	Contribution margin......................		$150,000
	Fixed costs:		
	Manufacturing	$40,000	
	Selling and administrative expenses	30,000	70,000
	Income from operations		$ 80,000

(Ending inventory of finished goods, 30,000 units @ $4 = $120,000)

A full costing partial income statement for Year 2 appears below:

HAMILTON CORPORATION LTD.
Partial Income Statement—Full Costing
Year 2

Fixed factory overhead costs included in inventory— Year 2	Sales (30,000 @ $10)........................	$300,000
	Cost of goods sold*........................	146,000
	Gross profit on sales	$154,000
	Selling and administrative expenses (fixed and variable)...........	60,000
	Income from operations	$ 94,000

*Computation of cost of goods sold:

Beginning inventory, 10,000 units (from Year 1)	$ 50,000
Add: Variable manufacturing costs (50,000 units @ $4).	200,000
Fixed manufacturing costs, Year 2	40,000
Goods available for sale (60,000 units)	$290,000
Less: Ending inventory on fifo basis, 30,000 units @ $4.80	
($240,000 ÷ 50,000 units).	144,000
Cost of goods sold (30,000 units)	$146,000

Briefly, we can summarize the results for the two years using variable costing and full costing as follows:

Results using variable and full costing compared		Income from Operations			Ending Inventory		
		Sales	Variable Costing	Full Costing	Variable Costing	Full Costing	Difference
Year 1		$300,000	$80,000	$90,000	$ 40,000	$ 50,000	$10,000*
Year 2		300,000	80,000	94,000	120,000	144,000	24,000†

*Income for the first year was $10,000 higher under full costing because ending inventory is higher by this amount.
†Two-year income in total is $24,000 higher under full costing because cumulative ending inventory is higher by this amount.

When variable costing is used, the income from operations for Year 2 remained unchanged at $80,000—a perfectly logical result since sales volume, selling price, variable costs per unit, and fixed costs were all unchanged. Using full costing, however, the income from operations increased from $90,000 in Year 1 to $94,000 in Year 2, *despite the fact that the sales volume remained at the same level* as in Year 1. This apparently illogical result probably represents a strong argument in favor of the use of variable costing for decision-making purposes by management; *when variable costing is used, income from operations changes in concert with changes in sales volume rather than with changes in production volume.*

Proponents of variable costing also argue that fixed manufacturing costs are not a part of the cost of goods produced during a given period but are the *costs of having the capacity to produce.* They believe that fixed manufacturing costs are *period* or *capacity* costs which should be charged against the revenues of the period in which they are incurred, without regard to the level of production. Critics of variable costing, however, point out that fixed manufacturing costs *add value to the goods produced* and are no less essential in the production of goods than variable costs. They argue that a profit on the sale of any product emerges only after recovery of the total cost of bringing that product to the point of sale.

Segregating variable and fixed costs in the accounts produces data that are useful to management in studying cost-volume-earnings relationships and in arriving at decisions involving pricing, production planning, and cost control. On the other hand, exclusion of fixed manufacturing costs from inventory valuation understates the full cost of inventories and makes variable costing of doubtful validity for income measurement purposes. For this reason, *variable costing is not an accepted procedure for income determination.*[4] When variable costing is used for internal decision-making purposes, inventory costs must be restated on a full cost basis for external reporting and for income tax purposes.

Summary of advantages and disadvantages of variable costing

Some of the advantages and disadvantages generally associated with the use of variable costing procedures may be summarized as follows:

[4] American Institute of Certified Public Accountants, *Accounting Research and Terminology Bulletins,* Final Edition (New York: 1961), pp. 28–29.

Advantages	*Disadvantages*
1 Installation of a variable costing system requires a careful analysis of costs and this may result in more effective planning and cost control throughout the entire organization.	1 Financial statements prepared on the variable costing basis are not acceptable for financial reporting or income tax purposes.
2 Information needed for cost-volume-earnings analysis is readily available from statements prepared on a variable costing basis.	2 Inventories, working capital, and stockholders' equity tend to be understated when variable costing is used for financial reporting purposes.
3 Because variable and fixed costs are segregated, the variable costing income statement may be more useful to management in arriving at certain decisions.	3 Segregation of factory overhead costs into fixed and variable components is often difficult.
4 Since fixed costs are not allocated to departments or products under variable costing, it is easier for management to determine the contribution margin on product lines and sales territories.	4 Exclusion of fixed factory overhead costs from inventory tends to make long-run pricing decisions less effective because prices may be set at a level sufficient to recover the variable costs but not all the fixed costs. Net income can only result after all costs are recovered.
5 Operating income under variable costing will generally increase when sales increase and decreases when sales decrease; this may not be true when full costing is used.	

Concluding comments

The information needed by managers is sometimes significantly different from that collected in the ordinary processes of financial accounting. Managers are primarily concerned with the possible outcomes of future courses of action. This means that they must have reliable estimates of costs which will be incurred and revenue which will be earned as a result of a business decision. Effective decision making generally includes the following steps:

1 A clear definition of the problem or proposed action is prepared, and the relevant information (both quantitative and subjective) is gathered.

2 The decision is made and the actions and resources required to carry out the decision are spelled out.

3 A feedback system is designed which will evaluate the decision against actual results.

Although managers are responsible for making decisions, accountants provide inputs needed to implement each of these steps. Examples of business decisions which would not require some form of accounting information are not easy to find.

Obviously we have merely scratched the surface in discussing the possible kinds of analyses that might be prepared in making decisions. The brief treatment in this chapter, however, has been sufficient to establish the basic principles that lie behind such analyses. The most profitable course of action is determined by studying the costs, revenues, and investments that are incremental to the particular alternatives under consideration. The relevant information is often difficult to obtain and always involves making estimates about the future. As a result, such information is generally subject to some degree of error. Finally, there are always important intangible factors that defy quantification which should be brought into the decision picture only after the quantitative analysis has been made.

QUESTIONS

1 What characteristics should reports submitted to management have in order to be most effective?

2 Give three examples of reports that management may find helpful in controlling day-to-day activities.

3 What are the three areas of managerial activity where quantitative information may be useful?

4 Differentiate between *marginal* and *incremental costs.* Are *differential costs* more like marginal costs or incremental costs?

5 What is the difference between a *sunk cost* and an *out-of-pocket cost?*

6 Define *opportunity costs* and explain why they represent a common source of error in making cost analyses.

7 The Perfidy Manufacturing Company Ltd. produced 1,000 units at a total cost of $80,000, including $25,000 of depreciation and amortization of patents. These units are on hand at the end of the accounting period. Did the company's working capital increase or decrease as a result of producing these units and by how much?

8 List the four steps that may be followed in arriving at a solution of an alternative-choice problem.

9 Briefly discuss the type of information you would want before deciding to discontinue the production of a major line of products.

10 Explain why the book value of existing equipment is not relevant in deciding whether the equipment should be scrapped (without realizing any proceeds) or continued in use.

11 The Calcutta Corporation Ltd. produces a large number of products. The costs per unit of one of its products, Maxad, is shown below:

Prime costs (direct materials and direct labor)	$7.00
Variable factory overhead	4.00
Fixed factory overhead	2.00

The company recently decided to buy 10,000 Maxads from another manufacturer for $12.50 per unit because "it was cheaper than our cost of $13.00 per unit." Evaluate the decision only on the basis of the cost data given.

12 A company regularly sells 100,000 washing machines at an average price of $250. The average cost of producing these machines is $180. Under what circumstances might the company accept an order for 20,000 washing machines at $175 per machine?

13 List the three basic features of *variable (direct) costing.*

14 During the current year the inventory of finished product of a manufacturing firm declined. In which case would the company's reported income be larger: if it used variable costing, or if it used full costing? Explain your reasoning.

15 The Bombay Company Ltd. reports an amount labeled *manufacturing margin* in its income statement. The income statement is stamped "for management's use only." Explain what is meant by "manufacturing margin" and why the income statement containing this term is not issued to outsiders.

16 List three advantages and three disadvantages of using variable (direct) costing.

17 List the three characteristics of effective decision making.

18 Comment on the following position taken by a business executive: "Since relevant quantitative information is difficult to obtain and is subject to some degree of error, I'd rather make decisions on the basis of subjective factors and my many years of business experience."

EXERCISES

Ex. 28-1 The controller of Conglom Ltd., presents the following statement (in thousands of dollars) to the president and suggests that the Hat Division be eliminated:

	All Other Divisions	Hat Division	Total
Sales	$100,000	$ 5,000	$105,000
Cost of goods sold:			
Variable	(35,000)	(3,000)	(38,000)
Fixed	(10,000)	(1,000)	(11,000)
Gross profit on sales	$ 55,000	$ 1,000	$ 56,000
Operating expenses:			
Variable	(25,000)	(1,500)	(26,500)
Fixed	(15,000)	(2,000)	(17,000)
Income or (loss)	$ 15,000	$(2,500)	$ 12,500

Do you agree with the controller? Prepare a schedule in support of your answer. You may assume that fixed costs and expenses would not be affected by the elimination of the Hat Division.

Ex. 28-2 The Ruppert Corporation Ltd. is considering the replacement of machine A with machine B. Information relating to the two machines follows:

	Machine A	Machine B
Cost	$60,000	$75,000
Accumulated depreciation	30,000	—
Current scrap value	10,000	—
Estimated annual cost savings if machine B is purchased .	—	20,500
Remaining years of useful life	3 years	3 years

Prepare an analysis over a three-year period which shows the advantage or disadvantage that would accrue to the Ruppert Corporation Ltd. if machine B is purchased. Ignore income taxes and the time value of money.

Ex. 28-3 The Ceramic Toys Company Ltd. sells 600,000 widgets per year at $3.00 each. The current unit cost of the widgets is broken down as follows:

Direct materials	$0.50
Direct labor.	0.90
Variable factory overhead	0.20
Fixed factory overhead.	0.40
Total	$2.00

At the beginning of the current year the company receives a special order for 10,000 widgets per month *for one year only* at $1.80 per unit. A new machine with an estimated life of five years would have to be purchased for $10,000 to produce the additional widgets. Management thinks that it will not be able to use the new machine beyond one year and that it will have to be sold for approximately $6,500. Compute the estimated gain or loss that the company would realize if the special order is accepted.

Ex. 28-4 Brass & Metal, Ltd., has 20,000 units of a defective product on hand which cost $36,000 to manufacture. The company can either sell this product as scrap for $0.90 per unit or it can sell the product for $3.50 per unit by reworking the units and correcting the defects at a cost of $22,000. What should the company do? Prepare a schedule in support of your recommendation.

Ex. 28-5 It costs $60,000 (fixed and variable) to produce 10,000 units of part A. Fixed factory overhead is 50% of total variable costs. The company can buy the part from an outside supplier for $4.50 per unit, although the regular price of the part is $5.75 per unit. If the company buys the part, the fixed factory overhead now allocated to the part will remain unchanged, and another product would be produced which would bring in $12,000 of contribution margin. Should the company buy the part or continue to manufacture it? Prepare a comparative schedule in good form.

Ex. 28-6 Given below is sales and cost information for Year 1 relating to two products manufactured by Ecological Products Corporation Ltd.

	Purifier	*Analyzer*
Sales	$300,000	$600,000
Variable manufacturing costs (% of sales)	40%	55%
Variable operating expenses traceable to each product	$ 50,000	$ 80,000
Fixed costs and expenses directly traceable to each product .	30,000	145,000
Fixed costs and expenses not directly traceable to products		
($120,000).	?	?

Which product is more profitable? In arriving at your answer, compute the total contribution margin and the amount of the common fixed costs of $120,000 defrayed by each product.

Ex. 28-7 Given below are the production and sales data for the Motown Corporation Ltd. at the end of its first year of operations:

Sales (6,000 units × $11)	$66,000
Production costs (10,000 units):	
Variable	50,000
Fixed	30,000
Selling and administrative expenses (all fixed).	10,000

Compute income from operations for the year using (*a*) full costing and (*b*) variable costing.

PROBLEMS

Group A

28A-1 The Space Metals Company Ltd. manufactures a single product and has a normal capacity of 100,000 units per year. Variable manufacturing costs are $6 per unit. Fixed factory overhead is $200,000 per year. Variable selling and administrative expenses are $3 per unit and fixed selling and administrative expenses are $150,000 per year. The unit sales price is $15.

The operating results for Year 1 are sales, 80,000 units, and production, 100,000 units. The beginning inventory amounted to 10,000 units at a total cost of $80,000, including $20,000 of fixed manufacturing costs.

Instructions
a Prepare formal income statements (through income from operations) for Year 1 using:
  (*1*) Variable (direct) costing
  (*2*) Full costing
b Briefly explain the difference in the income from operations between the two income statements.

28A-2 The directors of the Dilemma Corporation Ltd. have been studying the income statements for 1973 and 1974 in which pretax income (income from operations) of $65,000 and $55,000 are shown. The directors do not understand how income could decrease by $10,000 when sales increased by 50%. The cost accountant explains that underapplied fixed factory overhead of $60,000 was charged to 1974 operations because the plant worked at only 66 $\frac{2}{3}$% of normal capacity. His income statement was based on the following information:

	1974	1973
Sales ($16 per unit)	$480,000	$320,000
Total fixed factory overhead	180,000	180,000
Selling and administrative expenses (all fixed)	35,000	35,000
Inventory of finished goods (10,000 units at standard cost)	None	110,000
Unit-cost information (at standard):		
Variable manufacturing cost	$5	$5
Fixed factory overhead	6	6

In 1974, the plant produced 20,000; in 1973, a total of 30,000 units were produced. There was no inventory of finished goods at the beginning of 1973.

Instructions
a Prepare a comparative income statement for the two years using full (absorption) costing. Inventory should be valued at standard cost and the idle capacity cost of $60,000 should be added to the cost of goods sold.
b Prepare a comparative income statement for the two years using variable (direct) costing.
c Comment on the results obtained in parts (*a*) and (*b*).

28A-3 The owner of Opportunity Wholesalers presents you with the comparison of the performance for two salesmen who are paid a commission of 6% of gross sales:

	Jacob	Stan
Gross sales	$425,000	$205,000
Sales returns	25,000	5,000
Cost of goods sold, excluding returns	280,000	120,000

Reimbursed entertainment and other direct expenses	$ 7,500	$ 3,000
Samples distributed	6,200	1,100
Allocated indirect expenses	5,000	2,500

Both salesmen handle similar products in comparable territories in different parts of Alberta. Each is given authority to offer discounts to customers within broad guidelines established by the owner.

Instructions

a Compute the contribution margin generated by each salesman (after commissions) and compute the percentage that the contribution margin generated by each salesman bears to net sales.

b What percentage of contribution margin (before commissions) is paid out to each salesman in the form of commissions?

c Briefly evaluate the relative performance of the two salesmen and suggest possible reasons why Jacob's performance may be viewed as favorable or unfavorable from the owner's standpoint.

28A-4 Management of Farm Equipment Company Ltd. has asked for your assistance in arriving at a decision whether to continue manufacturing a small motor called Motora or to buy it from an outside supplier. The Motora is used by the Farm Equipment Company Ltd. in assembling a line of spraying and pruning equipment.

Your investigation yields the following data as being typical of the company's operations:

(1) The annual requirement for Motoras is 6,000 units. The lowest bid received from an outside supplier is for a price of $10.50 per unit.

(2) Motoras have been manufactured by the Farm Equipment Company Ltd. in its machine shop. If Motoras are purchased from an outside supplier, certain machinery will be sold at book value.

(3) Following are the total costs of the machine shop during the year when 6,000 Motoras were manufactured:

Direct materials	$80,000
Direct labor	60,000
Indirect labor	40,000
Heat, light and power	9,000
Depreciation on building and machinery	10,000
Property taxes and insurance	8,000
Payroll taxes and other fringe benefits—15% of total labor costs	15,000
Other factory overhead costs	4,800

(4) The following costs of the machine shop were directly identified with the production of Motoras: direct materials, $30,000; direct labor, $27,000; indirect labor, $10,000; power, $400; other factory overhead costs, $800. The sale of the equipment in the manufacture of Motoras would reduce the fixed factory overhead by $2,000 for depreciation and $300 for property taxes and insurance.

(5) The following additional costs would be incurred if Motoras were purchased from an outside supplier: freight, $0.50 per unit; indirect labor for receiving, handling, and inspection (before payroll taxes and fringe benefits), $2,200.

Instructions Prepare a schedule showing whether Motoras should continue to be manufactured by the Farm Equipment Company Ltd. or should be purchased from an outside supplier.

28A-5 You have been asked to assist the management of the Southern Corporation Ltd. in arriving at certain decisions. The corporation has its home office in

Toronto and leases plant facilities in Kingston and Windsor. The same product is manufactured in both plants. Given below is the summary of operating results for the latest fiscal year:

	Total	Kingston	Windsor
Sales	$900,000	$600,000	$300,000
Fixed costs:			
Factory overhead	$200,000	$125,000	$ 75,000
General and administrative	66,000	41,000	25,000
Variable factory overhead and other costs . .	480,000	300,000	180,000
Allocated home office expenses	54,000	36,000	18,000
Total.	$800,000	$502,000	$298,000
Income from operations	$100,000	$ 98,000	$ 2,000

Home office expenses are allocated on the basis of units sold. The sales price is $10 per unit sold.

Management is undecided whether to renew the lease of the Windsor plant, which expires in a few months and calls for a rental increase of $15,000 per year if renewed.

If the Windsor plant is shut down, the Southern Corporation Ltd. can continue to serve customers of the Windsor plant in one of the following alternative ways:

(1) Expand the Kingston plant at an estimated cost of $50,000. This would increase the fixed factory overhead (including depreciation) of the Kingston plant by 20%. Assume that there would be no change in general and administrative expenses. Additional shipping expense of $2 per unit will be incurred in shipping the increased production of the Kingston plant to customers. Variable factory overhead and other costs at the Kingston plant would remain unchanged at $5 per unit ($300,000 ÷ 60,000).

(2) Enter into a long-term contract with Ginn & Co. to serve the customers of the Windsor plant in return for a royalty of $1.25 per unit sold.

Under either of these alternatives, the total amount of home office expenses incurred by the Southern Corporation Ltd. would not change.

Instructions
a Prepare a schedule showing the total estimated annual income from operations for the Southern Corporation Ltd. under each of the following alternatives:
(1) Close the Windsor plant and expand the Kingston plant.
(2) Close the Windsor plant and sign a long-term contract calling for a royalty of $1.25 per unit to be paid to the Southern Corporation Ltd. on sales made by Ginn & Co. Ltd. to former customers of the Windsor plant.
b Comment on the relative merits of renewing the lease, expanding the Kingston plant, or entering into a long-term royalty contract with Ginn & Co. Ltd.

Group B

28B-1 A partial income statement for the New Brunswick Distilling Corporation Ltd. for the first year of its operations prepared in conventional (full costing) form is shown on page 878.

Instructions
a Revise the statement using the variable (direct) costing approach. Briefly explain the difference in the income from operations reported in the two statements.
b Prepare a schedule showing whether it would be profitable for the New Brunswick Distilling Corporation Ltd. to accept an offer from a foreign customer to

Income Statement
For First Year of Operations (in Thousands)

Sales (100,000 units at $100 per unit)		$10,000
Cost of goods sold:		
Direct material	$3,500	
Direct labor	2,750	
Variable factory overhead	250	
Fixed factory overhead	2,000	
Total manufacturing costs	$8,500	
Less: Ending finished goods inventory (25,000 units)	1,700	
Cost of goods sold ($68 per unit)		6,800
Gross profit on sales		$ 3,200
Less: Operating expenses:		
Variable	$1,000	
Fixed	1,200	
Total operating expenses		2,200
Income from operations		$ 1,000

purchase 25,000 units for $60 per unit. This special order would have no effect on fixed factory overhead or on operating expenses.

28B-2 At the beginning of the current year, the Afro Manufacturing Company Ltd. opened its Benton plant to manufacture and assemble a special picnic kit. During the year the Benton Plant sold 50,000 picnic kits at an average price of $6 per unit. At the end of the year, there were 10,000 finished picnic kits on hand. There was no goods in process inventory at the end of the year. During the year the Benton Plant reported the following costs charged to the Goods in Process account:

Direct materials	$90,000
Direct labor	72,000
Variable factory overhead	30,000
Fixed factory overhead	60,000

Operating expenses for the year are analyzed below:

	Fixed	Variable (per Unit Sold)
Selling expenses	$30,000	$0.45
Administrative expenses	20,000	0.20

The plant manager prepared an income statement for the current year showing an income from operations for the plant of $7,500, based on a full costing assumption. The company controller, who is an advocate of variable costing, insists that on a variable costing basis the plant did not cover the fixed costs incurred for the year.

Instructions
a Prepare an income statement under the full (absorption) costing assumption as it must have been made by the plant manager.
b Prepare an income statement such as the controller had in mind, using the variable (direct) costing assumption.

28B-3 Plaza Leasing Company Ltd. owns a downtown office building, and is considering the installation of certain concessions in the main lobby. If the company operates the concessions for its own account, the following annual costs and revenue may be expected:

Cost of goods sold	$58,000
Salaries	15,000
Licenses and payroll taxes	1,300
Share of heating and lighting expense which would be allocated to the concessions	700
Pro rata building depreciation and maintenance	1,600
Concession advertising ($100 per month)	1,200
Share of administrative expense which would be allocated to the concessions	1,800
Estimated net sales (all on cash basis)	80,000

The investment in display equipment for the concessions would be $5,000; the display equipment would be depreciated on a straight-line basis over a 10-year period. The average inventory of concession merchandise would have a cost of approximately $3,500.

As an alternative, a local businessman offered to lease the space in the lobby for $1,500 per year for 10 years. He would install and operate concessions similar to those planned by Plaza Leasing Company Ltd. at no out-of-pocket cost to Plaza Leasing Company Ltd., except that heating and lighting would be furnished by the office building at no additional charge to the businessman.

Instructions Prepare a schedule of estimated annual results supporting your recommendation whether Plaza Leasing Company Ltd. should lease the concession to the businessman or operate the concession for its own account. If you recommend that the company operate the concession, indicate the approximate rate of return that it would realize on the average investment in concession equipment and inventory. You may assume that the average investment in the display equipment over the 10-year period would be $2,500, the average book value of the equipment.

28B-4 The Heavy Equipment Company Ltd. requests your assistance in deciding whether it should continue to manufacture GAMS or whether it should purchase this part. The annual requirement for GAMS is 5,000 units and the part is currently available from Axel Corporation Ltd. at $7.00 per unit.

The following information is available for your consideration:

(1) If GAMS were purchased, some of the machinery used to produce GAMS would be used to help out in the production of other products now being manufactured and some of the machinery would be idle for the time being because it has no current resale value. The machinery used to produce GAMS cost $20,000, has a book value of $9,000, and has a remaining life of five years (no residual value) based on the existing depreciation schedule. Property taxes and insurance on this machinery amount to $400 per year.

(2) The company has devoted approximately 10% of its factory capacity to the production of GAMS. Direct material and labor costs could be reduced without affecting other operations if GAMS were purchased.

(3) During the latest year, in which 5,000 GAMS were produced, the total factory costs and the portion of these costs allocated to GAMS were as follows:

	Total Factory Costs	Costs Allocated to GAMS
Direct materials	$ 90,000	$18,400
Direct labor (including payroll taxes)	100,000	13,000
Indirect labor (including payroll taxes)	30,000	3,000

Heat and light (allocated on basis of capacity devoted to		
production of GAMS)	$ 10,000	$?
Depreciation (straight-line method)	28,000	3,200
Property taxes and insurance	12,000	1,200
Factory supplies used.	6,000	1,000
Total	$276,000	$?

(4) Direct materials, direct labor, and factory supplies used may be considered variable costs. One-half of the indirect labor cost allocated to GAMS is variable and the other one-half is fixed; all other costs are completely fixed.

(5) If GAMS were purchased, the Heavy Equipment Company Ltd. would incur added costs of $0.40 per unit for freight and $800 per year for receiving, handling, and inspection.

Instructions

a Prepare a three-column schedule showing (1) the total annual cost now allocated to GAMS, (2) the annual *incremental* cost that has been incurred in producing GAMS, and (3) the estimated annual cost of purchasing GAMS from the Axel Corporation Ltd.

b **List** some other factors that management of the Heavy Equipment Company Ltd. should take into account in arriving at a decision whether to purchase GAMS or continue to manufacture them. **You need not discuss the factors listed.**

28B-5 The Valley Mfg. Company Ltd. produces an agricultural tool called Disc-X which has a stable selling price of $35.00 per unit. It has been operating for many months at 50% of its operating capacity and has sold its entire production of 80,000 units per month. The head of the sales department presents the following two alternatives to management:

Alternative A An exporter has offered to buy 60,000 units of Disc-X per month for at least a two-year period at $25.00 per unit. These units would be sold outside of the company's regular sales territory and would not reduce the current sales volume. No costs other than manufacturing costs would be incurred on this special order.

Alternative B The company's advertising agency advises that sales volume can be increased from the current level of 80,000 units per month to a level of 140,000 units per month. In order to achieve this volume, however, the sales price must be reduced from $35 to $30 per unit, and $150,000 must be spent on special promotional advertising each month. Variable selling and administrative expenses would remain unchanged at $2.25 per unit.

You are asked to assist the board of directors to evaluate these two proposals. The accounting staff of the company has accumulated the following information for the latest month:

	Standard Costs per Unit	Actual Costs per Unit
Unit manufacturing costs:		
Direct materials	$15.20	$14.00
Direct labor.	4.80	5.30
Factory overhead	6.00	8.65
Total unit manufacturing costs	$26.00	$27.95

Factory overhead incurred:	
Fixed ($5.00 per unit)	$400,000
Variable ($3.65 per unit)	292,000
Selling and administrative expenses (40% of which are fixed)	300,000

Actual unit costs for direct materials, direct labor, and variable factory overhead are not expected to change significantly during the next two years.

Instructions

a Prepare a statement showing probable monthly income from operations under each of the two proposals compared to the income from operations earned in the current month. Disregard income taxes, and assume that the entire monthly production will be sold. Use the following three column headings for your statement: Current Month, Alternative A, and Alternative B.

b Reconcile the difference between the income from operations that would be attained under Alternative B and the actual income from operations for the current month. Use the following format:

Loss of contribution margin on existing sales as a result of price		
reduction: 80,000 × $5.00 ($35.00 − $30.00)	$	?
Special promotional advertising		?
Total reduction in income from operations	$	?
Increase in contribution margin from sale of additional units:		
60,000 × $4.80 ($30.00 − $25.20 total variable costs)		?
Net decrease in income from operations if Alternative B is adopted . . .	$	?

BUSINESS DECISION PROBLEM 28

The Innovative Gadget Company Ltd. is engaged in manufacturing a breakfast cereal. You are asked to advise management on sales policy for the coming year.

Two proposals are being considered by management which will (*1*) increase the volume of sales, (*2*) reduce the ratio of selling expense to sales, and (*3*) decrease manufacturing cost per unit. These proposals are as follows:

Proposal no. 1: increase advertising expenditures by offering premium stamps
It is proposed that each package of cereal will contain premium stamps which will be redeemed for cash prizes. The estimated cost of this premium plan for a sales volume of over 500,000 boxes is estimated at $60 per 1,000 boxes sold. The new advertising plan will take the place of all existing advertising expenditures and the current selling price of 70 cents per unit will be maintained.

Proposal no. 2: reduce selling price of product
It is proposed that the selling price of the cereal be reduced by 5% and that advertising expenditures be increased over those of the current year. This plan is an alternative to Proposal No. 1, and only one will be adopted by management.

Management has provided you with the following information as to the current year's operations:

Quantity sold	*500,000 boxes*
Selling price per unit	*$0.70*
Manufacturing cost per unit	*$0.40*
Selling expenses, 20% of sales (one-fourth of which was	
for newspaper advertising)	
Administrative expenses, 6% of sales	

Estimates for the coming year for each proposal are shown on page 882.

	Proposal No. 1	Proposal No. 2
Increase in unit sales volume	50%	30%
Decrease in manufacturing cost per unit	10%	5%
Newspaper advertising	None	10% of sales
Other selling expenses	8% of sales	8% of sales
Premium plan expense	$.06 per box	None
Administrative expenses	5% of sales	10% of sales

Instructions Which of the two proposals should management select? In support of your recommendation prepare a statement comparing the income from operations for the current year with the anticipated income from operations for the coming year under Proposal No. 1 and under Proposal No. 2. In preparing the statement use the following column headings: Current Year, Proposal No. 1, and Proposal No. 2.

SOLUTIONS TO
DEMONSTRATION
PROBLEMS

Chapter 1

WILSON COMPANY

a

WILSON COMPANY
Balance Sheet
September 30, 19___

Assets		Liabilities & Owner's Equity	
Cash	$ 8,500	Liabilities:	
Notes receivable	1,400	Notes payable	$35,000
Accounts receivable	16,400	Accounts payable	18,100
Land	24,000	Total liabilities	$53,100
Building	39,200	Owner's equity:	
Office equipment	4,800	Ralph Wilson, capital	44,200
Delivery truck	3,000		
	$97,300		$97,300

b

WILSON COMPANY
Balance Sheet
October 1, 19___

Assets		Liabilities & Owner's Equity	
Cash	$ 5,500	Liabilities:	
Notes receivable	7,400	Notes payable	$35,000
Accounts receivable	16,400	Accounts payable	11,100
Land	18,000	Total liabilities	$46,100
Building	39,200	Owner's equity:	
Office equipment	5,800	Ralph Wilson, capital	49,200
Delivery truck	3,000		
	$95,300		$95,300

Chapter 2

DRILL COMPANY

a   General Journal   *Page 1*

Date		Account Titles and Explanations	LP	Debit	Credit
19___					
July	1	Cash	1	50,000	
		Howard Drill, Capital	50		50,000
		Howard Drill opened a bank account in the name of the business by making a deposit of his personal funds.			
	2	Land	20	30,000	
		Cash	1		10,000
		Notes Payable	30		20,000
		Purchased land. Paid one-third cash and issued a note payable for the balance.			
	5	Building	22	12,000	
		Cash	1		12,000
		Purchased a small portable building for cash. The price included installation on Drill Company's lot.			
	12	Office Equipment.................	25	2,500	
		Accounts Payable	32		2,500
		Purchased office equipment on credit from Suzuki & Co. Ltd.			
	28	Accounts Payable	32	1,000	
		Cash	1		1,000
		Paid part of account payable to Suzuki & Co. Ltd.			

b

Cash
Account No. 1

Date	Explanation	Ref	Debit	Credit	Balance
19— July 1		1	50 000 00		50 000 00
2		1		10 000 00	40 000 00
5		1		12 000 00	28 000 00
28		1		1 000 00	27 000 00

Land
Account No. 20

Date	Explanation	Ref	Debit	Credit	Balance
19— July 2		1	30 000 00		30 000 00

Building
Account No. 22

Date	Explanation	Ref	Debit	Credit	Balance
19— July 5		1	12 000 00		12 000 00

Office Equipment
Account No. 25

Date	Explanation	Ref	Debit	Credit	Balance
19— July 12		1	2 500 00		2 500 00

Notes Payable
Account No. 30

Date	Explanation	Ref	Debit	Credit	Balance
19— July 2		1		20 000 00	20 000 00

Accounts Payable
Account No. 32

Date	Explanation	Ref	Debit	Credit	Balance
19— July 12		1		2 500 00	2 500 00
28		1	1 000 00		1 500 00

Howard Drill, Capital Account No. *50*

Date	Explanation	Ref	Debit	Credit	Balance
19— July /		/		50 000 00	50 000 00

c

DRILL COMPANY
Trial Balance
July 31, 19____

Cash	$27,000	
Land	30,000	
Building	12,000	
Office equipment	2,500	
Notes payable		$20,000
Accounts payable		1,500
Howard Drill, capital		50,000
	$71,500	$71,500

Chapter 3

LANE INSURANCE AGENCY

a Adjusting journal entry:

Depreciation Expense: Office Equipment *50*

    Accumulated Depreciation: Office Equipment *50*

To record depreciation for June ($6,000 ÷ 120).

b

LANE INSURANCE AGENCY
Adjusted Trial Balance
June 30, 19___

Cash	$ 1,275	
Accounts receivable	605	
Office equipment	6,000	
Accumulated depreciation: office equipment		$ 150
Accounts payable		1,260
Richard Lane, capital		6,500
Richard Lane, drawing	1,000	
Commissions earned		3,710
Advertising expense	500	
Rent expense	370	
Telephone expense	120	
Salaries expense	1,700	
Depreciation expense: office equipment	50	
	$11,620	$11,620

c

LANE INSURANCE AGENCY
Income Statement
For the Month Ended June 30, 19___

Commissions earned		$3,710
Expenses:		
Advertising expense	$ 500	
Rent expense	370	
Telephone expense	120	
Salaries expense	1,700	
Depreciation expense: office equipment	50	2,740
Net income		$ 970

LANE INSURANCE AGENCY
Balance Sheet
June 30, 19___

Assets

Cash		*$1,275*
Accounts receivable		605
Office equipment	*$6,000*	
Less: Accumulated depreciation	150	5,850
		$7,730

Liabilities & Owner's Equity

Liabilities:		
Accounts payable		*$1,260*
Owner's equity:		
Richard Lane, capital, May 31, 19___	*$6,500*	
Net income for June	970	
Subtotal	*$7,470*	
Less: Withdrawals	1,000	
Richard Lane, capital, June 30, 19___		6,470
		$7,730

Chapter 9

BART CORPORATION LTD.

a
Journal

Date		Account Titles and Explanations	LP	Debit	Credit
1974					
Jan.	3	Notes Receivable		5,040.00	
		Accounts Receivable, A. B. Cole			5,040.00
		Received a 30-day, 5% note from A. B. Cole in settlement of his account.			
	14	Cash		3,000.00	
		Notes Receivable		4,600.00	
		Accounts Receivable, M. E. White			7,600.00
		Received cash and 60-day, 4% note in full settlement of M. E. White account.			
	23	Cash		157.80	
		Notes Receivable		20,000.00	
		Notes Receivable			20,000.00
		Interest Earned......................			157.80
		Received 30-day, 6% note from R. K. Rogers renewing old note and cheque to cover interest to date.			
	27	Cash		5,054.02	
		Notes Receivable			5,040.00
		Interest Earned......................			14.02
		Discounted the A. B. Cole note @ 7%. Proceeds computed as follows:			
		Maturity value $5,062.78			
		Discount ($5,062.78 × 0.07 × $\frac{9}{365}$) 8.76			
		Proceeds $5,054.02			
	30	Cash		1,590.00	
		Unearned Interest		90.00	
		Installment Contracts Receivable..........			1,590.00
		Interest Earned......................			90.00
		To record collection of monthly payment on L. D. Harris contract and record earned interest income. Original amount of contract was 12 × $1,590 monthly payments, or $19,080, which included 6% interest charge. ($19,080 ÷ 1.06 = $18,000 principal amount; interest = $19,080 ÷ $18,000 = $1,080.) Equal monthly amounts for interest would therefore be $1,080 ÷ 12 = $90.			

Date		Account Titles and Explanations	LP	Debit	Credit
1974		*Adjusting Entries*			
Jan.	*31*	**Accrued Interest Receivable**		*75.31*	
		Interest Earned			*75.31*
		To record accrued interest on notes as follows:			
		White note ($4,600 × .04 × $\frac{17}{365}$) = $ 8.57			
		Rogers note ($20,000 × .06 × $\frac{11}{365}$) = 36.16			
		King note ($8,000[3] × .045 × $\frac{31}{365}$) = 30.58			
		$75.31			

b

BART CORPORATION LTD.

Partial Balance Sheet

January 31, 1974

Current assets:

Accounts receivable		*$17,200.00*
*Notes receivable**		*32,600.00*
Installment contracts receivable	*$9,540.00*	
Less: Unearned interest	*540.00*	*9,000.00*
Accrued interest receivable		*75.31*
Total current assets		*$58,875.31*

*On Jan. 31, 1974, the company was contingently liable on a note receivable discounted in the amount of $5,040.

Chapter 15

BISON COMPANY LTD.

a The difficulty stems from the fact that the partnership agreement does not clearly specify the agreed meaning of the term *invested capital.* Since Partner B has added capital during the year while Partner S has withdrawn capital, neither the capital at the beginning nor that at the end of the year is representative of their investment throughout the year. A reasonable decision would be to compute the "investment allowance" by taking 20% of a weighted average of capital invested throughout the year. An average daily capital could be computed, but for the purpose at hand an average by months is sufficiently precise. The partnership agreement should be amended to specify the meaning of the term *invested capital* that the partners intend to apply in future years.

b Journal entries to complete closing as of Dec. 31:

Income Summary	*19,800*	
B, *Capital*		*9,000*
S, *Capital*		*10,800*

To credit each partner with salary allowance.

Income Summary	*21,500*	
B, *Capital*		*11,700*
S, *Capital*		*9,800*

To credit each partner with allowance of 20% on average capital, computed as follows:

B: *Dollar-months*

$54,000 invested for 10 months . . .	*$540,000*
$81,000 invested for 2 months	*162,000*
Total dollar-months invested	*$702,000*
Average investment (divide by 12) .	*$ 58,500*
20% of average investment	*$ 11,700*

S:

$54,000 invested for 7 months	*$378,000*
$42,000 invested for 5 months	*210,000*
Total dollar-months invested	*$588,000*
Average investment (divide by 12) .	*$ 49,000*
20% of average investment	*$ 9,800*

B, Capital	*1,650*	
S, Capital	*1,650*	
Income Summary		*3,300*

To divide excess of salary and interest allowances over
income among partners equally:

Salaries	*$19,800*
Interest on capital .	*21,500*
Total	*$41,300*
Income for year . .	*38,000*
Excess	*$ 3,300*

B, Capital	*9,000*	
S, Capital	*10,800*	
B, Drawing		*9,000*
S, Drawing		*10,800*

To close partners' drawing accounts.

Chapter 17

MATHEWSON CORPORATION LTD.

a

MATHEWSON CORPORATION LTD.
Stockholders' Equity
December 31, 1974

Common stock, par value $60, issued 12,000*	$ 720,000
Premium on common stock	134,000
Retained earnings†	166,000
Total stockholders' equity‡	$1,020,000

*24,000 shares issued after stock split of 2 for 1. 24,000 ÷ 2 = 12,000 shares issued before stock split.
† $1,020,000 − (common stock and contributed surplus) $854,000 = $166,000
‡ 12,000 shares × $85 = $1,020,000

b

MATHEWSON CORPORATION LTD.
Stockholders' Equity
December 31, 1973

Common stock, par value $60, issued 10,000*	$ 600,000
Additional paid-in capital†	100,000
Retained earnings‡	300,000
Total stockholders' equity§	$1,000,000

*12,000 ÷ 120% = 10,000 shares issued before 20% stock dividend.
† Amount capitalized per share on 2,000-share stock dividend = $77 (market value).

Premium on common stock at Dec. 31, 1974	$134,000
Increase in Premium on common stock (77 − $60 × 2,000)	34,000
Premium on common stock at Dec. 31, 1973	$100,000

‡ $1,000,000 − common stock plus total premium $700,000 = $300,000
§ 10,000 shares × $100 = $1,000,000

c Computation of net income:

	1973	1974	1975
Retained earnings at end of year	$300,000	$166,000	$240,000
Add back:			
Cash dividends: *1973: 10,000 × $1.40 .	14,000		
1974: 12,000 × $1.50 .		18,000	
1975: 24,000 × $1.00 .			24,000
Stock dividend ($77 × 2,000)		154,000	
Retained earnings at end of year			
(before dividends)	$314,000	$338,000	$264,000
Retained earnings at beginning of year ...	280,000	300,000	166,000
Net income for year	$ 34,000	$ 38,000	$ 98,000

* Cash dividends per share:

	Shares Owned by Sydney	Dividends Received by Sydney	Dividends Paid per Share
Dec. 31, 1973	200	$280	$1.40
Dec. 31, 1974	240	360	1.50
Dec. 31, 1975	480	480	1.00

Chapter 21

KNIGHT COMPANY LTD.

	Year 2	Year 1
(1) Quick ratio:		
$126,000 ÷ $145,000	.9 to 1	
$115,000 ÷ $71,000		1.6 to 1
(2) Current ratio:		
$290,000 ÷ $145,000	2 to 1	
$260,000 ÷ $71,000		3.7 to 1
(3) Equity ratio:		
$571,400 ÷ $1,000,000	57%	
$445,000 ÷ $800,000		56%
(4) Debt ratio:		
$428,600 ÷ $1,000,000	43%	
$355,000 ÷ $800,000		44%
(5) Book value per share of stock:		
$571,400 ÷ 33,000 shares	$17.32	
$445,000 ÷ 33,000 shares		$13.48
(6) Earnings per share (including extraordinary item):		
$166,400 ÷ 33,000 shares	$5.04	
$80,000 ÷ 33,000* shares		$2.42
(7) Price-earnings ratio:		
$86 ÷ $5.04	17 times	
$43.50 ÷ 1.5* = $29, adjusted price. $29 ÷ $2.42 . .		12 times
(8) Gross profit percentage:		
$594,000 ÷ $2,200,000	27%	
$480,000 ÷ $1,600,000		30%
(9) Operating expense ratio:		
$330,000 ÷ $2,200,000	15%	
$352,000 ÷ $1,600,000		22%
(10) Income before extraordinary item as a percentage of net sales:		
$154,000 ÷ $2,200,000	7%	
$ 80,000 ÷ $1,600,000		5%
(11) Inventory turnover:		
$1,606,000 ÷ $150,000	10.7 times	
$1,120,000 ÷ $150,000		7.5 times
(12) Accounts receivable turnover:		
$2,200,000 ÷ $90,500	24.3 times	
$1,600,000 ÷ $90,000		17.8 times
(13) Times bond interest earned:		
($166,400 + $22,400) ÷ $22,400	8.4 times	
($ 80,000 + $22,400) ÷ $22,400		4.6 times

* Adjusted for 50% stock dividend.

Chapter 22

LIQUID GAS COMPANY LTD.

		As of December 31	
a		*Year 2*	*Year 1*
Computation of decrease in working capital:			
Current assets		*$112,400*	*$ 81,000*
Less: Current liabilities		*79,200*	*40,000*
Working capital		*$ 33,200*	*$ 41,000*
Decrease in working capital during Year 2		*7,800*	
		$ 41,000	*$ 41,000*

b Working papers appear on the next page.

c

LIQUID GAS COMPANY LTD.
Statement of Changes in Financial Position
Year 2

Sources of working capital:		
Operations:		
Income before extraordinary loss		*$ 68,000*
Add: Expense not requiring the use of working		
capital—depreciation	*$ 51,000*	
Less: Increase in net income which did not		
provide working capital—amortization of premium		
on bonds payable	*200*	*50,800*
Total working capital provided by operations		*$118,800*
Sale of land		*8,000*
Total sources of working capital		*$126,800*
Uses of working capital:		
Payment of cash dividends	*$ 56,000*	
Purchase of buildings	*20,000*	
Purchase of equipment	*28,600*	
Redemption of preferred stock	*30,000*	
Total uses of working capital		*134,600*
Decrease in working capital		*$ 7,800*

b

LIQUID GAS COMPANY LTD.
Working Papers for Statement of Changes in Financial Position
Year 2

Debits	Account Balances Dec. 31, Year 1	Analysis of Transactions for Year 2		Account Balances Dec. 31, Year 2
		Debit	Credit	
Working capital.	41,000		(x) 7,800	33,200
Land	19,000		(5) 10,000	9,000
Buildings.	250,000	(6) 20,000		270,000
Equipment	450,000	(7) 28,600		478,600
Total debits	760,000			790,800
Credits				
Accumulated depreciation: buildings	77,000		(2) 18,000	95,000
Accumulated depreciation: equipment.	120,000		(2) 33,000	153,000
Bonds payable	90,000			90,000
Premium on bonds payable	3,000	(8) 200		2,800
Preferred stock, $100 par	100,000	(9) 30,000		70,000
Common stock, $25 par	250,000		(3) 10,000	260,000
Premium on common stock	40,000		(3) 5,000	45,000
Retained earnings	80,000	(3) 15,000	(1) 66,000⎫	75,000
		(4) 56,000	⎬	
Total credits	760,000			790,800
Sources of working capital:				
Operations—net income		(1) 66,000	⎫	
Add: Depreciation		(2) 51,000	⎪	(From
Loss on sale of land		(5) 2,000	⎬	operations,
Less: Amortization of premium on			⎪	$118,800)
bonds payable			(8) 200⎭	
Sale of land.		(5) 8,000		
Uses of working capital:				
Payment of cash dividends			(4) 56,000	
Purchase of buildings			(6) 20,000	
Purchase of equipment			(7) 28,600	
Redemption of preferred stock			(9) 30,000	
Total sources and uses of				
working capital		127,000	134,800	
Decrease in working capital		(x) 7,800		
		134,800	134,800	

Explanation of transactions for Year 2:
(1) Net income, $66,000, including extraordinary loss of $2,000, transferred to Retained Earnings.
(2) Depreciation for the year, $51,000 (buildings, $18,000, and equipment, $33,000) is added to net income because it is an expense which did not reduce working capital.
(3) Entry to record 4% stock dividend; no effect on working capital.
(4) Cash dividends declared, $56,000, (preferred stock, $6,000, and common, $50,000).
(5) To record sale of land for $8,000; the loss is added to net income because the loss reduced net income but had no effect on working capital.
(6) To record working capital used for purchase of buildings.
(7) To record working capital used for purchase of equipment.
(8) To record amortization of premium on bonds payable; the amortization increased net income but had no effect on working capital.
(9) To record working capital applied to retirement of preferred stock.
(x) Balancing figure—decrease in working capital during Year 2.

d

LIQUID GAS COMPANY LTD.

Cash Flow Statement

Year 2

Cash receipts:

Cash generated from operations (see Schedule A)		$150,020
Sale of land.		8,000
Total cash receipts		$158,020
Cash payments:		
Payment of cash dividends	$ 56,000	
Purchase of buildings	20,000	
Purchase of equipment	28,600	
Redemption of preferred stock	30,000	
Total cash payments		134,600
Increase in cash during the year ($39,220 − $15,800)		$ 23,420
Schedule A—Cash generated from operations:		
Working capital provided by operations—part (c)		$118,800
Add: Decrease in inventories	$ 9,200	
Decrease in prepaid expenses	220	
Increase in accounts payable	29,200	
Increase in accrued liabilities	10,000	48,620
Less: Increase in receivables		(17,400)
Cash generated from operations		$150,020

Chapter 23

SUBURB OUTLET COMPANY LTD.

SUBURB OUTLET COMPANY LTD.
Working Papers
September 30, Current Year

	Adjusted Trial Balance		Income Statements — Department A		Department B		Unallocated		Balance Sheet	
	Dr	Cr	Dr	Cr	Dr	Cr	Dr	Cr	Dr	Cr
Administrative expense	43,600		12,300		5,900		25,400			
Advertising expense	40,600		12,400		12,200		16,000			
Accumulated depreciation		72,000								72,000
Buildings and equipment	167,000								167,000	
Bldg. occupancy expense	18,000		2,800		4,000		11,200			
Buying expense	25,600		10,300		5,600		9,700			
Capital stock		50,000								50,000
Cost of goods sold	368,500		218,500		150,000					
Current assets	166,000								166,000	
Current liabilities		84,400								84,400
Goodwill	25,000								25,000	
Interest expense	5,500						5,500			
Interest earned		1,200		500		700				
Land	42,000								42,000	
Long-term notes payable		80,000								80,000
Net sales		578,600		360,000		218,600				
Retained earnings		70,600								70,600
Sales salaries	35,000		18,000		9,000		8,000			
	936,800	936,800	274,300	360,500	186,700	219,300	75,800	118,800	400,000	400,000
Departmental contribution to indirect expenses			86,200		32,600			118,800		
			360,500	360,500	219,300	219,300				
Income taxes°							14,140			14,140
Net income for current year							28,860			28,860
							118,800	118,800	400,000	400,000

° Computation of income taxes:

Departmental contribution to indirect expenses	$118,800
Less: Unallocated expenses	75,800
Income before income taxes	$ 43,000
Income tax on first $25,000 of taxable income, 22%	$ 5,500
Income tax on taxable income in excess of $25,000 (48% × $18,000)	8,640
Income taxes	$ 14,140

Chapter 25

DIVERSIFIED MFG. COMPANY LTD.

a *(1)* *Materials Inventory*   40,000
  Accounts Payable   40,000
 To record purchase of materials.

 Goods in Process: Foundry Department   13,000
 Goods in Process: Blending Department   23,000
  Materials Inventory   36,000
 To record requisitions of materials.

(2) *Factory Payroll*   56,800
 Factory Overhead   43,600
  Cash, Accounts Payable, etc.   100,400
 To record factory payroll and overhead costs.

 Goods in Process: Foundry Department   36,000
 Goods in Process: Blending Department   64,400
  Factory Payroll   56,800
  Factory Overhead   43,600
 To allocate factory payroll and overhead costs to
 productive departments.

b   Cost of jobs in process in Foundry Department at January 31:

	Total	*Job No. 9*	*Job No. 10*
Materials	$1,180	$ 600	$ 580
Direct labor	900	400	500
Factory overhead, 80% of direct labor . .	720	320	400
	$2,800	$1,320	$1,480

(1) *Finished Goods Inventory*   46,200
  Goods in Process: Foundry Department   46,200
 To record cost of jobs completed: Total debits to
 Foundry Department, $49,000, less cost of jobs in
 process, $2,800 = $46,200.

(2) *Accounts Receivable*   60,000
  Sales   60,000
 To record sale of goods completed in Foundry
 Department.

 Cost of Goods Sold   46,200
  Finished Goods Inventory   46,200
 To record cost of goods sold from Foundry
 Department.

c

Blending Department
Cost Report for January

	Total Units	Total Costs	÷ Equivalent Full Units*	= Unit Cost
Inputs:				
Materials	95,000	$23,000	92,000	$0.25
Direct labor		36,800	92,000	0.40
Factory overhead		27,600	92,000	0.30
Total inputs—units and costs	95,000	$87,400		
Unit cost for January				$0.95
Outputs:				
Transferred to Finished Goods				
Inventory ($0.95 per unit)	80,000	$76,000		
Units in process at end of month				
(80% complete as to materials and				
conversion costs), 12,000 @ $.95	15,000	11,400		
Total outputs—units and costs	95,000	$87,400		

* Computation of equivalent full units:

Units completed during January	80,000
Add: Full units of work done in January on ending inventory in process	
(15,000 × 80%)	12,000
Output in January in terms of equivalent full units	92,000

(1) Finished Goods Inventory	76,000	
Goods in Process: Blending Department		76,000
To record cost of finished product.		
(2) Accounts Receivable	92,500	
Sales		92,500
To record sales from Blending Department.		
Cost of Goods Sold	66,500	
Finished Goods Inventory		66,500
To record cost of goods sold from Blending Department,		
70,000 units @ $0.95 per unit.		

d

DIVERSIFIED MFG. COMPANY LTD.
Income Statement
For January

Sales ($60,000 + $92,500)		$152,500
Cost of goods sold ($46,200 + $66,500)		112,700
Gross profit on sales		$ 39,800
Operating expenses:		
Selling expenses	$14,250	
General and administrative expenses	12,500	26,750
Operating income		$ 13,050

Chapter 26

MODERN TOY COMPANY LTD.

a

MODERN TOY COMPANY LTD.

Projected Income Statement

For Year 5

Sales, 180,000 @ $2.40		$432,000
Cost of goods sold:		
Cost of goods manufactured (see Schedule A)	$314,000	
Less: Finished goods, Dec. 31		
(20,000 units @ $1.57 per unit)	31,400	
Cost of goods sold		282,600
Gross profit on sales		$149,400
Operating expenses [$15,500 + (180,000 units sold × $.30)]		69,500
Operating income (taxable income)		$ 79,900
Income taxes (40% of taxable income)		31,960
Net income		$ 47,940

MODERN TOY COMPANY LTD.

Projected Statement of Cost of Goods Manufactured

For Year 5

Schedule A

Direct materials used*		$ 19,500
Direct labor (given)		125,000
Factory overhead:		
Depreciation: building	$ 4,600	
Depreciation: machinery	9,500	
Salary of plant manager	11,500	
Insurance and property taxes	2,900	
Indirect labor (30,000 direct labor hours × $1.50)	45,000	
Indirect materials and supplies (200,000 × $.15)	30,000	
Miscellaneous factory costs (30,000 direct labor		
hours × $.22)	66,000	
Total factory overhead		169,500
Cost of goods manufactured		$314,000

Cost per unit: $314,000 ÷ 200,000 = $1.57 per unit

* Sheet metal, 80,000 pounds @ $0.20	$16,000
Paint, 700 gallons @ $5.00	3,500
Total direct materials used	$19,500

Total factory overhead (see Schedule A)	$169,500
Total direct labor hours (20,000 + 10,000)	30,000
Planned factory overhead rate per direct labor hour,	
$169,500 ÷ 30,000	$ 5.65

Chapter 27

FRESNO PROCESSING COMPANY LTD.

a Computation of average maximum amount that the company can afford to pay for a ton of cottonseed:

Total revenue per ton of cottonseed		$90
Less: Variable costs other than cottonseed:		
Processing	$13	
Marketing, 90% of $30	27	40
Balance, maximum amount that can be paid for a ton of		
cottonseed		$50

By paying $50 per ton of cottonseed, there would be no contribution margin per ton of cottonseed processed and the company would not incur losses greater when operating than when closed down.

b Computation of number of tons that must be processed and sold in order to break even, if cottonseed is purchased for $30 per ton:

Total revenue per ton of cottonseed		$90
Less: Variable costs:		
Processing	$13	
Marketing	27	
Cottonseed	30	70
Contribution margin per ton		$20

Break-even sales volume:

Fixed costs, $190,000 ($120,000 processing costs + $70,000 administrative costs) ÷ $20 contribution margin per ton = 9,500 tons.

c Sales volume necessary to earn $8 per share:

Fixed costs, $120,000 + $70,000	$190,000
Required pretax income, (10,000 × $8) ÷ .5	160,000
Total contribution margin required	$350,000
Contribution margin per ton—see part (b)	$20

Number of tons that must be processed and sold in order to earn $8 per share: $350,000 ÷ $20 = 17,500 tons.

APPENDIX

SELECTED

FINANCIAL

STATEMENTS

OF WELL-KNOWN

CORPORATIONS

Four samples of corporate financial statements are presented in the following pages. These "real-world" financial statements, taken from the annual reports of the four companies, will give the student a better idea of financial reporting practices of large companies.

In addition to financial statements and the auditors' opinion on them, annual reports generally include the following:

1 Summary of the financial and operating highlights for the preceding year
2 Letter to stockholders from the chairman of the board and the president
3 List of directors and officers
4 Financial review
5 Ten-year summary of financial trends and other miscellaneous data
6 Information about other key developments or plans.

Brief comments relating to the four selected financial statements follow:

FORD MOTOR COMPANY OF CANADA, LIMITED Retained earnings comprise over 95% of shareholders' equity.

HUDSON BAY MINING AND SMELTING COMPANY LIMITED This is an example of an increasingly acceptable Canadian practice of the *financial position form* of balance sheet in which current liabilities are deducted from current assets to arrive at working capital. The highly risky nature of the mining industry is apparent from the extraordinary loss on a mine which had been in production for only one year.

IMASCO LIMITED Similar to Hudson Bay Mining and Smelting Company, the annual report of Imasco contains the financial position form of balance sheet. The formal financial statements are a concise presentation of the company's financial results for the year with detailed information presented in the notes to the statements.

STEINBERGS LIMITED Four classes of capital stock are outstanding. Inventories are a high percentage (over 40%) of assets employed in the retailing and manufacturing operations.

FORD MOTOR COMPANY OF CANADA, LIMITED
AND OVERSEAS SUBSIDIARIES
Consolidated Statement of Income

For the years ended December 31	1971	1970
	(in thousands of dollars)	
Sales(note 2)	$1,458,400	$1,351,800
Operating Costs:		
Costs, excluding items listed below (note 3)	1,140,200	1,051,800
Marketing and administrative (note 4)	95,200	86,100
Amortization of special tools (note 5).	32,600	37,500
Depreciation (note 5)	27,600	26,100
Employee retirement plans (note 6)	16,200	11,300
	1,311,800	1,212,800
Operating Income	146,600	139,000
Other Income and (Expense):		
Interest income	11,200	10,300
Interest expense—short term debt	(6,000)	(5,100)
—long term debt	(2,000)	(2,900)
Revaluations of foreign currency net assets (note 1) . .	(300)	(1,100)
Other	2,700	4,000
	5,600	5,200
Income Before Income Taxes	152,200	144,200
Income Taxes (note 7)	76,400	74,800
Net Income	$ 75,800	$ 69,400
Net Income Per Share (in dollars)	$ 9.14	$ 8.37

Consolidated Statement of Earnings Retained for
Use in the Business

For the years ended December 31	1971	1970
	(in thousands of dollars)	
Balance at January 1	$ 450,100	$ 397,300
Net Income	75,800	69,400
Dividends:		
($3.00 per share in 1971)	(24,900)	
($2.00 per share in 1970)		(16,600)
Balance at December 31	$ 501,000	$ 450,100

The accompanying notes are part of the financial statements.

FORD MOTOR COMPANY OF CANADA, LIMITED
AND OVERSEAS SUBSIDIARIES
Consolidated Statement of Financial Position

At December 31	1971	1970
	(in thousands of dollars)	
Current Assets:		
Cash	$ 200	$ 700
Short term investments	68,800	64,100
Receivables	123,700	132,300
Inventories (note 8)	304,300	265,500
Prepaid income taxes (note 7)	20,000	19,600
Prepaid expenses and other current assets	2,500	2,100
	519,500	484,300
Deduct:		
Current Liabilities:		
Payables and accrued liabilities	248,500	233,500
Income and other taxes payable	93,800	77,900
Debt payable within one year	54,000	35,600
	396,300	347,000
Working Capital	123,200	137,300
Add:		
Investments and Other Assets:		
Equity in dealership subsidiaries (note 1)	11,600	10,900
Noncurrent loans and receivables (note 10)	47,600	18,500
Deferred pension costs	18,500	21,300
	77,700	50,700
Add:		
Fixed Assets (note 5):		
Land, buildings and equipment, net of depreciation	314,200	295,900
Unamortized special tools	75,600	62,800
	389,800	358,700
Deduct:		
Long Term Liabilities and Deferred Credit		
Accrued liabilities	19,200	21,600
Long term debt (note 9)	21,400	26,500
Deferred income taxes (note 7)	35,700	35,100
	76,300	83,200
	$514,400	$463,500
Shareholders' Equity		
Consisting of:		
Capital		
Authorized—10,000,000 common shares, no par value		
Issued—8,294,800 shares	$ 13,400	$ 13,400
Earnings retained for use in the business	501,000	450,100
	$514,400	$463,500

On behalf of the Board: Roy F. Bennett, Director
Lee A. Iacocca, Director
The accompanying notes are part of the financial statements.

FORD MOTOR COMPANY OF CANADA, LIMITED
AND OVERSEAS SUBSIDIARIES
Consolidated Statement of Changes in Working Capital

For the years ended December 31	1971	1970
	(in thousands of dollars)	
Source of Funds:		
Net Income	$ 75,800	$ 69,400
Charges to income which did not require an outlay of funds		
Amortization of special tools	32,600	37,500
Depreciation	27,600	26,100
Other—net	1,000	2,800
Total funds from operations	137,000	135,800
Use of Funds:		
Dividends	24,900	16,600
Additions to land, buildings and equipment	45,900	42,200
Additions to special tools	45,400	49,600
Increase in noncurrent loans and receivables	29,100	6,500
Decrease in long term debt	5,100	8,800
Increase in equity in dealership subsidiaries	700	1,300
Total funds used	151,100	125,000
Working Capital:		
Increase (decrease) during year	(14,100)	10,800
Balance at January 1	137,300	126,500
Balance at December 31	$123,200	$137,300

The accompanying notes are part of the financial statements.

AUDITORS' REPORT

To the Shareholders of
Ford Motor Company of Canada, Limited:

We have examined the consolidated statement of financial position of Ford Motor Company of Canada, Limited and overseas subsidiaries as at December 31, 1971 and the consolidated statements of income, earnings retained for use in the business and changes in working capital for the year then ended. Our examination was made in accordance with generally accepted auditing standards, and accordingly included such tests of the accounting records and such other auditing procedures as we considered necessary in the circumstances. We previously examined and reported upon the consolidated financial statements of Ford Motor Company of Canada, Limited and overseas subsidiaries for the year ended December 31, 1970.

In our opinion, these consolidated financial statements present fairly the financial position of the companies as at December 31, 1971 and 1970, and the results of their operations and the changes in working capital for the years then ended, in conformity with generally accepted accounting principles applied on a consistent basis.

Clarkson, Gordon & Co.
Chartered Accountants
Toronto, Canada
January 31, 1972

Note 1: Principles of Consolidation The consolidated financial statements include the accounts of Ford of Canada and all of its overseas subsidiaries (collectively called the "companies"). Dealership subsidiaries are reflected on an equity basis because they are subject to sale to dealer principals.

In the translation of the accounts of overseas subsidiaries to Canadian dollars, the company uses bookkeeping rates which are adjusted periodically to closely approximate actual rates of exchange. The general policy followed is to translate fixed assets at rates in effect on the dates of acquisition of the assets. Other assets and liabilities are translated at year-end rates. Revenues and expenses are translated at rates prevailing during the years, adjusted to reflect depreciation and amortization at historical dollar costs and the effects of currency revaluations.

Investment in net assets at the end of 1971 was $283.8 million in Canada and $230.6 million overseas; these compare with the 1970 levels of $273.5 million in Canada and $190 million overseas.

Note 2: Sales Consistent with the accounting practice of previous years, sales to Ford Motor Company (U.S.) have been excluded from reported sales and netted against purchases from Ford U.S. Sales to Ford Motor Company in 1971 totalled $1,009 million, compared to $1,034 million in 1970.

Note 3: Costs, Excluding Items Listed Below These costs consist primarily of material, labour, production overhead, warranty and engineering costs. The companies follow the accounting practices of accruing estimated total warranty costs for a vehicle at the time of sale, and of expensing engineering costs as incurred.

Note 4: Marketing and Administrative These costs include advertising, sales promotion, and special merchandising programs except those which result in price reductions to dealers, which are netted against sales revenue. Also included are salaries and wages, fringe benefits and other expenses related to the companies' selling, administrative and parts depot operations.

Note 5: Fixed Assets, Depreciation, Amortization Fixed assets are recorded on the companies' books at acquisition cost, including transportation and installation charges. Generally, depreciation is determined using the declining balance method, commencing with the month in which the assets are put into use. This results in accumulated depreciation of approximately two-thirds of the cost of an asset during the first half of its estimated useful life.

Special tools are dies, jigs, molds, patterns, etc. which are used for the manufacture of a specific product, and whose useful life is limited to the life of that product. The amortization period, not more than four years, reflects the comparatively short productive use of these tools.

At December 31, 1971, the companies had approved programs which upon completion will result in additions of $69 million to fixed assets. At that date, commitments of $32 million were outstanding under these programs. Land, buildings and equipment at December 31, are summarized as follows (in millions of dollars):

			1971	1970
	Cost	Accumulated Depreciation	Net Book Value	Net Book Value
Land	$ 49	$ —	$ 49	$ 45
Land improvements and buildings	226	(83)	143	136
Machinery and equipment	247	(136)	111	96
Construction in progress	11	—	11	19
	$533	($219)	$314	$296

Note 6: Employee Retirement Plans The companies have retirement plans covering substantially all employees.

Current service costs are expensed and funded during the year. In 1971, the unamortized obligations for past service costs were revalued by independent actuaries to reflect changes in actuarial assumptions. Past service costs to be amortized in the period 1972 through 1989 are projected at $110 million.

Note 7: Income Taxes The companies follow the deferred tax accounting practice.

Net income has not been reduced for additional taxes that might result from the distribution to the company of unremitted income of overseas subsidiaries; the major portion of such unremitted income has been invested by the subsidiaries in facilities and other operating assets. If all 1971 and 1970 incomes had been distributed, the amount of additional withholding taxes would have been $2.2 million and $4.6 million, respectively.

Note 8: Inventories Inventories are valued at the lower of cost and net realizable value. Cost is determined principally on a first-in first-out basis. At December 31, inventories consisted of the following (in millions of dollars):

	1971	1970
Work in process and supplies	$180	$158
Vehicles, service parts and other finished product	124	108
	$304	$266

Note 9: Long Term Debt At December 31, the companies had debt not due within one year as follows (in millions of dollars):

	1971	1970
Ford Canada		
6-¾% loans due 1972	$—	$ 3
7-½% loans due 1978	—	6
Ford Australia (payable in Australian currency)		
7-¼% debentures due 1973	6	6
7-½% debentures due 1977	12	12
Ford South Africa (payable in South African currency)		
9-½% loan due 1976	3	—
	$21	$27

Note 10: Remuneration of Officers and Directors of the Company During 1971, the company employed nine officers. Their aggregate remuneration as officers was $524,000. Four of the nine officers also served as directors but received no additional remuneration. Nine other persons, not employed by Ford Canada, also served as directors during the year. Their aggregate remuneration as directors of the company was $20,000.

HUDSON BAY MINING AND SMELTING CO., LIMITED
AND SUBSIDIARY COMPANIES
Consolidated Statement of Financial Position

	As at December 31	
	1972	**1971**
Current assets:		
Cash	$ 301,681	$ 362,043
Short-term securities	20,895,400	14,070,000
Accounts receivable	17,087,999	11,084,565
Inventories (note 3)	25,398,245	21,755,088
Materials and supplies—at cost	6,309,262	6,369,015
Total current assets	69,992,587	53,640,711
Deduct:		
Current liabilities:		
Accounts payable and accrued liabilities	18,574,020	10,530,563
Income and other taxes payable	1,213,073	843,554
Dividend payable	1,808,286	904,083
Current portion of long-term debt	576,000	576,000
Total current liabilities	22,171,379	12,854,200
Working capital	47,821,208	40,786,511
Add:		
Marketable securities—at cost		
(Market value 1972—$1,955,469;		
1971—$1,953,594)	2,541,190	2,541,190
Investments in other companies—at cost		
Quoted (Market value 1972—$546,500;		
1971—$1,439,421)	1,479,149	3,564,269
Unquoted	18,367,810	15,281,390
	19,846,959	18,845,659
Less provision for future write-offs	7,404,895	7,991,850
	12,442,064	10,853,809
Property, plant and equipment (note 4)	89,350,948	100,391,128
Other assets:		
Unamortized mine development expenditures (note 5)	37,717,772	42,688,375
Sundry assets and deferred charges—at cost	4,386,912	5,541,520
	42,104,684	48,229,895
Capital employed	194,260,094	202,802,533
Deduct:		
Long-term debt (note 6)	27,778,000	28,354,000
Deferred income taxes (note 7)	16,687,000	19,987,000
Minority interests in subsidiaries	5,716,477	6,021,912
	50,181,477	54,362,912
Shareholders' investment	$144,078,617	$148,439,621

Investment evidenced by

Capital stock (note 8)

Authorized—12,000,000 shares of no par value

Issued and fully paid—9,041,433 shares	$ 45,936,356	$ 45,925,526
Retained earnings	98,142,261	102,514,095
Total shareholders' equity	$144,078,617	$148,439,621

Approved by the Board of Directors

Director: Gavin W. H. Relly

Director: W. A. Morrice

The accompanying notes are an integral part of the financial statements.

HUDSON BAY MINING AND SMELTING CO., LIMITED
AND SUBSIDIARY COMPANIES
Consolidated Statement of Earnings

	For the year ended	
	1972	1971
Revenue:		
Sales of product	$107,843,689	$ 60,606,500
Less freight, refining and selling expenses	11,967,251	6,946,619
	95,876,438	53,659,881
Interest and other income (note 9)	2,783,835	2,148,263
	98,660,273	55,808,144
Cost and expenses:		
Production costs	63,485,080	37,801,452
Amortization of mine development expenditures . . .	6,882,065	3,796,088
Depreciation and depletion	6,557,975	4,559,887
Exploration expenses	2,759,016	3,045,171
General administrative expenses	2,292,265	2,303,833
Interest and other long-term debt expense	2,535,224	1,272,819
	84,511,625	52,779,250
Income taxes and provincial mining taxes:		
Income taxes	927,000	(1,330,000)
Provincial mining taxes	1,572,566	125,858
	2,499,566	(1,204,142)
Earnings from operations	11,649,082	4,233,036
Other deductions:		
Provision for future write-offs of investments	—	812,500
Earnings before minority interests	11,649,082	3,420,536
Minority interests in earnings of subsidiaries	269,770	411,559
Earnings before extraordinary item	11,379,312	3,008,977
Estimated loss on investment in Wellgreen Mine		
(less applicable income tax reduction $4,847,000)		
(note 11)	8,518,000	—
Net earnings for the year	$ 2,861,312	$ 3,008,977
Earnings per share:		
Before extraordinary item	$1.26	$0.33
After extraordinary item	$0.32	$0.33

Consolidated Statement of Retained Earnings

Retained earnings at beginning of the year	$102,514,095	$104,025,535
Net earnings for the year	2,861,312	3,008,977
	105,375,407	107,034,512
Dividends:		
80¢ per share (1971—50¢)	7,233,146	4,520,417
Retained earnings at end of the year	$ 98,142,261	$102,514,095

The accompanying notes are an integral part of the financial statements.

HUDSON BAY MINING AND SMELTING CO., LIMITED
AND SUBSIDIARY COMPANIES
Consolidated Statement of Source and
Application of Funds

	For the year ended	
	1972	1971
Source of funds:		
Operations:		
Earnings from operations	$11,649,082	$ 4,233,036
Depreciation, depletion and amortization of mine		
development expenditures	13,440,040	8,355,975
Deferred income taxes	1,547,000	(2,809,000)
	26,636,122	9,780,011
Contribution from Wellgreen operations	1,062,972	—
	27,699,094	9,780,011
Proceeds from long-term debt	—	29,000,000
Sale of investment	1,571,580	—
Issue of shares under options	10,830	—
Decrease in sundry assets	1,154,608	(828,860)
	30,436,112	37,951,151
Application of funds:		
Dividends	7,233,146	4,520,417
Investments in other companies	3,159,835	1,608,645
Additions to property, plant and equipment	6,232,573	15,470,625
Mine development expenditures	6,049,893	6,507,445
Reduction of long-term debt	576,000	646,000
Decrease in minority interests	149,968	358,967
	23,401,415	29,112,099
Increase in working capital	7,034,697	8,839,052
Working capital at beginning of the year	40,786,511	31,947,459
Working capital at end of the year	$47,821,208	$40,786,511

The accompanying notes are an integral part of the financial statements.

HUDSON BAY MINING AND SMELTING CO., LIMITED
AND SUBSIDIARY COMPANIES

Notes to the consolidated financial statements
December 31, 1972

1. Principles of consolidation The consolidated financial statements include the accounts of Hudson Bay Mining and Smelting Co., Limited and of all its subsidiaries.

2. Inventories Inventories comprise the following:

	1972	1971
Metals, at estimated sales value	$ 17,807,215	$ 14,877,534
Metals in process, at cost	2,027,774	1,648,181
Manufactured and other products (finished, in process and raw materials), at cost or net realizable value, whichever is the lower	5,563,256	5,229,373
	$ 25,398,245	$ 21,755,088

3. Property plant and equipment (a) The following is a summary of property, plant and equipment at cost by major category.

These costs were reduced during 1972 by the write-off of the assets of the Wellgreen Mine.

	1972	1971
Mineral properties	$ 19,410,140	$ 22,555,867
Base-metal plant and equipment	77,839,926	82,716,577
Industrial mineral plant and equipment	45,402,181	43,971,643
Oil and gas properties, plant and equipment	24,138,188	22,333,483
Other property, plant and equipment.	8,040,694	7,735,764
Total cost.	174,831,129	179,313,334
Less accumulated depreciation and depletion	85,480,181	78,922,206
	$ 89,350,948	$100,391,128

Mineral properties include all exploration costs with respect to mines operating or in the development stage. Oil and gas properties are accounted for on the full-cost basis whereby all costs relating to the exploration for and development of oil and gas resources are capitalized whether productive or unproductive.

(b) Depreciation of base-metal plant and equipment and depletion of mineral and oil and gas properties are charged to operations by the unit of production method based on estimated recoverable reserves. Depreciation on industrial mineral and other plant and equipment is charged to

operations on a straight-line basis over the estimated useful lives of the plant and equipment.

4. Amortization of mine development expenditures Mine development expenditures are charged to operations on a unit-of-production basis based on estimated recoverable reserves. Unamortized mine development expenditures were reduced during 1972 by the write-off of the development costs of the Wellgreen Mine.

5. Long-term debt Long-term debt comprises the following:

	1972	1971
9% unsecured debentures maturing June 15, 1991 . . .	$ 25,000,000	$ 25,000,000
Bank production loans of subsidiary, Francana Oil & Gas Ltd.	3,354,000	3,930,000
	28,354,000	28,930,000
Less amount included in current liabilities	576,000	576,000
	$ 27,778,000	$ 28,354,000

(a) Under the trust indenture covering the 9% unsecured debentures, sinking-fund payments sufficient to retire $800,000 of principal amount each year from 1977 to 1990 inclusive are required. The Company has the option to redeem the debentures at prices ranging downward from 108.45% currently to 100% in 1989 and thereafter. Debentures redeemed through the operations of the sinking-fund are callable at par.

(b) The production loans are repayable in monthly installments of $48,000, plus interest at rates approximating prime bank rate. The loans are secured by an assignment of the subsidiary's interest in certain producing properties.

6. Deferred income taxes Deferred income taxes represent tax reductions for expenditures on mine development, mineral and oil properties, cost of participation in certain mining companies, and depreciation deducted in the determination of taxable income but not charged to earnings. The reduction in deferred income taxes in the current year results from the loss on the investment in the Wellgreen Mine.

7. Share option plan Under the Company's Share Option Plan for Full Time Officers and Key Employees, 168,000 unissued shares were reserved for granting of options at prices not less than 95% of the market value (full market value in the case of United States citizens) on the day the option is granted.

During 1972 options were granted for 81,365 shares (officers 15,940 shares) and options for 42,375 shares granted in 1970 were terminated. Options were exercised in respect of 600 shares granted in 1968 for which the Company received $10,830 cash.

As of December 31, 1972, 6,010 shares were available for future grants and 86,390 shares were subject to outstanding options as follows:

Date of Grant	Option Price Per Share	Shares For Officers	Total Shares
January 23, 1970	$27.01	750	5,025
December 14, 1972	$19.65	15,940	81,365

The options granted in 1970 are exercisable until January 22, 1975, and the options granted in 1972 are exercisable from January 23, 1975, to December 13, 1977.

8. Interest and other income This amount includes interest on short-term securities, sales of power, revenue from custom treatment of concentrates, and miscellaneous investment income.

9. Operations in 1971 The mining and metallurgical operations at Flin Flon and Snow Lake were shut down by a strike from January 27 to June 21.

10. Extraordinary item The Wellgreen Mine in the Yukon, entirely financed by the Company, came into production in May, 1972, and will be closed early in 1973.

It is estimated that of the total investment in this property an amount of $8,518,000, which is net of an applicable tax reduction of $4,847,000, will not be recovered.

11. Pension fund The unfunded past service pension liability at December 31, 1972, approximates $5,000,000 and is being funded over the next 16 years as recommended by the actuaries.

12. Remuneration of directors and officers
The Company has 10 directors and 11 officers; two of the officers are also directors. The aggregate remuneration paid to the directors and officers as such was as follows:

	1972	1971
Directors	$ 27,400	$ 30,733
Officers	$578,194	$585,291

AUDITORS' REPORT

To the shareholders of
Hudson Bay Mining and Smelting Co., Limited:

We have examined the consolidated statement of financial position of Hudson Bay Mining and Smelting Co., Limited and subsidiary companies as at December 31, 1972, and the consolidated statements of earnings, retained earnings and source and application of funds for the year then ended. Our examination was made in accordance with generally accepted auditing standards, and accordingly included such tests of the accounting records and such other auditing procedures as we considered necessary in the circumstances.

In our opinion these consolidated financial statements present fairly the financial position of the companies as at December 31, 1972, and the results of their operations and the source and application of their funds for the year then ended, in accordance with generally accepted accounting principles applied on a basis consistent with that of the preceding year.

Deloitte, Haskins & Sells
Chartered Accountants
Toronto, Canada, February 19, 1973.

IMASCO LIMITED AND SUBSIDIARY COMPANIES
Year ended December 31, 1972

Consolidated Statement of Earnings	1972	1971
	Thousands of dollars	
Sales (Note 2)	625,613	569,629
Sales and excise taxes	246,082	242,356
	379,531	327,273
Operating costs	335,020	289,832
Earnings from operations (Note 2)	44,511	37,441
Income from investments	62	582
Interest expense	(3,812)	(3,847)
Earnings before income taxes	40,761	34,176
Income taxes	18,536	16,349
	22,225	17,827
Minority interest	63	166
Net earnings before extraordinary items	22,162	17,661
Extraordinary items (Note 3)	—	(122)
Net earnings after extraordinary items	22,162	17,539
Earnings per common share		
Before extraordinary items	$2.26	$1.79
After extraordinary items	$2.26	$1.78

Consolidated Statement of Retained Earnings

Retained earnings, beginning of year	75,173	70,648
Net earnings after extraordinary items	22,162	17,539
Goodwill on consolidation of subsidiaries (Note 1)	(11,520)	(2,995)
Dividends (Note 8)	(10,986)	(10,019)
Retained earnings, end of year	74,829	75,173

The attached notes form an integral part of these statements.

IMASCO LIMITED AND SUBSIDIARY COMPANIES
December 31, 1972

Consolidated Balance Sheet	1972	1971
	Thousands of dollars	
Current assets		
Cash and term deposits	3,346	861
Accounts and notes receivable	52,943	47,019
Inventories (Note 4)	128,479	124,883
Prepaid expenses	1,690	1,467
Total current assets	186,458	174,230
Current liabilities:		
Bank indebtedness	37,958	21,276
Accounts payable and accrued liabilities	26,982	19,595
Income, excise and other taxes	19,761	24,950
Current portion of long term debt (Note 7)	2,558	2,099
Dividends payable	1,934	967
Total current liabilities	89,193	68,887
Working capital (net current assets)	97,265	105,343
Other assets:		
Notes receivable and other investments	9,237	11,657
Deferred charges	6,084	1,254
Fixed assets (Note 6)	61,748	56,087
Goodwill, trademarks and patents	1	1
Excess of assets over current liabilities	174,335	174,342
Other liabilities:		
Long term debt (Note 7)	36,667	37,349
Deferred income taxes	6,381	5,231
Minority interest	75	206
	43,123	42,786
Excess of assets over liabilities	131,212	131,556
Shareholders' equity:		
Capital stock (Note 9)	54,153	54,153
Capital surplus (Note 5)	2,230	2,230
Retained earnings	74,829	75,173
	131,212	131,556

Approved by the Board, Paul Paré, Director G. G. Ross, Director
The attached notes form an integral part of these statements.

IMASCO LIMITED AND SUBSIDIARY COMPANIES
Year ended December 31, 1972

Consolidated Statement of Source and Application of Funds	1972	1971
	Thousands of dollars	
Source of funds:		
Net earnings before extraordinary items	22,162	17,661
Depreciation	5,337	4,431
Deferred income taxes	1,785	(296)
Other non-cash items	128	667
Funds provided from operations	29,412	22,463
Sale of fixed assets	3,334	325
Proceeds from issue of debentures	—	34,284
Notes receivable and other investments	2,420	3,316
	35,166	60,388
Application of funds:		
Purchase of subsidiaries	20,764	5,087
Dividends	10.986	10,019
Past service pension liability (Note 5)	4,310	—
Fixed assets	4,878	6,642
Long term debt	2,080	32,127
Other	226	257
	43,244	54,132
Working capital:		
Increase (decrease) in working capital	(8,078)	6,256
Beginning of year	105,343	99,087
End of year	97,265	105,343

The attached notes form an integral part of these statements.

IMASCO LIMITED AND SUBSIDIARY COMPANIES

Notes to the Consolidated Financial Statements	1972	1971
	Thousands of dollars	

1. **Principles of consolidation and related information:**
   The consolidated financial statements include the accounts of all subsidiaries. Included are Grissol Foods Limited from its effective date of acquisition, May 1, 1972 and certain retailing and automatic vending businesses acquired by the Imasco Associated Products Division during 1972.

   United States dollar amounts have been translated to Canadian dollars at the following exchange rates: net fixed assets and depreciation at rates in effect at the appropriate acquisition dates; all other assets and liabilities at rates in effect at December 31st; all earnings accounts, other than depreciation, at average exchange rates for the year.

   It is the Company's practice to charge directly to retained earnings the excess of the purchase price of the subsidiaries over the value of their net assets at dates of acquisition. In 1972, this excess was reduced by $586 as a result of income tax savings permitted by United States tax laws.

2. **Operations by type of business:**

	1972	1971
Sales		
Imperial Tobacco Products Division	430,372	418,049
Imasco Food Division	135,772	112,349
Imasco Associated Products Division		
Retail and other services	66,780	44,247
Wine	7,176	6,546
Interdivisional transactions	(14,487)	(11,562)
	625,613	569,629
Earnings from operations		
Imperial Tobacco Products Division	40,360	35,865
Imasco Food Division	4,725	2,862
Imasco Associated Products Division		
Retail and other services	2,015	977
Wine	1,021	937
	48,121	40,641
General administration	(2,930)	(2,325)
Non-recurring items	(680)	(875)
	44,511	37,441
Non-recurring items are made up of:		
Imperial Tobacco Products Division		
Plant closing expenses	(1,805)	—
Gain on sale of real estate	760	—

IMASCO LIMITED AND SUBSIDIARY COMPANIES

Notes to the Consolidated Financial Statements	*1972*	*1971*
	Thousands of dollars	
Imasco Associated Products Division		
Gain on sale of real estate	*365*	*—*
Imasco Food Division		
Start-up costs	*—*	*(875)*
	(680)	*(875)*

3. Extraordinary items:

Foreign exchange gain realized on repayment of U.S. bank		
loans	*—*	*2,294*
Unrealized foreign exchange loss on consolidation of U.S.		
subsidiaries	*—*	*(1,700)*
Cost of debenture issue	*—*	*(716)*
	—	*(122)*

4. Inventories:

Inventories by division, valued principally at average cost which does not exceed realizable value, are:

Imperial Tobacco Products Division	*79,360*	*89,453*
Imasco Food Division	*35,626*	*27,928*
Imasco Associated Products Division		
Retail and other services	*9,048*	*4,037*
Wine	*4,445*	*3,465*
	128,479	*124,883*

5. Statutory information:

The following items have been charged (credited) in deter-mining net earnings:

Depreciation	*5,337*	*4,431*
Interest on long term debt	*3,065*	*2,973*
Deferred income taxes	*1,785*	*(296)*

Remuneration of directors and senior officers

Directors, all of whom are officers

  Number at December 31st: 1972, 8; 1971, 9

  Number during the year: 1972, 10; 1971, 10

Officers

  Number at December 31st: 1972, 17; 1971, 17

  Number during the year: 1972, 19; 1971, 18

Aggregate remuneration as officers	*1,555*	*1,249*

Pension plans

The unfunded liability for past service pension costs at December 29, 1972 amounting to $4,310 was paid into the pension fund on that date and is included in deferred charges. In addition, certain changes in pension benefits

IMASCO LIMITED AND SUBSIDIARY COMPANIES

Notes to the Consolidated Financial Statements	*1972*	*1971*
	Thousands of dollars	

which will become effective March 1, 1973 will create an additional past service liability of approximately $14,500. These amounts will be charged to earnings over a period not to exceed nineteen years.

Long term leases
The Company has outstanding commitments with respect to long term real estate leases with expiry dates extending to 1996.
Rental expenses for the year amounted to $3,239 (1971 $2,591) and the minimum annual rental under such leases amounts to approximately $2,617 before giving effect to escalation and percentage of sales clauses in certain of the leases.

Other commitments
The Company is negotiating for the purchase of certain businesses. The expected cost of these acquisitions amounts to approximately $2,800.

Capital surplus
Capital surplus consists of amounts transferred from retained earnings as required by the Canada Corporations Act in respect of 6% cumulative preference shares purchased and cancelled.

6. Fixed assets and depreciation:

	1972	1971
Land	*5,189*	*5,242*
Buildings	*41,309*	*38,769*
Equipment	*70,315*	*60,552*
	116,813	*104,563*
Accumulated depreciation	*55,065*	*48,476*
Net fixed assets	*61,748*	*56,087*

Fixed assets are stated at cost. Depreciation has been calculated on the straight line basis over the estimated useful lives of the assets.

7. Long term debt:

	1972	1971
8½% Sinking Fund Debentures Series A due March 15, 1991	*33,950*	*35,000*
Less held in treasury	*700*	*700*
	33,250	*34,300*

IMASCO LIMITED AND SUBSIDIARY COMPANIES

Notes to the Consolidated Financial Statements	1972	1971
	Thousands of dollars	

	1972	1971
U.S. dollar loan, payable in three annual instalments commencing March 31, 1973 bearing interest at New York prime bank rate less 1%	2,881	3,955
Other long term obligations	3,094	1,193
	39,225	39,448
Less current portion	2,558	2,099
	36,667	37,349

Required payments during the next five years including $1,050 annual sinking fund payments on the 8½% sinking fund debentures amount to: 1973 $2,558; 1974 $2,437; 1975 $2,368; 1976 $1,304; 1977 $1,276.

8. Dividends:

	1972	1971
On 6% cumulative preference shares	348	348
On common shares	10,638	9,671
	10,986	10,019

9. Capital stock:

6% cumulative preference shares,
par value $4.86⅔ each

		1972	1971
Authorized and issued	1,650,000 shares		
Less purchased and cancelled	458,112 shares		
Outstanding	1,191,888 shares	5,800	5,800

Redeemable sinking fund preference shares, par value $25 each

Authorized	200,000 shares
Issued	Nil

Common shares, no par value

		1972	1971
Authorized	10,800,000 shares		
Issued	9,670,532 shares	48,353	48,353
		54,153	54,153

10. Subsequent events:

The Company has agreed to sell its wine business for a price of $10,500 which approximates its investment therein.

IMASCO LIMITED AND SUBSIDIARY COMPANIES

Auditors' Report
To the Shareholders of Imasco Limited

We have examined the consolidated balance sheet of Imasco Limited and subsidiary companies as at December 31, 1972 and the consolidated statements of earnings, retained earnings and source and application of funds for the year then ended. Our examination included a general review of the accounting procedures and such tests of accounting records and other supporting evidence as we considered necessary in the circumstances.

In our opinion, these financial statements present fairly the financial position of the companies as at December 31, 1972 and the results of their operations and the source and application of their funds for the year then ended, in accordance with generally accepted accounting principles applied on a basis consistent with that of the preceding year.

Deloitte, Haskins & Sells
Chartered Accountants
930 Sun Life Building
Montreal 110, Canada
February 23, 1973

STEINBERG'S LIMITED AND SUBSIDIARY COMPANIES
Consolidated Statement of Earnings

for the year ended July 29, 1972
(expressed in thousands of dollars)

	1972 $	1971 $
Sales and Operating Revenue	881,575	792,821
Expenses:		
Cost of sales and other operating and administrative expenses	712,408	644,143
Wages and employee benefits	113,827	101,774
Directors' and officers' remuneration	823	801
Rentals and lease purchase payments	11,426	11,350
Depreciation and amortization (note 9)	11,511	10,674
	849,995	768,742
Earnings from Operations	31,580	24,079
Financial (Income) and Expenses:		
Interest and amortization of discount on long-term debt	5,890	5,432
Other interest	1,003	1,597
Investment income, including interest earned and gain on redemption of long-term debt	(1,102)	(1,581)
	5,791	5,448
Earnings before Income Taxes	25,789	18,631
Income Taxes:		
Current	10,067	9,111
Deferred	552	(111)
	10,619	9,000
Earnings before Minority Interest:	15,170	9,631
Minority Interest	198	172
Net Earnings for the Year	14,972	9,459
Net Earnings per Class "A" and Common Share (note 10)	$ 2.16	$ 1.37
Represented by:		
Retail and manufacturing companies (after eliminating dividends from Ivanhoe Corporation of $750,000 in each year)	11,352	8,136
Real estate companies	3,620	1,323
	14,972	9,459

STEINBERG'S LIMITED AND SUBSIDIARY COMPANIES
Consolidated Balance Sheet

as at July 29, 1972

(expressed in thousands of dollars)

Assets		1972 $	1971 $
Current Assets:			
Cash		8,650	9,788
Marketable investments—at cost (approximately market value)		509	356
Accounts receivable		5,809	6,020
Inventories—at the lower of cost or market		68,440	59,011
Prepaid expenses		3,836	2,634
		87,244	77,809
Investments			
Sundry investments—at cost (note 2)		1,524	1,589
Assets of Real Estate Operations:			
Property—			
Undeveloped land—at cost plus carrying charges		16,572	18,213
Land, buildings and parking areas— at cost	$123,543		
Less: Accumulated depreciation	25,407	98,136	87,321
		114,708	105,534
Investments—at cost		4,006	2,958
Other assets—principally amounts recoverable on land transactions		2,567	3,392
		121,281	111,884

Fixed Assets—Retail and Manufacturing Operations:	Cost	Accumulated depreciation		
Land and buildings	$ 5,089	$ 779	4,310	7,637
Equipment	95,687	51,910	43,777	39,716
	$100,776	$52,689	48,087	47,353
Leasehold improvements—at cost, less amortization			12,683	11,646
			60,770	58,999
Intangible Assets:				
Unamortized discount on long-term debt			1,570	1,222
Excess of cost of shares in subsidiary companies over net book values at date of acquisition			15,459	15,182
			17,029	16,404
			287,848	266,685

	1972	1971
Liabilities	$	$
Current Liabilities:		
Notes payable	4,130	20,707
Accounts payable and accrued liabilities	53,953	45,964
Dividends payable on preferred shares	39	41
Income taxes	2,627	1,811
Current portion of long-term debt (note 3)	292	307
	61,041	68,830
Long-term Debt and Other Obligations (note 3)		
Real estate operations	57,081	59,085
Retail and manufacturing operations	42,147	23,858
	99,228	82,943
Deferred Income Taxes	8,575	8,004
Minority Interest		
(including preferred shares: 1972—$723,200;		
1971—$1,132,000)	1,593	2,420

Capital Stock (note 4)

  Authorized—

    80,866 cumulative redeemable preferred shares of the
      par value of $100 each

    102,000 2½% non-cumulative subordinated preferred shares
      redeemable at their par value of $98 each

    4,500,000 Class "A" shares without par value—non-voting

    3,500,000 common shares without par value

  Issued and fully paid—

	1972	1971
29,658 5¼% preferred shares—Series "A"	2,966	3,087
102,000 subordinated preferred shares	9,996	9,996
3,873,161 Class "A" shares	4,913	4,250
3,000,000 common shares	1,500	1,500
	19,375	18,833
Contributed Surplus (note 5)	10,515	10,486
Retained Earnings	87,521	75,169
	117,411	104,488
	287,848	266,685

Signed on behalf of the board
Sam Steinberg, Director
Mel Dobrin, Director

STEINBERG'S LIMITED AND SUBSIDIARY COMPANIES

Consolidated Statement of Retained Earnings

for the year ended July 29, 1972

(expressed in thousands of dollars)

	1972	1971
	$	$
Balance—Beginning of Year	75,169	68,318
Net earnings for the year	14,972	9,459
	90,141	77,777
Dividends—5¼% preferred shares	158	164
—Class "A" and common shares	2,462	2,444
	2,620	2,608
Balance—End of Year	87,521	75,169

STEINBERG'S LIMITED AND SUBSIDIARY COMPANIES

Notes to Consolidated Financial Statements

for the year ended July 29, 1972

1. Principles of Consolidation The consolidated financial statements include the accounts of all companies in which Steinberg's Limited has a controlling interest, including those of Ivanhoe Corporation and its subsidiaries.

2. Investments Sundry investments include a minority interest (49%) amounting to $973,000 in Supermarchés Montréal, a French company which currently operates four stores in the Paris area.

Steinberg's Limited has also guaranteed loans to Supermarchés Montréal and its subsidiaries up to a total amount of 8,600,000 French francs, or their approximate equivalent of $1,720,000 (1971—$1,700,000).

To February 28, 1972, this company has incurred gross cumulative losses of $4,155,000 in its operations. The share of Steinberg's Limited in this deficit amounts to $2,036,000 exclusive of future tax reductions.

No reduction in the book value of the investment has been made to reflect these losses.

Subsequent to July 29, 1972 the company has made arrangements for the sale of its interest in Supermarchés Montréal at the approximate cost of the investment and for the removal of its guarantees of that company's loans.

3. Capital Stock

a) The 2½% subordinated preferred shares are subject to restrictions that no dividend will be payable thereon prior to August 1, 1972 and none of the shares may be retired prior to August 1, 1972. Thereafter, the company may redeem such shares to a maximum of $1,000,000 in each year. Subsequent to July 29, 1972, the company redeemed 10,200 shares at par for a consideration of $1,000,000.

b) The company has reserved 257,328 Class "A" shares as follows:

	Number of Shares	Price per Share
Options to senior employees—		
Exercisable to November 30, 1973	*10,775*	*$10*
November 30, 1978	*138,925*	*$12*
November 30, 1978	*3,750*	*$14*
November 30, 1978	*5,000*	*$19*
Reserved for future allocation at a price to be determined by the Board of Directors but not less than 90% of the market value at the time of allocation	*65,600*	—
Subscription rights under the Employee Stock Purchase Plan—1970 which will be in effect until		
February 28, 1973	*19,388*	*$12*
February 28, 1973	*4,410*	*$14*
February 28, 1973	*9,480*	*$22*
	257,328	

c) During the year 55,729 Class "A" shares were issued to employees for cash of $663,000. In addition 1,208 5¼% preferred shares—Series "A" were redeemed and retained earnings include an amount of $120,800 set aside according to law equal to the par value of the shares redeemed.

4. Contributed Surplus The contributed surplus as at July 29, 1972 consists of a premium on issue and conversion of shares and gains on redemption of 5¼% preferred shares amounting to $10,486,000 with respect to prior years and of a gain on redemption of 5¼% preferred shares amounting to $29,000 during 1972.

5. Retirement Plan There is an obligation for past service pension benefits amounting to $430,000 in accordance with an actuarial estimate as at December 31, 1971. This obligation is being satisfied by annual payments of $33,000 with the final payment to be made in 1990.

6. Long-term Leases The aggregate minimum rentals, exclusive of additional amounts based on percentage of sales, taxes, insurance and other occupancy charges under long-term leases in effect July 29, 1972 for each of the periods shown are as follows:

	Payable to Ivanhoe Corporation and subsidiaries $	Payable to others $
1973–77	*26,364,000*	*49,809,000*
1978–82	*22,611,000*	*45,884,000*
1983–87	*17,200,000*	*39,764,000*
1988–92	*13,058,000*	*29,971,000*
After 1992	*4,132,000*	*27,693,000*
	83,365,000	*193,121,000*

7. Contingent Liabilities

a) Legal action

A legal action claiming $1,000,000 was instituted in 1965 against Ivanhoe Corporation for an alleged breach of sale agreement in connection with a property transaction. Counsel for the company has advised that Ivanhoe Corporation has a valid defense but that even if the action were successful, damages awarded should not exceed $25,000. The action has not yet been tried.

b) Income taxes

As reported in prior years, the Deputy Minister of Revenue of the Province of Quebec instituted legal action against the company claiming taxes for the years 1951 to 1963 inclusive, aggregating $902,000 including interest to date of the action, on profits made through the disposition of capital assets. Judgement was awarded in favour of the company in the Quebec Superior Court; however, the Deputy Minister of Revenue has appealed the judgement to the Quebec Court of Appeal. The appeal has not yet been heard.

c) Guarantee

Ivanhoe Corporation has guaranteed bank loans, amounting to $560,000 of companies in which it has ownership interests.

8. Depreciation and Amortization Depreciation of fixed assets is computed on the straight-line method at rates which are sufficient to amortize the costs over their estimated useful lives.

9. Net Earnings per Class "A" and Common Share Exercise of the outstanding options and subscription rights to purchase Class "A" shares would not have a significant dilutive effect on earnings per Class "A" and common share.

AUDITOR'S REPORT TO THE SHAREHOLDERS

We have examined the consolidated balance sheet of Steinberg's Limited and its subsidiaries as at July 29, 1972 and the consolidated statements of earnings (including the consolidated statements of earnings of Steinberg's Limited and its retail and manufacturing subsidiaries and the consolidated statements of earnings and cash flow of Ivanhoe Corporation and its subsidiaries), retained earnings and source and use of working capital for the year then ended. Our examination included a general review of the accounting procedures and such tests of accounting records and other supporting evidence as we considered necessary in the circumstances.

In our opinion these consolidated financial statements present fairly the financial position of the companies as at July 29, 1972 and the results of their operations and the source and use of their working capital for the year then ended, in accordance with generally accepted accounting principles applied on a basis consistent with that of the preceding year.

Coopers & Lybrand*

Montreal, October 30, 1972   Chartered Accountants

*Successors to McDonald Currie & Company